LITERATURE

A COLLEGE ANTHOLOGY

LITERATURE
A COLLEGE ANTHOLOGY

PATRICK W. SHAW
TEXAS TECH UNIVERSITY

HOUGHTON MIFFLIN CO.
BOSTON
ATLANTA
DALLAS
GENEVA, ILL.
HOPEWELL, N.J.
PALO ALTO
LONDON

Printed in the U.S.A.

Library of Congress Catalog Card Number: 76-19905

ISBN: 0-395-24841-8

Credits

Edward Albee. *The American Dream.* Reprinted by permission of Coward, McCann & Geoghegan, Inc. Copyright © 1960, 1961 by Edward Albee. *The American Dream* is the sole property of the author and is fully protected by copyright. It may not be acted whether by professionals or amateurs without written consent. Public readings, radio and television broadcasts likewise are forbidden. All inquiries concerning these rights should be addressed to the William Morris Agency, 1350 Avenue of the Americas, NYC 10019. **W. H. Auden.** "As I Walked Out One Evening," "Musée des Beaux Arts," and "The Unknown Citizen." Copyright 1940 and renewed 1968 by W. H. Auden. Reprinted from *Collected Shorter Poems 1927–1957,* by W. H. Auden, by permission of Random House, Inc. and Faber and Faber Ltd. **James Baldwin.** "Sonny's Blues." Copyright © 1957 by James Baldwin. Originally appeared in *Partisan Review.* Reprinted from *Going to Meet the Man* by James Baldwin with permission of The Dial Press. **John Barth.** "Lost in the Funhouse." Copyright © 1967 by The Atlantic Monthly Company from the book *Lost in the Funhouse* by John Barth. Reprinted by permission of Doubleday & Co., Inc. **Elizabeth Bishop.** "The Fish," "The Man-Moth," and "Some Dreams They Forgot," reprinted with the permission of Farrar, Straus & Giroux, Inc. from *The Complete Poems* by Elizabeth Bishop. Copyright © 1933, 1935, 1936, 1937, 1938, 1939, 1940, 1941, 1944, 1945, 1946, 1947, 1948, 1949, 1951, 1952, 1955, 1956, 1957, 1958, 1959, 1960, 1961, 1962, 1963, 1964, 1965, 1966, 1967, 1968, 1969 by Elizabeth Bishop. **Jorge Luis Borges.** "The Shape of the Sword," Jorge Luis Borges, *Labyrinths.* Copyright © 1962 by New Directions Publishing Corporation. Reprinted by permission of New Directions Publishing Corporation. Translated by Donald A. Yates. **Ray Bradbury.** "August 2026: There Will Come Soft Rains." Copyright 1950 by Ray Bradbury. Reprinted by permission of Harold Matson Company, Inc. **Bertolt Brecht.** *The Caucasian Chalk Circle.* Eric Bentley, Translator. *Parables for the Theatre* by Bertolt Brecht. University of Minnesota Press, Minneapolis. *The Caucasian Chalk Circle.* Copyright by Eric Bentley, 1947, as an unpublished MS, Registration No. D-12018. © Copyright 1961, 1963, by Eric Bentley. Prologue © Copyright by Eric Bentley. **Gwendolyn Brooks.** From *The World of Gwendolyn Brooks* (1971) by Gwendolyn Brooks: "The Birth in a Room" and "Pygmies are Pygmies Still, Though Percht on Alps," copyright 1949 by Gwendolyn Brooks Blakely; "We Real Cool: The Pool Players. Seven at the Golden Shovel," copyright 1959 by Gwendolyn Brooks. All reprinted by permission of Harper & Row, Publishers, Inc. **Ed Bullins.** *A Son, Come Home,* from *Five Plays by Ed Bullins,* copyright © 1968 by Ed Bullins, reprinted by permission of the publisher, The Bobbs-Merrill Company, Inc. **Albert Camus.** "The Guest," from *Exile and the Kingdom,* by Albert Camus, translated by Justin O'Brien. Copyright © 1957, 1958 by Alfred A. Knopf, Inc. Reprinted by permission of Alfred A. Knopf, Inc. **e. e. cummings.** "All in green went my love riding." Copyright, 1923, 1951, by e. e. cummings. "anyone lived in a pretty how town." Copyright, 1940, by e. e. cummings; copyright, 1968, by Marion Morehouse Cummings. "Buffalo Bill's." Copyright, 1923, 1951, by e. e. cummings. "somewhere i have never travelled." Copyright, 1931, 1959, by e. e. cummings. Reprinted from his volume, *Complete Poems 1913–1962,* by permission of Harcourt Brace Jovanovich, Inc. **Emily Dickinson.** Poem 712 "Because I could not stop for Death—," Poem 465 "I heard a Fly buzz—when I died—," Poem 585 "I like to see it lap the Miles—," Poem 520 "I started Early—Took my Dog," Poem 214 "I taste a liquor never brewed," Poem 435 "Much Madness is divinest Sense—," Poem 986 "A narrow Fellow in the Grass," and Poem 258 "There's a certain Slant of light." Reprinted by permission of the publishers and the Trustees of Amherst College from *The Poems of Emily Dickinson,* edited by Thos. H. Johnson, Cambridge, Massachusetts: The Belknap Press of Harvard University Press, Copyright © 1951, 1955 by the President and Fellows of Harvard College. **T. S. Eliot.** "The Hippopotamus" and "The Love Song of J. Alfred Prufrock," from *Collected Poems 1909–1962* by T. S. Eliot. Copyright, 1936, by Harcourt Brace Jovanovich, Inc.; copyright © 1963, 1964 by T. S. Eliot. Reprinted by permission of Harcourt Brace Jovanovich, Inc. and Faber and Faber Ltd. **Ralph Ellison.** "King of the Bingo Game," reprinted by permission of William Morris Agency, Inc., on behalf of author. Copyright © 1944 (renewed) by Ralph Ellison. **William Faulkner.** "Barn Burning." Copyright 1939 and renewed 1967 by Estelle Faulkner and Jill Faulkner Summers. Reprinted from *Collected Stories of William Faulkner,* by permission of Random House, Inc. **F. Scott Fitzgerald.** "Babylon Revisited" (Copyright 1931 The Curtis Publishing Company) is reprinted by permission of Charles Scribner's Sons from *Taps At Reveille* by F. Scott Fitzgerald. **Robert Frost.** "Acquainted with the Night," "Mending Wall," and "Stopping by Woods on a Snowy Evening," from *The Poetry of Robert Frost* edited by Edward Connery Lathem. Copyright

For Pat, Allison, and Erin

CONTENTS

THE POEM   953

PREFACE

This text is intended for use in an "introduction to literature" course. Physically, the book is divided by genres—short stories, novellas, plays, and poems; within each genre the arrangement is chronological. My objective in using these selections is to present a wide range of works; each work was chosen in accordance with how well it represents the author, how well it represents the genre, how firmly it is established—both critically and popularly, and—perhaps most important—how well it lends itself to teaching. No selection from any writer or genre is included simply because it is "different" or has not been anthologized before. My hope is that each selection best meets these criteria, while suiting the anthology format.

The text has deliberately been kept relatively clean of editorial paraphernalia, because I do not believe that the English department or individual teacher wishes to have an editor package a course. In many cases instructors prefer to have the selections presented in such a way that they can use them as they see fit. Consequently no attempt has been made to arrange the selections by any thematic or "critical" system. However, the first section, "An Introduction to Reading Literature," does present an overview of the terminologies and approaches the novice reader will need in such a course; the remainder of the text is free from editorial prodding. Throughout the text study questions and possible writing topics follow the selections, but these are only suggestions and do not force the student or teacher into any particular interpretation. The final section, a supplementary "Guide to Literary Terms," offers definitions and examples of basic terms not discussed in the introductory chapter but which the student may need in reading and discussing the various selections.

My overall goal has been to make the book a teacher-student text, not an editor's text. Its impetus is traditional rather than revolutionary, for I think that the trend in teaching has moved away from fads and frills, toward a sound reading of works that have proved of value or that show definite promise of establishing themselves as enduring literature.

In developing this anthology, I have been most grateful for the help provided by the following reviewers: Ben Collins, University of North Dakota; Marvin Garfinkel, Erie Community College; Leon Gatlin, University of North Carolina, Charlotte; John Lucarelli, Community College of Allegheny County; and David Skwire, Cuyahoga Community College.

AN
INTRODUCTION
TO READING
LITERATURE

In this book, you will discover four genres *a designation of types of literature* of fiction. Before discussing these genres, however, we need to mention a fifth genre, criticism—for your purpose in using this text is to sharpen your critical powers so that you can better understand and enjoy short stories, novellas, plays, and poems. Numerous forms of criticism exist, but our interest here is with literary criticism. In this sense, the word "criticize" means to use one's knowledge and insight in evaluating a work of literature in order to discern facets of the work that might otherwise be overlooked. Ezra Pound once observed that literature is language charged with meaning. What he meant was that a work of literature offers a wide range of values and interpretations; it offers great potential for pleasure and enlightenment. Criticism—yours and others—allows you to discover the meanings with which literature is "charged," and thus increases your enjoyment of a story, play, or poem. In short, criticism is your way of approaching a work of literature, of discovering values within that work, and of articulating your discoveries to yourself and others.

There are numerous critical methods that writers use in evaluating literature. Some critical essays concern specific works; others concern more general aspects of literature. Each method, however, is a form of literary criticism. In conjunction with your study of this text, your instructor may ask you to read some literary criticism. You will agree with some of the critical essays and disagree with others—but that, in part, is precisely the purpose of such criticism. There is no "one right meaning" of any literary work, nor is there any "one thing" that literature means to all people. Your interpretation of a story or poem or play can be as valid as anyone else's, so long as you base your interpretation on the facts present in the work and use reason in applying those facts to substantiate your opinions. The purpose of your literary criticism is therefore twofold: (1) to enlighten others by adding your opinions to their own; and (2) to convince others that your interpretation is sound and feasible.

What is meant by "reason" and "facts"? You may understand "reason" to mean common sense, and "facts" to mean that which is literally said in the poem, play, or story. Ralph Ellison begins "King of the Bingo Game" (page 241) by stating: "The woman in front of him was eating roasted peanuts. . . ." Immediately, you know three facts: (1) a male—probably the main character—is sitting or standing somewhere; (2) a female is in front of him; and (3) she is eating roasted peanuts. This information cannot be altered or denied, no matter what your ultimate interpretation of the story is.

Common sense is the knowledge that you already possess and can use as your basis for comprehending and enjoying literature. To grasp the meanings of fiction requires no occult systems or methods. Bernard Shaw or your instructor may seem to be able to present "better" commentaries than yours; they may seem to arrive at their interpretations more easily and more quickly than you. This is true, primarily, because both Bernard Shaw and your instructor are more experienced than you in literary matters. Reading and interpreting literature are learned processes. The more you learn about literature, the broader and deeper its meanings become to you, and the more easily you can move from one work to another with increased understanding and enjoyment. As in anything else that you learn, this process begins with very practical matters. You know how to read, you have an understanding of people, and you have had some experience in life. Literature, among other things, is about people living their lives. So, you already have the essentials for reading and criticizing literature.

You may never have nailed two boards together, but if you had to do so at this moment, you would know that you need a hammer and nails; that you aim those nails sharp-end first into the board; and that you strike the other end with the hammer. In literature, the "facts" are the hammer, the nails, and the boards; the "reason" is your common sense, which tells you how to begin constructing a meaning for a literary work. The following discussion will supply you with more tools and experience.

The Vocabulary of Literary Criticism

As in any other field of study, there is a working vocabulary that you must understand before you can effectively discuss stories, plays, and poems. The basic terminology is neither complex nor extensive. Let us begin by discussing fiction in general.

Fiction is writing that is produced more from the writer's imagination than from actual events. This does not imply that fiction *cannot* contain historical truth or statistically verifiable information, but it does mean that these aspects of fiction are of secondary importance. Stephen Crane's "The Open Boat" (page 112) is based on an actual shipwreck—an

event that Crane himself experienced and that is historically document-
ed. Yet Crane's story is not primarily concerned with the shipwreck, but
rather with the relationship of people and nature. Tolstoi's *War and
Peace* relies heavily on the facts of the Napoleonic Wars, but, ultimately,
that is not what the novel is "about." The point is that the writer of
fiction is not controlled by history or objective reality, and may even
twist both in outrageous fashion to obtain a goal. If you have read the
novel *Little Big Man*, by Thomas Berger, or have seen the movie, you
have experienced a writer using history pretty much as the writer wishes.
In *Little Big Man*, Jack Crabb, the *protagonist*,[1] meets a number of
famous historical figures—Wyatt Earp, George Custer, Wild Bill Hickok,
Calamity Jane, and numerous others. These people did indeed live; but
there is no historical evidence that they ever did many of the things
Crabb sees them do, or that they ever were in some of the places Crabb
meets them. Berger brings his imagination to bear on history; and he
manipulates history at will to develop the theme of his novel, neither
expecting nor desiring that the reader take him literally. Historical
accuracy is not the point of the novel; the imaginative development of
character and social commentary is. Fiction, therefore, is that form of
literature in which the reader is expected to look for something more
than mere facts or information, and in which the writer's imagination is
the dominant force at work.

Fiction Genres

Short stories, novels or novellas, plays, and poems are the fiction
genres. Some commentators believe that narrative poetry is the only
form of poetry that is true fiction. This contention is a technical one, and,
for practical purposes, you may consider all poetry as fiction. In any case,
how do you distinguish these kinds of fiction from one another?

The Short Story The short story is a form of prose fiction that is
controlled by length and construction. Beyond a certain length a short
story loses its distinguishing characteristics, and becomes a novella or
novel. A short story is to a novel as a well-built cabin is to a castle. Every
part of a short story must be functional, must work directly to further the
author's purpose—with no fancy decorations or hallways. Usually, the
purpose of the short story is to expose the human personality at work in
one specific situation. This exposure is most often brought about through
action and dialogue that show the main character in immediate conflict
with an opposing force. The length of the story does not allow for any
complex plot development and, in comparison with the novel, the short
story has a highly-structured plot—one that moves clearly from a

---

1. Italicized terms can be found in the Guide to Literary Terms, which begins on page 1237.

beginning to an end. Ultimately, however, about the only definition of a short story that can be given is that it is a form of prose fiction that does not exceed ten or fifteen thousand words in length. Despite its length restriction, the short story can take on a diversity of forms.

The Novel or Novella The novel is a form of prose fiction of any length greater than that of a short story. It is a highly flexible genre, and a discussion of "What is a novel?" could extend throughout a book longer than this one, without arriving at any definite answer. The novella is actually a short novel. For your purposes, think of the novel, or novella, as an extended piece of prose fiction. It differs from a short story in that it can concern itself with more characters and situations. Instead of being limited to only one or two scenes, as is the short story, the novel can place a protagonist in numerous situations. This gives the reader an opportunity to observe the protagonist reacting to different pressures and problems. Consequently, the reader has more information about the characters of a novel than about the characters of a short story, and is able to make a more thorough evaluation of the characters' personalities.

Also, since the writer of a novel has a much greater field in which to work, the novel can develop more *themes* than can a short story. Even in a short, relatively structured novel such as *Goodbye, Columbus* (page 359), you can readily note the number of different themes or ideas that are introduced, especially in comparison to a short story such as Edith Wharton's "Roman Fever" (page 102). In a sense, the novelist is more at leisure than is the short-story writer. Some novels are of monumental length, and, as Stephen Crane said of *War and Peace*, they just seem to go on and on forever, like Texas. Laurence Sterne's *Tristram Shandy* is a novel that ambles along; it never reaches a climax, just stops. Then, without protracting our definition too much, we can see that the novel is a much broader, looser form of prose fiction than the short story. The novel contains more action, more dialogue, more themes, and more thoroughly developed characters than does the short story.

Poetry Any attempt to define poetry would hinder more than help; it would, in fact, probably scare you so badly that you would throw up your hands and say "To hell with it!" Almost all well-known poets and critics of poetry have attempted to define it; but, ultimately, what they have done is to explain how they feel about poetry. They have neither clarified the meaning of poetry nor shown how it differs from prose fiction. Thomas Carlyle viewed poetry as "musical Thought"; Edgar Allan Poe, as the "rhythmical creation of beauty"; and William Wordsworth, as "the spontaneous overflow of powerful feelings recollected in tranquility." Each of these definitions is highly subjective. Howard Nemerov has suggested, only half-humorously, that the distinction between poetry and prose is that poetry does not go all the way to the right-hand margin of the page. This, perhaps, is a far more objective and honest definition of poetry than the others. In any event, you can call into play your aforementioned common sense. Quite frankly, you needn't worry too much about defining poetry, but rather about how to read it and interpret its meanings.

Poetry, more than any other form of fiction, demands careful reading. Still you must first read a poem just as you would read prose. Don't stop reading when you reach the end of a line of poetry—unless that line ends with a period, a question mark, or some other form of end-stop punctuation. When first reading a poem, read it sentence by sentence, just as you have read this paragraph, sentence by sentence. In subsequent readings, you may read the poem for rhyme or meter or symbol or whatever, but first make sure that you know what the poem says—before you try to decide what it means.

For example, take this stanza from a nonsense poem by Ogden Nash:

> I'll bet that the poet Herrick
> With Corinna gone a-Maying,
> Had to run like a rabbit
> To catch what she was saying.[2]

As you can see, there are four lines of poetry here. However, these four lines make but one sentence. Only after you have recognized and read this "sentence" should you go back and notice the *allusion* to Herrick's poem (page 984), the rhyme of "a-Maying" and "saying," and the *simile* "like a rabbit." Of course Nash's is a very simple example of poetry; but as you begin to read more complex poems, you should remember that a poem, like prose, conforms to some kind of grammatical logic. This is true even of unusual poetry, such as that of e. e. cummings, which foregoes the conventions of punctuation and capitalization. But with practice in reading you will see that cummings's poetry is written in complete sentences expressing complete thoughts. To prove the point, read these lines from "All in green went my love riding" (page 1193):

> All in green went my love riding
> on a great horse of gold
> into the silver dawn.
>
> four lean hounds crouched low and smiling
> the merry deer ran before.

At first glance, these two stanzas may seem confusing. Notice, however, that they are in fact quite logical in arrangement: "All in green went my

---

2. Ogden Nash, "How Can Echo Answer What Echo Cannot Hear?" in *Marriage Lines*, Little, Brown and Company, Boston, 1964, pp. 87–88.

love, riding on a great horse of gold into the silver dawn. Four lean hounds crouched low; and, smiling, the merry deer ran before." Although the question of interpretation is still wide open, the insertion of punctuation and capitalization has made the factual meaning much clearer.

Poetry also demands a closer attention to word meaning than does any other form of fiction. You can safely read short stories, novels, or plays without needing to define each and every word you encounter. You can, in fact, usually "skip" words that you do not know and still understand what you have read. With poetry, however, you cannot run this risk. Since poetry is much more compact than prose, it demands that each word carry maximum weight. Consequently, you should know the meaning of every word in a poem; if there is some doubt about which meaning or meanings the poet intends, you must decide which is the most logical. To do this, consider not only the denotation of a word but its connotation as well. The "denotation" of a word is its dictionary meaning. The "connotation" of a word is its abstract associations—those things that the reader thinks of when he or she sees the word and that are independent of the word's denotation. A prime example of connotation is "Watergate," a word that, until 1972 or 1973, was merely the name of an apartment complex, or meant a gate through which water passed. Because of political happenings, however, "Watergate" has become so closely associated with morally questionable practices that you could never again think of it as simply an apartment complex.

Consider the opening lines of Andrew Marvell's "To His Coy Mistress" (page 990):

Had we but world enough, and time,
This coyness, lady, were no crime.

Substitute "girly" for "lady" and see how your impression of the lines is altered. Though both terms denote "female," they obviously do not have the same meaning because of their differing connotations. Many words can be synonymous, or near-synonymous, and still convey entirely different values. In fact, one of the things that differentiates fiction (especially poetry) from nonfiction is that writers of fiction depend more upon connotation than do writers of nonfiction.

Thus, one of the prime requisites for reading poetry is that you know what the words of the poem mean, in both their denotative and connotative senses. The first way to arrive at a word's connotation is to think of those ideas or events that you personally associate with the word. An unabridged dictionary, such as *Webster's Third New International*, can give you further connotations of words.

Also, context can help determine the meaning of a word. "Context" is the other words and sentences that surround the word. Just as you and I are shaped in part by our environment, so too is a word. What, for instance, would be your reaction on seeing this word printed alone, surrounded by nothing but white space?

Death

You can easily give the denotation of death; and its connotation—though perhaps different for each of us—is generally unpleasant and ominous. Yet, place the word within the context of Emily Dickinson's "Poem 712" (page 1155):

> Because I could not stop for Death—
> He kindly stopped for me—
> The Carriage held but just Ourselves—
> And Immortality.

In this context, does the word "Death" have the same value or meaning that it has when presented alone? In Dickinson's poem the word is neither ominous nor totally unpleasant. As a matter of fact, Dickinson gives the word a rather comforting, gentlemanly value. Note the same word as it appears in other poetic contexts, such as in Donne's "Holy Sonnet 10" (page 981) or in Keats's "Ode to a Nightingale" (page 1086). Clearly, then, context is a factor that must be given some consideration in determining the meanings of words.

There are additional terms that apply to poetry—conceit, foot, rhyme, scheme, and numerous others. However, you do not need to know these terms in order to analyze, understand, and enjoy poetry, just as you do not need to know the names of instruments or the techniques of music in order to understand and enjoy a song. You should be aware of these terms, but in the early stages of reading poetry you need not worry about the complexities that such terms often present.

Plays Drama is a story performed on stage by actors who impersonate other people. Usually, much of the story is told through the use of *dialogue*, reinforced by action; but it is possible to have a play in which there is little or no dialogue, or a play in which there is nothing but dialogue. Also, drama can be of almost any length, though most often the duration of a play conforms to the realistic limitations of an audience's interest span. You can quickly see the diversity of length in drama by comparing the brevity of *The American Dream* (page 912) to the lengthiness of *Hamlet* (page 474). The first is so brief that it is usually performed in conjunction with other short plays; the latter is so long that, despite its greatness, it is seldom performed in its entirety.

You might think of drama as being the three-dimensional, five-senses genre of fiction because it is meant to be performed in front of an audience. Consequently, it can and does make use of all the visual potential of lighting, stage props, and actors' movement. Moreover, drama can employ just about any sound effect needed to further the purpose of the play. Some of the avant-garde plays have even used the senses of touch and smell. The point is that drama is fiction come to life. When you read plays, keep in mind that you are missing much of their effect. Reading a play is somewhat akin to listening to the Super Bowl on the radio. In the theater you can see the mood-setting colors, hear the suggestive music, and tell when an actor speaks a line sarcastically or sincerely. But in reading, you do not have the benefits of these effects. Consequently, you must read carefully and with an active imagination— you must be your own director, actor, and audience.

Nonetheless, reading plays can have its advantages. Since reading requires an active imagination and close attention to detail, you can, in fact, become personally involved with the play. You are not bothered by the problem of hearing lines; and you are freer to bring your own interpretation to stage directions and dialogue. (Of course, here again, you must use reason and facts as the basis of your interpretation.) So, even though drama is created as a viewer's medium, it can function very well as a reader's medium.

Traditionally, drama is divided into two major types: comedy and tragedy. Comedy, in contrast to tragedy, is less serious in content. Because its primary purpose is to amuse, comedy seldom presents characters who face great adversity. The characters may have problems and conflicts, but these troubles are seldom devastating, and ultimately the situation is resolved in favor of the protagonists. In short, comedies have "happy" endings. Yet, you should not assume that comedies have no serious purpose. Laughter and tears are often closely related; the writer of comedy may well have serious intent in mind. Molière's *The Misanthrope* (page 584), for instance, is a comedy, but it is quite serious in its *satire* of society's shortcomings; Molière wants the viewer or reader to understand that society is unjust and that its faults should be corrected.

Tragedy deals with problems more serious than those of comedy. In tragedy, the protagonist is placed in a life or death situation. Because of some great error or fatal flaw in character, the protagonist is unable to avoid a death that is violent and premature or, at the least, a life of catastrophe and misery. In *Oedipus Rex* (page 433), for instance, Oedipus is not killed, but is left blind and suffering. Shakespeare's Hamlet, though still a very young man, is killed violently. According to traditional definitions, the purpose of tragedy is to create in the audience a feeling of fear and pity, causing a *catharsis* for the viewer or reader.

There are numerous subdivisions of comedy and tragedy, several of which are discussed in the Guide to Literary Terms. (See, for instance, *comedy of humors, comedy of manners,* and *melodrama.*) The definitions given above for comedy and tragedy apply primarily to classic drama. Through the years, the distinctions between comedy and tragedy, and the distinctions among the various subdivisions, have become increasingly blurred; it is often an artificial limitation to discuss plays merely in terms of comedy and tragedy. This is particularly true of modern drama. Tennessee Williams's *The Glass Menagerie* (page 859) is by strict definition a comedy—yet it obviously has very tragic undertones. Albee's *The American Dream* (page 912) is a comedy—none of the main characters gets killed or faces any drastic problems that threaten his or her life—yet some of the actions described in the play are bloodier and far more horrible than those in such classic tragedies as *Oedipus Rex* and *Hamlet.*

Therefore, read the modern plays with an awareness that they will not fit easily into the classical definitions, as do *Oedipus Rex, The Misanthrope,* and *Hamlet.* Yet, the distinctions of comedy and tragedy are convenient starting places. By using them, you can perhaps better understand how not only drama itself has changed, but how the life that drama seeks to represent has changed.

Literary Vocabulary

Now that you can distinguish one form of fiction from another, you can begin to familiarize yourself with the general vocabulary needed to discuss the various genres.

Plot If someone asks you to give the plot of a story or play, you no doubt respond by relating what *happens* in the work. This is, for the most part, a valid interpretation of "plot." More precisely, plot refers to the systematized action in a piece of fiction. A plot may be simple and unified, as it usually is in a short story. "Roman Fever" (page 102), for instance, has a plot that moves in a straight line; it begins with the innocent conversation of two aging women and culminates with the final ironic revelation. On the other hand, a plot may be complex. *Hamlet* contains plots within plots (*subplots*). And if you have ever read some of Charles Dickens's long novels, such as *Bleak House,* you know how truly convoluted plots can be. From any work, however, you can expect that all plots and subplots will be resolved or brought to a reasonable stage of explanation.

In some fiction there is no plot; short poems do not usually have plots, though plots can be found in long poems such as *The Rime of the Ancient Mariner* (page 1034) or *Don Juan* (page 1052). Stories and plays, particularly some of the modern works, may appear to have no plots, or at least not to emphasize plot. Albee's *The American Dream,* for instance, is really not too concerned with plot; and the plot of Barth's "Lost in the Funhouse" (page 291), a short story, is insignificant—if not completely lacking. Such works depend on factors other than plot for their impact. Most often, however, plot is an important part of any work of fiction; and you may safely begin your appraisal of a piece of literature by asking yourself "What is the plot?" In writing literary criticism, by the way, you usually assume that your reader is familiar with the work you are discussing; therefore, do not include a plot summary as part of your criticism. However, if the work has little or no plot, and you feel that this is an intentional device used by the author, then of course you may write about that fact.

Character and Characterization   The character in a piece of fiction is the carrier of the action, the fictional "person" who conveys the plot. Usually, a work will have only one main character, but there is no limitation on how many characters a work may have. Bradbury's "August 2026: There Will Come Soft Rains" (page 255) contains no human characters; Roth's *Goodbye, Columbus* contains two main characters and several other important characters. One work is a short story and the other a novella; naturally that has some effect on the number of characters involved. But even a long novel can limit itself to one character. For the most part, Daniel Defoe's *Robinson Crusoe* has only one character. The main character in a piece of fiction is called the hero or protagonist; the opposing person is called the *antagonist*. It is often the *conflict* that develops between these two that forms much of the plot and that helps reveal the personalities of both parties. (Check the terms *protagonist*, *antagonist*, and *conflict* in the Guide to Literary Terms.)

Characterization is the ways in which a character's personality is revealed to the reader. Anything you are told or can safely surmise about a character is part of characterization—age, size, physical appearance, manner of speech, geographical background, likes and dislikes, and so forth. One particular aspect of characterization is motivation. *Why* does a character act in a certain way? Why, for instance, does Hamlet think so much about suicide? Why does Daru in "The Guest" (page 231) let his prisoner go free? Why does Goodman Brown leave his wife to go into the woods? If a writer does not give you enough information to answer the question of motivation—or at least enough information to allow you to arrive at a feasible hypothesis—then the work is weak in a vital area. You can expect the motivation in a piece of fiction to be both explainable and consistent. This does not mean that you can demand simplemindedness or stereotyping—in fiction as in life the motivations may be far from overt. (Why does the ancient mariner suddenly shoot the albatross? Why does Prufrock fear women so?) It does mean, however, that a character should not suddenly change personality in mid-plot and commence to act in ways that contradict an established personality.

Point of View   Through whose eyes is the reader viewing the action of the story? If you can answer this, then you have pretty well answered the question of point of view. There are three kinds of point of view: omniscient, first person, and central character.

Omniscient point of view means that the author of the work is speaking directly to the reader, revealing any or all facts about the characters or situations in the work. In a way, the author plays God, giving and withholding whatever he or she wishes. Crane's "The Open Boat" (page 112) is a good example of the omniscient point of view. In this story, the author seems to stand apart from the action, giving the reader a rather objective account of what is happening to the men on the ocean. In omniscient point of view, no person in the story itself tells the reader what is taking place.

First-person point of view means that a major character (usually the protagonist) narrates the action, telling the reader what the author wants the reader to know. The first-person pronouns "I," "my," "we," and "us" are clues that this is first-person point of view. When John Updike states, in the second line of "A & P" (page 307), that "I'm in the third checkout slot," you are fairly certain that Updike is using the first-person point of view. Of course, you should ask "How trustworthy is the narrator?" The first-person narrator is the character who guides you and tells you what that character wants you to know about other people and events in the story. In the process he or she will reveal, either intentionally or inadvertently, much about him or herself. So, you must first decide whether you trust the narrator. You must evaluate the narrator's characterization before that of any other person in the story. If it reveals the narrator to be unreliable, bigoted, or somehow shortsighted, then you should consider these limitations in your thinking about the other characters in the story. If, on the other hand, you decide that the narrator is honest and dependable, you may of course assume that you are receiving reliable information.

The central-character point of view differs from first-person point of view. The main character does not tell the story; however, the action centers on her or him, and, therefore, the reader is limited by what happens to this character. In addition, the reader knows nothing that the central character does not know, although occasionally the reader learns what the character is thinking about certain events. Fitzgerald's "Babylon Revisited" (page 158) and Camus's "The Guest" (page 231) are examples of this point of view. As with the first-person point of view, you must carefully evaluate the trustworthiness of the central character.

Understanding the point of view is of primary importance in reading and evaluating a work of fiction. The point of view is, perhaps, the first aspect that the author of a work of fiction must determine. The point of view affects every other aspect of the work—the *style*, the *tone*, the information that can be given to the reader, and, particularly, how the reader will respond to the characters and events. Philip Roth, for example, presents *Goodbye, Columbus* from the first-person point of view. Among other things, this point of view gives the reader a sense of personal involvement with Neil Klugman's life; it brings to the novella a kind of confessional quality. In short, no other narrator could give the reader the same intimate knowledge of Neil's experiences that Neil himself can give. You may still question Neil's reliability as a narrator; in

fact, you must consider his close personal involvement as being, perhaps, a prejudicing factor. Nonetheless, you should realize that no other
"eyes" can reveal the same information that Neil gives. On the other
hand, you will see that in Crane's "The Open Boat," the use of the
first-person narrator would have changed the entire quality of the story.
Crane strives for a removed, objective—almost scientific—analysis of the
men in the boat. If Crane had used any point of view other than the
omniscient, he would have had great difficulty in maintaining the objectivity; the story would have been something other than what it is.

Particularly in longer works of fiction, you will find combinations
and variations of these three points of view. As a rule, however, these are
the three that you should learn to recognize. Again, the point of view is
an important aspect of any piece of fiction. In a sense, the point of view is
the lens through which you view the action.

Symbol The dictionary defines "symbol" as something that
stands for something else, or something visible that suggests something
invisible. Quite literally, any thing can be used symbolically: a pair of
empty shoes quickly reminds you of the person who is not in them; a
scar on your forehead reminds you of the time you forgot to duck in the
rock fight; and a red traffic light not only warns you to stop, but also
suggests rather vividly what can happen to you if you do not stop. But in
literature we usually think of symbols as being applied somewhat more
selectively than this. There are only two types of literary symbols:
universal and private. The universal symbol is one that is so well known,
nearly everyone in the world (or at least everyone within a certain social
order) recognizes its significance. A writer using a universal symbol
knows with some certainty how readers will react to it. For those of us
living in Christian countries, the cross is perhaps the most famous
universal symbol. Literally, the cross is no more than two pieces of wood
joined together to form a T-shaped frame; but because of what happened
to Jesus, the cross has come to symbolize all of Christian life. It is
something visible that suggests all the psychological, social, and religious associations that the crucifixion of Christ has acquired. Water,
wedding bands, flags, doves, and the sun are other universal symbols.
Moreover, certain colors have universal significance—red for violence,
green for fertility, white for purity, black for evil.

Private symbols are those things that assume symbolic value for
an individual or a small group of individuals. You, no doubt, have several
private symbols—your class ring, the sea shell you picked up when you
were seven, the flower pressed somewhere between the pages of a book;
authors, too, can bring private symbols into a work. Things that have
little or no universal symbolism can be made symbolic within the context
of a story, poem, or play. You can usually spot these symbols by the
prominence or frequency of their mention. For instance, notice how

often in Part I of *The Rime of the Ancient Mariner* Coleridge mentions the albatross, and how he ends the final stanza with the line "I shot the ALBATROSS" (page 1036). Coleridge's emphasis is apparent, and should let you know immediately that the albatross has some symbolic value in the poem. Also, in "Young Goodman Brown" Hawthorne uses a pink ribbon. A pink ribbon has no universal significance—that is, there is no distinct set of associations that it would elicit from a large number of people. Yet, count the number of times that a pink ribbon appears in Hawthorne's short story; after its second mention, you can be fairly certain that Hawthorne is using it as a symbol. Because of the context in which the ribbon appears, however, it should not be difficult for you to suggest possible meanings for the symbol.

In poetry, particularly, you will find symbols. We have already mentioned the fact that poetry, more than any other form of fiction, depends on compact language. Consequently, poetry—especially the short poem—lends itself more readily to symbolism. Certainly, this does not imply that short stories, novels, and plays cannot be replete with symbols; but it is true that symbols are often more apparent in a poem—just as a single deer would be more apparent in a small pen than in a forest.

One of the frequent comments about recent poetry is that often the poetic symbols are so personal with the author that the reader is unable to affix any real meaning to the poem. This may or may not be a valid criticism. In any case, you as the reader have the right (perhaps even the obligation) to expect the ultimate content of a poem to be worth your examination. This does not mean that you should scan a poem, shrug, and throw up your hands in defeat. It does mean, however, that since the poet is asking you to be his or her audience (and all poets are doing that, or else they wouldn't struggle so hard to publish), he or she should at least communicate in such a way that an intelligent person can understand, at least partially, what is being said. So, if after checking word denotation, connotation, and allusion, you still have no idea what a particular poem is talking about, then you can safely question how "good" the poem is and whether it is worthy of your efforts.

Look at "The Second Coming" (page 1169). For the amateur reader this can be a perplexing poem, particularly if the reader does not know that Yeats developed a complex, highly esoteric set of private symbols and theories by which he tried to interpret history and civilization. For example, "gyre" is a symbol referring to the cone, the cone, in turn, refers to Yeats's cyclical view of history. Generally speaking, Yeats saw history as being divided into two-thousand-year cycles, each cycle or "cone" interpenetrating the next. The term *"Spiritus Mundi"* refers to Yeats's concept of a "great memory" that pervades all life and from which the individual receives inexplicable visions. Other symbols in the poem, such as the "rough beast" (the Sphinx) and the falcon, have meanings that are circumscribed if not totally personal. Once you know about the poet's private interpretation of the universe, you may be able to uncover an almost endless series of meanings for the poem. It may become one of those poems that you can peel layer after layer like an onion, revealing a complexity of values. Nonetheless, you retain the prerogative of asking whether the tears you shed during the process are worth the trouble.

A final word of caution. We have said that symbols can be defined as visible things that suggest invisible things. This of course is true, but do not take it too literally. Often, sounds can be used to suggest something else. In "Ode to a Nightingale" (page 1086) you will find a prime example of sound used symbolically; the bird's song is the main symbol in the poem, and though technically the bird can be "seen," the song cannot. Wallace Stevens uses this "sound" symbol in "The Idea of Order at Key West" (page 1182), when he speaks of the girl who "sang beyond the genius of the sea." So a better working definition of symbol might be: any one thing that human senses can perceive and that, in turn, suggests extrasensory things.

Images and Imagery Images are often confused with symbols, and imagery with symbolism. The distinction between image and symbol is that images depend more on words than on a single thing. That is, a series of words is needed to create an image, whereas a symbol is only one thing. But like a symbol, an image creates a reaction in the reader that is above and beyond the image itself. It causes the reader to form a mental picture—to taste or feel or hear something that is not literally present. In his poem "The Eve of St. Agnes," Keats has these lines (page 1076):

> And still she slept an azure-lidded sleep,
> In blanchéd linen, smooth, and lavendered,
> While he from forth the closet brought a heap
> Of candied apple, quince, and plum, and gourd;
> With jellies soother than the creamy curd,
> And lucent syrups, tinct with cinnamon;
> Manna and dates, in argosy transferred
> From Fez; and spicéd dainties, every one,
> From silken Samarcand to cedared Lebanon.

Here, all of the poet's description evokes images. You see the sleeping girl beneath her undisturbed, pale perfumed sheets; you see her lover surrounding her with exotic fruits and foods, giving a hedonistic offering to her beauty. It is difficult to read these lines—particularly if you are hungry—without salivating, without tasting candied apples and lucent syrups. In short, you as the reader experience what is going on in the poem. Through the distinct images, you participate almost literally in a nonliteral happening; your mind takes you to places and causes you to enjoy things that your body does not share. Keats meant for the poem to be sensual and sensuous, and by careful construction of images, he succeeded quite well.

Image, then, may be thought of as a unit larger than a symbol. An entire poem (or at least large segments of a poem) may be an image, but seldom, if ever, can an entire poem be a symbol. Williams's "The Red Wheelbarrow" (page 1185) is a good example of a poem that is an image. In this poem, Williams seems to use a verbal Polaroid camera to capture a rather insignificant scene. The power of the poem comes from its suddenness; the poem implants a very distinct picture on your mind, almost before you are aware that you have read the poem. You may or may not interpret the wheelbarrow, the chicken, and the rain as being symbols. But even if these objects are used symbolically, the symbols remain a part of the larger unit—the image.

I hope this discussion has given you the fundamentals you'll need for working critically and pleasurably with literature. There are, of course, other terms that come within the literary vocabulary; some of the most common of these are given in the Guide to Literary Terms. In addition, a good handbook to literature can furnish you with further definitions and discussions of a much broader range of literary topics. Do not hesitate to use any source that you feel will enhance your understanding of literature. On the other hand, do not forget that you, as the reader, provide fifty percent of the meaning of any poem or play or story; the author provides the other fifty percent. Critical terminology should give you the methods of articulating your reactions to a work of literature; the terminology should never dictate what that reaction should be. So, if you are somewhat intimidated by symbols and images and characterization, forget them for the time being. Just begin to read the following selections with an open, inquisitive mind. Through your own efforts and with the help of your instructor, you will soon pick up the terminology.

THE
SHORT
STORY

Edgar Allan Poe [1809–1849]

Poe was born in Boston, Massachusetts, the child of poor itinerant actors. After his father deserted the family and his mother died, he lived with John Allan, a merchant in Richmond, Virginia. Poe's education was sporadic—he studied in England, at the University of Virginia, and at West Point. In 1836 he married his thirteen-year-old cousin, Virginia Clemm, who died eleven years later. Poe's life could be described as "desperate." It was marked by a seldom happy relationship with John Allan; alcoholism and a number of physical and psychological illnesses; and the rejection by society of both his lifestyle and writing. Even today, opinion about his work is polarized. Yet, at its best, Poe's writing powerfully explores human psychology. Among his publications are *Tamerlane and Other Poems* (1827) and *Tales of the Grotesque and Arabesque* (1839).

The Cask of Amontillado

The thousand injuries of Fortunato I had borne as I best could, but when he ventured upon insult I vowed revenge. You, who so well know the nature of my soul, will not suppose, however, that I gave utterance to a threat. *At length* I would be avenged; this was a point definitely settled—but the very definitiveness with which it was resolved precluded the idea of risk. I must not only punish but punish with impunity. A wrong is unredressed when retribution overtakes its redresser. It is equally unredressed when the avenger fails to make himself felt as such to him who has done the wrong.

It must be understood that neither by word nor deed had I given Fortunato cause to doubt my good will. I continued, as was my wont, to smile in his face, and he did not perceive that my smile *now* was at the thought of his immolation.

He had a weak point—this Fortunato—although in other regards he was a man to be respected and even feared. He prided himself on his connoisseurship in wine. Few Italians have the true virtuoso spirit. For the most part their enthusiasm is adopted to suit the time and opportunity, to practise imposture upon the British and Austrian *millionaires*. In painting and gemmary, Fortunato, like his countrymen, was a quack, but in the matter of old wines he was sincere. In this respect I did not differ from him materially;—I was skilful in the Italian vintages myself, and bought largely whenever I could.

It was about dusk, one evening during the supreme madness of the carnival season, that I encountered my friend. He accosted me with excessive warmth, for he had been drinking much. The man wore motley. He had on a tight-fitting parti-striped dress, and his head was surmounted by the conical cap and bells. I was so pleased to see him that I thought I should never have done wringing his hand.

I said to him—"My dear Fortunato, you are luckily met. How remarkably well you are looking to-day. But I have received a pipe of what passes for Amontillado, and I have my doubts."

"How?" said he. "Amontillado? A pipe? Impossible! And in the middle of the carnival!"

"I have my doubts," I replied; "and I was silly enough to pay the full Amontillado price without consulting you in the matter. You were not to be found, and I was fearful of losing a bargain."

"Amontillado!"

"I have my doubts."

"Amontillado!"

"And I must satisfy them."

"Amontillado!"

"As you are engaged, I am on my way to Luchresi. If any one has a critical turn it is he. He will tell me——"

"Luchresi cannot tell Amontillado from Sherry."

"And yet some fools will have it that his taste is a match for your own."

"Come, let us go."

"Whither?"

"To your vaults."

"My friend, no; I will not impose upon your good nature. I perceive you have an engagement. Luchresi——"

"I have no engagement;—come."

"My friend, no. It is not the engagement, but the severe cold with which I perceive you are afflicted. The vaults are insufferably damp. They are encrusted with nitre."

"Let us go, nevertheless. The cold is merely nothing. Amontillado! You have been imposed upon. And as for Luchresi, he cannot distinguish Sherry from Amontillado."

Thus speaking, Fortunato possessed himself of my arm; and putting on a mask of black silk and drawing a *roquelaire*[1] closely about my person, I suffered him to hurry me to my palazzo.

There were no attendants at home; they had absconded to make merry in honour of the time. I had told them that I should not return until the morning, and had given them explicit orders not to stir from the house. These orders were sufficient, I well knew, to insure their immediate disappearance, one and all, as soon as my back was turned.

I took from their sconces two flambeaux, and giving one to Fortunato, bowed him through several suites of rooms to the archway that led into the vaults. I passed down a long and winding staircase, requesting him to be cautious as he followed. We came at length to the foot of the descent, and stood together upon the damp ground of the catacombs of the Montresors.

The gait of my friend was unsteady, and the bells upon his cap jingled as he strode.

"The pipe," he said.

"It is farther on," said I; "but observe the white web-work which gleams from these cavern walls."

He turned towards me, and looked into my eyes with two filmy orbs that distilled the rheum of intoxication.

1. A short cloak.

"Nitre?" he asked at length.

"Nitre," I replied. "How long have you had that cough?"

"Ugh! ugh! ugh!—ugh! ugh! ugh!—ugh! ugh! ugh!—ugh! ugh! ugh!—ugh! ugh! ugh!"

My poor friend found it impossible to reply for many minutes.

"It is nothing," he said at last.

"Come," I said, with decision, "we will go back; your health is precious. You are rich, respected, admired, beloved; you are happy, as once I was. You are a man to be missed. For me it is no matter. We will go back; you will be ill, and I cannot be responsible. Besides, there is Luchresi——"

"Enough," he said; "the cough is a mere nothing; it will not kill me. I shall not die of a cough."

"True—true," I replied; "and, indeed, I had no intention of alarming you unnecessarily—but you should use all proper caution. A draught of this Medoc will defend us from the damps."

Here I knocked off the neck of a bottle which I drew from a long row of its fellows that lay upon the mould.

"Drink," I said, presenting him the wine.

He raised it to his lips with a leer. He paused and nodded to me familiarly, while his bells jingled.

"I drink," he said, "to the buried that repose around us."

"And I to your long life."

He again took my arm, and we proceeded.

"These vaults," he said, "are extensive."

"The Montresors," I replied, "were a great and numerous family."

"I forget your arms."

"A huge human foot d'or, in a field azure; the foot crushes a serpent rampant whose fangs are imbedded in the heel."

"And the motto?"

"*Nemo me impune lacessit.*"[2]

"Good!" he said.

The wine sparkled in his eyes and the bells jingled. My own fancy grew warm with the Medoc. We had passed through long walls of piled skeletons, with casks and puncheons intermingling, into the inmost recesses of the catacombs. I paused again, and this time I made bold to sieze Fortunato by an arm above the elbow.

"The nitre!" I said; "see, it increases. It hangs like moss upon the vaults. We are below the river's bed. The drops of moisture trickle among the bones. Come, we will go back ere it is too late. Your cough——"

"It is nothing," he said; "let us go on. But first, another draught of the Medoc."

I broke and reached him a flagon of De Grâve. He emptied it at a breath. His eyes flashed with a fierce light. He laughed and threw the bottle upwards with a gesticulation I did not understand.

I looked at him in surprise. He repeated the movement—a grotesque one.

"You do not comprehend?" he said.

2. "No one attacks me with impunity."

"Not I," I replied.

"Then you are not of the brotherhood."

"How?"

"You are not of the masons."

"Yes, yes," I said; "yes, yes."

"You? Impossible! A mason?"

"A mason," I replied.

"A sign," he said, "a sign."

"It is this," I answered, producing from beneath the folds of my *roquelaire* a trowel.

"You jest," he exclaimed, recoiling a few paces. "But let us proceed to the Amontillado."

"Be it so," I said, replacing the tool beneath the cloak and again offering him my arm. He leaned upon it heavily. We continued our route in search of the Amontillado. We passed through a range of low arches, descended, passed on, and descending again, arrived at a deep crypt, in which the foulness of the air caused our flambeaux rather to glow than flame.

At the most remote end of the crypt there appeared another less spacious. Its walls had been lined with human remains, piled to the vault overhead, in the fashion of the great catacombs of Paris. Three sides of this interior crypt were still ornamented in this manner. From the fourth side the bones had been thrown down, and lay promiscuously upon the earth, forming at one point a mound of some size. Within the wall thus exposed by the displacing of the bones, we perceived a still interior crypt or recess, in depth about four feet, in width three, in height six or seven. It seemed to have been constructed for no especial use within itself, but formed merely the interval between two of the colossal supports of the roof of the catacombs, and was backed by one of their circumscribing walls of solid granite.

It was in vain that Fortunato, uplifting his dull torch, endeavoured to pry into the depth of the recess. Its termination the feeble light did not enable us to see.

"Proceed," I said; "herein is the Amontillado. As for Luchresi——"

"He is an ignoramus," interrupted my friend, as he stepped unsteadily forward, while I followed immediately at his heels. In an instant he had reached the extremity of the niche, and finding his progress arrested by the rock, stood stupidly bewildered. A moment more and I had fettered him to the granite. In its surface were two iron staples, distant from each other about two feet, horizontally. From one of these depended a short chain, from the other a padlock. Throwing the links about his waist, it was but the work of a few seconds to secure it. He was too much astounded to resist. Withdrawing the key I stepped back from the recess.

"Pass your hand," I said, "over the wall; you cannot help feeling the nitre. Indeed, it is *very* damp. Once more let me *implore* you to return. No? Then I must positively leave you. But I must first render you all the little attentions in my power."

"The Amontillado!" ejaculated my friend, not yet recovered from his astonishment.

"True," I replied; "the Amontillado."

As I said these words I busied myself among the pile of bones of which I have before spoken. Throwing them aside, I soon uncovered a quantity of building stone and mortar. With these materials and with the aid of my trowel, I began vigorously to wall up the entrance of the niche.

I had scarcely laid the first tier of the masonry when I discovered that the intoxication of Fortunato had in a great measure worn off. The earliest indication I had of this was a low moaning cry from the depth of the recess. It was *not* the cry of a drunken man. There was a long and obstinate silence. I laid the second tier, and the third, and the fourth; and then I heard the furious vibrations of the chain. The noise lasted for several minutes, during which, that I might hearken to it with the more satisfaction, I ceased my labours and sat down upon the bones. When at last the clanking subsided, I resumed the trowel, and finished without interruption the fifth, the sixth, and the seventh tier. The wall was now nearly upon a level with my breast. I again paused, and holding the flambeaux over the mason-work, threw a few feeble rays upon the figure within.

A succession of loud and shrill screams, bursting suddenly from the throat of the chained form, seemed to thrust me violently back. For a brief moment I hesitated, I trembled. Unsheathing my rapier, I began to grope with it about the recess; but the thought of an instant reassured me. I placed my hand upon the solid fabric of the catacombs, and felt satisfied. I reapproached the wall; I replied to the yells of him who clamoured. I re-echoed, I aided, I surpassed them in volume and in strength. I did this, and the clamourer grew still.

It was now midnight, and my task was drawing to a close. I had completed the eighth, the ninth and the tenth tier. I had finished a portion of the last and the eleventh; there remained but a single stone to be fitted and plastered in. I struggled with its weight; I placed it partially in its destined position. But now there came from out the niche a low laugh that erected the hairs upon my head. It was succeeded by a sad voice, which I had difficulty in recognizing as that of the noble Fortunato. The voice said—

"Ha! ha! ha!—he! he! he!—a very good joke, indeed—an excellent jest. We will have many a rich laugh about it at the palazzo—he! he! he!— over our wine—he! he! he!"

"The Amontillado!" I said.

"He! he! he!—he! he! he!—yes, the Amontillado. But is it not getting late? Will not they be awaiting us at the palazzo, the Lady Fortunato and the rest? Let us be gone."

"Yes," I said, "let us be gone."

"*For the love of God, Montresor!*"

"Yes," I said, "for the love of God."

But to these words I hearkened in vain for a reply. I grew impatient. I called aloud—

"Fortunato!"

No answer. I called again—

"Fortunato!"

No answer still. I thrust a torch through the remaining aperture and let it fall within. There came forth in return only a jingling of the bells. My heart grew sick; it was the dampness of the catacombs that made it so. I hastened to make an end of my labour. I forced the last stone into its position; I plastered it up.

Against the new masonry I re-erected the old rampart of bones. For the half of a century no mortal has disturbed them. *In pace requiescat!*[3]

3. "May he rest in peace."

Fact Questions and Exercises

[handwritten: prided himself on his connoisseurship of wine. He likes wine]

1. What is Fortunato's "weak point"? Why does it make him vulnerable to the speaker's revenge?   *He likes wine too much*
2. In one or two brief sentences, state the plot of the story.   *Maneuvering Fortunato to meet his death.*
3. Who or what is "Amontillado"?   *Wine*
4. During what season of the year and in what country does the story take place? What facts give you this information?   *Carnival season, Italy*
5. Describe the way in which Fortunato is dressed.   *Costume*
6. Describe the speaker's coat of arms.
7. On page 22, the speaker pulls a trowel from beneath his cloak and makes a joke about "masons." What is the speaker's real reason for having the trowel with him?   *To brick the entry way*
8. Describe the place to which the speaker leads Fortunato.   *Crypt*
9. Which line in the story lets you know that the speaker's crime is not discovered and that he escapes retribution?   *Next to last*
10. In the context of the story, what do these words mean—immolation, pipe, nitre, catacombs?

For Discussion and Writing

1. Analyze the speaker's character. Is he subtle and intelligent? Is he obvious and uneducated? What are his motives for revenge? Which passages give clues to what the speaker hates about Fortunato? Which passages reveal that the speaker knows how to take advantage of other people's weaknesses? How does he lead Fortunato into the trap? Does the story reveal the speaker's age and physical appearance? Are these facts important? Why or why not?
2. Discuss some of the things that Poe might be using as symbols in the story. How, for instance, does the Montresors' coat of arms relate to the story? Are the skeletons and catacombs symbols, or are they simply part of an appropriate setting? What is the significance of the way in which Fortunato is dressed? Are the symbols very important to the story?
3. Analyze some of the factors that make you enjoy or dislike the story. Is the plot important? Does the setting create an interesting atmosphere or mood? Is there any suspense for the reader, or do you know from the beginning what is going to happen in the story? Does the character of the speaker intrigue you? Do you like him? Does the fact that "revenge" is a more or less universal feeling have any bearing on your reaction to the story? How so?
4. Is Poe's writing style straightforward and easy to understand? Does it sometimes get in your way in trying to read the story? Explain.

Nathaniel Hawthorne [1804–1864]

Hawthorne was born in Salem, Massachusetts, the son of a sea captain. He attended Bowdoin College from 1821 to 1825. Thereafter, until 1839, he lived in near-seclusion in Salem. His first novel, *Fanshawe* (1828), was a complete failure; not until years later would Hawthorne establish his reputation as a significant writer. *The Scarlet Letter* (1850) and subsequent novels brought him fame, and from 1853 to 1857 he served as United States Consul at Liverpool, England. In his fiction Hawthorne uses symbols to explore the mind or soul. Some see the resulting ambiguity as a defect in Hawthorne's art, others as a source of power and meaning. Among his works are *The House of the Seven Gables* (1851), *The Blithedale Romance* (1853), and *The Marble Faun* (1860).

Young Goodman Brown

Young Goodman Brown came forth at sunset, into the street of Salem village, but put his head back, after crossing the threshold, to exchange a parting kiss with his young wife. And Faith, as the wife was aptly named, thrust her own pretty head into the street, letting the wind play with the pink ribbons of her cap, while she called to Goodman Brown.

"Dearest heart," whispered she, softly and rather sadly, when her lips were close to his ear, "prithee, put off your journey until sunrise, and sleep in your own bed to-night. A lone woman is troubled with such dreams and such thoughts, that she's afeard of herself, sometimes. Pray, tarry with me this night, dear husband, of all nights in the year!" *[foreshadowing]*

"My love and my Faith," replied young Goodman Brown, "of all nights in the year, this one night must I tarry away from thee. My journey, as thou callest it, forth and back again, must needs be done 'twixt now and sunrise. What, my sweet, pretty wife, dost thou doubt me already, and we but three months married!"

"Then God bless you!" said Faith with the pink ribbons, "and may you find all well, when you come back." *[?]*

"Amen!" cried Goodman Brown. "Say thy prayers, dear Faith, and go to bed at dusk, and no harm will come to thee."

So they parted; and the young man pursued his way, until, being about to turn the corner by the meeting-house, he looked back and saw the head of Faith still peeping after him, with a melancholy air, in spite of her pink ribbons.

"Poor little Faith!" thought he, for his heart smote him. "What a wretch am I, to leave her on such an errand! She talks of dreams, too. Methought, as she spoke, there was trouble in her face, as if a dream had warned her what work is to be done to-night. But no, no! 't would kill her to think it. Well; she's a blessed angel on earth; and after this one night, I'll cling to her skirts and follow her to Heaven." *[Resolve for the future]*

With this excellent resolve for the future, Goodman Brown felt himself justified in making more haste on his present evil purpose. He had taken a dreary road, darkened by all the gloomiest trees of the forest, which barely stood aside to let the narrow path creep through, and closed immediately behind. It was as lonely as could be; and there is this peculiarity in such a solitude, that the traveller knows not who may be concealed by the innumerable trunks and the thick boughs overhead; so that, with lonely footsteps, he may yet be passing through an unseen multitude.

"There may be a devilish Indian behind every tree," said Goodman Brown to himself; and he glanced fearfully behind him, as he added, "What if the devil himself should be at my very elbow!"

His head being turned back, he passed a crook of the road, and looking forward again, behind the figure of a man, in grave and decent attire, seated at the foot of an old tree. He arose at Goodman Brown's approach, and walked onward, side by side with him.

"You are late, Goodman Brown," said he. "The clock of the Old South was striking, as I came through Boston; and that is full fifteen minutes agone."

"Faith kept me back awhile," replied the young man, with a tremor in his voice, caused by the sudden appearance of his companion, though not wholly unexpected.

It was now deep dusk in the forest, and deepest in that part of it where these two were journeying. As nearly as could be discerned, the second traveller was about fifty years old, apparently in the same rank of life as Goodman Brown, and bearing a considerable resemblance to him, though perhaps more in expression than features. Still, they might have been taken for father and son. And yet, though the elder person was as simply clad as the younger, and as simple in manner too, he had an indescribable air of one who knew the world, and would not have felt abashed at the governor's dinner-table, or in King William's[1] court, were it possible that his affairs should call him thither. But the only thing about him that could be fixed upon as remarkable, was his staff, which bore the likeness of a great black snake, so curiously wrought, that it might almost be seen to twist and wriggle itself like a living serpent. This, of course, must have been an ocular deception, assisted by the uncertain light.

"Come, Goodman Brown!" cried his fellow-traveller, "this is a dull pace for the beginning of a journey. Take my staff, if you are so soon weary."

"Friend," said the other, exchanging his slow pace for a full stop, "having kept covenant by meeting thee here, it is my purpose now to return whence I came. I have scruples, touching the matter thou wot'st of."

"Sayest thou so?" replied he of the serpent, smiling apart. "Let us walk on, nevertheless, reasoning as we go, and if I convince thee not, thou shalt turn back. We are but a little way in the forest, yet."

"Too far, too far!" exclaimed the goodman, unconsciously resuming his walk. "My father never went into the woods on such an errand, nor his father before him. We have been a race of honest men and good Christians, since the days of the martyrs. And shall I be the first of the name of Brown that ever took this path and kept—"

"Such company, thou wouldst say," observed the elder person, interrupting his pause. "Well said, Goodman Brown! I have been as well acquainted with your family as with ever a one among the Puritans; and that's no trifle to say. I

---

1. King William III, who reigned in England from 1689 to 1702.

helped your grandfather, the constable, when he lashed the Quaker woman so smartly through the streets of Salem. And it was I that brought your father a pitch-pine knot, kindled at my own hearth, to set fire to an Indian village, in King Philip's war.[2] They were my good friends, both; and many a pleasant walk have we had along this path, and returned merrily after midnight. I would fain be friends with you, for their sake."

"If it be as thou sayest," replied Goodman Brown, "I marvel they never spoke of these matters. Or, verily, I marvel not, seeing that the least rumor of the sort would have driven them from New England. We are a people of prayer, and good works to boot, and abide no such wickedness."

"Wickedness or not," said the traveller with the twisted staff, "I have a very general acquaintance here in New England. The deacons of many a church have drunk the communion wine with me; the selectmen, of divers towns, make me their chariman; and a majority of the Great and General Court are firm supporters of my interest. The governor and I, too—but these are state secrets."

"Can this be so!" cried Goodman Brown, with a stare of amazement at his undisturbed companion. "Howbeit, I have nothing to do with the governor and council; they have their own ways, and are no rule for a simple husbandman like me. But, were I to go on with thee, how should I meet the eye of that good old man, our minister, at Salem village? Oh, his voice would make me tremble, both Sabbath-day and lecture-day!"

Thus far, the elder traveller had listened with due gravity, but now burst into a fit of irrepressible mirth, shaking himself so violently, that his snakelike staff actually seemed to wriggle in sympathy.

"Ha, ha, ha!" shouted he, again and again; then composing himself, "Well, go on, Goodman Brown, go on; but, prithee, don't kill me with laughing!"

"Well, then, to end the matter at once," said Goodman Brown, considerably nettled, "there is my wife, Faith. It would break her dear little heart; and I'd rather break my own!"

"Nay, if that be the case," answered the other, "e'en go thy ways, Goodman Brown. I would not, for twenty old women like the one hobbling before us, that Faith should come to any harm."

As he spoke, he pointed his staff at a female figure on the path, in whom Goodman Brown recognized a very pious and exemplary dame, who had taught him his catechism in youth, and was still his moral and spiritual adviser, jointly with the minister and Deacon Gookin.

"A marvel, truly, that Goody Cloyse should be so far in the wilderness, at nightfall!" said he. "But, with your leave, friend, I shall take a cut through the woods, until we have left this Christian woman behind. Being a stranger to you, she might ask whom I was consorting with, and whither I was going."

"Be it so," said his fellow-traveller. "Betake you to the woods, and let me keep the path."

Accordingly, the young man turned aside, but took care to watch his companion, who advanced softly along the road, until he had come within a staff's length of the old dame. She, meanwhile, was making the best of her way, with singular speed for so aged a woman, and mumbling some indistinct words, a

2. Metacomet (King Philip) led the last Indian resistance in New England.

prayer, doubtless, as she went. The traveller put forth his staff, and touched her withered neck with what seemed the serpent's tail.

"The devil!" screamed the pious old lady.

"Then Goody Cloyse knows her old friend?" observed the traveller, confronting her, and leaning on his writhing stick.

"Ah, forsooth, and is it your worship, indeed?" cried the good dame. "Yea, truly is it, and in the very image of my old gossip, Goodman Brown, the grandfather of the silly fellow that now is. But, would your worship believe it? My broomstick hath strangely disappeared, stolen, as I suspect, by that unhanged witch, Goody Cory, and that, too, when I was all anointed with the juice of smallage and cinque-foil and wolf's-bane—"

"Mingled with fine wheat and the fat of a new-born babe," said the shape of old Goodman Brown.

"Ah, your worship knows the recipe," cried the old lady, cackling aloud. "So, as I was saying, being all ready for the meeting, and no horse to ride on, I made up my mind to foot it; for they tell me there is a nice young man to be taken into communion to-night. But now your good worship will lend me your arm, and we shall be there in a twinkling."

"That can hardly be," answered her friend. "I may not spare you my arm, Goody Cloyse, but here is my staff, if you will."

So saying, he threw it down at her feet, where, perhaps, it assumed life, being one of the rods which its owner had formerly lent to the Egyptian Magi. Of this fact, however, Goodman Brown could not take cognizance. He had cast his eyes in astonishment, and looking down again, beheld neither Goody Cloyse nor the serpentine staff, but his fellow-traveller alone, who waited for him as calmly as if nothing had happened.

"That old woman taught me my catechism!" said the young man; and there was a world of meaning in this simple comment.

They continued to walk onward, while the elder traveller exhorted his companion to make good speed and persevere in the path, discoursing so aptly, that his arguments seemed rather to spring up in the bosom of his auditor, than to be suggested by himself. As they went he plucked a branch of maple, to serve for a walking-stick, and began to strip it of the twigs and little boughs, which were wet with evening dew. The moment his fingers touched them, they became strangely withered and dried up, as with a week's sunshine. Thus the pair proceeded, at a good free pace, until suddenly, in a gloomy hollow of the road, Goodman Brown sat himself down on the stump of a tree, and refused to go any farther.

"Friend," said he, stubbornly, "my mind is made up. Not another step will I budge on this errand. What if a wretched old woman do choose to go to the devil, when I thought she was going to Heaven! Is that any reason why I should quit my dear Faith, and go after her?"

"You will think better of this by and by," said his acquaintance, composedly. "Sit here and rest yourself awhile; and when you feel like moving again, there is my staff to help you along."

Without more words, he threw his companion the maple stick, and was as speedily out of sight as if he had vanished into the deepening gloom. The young man sat a few moments by the roadside, applauding himself greatly, and thinking with how clear a conscience he should meet the minister, in his morning walk, nor shrink from the eye of good old Deacon Gookin. And what calm sleep would be his, that very night, which was to have been spent so wickedly, but purely and sweetly now, in the arms of Faith! Amidst these pleasant and praiseworthy meditations, Goodman Brown heard the tramp of horses along the road, and deemed it advisable to conceal himself within the verge of the forest, conscious of the guilty purpose that had brought him thither, though now so happily turned from it.

On came the hoof-tramps and the voices of the riders, two grave old voices, conversing soberly as they drew near. These mingled sounds appeared to pass along the road, within a few yards of the young man's hiding-place; but owing, doubtless, to the depth of the gloom, at that particular spot, neither the travellers nor their steeds were visible. Though their figures brushed the small boughs by the wayside, it could not be seen that they intercepted, even for a moment, the faint gleam from the strip of bright sky, athwart which they must have passed. Goodman Brown alternately crouched and stood on tiptoe, pulling aside the branches, and thrusting forth his head as far as he durst, without discerning so much as a shadow. It vexed him the more, because he could have sworn, were such a thing possible, that he recognized the voices of the minister and Deacon Gookin, jogging along quietly, as they were wont to do, when bound to some ordination or ecclesiastical council. While yet within hearing, one of the riders stopped to pluck a switch.

"Of the two, reverend Sir," said the voice like the deacon's, "I had rather miss an ordination dinner than to-night's meeting. They tell me that some of our community are to be here from Falmouth and beyond, and others from Connecticut and Rhode Island; besides several of the Indian powwows, who, after their fashion, know almost as much deviltry as the best of us. Moreover, there is a goodly young woman to be taken into communion."

"Mighty well, Deacon Gookin!" replied the solemn old tones of the minister. "Spur up, or we shall be late. Nothing can be done, you know, until I get on the ground."

The hoofs clattered again, and the voices, talking so strangely in the empty air, passed on through the forest, where no church had ever been gathered, nor solitary Christian prayed. Whither, then, could these holy men be journeying, so deep into the heathen wilderness? Young Goodman Brown caught hold of a tree, for support, being ready to sink down on the ground, faint and over-burthened with the heavy sickness of his heart. He looked up to the sky, doubting whether there really was a Heaven above him. Yet, there was the blue arch, and the stars brightening in it.

"With Heaven above, and Faith below, I will yet stand firm against the devil!" cried Goodman Brown.

While he still gazed upward, into the deep arch of the firmament, and had lifted his hands to pray, a cloud, though no wind was stirring, hurried across the zenith, and hid the brightening stars. The blue sky was still visible, except directly overhead, where this black mass of cloud was sweeping swiftly northward. Aloft in the air, as if from the depths of the cloud, came a confused and doubtful sound of voices. Once, the listener fancied that he could distinguish the accents of townspeople of his own, men and women, both pious and ungodly, many of whom he had met at the communion-table, and had seen others rioting at the tavern. The next moment, so indistinct were the sounds, he doubted whether he had heard aught but the murmur of the old forest, whispering without a wind. Then came a stronger swell of those familiar tones, heard daily in the sunshine, at Salem village, but never, until now, from a cloud at night. There was one voice, of a young woman, uttering lamentations, yet with an uncertain sorrow, and entreating for some favor, which, perhaps, it would grieve her to obtain. And all the unseen multitude, both saints and sinners, seemed to encourage her onward.

"Faith!" shouted Goodman Brown, in a voice of agony and desperation; and the echoes of the forest mocked him, crying—"Faith! Faith!" as if bewildered wretches were seeking her, all through the wilderness.

The cry of grief, rage, and terror was yet piercing the night, when the unhappy husband held his breath for a response. There was a scream, drowned immediately in a louder murmur of voices fading into far-off laughter, as the dark cloud swept away, leaving the clear and silent sky above Goodman Brown. But something fluttered lightly down through the air, and caught on the branch of a tree. The young man seized it and beheld a pink ribbon.

"My Faith is gone!" cried he, after one stupefied moment. "There is no good on earth, and sin is but a name. Come, devil! for to thee is this world given."

And maddened with despair, so that he laughed loud and long, did Goodman Brown grasp his staff and set forth again, at such a rate, that he seemed to fly along the forest path, rather than to walk or run. The road grew wilder and drearier, and more faintly traced, and vanished at length, leaving him in the heart of the dark wilderness, still rushing onward, with the instinct that guides mortal man to evil. The whole forest was peopled with frightful sounds: the creaking of the trees, the howling of wild beasts, and the yell of Indians; while, sometimes, the wind tolled like a distant church bell, and sometimes gave a broad roar around the traveller, as if all Nature was laughing him to scorn. But he was himself the chief horror of the scene, and shrank not from its other horrors.

"Ha! ha! ha!" roared Goodman Brown, when the wind laughed at him. "Let us hear which will laugh loudest! Think not to frighten me with your deviltry! Come witch, come wizard, come Indian powwow, come devil himself! and here comes Goodman Brown. You may as well fear him as he fear you!"

In truth, all through the haunted forest, there could be nothing more frightful than the figure of Goodman Brown. On he flew, among the black pines, brandishing his staff with frenzied gestures, now giving vent to an inspiration of horrid blasphemy, and now shouting forth such laughter, as set all the echoes of the forest laughing like demons around him. The fiend in his own shape is less hideous, than when he rages in the breast of man. Thus sped the demoniac on his course, until, quivering among the tress, he saw a red light before him, as when the felled trunks and branches of a clearing have been set on fire, and throw up their lurid blaze against the sky, at the hour of midnight. He paused, in a lull of the tempest that had driven him onward, and heard the swell of what seemed a hymn, rolling solemnly from a distance, with the weight of many voices. He knew the tune. It was a familiar one in the choir of the village meeting-house. The verse died heavily away, and was lengthened by a chorus, not of human voices, but of all the sounds of the benighted wilderness, pealing in awful harmony together. Goodman Brown cried out; and his cry was lost to his own ear, by its unison with the cry of the desert.

In the interval of silence, he stole forward, until the light glared full upon his eyes. At one extremity of an open space, hemmed in by the dark wall of the forest, arose a rock, bearing some rude, natural resemblance either to an altar or a pulpit, and surrounded by four blazing pines, their tops aflame, their stems untouched, like candles at an evening meeting. The mass of foliage, that had overgrown the summit of the rock, was all on fire, blazing high into the night, and fitfully illuminating the whole field. Each pendent twig and leafy festoon was in a blaze. As the red light arose and fell, a numerous congregation alternately shone forth, then disappeared in shadow, and again grew, as it were, out of the darkness, peopling the heart of the solitary woods at once.

"A grave and dark-clad company!" quoth Goodman Brown.

In truth, they were such. Among them, quivering to-and-fro, between gloom and splendor, appeared faces that would be seen, next day, at the council-board of the province, and others which, Sabbath after Sabbath, looked devoutly heavenward, and benignantly over the crowded pews, from the holiest pulpits in the land. Some affirm, that the lady of the governor was there. At least, there were high dames well known to her, and wives of honored husbands, and widows a great multitude, and ancient maidens, all of excellent repute, and fair young girls, who trembled lest their mothers should espy them. Either the sudden gleams of light, flashing over the obscure field, bedazzled Goodman Brown, or he recognized a score of the church members of Salem village, famous for their especial sanctity. Good old Deacon Gookin had arrived, and waited at the skirts of that venerable saint, his reverend pastor. But, irreverently consorting with these grave, reputable, and pious people, these elders of the church, these chaste dames and dewy virgins, there were men of dissolute lives and women of spotted fame, wretches given over to all mean and filthy vice, and suspected even of horrid crimes. It was strange to see, that the good shrank not from the wicked, nor were the sinners abashed by the saints. Scattered, also, among their pale-faced enemies, were the Indian priests, or powwows, who had often scared their native forest with more hideous incantations than any known to English witchcraft.

"But, where is Faith?" thought Goodman Brown; and, as hope came into his heart, he trembled.

Another verse of the hymn arose, a slow and mournful strain, such as the pious love, but joined to words which expressed all that our nature can conceive of sin, and darkly hinted at far more. Unfathomable to mere mortals is the lore of fiends. Verse after verse was sung, and still the chorus of the desert swelled between, like the deepest tone of a mighty organ. And, with the final peal of that dreadful anthem, there came a sound, as if the roaring wind, the rushing streams, the howling beasts, and every other voice of the unconverted wilderness were mingling and according with the voice of guilty man, in homage to the prince of all. The four blazing pines threw up a loftier flame, and obscurely discovered shapes and visages of horror on the smoke-wreaths, above the impious assembly. At the same moment, the fire on the rock shot redly forth, and formed a glowing arch above its base, where now appeared a figure. With reverence be it spoken, the apparition bore no slight similitude, both in garb and manner, to some grave divine of the New England churches.

"Bring forth the converts!" cried a voice, that echoed through the field and rolled into the forest.

At the word, Goodman Brown stepped forth from the shadow of the trees, and approached the congregation, with whom he felt a loathful brotherhood, by the sympathy of all that was wicked in his heart. He could have well-nigh sworn, that the shape of his own dead father beckoned him to advance, looking downward from a smoke-wreath, while a woman, with dim features of despair, threw out her hand to warn him back. Was it his mother? But he had no power to retreat one step, nor to resist, even in thought, when the minister and good old Deacon Gookin seized his arms, and led him to the blazing rock. Thither came also the slender form of a veiled female, led between Goody Cloyse, that pious teacher of the catechism, and Martha Carrier, who had received the devil's promise to be queen of hell. A rampant hag was she! And there stood the proselytes, beneath the canopy of fire.

"Welcome, my children," said the dark figure, "to the communion of your race! Ye have found, thus young, your nature and your destiny. My children, look behind you!"

They turned; and flashing forth, as it were, in a sheet of flame, the fiend-worshippers were seen; the smile of welcome gleamed darkly on every visage.

"There," resumed the sable form, "are all whom ye have reverenced from youth. Ye deemed them holier than yourselves, and shrank from your own sin, contrasting it with their lives of righteousness and prayerful aspirations heavenward. Yet, here are they all, in my worshipping assembly! This night it shall be granted you to know their secret deeds; how hoary-bearded elders of the church have whispered wanton words to the young maids of their households; how many a woman, eager for widow's weeds, has given her husband a drink at bedtime, and let him sleep his last sleep in her bosom; how beardless youths have made haste to inherit their father's wealth; and how fair damsels—blush not, sweet ones!—have dug little graves in the garden, and bidden me, the sole guest, to an infant's funeral. By the sympathy of your human hearts for sin, ye shall scent out all the places—whether in church, bedchamber, street, field, or forest—where crime has been committed, and shall exult to behold the whole earth one stain of guilt, one mighty blood-spot. Far more than this! It shall be yours to penetrate, in every bosom, the deep mystery of sin, the fountain of all wicked arts, and which inexhaustibly supplies more evil impulses than human power—than my power, at its utmost!—can make manifest in deeds. And now, my children, look upon each other."

They did so; and by the blaze of the hell-kindled torches, the wretched man beheld his Faith, and the wife her husband, trembling before that unhallowed altar.

"Lo! there ye stand, my children," said the figure, in a deep and solemn tone, almost sad, with its despairing awfulness, as if his once angelic nature could yet mourn for our miserable race. "Depending upon one another's hearts, ye had still hoped that virtue were not all a dream! Now are ye undeceived!—Evil is the nature of mankind. Evil must be your only happiness. Welcome, again, my children, to the communion of your race!"

"Welcome!" repeated the fiend-worshippers, in one cry of despair and triumph.

And there they stood, the only pair, as it seemed, who were yet hesitating on the verge of wickedness, in this dark world. A basin was hollowed, naturally, in the rock. Did it contain water, reddened by the lurid light? or was it blood? or, perchance, a liquid flame? Herein did the Shape of Evil dip his hand, and prepare to lay the mark of baptism upon their foreheads, that they might be partakers of the mystery of sin, more conscious of the secret guilt of others, both in deed and thought, than they could now be of their own. The husband cast one look at his pale wife, and Faith at him. What polluted wretches would the next glance show them to each other, shuddering alike at what they disclosed and what they saw!

"Faith! Faith!" cried the husband. "Look up to Heaven, and resist the Wicked One!"

Whether Faith obeyed, he knew not. Hardly had he spoken, when he found himself amid calm night and solitude, listening to a roar of the wind, which died heavily away through the forest. He staggered against the rock, and felt it chill and damp, while a hanging twig, that had been all on fire, besprinkled his cheek with the coldest dew.

The next morning, young Goodman Brown came slowly into the street of Salem village staring around him like a bewildered man. The good old minister was taking a walk along the grave-yard, to get an appetite for breakfast and meditate his sermon, and bestowed a blessing, as he passed, on Goodman Brown. He shrank from the venerable saint, as if to avoid an anathema. Old Deacon Gookin was at domestic worship, and the holy words of his prayer were heard through the open window. "What God doth the wizard pray to?" quoth Goodman Brown. Goody Cloyse, that excellent old Christian, stood in the early sunshine, at her own lattice, catechising a little girl, who had brought her a pint of morning's milk. Goodman Brown snatched away the child, as from the grasp of the fiend himself. Turning the corner by the meetinghouse, he spied the head of Faith, with the pink ribbons, gazing anxiously forth, and bursting into such joy at sight of him that she skipt along the street, and almost kissed her husband before the whole village. But Goodman Brown looked sternly and sadly into her face, and passed on without a greeting.

Had Goodman Brown fallen asleep in the forest, and only dreamed a wild dream of a witch-meeting?

Be it so, if you will. But, alas! it was a dream of evil omen for young Goodman Brown. A stern, a sad, a darkly meditative, a distrustful, if not a desperate man did he become, from the night of that fearful dream. On the Sabbath day, when the congregation were singing a holy psalm, he could not listen, because an anthem of sin rushed loudly upon his ear, and drowned all the blessed strain. When the minister spoke from the pulpit, with power and fervid eloquence, and with his hand on the open Bible, of the sacred truths of our religion, and of saint-like lives and triumphant deaths, and of future bliss or misery unutterable, then did Goodman Brown turn pale, dreading lest the roof should thunder down upon the gray blasphemer and his hearers. Often, awaking suddenly at midnight, he shrank from the bosom of Faith, and at morning or eventide, when the family knelt down at prayer, he scowled, and muttered to himself, and gazed sternly at his wife, and turned away. And when he had lived long, and was borne to his grave, a hoary corpse, followed by Faith, an aged woman, and children and grand-children, a goodly procession, besides neighbors not a few, they carved no hopeful verse upon his tombstone; for his dying hour was gloom.

Fact Questions and Exercises

1. In what village do Goodman and Faith live? When does the story take place?
2. What color is the ribbon in Faith's hair? Does this ribbon appear later in the story?
3. How long have Faith and Goodman been married?
4. Describe the man Goodman meets in the forest and who is to accompany him on his journey.
5. Hawthorne refers at one point to Goodman's ancestors. What have these ancestors done?
6. Who else do Goodman and the "second traveller" meet as they walk through the forest?
7. Who attends the meeting in the forest?
8. How does Goodman react to his experience in the forest?

For Discussion and Writing

1. What are the opposing forces causing the conflict in Goodman Brown? How does Hawthorne make one aware of these forces? Why does he never state clearly whether Goodman is dreaming?
2. Check the meaning of "allegory" in the Guide to Literary Terms. What allegorical qualities are found in "Young Goodman Brown"? Do the names of the characters offer any clues?
3. Faith and Goodman have been married for only a short while—they are still on their honeymoon, so to speak. How, then, can Faith's statement in paragraph two be interpreted? Also, in paragraph four, is Faith being sarcastic? How does the interpretation of these passages influence the overall interpretation of the story?
4. What are some of the dominant symbols in the story? How do you know that Hawthorne intends for the reader to see them as symbols? How do these symbols affect your interpretation of the story?
5. In one or two sentences, state the plot of "Young Goodman Brown." Does the statement reveal what the story is actually about?
6. "Had Goodman Brown fallen asleep in the forest, and only dreamed a wild dream of a witch-meeting?" By asking this question, Hawthorne expands the possible interpretations of the story. Do you think that Goodman's encounter with the witches was a "wild dream"? If so, what has driven Goodman to having such nightmares? What is the result of his "dream"?

Herman Melville [1819–1891]

Melville was born in New York City, the son of a successful businessman. After suffering financial reverses, the family moved to Albany, where Melville worked as a store clerk and school teacher. In 1841 he sailed on a whaling ship; a year later, he jumped ship and lived for a while among the natives of the Marquesas Islands. His experiences on the islands were the basis of his first novels: *Typee* (1846), *Omoo* (1847), and *Mardi* (1849). These early works brought Melville acclaim, but his masterpiece *Moby-Dick* (1851) was not popularly accepted and, in fact, alienated the reading public. He spent the remainder of his life in obscurity, working as a customs inspector on the New York docks. *Moby-Dick*, an allegorical tale of good and evil, is now considered to be a classic American novel.

Bartleby, the Scrivener

I am a rather elderly man. The nature of my avocations, for the last thirty years, has brought me into more than ordinary contact with what would seem an interesting and somewhat singular set of men, of whom, as yet, nothing, that I know of, has ever been written—I mean, the law-copyists, or scriveners. I have known very many of them, professionally and privately, and, if I pleased, could relate divers histories, at which good-natured gentlemen might smile, and sentimental souls might weep. But I waive the biographies of all other scriveners, for a few passages in the life of Bartleby, who was a scrivener, the strangest I ever saw, or heard of. While, of other law-copyists, I might write the complete life, of Bartleby nothing of that sort can be done. I believe that no materials exist, for a full and satisfactory biography of this man. It is an irreparable loss to literature. Bartleby was one of those beings of whom nothing is ascertainable, except from the original sources, and, in his case, those are very small. What my own astonished eyes saw of Bartleby, *that* is all I know of him, except, indeed, one vague report, which will appear in the sequel.

Ere introducing the scrivener, as he first appeared to me, it is fit I make some mention of myself, my employés, my business, my chambers, and general surroundings; because some such description is indispensable to an adequate understanding of the chief character about to be presented. Imprimis: I am a man who, from his youth upward, has been filled with a profound conviction that the easiest way of life is the best. Hence, though I belong to a profession proverbially energetic and nervous, even to turbulence, at times, yet nothing of that sort have I ever suffered to invade my peace. I am one of those unambitious lawyers who never addresses a jury, or in any way draws down public applause; but, in the cool tranquillity of a snug retreat, do a snug business among rich men's bonds, and mortgages, and title-deeds. All who know me, consider me an eminently safe man. The late John Jacob Astor, a personage little given to poetic enthusiasm, had no hesitation in pronouncing my first grand point to be prudence; my next, method. I do not speak it in vanity, but simply record the fact, that I was not unemployed in my profession by the late John Jacob Astor; a name which, I admit, I love to repeat; for it hath a rounded and orbicular sound to it, and rings like unto bullion. I will freely add, that I was not insensible to the late John Jacob Astor's good opinion.

Some time prior to the period at which this little history begins, my avocations had been largely increased. The good old office, now extinct in the State of New York, of a Master in Chancery, had been conferred upon me. It was not a very arduous office, but very pleasantly remunerative. I seldom lose my temper; much more seldom indulge in dangerous indignation at wrongs and outrages; but, I must be permitted to be rash here, and declare, that I consider the sudden and violent abrogation of the office of Master in Chancery, by the new Constitution, as a—premature act; inasmuch as I had counted upon a life-lease of the profits, whereas I only received those of a few short years. But this is by the way.

My chambers were upstairs, at No. — Wall Street. At one end, they looked upon the white wall of the interior of a spacious skylight shaft, penetrating the building from top to bottom.

This view might have been considered rather tame than otherwise, deficient in what landscape painters call "life." But, if so, the view from the other end of my chambers offered, at least, a contrast, if nothing more. In that direction, my windows commanded an unobstructed view of a lofty brick wall, black by age and everlasting shade; which wall required no spy-glass to bring out its lurking beauties, but, for the benefit of all near-sighted spectators, was pushed up to within ten feet of my window panes. Owing to the great height of the surrounding buildings, and my chambers being on the second floor, the interval between this wall and mine not a little resembled a huge square cistern.

At the period just preceding the advent of Bartleby, I had two persons as copyists in my employment, and a promising lad as an office-boy. First, Turkey; second, Nippers; third, Ginger Nut. These may seem names, the like of which are not usually found in the Directory. In truth, they were nicknames, mutually conferred upon each other by my three clerks, and were deemed expressive of their respective persons or characters. Turkey was a short, pursy Englishman, of about my own age—that is, somewhere not far from sixty. In the morning, one might say, his face was of a fine florid hue, but after twelve o'clock, meridian— his dinner hour—it blazed like a grate full of Christmas coals; and continued blazing—but, as it were, with a gradual wane—till six o'clock, P.M., or therea-bouts; after which, I saw no more of the proprietor of the face, which, gaining its meridian with the sun, seemed to set with it, to rise, culminate, and decline the following day, with the like regularity and undiminished glory. There are many singular coincidences I have known in the course of my life, not the least among which was the fact, that, exactly when Turkey displayed his fullest beams from his red and radiant countenance, just then, too, at that critical moment, began the daily period when I considered his business capacities as seriously disturbed for the remainder of the twenty-four hours. Not that he was absolutely idle, or averse to business, then; far from it. The difficulty was, he was apt to be altogether too energetic. There was a strange, inflamed, flurried, flighty reckless-ness of activity about him. He would be incautious in dipping his pen into his inkstand. All his blots upon my documents were dropped there after twelve o'clock, meridian. Indeed, not only would he be reckless, and sadly given to making blots in the afternoon, but, some days, he went further, and was rather noisy. At such times, too, his face flamed with augmented blazonry, as if cannel coal had been heaped on anthracite. He made an unpleasant racket with his chair; spilled his sand-box; in mending his pens, impatiently split them all to pieces, and threw them on the floor in a sudden passion; stood up, and leaned over his table, boxing his papers about in a most indecorous manner, very sad to behold in an elderly man like him. Nevertheless, as he was in many ways a most valuable person to me, and all the time before twelve o'clock, meridian, was the quickest, steadiest creature, too, accomplishing a great deal of work in a style not easily to be matched—for these reasons, I was willing to overlook his eccentricities, though, indeed, occasionally, I remonstrated with him. I did this very gently, however, because, though the civilest, nay, the blandest and most reverential of men in the morning, yet, in the afternoon, he was disposed, upon provocation, to be slightly rash with his tongue—in fact, insolent. Now, valuing his morning services as I did, and resolved not to lose them—yet, at the same time, made uncomfortable by his inflamed ways after twelve o'clock—and being a man of peace, unwilling by my admonitions to call forth unseemly retorts from him, I took upon me, one Saturday noon (he was always worse on Saturdays) to hint to him, very kindly, that, perhaps, now that he was growing old, it might be well to abridge his labours; in short, he need not come to my chambers after twelve o'clock, but, dinner over, had best go home to his lodgings, and rest himself till tea-time. But no; he insisted upon his afternoon devotions. His countenance became intolerably fervid, as he oratorically assured me— gesticulating with a long ruler at the other end of the room—that if his services in the morning were useful, how indispensable, then, in the afternoon?

"With submission, sir," said Turkey, on this occasion, "I consider myself your right-hand man. In the morning I but marshal and deploy my columns; but in the afternoon I put myself at their head, and gallantly charge the foe, thus"—and he made a violent thrust with the ruler.

"But the blots, Turkey," intimated I.

"True; but, with submission, sir, behold these hairs! I am getting old. Surely, sir, a blot or two of a warm afternoon is not to be severely urged against gray hairs. Old age—even if it blot the page—is honourable. With submission, sir we *both* are getting old."

This appeal to my fellow-feeling was hardly to be resisted. At all events, I saw that go he would not. So, I made up my mind to let him stay, resolving, nevertheless, to see to it that, during the afternoon, he had to do with my less important papers.

Nippers, the second on my list, was a whiskered, sallow, and, upon the whole, rather piratical-looking young man, of about five-and-twenty. I always deemed him the victim of two evil powers—ambition and indigestion. The ambition was evinced by a certain impatience of the duties of a mere copyist, an unwarrantable usurpation of strictly professional affairs, such as the original drawing up of legal documents. The indigestion seemed betokened in an occasional nervous testiness and grinning irritability, causing the teeth to audibly grind together over mistakes committed in copying; unnecessary maledictions, hissed, rather than spoken, in the heat of business; and especially by a continual discontent with the height of the table where he worked. Though of a very ingenious mechanical turn, Nippers could never get this table to suit him. He put chips under it, blocks of various sorts, bits of pasteboard, and at last went so far as to attempt an exquisite adjustment, by final pieces of folded blotting-paper. But no invention would answer. If, for the sake of easing his back, he brought the

Nippers

Ambitious

table lid at a sharp angle well up toward his chin, and wrote there like a man using the steep roof of a Dutch house for his desk, then he declared that it stopped the circulation in his arms. If now he lowered the table to his waistbands, and stooped over it in writing, then there was a sore aching in his back. In short, the truth of the matter was, Nippers knew not what he wanted. Or, if he wanted anything, it was to be rid of a scrivener's table altogether. Among the manifestations of his diseased ambition was a fondness he had for receiving visits from certain ambiguous-looking fellows in seedy coats, whom he called his clients. Indeed, I was aware that not only was he, at times, considerable of a ward-politician, but he occasionally did a little business at the Justices' courts, and was not unknown on the steps of the Tombs. I have good reason to believe, however, that one individual who called upon him at my chambers, and who, with a grand air, he insisted was his client, was no other than a dun, and the alleged title-deed, a bill. But, with all his failings, and the annoyances he caused me, Nippers, like his compatriot Turkey, was a very useful man to me; wrote a neat, swift hand; and, when he chose, was not deficient in a gentlemanly sort of deportment. Added to this, he always dressed in a gentlemanly sort of way; and so, incidentally, reflected credit upon my chambers. Whereas, with respect to Turkey, I had much ado to keep him from being a reproach to me. His clothes were apt to look oily, and smell of eating-houses. He wore his pantaloons very loose and baggy in summer. His coats were execrable; his hat not to be handled. But while the hat was a thing of indifference to me, inasmuch as his natural civility and deference, as a dependent Englishman, always led him to doff it the moment he entered the room, yet his coat was another matter. Concerning his coats, I reasoned with him; but with no effect. The truth was, I suppose, that a man with so small an income could not afford to sport such a lustrous face and a lustrous coat at one and the same time. As Nippers once observed, Turkey's money went chiefly for red ink. One winter day, I presented Turkey with a highly respectable-looking coat of my own—a padded gray coat, of a most comfortable warmth, and which buttoned straight up from the knee to the neck. I thought Turkey would appreciate the favour, and abate his rashness and obstreperousness of afternoons. But no; I verily believe that buttoning himself up in so downy and blanket-like a coat had a pernicious effect upon him—upon the same principle that too much oats are bad for horses. In fact, precisely as a rash, restive horse is said to feel his oats, so Turkey felt his coat. It made him insolent. He was a man whom prosperity harmed.

Though, concerning the self-indulgent habits of Turkey, I had my own private surmises, yet, touching Nippers, I was well persuaded that, whatever might be his faults in other respects, he was, at least, a temperate young man. But, indeed, nature herself seemed to have been his vintner, and, at his birth, charged him so thoroughly with an irritable, brandy-like disposition, that all subsequent potations were needless. When I consider how, amid the stillness of my chambers, Nippers would sometimes impatiently rise from his seat, and stooping over his table, spread his arms wide apart, seize the whole desk, and move it, and jerk it, with a grim, grinding motion on the floor, as if the table were a perverse voluntary agent, intent on thwarting and vexing him, I plainly perceive that, for Nippers, brandy-and-water were altogether superfluous.

It was fortunate for me that, owing to its peculiar cause—indigestion—the irritability and consequent nervousness of Nippers were mainly observable in the morning, while in the afternoon he was comparatively mild. So that, Turkey's paroxysms only coming on about twelve o'clock, I never had to do with their eccentricities at one time. Their fits relieved each other, like guards. When Nippers's was on, Turkey's was off; and *vice versa*. This was a good natural arrangement, under the circumstances.

Ginger Nut, the third on my list, was a lad, some twelve years old. His father was a carman, ambitious of seeing his son on the bench instead of a cart, before he died. So he sent him to my office, as student at law, errand-boy, cleaner and sweeper, at the rate of one dollar a week. He had a little desk to himself, but he did not use it much. Upon inspection, the drawer exhibited a great array of the shells of various sorts of nuts. Indeed, to this quick-witted youth, the whole noble science of the law was contained in a nutshell. Not the least among the employments of Ginger Nut, as well as one which he discharged with the most alacrity, was his duty as cake and apple purveyor for Turkey and Nippers. Copying law-papers being proverbially a dry, husky sort of business, my two scriveners were fain to moisten their mouths very often with Spitzenbergs, to be had at the numerous stalls nigh the Custom House and Post Office. Also, they sent Ginger Nut very frequently for that peculiar cake—small, flat, round, and very spicy—after which he had been named by them. Of a cold morning, when business was but dull, Turkey would gobble up scores of these cakes, as if they were mere wafers—indeed, they sell them at the rate of six or eight for a penny—the scrape of his pen blending with the crunching of the crisp particles in his mouth. Of all the fiery afternoon blunders and flurried rashnesses of Turkey, was his once moistening a ginger-cake between his lips, and clapping it on to a mortgage, for a seal. I came within an ace of dismissing him then. But he mollified me by making an oriental bow, and saying—"With submission, sir, it was generous of me to find you in stationery on my own account."

Now my original business—that of a conveyancer and title-hunter, and drawer-up of recondite documents of all sorts—was considerably increased by receiving the master's office. There was now great work for scriveners. Not only must I push the clerks already with me, but I must have additional help.

In answer to my advertisement, a motionless young man one morning stood upon my office threshold, the door being open, for it was summer. I can see that figure now—pallidly neat, pitiably respectable, incurably forlorn! It was Bartleby. *(pale)*

After a few words touching his qualifications, I engaged him, glad to have among my corps of copyists a man of so singularly sedate an aspect, which I thought might operate beneficially upon the flighty temper of Turkey, and the fiery one of Nippers.

I should have stated before that ground-glass folding doors divided my premises into two parts, one of which was occupied by my scriveners, the other by myself. According to my humour, I threw open these doors, or closed them. I resolved to assign Bartleby a corner by the folding-doors, but on my side of them, so as to have this quiet man within easy call, in case any trifling thing was to be done. I placed his desk close up to a small side-window in that part of the room, a window which originally had afforded a lateral view of certain grimy back-yards and bricks, but which, owing to subsequent erections, commanded at present no view at all, though it gave some light. Within three feet of the panes was a wall, and the light came down from far above, between two lofty buildings, as from a

[margin annotation: Bartleby is closed behind walls also]

very small opening in a dome. Still further to a satisfactory arrangement, I procured a high green folding-screen, which might entirely isolate Bartleby from my sight, though not remove him from my voice. And thus, in a manner, privacy and society were conjoined.

At first, Bartleby did an extraordinary quantity of writing. As if long famishing for something to copy, he seemed to gorge himself on my documents. There was no pause for digestion. He ran a day and night line, copying by sun-light and by candle-light. I should have been quite delighted with his application, had he been cheerfully industrious. But he wrote on silently, palely, mechanically.

It is, of course, an indispensable part of a scrivener's business to verify the accuracy of his copy, word by word. Where there are two or more scriveners in an office, they assist each other in this examination, one reading from the copy, the other holding the original. It is a very dull, wearisome, and lethargic affair. I can readily imagine that, to some sanguine temperaments, it would be altogether intolerable. For example, I cannot credit that the mettlesome poet, Byron, would have contentedly sat down with Bartleby to examine a law document, of say, five hundred pages, closely written in a crimpy hand.

Now and then, in the haste of business, it had been my habit to assist in comparing some brief document myself, calling Turkey or Nippers for this purpose. One object I had, in placing Bartleby so handy to me behind the screen, was, to avail myself of his services on such trivial occasions. It was on the third day, I think, of his being with me, and before any necessity had arisen for having his own writing examined, that, being much hurried to complete a small affair I had in hand, I abruptly called to Bartleby. In my haste and natural expectancy of instant compliance, I sat with my head bent over the original on my desk, and my right hand sideways, and somewhat nervously extended with the copy, so that, immediately upon emerging from his retreat, Bartleby might snatch it and proceed to business without the least delay.

In this very attitude did I sit when I called to him, rapidly stating what it was I wanted him to do—namely, to examine a small paper with me. Imagine my surprise, nay, my consternation, when, without moving from his privacy, Bartleby, in a singularly mild, firm voice, replied, "I would prefer not to."

I sat a while in perfect silence, rallying my stunned faculties. Immediately it occurred to me that my ears had deceived me, or Bartleby had entirely misunderstood my meaning. I repeated my request in the clearest tone I could assume; but in quite as clear a one came the previous reply, "I would prefer not to."

"Prefer not to," echoed I, rising in high excitement, and crossing the room with a stride. "What do you mean? Are you moon-struck? I want you to help me compare this sheet here—take it," and I thrust it toward him.

"I would prefer not to," said he.

I looked at him steadfastly. His face was leanly composed; his gray eye dimly calm. Not a wrinkle of agitation rippled him. Had there been the least uneasiness, anger, impatience, or impertinence in his manner; in other words, had there been anything ordinarily human about him, doubtless I should have violently dismissed him from the premises. But as it was, I should have as soon thought of turning my pale plaster-of-paris bust of Cicero out of doors. I stood gazing at him a while, as he went on with his own writing, and then reseated myself at my desk. This is very strange, thought I. What had one best do? But my business hurried me. I concluded to forget the matter for the present, reserving it for my future leisure. So calling Nippers from the other room, the paper was speedily examined.

A few days after this, Bartleby concluded four lengthy documents, being quadruplicates of a week's testimony taken before me in my High Court of Chancery. It became necessary to examine them. It was an important suit, and great accuracy was imperative. Having all things arranged, I called Turkey, Nippers, and Ginger Nut, from the next room, meaning to place the four copies in the hands of my four clerks, while I should read from the original. Accordingly, Turkey, Nippers, and Ginger Nut had taken their seats in a row, each with his document in his hand, when I called to Bartleby to join this interesting group.

"Bartleby! quick, I am waiting."

I heard a slow scrape of his chair legs on the uncarpeted floor, and soon he appeared standing at the entrance of his hermitage.

"What is wanted?" said he mildly.

"The copies, the copies," said I hurriedly. "We are going to examine them. There"—and I held toward him the fourth quadruplicate.

"I would prefer not to," he said, and gently disappeared behind the screen.

For a few moments I was turned into a pillar of salt, standing at the head of my seated column of clerks. Recovering myself, I advanced toward the screen, and demanded the reason for such extraordinary conduct.

"*Why* do you refuse?"

"I would prefer not to."

With any other man I should have flown outright into a dreadful passion, scorned all further words, and thrust him ignominiously from my presence. But there was something about Bartleby that not only strangely disarmed me, but, in a wonderful manner, touched and disconcerted me. I began to reason with him.

"These are your own copies we are about to examine. It is labour saving to you, because one examination will answer for your four papers. It is common usage. Every copyist is bound to help examine his copy. Is it not so? Will you not speak? Answer!"

"I prefer not to," he replied in a flute-like tone. It seemed to me that, while I had been addressing him, he carefully revolved every statement that I made; fully comprehended the meaning; could not gainsay the irresistible conclusion; but, at the same time, some paramount consideration prevailed with him to reply as he did.

"You are decided, then, not to comply with my request—a request made according to common usage and common sense?"

He briefly gave me to understand, that on that point my judgment was sound. Yes: his decision was irreversible.

It is not seldom the case that, when a man is browbeaten in some unprecedented and violently unreasonable way, he begins to stagger in his own plainest faith. He begins, as it were, vaguely to surmise that, wonderful as it may be, all the justice and all the reason is on the other side. Accordingly, if any disinterested persons are present, he turns to them for some reinforcement for his own faltering mind.

He liked Bartleby 'cause they had things in common

"Turkey," said I, "what do you think of this? Am I not right?"

"With submission, sir," said Turkey, in his blandest tone, "I think that you are."

"Nippers," said I, "what do *you* think of it?"

"I think I should kick him out of the office."

(The reader, of nice perceptions, will here perceive that, it being morning, Turkey's answer is couched in polite and tranquil terms, but Nippers's replies in ill-tempered ones. Or, to repeat a previous sentence, Nippers's ugly mood was on duty, and Turkey's off.)

"Ginger Nut," said I, willing to enlist the smallest suffrage in my behalf, "what do *you* think of it?"

"I think, sir, he's a little *luny*," replied Ginger Nut, with a grin.

"You hear what they say," said I, turning toward the screen, "come forth and do your duty."

But he vouchsafed no reply. I pondered a moment in sore preplexity. But once more business hurried me. I determined again to postpone the consideration of this dilemma to my future leisure. With a little trouble we made out to examine the papers without Bartleby, though at every page of two Turkey deferentially dropped his opinion, that this proceeding was quite out of the common; while Nippers, twitching in his chair with a dyspeptic nervousness, ground out, between his set teeth, occasional hissing maledictions against the stubborn oaf behind the screen. And for his (Nippers's) part, this was the first and the last time he would do another man's business without pay.

Meanwhile Bartleby sat in his hermitage, oblivious to everything but his own peculiar business there.

Some days passed, the scrivener being employed upon another lengthy work. His late remarkable conduct led me to regard his ways narrowly. I observed that he never went to dinner; indeed, that he never went anywhere. As yet I had never, of my personal knowledge, known him to be outside of my office. He was a perpetual sentry in the corner. At about eleven o'clock though, in the morning, I noticed that Ginger Nut would advance toward the opening in Bartleby's screen, as if silently beckoned thither by a gesture invisible to me where I sat. The boy would then leave the office, jingling a few pence, and reappear with a handful of ginger-nuts, which he delivered in the hermitage, receiving two of the cakes for his trouble.

He lives, then, on ginger-nuts, thought I; never eats a dinner, properly speaking; he must be a vegetarian, then; but no; he never eats even vegetables, he eats nothing but ginger-nuts. My mind then ran on in reveries concerning the probable effects upon the human constitution of living entirely on ginger-nuts. Ginger-nuts are so called, because they contain ginger as one of their peculiar constituents, and the final flavouring one. Now, what was ginger? A hot, spicy thing. Was Bartleby hot and spicy? Not at all. Ginger, then, had no effect upon Bartleby. Probably he preferred it should have none.

Nothing so aggravates an earnest person as a passive resistance. If the individual so resisted be of a not inhumane temper, and the resisting one perfectly harmless in his passivity, then, in the better moods of the former, he will endeavour charitably to construe to his imagination what proves impossible to be solved by his judgment. Even so, for the most part, I regarded Bartleby and his ways. Poor fellow! thought I, he means no mischief; it is plain he intends no insolence; his aspect sufficiently evinces that his eccentricities are involuntary. He is useful to me. I can get along with him. If I turn him away, the chances are he will fall in with some less-indulgent employer, and then he will be rudely treated, and perhaps driven forth miserably to starve. Yes. Here I can cheaply purchase a delicious self-approval. To befriend Bartleby; to humour him in his strange wilfulness, will cost me little or nothing, while I lay up in my soul what will eventually prove a sweet morsel for my conscience. But this mood was not invariable with me. The passiveness of Bartleby sometimes irritated me. I felt strangely goaded on to encounter him in new opposition—to elicit some angry spark from him answerable to my own. But, indeed, I might as well have essayed to strike fire with my knuckles against a bit of Windsor soap. But one afternoon the evil impulse in me mastered me, and the following little scene ensued:—

"Bartleby," said I, "when those papers are all copied, I will compare them with you."

"I would prefer not to."

"How? Surely you do not mean to persist in that mulish vagary?"

No answer.

I threw open the folding-doors near by, and turning upon Turkey and Nippers, exclaimed:

"Bartleby a second time says, he won't examine his papers. What do you think of it, Turkey?"

It was afternoon, be it remembered. Turkey sat glowing like a brass boiler; his bald head steaming; his hands reeling among his blotted papers.

"Think of it?" roared Turkey; "I think I'll just step behind his screen, and black his eyes for him!"

So saying, Turkey rose to his feet and threw his arms into a pugilistic position. He was hurrying away to make good his promise, when I detained him, alarmed at the effect of incautiously rousing Turkey's combativeness after dinner.

"Sit down, Turkey," said I, "and hear what Nippers has to say. What do you think of it, Nippers? Would I not be justified in immediately dismissing Bartleby?"

"Excuse me, that is for you to decide, sir. I think his conduct quite unusual, and, indeed, unjust, as regards Turkey and myself. But it may only be a passing whim."

"Ah," exclaimed I, "you have strangely changed your mind, then—you speak very gently of him now."

"All beer," cried Turkey; "gentleness is effects of beer—Nippers and I dined together to-day. You see how gentle I am, sir. Shall I go and black his eyes?"

"You refer to Bartleby, I suppose. No, not to-day, Turkey," I replied; "pray, put up your fists."

I closed the doors, and again advanced toward Bartleby. I felt additional incentives tempting me to my fate. I burned to be rebelled against again. I remembered that Bartleby never left the office.

"Bartleby," said I, "Ginger Nut is away; just step around to the Post Office, won't you? (it was but a three minutes' walk), and see if there is anything for me."

"I would prefer not to."

"You *will* not?"

"I *prefer* not."

I staggered to my desk, and sat there in a deep study. My blind inveteracy returned. Was there any other thing in which I could procure myself to be ignominiously repulsed by this lean, penniless wight?—my hired clerk? What added thing is there, perfectly reasonable, that he will be sure to refuse to do?

"Bartleby!"

No answer.

"Bartleby," in a louder tone.

No answer.

"Bartleby," I roared.

Like a very ghost, agreeably to the laws of magical invocation, at the third summons, he appeared at the entrance of his hermitage.

"Go to the next room, and tell Nippers to come to me."

"I prefer not to," he respectfully and slowly said, and mildly disappeared.

"Very good, Bartleby," said I, in a quiet sort of serenely-severe self-possessed tone, intimating the unalterable purpose of some terrible retribution very close at hand. At the moment I half intended something of the kind. But upon the whole, as it was drawing toward my dinner-hour, I thought it best to put on my hat and walk home for the day, suffering much from perplexity and distress of mind.

Shall I acknowledge it? The conclusion of this whole business was, that it soon became a fixed fact of my chambers, that a pale young scrivener, by the name of Bartleby, had a desk there; that he copied for me at the usual rate of four cents a folio (one hundred words); but he was permanently exempt from examining the work done by him, that duty being transferred to Turkey and Nippers, out of compliment, doubtless, to their superior acuteness; moreover, said Bartleby was never, on any account, to be dispatched on the most trivial errand of any sort; and that even if entreated to take upon him such a matter, it was generally understood that he would "prefer not to"—in other words, that he would refuse point-blank.

As days passed on, I became considerably reconciled to Bartleby. His steadiness, his freedom from all dissipation, his incessant industry (except when he chose to throw himself into a standing revery behind his screen), his great stillness, his unalterableness of demeanour under all circumstances, made him a valuable acquisition. One prime thing was this—*he was always there*—first in the morning, continually through the day, and the last at night. I had a singular confidence in his honesty. I felt my most precious papers perfectly safe in his hands. Sometimes, to be sure, I could not, for the very soul of me, avoid falling into sudden spasmodic passions with him. For it was exceeding difficult to bear in mind all the time those strange peculiarities, privileges, and unheard-of exemptions, forming the tacit stipulations on Bartleby's part under which he remained in my office. Now and then, in the eagerness of dispatching pressing business, I would inadvertently summon Bartleby, in a short, rapid tone, to put his finger, say, on the incipient tie of a bit of red tape with which I was about compressing some papers. Of course, from behind the screen the usual answer, "I prefer not to," was sure to come; and then, how could a human creature, with the common infirmities of our nature, refrain from bitterly exclaiming upon such perverseness—such unreasonableness. However, every added repulse of this sort which I received only tended to lessen the probability of my repeating the inadvertence.

Here it must be said, that according to the custom of most legal gentlemen occupying chambers in densely populated lawbuildings, there were several keys to my door. One was kept by a woman residing in the attic, which person weekly scrubbed and daily swept and dusted my apartments. Another was kept by Turkey for convenience sake. The third I sometimes carried in my own pocket. The fourth I knew not who had.

Now, one Sunday morning I happened to go to Trinity Church, to hear a celebrated preacher, and finding myself rather early on the ground I thought I would walk round to my chambers for a while. Luckily I had my key with me; but upon applying it to the lock, I found it resisted by something inserted from the inside. Quite surprised, I called out; when to my consternation a key was turned from within; and thrusting his lean visage at me, and holding the door ajar, the apparition of Bartleby appeared, in his shirt-sleeves, and otherwise in a strangely tattered dishabille, saying quietly that he was sorry, but he was deeply engaged just then, and—preferred not admitting me at present. In a brief word or two, he moreover added, that perhaps I had better walk round the block two or three times, and by that time he would probably have concluded his affairs.

Now, the utterly unsurmised appearance of Bartleby, tenanting my law-chambers of a Sunday morning, with his cadaverously gentlemanly noncha-lance, yet withal firm and self-possesed, had such a strange effect upon me, that incontinently I slunk away from my own door, and did as desired. But not without sundry twinges of impotent rebellion against the mild effrontery of this unaccountable scrivener. Indeed, it was his wonderful mildness chiefly, which not only disarmed me, but unmanned me as it were. For I consider that one, for the time, is a sort of unmanned when he tranquilly permits his hired clerk to dictate to him, and order him away from his own premises. Furthermore, I was full of uneasiness as to what Bartleby could possibly be doing in my office in his shirt sleeves, and in an otherwise dismantled condition of a Sunday morning. Was anything amiss going on? Nay, that was out of the question. It was not to be thought of for a moment that Bartleby was an immoral person. But what could he be doing there?—copying? Nay again, whatever might be his eccentricities, Bartleby was an eminently decorous person. He would be the last man to sit down to his desk in any state approaching to nudity. Besides, it was Sunday; and there was something about Bartleby that forbade the supposition that he would by any secular occupation violate the proprieties of the day.

Nevertheless, my mind was not pacified; and full of a restless curiosity, at last I returned to the door. Without hindrance I inserted my key, opened it, and entered. Bartleby was not to be seen. I looked round anxiously, peeped behind his screen; but it was very plain that he was gone. Upon more closely examining the place, I surmised that for an indefinite period Bartleby must have ate, dressed, and slept in my office, and that, too, without plate, mirror, or bed. The cushioned seat of a rickety old sofa in one corner bore the faint impress of a lean, reclining form. Rolled away under his desk, I found a blanket; under the empty grate a blacking box and brush; on a chair, a tin basin, with soap and a ragged towel; in a newspaper a few crumbs of ginger-nuts and a morsel of cheese. Yes, thought I, it is evident enough that Bartleby has been making his home here, keeping bachelor's hall all by himself. Immediately then the thought came sweeping across me, what miserable friendlessness and loneliness are here revealed! His poverty is great; but his solitude, how horrible! Think of it. Of a Sunday, Wall Street is deserted as Petra;[1] and every night of every day it is an emptiness. This building, too, which of week-days hums with industry and life, at nightfall echoes with sheer vacancy, and all through Sunday is forlorn. And here Bartleby makes his home; sole spectator of a solitude which he has seen all-populous—a sort of innocent and transformed Marius[2] brooding among the ruins of Carthage!

For the first time in my life a feeling of overpowering stinging melancholy seized me. Before, I had never experienced aught but a not unpleasing sadness. The bond of a common humanity now drew me irresistibly to gloom. A fraternal melancholy! For both I and Bartleby were sons of Adam. I remembered the bright silks and sparkling faces I had seen that day, in gala trim, swan-like sailing down the Mississippi of Broadway; and I contrasted them with the pallid copyist, and thought to myself, Ah, happiness courts the light, so we deem the world is gay; but misery hides aloof, so we deem that misery there is none. These sad fancyings—chimeras, doubtless, of a sick and silly brain—led on to other and more special thoughts, concerning the eccentricities of Bartleby. Presentiments of strange discoveries hovered round me. The scrivener's pale form appeared to me laid out, among uncaring strangers, in its shivering winding-sheet.

Suddenly I was attracted by Bartleby's closed desk, the key in open sight left in the lock.

I mean no mischief, seek the gratification of no heartless curiosity, thought I; besides, the desk is mine, and its contents, too, so I will make bold to look within. Everything was methodically arranged, the papers smoothly placed. The pigeonholes were deep, and removing the files of documents, I groped into their recesses. Presently I felt something there, and dragged it out. It was an old bandanna handkerchief, heavy and knotted. I opened it, and saw it was a savings-bank.

I now recalled all the quiet mysteries which I had noted in the man. I remembered that he never spoke but to answer; that, though at intervals he had considerable time to himself, yet I had never seen him reading—no, not even a newspaper; that for long periods he would stand looking out, at his pale window behind the screen, upon the dead brick wall; I was quite sure he never visited any refectory or eating-house; while his pale face clearly indicated that he never drank beer like Turkey, or tea and coffee even, like other men; that he never went anywhere in particular that I could learn; never went out for a walk, unless, indeed, that was the case at present; that he had declined telling who he was, or whence he came, or whether he had any relatives in the world; that though so thin and pale, he never complained of ill health. And more than all, I remembered a certain unconscious air of pallid—how shall I call it?—of pallid haughtiness, say, or rather an austere reserve about him which had positively awed me into my tame compliance with his eccentricities, when I had feared to ask him to do the slightest incidental thing for me, even though I might know,

1. A city in Palestine. Petra was not rediscovered until 1812, after having been lost since biblical times.
2. Caius Marius (155–86 B.C.), a Roman general who was sent into exile by his superiors.

from his long-continued motionlessness, that behind his screen he must be standing in one of those dead-wall reveries of his.

Revolving all these things, and coupling them with the recently discovered fact, that he made my office his constant abiding-place and home, and not forgetful of his morbid moodiness; revolving all these things, a prudential feeling began to steal over me. My first emotions had been those of pure melancholy and sincerest pity; but just in proportion as the forlornness of Bartleby grew and grew to my imagination, did that same melancholy merge into fear, that pity into repulsion. So true it is, and so terrible, too, that up to a certain point the thought or sight of misery enlists our best affections; but, in certain special cases, beyond that point it does not. They err who would assert that invariably this is owing to the inherent selfishness of the human heart. It rather proceeds from a certain hopelessness of remedying excessive and organic ill. To a sensitive being, pity is not seldom pain. And when at last it is perceived that such pity cannot lead to effectual succour, commonsense bids the soul be rid of it. What I saw that morning persuaded me that the scrivener was the victim of innate and incurable disorder. I might give alms to his body; but his body did not pain him; it was his soul that suffered, and his soul I could not reach.

I did not accomplish the purpose of going to Trinity Church that morning. Somehow, the things I had seen disqualified me for the time from church-going. I walked homeward, thinking what I would do with Bartleby. Finally, I resolved upon this—I would put certain calm questions to him the next morning, touching his history, etc., and if he declined to answer them openly and unreservedly (and I supposed he would prefer not), then to give him a twenty-dollar bill over and above whatever I might owe him, and tell him his services were no longer required; but that if in any other way I could assist him, I would be happy to do so, especially if he desired to return to his native place, wherever that might be, I would willingly help to defray the expenses. Moreover, if, after reaching home, he found himself at any time in want of aid, a letter from him would be sure of a reply.

The next morning came.

"Bartleby," said I, gently calling to him behind his screen.

No reply.

"Bartleby," said I, in a still gentler tone, "come here; I am not going to ask you to do anything you would prefer not to do—I simply wish to speak to you."

Upon this he noiselessly slid into view.

"Will you tell me, Bartleby, where you were born?"

"I would prefer not to."

"Will you tell me *anything* about yourself?"

"I would prefer not to."

"But what reasonable objection can you have to speak to me? I feel friendly toward you."

He did not look at me while I spoke, but kept his glance fixed upon my bust of Cicero, which, as I then sat, was directly behind me, some six inches above my head.

"What is your answer, Bartleby?" said I, after waiting a considerable time for a reply, during which his countenance remained immovable, only there was the faintest conceivable tremor of the white attenuated mouth.

"At present I prefer to give no answer," he said, and retired into his hermitage.

It was rather weak in me, I confess, but his manner, on this occasion, nettled me. Not only did there seem to lurk in it a certain calm disdain, but his perverseness seemed ungrateful, considering the undeniable good usage and indulgence he had received from me.

Again I sat ruminating what I should do. Mortified as I was at his behaviour, and resolved as I had been to dismiss him when I entered my office, nevertheless I strangely felt something superstitious knocking at my heart, and forbidding me to carry out my purpose, and denouncing me for a villain if I dared to breathe one bitter word against this forlornest of mankind. At last, familiarly drawing my chair behind his screen, I sat down and said: "Bartleby, never mind, then, about revealing your history; but let me entreat you, as a friend, to comply as far as may be with the usages of this office. Say now, you will help to examine papers to-morrow or next day: in short, say now, that in a day or two you will begin to be a little reasonable:—say so, Bartleby."

"At present I would prefer not to be a little reasonable," was his mildly cadaverous reply.

Just then the folding doors opened, and Nippers approached. He seemed suffering from an unusually bad night's rest, induced by severer indigestion than common. He overheard those final words of Bartleby.

"*Prefer not*, eh?" gritted Nippers—"I'd *prefer* him, if I were you, sir" addressing me—"I'd *prefer* him; I'd give him preferences, the stubborn mule! What is it, sir, pray, that he *prefers* not to do now?"

Bartleby moved not a limb.

"Mr. Nippers," said I, "I'd prefer that you would withdraw for the present."

Somehow, of late, I had got into the way of involuntarily using this word "prefer" upon all sorts of not exactly suitable occasions. And I trembled to think that my contact with the scrivener had already and seriously affected me in a mental way. And what further and deeper aberration might it not yet produce? This apprehension had not been without efficacy in determining me to summary measures.

As Nippers, looking very sour and sulky, was departing, Turkey blandly and deferentially approached.

"With submission, sir," said he, "yesterday I was thinking about Bartleby here, and I think that if he would but prefer to take a quart of good ale every day, it would do much toward mending him, and enabling him to assist in examining his papers."

"So you have got the word too," said I, slightly excited.

"With submission, what word, sir," asked Turkey, respectfully crowding himself into the contracted space behind the screen, and by so doing, making me jostle the scrivener. "What word, sir?"

"I would prefer to be left alone here," said Bartleby, as if offended at being mobbed in his privacy.

"*That's* the word, Turkey," said I—"*that's* it."

"Oh, *prefer*? oh yes—queer word. I never use it myself. But, sir, as I was saying, if he would but prefer——"

"Turkey," interrupted I, "you will please withdraw."

"Oh certainly, sir, if you prefer that I should."

As he opened the folding-door to retire, Nippers at his desk caught a glimpse of me, and asked whether I would prefer to have a certain paper copied on blue paper or white. He did not in the least roguishly accent the word prefer. It was plain that it involuntarily rolled from his tongue. I thought to myself, surely I must get rid of a demented man, who already has in some degree turned the tongues, if not the heads of myself and clerks. But I thought it prudent not to break the dismission at once.

The next day I noticed that Bartleby did nothing but stand at his window in his dead-wall revery. Upon asking him why he did not write, he said that he had decided upon doing no more writing.

"Why, how now? what next?" exclaimed I, "do no more writing?"

"No more."

"And what is the reason?"

"Do you not see the reason for yourself?" he indifferently replied.

I looked steadfastly at him, and perceived that his eyes looked dull and glazed. Instantly it occurred to me, that his unexampled diligence in copying by his dim window for the first few weeks of his stay with me might have temporarily impaired his vision.

I was touched. I said something in condolence with him. I hinted that of course he did wisely in abstaining from writing for a while; and urged him to embrace that opportunity of taking wholesome exercise in the open air. This, however, he did not do. A few days after this, my other clerks being absent, and being in a great hurry to dispatch certain letters by the mail, I thought that having nothing else earthly to do, Bartleby would surely be less inflexible than usual, and carry these letters to the Post Office. But he blankly declined. So, much to my inconvenience, I went myself.

Still added days went by. Whether Bartleby's eyes improved or not, I could not say. To all appearance, I thought they did. But when I asked him if they did, he vouchsafed no answer. At all events, he would do no copying. At last, in reply to my urgings, he informed me that he had permanently given up copying.

"What!" exclaimed I; "suppose your eyes should get entirely well—better than ever before—would you not copy then?"

"I have given up copying," he answered, and slid aside.

He remained as ever, a fixture in my chamber. Nay—if that were possible—he became still more of a fixture than before. What was to be done? He would do nothing in the office; why should he stay there? In plain fact, he had now become a millstone to me, not only useless as a necklace, but afflictive to bear. Yet I was sorry for him. I speak less than truth when I say that, on his own account, he occasioned me uneasiness. If he would but have named a single relative or friend, I would instantly have written, and urged their taking the poor fellow away to some convenient retreat. But he seemed alone, absolutely alone in the universe. A bit of wreck in the mid-Atlantic. At length, necessities connected with my business tyrannised over all other considerations. Decently as I could, I told Bartleby that in six days' time he must unconditionally leave the office. I warned him to take measures, in the interval, for procuring some other abode. I offered to assist him in this endeavour, if he himself would but take the first step toward a removal. "And when you finally quit me, Bartleby," added I, "I shall see that you go not away entirely unprovided. Six days from this hour, remember."

At the expiration of that period, I peeped behind the screen, and lo! Bartleby was there.

I buttoned up my coat, balanced myself; advanced slowly toward him, touched his shoulder, and said, "The time has come; you must quit this place; I am sorry for you; here is money; but you must go."

"I would prefer not," he replied, with his back still toward me.

"You *must*."

He remained silent.

Now I had an unbounded confidence in this man's common honesty. He had frequently restored to me sixpences and shillings carelessly dropped upon the floor, for I am apt to be very reckless in such shirt-button affairs. The proceeding, then, which followed will not be deemed extraordinary.

"Bartleby," said I, "I owe you twelve dollars on account; here are thirty-two; the odd twenty are yours—Will you take it?" and I handed the bills toward him.

But he made no motion.

"I will leave them here, then," putting them under a weight on the table. Then taking my hat and cane and going to the door, I tranquilly turned and added—"After you have removed your things from these offices, Bartleby, you will of course lock the door—since everyone is now gone for the day but you—and if you please, slip your key underneath the mat, so that I may have it in the morning. I shall not see you again; so good-bye to you. If, hereafter, in your new place of abode, I can be of any service to you, do not fail to advise me by letter. Good-bye, Bartleby, and fare you well."

But he answered not a word; like the last column of some ruined temple, he remained standing mute and solitary in the middle of the otherwise deserted room.

As I walked home in a pensive mood, my vanity got the better of my pity. I could not but highly plume myself on my masterly management in getting rid of Bartleby. Masterly I call it, and such it must appear to any dispassionate thinker. The beauty of my procedure seemed to consist in its perfect quietness. There was no vulgar bullying, no bravado of any sort, no choleric hectoring, and striding to and fro across the apartment, jerking out vehement commands for Bartleby to bundle himself off with his beggarly traps. Nothing of the kind. Without loudly bidding Bartleby depart—as an inferior genius might have done—I *assumed* the ground that depart he must; and upon that assumption built all I had to say. The more I thought over my procedure, the more I was charmed with it. Nevertheless, next morning, upon awakening, I had my doubts—I had somehow slept off the fumes of vanity. One of the coolest and wisest hours a man has, is just after he awakes in the morning. My procedure seemed as sagacious as ever—but only in theory. How it would prove in practice—there was the rub. It was truly a beautiful thought to have assumed Bartleby's departure; but, after all, that assumption was simply my own, and none of Bartleby's. The great point was, not whether I had assumed that he would quit me, but whether he would prefer so to do. He was more a man of preferences than assumptions.

After breakfast, I walked down town, arguing the probabilities *pro* and *con.* One moment I thought it would prove a miserable failure, and Bartleby would be found all alive at my office as usual; the next moment it seemed certain that I should find his chair empty. And so I kept veering about. At the corner of Broadway and Canal Street, I saw quite an excited group of people standing in earnest conversation.

"I'll take odds he doesn't," said a voice as I passed.

"Doesn't go?—done!" said I; "put up your money."

I was instinctively putting my hand in my pocket to produce my own, when I remembered that this was an election day. The words I had overheard bore no reference to Bartleby, but to the success or non-success of some candidate for the mayoralty. In my intent frame of mind, I had, as it were, imagined that all Broadway shared in my excitement, and were debating the same question with me. I passed on, very thankful that the uproar of the street screened my momentary absent-mindedness.

As I had intended, I was earlier than usual at my office door. I stood listening for a moment. All was still. He must be gone. I tried the knob. The door was locked. Yes, my procedure had worked to a charm; he indeed must be vanished. Yet a certain melancholy mixed with this: I was almost sorry for my brilliant success. I was fumbling under the doormat for the key, which Bartleby was to have left there for me, when accidentally my knee knocked against a panel, producing a summoning sound, and in response a voice came to me from within—"Not yet; I am occupied."

It was Bartleby.

I was thunderstruck. For an instant I stood like the man who, pipe in mouth, was killed one cloudless afternoon long ago in Virginia, by summer lightning; at his own warm open window he was killed, and remained leaning out there upon the dreamy afternoon, till someone touched him, when he fell.

"Not gone!" I murmured at last. But again obeying that wondrous ascendency which the inscrutable scrivener had over me, and from which ascendency, for all my chafing, I could not completely escape, I slowly went downstairs and out into the street, and while walking round the block, considered what I should next do in this unheard-of perplexity. Turn the man out by an actual thrusting I could not; to drive him away by calling him hard names would not do; calling in the police was an unpleasant idea; and yet, permit him to enjoy his cadaverous triumph over me—this, too, I could not think of. What was to be done? or, if nothing could be done, was there anything further that I could *assume* in the matter? Yes, as before I had prospectively assumed that Bartleby would depart, so now I might retrospectively assume that departed he was. In the legitimate carrying out of this assumption, I might enter my office in a great hurry, and pretending not to see Bartleby at all, walk straight against him as if he were air. Such a proceeding would in a singular degree have the appearance of a home-thrust. It was hardly possible that Bartleby could withstand such an application of the doctrine of assumptions. But upon second thoughts the success of the plan seemed rather dubious. I resolved to argue the matter over with him again.

"Bartleby," said I, entering the office, with a quietly severe expression, "I am seriously displeased. I am pained, Bartleby. I had thought better of you. I had imagined you of such a gentlemanly organisation, that in any delicate dilemma a slight hint would suffice—in short, an assumption. But it appears I am deceived. Why," I added, unaffectedly starting, "you have not even touched that money yet," pointing to it, just where I had left it the evening previous.

He answered nothing.

"Will you, or will you not, quit me?" I now demanded in a sudden passion, advancing close to him.

"I would prefer *not* to quit you," he replied, gently emphasising the *not.*

"What earthly right have you to stay here? Do you pay any rent? Do you pay my taxes? Or is this property yours?"

He answered nothing.

"Are you ready to go on and write now? Are your eyes recovered? Could you copy a small paper for me this morning? or help examine a few lines? or step round to the Post Office? In a word, will you do anything at all, to give a colouring to your refusal to depart the premises?"

He silently retired into his hermitage.

I was now in such a state of nervous resentment that I thought it but prudent to check myself at present from further demonstrations. Bartleby and I were alone. I remembered the tragedy of the unfortunate Adams and the still more unfortunate Colt in the solitary office of the latter;[3] and how poor Colt, being dreadfully incensed by Adams, and imprudently permitting himself to get wildly excited, was at unawares hurried into his fatal act—an act which certainly no man could possibly deplore more than the actor himself. Often it had occurred to me in my ponderings upon the subject, that had that altercation taken place in the public street, or at a private residence, it would not have terminated as it did. It was the circumstance of being alone in a solitary office, upstairs, of a building entirely unhallowed by humanising domestic associations—an uncarpeted office, doubtless, of a dusty, haggard sort of appearance—this it must have been, which greatly helped to enhance the irritable desperation of the hapless Colt.

But when this old Adam of resentment rose in me and tempted me concerning Bartleby, I grappled him and threw him. How? Why, simply by recalling the divine injunction: "A new commandment give I unto you, that ye love one another." Yes, this it was that saved me. Aside from higher considerations, charity often operates as a vastly wise and prudent principle—a great safeguard to its possessor. Men have committed murder for jealousy's sake, and anger's sake, and hatred's sake, and selfishness' sake, and spiritual pride's sake; but no man, that ever I heard of, ever committed a diabolical murder for sweet charity's sake. Mere self-interest, then, if no better motive can be enlisted, should, especially with high-tempered men, prompt all beings to charity and philanthropy. At any rate, upon the occasion in question, I strove to drown my exasperated feelings toward the scrivener by benevolently construing his conduct. Poor fellow, poor fellow! thought I, he don't mean anything; and besides, he has seen hard times, and ought to be indulged.

I endeavoured, also, immediately to occupy myself, and at the same time to comfort my despondency. I tried to fancy, that in the course of the morning, at such time as might prove agreeable to him, Bartleby, of his own free accord,

---

3. In 1842 John Colt murdered Samuel Adams in a fight concerning a woman. Colt committed suicide before he could be hanged.

would emerge from his hermitage and take up some decided line of march in the direction of the door. But no. Half-past twelve o'clock came; Turkey began to glow in the face, overturn his inkstand, and become generally obstreperous; Nippers abated down into quietude and courtesy; Ginger Nut munched his noon apple; and Bartleby remained standing at his window in one of his profoundest dead-wall reveries. Will it be credited? Ought I to acknowledge it? That afternoon I left the office without saying one further word to him.

Some days now passed, during which, at leisure intervals, I looked a little into "Edwards on the Will," and "Priestley on Necessity." Under the circumstances, those books induced a salutary feeling. Gradually I slid into the persuasion that these troubles of mine touching the scrivener, had been all predestinated from eternity, and Bartleby was billeted upon me for some mysterious purpose of an all-wise Providence, which it was not for a mere mortal like me to fathom. Yes, Bartleby, stay there behind your screen, thought I; I shall persecute you no more; you are harmless and noiseless as any of these old chairs; in short, I never feel so private as when I know you are here. At last I see it, I feel it; I penetrate to the predestinated purpose of my life. I am content. Others may have loftier parts to enact; but my mission in this world, Bartleby, is to furnish you with office-room for such period as you may see fit to remain.

I believe that this wise and blessed frame of mind would have continued with me, had it not been for the unsolicited and uncharitable remarks obtruded upon me by my professional friends who visited the rooms. But thus it often is, that the constant friction of illiberal minds wears out at last the best resolves of the more generous. Though to be sure, when I reflected upon it, it was not strange that people entering my office should be struck by the peculiar aspect of the unaccountable Bartleby, and so be tempted to throw out some sinister observations concerning him. Sometimes an attorney, having business with me, and calling at my office, and finding no one but the scrivener there, would undertake to obtain some sort of precise information from him touching my whereabouts; but without heeding his idle talk, Bartleby would remain standing immovable in the middle of the room. So after contemplating him in that position for a time, the attorney would depart, no wiser than he came.

Also, when a reference was going on, and the room full of lawyers and witnesses, and business driving fast, some deeply occupied legal gentleman present, seeing Bartleby wholly unemployed, would request him to run round to his (the legal gentleman's) office and fetch some papers for him. Thereupon, Bartleby would tranquilly decline, and yet remain idle as before. Then the lawyer would give a great stare, and turn to me. And what could I say? At last I was made aware that all through the circle of my professional acquaintance, a whisper of wonder was running round, having reference to the strange creature I kept at my office. This worried me very much. And as the idea came upon me of his possibly turning out a long-lived man, and keep occupying my chambers, and denying my authority; and perplexing my visitors; and scandalising my professional reputation; and casting a general gloom over the premises; keeping soul and body together to the last upon his savings (for doubtless he spent but half a dime a day), and in the end perhaps outlive me, and claim possession of my office by right of his perpetual occupancy: as all these dark anticipations crowded upon me more and more, and my friends continually intruded their relentless remarks upon the apparition in my room; a great change was wrought in me. I resolved to gather all my faculties together, and forever rid me of this intolerable incubus.

Ere revolving any complicated project, however, adapted to this end, I first simply suggested to Bartleby the propriety of his permanent departure. In a calm and serious tone, I commended the idea to his careful and mature consideration. But, having taken three days to meditate upon it, he apprised me, that his original determination remained the same; in short, that he still preferred to abide with me.

What shall I do? I now said to myself, buttoning up my coat to the last button. What shall I do? what ought I to do? what does conscience say I *should* do with this man, or rather, ghost. Rid myself of him, I must; go, he shall. But how? You will not thrust him, the poor, pale, passive mortal—you will not thrust such a helpless creature out of your door? you will not dishonour yourself by such cruelty? No, I will not, I cannot do that. Rather would I let him live and die here, and then mason up his remains in the wall. What, then, will you do? For all your coaxing, he will not budge. Bribes he leaves under your own paperweight on your table; in short, it is quite plain that he prefers to cling to you.

Then something severe, something unusual must be done. What! surely you will not have him collared by a constable, and commit his innocent pallor to the common jail? And upon what ground could you procure such a thing to be done?—a vagrant, is he? What! he a vagrant, a wanderer, who refuses to budge? It is because he will *not* be a vagrant, then, that you seek to count him *as a* vagrant. That is too absurd. No visible means of support; there I have him. Wrong again: for indubitably he *does* support himself, and that is the only unanswerable proof that any man can show of his possessing the means so to do. No more, then. Since he will not quit me, I must quit him. I will change my offices; I will move elsewhere, and give him fair notice, that if I find him on my new premises I will then proceed against him as a common trespasser.

Acting accordingly, next day I thus addressed him: "I find these chambers too far from the City Hall; the air is unwholesome. In a word, I propose to remove my offices next week, and shall no longer require your services. I tell you this now, in order that you may seek another place."

He made no reply, and nothing more was said.

On the appointed day I engaged carts and men, proceeded to my chambers, and, having but little furniture, everything was removed in a few hours. Throughout, the scrivener remained standing behind the screen, which I directed to be removed the last thing. It was withdrawn; and, being folded up like a huge folio, left him the motionless occupant of a naked room. I stood in the entry watching him a moment, while something from within me upbraided me.

I re-entered, with my hand in my pocket—and—and my heart in my mouth.

"Good-bye, Bartleby; I am going—good-bye, and God some way bless you; and take that," slipping something in his hand. But it dropped upon the floor, and then—strange to say—I tore myself from him whom I had so longed to be rid of.

Established in my new quarters, for a day or two I kept the door locked, and started at every footfall in the passages. When I returned to my rooms, after any little absence, I would pause at the threshold for an instant, and attentively listen ere applying my key. But these fears were needless. Bartleby never came nigh me.

I thought all was going well, when a perturbed-looking stranger visited me, inquiring whether I was the person who had recently occupied rooms at No. — Wall Street.

Full of forebodings, I replied that I was.

"Then, sir," said the stranger, who proved a lawyer, "you are responsible for the man you left there. He refuses to do any copying; he refuses to do anything; he says he prefers not to; and he refuses to quit the premises."

"I am very sorry, sir," said I, with assumed tranquillity, but an inward tremor, "but, really, the man you allude to is nothing to me—he is no relation or apprentice of mine, that you should hold me responsible for him."

"In mercy's name, who is he?"

"I certainly cannot inform you. I know nothing about him. Formerly I employed him as a copyist; but he has done nothing for me now for some time past."

"I shall settle him, then—good morning, sir."

Several days passed, and I heard nothing more; and, though I often felt a charitable prompting to call at the place and see poor Bartleby, yet a certain squeamishness, of I know not what, withheld me.

All is over with him, by this time, thought I at last, when, through another week, no further intelligence reached me. But, coming to my room the day after, I found several persons waiting at my door in a high state of nervous excitement.

"That's the man—here he comes," cried the foremost one, whom I recognised as the lawyer who had previously called upon me alone.

"You must take him away, sir, at once," cried a portly person among them, advancing upon me, and whom I knew to be the landlord of No. — Wall Street. "These gentlemen, my tenants, cannot stand it any longer; Mr. B——," pointing to the lawyer, "has turned him out of his room, and he now persists in haunting the building generally, sitting upon the banisters of the stairs by day, and sleeping in the entry by night. Everybody is concerned; clients are leaving the offices; some fears are entertained of a mob; something you must do, and that without delay."

Aghast at this torrent, I fell back before it, and would fain have locked myself in my new quarters. In vain I persisted that Bartleby was nothing to me—no more than to anyone else. In vain—I was the last person known to have anything to do with him, and they held me to the terrible account. Fearful, then, of being exposed in the papers (as one person present obscurely threatened), I considered the matter, and, at length, said, that if the lawyer would give me a confidential interview with the scrivener, in his (the lawyer's) own room, I would, that afternoon, strive my best to rid them of the nuisance they complained of.

Going upstairs to my old haunt, there was Bartleby silently sitting upon the banister at the landing.

"What are you doing here, Bartleby?" said I.

"Sitting upon the banister," he mildly replied.

I motioned him into the lawyer's room, who then left us.

"Bartleby," said I, "are you aware that you are the cause of great tribulation to me, by persisting in occupying the entry after being dismissed from the office?"

No answer.

"Now one of two things must take place. Either you must do something, or something must be done to you. Now what sort of business would you like to engage in? Would you like to re-engage in copying for someone"

"No; I would prefer not to make any change."

"Would you like a clerkship in a drygoods store?"

"There is too much confinement about that. No, I would not like a clerkship; but I am not particular."

"Too much confinement," I cried, "why, you keep yourself confined all the time!"

"I would prefer not to take a clerkship," he rejoined, as if to settle that little item at once.

"How would a bar-tender's business suit you? There is no trying of the eyesight in that."

"I would not like it at all; though, as I said before, I am not particular."

His unwonted wordiness inspirited me. I returned to the charge.

"Well, then, would you like to travel through the country collecting bills for the merchants? That would improve your health."

"No, I would prefer to be doing something else."

"How, then, would going as a companion to Europe, to entertain some young gentleman with your conversation—how would that suit you?"

"Not at all. It does not strike me that there is anything definite about that. I like to be stationary. But I am not particular."

"Stationary you shall be, then," I cried, now losing all patience, and, for the first time in all my exasperating connection with him, fairly flying into a passion. "If you do not go away from these premises before night, I shall feel bound—indeed, I *am* bound—to—to quit the premises myself!" I rather absurdly concluded, knowing not with what possible threat to try to frighten his immobility into compliance. Despairing of all further efforts, I was precipitately leaving him, when a final thought occurred to me—one which had not been wholly unindulged before.

"Bartleby," said I, in the kindest tone I could assume under such exciting circumstances, "will you go home with me now —not to my office, but my dwelling—and remain there till we can conclude upon some convenient arrangement for you at our leisure? Come, let us start now, right away."

"No; at present I would prefer not to make any change at all."

I answered nothing; but, effectually dodging everyone by the suddenness and rapidity of my flight, rushed from the building, ran up Wall Street toward Broadway, and, jumping into the first omnibus, was soon removed from pursuit. As soon as tranquillity returned, I distinctly perceived that I had now done all that I possibly could, both in respect to the demands of the landlord and his tenants, and with regard to my own desire and sense of duty, to benefit Bartleby, and shield him from rude persecution. I now strove to be entirely carefree and quiescent; and my conscience justified me in the attempt; though, indeed, it was not so successful as I could have wished. So fearful was I of being again hunted out by the incensed landlord and his exasperated tenants, that, surrendering my business to Nippers, for a few days, I drove about the upper part of the town and through the suburbs, in my rockaway; crossed over to Jersey City and Hoboken, and paid fugitive visits to Manhattanville and Astoria. In fact, I almost lived in my rockaway for the time.

When again I entered my office, lo, a note from the landlord lay upon the desk. I opened it with trembling hands. It informed me that the writer had sent to the police, and had Bartleby removed to the Tombs as a vagrant. Moreover, since I knew more about him than anyone else, he wished me to appear at that place, and make a suitable statement of the facts. These tidings had a conflicting effect upon me. At first I was indignant; but, at last, almost approved. The landlord's energetic summary disposition had led him to adopt a procedure which I do not think I would have decided upon myself; and yet, as a last resort, under such peculiar circumstances, it seemed the only plan.

As I afterward learned, the poor scrivener, when told that he must be conducted to the Tombs, offered not the slightest obstacle, but, in his pale, unmoving way, silently acquiesced.

Some of the compassionate and curious bystanders joined the party; and headed by one of the constables arm in arm with Bartleby, the silent procession filed its way through all the noise, and heat, and joy of the roaring thoroughfares at noon.

The same day I received the note, I went to the Tombs, or, to speak more properly, the Halls of Justice. Seeking the right officer, I stated the purpose of my call, and was informed that the individual I described was, indeed, within. I then assured the functionary that Bartleby was a perfectly honest man, and greatly to be compassionated, however unaccountably eccentric. I narrated all I knew, and closed by suggesting the idea of letting him remain in as indulgent confinement as possible, till something less harsh might be done—though, indeed, I hardly knew what. At all events, if nothing else could be decided upon, the almshouse must receive him. I then begged to have an interview.

Being under no disgraceful charge, and quite serene and harmless in all his ways, they had permitted him freely to wander about the prison, and, especially, in the enclosed grass-platted yards thereof. And so I found him there, standing all alone in the quietest of the yards, his face toward a high wall, while all around, from the narrow slits of the jail windows, I thought I saw peering out upon him the eyes of murderers and thieves.

"Bartleby!"

"I know you," he said, without looking round—"and I want nothing to say to you."

"It was not I that brought you here, Bartleby," said I, keenly pained at his implied suspicion. "And to you, this should not be so vile a place. Nothing reproachful attaches to you by being here. And see, it is not so sad a place as one might think. Look, there is the sky, and here is the grass."

"I know where I am," he replied, but would say nothing more, and so I left him.

As I entered the corridor again, a broad meat-like man, in an apron, accosted me, and, jerking his thumb over his shoulder, said, "Is that your friend?"

"Yes."

"Does he want to starve? If he does, let him live on the prison fare, that's all."

"Who are you?" asked I, not knowing what to make of such an unofficially speaking person in such a place.

"I am the grub-man. Such gentlemen as have friends here, hire me to provide them with something good to eat."

"Is this so?" said I, turning to the turnkey.

He said it was.

"Well, then," said I, slipping some silver into the grub-man's hands (for so they called him), "I want you to give particular attention to my friend there; let him have the best dinner you can get. And you must be as polite to him as possible."

"Introduce me, will you?" said the grub-man, looking at me with an expression which seemed to say he was all impatience for an opportunity to give a specimen of his breeding.

Thinking it would prove of benefit to the scrivener, I acquiesced; and, asking the grub-man his name, went up with him to Bartleby.

"Bartleby, this is a friend; you will find him very useful to you."

"Your sarvant, sir, your sarvant," said the grub-man, making a low salutation behind his apron. "Hope you find it pleasant here, sir; nice grounds— cool apartments—hope you'll stay with us some time—try to make it agreeable. What will you have for dinner to-day?"

"I prefer not to dine to-day," said Bartleby, turning away. "It would disagree with me; I am unused to dinners." So saying, he slowly moved to the other side of the enclosure, and took up a position fronting the dead-wall.

"How's this?" said the grub-man, addressing me with a stare of astonishment. "He's odd, ain't he?"

"I think he is a little deranged," said I sadly.

"Deranged? deranged is it? Well, now, upon my word, I thought that friend of yourn was a gentleman forger; they are always pale and genteel-like, them forgers. I can't help pity 'em—can't help it, sir. Did you know Monroe Edwards?" he added touchingly, and paused. Then, laying his hand piteously on my shoulder, sighed, "he died of consumption at Sing-Sing. So you weren't acquainted with Monroe?"

"No, I was never socially acquainted with any forgers. But I cannot stop longer. Look to my friend yonder. You will not lose by it. I will see you again."

Some few days after this, I again obtained admission to the Tombs, and went through the corridors in quest of Bartleby; but without finding him.

"I saw him coming from his cell not long ago," said a turnkey, "maybe he's gone to loiter in the yards."

So I went in that direction.

"Are you looking for the silent man?" said another turnkey, passing me. "Yonder he lies—sleeping in the yard there. 'Tis not twenty minutes since I saw him lie down."

The yard was entirely quiet. It was not accessible to the common prisoners. The surrounding walls, of amazing thickness, kept off all sounds behind them. The Egyptian character of the masonry weighed upon me with its gloom. But a soft imprisoned turf grew under foot. The heart of the eternal pyramids, it seemed, wherein, by some strange magic, through the clefts, grass-seed, dropped by birds, had sprung.

Strangely huddled at the base of the wall, his knees drawn up, and lying on his side, his head touching the cold stones, I saw the wasted Bartleby. But nothing stirred. I paused; then went close up to him; stooped over, and saw that his dim eyes were open; otherwise he seemed profoundly sleeping. Something prompted me to touch him. I felt his hand, when a tingling shiver ran up my arm and down my spine to my feet.

The round face of the grub-man peered upon me now. "His dinner is ready. Won't he dine to-day, either? Or does he live without dining?"

"Lives without dining," said I, and closed the eyes.

"Eh!—He's asleep, ain't he?"

"With kings and counsellors," murmured I.

There would seem little need for proceeding further in this history. Imagination will readily supply the meagre recital of poor Bartleby's interment. But, ere parting with the reader, let me say, that if this little narrative has sufficiently interested him, to awaken curiosity as to who Bartleby was, and what manner of life he led prior to the present narrator's making his acquaintance, I can only reply, that in such curiosity I fully share, but am wholly unable to gratify it. Yet here I hardly know whether I should divulge one little item of rumour, which came to my ear a few months after the scrivener's decease. Upon what basis it rested I could never ascertain; and hence, how true it is I cannot now tell. But, inasmuch as this vague report has not been without a certain suggestive interest to me, however sad, it may prove the same with some others; and so I will briefly mention it. The report was this: that Bartleby had been a subordinate clerk in the Dead Letter Office at Washington, from which he had been suddenly removed by a change in the administration. When I think over this rumour, hardly can I express the emotions which seize me. Dead letters! does it not sound like dead men? Conceive a man by nature and misfortune prone to a pallid hopelessness, can any business seem more fitted to heighten it than that of continually handling these dead letters, and assorting them for the flames? For by the cartload they are annually burned. Sometimes from out the folded paper the pale clerk takes a ring—the finger it was meant for, perhaps, moulders in the grave; a bank-note sent in swiftest charity—he whom it would relieve, nor eats nor hungers any more; pardon for those who died despairing; hope for those who died unhoping; good tidings for those who died stifled by unrelieved calamaties. On errands of life, these letters speed to death.

Ah, Bartleby! Ah, humanity!

[margin note: never able to communicate]

Fact Questions and Exercises   *[margin note: 1st person]*

1. What is the point of view of the story? Who is the narrator?
2. What does the word "scrivener" mean?   *[margin note: Scribe, law-copyist]*
3. How is Bartleby's desk arranged in relation to the rest of the office?   *[margin note: shows relation w/ narrator]*
4. What phrase does Bartleby repeat each time he is asked to perform a task?   *[margin note: I would prefer not to.]*
5. What does Bartleby eat most of the time? What does he do with his money?
6. Where does Bartleby live? Where is he from? What is his first (or last) name?
7. Point out some specific facts that suggest Bartleby's influence on the narrator's personality.
8. Ultimately, what does the narrator do to rid his offices of Bartleby?

9. Where is Bartleby when he dies?
10. What is the "rumour" that the narrator hears after Bartleby's death?

For Discussion and Writing

1. Characterize the narrator. What is his profession? How old is he? What does he mean when he says that he is "an eminently *safe* man"? Do you accept him as a reliable narrator? If so, when? If not, when?
2. Contrast Bartleby with the other copyists. Does this contrast help make Bartleby's character more understandable? Could Melville have said less about the other copyists?
3. The narrator comments that Bartleby's "poverty is great; but his solitude, how horrible!" Could this phrase serve as a possible theme of the story? How? Why does the narrator feel "a fraternal melancholy" for Bartleby?
4. In an essay, develop your interpretation of the story. Are there themes not suggested in the preceding questions? What symbols or events help convey these themes? What are some of the conflicts that Melville suggests?

Mark Twain
(Samuel Langhorne Clemens) [1835–1910]

Twain was born in rural Missouri, and began to work as a printer's helper at the age of thirteen. He received practically no formal education, and worked at a variety of trades before establishing himself as a writer. One of the most important of his jobs was a stint as a riverboat pilot on the Mississippi, from 1857 to 1861. His fame as a writer came from a series of humorous sketches, essays, and novels, such as *The Innocents Abroad* (1869) and *The Adventures of Tom Sawyer* (1876). After 1890, however, following a number of personal misfortunes and sorrows, Twain's view of the world darkened. This increasing skepticism is expressed in his later works, such as *The Mysterious Stranger* (1916) and "The Man That Corrupted Hadleyburg" (1900). During his lifetime, Twain was an immensely popular writer, and even today he is considered by many to be America's greatest writer. His most famous and critically examined novel, *The Adventures of Huckleberry Finn*, was published in 1885.

The Man That Corrupted Hadleyburg

It was many years ago. Hadleyburg was the most honest and upright town in all the region round about. It had kept that reputation unsmirched during three generations, and was prouder of it than of any other of its possessions. It was so proud of it, and so anxious to insure its perpetuation, that it began to teach the principles of honest dealing to its babies in the cradle, and made the like teachings the staple of their culture thenceforward through all the years devoted to their education. Also, throughout the formative years temptations were kept out of the way of the young people, so that their honesty could have every chance to harden and solidify, and become a part of their very bone. The neighboring towns were jealous of this honorable supremacy, and affected to sneer at Hadleyburg's pride in it and call it vanity; but all the same they were obliged to acknowledge that Hadleyburg was in reality an incorruptible town; and if pressed they would also acknowledge that the mere fact that a young man hailed from Hadleyburg was all the recommendation he needed when he went forth from his natal town to seek for responsible employment.

But at last, in the drift of time, Hadleyburg had the ill luck to offend a passing stranger—possibly without knowing it, certainly without caring, for Hadleyburg was sufficient unto itself, and cared not a rap for strangers or their opinions. Still, it would have been well to make an exception in this one's case, for he was a bitter man and revengeful. All through his wanderings during a whole year he kept his injury in mind, and gave all his leisure moments to trying to invent a compensating satisfaction for it. He contrived many plans, and all of them were good, but none of them was quite sweeping enough; the poorest of them would hurt a great many individuals, but what he wanted was a plan which would comprehend the entire town, and not let so much as one person escape unhurt. At last he had a fortunate idea, and when it fell into his brain it lit up his whole head with an evil joy. He began to form a plan at once, saying to himself, "That is the thing to do—I will corrupt the town."

Six months later he went to Hadleyburg, and arrived in a buggy at the house of the old cashier of the bank about ten at night. He got a sack out of the buggy, shouldered it, and staggered with it through the cottage yard, and knocked at the door. A woman's voice said "Come in," and he entered, and set his sack behind the stove in the parlor, saying politely to the old lady who sat reading the *Missionary Herald* by the lamp:

"Pray keep your seat, madam, I will not disturb you. There—now it is pretty well concealed; one would hardly know it was there. Can I see your husband a moment, madam?"

No, he was gone to Brixton, and might not return before morning.

"Very well, madam, it is no matter. I merely wanted to leave that sack in his care, to be delivered to the rightful owner when he shall be found. I am a stranger; he does not know me; I am merely passing through the town to-night to discharge a matter which has been long in my mind. My errand is now completed, and I go pleased and a little proud, and you will never see me again. There is a paper attached to the sack which will explain everything. Good night, madam."

The old lady was afraid of the mysterious big stranger, and was glad to see him go. But her curiosity was roused, and she went straight to the sack and brought away the paper. It began as follows:

> To be published; or, the right man sought out by private inquiry—either will answer. This sack contains gold coin weighing a hundred and sixty pounds four ounces—

"Mercy on us, and the door not locked!"

Mrs. Richards flew to it all in a tremble and locked it, then pulled down the window-shades and stood frightened, worried, and wondering if there was anything else she could do toward making herself and the money more safe. She listened awhile for burglars, then surrendered to curiosity and went back to the lamp and finished reading the paper:

I am a foreigner, and am presently going back to my own country, to remain there permanently. I am greatful to America for what I have received at her hands during my long stay under her flag; and to one of her citizens—a citizen of Hadleyburg—I am especially grateful for a great kindness done me a year or two ago. Two great kindnesses, in fact. I will explain. I was a gambler. I say I *was*. I was a ruined gambler. I arrived in this village at night, hungry and without a penny. I asked for help—in the dark; I was ashamed to beg in the light. I begged of the right man. He gave me twenty dollars—that is to say, he gave me life, as I considered it. He also gave me fortune; for out of that money I have made myself rich at the gaming-table. And finally, a remark which he made to me has remained with me to this day, and has at last conquered me; and in conquering has saved the remnant of my morals; I shall gamble no more. Now I have no idea who that man was, but I want him found, and I want him to have this money, to give away, throw away, or keep, as he pleases. It is merely my way of testifying my gratitude to him. If I could stay, I would find him myself; but no matter, he will be found. This is an honest town, an incorruptible town, and I know I can trust it without fear. This man can be identified by the remark which he made to me; I feel persuaded that he will remember it.

And now my plan is this: If you prefer to conduct the inquiry privately, do so. Tell the contents of this present writing to any one who is likely to be the right man. If he shall answer, "I am the man; the remark I made was so-and-so," apply the test—to wit: open the sack, and in it you will find a sealed envelope containing that remark. If the remark mentioned by the candidate tallies with it give him the money, and ask no further questions, for he is certainly the right man.

But if you shall prefer a public inquiry, then publish this present writing in the local paper—with these instructions added, to wit: Thirty days from now, let the candidate appear at the town-hall at eight in the evening (Friday), and hand his remark, in a sealed envelope, to the Rev. Mr. Burgess (if he will be kind enough to act); and let Mr. Burgess there and then destroy the seals of the sack, open it, and see if the remark is correct; if correct, let the money be delivered, with my sincere gratitude, to my benefactor thus identified.

Mrs. Richards sat down, gently quivering with excitement, and was soon lost in thinkings—after this pattern: "What a strange thing it is! . . . And what a fortune for that kind man who set his bread afloat upon the waters! . . . If it had only been my husband that did it!—for we are so poor, so old and poor! . . ." Then, with a sigh—"but it was not my Edward; no, it was not he that gave a stranger twenty dollars. It is a pity, too; I see it now. . . ." Then, with a shudder—"But it is *gambler's* money! the wages of sin: we couldn't take it; we couldn't touch it. I don't like to be near it; it seems a defilement." She moved to a farther chair. . . . "I wish Edward would come and take it to the bank; a burglar might come at any moment; it is dreadful to be here all alone with it."

At eleven Mr. Richards arrived, and while his wife was saying, "I am *so* glad you've come!" he was saying, "I'm so tired—tired clear out; it is dreadful to be poor, and have to make these dismal journeys at my time of life. Always at the grind, grind, grind, on a salary—another man's slave, and he sitting at home in his slippers, rich and comfortable."

"I am so sorry for you, Edward, you know that; but be comforted: we have our livelihood; we have our good name—"

"Yes, Mary, and that is everything. Don't mind my talk—it's just a moment's irritation and doesn't mean anything. Kiss me—there, it's all gone now, and I am not complaining any more. What have you been getting? What's in the sack?"

Then his wife told him the great secret. It dazed him for a moment; then he said: "It weighs a hundred and sixty pounds? Why, Mary, it's for-ty thousand dollars—think of it—a whole fortune! Not ten men in this village are worth that much. Give me the paper."

He skimmed through it and said:

"Isn't it an adventure! Why it's a romance; it's like the impossible things one reads about in books, and never sees in life." He was well stirred up now; cheerful, even gleeful. He tapped his old wife on the cheek, and said, humorously, "Why, we're rich, Mary, rich; all we've got to do is to bury the money and burn the papers. If the gambler ever comes to inquire, we'll merely look coldly upon him and say: 'What is this nonsense you are talking? We have never heard of you and your sack of gold before'; and then he would look foolish, and—"

"And in the meantime, while you are running on with your jokes, the money is still here, and it is fast getting along toward burglar-time."

"True. Very well, what shall we do—make the inquiry private? No, not that: it would spoil the romance. The public method is better. Think what a noise it will make! And it will make all the other towns jealous; for no stranger would trust such a thing to any town but Hadleyburg, and they know it. It's a great card for us. I must get to the printing-office now, or I shall be too late."

"But stop—stop—don't leave me here alone with it, Edward!"

But he was gone. For only a little while, however. Not far from his own house he met the editor-proprietor of the paper, and gave him the document, and said, "Here is a good thing for you, Cox—put it in."

"It may be too late, Mr. Richards, but I'll see."

At home again he and his wife sat down to talk the charming mystery over; they were in no condition for sleep. The first question was, Who could the citizen have been who gave the stranger the twenty dollars? It seemed a simple one; both answered it in the same breath:

"Barclay Goodson."

"Yes," said Richards, "he could have done it, and it would have been like him, but there's not another in the town."

"Everybody will grant that, Edward—grant it privately, anyway. For six months, now, the village has been its own proper self once more—honest, narrow, self-righteous, and stingy."

"It is what he always called it, to the day of his death—said it right out publicly, too."

"Yes, and he was hated for it."

"Oh, of course; but he didn't care. I reckon he was the best-hated man among us, except the Reverend Burgess."

"Well, Burgess deserves it—he will never get another congregation here. Mean as the town is, it knows how to estimate *him*. Edward, doesn't it seem odd that the stranger should appoint Burgess to deliver the money?"

"Well, yes—it does. That is—that is—"

"Why so much that-*is*-ing? Would *you* select him?"

"Mary, maybe the stranger knows him better than this village does."

"Much *that* would help Burgess!"

The husband seemed preplexed for an answer; the wife kept a steady eye upon him, and waited. Finally Richards said, with the hesitancy of one who is making a statement which is likely to encounter doubt:

"Mary, Burgess is not a bad man."

His wife was certainly surprised.

"Nonsense!" she exclaimed.

"He is not a bad man. I know. The whole of his unpopularity had its foundation in that one thing—the thing that made so much noise."

"That 'one thing,' indeed! As if that 'one thing' wasn't enough, all by itself."

"Plenty. Plenty. Only he wasn't guilty of it."

"How you talk! Not guilty of it! Everybody knows he *was* guilty."

"Mary, I give you my word—he was innocent."

"I can't believe it, and I don't. How do you know?"

"It is a confession. I am ashamed, but I will make it. I was the only man who knew he was innocent. I could have saved him, and—and—well, you know how the town was wrought up—I hadn't the pluck to do it. I would have turned everybody against me. I felt mean, ever so mean; but I didn't dare; I hadn't the manliness to face that."

Mary looked troubled, and for a while was silent. Then she said, stammeringly:

"I—I don't think it would have done for you to—to—One musn't—er— public opinion—one has to be so careful—so—" It was a difficult road, and she got mired; but after a little she got started again. "It was a great pity, but—Why, we couldn't afford it, Edward—we couldn't indeed. Oh, I wouldn't have had you do it for anything!"

"It would have lost us the good will of so many people, Mary; and then—and then—"

"What troubles me now is, what *he* thinks of us, Edward."

"He? *He* doesn't suspect that I could have saved him."

"Oh," exclaimed the wife, in a tone of relief, "I am glad of that! As long as he doesn't know that you could have saved him, he—he—well, that makes it a great deal better. Why, I might have known he didn't know, because he is always trying to be friendly with us, as little encouragement as we give him. More than once people have twitted me with it. There's the Wilsons, and the Wilcoxes, and the Harknesses, they take a mean pleasure in saying, '*Your friend* Burgess,' because they know it pesters me. I wish he wouldn't persist in liking us so; I can't think why he keeps it up."

"I can explain it. It's another confession. When the thing was new and hot, and the town made a plan to ride him on a rail, my conscience hurt me so that I couldn't stand it, and went privately and gave him notice, and he got out of the town and staid out till it was safe to come back."

"Edward! If the town had found it out—"

"*Don't!* It scares me yet, to think of it. I repented of it the minute it was done; and I was even afraid to tell you, lest your face might betray it to somebody. I didn't sleep any that night, for worrying. But after a few days I saw that no one was going to suspect me, and after that I got to feeling glad I did it. And I feel glad yet, Mary—glad through and through."

"So do I, now, for it would have been a dreadful way to treat him. Yes, I'm glad; for really you did owe him that, you know. But, Edward, suppose it should come out yet, some day!"

"It won't."

"Why?"

"Because everybody thinks it was Goodson."

"Of course they would!"

"Certainly. And of course he didn't care. They persuaded poor old Sawlsberry to go and charge it on him, and he went blustering over there and did it. Goodson looked him over, like as if he was hunting for a place on him that he could despise the most, then he says, 'So you are the Committee of Inquiry, are you?' Sawlsberry said that was about what he was. 'Hm. Do they require particulars, or do you reckon a kind of a *general* answer will do?' 'If they require particulars, I will come back, Mr. Goodson; I will take the general answer first.' 'Very well, then, tell them to go to hell—I reckon that's general enough. And I'll give you some advice, Sawlsberry; when you come back for the particulars, fetch a basket to carry the relics of yourself home in.'"

"Just like Goodson; it's got all the marks. He had only one vanity: he thought he could give advice better than any other person."

"It settled the business, and saved us, Mary. The subject was dropped."

"Bless you, I'm not doubting *that.*"

Then they took up the gold-sack mystery again, with strong interest. Soon the conversation began to suffer breaks—interruptions caused by absorbed thinkings. The breaks grew more and more frequent. At last Richards lost himself wholly in thought. He sat long, gazing vacantly at the floor, and by and by he began to punctuate his thoughts with little nervous movements of his hands that seemed to indicate vexation. Meantime his wife too had relapsed into a thoughtful silence, and her movements were beginning to show a troubled discomfort. Finally Richards got up and strode aimlessly about the room, plowing his hands through his hair, much as a somnambulist might do who was having a bad dream. Then he seemed to arrive at a definite purpose; and without a word he put on his hat and passed quickly out of the house. His wife sat brooding, with a drawn face, and did not seem to be aware that she was alone. Now and then she murmured. "Lead us not into t- . . . but-but-we are so poor, so poor! . . . Lead us not into . . . Ah, who would be hurt by it?—and no one would ever know . . . Lead us . . ." The voice died out in mumblings. After a little while she glanced up and muttered in a half-frightened, half-glad way:

"He is gone! But, oh dear, he may be too late—too late. . . . Maybe not—maybe there is still time." She rose and stood thinking, nervously clasping and unclasping her hands. A slight shudder shook her frame, and she said, out of a dry throat, "God forgive me—it's awful to think such things—but . . . Lord, how we are made—how strangely we are made!"

She turned the light low, and slipped stealthily over and kneeled down by the sack and felt of its ridgy sides with her hands, and fondled them lovingly; and there was a gloating light in her poor old eyes. She fell into fits of absence; and came half out of them at times to mutter, "If we had only waited!—oh, if we had only waited a little, and not been in such a hurry!"

Meantime Cox had gone home from his office and told his wife all about the strange thing that had happened, and they had talked it over eagerly, and guessed that the late Goodson was the only man in the town who could have helped a suffering stranger with so noble a sum as twenty dollars. Then there was a pause, and the two became thoughtful and silent. And by and by nervous and fidgety. At last the wife said, as if to herself:

"Nobody knows this secret but the Richardses . . . and us . . . nobody."

The husband came out of his thinkings with a slight start, and gazed wistfully at his wife, whose face was become very pale; then he hesitatingly rose, and glanced furtively at his hat, then at his wife—a sort of mute inquiry. Mrs. Cox swallowed once or twice, with her hand at her throat, then in place of speech she nodded her head. In a moment she was alone, and mumbling to herself.

And now Richards and Cox were hurrying through the deserted streets, from opposite directions. They met, panting, at the foot of the printing-office stairs; by the night light there they read each other's face. Cox whispered:

"Nobody knows about this but us?"

The whispered answer was,

"Not a soul—on honor, not a soul!"

"If it isn't too late to—"

The men were starting up-stairs; at this moment they were overtaken by a boy, and Cox asked:

"Is that you, Johnny?"

"Yes, sir."

"You needn't ship the early mail—nor *any* mail; wait till I tell you."

"It's already gone, sir."

"*Gone?*" It had the sound of unspeakable disappointment in it.

"Yes, sir. Time-table for Brixton and all the towns beyond changed to-day, sir—had to get the papers in twenty minutes earlier than common. I had to rush; if I had been two minutes later—"

The men turned and walked slowly away, not waiting to hear the rest. Neither of them spoke during ten minutes; then Cox said, in a vexed tone:

"What possessed you to be in such a hurry, *I* can't make out."

The answer was humble enough:

["I see it now, but somehow I never thought, you know, until it was too late. But the next time—"]

"Next time be hanged! It won't come in a thousand years."

Then the friends separated without a good night, and dragged themselves home with a gait of mortally stricken men. At their homes their wives sprang up with an eager "Well?"—then saw the answer with their eyes and sank down sorrowing, without waiting for it to come in words[. In both houses a discussion followed of a heated sort—a new thing; there had been discussions before, but not heated ones, not ungentle ones. The discussions to-night were a sort of seeming plagiarisms of each other.] Mrs. Richards said,

"If you had only waited, Edward—if you had only stopped to think; but no, you must run straight to the printing-office and spread it all over the world."

"It *said* publish it."

"That is nothing; it also said do it privately, if you liked. There, now—is that true, or not?"

"Why, yes—yes, it is true; but when I thought what a stir it would make, and what a compliment it was to Hadleyburg that a stranger should trust it so—"

"Oh, certainly, I know all that; but if you had only stopped to think, you would have seen that you *couldn't* find the right man, because he is in his grave, and hasn't left chick nor child nor relation behind him; and as long as the money went to somebody that awfully needed it, and nobody would be hurt by it, and—and—"

[margin handwriting: LOGICAL EXCUSES for doing WRONG ↓]

She broke down, crying. Her husband tried to think of some comforting thing to say, and presently came out with this:

"But after all, Mary, it must be for the best—it *must* be; we know that. And we must remember that it was so ordered—"

[margin handwriting: L.E. for doing right ↓]

"Ordered! Oh, everything's *ordered*, when a person has to find some way out when he has been stupid. Just the same, it was *ordered* that the money should come to us in this special way, and it was you that must take it on yourself to go meddling with the designs of Providence—and who gave you the right? It was wicked, that is what it was—just blasphemous presumption, and no more becoming to a meek and humble professor of—"

[margin handwriting: doing wrong]

"But, Mary, you know how we have been trained all our lives long, like the whole village, till it is absolutely second nature to us to stop not a single moment to think when there's an honest thing to be done—"

[margin handwriting: even the best of training is sometimes insuffic...]

"Oh, I know it, I know it—it's been one everlasting training and training and training in honesty—honesty shielded, from the very cradle, against every possible temptation, and so it's *artificial* honesty, and weak as water when temptation comes, as we have seen this night. God knows I never had shade nor shadow of a doubt of my petrified and indestructible honesty until now—and now, under the very first big and real temptation, I—Edward, it is my belief that this town's honesty is as rotten as mine is; as rotten as yours is. It is a mean town, a hard, stingy town, and hasn't a virtue in the world but this honesty it is so celebrated for and so conceited about; and so help me, I do believe that if ever the day comes that its honesty falls under great temptation, its grand reputation will go to ruin like a house of cards. There, now, I've made confession, and I feel better; I am a humbug, and I've been one all my life, without knowing it. Let no man call me honest again—I will not have it."

"I—well, Mary, I feel a good deal as you do; I certainly do. It seems strange, too, so strange. I never could have believed it—never."

A long silence followed; both were sunk in thought. At last the wife looked up and said:

"I know what you are thinking, Edward."

Richards had the embarrassed look of a person who is caught.

"I am ashamed to confess it, Mary, but—"

"It's no matter, Edward, I was thinking the same question myself."

"I hope so. State it."

"You were thinking, if a body could only guess out *what the remark was* that Goodson made to the stranger."

"It's perfectly true. I feel guilty and ashamed. And you?"

"I'm past it. Let us make a pallet here; we've got to stand watch till the bank vault opens in the morning and admits the sack. . . . Oh dear, oh dear—if we hadn't made the mistake!"

The pallet was made, and Mary said:

"The open sesame—what could it have been? I do wonder what that remark could have been? But come; we will get to bed now."

"And sleep?"

"No: think."

"Yes, think."

By this time the Coxes too had completed their spat and their reconciliation, and were turning in—to think, to think, and toss, and fret, and worry over what the remark could possibly have been which Goodson made to the stranded derelict; that golden remark; that remark worth forty thousand dollars, cash.

The reason that the village telegraph-office was open later than usual that night was this: The foreman of Cox's paper was the local representative of the Associated Press. One might say its honorary representative, for it wasn't four times a year that he could furnish thirty words that would be accepted. But this time it was different. His dispatch stating what he had caught got an instant answer:

Send the whole thing—all the details—twelve hundred words.

A colossal order! The foreman filled the bill; and he was the proudest man in the State. By breakfast-time the next morning the name of Hadleyburg the Incorruptible was on every lip in America, from Montreal to the Gulf, from the glaciers of Alaska to the orange-groves of Florida; and millions and millions of people were discussing the stranger and his money-sack, and wondering if the right man would be found, and hoping some more news about the matter would come soon—right away.

II

Hadleyburg village woke up world-celebrated—astonished—happy—vain. Vain beyond imagination. Its nineteen principal citizens and their wives went about shaking hands with each other, and beaming, and smiling, and congratulating, and saying *this* thing adds a new word to the dictionary—*Hadleyburg,* synonym for *incorruptible*—destined to live in dictionaries forever! And the minor and unimportant citizens and their wives went around acting in much the same way. Everybody ran to the bank to see the gold-sack; and before noon grieved and envious crowds began to flock in from Brixton and all neighboring towns; and that afternoon and next day reporters began to arrive from everywhere to verify the sack and its history and write the whole thing up anew, and make dashing free-hand pictures of the sack, and of Richards's house, and the bank, and the Presbyterian church, and the Baptist church, and the public square, and the town-hall where the test would be applied and the money delivered; and damnable portraits of the Richardses, and Pinkerton the banker, and Cox, and the foreman, and Reverend Burgess, and the postmaster—and even of Jack Halliday, who was the loafing, good-natured, no-account, irreverent fisherman, hunter, boys' friend, stray-dogs' friend, typical "Sam Lawson" of the town. The little, mean, smirking, oily Pinkerton showed the sack to all comers, and rubbed his sleek palms together pleasantly, and enlarged upon the town's fine old reputation for honesty and upon this wonderful indorsement of it, and hoped and believed that the example would now spread far and wide over the American world, and be epoch-making in the matter of moral regeneration. And so on, and so on.

By the end of a week things had quieted down again; the wild intoxication of pride and joy had sobered to a soft, sweet, silent delight—a sort of deep, nameless, unutterable content. All faces bore a look of peaceful, holy happiness.

Then a change came. It was a gradual change; so gradual that its beginnings were hardly noticed; maybe were not noticed at all, except by Jack Halliday, who always noticed everything; and always made fun of it, too, no matter what it was. He began to throw out chaffing remarks about people not looking quite so happy as they did a day or two ago; and next he claimed that the new aspect was deepening to positive sadness; next, that it was taking on a sick look; and finally he said that everybody was become so moody, thoughtful, and absent-minded that he could rob the meanest man in town of a cent out of the bottom of his breeches pocket and not disturb his revery.

At this stage—or about this stage—a saying like this was dropped at bedtime—with a sigh, usually—by the head of each of the nineteen principal households: "Ah, what *could* have been the remark that Goodson made?"

And straightaway—with a shudder—came this, from the man's wife:

"Oh, *don't*! What horrible thing are you mulling in your mind? Put it away from you, for God's sake!"

But that question was wrung from those men again the next night—and got the same retort. But weaker.

And the third night the men uttered the question yet again—with anguish, and absently. This time—and the following night—the wives fidgeted feebly, and tried to say something. But didn't.

And the night after that they found their tongues and responded *4th night* longingly:

"Oh, if we *could* only guess!"

Halliday's comments grew daily more and more sparkingly disagreeable and disparaging. He went diligently about, laughing at the town, individually and in mass. But his laugh was the only one left in the village: it fell upon a hollow and mournful vacancy and emptiness. Not even a smile was findable anywhere. Halliday carried a cigar-box around on a tripod, playing that it was a camera, and halted all passers and aimed the thing and said, "Ready!—now look pleasant, please," but not even this capital joke could surprise the dreary faces into any softening.

So three weeks passed—one week was left. It was Saturday evening—after supper. Instead of the aforetime Saturday-evening flutter and bustle and shopping and larking, the streets were empty and desolate. Richards and his old wife sat apart in their little parlor—miserable and thinking. This was become their evening habit now: the lifelong habit which had preceded it, of reading, knitting, and contented chat, or receiving or paying neighborly calls, was dead and gone and forgotten, ages ago—two or three weeks ago; nobody talked now, nobody read, nobody visited—the whole village sat at home, sighing, worrying, silent. Trying to guess out that remark.

The postman left a letter. Richards glanced listlessly at the superscription and the postmark—unfamiliar, both—and tossed the letter on the table and resumed his might-have-beens and his hopeless dull miseries where he had left them off. Two or three hours later his wife got wearily up and was going away to bed without a good night—custom now—but she stopped near the letter and eyed it awhile with a dead interest, then broke it open, and began to skim it over. Richards, sitting there with his chair tilted back against the wall and his chin between his knees, heard something fall. It was his wife. He sprang to her side, but she cried out:

"Leave me alone, I am too happy. Read the letter—read it!"

He did. He devoured it, his brain reeling. The letter was from a distant state, and it said:

I am a stranger to you, but no matter: I have something to tell. I have just arrived home from Mexico, and learned about that episode. Of course you do not know who made that remark, but I know, and I am the only person living who does know. It was *Goodson.* I knew him well, many years ago. I passed through your village that very night, and was his guest till the midnight train came along. I overheard him make that remark to the stranger in the dark—it was in Hale Alley. He and I talked of it the rest of the way home, and while smoking in his house. He mentioned many of your villagers in the course of his talk—most of them in a very uncomplimentary way, but two or three favorably; among these latter yourself. I say "favorably"—nothing stronger. I remember his saying he did not actually *like* any person in the town—not one; but that you—I *think* he said you—am almost sure—had done him a very great service once, possibly without knowing the full value of it, and he wished he had a fortune, he would leave it to you when he died, and a curse apiece for the rest of the citizens. Now, then, if it was you that did him that service, you are his legitimate heir, and entitled to the sack of gold. I know that I can trust to your honor and honesty, for in a citizen of Hadleyburg these virtues are an unfailing inheritance, and so I am going to reveal to you the remark, well satisfied that if you are not the right man you will seek and find the right one and see that poor Goodson's debt of gratitude for the service referred to is paid. This is the remark: "*You are far from being a bad man: go, and reform.*"

Howard L. Stephenson

"Oh, Edward, the money is ours and I am so grateful, *oh,* so grateful— kiss me, dear, it's forever since we kissed—and we needed it so—the money— and now you are free of Pinkerton and his bank, and nobody's slave any more; it seems to me I could fly for joy."

It was a happy half-hour that the couple spent there on the settee caressing each other; it was the old days come again—days that had begun with their courtship and lasted without a break till the stranger brought the deadly money. By and by the wife said:

"Oh, Edward, how lucky it was you did him that grand service, poor Goodson! I never liked him, but I love him now. And it was fine and beautiful of you never to mention it or brag about it." Then, with a touch of reproach, "But you ought to have told *me,* Edward, you ought to have told your wife, you know."

"Well, I—er—well, Mary, you see—"

"Now stop hemming and hawing, and tell me about it, Edward. I always loved you, and now I'm proud of you. Everybody believes there was only one good generous soul in this village, and now it turns out that you—Edward, why don't you tell me?"

"Well—er—er—Why, Mary, I can't!"

"You *can't*? *Why* can't you?"

"You see, he—well, he—he made me promise I wouldn't."

The wife looked him over, and said, very slowly:

"Made—you—promise? Edward, what do you tell me that for?"

"Mary, do you think I would lie?"

She was troubled and silent for a moment, then she laid her hand within his and said:

"No . . . no. We have wandered far enough from our bearings—God spare us that! In all your life you have never uttered a lie. But now—now that the foundations of things seem to be crumbling from under us, we—we—" She lost her voice for a moment, then said, brokenly, "Lead us not into temptation . . . . I think you made the promise, Edward. Let it rest so. Let us keep away from that ground. Now—that is all gone by; let us be happy again; it is no time for clouds."

Edward found it something of an effort to comply, for his mind kept wandering—trying to remember what the service was that he had done Goodson.

The couple lay awake the most of the night, Mary happy and busy, Edward busy but not so happy. Mary was planning what she would do with the money. Edward was trying to recall that service. At first his conscience was sore on account of the lie he had told Mary—if it was a lie. After much reflection—suppose it *was* a lie? What then? Was it such a great matter? Aren't we always *acting* lies? Then why not *tell* them? Look at Mary—look what she had done. While he was hurrying off on his honest errand, what was she doing? Lamenting because the papers hadn't been destroyed and the money kept! Is theft better than lying?

That point lost its sting—the lie dropped into the background and left comfort behind it. The next point came to the front: *Had* he rendered that service? Well, here was Goodson's own evidence as reported in Stephenson's letter; there could be no better evidence than that—it was even *proof* that he had rendered it. Of course. So that point was settled . . . . No, not quite. He recalled with a wince that this unknown Mr. Stephenson was just a trifle unsure as to whether the performer of it was Richards or some other—and, oh dear, he had put Richards on his honor! He must himself decide whither that money must go—and Mr. Stephenson was not doubting that if he was the wrong man he would go honorably and find the right one. Oh, it was odious to put a man in such a situation—ah, why couldn't Stephenson have left out that doubt! What did he want to intrude that for?

Further reflection. How did it happen that *Richards'* name remained in Stephenson's mind as indicating the right man, and not some other man's name? That looked good. Yes, that looked very good. In fact, it went on looking better and better, straight along—until by and by it grew into positive *proof*. And then Richards put the matter at once out of his mind, for he had a private instinct that a proof once established is better left so.

He was feeling reasonably comfortable now, but there was still one other detail that kept pushing itself on his notice: of course he had done that

Contemplation

service—that was settled; but what *was* that service? He must recall it—he would not go to sleep till he had recalled it; it would make his peace of mind perfect. And so he thought and thought. He thought of a dozen things—possible services, even probable services—but none of them seemed adequate, none of them seemed large enough, none of them seemed worth the money—worth the fortune Goodson had wished he could leave in his will. And besides, he couldn't remember having done them, anyway. Now, then—now, then—what *kind* of a service would it be that would make a man so inordinately grateful? Ah—the saving of his soul! That must be it. Yes, he could remember, now, how he once set himself the task of converting Goodson, and labored at it as much as—he was going to say three months; but upon closer examination it shrunk to a month, then to a week, then to a day, then to nothing. Yes, he remembered now, and with unwelcome vividness, that Goodson had told him to go to thunder and mind his own business—*he* wasn't hankering to follow Hadleyburg to heaven!

So that solution was a failure—he hadn't saved Goodson's soul. Richards was discouraged. Then after a little came another idea: had he saved Goodson's property? No, that wouldn't do—he hadn't any. His life? That is it! Of course. Why, he might have thought of it before. This time he was on the right track, sure. His imagination-mill was hard at work in a minute, now.

Thereafter during a stretch of two exhausting hours he was busy saving Goodson's life. He saved it in all kinds of difficult and perilous ways. In every case he got it saved satisfactorily up to a certain point; then, just as he was beginning to get well persuaded that it had really happened, a troublesome detail would turn up which made the whole thing impossible. As in the matter of drowning, for instance. In that case he had swum out and tugged Goodson ashore in an unconscious state with a great crowd looking on and applauding, but when he had got it all thought out and was just beginning to remember all about it, a whole swarm of disqualifying details arrived on the ground: the town would have known of the circumstance, Mary would have known of it, it would glare like a limelight in his own memory instead of being an inconspicuous service which he had possibly rendered "without knowing its full value." And at this point he remembered that he couldn't swim, anyway.

Ah—*there* was a point which he had been overlooking from the start: it had to be a service which he had rendered "possibly without knowing the full value of it." Why, really, that ought to be an easy hunt—much easier than those others. And sure enough, by and by he found it. Goodson, years and years ago, came near marrying a very sweet and pretty girl, named Nancy Hewitt, but in some way or other the match had been broken off; the girl died, Goodson remained a bachelor, and by and by became a soured one and a frank despiser of the human species. Soon after the girl's death the village found out, or thought it had found out, that she carried a spoonful of negro blood in her veins. Richards worked at these details a good while, and in the end he thought he remembered things concerning them which must have gotten mislaid in his memory through long neglect. He seemed to dimly remember that it was *he* that found out about the negro blood; that it was he that told the village; that the village told Goodson where they got it; that he thus saved Goodson from marrying the tainted girl; that he had done him this great service "without knowing the full value of it," in fact without knowing that he was doing it; but that Goodson knew the value of it, and what a narrow escape he had had, and so went to his grave grateful to his benefactor and wishing he had a fortune to leave him. It was all clear and simple now, and the more he went over it the more luminous and certain it grew; and at last, when he nestled to sleep satisfied and happy, he remembered the whole thing just as if it had been yesterday. In fact, he dimly remembered Goodson's *telling* him his gratitude once. Meantime Mary had spent six thousand dollars on a new house for herself and a pair of slippers for her pastor, and then had fallen peacefully to rest.

That same Saturday evening the postman had delivered a letter to each of the other principal citizens—nineteen letters in all. No two of the envelopes were alike, and no two of the superscriptions were in the same hand, but the letters inside were just like each other in every detail but one. They were exact copies of the letter received by Richards—handwriting and all—and were all signed by Stephenson, but in place of Richards's name each receiver's own name appeared.

All night long eighteen principal citizens did what their caste-brother Richards was doing at the same time—they put in their energies trying to remember what notable service it was that they had unconsciously done Barclay Goodson. In no case was it a holiday job; still they succeeded.

And while they were at this work, which was difficult, their wives put in the night spending the money, which was easy. During that one night the nineteen wives spent an average of seven thousand dollars each out of the forty thousand in the sack—a hundred and thirty-three thousand altogether.

Next day there was a surprise for Jack Halliday. He noticed that the faces of the nineteen chief citizens and their wives bore that expression of peaceful and holy happiness again. He could not understand it, neither was he able to invent any remarks about it that could damage it or disturb it. And so it was his turn to be dissatisfied with life. His private guesses at the reasons for the happiness failed in all instances, upon examination. When he met Mrs. Wilcox and noticed the placid ecstasy in her face, he said to himself, "Her cat has had kittens"—and went and asked the cook: it was not so; the cook had detected the happiness, but did not know the cause. When Halliday found the duplicate ecstasy in the face of "Shadbelly" Billson (village nickname), he was sure some neighbor of Billson's had broken his leg, but inquiry showed that this had not happened. The subdued ecstasy in Gregory Yates's face could mean but one thing—he was a mother-in-law short: it was another mistake. "And Pinkerton—Pinkerton—he has collected ten cents that he thought he was going to lose." And so on, and so on. In some cases the guesses had to remain in doubt, in the others they proved distinct errors. In the end Halliday said to himself, "Anyway it foots up that there's nineteen Hadleyburg families temporarily in heaven: I don't know how it happened; I only know Providence is off duty to-day."

An architect and builder from the next state had lately ventured to set up a small business in this unpromising village, and his sign had now been hanging out a week. Not a customer yet; he was a discouraged man, and sorry he had come. But his weather changed suddenly now. First one and then another chief citizen's wife said to him privately:

"Come to my house Monday week—but say nothing about it for the present. We think of building."

He got eleven invitations that day. That night he wrote his daughter and broke off her match with her student. He said she could marry a mile higher than that.

Pinkerton the banker and two or three other well-to-do men planned country-seats—but waited. [That kind don't count their chickens until they are hatched.]

The Wilsons devised a grand new thing—a fancy-dress ball. They made no actual promises, but told all their acquaintanceship in confidence that they were thinking the matter over and thought they should give it—"and if we do, you will be invited, of course." People were surprised, and said, one to another, "Why, they are crazy, those poor Wilsons, they can't afford it." Several among the nineteen said privately to their husbands, ["It is a good idea: we will keep still till their cheap thing is over, then *we* will give one that will make it sick."]

try to out-do the "Jones"

The days drifted along, and the bill of future squandering rose higher and higher, wilder and wilder, more and more foolish and reckless. It began to look as if every member of the nineteen would not only spend his whole forty thousand dollars before receiving-day, but be actually in debt by the time he got the money. In some cases light-headed people did not stop with planning to spend, they really spent—on credit. They bought land, mortgages, farms, speculative stocks, fine clothes, horses, and various other things, paid down the bonus, and made themselves liable for the rest—at ten days. Presently the sober second thought came, and Halliday noticed a ghastly anxiety was beginning to show up in a good many faces. Again he was puzzled, and didn't know what to make of it. "The Wilcox kittens aren't dead, for they weren't born; nobody's broken a leg; there's no shrinkage in mother-in-laws; *nothing* has happened—it is an unsolvable mystery."

There was another puzzled man, too—the Rev. Mr. Burgess. For days, wherever he went, people seemed to follow him or to be watching out for him; and if he ever found himself in a retired spot, a member of the nineteen would be sure to appear, thrust an envelope privately into his hand, whisper "To be opened at the town-hall Friday evening," then vanish away like a guilty thing. He was expecting that there might be one claimant for the sack—doubtful, however, Goodson being dead—but it never occurred to him that all this crowd might be claimants. When the great Friday came at last, he found that he had nineteen envelopes.

III

The town hall had never looked finer. The platform at the end of it was backed by a showy draping of flags; at intervals along the walls were festoons of flags; the gallery fronts were clothed in flags; the supporting columns were swathed in flags; all this was to impress the stranger, for he would be there in considerable force, and in a large degree he would be connected with the press. The house was full. The 412 fixed seats were occupied; also the 68 extra chairs which had been packed into the aisles; the steps of the platform were occupied; some distinguished strangers were given seats on the platform; at the horseshoe of tables which fenced the front and sides of the platform sat a strong force of special correspondents who had come from everywhere. It was the best-dressed house the town had ever produced (There were some tolerably expensive toilets there, and in several cases the ladies who wore them had the look of being unfamiliar with that kind of clothes.) At least the town thought they had that look, but the notion could have arisen from the town's knowledge of the fact that these ladies had never inhabited such clothes before.

The gold sack stood on a little table at the front of the platform where all the house could see it. The bulk of the house gazed at it with a burning interest, a mouth-watering interest, a wistful and pathetic interest; a minority of nineteen couples gazed at it tenderly, lovingly, proprietarily, and the male half of this minority kept saying over to themselves the moving little impromptu speeches of thankfulness for the audience's applause and congratulations which they were presently going to get up and deliver. Every now and then one of these got a piece of paper out of his vest pocket and privately glanced at it to refresh his memory.

counting chickens before they hatch

Of course there was a buzz of conversation going on—there always is; but at last when the Rev. Mr. Burgess rose and laid his hand on the sack he could hear his microbes gnaw, the place was so still. He related the curious history of the sack, then went on to speak in warm terms of Hadleyburg's old and well-earned reputation for spotless honesty, and of the town's just pride in this reputation. He said that this reputation was a treasure of priceless value; that under Providence its value had now become inestimably enhanced, for the recent episode had spread this fame far and wide, and thus had focused the eyes of the American world upon this village, and made its name for all time, as he hoped and believed, a synonym for commercial incorruptibility. [*Applause.*]"And who is to be the guardian of this noble treasure—the community as a whole? No! The responsibility is individual, not communal. From this day forth each and every one of you is in his own person its special guardian, and individually responsible that no harm shall come to it. Do you—does each of you—accept this great trust? [*Tumultuous assent*] Then all is well. Transmit it to your children and to your children's children. To-day your purity is beyond reproach—see to it that it shall remain so. To-day there is not a person in your community who could be beguiled to touch a penny not his own—see to it that you abide in this grace. [*"We will! we will!"*] This is not the place to make comparisons between ourselves and other communities—some of them ungracious toward us; they have their ways, we have ours; let us be content. [*Applause.*] I am done. Under my hand, my friends, rests a stranger's eloquent recognition of what we are; through him the world will always henceforth know what we are. We do not know who he is, but in your name I utter your gratitude, and ask you to raise your voices in indorsement."

The house rose in a body and made the walls quake with the thunders of its thankfulness for the space of a long minute. Then it sat down, and Mr. Burgess took an envelope out of his pocket. The house held its breath while he slit the envelope open and took from it a slip of paper. He read its contents— slowly and impressively—the audience listening with tranced attention to this magic document, each of whose words stood for an ingot of gold:

"'The remark which I made to the distressed stranger was this: "You are very far from being a bad man: go, and reform."'" Then he continued:

"We shall know in a moment now whether the remark here quoted corresponds with the one concealed in the sack; and if that shall prove to be so—and it undoubtedly will—this sack of gold belongs to a fellow-citizen who will henceforth stand before the nation as the symbol of the special virtue which has made our town famous throughout the land—Mr. Billson!"

The house had gotten itself all ready to burst into the proper tornado of applause; but instead of doing it, it seemed stricken with a paralysis; there was a deep hush for a moment or two, then a wave of whispered murmurs swept the place—of about this tenor: "*Billson!* oh, come, this is *too* thin! Twenty dollars to a stranger—or *anybody—Billson!* Tell it to the marines!" And now at this point the house caught its breath all of a sudden in a new access of astonishment, for it discovered that whereas in one part of the hall Deacon Billson was standing up with his head meekly bowed, in another part of it Lawyer Wilson was doing the same. There was a wondering silence now for a while.

Everybody was puzzled, and nineteen couples were surprised and indignant.

Billson and Wilson turned and stared at each other. Billson asked, bitingly:

"Why do *you* rise, Mr. Wilson?"

"Because I have a right to. Perhaps you will be good enough to explain to the house why *you* rise?"

"With great pleasure. Because I wrote that paper."

"It is an impudent falsity! I wrote it myself."

It was Burgess's turn to be paralyzed. He stood looking vacantly at first one of the men and then the other, and did not seem to know what to do. The house was stupefied. Lawyer Wilson spoke up, now, and said:

"I asked the Chair to read the name signed to that paper."

That brought the Chair to itself, and it read out the name:

"'John Wharton *Billson.*'"

"There!" shouted Billson, "what have you got to say for yourself, now? And what kind of apology are you going to make to me and to this insulted house for the imposture which you have attempted to play here?"

"No apologies are due, sir; and as for the rest of it, I publicly charge you with pilfering my note from Mr. Burgess and substituting a copy of it signed with your own name. There is no other way by which you could have gotten hold of the test-remark; I alone, of living men, possessed the secret of its wording."

There was likely to be a scandalous state of things if this went on; everybody noticed with distress that the short-hand scribes were scribbling like mad; many people were crying "Chair, Chair! Order! order!" Burgess rapped with his gavel and said:

"Let us not forget the proprieties due. There has evidently been a mistake somwhere, but surely that is all. If Mr. Wilson gave me an envelope—and I remember now that he did—I still have it."

He took one out of his pocket, opened it, glanced at it, looked surprised and worried, and stood silent a few moments. Then he waved his hand in a wandering and mechanical way, and made an effort or two to say something, then gave it up, despondently. Several voices cried out:

"Read it! read it! What is it?"

So he began in a dazed and sleep-walker fashion:

"'*The remark which I made to the unhappy stranger was this: "You are far from being a bad man.* [The house gazed at him, marvelling.] *Go, and reform.*"' [*Murmurs:* "Amazing! what can this mean?"] This one," said the Chair, "is signed Thurlow G. Wilson."

"There!" cried Wilson. "I reckon that settles it! I knew perfectly well my note was purloined."

"Purloined!" retorted Billson. "I'll let you know that neither you nor any man of your kidney must venture to—"

The Chair: "Order, gentlemen, order! Take your seats, both of you, please."

They obeyed, shaking their heads and grumbling angrily. The house was profoundly puzzled; it did not know what to do with this curious emergency. Presently Thompson got up. Thompson was the hatter. He would have liked to be a Nineteener; but such was not for him: his stock of hats was not considerable enough for the position. He said:

"Mr. Chairman, if I may be permitted to make a suggestion, can both of these gentlemen be right? I put it to you, sir, can both have happened to say the very same words to the stranger? It seems to me—"

The tanner got up and interrupted him. The tanner was a disgruntled man; he believed himself entitled to be a Nineteener, but he couldn't get recognition. It made him a little unpleasant in his ways and speech. Said he:

"Sho, *that's* not the point! *That* could happen—twice in a hundred years—but not the other thing. *Neither* of them gave the twenty dollars!"

[*A ripple of applause.*]

Billson: "*I* did!"

Wilson: "*I* did!"

Then each accused the other of pilfering.

The Chair: "Order! Sit down, if you please—both of you. Neither of the notes has been out of my possession at any moment."

A voice: "Good—that settles *that*!"

The Tanner: "Mr. Chairman, one thing is now plain: one of these men has been eavesdropping under the other one's bed, and filching family secrets. If it is not unparliamentary to suggest it, I will remark that both are equal to it. [*The Chair*: "Order! order!"] I withdraw the remark, sir, and will confine myself to suggesting that *if* one of them has overheard the other reveal the test-remark to his wife, we shall catch him now."

A Voice: "How?"

The Tanner: "Easily. The two have not quoted the remark in exactly the same words. You would have noticed that, if there hadn't been a considerable stretch of time and an exciting quarrel inserted between the two readings."

A Voice: "Name the difference."

The Tanner: "The word *very* is in Billson's note, and not in the other."

Many Voices: "That's so—he's right!"

The Tanner: "And so, if the Chair will examine the test-remark in the sack, we shall know which of these two frauds—[*The Chair*: "Order!"]—which of these two adventurers—[*The Chair*: "Order! order!"]—which of these two gentlemen [*laughter and applause*]—is entitled to wear the belt as being the first dishonest blatherskite ever bred in this town—which he has dishonored, and which will be a sultry place for him from now out!" [*Vigorous applause.*]

Many Voices: "Open it!—Open the sack!"

Mr Burgess made a slit in the sack, slid his hand in and brought out an envelope. In it were a couple of folded notes. He said:

"One of these is marked, 'Not to be examined until all written communications which have been addressed to the Chair—if any—shall have been read.' The other is marked '*The Test*.' Allow me. It is worded—to wit:

" 'I do not require that the first half of the remark which was made to me by my benefactor shall be quoted with exactness, for it was not striking, and could be forgotten; but its closing fifteen words are quite striking, and I think easily rememberable; unless *these* shall be accurately reproduced, let the applicant be regarded as an impostor. My benefactor began by saying he seldom gave advice to any one, but that it always bore the hall-mark of high value when he did give it. Then he said this—and it has never faded from my memory: *"You are far from being a bad man—"* ' "

Fifty Voices: "That settles it—the money's Wilson's! Wilson! Wilson! Speech! Speech!"

People jumped up and crowded around Wilson, wringing his hand and congratulating fervently—meantime the Chair was hammering with the gavel and shouting:

"Order, gentlemen! Order! Order! Let me finish reading, please." When quiet was restored, the reading was resumed—as follows:

" ' *"Go, and reform—or, mark my words—some day, for your sins, you will die and go to hell or Hadleyburg—try and make it the former."* ' "

A ghastly silence followed. First an angry cloud began to settle darkly upon the faces of the citizenship; after a pause the cloud began to rise, and a tickled expression tried to take its place; tried so hard that it was only kept under with great and painful difficulty; the reporters, the Brixtonites, and other strangers bent their heads down and shielded their faces with their hands, and managed to hold in by main strength and heroic courtesy. At this most inopportune time burst upon the stillness the roar of a solitary voice—Jack Halliday's:

"*That's* got the hall-mark on it!"

Then the house let go, strangers and all. Even Mr. Burgess's gravity broke down presently, then the audience considered itself officially absolved from all restraint, and it made the most of its privilege. It was a good long laugh, and a tempestuously whole-hearted one, but it ceased at last—long enought for Mr. Burgess to try to resume, and for the people to get their eyes partially wiped; then it broke out again; and afterward yet again; then at last Burgess was able to get out these serious words:

"It is useless to try to disguise the fact—we find ourselves in the presence of a matter of grave import. It involves the honor of your town, it strikes at the town's good name. The difference of a single word between the test-remarks offered by Mr. Wilson and Mr. Billson was itself a serious thing, since it indicated that one or the other of these gentlemen had committed a theft—"

The two men were sitting limp, nerveless, crushed; but at these words, both were electrified into movement, and started to get up—

"Sit down!" said the Chair, sharply, and they obeyed. "That, as I have said, was a serious thing. And it was—but for only one of them. But the matter has become graver; for the honor of *both* is now in formidable peril. Shall I go even further, and say in inextricable peril? *Both* left out the crucial fifteen words." He paused. During several moments he allowed the pervading stillness to gather and deepen its impressive effects, then added: "There would seem to be but one way whereby this could happen. I ask these gentlemen—Was there *collusion?—agreement?*"

A low murmur sifted through the house; its import was, "He's got them both."

Billson was not used to emergencies; he sat in a helpless collapse. But Wilson was a lawyer. He struggled to his feet, pale and worried, and said:

"I ask the indulgence of the house while I explain this most painful matter. I am sorry to say what I'm about to say, since it must inflict irreparable injury upon Mr. Billson, whom I have always esteemed and respected until now, and in whose invulnerability to temptation I entirely believed—as did you all. But for the preservation of my own honor I must speak—and with frankness. I confess with shame—and I now beseech your pardon for it—that I said to the ruined stranger all of the words contained in the test-remark, including the disparaging fifteen. [*Sensation.*] When the late publication was made I recalled them, and I resolved to claim the sack of coin, for by every right I was entitled to it. Now I will ask you to consider this point, and weigh it well: that stranger's gratitude to me that night knew no bounds; he said himself that he could find no words for it that were adequate, and that if he should ever be able he would repay me a thousandfold. Now, then, I ask you this: Could I expect—could I believe—could I even remotely imagine—that, feeling as he did, he would do so ungrateful a thing as to add those quite unnecessary fifteen words to his test?—set a trap for me?—expose me as a slanderer of my own town before my own people assembled in a public hall? It was preposterous; it was impossible. His test would contain only the kindly opening clause of my remark. Of that I had no shadow of doubt. You would have thought as I did. You would not have expected a base betrayal from one whom you had befriended and against whom you had committed no offense. And so, with perfect confidence, perfect trust, I wrote on a piece of paper the opening words—ending with 'Go, and reform,'— and signed it. When I was about to put it in an envelope I was called into my back office, and without thinking I left the paper lying open on my desk." He stopped, turned his head slowly toward Billson, waited a moment, then added: "I ask you to note this: when I returned, a little later, Mr. Billson was retiring by my street door." [*Sensation.*]

In a moment Billson was on his feet and shouting:

"It's a lie! It's an infamous lie!"

The Chair: "Be seated, sir! Mr. Wilson has the floor."

Billson's friends pulled him into his seat and quieted him, and Wilson went on:

"Those are the simple facts. My note was now lying in a different place on the table from where I had left it. I noticed that, but attached no importance to it, thinking a draught had blown it there. That Mr. Billson would read a private paper was a thing which could not occur to me; he was an honorable man, and he would be above that. If you will allow me to say it, I think his extra word '*very*' stands explained; it is attributable to a defect of memory. I was the only man in the world who could furnish here any detail of the test remark—by *honorable* means. I have finished."

There is nothing in the world like a persuasive speech to fuddle the mental apparatus and upset the convictions and debauch the emotions of an audience not practised in the tricks and delusions of oratory. Wilson sat down victorious. The house submerged him in tides of approving applause; friends swarmed to him and shook him by the hand and congratulated him, and Billson was shouted down and not allowed to say a word. The Chair hammered and hammered with its gavel, and kept shouting:

"But let us proceed, gentlemen, let us proceed!"

At last there was a measurable degree of quiet, and the hatter said; "But what is there to proceed with, sir, but to deliver the money?"

Voices: "That's it! That's it! Come forward, Wilson!"

The Hatter: "I move three cheers for Mr. Wilson, Symbol of the special virtue which—"

The cheers burst forth before he could finish; and in the midst of them—and in the midst of the clamor of the gavel also—some enthusiasts mounted Wilson on a big friend's shoulder and were going to fetch him in triumph to the platform. The Chair's voice now rose above the noise—

"Order! To your places! You forget that there is still a document to be read." When quiet had been restored he took up the document, and was going to read it, but laid it down again, saying: "I forgot; this is not to be read until all written communications received by me have first been read." He took an envelope out of his pocket, removed its inclosure, glanced at it—seemed astonished—held it out and gazed at it—stared at it.

Twenty or thirty voices cried out:

"What is it? Read it! read it!"

And he did—slowly, and wondering:

"'*The remark which I made to the stranger*—[*Voices*: "Hello! how's this?"]—*was this*: "*You are far from being a bad man.* [*Voices*: "Great Scott!"] *Go, and reform*"' [*Voices*: "Oh, saw my leg off!"] Signed by Mr. Pinkerton, the banker."

The <u>pandemonium</u> of delight which turned itself loose now was of a sort to make the <u>judicious</u> weep. Those whose withers were unwrung laughed till the tears ran down; the reporters, in throes of laughter, set down disordered pothooks which would never in the world be decipherable; and a sleeping dog jumped up, scared out of its wits, and barked itself crazy at the turmoil. All manner of cries were scattered through the din: "We're getting rich—*two* Symbols of Incorruptibility!—without counting Billson!" "*Three!*—count Shadbelly in—we can't have too many!" "All right—Billson's elected!" "Alas, poor Wilson—victim of *two* thieves!"

A Powerful Voice: "Silence! The Chair's fished up something more out of his pocket."

Voices: "Hurrah! Is it something fresh? Read it! read it! read!"

The Chair [*reading*]: "'*The remark which I made,*' etc.: '"*You are far from being a bad man. Go,*"' etc. Signed, 'Gregory Yates.'"

Tornado of Voices: "Four Symbols!" "'Rah for Yates!" "Fish again!"

The house was in a roaring humor now, and ready to get all the fun out of the occasion that might be in it. Several Nineteeners, looking pale and distressed, got up and began to work their way toward the aisles, but a score of shouts went up:

"The doors, the doors—close the doors; no Incorruptible shall leave this place! Sit down, everybody!"

The mandate was obeyed.

"Fish again! Read! read!"

The Chair fished again, and once more the familiar words began to fall from its lips—"'*You are far from being a bad man.*'"

"Name! name! What's his name?"

"'L. Ingoldsby Sargent.'"

"Five elected! Pile up the Symbols! Go on, go on!"

"'*You are far from being a bad—*'"

"Name! name!"

"'Nicholas Whitworth.'"

"Hooray! hooray! it's a symbolical day!"

Somebody wailed in, and began to sing this rhyme (leaving out "it's") to the lovely "Mikado" tune of "When a man's afraid, a beautiful maid—"; the audience joined in, with joy; then, just in time somebody contributed another line—

And don't you this forget—

The house roared it out. A third line was at once furnished—

Corruptibles far from Hadleyburg are—

The house roared that one too. As the last note died, Jack Halliday's voice rose high and clear, freighted with a final line—

But the Symbols are here, you bet!

That was sung, with booming enthusiasm. Then the happy house started in at the beginning and sang the four lines through twice, with immense swing and dash, and finished up with a crashing three-times-three and a tiger for "Hadleyburg the Incorruptible and all Symbols of it which we shall find worthy to receive the hall-mark to-night."

Then the shoutings at the Chair began again, all over the place:

"Go on! go on! Read! read some more! Read all you've got!"

"That's it—go on! We are winning eternal celebrity!"

A dozen men got up now and began to protest. They said that this farce was the work of some abandoned joker, and was an insult to the whole community. Without a doubt these signatures were all forgeries—

"Sit down! sit down! Shut up! You are confessing. We'll find *your* names in the lot."

"Mr. Chairman, how many of those envelopes have you got?"

The chair counted.

"Together with those that have been already examined, there are nineteen."

A storm of derisive applause broke out.

"Perhaps they all contain the secret. I move that you open them all and read every signature that is attached to a note of that sort—and read also the first eight words of the note."

"Second the motion!"

It was put and carried—uproariously. Then poor old Richards got up, and his wife rose and stood at his side. Her head was bent down, so that none might see that she was crying. Her husband gave her his arm, and so supporting her, he began to speak in a quavering voice:

"My friends, you have known us two—Mary and me—all our lives, and I think you have liked us and respected us—"

The Chair interrupted him:

"Allow me. It is quite true—that which you are saying, Mr. Richards: this town *does* know you two; it *does* like you; it *does* respect you; more—it honors you and *loves* you—"

Halliday's voice rang out:

"That's the hall-marked truth, too! If the Chair is right, let the house speak up and say it. Rise! Now, then—hip! hip! hip!—all together!"

The house rose in mass, faced toward the old couple eagerly, filled the air with a snow-storm of waving handkerchiefs, and delivered the cheers with all its affectionate heart.

The Chair then continued:

"What I was going to say is this: We know your good heart, Mr. Richards, but this is not a time for the exercise of charity toward offenders. [*Shouts of "Right! right!"*] I see your generous purpose in your face, but I cannot allow you to plead for these men—"

"But I was going to—"

"Please take your seat, Mr. Richards. We must examine the rest of these notes—simple fairness to the men who have already been exposed requires this. As soon as that has been done—I give you my word for this—you shall be heard."

Many Voices: "Right—the Chair is right—no interruption can be permitted at this stage! Go on—the names! the names!—according to the terms of the motion!"

The old couple sat reluctantly down, and the husband whispered to the wife, "It is pitifully hard to have to wait; the shame will be greater than ever when they find we were only going to plead for *ourselves*."

Straightaway the jollity broke loose again with the reading of the names.

"'*You are far from being a bad man*—' Signature, 'Robert J. Titmarsh.'"

"'*You are far from being a bad man*—' Signature, 'Eliphalet Weeks.'"

"'*You are far from being a bad man*—' Signature, 'Oscar B. Wilder.'"

At this point the house lit upon the idea of taking the eight words out of the Chairman's hands. He was not unthankful for that. Thenceforward he held up each note in its turn and waited. The house droned out the eight words in a massed and measured and musical deep volume of sound (with a daringly close resemblance to a well-known church chant)—"'You are f-a-r from being a b-a-a-a-d man.'" Then the Chair said, "Signature, 'Archibald Wilcox.'" And so on, and so on, name after name, and everybody had an increasingly and gloriously good time except the wretched Nineteen. Now and then, when a particularly shining name was called, the house made the Chair wait while it chanted the whole of the test-remark from the beginning to the closing words, "And go to hell or Hadleyburg—try and make it the for-or-m-e-r!" and in these special cases they added a grand and agonized and imposing "A-a-a-a-men!"

The list dwindled, dwindled, dwindled, poor old Richards keeping tally of the count, wincing when a name resembling his own was pronounced, and waiting in miserable suspense for the time to come when it would be his humiliating privilege to rise with Mary and finish his plea, which he was intending to word thus: ". . . for until now we have never done any wrong thing, but have gone our humble way unreproached. We are very poor, we are old, and have no chick nor child to help us; we were sorely tempted, and we fell. It was my purpose when I got up before to make confession and beg that my name might not be read out in this public place, for it seemed to us that we could not bear it; but I was prevented. It was just; it was our place to suffer with the rest. It has been hard for us. It is the first time we have ever heard our name fall from any one's lips—sullied. Be merciful—for the sake of the better days; make our shame as light to bear as in your charity you can." At this point in his revery Mary nudged him, perceiving that his mind was absent. The house was chanting, "You are f-a-r," etc.

"Be ready," Mary whispered. "Your name comes now; he has read eighteen."

The chant ended.

"Next! next! next!" came volleying from all over the house.

Burgess put his hand into his pocket. The old couple, trembling, began to rise. Burgess fumbled a moment, then said,

"I find I have read them all."

Faint with joy and surprise, the couple sank into their seats, and Mary whispered:

"Oh, bless God, we are saved!—he has lost ours—I wouldn't give this for a hundred of those sacks!"

The house burst out with its "Mikado" travesty, and sang it three times with ever-increasing enthusiasm, rising to its feet when it reached for the third time the closing line—

But the Symbols are here, you bet!

and finishing up with cheers and a tiger for "Hadleyburg purity and our eighteen immortal representatives of it."

Then Wingate, the saddler, got up and proposed cheers "for the cleanest man in town, the one solitary important citizen in it who didn't try to steal that money—Edward Richards."

They were given with great and moving heartiness; then somebody proposed that Richards be elected sole guardian and Symbol of the now Sacred Hadleyburg Tradition, with power and right to stand up and look the whole sarcastic world in the face.

Passed, by acclamation; then they sang the "Mikado" again, and ended it with:

And there's *one* Symbol left, you bet!

There was a pause; then—

A Voice: "Now, then, who's to get the sack?"

The Tanner: [*with bitter sarcasm*] "That's easy. The money has to be divided among the eighteen Incorruptibles. They gave the suffering stranger twenty dollars apiece—and that remark—each in his turn—it took twenty-two minutes for the procession to move past. Staked the stranger—total contribution, $360. All they want is just the loan back—and interest—forty thousand dollars altogether."

Many Voices: [*derisively*] "That's it! Divvy! divvy! Be kind to the poor—don't keep them waiting!"

The Chair: "Order! I now offer the stranger's remaining document. It says: 'If no claimant shall appear [*grand chorus of groans*] I desire that you open the sack and count out the money to the principal citizens of your town, they to take it in trust [*cries of "Oh! Oh! Oh"*], and use it in such ways as to them shall seem best for the propagation and preservation of your community's noble reputation for incorruptible honesty [*more cries*]—a reputation to which their names and their efforts will add a new and far-reaching luster.' [*Enthusiastic outburst of sarcastic applause.*] That seems to be all. No—here is a postscript:

" 'P.S.—Citizens of Hadleyburg. There *is* no test-remark—nobody made one. [*Great sensation.*] There wasn't any pauper stranger, nor any twenty-dollar contribution, nor any accompanying benediction and compliment—these are all inventions. [*General buzz and hum of astonishment and delight.*] Allow me to tell my story—it will take but a word or two. I passed through your town at a certain time, and received a deep offense which I had not earned. Any other man would have been content to kill one or two of you and call it square, but to me that would have been a trivial revenge, and inadequate; for the dead do not *suffer.* Besides, I could not kill you all—and, anyway, made as I am, even that would not have satisfied me. I wanted to damage every man in the place, and every woman—and not in their bodies or in their estate, but in their vanity—the place where feeble and foolish people are most vulnerable. So I disguised myself and came back and studied you. You were easy game. You had an old and lofty reputation for honesty, and naturally you were proud of it—it was your treasure of treasures, the very apple of your eye. As soon as I found out that you carefully and vigilantly kept yourselves and your children *out of temptation,* I knew how to proceed. Why, you simple creatures, the weakest of all weak things is a virtue which has not been tested in the fire. I laid a plan, and gathered a list of names. My project was to corrupt Hadleyburg the Incorruptible. My idea was to make liars and thieves of nearly half a hundred smirchless men and women who had never in their lives uttered a lie or stolen a penny. I was afraid of Goodson. He was neither born nor reared in Hadleyburg. I was afraid that if I started to operate my scheme by getting my letter laid before you, you would say to yourselves, "Goodson is the only man among us who would give away twenty dollars to a poor devil"—and then you might not bite at my bait. But Heaven took Goodson; then I knew I was safe, and I set my trap and baited it. It may be that I shall not catch all the men to whom I mailed the pretended test secret, but I shall catch the most of them, if I know Hadleyburg nature. [*Voices:* "Right—he got every last one of them."] I believe they will even steal ostensible *gamble*-money, rather than miss, poor, tempted, and mistrained fellows. I am hoping to eternally and everlastingly squelch your vanity and give Hadleyburg a new renown—one that will *stick*—and spread far. If I have succeeded, open the sack and summon the Committee on Propagation and Preservation of the Hadleyburg Reputation.' "

A *Cyclone of Voices*: "Open it! Open it! The Eighteen to the front! Committee on Propagation of the Tradition! Forward—the Incorruptibles!"

The Chair ripped the sack wide, and gathered up a handful of bright, broad, yellow coins, shook them together, then examined them—

"Friends they are only gilded disks of lead!"

There was a crashing outbreak of delight over this news, and when the noise had subsided, the tanner called out:

"By right of apparent seniority in this business, Mr. Wilson is Chairman of the Committee on Propagation of the Tradition. I suggest that he step forward on behalf of his pals, and receive in trust the money."

A *Hundred Voices*: "Wilson! Wilson! Wilson! Speech! Speech!"

Wilson: [*in a voice trembling with anger*] "You will allow me to say, and without apologies for my language, *damn* the money!"

A *Voice*: "Oh, and him a Baptist!"

A *Voice*: "Seventeen Symbols left! Step up, gentlemen, and assume your trust!"

There was a pause—no response.

The Saddler: "Mr. Chairman, we've got *one* clean man left, anyway, out of the late aristocracy; and he needs money, and deserves it. I move that you appoint Jack Halliday to get up there and auction off that sack of gilt twenty-dollar pieces, and give the result to the right man—the man whom Hadleyburg delights to honor—Edward Richards."

This was received with great enthusiasm, the dog taking a hand again; the saddler started the bids at a dollar, the Brixton folk and Barnum's representative fought hard for it, the people cheered every jump that the bids made, the excitement climbed moment by moment higher and higher, the bidders got on their mettle and grew steadily more and more daring, more and more determined, the jumps went from a dollar up to five, then to ten, then to twenty, then fifty, then to a hundred, then—

At the beginning of the auction Richards whispered in distress to his wife: "O Mary, can we allow it? It—it—you see, it is an honor-reward, a testimonial to purity of character, and—and—can we allow it? Hadn't I better get up and—O Mary, what ought we to do?—what do you think we—[*Halliday's voice: "Fifteen I'm bid—fifteen for the sack!—twenty!—ah, thanks!—thirty—thanks again! Thirty, thirty, thirty!—do I hear forty?—forty it is! Keep the ball rolling gentlemen, keep it rolling!—fifty! thanks, noble Roman! going at fifty, fifty, fifty!—seventy! ninety! splendid!—a hundred! pile it up, pile it up!—hundred and twenty—forty!—just in time!—hundred and fifty!—Two hundred!—superb! Do I hear two h—thanks!—two hundred and fifty!—"*]

"It is another temptation, Edward—I'm all in a tremble—but, oh, we've escaped one temptation, and that ought to warn us to—[*"Six did I hear?—thanks!—six-fifty, six-f—seven hundred!"*] And yet, Edward, when you think—nobody susp—[*"Eight hundred dollars!—hurrah!—make it nine!—Mr. Parsons, did I hear you say—thanks—nine!—this noble sack of virgin lead going at only nine hundred dollars, gilding and all—come! do I hear—a thousand!—gratefully yours!—did someone say eleven?—a sack which is going to be the most celebrated in the whole Uni—"*] O Edward" (beginning to sob), "we are *so* poor!—but—but do as you think best—do as you think best."

Edward fell—that is, he sat still; sat with a conscience which was not satisfied, but which was overpowered by circumstances.

Meantime a stranger, who looked like an amateur detective gotten up as an impossible English earl, had been watching the evening's proceedings with manifest interest, and with a contented expression in his face; and he had been privately commenting to himself. He was now soliloquizing somewhat like this: "None of the Eighteen are bidding; that is not satisfactory; I must change that—the dramatic unities require it; they must buy the sack they tried to steal; they must pay a heavy price, too—some of them are rich. And another thing, when I make a mistake in Hadleyburg nature the man that puts that error upon me is entitled to a high honorarium, and some one must pay it. This poor old Richards has brought my judgment to shame; he is an honest man:—I don't understand it, but I acknowledge it. Yes, he saw my deuces *and* with a straight flush, and by rights the pot is his. And it shall be a jackpot, too, if I can manage it. He disappointed me, but let that pass."

He was watching the bidding. At a thousand, the market broke; the prices tumbled swiftly. He waited—and still watched. One competitor dropped out; then another, and another. He put in a bid or two now. When the bids had sunk to ten dollars, he added a five; some one raised him a three; he waited a moment, then flung in a fifty-dollar jump, and the sack was his—at $1,282. The house broke out in cheers—then stopped; for he was on his feet, and had lifted his hand. He began to speak.

"I desire to say a word, and ask a favor. I am a speculator in rarities, and I have dealings with persons interested in numismatics all over the world. I can make a profit on this purchase, just as it stands; but there is a way, if I can get your approval, whereby I can make every one of these leaden twenty-dollar pieces worth its face in gold, and perhaps more. Grant me that approval, and I will give part of my gains to your Mr. Richards, whose invulnerable probity you have so justly and so cordially recognized to-night; his share shall be ten thousand dollars, and I will hand him the money to-morrow. [*Great applause from the house.* But the "invulnerable probity" made the Richardses blush prettily; however, it went for modesty, and did no harm.] If you will pass my proposition by a good majority—I would like a two-thirds vote—I will regard that as the town's consent, and that is all I ask. Rarities are always helped by any device which will rouse curiosity and compel remark. Now if I may have your permission to stamp upon the faces of each of these ostensible coins the names of the eighteen gentlemen who—"

Nine-tenths of the audience were on their feet in a moment—dog and all—and the proposition was carried with a whirlwind of approving applause and laughter.

They sat down, and all the Symbols except "Dr." Clay Harkness got up, violently protesting against the proposed outrage, and threatening to—

"I beg you not to threaten me," said the stranger calmly. "I know my legal rights, and am not accustomed to being frightened at bluster." [*Applause.*] He sat down. "Dr." Harkness saw an opportunity here. He was one of the two very rich men of the place, and Pinkerton was the other. Harkness was proprietor of a mint; that is to say, a popular patent medicine. He was running for the legislature on one ticket, and Pinkerton on the other. It was a close race and a hot one, and getting hotter every day. Both had strong appetites for money; each had bought a great tract of land, with a purpose; there was going to be a new railway, and each wanted to be in the legislature and help locate the route to his own advantage; a single vote might make the decision, and with it two or three fortunes. The stake was large, and Harkness was a daring speculator. He was sitting close to the stranger. He leaned over while one or another of the other Symbols was entertaining the house with protests and appeals, and asked, in a whisper.

"What is your price for the sack?"

"Forty thousand dollars."

"I'll give you twenty."

"No."

"Twenty-five."

"No."

"Say Thirty."

"The price is forty thousand dollars; not a penny less."

"All right, I'll give it. I will come to the hotel at ten in the morning. I don't want it known: will see you privately."

"Very good." Then the stranger got up and said to the house:

"I find it late. The speeches of these gentlemen are not without merit, not without interest, not without grace; yet if I may be excused I will take my leave. I thank you for the great favor which you have shown me in granting my petition. I ask the Chair to keep the sack for me until to-morrow, and to hand these three five-hundred-dollar notes to Mr. Richards." They were passed up to the Chair. "At nine I will call for the sack, and at eleven will deliver the rest of the ten thousand to Mr. Richards in person, at his home. Good night."

Then he slipped out, and left the audience making a vast noise, which was composed of a mixture of cheers, the "Mikado" song, dog-disapproval, and the chant, "You are f-a-r from being a b-a-a-d man—a-a-a-a-men!"

IV

At home the Richardses had to endure congratulations and compliments until midnight. Then they were left to themselves. They looked a little sad, and they sat silent and thinking. Finally Mary sighed and said:

"Do you think we are to blame, Edward—*much* to blame?" and her eyes wandered to the accusing triplet of big banknotes lying on the table, where the congratulators had been gloating over them and reverently fingering them. Edward did not answer at once; then he brought out with a sigh and said, hesitatingly:

"We—we couldn't help it, Mary. It—well, it was ordered. *All* things are."

Mary glanced up and looked at him steadily, but he didn't return the look. Presently she said:

"I thought congratulations and praises always tasted good. But—it seems to me, now—Edward?"

"Well?"

"Are you going to stay in the bank?"

"N-n-o-no."

"Resign?"

"In the morning—by note."

"It does seem best."

Richards bowed his head in his hands and muttered:

"Before, I was not afraid to let oceans of people's money pour through my hands, but—Mary, I am so tired, so tired—"

"We will go to bed."

At nine in the morning the stranger called for the sack and took it to the hotel in a cab. At ten Harkness had a talk with him privately. The stranger asked for and got five checks on a metropolitan bank—drawn to "Bearer"—four for $1,500 each, and one for $34,000. He put one of the former in his pocketbook, and the remainder, representing $38,500, he put in an envelope, and with these he added a note, which he wrote after Harkness was gone. At eleven he called at the Richards house and knocked. Mrs. Richards peeped through the shutters, then went and received the envelope, and the stranger disappeared without a word. She came back flushed and a little unsteady on her legs, and gasped out:

"I am sure I recognized him! Last night it seemed to me that maybe I had seen him somewhere before."

"He is the man that brought the sack here?"

"I am almost sure of it."

"Then he is the ostensible Stephenson, too, and sold every important citizen in this town with his bogus secret. Now if he has sent checks instead of money, we are sold, too, after we thought we had escaped. I was beginning to feel fairly comfortable once more, after my night's rest, but the look of that envelope makes me sick. It isn't fat enough; $8,500 in even the largest bank-notes makes more bulk than that."

"Edward, why do you object to checks?"

"Checks signed by Stephenson! I am resigned to take the $8,500 if it could come in bank-notes—for it does seem that it was so ordered, Mary—but I have never had much courage, and I have not the pluck to try to market a check signed with that disastrous name. It would be a trap. That man tried to catch me; we escaped somehow or other; and now he is trying a new way. If it is checks—"

"Oh, Edward, it is *too* bad!" and she held up the checks and began to cry.

"Put them in the fire! quick! we musn't be tempted. It is a trick to make the world laugh at *us,* along with the rest, and—Give them to *me,* since you can't do it!" He snatched them and tried to hold his grip till he could get to the stove; but he was human, he was a cashier, and he stopped a moment to make sure of the signature. Then he came near to fainting.

"Fan me, Mary, fan me! They are the same as gold!"

"Oh, how lovely, Edward! Why?"

"Signed by Harkness. What can the mystery of that be, Mary?"

"Edward, do you think—"

"Look here—look at this! Fifteen—fifteen—fifteen—thirty-four. Thirty-eight thousand five hundred! Mary, the sack isn't worth twelve dollars, and Harkness—apparently—has paid about par for it."

"And does it all come to us, do you think—instead of the ten thousand?"

"Why, it looks like it. And the checks are made to 'Bearer,' too."

"Is that good, Edward? What is it for?"

"A hint to collect them at some distant bank, I reckon. Perhaps Harkness doesn't want the matter known. What is that—a note?"

"Yes. It was with the checks."

It was in the "Stephenson" handwriting, but there was no signature. It said:

"I am a disappointed man. Your honesty is beyond the reach of temptation. I had a different idea about it, but I wronged you in that, and I beg pardon, and do it sincerely. I honor you—and that is sincere too. This town is not worthy to kiss the hem of your garment. Dear sir, I made a square bet with myself that there were nineteen debauchable men in your self-righteous community. I have lost. Take the whole pot, you are entitled to it."

Richards drew a deep sigh, and said:

"It seems written with fire—it burns so. Mary—I am miserable again."

"I, too. Ah, dear, I wish—"

"To think, Mary—he *believes* in me."

"Oh, don't Edward—I can't bear it."

"If those beautiful words were deserved, Mary—and God knows I believed I deserved them once—I think I could give the forty thousand dollars for them. And I would put that paper away, as representing more than gold and jewels, and keep it always. But now— We could not live in the shadow of its accusing presence, Mary."

He put it in the fire.

A messenger arrived and delivered an envelope.

Richards took from it a note and read it; it was from Burgess.

"You saved me, in a difficult time. I saved you last night. It was at cost of a lie, but I made the sacrifice freely, and out of a grateful heart. None in this village knows so well as I know how brave and good and noble you are. At bottom you cannot respect me, knowing as you do of that matter of which I am accused, and by the general voice condemned; but I beg that you will at least believe that I am a grateful man; it will help me to bear my burden."

[SIGNED] *Burgess*

"Saved, once more. And on such terms!" He put the note in the fire. "I—I wish I were dead, Mary, I wish I were out of it all."

"Oh, these are bitter, bitter days, Edward. The stabs, through their generosity, are so deep—and they come so fast!"

Three days before the election each of two thousand voters suddenly found himself in possession of a prized memento—one of the renowned bogus double-eagles. Around one of its faces was stamped these words: "The Remark I made To The Poor Stranger Was—" Around the other face was stamped these: "Go, And Reform. [Signed] Pinkerton." Thus the entire remaining refuse of the renowned joke was emptied upon a single head, and with calamitous effect. It revived the recent vast laugh and concentrated it upon Pinkerton; and Harkness's election was a walkover.

Within twenty-four hours after the Richardses had received their checks their consciences were quieting down, discouraged; the old couple were learning to reconcile themselves to the sin which they had committed. But they were to learn, now, that a sin takes on new and real terrors when there seems a chance that it is going to be found out. This gives it a fresh and most substantial and important aspect. At church the morning sermon was of the usual pattern; it was the same old things said in the same old way; they had heard them a thousand times and found them innocuous, next to meaningless, and easy to sleep under; but now it was different: the sermon seemed to bristle with accusations; it seemed aimed straight and specially at people who were concealing deadly sins. After church they got away from the mob of congratulators as soon as they could, and hurried homeward, chilled to the bone at they did not know what—vague, shadowy, indefinite fears. And by chance they caught a glimpse of Mr. Burgess as he turned a corner. He paid no attention to their nod of recognition! He hadn't seen it; but they did not know that. What could his conduct mean? It might mean—it might mean—oh, a dozen dreadful things. Was it possible that he knew that Richards could have cleared him of guilt in that bygone time, and had been silently waiting for a chance to even up accounts? At home, in their distress they got to imagining that their servant might have been in the next room listening when Richards revealed the secret to his wife that he knew of Burgess's innocence; next, Richards began to imagine that he had heard the swish of a gown in there at that time; next, he was sure he *had* heard it. They would call Sarah in, on a pretext, and watch her face: if she had been betraying them to Mr.

Burgess, it would show in her manner. They asked her some questions—questions which were so random and incoherent and seemingly purposeless that the girl felt sure that the old people's minds had been affected by their sudden good fortune; the sharp and watchful gaze which they bent upon her frightened her, and that completed the business. She blushed, she became nervous and confused, and to the old people these were plain signs of guilt—guilt of some fearful sort or other—without doubt she was a spy and a traitor. When they were alone again they began to piece many unrelated things together and get horrible results out of the combination. When things had got about to the worst, Richards was delivered of a sudden gasp, and his wife asked:

"Oh, what is it?—what is it?"

"The note—Burgess's note! Its language was sarcastic, I see it now." He quoted: " 'At bottom you cannot respect me, *knowing,* as you do, of *that matter* of which I am accused'—oh, it is perfectly plain, now, God help me! He knows that I know! You see the ingenuity of the phrasing. It was a trap—and like a fool, I walked into it. And Mary—?"

"Oh, it is dreadful—I know what you are going to say—he didn't return your transcript of the pretended test-remark."

"No—kept it to destroy us with. Mary, he has exposed us to some already. I know it—I know it well. I saw it in a dozen faces after church. Ah, he wouldn't answer our nod of recognition—*he* knew what he had been doing!"

In the night the doctor was called. The news went around in the morning that the old couple were rather seriously ill—prostrated by the exhausting excitement growing out of their great windfall, the congratulations, and the late hours, the doctor said. The town was sincerely distressed; for these old people were about all it had left to be proud of, now.

Two days later the news was worse. The old couple were delirious, and were doing strange things. By witness of the nurses, Richards had exhibited checks—for $8,500? No—for an amazing sum—$38,500! What could be the explanation of this gigantic piece of luck?

The following day the nurses had more news—and wonderful. They had concluded to hide the checks, lest harm come to them; but when they searched they were gone from under the patient's pillow—vanished away. The patient said:

"Let the pillow alone; what do you want?"

"We thought it best that the checks—"

"You will never see them again—they are destroyed. They came from Satan. I saw the hell-brand on them, and I knew they were sent to betray me to sin." Then he fell to gabbling strange and dreadful things which were not clearly understandable, and which the doctor admonished them to keep to themselves.

Richards was right; the checks were never seen again.

A nurse must have talked in her sleep, for within two days the forbidden gabblings were the property of the town; and they were of a surprising sort. They seemed to indicate that Richards had been a claimant for the sack himself, and that Burgess had concealed that fact and then maliciously betrayed it.

Burgess was taxed with this and stoutly denied it. And he said it was not fair to attach weight to the chatter of a sick old man who was out of his mind. Still, suspicion was in the air, and there was much talk.

After a day or two it was reported that Mrs. Richards' delirious deliveries were getting to be duplicates of her husband's. Suspicion flamed up into conviction, now, and the town's pride in the purity of its one undiscredited important citizen began to dim down and flicker toward extinction.

Six days passed, then came more news. The old couple were dying. Richards' mind cleared in his latest hour, and he sent for Burgess. Burgess said:

"Let the room be cleared. I think he wishes to say something in privacy."

"No!" said Richards: "I want witnesses. I want you all to hear my confession, so that I may die a man, and not a dog. I was clean—artificially—like the rest; and like the rest I fell when temptation came. I signed a lie, and claimed the miserable sack. Mr. Burgess remembered that I had done him a service, and in gratitude (and ignorance) he suppressed my claim and saved me. You know the thing that was charged against Burgess years ago. My testimony, and mine alone, could have cleared him, and I was a coward, and left him to suffer disgrace—"

"No—no—Mr. Richards, you—"

"My servant betrayed my secret to him—"

"No one has betrayed anything to me—"

—"and then he did a natural and justifiable thing, he repented of the saving kindness which he had done me, and he *exposed* me—as I deserved—"

"Never!—I make oath—"

"Out of my heart I forgive him."

Burgess's impassioned protestations fell upon deaf ears; the dying man passed away without knowing that once more he had done poor Burgess a wrong. The old wife died that night.

The last of the sacred Nineteen had fallen a prey to the fiendish sack; the town was stripped of the last rag of its ancient glory. Its mourning was not showy, but it was deep.

By act of the Legislature—upon prayer and petition—Hadleyburg was allowed to change its name to (never mind what—I will not give it away), and leave one word out of the motto that for many generations had graced the town's official seal.

It is an honest town once more, and the man will have to rise early that catches it napping again.

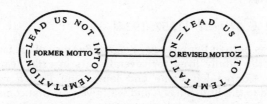

Fact Questions and Exercises

1. What is the gist of the note attached to the outside of the sack?
2. According to Mr. Richards, how many dollars is the "sack of gold" worth?

3. What is the "one thing" that Reverend Burgess has been accused of? Is he guilty? *story does not say - 870*
4. How do "millions and millions of people" throughout America learn the story about the gold and Hadleyburg? *Through Cox's (the newspaper owner)*
5. Identify Jack Halliday. *loafer, the Sam Foreman "Lawson" type?*
6. According to the letter from "Howard L. Stephenson," what was the "remark" that the good samaritan was supposed to have made? *you are far from being a bad man, go, & reform*

Build houses, balls, country seats

7. After the nineteen leading citizens received copies of the Stephenson letter, what were some of the things that they planned to do with the money?
8. What is the actual "remark" written on the note in the sack of gold? How do the townspeople react to the note? *"you are far from being a bad man, go, & reform or mark my words - some day, for your own sake,*

Rev. Burgess is repaying a debt of gratitude.
They are eaten up w/ guilt.
gilded disks of lead

9. Why isn't the Richards' note read along with the eighteen other notes? What happens to the Richards because the note is left unread? *will die & go to hell w/*
10. What is actually in the sack that the stranger has left in Hadleyburg?
11. How does the new town motto differ from the old motto? *The word "not" is left out* *Hadleyburg — try and make it the former."*

For Discussion and Writing

1. Examine the first paragraph of the story. Is there a parable or fairy-tale quality to the paragraph? If so, how does the paragraph serve as an effective introduction to the story? *yes, sets the plot for the basis of whole story*
2. In one of his essays, John Milton speaks against "cloistered virtue"—or the preservation of good by avoiding evil or temptation. Does Twain make the same point in this story? What, then, is Twain's idea of true virtue? How has the stranger "corrupted" the town into virtue? *yes, honesty from the heart. By making them realize the vannes of incorrupt*
3. There is considerable irony in the story. Point out several instances of this, particularly cases in which people convince themselves that they have done good deeds, when in fact their actions have been unkind or harmful.
4. Point out several of the traditional institutions or values that Twain comments on—such as law and an emphasis on material things. How does Twain feel about these values? Which human qualities and values does he seem to admire or promote? *① Incorruptible - treasure of all treasures ② Not true ③ Honesty & truth*

Joseph Conrad [1857–1924]

Conrad was born in Berdycezew, Poland. Because of his father's political activities, the family lived for several years in exile near Moscow. At seventeen Conrad left home and joined the French navy; later he transferred to the British navy, and was given his first command in 1888. In 1894 he left the sea to devote his life to writing. His fiction is written in English, and he is usually considered to be an "English" writer. His work is noted for its use of symbols, its narrative technique, and its exploration of the moral and psychological questions that underlie human action. Among his best-known novels are *Lord Jim* (1900), *Nostromo* (1904), and *Chance* (1913). His famous short novel, *Heart of Darkness,* was published in 1899.

The Lagoon

The white man, leaning with both arms over the roof of the little house in the stern of the boat, said to the steersman—

"We will pass the night in Arsat's clearing. It is late."

The Malay only grunted, and went on looking fixedly at the river. The white man rested his chin on his crossed arms and gazed at the wake of the boat. At the end of the straight avenue of forests cut by the intense glitter of the river, the sun appeared unclouded and dazzling, poised low over the water that shone smoothly like a band of metal. The forests, sombre and dull, stood motionless and silent on each side of the broad stream. At the foot of big, towering trees, trunkless nipa palms rose from the mud of the bank, in bunches of leaves enormous and heavy, that hung unstirring over the brown swirl of eddies. In the stillness of the air every tree, every leaf, every bough, every tendril of creeper and every petal of minute blossoms seemed to have been bewitched into an immobility perfect and final. Nothing moved on the river but the eight paddles that rose flashing regularly, dipped together with a single splash; while the steersman swept right and left with a periodic and sudden flourish of his blade describing a glinting semicircle above his head. The churned-up water frothed alongside with a confused murmur. And the white man's canoe, advancing upstream in the short-lived disturbance of its own making, seemed to enter the portals of a land from which the very memory of motion had forever departed.

The white man, turning his back upon the setting sun, looked along the empty and broad expanse of the sea-reach. For the last three miles of its course the wandering, hesitating river, as if enticed irresistibly by the freedom of an open horizon, flows straight into the sea, flows straight to the east—to the east that harbours both light and darkness. Astern of the boat the repeated call of some bird, a cry discordant and feeble, skipped along over the smooth water and lost itself, before it could reach the other shore, in the breathless silence of the world.

The steersman dug his paddle into the stream, and held hard with stiffened arms, his body thrown forward. The water gurgled aloud; and suddenly the long straight reach seemed to pivot on its centre, the forests swung in a semicircle, and the slanting beams of sunset touched the broadside of the canoe with a fiery glow, throwing the slender and distorted shadows of its crew upon the streaked glitter of the river. The white man turned to look ahead. The course of the boat had been altered at right-angles to the stream, and the carved dragon-head of its prow was pointing now at a gap in the fringing bushes of the bank. It glided through, brushing the overhanging twigs, and disappeared from the river like some slim and amphibious creature leaving the water for its lair in the forests.

The narrow creek was like a ditch: tortuous, fabulously deep; filled with gloom under the thin strip of pure and shining blue of the heaven. Immense trees soared up, invisible behind the festooned draperies of creepers. Here and there, near the glistening blackness of the water, a twisted root of some tall tree showed amongst the tracery of small ferns, black and dull, writhing and motionless, like an arrested snake. The short words of the paddlers reverberated loudly between the thick and sombre walls of vegetation. Darkness oozed out from between the trees, through the tangled maze of the creepers, from behind the great fantastic and unstirring leaves; the darkness, mysterious and invincible; the darkness scented and poisonous of impenetrable forests.

The men poled in the shoaling water. The creek broadened, opening out into a wide sweep of a stagnant lagoon. The forests receded from the marshy bank, leaving a level strip of bright green, reedy grass to frame the reflected blueness of the sky. A fleecy pink cloud drifted high above, trailing the delicate colouring of its image under the floating leaves and the silvery blossoms of the lotus. A little house, perched on high piles, appeared black in the distance. Near it, two tall nibong palms, that seemed to have come out of the forests in the background, leaned slightly over the ragged roof, with a suggestion of sad tenderness and care in the droop of their leafy and soaring heads.

The steersman, pointing with his paddle, said, "Arsat is there. I see his canoe fast between the piles."

The polers ran along the sides of the boat glancing over their shoulders at the end of the day's journey. They would have preferred to spend the night somewhere else than on this lagoon of weird aspect and ghostly reputation. Moreover, they disliked Arsat, first as a stranger, and also because he who repairs a ruined house, and dwells in it, proclaims that he is not afraid to live amongst the spirits that haunt the places abandoned by mankind. Such a man can disturb the course of fate by glances or words; while his familiar ghosts are not easy to propitiate by casual wayfarers upon whom they long to wreak the malice of their human master. White men care not for such things, being unbelievers and in league with the Father of Evil, who leads them unharmed through the invisible dangers of this world. To the warnings of the righteous they oppose an offensive pretence of disbelief. What is there to be done?

So they thought, throwing their weight on the end of their long poles. The big canoe glided on swiftly, noiselessly, and smoothly, towards Arsat's clearing, till, in a great rattling of poles thrown down, and the loud murmurs of "Allah be praised!" it came with a gentle knock against the crooked piles below the house.

The boatmen with uplifted faces shouted discordantly, "Arsat! O Arsat!" Nobody came. The white man began to climb the rude ladder giving access to the bamboo platform before the house. The juragan of the boat said sulkily, "We will cook in the sampan, and sleep on the water."

"Pass my blankets and the basket," said the white man, curtly.

He knelt on the edge of the platform to receive the bundle. Then the boat shoved off, and the white man, standing up, confronted Arsat, who had come out through the low door of his hut. He was a man young, powerful, with broad chest and muscular arms. He had nothing on but his sarong. His head was bare. His big, soft eyes stared eagerly at the white man, but his voice and demeanour were composed as he asked, without any words of greeting—

"Have you medicine, Tuan?"

"No," said the visitor in a startled tone. "No, why? Is there sickness in the house?"

"Enter and see," replied Arsat, in the same calm manner, and turning short round, passed again through the small doorway. The white man, dropping his bundles, followed.

In the dim light of the dwelling he made out on a couch of bamboos a woman stretched on her back under a broad sheet of red cotton cloth. She lay still, as if dead; but her big eyes, wide open, glittered in the gloom, staring upwards at the slender rafters, motionless and unseeing. She was in a high fever, and evidently unconscious. Her cheeks were sunk slightly, her lips were partly open, and on the young face there was the ominous and fixed expression—the absorbed, contemplating expression of the unconscious who are going to die. The two men stood looking down at her in silence.

"Has she been long ill?" asked the traveller.

"I have not slept for five nights," answered the Malay, in a deliberate tone. "At first she heard voices calling her from the water and struggled against me who held her. But since the sun of to-day rose she hears nothing—she hears not me. She sees nothing. She sees not me—me!"

He remained silent for a minute, then asked softly—

"Tuan, will she die?"

"I fear so," said the white man, sorrowfully. He had known Arsat years ago, in a far country in times of trouble and danger, when no friendship is to be despised. And since his Malay friend had come unexpectedly to dwell in the hut on the lagoon with a strange woman, he had slept many times there, in his journeys up and down the river. He liked the man who knew how to keep faith in council and how to fight without fear by the side of his white friend. He liked him—not so much perhaps as a man likes his favourite dog—but still he liked him well enough to help and ask no questions, to think sometimes vaguely and hazily in the midst of his own pursuits, about the lonely man and the long-haired woman with audacious face and triumphant eyes, who lived together hidden by the forests—alone and feared.

The white man came out of the hut in time to see the enormous conflagration of sunset put out by the swift and stealthy shadows that, rising like a black and impalpable vapour above the tree-tops, spread over the heaven, extinguishing the crimson glow of floating clouds and the red brilliance of departing daylight. In a few moments all the stars came out above the intense blackness of the earth and the great lagoon gleaming suddenly with reflected lights resembled an oval patch of night sky flung down into the hopeless and abysmal night of the wilderness. The white man had some supper out of the basket, then collecting a few sticks that lay about the platform, made up a small fire, not for warmth, but for the sake of the smoke, which would keep off the mosquitos. He wrapped himself in the blankets and sat with his back against the reed wall of the house, smoking thoughtfully.

Arsat came through the doorway with noiseless steps and squatted down by the fire. The white man moved his outstretched legs a little.

"She breathes," said Arsat in a low voice, anticipating the expected question. "She breathes and burns as if with a great fire. She speaks not; she hears not—and burns!"

He paused for a moment, then asked in a quiet, incurious tone—

"Tuan . . . will she die?"

The white man moved his shoulders uneasily and muttered in a hesitating manner—

"If such is her fate."

"No, Tuan," said Arsat, calmly. "If such is my fate. I hear, I see, I wait. I remember . . . Tuan, do you remember the old days? Do you remember my brother?"

"Yes," said the white man. The Malay rose suddenly and went in. The other, sitting still outside, could hear the voice in the hut. Arsat said: "Hear me! Speak!" His words were succeeded by a complete silence. "O Diamelen!" he cried, suddenly. After that cry there was a deep sigh. Arsat came out and sank down again in his old place.

They sat in silence before the fire. There was no sound within the house, there was no sound near them; but far away on the lagoon they could hear the voices of the boatmen ringing fitful and distinct on the calm water. The fire in the bows of the sampan shone faintly in the distance with a hazy red glow. Then it died out. The voices ceased. The land and the water slept invisible, unstirring and mute. It was as though there had been nothing left in the world but the glitter of stars streaming, ceaseless and vain, through the black stillness of the night.

The white man gazed straight before him into the darkness with wide-open eyes. The fear and fascination, the inspiration and the wonder of death—of death, near, unavoidable, and unseen, soothed the unrest of his race and stirred the most indistinct, the most intimate of his thoughts. The ever-ready suspicion of evil, the gnawing suspicion that lurks in our hearts, flowed out into the stillness round him—into the stillness profound and dumb, and made it appear untrustworthy and infamous, like the placid and impenetrable mask of an unjustifiable violence. In that fleeting and powerful disturbance of his being the earth enfolded in the starlight peace became a shadowy country of inhuman strife, a battle-field of phantoms terrible and charming, august or ignoble, struggling ardently for the possession of our helpless hearts. An unquiet and mysterious country of inextinguishable desires and fears.

A plaintive murmur rose in the night; a murmur saddening and startling, as if the great solitudes of surrounding woods had tried to whisper into his ear the wisdom of their immense and lofty indifference. Sounds hesitating and vague floated in the air round him, shaped themselves slowly into words; and at last flowed on gently in a murmuring stream of soft and monotonous sentences. He stirred like a man waking up and changed his position slightly. Arsat, motionless and shadowy, sitting with bowed head under the stars, was speaking in a low and dreamy tone—

". . . for where can we lay down the heaviness of our trouble but in a friend's heart? A man must speak of war and of love. You, Tuan, know what war is, and you have seen me in time of danger seek death as other men seek life! A writing may be lost; a lie may be written; but what the eye has seen is truth and remains in the mind!"

"I remember," said the white man, quietly. Arsat went on with mournful composure—

"Therefore I shall speak to you of love. Speak in the night. Speak before both night and love are gone—and the eye of day looks upon my sorrow and my shame; upon my blackened face; upon my burnt-up heart."

A sigh, short and faint, marked an almost imperceptible pause, and then his words flowed on, without a stir, without a gesture.

"After the time of trouble and war was over and you went away from my country in the pursuit of your desires, which we, men of the islands, cannot understand, I and my brother became again, as we had been before, the sword-bearers of the Ruler. You know we were men of family, belonging to a ruling race, and more fit than any to carry on our right shoulder the emblem of power. And in the time of prosperity Si Dendring showed us favour, as we, in time of sorrow, had showed to him the faithfulness of our courage. It was a time of peace. A time of deer-hunts and cock-fights; of idle talks and foolish squabbles between men whose bellies are full and weapons are rusty. But the sower watched the young rice-shoots grow up without fear, and the traders came and went, departed lean and returned fat into the river of peace. They brought news, too. Brought lies and truth mixed together, so that no man knew when to rejoice and when to be sorry. We heard from them about you also. They had seen you here and had seen you there. And I was glad to hear, for I remembered the stirring times, and I always remembered you, Tuan, till the time came when my eyes could see nothing in the past, because they had looked upon the one who is dying here—in the house."

He stopped to exclaim in an intense whisper, "O Mara Bahia! O Calamity!" then went on speaking a little louder:

"There's no worse enemy and no better friend than a brother, Tuan, for one brother knows another, and in perfect knowledge is strength for good or evil. I loved my brother. I went to him and told him that I could see nothing but one face, hear nothing but one voice. He told me: 'Open your heart so that she can see what is in it—and wait. Patience is wisdom. Inchi Midah may die or our Ruler may throw off his fear of a woman!' . . . I waited! . . . You remember the lady with the veiled face, Tuan, and the fear of our Ruler before her cunning and temper. And if she wanted her servant, what could I do? But I fed the hunger of my heart on short glances and stealthy words. I loitered on the path to the bath-houses in the daytime, and when the sun had fallen behind the forest I crept along the jasmine hedges of the woman's courtyard. Unseeing, we spoke to one another through the scent of flowers, through the veil of leaves, through the blades of long grass that stood still before our lips; so great was our prudence, so faint was the murmur of our great longing. The time passed swiftly . . . and there were whispers amongst women—and our enemies watched—my brother was gloomy, and I began to think of killing and of a fierce death. . . . We are of a people who take what they want—like you whites. There is a time when a man should forget loyalty and respect. Might and authority are given to rulers, but to all men is given love and strength and courage. My brother said, 'You shall take her from their midst. We are two who are like one.' And I answered, 'Let it be soon, for I find no warmth in sunlight that does not shine upon her.' Our time came when the Ruler and all the great people went to the mouth of the river to fish by torchlight. There were hundreds of boats, and on the white sand, between the water and the forests, dwellings of leaves were built for the households of the Rajah. The smoke of cooking-fires was like a blue mist of the evening, and many voices rang in it joyfully. While they were making the boats ready to beat up the fish, my brother came to me and said, 'To-night!' I looked to my weapons, and when the time came our canoe took its place in the circle of boats carrying the torches. The lights blazed on the water, but behind the boats there was darkness. When the shouting began and the excitement made them like mad we dropped out. The water shallowed our fire, and we floated back to the shore that was dark with only here and there the glimmer of embers. We could hear the talk of slave-girls amongst the sheds. Then we found a place deserted and silent. We waited there. She came. She came running along the shore, rapid and leaving no trace, like a leaf driven by the wind into the sea. My brother said gloomily, 'Go and take her; carry her into our boat.' I lifted her in my arms. She panted. Her heart was beating against my breast. I said, 'I take you from those people. You came to the cry of my heart, but my arms take you into my boat against the will of the great!' 'It is right,' said my brother. 'We are men who take what we want and can hold it against many. We should have taken her in daylight.' I said, 'Let us be off'; for since she was in my boat I began to think of our Ruler's many men. 'Yes. Let us be off,' said my brother. 'We are cast out and this boat is our country now—and the sea is our refuge.' He lingered with his foot on the shore, and I entreated him to hasten, for I remembered the strokes of her heart against my breast and thought that two men cannot withstand a hundred. We left, paddling downstream close to the bank; and as we passed by the creek where they were fishing, the great shouting had ceased, but the murmur of voices was loud like the humming of insects flying at noonday. The boats floated, clustered together, in the red light of torches, under a black roof of smoke; and men talked of their sport. Men that boasted, and praised, and jeered—men that would have been our friends in the morning, but on that night were already our enemies. We paddled swiftly past. We had no more friends in the country of our birth. She sat in the middle of the canoe with covered face; silent as she is now; unseeing as she is now—and I had no regret at what I was leaving because I could hear her breathing close to me—as I can hear her now."

He paused, listened with his ear turned to the doorway, then shook his head and went on:

"My brother wanted to shout the cry of challenge—one cry only—to let the people know we were freeborn robbers who trusted our arms and the great sea. And again I begged him in the name of our love to be silent. Could I not hear her breathing close to me? I knew the pursuit would come quick enough. My brother loved me. He dipped his paddle without a splash. He only said, 'There is half a man in you now—the other half is in that woman. I can wait. When you are a whole man again, you will come back with me here to shout defiance. We are sons of the same mother.' I made no answer. All my strength and all my spirit were in my hands that held the paddle—for I longed to be with her in a safe place beyond the reach of men's anger and of women's spite. My love was so great, that I thought it could guide me to a country where death was unknown, if I could only escape from Inchi Midah's fury and from our Ruler's sword. We paddled with haste, breathing through our teeth. The blades bit deep into the smooth water. We passed out of the river; we flew in clear channels amongst the shallows. We skirted the black coast; we skirted the sand beaches where the sea speaks in whispers to the land; and the gleam of white sand flashed back past our boat, so swiftly she ran upon the water. We spoke not. Only once I said, 'Sleep, Diamelen, for soon you may want all your strength.' I heard the sweetness of her voice, but I never turned my head. The sun rose and still we went on. Water fell from my face like rain from a cloud. We flew in the light and heat. I never looked back, but I knew that my brother's eyes, behind me, were looking steadily ahead, for the boat went as straight as a bushman's dart, when it leaves the end of the sumpitan. There was no better paddler, no better steersman than my brother. Many times, together, we had won races in that canoe. But we never had put out our strength as we did then—then, when for the last time we paddled together! There was no braver or stronger man in our country than my brother. I could not spare the strength to turn my head and look at him, but every moment I heard the hiss of his breath getting louder behind me. Still he did not speak. The sun was high. The heat clung to my back like a flame of fire. My ribs were ready to burst, but I could no longer get enough air into my chest. And then I felt I must cry out with my last breath, 'Let us rest!' . . . 'Good!' he answered; and his voice was firm. He was strong. He was brave. He knew not fear and no fatigue . . . My brother!"

A murmur powerful and gentle, a murmur vast and faint; the murmur of trembling leaves, of stirring boughs, ran through the tangled depths of the forests, ran over the starry smoothness of the lagoon, and the water between the piles lapped the slimy timber once with a sudden splash. A breath of warm air touched the two men's faces and passed on with a mournful sound—a breath loud and short like an uneasy sigh of the dreaming earth.

Arsat went on in an even, low voice.

"We ran our canoe on the white beach of a little bay close to a long tongue of land that seemed to bar our road; a long wooded cape going far into the sea. My brother knew that place. Beyond the cape a river has its entrance, and through the jungle of that land there is a narrow path. We made a fire and cooked rice. Then we lay down to sleep on the soft sand in the shade of our canoe, while she watched. No sooner had I closed my eyes than I heard her cry of alarm. We leaped up. The sun was halfway down the sky already, and coming in sight in the opening of the bay we saw a prau manned by many paddlers. We knew it at once; it was one of our Rajah's praus. They were watching the shore, and saw us. They beat the gong, and turned the head of the prau into the bay. I felt my heart become weak within my breast. Diamelen sat on the sand and covered her face. There was no escape by sea. My brother laughed. He had the gun you had given him, Tuan, before you went away, but there was only a handful of powder. He spoke to me quickly: 'Run with her along the path. I shall keep them back, for they have no firearms, and landing in the face of a man with a gun is certain death for some. Run with her. On the other side of that wood there is a fisherman's house—and a canoe. When I have fired all the shots I will follow. I am a great runner, and before they can come up we shall be gone. I will hold out as long as I can, for she is but a woman—that can neither run nor fight, but she has your heart in her weak hands.' He dropped behind the canoe. The prau was coming. She and I ran, and as we rushed along the path I heard shots. My brother fired—once—twice—and the booming of the gong ceased. There was silence behind us. That neck of land is narrow. Before I heard my brother fire the third shot I saw the shelving shore, and I saw the water again; the mouth of a broad river. We crossed a grassy glade. We ran down to the water. I saw a low hut above the black mud, and a small canoe hauled up. I heard another shot behind me. I thought, 'That is his last charge.' We rushed down to the canoe; a man came running from the hut, but I leaped on him, and we rolled together in the mud. Then I got up, and he lay still at my feet. I don't know whether I had killed him or not. I and Diamelen pushed the canoe afloat. I heard yells behind me, and I saw my brother run across the glade. Many men were bounding after him, I took her in my arms and threw her into the boat, then leaped in myself. When I looked back I saw that my brother had fallen. He fell and was up again, but the men were closing round him. He shouted, 'I am coming!' The men were close to him. I looked. Many men. Then I looked at her. Tuan, I pushed the canoe! I pushed it into deep water. She was kneeling forward looking at me, and I said, 'Take your paddle,' while I struck the water with mine. Tuan, I heard him cry. I heard him cry my name twice; and I heard voices shouting, 'Kill! Strike!' I never turned back. I heard him calling my name again with a great shriek, as when life is going out together with the voice—and I never turned my head. My own name! . . . My brother! Three times he called—but I was not afraid of life. Was she not there in that canoe? And could I not with her find a country where death is forgotten—where death is unknown!"

The white man sat up. Arsat rose and stood, an indistinct and silent figure above the dying embers of the fire. Over the lagoon a mist drifting and low had crept, erasing slowly the glittering images of the stars. And now a great expanse of white vapour covered the land: it flowed cold and gray in the darkness, eddied in noiseless whirls round the tree-trunks and about the platform of the house, which seemed to float upon a restless and impalpable illusion of a sea. Only far away the tops of the trees stood outlined on the twinkle of heaven, like a sombre and forbidding shore—a coast deceptive, pitiless and black.

Arsat's voice vibrated loudly in the profound peace.

"I had her there! I had her! To get her I would have faced all mankind. But I had her—and—"

His words went out ringing into the empty distances. He paused, and seemed to listen to them dying away very far—beyond help and beyond recall. Then he said quietly—

"Tuan, I loved my brother."

A breath of wind made him shiver. High above his head, high above the silent sea of mist the drooping leaves of the palms rattled together with a mournful and expiring sound. The white man stretched his legs. His chin rested on his chest, and he murmured sadly without lifting his head—

"We all love our brothers."

Arsat burst out with an intense whispering violence—

"What did I care who died? I wanted peace in my own heart."

He seemed to hear a stir in the house—listened—then stepped in noiselessly. The white man stood up. A breeze was coming in fitful puffs. The stars shone paler as if they had retreated into the frozen depths of immense space. After a chill gust of wind there were a few seconds of perfect calm and absolute silence. Then from behind the black and wavy line of the forests a column of golden light shot up into the heavens and spread over the semicircle of the eastern horizon. The sun had risen. The mist lifted, broke into drifting patches, vanished into thin flying wreaths; and the unveiled lagoon lay, polished and black, in the heavy shadows at the foot of the wall of trees. A white eagle rose over it with a slanting and ponderous flight, reached the clear sunshine and appeared dazzlingly brilliant for a moment, then soaring higher, became a dark and motionless speck before it vanished into the blue as if it had left the earth forever. The white man, standing gazing upwards before the doorway, heard in the hut a confused and broken murmur of distracted words ending with a loud groan. Suddenly Arsat stumbled out with outstretched hands, shivered and stood still for some time with fixed eyes. Then, he said—

"She burns no more."

Before his face the sun showed its edge above the treetops rising steadily. The breeze freshened; a great brilliance burst upon the lagoon, sparkled on the rippling water. The forests came out of the clear shadows of the morning, became distinct, as if they had rushed nearer—to stop short in a great stir of leaves, of nodding boughs, of swaying branches. In the merciless sunshine the whisper of unconscious life grew louder, speaking in an incomprehensible voice round the dumb darkness of that human sorrow. Arsat's eyes wandered slowly, then stared at the rising sun.

"I can see nothing," he said half aloud to himself.

"There is nothing," said the white man, moving to the edge of the platform and waving his hand to his boat. A shout came faintly over the lagoon and the sampan began to glide towards the abode of the friend of ghosts.

"If you want to come with me, I will wait all the morning," said the white man, looking away upon the water.

"No, Tuan," said Arsat, softly. "I shall not eat or sleep in this house, but I must first see my road. Now I can see nothing—see nothing! There is no light and no peace in the world; but there is death—death for many. We are sons of the same mother—and I left him in the midst of enemies; but I am going back now."

He drew a long breath and went on in a dreamy tone:

"In a little while I shall see clear enough to strike—to strike. But she has died, and . . . now . . . darkness."

He flung his arms wide open, let them fall along his body, then stood still with unmoved face and stony eyes, staring at the sun. The white man got down into his canoe. The polers ran smartly along the sides of the boat, looking over their shoulders at the beginning of a weary journey. High in the stern, his head muffled up in white rags, the juragan sat moody, letting his paddle trail in the water. The white man, leaning with both arms over the grass roof of the little cabin, looked back at the shining ripple of the boat's wake. Before the sampan passed out of the lagoon into the creek he lifted his eyes. Arsat had not moved. He stood lonely in the searching sunshine; and he looked beyond the great light of a cloudless day into the darkness of a world of illusions.

Fact Questions and Exercises

1. What is a lagoon and why is a lagoon an appropriate setting for this story?
2. Identify Arsat.
3. How does Arsat take Diamelen? From whom does he take her?
4. What happens to Arsat's brother?
5. What happens to Diamelen?
6. Who is the narrator of the story?

For Discussion and Writing

1. Light and darkness are introduced early in the story. How does Conrad develop them as themes or symbols throughout "The Lagoon"?
2. Characterize Arsat. What do the native boatmen think of him? What is his relationship with the white man? What has he sacrificed in order to have Diamelen?

3. Why does Conrad refer to the Englishman as the "white man"? How is this an allegorical device? Are there any other suggestions of allegory in the story? If so, what are they?

Edith Wharton [1862–1937]

Wharton was born in New York City, the daughter of a fashionable, wealthy family. After the Civil War, however, she saw the manners and standards of her world replaced by those of a financial-industrial society. When she was twenty-three, Wharton married a Boston banker. The marriage ended disastrously, and she went to Europe, eventually becoming a resident of France. Her fiction often reflects the pressures that result from social, economic, and personal conflicts. Among her best-known works are *The House of Mirth* (1905), *Ethan Frome* (1911), and *The Age of Innocence* (1920). *The Writing of Fiction* (1925) is her commentary on the art of fiction.

Roman Fever

I

From the table at which they had been lunching two American ladies of ripe but well-cared-for middle age moved across the lofty terrace of the Roman restaurant and, leaning on its parapet, looked first at each other, and then down on the outspread glories of the Palatine and the Forum, with the same expression of vague but benevolent approval.

As they leaned there a girlish voice echoed up gaily from the stairs leading to the court below. "Well, come along then," it cried, not to them but to an invisible companion, "and let's leave the young things to their knitting"; and a voice as fresh laughed back: "Oh, look here, Babs, not actually *knitting*—" "Well, I mean figuratively," rejoined the first. "After all, we haven't left our poor parents much else to do. . . ." and at that point the turn of the stairs engulfed the dialogue.

The two ladies looked at each other again, this time with a tinge of smiling embarrassment, and the smaller and paler one shook her head and colored slightly.

"Barbara!" she murmured, sending an unheard rebuke after the mocking voice in the stairway.

The other lady, who was fuller, and higher in color, with a small determined nose supported by vigorous black eyebrows, gave a good-humored laugh. "That's what our daughters think of us!"

Her companion replied by a deprecating gesture. "Not of us individually. We must remember that. It's just the collective modern idea of Mothers. And you see—" Half-guiltily she drew from her handsomely mounted black handbag a twist of crimson silk run through by two fine knitting needles. "One never knows," she murmured. "The new system has certainly given us a good deal of time to kill; and sometimes I get tired just looking—even at this." Her gesture was now addressed to the stupendous scene at their feet.

The dark lady laughed again, and they both relapsed upon the view, contemplating it in silence, with a sort of diffused serenity which might have been borrowed from the spring effulgence of the Roman skies. The luncheon-hour was long past, and the two had their end of the vast terrace to themselves. At this opposite extremity a few groups, detained by a lingering look at the outspread city, were gathering up guide-books and fumbling for tips. The last of them scattered, and the two ladies were alone on the air-washed height.

"Well, I don't see why we shouldn't just stay here," said Mrs. Slade, the lady of the high colour and energetic brows. Two derelict basket-chairs stood near, and she pushed them into the angle of the parapet, and settled herself in one, her gaze upon the Palatine. "After all, it's still the most beautiful view in the world."

"It always will be, to me," assented her friend Mrs. Ansley, with so slight a stress on the "me" that Mrs. Slade, though she noticed it, wondered if it were not merely accidental, like the random underlinings of old-fashioned letter-writers.

"Grace Ansley was always old-fashioned," she thought; and added aloud, with a retrospective smile: "It's a view we've both been familiar with for a good many years. When we first met here we were younger than our girls are now. You remember?"

"Oh, yes, I remember," murmured Mrs. Ansley, with the same undefinable stress.—"There's that head-waiter wondering," she interpolated. She was evidently far less sure than her companion of herself and of her rights in the world.

"I'll cure him of wondering," said Mrs. Slade, stretching her hand toward a bag as discreetly opulent-looking as Mrs. Ansley's. Signing to the head-waiter, she explained that she and her friend were old lovers of Rome, and would like to spend the end of the afternoon looking down on the view—that is, if it did not disturb the service? The head-waiter, bowing over her gratuity, assured her that the ladies were most welcome, and would be still more so if they would condescend to remain for dinner. A full moon night, they would remember . . . .

Mrs. Slade's black brows drew together, as though references to the moon were out-of-place and even unwelcome. But she smiled away her frown as the head-waiter retreated. "Well, why not? We might do worse. There's no knowing, I suppose, when the girls will be back. Do you even know back from *where?* I don't"

Mrs. Ansley again coloured slightly. "I think those young Italian aviators we met at the Embassy invited them to fly to Tarquinia for tea. I suppose they'll want to wait and fly back by moonlight."

"Moonlight—moonlight! What a part it still plays. Do you suppose they're as sentimental as we were?"

"I've come to the conclusion that I don't in the least know what they are," said Mrs. Ansley. "And perhaps we didn't know much more about each other."

"No; perhaps we didn't."

Her friend gave her a shy glance. "I never should have supposed you were sentimental, Alida."

"Well, perhaps I wasn't." Mrs. Slade drew her lids together in retrospect; and for a few moments the two ladies, who had been intimate since childhood, reflected how little they knew each other. Each one, of course, had a label ready to attach to the other's name; Mrs. Delphin Slade, for instance, would have told herself, or any one who asked her, that Mrs. Horace Ansley, twenty-five years ago, had been exquisitely lovely—no, you wouldn't believe it, would you? . . . though, of course, still charming, distinguished . . . Well, as a girl she had been exquisite; far more beautiful than her daughter Barbara, though certainly Babs, according to the new standards at any rate, was more effective—had more edge, as they say. Funny where she got it, with those two nullities as parents. Yes; Horace Ansley was—well, just the duplicate of his wife. Museum specimens of old New York. Good-looking, irreproachable, exemplary. Mrs. Slade and Mrs. Ansley had lived opposite each other—actually as well as figuratively—for years. When the drawing-room curtains in No. 20 East 73rd Street were renewed, No. 23, across the way, was always aware of it. And of all the movings, buyings, travels, anniversaries, illnesses—the tame chronicle of an estimable pair. Little of it escaped Mrs. Slade. But she had grown bored with it by the time her husband made his big *coup* in Wall Street, and when they bought in upper Park Avenue had already begun to think: "I'd rather live opposite a speakeasy for a change; at least one might see it raided." The idea of seeing Grace raided was so amusing that (before the move) she launched it at a woman's lunch. It made a hit, and went the rounds—she sometimes wondered if it had crossed the street, and reached Mrs. Ansley. She hoped not, but didn't much mind. Those were the days when respectability was at a discount, and it did the irreproachable no harm to laugh at them a little.

A few years later, and not many months apart, both ladies lost their husbands. There was an appropriate exchange of wreaths and condolences, and a brief renewal of intimacy in the half-shadow of their mourning; and now, after another interval, they had run across each other in Rome, at the same hotel, each of them the modest appendage of a salient daughter. The similarity of their lot had again drawn them together, lending itself to mild jokes, and the mutual confession that, if in old days it must have been tiring to "keep up" with daughters, it was now, at times, a little dull not to.

No doubt, Mrs. Slade reflected, she felt her unemployment more than poor Grace ever would. It was a big drop from being the wife of Delphin Slade to being his widow. She had always regarded herself (with a certain conjugal pride) as his equal in social gifts, as contributing her full share to the making of the exceptional couple they were: but the difference after his death was irremediable. As the wife of the famous corporation lawyer, always with an international case or two on hand, every day brought its exciting and unexpected obligation: the impromptu entertaining of eminent colleagues from abroad, the hurried dashes on legal business to London, Paris or Rome, where the entertaining was so handsomely reciprocated; the amusement of hearing in her wake: "What, that handsome woman with the good clothes and the eyes is Mrs. Slade—*the* Slade's wife? Really? Generally the wives of celebrities are such frumps."

Yes; being *the* Slade's widow was a dullish business after that. In living up to such a husband all her faculties had been engaged; now she had only her daughter to live up to, for the son who seemed to have inherited his father's gifts had died suddenly in boyhood. She had fought through that agony because her husband was there, to be helped and to help; now, after the father's death, the thought of the boy had become unbearable. There was nothing left but to mother her daughter; and dear Jenny was such a perfect daughter that she needed no excessive mothering. "Now with Babs Ansley I don't know that I *should* be so quiet," Mrs. Slade sometimes half-enviously reflected; but Jenny, who was younger than her brilliant friend, was that rare accident, an extremely pretty girl who somehow made youth and prettiness seem as safe as their absence. It was all perplexing—and to Mrs. Slade a little boring. She wished that Jenny would fall in love—with the wrong man, even; that she might have to be watched, out-maneuvered, rescued. And instead, it was Jenny who watched her mother, kept her out of draughts, made sure that she had taken her tonic . . .

Mrs. Ansley was much less articulate than her friend, and her mental portrait of Mrs. Slade was slighter, and drawn with fainter touches. "Alida Slade's awfully brilliant; but not as brilliant as she thinks," would have summed it up; though she would have added, for the enlightenment of strangers, that Mrs. Slade had been an extremely dashing girl; much more so than her daughter, who was pretty, of course, and clever in a way, but had none of her mother's—well, "vividness," some one had once called it. Mrs. Ansley would take up current words like this, and cite them in quotation marks, as unheard-of audacities. No; Jenny was not like her mother. Sometimes Mrs. Ansley thought Alida Slade was disappointed; on the whole she had had a sad life. Full of failures and mistakes; Mrs. Ansley had always been rather sorry for her . . .

So these two ladies visualized each other, each through the wrong end of her little telescope.

II

For a long time they continued to sit side by side without speaking. It seemed as though, to both, there was a relief in laying down their somewhat futile activities in the presence of the vast Memento Mori which faced them. Mrs. Slade sat quite still, her eyes fixed on the golden slope of the Palace of the Caesars, and after a while Mrs. Ansley ceased to fidget with her bag, and she too sank into meditation. Like many intimate friends, the two ladies had never before had occasion to be silent together, and Mrs. Ansley was slightly embarrassed by what seemed, after so many years, a new stage in their intimacy, and one with which she did not yet know how to deal.

Suddenly the air was full of that deep clangor of bells which periodically covers Rome with a roof of silver. Mrs. Slade glanced at her wristwatch. "Five o'clock already," she said, as though surprised.

Mrs. Ansley suggested interrogatively: "There's bridge at the Embassy at five." For a long time Mrs. Slade did not answer. She appeared to be lost in contemplation, and Mrs. Ansley thought the remark had escaped her. But after a while she said, as if speaking out of a dream: "Bridge, did you say? Not unless you want to . . . But I don't think I will, you know."

"Oh, no," Mrs. Ansley hastened to assure her. "I don't care to at all. It's so lovely here; and so full of old memories, as you say." She settled herself in her chair, and almost furtively drew forth her knitting. Mrs. Slade took sideway note of this activity, but her own beautifully cared-for hands remained motionless on her knee.

"I was just thinking," she said slowly, "what different things Rome stands for to each generation of travelers. To our grandmothers, Roman fever; to our mothers, sentimental dangers—how we used to be guarded!—to our daughters, no more dangers than the middle of Main Street. They don't know it—but how much they're missing!"

The long golden light was beginning to pale, and Mrs. Ansley lifted her knitting a little closer to her eyes. "Yes; how we were guarded!"

"I always used to think," Mrs. Slade continued, "that our mothers had a much more difficult job than our grandmothers. When Roman fever stalked the streets it must have been comparatively easy to gather in the girls at the danger hour; but when you and I were young, with such beauty calling us, and the spice of disobedience thrown in, and no worse risk than catching cold during the cool hour after sunset, the mothers used to be put to it to keep us in—didn't they?"

She turned again toward Mrs. Ansley, but the latter had reached a delicate point in her knitting. "One, two three—slip two; yes, they must have been," she assented, without looking up.

Mrs. Slade's eyes rested on her with a deepened attention. "She can knit—in the face of *this*! How like her . . ."

Mrs. Slade leaned back, brooding, her eyes ranging from the ruins which faced her to the long green hollow of the Forum, the fading glow of the church fronts beyond it, and the outlying immensity of the Colosseum. Suddenly she thought: "It's all very well to say that our girls have done away with sentiment and moonlight. But if Babs Ansley isn't out to catch that young aviator—the one who's a Marchese—then I don't know anything. And Jenny has no chance beside her. I know that too. I wonder if that's why Grace Ansley likes the two girls to go everywhere together? My poor Jenny as a foil—!" Mrs. Slade gave a hardly audible laugh, and at the sound Mrs. Ansley dropped her knitting.

"Yes—?"

"I—oh, nothing. I was only thinking how your Babs carries everything before her. That Campolieri boy is one of the best matches in Rome. Don't look so innocent, my dear—you know he is. And I was wondering, ever so respectfully, you understand . . . wondering how two such exemplary characters as you and Horace had managed to produce anything quite so dynamic." Mrs. Slade laughed again, with a touch of asperity.

Mrs. Ansley's hands lay inert across her needles. She looked straight out at the great accumulated wreckage of passion and splendour at her feet. But her small profile was almost expressionless. At length she said: "I think you overrate Babs, my dear."

Mrs. Slade's tone grew easier. "No; I don't. I appreciate her. And perhaps envy you. Oh, my girl's perfect; if I were a chronic invalid I'd—well, I think I'd rather be in Jenny's hands. There must be times . . . but there! I always wanted a brilliant daughter . . . and never quite understood why I got an angel instead."

Mrs. Ansley echoed her laugh in a faint murmur. "Babs is an angel too."

"Of course—of course! But she's got rainbow wings. Well, they're wandering by the sea with their young men; and here we sit . . . and it all brings back the past a little too acutely."

Mrs. Ansley had resumed her knitting. One might almost have imagined (if one had known her less well, Mrs. Slade reflected) that, for her also, too many memories rose from the lengthening shadows of those august ruins. But no; she was simply absorbed in her work. What was there for her to worry about? She knew that Babs would almost certainly come back engaged to the extremely eligible Campolieri. "And she'll sell the New York house, and settle down near them in Rome, and never be in their way . . . she's much too tactful. But she'll have an excellent cook, and just the right people in for bridge and cocktails . . . and a perfectly peaceful old age among her grandchildren."

Mrs. Slade broke off this prophetic flight with a recoil of self-disgust. There was no one of whom she had less right to think unkindly than of Grace Ansley. Would she never cure herself of envying her? Perhaps she had begun too long ago.

Slade feels guilty & is disgusted of herself

She stood up and leaned against the parapet, filling her troubled eyes with the tranquilizing magic of the hour. But instead of tranquilizing her the sight seemed to increase her exasperation. Her gaze turned toward the Colosseum. Already its golden flank was drowned in purple shadow, and above it the sky curved crystal clear, without light or color. It was the moment when afternoon and evening hang balanced in mid-heaven.

Mrs. Slade turned back and laid her hand on her friend's arm. The gesture was so abrupt that Mrs. Ansley looked up, startled.

"The sun's set. You're not afraid, my dear?"

"Afraid—?"

"Of Roman fever or pneumonia? I remember how ill you were that winter. As a girl you had a very delicate throat, hadn't you?"

Story title

"Oh, we're all right up here. Down below, in the Forum, it does get deathly cold, all of a sudden . . . but not here."

"Ah, of course you know because you had to be so careful." Mrs. Slade turned back to the parapet. She thought: "I must make one more effort not to hate her." Aloud she said: "Whenever I look at the Forum from up here, I remember that story about a great-aunt of yours, wasn't she? A dreadfully wicked great-aunt?"

GREAT-AUNT HARRIET

"Oh, yes; great-aunt Harriet. The one who was supposed to have sent her young sister out to the Forum after sunset to gather a night-blooming flower for her album. All our great-aunts and grandmothers used to have albums of dried flowers."

Mrs. Slade nodded. "But she really sent her because they were in love with the same man—"

"Well, that was the family tradition. They said Aunt Harriet confessed it years afterward. At any rate, the poor little sister caught the fever and died. Mother used to frighten us with the story when we were children."

"And you frightened *me* with it, that winter when you and I were here as girls. The winter I was engaged to Delphin."

Mrs. Ansley gave a faint laugh. "Oh, did I? Really frightened you? I don't believe you're easily frightened."

"Not often; but I was then. I was easily frightened because I was too happy. I wonder if you know what that means?"

"I—yes . . ." Mrs. Ansley faltered.

"Well, I suppose that was why the story of your wicked aunt made such an impression on me. And I thought: 'There's no more Roman fever, but the Forum is deathly cold after sunset—especially after a hot day. And the Colosseum's even colder and damper.'"

"The Colosseum—?"

"Yes. It wasn't easy to get in, after the gates were locked for the night. Far from easy. Still, in those days it could be managed; it was managed, often. Lovers met there who couldn't meet elsewhere. You knew that?"

"I—I daresay. I don't remember."

"You don't remember? You don't remember going to visit some ruins or other one evening, just after dark, and catching a bad chill? You were supposed to have gone to see the moon rise. People always said that expedition was what caused your illness."

There was a moment's silence; then Mrs. Ansley rejoined: "Did they? It was all so long ago."

"Yes. And you got well again—so it didn't matter. But I suppose it struck your friends—the reason given for your illness, I mean—because everybody knew you were so prudent on account of your throat, and your mother took such care of you . . . You *had* been out late sightseeing, hadn't you, that night?"

"Perhaps I had. The most prudent girls aren't always prudent. What made you think of it now?"

Mrs. Slade seemed to have no answer ready. But after a moment she broke out: "Because I simply can't bear it any longer—!"

Mrs. Ansley lifted her head quickly. Her eyes were wide and very pale. "Can't bear what?"

"Why—your not knowing that I've always known why you went."

"Why I went—?"

"Yes. You think I'm bluffing, don't you? Well, you went to meet the man I was engaged to—and I can repeat every word of the letter that took you there."

While Mrs. Slade spoke Mrs. Ansley had risen unsteadily to her feet. Her bag, her knitting and gloves, slid in a panic-stricken heap to the ground. She looked at Mrs. Slade as though she were looking at a ghost.

"No, no—don't," she faltered out.

"Why not? Listen, if you don't believe me. 'My one darling, things can't go on like this. I must see you alone. Come to the Colosseum immediately after dark tomorrow. There will be somebody to let you in. No one whom you need fear will suspect'—but perhaps you've forgotten what the letter said?"

Mrs. Ansley met the challenge with an unexpected composure. Steadying herself against the chair she looked at her friend, and replied: "No; I know it by heart too."

"And the signature? 'Only *your* D.S.' Was that it? I'm right, am I? That was the letter that took you out that evening after dark?"

Mrs. Ansley was still looking at her. It seemed to Mrs. Slade that a slow struggle was going on behind the voluntarily controlled mask of her small quiet face. "I shouldn't have thought she had herself so well in hand," Mrs. Slade reflected, almost resentfully. But at this moment Mrs. Ansley spoke. "I don't know how you knew. I burnt that letter at once."

"Yes; you would, naturally—you're so prudent!" The sneer was open now. "And if you burnt the letter you're wondering how on earth I know what was in it. That's it, isn't it?"

Mrs. Slade waited, but Mrs. Ansley did not speak.

"Well, my dear, I know what was in that letter because I wrote it!"

"You wrote it?"

"Yes."

The two women stood for a minute staring at each other in the last golden light. Then Mrs. Ansley dropped back into her chair. "Oh," she murmured, and covered her face with her hands.

Mrs. Slade waited nervously for another word or movement. None came, and at length she broke out: "I horrify you."

Mrs. Ansley's hands dropped to her knee. The face they uncovered was streaked with tears. "I wasn't thinking of you. I was thinking—it was the only letter I ever had from him!"

"And I wrote it. Yes; I wrote it! But I was the girl he was engaged to. Did you happen to remember that?"

Mrs. Ansley's head drooped again. "I'm not trying to excuse myself . . . I remembered. . . ."

"And still you went?"

"Still I went."

Mrs. Slade stood looking down on the small bowed figure at her side. The flame of her wrath had already sunk, and she wondered why she had ever thought there would be any satisfaction in inflicting so purposeless a wound on her friend. But she had to justify herself.

"You do understand? I'd found out—and I hated you, hated you. I knew you were in love with Delphin—and I was afraid; afraid of you, of your quiet ways, your sweetness . . . your . . . well, I wanted you out of the way, that's all. Just for a few weeks; just till I was sure of him. So in a blind fury I wrote that letter . . . I don't know why I'm telling you now."

"I suppose," said Mrs. Ansley slowly, "it's because you've always gone on hating me."

"Perhaps. Or because I wanted to get the whole thing off my mind." She paused. "I'm glad you destroyed the letter. Of course I never thought you'd die."

Mrs. Ansley relapsed into silence, and Mrs. Slade, leaning above her, was conscious of a strange sense of isolation, of being cut off from the warm current of human communion. "You think me a monster!"

"I don't know . . . It was the only letter I had, and you say he didn't write it?"

"Ah, how you care for him still!"

"I cared for that memory," said Mrs. Ansley.

Mrs. Slade continued to look down on her. She seemed physically reduced by the blow—as if, when she got up, the wind might scatter her like a puff of dust. Mrs. Slade's jealousy suddenly leapt up again at the sight. All these years the woman had been living on that letter. How she must have loved him, to treasure the mere memory of its ashes! The letter of the man her friend was engaged to. Wasn't it she who was the monster?

"You tried your best to get him away from me, didn't you? But you failed; and I kept him. That's all."

"Yes. That's all."

"I wish now I hadn't told you. I'd no idea you'd feel about it as you do; I thought you'd be amused. It all happened so long ago, as you say; and you must do me the justice to remember that I had no reason to think you'd ever taken it seriously. How could I, when you were married to Horace Ansley two months afterward? As soon as you could get out of bed your mother rushed you off to Florence and married you. People were rather surprised—they wondered at its being done so quickly; but I thought I knew. I had an idea you did it out of *pique*—to be able to say you'd got ahead of Delphin and me. Girls have such silly reasons for doing the most serious things. And your marrying so soon convinced me that you'd never really cared."

"Yes, I suppose it would," Mrs. Ansley assented.

The clear heaven overhead was emptied of all its gold. Dusk spread over it, abruptly darkening the Seven Hills. Here and there lights began to twinkle through the foliage at their feet. Steps were coming and going on the deserted terrace—waiters looking out of the doorway at the head of the stairs, then reappearing with trays and napkins and flasks of wine. Tables were moved, chairs straightened. A feeble string of electric lights flickered out. Some vases of faded flowers were carried away, and brought back replenished. A stout lady in a dust-coat suddenly appeared, asking in broken Italian if any one had seen the elastic band which held together her tattered Baedeker. She poked with her stick under the table at which she had lunched, the waiters assisting.

The corner where Mrs. Slade and Mrs. Ansley sat was still shadowy and deserted. For a long time neither of them spoke. At length Mrs. Slade began again: "I suppose I did it as a sort of joke—"

"A joke?"

"Well, girls are ferocious sometimes, you know. Girls in love especially. And I remember laughing to myself all that evening at the idea that you were waiting around there in the dark, dodging out of sight, listening for every sound, trying to get in—. Of course I was upset when I heard you were so ill afterward."

Mrs. Ansley had not moved for a long time. But now she turned slowly to her companion. "But I didn't wait. He'd arranged everything. He was there. We were let in at once," she said.

Mrs. Slade sprang up from her leaning position. "Delphin there? They let you in?—Ah, now you're lying!" she burst out with violence.

Mrs. Ansley's voice grew clearer, and full of surprise. "But of course he was there. Naturally he came—"

"Came? How did he know he'd find you there? You must be raving!"

Mrs. Ansley hesitated, as though reflecting. "But I answered the letter. I told him I'd be there. So he came."

Mrs. Slade flung her hands up to her face. "Oh, God—you answered! I never thought of your answering . . ."

"It's odd you never thought of it, if you wrote the letter."

"Yes. I was blind with rage."

Mrs. Ansley rose, and drew her fur scarf about her. "It is cold here. We'd better go . . . I'm sorry for you," she said, as she clasped the fur about her throat.

The unexpected words sent a pang through Mrs. Slade. "Yes; we'd better go." She gathered up her bag and cloak. "I don't know why you should be sorry for me," she muttered.

Mrs. Ansley stood looking away from her toward the dusky secret mass of the Colosseum. "Well—because I didn't have to wait that night."

Mrs. Slade gave an unquiet laugh. "Yes; I was beaten there. But I oughtn't to begrudge it to you, I suppose. At the end of all these years. After all, I had everything; I had him for twenty-five years. And you had nothing but that one letter that he didn't write."

Mrs. Ansley was again silent. At length she turned toward the door of the terrace. She took a step, and turned back, facing her companion.

"I had Barbara," she said, and began to move ahead of Mrs. Slade toward the stairway.

Fact Questions and Exercises

1. Early in the story, Mrs. Ansley refers to the "new system." What does she mean by this? *a new generation of people and ideas*
2. What is the meaning of the story's title? *Rome is a place to for romance –*
3. How do the comments about great-aunt Harriet (page 107) foreshadow Mrs. Slade's revelation? *She's thinking of the similarity of her own situation.*
4. Why did Mrs. Ansley's mother "rush" her off to Florence to marry Horace Ansley? *Because she was pregnant*
5. What is the story's time setting? Which details establish this setting? *Spring or Summer*
6. Point out details that show how the two daughters differ from each other. *Jenny is sweet, an angel, perfect – Babs is brilliant and perfect*

For Discussion and Writing

1. Does Wharton present a more favorable characterization of Mrs. Slade or of Mrs. Ansley? With which of the two women do you sympathize? Which do you find less morally reprehensible? *Slade* In the conventional sense, which woman has committed the greatest sin? *Slade* *yes*
2. Does the end of the story come as a surprise? Or does Wharton present foreshadowings throughout to lead logically to this ending? If so, point out several facts in the story that lead to the revelation that Mr. Slade is the father of Mrs. Ansley's daughter.

Stephen Crane [1871–1900]

Crane was born in Newark, New Jersey, the fourteenth and last child of a Methodist preacher. Crane attended private secondary schools and Syracuse University. He made his living as a newspaper journalist— particularly as a war correspondent—and his fiction is noticeably influenced by the sparse style of journalism. His classic story of the American Civil War, *The Red Badge of Courage* (1895), captures the realism of battle, although Crane himself had never served in the military. His earlier novel, *Maggie: A Girl of the Streets* (1893), is a realistic/naturalistic account of prostitution and slum life in New York. *The Open Boat and Other Tales of Adventure* was published in 1898. Crane died from tuberculosis, a condition caused by the hardships of his vagabond life as a war correspondent.

The Open Boat

A Tale Intended to be after the Fact: Being the Experience of Four Men from the Sunk Steamer "Commodore"

I

None of them knew the color of the sky. Their eyes glanced level, and were fastened upon the waves that swept toward them. These waves were of the hue of slate, save for the tops, which were of foaming white, and all of the men knew the colors of the sea. The horizon narrowed and widened, and dipped and rose, and at all times its edge was jagged with waves that seemed thrust up in points like rocks.

Many a man ought to have a bathtub larger than the boat which here rode upon the sea. These waves were most wrongfully and barbarously abrupt and tall, and each froth-top was a problem in small-boat navigation.

The cook squatted in the bottom, and looked with both eyes at the six inches of gunwale which separated him from the ocean. His sleeves were rolled over his fat forearms, and the two flaps of his unbottoned vest dangled as he bent to bail out the boat. Often he said, "Gawd! that was a narrow clip." As he remarked it he invariably gazed eastward over the broken sea.

The oiler, steering with one of the two oars in the boat, sometimes raised himself suddenly to keep clear of water that swirled in over the stern. It was a thin little oar, and it seemed often ready to snap.

The correspondent, pulling at the other oar, watched the waves and wondered why he was there.

The injured captain, lying in the bow, was at this time buried in that profound dejection and indifference which comes, temporarily at least, to even the bravest and most enduring when, willy-nilly, the firm fails, the army loses, the ship goes down. The mind of the master of a vessel is rooted deep in the timbers of her, though he command for a day or a decade; and this captain had on him the stern impression of a scene in the grays of dawn of seven turned faces, and later a stump of a topmast with a white ball on it, that slashed to and fro at the waves, went low and lower, and down. Thereafter there was something strange in his voice. Although steady, it was deep with mourning, and of a quality beyond oration or tears.

"Keep 'er a little more south, Billie," said he.

"A little more south, sir," said the oiler in the stern.

A seat in this boat was not unlike a seat upon a bucking broncho, and, by the same token, a broncho is not much smaller. The craft pranced and reared and plunged like an animal. As each wave came, and she rose for it, she seemed like a horse making at a fence outrageously high. The manner of her scramble over these walls of water is a mystic thing, and, moreover, at the top of them were ordinarily these problems in white water, the foam racing down from the summit of each wave requiring a new leap, and a leap from the air. Then, after scornfully bumping a crest, she would slide and race and splash down a long incline, and arrive bobbing and nodding in front of the next menace.

A singular disadvantage of the sea lies in the fact that, after successfully surmounting one wave, you discover that there is another behind it just as important and just as nervously anxious to do something effective in the way of swamping boats. In a ten-foot dinghy one can get an idea of the resources of the sea in the line of waves that is not probable to the average experience, which is never at sea in a dinghy. As each slaty wall of water approached, it shut all else from the view of the men in the boat, and it was not difficult to imagine that this particular wave was the final outburst of the ocean, the last effort of the grim water. There was a terrible grace in the move of the waves, and they came in silence, save for the snarling of the crests.

In the wan light the faces of the men must have been gray. Their eyes must have glinted in strange ways as they gazed steadily astern. Viewed from a balcony, the whole thing would, doubtless, have been weirdly picturesque. But the men in the boat had no time to see it, and if they had had leisure, there were other things to occupy their minds. The sun swung steadily up the sky, and they knew it was broad day because the color of the sea changed from slate to emerald-green streaked with amber lights, and the foam was like tumbling snow. The process of the breaking day was unknown to them. They were aware only of this effect upon the color of the waves that rolled toward them.

In disjointed sentences the cook and the correspondent argued as to the difference between a life-saving station and a house of refuge. The cook had said: "There's a house of refuge just north of the Mosquito Inlet Light, and as soon as they see us they'll come off in their boat and pick us up."

"As soon as who see us?" said the correspondent.

"The crew," said the cook.

"Houses of refuge don't have crews," said the correspondent. "As I understand them, they are only places where clothes and grub are stored for the benefit of shipwrecked people. They don't carry crews."

"Oh, yes, they do," said the cook.

"No, they don't," said the correspondent.

"Well, we're not there yet, anyhow," said the oiler in the stern.

"Well," said the cook, "perhaps it's not a house of refuge that I'm thinking of as being near Mosquito Inlet Light; perhaps it's a life-saving station."

"We're not there yet," said the oiler in the stern.

II

As the boat bounced from the top of each wave the wind tore through the hair of the hatless men, and as the craft plopped her stern down again the spray slashed past them. The crest of each of these waves was a hill, from the top of which the men surveyed for a moment a broad, tumultuous expanse, shining and wind-riven. It was probably splendid, it was probably glorious, this play of the free sea, wild with lights of emerald and white and amber.

"Bully good thing it's an on-shore wind," said the cook. "If not, where would we be? Wouldn't have a show."

"That's right," said the correspondent.

The busy oiler nodded his assent.

Then the captain, in the bow, chuckled in a way that expressed humor, contempt, tragedy, all in one. "Do you think we've got much of a show now, boys?" said he.

Whereupon the three were silent, save for a trifle of hemming and hawing. To express any particular optimism at this time they felt to be childish and stupid, but they all doubtless possessed this sense of the situation in their minds. A young man thinks doggedly at such times. On the other hand, the ethics of their condition was decidedly against any open suggestion of hopelessness. So they were silent.

"Oh, well," said the captain, soothing his children, "we'll get ashore all right."

But there was that in his tone which made them think; so the oiler quoth, "Yes! if this wind holds."

The cook was bailing. "Yes! if we don't catch hell in the surf."

Canton-flannel gulls flew near and far. Sometimes they sat down on the sea, near patches of brown seaweed that rolled over the waves with a movement like carpets on a line in a gale. The birds sat comfortably in groups, and they were envied by some in the dinghy, for the wrath of the sea was no more to them than it was to a covey of prairie chickens a thousand miles inland. Often they came very close and stared at the men with black, bead-like eyes. At these times they were uncanny and sinister in their unblinking scrutiny, and the men hooted angrily at them, telling them to be gone. One came, and evidently decided to alight on the top of the captain's head. The bird flew parallel to the boat and did not circle, but made short sidelong jumps in the air in chicken fashion. His black eyes were wistfully fixed upon the captain's head. "Ugly brute," said the oiler to the bird. "You look as if you were made with a jackknife." The cook and the correspondent swore darkly at the creature. The captain naturally wished to knock it away with the end of the heavy painter, but he did not dare do it, because anything resembling an emphatic gesture would have capsized this freighted boat; and so, with his open hand, the captain gently and carefully waved the gull away. After it had been discouraged from the pursuit the captain breathed easier on account of his hair, and others breathed easier because the bird struck their minds at this time as being somehow gruesome and ominous.

In the meantime the oiler and the correspondent rowed; and also they rowed. They sat together in the same seat, and each rowed an oar. Then the oiler took both oars; then the correspondent took both oars, then the oiler; then the correspondent. They rowed and they rowed. The very ticklish part of the business was when the time came for the reclining one in the stern to take his turn at the oars. By the very last star of truth, it is easier to steal eggs from under a hen than it was to change seats in the dinghy. First the man in the stern slid his hand along the thwart and moved with care, as if he were of Sèvres.[1] Then the man in the rowing-seat slid his hand along the other thwart. It was all done with the most extraordinary care. As the two sidled past each other, the whole party kept watchful eyes on the coming wave, and the captain cried: "Look out, now! Steady, there!"

The brown mats of seaweed that appeared from time to time were like islands, bits of earth. They were travelling, apparently, neither one way nor the other. They were, to all intents, stationary. They informed the men in the boat that it was making progress slowly toward the land.

The captain, rearing cautiously in the bow after the dinghy soared on a great swell, said that he had seen the lighthouse at Mosquito Inlet. Presently the cook remarked that he had seen it. The correspondent was at the oars then, and for some reason he too wished to look at the lighthouse; but his back was toward the far shore, and the waves were important, and for some time he could not seize an opportunity to turn his head. But at last there came a wave more gentle than the others, and when at the crest of it he swifty scoured the western horizon.

"See it?" said the captain.

"No," said the correspondent, slowly; "I didn't see anything."

"Look again," said the captain. He pointed. "It's exactly in that direction."

At the top of another wave the correspondent did as he was bid, and this time his eyes chanced on a small, still thing on the edge of the swaying horizon. It was precisely like the point of a pin. It took an anxious eye to find a lighthouse so tiny.

"Think we'll make it, Captain?"

"If this wind holds and the boat don't swamp, we can't do much else," said the captain.

The little boat, lifted by each towering sea and splashed viciously by the crests, made progress that in the absence of seaweed was not apparent to those in her. She seemed just a wee thing wallowing, miraculously top up, at the mercy of five oceans. Occasionally a great spread of water, like white flames, swarmed into her.

"Bail her, cook," said the captain, serenely.

"All right, Captain," said the cheerful cook.

III

It would be difficult to describe the subtle brotherhood of men that was here established on the seas. No one said that it was so. No one mentioned it. But it dwelt in the boat, and each man felt it warm him. They were a captain, an oiler, a cook, and a correspondent, and they were friends—friends in a more curiously iron-bound degree than may be common. The hurt captain, lying against the water jar in the bow, spoke always in a low voice and calmly; but he could never command a more ready and swiftly obedient crew than the motley three of the dinghy. It was more than a mere recognition of what was best for the common

1. Fine French porcelain.

safety. There was surely in it a quality that was personal and heartfelt. And after this devotion to the commander of the boat, there was this comradeship, that the correspondent, for instance, who had been taught to be cynical of men, knew even at the time was the best experience of his life. But no one said that it was so. No one mentioned it.

"I wish we had a sail," remarked the captain. "We might try my overcoat on the end of an oar, and give you two boys a chance to rest." So the cook and the correspondent held the mast and spread wide the overcoat; the oiler steered; and the little boat made good way with her new rig. Sometimes the oiler had to scull sharply to keep a sea from breaking into the boat, but otherwise sailing was a success.

Meanwhile the lighthouse had been growing slowly larger. It had now almost assumed color, and appeared like a little gray shadow on the sky. The man at the oars could not be prevented from turning his head rather often to try for a glimpse of this little gray shadow.

At last, from the top of each wave, the men in the tossing boat could see land. Even as the lighthouse was an upright shadow on the sky, this land seemed but a long black shadow on the sea. It certainly was thinner than paper. "We must be about opposite New Smyrna," said the cook, who had coasted this shore often in schooners. "Captain, by the way, I believe they abandoned that life-saving station there about a year ago."

"Did they?" said the captain.

The wind slowly died away. The cook and the correspondent were not now obliged to slave in order to hold high the oar, but the waves continued their old impetuous swooping at the dinghy, and the little craft, no longer under way, struggled woundily over them. The oiler or the correspondent took the oars again.

Shipwrecks are *apropos* of nothing. If men could only train for them and have them occur when the men had reached pink condition, there would be less drowning at sea. Of the four in the dinghy none had slept any time worth mentioning for two days and two nights previous to embarking in the dinghy, and in the excitement of clambering about the deck of a foundering ship they had also forgotten to eat heartily.

For these reasons, and for others, neither the oiler nor the correspondent was fond of rowing at this time. The correspondent wondered ingenuously how in the name of all that was sane could there be people who thought it amusing to row a boat. It was not an amusement; it was a diabolical punishment, and even a genius of mental aberrations could never conclude that it was anything but a horror to the muscles and a crime against the back. He mentioned to the boat in general how the amusement of rowing struck him, and the weary-faced oiler smiled in full sympathy. Previously to the foundering, by the way, the oiler had worked double watch in the engine-room of the ship.

"Take her easy now boys," said the captain. "Don't spend yourselves. If we have to run a surf you'll need all your strength, because we'll sure have to swim for it. Take your time."

Slowly the land arose from the sea. From a black line it became a line of black and a line of white—trees and sand. Finally the captain said that he could make out a house on the shore. "That's the house of refuge, sure," said the cook. "They'll see us before long, and come out after us."

The distant lighthouse reared high. "The keeper ought to be able to make us out now, if he's looking through a glass," said the captain. "He'll notify the life-saving people."

"None of those other boats could have got ashore to give word of the wreck," said the oiler, in a low voice, "else the life boat would be out hunting us."

Slowly and beautifully the land loomed out of the sea. The wind came again. It had veered from the northeast to the southeast. Finally a new sound struck the ears of the men in the boat. It was the low thunder of the surf on the shore. "We'll never be able to make the lighthouse now," said the captain. "Swing her head a little more north, Billie."

"A little more north, sir," said the oiler.

Whereupon the little boat turned her nose once more down the wind, and all but the oarsman watched the shore grow. Under the influence of this expansion doubt and direful apprehension were leaving the minds of the men. The management of the boat was still most absorbing, but it could not prevent a quiet cheerfulness. In an hour, perhaps, they would be ashore.

Their backbones had become thoroughly used to balancing in the boat, and they now rode this wild colt of a dinghy like circus men. The correspondent thought that he had been drenched to the skin, but happening to feel in the top of his coat, he found therein eight cigars. Four of them were soaked with sea water; four were perfectly scatheless. After a search, somebody produced three dry matches; thereupon the four waifs rode in their little boat and, with an assurance of an impending rescue shining in their eyes, puffed at the big cigars, and judged well and ill of all men. Everybody took a drink of water.

IV

"Cook," remarked the captain, "there don't seem to be any signs of life about your house of refuge."

"No," replied the cook. "Funny they don't see us!"

A broad stretch of lowly coast lay before the eyes of the men. It was of low dunes topped with dark vegetation. The roar of the surf was plain, and sometimes they could see the white lip of a wave as it spun up the beach. A tiny house was blocked out black upon the sky. Southward, the slim lighthouse lifted its little gray length.

Tide, wind, and waves were swinging the dinghy northward. "Funny they don't see us," said the men.

The surf's roar was here dulled, but its tone was nevertheless thunderous and mighty. As the boat swam over the great rollers the men sat listening to this roar. "We'll swamp sure," said everybody.

It is fair to say here that there was not a life-saving station within twenty miles in either direction; but the men did not know this fact, and in consequence they made dark and opprobrious remarks concerning the eyesight of the nation's life savers. Four scowling men sat in the dinghy and surpassed records in the invention of epithets.

"Funny they don't see us."

The light-heartedness of a former time had completely faded. To their sharpened minds it was easy to conjure pictures of all kinds of incompetency and blindness and, indeed, cowardice. There was the shore of the populous land, and it was bitter and bitter to them that from it came no sign.

"Well," said the captain, ultimately, "I suppose we'll have to make a try for ourselves. If we stay out here too long, we'll none of us have strength left to swim after the boat swamps."

And so the oiler, who was at the oars, turned the boat straight for the shore. There was a sudden tightening of muscles. There was some thinking.

"If we don't all get ashore," said the captain—"If we don't all get ashore, I suppose you fellows know where to send news of my finish?"

They then briefly exchanged some addresses and admonitions. As for the reflections of the men, there was a great deal of rage in them. Perchance they might be formulated thus: "If I am going to be drowned—if I am going to be drowned—if I am going to be drowned, why, in the name of the seven mad gods who rule the sea, was I allowed to come thus far and contemplate sand and trees? Was I brought here merely to have my nose dragged away as I was about to nibble the sacred cheese of life? It is preposterous! If this old ninny woman, Fate, cannot do better than this, she should be deprived of the management of men's fortunes. She is an old hen who knows not her intention. If she has decided to drown me, why did she not do it in the beginning and save me all this trouble? The whole affair is absurd. . . . But no; she cannot mean to drown me. She dare not drown me. She cannot drown me. Not after all this work!" Afterward the man might have had an impulse to shake his fist at the clouds. "Just you drown me, now, and then hear what I call you!"

The billows that came at this time were more formidable. They seemed always just about to break and roll over the little boat in a turmoil of foam. There was a preparatory and long growl in the speech of them. No mind unused to the sea would have concluded that the dinghy could ascend these sheer heights in time. The shore was still afar. The oiler was a wily surfman. "Boys," he said swiftly, "she won't live three minutes more, and we're too far out to swim. Shall I take her to sea again, Captain?"

"Yes; go ahead!" said the captain.

This oiler, by a series of quick miracles and fast and steady oarsmanship, turned the boat in the middle of the surf and took her safely to sea again.

There was a considerable silence as the boat bumped over the furrowed sea to deeper water. Then somebody in gloom spoke: "Well, anyhow, they must have seen us from the shore by now."

The gulls went in slanting flight up the wind toward the gray, desolate east. A squall, marked by dingy clouds and clouds brick-red, like smoke from a burning building, appeared from the southeast.

"What do you think of those life-saving people? Ain't they peaches?"

"Funny they haven't seen us."

"Maybe they think we're out here for sport! Maybe they think we're fishin'. Maybe they think we're damned fools."

It was a long afternoon. A changed tide tried to force them southward, but wind and wave said northward. Far ahead, where coast-line, sea, and sky formed their mighty angle, there were little dots which seemed to indicate a city on the shore.

"St. Augustine?"

The captain shook his head. "Too near Mosquito Inlet."

And the oiler rowed, and then the correspondent rowed; then the oiler rowed. It was a weary business. The human back can become the seat of more aches and pains than are registered in books for the composite anatomy of a regiment. It is a limited area, but it can become the theater of innumerable muscular conflicts, tangles, wrenches, knots, and other comforts.

"Did you ever like to row, Billie?" asked the correspondent.

"No," said the oiler; "hang it!"

When one exchanged the rowing-seat for a place in the bottom of the boat, he suffered a bodily depression that caused him to be careless of everything save an obligation to wiggle one finger. There was cold sea water swashing to and fro in the boat, and he lay in it. His head, pillowed on a thwart, was within an inch of the swirl of a wave crest, and sometimes a particularly obstreperous sea came inboard and drenched him once more. But these matters did not annoy him. It is almost certain that if the boat had capsized he would have tumbled comfortably out upon the ocean as if he felt sure that it was a great, soft mattress.

"Look! There's a man on the shore!"

"Where?"

"There! See 'im? See'im?"

Yes, sure! He's walking along."

"Now he's stopped. Look! He's facing us!"

"He's waving at us!"

"So he is! By thunder!"

"Ah, now we're all right! Now we're all right! There'll be a boat out here for us in half an hour."

"He's going on. He's running. He's going up to that house there."

The remote beach seemed lower than the sea, and it required a searching glance to discern the little black figure. The captain saw a floating stick, and they rowed to it. A bath towel was by some weird chance in the boat, and, tying this on the stick, the captain waved it. The oarsman did not dare turn his head, so he was obliged to ask questions.

"What's he doing now?"

"He's standing still again. He's looking, I think. . . . There he goes again—toward the house. . . . Now he's stopped again."

"Is he waving at us?"

"No, not now; he was though."

"Look! There comes another man!"

"He's running."

"Look at him go, would you!"

"Why, he's on a bicycle. Now he's met the other man. They're both waving at us. Look!"

"There comes something up the beach."

"What the devil is that thing?"

"Why, it looks like a boat."

"Why, certainly, it's a boat."

"No; it's on wheels."

"Yes, so it is. Well, that must be the life boat. They drag them along shore on a wagon."

"That's the life boat, sure."

"No, by —— , it's—it's an omnibus."

"I tell you it's a life boat."

"It is not! It's an omnibus. I can see it plain. See? One of these big hotel omnibuses."

"By thunder, you're right. It's an omnibus, sure as fate. What do you suppose they are doing with an omnibus? Maybe they are going around collecting the life crew, hey?"

"That's it, likely. Look! There's a fellow waving a little black flag. He's standing on the steps of the omnibus. There come those other two fellows. Now they're all talking together. Look at the fellow with the flag. Maybe he ain't waving it!"

"That ain't a flag, is it? That's his coat. Why, certainly, that's his coat."

"So it is; it's his coat. He's taken it off and is waving it around his head. But would you look at him swing it!"

"Oh, say, there isn't any life-saving station there. That's just a winter-resort hotel omnibus that has brought over some of the boarders to see us drown."

"What's that idiot with the coat mean? What's he signalling, anyhow?"

"It looks as if he were trying to tell us to go north. There must be a life-saving station up there."

"No; he thinks we're fishing. Just giving us a merry hand. See? Ah, there, Willie!"

"Well, I wish I could make something out of those signals. What do you suppose he means?"

"He don't mean anything; he's just playing."

"Well, if he'd just signal us to try the surf again, or to go to sea and wait, or go north, or south, or go to hell, there would be some reason in it. But look at him! He just stands there and keeps his coat revolving like a wheel. The ass!"

"There come more people."

"Now there's quite a mob. Look! Isn't that a boat?"

"Where? Oh, I see where you mean. No, that's no boat."

"That fellow is still waving his coat."

"He must think we like to see him do that. Why don't he quit it? It don't mean anything."

"I don't know. I think he is trying to make us go north. It must be that there's a life-saving station there somewhere."

"Say, he ain't tired yet. Look at 'im wave!"

"Wonder how long he can keep that up. He's been revolving his coat ever since he caught sight of us. He's an idiot. Why aren't they getting men to bring a boat out? A fishing boat—one of those big yawls—could come out here all right. Why don't he do something?"

"Oh, it's all right now."

"They'll have a boat out here for us in less than no time, now that they've seen us."

A faint yellow tone came into the sky over the low land. The shadows on the sea slowly deepened. The wind bore coldness with it, and the men began to shiver.

"Holy smoke!" said one, allowing his voice to express his impious mood, "if we keep on monkeying out here! If we've got to flounder out here all night!"

"Oh, we'll never have to stay here all night! Don't you worry. They've seen us now, and it won't be long before they'll come chasing out after us."

The shore grew dusky. The man waving a coat blended gradually into this gloom, and it swallowed in the same manner the omnibus and the group of people. The spray, when it dashed uproariously over the side, made the voyagers shrink and swear like men who were being branded.

"I'd like to catch the chump who waved the coat. I feel like soaking him one, just for luck."

"Why? What did he do?"

"Oh, nothing, but then he seemed so damned cheerful."

In the meantime the oiler rowed, and then the correspondent rowed, and then the oiler rowed. Gray-faced and bowed forward, they mechanically, turn by turn, plied the leaden oars. The form of the lighthouse had vanished from the southern horizon, but finally a pale star appeared, just lifting from the sea. The streaked saffron in the west passed before the all-merging darkness, and the sea to the east was black. The land had vanished, and was expressed only by the low and drear thunder of the surf.

"If I am going to be drowned—if I am going to be drowned—If I am going to be drowned, why, in the name of the seven mad gods who rule the sea, was I allowed to come thus far and contemplate sand and trees? Was I brought here merely to have my nose dragged away as I was about to nibble the sacred cheese of life?"

The patient captain, drooped over the water jar, was sometimes obliged to speak to the oarsman.

"Keep her head up! Keep her head up!"

"Keep her head up, sir." The voices were weary and low.

This was surely a quiet evening. All save the oarsman lay heavily and listlessly in the boat's bottom. As for him, his eyes were just capable of noting the tall black waves that swept forward in a most sinister silence, save for an occasional subdued growl of a crest.

The cook's head was on a thwart, and he looked without interest at the water under his nose. He was deep in other scenes. Finally he spoke. "Billie," he murmured dreamfully, "what kind of pie do you like best?"

V

"Pie!" said the oiler and the correspondent, agitatedly. "Don't talk about those things, blast you!"

"Well," said the cook, "I was just thinking about ham sandwiches, and—"

A night on the sea in an open boat is a long night. As darkness settled finally, the shine of the light, lifting from the sea in the south, changed to full gold. On the northern horizon a new light appeared, a small bluish gleam on the edge of the waters. These two lights were the furniture of the world. Otherwise there was nothing but waves.

Two men huddled in the stern, and distances were so magnificent in the dinghy that the rower was enabled to keep his feet partly warm by thrusting them under his companions. Their legs indeed extended far under the rowing-seat until they touched the feet of the captain forward. Sometimes, despite the efforts of the tired oarsman, a wave came piling into the boat, an icy wave of the night, and the chilling water soaked them anew. They would twist their bodies for a moment and groan, and sleep the dead sleep once more, while the water in the boat gurgled about them as the craft rocked.

The plan of the oiler and the correspondent was for one to row until he lost the ability, and then arouse the other from his sea-water couch in the bottom of the boat.

The oiler plied the oars until his head drooped forward and the overpowering sleep blinded him; and he rowed yet afterward. Then he touched a man in the bottom of the boat, and called his name. "Will you spell me for a little while?" he said meekly.

"Sure, Billie," said the correspondent, awaking and dragging himself to a sitting position. They exchanged places carefully, and the oiler, cuddling down in the sea water at the cook's side, seemed to go to sleep instantly.

The particular violence of the sea had ceased. The waves came without snarling. The obligation of the man at the oars was to keep the boat headed so that the tilt of the rollers would not capsize her, and to preserve her from filling when the crests rushed past. The black waves were silent and hard to be seen in the darkness. Often one was almost upon the boat before the oarsman was aware.

In a low voice the correspondent addressed the captain. He was not sure that the captain was awake, although this iron man seemed to be always awake. "Captain, shall I keep her making for that light north, sir?"

The same steady voice answered him. "Yes. Keep it about two points off the port bow."

The cook had tied a life belt around himself in order to get even the warmth which this clumsy cork contrivance could donate, and he seemed almost stove-like when a rower, whose teeth invariably chattered wildly as soon as he ceased his labor, dropped down to sleep.

The correspondent, as he rowed, looked down at the two men sleeping underfoot. The cook's arm was around the oiler's shoulders, and, with their fragmentary clothing and haggard faces, they were the babes of the sea—a grotesque rendering of the old babes in the wood.

Later he must have grown stupid at his work, for suddenly there was a growling of water, and a crest came with a roar and a swash into the boat, and it was a wonder that it did not set the cook afloat in his life belt. The cook continued to sleep, but the oiler sat up, blinking his eyes and shaking with the new cold.

"Oh, I'm awful sorry, Billie," said the correspondent, contritely.

"That's all right, old boy," said the oiler, and lay down again and was asleep.

Presently it seemed that even the captain dozed, and the correspondent thought that he was the one man afloat on all the oceans. The wind had a voice as it came over the waves, and it was sadder than the end.

There was a long, loud swishing astern of the boat, and a gleaming trail of phosphorescence, like blue flame, was furrowed on the black waters. It might have been made by a monstrous knife.

Then there came a stillness, while the correspondent breathed with open mouth and looked at the sea.

Suddenly there was another swish and another long flash of bluish light, and this time it was alongside the boat, and might almost have been reached with an oar. The correspondent saw an enormous fin speed like a shadow through the water, hurling the crystalline spray and leaving the long glowing trail.

The correspondent looked over his shoulder at the captain. His face was hidden, and he seemed to be asleep. He looked at the babes of the sea. They certainly were asleep. So, being bereft of sympathy, he leaned a little way to one side and swore softly into the sea.

But the thing did not then leave the vicinity of the boat. Ahead or astern, on one side or the other, at intervals long or short, fled the long sparkling streak, and there was to be heard the *whiroo* of the dark fin. The speed and power of the thing was greatly to be admired. It cut the water like a gigantic and keen projectile.

The presence of this biding thing did not affect the man with the same horror that it would if he had been a picnicker. He simply looked at the sea dully and swore in an undertone.

Nevertheless, it is true that he did not wish to be alone with the thing. He wished one of his companions to awake by chance and keep him company with it. But the captain hung motionless over the water jar, and the oiler and the cook in the bottom of the boat were plunged in slumber.

VI

"If I am going to be drowned—if I am going to be drowned—if I am going to be drowned, why, in the name of the seven mad gods who rule the sea, was I allowed to come thus far and contemplate sand and trees?"

During this dismal night, it may be remarked that a man would conclude that it was really the intention of the seven mad gods to drown him, despite the abominable injustice of it. For it was certainly an abominable injustice to drown a man who had worked so hard, so hard. The man felt it would be a crime most unnatural. Other people had drowned at sea since galleys swarmed with painted sails, but still—

When it occurs to a man that nature does not regard him as important, and that she feels she would not maim the universe by disposing of him, he at first wishes to throw bricks at the temple, and he hates deeply the fact that there are no bricks and no temples. Any visible expression of nature would surely be pelleted with his jeers.

Then, if there be no tangible thing to hoot, he feels, perhaps, the desire to confront a personification and indulge in pleas, bowed to one knee, and with hands supplicant, saying, "Yes, but I love myself."

A high cold star on a winter's night is the word he feels that she says to him. Thereafter he knows the pathos of his situation.

The men in the dinghy had not discussed these matters, but each had, no doubt, reflected upon them in silence and according to his mind. There was seldom any expression upon their faces save the general one of complete weariness. Speech was devoted to the business of the boat.

To chime the notes of his emotion, a verse mysteriously entered the correspondent's head. He had even forgotten that he had forgotten this verse, but it suddenly was in his mind.

A soldier of the Legion lay dying in Algiers;
There was lack of woman's nursing, there was dearth of woman's tears;
But a comrade stood beside him, and he took the comrade's hand,
And he said, "I never more shall see my own, my native land."

In his childhood the correspondent had been made acquainted with the fact that a soldier of the Legion lay dying in Algiers, but he had never regarded it as important. Myriads of his school-fellows had informed him of the soldier's plight, but the dinning had naturally ended by making him perfectly indifferent. He had never considered it his affair that a soldier of the Legion lay dying in Algiers, nor had it appeared to him as a matter for sorrow. It was less to him than breaking a pencil's point.

Now, however, it quaintly came to him as a human, living thing. It was no longer merely a picture of a few throes in the breast of a poet, meanwhile drinking tea and warming his feet at the grate; it was an actuality—stern, mournful, and fine.

The correspondent plainly saw the soldier. He lay on the sand with his feet out straight and still. While his pale left hand was upon his chest in an attempt to thwart the going of his life, the blood came between his fingers. In the far Algerian distance, a city of low square forms was set against a sky that was faint with the last sunset hues. The correspondent, plying the oars and dreaming of the slow and slower movements of the lips of the soldier, was moved by a profound and perfectly impersonal comprehension. He was sorry for the soldier of the Legion who lay dying in Algiers.

The thing which had followed the boat and waited had evidently grown bored at the delay. There was no longer to be heard the slash of the cutwater, and there was no longer the flame of the long trail. The light in the north still glimmered, but it was apparently no nearer to the boat. Sometimes the boom of the surf rang in the correspondent's ears, and he turned the craft seaward then and rowed harder. Southward, some one had evidently built a watch fire on the beach. It was too low and too far to be seen, but it made a shimmering, roseate reflection upon the bluff back of it, and this could be discerned from the boat. The wind came stronger, and sometimes a wave suddenly raged out like a mountain cat, and there was to be seen the sheen and sparkle of a broken crest.

The captain, in the bow, moved on his water jar and sat erect. "Pretty long night," he observed to the correspondent. He looked at the shore. "Those life-saving people take their time."

"Did you see that shark playing around?"

"Yes, I saw him. He was a big fellow, all right."

"Wish I had known you were awake."

Later the correspondent spoke into the bottom of the boat. "Billie!" There was a slow and gradual disentanglement. "Billie, will you spell me?"

"Sure," said the oiler.

As soon as the correspondent touched the cold, comfortable sea water in the bottom of the boat and had huddled close to the cook's life belt he was deep in sleep, despite the fact that his teeth played all the popular airs. This sleep was so good to him that it was but a moment before he heard a voice call his name in a tone that demonstrated the last stages of exhaustion. "Will you spell me?"

"Sure, Billie."

The light in the north had mysteriously vanished, but the correspondent took his course from the wide-awake captain.

Later in the night they took the boat farther out to sea, and the captain directed the cook to take one oar at the stern and keep the boat facing the seas. He was to call out if he should hear the thunder of the surf. This plan enabled the oiler and the correspondent to get respite together. "We'll give those boys a chance to get into shape again," said the captain. They curled down and, after a few preliminary chatterings and trembles, slept once more the dead sleep. Neither knew they had bequeathed to the cook the company of another shark, or perhaps the same shark.

As the boat caroused on the waves, spray occasionally bumped over the side and gave them a fresh soaking, but this had no power to break their repose. The ominous slash of the wind and the water affected them as it would have affected mummies.

"Boys," said the cook, with the notes of every reluctance in his voice, "She's drifted in pretty close. I guess one of you had better take her to sea again." The correspondent, aroused, heard the crash of the toppled crests.

As he was rowing, the captain gave him some whiskey and water, and this steadied the chills out of him. "If I ever get ashore and anybody shows me even a photograph of an oar—"

At last there was a short conversation.

"Billie! . . . Billie, will you spell me?"

"Sure," said the oiler.

VII

When the correspondent again opened his eyes, the sea and the sky were each of the gray hue of the dawning. Later, carmine and gold was painted upon the waters. The morning appeared finally, in its splendor, with a sky of pure blue, and the sunlight flamed on the tips of the waves.

On the distant dunes were set many little black cottages, and a tall white windmill reared above them. No man, nor dog, nor bicycle appeared on the beach. The cottages might have formed a deserted village.

The voyagers scanned the shore. A conference was held in the boat. "Well," said the captain, "if no help is coming, we might better try a run through the surf right away. If we stay out here much longer we will be too weak to do anything for ourselves at all." The others silently acquiesced in this reasoning. The boat was headed for the beach. The correspondent wondered if none ever ascended the tall wind-tower, and if then they never looked seaward. This tower was a giant, standing with its back to the plight of the ants. It represented in a degree, to the correspondent, the serenity of nature amid the struggles of the individual—nature in the wind, and nature in the vision of men. She did not seem cruel to him then, nor beneficent, nor treacherous, nor wise. But she was indifferent, flatly indifferent. It is, perhaps, plausible that a man in this situation, impressed with the unconcern of the universe, should see the innumerable flaws of his life and have them taste wickedly in his mind, and wish for another chance. A distinction between right and wrong seems absurdly clear to him, then, in this new ignorance of the grave-edge, and he understands that if he were given another opportunity he would mend his conduct and his words, and be better and brighter during an introduction or at a tea.

"Now, boys," said the captain, "she is going to swamp sure. All we can do is to work her in as far as possible, and then when she swamps, pile out and scramble for the beach. Keep cool now, and don't jump until she swamps sure."

The oiler took the oars. Over his shoulders he scanned the surf. "Captain," he said, "I think I'd better bring her about and keep her head-on to the seas, and back her in."

"All right, Billie," said the captain. "Back her in." The oiler swung the boat then, and seated in the stern, the cook and the correspondent were obliged to look over their shoulders to contemplate the lonely and indifferent shore.

The monstrous inshore rollers heaved the boat high until the men were again enabled to see the white sheets of water scudding up the slanted beach. "We won't get in very close," said the captain. Each time a man could wrest his attention from the roller, he turned his glance towards the shore, and in the expression of the eyes during this contemplation there was a singular quality. The correspondent, observing the others, knew that they were not afraid, but the full meaning of their glances was shrouded.

As for himself, he was too tired to grapple fundamentally with the fact. He tried to coerce his mind into thinking of it, but the mind was dominated at this time by the muscles, and the muscles said they did not care. It merely occurred to him that if he should drown it would be a shame.

There were no hurried words, no pallor, no plain agitation. The men simply looked at the shore. "Now, remember to get well clear of the boat when you jump," said the captain.

Seaward the crest of a roller suddenly fell with a thunderous crash, and the long white comber came roaring down upon the boat.

"Steady now," said the captain. The men were silent. They turned their eyes from the shore to the comber and waited. The boat slid up the incline, leaped at the furious top, bounced over it, and swung down the long back of the wave. Some water had been shipped, and the cook bailed it out.

But the next crest crashed also. The tumbling, boiling flood of white water caught the boat and whirled it almost perpendicular. Water swarmed in from all sides. The correspondent had his hands on the gunwale at this time, and when the water entered at that place he swiftly withdrew his fingers, as if he objected to wetting them.

The little boat, drunken with this weight of water, reeled and snuggled deeper into the sea.

"Bail her out, cook! Bail her out!" said the captain.

"All right, Captain," said the cook.

"Now, boys, the next one will do for us sure," said the oiler. "Mind to jump clear of the boat."

The third wave moved forward, huge, furious, implacable. It fairly swallowed the dinghy, and almost simultaneously the men tumbled into the sea. A piece of life belt had lain in the bottom of the boat, and as the correspondent went overboard he held this to his chest with his left hand.

The January water was icy, and he reflected immediately that it was colder than he had expected to find it off the coast of Florida. This appeared to his dazed mind as a fact important enough to be noted at the time. The coldness of the water was sad; it was tragic. This fact was somehow mixed and confused with his opinion of his own situation so that it seemed almost a proper reason for tears. The water was cold.

When he came to the surface he was conscious of little but the noisy water. Afterward he saw his companions in the sea. The oiler was ahead in the race. He was swimming strongly and rapidly. Off to the correspondent's left, the cook's great white and corked back bulged out of the water; and in the rear the captain was hanging with one good hand to the keel of the overturned dinghy.

There is a certain immovable quality to a shore, and the correspondent wondered at it amid the confusion of the sea.

It seemed also very attractive; but the correspondent knew that it was a long journey, and he paddled leisurely. The piece of life preserver lay under him, and sometimes he whirled down the incline of a wave as if he were on a hand-sled.

But finally he arrived at a place in the sea where the travel was beset with difficulty. He did not pause swimming to inquire what manner of current had caught him, but there his progress ceased. The shore was set before him like a bit of scenery on a stage, and he looked at it, and understood with his eyes each detail of it.

As the cook passed, much farther to the left, the captain was calling to him, "Turn over on your back, cook! Turn over on your back and use the oar."

"All right, sir." The cook turned on his back, and, paddling with an oar, went ahead as if he were a canoe.

Presently the boat also passed to the left of the correspondent, with the captain clinging with one hand to the keel. He would have appeared like a man raising himself to look over a board fence if it were not for the extraordinary gymnastics of the boat. The correspondent marvelled that the captain could still hold to it.

They passed on nearer to shore—the oiler, the cook, the captain—and following them went the water jar, bouncing gaily over the seas.

The correspondent remained in the grip of this strange new enemy, a current. The shore, with its white slope of sand and its green bluff, topped with little silent cottages, was spread like a picture before him. It was very near to him then, but he was impressed as one who, in a gallery, looks at a scene from Britanny or Algiers.

He thought: "I am going to drown? Can it be possible? Can it be possible? Can it be possible?" Perhaps an individual must consider his own death to be the final phenomenon of nature.

But later a wave perhaps whirled him out of this small deadly current, for he found suddenly that he could again make progress towards the shore. Later still he was aware that the captain, clinging with one hand to the keel of the dinghy, had his face turned away from the shore and towards him and was calling his name. "Come to the boat! Come to the boat!"

In his struggle to reach the captain and the boat, he reflected that when one gets properly wearied drowning must really be a comfortable arrangement—a cessation of hostilities accompanied by a large degree of relief; and he was glad of it, for the main thing in his mind for some moments had been horror of the temporary agony; he did not wish to be hurt.

Presently he saw a man running along the shore. He was undressing with most remarkable speed. Coat, trousers, shirt, everything flew magically off him.

"Come to the boat!" called the captain.

"All right, Captain." As the correspondent paddled, he saw the captain let himself down to bottom and leave the boat. Then the correspondent performed his one little marvel of the voyage. A large wave caught him and flung him with ease and supreme speed completely over the boat and far beyond it. It struck him even then as an event in gymnastics and a true miracle of the sea. An overturned boat in the surf is not a plaything to a swimming man.

The correspondent arrived in water that reached only to his waist, but his condition did not enable him to stand for more than a moment. Each wave knocked him into a heap, and the undertow pulled at him.

Then he saw the man who had been running and undressing, and undressing and running, come bounding into the water. He dragged ashore the cook, and then waded toward the captain; but the captain waved him away and sent him to the correspondent. He was naked—naked as a tree in winter; but a halo was about his head, and he shone like a saint. He gave a strong pull, and a long drag, and a bully heave at the correspondent's hand. The correspondent, schooled in the minor formulae, said, "Thanks, old man." But suddenly the man cried, "What's that?" He pointed a swift finger. The correspondent said, "Go."

In the shallows, face downward, lay the oiler. His forehead touched sand that was periodically, between each wave, clear of the sea.

The correspondent did not know all that transpired afterward. When he achieved safe ground he fell, striking the sand with each particular part of his body. It was as if he had dropped from a roof, but the thud was grateful to him.

It seems that instantly the beach was populated with men with blankets, clothes, and flasks, and women with coffee pots and all the remedies sacred to their minds. The welcome of the land to the men from the sea was warm and generous; but a still and dripping shape was carried slowly up the beach, and the land's welcome for it could only be the different and sinister hospitality of the grave.

When it came night, the white waves paced to and fro in the moonlight, and the wind brought the sound of the great sea's voice to the men on the shore, and they felt that they could then be interpreters.

Fact Questions and Exercises

1. How many of the men in the boat are given names?
2. Throughout most of the story, is the boat far out to sea or relatively close to land? Cite facts that support your answer.
3. What is it that almost perches on the captain's head? Why does it strike the men as "being somehow gruesome and ominous"?
4. In the boat, the correspondent recalls a poem. What is the gist of this poem?
5. The story contains a passage that is repeated several times (a *refrain*). What is this refrain? How does it change each time it is repeated?
6. In what body of water is the boat located? In what American state do the men land?
7. Describe how the men finally get to shore.
8. Which of the men drowns before reaching shore?

For Discussion and Writing

1. Crane is careful to avoid unqualified descriptions and statements. Point out some of the ways in which Crane manages to do this. What is the purpose of his attempted objectivity?

2. Crane uses the term "brotherhood" several times in the story. What kind of brotherhood is it that the men come to feel? Which events lead the men to this brotherhood? How does the poem about the Algerian soldier relate to this?

3. At the end of the story, Crane says that the men now feel that they can be "interpreters." What does he mean by this? What can they now interpret?

4. This story is considered to be a good example of naturalism. Check the meaning of naturalism in the Guide to Literary Terms. How does the story support the definition of naturalism? Are the men at the mercy of forces beyond their control? If so, what are these forces? Does nature seem to pay special favor to the men, or are the men treated merely as another kind of animal? How does the fact that only the oiler drowns relate to this?

5. What role do the people on shore play? Do they seem to comprehend the situation faced by the men in the boat? What do the men in the boat think of the people? Does this attitude change once the men are ashore? If so, how? Do the people ashore share the "brotherhood" (Question 2) with the men in the boat? Explain.

James Joyce [1882–1941]

Joyce was born in Dublin, Ireland—which serves as the setting for most of his fiction. He was reared a Catholic and educated at University College. In 1904, however, he abandoned the Church, his family, and his country, and moved to the Continent. His first collection of fiction, *Dubliners* (1914), is a realistic rendering of his life in Dublin. His first novel, *A Portrait of the Artist as a Young Man* (1916), is a further autobiographical account of his childhood. Joyce's fame rests primarily on *Ulysses* (1922), a novel set in Dublin on one June day. It employs a stream-of-consciousness technique, mixes reality with myth, and demonstrates a highly original prose style. *Ulysses* has had an incalculable influence on later writers, particularly such novelists as William Faulkner and John Barth.

Counterparts

The bell rang furiously and, when Miss Parker went to the tube, a furious voice called out in a piercing North of Ireland accent:

"Send Farrington here!"

Miss Parker returned to her machine, saying to a man who was writing at a desk:

"Mr. Alleyne wants you upstairs."

The man muttered *"Blast* him!" under his breath and pushed back his chair to stand up. When he stood up he was tall and of great bulk. He had a hanging face, dark wine-coloured, with fair eyebrows and moustache: his eyes bulged forward slightly and the whites of them were dirty. He lifted up the counter and, passing by the clients, went out of the office with a heavy step.

He went heavily upstairs until he came to the second landing, where a door bore a brass plate with the inscription *Mr. Alleyne.* Here he halted, puffing with labour and vexation, and knocked. The shrill voice cried:

"Come in!"

The man entered Mr. Alleyne's room. Simultaneously Mr. Alleyne, a little man wearing gold-rimmed glasses on a clean-shaven face, shot his head up over a pile of documents. The head itself was so pink and hairless it seemed like a large egg reposing on the papers. Mr. Alleyne did not lose a moment:

"Farrington? What is the meaning of this? Why have I always to complain of you? May I ask you why you haven't made a copy of that contract between Bodley and Kirwan? I told you it must be ready by four o'clock."

"But Mr. Shelley said, sir—"

"*Mr. Shelley said, sir.* . . . Kindly attend to what I say and not to what *Mr. Shelley says, sir.* You have always some excuse or another for shirking work. Let me tell you that if the contract is not copied before this evening I'll lay the matter before Mr. Crosbie. . . . Do you hear me now?"

"Yes, sir."

"Do you hear me now? . . . Ay and another little matter! I might as well be talking to the wall as talking to you. Understand once for all that you get a half an hour for your lunch and not an hour and a half. How many courses do you want, I'd like to know. . . . Do you mind me now?"

"Yes, sir."

Mr. Alleyne bent his head again upon his pile of papers. The man stared fixedly at the polished skull which directed the affairs of Crosbie & Alleyne, gauging its fragility. A spasm of rage gripped his throat for a few moments and then passed, leaving after it a sharp sensation of thirst. The man recognized the sensation and felt that he must have a good night's drinking. The middle of the month was passed and, if he could get the copy done in time, Mr. Alleyne might give him an order on the cashier. He stood still, gazing fixedly at the head upon the pile of papers. Suddenly Mr. Alleyne began to upset all the papers, searching for something. Then, as if he had been unaware of the man's presence till that moment, he shot up his head again, saying:

"Eh? Are you going to stand there all day? Upon my word, Farrington, you take things easy!"

"I was waiting to see . . ."

"Very good, you needn't wait to see. Go downstairs and do your work."

The man walked heavily towards the door and, as he went out of the room, he heard Mr. Alleyne cry after him that if the contract was not copied by evening Mr. Crosbie would hear of the matter.

He returned to his desk in the lower office and counted the sheets which remained to be copied. He took up his pen and dipped it in the ink but he continued to stare stupidly at the last words he had written: *In no case shall the said Bernard Bodley be* . . . The evening was falling and in a few minutes they would be lighting the gas: then he could write. He felt that he must slake the thirst in his throat. He stood up from his desk and, lifting the counter as before, passed out of the office. As he was passing out the chief clerk looked at him inquiringly.

"It's all right, Mr. Shelley," said the man, pointing his finger to indicate the objective of his journey.

The chief clerk glanced at the hat-rack, but, seeing the row complete, offered no remark. As soon as he was on the landing the man pulled a shepherd's plaid cap out of his pocket, put it on his head and ran quickly down the rickety stairs. From the street door he walked on furtively on the inner side of the path towards the corner and all at once dived into a doorway. He was now safe in the dark snug of O'Neill's shop, and filling up the little window that looked into the bar with his inflamed face, the colour of dark wine or dark meat, he called out:

"Here, Pat, give us a g.p., like a good fellow."

The curate brought him a glass of plain porter. The man drank it at a gulp and asked for a caraway seed. He put his penny on the counter and, leaving the curate to grope for it in the gloom, retreated out of the snug as furtively as he had entered it.

Darkness, accompanied by a thick fog, was gaining upon the dusk of February and the lamps in Eustace Street had been lit. The man went up by the houses until he reached the door of the office, wondering whether he could finish his copy in time. On the stairs a moist pungent odour of perfumes saluted his nose: evidently Miss Delacour had come while he was out in O'Neill's. He crammed his cap back again into his pocket and reentered the office, assuming an air of absentmindedness.

"Mr. Alleyne has been calling for you," said the chief clerk severely. "Where were you?"

The man glanced at the two clients who were standing at the counter as if to intimate that their presence prevented him from answering. As the clients were both male the chief clerk allowed himself a laugh.

"I know that game," he said. "Five times in one day is a little bit . . . Well, you better look sharp and get a copy of our correspondence in the Delacour case for Mr. Alleyne."

This address in the presence of the public, his run upstairs and the porter he had gulped down so hastily confused the man and, as he sat down at his desk to get what was required, he realised how hopeless was the task of finishing his copy of the contract before half past five. The dark damp night was coming and he longed to spend it in the bars, drinking with his friends amid the glare of gas and the clatter of glasses. He got out the Delacour correspondence and passed out of the office. He hoped Mr. Alleyne would not discover that the last two letters were missing.

The moist pungent perfume lay all the way up to Mr. Alleyne's room. Miss Delacour was a middle-aged woman of Jewish appearance. Mr. Alleyne was said to be sweet on her or on her money. She came to the office often and stayed a long time when she came. She was sitting beside his desk now in an aroma of perfumes, smoothing the handle of her umbrella and nodding the great black feather in her hat. Mr. Alleyne had swivelled his chair round to face her and thrown his right foot jauntily upon his left knee. The man put the correspondence on the desk and bowed respectfully but neither Mr. Alleyne nor Miss Delacour took any notice of his bow. Mr. Alleyne tapped a finger on the correspondence and then flicked it towards him as if to say: *"That's all right: you can go."*

The man returned to the lower office and sat down again at his desk. He stared intently at the incomplete phrase: *In no case shall the said Bernard Bodley be . . .* and thought how strange it was that the last three words began with the same letter. The chief clerk began to hurry Miss Parker, saying she would never have the letters typed in time for post. The man listened to the clicking of the machine for a few minutes and then set to work to finish his copy. But his head was not clear and his mind wandered away to the glare and rattle of the public-house. It was a night for hot punches. He struggled on with his copy, but when the clock struck five he had still fourteen pages to write. Blast it! He couldn't finish it in time. He longed to execrate aloud, to bring his fist down on something violently. He was so enraged that he wrote *Bernard Bernard* instead of *Bernard Bodley* and had to begin again on a clean sheet.

He felt strong enough to clear out the whole office singlehanded. His body ached to do something, to rush out and revel in violence. All the indignities of his life enraged him. . . . Could he ask the cashier privately for an advance? No, the cashier was no good, no damn good; he wouldn't give an advance. . . . He knew where he would meet the boys: Leonard and O'Halloran and Nosey Flynn. The barometer of his emotional nature was set for a spell of riot.

His imagination had so abstracted him that his name was called twice before he answered. Mr. Alleyne and Miss Delacour were standing outside the counter and all the clerks had turned round in anticipation of something. The man got up from his desk. Mr. Alleyne began a tirade of abuse, saying that two letters were missing. The man answered that he knew nothing about them, that he had made a faithful copy. The tirade continued: it was so bitter and violent that the man could hardly restrain his fist from descending upon the head of the manikin before him:

"I know nothing about any other two letters," he said stupidly.

"*You—know—nothing.* Of course you know nothing," said Mr. Alleyne. "Tell me," he added, glancing first for approval to the lady beside him, "do you take me for a fool? Do you think me an utter fool?"

The man glanced from the lady's face to the little egg-shaped head and back again; and, almost before he was aware of it, his tongue had found a felicitous moment:

"I don't think, sir," he said, "that that's a fair question to put to me."

There was a pause in the very breathing of the clerks. Everyone was astounded (the author of the witticism no less than his neighbours) and Miss Delacour, who was a stout amiable person, began to smile broadly. Mr. Alleyne flushed to the hue of a wild rose and his mouth twitched with a dwarf's passion. He shook his fist in the man's face till it seemed to vibrate like the knob of some electric machine:

"You impertinent ruffian! You impertinent ruffian! I'll make short work of you! Wait till you see! You'll apologise to me for your impertinence or you'll quit the office instanter! You'll quit this, I'm telling you, or you'll apologise to me!"

He stood in a doorway opposite the office watching to see if the cashier would come out alone. All the clerks passed out and finally the cashier came out with the chief clerk. It was no use trying to say a word to him when he was with the chief clerk. The man felt that his position was bad enough. He had been obliged to offer an abject apology to Mr. Alleyne for his impertinence but he knew what a hornet's nest the office would be for him. He could remember the way in which Mr. Alleyne had hounded little Peake out of the office in order to make room for his own nephew. He felt savage and thirsty and revengeful, annoyed with himself and with everyone else. Mr. Alleyne would never give him an hour's rest; his life would be a hell to him. He had made a proper fool of himself this time. Could he not keep his tongue in his cheek? But they had never pulled together from the first, he and Mr. Alleyne, ever since the day Mr. Alleyne had overheard him mimicking his North of Ireland accent to amuse Higgins and Miss Parker: that had been the beginning of it. He might have tried Higgins for the money, but sure Higgins never had anything for himself. A man with two establishments to keep up, of course he couldn't. . . .

He felt his great body again aching for the comfort of the public-house. The fog had begun to chill him and he wondered could he touch Pat in O'Neill's. He could not touch him for more than a bob—and a bob was no use. Yet he must get money somewhere or other: he had spent his last penny for the g.p. and soon it would be too late for getting money anywhere. Suddenly, as he was fingering his watch-chain, he thought of Terry Kelly's pawn-office in Fleet Street. That was the dart! Why didn't he think of it sooner?

He went through the narrow alley of Temple Bar quickly, muttering to himself that they could all go to hell because he was going to have a good night of it. The clerk in Terry Kelly's said *A crown!* but the consignor held out for six shillings; and in the end the six shillings was allowed him literally. He came out of the pawn-office joyfully, making a little cylinder of the coins between his thumb and fingers. In Westmoreland Street the footpaths were crowded with young men and women returning from business and ragged urchins ran here and there yelling out the names of the evening editions. The man passed through the crowd, looking on the spectacle generally with proud satisfaction and staring masterfully at the office-girls. His head was full of the noises of tram-gongs and swishing trolleys and his nose already sniffed the curling fumes of punch. As he walked on he preconsidered the terms in which he would narrate the incident to the boys:

"So, I just looked at him—coolly, you know, and looked at her. Then I looked back at him again—taking my time, you know. 'I don't think that that's a fair question to put to me,' says I."

Nosey Flynn was sitting up in his usual corner of Davy Byrne's and, when he heard the story, he stood Farrington a half-one, saying it was as smart a thing as ever he heard. Farrington stood a drink in his turn. After a while O'Halloran and Paddy Leonard came in and the story was repeated to them. O'Halloran stood tailors of malt, hot, all round and told the story of the retort he had made to the chief clerk when he was in Callan's of Fownes's Street; but, as the retort was after the manner of the liberal shepherds in the eclogues, he had to admit that it was not as clever as Farrington's retort. At this Farrington told the boys to polish off that and have another.

Just as they were naming their poisons who should come in but Higgins! Of course he had to join in with the others. The men asked him to give his version of it, and he did so with great vivacity for the sight of five small hot whiskies was very exhilarating. Everyone roared laughing when he showed the way in which Mr. Alleyne shook his fist in Farrington's face. Then he imitated Farrington, saying, "*And here was my nabs, as cool as you please,*" while Farrington looked at the company out of his heavy dirty eyes, smiling and at times drawing forth stray drops of liquor from his moustache with the aid of his lower lip.

When that round was over there was a pause. O'Halloran had money but neither of the other two seemed to have any; so the whole party left the shop somewhat regretfully. At the corner of Duke Street Higgins and Nosey Flynn bevelled off to the left while the other three turned back towards the city. Rain was drizzling down on the cold streets and, when they reached the Ballast Office, Farrington suggested the Scotch House. The bar was full of men and loud with the noise of tongues and glasses. The three men pushed past the whining match-sellers at the door and formed a little party at the corner of the counter. They began to exchange stories. Leonard introduced them to a young fellow named Weathers who was performing at the Tivoli as an acrobat and knockabout *artiste*. Farrington stood a drink all round. Weathers said he would take a small Irish and Apollinaris. Farrington, who had definite notions of what was what, asked the boys would they have an Apollinaris too; but the boys told Tim to make theirs hot. The talk became theatrical. O'Halloran stood a round and then Farrington stood another round, Weathers protesting that the hospitality was too Irish. He promised to get them in behind the scenes and introduce them to some nice girls. O'Halloran said that he and Leonard would go, but that Farrington wouldn't go because he was a married man; and Farrington's heavy dirty eyes leered at the company in token that he understood he was being chaffed. Weathers made them all have just one little tincture at his expense and promised to meet them later on at Mulligan's in Poolbeg Street.

When the Scotch House closed they went round to Mulligan's. They went into the parlour at the back and O'Halloran ordered small hot specials all round. They were all beginning to feel mellow. Farrington was just standing another round when Weathers came back. Much to Farrington's relief he drank a glass of bitter this time. Funds were getting low but they had enough to keep them going. Presently two young women with big hats and a young man in a check suit came in and sat at a table close by. Weathers saluted them and told the company that they were out of the Tivoli. Farrington's eyes wandered at every moment in the direction of one of the young women. There was something striking in her appearance. An immense scarf of peacock-blue muslin was wound round her hat and knotted in a great bow under her chin; and she wore bright yellow gloves, reaching to the elbow. Farrington gazed admiringly at the plump arm which she moved very often and with much grace; and when, after a little time, she answered his gaze he admired still more her large dark brown eyes. The oblique staring expression in them fascinated him. She glanced at him once or twice and, when the party was leaving the room, she brushed against his chair and said "O, pardon!" in a London accent. He watched her leave the room in the hope that she would look back at him, but he was disappointed. He cursed his want of money and cursed all the rounds he had stood, particularly to all the whiskies and Apollinaris which he had stood to Weathers. If there was one thing that he hated it was a sponge. He was so angry that he lost count of the conversation of his friends.

When Paddy Leonard called him he found that they were talking about feats of strength. Weathers was showing his biceps muscle to the company and boasting so much that the other two had called on Farrington to uphold the national honour. Farrington pulled up his sleeve accordingly and showed his biceps muscle to the company. The two arms were examined and compared and finally it was agreed to have a trial of strength. The table was cleared and the two men rested their elbows on it, clasping hands. When Paddy Leonard said *"Go!"* each was to try to bring down the other's hand on to the table. Farrington looked very serious and determined.

The trial began. After about thirty seconds Weathers brought his opponent's hand slowly down on to the table. Farrington's dark wine-coloured face flushed darker still with anger and humiliation at having been defeated by such a stripling.

"You're not to put the weight of your body behind it. Play fair," he said.

"Who's not playing fair?" said the other.

"Come on again. The two best out of three."

The trial began again. The veins stood out on Farrington's forehead, and the pallor of Weathers' complexion changed to peony. Their hands and arms trembled under the stress. After a long struggle Weathers again brought his opponent's hand slowly on to the table. There was a murmur of applause from the spectators. The curate, who was standing beside the table, nodded his red head towards the victor and said with stupid familiarity:

"Ah! that's the knack!"

"What the hell do you know about it?" said Farrington fiercely, turning on the man. "What do you put in your gab for?"

"Sh, sh!" said O'Halloran, observing the violent expression of Farrington's face. "Pony up, boys, We'll have just one little smahan more and then we'll be off."

A very sullen-faced man stood at the corner of O'Connell Bridge waiting for the little Sandymount tram to take him home. He was full of smouldering anger and revengefulness. He felt humiliated and discontented; he did not even feel drunk; and he had only twopence in his pocket. He cursed everything. He had done for himself in the office, pawned his watch, spent all his money; and he had not even got drunk. He began to feel thirsty again and he longed to be back again in the hot reeking public-house. He had lost his reputation as a strong man, having been defeated twice by a mere boy. His heart swelled with fury and, when he thought of the woman in the big hat who had brushed against him and said *Pardon!* his fury nearly choked him.

His tram let him down at Shelbourne Road and he steered his great body along in the shadow of the wall of the barracks. He loathed returning to his home. When he went in by the side-door he found the kitchen empty and the kitchen fire nearly out. He bawled upstairs:

"Ada! Ada!"

His wife was a little sharp-faced woman who bullied her husband when he was sober and was bullied by him when he was drunk. They had five children. A little boy came running down the stairs.

"Who is that?" said the man, peering through the darkness.

"Me, pa."

"Who are you? Charlie?"

"No, pa. Tom."

"Where's your mother?"

"She's out at the chapel."

"That's right. . . . Did she think of leaving any dinner for me?"

"Yes, pa. I—"

"Light the lamp. What do you mean by having the place in darkness? Are the other children in bed?"

The man sat down heavily on one of the chairs while the little boy lit the lamp. He began to mimic his son's flat accent, saying half to himself: "*At the chapel. At the chapel, if you please!*" When the lamp was lit he banged his fist on the table and shouted:

"What's for my dinner?"

"I'm going . . . to cook it, pa," said the little boy.

The man jumped up furiously and pointed to the fire.

"On that fire! You let the fire out! By God, I'll teach you to do that again!"

He took a step to the door and seized the walking-stick which was standing behind it.

"I'll teach you to let the fire out!" he said, rolling up his sleeve in order to give his arm free play.

The little boy cried "*O pa!*" and ran whimpering round the table, but the man followed him and caught him by the coat. The little boy looked about him wildly but, seeing no way of escape, fell upon his knees.

"Now, you'll let the fire out the next time!" said the man, striking at him vigorously with the stick. "Take that, you little whelp!"

The boy uttered a squeal of pain as the stick cut his thigh. He clasped his hands together in the air and his voice shook with fright.

"O, pa!" he cried. "Don't beat me, pa! And I'll . . . I'll say a *Hail Mary* for you. . . . I'll say a *Hail Mary* for you, pa, if you don't beat me. . . . I'll say a *Hail Mary.* . . ."

Fact Questions and Exercises

1. What does the word "counterpart" mean? How does it apply to Farrington's profession?
2. Identify Mr. Alleyne. Point out specific lines that indicate how Mr. Alleyne feels toward Farrington.
3. Who in the story wears "moist pungent perfume" and a "great black feather in her hat"?
4. Why does Farrington visit Terry Kelly's pawn office? What does he pawn there?
5. The story is set in Dublin. Point out specific facts that reveal this setting.
6. Describe the woman who brushes against Farrington in Mulligan's.
7. Farrington and Weathers engage in an arm-wrestling match. What is the outcome?
8. What does Farrington's son promise to do if his father will not beat him?

For Discussion and Writing

1. Characterize Farrington. What are his motivations? For instance, why does he drink even when he is supposed to be working? Why does he become angry with his friends at the end of the story? Why does he beat his son? Why is he "full of smouldering anger and revengefulness"? What is his social status? Is

his job exciting? challenging? mundane? Which scenes or passages support your interpretation of Farrington?

2. How does the final scene relate to the rest of the story? Does it logically develop from the actions that take place in the office and taverns? What is the significance of the son promising to pray for his father?

3. Analyze some of the secondary characters in the story—Mr. Alleyne, the woman in the bar, Farrington's friends, Farrington's wife. How do these various characters affect Farrington? How does his relationship with them help explain his own character? Choose two or three of the minor characters and concentrate your discussion on them.

D. H. Lawrence [1885–1930]

Lawrence was born in Nottinghamshire, England, where his father worked as a coal miner. Although Lawrence received a limited formal education, he worked for a short time as a schoolmaster. His first novel, *Sons and Lovers* (1913), concerns his early life in Nottinghamshire. Because of his moral and political views—and partially because he was married to a German—Lawrence was not appreciated by the British government and public. Consequently, he lived in various countries— Mexico, France, America—trying to find a place to settle. Lawrence's work is well known for its frank appraisal of human sexuality, a theme which has involved his novels in much controversy. Among his best-known novels are *The Rainbow* (1915), *Women in Love* (1920), and *Lady Chatterly's Lover* (1928).

Lawrence thinks people have lost touch w/ anything human. Sees Technology as a villan.

The Rocking-Horse Winner

There was a woman who was beautiful, who started with all the advantages, yet she had no luck. She married for love, and the love turned to dust. She had bonny children, yet she felt they had been thrust upon her, and she could not love them. They looked at her coldly, as if they were finding fault with her. And hurriedly she felt she must cover up some fault in herself. Yet what it was that she must cover up she never knew. Nevertheless, when her children were present, she always felt the centre of her heart go hard. This troubled her, and in her manner she was all the more gentle and anxious for her children, as if she loved them very much. Only she herself knew that at the centre of her heart was a hard little place that could not feel love, no, not for anybody. Everybody else said of her: "She is such a good mother. She adores her children." Only she herself, and her children themselves, knew it was not so. They read it in each other's eyes.

There were a boy and two little girls. They lived in a pleasant house, with a garden, and they had discreet servants, and felt themselves superior to anyone in the neighbourhood.

attraction
of
son to
mother

Although they lived in style, they felt always an anxiety in the house. There was never enough money. The mother had a small income, and the father had a small income, but not nearly enough for the social position which they had to keep up. The father went into town to some office. But though he had good prospects, these prospects never materialized. There was always the grinding sense of the shortage of money, though the style was always kept up.

At last the mother said: "I will see if I can't make something." But she did not know where to begin. She racked her brains, and tried this thing and the other, but could not find anything successful. The failure made deep lines come into her face. Her children were growing up, they would have to go to school. There must be more money, there must be more money. The father, who was always very handsome and expensive in his tastes, seemed as if he never would be able to do anything worth doing. And the mother, who had a great belief in herself, did not succeed any better, and her tastes were just as expensive.

And so the house came to be haunted by the unspoken phrase: There must be more money! There must be more money! The children could hear it all the time, though nobody said it aloud. They heard it at Christmas, when the expensive and splendid toys filled the nursery. Behind the shining modern rocking horse, behind the smart doll's-house, a voice would start whispering: "There must be more money! There must be more money!" And the children would stop playing, to listen for a moment. They would look into each other's eyes, to see if they had all heard. And each one saw in the eyes of the other two that they too had heard. "There must be more money! There must be more money!"

It came whispering from the springs of the still-swaying rocking horse, and even the horse, bending his wooden, champing head, heard it. The big doll, sitting so pink and smirking in her new pram, could hear it quite plainly, and seemed to be smirking all the more self-consciously because of it. The foolish puppy, too, that took the place of the Teddy bear, he was looking so extraordinarily foolish for no other reason but that he heard the secret whisper all over the house: "There must be more money!"

Yet nobody ever said it aloud. The whisper was everywhere, and therefore no one spoke it. Just as no one ever says: "We are breathing!" in spite of the fact that breath is coming and going all the time.

"Mother," said the boy Paul one day, "why don't we keep a car of our own? Why do we always use uncle's, or else a taxi?"

"Because we're the poor members of the family," said the mother.

"But why are we, mother?"

"Well—I suppose," she said slowly and bitterly, "it's because your father has no luck."

The boy was silent for some time.

"Is luck money, mother?" he asked, rather timidly.

"No, Paul. Not quite. It's what causes you to have money."

"Oh!" said Paul vaguely. "I thought when Uncle Oscar said filthy lucker, riches it meant money." money

"Filthy lucre does mean money," said the mother. "But it's lucre, not luck."

"Oh!" said the boy. "Then what is luck, mother?"

"It's what causes you to have money. If you're lucky you have money. That's why it's better to be born lucky than rich. If you're rich, you may lose your money. But if you're lucky, you will always get more money."

"Oh! Will you? And is father not lucky?"

"Very unlucky, I should say," she said bitterly.

The boy watched her with unsure eyes.

"Why?" he asked.

"I don't know. Nobody ever knows why one person is lucky and another unlucky."

"Don't they? Nobody at all? Does nobody know?"

"Perhaps God. But He never tells."

"He ought to, then. And aren't you lucky either, mother?"

"I can't be, if I married an unlucky husband."

"But by yourself, aren't you?"

"I used to think I was, before I married. Now I think I am very unlucky indeed."

"Why?"

"Well—never mind! Perhaps I'm not really," she said.

The child looked at her, to see if she meant it. But he saw, by the lines of her mouth, that she was only trying to hide something from him.

"Well, anyhow," he said stoutly, "I'm a lucky person."

"Why?" said his mother, with a sudden laugh.

He stared at her. He didn't even know why he had said it.

"God told me," he asserted, brazening it out.

"I hope He did, dear!" she said, again with a laugh, but rather bitter.

"He did, mother!"

"Excellent!" said the mother, using one of her husband's exclamations.

The boy saw she did not believe him; or, rather, that she paid no attention to his assertion. This angered him somewhat, and made him want to compel her attention.

He went off by himself, vaguely, in a childish way, seeking for the clue to "luck." Absorbed, taking no heed of other people, he went about with a sort of stealth, seeking inwardly for luck. He wanted luck, he wanted it, he wanted it. When the two girls were playing dolls in the nursery, he would sit on his big rocking horse, charging madly into space, with a frenzy that made the little girls peer at him uneasily. Wildly the horse careered, the waving dark hair of the boy tossed, his eyes had a strange glare in them. The little girls dared not speak to him.

When he had ridden to the end of his mad little journey, he climbed down and stood in front of his rocking horse, staring fixedly into its lowered face. Its red mouth was slightly open, its big eye was wide and glassy-bright.

"Now!" he would silently command the snorting steed. "Now, take me to where there is luck! Now take me!"

And he would slash the horse on the neck with the little whip he had asked Uncle Oscar for. He knew the horse could take him to where there was luck, if only he forced it. So he would mount again, and start on his furious ride, hoping at last to get there. He knew he could get there.

"You'll break your horse, Paul!" said the nurse.

"He's always riding like that! I wish he'd leave off!" said his elder sister Joan.

But he only glared down on them in silence. Nurse gave him up. She could make nothing of him. Anyhow he was growing beyond her.

One day his mother and his Uncle Oscar came in when he was on one of his furious rides. He did not speak to them.

"Hallo, you young jockey! Riding a winner?" said his uncle.

"Aren't you growing too big for a rocking horse? You're not a very little boy any longer, you know," said his mother.

But Paul only gave a blue glare from his big, rather close-set eyes. He would speak to nobody when he was in full tilt. His mother watched him with an anxious expression on her face.

At last he suddenly stopped forcing his horse into the mechanical gallop, and slid down.

"Well, I got there!" he announced fiercely, his blue eyes still flaring, and his sturdy long legs straddling apart.

"Where did you get to?" asked his mother.

"Where I wanted to go," he flared back at her.

"That's right, son!" said Uncle Oscar. "Don't you stop till you get there. What's the horse's name?"

"He doesn't have a name," said the boy.

"Gets on without all right?" asked the uncle.

"Well, he has different names. He was called Sansovino last week."

"Sansovino, eh? Won the Ascot. How did you know his name?"

"He always talks about horse races with Bassett," said Joan.

The uncle was delighted to find that his small nephew was posted with all the racing news. Bassett, the young gardener, who had been wounded in the left foot in the war and had got his present job through Oscar Cresswell, whose batman he had been, was a perfect blade of the "turf." He lived in the racing events, and the small boy lived with him.

Oscar Cresswell got it all from Bassett.

"Master Paul comes and asks me, so I can't do more than tell him, sir," said Bassett, his face terribly serious, as if he were speaking of religious matters.

"And does he ever put anything on a horse he fancies?"

"Well—I don't want to give him away—he's a young sport, a fine sport, sir. Would you mind asking him yourself? He sort of takes a pleasure in it, and perhaps he'd feel I was giving him away, sir, if you don't mind."

Bassett was serious as a church.

The uncle went back to his nephew, and took him off for a ride in the car.

"Say, Paul, old man, do you ever put anything on a horse?" the uncle asked.

The boy watched the handsome man closely.

"Why, do you think I oughtn't to?" he parried.

"Not a bit of it! I thought perhaps you might give me a tip for the Lincoln."

The car sped on into the country, going down to Uncle Oscar's place in Hampshire.

"Honour bright?" said the nephew.

"Honour bright, son!" said the uncle.

"Well, then, Daffodil."

"Daffodil! I doubt it, sonny. What about Mirza?"

"I only know the winner," said the boy. "That's Daffodil."

"Daffodil, eh?"

There was a pause. Daffodil was an obscure horse comparatively.

"Uncle!"

"Yes, son?"

"You won't let it go any further, will you? I promised Bassett."

"Bassett be damned, old man! What's he got to do with it?"

"We're partners. We've been partners from the first. Uncle, he lent me my first five shillings, which I lost. I promised him, honour bright, it was only between me and him; only you gave me that ten-shilling note I started winning with, so I thought you were lucky. You won't let it go any further, will you?"

The boy gazed at his uncle from those big, hot, blue eyes, set rather close together. The uncle stirred and laughed uneasily.

"Right you are, son! I'll keep your tip private. Daffodil, eh? How much are you putting on him?"

"All except twenty pounds," said the boy. "I keep that in reserve."

The uncle thought it a good joke.

"You keep twenty pounds in reserve, do you, you young romancer? What are you betting, then?"

"I'm betting three hundred," said the boy gravely. "But it's between you and me, Uncle Oscar! Honour bright?"

The uncle burst into a roar of laughter.

"It's between you and me all right, you young Nat Gould," he said, laughing. "But where's your three hundred?"

"Bassett keeps it for me. We're partners."

"You are, are you! And what is Bassett putting on Daffodil?"

"He won't go quite as high as I do, I expect. Perhaps he'll go a hundred and fifty."

"What, pennies?" laughed the uncle.

"Pounds," said the child, with a surprised look at his uncle. "Bassett keeps a bigger reserve than I do."

Between wonder and amusement Uncle Oscar was silent. He pursued the matter no further, but he determined to take his nephew with him to the Lincoln races.

"Now, son," he said, "I'm putting twenty on Mirza, and I'll put five for you on any horse you fancy. What's your pick?"

"Daffodil, uncle."

"No, not the fiver on Daffodil!"

"I should if it was my own fiver," said the child.

"Good! Good! Right you are! A fiver for me and a fiver for you on Daffodil."

The child had never been to a race meeting before, and his eyes were blue fire. He pursed his mough tight, and watched. A Frenchman just in front had put his money on Lancelot. Wild with excitement, he flayed his arms up and down, yelling "Lancelot! Lancelot!" in his French accent.

Daffodil came in first, Lancelot second, Mirza third. The child, flushed and with eyes blazing, was curiously serene. His uncle brought him four five-pound notes, four to one.   *quiet, calm*

"What am I to do with these?" he cried, waving them before the boy's eyes.

"I suppose we'll talk to Bassett," said the boy. "I expect I have fifteen hundred now; and twenty in reserve; and this twenty."

His uncle studied him for some moments.

"Look here, son!" he said. "You're not serious about Bassett and that fifteen hundred, are you?"

"Yes, I am. But it's between you and me, uncle. Honour bright!"

"Honour bright all right, son! But I must talk to Bassett."

"If you'd like to be a partner, uncle, with Bassett and me, we could all be partners. Only, you'd have to promise, honour bright, uncle, not to let it go beyond us three. Bassett and I are lucky, and you must be lucky, because it was your ten shillings I started winning with. . . ."

Uncle Oscar took both Bassett and Paul into Richmond Park for an afternoon, and there they talked.

"It's like this, you see, sir," Bassett said. "Master Paul would get me talking about racing events, spinning yarns, you know, sir. And he was always keen on knowing if I'd made or if I'd lost. It's about a year since, now, that I put five shillings on Blush of Dawn for him—and we lost. Then the luck turned, with that ten shillings he had from you, that we put on Singhalese. And since that time, it's been pretty steady, all things considering. What do you say, Master Paul?"

"We're all right when we're sure," said Paul, "It's when we're not quite sure that we go down."

"Oh, but we're careful then," said Bassett.

"But when are you sure?" smiled Uncle Oscar.

"It's Master Paul, sir," said Bassett, in a secret, religious voice. "It's as if he had it from heaven. Like Daffodil, now, for the Lincoln. That was as sure as eggs."

"Did you put anything on Daffodil?" asked Oscar Cresswell.

"Yes, sir, I made my bit."

"And my nephew?"

Bassett was obstinately silent, looking at Paul.

"I made twelve hundred, didn't I, Bassett? I told uncle I was putting three hundred on Daffodil."

"That's right," said Bassett, nodding.

"But where's the money?" asked the uncle.

"I keep it safe locked up, sir. Master Paul can have it any minute he likes to ask for it."

"What, fifteen hundred pounds?"

"And twenty! and forty, that is, with the twenty he made on the course."

"It's amazing!" said the uncle.

"If Master Paul offers you to be partners, sir, I would, if I were you; if you'll excuse me," said Bassett.

Oscar Cresswell thought about it.

"I'll see the money," he said.

They drove home again, and sure enough, Bassett came round to the garden-house with fifteen hundred pounds in notes. The twenty pounds reserve was left with Joe Glee, in the Turf Commission deposit.

"You see, it's all right, uncle, when I'm sure! Then we go strong, for all we're worth. Don't we, Bassett?"

"We do that, Master Paul."

"And when are you sure?" said the uncle, laughing.

"Oh, well, sometimes I'm absolutely sure, like about Daffodil," said the boy; "and sometimes I have an idea; and sometimes I haven't even an idea, have I, Bassett? Then we're careful, because we mostly go down."

"You do, do you? And when you're sure, like about Daffodil, what makes you sure, sonny?"

"Oh, well, I don't know," said the boy uneasily. "I'm sure, you know, uncle; that's all."

"It's as if he had it from heaven, sir," Bassett reiterated. _repeated_

"I should say so!" said the uncle.

But he became a partner. And when the Leger was coming on, Paul was "sure" about Lively Spark, which was a quite inconsiderable horse. The boy insisted on putting a thousand on the horse, Bassett went for five hundred, and Oscar Cresswell two hundred. Lively Spark came in first, and the betting had been ten to one against him. Paul had made ten thousand.

"You see," he said, "I was absolutely sure of him."

Even Oscar Cresswell had cleared two thousand.

"Look here, son," he said, "this sort of thing makes me nervous."

"It needn't, uncle! Perhaps I shan't be sure again for a long time."

"But what are you going to do with your money?" asked the uncle.

"Of course," said the boy, "I started it for mother. She said she had no luck, because father is unlucky, so I thought if I was lucky, it might stop whispering."

"What might stop whispering?"

"Our house. I hate our house for whispering."

"What does it whisper?"

"Why—why"—the boy fidgeted—"why, I don't know. But it's always short of money, you know, uncle."

"I know it, son, I know it."

"You know people send mother writs, don't you, uncle?"

"I'm afraid I do," said the uncle.

"And then the house whispers, like people laughing at you behind your back. It's awful, that is! I thought if I was lucky. . . ."

"You might stop it," added the uncle.

The boy watched him with the big blue eyes that had an uncanny cold fire in them, and he said never a word.

"Well, then!" said the uncle. "What are we doing?"

"I shouldn't like mother to know I was lucky," said the boy.

"Why not, son?"

"She'd stop me."

"I don't think she would."

"Oh?"—and the boy writhed in an odd way—"I don't want her to know, uncle."

"All right, son! We'll manage it without her knowing."

They managed it very easily. Paul, at the other's suggestion, handed over five thousand pounds to his uncle, who deposited it with the family lawyer, who was then to inform Paul's mother that a relative had put five thousand pounds into his hands, which sum was to be paid out a thousand pounds at a time, on the mother's birthday, for the next five years.

"So she'll have a birthday present of a thousand pounds for five successive years," said Uncle Oscar. "I hope it won't make it all the harder for her later."

Paul's mother had her birthday in November. The house had been "whispering" worse than ever lately, and, even in spite of his luck, Paul could not bear up against it. He was very anxious to see the effect of the birthday letter, telling his mother about the thousand pounds.

When there were no visitors, Paul now took his meals with his parents, as he was beyond the nursery control. His mother went into town nearly every day. She had discovered that she had an odd knack of sketching furs and dress materials, so she worked secretly in the studio of a friend who was the chief "artist" for the leading drapers. She drew the figures of ladies in furs and ladies in silk and sequins for the newspaper advertisements. This young woman artist earned several thousand pounds a year, but Paul's mother only made several hundreds, and she was again dissatisfied. She so wanted to be first in something, and she did not succeed, even in making sketches for drapery advertisements.

She was down to breakfast on the morning of her birthday. Paul watched her face as she read her letters. He knew the lawyer's letter. As his mother read it, her face hardened and became more expressionless. Then a cold, determined look came on her mouth. She hid the letter under the pile of others, and said not a word about it.

"Didn't you have anything nice in the post for your birthday, mother?" said Paul.

"Quite moderately nice," she said, her voice cold and absent.

She went away to town without saying more.

But in the afternoon Uncle Oscar appeared. He said Paul's mother had had a long interview with the lawyer, asking if the whole five thousand could be advanced at once, as she was in debt.

"What do you think, uncle?" said the boy.

"I leave it to you, son."

"Oh, let her have it, then! We can get some more with the other," said the boy.

"A bird in the hand is worth two in the bush, laddie!" said Uncle Oscar.

"But I'm sure to know for the Grand National; or the Lincolnshire; or else the Derby. I'm sure to know for one of them," said Paul.

So Uncle Oscar signed the agreement, and Paul's mother touched the whole five thousand. Then something very curious happened. The voices in the house suddenly went mad, like a chorus of frogs on a spring evening. There were certain new furnishings, and Paul had a tutor. He was really going to Eton, his father's school, in the following autumn. There were flowers in the winter, and a blossoming of the luxury Paul's mother had been used to. And yet the voices in the house, behind the sprays of mimosa and almond blossom, and from under the piles of iridescent cushions, simply trilled and screamed in a sort of ecstasy: "There must be more money! Oh-h, there must be more money. Oh, now, now-w! Now-w-w—there must be more money!—more than ever! More than ever!"

It frightened Paul terribly. He studied away at his Latin and Greek with his tutors. But his intense hours were spent with Bassett. The Grand National had gone by: he had not "known," and had lost a hundred pounds. Summer was at hand. He was in agony for the Lincoln. But even for the Lincoln he didn't "know" and he lost fifty pounds. He became wild-eyed and strange, as if something were going to explode in him.

"Let it alone, son! Don't you bother about it!" urged Uncle Oscar. But it was as if the boy couldn't really hear what his uncle was saying.

"I've got to know for the Derby! I've got to know for the Derby!" the child reiterated, his big blue eyes blazing with a sort of madness.

His mother noticed how overwrought he was.

"You'd better go to the seaside. Wouldn't you like to go now to the seaside, instead of waiting? I think you'd better," she said, looking down at him anxiously, her heart curiously heavy because of him.

But the child lifted his uncanny blue eyes.

"I couldn't possibly go before the Derby, mother!" he said. "I couldn't possibly!"

"Why not?" she said, her voice becoming heavy when she was opposed. "Why not? You can still go from the seaside to see the Derby with your Uncle Oscar, if that's what you wish. No need for you to wait here. Besides, I think you care too much about these races. It's a bad sign. My family has been a gambling family, and you won't know till you grow up how much damage it has done. But it has done damage. I shall have to send Bassett away, and ask Uncle Oscar not to talk racing to you, unless you promise to be reasonable about it; go away to the seaside and forget it. You're all nerves!"

"I'll do what you like, mother, so long as you don't send me away till after the Derby," the boy said.

"Send you away from where? Just from this house?"

"Yes," he said, gazing at her.

"Why, you curious child, what makes you care about this house so much, suddenly? I never knew you loved it."

He gazed at her without speaking. He had a secret within a secret, something he had not divulged, even to Bassett or to his Uncle Oscar.

But his mother, after standing undecided and a little bit sullen for some moments, said:

"Very well, then! Don't go to the seaside till after the Derby, if you don't wish it. But promise me you won't let your nerves go to pieces. Promise you won't think so much about horse racing and events, as you call them!"

"Oh, no," said the boy casually. "I won't think much about them, mother. You needn't worry. I wouldn't worry, mother, if I were you."

"If you were me and I were you," said his mother, "I wonder what we should do!"

"But you know you needn't worry, mother, don't you?" the boy repeated.

"I should be awfully glad to know it," she said wearily.

"Oh, well, you can, you know. I mean, you ought to know you needn't worry," he insisted.

"Ought I? Then I'll see about it," she said.

Paul's secret of secrets was his wooden horse, that which had no name. Since he was emancipated from a nurse and a nursery-governess, he had had his rocking horse removed to his own bedroom at the top of the house.

"Surely, you're too big for a rocking horse!" his mother had remonstrated.

"Well, you see, mother, till I can have a real horse, I like to have some sort of animal about," had been his quaint answer.

"Do you feel he keeps you company?" she laughed.

"Oh, yes! He's very good, he always keeps me company, when I'm there," said Paul.

So the horse, rather shabby, stood in an arrested prance in the boy's bedroom.

The Derby was drawing near, and the boy grew more and more tense. He hardly heard what was spoken to him, he was very frail, and his eyes were really uncanny. His mother had sudden seizures of uneasiness about him. Sometimes, for half-an-hour, she would feel a sudden anxiety about him that was almost anguish. She wanted to rush to him at once, and know he was safe.

Two nights before the Derby, she was at a big party in town, when one of her rushes of anxiety about her boy, her first-born, gripped her heart till she could hardly speak. She fought with the feeling, might and main, for she believed in common sense. But it was too strong. She had to leave the dance and go downstairs to telephone to the country. The children's nursery-governess was terribly surprised and startled at being rung up in the night.

"Are the children all right, Miss Wilmot?"

"Oh, yes, they are quite all right."

"Master Paul? Is he all right?"

"He went to bed as right as a trivet. Shall I run up and look at him?"

"No," said Paul's mother reluctantly. "No! Don't trouble. It's all right. Don't sit up. We shall be home fairly soon." She did not want her son's privacy intruded upon.

"Very good," said the governess.

It was about one o'clock when Paul's mother and father drove up to their house. All was still. Paul's mother went to her room and slipped off her white fur coat. She had told her maid not to wait up for her. She heard her husband downstairs, mixing a whisky-and-soda.

And then, because of the strange anxiety at her heart, she stole upstairs to her son's room. Noiselessly she went along the upper corridor. Was there a faint noise? What was it?

She stood, with arrested muscles, outside his door, listening. There was a strange, heavy, and yet not loud noise. Her heart stood still. It was a soundless noise, yet rushing and powerful. Something huge, in violent, hushed motion. What was it? What in God's name was it? She ought to know. She felt that she knew the noise. She knew what it was.

Yet she could not place it. She couldn't say what it was. And on and on it went, like a madness.

Softly, frozen with anxiety and fear, she turned the door handle.

The room was dark. Yet in the space near the window, she heard and saw something plunging to and fro. She gazed in fear and amazement.

Then suddenly she switched on the light, and saw her son, in his green pyjamas, madly surging on the rocking horse. The blaze of light suddenly lit him up, as he urged the wooden horse, and lit her up, as she stood, blonde, in her dress of pale green and crystal, in the doorway.

"Paul!" she cried. "Whatever are you doing?"

"It's Malabar!" he screamed, in a powerful, strange voice. "It's Malabar."

His eyes blazed at her for one strange and senseless second, as he ceased urging his wooden horse. Then he fell with a crash to the ground, and she, all her tormented motherhood flooding upon her, rushed to gather him up.

But he was unconscious, and unconscious he remained, with some brain-fever. He talked and tossed, and his mother sat stonily by his side.

"Malabar! It's Malabar! Bassett, Bassett, I know! It's Malabar!"

So the child cried, trying to get up and urge the rocking horse that gave him his inspiration.

"What does he mean by Malabar?" asked the heart-frozen mother.

"I don't know," said the father stonily.

"What does he mean by Malabar?" she asked her brother Oscar.

"It's one of the horses running for the Derby," was the answer.

And, in spite of himself, Oscar Cresswell spoke to Bassett, and himself put a thousand on Malabar: at fourteen to one.

The third day of the illness was critical: they were waiting for a change. The boy, with his rather long, curly hair, was tossing ceaselessly on the pillow. He neither slept nor regained consciousness, and his eyes were like blue stones. His mother sat, feeling her heart had gone, turned actually into a stone.

In the evening, Oscar Cresswell did not come, but Bassett sent a message, saying could he come up for one moment, just one moment? Paul's mother was very angry at the intrusion, but on second thought she agreed. The boy was the same. Perhaps Bassett might bring him to consciousness.

The gardener, a shortish fellow with a little brown moustache, and sharp little brown eyes, tiptoed into the room, touched his imaginary cap to Paul's mother, and stole to the bedside, staring with glittering, smallish eyes, at the tossing, dying child.

"Master Paul!" he whispered. "Master Paul! Malabar came in first all right, a clean win. I did as you told me. You've made over seventy thousand pounds, you have; you've got over eighty thousand. Malabar came in all right, Master Paul."

"Malabar! Malabar! Did I say Malabar, mother? Did I say Malabar? Do you think I'm lucky, mother? I knew Malabar, didn't I? Over eighty thousand pounds! I call that lucky, don't you, mother? Over eighty thousand pounds! I knew, didn't I know I knew? Malabar came in all right. If I ride my horse till I 'm sure, then I tell you, Bassett, you can go as high as you like. Did you go for all you were worth, Bassett?"

"I went a thousand on it, Master Paul."

"I never told you, mother, that if I can ride my horse, and get there, then I'm absolutely sure—oh, absolutely! Mother, did I ever tell you? I am lucky."

"No, you never did," said the mother.

But the boy died in the night.

And even as he lay dead, his mother heard her brother's voice saying to her: "My God, Hester, you're eighty-odd thousand to the good and a poor devil of a son to the bad. But, poor devil, poor devil, he's best gone out of a life where he rides his rocking horse to find a winner."

Fact Questions and Exercises

1. What is the phrase or refrain that the house seems to whisper?
2. What does Paul think the term "filthy lucre" means? How does he pronounce it?
3. Where does Paul want his toy horse to take·him?
4. How does Paul make the money that his mother desires?
5. After Paul's mother returns from the party and goes to his room, what does she find him doing?
6. Identify Malabar.
7. How old is Paul? What facts does the story give about his physical appearance?
8. What happens to Paul?

For Discussion and Writing

1. Characterize the mother. What are her values? What does she feel toward her husband? What is her attitude toward her children? Does she love Paul, or is he merely a means to an end?
2. Look at the first paragraph of the story. What details in this paragraph give it a fairy-tale quality? How does Lawrence change the traditional fairy-tale plot to make a point about materialism and modern society? Compare the story to a fairy tale—Grimms' "Hansel and Gretel," for example.
3. Numerous critics see sexual or Freudian symbolism as being of central importance to this story. Do you share this view? If so, what are some of the symbols or themes that support this idea? If not, suggest other interpretations and give facts to support your opinion.

Katherine Anne Porter [1890–   ]

Porter was born in Indian Creek, Texas, the daughter of an old Southern family that counted Daniel Boone among its ancestors. She attended convent schools in Texas and Louisiana, and at the age of sixteen ran away to get married. The marriage was short-lived; after it ended, Porter went to Chicago, where she worked as a newspaper reporter and acted in several movies. In 1921 she taught dancing in a girl's school in Mexico. Her first short story was published in 1922; thereafter she devoted most of her time to writing. She has published only one novel, *Ship of Fools* (1962), and is noted primarily as a short-story writer. Among her collections are *Flowering Judas and Other Stories* (1930), *Pale, Horse, Pale Rider* (1939), and *The Leaning Tower and Other Stories* (1944).

Flowering Judas   *Judas in Bible -traitor*

Braggioni sits heaped upon the edge of a straight-backed chair much too small for him, and sings to Laura in a furry, mournful voice. Laura has begun to find reasons for avoiding her own house until the latest possible moment, for Braggioni is there almost every night. No matter how late she is, he will be sitting there with a surly, waiting expression, pulling at his kinky yellow hair, thumbing the strings of his guitar, snarling a tune under his breath. Lupe the Indian maid meets Laura at the door, and says with a flicker of a glance towards the upper room, "He waits."

Laura wishes to lie down, she is tired of her hairpins and the feel of her long tight sleeves, but she says to him, "Have you a new song for me this evening?" If he says yes, she asks him to sing it. If he says no, she remembers his favorite one, and asks him to sing it again. Lupe brings her a cup of chocolate and a plate of rice, and Laura eats at the small table under the lamp, first inviting Braggioni, whose answer is always the same: "I have eaten, and besides, chocolate thickens the voice."

Laura says, "Sing, then," and Braggioni heaves himself into song. He scratches the guitar familiarly as though it were a pet animal, and sings passionately off key, taking the high notes in a prolonged painful squeal. Laura, who haunts the markets listening to the ballad singers, and stops every day to hear the blind boy playing his reed-flute in Sixteenth of September Street, listens to Braggioni with pitiless courtesy, because she dares not smile at his miserable performance. Nobody dares to smile at him. Braggioni is cruel to everyone, with a kind of specialized insolence, but he is so vain of his talents, and so sensitive to slights, it would require a cruelty and vanity greater than his own to lay a finger on the vast cureless wound of his self-esteem. It would require courage, too, for it is dangerous to offend him, and nobody has this courage.

Braggioni loves himself with such tenderness and amplitude and eternal charity that his followers—for he is a leader of men, a skilled revolutionist, and his skin has been punctured in honorable warfare—warm themselves in a reflected glow, and say to each other: "He has a real nobility, a love of humanity raised above mere personal affections." The excess of this self-love has flowed out, inconveniently for her, over Laura, who, with so many others, owes her comfortable situation and her salary to him. When he is in a very good humor, he tells her, "I am tempted to forgive you for being a *gringa. Gringita!*"[1] and Laura, burning, imagines herself leaning forward suddenly, and with a sound back-handed slap wiping the suety smile from his face. If he notices her eyes at these moments he gives no sign.

Leader, skilled Revolutionist

She knows what Braggioni would offer her, and she must resist tena-ciously without appearing to resist, and if she could avoid it she would not admit even to herself the slow drift of his intention. During these long evenings which have spoiled a long month for her, she sits in her deep chair with an open book on her knees, resting her eyes on the consoling rigidity of the printed page when the sight and sound of Braggioni singing threaten to identify themselves with all her remembered afflictions and to add their weight to her uneasy premonitions of the future. The gluttonous bulk of Braggioni has become a symbol of her many

---

1. Little foreign girl.

disillusions, for a revolutionist should be lean, animated by heroic faith, a vessel of abstract virtues. This is nonsense, she knows it now and is ashamed of it. Revolution must have leaders, and leadership is a career for energetic men. She is, her comrades tell her, full of romantic error, for what she defines as cynicism in them is merely "a developed sense of reality." She is almost too willing to say, "I am wrong, I suppose I don't really understand the principles," and afterward she makes a secret truce with herself, determined not to surrender her will to such expedient logic. But she cannot help feeling that she has been betrayed irreparably by the disunion between her way of living and her feeling of what life should be, and at times she is almost contented to rest in this sense of grievance as a private store of consolation. Sometimes she wishes to run away, but she stays. Now she longs to fly out of this room, down the narrow stairs, and into the street where the houses lean together like conspirators under a single mottled lamp, and leave Braggioni singing to himself.

Instead she looks at Braggioni, frankly and clearly, like a good child who understands the rules of behavior. Her knees cling together under sound blue serge, and her round white collar is not purposely nun-like. She wears the uniform of an idea, and has renounced vanities. She was born Roman Catholic, and in spite of her fear of being seen by someone who might make a scandal of it, she slips now and again into some crumbling little church, kneels on the chilly stone, and says a Hail Mary on the gold rosary she bought in Tehuantepec. It is no good and she ends by examining the altar with its tinsel flowers and ragged brocades, and feels tender about the battered doll-shape of some male saint whose white, lace-trimmed drawers hang limply around his ankles below the hieratic dignity of his velvet robe. She has encased herself in a set of principles derived from her early training, leaving no detail of gesture or of personal taste untouched, and for this reason she will not wear lace made on machines. This is her private heresy, for in her special group the machine is sacred, and will be the salvation of the workers. She loves fine lace, and there is a tiny edge of fluted cobweb on this collar, which is one of twenty precisely alike, folded in blue tissue paper in the upper drawer of her clothes chest.

Braggioni catches her glance solidly as if he had been waiting for it, leans forward, balancing his paunch between his spread knees, and sings with tremendous emphasis, weighing his words. He has, the song relates, no father and no mother, nor even a friend to console him; lonely as a wave of the sea he comes and goes, lonely as a wave. His mouth opens round and yearns sideways, his balloon cheeks grow oily with the labor of song. He bulges marvelously in his expensive garments. Over his lavender collar, crushed upon a purple necktie, held by a diamond hoop: over his ammunition belt of tooled leather worked in silver, buckled cruelly around his gasping middle: over the tops of his glossy yellow shoes Braggioni swells with ominous ripeness, his mauve silk hose stretched taut, his ankles bound with the stout leather thongs of his shoes.

When he stretches his eyelids at Laura she notes again that his eyes are the true tawny yellow cat's eyes. He is rich, not in money, he tells her, but in power, and this power brings with it the blameless ownership of things, and the right to indulge his love of small luxuries. "I have a taste for the elegant refinements," he said once, flourishing a yellow silk handkerchief before her nose. "Smell that? It is Jockey Club, imported from New York" Nonetheless he is wounded by life. He will say so presently. "It is true everything turns to dust in the hand, to gall on the tongue." He sighs and his leather belt creaks like a saddle girth. "I am disappointed in everything as it comes. Everything." He shakes his head. "You, poor thing, you will be disappointed too. You are born for it. We are more alike than you realize in some things. Wait and see. Some day you will remember what I have told you, you will know that Braggioni was your friend."

Laura feels a slow chill, a purely physical sense of danger, a warning in her blood that violence, mutilation, a shocking death, wait for her with lessening patience. She has translated this fear into something homely, immediate, and sometimes hesitates before crossing the street. "My personal fate is nothing, except as the testimony of a mental attitude," she reminds herself, quoting from some forgotten philosophic primer, and is sensible enough to add, "Anyhow, I shall not be killed by an automobile if I can help it."

"It may be true I am as corrupt, in another way, as Braggioni," she thinks in spite of herself, "as callous, as incomplete," and if this is so, any kind of death seems preferable. Still she sits quietly, she does not run. Where could she go? Uninvited she has promised herself to this place: she can no longer imagine herself as living in another country, and there is no pleasure in remembering her life before she came here.

Precisely what is the nature of this devotion, its true motives, and what are its obligations? Laura cannot say. She spends part of her days in Xochimilco, near by, teaching Indian children to say in English, "The cat is on the mat." When she appears in the classroom they crowd about her with smiles on their wise, innocent, clay-colored faces, crying, "Good morning, my titcher!" in immaculate voices, and they make of her desk a fresh garden of flowers every day.

During her leisure she goes to union meetings and listens to busy important voices quarreling over tactics, methods, internal politics. She visits the prisoners of her own political faith in their cells, where they entertain themselves with counting cockroaches, repenting of their indiscretions, composing their memoirs, writing out manifestoes and plans for their comrades who are still walking about free, hands in pockets, sniffing fresh air. Laura brings them food and cigarettes and a little money, and she brings messages disguised in equivocal phrases from the men outside who dare not set foot in the prison for fear of disappearing into the cells kept empty for them. If the prisoners confuse night and day, and complain, "Dear little Laura, time doesn't pass in this infernal hole, and I won't know when it is time to sleep unless I have a reminder," she brings them their favorite narcotics, and says in a tone that does not wound them with pity, "Tonight will really be night for you," and though her Spanish amuses them, they find her comforting, useful. If they lose patience and all faith, and curse the slowness of their friends in coming to their rescue with money and influence, they trust her not to repeat everything, and if she inquires, "Where do you think we can find money, or influence?" they are certain to answer, "Well, there is Braggioni, why doesn't he do something?"

She smuggles letters from headquarters to men hiding from firing squads in back streets in mildewed houses, where they sit in tumbled beds and talk bitterly as if all Mexico were at their heels, when Laura knows positively they might appear at the band concert in the Alameda[2] on Sunday morning, and no one would notice them. But Braggioni says, "Let them sweat a little. The next time they may be careful. It is very restful to have them out of the way for a

2. A park in Mexico City.

while." She is not afraid to knock on any door in any street after midnight, and enter in the darkness, and say to one of these men who is really in danger: "They will be looking for you—seriously—tomorrow morning after six. Here is some money from Vicente. Go to Vera Cruz and wait."

She borrows money from the Roumanian agitator to give to his bitter enemy the Polish agitator. The favor of Braggioni is their disputed territory, and Braggioni holds the balance nicely, for he can use them both. The Polish agitator talks love to her over café tables, hoping to exploit what he believes is her secret sentimental preference for him, and he gives her misinformation which he begs her to repeat as the solemn truth to certain persons. The Roumanian is more adroit. He is generous with his money in all good causes, and lies to her with an air of ingenuous candor, as if he were her good friend and confidant. She never repeats anything they may say. Braggioni never asks questions. He has other ways to discover all that he wishes to know about them.

Nobody touches her, but all praise her gray eyes, and the soft, round under lip which promises gayety, yet is always grave, nearly always firmly closed: and they cannot understand why she is in Mexico. She walks back and forth on her errands, with puzzled eyebrows, carrying her little folder of drawings and music and school papers. No dancer dances more beautifully than Laura walks, and she inspires some amusing, unexpected ardors, which cause little gossip, because nothing comes of them. A young captain who had been a soldier in Zapata's[3] army attempted, during a horseback ride near Cuernavaca, to express his desire for her with the noble simplicity befitting a rude folk hero: but gently, because he was gentle. This gentleness was his defeat, for when he alighted, and removed her foot from the stirrup, and essayed to draw her down into his arms, her horse, ordinarily a tame one, shied fiercely, reared and plunged away. The young hero's horse careered blindly after his stable-mate, and the hero did not return to the hotel until rather late that evening. At breakfast he came to her table in full charro dress, gray buckskin jacket and trousers with strings of silver buttons down the leg, and he was in a humorous, careless mood. "May I sit with you?" and "You are a wonderful rider. I was terrified that you might be thrown and dragged. I should never have forgiven myself. But I cannot admire you enough for your riding!"

"I learned to ride in Arizona," said Laura.

"If you will ride with me again this morning, I promise you a horse that will not shy with you," he said. But Laura remembered that she must return to Mexico City at noon.

Next morning the children made a celebration and spent their playtime writing on the blackboard, "We lov ar ticher," and with tinted chalks they drew wreaths of flowers around the words. The young hero wrote her a letter: "I am a very foolish, wasteful, impulsive man. I should have first said I love you, and then you would not have run away. But you shall see me again." Laura thought, "I must send him a box of colored crayons," but she was trying to forgive herself for having spurred her horse at the wrong moment.

A brown, shock-haired youth came and stood in her patio one night and sang like a lost soul for two hours, but Laura could think of nothing to do about it. The moonlight spread a wash of gauzy silver over the clear spaces of the garden,

American

---

3. Emiliano Zapata was a famous general and leader of the Mexican revolution.

and the shadows were cobalt blue. The scarlet blossoms of the Judas tree were dull purple, and the names of the colors repeated themselves automatically in her mind, while she watched not the boy, but his shadow, fallen like a dark garment across the fountain rim, trailing in the water. Lupe came silently and whispered expert counsel in her ear: "If you will throw him one little flower, he will sing another song or two and go away." Laura threw the flower, and he sang a last song and went away with the flower tucked in the band of his hat. Lupe said, "He is one of the organizers of the Typographers Union, and before that he sold corridos[4] in the Merced market, and before that, he came from Guanajuato, where I was born. I would not trust any man, but I trust least those from Guanajuato."

She did not tell Laura that he would be back again the next night, and the next, nor that he would follow her at a certain fixed distance around the Merced market, through the Zócalo,[5] up Francisco I. Madero Avenue, and so along the Paseo de la Reforma to Chapultepec Park, and into the Philosopher's Footpath, still with that flower withering in his hat, and an indivisible attention in his eyes.

Now Laura is accustomed to him, it means nothing except that he is nineteen years old and is observing a convention with all propriety, as though it were founded on a law of nature, which in the end it might well prove to be. He is beginning to write poems which he prints on a wooden press, and he leaves them stuck like handbills in her door. She is pleasantly disturbed by the abstract, unhurried watchfulness of his black eyes which will in time turn easily towards another object. She tells herself that throwing the flower was a mistake, for she is twenty-two years old and knows better; but she refuses to regret it, and persuades herself that her negation of all external events as they occur is a sign that she is gradually perfecting herself in the stoicism she strives to cultivate against that disaster she fears, though she cannot name it.

She is not at home in the world. Every day she teaches children who remain strangers to her, though she loves their tender round hands and their charming opportunist savagery. She knocks at unfamiliar doors not knowing whether a friend or a stranger shall answer, and even if a known face emerges from the sour gloom of that unknown interior, still it is the face of a stranger. No matter what this stranger says to her, nor what her message to him, the very cells of her flesh reject knowledge and kinship in one monotonous word. No. No. No. She draws her strength from this one holy talismanic word which does not suffer her to be led into evil. Denying everything, she may walk anywhere in safety, she looks at everything without amazement.

No, repeats this firm unchanging voice of her blood; and she looks at Braggioni without amazement. He is a great man, he wishes to impress this simple girl who covers her great round breasts with thick dark cloth, and who hides long, invaluably beautiful legs under a heavy skirt. She is almost thin except for the incomprehensible fullness of her breasts, like a nursing mother's, and Braggioni, who considers himself a judge of women, speculates again on the puzzle of her notorious virginity, and takes the liberty of speech which she permits without a sign of modesty, indeed, without any sort of sign, which is disconcerting.

4. Songs or ballads.
5. Constitution Square in Mexico City.

"You think you are so cold, *gringita!* Wait and see. You will surprise yourself some day! May I be there to advise you!" He stretches his eyelids at her, and his ill-humored cat's eyes waver in a separate glance for the two points of light marking the opposite ends of a smoothly drawn path between the swollen curve of her breasts. He is not put off by that blue serge, nor by her resolutely fixed gaze. There is all the time in the world. His cheeks are bellying with the wind of song "O girl with the dark eyes," he sings, and reconsiders. "But yours are not dark. I can change all that. O girl with the green eyes, you have stolen my heart away!" then his mind wanders to the song, and Laura feels the weight of his attention being shifted elsewhere. Singing thus, he seems harmless, he is quite harmless, there is nothing to do but sit patiently and say "No," when the moment comes. She draws a full breath, and her mind wanders also, but not far. She dares not wander too far.

Not for nothing has Braggioni taken pains to be a good revolutionist and a professional lover of humanity. He will never die of it. He has the malice, the cleverness, the wickedness, the sharpness of wit, the hardness of heart, stipulated for loving the world profitably. *He will never die of it.* He will live to see himself kicked out from his feeding trough by other hungry world-saviors. Traditionally he must sing in spite of his life which drives him to bloodshed, he tells Laura, for his father was a Tuscany peasant who drifted to Yucatan and married a Maya woman: a woman of race, an aristocrat. They gave him the love and knowledge of music, thus: and under the rip of his thumbnail, the strings of the instrument complain like exposed nerves.

Once he was called Delgadito[6] by all the girls and married women who ran after him; he was so scrawny all his bones showed under his thin cotton clothing, and he could squeeze his emptiness to the very backbone with his two hands. He was a poet and the revolution was only a dream then; too many women loved him and sapped away his youth, and he could never find enough to eat anywhere, anywhere! Now he is a leader of men, crafty men who whisper in his ear, hungry men who wait for hours outside his office for a word with him, emaciated men with wild faces who waylay him at the street gate with a timid, "Comrade, let me tell you . . ." and they blow the foul breath from their empty stomachs in his face.

He is always sympathetic. He gives them handfuls of small coins from his own pocket, he promises them work, there will be demonstrations, they must join the unions and attend the meetings, above all they must be on the watch for spies. They are closer to him than his own brothers, without them he can do nothing—until tomorrow, comrade!

Until tomorrow. "They are stupid, they are lazy, they are treacherous, they would cut my throat for nothing," he says to Laura. He has good food and abundant drink, he hires an automobile and drives in the Paseo on Sunday morning, and enjoys plenty of sleep in a soft bed beside a wife who dares not disturb him; and he sits pampering his bones in easy billows of fat, singing to Laura, who knows and thinks these things about him. When he was fifteen, he tried to drown himself because he loved a girl, his first love, and she laughed at him. "A thousand women have paid for that," and his tight little mouth turns down at the corners. Now he perfumes his hair with Jockey Club, and confides to

---

6. Scrawny or skinny.

Laura: "One woman is really as good as another for me, in the dark. I prefer them all."

His wife organizes unions among the girls in the cigarette factories, and walks in picket lines, and even speaks at meetings in the evening. But she cannot be brought to acknowledge the benefits of true liberty. "I tell her I must have my freedom, net. She does not understand my point of view." Laura has heard this many times. Braggioni scratches the guitar and meditates. "She is an instinctively virtuous woman, pure gold, no doubt of that. If she were not, I should lock her up, and she knows it."

His wife, who works so hard for the good of the factory girls employs part of her leisure lying on the floor weeping because there are so many women in the world, and only one husband for her, and she never knows where nor when to look for him. He told her: "Unless you can learn to cry when I am not here, I must go away for good." That day he went away and took a room at the Hotel Madrid.

It is this month of separation for the sake of higher principles that has been spoiled not only for Mrs. Braggioni, whose sense of reality is beyond criticism, but for Laura, who feels herself bogged in a nightmare. Tonight Laura envies Mrs. Braggioni, who is alone, and free to weep as much as she pleases about a concrete wrong. Laura has just come from a visit to the prison, and she is waiting for tomorrow with a bitter anxiety as if tomorrow may not come, but time may be caught immovably in this hour, with herself transfixed, Braggioni singing on forever, and Eugenio's body not yet discovered by the guard.

Braggioni says: "Are you going to sleep?" Almost before she can shake her head, he begins telling her about the May-day disturbances coming on in Morelia, for the Catholics hold a festival in honor of the Blessed Virgin, and the Socialists celebrate their martyrs on that day. "There will be two independent processions, starting from either end of town, and they will march until they meet, and the rest depends . . ." He asks her to oil and load his pistols. Standing up, he unbuckles his ammunition belt, and spreads it laden across her knees. Laura sits with the shells slipping through the cleaning cloth dipped in oil, and he says again he cannot understand why she works so hard for the revolutionary idea unless she loves some man who is in it. "Are you not in love with someone?" "No," says Laura. "And no one is in love with you?" "No." "Then it is your own fault. No woman need go begging. Why, what is the matter with you? The legless beggar woman in the Alameda has a perfectly faithful lover. Did you know that?"

Laura peers down the pistol barrel and says nothing, but a long, slow faintness rises and subsides in her; Braggioni curves his swollen fingers around the throat of the guitar and softly smothers the music out of it, and when she hears him again he seems to have forgotten her, and is speaking in the hypnotic voice he uses when talking in small rooms to a listening, close-gathered crowd. Some day this world, now seemingly so composed and eternal, to the edges of every sea shall be merely a tangle of gaping trenches, of crashing walls and broken bodies. Everything must be torn from its accustomed place where it has rotted for centuries, hurled skyward and distributed, cast down again clean as rain, without separate identity. Nothing shall survive that the stiffened hands of poverty have created for the rich and no one shall be left alive except the elect spirits destined to procreate a new world cleansed of cruelty and injustice, ruled by benevolent anarchy: "Pistols are good, I love them, cannon are even better, but in the end I pin my faith to good dynamite," he concludes, and strokes the pistol lying in her hands. "Once I dreamed of destroying this city, in case it offered resistance to General Ortíz, but it fell into his hands like an over-ripe pear."

He is made restless by his own words, rises and stands waiting. Laura holds up the belt to him: "Put that on, and go kill somebody in Morelia, and you will be happier," she says softly. The presence of death in the room makes her bold. "Today, I found Eugenio going into a stupor. He refused to allow me to call the prison doctor. He had taken all the tablets I brought him yesterday. He said he took them because he was bored."

"He is a fool, and his death is his own business," says Braggioni, fastening his belt carefully.

"I told him if he had waited only a little while longer, you would have got him set free," says Laura. "He said he did not want to wait."

"He is a fool and we are well rid of him," says Braggioni, reaching for his hat.

He goes away. Laura knows his mood has changed, she will not see him any more for a while. He will send word when he needs her to go on errands into strange streets, to speak to the strange faces that will appear, like clay masks with the power of human speech, to mutter their thanks to Braggioni for his help. Now she is free, and she thinks, I must run while there is time. But she does not go.

Braggioni enters his own house where for a month his wife has spent many hours every night weeping and tangling her hair upon her pillow. She is weeping now, and she weeps more at the sight of him, the cause of all her sorrows. He looks about the room. Nothing is changed, the smells are good and familiar, he is well acquainted with the woman who comes toward him with no reproach except grief on her face. He says to her tenderly: "You are so good, please don't cry any more, you dear good creature." She says, "Are you tired, my angel? Sit here and I will wash your feet." She brings a bowl of water, and kneeling, unlaces his shoes, and when from her knees she raises her sad eyes under her blackened lids, he is sorry for everything, and bursts into tears. "Ah, yes, I am hungry, I am tired, let us eat something together," he says, between sobs. His wife leans her head on his arm and says, "Forgive me!" and this time he is refreshed by the solemn, endless rain of her tears.

Laura takes off her serge dress and puts on a white linen nightgown and goes to bed. She turns her head a little to one side, and lying still, reminds herself that it is time to sleep. Numbers tick in her brain like little clocks, soundless doors close of themselves around her. If you would sleep, you must not remember anything, the children will say tomorrow, good morning, my teacher, the poor prisoners who come every day bringing flowers to their jailor. 1-2-3-4-5—it is monstrous to confuse love with revolution, night with day, life with death—ah, Eugenio!

The tolling of the midnight bell is a signal, but what does it mean? Get up, Laura, and follow me: come out of your sleep, out of your bed, out of this strange house. What are you doing in this house? Without a word, without fear she rose and reached for Eugenio's hand, but he eluded her with a sharp, sly smile and drifted away. This is not all, you shall see—Murderer, he said, follow me, I will show you a new country, but it is far away and we must hurry. No, said Laura, not unless you take my hand, no; and she clung first to the stair rail, and then to the topmost branch of the Judas tree that bent down slowly and set her upon the earth, and then to the rocky ledge of a cliff, and then to the jagged wave of a sea that was not water but a desert of crumbling stone. Where are you taking me, she asked in wonder but without fear. To death, and it a long way off, and we must hurry, said Eugenio. No, said Laura, not unless you take my hand. Then eat these flowers, poor prisoner, said Eugenio in a voice of pity, take and eat: and from the Judas tree he stripped the warm bleeding flowers, and held them to her lips. She saw that his hand was fleshless, a cluster of small white petrified branches, and his eye sockets were without light, but she ate the flowers greedily for they satisfied both hunger and thirst. Murderer! said Eugenio, and Cannibal! This is my body and my blood. Laura cried No! and at the sound of her own voice, she awoke trembling, and was afraid to sleep again. (Judas) aura betrayed Eugenio & herself – her emotions.

Fact Questions and Exercises

1. What is the name of the "cruel" man who sings off key to Laura? Braggioni
2. What tasks does Laura perform for the revolutionists?
3. Point out details that indicate Laura's physical appearance. How old is she? 22
4. What nationality is Laura? Where does the story take place? Mexico
5. What does Laura give to the "brown, shock-haired youth" who comes and sings in her patio? flower
6. What is the "one holy talismanic" word that Laura thinks protects her from evil? No
7. Identify Eugenio.
8. Describe Laura's dream at the end of the story.

For Discussion and Writing

1. Analyze Braggioni. In what ways is he "a symbol of [Laura's] many disillusions"? What is his attitude toward Laura? How has he changed since he was young?
2. Analyze Laura. How does her physical appearance contrast with her moral attitudes? Why does she dress like a nun? Why does she think a scandal would result if she were seen entering the church to pray? Why does she insist upon saying no so often? What does her dream reveal about her true motives?
3. Some readers see the story as a revelation of Laura's sexual and religious conflicts. Do you agree? Are there sexual symbols and themes in the story? What, for instance, does the Judas tree represent? Why does Laura react as she does to the pistol? Which incidents or symbols represent the religious side of Laura's conflict?

F. Scott Fitzgerald [1896–1940]

Francis Scott Key Fitzgerald was born in St. Paul, Minnesota, and attended Princeton University. In 1920 he published his first novel, *This Side of Paradise*, and married Zelda Sayre, the woman who would figure so prominently in his life and fiction. The novel brought him instant fame and, along with his short stories, established Fitzgerald as the spokesman of the Jazz Age—that wild, carefree period of the twenties. Fitzgerald and Zelda spent a lot ot time in Europe, made and wasted great amounts of money, and led a hectic and ultimately tragic life. (Zelda would subsequently die in a fire at an insane asylum; Fitzgerald would die with his works unread and a reputation as an alcoholic.) The tensions ot their life are reflected in his writings, such as the novel *Tender is the Night* (1934) and "Babylon Revisited" (1931). Since Fitzgerald's death, regard for his work has greatly increased. His most famous novel, *The Great Gatsby* (1925) is now considered an American classic.

Babylon Revisited

"And where's Mr. Campbell?" Charlie asked.

"Gone to Switzerland. Mr. Campbell's a pretty sick man, Mr. Wales."

"I'm sorry to hear that. And George Hardt?" Charlie inquired.

"Back in America, gone to work."

"And where is the Snow Bird?"[1]

"He was in here last week. Anyway, his friend, Mr. Schaeffer, is in Paris."

Two familiar names from the long list of a year and a half ago. Charlie scribbled an address in his notebook and tore out the page.

"If you see Mr. Schaeffer, give him this," he said. "It's my brother-in-law's address. I haven't settled on a hotel yet."

He was not really disappointed to find Paris so empty. But the stillness in the Ritz bar was strange and portentous. It was not an American bar any more—he felt polite in it, and not as if he owned it. It had gone back into France. He felt the stillness from the moment he got out of the taxi and saw the doorman, usually in a frenzy of activity at this hour, gossiping with a *chasseur*[2] by the servants' entrance.

Passing through the corridor, he heard only a single, bored voice in the once-clamorous women's room. When he turned into the bar he travelled the twenty feet of green carpet with his eyes fixed straight ahead by old habit; and then, with his foot firmly on the rail, he turned and surveyed the room, encountering only a single pair of eyes that fluttered up from a newspaper in the corner. Charlie asked for the head barman, Paul, who in the latter days of the bull market had come to work in his own custom-built car—disembarking, however, with due nicety at the nearest corner. But Paul was at his country house today and Alix giving him information.

1. "Snow Bird" means a heroin addict.
2. A doorman or porter.

"No, no more," Charlie said. "I'm going slow these days."

Alix congratulated him: "You were going pretty strong a couple of years ago."

"I'll stick to it all right," Charlie assured him. "I've stuck to it for over a year and a half now."

"How do you find conditions in America?"

"I haven't been to America for months. I'm in business in Prague, representing a couple of concerns there. They don't know about me down there."

Alix smiled.

"Remember the night of George Hardt's bachelor dinner here?" said Charlie. "By the way, what's become of Claude Fessenden?"

Alix lowered his voice confidentially: "He's in Paris, but he doesn't come here any more. Paul doesn't allow it. He ran up a bill of thirty thousand francs, charging all his drinks and his lunches, and usually his dinner, for more than a year. And when Paul finally told him he had to pay, he gave him a bad check."

Alix shook his head sadly.

"I don't understand it, such a dandy fellow. Now he's all bloated up—" He made a plump apple of his hands.

Charlie watched a group of strident queens installing themselves in a corner.

"Nothing affects them," he thought. "Stocks rise and fall, people loaf or work, but they go on forever." The place oppressed him. He called for the dice and shook with Alix for the drink.

"Here for long, Mr. Wales?"

"I'm here for four or five days to see my little girl."

"Oh-h! You have a little girl?"

Outside, the fire-red, gas-blue, ghost-green signs shone smokily through the tranquil rain. It was late afternoon and the streets were in movement; the *bistros* gleamed. At the corner of the Boulevard des Capucines he took a taxi. The Place de la Concorde moved by in pink majesty; they crossed the logical Seine, and Charlie felt the sudden provincial quality of the left bank.

Charlie directed his taxi to the Avenue de l'Opéra, which was out of his way. But he wanted to see the blue hour spread over the magnificent facade, and imagine that the cab horns, playing endlessly the first few bars of *La Plus que Lente*,[3] were the trumpets of the Second Empire. They were closing the iron grill in front of Brentano's Bookstore, and people were already at dinner behind the trim little Bourgeois hedge of Duval's. He had never eaten at a really cheap restaurant in Paris. Five-course dinner, four francs fifty, eighteen cents, wine included. For some odd reason he wished that he had.

As they rolled on to the Left Bank and he felt its sudden provincialism, he thought, "I spoiled this city for myself. I didn't realize it, but the days came along one after another, and then two years were gone, and everything was gone, and I was gone."

He was thirty-five, and good to look at. The Irish mobility of his face was sobered by a deep wrinkle between his eyes. As he rang his brother-in-law's bell in the Rue Palatine, the wrinkle deepened till it pulled down his brows; he felt a cramping sensation in his belly. From behind the maid who opened the door

3. A waltz by Debussy.

darted a lovely little girl of nine, who shrieked "Daddy!" and flew up, struggling like a fish, into his arms. She pulled his head around by one ear and set her cheek against his.

"My old pie," he said.

"Oh, daddy, daddy, daddy, daddy, dads, dads, dads!"

She drew him into the salon, where the family waited, a boy and girl his daughter's age, his sister-in-law and her husband. He greeted Marion with his voice pitched carefully to avoid either feigned enthusiasm or dislike, but her response was more frankly tepid, though she minimized her expression of unalterable distrust by directing her regard toward his child. The two men clasped hands in a friendly way and Lincoln Peters rested his for a moment on Charlie's shoulder.

The room was warm and comfortably American. The three children moved intimately about, playing through the yellow oblongs that led to other rooms; the cheer of six o'clock spoke in the eager smacks of the fire and the sounds of French activity in the kitchen. But Charlie did not relax; his heart sat up rigidly in his body and he drew confidence from his daughter, who from time to time came close to him, holding in her arms the doll he had brought.

"Really extremely well," he declared in answer to Lincoln's question. "There's a lot of business there that isn't moving at all, but we're doing even better than ever. In fact, damn well. I'm bringing my sister over from America next month to keep house for me. My income last year was bigger than it was when I had money. You see, the Czechs——"

His boasting was for a specific purpose; but after a moment, seeing a faint restiveness in Lincoln's eyes, he changed the subject:

"Those are fine children of yours, well brought up, good manners."

"We think Honoria's a great little girl too."

Marion Peters came back from the kitchen. She was a tall woman with worried eyes, who had once possessed a fresh American loveliness. Charlie had never been sensitive to it and was always surprised when people spoke of how pretty she had been. From the first there had been an instinctive antipathy between them.

"Well, how do you find Honoria?" she asked.

"Wonderful. I was astonished how much she's grown in ten months. All the children are looking well."

"We haven't had a doctor for a year. How do you like being back in Paris?"

"It seems very funny to see so few Americans around."

"I'm delighted," Marion said vehemently. "Now at least you can go into the store without their assuming you're a millionaire. We've suffered like everybody, but on the whole it's a good deal pleasanter."

"But it was nice while it lasted," said Charlie. "We were a sort of royalty, almost infallible, with a sort of magic around us. In the bar this afternoon"—he stumbled, seeing his mistake—"there wasn't a man I knew."

She looked at him keenly. "I should think you'd have had enough of bars."

"I only stayed a minute. I take one drink every afternoon, and no more."

"Don't you want a cocktail before dinner?" Lincoln asked.

"I take only one drink every afternoon, and I've had that."

"I hope you keep to it," said Marion.

Her dislike was evident in the coldness with which she spoke, but Charlie only smiled; he had larger plans. Her very aggressiveness gave him an advantage, and he knew enough to wait. He wanted them to initiate the discussion of what they knew had brought him to Paris.

At dinner he couldn't decide whether Honoria was most like him or her mother. Fortunate if she didn't combine the traits of both that had brought them to disaster. A great wave of protectiveness went over him. He thought he knew what to do for her. He believed in character; he wanted to jump back a whole generation and trust in character again as the eternally valuable element. Everything else wore out.

He left soon after dinner, but not to go home. He was curious to see Paris by night with clearer and more judicious eyes than those of other days. He bought a *strapontin*[4] for the Casino and watched Josephine Baker go through her chocolate arabesques.

After an hour he left and strolled toward Montmartre, up the Rue Pigalle into the Place Blanche. The rain had stopped and there were a few people in evening clothes disembarking from taxis in front of cabarets, and *cocottes*[5] prowling singly or in pairs, and many Negroes. He passed a lighted door from which issued music, and stopped with the sense of familiarity; it was Bricktop's, where he had parted with so many hours and so much money. A few doors farther on he found another ancient rendezvous and incautiously put his head inside. Immediately an eager orchestra burst into sound, a pair of professional dancers leaped to their feet and a maitre d'hôtel swooped toward him, crying, "Crowd just arriving, sir!" But he withdrew quickly.

"You have to be damn drunk," he thought.

Zelli's was closed, the bleak and sinister cheap hotels surrounding it were dark; up in the Rue Blanche there was more light and a local, colloquial French crowd. The Poet's Cave had disappeared, but the two great mouths of the Café of Heaven and the Café of Hell still yawned—even devoured, as he watched, the meager contents of a tourist bus—a German, a Japanese, and an American couple who glanced at him with frightened eyes.

So much for the effort and ingenuity of Montmartre. All the catering to vice and waste was on an utterly childish scale, and he suddenly realized the meaning of the word "dissipate"—to dissipate into thin air; to make nothing out of something. In the little hours of the night every move from place to place was an enormous human jump, an increase of paying for the privilege of slower and slower motion.

He remembered thousand-franc notes given to an orchestra for playing a single number, hundred-franc notes tossed to a doorman for calling a cab.

But it hadn't been given for nothing.

It had been given, even the most wildly squandered sum, as an offering to destiny that he might not remember the things most worth remembering, the things that now he would always remember—his child taken from his control, his wife escaped to a grave in Vermont.

4. An inexpensive seat.
5. Prostitutes.

In the glare of a *brasserie*[6] a woman spoke to him. He bought her some eggs and coffee, and then, eluding her encouraging stare, gave her a twenty-note franc and took a taxi to his hotel.

II

He woke up on a fine fall day—football weather. The depression of yesterday was gone and he liked the people on the streets. At noon he sat opposite Honoria at Le Grand Vatel, the only restaurant he could think of not reminiscent of champagne dinners and long luncheons that began at two and ended in a blurred and vague twilight.

"Now, how about vegetables? Oughtn't you to have some vegetables?"

"Well, yes."

"Here's *épinards* and *chou-fleur* and carrots and *haricots*."[7]

I'd like *chou-fleur*."

Wouldn't you like to have two vegetables?"

"I usually have only one at lunch."

The waiter was pretending to be inordinately fond of children. *"Qu'elle est mignonne, la petite! Elle parle exactement comme une française."*[8]

"How about dessert? Shall we wait and see?"

The waiter disappeared. Honoria looked at her father expectantly.

"What are we going to do?"

"First, we're going to that toy store in the Rue Saint-Honoré and buy you anything you like. And then we're going to the vaudeville at the Empire."

She hesitated. "I like it about the vaudeville, but not the toy store."

"Why not?"

"Well, you brought me this doll." She had it with her. "And I've got lots of things. And we're not rich any more, are we?"

"We never were. But today you are to have anything you want."

"All right," she agreed resignedly.

When there had been her mother and a French nurse he had been inclined to be strict; now he extended himself, reached out for a new tolerance; he must be both parents to her and not shut any of her out of communication.

"I want to get to know you," he said gravely. "First let me introduce myself. My name is Charles J. Wales, of Prague."

"Oh, daddy!" her voice cracked with laughter.

"And who are you, please?" he persisted, and she accepted a rôle immediately: "Honoria Wales, Rue Palatine, Paris."

"Married or single?"

"No, not married. Single."

He indicated the doll. "But I see you have a child, madame."

Unwilling to disinherit it, she took it to her heart and thought quickly: "Yes, I've been married, but I'm not married now. My husband is dead."

He went on quickly, "And the child's name?"

"Simone. That's after my best friend at school."

6. A restaurant that sells beer.

7 "Here's spinach and cauliflower and carrots and beans."

8. "She is charming, the little one! She speaks exactly like a French girl."

"I'm very pleased that you're doing so well at school."

"I'm third this month," she boasted. "Elsie"—that was her cousin—"is only about eighteenth, and Richard is about at the bottom."

"You like Richard and Elsie, don't you?"

"Oh, yes. I like them all right."

Cautiously and casually he asked: "And Aunt Marion and Uncle Lincoln—which do you like best?"

"Oh, Uncle Lincoln, I guess."

He was increasingly aware of her presence. As they came in, a murmur of ". . . adorable" followed them, and now the people at the next table bent all their silences upon her, staring as if she were something no more conscious than a flower.

"Why don't I live with you?" she asked suddenly. "Because mamma's dead?"

"You must stay here and learn more French. It would have been hard for daddy to take care of you so well."

"I don't really need much taking care of any more. I do everything for myself."

Going out of the restaurant, a man and a woman unexpectedly hailed him.

"Well, the old Wales!"

"Hello there, Lorraine . . . Dunc."

Sudden ghosts out of the past: Duncan Schaeffer, a friend from college. Lorraine Quarles, a lovely, pale blonde of thirty; one of a crowd who had helped them make months into days in the lavish times of three years ago.

"My husband couldn't come this year," she said, in answer to his question. "We're poor as hell. So he gave me two hundred a month, and told me I could do my worst on that. . . . This your little girl?"

"What about coming back and sitting down?" Duncan asked.

"Can't do it." He was glad for an excuse. As always, he felt Lorraine's passionate, provocative attraction, but his own rhythm was different now.

"Well, how about dinner?" she asked.

"I'm not free. Give me your address and let me call you."

"Charlie, I believe you're sober," she said judicially. "I honestly believe he's sober, Dunc. Pinch him and see if he's sober."

Charlie indicated Honoria with his head. They both laughed.

"What's your address?" said Duncan skeptically.

He hesitated, unwilling to give the name of his hotel.

"I'm not settled yet. I'd better call you. We're going to see the vaudeville at the Empire."

"There! That's what I want to do," Lorraine said. "I want to see some clowns and acrobats and jugglers. That's just what we'll do, Dunc."

"We've got to do an errand first," said Charlie. "Perhaps we'll see you there."

"All right, you snob. . . . Good-by, beautiful little girl."

"Good-by."

Honoria bobbed politely.

Somehow, an unwelcome encounter. They liked him because he was functioning, because he was serious; they wanted to see him, because he was stronger than they were now, because they wanted to draw a certain sustenance from his strength.

At the Empire, Honoria proudly refused to sit upon her father's folded coat. She was already an individual with a code of her own, and Charlie was more and more absorbed by the desire of putting a little of himself into her before she crystallized utterly. It was hopeless to try to know her in so short a time.

Between the acts they came upon Duncan and Lorraine in the lobby where the band was playing.

"Have a drink?"

"All right, but not up at the bar. We'll take a table."

"The perfect father."

Listening abstractedly to Lorraine, Charlie watched Honoria's eyes leave their table, and he followed them wistfully about the room, wondering what they saw. He met her glance and she smiled.

"I liked that lemonade," she said.

What had she said? What had he expected? Going home in a taxi afterward, he pulled her over until her head rested against his chest.

"Darling, do you ever think about your mother?"

"Yes, sometimes," she answered vaguely.

"I don't want you to forget her. Have you got a picture of her?"

"Yes, I think so. Anyhow, Aunt Marion has. Why don't you want me to forget her?"

"She loved you very much."

"I loved her too."

They were silent for a moment.

"Daddy, I want to come and live with you," she said suddenly.

His heart leaped; he had wanted it to come like this.

"Aren't you perfectly happy?"

"Yes, but I love you better than anybody. And you love me better than anybody, don't you, now that mummy's dead?"

"Of course I do. But you won't always like me best, honey. You'll grow up and meet somebody your own age and go marry him and forget you ever had a daddy."

"Yes, that's true," she agreed tranquilly.

He didn't go in. He was coming back at nine o'clock and he wanted to keep himself fresh and new for the thing he must say then.

"When you're safe inside, just show yourself in that window."

"All right. Good-by, dads, dads, dads, dads."

He waited in the dark street until she appeared, all warm and glowing, in the window above and kissed her fingers out into the night.

III

They were waiting. Marion sat behind the coffee service in a dignified black dinner dress that just faintly suggested mourning. Lincoln was walking up and down with the animation of one who had already been talking. They were as anxious as he was to get into the question. He opened it almost immediately:

"I suppose you know what I want to see you about—why I really came to Paris."

Marion played with the black stars on her necklace and frowned.

"I'm awfully anxious to have a home," he continued. "And I'm awfully anxious to have Honoria in it. I appreciate your taking in Honoria for her mother's sake, but things have changed now"—he hesitated and then continued more forcibly—"changed radically with me, and I want to ask you to reconsider the matter. It would be silly for me to deny that about three years ago I was acting badly—"

Marion looked up at him with hard eyes.

"—But all that's over. As I told you, I haven't had more than a drink a day for over a year, and I take that drink deliberately, so that the idea of alcohol won't get too big in my imagination. You see the idea?"

"No," said Marion succinctly.

"It's a sort of stunt I set myself. It keeps the matter in proportion."

"I get you," said Lincoln. "You don't want to admit it's got any attraction for you."

"Something like that. Sometimes I forget and don't take it. But I try to take it. Anyhow, I couldn't afford to drink in my position. The people I represent are more than satisfied with what I've done, and I'm bringing my sister over from Burlington to keep house for me, and I want awfully to have Honoria too. You know that even when her mother and I weren't getting along well we never let anything that happened touch Honoria. I know she's fond of me and I know I'm able to take care of her—well, there you are. How do you feel about it?"

He knew that now he would have to take a beating. It would last an hour or two hours, and it would be difficult, but if he modulated his inevitable resentment to the chastened attitude of the reformed sinner, he might win his point in the end.

Keep your temper, he told himself. You don't want to be justified. You want Honoria.

Lincoln spoke first: "We've been talking it over ever since we got your letter last month. We're happy to have Honoria here. She's a dear little thing, and we're glad to be able to help her, but of course that isn't the question—"

Marion interrupted suddenly. "How long are you going to stay sober, Charlie?" she asked.

"Permanently, I hope."

"How can anybody count on that?"

"You know I never did drink heavily until I gave up business and came over here with nothing to do. Then Helen and I began to run around with—"

"Please leave Helen out of it. I can't bear to hear you talk about her like that."

He stared at her grimly; he had never been certain how fond of each other the sisters were in life.

"My drinking only lasted about a year and a half—from the time we came over until I—collapsed."

"It was time enough."

"It was time enough," he agreed.

"My duty is entirely to Helen," she said. "I try to think what she would have wanted me to do. Frankly, from the night you did that terrible thing you haven't really existed for me. I can't help that. She was my sister."

"Yes."

"When she was dying she asked me to look out for Honoria. If you hadn't been in a sanitarium then, it might have helped matters."

He had no answer.

"I'll never in my life be able to forget the morning when Helen knocked at my door, soaked to the skin and shivering, and said you'd locked her out."

Charlie gripped the sides of the chair. This was more difficult than he expected: he wanted to launch out into a long expostulation and explanation, but he only said: "The night I locked her out—" and she interrupted, "I don't feel up to going over that again."

After a moment's silence Lincoln said: "We're getting off the subject. You want Marion to set aside her legal guardianship and give you Honoria. I think the main point for her is whether she has confidence in you or not."

"I don't blame Marion," Charlie said slowly, "but I think she can have entire confidence in me. I had a good record up to three years ago. Of course, it's within human possibilities I may go wrong again. But if we wait much longer I'll lose Honoria's childhood and my chance for a home." He shook his head. "I'll simply lose her, don't you see?"

"Yes, I see," said Lincoln.

"Why didn't you think of all this before?" Marion asked.

"I suppose I did, from time to time, but Helen and I were getting along badly. When I consented to the guardianship, I was flat on my back in a sanitarium, and the market had cleaned me out. I knew I'd acted badly, and I thought if it would bring any peace to Helen, I'd agree to anything. But now it's different. I'm functioning, I'm behaving damn well, so far as—"

"Please don't swear at me," Marion said.

He looked at her, startled. With each remark the force of her dislike became more and more apparent. She had built up all her fear of life into one wall and faced it toward him. This trivial reproof was possibly the result of some trouble with the cook several hours before. Charlie became increasingly alarmed at leaving Honoria in this atmosphere of hostility against himself; sooner or later it would come out, in a word here, a shake of the head there, and some of that distrust would be irrevocably implanted in Honoria. But he pulled his temper down out of his face and shut it up inside him; he had won a point, for Lincoln realized the absurdity of Marion's remark, and asked her lightly since when she had objected to the word "damn."

"Another thing," Charlie said: "I'm able to give her certain advantages now. I'm going to take a French governess to Prague with me. I've got a lease on a new apartment—"

He stopped, realizing that he was blundering. They couldn't be expected to accept with equanimity the fact that his income was again twice as large as their own.

"I suppose you can give her more luxuries than we can," said Marion. "When you were throwing away money we were living along watching every ten francs. . . . I suppose you'll start doing it again."

"Oh, no," he said. "I've learned. I worked hard for ten years, you know—until I got lucky in the market, like so many people. Terribly lucky. It didn't seem any use working any more, so I quit. It won't happen again."

There was a long silence. All of them felt their nerves straining, and for the first time in a year Charlie wanted a drink. He was sure now that Lincoln Peters wanted him to have his child.

Marion shuddered suddenly; part of her saw that Charlie's feet were planted on the earth now, and her own maternal feeling recognized the naturalness of his desire; but she had lived for a long time with a prejudice—a prejudice founded on a curious disbelief in her sister's happiness, which, in the shock of one terrible night, had turned to hatred for him. It had all happened at a point in her life where the discouragement of ill health and adverse circumstances made it necessary for her to believe in tangible villainy and a tangible villain.

"I can't help what I think!" she cried out suddenly. "How much you were responsible for Helen's death, I don't know. It's something you'll have to square with your own conscience."

An electric current of agony surged through him; for a moment he was almost on his feet, an unuttered sound echoing in his throat. He hung on to himself for a moment, another moment.

"Hold on there," said Lincoln uncomfortably, "I never thought you were responsible for that."

"Helen died of heart trouble," Charlie said dully.

"Yes, heart trouble." Marion spoke as if the phrase had another meaning for her.

Then, in the flatness that followed her outburst, she saw him plainly and she knew he had somehow arrived at control over the situation. Glancing at her husband, she found no help from him, and as abruptly as if it were a matter of no importance, she threw up the sponge.

"Do what you like!" she cried, springing up from her chair. "She's your child. I'm not the person to stand in your way. I think if it were my child I'd rather see her—" She managed to check herself. "You two decide it. I can't stand this. I'm sick. I'm going to bed."

She hurried from the room; after a moment Lincoln said:

"This has been a hard day for her. You know how strongly she feels—" His voice was almost apologetic: "When a woman gets an idea in her head."

"Of course."

"It's going to be all right. I think she sees now that you—can provide for the child, and so we can't very well stand in your way or Honoria's way."

"Thank you, Lincoln."

"I'd better go along and see how she is."

"I'm going."

He was still trembling when he reached the street, but a walk down the Rue Bonaparte to the quais set him up, and as he crossed the Seine, fresh and new by the quai lamps, he felt exultant. But back in his room he couldn't sleep. The image of Helen haunted him. Helen whom he had loved so until they had senselessly begun to abuse each other's love, tear it into shreds. On that terrible February night that Marion remembered so vividly, a slow quarrel had gone on for hours. There was a scene at the Florida, and then he attempted to take her home, and then she kissed young Webb at a table; after that there was what she had hysterically said. When he arrived home alone he turned the key in the lock in wild anger. How could he know she would arrive an hour later alone, that there would be a snowstorm in which she wandered about in slippers, too confused to find a taxi? Then the aftermath, her escaping pneumonia by a miracle, and all the attendant horror. They were "reconciled," but that was the beginning of the end, and Marion, who had seen with her own eyes and who imagined it to be one of many scenes from her sister's martyrdom, never forgot.

Going over it again brought Helen nearer, and in the white, soft light that steals upon half sleep near morning he found himself talking to her again. She said that he was perfectly right about Honoria and that she wanted Honoria to be with him. She said she was glad he was being good and doing better. She said a lot of other things—very friendly things—but she was in a swing in a white dress, and swinging faster and faster all the time, so that at the end he could not hear clearly all that she said.

IV

He woke up feeling happy. The door of the world was open again. He made plans, vistas, futures for Honoria and himself, but suddenly he grew sad, remembering all the plans he and Helen had made. She had not planned to die. The present was the thing—work to do, and some one to love. But not to love too much, for he knew the injury that a father can do to a daughter or a mother to a son by attaching them too closely; afterward, out in the world, the child would seek in the marriage partner the same blind tenderness and, failing probably to find it, turn against love and life.

It was another bright, crisp day. He called Lincoln Peters at the bank where he worked and asked if he could count on taking Honoria when he left for Prague. Lincoln agreed that there was no reason for delay. One thing—the legal guardianship. Marion wanted to retain that a while longer. She was upset by the whole matter, and it would oil things if she felt that the situation was still in her control for another year. Charlie agreed, wanting only the tangible, visible child.

Then the question of a governess. Charlie sat in a gloomy agency and talked to a cross Bernaise and to a buxom Breton peasant, neither of whom he could have endured. There were others whom he would see tomorrow.

He lunched with Lincoln Peters at Griffons, trying to keep down his exultation.

"There's nothing quite like your own child," Lincoln said. "But you understand how Marion feels too."

"She's forgotten how hard I worked for seven years there," Charlie said. "She just remembers one night."

"There's another thing," Lincoln hesitated. "While you and Helen were tearing around Europe throwing money away, we were just getting along. I didn't touch any of the prosperity because I never got ahead enough to carry anything but my insurance. I think Marion felt there was some kind of injustice in it—you not even working toward the end, and getting richer and richer."

"It went just as quick as it came," said Charlie.

"Yes, a lot of it stayed in the hands of *chasseurs* and saxophone players and maîtres d'hôtel—well, the big party's over now. I just said that to explain Marion's feeling about those crazy years. If you drop in about six o'clock tonight before Marion's too tired, we'll settle the details on the spot."

Back at his hotel, Charlie found a *pneumatique*[9] that had been redirected from the Ritz bar where Charlie had left his address for the purpose of finding a certain man.

> DEAR CHARLIE:
> You were so strange when we saw you the other day that I wondered if I did something to offend you. If so, I'm not conscious of it. In fact, I have thought about you too much for the last year, and it's always been in the back of my mind that I might see you if I came over here. We *did* have such good times that crazy spring, like the night you and I stole the butcher's tricycle, and the time we tried to call on the president and you had the old derby rim and the wire cane. Everybody seems so old lately, but I don't feel old a bit. Couldn't we get together some time today for old time's sake? I've got a vile hang-over for the moment, but will be feeling better this afternoon and will look for you about five in the sweet-shop at the Ritz.
>
> Always devotedly,
LORRAINE.

His first feeling was one of awe that he had actually, in his mature years, stolen a tricycle and pedalled Lorraine all over the Étoile[10] between the small hours and dawn. In retrospect it was a nightmare. Locking out Helen didn't fit in with any other act of his life, but the tricycle incident did—it was one of many. How many weeks or months of dissipation to arrive at that condition of utter irresponsibility?

He tried to picture how Lorraine had appeared to him then—very attractive; Helen was unhappy about it, though she said nothing. Yesterday, in the restaurant, Lorraine had seemed trite, blurred, worn away. He emphatically did not want to see her, and he was glad Alix had not given away his hotel address. It was a relief to think, instead, of Honoria, to think of Sundays spent with her and of saying good morning to her and of knowing she was there in his house at night, drawing her breath in the darkness.

At five he took a taxi and bought presents for all the Peters—a piquant cloth doll, a box of Roman soldiers, flowers for Marion, big linen handkerchiefs for Lincoln.

He saw, when he arrived in the apartment, that Marion had accepted the inevitable. She greeted him now as though he were a recalcitrant member of the family, rather than a menacing outsider. Honoria had been told she was going; Charlie was glad to see that her tact made her conceal her excessive happiness. Only on his lap did she whisper her delight and the question "When?" before she slipped away with the other children.

He and Marion were alone for a minute in the room, and on an impulse he spoke out boldly:

"Family quarrels are bitter things. They don't go according to any rules. They're not like aches or wounds; they're more like splits in the skin that won't heal because there's not enough material. I wish you and I could be on better terms."

9. A message.

10. A square or park in Paris.

"Some things are hard to forget," she answered. "It's a question of confidence." There was no answer to this and presently she asked, "When do you propose to take her?"

"As soon as I can get a governess. I hoped the day after tomorrow."

"That's impossible. I've got to get her things in shape. Not before Saturday."

He yielded. Coming back into the room, Lincoln offered him a drink. "I'll take my daily whisky," he said.

It was warm here, it was a home, people together by a fire. The children felt very safe and important; the mother and father were serious, watchful. They had things to do for the children more important than his visit here. A spoonful of medicine was, after all, more important than the strained relations between Marion and himself. They were not dull people, but they were very much in the grip of life and circumstances. He wondered if he couldn't do something to get Lincoln out of his rut at the bank.

A long peal at the door-bell; the *bonne à tout faire*[11] passed through and went down the corridor. The door opened upon another long ring, and then voices, and the three in the salon looked up expectantly; Richard moved to bring the corridor within his range of vision, and Marion rose. Then the maid came back along the corridor, closely followed by the voices, which developed under the light into Duncan Schaeffer and Lorraine Quarles.

They were gay, they were hilarious, they were roaring with laughter. For a moment Charlie was astounded; unable to understand how they had ferreted out the Peters' address.

"Ah-h-h!" Duncan wagged his finger roguishly at Charlie. "Ah-h-h!"

They both slid down another cascade of laughter. Anxious and at a loss, Charlie shook hands with them quickly and presented them to Lincoln and Marion. Marion nodded, scarcely speaking. She had drawn back a step toward the fire; her little girl stood beside her, and Marion put an arm about her shoulder.

With growing annoyance at the intrusion, Charlie waited for them to explain themselves. After some concentration Duncan said:

"We came to invite you out to dinner. Lorraine and I insist that all this shishi business 'bout your address got to stop."

Charlie came closer to them, as if to force them backward down the corridor.

"Sorry, but I can't. Tell me where you'll be and I'll phone you in half an hour."

This made no impression. Lorraine sat down suddenly on the side of a chair, and focussing her eyes on Richard, cried, "Oh, what a nice little boy! Come here, little boy." Richard glanced at his mother, but did not move. With a perceptible shrug of her shoulders, Lorraine turned back to Charlie:

"Come and dine. Sure your cousins won' mine. See you so sel'om. Or solemn."

"I can't," said Charlie sharply. "You two have dinner and I'll phone you."

11. A maid.

Her voice became suddenly unpleasant. "All right, we'll go. But I remember once when you hammered on my door at four A.M. I was enough of a good sport to give you a drink. Come on, Dunc." Still in slow motion, with blurred, angry faces, with uncertain feet, they retired along the corridor.

"Good night," Charlie said.

"Good night!" responded Lorraine emphatically.

When he went back into the salon Marion had not moved, only now her son was standing in the circle of her other arm. Lincoln was still swinging Honoria back and forth like a pendulum from side to side.

"What an outrage!" Charlie broke out. "What an absolute outrage!"

Neither of them answered. Charlie dropped into an armchair, picked up his drink, set it down again and said:

"People I haven't seen for two years having the colossal nerve—"

He broke off. Marion had made the sound "Oh!" in one swift, furious breath, turned her body from him with a jerk and left the room.

Lincoln set down Honoria carefully.

"You children go in and start your soup," he said, and when they obeyed, he said to Charlie:

"Marion's not well and she can't stand shocks. That kind of people make her really physically sick."

"I didn't tell them to come here. They wormed your name out of somebody. They deliberately—"

"Well, it's too bad. It doesn't help matters. Excuse me a minute."

Left alone, Charlie sat tense in his chair. In the next room he could hear the children eating, talking in monosyllables, already oblivious to the scene between their elders. He heard a murmur of conversation from a farther room and then the ticking bell of a telephone receiver picked up, and in a panic he moved to the other side of the room and out of earshot.

In a minute Lincoln came back. "Look here, Charlie. I think we'd better call off dinner for tonight. Marion's in bad shape."

"Is she angry with me?"

"Sort of," he said, almost roughly. "She's not strong and—"

"You mean she's changed her mind about Honoria."

"She's pretty bitter right now. I don't know. You phone me at the bank tomorrow."

"I wish you'd explain to her I never dreamed these people would come here. I'm just as sore as you are."

"I couldn't explain anything to her now."

Charlie got up. He took his coat and hat and started down the corridor. Then he opened the door of the dining room and said in a strange voice, "Good night, children."

Honoria rose and ran around the table to hug him.

"Good night, sweetheart," he said vaguely, and then trying to make his voice more tender, trying to conciliate something, "Good night, dear children."

V

Charlie went directly to the Ritz bar with the furious idea of finding Lorraine and Duncan, but they were not there, and he realized that in any case there was nothing he could do. He had not touched his drink at the Peters', and now he ordered a whisky-and-soda. Paul came over to say hello.

"It's a great change," he said sadly. "We do about half the business we did. So many fellows I hear about back in the States lost everything, maybe not in the first crash, but then in the second. Your friend George Hardt lost every cent, I hear. Are you back in the States?"

"No. I'm in business in Prague."

"I heard that you lost a lot in the crash."

"I did," and he added grimly, "but I lost everything I wanted in the boom."

"Selling short?"

"Something like that."

Again the memory of those days swept over him like a nightmare—the people they had met travelling; the people who couldn't add a row of figures or speak a coherent sentence. The little man Helen had consented to dance with at the ship's party, who had insulted her ten feet from the table; the women and girls carried screaming with drink or drugs out of public places . . . the men who locked their wives out in the snow, because the snow of '29 wasn't real snow. If you didn't want it to be snow, you just paid some money.

He went to the phone and called the Peters apartment; Lincoln answered.

"I called up because this thing is on my mind. Has Marion said anything definite?"

"Marion's sick," Lincoln answered shortly. "I know this thing isn't altogether your fault, but I can't have her go to pieces about it. I'm afraid we'll have to let it slide for six months; I can't take the chance of working her up to this state again."

"I see."

"I'm sorry, Charlie."

He went back to his table. His whisky glass was empty, but he shook his head when Alix looked at it questioningly. There wasn't much he could do now except send Honoria some things; he would send her a lot of things tomorrow. He thought rather angrily that this was just money—he had given so many people money. . . .

"No, no more," he said to another waiter. "What do I owe you?"

He would come back some day; they couldn't make him pay forever. But he wanted his child, and nothing was much good now, beside that fact. He wasn't young any more, with a lot of nice thoughts and dreams to have by himself. He was absolutely sure Helen wouldn't have wanted him to be so alone.

Fact Questions and Exercises

1. Point out details from the first few pages of the story that suggest the deterioration or decadence that had been part of Charlie's life.
2. What city is the setting for the story? Why has Charlie returned to the city?
3. Identify Marion.
4. Identify Honoria.
5. What happened to Charlie's wife?
6. Which restaurants are named in the story?

7. Who are the two people that Charlie meets again and who later show up at an inopportune time?
8. Point out details that suggest that Charlie is trying to avoid the life of "vice and waste."

For Discussion and Writing

1. The title of the story suggests a parallel between ancient Babylon and modern Paris. Is this an appropriate comparison? How does it help to explain the meaning of the story?
2. Charlie says at one point that he "lost everything I wanted in the boom." What does he mean? What has he lost? What is the boom? How have his values changed since his first "visit" to Paris?
3. Are there details in the story that suggest that Charlie (or people in general) cannot escape the past? What are these details? How does Fitzgerald show that the present cannot be separated from the past? What are the implications of this?
4. How do the names Café of Heaven and Café of Hell fit the general theme of the story? How do these names reflect the way in which Charlie is trying to redeem himself? What other symbols does Fitzgerald use in the story? Note, for instance, the fact that Marion dresses in black and wears a black necklace.

William Faulkner [1897–1962]

Faulkner was born in New Albany, Mississippi, but spent most of his life in Oxford, Mississippi. Faulkner never graduated from high school; yet after World War I he briefly attended the University of Mississippi, while serving as the postmaster of Oxford. It was not long, however, before his interest turned completely to writing. With his novels *Sartoris* and *The Sound and the Fury* (both published in 1929), Faulkner began to create the mythical world of Yoknapatawpha County. By 1942 he had published eight novels and four short-story collections in which he further explored the inhabitants and history of his fictional world. Although Faulkner's work is distinctly "Southern," it easily transcends locality through its mythic and symbolic handling of people and events. Faulkner is noted as a significant prose stylist; his writing is balanced between a realistic, humorous use of dialect and a poetic, complex use of rhetoric. Among his best-known works are *Go Down, Moses* (1942), *Absalom, Absalom!* (1936), and *Light in August* (1932). He won the Nobel Prize in 1950.

Barn Burning

The store in which the Justice of the Peace's court was sitting smelled of cheese. The boy, crouched on his nail keg at the back of the crowded room, knew he smelled cheese, and more: from where he sat he could see the ranked shelves close-packed with the solid, squat, dynamic shapes of tin cans whose labels his stomach read, not from the lettering which meant nothing to his mind but from the scarlet devils and the silver curve of fish—this, the cheese which he knew he smelled and the hermetic meat which his intestines believed he smelled coming in intermittent gusts momentary and brief between the other constant one, the smell and sense just a little of fear because mostly of despair and grief, the old fierce pull of blood. He could not see the table where the Justice sat and before which his father and his father's enemy (*our enemy* he thought in that despair; *ourn! mine and hisn both! He's my father!*) stood, but he could hear them, the two of them that is, because his father had said no word yet:

"But what proof have you, Mr. Harris?"

"I told you. The hog got into my corn. I caught it up and sent it back to him. He had no fence that would hold it. I told him so, warned him. The next time I put the hog in my pen. When he came to get it I gave him enough wire to patch up his pen. The next time I put the hog up and kept it. I rode down to his house and saw the wire I gave him still rolled on to the spool in his yard. I told him he could have the hog when he paid me a dollar pound fee. That evening a nigger came with the dollar and got the hog. He was a strange nigger. He said, 'He say to tell you wood and hay kin burn.' I said, 'What?' 'That whut he say to tell you,' the nigger said. 'Wood and hay kin burn.' That night my barn burned. I got the stock out but I lost the barn."

"Where is the nigger? Have you got him?"

"He was a strange nigger, I tell you. I don't know what became of him."

"But that's not proof. Don't you see that's not proof?"

"Get that boy up here. He knows." For a moment the boy thought too that the man meant his older brother until Harris said, "Not him. The little one. The boy," and, crouching, small for his age, small and wiry like his father, in patched and faded jeans even too small for him, with straight, uncombed, brown hair and eyes gray and wild as storm scud, he saw the men between himself and the table part and become a lane of grim faces, at the end of which he saw the Justice, a shabby, collarless, graying man in spectacles, beckoning him. He felt no floor under his bare feet; he seemed to walk beneath the palpable weight of the grim turning faces. His father, stiff in his black Sunday coat donned not for the trial but for the moving, did not even look at him. *He aims for me to lie,* he thought, again with that frantic grief and despair. *And I will have to do hit.*

"What's your name, boy?" the Justice said.

"Colonel Sartoris Snopes," the boy whispered.

"Hey?" the Justice said. "Talk louder. Colonel Sartoris? I reckon anybody named for Colonel Sartoris in this country can't help but tell the truth, can they?" The boy said nothing. *Enemy! Enemy!* he thought; for a moment he could not even see, could not see that the Justice's face was kindly nor discern that his voice was troubled when he spoke to the man named Harris: "Do you want me to question this boy?" But he could hear, and during those subsequent long seconds while there was absolutely no sound in the crowded little room save that of quiet and intent breathing it was as if he had swung outward at the end of a grape vine, over a ravine, and at the top of the swing had been caught in a prolonged instant of mesmerized gravity, weightless in time.

"Now!" Harris said violently, explosively. "Damnation! Send him out of here!" Now time, the fluid world, rushed beneath him again, the voices coming to him again through the smell of cheese and sealed meat, the fear and despair and the old grief of blood: ✗

"This case is closed. I can't find against you, Snopes, but I can give you advice. Leave this country and don't come back to it."

His father spoke for the first time, his voice cold and harsh, level, without emphasis: "I aim to. I don't figure to stay in a country among people who . . ." he said something unprintable and vile, addressed to no one.

"That'll do," the Justice said. "Take your wagon and get out of this country before dark. Case dismissed."

His father turned, and he followed the stiff black coat, the wiry figure walking a little stiffly from where a Confederate provost's man's musket ball had taken him in the heel on a stolen horse thirty years ago, followed the two backs now, since his older brother had appeared from somewhere in the crowd, no taller than the father but thicker, chewing tobacco steadily, between the two lines of grim-faced men and out of the store and across the worn gallery and down the sagging steps and among the dogs and half-grown boys in the mild May dust, where as he passed a voice hissed:

Abner was a horse thief, has no sense of right & wrong

"Barn burner!"

Again he could not see, whirling; there was a face in a red haze, moonlike, bigger than the full moon, the owner of it half again his size, he leaping in the red haze toward the face, feeling no blow, feeling no shock when his head struck the earth, scrabbling up and leaping again, feeling no blow this time either and tasting no blood, scrabbling up to see the other boy in full flight and himself already leaping into pursuit as his father's hand jerked him back, the harsh, cold voice speaking above him: "Go get in the wagon."

It stood in a grove of locusts and mulberries across the road. His two hulking sisters in their Sunday dresses and his mother and her sister in calico and sunbonnets were already in it, sitting on and among the sorry residue of the dozen and more movings which even the boy could remember—the battered stove, the broken beds and chairs, the clock inlaid with mother-of-pearl, which would not run, stopped at some fourteen minutes past two o'clock of a dead and forgotten day and time, which had been his mother's dowry. She was crying, though when she saw him she drew her sleeve across her face and began to descend from the wagon. "Get back," the father said.

"He's hurt. I got to get some water and wash his . . ."

"Get back in the wagon," his father said. He got in too, over the tailgate. His father mounted to the seat where the older brother already sat and struck the gaunt mules two savage blows with the peeled willow, but without heat. It was not even sadistic; it was exactly that same quality which in later years would cause his descendants to over-run the engine before putting a motor car into motion, striking and reining back in the same movement. The wagon went on, the store with its quiet crowd of grimly watching men dropped behind; a curve in the road hid it. *Forever,* he thought. *Maybe he's done satisfied now, now that he has . . .* stopping himself, not to say it aloud even to himself. His mother's hand touched his shoulder.

beats mules just ~~kind~~ of man he was.

"Does hit hurt?" she said.

"Naw," he said. "Hit don't hurt. Lemme be."

"Can't you wipe some of the blood off before hit dries?"

"I'll wash to-night," he said. "Lemme be, I tell you."

The wagon went on. He did not know where they were going. None of them ever did or ever asked, because it was always somewhere, always a house of sorts waiting for them a day or two days or even three days away. Likely his father had already arranged to make a crop on another farm before he . . . Again he had to stop himself. He (the father) always did. There was something about his wolflike independence and even courage when the advantage was at least neutral which impressed strangers, as if they got from his latent ravening ferocity not so much a sense of dependability as a feeling that his ferocious conviction in the rightness of his own actions would be of advantage to all whose interest lay with his.

That night they camped, in a grove of oaks and beeches where a spring ran. The nights were still cool and they had a fire against it, of a rail lifted from a nearby fence and cut into lengths—a small fire, neat, niggard almost, a shrewd fire; such fires were his father's habit and custom always, even in freezing weather. Older, the boy might have remarked this and wondered why not a big one; why should not a man who had not only seen the waste and extravagance of war, but who had in his blood an inherent voracious prodigality with material not his own, have burned everything in sight? Then he might have gone a step farther and thought that that was the reason: that niggard blaze was the living fruit of nights passed during those four years in the woods hiding from all men, blue or gray, with his strings of horses (captured horses, he called them). And older still, he might have divined the true reason: that the element of fire spoke to some deep mainspring of his father's being, as the element of steel or of powder spoke to other men, as the one weapon for the preservation of integrity, else breath were not worth the breathing, and hence to be regarded with respect and used with discretion.

But he did not think this now and he had seen those same niggard blazes all his life. He merely ate his supper beside it and was already half asleep over his iron plate when his father called him, and once more he followed the stiff back, the stiff and ruthless limp, up the slope and on to the starlit road where, turning, he could see his father against the stars but without face of depth—a shape black, flat, and bloodless as though cut from tin in the iron folds of the frockcoat which had not been made for him, the voice harsh like tin and without heat like tin:

"You were fixing to tell them. You would have told him." He didn't answer. His father struck him with the flat of his hand on the side of the head, hard but without heat, exactly as he had struck the two mules at the store, exactly as he would strike either of them with any stick in order to kill a horsefly, his voice still without heat or anger: "You're getting to be a man. You got to learn. You got to learn to stick to your own blood or you ain't going to have any blood to stick to you. Do you think either of them, any man there this morning, would? Don't you know all they wanted was a chance to get at me because they knew I had them beat? Eh?" Later, twenty years later, he was to tell himself, "If I had said they wanted only truth, justice, he would have hit me again." But now he said nothing. He was not crying. He just stood there. "Answer me," his father said.

"Yes," he whispered. His father turned.

"Get on to bed. We'll be there to-morrow."

To-morrow they were there. In the early afternoon the wagon stopped before a paintless two-room house identical almost with the dozen others it had stopped before even in the boy's ten years, and again, as on the other dozen occasions, his mother and aunt got down and began to unload the wagon, *2 sisters* *1 brother* although his two sisters and his father and brother had not moved.

"Likely hit ain't fitten for hawgs," one of the sisters said.

"Nevertheless, fit it will and you'll hog it and like it," his father said. "Get out of them chairs and help your Ma unload."

The two sisters got down, big, bovine, in a flutter of cheap ribbons; one of them drew from the jumbled wagon bed a battered lantern, the other a worn broom. His father handed the reins to the older son and began to climb stiffly over the wheel. "When they get unloaded, take the team to the barn and feed them." Then he said, and at first the boy thought he was still speaking to his brother: "Come with me."

"Me?" he said.

"Yes," his father said. "You."

"Abner," his mother said. His father paused and looked back—the harsh level stare beneath the shaggy, graying, irascible brows.

"I reckon I'll have a word with the man that aims to begin to-morrow owning me body and soul for the next eight months."

They went back up the road. A week ago—or before last night, that is—he would have asked where they were going, but not now. His father had struck him before last night but never before had he paused afterward to explain why; it was as if the blow and the following calm, outrageous voice still rang, repercussed, divulging nothing to him save the terrible handicap of being young, the light weight of his few years, just heavy enough to prevent his soaring free of the world as it seemed to be ordered but not heavy enough to keep him footed solid in it, to resist it and try to change the course of its events.

Presently he could see the grove of oaks and cedars and the other flowering trees and shrubs where the house would be, though not the house yet. They walked beside a fence massed with honeysuckle and Cherokee roses and came to a gate swinging open between two brick pillars, and now, beyond a sweep of drive, he saw the house for the first time and at that instant he forgot his father and the terror and despair both, and even when he remembered his father again (who had not stopped) the terror and despair did not return. Because, for all the twelve movings, they had sojourned until now in a poor country, a land of small farms and fields and houses, and he had never seen a house like this before. *Hit's big as a courthouse,* he thought quietly, with a surge of peace and joy whose reason he could not have thought into words, being too young for that: *They are safe from him. People whose lives are a part of this peace and dignity are beyond his touch, he no more to them than a buzzing wasp: capable of stinging for a little moment but that's all; the spell of this peace and dignity rendering even the barns and stable and cribs which belong to it impervious to the puny flames he might contrive . . .* this, the peace and joy, ebbing for an instant as he looked again at the stiff black back, the stiff and implacable limp of the figure which was not dwarfed by the house, for the reason that it had never looked big anywhere and which now, against the serene columned backdrop, had more than ever that impervious quality of something cut ruthlessly from tin, depthless, as though, sidewise to the sun, it would cast no shadow. Watching him, the boy remarked the absolutely undeviating course which his father held and saw the stiff foot come squarely down in a pile of fresh droppings where a horse had stood in the drive and which his father could have avoided by a simple change of stride. But it ebbed only for a moment, though he could not have thought this into words

either, walking on in the spell of the house, which he could even want but
without envy, without sorrow, certainly never with that ravening and jealous
rage which unknown to him walked in the ironlike black coat before him: *Maybe
he will feel it too. Maybe it will even change him now from what maybe he couldn't
help but be.*

They crossed the portico. Now he could hear his father's stiff foot as it
came down on the boards with clocklike finality, a sound out of all proportion to
the displacement of the body it bore and which was not dwarfed either by the
white door before it, as though it had attained to a sort of vicious and ravening
minimum not to be dwarfed by anything—the flat, wide, black hat, the formal
coat of broadcloth which had once been black but which had now that
friction-glazed greenish cast of the bodies of old house flies, the lifted sleeve
which was too large, the lifted hand like a curled claw. The door opened so
promptly that the boy knew the Negro must have been watching them all the
time, an old man with neat grizzled hair, in a linen jacket, who stood barring the
door with his body, saying, "Wipe yo foots, white man, fo you come in here.
Major ain't home nohow."

"Get out of my way, nigger," his father said, without heat too, flinging
the door back and the Negro also and entering, his hat still on his head. And now
the boy saw the prints of the stiff foot on the doorjamb and saw them appear on
the pale rug behind the machinelike deliberation of the foot which seemed to
bear (or transmit) twice the weight which the body compassed. The Negro was
shouting "Miss Lula! Miss Lula!" somewhere behind them, then the boy,
deluged as though by a warm wave by a suave turn of carpeted stair and a
pendant glitter of chandeliers and a mute gleam of gold frames, heard the swift
feet and saw her too, a lady—perhaps he had never seen her like before
either—in a gray, smooth gown with lace at the throat and an apron tied at the
waist and the sleeves turned back, wiping cake or biscuit dough from her hands
with a towel as she came up the hall, looking not at his father at all but at the
track on the blond rug with an expression of incredulous amazement.

"I tried," the Negro cried. "I tole him to . . ."

"Will you please go away?" she said in a shaking voice. "Major de Spain
is not at home. Will you please go away?"

His father had not spoken again. He did not speak again. He did not even
look at her. He just stood stiff in the center of the rug, in his hat, the shaggy
iron-gray brows twitching slightly above the pebble-colored eyes as he appeared
to examine the house with brief deliberation. Then with the same deliberation he
turned; the boy watched him pivot on the good leg and saw the stiff foot drag
round the arc of the turning, leaving a final long and fading smear. His father
never looked at it, he never once looked down at the rug. The Negro held the
door. It closed behind them, upon the hysteric and indistinguishable woman-
wail. His father stopped at the top of the steps and scraped his boot clean on the
edge of it. At the gate he stopped again. He stood for a moment, planted stiffly on
the stiff foot, looking back at the house. "Pretty and white, ain't it?" he said.
"That's sweat. Nigger sweat. Maybe it ain't white enough yet to suit him. Maybe
he wants to mix some white sweat with it."

Two hours later the boy was chopping wood behind the house within
which his mother and aunt and the two sisters (the mother and aunt, not the two
girls, he knew that; even at this distance and muffled by walls the flat loud voices
of the two girls emanated an incorrigible idle inertia) were setting up the stove to

prepare a meal, when he heard the hooves and saw the linen-clad man on a fine sorrel mare, whom he recognized even before he saw the rolled rug in front of the Negro youth following on a fat bay carriage horse—a suffused, angry face vanishing, still at full gallop, beyond the corner of the house where his father and brother were sitting in the two tilted chairs; and a moment later, almost before he could have put the axe down, he heard the hooves again and watched the sorrel mare go back out of the yard, already galloping again. Then his father began to shout one of the sisters' names, who presently emerged backward from the kitchen door dragging the rolled rug along the ground by one end while the other sister walked behind it.

"If you ain't going to tote, go on and set up the wash-pot," the first said.

"You, Sarty!" the second shouted. "Set up the wash-pot!" His father appeared at the door, framed against that shabbiness, as he had been against that other bland perfection, impervious to either, the mother's anxious face at his shoulder.

"Go on," the father said. "Pick it up." The two sisters stooped, broad, lethargic; stooping, they presented an incredible expanse of pale cloth and a flutter of tawdry ribbons.

"If I thought enough of a rug to have to git hit all the way from France I wouldn't keep hit where folks coming in would have to tromp on hit," the first said. They raised the rug.

"Abner," the mother said. "Let me do it."

"You go back and git dinner," his father said. "I'll tend to this."

From the woodpile through the rest of the afternoon the boy watched them, the rug spread flat in the dust beside the bubbling wash-pot, the two sisters stooping over it with that profound and lethargic reluctance, while the father stood over them in turn, implacable and grim, driving them though never raising his voice again. He could smell the harsh home-made lye they were using; he saw his mother come to the door once and look toward them with an expression not anxious now but very like despair; he saw his father turn, and he fell to with the axe and saw from the corner of his eye his father raise from the ground a flattish fragment of field stone and examine it and return to the pot, and this time his mother actually spoke: "Abner. Abner. Please don't. Please, Abner."

Then he was done too. It was dusk; the whippoorwills had already begun. He could smell coffee from the room where they would presently eat the cold food remaining from the mid-afternoon meal, though when he entered the house he realized they were having coffee again probably because there was a fire on the hearth, before which the rug now lay spread over the backs of the two chairs. The tracks of his father's foot were gone. Where they had been were now long, water-cloudy scorifications resembling the sporadic course of a lilliputian mowing machine.

It still hung there while they ate the cold food and then went to bed, scattered without order or claim up and down the two rooms, his mother in one bed, where his father would later lie, the older brother in the other, himself, the aunt, and the two sisters on pallets on the floor. But his father was not in bed yet. The last thing the boy remembered was the depthless, harsh silhouette of the hat and coat bending over the rug and it seemed to him that he had not even closed his eyes when the silhouette was standing over him, the fire almost dead behind it, the stiff foot prodding him awake. "Catch up the mule," his father said.

When he returned with the mule his father was standing in the black door, the rolled rug over his shoulder. "Ain't you going to ride?" he said.

"No, Give me your foot."

He bent his knee into his father's hand, the wiry, surprising power flowed smoothly, rising, he rising with it, on to the mule's bare back (they had owned a saddle once; the boy could remember it though not when or where) and with the same effortlessness his father swung the rug up in front of him. Now in the starlight they retraced the afternoon's path, up the dusty road rife with honeysuckle, through the gate and up the black tunnel of the drive to the lightless house, where he sat on the mule and felt the rough warp of the rug drag across his thighs and vanish.

"Don't you want me to help?" he whispered. His father did not answer and now he heard again that stiff foot striking the hollow portico with that wooden and clocklike deliberation, that outrageous overstatement of the weight it carried. The rug, hunched, not flung (the boy could tell that even in the darkness) from his father's shoulder struck the angle of wall and floor with a sound unbelievably loud, thunderous, then the foot again, unhurried and enormous; a light came on in the house and the boy sat, tense, breathing steadily and quietly and just a little fast, though the foot itself did not increase its beat at all, descending the steps now; now the boy could see him.

"Don't you want to ride now?" he whispered. "We kin both ride now," the light within the house altering now, flaring up and sinking. *He's coming down the stairs now,* he thought. He had already ridden the mule up beside the horse block; presently his father was up behind him and he doubled the reins over and slashed the mule across the neck, but before the animal could begin to trot the hard, thin arm came round him, the hard, knotted hand jerking the mule back to a walk.

In the first red rays of the sun they were in the lot, putting plow gear on the mules. This time the sorrel mare was in the lot before he heard it at all, the rider collarless and even bareheaded, trembling, speaking in a shaking voice as the woman in the house had done, his father merely looking up once before stooping again to the hame he was buckling, so that the man on the mare spoke to his stooping back:

"You must realize you have ruined that rug. Wasn't there anybody here, any of your women . . ." he ceased, shaking, the boy watching him, the older brother leaning now in the stable door, chewing, blinking slowly and steadily at nothing apparently. "It cost a hundred dollars. But you never had a hundred dollars. You never will. So I'm going to charge you twenty bushels of corn against your crop. I'll add it in your contract and when you come to the commissary you can sign it. That won't keep Mrs. de Spain quiet but maybe it will teach you to wipe your feet off before you enter her house again."

Then he was gone. The boy looked at his father, who still had not spoken or even looked up again, who was now adjusting the loggerhead in the hame.

"Pap," he said. His father looked at him—the inscrutable face, the shaggy brows beneath which the gray eyes glinted coldly. Suddenly the boy went toward him, fast, stopping as suddenly. "You done the best you could!" he cried. "If he wanted hit done different why didn't he wait and tell you how? He won't git no twenty bushels! He won't git none! We'll gether hit and hide hit! I kin watch . . ."

"Did you put the cutter back in that straight stock like I told you?"

"No, sir," he said.

"Then go do it."

That was Wednesday. During the rest of that week he worked steadily, at what was within his scope and some which was beyond it, with an industry that did not need to be driven nor even commanded twice; he had this from his mother, with the difference that some at least of what he did he liked to do, such as splitting wood with the half-size axe which his mother and aunt had earned, or saved money somehow, to present him with at Christmas. In company with the two older women (and on one afternoon, even one of the sisters), he built pens for the shoat and the cow which were a part of his father's contract with the landlord, and one afternoon, his father being absent, gone somewhere on one of the mules, he went to the field.

They were running a middle buster now, his brother holding the plow straight while he handled the reins, and walking beside the straining mule, the rich black soil shearing cool and damp against his bare ankles, he thought *Maybe this is the end of it. Maybe even that twenty bushels that seems hard to have to pay for just a rug will be a cheap price for him to stop forever and always from being what he used to be;* thinking, dreaming now, so that his brother had to speak sharply to him to mind the mule: *Maybe he even won't collect the twenty bushels. Maybe it will all add up and balance and vanish—corn, rug, fire; the terror and grief, the being pulled two ways like between two teams of horses—gone, done with forever and ever.*

Then it was Saturday; he looked up from beneath the mule he was harnessing and saw his father in the black coat and hat. "Not that," his father said. "The wagon gear." And then, two hours later, sitting in the wagon bed behind his father and brother on the seat, the wagon accomplished a final curve, and he saw the weathered paintless store with its tattered tobacco and patent-medicine posters and the tethered wagons and saddle animals below the gallery. He mounted the gnawed steps behind his father and brother, and there again was the lane of quiet, watching faces for the three of them to walk through. He saw the man in spectacles sitting at the plank table and he did not need to be told this was a Justice of the Peace; he sent one glare of fierce, exultant, partisan defiance at the man in collar and cravat now, whom he had seen but twice before in his life, and that on a galloping horse, who now wore on his face an expression not of rage but of amazed unbelief which the boy could not have known was at the incredible circumstance of being sued by one of his own tenants, and came and stood against his father and cried at the Justice: "He ain't done it! He ain't burnt . . ."

"Go back to the wagon," his father said.

"Burnt?" the Justice said. "Do I understand this rug was burned too?"

"Does anybody here claim it was?" his father said. "Go back to the wagon." But he did not, he merely retreated to the rear of the room, crowded as that other had been, but not to sit down this time, instead, to stand pressing among the motionless bodies, listening to the voices:

"And you claim twenty bushels of corn is too high for the damage you did to the rug?"

"He brought the rug to me and said he wanted the tracks washed out of it. I washed the tracks out and took the rug back to him."

"But you didn't carry the rug back to him in the same condition it was in before you made the tracks on it."

His father did not answer, and now for perhaps half a minute there was no sound at all save that of breathing, the faint, steady suspiration of complete and intent listening.

"You decline to answer that, Mr. Snopes?" Again his father did not answer. "I'm going to find against you, Mr. Snopes. I'm going to find that you were responsible for the injury to Major de Spain's rug and hold you liable for it. But twenty bushels of corn seems a little high for a man in your circumstances to have to pay. Major de Spain claims it cost a hundred dollars. October corn will be worth about fifty cents. I figure that if Major de Spain can stand a ninety-five dollar loss on something he paid cash for, you can stand a five-dollar loss you haven't earned yet. I hold you in damages to Major de Spain to the amount of ten bushels of corn over and above your contract with him, to be paid to him out of your crop at gathering time. Court adjourned."

It had taken no time hardly, the morning was but half begun. He thought they would return home and perhaps back to the field, since they were late, far behind all other farmers. But instead his father passed on behind the wagon, merely indicating with his hand for the older brother to follow with it, and crossed the road toward the blacksmith shop opposite, pressing on after his father, overtaking him, speaking, whispering up at the harsh, calm face beneath the weathered hat: "He won't git no ten bushels neither. He won't git one. We'll . . ." until his father glanced for an instant down at him, the face absolutely calm, the grizzled eyebrows tangled above the cold eyes, the voice almost pleasant, almost gentle:

"You think so? Well, we'll wait till October anyway."

The matter of the wagon—the setting of a spoke or two and the tightening of the tires—did not take long either, the business of the tires accomplished by driving the wagon into the spring branch behind the shop and letting it stand there, the mules nuzzling into the water from time to time, and the boy on the seat with the idle reins, looking up the slope and through the sooty tunnel of the shed where the slow hammer rang and where his father sat on an upended cypress bolt, easily, either talking or listening, still sitting there when the boy brought the dripping wagon up out of the branch and halted it before the door.

"Take them on to the shade and hitch," his father said. He did so and returned. His father and the smith and a third man squatting on his heels inside the door were talking, about crops and animals; the boy, squatting too in the ammoniac dust and hoof-parings and scales of rust, heard his father tell a long and unhurried story out of the time before the birth of the older brother even when he had been a professional horse-trader. And then his father came up beside him where he stood before a tattered last year's circus poster on the other side of the store, gazing rapt and quiet at the scarlet horses, the incredible poisings and convolutions of tulle and tights and the painted leers of comedians, and said, "It's time to eat."

But not at home. Squatting beside his brother against the front wall, he watched his father emerge from the store and produce from a paper sack a segment of cheese and divide it carefully and deliberately into three with his pocket knife and produce crackers from the same sack. They all three squatted on the gallery and ate, slowly, without talking; then in the store again, they drank from a tin dipper tepid water smelling of the cedar bucket and of living beech trees. And still they did not go home. It was a horse lot this time, a tall rail fence upon and along which men stood and sat and out of which one by one horses were led, to be walked and trotted and then cantered back and forth along the road while the slow swapping and buying went on and the sun began to slant westward, they—the three of them—watching and listening, the older brother with his muddy eyes and his steady, inevitable tobacco, the father commenting now and then on certain of the animals, to no one in particular.

It was after sundown when they reached home. They ate supper by lamplight, then, sitting on the doorstep, the boy watched the night fully accomplish, listening to the whippoorwills and the frogs, when he heard his mother's voice: "Abner! No! No! Oh, God. Oh, God. Abner!" and he rose, whirled, and saw the altered light through the door where a candle stub now burned in a bottleneck on the table and his father, still in the hat and coat, at once formal and burlesque as though dressed carefully for some shabby and ceremonial violence, emptying the reservoir of the lamp back into the five-gallon kerosene can from which it had been filled, while the mother tugged at his arm until he shifted the lamp to the other hand and flung her back, not savagely or viciously, just hard, into the wall, her hands flung out against the wall for balance, her mouth open and in her face the same quality of hopeless despair as had been in her voice. Then his father saw him standing in the door.

"Go to the barn and get that can of oil we were oiling the wagon with," he said. The boy did not move. Then he could speak.

"What . . ." he cried. "What are you . . ."

"Go get that oil," his father said. "Go."

Then he was moving, running, outside the house, toward the stable: this the old habit, the old blood which he had not been permitted to choose for himself, which had been bequeathed him willy nilly and which had run for so long (and who knew where, battening on what of outrage and savagery and lust) before it came to him. *I could keep on,* he thought. *I could run on and on and never look back, never need to see his face again. Only I can't. I can't,* the rusted can in his hand now, the liquid sploshing in it as he ran back to the house and into it, into the sound of his mother's weeping in the next room, and handed the can to his father.

"Ain't you going to even send a nigger?" he cried. "At least you sent a nigger before!"

This time his father didn't strike him. The hand came even faster than the blow had, the same hand which had set the can on the table with almost excruciating care flashing from the can toward him too quick for him to follow it, gripping him by the back of his shirt and on to tiptoe before he had seen it quit the can, the face stooping at him in breathless and frozen ferocity, the cold, dead voice speaking over him to the older brother who leaned against the table, chewing with that steady, curious, sidewise motion of cows.

"Empty the can into the big one and go on. I'll catch up with you."

"Better tie him up to the bedpost," the brother said.

"Do like I told you," the father said. Then the boy was moving, his bunched shirt and the hard, bony hand between his shoulder-blades, his toes just touching the floor, across the room and into the other one, past the sisters sitting with spread heavy thighs in the two chairs over the cold hearth, and to where his mother and aunt sat side by side on the bed, the aunt's arms about his mother's shoulders.

"Hold him," the father said. The aunt made a startled movement. "Not you," the father said. "Lennie. Take hold of him. I want to see you do it." His mother took him by the wrist. "You'll hold him better than that. If he gets loose don't you know what he is going to do? He will go up yonder." He jerked his head toward the road. "Maybe I'd better tie him."

"I'll hold him," his mother whispered.

"See you do then." Then his father was gone, the stiff foot heavy and measured upon the boards, ceasing at last.

Then he began to struggle. His mother caught him in both arms, he jerking and wrenching at them. He would be stronger in the end, he knew that. But he had no time to wait for it. "Lemme go!" he cried. "I don't want to have to hit you!"

"Let him go!" the aunt said. "If he don't go, before God, I am going up there myself!"

"Don't you see I can't" his mother cried. "Sarty! Sarty! No! No! Help me, Lizzie!"

Then he was free. His aunt grasped at him but it was too late. He whirled, running, his mother stumbled forward onto her knees behind him, crying to the nearer sister: "Catch him, Net! Catch him!" But that was too late too, the sister (the sisters were twins, born at the same time, yet either of them now gave the impression of being, encompassing as much living meat and volume and weight as any other two of the family) not yet having begun to rise from the chair, her head, face, alone merely turned, presenting to him in the flying instant an astonishing expanse of young female features untroubled by any surprise even, wearing only an expression of bovine interest. Then he was out of the room, out of the house, in the mild dust of the starlit road and the heavy rifeness of honeysuckle, the pale ribbon unspooling with terrific slowness under his running feet, reaching the gate at last and turning in, running, his heart and lungs drumming, on up the drive toward the lighted house, the lighted door. He did not knock, he burst in, sobbing for breath, incapable for the moment of speech; he saw the astonished face of the Negro in the linen jacket without knowing when the Negro had appeared.

"De Spain!" he cried, panted. "Where's . . ." then he saw the white man too emerging from a white door down the hall. "Barn!" he cried. "Barn!"

"What?" the white man said. "Barn?"

"Yes!" the boy cried. "Barn!"

"Catch him!" the white man shouted.

But it was too late this time too. The Negro grasped his shirt, but the entire sleeve, rotten with washing, carried away, and he was out that door too and in the drive again, and had actually never ceased to run even while he was screaming into the white man's face.

Behind him the white man was shouting, "My horse! Fetch my horse!" and he thought for an instant of cutting across the park and climbing the fence into the road, but he did not know the park nor how high the vine-massed fence might be and he dared not risk it. So he ran on down the drive, blood and breath roaring; presently he was in the road again though he could not see it. He could not hear either: the galloping mare was almost upon him before he heard her, and even then he held his course, as if the very urgency of his wild grief and need must in a moment more find him wings, waiting until the ultimate instant to hurl himself aside and into the weed-choked roadside ditch as the horse thundered past and on, for an instant in furious silhouette against the stars, the tranquil early summer night sky which, even before the shape of the horse and rider vanished, stained abruptly and violently upward: a long, swirling roar incredible and soundless, blotting the stars, and he springing up and into the road again, running again, knowing it was too late yet still running even after he heard the shot and, an instant later, two shots, pausing now without knowing he had ceased to run, crying "Pap! Pap!," running again before he knew he had begun to run, stumbling, tripping over something and scrabbling up again without ceasing to run, looking backward over his shoulder at the glare as he got up, running on among the invisible trees, panting, sobbing, "Father! Father!"

At midnight he was sitting on the crest of a hill. He did not know it was midnight and he did not know how far he had come. But there was no glare behind him now and he sat now, his back toward what he had called home for four days anyhow, his face toward the dark woods which he would enter when breath was strong again, small, shaking steadily in the chill darkness, hugging himself into the remainder of his thin, rotten shirt, the grief and despair now no longer terror and fear but just grief and despair. *Father. My father,* he thought. "He was brave!" he cried suddenly, aloud but not loud, no more than a whisper: "He was! He was in the war! He was in Colonel Sartoris' cav'ry!" not knowing that his father had gone to that war a private in the fine old European sense, wearing no uniform, admitting the authority of and giving fidelity to no man or army or flag, going to war as Malbrouck himself did: for booty—it meant nothing and less than nothing to him if it were enemy booty or his own.

The slow constellations wheeled on. It would be dawn and then sun-up after a while and he would be hungry. But that would be to-morrow and now he was only cold, and walking would cure that. His breathing was easier now and he decided to get up and go on, and then he found that he had been asleep because he knew it was almost dawn, the night almost over. He could tell that from the whippoorwills. They were everywhere now among the dark trees below him, constant and inflectioned and ceaseless, so that, as the instant for giving over to the day birds drew nearer and nearer, there was no interval at all between them. He got up. He was a little stiff, but walking would cure that too as it would the cold, and soon there would be the sun. He went on down the hill, toward the dark woods within which the liquid silver voices of the birds called unceasing—the rapid and urgent beating of the urgent and quiring heart of the late spring night. He did not look back.

Fact Questions and Exercises

1. How do you know that Sarty cannot read?
2. Sarty and his father go to court twice in the story. What are the reasons for each court appearance? What are the results?
3. What is Sarty's full name? For whom has he been named?
4. How did Snopes receive the wound that causes his limp?

ximately when does the story take place?

does Snopes soil Major de Spain's rug? Ultimately, how does he ruin
g?

does Snopes want to tie Sarty to the bedpost?

warns de Spain that Snopes is about to burn the barn?

Snopes succeed in burning de Spain's barn? What apparently happens
to Snopes when he comes to burn the barn?

10. What happens to Sarty at the end of the story?

For Discussion and Writing

1. Note the italicized passages; these indicate Sarty's unspoken thoughts or
interior monologues. Do these passages form any particular pattern? How do
they compare with what Sarty actually says and does? Are they appropriate
for an illiterate boy? Why?

2. Characterize Abner Snopes. Does Faulkner totally condemn Snopes? Are
there any indications that Faulkner has some admiration for Snopes? If so,
what are they? How does Sarty feel toward his father?

3. Which two forces create the conflict in Sarty? Does Sarty himself symbolize
these forces in any way? If so, how does Faulkner make this known?

4. Why, on page 179, does Sarty's mother say "Abner. Abner. Please don't.
Please, Abner."? Does she know at this point what Snopes intends to do? If
so, how has she discovered his intentions? Are there other instances in the
story where she exhibits similar knowledge about Snopes?

Limited
omniscient perspective

Ernest Hemingway [1898–1961]

Hemingway was born in Oak Park, Illinois, near Chicago. After graduating from high school in 1917, Hemingway worked briefly as a reporter for
the Kansas City *Star.* When World War I began, he volunteered and
served with the ambulance corps in Italy, where he was severely
wounded. After the war he again worked as a newspaper correspondent,
eventually settling in Paris. He published his first significant collection of
stories, *In Our Time*, in 1925, and became famous a year later with the
publication of the novel *The Sun Also Rises*. Hemingway is best remembered for the fiction he wrote during the 1920s and 1930s. That fiction best
exemplifies his famous terse, clean style—a style derived in part from his
journalistic background. Among his best known works are *A Farewell to
Arms* (1929), *For Whom the Bell Tolls* (1940), and *The Old Man and the
Sea* (1952). Hemingway was awarded the Nobel Prize in 1952.

The Snows of Kilimanjaro

Kilimanjaro is a <u>snow covered mountain 19,710 feet</u> high, and is said to be the <u>highest mountain in Africa.</u> Its western summit is called the Masai "Ngàje Ngài," the <u>House of God.</u> Close to the western summit there is the <u>dried and frozen</u> carcass of a leopard. No one has explained what the leopard was seeking at that altitude.

"The marvellous thing is that it's painless," he said. "That's how you know when it starts."

"Is it really?"

"Absolutely. I'm awfully sorry about the odor though. That must bother you."

"Don't! Please don't."

"Look at them," he said. "Now is it sight or is it scent that brings them like that?"

The cot the man lay on was in the wide shade of a mimosa tree and as he looked out past the shade onto the glare of the plain there were three of the big birds squatted obscenely, while in the sky a dozen more sailed, making quick-moving shadows as they passed.

"They've been there since the day the truck broke down," he said. "Today's the first time any have lit on the ground. I watched the way they sailed very carefully at first in case I ever wanted to use them in a story. That's funny now."

"I wish you wouldn't," she said.

"I'm only talking," he said. "It's much easier if I talk. But I don't want to bother you."

"You know it doesn't bother me," she said. "It's that I've gotten so very nervous not being able to do anything. I think we might make it as easy as we can until the plane comes."

"Or until the plane doesn't come."

"Please tell me what I can do. There must be something I can do."

"You can take the leg off and that might stop it, though I doubt it. Or you can shoot me. You're a good shot now. I taught you to shoot didn't I?"

"Please don't talk that way. Couldn't I read to you?"

"Read what?"

"Anything in the book bag that we haven't read."

"I can't listen to it," he said. "Talking is the easiest. We quarrel and that makes the time pass."

"I don't quarrel. I never want to quarrel. Let's not quarrel any more. No matter how nervous we get. Maybe they will be back with another truck today. Maybe the plane will come."

"I don't want to move," the man said. "There is no sense in moving now except to make it easier for you."

"That's cowardly."

"Can't you let a man die as comfortably as he can without calling him names? What's the use of slanging me?"

"You're not going to die."

"Don't be silly. I'm dying now. Ask those bastards." He looked over to where the huge, filthy birds sat, their naked heads sunk in the hunched feathers. A fourth planed down, to run quick-legged and then waddle slowly toward the others.

"They are around every camp. You never notice them. You can't die if you don't give up."

"Where did you read that? You're such a bloody fool."

"You might think about some one else."

"For Christ's sake," he said, "That's been my trade."

He lay then and was quiet for a while and looked across the heat shimmer of the plain to the edge of the bush. There were a few Tommies that showed minute and white against the yellow and, far off, he saw a herd of zebra, white against the green of the bush. This was a pleasant camp under big trees against a hill, with good water, and close by, a nearly dry water hole where sand grouse flighted in the mornings.

"Wouldn't you like me to read?" she asked. She was sitting on a canvas chair beside his cot. "There's a breeze coming up."

"No thanks."

"Maybe the truck will come."

"I don't give a damn about the truck."

"I do."

"You give a damn about so many things that I don't."

"Not so many, Harry."

"What about a drink?"

"It's supposed to be bad for you. It said in Black's to avoid all alcohol. You shouldn't drink."

"Molo!" he shouted.

"Yes Bwana."

"Bring whiskey-soda."

"Yes Bwana."

"You shouldn't," she said. "That's what I mean by giving up. It says it's bad for you. I know it's bad for you."

"No," he said. "It's good for me."

So now it was all over, he thought. So now he would never have a chance to finish it. So this was the way it ended in a bickering over a drink. Since the gangrene started in his right leg he had no pain and with the pain the horror had gone and all he felt now was a great tiredness and anger that this was the end of it. For this, that now was coming, he had very little curiosity. For years it had obsessed him; but now it meant nothing in itself. It was strange how easy being tired enough made it.

Now he would never write the things that he had saved to write until he knew enough to write them well. Well, he would not have to fail at trying to write them either. Maybe you could never write them, and that was why you put them off and delayed the starting. Well he would never know, now.

"I wish we'd never come," the woman said. She was looking at him holding the glass and biting her lip. "You never would have gotten anything like this in Paris. You always said you loved Paris. We could have stayed in Paris or gone anywhere. I'd have gone anywhere. I said I'd go anywhere you wanted. If you wanted to shoot we could have gone shooting in Hungary and been comfortable."

"Your bloody money," he said.

"That's not fair," she said. "It was always yours as much as mine. I left everything and I went wherever you wanted to go and I've done what you wanted to do. But I wish we'd never come here."

"You said you loved it."

"I did when you were all right. But now I hate it. I don't see why that had to happen to your leg. What have we done to have that happen to us?"

"I suppose what I did was to forget to put iodine on it when I first scratched it. Then I didn't pay any attention to it because I never infect. Then, later, when it got bad, it was probably using that weak carbolic solution when the other antiseptics ran out that paralyzed the minute blood vessels and started the gangrene." He looked at her, "What else?"

[handwritten margin note: Tells: What was the injury]

"I don't mean that."

"If we would have hired a good mechanic instead of a half baked kikuyu[1] driver, he would have checked the oil and never burned out that bearing in the truck."

"I don't mean that."

"If you hadn't left your own people, your goddamned Old Westbury, Saratoga, Palm Beach people to take me on——"

[handwritten margin note: profanity]

"Why, I loved you. That's not fair. I love you now. I'll always love you. Don't you love me?"

"No," said the man. "I don't think so. I never have."

"Harry, what are you saying? You're out of your head."

"No. I haven't any head to go out of."

"Don't drink that," she said. "Darling, please don't drink that. We have to do everything we can."

"You do it," he said. "I'm tired."

Now in his mind he saw a railway station at Karagatch and he was standing with his pack and that was the headlight of the Simplon-Orient cutting the dark now and he was leaving Thrace then after the retreat. That was one of the things he had saved to write, with, in the morning at breakfast, looking out the window and seeing snow on the mountains in Bulgaria and Nansen's Secretary asking the old man if it were snow and the old man looking at it and saying, No, that's not snow. It's too early for snow. And the Secretary repeating to the other girls, No, You see. It's not snow and them all saying, It's not snow we were mistaken. But it was the snow all right and he sent them on into it when he evolved exchange of populations. And it was snow they tramped along in until they died that winter.

It was snow too that fell all Christmas week that year up in the Gauertal, that year they lived in the woodcutter's house with the big square porcelain stove

1. A member of the Bantu-speaking tribe of Kenya, Africa.

that filled half the room, and they slept on mattresses filled with beech leaves, the time the deserter came with his feet bloody in the snow. He said the police were right behind him and they gave him woolen socks and held the gendarmes talking until the tracks had drifted over.

In Schrunz, on Christmas day, the snow was so bright it hurt your eyes when you looked out from the weinstube[2] and saw every one coming home from church. That was where they walked up the sleigh-smoothed urine-yellowed road along the river with the steep pine hills, skis heavy on the shoulder, and where they ran that great run down the glacier above the Madlener-haus, the snow as smooth to see as cake frosting and as light as powder and he remembered the noiseless rush the speed made as you dropped down like a bird.

They were snow-bound a week in the Madlener-haus that time in the blizzard playing cards in the smoke by the lantern light and the stakes were higher all the time as Herr Lent lost more. Finally he lost it all. Everything, the skischule money and all the season's profit and then his capital. He could see him with his long nose, picking up the cards and then opening, "Sans Voir."[3] There was always gambling then. When there was no snow you gambled and when there was too much you gambled. He thought of all the time in his life he had spent gambling.

But he had never written a line of that, nor of that cold, bright Christmas day with the mountains showing across the plain that Barker had flown across the lines to bomb the Austrian officers' leave train, machine-gunning them as they scattered and ran. He remembered Barker afterwards coming into the mess and starting to tell about it. And how quiet it got and then somebody saying, "You bloody murderous bastard."

Those were the same Austrians they killed then that he skied with later. No not the same. Hans, that he skied with all that year, had been in the Kaiser-Jägers[4] and when they went hunting hares together up the little valley above the saw-mill they had talked of the fighting on Pasubio and of the attack on Pertica and Asalone and he had never written a word of that. Nor of Monte Corno, nor the Siete Commum, nor of Arsiedo.

How many winters had he lived in the Voralberg and the Arlberg? It was four and then he remembered the man who had the fox to sell when they had walked into Bludenz, that time to buy presents, and the cherry-pit taste of good kirsch, the fast-slipping rush of running powder-snow on crust, singing "Hi! Ho! said Rolly!" as you ran down the last stretch to the steep drop, taking it straight, then running the orchard in three turns and out across the ditch and onto the icy road behind the inn. Knocking your bindings loose, kicking the skis free and leaning them up against the wooden wall of the inn, the lamplight coming from the window, where inside, in the smoky, new-wine smelling warmth, they were playing the accordion.

"Where did we stay in Paris?" he asked the woman who was sitting by him in a canvas chair, now, in Africa.

"At the Crillon. You know that."

"Why do I know that?"

"That's where we always stayed."

2. A tavern.

3. That is, without looking at the cards.

4. The Kaiser's Riflemen, a special military unit.

"No. Not always."

"There and at the Pavillion Henri-Quatre in St. Germain. You said you loved it there."

"Love is a dunghill," said Harry. "And I'm the cock that gets on it to crow."

"If you have to go away," she said, "is it absolutely necessary to kill off everything you leave behind? I mean do you have to take away everything? Do you have to kill your horse, and your wife and burn your saddle and your armour?"

"Yes," he said. "Your damned money was my armour. My Swift and my Armour."

"Don't."

"All right. I'll stop that. I don't want to hurt you."

"It's a little bit late now."

"All right then. I'll go on hurting you. It's more amusing. The only thing I ever really liked to do with you I can't do now."

"No, that's not true. You liked to do many things and everything you wanted to do I did."

"Oh, for Christ sake stop bragging, will you?"

He looked at her and saw her crying.

"Listen," he said. "Do you think that it is fun to do this? I don't know why I'm doing it. It's trying to kill to keep yourself alive, I imagine. I was all right when we started talking. I didn't mean to start this, and now I'm crazy as a coot and being as cruel to you as I can be. Don't pay any attention, darling, to what I say. I love you, really. You know I love you. I've never loved any one else the way I love you."

He slipped into the familiar lie he made his bread and butter by.

"You're sweet to me."

"You bitch," he said. "You rich bitch. That's poetry. I'm full of poetry now. Rot and poetry. Rotten poetry."

"Stop it. Harry, why do you have to turn into a devil now?"

"I don't like to leave anything," the man said. "I don't like to leave things behind."

It was evening now and he had been asleep. The sun was gone behind the hill and there was a shadow all across the plain and the small animals were feeding close to camp; quick dropping heads and switching tails, he watched them keeping well out away from the bush now. The birds no longer waited on the ground. They were all perched heavily in a tree. There were many more of them. His personal boy was sitting by the bed.

"Memsahib's gone to shoot," the boy said. "Does Bwana want?"

"Nothing."

She had gone to kill a piece of meat and, knowing how he liked to watch the game, she had gone well away so she would not disturb this little pocket of the plain that he could see. She was always thoughtful, he thought. On anything she knew about, or had read, or that she had ever heard.

It was not her fault that when he went to her he was already over. How could a woman know that you meant nothing that you said; that you spoke only from habit and to be comfortable? After he no longer meant what he said, his lies were more successful with women than when he had told them the truth.

It was not so much that he lied as that there was no truth to tell. He had had his life and it was over and then he went on living it again with different people and more money, with the best of the same places, and some new ones.

You kept from thinking and it was all marvellous. You were equipped with good insides so that you did not go to pieces that way, the way most of them had, and you made an attitude that you cared nothing for the work you used to do, now that you could no longer do it. But, in yourself, you said that you would write about these people; about the very rich; that you were really not of them but a spy in their country; that you would leave it and write of it and for once it would be written by some one who knew what he was writing of. But he would never do it, because each day of not writing, of comfort, of being that which he despised, dulled his ability and softened his will to work so that, finally, he did no work at all. The people he knew now were all much more comfortable when he did not work. Africa was where he had been happiest in the good time of his life, so he had come out here to start again. They had made this safari with the minimum of comfort. There was no hardship; but there was no luxury and he had thought that he could get back into training that way. That in some way he could work the fat off his soul the way a fighter went into the mountains to work and train in order to burn it out of his body.

She had liked it. She said she loved it. She loved anything that was exciting, that involved a change of scene, where there were new people and where things were pleasant. And he had felt the illusion of returning strength of will to work. Now if this was how it ended, and he knew it was, he must not turn like some snake biting itself because its back was broken. It wasn't this woman's fault. If it had not been she it would have been another. If he lived by a lie he should try to die by it. He heard a shot beyond the hill.

She shot very well this good, this rich bitch, this kindly caretaker and destroyer of his talent. Nonsense. He had destroyed his talent himself. Why should he blame this woman because she kept him well? He had destroyed his talent by not using it, by betrayals of himself and what he believed in, by drinking so much that he blunted the edge of his perceptions, by laziness, by sloth, and by snobbery, by pride and by prejudice, by hook and by crook. What was this? A catalogue of old books? What was his talent anyway? It was a talent all right but instead of using it, he had traded on it. It was never what he had done, but always what he could do. And he had chosen to make his living with something else instead of a pen or a pencil. It was strange, too, wasn't it, that when he fell in love with another woman, that woman should always have more money than the last one? But when he no longer was in love, when he was only lying, as to this woman, now, who had the most money of all, who had all the money there was, who had had a husband and children, who had taken lovers and been dissatisfied with them, and who loved him dearly as a writer, as a man, as a companion and as a proud possession; it was strange that when he did not love her at all and was lying, that he should be able to give her more for her money than when he had really loved.

We must all be cut out for what we do, he thought. However you make your living is where your talent lies. He had sold vitality, in one form or another, all his life and when your affections are not too involved you give much better

profanity

value for the money. He had found that out but he would never write that, now, either. No, he would not write that, although it was well worth writing.

Now she came in sight, walking across the open toward the camp. She was wearing jodphurs and carrying her rifle. The two boys had a Tommie slung and they were coming along behind her. She was still a good-looking woman, he thought, and she had a pleasant body. She had a great talent and appreciation for the bed, she was not pretty, but he liked her face, she read enormously, liked to ride and shoot and, certainly, she drank too much. Her husband had died when she was still a comparatively young woman and for a while she had devoted herself to her two just-grown children, who did not need her and were embarrassed at having her about, to her stable of horses, to books, and to bottles. She liked to read in the evening before dinner and she drank Scotch and soda while she read. By dinner she was fairly drunk and after a bottle of wine at dinner she was usually drunk enough to sleep.

That was before the lovers. After she had the lovers she did not drink so much because she did not have to be drunk to sleep. But the lovers bored her. She had been married to a man who had never bored her and these people bored her very much.

Then one of her two children was killed in a plane crash and after that was over she did not want the lovers, and drink being no anaesthetic she had to make another life. Suddenly, she had been acutely frightened of being alone. But she wanted some one that she respected with her.

It had begun very simply. She liked what he wrote and she had always envied the life he led. She thought he did exactly what he wanted to. The steps by which she had acquired him and the way in which she had finally fallen in love with him were all part of a regular progression in which she had built herself a new life and he had traded away what remained of his old life.

He had traded it for security, for comfort too, there was no denying that, and for what else? He did not know. She would have bought him anything he wanted. He knew that. She was a damned nice woman too. He would as soon be in bed with her as any one; rather with her, because she was richer, because she was very pleasant and appreciative and because she never made scenes. And now this life that she had built again was coming to a term because he had not used iodine two weeks ago when a thorn had scratched his knee as they moved forward trying to photograph a herd of waterbuck standing, their heads up, peering while their nostrils searched the air, their ears spread wide to hear the first noise that would send them rushing into the bush. They had bolted, too, before he got the picture.

Here she came now.

He turned his head on the cot to look toward her. "Hello," he said.

"I shot a Tommy ram " she told him. "He'll make you good broth and I'll have them mash some potatoes with the Klim. How do you feel?"

"Much better."

"Isn't that lovely? You know I thought perhaps you would. You were sleeping when I left."

"I had a good sleep. Did you walk far?"

"No. Just around behind the hill. I made quite a good shot on the Tommy."

"You shoot marvellously, you know."

"I love it. I've loved Africa. Really, If *you're* all right it's the most fun that I've ever had. You don't know the fun it's been to shoot with you. I've loved the country."

"I love it too."

"Darling, you don't know how marvellous it is to see you feeling better. I couldn't stand it when you felt that way. You won't talk to me like that again, will you? Promise me?"

"No," he said. "I don't remember what I said."

"You don't have to destroy me. Do you? I'm only a middle-aged woman who loves you and wants to do what you want to do. I've been destroyed two or three times already. You wouldn't want to destroy me again, would you?"

"I'd like to destroy you a few times in bed," he said.

"Yes. That's the good destruction. That's the way we're made to be destroyed. The plane will be here tomorrow."

"How do you know?"

"I'm sure. It's bound to come. The boys have the wood all ready and the grass to make the smudge. I went down and looked at it again today. There's plenty of room to land and we have the smudges ready at both ends."

"What makes you think it will come tomorrow?"

"I'm sure it will. It's overdue now. Then, in town, they will fix up your leg and then we will have some good destruction. Not that dreadful talking kind."

"Should we have a drink? The sun is down."

"Do you think you should?"

"I'm having one."

"We'll have one together. *Molo, letti dui whiskey-soda!*" she called.

"You'd better put on your mosquito boots," he told her.

"I'll wait till I bathe . . ."

While it grew dark they drank and just before it was dark and there was no longer enough light to shoot, a hyena crossed the open on his way around the hill.

"That bastard crosses there every night," the man said. "Every night for two weeks."

"He's the one makes the noise at night. I don't mind it. They're a filthy animal though."

Drinking together, with no pain now except the discomfort of lying in the one position, the boys lighting a fire, its shadow jumping on the tents, he could feel the return of acquiescence in this life of pleasant surrender. She *was* very good to him. He had been cruel and unjust in the afternoon. She was a fine woman, marvellous really. And just then it occurred to him that he was going to die.

It came with a rush; not as a rush of water nor of wind; but of a sudden evil-smelling emptiness and the odd thing was that the hyena slipped lightly along the edge of it.

"What is it, Harry?" she asked him.

"Nothing," he said. "You had better move over to the other side. To windward."

"Did Molo change the dressing?"

"Yes. I'm just using the boric now."

"How do you feel?"

"A little wobbly."

"I'm going in to bathe," she said. "I'll be right out. I'll eat with you and then we'll put the cot in."

So, he said to himself, we did well to stop the quarrelling. He had never quarrelled much with this woman, while with the women that he loved he had quarrelled so much they had finally, always, with the corrosion of the quarrelling, killed what they had together. He had loved too much, demanded too much, and he wore it all out.

He thought about alone in Constantinople that time, having quarrelled in Paris before he had gone out. He had whored the whole time and then, when that was over, and he had failed to kill his loneliness, but only made it worse, he had written her, the first one, the one who left him, a letter telling her how he had never been able to kill it. . . . How when he thought he saw her outside the Regence one time it made him go all faint and sick inside, and that he would follow a woman who looked like her in some way, along the Boulevard, afraid to see it was not she, afraid to lose the feeling it gave him. How every one he had slept with had only made him miss her more. How what she had done could never matter since he knew he could not cure himself of loving her. He wrote this letter at the Club, cold sober, and mailed it to New York asking her to write him at the office in Paris. That seemed safe. And that night missing her so much it made him feel hollow sick inside, he wandered up past Taxim's, picked a girl up and took her out to supper. He had gone to a place to dance with her afterward, she danced badly, and left her for a hot Armenian slut, that swung her belly against him so it almost scalded. He took her away from a British gunner subaltern after a row. The gunner asked him outside and they fought in the street on the cobbles in the dark. He'd hit him twice, hard, on the side of the jaw and when he didn't go down he knew he was in for a fight. The gunner hit him in the body, then beside his eye. He swung with his left again and landed and the gunner fell on him and grabbed his coat and tore the sleeve off and he clubbed him twice behind the ear and then smashed him with his right as he pushed him away. When the gunner went down his head hit first and he ran with the girl because they heard the M. P.'s coming. They got into a taxi and drove out to Rimmily Hissa along the Bosphorus, and around, and back in the cool night and went to bed and she felt as over-ripe as she looked but smooth, rose-petal, syrupy, smooth-bellied, big-breasted and needed no pillow under her buttocks, and he left her before she was awake looking blousy enough in the first daylight and turned up at the Pera Palace with a black eye, carrying his coat because one sleeve was missing.

That same night he left for Anatolia and he remembered, later on that trip, riding all day through fields of the poppies that they raised for opium and how strange it made you feel, finally, and all the distances seemed wrong, to where they had made the attack with the newly arrived Constantine officers, that did not know a god-damned thing, and the artillery had fired into the troops and the British observer had cried like a child.

That was the day he'd first seen dead men wearing white ballet skirts and upturned shoes with pompons on them. The Turks had come steadily and lumpily and he had seen the skirted men running and the officers shooting into them and running then themselves and he and the British observer had run too until his lungs ached and his mouth was full of the taste of pennies and they stopped behind some rocks and there were the Turks coming as lumpily as ever. Later he had seen the things that he could never think of and later still he had seen much worse. So when he got back to Paris that time he could not talk about it or stand to have it mentioned. And there in the café as he passed was that American poet with a pile of saucers in front of him and a stupid look on his potato face talking about the Dada movement with a Roumanian who said his name was Tristan Tzara, who always wore a monocle and had a headache, and, back at the apartment with his wife that now he loved again, the quarrel all over, the madness all over, glad to be home, the office sent his mail up to the flat. So then the letter in answer to the one he'd written came in on a platter one morning and when he saw the handwriting he went cold all over and tried to slip the letter underneath another. But his wife said, "Who is that letter from, dear?" and that was the end of the beginning of that.

He remembered the good times with them all, and the quarrels. They always picked the finest places to have the quarrels. And why had they always quarrelled when he was feeling best? He had never written any of that because, at first, he never wanted to hurt any one and then it seemed as though there was enough to write without it. But he had always thought that he would write it finally. There was so much to write. He had seen the world change; not just the events; although he had seen many of them and had watched the people, but he had seen the subtler change and he could remember how the people were at different times. He had been in it and he had watched it and it was his duty to write of it; but now he never would.

"How do you feel?" she said. She had come out from the tent now after her bath.

"All right."

"Could you eat now?" He saw Molo behind her with the folding table and the other boy with the dishes.

"I want to write," he said.

"You ought to take some broth to keep your strength up."

"I'm going to die tonight," he said. "I don't need my strength up."

"Don't be melodramatic, Harry, please," she said.

"Why don't you use your nose? I'm rotted half way up my thigh now. What the hell should I fool with broth for? Molo bring whiskey-soda."

"Please take the broth," she said gently.

"All right."

The broth was too hot. He had to hold it in the cup until it cooled enough to take it and then he just got it down without gagging.

"You're a fine woman," he said. "Don't pay any attention to me."

She looked at him with her well-known, well-loved face from *Spur* and *Town and Country,* only a little the worse for drink, only a little the worse for bed, but *Town and Country* never showed those good breasts and those useful thighs and those lightly small-of-back-caressing hands, and as he looked and saw her well-known pleasant smile, he felt death come again. This time there was no rush. It was a puff, as of a wind that makes a candle flicker and the flame go tall.

"They can bring my net out later and hang it from the tree and build the fire up. I'm not going in the tent tonight. It's not worth moving. It's a clear night. There won't be any rain."

So this was how you died, in whispers that you did not hear. Well, there would be no more quarrelling. He could promise that. The one experience that he had never had he was not going to spoil now. He probably would. You spoiled everything. But perhaps he wouldn't.

"You can't take dictation, can you?"

"I never learned," she told him.

"That's all right."

There wasn't time, of course, although it seemed as though it telescoped so that you might put it all into one paragraph if you could get it right.

There was a log house, chinked white with mortar, on a hill above the lake. There was a bell on a pole by the door to call the people in to meals. Behind the house were fields and behind the fields was the timber. A line of lombardy poplars ran from the house to the dock. Other poplars ran along the point. A road went up to the hills along the edge of the timber and along that road he picked blackberries. Then that log house was burned down and all the guns that had been on deer foot racks above the open fire place were burned and afterwards their barrels, with the lead melted in the magazines, and the stocks burned away, lay out on the heap of ashes that were used to make lye for the big iron soap kettles, and you asked Grandfather if you could have them to play with, and he said, no. You see they were his guns still and he never bought any others. Nor did he hunt any more. The house was rebuilt in the same place out of lumber now and painted white and from its porch you saw the poplars and the lake beyond; but there were never any more guns. The barrels of the guns that had hung on the deer feet on the wall of the log house lay out there on the heap of ashes and no one ever touched them.

In the Black Forest, after the war, we rented a trout stream and there were two ways to walk to it. One was down the valley from Triberg and around the valley road in the shade of the trees that bordered the white road, and then up a side road that went up through the hills past many small farms, with the big Schwarzwald houses, until that road crossed the stream. That was where our fishing began.

The other way was to climb steeply up to the edge of the woods and then go across the top of the hills through the pine woods, and then out to the edge of a meadow and down across this meadow to the bridge. There were birches along the stream and it was not big, but narrow, clear and fast, with pools where it had cut under the roots of the birches. At the Hotel in Triberg the proprietor had a fine season. It was very pleasant and we were all great friends. The next year came the inflation and the money he had made the year before was not enough to buy supplies to open the hotel and he hanged himself.

You could dictate that, but you could not dictate the Place Contrescarpe where the flower sellers dyed their flowers in the street and the dye ran over the paving where the autobus started and the old men and the women, always drunk on wine and bad marc; and the children with their noses running in the cold; the smell of dirty sweat and poverty and drunkenness at the Café des Amateurs and the whores at the Bal Musette they lived above. The Concierge who entertained the trooper of the Garde Republicaine in her loge, his horse-hair-plumed helmet on a chair. The locataire[5] *across the hall whose husband was a bicycle racer and her joy*

5. One who rents, a roomer.

that morning at the Cremerie when she had opened L'Auto and seen where he placed third in Paris-Tours, his first big race. She had blushed and laughed and then gone upstairs crying with the yellow sporting paper in her hand. The husband of the woman who ran the Bal Musette drove a taxi and when he, Harry, had to take an early plane the husband knocked upon the door to wake him and they each drank a glass of white wine at the zinc of the bar before they started. He knew his neighbors in that quarter then because they all were poor.

Around that Place *there were two kinds; the drunkards and the sportifs. The drunkards killed their poverty that way; the sportifs took it out in exercise. They were the descendants of the Communards and it was no struggle for them to know their politics. They knew who had shot their fathers, their relatives, their brothers, and their friends when the Versailles troops came in and took the town after the Commune and executed any one they could catch with calloused hands, or who wore a cap, or carried any other sign he was a working man. And in that poverty, and in that quarter across the street from a Boucherie Chevaline and a wine co-operative he had written the start of all he was to do. There never was another part of Paris that he loved like that, the sprawling trees, the old white plastered houses painted brown below, the long green of the autobus in that round square, the purple flower dye upon the paving, the sudden drop down the hill of the rue Cardinal Lemoine to the River, and the other way the narrow crowded world of the rue Mouffetard. The street that ran up toward the Pantheon and the other that he always took with the bicycle, the only asphalted street in all that quarter, smooth under the tires, with the high narrow houses and the cheap tall hotel where Paul Verlaine had died. There were only two rooms in the apartments where they lived and he had a room on the top floor of that hotel that cost him sixty francs a month where he did his writing, and from it he could see the roofs and chimney pots and all the hills of Paris.*

From the apartment you could only see the wood and coal man's place. He sold wine too, bad wine. The golden horse's head outside the Boucherie Chevaline where the carcasses hung yellow gold and red in the open window, and the green painted co-operative where they bought their wine; good wine and cheap. The rest was plaster walls and the windows of the neighbors. The neighbors who, at night, when some one lay drunk in the street, moaning and groaning in that typical French ivresse[6] that you were propaganded to believe did not exist, would open their windows and then the murmur of talk.

"Where is the policeman? When you don't want him the bugger is always there. He's sleeping with some concierge. Get the Agent." Till some one threw a bucket of water from a window and the moaning stopped. "What's that? Water. Ah, that's intelligent." And the windows shutting. Marie, his femme de menage,[7] protesting against the eight-hour day saying, "If a husband works until six he gets only a little drunk on the way home and does not waste too much. If he works only until five he is drunk every night and one has no money. It is the wife of the working man who suffers from this shortening of hours."

"Wouldn't you like some more broth?" the woman asked him now.

---

6. Drunkenness.

7. Mistress.

"No, thank you very much. It is awfully good."

"Try just a little."

"I would like a whiskey-soda."

"It's not good for you."

"No. It's bad for me. Cole Porter wrote the words and the music. This knowledge that you're going mad for me."

"You know I like you to drink."

"Oh yes. Only it's bad for me."

When she goes, he thought. I'll have all I want. Not all I want but all there is. Ayee he was tired. Too tired. He was going to sleep a little while. He lay still and death was not there. It must have gone around another street. It went in pairs, on bicycles, and moved absolutely silently on the pavements.

No, he had never written about Paris. Not the Paris that he cared about. But what about the rest that he had never written?

What about the ranch and the silvered gray of the sage brush, the quick, clear water in the irrigation ditches, and the heavy green of the alfalfa. The trail went up into the hills and the cattle in the summer were shy as deer. The bawling and the steady noise and slow moving mass raising a dust as you brought them down in the fall. And behind the mountains, the clear sharpness of the peak in the evening light and, riding down along the trail in the moonlight, bright across the valley. Now he remembered coming down through the timber in the dark holding the horse's tail when you could not see and all the stories that he meant to write.

About the half-wit chore boy who was left at the ranch that time and told not to let any one get any hay, and that old bastard from the Forks who had beaten the boy when he had worked for him stopping to get some feed. The boy refusing and the old man saying he would beat him again. The boy got the rifle from the kitchen and shot him when he tried to come into the barn and when they came back to the ranch he'd been dead a week, frozen in the corral, and the dogs had eaten part of him. But what was left you packed on a sled wrapped in a blanket and roped on and you got the boy to help you haul it, and the two of you took it out over the road on skis, and sixty miles down to town to turn the boy over. He having no idea that he would be arrested. Thinking he had done his duty and that you were his friend and he would be rewarded. He'd helped to haul the old man in so everybody could know how bad the old man had been and how he'd tried to steal some feed that didn't belong to him, and when the sheriff put the handcuffs on the boy he couldn't believe it. Then he'd started to cry. That was one story he had saved to write. He knew at least twenty good stories from out there and he had never written one. Why?

"You tell them why," he said.

"Why what, dear?"

"Why nothing."

She didn't drink so much, now, since she had him. But if he lived he would never write about her, he knew that now. Nor about any of them. The rich were dull and they drank too much, or they played too much backgammon. They were dull and they were repetitious. He remembered poor Julian and his romantic awe of them and how he had started a story once that began, "The very rich are different from you and me." And how some one had said to Julian, Yes, they have more money. But that was not humorous to Julian. He thought they were a special glamorous race and when he found they weren't it wrecked him just as much as any other thing that wrecked him.

He had been contemptuous of those who wrecked. You did not have to like it because you understood it. He could beat anything, he thought, because no thing could hurt him if he did not care.

All right. Now he would not care for death. One thing he had always dreaded was the pain. He could stand pain as well as any man, until it went on too long, and wore him out, but here he had something that had hurt frightfully and just when he had felt it breaking him, the pain had stopped.

He remembered long ago when Williamson, the bombing officer, had been hit by a stick bomb some one in a German patrol had thrown as he was coming in through the wire that night and, screaming, had begged every one to kill him. He was a fat man, very brave, and a good officer, although addicted to fantastic shows. But that night he was caught in the wire, with a flare lighting him up and his bowels spilled out into the wire, so when they brought him in, alive, they had to cut him loose. Shoot me, Harry. For Christ sake shoot me. They had had an argument one time about our Lord never sending you anything you could not bear and some one's theory had been that meant that at a certain time the pain passed you out automatically. But he had always remembered Williamson, that night. Nothing passed out Williamson until he gave him all his morphine tablets that he had always saved to use himself and then they did not work right away.

Still this now, that he had, was very easy; and if it was no worse as it went on there was nothing to worry about. Except that he would rather be in better company.

He thought a little about the company that he would like to have.

No, he thought, when everything you do, you do too long, and do too late, you can't expect to find the people still there. The people all are gone. The party's over and you are with your hostess now.

I'm getting as bored with dying as with everything else, he thought.

"It's a bore," he said out loud.

"What is, my dear?"

"Anything you do too bloody long."

He looked at her face between him and the fire. She was leaning back in the chair and the firelight shone on her pleasantly lined face and he could see that she was sleepy. He heard the hyena make a noise just outside the range of the fire.

"I've been writing," he said. "But I got tired."

"Do you think you will be able to sleep?"

"Pretty sure. Why don't you turn in?"

"I like to sit here with you."

"Do you feel anything strange?" he asked her.

"No. Just a little sleepy."

"I do," he said.

He had just felt death come by again.

"You know the only thing I've never lost is curiosity," he said to her.

"You've never lost anything. You're the most complete man I've ever known."

"Christ," he said. "How little a woman knows. What is that? Your intuition?"

Because, just then, death had come and rested its head on the foot of the cot and he could smell its breath.

"Never believe any of that about a scythe and a skull," he told her. "It can be two bicycle policemen as easily, or be a bird. Or it can have a wide snout like a hyena."

It had moved up on him now, but it had no shape any more. It simply occupied space.

"Tell it to go away."

It did not go away but moved a little closer.

"You've got a hell of a breath," he told it. "You stinking bastard."   *Talking to Death*

It moved up closer to him still and now he could not speak to it, and when it saw he could not speak it came a little closer, and now he tried to send it away without speaking, but it moved in on him so its weight was all upon his chest, and while it crouched there and he could not move, or speak, he heard the woman say, "Bwana is asleep now. Take the cot up very gently and carry it into the tent."   *Dying*

He could not speak to tell her to make it go away and it crouched now, heavier, so he could not breathe. And then, while they lifted the cot, suddenly it was all right and the weight went from his chest.

It was morning and had been morning for some time and he heard the plane. It showed very tiny and then made a wide circle and the boys ran out and lit the fires, using kerosene, and piled on grass so there were two big smudges at each end of the level place and the morning breeze blew them toward the camp and the plane circled twice more, low this time, and then glided down and levelled off and landed smoothly and, coming walking toward him, was old Compton in slacks, a tweed jacket and a brown felt hat.

"What's the matter, old cock?" Compton said.

"Bad leg," he told him. "Will you have some breakfast?"

"Thanks. I'll just have some tea. It's the Puss Moth you know. I won't be able to take the Memsahib. There's only room for one. Your lorry is on the way."

Helen had taken Compton aside and was speaking to him. Compton came back more cheery than ever.

"We'll get you right in," he said. "I'll be back for the Mem. Now I'm afraid I'll have to stop at Arusha to refuel. We'd better get going."

"What about the tea?"

"I don't really care about it you know."

The boys had picked up the cot and carried it around the green tents and down along the rock and out onto the plain and along past the smudges that were burning brightly now, the grass all consumed, and the wind fanning the fire, to the little plane. It was difficult getting him in, but once in he lay back in the leather seat, and the leg was stuck straight out to one side of the seat where Compton sat. Compton started the motor and got in. He waved to Helen and to   *wife now*
the boys and, as the clatter moved into the old familiar roar, they swung around

with Compie watching for wart-hog holes and roared, bumping, along the stretch between the fires and with the last bump rose and he saw them all standing below, waving, and the camp beside the hill, flattening now, and the plain spreading, clumps of trees, and the bush flattening, while the game trails ran now smoothly to the dry waterholes, and there was a new water that he had never known of. The zebra, small rounded backs now, and the wildebeeste, big-headed dots seeming to climb as they moved in long fingers across the plain, now scattering as the shadow came toward them, they were tiny now, and the movement had no gallop, and the plain as far as you could see, gray-yellow now and ahead old Compie's tweed back and the brown felt hat. Then they were over the first hills and the wildebeeste were trailing up them, and then they were over mountains with sudden depths of green-rising forest and the solid bamboo slopes, and then the heavy forest again, sculptured into peaks and hollows until they crossed, and hills sloped down and then another plain, hot now, and purple brown, bumpy with heat and Compie looking back to see how he was riding. Then there were other mountains dark ahead.

And then instead of going on to Arusha they turned left, he evidently figured that they had the gas, and looking down he saw a pink sifting cloud, moving over the ground, and in the air, like the first snow in a blizzard, that comes from nowhere, and he knew the locusts were coming up from the South. Then they began to climb and they were going to the East it seemed, and then it darkened and they were in a storm, the rain so thick it seemed like flying through a waterfall, and then they were out and Compie turned his head and grinned and pointed and there, ahead, all he could see, as wide as all the world, great, high, and unbelievably white in the sun, was the square top of Kilimanjaro. And then he knew that there was where he was going.

Just then the hyena stopped whimpering in the night and started to make a strange, human, almost crying sound. The woman heard it and stirred uneasily. She did not wake. In her dream she was at the house on Long Island and it was the night before her daughter's début. Somehow her father was there and he had been very rude. Then the noise the hyena made was so loud she woke and for a moment she did not know where she was and she was very afraid. Then she took the flashlight and shone it on the other cot that they had carried in after Harry had gone to sleep. She could see his bulk under the mosquito bar but somehow he had gotten his leg out and it hung down alongside the cot. The dressings had all come down and she could not look at it.

"Molo," she called, "Molo! Molo!"

Then she said, "Harry, Harry!" Then her voice rising, "Harry! Please, Oh Harry!"

There was no answer and she could not hear him breathing.

Outside the tent the hyena made the same strange noise that had awakened her. But she did not hear him for the beating of her heart.

Fact Questions and Exercises

1. What kind of animal's "dried and frozen carcass" is on Mt. Kilimanjaro?

[handwritten: Africa]

2. In what country does the story take place? At what time? Cite specific details to support your answers.

3. What is happening to Harry in the story? *[handwritten: dying]* Why is it important that a truck or plane arrive soon? *[handwritten: help]*

4. Explain the pun on page 191, where Harry says "Your damned money was my armour. My Swift and my Armour."

5. Describe the circumstances under which Harry married his present wife.

6. What is Harry's profession? What does he regret about it? *[handwritten: Writer]*

7. Two kinds of animals are waiting about the camp. What are they? *[handwritten: Hyena]*

8. What has "a hell of a breath" and "rested its head on the foot of the cot"? *[handwritten: Death]*

For Discussion and Writing

1. Note the italicized passages. What do these represent? Is there any pattern to these passages? How do they make Harry's present condition more vivid or poignant? How, in general, do the passages add to the development of the story, insofar as symbols, themes, or characterizations are concerned?

2. Analyze Harry's character. What is his attitude toward love? Toward dying? Is his treatment of his wife justified? What is his attitude toward women in general? Do you like Harry?

3. One of the themes of the story is that money is the root of all evil, or that somehow money corrupts. How does Hemingway develop this theme? What values does he offer in lieu of money values?

4. Note the final paragraphs of the story, beginning on page 201 with the phrase "It was morning. . . ." How do you explain what happens in these concluding paragraphs? Is Harry dead at the beginning of these passages? If so, what is the meaning of Harry's death vision?

5. Check the definition of "naturalism" in the Guide to Literary Terms. Does this story exhibit naturalistic qualities? If so, cite some specific examples.

Jorge Luis Borges [1899–   ]

Borges was born in Buenos Aires, Argentina, the son of a novelist and poet. Borges traveled throughout Europe, and developed a great knowledge of world literature—a knowledge reflected in his translation of many foreign novels into Spanish. He served as Director of the National Library of Buenos Aires, but his opposition to Hitler and Juan Péron caused his fall from political favor. After World War II and the eventual ouster of Péron, however, Borges regained his status; and in 1956 he was appointed a professor of English and American literature at the University of Buenos Aires. Among his best-known works are *Ficciones* (1962), *Labyrinths* (1962), and *Dr. Brodie's Report* (1972). His stories combine reality, myth, and parable, and are often Kafka-like in their presentation of life's haunting complexity.

The Shape of the Sword

A spiteful scar crossed his face: an ash-colored and nearly perfect arc that creased his temple at one tip and his cheek at the other. His real name is of no importance; everyone in Tacuarembó called him the "Englishman from La Colorada." Cardoso, the owner of those fields, refused to sell them: I understand that the Englishman resorted to an unexpected argument: he confided to Cardoso the secret of the scar. The Englishman came from the border, from Río Grande del Sur; there are many who say that in Brazil he had been a smuggler. The fields were overgrown with grass, the waterholes brackish; the Englishman, in order to correct those deficiencies, worked fully as hard as his laborers. They say that he was severe to the point of cruelty, but scrupulously just. They say also that he drank: a few times a year he locked himself into an upper room, not to emerge until two or three days later as if from a battle or from vertigo, pale, trembling, confused and as authoritarian as ever. I remember the glacial eyes, the energetic leanness, the gray mustache. He had no dealings with anyone; it is a fact that his Spanish was rudimentary and cluttered with Brazilian. Aside from a business letter or some pamphlet, he received no mail.

The last time I passed through the northern provinces, a sudden overflowing of the Caraguatá stream compelled me to spend the night at La Colorada. Within a few moments, I seemed to sense that my appearance was inopportune; I tried to ingratiate myself with the Englishman; I resorted to the least discerning of passions: patriotism. I claimed as invincible a country with such spirit as England's. My companion agreed, but added with a smile that he was not English. He was Irish, from Dungarvan. Having said this, he stopped short, as if he had revealed a secret.

After dinner we went outside to look at the sky. It had cleared up, but beyond the low hills the southern sky, streaked and gashed by lightning, was conceiving another storm. Into the cleared up dining room the boy who had served dinner brought a bottle of rum. We drank for some time, in silence.

I don't know what time it must have been when I observed that I was drunk; I don't know what inspiration or what exultation or tedium made me mention the scar. The Englishman's face changed its expression; for a few seconds I thought he was going to throw me out of the house. At length he said in his normal voice:

"I'll tell you the history of my scar under one condition: that of not mitigating one bit of the opprobrium, of the infamous circumstances."

I agreed. This is the story that he told me, mixing his English with Spanish, and even with Portuguese:

"Around 1922, in one of the cities of Connaught, I was one of the many who were conspiring for the independence of Ireland. Of my comrades, some are still living, dedicated to peaceful pursuits; others, paradoxically, are fighting on desert and sea under the English flag; another, the most worthy, died in the courtyard of a barracks, at dawn, shot by men filled with sleep; still others (not the most unfortunate) met their destiny in the anonymous and almost secret battles of the civil war. We were Republicans, Catholics; we were, I suspect, Romantics. Ireland was for us not only the utopian future and the intolerable present; it was a bitter and cherished mythology, it was the circular towers and the red marshes, it was the repudiation of Parnell and the enormous epic poems which sang of the robbing of bulls which in another incarnation were heroes and in others fish and mountains . . . One afternoon I will never forget, an affiliate from Munster joined us: one John Vincent Moon.

"He was scarcely twenty years old. He was slender and flaccid at the same time; he gave the uncomfortable impression of being invertebrate. He had studied with fervor and with vanity nearly every page of Lord knows what Communist manual; he made use of dialectical materialism to put an end to any discussion whatever. The reasons one can have for hating another man, or for loving him, are infinite: Moon reduced the history of the universe to a sordid economic conflict. He affirmed that the revolution was predestined to succeed. I told him that for a gentleman only lost causes should be attractive . . . Night had already fallen; we continued our disagreement in the hall, on the stairs, then along the vague streets. The judgments Moon emitted impressed me less than his irrefutable, apodictic note. The new comrade did not discuss: he dictated opinions with scorn and with a certain anger.

"As we were arriving at the outlying houses, a sudden burst of gunfire stunned us. (Either before or afterwards we skirted the blank wall of a factory or barracks.) We moved into an unpaved street; a soldier, huge in the firelight, came out of a burning hut. Crying out, he ordered us to stop. I quickened my pace; my companion did not follow. I turned around: John Vincent Moon was motionless, fascinated, as if eternized by fear. I then ran back and knocked the soldier to the ground with one blow, shook Vincent Moon, insulted him and ordered him to follow. I had to take him by the arm; the passion of fear had rendered him helpless. We fled, into the night pierced by flames. A rifle volley reached out for us, and a bullet nicked Moon's right shoulder; as we were fleeing amid pines, he broke out in weak sobbing.

"In that fall of 1923 I had taken shelter in General Berkeley's country house. The general (whom I had never seen) was carrying out some administrative assignment or other in Bengal; the house was less than a century old, but it was decayed and shadowy and flourished in puzzling corridors and in pointless antechambers. The museum and the huge library usurped the first floor: controversial and uncongenial books which in some manner are the history of the nineteenth century; scimitars from Nishapur, along whose captured arcs there seemed to persist still the wind and violence of battle. We entered (I seem to recall) through the rear. Moon, trembling, his mouth parched, murmured that the events of the night were interesting; I dressed his wound and brought him a cup of tea; I was able to determine that his 'wound' was superficial. Suddenly he stammered in bewilderment:

" 'You know, you ran a terrible risk.'

"I told him not to worry about it. (The habit of the civil war had incited me to act as I did; besides, the capture of a single member could endanger our cause.)

"By the following day Moon had recovered his poise. He accepted a cigarette and subjected me to a severe interrogation on the 'economic resources of our revolutionary party.' His questions were very lucid; I told him (truthfully) that the situation was serious. Deep bursts of rifle fire agitated the south. I told Moon our comrades were waiting for us. My overcoat and my revolver were in my room; when I returned, I found Moon stretched out on the sofa, his eyes closed. He imagined he had a fever; he invoked a painful spasm in his shoulder.

"At that moment I understood that his cowardice was irreparable. I clumsily entreated him to take care of himself and went out. This frightened man mortified me, as if I were the coward, not Vincent Moon. Whatever one man does, it is as if all men did it. For that reason it is not unfair that one disobedience in a garden should contaminate all humanity; for that reason it is not unjust that the crucifixion of a single Jew should be sufficient to save it. Perhaps Schopenhauer was right: I am all other men, any man is all men, Shakespeare is in some manner the miserable John Vincent Moon.

"Nine days we spent in the general's enormous house. Of the agonies and the successes of the war I shall not speak: I propose to relate the history of the scar that insults me. In my memory, those nine days form only a single day, save for the next to the last, when our men broke into a barracks and we were able to avenge precisely the sixteen comrades who had been machinegunned in Elphin. I slipped out of the house towards dawn, in the confusion of daybreak. At nightfall I was back. My companion was waiting for me upstairs: his wound did not permit him to descend to the ground floor. I recall him having some volume of strategy in his hand, F. N. Maude or Clausewitz. 'The weapon I prefer is the artillery,' he confessed to me one night. He inquired into our plans; he liked to censure them or revise them. He also was accustomed to denouncing 'our deplorable economic basis'; dogmatic and gloomy, he predicted the disastrous end. *'C'est une affaire flambée,'*[1] he murmured. In order to show that he was indifferent to being a physical coward, he magnified his mental arrogance. In this way, for good or for bad, nine days elapsed.

"On the tenth day the city fell definitely to the Black and Tans. Tall, silent horsemen patrolled the roads; ashes and smoke rode on the wind; on the corner I saw a corpse thrown to the ground, an impression less firm in my memory than that of a dummy on which the soldiers endlessly practiced their marksmanship,

---

1. "It is a risky affair." *Flambée* implies ignition or flames.

in the middle of the square . . . I had left when dawn was in the sky; before noon I returned. Moon, in the library, was speaking with someone; the tone of his voice told me he was talking on the telephone. Then I heard my name; then, that I would return at seven; then, the suggestion that they should arrest me as I was crossing the garden. My reasonable friend was reasonably selling me out. I heard him demand guarantees of personal safety.

"Here my story is confused and becomes lost. I know that I pursued the informer along the black, nightmarish halls and along deep stairways of dizziness. Moon knew the house very well, much better than I. One or two times I lost him. I cornered him before the soldiers stopped me. From one of the general's collections of arms I tore a cutlass: with that half moon I carved into his face forever a half moon of blood. Borges, to you, a stranger, I have made this confession. Your contempt does not grieve me so much."

Here the narrator stopped. I noticed that his hands were shaking.

"And Moon?" I asked him.

"He collected his Judas money and fled to Brazil. That afternoon, in the square, he saw a dummy shot up by some drunken men."

I waited in vain for the rest of the story. Finally I told him to go on.

Then a sob went through his body; and with a weak gentleness he pointed to the whitish curved scar.

"You don't believe me?" he stammered. "Don't you see that I carry written on my face the mark of my infamy? I have told you the story thus so that you would hear me to the end. I denounced the man who protected me: I am Vincent Moon. Now despise me."

To E. H. M.

Fact Questions and Exercises

1. What nationality is the "Englishman"?
2. What is the Englishman's outstanding physical feature?
3. The Englishman speaks of a civil war. In what country does this war take place?
4. What is the name of the communist whose life the Englishman "saves"?
5. Who, in fact, is the Englishman?

For Discussion and Writing

1. Examine the literary and historical allusions in the story. Explain each of these references. How do they help clarify the narrator's character? How do they help clarify the story's meaning?
2. Borges uses the story-within-a-story technique in "The Shape of the Sword." Why is this effective?
3. Is Borges, in part, presenting a Christian parable? If so, which details suggest this fact? What is the moral?

Thomas Wolfe [1900–1938]

Wolfe was born in Asheville, North Carolina, and was educated at the University of North Carolina and Harvard. Wolfe wanted to be a playwright, but could never conform his rambling, poetic prose style to drama. He taught English composition at New York University, but soon quit to travel and devote himself to writing. The major part of his work consists of four long, autobiographical novels: *Look Homeward, Angel* (1929), *Of Time and the River* (1935), *The Web and the Rock* (1939), and *You Can't Go Home Again* (1940). "The Hollow Men," in a slightly different form, is part of this last novel.

The Hollow Men

How often have we read the paper in America! How often have we seen it *blocked* against our doors! Little route-boys fold and block it, so to throw it—and so we find it and unfold it, crackling and ink-laden, at our doors. Sometimes we find it tossed there lightly with flat *plop*; sometimes we find it thrown with solid, whizzing *whack* against the clapboards (clapboards here, most often, in America); sometimes servants find just freshly folded sheets laid neatly down in doorways, and take them to the table for their masters. No matter how it got there, we always find it.

How we do love the paper in America! How we do love the paper, all!

Why do we love the paper in America? Why do we love the paper, all?

Mad masters, I will tell ye why.

Because the paper is "the news" here in America, and we love the *smell* of news. We love the smell of news that's "fit to print." We also love the smell of news *not* fit to print. We love, besides, the smell of *facts* that news is made of. Therefore we love the paper because the news is so fit-printable—so unprintable—and so fact-printable.

Is the news, then, like America? No, it's not—

The news is *not* America, nor is America the *news*—the news is *in* America. It is a kind of light at morning, and at evening, and at midnight in America. It is a kind of growth and record and excrescence of our life. It is not good enough—it does not tell our story—yet it is the news!

Take the following, for instance:

An unidentified man fell or jumped yesterday at noon from the twelfth story of the Admiral Francis Drake Hotel in Brooklyn. The man, who was about thirty-five years old, registered at the hotel about a week ago, according to the police, as C. Green. Police are of the opinion that this was an assumed name. Pending identification, the body is being held at the King's County Morgue.

This, then, is news. Is it also the whole story, Admiral Drake? No! Yet we do not supply the whole story—we who have known all the lights and weathers of America.

Well, then, it's news, and it happened in your own hotel, brave Admiral Drake, so, of course, you'll want to know what happened.

"An unidentified man"—well, then, this man was an American. "About thirty-five years old" with "an assumed name"—well, then, call him C. Green as he called himself ironically in the hotel register. C. Green, the unidentified American, "fell or jumped," then, "yesterday at noon . . . in Brooklyn"—worth six lines of print in today's *Times*—one of seven thousand who died yesterday upon this continent—one of three hundred and fifty who died yesterday in this very city (see dense, close columns of obituaries, page 15: begin with "Aaronson," so through the alphabet to "Zorn"). C. Green came here "a week ago"—

And came from where? From the deep South, or the Mississippi Valley, or the Middle West? From Minneapolis, Bridgeport, Boston, or a little town in Old Catawba? From Scranton, Toledo, St. Louis, or the desert whiteness of Los Angeles? From the pine barrens of the Atlantic coastal plain, or from the Pacific shore?

And so—was *what*, brave Admiral Drake? In what way an American? In what way different from the men *you* knew, old Drake?

When the ships bore home again and Cape St. Vincent blazed in Spaniard's eye—or when old Drake was returning with his men, beating coastwise from strange seas abreast, past the Scilly Isles toward the slant of evening fields, chalk cliffs, the harbor's arms, the town's sweet cluster and the spire—where was Green?

When, in red-oak thickets at the break of day, coon-skinned, the huntsmen of the wilderness lay for bear, heard arrows rattling in the laurel leaves, the bullets' whining *plunk*, and waited with cocked musket by the tree—where was Green?

Or when, with strong faces turning toward the setting sun, hawk-eyed and Indian-visaged men bore gunstocks on the western trails and sternly heard the fierce war-whoops around the Painted Buttes—where, then, was Green?

Was never there with Drake's men in the evening when the sails stood in from the Americas! Was never there beneath the Spaniard's swarthy eye at Vincent's Cape! Was never there in the red-oak thicket in the morning! Was never there to hear the war-cries round the Painted Buttes!

No, no. He was no voyager of unknown seas, no pioneer of western trails. He was life's little man, life's nameless cipher, life's manswarm atom, life's American—and now he lies disjected and exploded on a street in Brooklyn!

He was a dweller in mean streets, was Green, a man-mote in the jungle of the city, a resident of grimy steel and stone, a stunned spectator of enormous salmon-colored towers, hued palely with the morning. He was a waker in bleak streets at morning, an alarm-clock watcher, saying, "Jesus, I'll be late!"—a fellow who took shortcuts through the corner lot, behind the advertising signs; a fellow used to concrete horrors of hot day and blazing noon; a man accustomed to the tormented hodgepodge of our architectures, used to broken pavements, ash cans, shabby store fronts, dull green paint, the elevated structure, grinding traffic, noise, and streets betortured with a thousand bleak and dismal signs. He was accustomed to the gas tanks going out of town, he was an atom of machinery in an endless flow, going, stopping, going to the winking of the lights; he tore down concrete roads on Sundays, past the hot-dog stands and filling stations; he would return at darkness; hunger lured him to the winking splendor of chop-suey signs; and midnight found him in The Coffee Pot, to prowl above a mug of coffee, tear a coffee cake in fragments, and wear away the slow grey ash of time and boredom with other men in grey hats and with skins of tallow-grey, at Joe the Greek's.

C. Green could read (which Drake could not), but not too accurately; could write, too (which the Spaniard couldn't), but not too well. C. Green had trouble over certain words, spelled them out above the coffee mug at midnight, with a furrowed brow, slow-shaping lips, and "Jesus!" when news stunned him—for he read the news. Preferred the news "hot," straight from the shoulder—socko!—biff!—straight off the griddle, with lots of mustard, shapely legs, roadside wrecks and mutilated bodies, gangsters' molls and gunmen's hide-outs, tallow faces of the night that bluntly stare at flashlight lenses—this and talk of "heart-balm," "love-thief," "sex-hijacker"—all of this liked Green.

Yes, Green liked the news—and now, a bit of news himself (six lines of print in the *Times*), has been disjected and exploded on a Brooklyn pavement!

Behold him, Admiral Drake! Observe the scene now! Listen to the people! Here's something strange as the Armadas, the gold-laden cargoes of the bearded Spaniards, the vision of unfound Americas!

What do you see here, Admiral Drake?

Well, first, a building—your own hotel—a great block of masonry, grimy-white, fourteen stories tall, stamped in an unvarying pattern with many windows. Sheeted glass below, the store front piled with medicines and toilet articles, perfumes, cosmetics, health contrivances. Within, a soda fountain, Admiral Drake. The men in white with monkey caps, soda jerkers sullen with perpetual overdriven irritation. Beneath the counter, pools of sloppy water, filth, and unwashed dishes. Across the counter, women with fat, rouged lips consuming ice cream sodas and pimento sandwiches.

Outside upon the concrete sidewalk lies the form of our exploded friend, C. Green. A crowd has gathered round—taxi drivers, passersby, hangers-on about the subway station, people working in the neighborhood, and the police. No one has dared to touch exploded Green as yet—they stand there in a rapt and fascinated circle, looking at him.

Not much to look at either, Admiral Drake; not even those who trod your gory decks would call the sight a pretty one. Our friend has landed on his head—"taken a nose dive," as we say—and smashed his brains out at the iron base of the second lamp post from the corner.

So here Green lies, on the concrete sidewalk all disjected. No head is left, the head is gone now, head's exploded; only brains are left. The brains are pink, and almost bloodless, Admiral Drake. (There's not much blood here—we shall tell you why.) But brains exploded are somewhat like pale sausage meat, freshground. Brains are stuck hard to the lamp post, too; there is a certain driven emphasis about them, as if they had been shot hydraulically out of a force-hose against the post.

The head, as we have said, is gone completely; a few fragments of the skull are scattered round—but of the face, the features, forehead—nothing! They have all been blown out, as by some inner explosion. Nothing is left but the back of the skull, which curiously remains, completely hollowed out and vacant, and curved over, like the rounded handle of a walking stick.

The body, five feet eight or nine of it, of middling weight, is lying—we were going to say "face downward"; had we not better say "stomach downward"? —on the sidewalk. And save for a certain indefinable and curiously "disjected" quality, one could scarcely tell that every bone in it is broken. The hands are still spread out, half-folded and half-clenched, with a still-warm and startling eloquence of recent life. (It happened just four minutes ago!)

Well, where's the blood, then, Drake? You're used to blood; you'd like to know. Well, you've heard of casting bread upon the waters, Drake, and having it return—but never yet, I'll vow, of casting blood upon the streets—and having it run away—and then come back to you! But here it comes now, down the street now toward C. Green, the lamp post, and the crowd!—a young Italian youth, his black eyes blank with horror, tongue mumbling thickly, arm held firmly by a policeman, suit and shirt all drenched with blood, and face bespattered with it! A stir of sudden interest in the crowd, sharp nudges, low-toned voices whispering:

"Here he is! Th' guy that 'got it'! . . . He was standin' *deh* beside the post! Sure, *that's* the guy!—talkin' to another guy—he got it all! That's the reason you didn't see more blood—*this* guy got it!—Sure! The guy just missed him by six inches!—Sure! I'm tellin' you I *saw* it, ain't I! I looked up an' saw him in the air! He'd a hit this guy, but when he saw that he was goin' to hit the lamp post, he put out his hands an' tried to keep away! *That's* the reason that he didn't hit this guy! . . . But this guy heard him when he hit, an' turned around—and zowie!—he got all of it right in his face!"

And another, whispering and nudging, nodding toward the horror-blank, thick-mumbling Italian boy: "Jesus! Look at th' guy, will yuh! . . . He don't know what he's doing! . . . He don't know yet what happened to him! . . . Sure! He got it *all*. I tell yuh! An' when it happened—when he got it—he just stahted runnin' . . . He don't know yet what happened! . . . That's what I'm tellin' yuh—th' guy just stahted runnin' when he got it."

And the Italian youth, thick-mumbling: ". . . Jeez! W'at happened? . . . Jeez! . . . I was standin' talkin' to a guy—I heard it hit . . . Jeez! . . . W'at happened, anyway? . . . I got it all over me! . . . Jeez! . . . I just stahted runnin' . . . Jeez! I'm sick!"

Voices: "Here, take 'im into the drugstore! . . . Wash 'im off! . . . That guy needs a shot of liquor! . . . Sure! Take him into the drugstoeh *deh*! . . . *They'll* fix him up!"

The plump young man who runs the newsstand in the corridor, talking to everyone around him, excitedly and indignantly: ". . . Did I see it? Listen! I saw *everything!* I was coming across the street, looked up, and saw him in the air! . . . See it? . . . *Listen!* If someone had taken a big ripe watermelon and dropped it on the street from the fourteenth floor you'd have some idea what it was like! . . . See it! *I'll* tell the world I saw it! I don't want to see anything like *that* again!" Then excitedly, with a kind of hysterical indignation: "Shows no consideration for other people, that's all *I've* got to say! If a man is going to do a thing like that, why does he pick a place like *this*—one of the busiest corners in Brooklyn? . . . How did *he* know he wouldn't hit someone? Why, if that boy had been standing six inches nearer to the post, he'd have killed him, as sure as you live! . . . And here he does it right in front of all these people who have to look at it! It shows he had no consideration for other people! A man who'd do a thing like that. . . ."

(Alas, poor youth! As if C. Green, now past considering, had considered nice "considerations.")

A taxi driver, impatiently: "That's what I'm tellin' yuh! . . . I watched him for five minutes before he jumped. He crawled out on the window sill an' stood there for *five* minutes, makin' up his mind! . . . Sure, I saw him! Lots of people saw him!" Impatiently, irritably: "Why didn't we *do* somethin' to stop him? F'r Chri' sake, what was there to do? A guy who'd do a thing like that is nuts to start with! You don't think he'd listen to anything *we* had to say, do you? . . . Sure, we *did* yell at him! . . . Jesus! . . . We was almost *afraid* to yell at him—we made motions to him to get back—tried to hold his attention while the cops sneaked round the corner into the hotel. . . . Sure, the cops got there just a second after he jumped—I don't know if he jumped when he heard 'em comin', or what happened, but Christ!— he stood there gettin' ready for five minutes while we watched!"

Observe now, Admiral, with what hypnotic concentration the people are examining the grimy-white facade of your hotel. Watch their faces and expressions. Their eyes go traveling upward slowly—up—up—up until they finally arrive and come to rest with focal concentration on that single open window twelve floors up. It is no jot different from all the other windows, but now the vision of the crowd is fastened on it with a fatal and united interest. And after staring at it fixedly, the eyes come traveling slowly down again—down—down—down—the faces strained a little, mouths all slightly puckered as if something set the teeth on edge—and slowly, with fascinated measurement—down—down—down—until the eyes reach sidewalk, lamp post, and—the Thing again.

The pavement finally halts all, stops all, answers all. It is the American pavement, Admiral Drake, our universal city sidewalk, a wide, hard stripe of grey-white cement, blocked accurately with dividing lines. It is the hardest, coldest, cruellest, most impersonal pavement in the world: all of the indifference, the atomic desolation, the exploded nothingness of one hundred million nameless "Greens" is in it.

It came from the same place where all our sidewalks come from—from Standard Concentrated Production Units of America, No. 1. This is where all our streets and lamp posts (like the one on which Green's brains are spattered) come from, where all our white-grimy bricks (like those of which your hotel is constructed) come from, where the red facades of our standard-unit tobacco stores (like the one across the street) come from, where our motor cars come from, where our drugstores and our drugstore windows and displays come from, where our soda fountains (complete, with soda jerkers attached) come from, where our cosmetics, toilet articles, and the fat, rouged lips of our women come from, where our soda water, slops and syrups, steamed spaghetti, ice cream, and pimento sandwiches come from, where our clothes, our hats (neat, standard stamps of grey), our faces (also stamps of grey, not always neat), our language, conversation, sentiments, feelings, and opinions come from. All these things are made for us by Standard Concentrated Production Units of America, No. 1.

So here we are, then, Admiral Drake. You see the street, the sidewalk, the front of your hotel, the constant stream of motor cars, the cops in uniform, the people streaming in and out of the subway, the rusty, pale-hued jungle of the buildings, old and new, high and low. There is no better place to see it, Drake. For this is Brooklyn—which means ten thousand streets and blocks like this one.

Brooklyn, Admiral Drake, is the Standard Concentrated Chaos No. 1 of the Whole Universe. That is to say, it has no size, no shape, no heart, no joy, no hopes, no aspiration, no center, no eyes, no soul, no purpose, no direction, and no anything—just Standard Concentrated Units everywhere—exploding in all directions for an unknown number of square miles like a completely triumphant Standard Concentrated Blot upon the Face of the Earth. And here, right in the middle, upon a minute portion of this magnificent Standard Concentrated Blot, where all the Standard Concentrated Blotters can stare at him, and with the brains completely out of him—

    —Lies Green!

    And this is bad—most bad—oh, *very* bad—and should not be allowed! For, as our young news-vendor friend has just indignantly proclaimed, it "shows no consideration for other people"—which means, for other Standard Concentrated Blotters, Green has no right to go falling in this fashion in a public place. He has no business *being* where he is at all. A Standard Concentrated Blotter is not supposed to *be* places, but to *go* places.

    You see, dear Admiral, this sidewalk, this Standard Concentrated Mobway, is not a place to walk on, really. It is a place to swarm on, to weave on, to thrust and dodge on, to scurry past on, to crowd by on. One of the earliest precepts in a Concentrated Blotter's life is: "Move on there! Where th' hell d'you think you are, anyway—in a cow pasture?"

    And, most certainly, it is not a place to lie on, to sprawl out on.

    But look at Green! Just *look* at him! No wonder the plump youth is angry with him!

    Green has willfully and deliberately violated every Standard Concentrated Principle of Blotterdom. He has not only gone and dashed his brains out, but he has done it in a public place—upon a piece of Standard Concentrated Mobway. He has messed up the sidewalk, messed up another Standard Concentrated Blotter, stopped traffic, taken people from their business, upset the nerves of his fellow Blotters—and now *lies* there, all *sprawled* out, in a place where he has no right to *be*. And, to make his crime unpardonable, C. Green has—

    —Come to Life!

    What's that, Admiral? You do not understand it? Small wonder, though it's really very simple:

    For just ten minutes since, C. Green was a Concentrated Blotter like the rest of us, a nameless atom, swarming with the rest of us, just another "guy" like a hundred million other "guys." But now, observe him! No longer is he just "another guy"—already he has become a "special guy"—he has become "*The* Guy." C. Green at last has turned into a—*Man*!

Fact Questions and Exercises

1. Why, according to Wolfe, do Americans love the newspaper?
2. In which paragraph of the story is Wolfe quoting a newspaper article? How do you know Wolfe is quoting in this paragraph?
3. What is the name of the hotel from which C. Green jumps?
4. Wolfe uses the word "disjected" several times. What does this word mean?

5. Identify the "Italian youth."
6. What is the news vendor's reaction to Green's jumping onto a public sidewalk?
7. According to the taxi driver, how long did Green stand on the ledge before jumping?
8. How many different nationalities of people does Wolfe mention in the story? Name some of them.

For Discussion and Writing

1. Is there any significance in the name "C. Green"? Why does Wolfe use a phony name? Why does he keep Green's background vague? What characterization does he create for Green?
2. Is the name of the hotel important? What connection does Wolfe make between the hotel and the man for whom it is named? Does Wolfe convey an historical perspective of America? Numerous nationalities make up the "Americans" who gather at the scene. How does this variety help Wolfe characterize America?
3. How does Wolfe impart the horror of Green's suicide? Are his descriptions of Green's body ironic or sarcastic. If so, what is the point of his irony or sarcasm? Does he condemn America and its values? Does he praise any American values? In what sense has Green "turned into a—*Man!*"?

Robert Penn Warren [1905–   ]

Warren was born in rural Kentucky, and was educated at Vanderbilt University. He received a Rhodes Scholarship to Oxford University, and then returned to America to teach at several universities. He is still active as a teacher, scholar, and writer. Perhaps more respected as a literary critic than as a writer of fiction, Warren has nonetheless published some outstanding stories and novels, including *All the King's Men* (1946), *The Circus in the Attic* (1947), and *The Cave* (1959). *Understanding Poetry* (1938) and *Understanding Fiction* (1943), written with Cleanth Brooks, have been two of the most influential critical texts in American education.

When the Light Gets Green

My grandfather had a long white beard and sat under the cedar tree. The beard, as a matter of fact, was not very long and not white, only gray, but when I was a child and was away from him at school during the winter, I would think of him, not seeing him in my mind's eye, and say: He has a long white beard. Therefore, it was a shock to me, on the first morning back home, to watch him lean over the dresser toward the wavy green mirror, which in his always shadowy room reflected things like deep water riffled by a little wind, and clip his gray beard to a point. It is gray and pointed, I would say then, remembering what I had thought before.

He turned his face to the green wavy glass, first one side and then the other in quarter profile, and lifted the long shears which trembled a little, to cut the beard. His face being turned like that, with his good nose and pointed gray beard, he looked like General Robert E. Lee, without any white horse to ride. My grandfather had been a soldier, too, but now he wore blue-jean pants and when he leaned over like that toward the mirror, I couldn't help but notice how small his hips and backsides were. Only they weren't just small, they were shrunken. I noticed how the blue jeans hung loose from his suspenders and loose off his legs and down around his shoes. And in the morning when I noticed all this about his legs and backsides, I felt a tight feeling in my stomach like when you walk behind a woman and see the high heel of her shoe is worn and twisted and jerks her ankle every time she takes a step.

Always before my grandfather had finished clipping his beard, my Uncle Kirby came to the door and beat on it for breakfast. "I'll be down in just a minute, thank you, sir," my grandfather said. My uncle called him Mr. Barden. "Mr. Barden, breakfast is ready." It was because my Uncle Kirby was not my real uncle, having married my Aunt Lucy, who lived with my grandfather. Then my grandfather put on a black vest and put his gold watch and chain in the vest and picked up his cob pipe from the dresser top, and he and I went down to breakfast, after Uncle Kirby was already downstairs.

When he came into the dining room, Aunt Lucy was sitting at the foot of the table with the iron coffee pot on a plate beside her. She said, "Good morning, Papa."

"Good morning, Lucy," he said, and sat down at the head of the table, taking one more big puff off his pipe before laying it beside his plate.

"You've brought that old pipe down to breakfast again," my aunt said, while she poured the bright-looking coffee into the cups.

"Don't it stink," he always said.

My uncle never talked at breakfast, but when my granfather said that, my uncle always opened his lips to grin like a dog panting, and showed his hooked teeth. His teeth were yellow because he chewed tobacco, which my grandfather didn't do, although his beard was yellow around the mouth from smoking. Aunt Lucy didn't like my uncle to chew, that was the whole trouble. So she rode my grandfather for bringing his pipe down, all in fun at first before she got serious about it. But he always brought it down just the same, and said to her, "Don't it stink."

After we ate, my uncle got up and said, "I got to get going," and went out through the kitchen where the cook was knocking and sloshing around. If it had rained right and was a good tobacco-setting season, my grandfather went off with me down to the stable to get his mare, for he had to see the setting. We saddled up the mare and went across the lot, where limestone bunched out of the ground and cedar trees and blue grass grew out of the split rock. A branch of cold water with minnows in it went through the lot between rocks and under the cedar trees; it was where I used to play before I got big enough to go to the river with the niggers to swim.

My grandfather rode across the lot and over the rise back of the house. He sat up pretty straight for an old man, holding the bridle in his left hand, and in his right hand a long hickory tobacco stick whittled down to make a walking cane. I walked behind him and watched the big straw hat he wore waggle a little above his narrow neck, or how he held the stick in the middle, firm and straight up like something carried in a parade, or how smooth and slow the muscles in the mare's flanks worked as she put each hoof down in the ground, going up hill. Sassafras bushes and blackberry bushes grew thick along the lane over the rise. In summer, tufts of hay would catch and hang on the dry bushes and showed that the hay wagons had been that way; but when we went that way in setting time, just after breakfast, the blackberry blooms were hardly gone, only a few rusty patches of white left, and the sassafras leaves showed still wet with dew or maybe the rain.

From the rise we could look back on the house. The shingles were black with damp, and the whitewash grayish, except in spots where the sun already struck it and it was drying. The tops of the cedar trees, too, were below us, very dark green and quiet. When we crossed the rise, there were the fields going down toward the river, all checked off and ready for setting, very even, only for the gullies where brush was piled to stop the washing. The fields were reddish from the wet, not yet steaming. Across them, the green woods and the sycamores showing white far off told where the river was.

The hands were standing at the edge of the field under the trees when we got there. The little niggers were filling their baskets with the wet plants to drop, and I got me a basket and filled it. My Uncle Kirby gave me fifty cents for dropping plants, but he didn't give the little niggers that much, I remember. The hands and women stood around waiting a minute, watching Uncle Kirby, who always fumed around, waving his dibble, his blue shirt already sticking to his arms with sweat. "Get the lead out," he said. The little niggers filled faster, grinning with their teeth at him. "Goddam, get the lead out!" My grandfather sat on his mare under the trees, still holding the walking cane, and said, "Why don't you start 'em, sir?"

Then, all of a sudden, they all moved out into the field, scattering out down the rows, the droppers first, and after a minute the setters, who lurched along, never straightening up, down the rows toward the river. I walked down my row, separating out the plants and dropping them at the hills, while it got hotter and the ground steamed. The sun broke out now and then, making my shadow on the ground, then the cloud would come again, and I could see its shadow drifting at me on the red field.

My grandfather rode very slow along the edge of the field to watch the setting, or stayed still under the trees. After a while, maybe about ten o'clock, he would leave and go home. I could see him riding the mare up the rise and then go over the rise; or if I was working the other way toward the river, when I turned round at the end, the lane would be empty and nothing on top of the rise, with the cloudy, blue-gray sky low behind it.

The tobacco was all he cared about, now we didn't have any horses that were any real good. He had some silver cups, only one real silver one though, that his horses won at fairs, but all that was before I was born. The real silver one, the one he kept on his dresser and kept string and old minnie balls and pins and things in, had *1859* on it because his horse won it then before the War, when he was a young man. Uncle Kirby said horses were foolishness, and Grandfather said, yes, he reckoned horses were foolishness, all right. So what he cared about now was the tobacco. One time he was a tobacco-buyer for three years, but after he bought a lot of tobacco and had it in his sheds, the sheds burned up on him. He didn't have enough insurance to do any good and he was a ruined man. After that all his children, he had all girls and his money was gone, said about him, "Papa's just visionary, he tried to be a tobacco-buyer but he's too visionary and not practical." But he always said, "All tobacco-buyers are sons-of-bitches, and three years is enough of a man's life for him to be a son-of-a-bitch, I reckon." Now he was old, the corn could get the rust or the hay get rained on for all he cared, it was Uncle Kirby's worry, but all summer, off and on, he had to go down to the tobacco field to watch them sucker or plow or worm, and sometimes he pulled a few suckers himself. And when a cloud would blow up black in summer, he got nervous as a cat, not knowing whether it was the rain they needed or maybe a hail storm coming that would cut the tobacco up bad.

Mornings he didn't go down to the field, he went out under the cedar tree where his chair was. Most of the time he took a book with him along with his pipe, for he was an inveterate reader. His being an inveterate reader was one of the things made his children say he was visionary. He read a lot until his eyes went bad the summer before he had his stroke, then after that, I read to him some, but not as much as I ought. He used to read out loud some from Macaulay's *History of England* or Gibbon's *Decline and Fall*, about Flodden Field or about how the Janizaries took Constantinople amid great slaughter and how the Turk surveyed the carnage and quoted from the Persian poet about the lizard keeping the courts of the mighty. My grandfather knew some poetry, too, and he said it to himself when he didn't have anything else to do. I lay on my back on the ground, feeling the grass cool and tickly on the back of my neck, and looked upside down into the cedar tree where the limbs were tangled and black-green like big hairy fern fronds with the sky blue all around, while he said some poetry. Like the "Isles of Greece, the Isles of Greece, where burning Sappho loved and sung." Or like "Roll on, thou deep and dark blue ocean, roll."

But he never read poetry, he just said what he already knew. He only read history and *Napoleon and His Marshals*, having been a soldier and fought in the War himself. He rode off and joined the cavalry, but he never told me whether he took the horse that won the real silver cup or not. He was with Forrest before Forrest was a general. He said Forrest was a great general, and if they had done what Forrest wanted and cleaned the country ahead of the Yankees, like the Russians beat Napoleon, they'd whipped the Yankees sure. He told me about Fort Donelson, how they fought in the winter woods, and how they got away with Forrest at night, splashing through the cold water. And how the dead men looked in the river bottoms in winter, and I lay on my back on the grass, looking up in the thick cedar limbs, and thought how it was to be dead.

After Shiloh was fought and they pushed the Yankees down in the river, my grandfather was a captain, for he raised a cavalry company of his own out of West Tennessee. He was a captain, but he never got promoted after the War; when I was a little boy everybody still called him Captain Barden, though they called lots of other people in our section Colonel and Major. One time I said to him: "Grandpa, did you ever kill any Yankees?" He said: "God-a-Mighty, how do I know?" So, being little, I thought he was just a captain because he never killed anybody, and I was ashamed. He talked about how they took Fort Pillow, and the drunk niggers under the bluff. And one time he said niggers couldn't stand a charge or stand the cold steel, so I thought maybe he killed some of them. But then I thought, Niggers don't count, maybe.

He only talked much in the morning. Almost every afternoon right after dinner, he went to sleep in his chair, with his hands curled up in his lap, one of them holding the pipe that still sent up a little smoke in the shadow, and his head propped back on the tree trunk. His mouth hung open, and under the hairs of his mustache, all yellow with nicotine, you could see his black teeth and his lips that were wet and pink like a baby's. Usually I remember him that way, asleep.

I remember him that way, or else trampling up and down the front porch, nervous as a cat, while a cloud blew up and the trees began to rustle. He tapped his walking cane on the boards and whistled through his teeth with his breath and kept looking off at the sky where the cloud and sometimes the lightning was. Then of a sudden it came, and if it was rain he used to go up to his room and lie down; but if it came hail on the tobacco, he stayed on the front porch, not trampling any more, and watched the hail rattle off the roof and bounce soft on the grass. "God-a-Mighty," he always said, "bigger'n minnie balls," even when it wasn't so big.

In 1914, just before the war began, it was a hot summer with the tobacco mighty good but needing rain. And when the dry spell broke and a cloud blew up, my grandfather came out on the front porch, watching it like that. It was mighty still, with lightning way off, so far you couldn't hardly hear the thunder. Then the leaves began to ruffle like they do when the light gets green, and my grandfather said to me, "Son, it's gonna hail." And he stood still. Down in the pasture, that far off, you could see the cattle bunching up and the white horse charging across the pasture, looking bright, for the sun was shining bright before the cloud struck it all at once. "It's gonna hail," my grandfather said. It was dark, with jagged lightning and the thunder high and steady. And there the hail was.

He just turned around and went in the house. I watched the hail bouncing, then I heard a noise and my aunt yelled. I ran back in the dining room where the noise was, and my grandfather was lying on the floor with the old silver pitcher he dropped and a broken glass. We tried to drag him, but he was too heavy; then my Uncle Kirby came up wet from the stable and we carried my grandfather upstairs and put him on his bed. My aunt tried to call the doctor even if the lightning might hit the telephone. I stayed back in the dining room and picked up the broken glass and the pitcher and wiped up the floor with a rag. After a while Dr. Blake came from town; then he went away.

When Dr. Blake was gone, I went upstairs to see my grandfather. I shut the door and went in his room, which was almost dark, like always, and quiet because the hail didn't beat on the roof any more. He was lying on his back in the featherbed, with a sheet pulled up over him, lying there in the dark. He had his hands curled loose on his stomach, like when he went to sleep in his chair holding the pipe. I sat on a split-bottom chair by the bed and looked at him: he had his eyes shut and his mouth hung loose, but you couldn't hear his breathing. Then I quit looking at him and looked round the room, my eyes getting used to the shadow. I could see his pants on the floor, and the silver cup on the dresser by the mirror, which was green and wavy like water.

When he said something, I almost jumped out of my skin, hearing his voice like that. He said, "Son, I'm gonna die." I tried to say something, but I couldn't. And he waited, then he said, "I'm on borrowed time, it's time to die." I said, "No!" so sudden and loud I jumped. He waited a long time and said, "It's time to die. Nobody loves me." I tried to say, "Grandpa, I love you." And then I did say it all right, feeling like it hadn't been me said it, and knowing all of a sudden it was a lie, because I didn't feel anything. He just lay there; and I went downstairs.

It was sunshiny in the yard, the clouds gone, but the grass was wet. I walked down toward the gate, rubbing my bare feet over the slick cold grass. A hen was in the yard and she kept trying to peck up a piece of hail, like a fool chicken will do after it hails; but every time she pecked it, it bounced away from her over the green grass. I leaned against the gate, noticing the ground on one side the posts, close up, was still dry and dusty. I wondered if the tobacco was cut up bad, because Uncle Kirby had gone to see. And while I looked through the gate down across the pasture where everything in the sun was green and shiny with wet and the cattle grazed, I thought about my grandfather, not feeling anything. But I said out loud anyway, "Grandpa, I love you."

My grandfather lived four more years. The year after his stroke they sold the farm and moved away, so I didn't stay with them any more. My grandfather died in 1918, just before the news came that my Uncle Kirby was killed in France, and my aunt had to go to work in a store. I got the letter about my grandfather, who died of flu, but I thought about four years back, and it didn't matter much.

Fact Questions and Exercises

1. Who is the narrator of the story?
2. What crop (in which Mr. Barden is so interested) is cultivated on the farm?
3. What is the setting of the story? Point out details to support your answer.
4. What specific event causes Mr. Barden's financial ruin?
5. What types of books does Mr. Barden read? What are the titles of some of these books?
6. Why does Mr. Barden go to his room to die? Explain the circumstances.

For Discussion and Writing

1. Comment on the way in which Warren uses symbols. Note particularly the emphasis on colors. What do the various symbols represent? How do they help in understanding the meaning of the story?
2. Who is the most important person in the story—Mr. Barden or the narrator? Develop a character sketch of this person to support your choice.
3. In the story a grown man narrates events from his childhood. How effective is this dual-perspective form of narrative? Does the reader understand things about the grandfather that the boy-narrator does not?

dora Welty [1909–   ]

..y was born in Jackson, Mississippi, and was educated at the University of Wisconsin and Columbia University. She has spent most of her life in Mississippi, which serves as the background for her fiction. Welty, like Faulkner, is a distinctly Southern writer, but her fiction is universal because of its adept use of symbols, myth, and distinct characters. Welty has commented in depth about her own writing and fiction in general in an essay entitled "How I Write" (1955). Among her best-known works are *A Curtain of Green and other Stories* (1941), *Delta Wedding* (1946), and *The Ponder Heart* (1954).

A Worn Path

It was December—a bright frozen day in the early morning. Far out in the country there was an old Negro woman with her head tied in a red rag, coming along a path through the pinewoods. Her name was Phoenix Jackson. She was very old and small and she walked slowly in the dark pine shadows, moving a little from side to side in her steps, with the balanced heaviness and lightness of a pendulum in a grandfather clock. She carried a thin, small cane made from an umbrella, and with this she kept tapping the frozen earth in front of her. This made a grave and persistent noise in the still air, that seemed meditative, like the chirping of a solitary little bird.

She wore a dark striped dress reaching down to her shoetops, and an equally long apron of bleached sugar sacks, with a full pocket; all neat and tidy, but every time she took a step she might have fallen over her shoe-laces, which dragged from her unlaced shoes. She looked straight ahead. Her eyes were blue with age. Her skin had a pattern all its own of numberless branching wrinkles and as though a whole little tree stood in the middle of her forehead, but a golden color run underneath, and the two knobs of her cheeks were illuminated by a yellow burning under the dark. Under the red rag her hair came down on her neck in the frailest of ringlets, still black, and with an odor like copper.

Now and then there was a quivering in the thicket. Old Phoenix said, "Out of my way, all you foxes, owls, beetles, jack rabbits, coons, and wild animals! . . . Keep out from under these feet, little bobwhites. . . . Keep the big wild hogs out of my path. Don't let none of those come running my direction. I got a long way." Under her small black-freckled hand her cane, limber as a buggy whip, would switch at the brush as if to rouse up any hiding things.

On she went. The woods were deep and still. The sun made the pine needles almost too bright to look at, up where the wind rocked. The cones dropped as light as feathers. Down in the hollow was the mourning dove—it was not too late for him.

The path ran up a hill. "Seem like there is chains about my feet, time I get this far," she said, in the voice of argument old people keep to use with themselves. "Something always take a hold on this hill—pleads I should stay."

After she got to the top she turned and gave a full, severe look behind her where she had come. "Up through pines," she said at length. "Now down through oaks." *down hill*

Her eyes opened their widest and she started down gently. But before she got to the bottom of the hill a bush caught her dress.

Her fingers were busy and intent, but her skirts were full and long, so that before she could pull them free in one place they were caught in another. It was not possible to allow the dress to tear. "I in the thorny bush," she said. "Thorns, you doing your appointed work. Never want to let folks pass—no sir. Old eyes thought you was a pretty little green bush."

Finally, trembling all over, she stood free, and after a moment dared to stoop for her cane.

"Sun so high!" she cried, leaning back and looking, while the thick tears went over her eyes. "The time getting all gone here."

At the foot of this hill was a place where a log was laid across the creek. *cross log*

"Now comes the trial," said Phoenix.

Putting her right foot out, she mounted the log and shut her eyes. Lifting her skirt, levelling her cane fiercely before her, like a festival figure in some parade, she began to march across. Then she opened her eyes and she was safe on the other side.

"I wasn't as old as I thought," she said.

But she sat down to rest. She spread her skirts on the bank around her and folded her hands over her knees. Up above her was a tree in a pearly cloud of mistletoe. She did not dare to close her eyes, and when a little boy brought her a little plate with a slice of marble-cake on it she spoke to him. "That would be acceptable," she said. But when she went to take it there was just her own hand in the air.

So she left that tree, and had to go through a barbed-wire fence. There *through* she had to creep and crawl, spreading her knees and stretching her fingers like a *barbed-wire* baby trying to climb the steps. But she talked loudly to herself: she could not let *fence* her dress be torn now, so late in the day, and she could not pay for having her arm or her leg sawed off if she got caught fast where she was.

At last she was safe through the fence and risen up out in the clearing. Big dead trees, like black men with one arm, were standing in the purple stalks of the *withered* withered cotton field. There sat a buzzard. *cotton*

"Who you watching?" *field*

In the furrow she made her way along.

"Glad this not the season for bulls," she said, looking sideways, "and the good Lord made his snakes to curl up and sleep in the winter. A pleasure I don't see no two-headed snake coming around that tree, where it come once. It took a while to get by him, back in the summer."

She passed through the old cotton and went into a field of dead corn. It *dead corn* whispered and shook, and was taller than her head. "Through the maze now," she said, for there was no path.

Then there was something tall, black and skinny there, moving before her.

At first she took it for a man. It could have been a man dancing in the field. But she stood still and listened, and it did not make a sound. It was as silent as a ghost.

"Ghost," she said sharply, "who be you the ghost of? For I have heard of nary death close by."

But there was no answer, only the ragged dancing in the wind.

She shut her eyes, reached out her hand, and touched a sleeve. She found a coat and inside that an emptiness, cold as ice.

"You scarecrow," she said. Her face lighted. "I ought to be shut up for good," she said with laughter. "My senses is gone. I too old. I the oldest people I ever know. Dance, old scarecrow," she said, "while I dancing with you."

She kicked her foot over the furrow, and with mouth drawn down shook her head once or twice in a little strutting way. Some husks blew down and whirled in streamers about her skirts.

Then she went on, parting her way from side to side with the cane, through the whispering field. At last she came to the end, to a wagon track, where the silver grass blew between the red ruts. The quail were walking around like pullets, seeming all dainty and unseen.

wagon trail

"Walk pretty," she said. "This the easy place. This the easy going."

She followed the track, swaying through the quiet bare fields, through the little strings of trees silver in their dead leaves, past cabins silver from weather, with the doors and windows boarded shut, all like old women under a spell sitting there. "I walking in their sleep," she said, nodding her head vigorously.

ravine

In a ravine she went where a spring was silently flowing through a hollow log. Old Phoenix bent and drank. "Sweetgum makes the water sweet," she said, and drank more. "Nobody know who made this well, for it was here when I was born."

the road

The track crossed a swampy part where the moss hung as white as lace from every limb. "Sleep on, alligators, and blow your bubbles." Then the track went into the road.

Deep, deep the road went down between the high green-colored banks. Overhead the live-oaks met, and it was as dark as a cave.

A black dog with a lolling tongue came up out of the weeds by the ditch. She was meditating, and not ready, and when he came at her she only hit him a little with her cane. Over she went in the ditch, like a little puff of milk-weed.

Down there, her senses drifted away. A dream visited her, and she reached her hand up, but nothing reached down and gave her a pull. So she lay there and presently went to talking. "Old woman," she said to herself, "that black dog came up out of the weeds to stall you off, and now there he sitting on his fine tail, smiling at you."

the hunter

A white man finally came along and found her—a hunter, a young man, with his dog on a chain.

"Well, Granny!" he laughed. "What are you doing there?"

"Lying on my back like a June-bug waiting to be turned over, mister," she said, reaching up her hand.

He lifted her up, gave her a swing in the air, and set her down. "Anything broken, Granny?"

"No sir, them old dead weeds is springy enough," said Phoenix, when she had got her breath. "I thank you for your trouble."

"Where do you live, Granny?" he asked, while the two dogs were growling at each other.

"Away back yonder, sir, behind the ridge. You can't even see it from here."

"On your way home?"

"No, sir, I going to town."

"Why, that's too far! That's as far as I walk when I come out myself, and I get something for my trouble." He patted the stuffed bag he carried, and there hung down a little closed claw. It was one of the bobwhites, with its beak hooked bitterly to show it was dead. "Now you go on home, Granny!"

"I bound to go to town, mister," said Phoenix. "The time come around."   *foreshadowing*

He gave another laugh, filling the whole landscape. "I know you colored people! Wouldn't miss going to town to see Santa Claus!"

But something held Old Phoenix very still. The deep lines in her face went into a fierce and different radiation. Without warning she had seen with her own eyes a flashing nickel fall out of the man's pocket on to the ground.   *nickel*

"How old are you, Granny?" he was saying.

"There is no telling, mister," she said, "no telling."

Then she gave a little cry and clapped her hands, and said, "Git on away from here, dog! Look! Look at that dog!" She laughed as if in admiration. "He ain't scared of nobody. He a big black dog." She whispered, "Sick him!"

"Watch me get rid of that cur," said the man. "Sick him, Pete! Sick him!"

Phoenix heard the dogs fighting and heard the man running and throwing sticks. She even heard a gunshot. But she was slowly bending forward by that time, further and further forward, the lids stretched down over her eyes, as if she were doing this in her sleep. Her chin was lowered almost to her knees. The yellow palm of her hand came out from the fold of her apron. Her fingers slid down and along the ground under the piece of money with the grace and care they would have in lifting an egg from under a sitting hen. Then she slowly straightened up, she stood erect, and the nickel was in her apron pocket. A bird flew by. Her lips moved, "God watching me the whole time. I come to stealing."

The man came back, and his own dog panted about them. "Well, I scared him off that time," he said, and then he laughed and lifted his gun and pointed it at Phoenix.

She stood straight and faced him.

"Doesn't the gun scare you?" he said, still pointing it.

"No, sir. I seen plenty go off closer by, in my day, and for less than what I done," she said, holding utterly still.

He smiled, and shouldered the gun. "Well, Granny," he said, "you must be a hundred years old, and scared of nothing. I'd give you a dime if I had any money with me. But you take my advice and stay home, and nothing will happen to you."

"I bound to go on my way, mister," said Phoenix. She inclined her head in the red rag. Then they went in different directions, but she could hear the gun shooting again and again over the hill.

She walked on. The shadows hung from the oak trees to the road like curtains. Then she smelled wood-smoke, and smelled the river, and she saw a steeple and the cabins on their steep steps. Dozens of little black children whirled around her. There ahead was Natchez shining. Bells were ringing. She walked on.

In the paved city it was Christmas time. There were red and green electric lights strung and crisscrossed everywhere, and all turned on in the daytime. Old

Phoenix would have been lost if she had not distrusted her eyesight and depended on her feet to know where to take her.

She paused quietly on the sidewalk, where people were passing by. A lady came along in the crowd, carrying an armful of red-, green-, and silver-wrapped presents; she gave off perfume like the red roses in hot summer, and Phoenix stopped her.

"Please, missy, will you lace up my shoe?" She held up her foot.

"What do you want, Grandma?"

"See my shoe," said Phoenix. "Do all right for out in the country, but wouldn't look right to go in a big building."

"Stand still then, Grandma," said the lady. She put her packages down carefully on the sidewalk beside her and laced and tied both shoes tightly.

"Can't lace 'em with a cane," said Phoenix. "Thank you, missy. I doesn't mind asking a nice lady to tie up my shoe when I gets out on the street."

stone building Moving slowly and from side to side, she went into the stone building and into a tower of steps, where she walked up and around and around until her feet knew to stop.

She entered a door, and there she saw nailed up on the wall the document that had been stamped with the gold seal and framed in the gold frame which matched the dream that was hung up in her head.

"Here I be," she said. There was a fixed and ceremonial stiffness over her body.

"A charity case, I suppose," said an attendant who sat at the desk before her.

But Phoenix only looked above her head. There was sweat on her face; the wrinkles shone like a bright net.

"Speak up, Grandma," the woman said. "What's your name? We must have your history, you know. Have you been here before? What seems to be the trouble with you?"

Old Phoenix only gave a twitch to her face as if a fly were bothering her.

"Are you deaf?" cried the attendant.

But then the nurse came in.

"Oh, that's just old Aunt Phoenix," she said. "She doesn't come for herself—she has a little grandson. She makes these trips just as regular as clockwork. She lives away back off the Old Natchez Trace." She bent down. "Well, Aunt Phoenix, why don't you just take a seat? We won't keep you standing after your long trip." She pointed.

The old woman sat down, bolt upright in the chair.

"Now, how is the boy?" asked the nurse.

Old Phoenix did not speak.

"I said, how is the boy?"

But Phoenix only waited and stared straight ahead, her face very solemn and withdrawn into rigidity.

"Is his throat any better?" asked the nurse. "Aunt Phoenix, don't you hear me? Is your grandson's throat any better since the last time you came for the medicine?"

With her hand on her knees, the old woman waited, silent, erect and motionless, just as if she were in armour.

"You mustn't take up our time this way, Aunt Phoenix," the nurse said. "Tell us quickly about your grandson, and get it over. He isn't dead, is he?"

At last there came a flicker and then a flame of comprehension across her face, and she spoke.

"My grandson. It was my memory had left me. There I sat and forgot why I made my long trip."

"Forgot?" The nurse frowned. "After you came so far?"

Then Phoenix was like an old woman begging a dignified forgiveness for waking up frightened in the night. "I never did go to school—I was too old at the Surrender," she said in a soft voice. "I'm an old woman without an education. It was my memory fail me. My little grandson, he is just the same, and I forgot it in the coming."

"Throat never heals, does it?" said the nurse, speaking in a loud, sure voice to Old Phoenix. By now she had a card with something written on it, a little list. "Yes. Swallowed lye. When was it—January—two—three years ago—"

Phoenix spoke unasked now. "No, missy, he not dead, he just the same. Every little while his throat begin to close up again, and he not able to swallow. He not get his breath. He not able to help himself. So the time come around, and I go on another trip for the soothing-medicine."

"All right. The doctor said as long as you came to get it you could have it," said the nurse. "But it's an obstinate case."

"My little grandson, he sit up there in the house all wrapped up, waiting by himself," Phoenix went on. "We is the only two left in the world. He suffer and it don't seem to put him back at all. He got a sweet look. He going to last. He wear a little patch quilt and peep out, holding his mouth open like a little bird. I remembers so plain now, I not going to forget him again, no, the whole enduring time. I could tell him from all the others in creation."

"All right." The nurse was trying to hush her now. She brought her a bottle of medicine. "Charity," she said, making a check mark in a book.

Old Phoenix held the bottle close to her eyes and then carefully put it into her pocket.

"I thank you," she said.

"It's Christmas time, Grandma," said the attendant. "Could I give you a few pennies out of my purse?"

"Five pennies is a nickel," said Phoenix stiffly.

"Here's a nickel," said the attendant.

Phoenix rose carefully and held out her hand. She received the nickel and then fished the other nickel out of her pocket and laid it beside the new one. She stared at her palm closely, with her head on one side.

Then she gave a tap with her cane on the floor.

"This is what come to me to do," she said. "I going to the store and buy my child a little windmill they sells, made out of paper. He going to find it hard to believe there such a thing in the world. I'll march myself back where he waiting, holding it straight up in this hand."

She lifted her free hand, gave a little nod, turned round, and walked out of the doctor's office. Then her slow step began on the stairs, going down.

Fact Questions and Exercises

1. Where is Phoenix going?   *To Natchez*
2. What does she see in the field and mistake for a "ghost"?   *Scarecrow*

ow does she fall into the ditch? *Hitting at a dog*

1. How does Phoenix outsmart the white hunter? *By Distraction*
5. What city and state are the setting for the story? *Natchez Trace, Miss.*
6. During what season of the year does Phoenix make her journey? *winter (Dec.)*
7. What task does the lady on the street perform for Phoenix? *Ties her shoes*
8. How has the grandson been injured? ~~Swallowed~~ *Swallowed lye*
9. What is Phoenix going to buy for her grandson? *Windmill (toy)*

For Discussion and Writing

1. What is the significance of the name "Phoenix"? How does understanding the name help to explain the purpose of the story?
2. Characterize Phoenix Jackson. How old is she? Can she read and write? Is she superstitious? In what ways is she devoted to others? What seem to be her most outstanding personal traits?
3. What is the importance of the story taking place during the Christmas season? What other references or symbols does Welty use to convey the meaning of the story? For instance, what things in the story suggest death? Evil? How does Welty use colors?

Irwin Shaw [1913–   ]

Shaw was born in Brooklyn, New York. He is probably one of America's most popular contemporary writers, having produced a great number of successful novels, plays, and short stories. In general, his writing may be thought of as "living history"—it attempts to chronicle typical American people experiencing the events that shape their lives, both individually and nationally. For instance, *The Young Lions* (1948), perhaps Shaw's best-known novel, examines the effect that World War II has upon both the German and American soldiers who are caught up in the conflict. And *Rich Man, Poor Man* (1970) details the lives of the members of an American family adjusting to the problems of and changes in postwar America.

Basically objective w/ omniscient perspective at end.

The Girls in Their Summer Dresses

Fifth Avenue was shining in the sun when they left the Brevoort. The sun was warm, even though it was February, and everything looked like Sunday morning—the buses and the well-dressed people walking slowly in couples and the quiet buildings with the windows closed.

Michael held Frances' arm tightly as they walked toward Washington Square in the sunlight. They walked lightly, almost smiling, because they had slept late and had a good breakfast and it was Sunday. Michael unbuttoned his coat and let it flap around him in the mild wind.

"Look out," Frances said as they crossed Eighth Street. "You'll break your neck." Michael laughed and Frances laughed with him.

"She's not so pretty," Frances said. "Anyway, not pretty enough to take a chance of breaking your neck."

Michael laughed again. "How did you know I was looking at her?"

Frances cocked her head to one side and smiled at her husband under the brim of her hat. "Mike, darling," she said.

"O.K." he said. "Excuse me."

Frances patted his arm lightly and pulled him along a little faster toward Washington Square. "Let's not see anybody all day," she said. "Let's just hang around with each other. You and me. We're always up to our neck in people, drinking their Scotch or drinking our Scotch; we only see each other in bed. I want to go out with my husband all day long. I want him to talk only to me and listen only to me."

"What's to stop us?" Michael asked.

"The Stevensons. They want us to drop by around one o'clock and they'll drive us into the country."

"The cunning Stevensons," Mike said. "Transparent. They can whistle. They can go driving in the country by themselves."

"Is it a date?"

"It's a date."

Frances leaned over and kissed him on the tip of the ear.

"Darling," Michael said, "this is Fifth Avenue."

"Let me arrange a program," Frances said. "A planned Sunday in New York for a young couple with money to throw away."

"Go easy."

"First let's go to the Metropolitan Museum of Art," Frances suggested, because Michael had said during the week he wanted to go. "I haven't been there in three years and there're at least ten pictures I want to see again. Then we can take the bus down to Radio City and watch them skate. And later we'll go down to Cavanaugh's and get a steak as big as a blacksmith's apron, with a bottle of wine, and after that there's a French picture at the Filmarte that everybody says—say, are you listening to me?"

"Sure," he said. He took his eyes off the hatless girl with the dark hair, cut dancer-style like a helmet, who was walking past him.

"That's the program for the day," Frances said flatly. "Or maybe you'd just rather walk up and down Fifth Avenue."

"No," Michael said. "Not at all."

"You always look at other women," Frances said. "Everywhere. Every damned place we go."

"No, darling," Michael said, "I look at everything. God gave me eyes and I look at women and men in subway excavations and moving pictures and the little flowers of the field. I casually inspect the universe."

"You ought to see the look in your eye," Frances said, "as you casually inspect the universe on Fifth Avenue."

"I'm a happily married man." Michael pressed her elbow tenderly. "Example for the whole twentieth century—Mr. and Mrs. Mike Loomis. Hey, let's have a drink," he said, stopping.

"We just had breakfast."

"Now listen, darling," Mike said, choosing his words with care, "it's a nice day and we both felt good and there's no reason why we have to break it up. Let's have a nice Sunday."

"All right. I don't know why I started this. Let's drop it. Let's have a good time."

They joined hands consciously and walked without talking among the baby carriages and the old Italian men in their Sunday clothes and the young women with Scotties in Washington Square Park.

"At least once a year everyone should go to the Metropolitan Museum of Art," Frances said after a while, her tone a good imitation of the tone she had used at breakfast and at the beginning of their walk. "And it's nice on Sunday. There're a lot of people looking at the pictures and you get the feeling maybe Art isn't on the decline in New York City, after all—"

"I want to tell you something," Michael said very seriously. "I have not touched another woman. Not once. In all the five years."

"All right," Frances said.

"You believe that, don't you?"

"All right."

They walked between the crowded benches, under the scrubby city-park trees.

"I try not to notice it," Frances said, "but I feel rotten inside, in my stomach, when we pass a woman and you look at her and I see that look in your eye and that's the way you looked at me the first time. In Alice Maxwell's house. Standing there in the living room, next to the radio, with a green hat on and all those people."

"I remember the hat," Michael said.

"The same look," Frances said. "And it makes me feel bad. It makes me feel terrible."

"Sh-h-h, please, darling, sh-h-h."

"I think I would like a drink now," Frances said.

They walked over to a bar on Eighth Street, not saying anything, Mike automatically helping her over curbstones and guiding her past automobiles. They sat near a window in the bar and the sun streamed in and there was a small, cheerful fire in the fireplace. A little Japanese waiter came over and put down some pretzels and smiled happily at them.

"What do you order after breakfast?" Michael asked.

"Brandy, I suppose," Frances said.

"Courvoisier," Michael told the waiter. "Two Courvoisiers."

The waiter came with the glasses and they sat drinking the brandy in the sunlight. Michael finished half his and drank a little water.

"I look at women," he said. "Correct. I don't say it's wrong or right. I look at them. If I pass them on the street and I don't look at them, I'm fooling you, I'm fooling myself."

"You look at them as though you want them," Frances said, playing with her brandy glass. "Every one of them."

"In a way," Michael said, speaking softly and not to his wife, "in a way, that's true. I don't do anything about it, but it's true."

"I know it. That's why I feel bad."

"Another brandy," Michael called. "Waiter, two more brandies."

He sighed and closed his eyes and rubbed them gently with his fingertips. "I love the way women look. One of the things I like best about New York is the battalions of women. When I first came to New York from Ohio that was the first thing I noticed, the million wonderful women, all over the city. I walked around with my heart in my throat."

"A kid," Frances said. "That's a kid's feeling."

"Guess again," Michael said. "Guess again. I'm older now. I'm a man getting near middle age, putting on a little fat, and I still love to walk along Fifth Avenue at three o'clock on the east side of the street between Fiftieth and the Fifty-seventh Streets. They're all out then, shopping, in their furs and their crazy hats, everything all concentrated from all over the world into seven blocks—the best furs, the best clothes, the handsomest women, out to spend money and feeling good about it."

The Japanese waiter put the two drinks down, smiling with great happiness.

"Everything is all right?" he asked.

"Everything is wonderful," Michael said.

"If it's just a couple of fur coats," Frances said, "and forty-five dollar hats—"

"It's not the fur coats. Or the hats. That's just the scenery for that particular kind of women. Understand," he said, "you don't have to listen to this."

"I want to listen."

"I like the girls in the offices. Neat, with their eyeglasses, smart, chipper, knowing what everything is about. I like the girls on Forty-fourth Street at lunchtime, the actresses, all dressed up on nothing a week. I like the sales-girls in the stores, paying attention to you first because you're a man, leav-ing lady customers waiting. I got all this stuff accumulated in me because I've been thinking about it for ten years and now you've asked for it and here it is."

"Go ahead," Frances said.

"When I think of New York City, I think of all the girls on parade in the city. I don't know whether it's something special with me or whether every man in the city walks around with the same feeling inside him, but I feel as though I'm at a picnic in this city. I like to sit near the women in the theatres, the famous beauties who've taken six hours to get ready and look it. And the young girls at the football games, with the red cheeks, and when the warm weather comes, the girls in their summer dresses." He finished his drink. "That's the story."

Frances finished her drink and swallowed two or three times extra. "You say you love me?"

"I love you."

"I'm pretty, too," Frances said. "As pretty as any of them." *Defensive*

"You're beautiful," Michael said.

"I'm good for you," Frances said, pleading. "I've made a good wife, a good housekeeper, a good friend. I'd do any damn thing for you."

"I know," Michael said. He put his hand out and grasped hers.

"You'd like to be free to—" Frances said.

"Sh-h-h."

"Tell the truth." She took her hand away from under his.

Michael flicked the edge of his glass with his finger. "O.K.," he said gently. "Sometimes I feel I would like to be free."

"Well," Frances said, "any time you say."

"Don't be foolish." Michael swung his chair around to her side of the table and patted her thigh.

She began to cry silently into her handkerchief, bent over just enough so that nobody else in the bar would notice. "Someday," she said, crying, "you're going to make a move."

Michael didn't say anything. He sat watching the bartender slowly peel a lemon.

"Aren't you?" Frances asked harshly. "Come on, tell me. Talk. Aren't you?"

"Maybe." Michael said. He moved his chair back again. "How the hell do I know?"

"You know," Frances persisted. "Don't you know?"

"Yes," Michael said after a while, "I know."

Frances stopped crying then. Two or three snuffles into the handkerchief and she put it away and her face didn't tell anything to anybody. "At least do me one favor," she said.

"Sure."

"Stop talking about how pretty this woman is or that one. Nice eyes, nice breasts, a pretty figure, good voice." She mimicked his voice. Keep it to yourself. I'm not interested."

Michael waved to the waiter. "I'll keep it to myself," he said.

Frances flicked the corners of her eyes. "Another brandy," she told the waiter.

"Two," Michael said.

"Yes, Ma'am, yes, sir," said the waiter, backing away.

Frances regarded Michael coolly across the table. "Do you want me to call the Stevensons?" she asked. "It'll be nice in the country."

"Sure," Michael said. "Call them."

She got up from the table and walked across the room toward the telephone. Michael watched her walk, thinking what a pretty girl, what nice legs.

Fact Questions and Exercises

1. In what city does the story take place? What facts in the story support your answer? *New York City (Fifth Ave.*
2. What are the names of the husband and wife? *Mike & Frances Loomis*
3. What facts suggest the financial condition of the couple?
4. What facts suggest the condition of the couple's marriage? Are they happy? Dissatisfied? What?
5. Does the story take place in summer? If not, why does "summer" appear in the title?
6. What does the wife mean when she tells her husband "you're going to make a move"? *He's going to leave her*

For Discussion and Writing

1. In the story, Michael wants to "look at everything," while Frances wants to look at the pictures in the museum. Discuss these two forms of seeing.
2. Are there indications that the husband and wife are controlled to some extent by outside forces—biological or social forces, for example? Comment on this.

3. At first, Frances doesn't want to accompany the Stevensons to the country, but later she changes her mind. What does her change of mind indicate about her relationship with her husband? Analyze Frances's character and motivations. Why, for instance, does she insist upon knowing the "truth" and later tell her husband to keep his thoughts to himself?
4. Interpret the ending of the story. Is this conclusion a logical one? What foreshadowings in the story prepare you for this ending?

Albert Camus [1913–1960]

Camus was born in Algeria, a French colony in Africa. During World War II he served in the French underground, fighting against the Germans and writing as a war correspondent. His most famous novel, *The Stranger*, was published in 1942, and his noted essay on suicide, "The Myth of Sisyphus," was published in 1943. Camus is respected not only as a novelist but as a dramatist and philosopher as well. He is often associated with the philosophy of existentialism, though he preferred not to be classified as an existentialist. The term "absurdism" derives in part from his writing, and he is generally considered to be a leading proponent of absurdism. Camus won the Nobel Prize in 1957.

The Guest

The schoolmaster was watching the two men climb toward him. One was on horseback, the other on foot. They had not yet tackled the abrupt rise leading to the schoolhouse built on the hillside. They were toiling onward, making slow progress in the snow, among the stones, on the vast expanse of the high deserted plateau. From time to time the horse stumbled. Without hearing anything yet, he could see the breath issuing from the horse's nostrils. One of the men, at least, knew the region. They were following the trail although it had disappeared two days ago under a layer of dirty white snow. The schoolmaster calculated that it would take them half an hour to get onto the hill. It was cold; he went back into the school to get a sweater.

He crossed the empty, frigid classroom. On the blackboard the four rivers of France, drawn with four different colored chalks, had been flowing toward their estuaries for the past three days. Snow had suddenly fallen in mid-October after eight months of drought without the transition of rain, and the twenty pupils, more or less, who lived in the villages scattered over the plateau had stopped coming. With fair weather they would return. Daru now heated only the single room that was his lodging, adjoining the classroom and giving also onto the plateau to the east. Like the class windows, his window looked to the south too. On that side the school was a few kilometers from the point where the plateau began to slope toward the south. In clear weather could be seen the purple mass of the mountain range where the gap opened onto the desert.

Somewhat alarmed, Daru returned to the window from which he had first seen the two men. They were no longer visible. Hence they must have tackled the rise. The sky was not so dark, for the snow had stopped falling during the night. The morning had opened with a dirty light which had scarcely become brighter as the ceiling of clouds lifted. At two in the afternoon it seemed as if the day were merely beginning. But still this was better than those three days when the thick snow was falling amidst unbroken darkness with little gusts of wind that rattled the double door of the classroom. Then Daru had spent long hours in his room, leaving it only to go to the shed and feed the chickens or get some coal. Fortunately the delivery truck from Tadjid, the nearest village to the north, had brought his supplies two days before the blizzard. It would return in forty-eight hours.

Besides, he had enough to resist a siege, for the little room was cluttered with bags of wheat that the administration left as a stock to distribute to those of his pupils whose families had suffered from the drought. Actually they had all been victims because they were all poor. Every day Daru would distribute a ration to the children. They had missed it, he knew, during these bad days. Possibly one of the fathers or big brothers would come this afternoon and he could supply them with grain. It was just a matter of carrying them over to the next harvest. Now shiploads of wheat were arriving from France and the worst was over. But it would be hard to forget that poverty, that army of ragged ghosts wandering in the sunlight, the plateaus burned to a cinder month after month, the earth shriveled up little by little, literally scorched, every stone bursting into dust under one's foot. The sheep had died then by thousands and even a few men, here and there, sometimes without anyone's knowing.

In contrast with such poverty, he who lived almost like a monk in his remote schoolhouse, nonetheless satisfied with the little he had and with the rough life, had felt like a lord with his whitewashed walls, his narrow couch, his unpainted shelves, his well, and his weekly provision of water and food. And suddenly this snow, without warning, without the foretaste of rain. This is the way the region was, cruel to live in, even without men—who didn't help matters either. But Daru had been born here. Everywhere else, he felt exiled.

He stepped out onto the terrace in front of the schoolhouse. The two men were now halfway up the slope. He recognized the horseman as Balducci, the old gendarme he had known for a long time. Balducci was holding on the end of a rope an Arab who was walking behind him with hands bound and head lowered. The gendarme waved a greeting to which Daru did not reply, lost as he was in contemplation of the Arab dressed in a faded blue jellaba, his feet in sandals but covered with socks of heavy raw wool, his head surmounted by a narrow, short chèche. They were approaching. Balducci was holding back his horse in order not to hurt the Arab, and the group was advancing slowly.

Within earshot, Balducci shouted: "One hour to do the three kilometers from El Ameur!" Daru did not answer. Short and square in his thick sweater, he watched them climb. Not once had the Arab raised his head. "Hello," said Daru when they got up onto the terrace. "Come in and warm up." Balducci painfully got down from his horse without letting go the rope. From under his bristling mustache he smiled at the schoolmaster. His little dark eyes, deep-set under a tanned forehead, and his mouth surrounded with wrinkles made him look attentive and studious. Daru took the bridle, led the horse to the shed, and came back to the two men, who were now waiting for him in the school. He led them into his room. "I am going to heat up the classroom," he said. "We'll be more comfortable there." When he entered the room again, Balducci was on the couch.

He had undone the rope tying him to the Arab, who had squatted near the stove. His hands still bound, the *chèche* pushed back on his head, he was looking toward the window. At first Daru noticed only his huge lips, fat, smooth, almost Negroid; yet his nose was straight, his eyes were dark and full of fever. The *chèche* revealed an obstinate forehead and, under the weathered skin now rather discolored by the cold, the whole face had a restless and rebellious look that struck Daru when the Arab, turning his face toward him, looked him straight in the eyes. "Go into the other room," said the schoolmaster, "and I'll make you some mint tea." "Thanks," Balducci said. "What a chore! How I long for retirement." And addressing his prisoner in Arabic: "Come on, you." The Arab got up and, slowly, holding his bound wrists in front of him, went into the classroom.

With the tea, Daru brought a chair. But Balducci was already enthroned on the nearest pupil's desk and the Arab had squatted against the teacher's platform facing the stove, which stood between the desk and the window. When he held out the glass of tea to the prisoner, Daru hesitated at the sight of his bound hands. "He might perhaps be untied." "Sure," said Balducci. "That was for the trip." He started to get to his feet. But Daru, setting the glass on the floor, had knelt beside the Arab. Without saying anything, the Arab watched him with his feverish eyes. Once his hands were free, he rubbed his swollen wrists against each other, took the glass of tea, and sucked up the burning liquid in swift little sips.

"Good," said Daru. "And where are you headed?"

Balducci withdrew his mustache from the tea. "Here, son."

"Odd pupils! And you're spending the night?"

"No. I'm going back to El Ameur. And you will deliver this fellow to Tinguit. He is expected at police headquarters."

Balducci was looking at Daru with a friendly little smile.

"What's this story?" asked the schoolmaster. "Are you pulling my leg?"

"No, son. Those are the orders."

"The orders? I'm not . . ." Daru hesitated, not wanting to hurt the old Corsican. "I mean, that's not my job."

"What! What's the meaning of that? In wartime people do all kinds of jobs."

"Then I'll wait for the declaration of war!"

Balducci nodded.

"O.K. But the orders exist and they concern you too. Things are brewing, it appears. There is talk of a forthcoming revolt. We are mobilized, in a way."

Daru still had his obstinate look.

"Listen, son," Balducci said. "I like you and you must understand. There's only a dozen of us at El Ameur to patrol throughout the whole territory of a small department and I must get back in a hurry. I was told to hand this guy over to you and return without delay. He couldn't be kept there. His village was beginning to stir; they wanted to take him back. You must take him to Tinguit tomorrow before the day is over. Twenty kilometers shouldn't faze a husky fellow like you. After that, all will be over. You'll come back to your pupils and your comfortable life."

Behind the wall the horse could be heard snorting and pawing the earth. Daru was looking out the window. Decidedly, the weather was clearing and the light was increasing over the snowy plateau. When all the snow was melted, the sun would take over again and once more would burn the fields of stone. For days, still, the unchanging sky would shed its dry light on the solitary expanse where nothing had any connection with man.

"After all," he said, turning around toward Balducci, "what did he do?" And, before the gendarme had opened his mouth, he asked: "Does he speak French?"

"No, not a word. We had been looking for him for a month, but they were hiding him. He killed his cousin."

"Is he against us?"

"I don't think so. But you can never be sure."

"Why did he kill?"

"A family squabble, I think: One owed the other grain, it seems. It's not at all clear. In short, he killed his cousin with a billhook. You know, like a sheep, kreezk!"

Balducci made the gesture of drawing a blade across his throat and the Arab, his attention attracted, watched him with a sort of anxiety. Daru felt a sudden wrath against the man, against all men with their rotten spite, their tireless hates, their blood lust.

But the kettle was singing on the stove. He served Balducci more tea, hesitated, then served the Arab again, who, a second time, drank avidly. His raised arms made the jellaba fall open and the schoolmaster saw his thin, muscular chest.

"Thanks, kid," Balducci said. "And now, I'm off."

He got up and went toward the Arab, taking a small rope from his pocket.

"What are you doing?" Daru asked dryly.

Balducci, disconcerted, showed him the rope.

"Don't bother."

The old gendarme hesitated. "It's up to you. Of course, you are armed?"

"I have my shotgun."

"Where?"

"In the trunk."

"You ought to have it near your bed."

"Why? I have nothing to fear."

"You're crazy, son. If there's an uprising, no one is safe, we're all in the same boat."

"I'll defend myself. I'll have time to see them coming."

Balducci began to laugh, then suddenly the mustache covered the white teeth.

"You'll have time? O.K. That's just what I was saying. You have always been a little cracked. That's why I like you, my son was like that."

At the same time he took out his revolver and put it on the desk.

"Keep it; I don't need two weapons from here to El Ameur."

The revolver shone against the black paint of the table. When the gendarme turned toward him, the schoolmaster caught the smell of leather and horseflesh.

"Listen, Balducci," Daru said suddenly, "every bit of this disgusts me, and first of all your fellow here. But I won't hand him over. Fight, yes, if I have to. But not that."

The old gendarme stood in front of him and looked at him severely.

"You're being a fool," he said slowly. "I don't like it either. You don't get used to putting a rope on a man even after years of it, and you're even ashamed—yes, ashamed. But you can't let them have their way.

"I won't hand him over," Daru said again.

"It's an order, son, and I repeat it."

"That's right. Repeat to them what I've said to you: I won't hand him over."

Balducci made a visible effort to reflect. He looked at the Arab and at Daru. At last he decided.

"No, I won't tell them anything. If you want to drop us, go ahead; I'll not denounce you. I have an order to deliver the prisoner and I'm doing so. And now you'll just sign this paper for me."

"There's no need. I'll not deny that you left him with me."

"Don't be mean with me. I know you'll tell the truth. You're from hereabouts and you are a man. But you must sign, that's the rule."

Daru opened his drawer, took out a little square bottle of purple ink, the red wooden penholder with the "sergeant-major" pen he used for making models of penmanship, and signed. The gendarme carefully folded the paper and put in into his wallet. Then he moved toward the door.

"I'll see you off," Daru said.

"No," said Balducci. "There's no use being polite. You insulted me."

He looked at the Arab, motionless in the same spot, sniffed peevishly, and turned away toward the door. "Good-by, son," he said. The door shut behind him. Balducci appeared suddenly outside the window and then disappeared. His footsteps were muffled by the snow. The horse stirred on the other side of the wall and several chickens fluttered in fright. A moment later Balducci reappeared outside the window leading the horse by the bridle. He walked toward the little rise without turning around and disappeared from sight with the horse following him. A big stone could be heard bouncing down. Daru walked back toward the prisoner, who, without stirring, never took his eyes off him. "Wait," the schoolmaster said in Arabic and went toward the bedroom. As he was going through the door, he had a second thought, went to the desk, took the revolver, and stuck it in his pocket. Then, without looking back, he went into his room.

For some time he lay on his couch watching the sky gradually close over, listening to the silence. It was this silence that had seemed painful to him during the first few days here, after the war. He had requested a post in the little town at the base of the foothills separating the upper plateaus from the desert. There, rocky walls, green and black to the north, pink and lavender to the south, marked the frontier of eternal summer. He had been named to a post farther north, on the plateau itself. In the beginning, the solitude and the silence had been hard for him on these wastelands peopled only by stones. Occasionally, furrows suggested cultivation, but they had been dug to uncover a certain kind of stone good for building. The only plowing here was to harvest rocks. Elsewhere a thin layer of soil accumulated in the hollows would be scraped out to enrich paltry village gardens. This is the way it was: bare rock covered three quarters of the region. Towns sprang up, flourished, then disappeared; men came by, loved one another or fought bitterly, then died. No one in this desert, neither he nor his guest, mattered. And yet, outside this desert neither of them, Daru knew, could have really lived.

When he got up, no noise came from the classroom. He was amazed at the unmixed joy he derived from the mere thought that the Arab might have fled and that he would be alone with no decision to make. But the prisoner was there. He had merely stretched out between the stove and the desk. With eyes open, he was staring at the ceiling. In that position, his thick lips were particularly noticeable, giving him a pouting look. "Come," said Daru. The Arab got up and followed him. In the bedroom, the schoolmaster pointed to a chair near the table under the window. The Arab sat down without taking his eyes off Daru.

"Are you hungry?"

"Yes," the prisoner said.

Daru set the table for two. He took flour and oil, shaped a cake in a frying-pan, and lighted the little stove that functioned on bottled gas. While the cake was cooking, he went out to the shed to get cheese, eggs, dates, and condensed milk. When the cake was done he set it on the window sill to cool, heated some condensed milk diluted with water, and beat up the eggs into an omelette. In one of his motions he knocked against the revolver stuck in his right pocket. He set the bowl down, went into the classroom, and put the revolver in his desk drawer. When he came back to the room, night was falling. He put on the light and served the Arab. "Eat," he said. The Arab took a piece of the cake, lifted it eagerly to his mouth, and stopped short.

"And you?" he asked.

"After you. I'll eat too."

The thick lips opened slightly. The Arab hesitated, then bit into the cake determinedly.

The meal over, the Arab looked at the schoolmaster. "Are you the judge?"

"No, I'm simply keeping you until tomorrow."

"Why do you eat with me?"

"I'm hungry."

The Arab fell silent. Daru got up and went out. He brought back a folding bed from the shed, set it up between the table and the stove, perpendicular to his own bed. From a large suitcase which, upright in a corner, served as a shelf for papers, he took two blankets and arranged them on the camp bed. Then he stopped, felt useless, and sat down on his bed. There was nothing more to do or to get ready. He had to look at this man. He looked at him, therefore, trying to imagine his face bursting with rage. He couldn't do so. He could see nothing but the dark yet shining eyes and the animal mouth.

"Why did you kill him?" he asked in a voice whose hostile tone surprised him.

The Arab looked away.

"He ran away. I ran after him."

He raised his eyes to Daru again and they were full of a sort of woeful interrogation. "Now what will they do to me?"

"Are you afraid?"

He stiffened, turning his eyes away.

"Are you sorry?"

The Arab stared at him openmouthed. Obviously he did not understand.

Daru's annoyance was growing. At the same time he felt awkward and self-conscious with his big body wedged between the two beds.

"Lie down there," he said impatiently. "That's your bed."

The Arab didn't move. He called to Daru:

"Tell me!"

The schoolmaster looked at him.

"Is the gendarme coming back tomorrow?"

"I don't know."

"Are you coming with us?"

"I don't know. Why?"

The prisoner got up and stretched out on top of the blankets, his feet toward the window. The light from the electric bulb shone straight into his eyes, and he closed them at once.

"Why?" Daru repeated, standing beside the bed.

The Arab opened his eyes under the blinding light and looked at him, trying not to blink.

"Come with us," he said.

In the middle of the night, Daru was still not asleep. He had gone to bed after undressing completely; he generally slept naked. But when he suddenly realized that he had nothing on, he hesitated. He felt vulnerable and the temptation came to him to put his clothes back on. Then he shrugged his shoulders; after all, he wasn't a child and, if need be, he could break his adversary in two. From his bed he could observe him, lying on his back, still motionless with his eyes closed under the harsh light. When Daru turned out the light, the darkness seemed to coagulate all of a sudden. Little by little, the night came back to life in the window where the starless sky was stirring gently. The schoolmaster soon made out the body lying at his feet. The Arab still did not move, but his eyes seemed open. A faint wind was prowling around the schoolhouse. Perhaps it would drive away the clouds and the sun would reappear.

During the night the wind increased. The hens fluttered a little and then were silent. The Arab turned over on his side with his back to Daru, who thought he heard him moan. Then he listened for his guest's breathing, become heavier and more regular. He listened to that breath so close to him and mused without being able to go to sleep. In this room where he had been sleeping alone for a year, the presence bothered him. But it bothered him also by imposing on him a sort of brotherhood he knew well but refused to accept in the present circumstances. Men who share the same rooms, soldiers or prisoners, develop a strange alliance as if, having cast off their armor with their clothing, they fraternized every evening, over and above their differences, in the ancient community of dream and fatigue. But Daru shook himself; he didn't like such musings, and it was essential to sleep.

A little later, however, when the Arab stirred slightly, the schoolmaster was still not asleep. When the prisoner made a second move, he stiffened, on the alert. The Arab was lifting himself slowly on his arms with almost the motion of a sleepwalker. Seated upright in bed, he waited motionless without turning his head toward Daru, as if he were listening attentively. Daru did not stir; it had just occurred to him that the revolver was still in the drawer of his desk. It was better to act at once. Yet he continued to observe the prisoner, who, with the same slithery motion, put his feet on the ground, waited again, then began to stand up slowly. Daru was about to call out to him when the Arab began to walk, in a quite natural but extraordinarily silent way. He was heading toward the door at the end of the room that opened into the shed. He lifted the latch with precaution and went out, pushing the door behind him but without shutting it. Daru had not stirred. "He is running away," he merely thought. "Good riddance!" Yet he listened attentively. The hens were not fluttering; the guest must be on the plateau. A faint sound of water reached him, and he didn't know what it was until the Arab again stood framed in the doorway, closed the door carefully, and came back to bed without a sound. Then Daru turned his back on him and fell asleep. Still later he seemed, from the depths of his sleep, to hear furtive steps around the schoolhouse. "I'm dreaming! I'm dreaming!" he repeated to himself. And he went on sleeping.

When he awoke, the sky was clear; the loose window let in a cold, pure air. The Arab was asleep, hunched up under the blankets now, his mouth open, utterly relaxed. But when Daru shook him, he started dreadfully, staring at Daru with wild eyes as if he had never seen him and such a frightened expression that the schoolmaster stepped back. "Don't be afraid. It's me. You must eat." The Arab nodded his head and said yes. Calm had returned to his face, but his expression was vacant and listless.

The coffee was ready. They drank it seated together on the folding bed as they munched their pieces of the cake. Then Daru led the Arab under the shed and showed him the faucet where he washed. He went back into the room, folded the blankets and the bed, made his own bed and put the room in order. Then he went through the classroom and out onto the terrace. The sun was already rising in the blue sky; a soft, bright light was bathing the deserted plateau. On the ridge the snow was melting in spots. The stones were about to reappear. Crouched on the edge of the plateau, the schoolmaster looked at the deserted expanse. He thought of Balducci. He had hurt him, for he had sent him off in a way as if he didn't want to be associated with him. He could still hear the gendarme's farewell and, without knowing why, he felt strangely empty and vulnerable. At that moment, from the other side of the schoolhouse, the prisoner coughed. Daru listened to him almost despite himself and then, furious, threw a pebble that whistled through the air before sinking into the snow. That man's stupid crime revolted him, but to hand him over was contrary to honor. Merely thinking of it made him smart with humiliation. And he cursed at one and the same time his own people who had sent him this Arab and the Arab too who had dared to kill and not managed to get away. Daru got up, walked in a circle on the terrace, waited motionless, and then went back into the schoolhouse.

The Arab, leaning over the cement floor of the shed, was washing his teeth with two fingers. Daru looked at him and said: "Come." He went back into the room ahead of the prisoner. He slipped a hunting-jacket on over his sweater and put on walking-shoes. Standing, he waited until the Arab had put on his chèche and sandals. They went into the classroom and the schoolmaster pointed to the exit, saying: "Go ahead." The fellow didn't budge. "I'm coming," said Daru. The Arab went out. Daru went back into the room and made a package of pieces of rusk, dates, and sugar. In the classroom, before going out, he hesitated a second in front of his desk, then crossed the threshold and locked the door. "That's the way," he said. He started toward the east, followed by the prisoner.

But, a short distance from the schoolhouse, he thought he heard a slight sound behind them. He retraced his steps and examined the surroundings of the house; there was no one there. The Arab watched him without seeming to understand. "Come on," said Daru.

They walked for an hour and rested beside a sharp peak of limestone. The snow was melting faster and faster and the sun was drinking up the puddles at once, rapidly cleaning the plateau, which gradually dried and vibrated like the air itself. When they resumed walking, the ground rang under their feet. From time to time a bird rent the space in front of them with a joyful cry. Daru breathed in deeply the fresh morning light. He felt a sort of rapture before the vast familiar expanse, now almost entirely yellow under its dome of blue sky. They walked an hour more, descending toward the south. They reached a level height made up of crumbly rocks. From there on, the plateau sloped down, eastward, toward a low plain where there were a few spindly trees and, to the south, toward outcroppings of rock that gave the landscape a chaotic look.

Daru surveyed the two directions. There was nothing but the sky on the horizon. Not a man could be seen. He turned toward the Arab, who was looking at him blankly. Daru held out the package to him. "Take it," he said. "There are dates, bread, and sugar. You can hold out for two days. Here are a thousand francs too." The Arab took the package and the money but kept his full hands at chest level as if he didn't know what to do with what was being given him. "Now look," the schoolmaster said as he pointed in the direction of the east, "there's the way to Tinguit. You have a two-hour walk. At Tinguit you'll find the administration and the police. They are expecting you." The Arab looked toward the east, still holding the package and the money against his chest. Daru took his elbow and turned him rather roughly toward the south. At the foot of the height on which they stood could be seen a faint path. "That's the trail across the plateau. In a day's walk from here you'll find pasturelands and the first nomads. They'll take you in and shelter you according to their law." The Arab had now turned toward Daru and a sort of panic was visible in his expression. "Listen," he said. Daru shook his head: "No, be quiet. Now I'm leaving you." He turned his back on him, took two long steps in the direction of the school, looked hesitantly at the motionless Arab, and started off again. For a few minutes he heard nothing but his own step resounding on the cold ground and did not turn his head. A moment later, however, he turned around. The Arab was still there on the edge of the hill, his arms hanging now, and he was looking at the schoolmaster. Daru felt something rise in his throat. But he swore with impatience, waved vaguely, and started off again. He had already gone some distance when he again stopped and looked. There was no longer anyone on the hill.

Daru hesitated. The sun was now rather high in the sky and was beginning to beat down on his head. The schoolmaster retraced his steps, at first somewhat uncertainly, then with decision. When he reached the little hill, he was bathed in sweat. He climbed it as fast as he could and stopped, out of breath, at the top. The rock-fields to the south stood out sharply against the blue sky, but on the plain to the east a steamy heat was already rising. And in that slight haze, Daru, with heavy heart, made out the Arab walking slowly on the road to prison.

A little later, standing before the window of the classroom, the schoolmaster was watching the clear light bathing the whole surface of the plateau, but

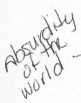

Absurdity of the world

he hardly saw it. Behind him on the blackboard, among the winding French rivers, sprawled the clumsily chalked up words he had just read: "You handed over our brother. You will pay for this." Daru looked at the sky, the plateau, and, beyond, the invisible lands stretching all the way to the sea. In this vast landscape he had loved so much, he was alone.

Fact Questions and Exercises

1. What is Daru's profession? *School teacher*
2. Identify Balducci.
3. What is the prisoner's nationality? Daru's nationality? *Arab,*
4. Identify Tinguit. *a city*
5. What crime has the prisoner committed? Why has he committed this crime? *Murder*
6. When Daru last sees him, where is the prisoner going? *to prison at Tinguit*
7. When Daru returns to the school, what is written on the blackboard?
8. Describe the story's setting.

For Discussion and Writing

1. Point out the ways in which Camus conveys Daru's isolation—physically and otherwise. Does this isolation help explain Daru's attitude toward the Arab? How? Why doesn't Daru take the Arab to prison? Why does the Arab choose to go to prison when let free? Is Daru also in a "prison"?
2. How many times are the four rivers of France mentioned? Why are these rivers important in the story? What do they symbolize, if anything? With what do they contrast?
3. List any details that indicate a brotherhood exists between Daru and the Arab, or between people in general. Does Camus imply that no such brotherhood is possible? Note the message that is scrawled on the blackboard when Daru returns from releasing the prisoner. Is this an ironic ending?
4. Check the definition of "existentialism" in the Guide to Literary Terms. How does this story expand the definition? Are there elements in the story that contradict the definition? If so, what are these elements?

Ralph Ellison [1914–   ]

Ellison was born in Oklahoma City, Oklahoma, and attended Tuskegee Institute. He originally wanted to be a composer of symphonies, but soon became interested in writing. His early stories usually involve the question of black racial identity within a white society. Ellison's work, however, is not characterized by the violence that is often associated with younger black writers. His only novel, *Invisible Man* (1952), is regarded as one of the best post-World War II American novels. Ellison's full name is Ralph Waldo Ellison—after the poet and philosopher Ralph Waldo Emerson. In *Invisible Man*, Ellison attempts to discover how Emerson's idea of self-reliance applies to the individual black man in American society.

King of the Bingo Game

The woman in front of him was eating roasted peanuts that smelled so good that he could barely contain his hunger. He could not even sleep and wished they'd hurry and begin the bingo game. There, on his right, two fellows were drinking wine out of a bottle wrapped in a paper bag, and he could hear soft gurgling in the dark. His stomach gave a low, gnawing growl. "If this was down South," he thought, "all I'd have to do is lean over and say, 'Lady, gimme a few of those peanuts, please ma'am,' and she'd pass me the bag and never think nothing of it." Or he could ask the fellows for a drink in the same way. Folks down South stuck together that way; they didn't even have to know you. But up here it was different. Ask somebody for something, and they'd think you were crazy. Well, I ain't crazy. I'm just broke, 'cause I got no birth certificate to get a job, and Laura 'bout to die 'cause we got no money for a doctor. But I ain't crazy. And yet a pinpoint of doubt was focused in his mind as he glanced toward the screen and saw the hero stealthily entering a dark room and sending the beam of a flashlight along a wall of bookcases. This is where he finds the trapdoor, he remembered. The man would pass abruptly through the wall and find the girl tied to a bed, her legs and arms spread wide, and her clothing torn to rags. He laughed softly to himself. He had seen the picture three times, and this was one of the best scenes.

On his right the fellow whispered wide-eyed to his companion, "Man, look ayonder!"

"Damn!"

"Wouldn't I like to have her tied up like that . . ."

"Hey! That fool's letting her loose!"

"Aw, man, he loves her."

"Love or no love!"

The man moved impatiently beside him, and he tried to involve himself in the scene. But Laura was on his mind. Tiring quickly of watching the picture he looked back to where the white beam filtered from the projection room above the balcony. It started small and grew large, specks of dust dancing in its whiteness as it reached the screen. It was strange how the beam always landed right on the screen and didn't mess up and fall somewhere else. But they had it all fixed. Everything was fixed. Now suppose when they showed that girl with her dress torn the girl started taking off the rest of her clothes, and when the guy came in he didn't untie her but kept her there and went to taking off his own clothes? *That* would be something to see. If a picture got out of hand like that those guys up there would go nuts. Yeah, and there'd be so many folks in here you couldn't find a seat for nine months! A strange sensation played over his skin. He shuddered. Yesterday he'd seen a bedbug on a woman's neck as they walked out into the bright street. But exploring his thigh through a hole in his pocket he found only goose pimples and old scars.

The bottle gurgled again. He closed his eyes. Now a dreamy music was accompanying the film and train whistles were sounding in the distance, and he was a boy again walking along a railroad trestle down South, and seeing the train coming, and running back as fast as he could go, and hearing the whistle blowing, and getting off the trestle to solid ground just in time, with the earth trembling beneath his feet, and feeling relieved as he ran down the cinder-strewn embankment onto the highway, and looking back and seeing with terror that the train had left the track and was following him right down the middle of the street, and all the white people laughing as he ran screaming . . .

"Wake up there, buddy! What the hell do you mean hollering like that? Can't you see we trying to enjoy this here picture?"

He stared at the man with gratitude.

"I'm sorry, old man," he said. "I musta been dreaming."

"Well, here, have a drink. And don't be making no noise like that, damn!"

His hands trembled as he tilted his head. It was not wine, but whiskey. Cold rye whiskey. He took a deep swoller, decided it was better not to take another, and handed the bottle back to its owner.

"Thanks, old man," he said.

Now he felt the cold whiskey breaking a warm path straight through the middle of him, growing hotter and sharper as it moved. He had not eaten all day, and it made him light-headed. The smell of the peanuts stabbed him like a knife, and he got up and found a seat in the middle aisle. But no sooner did he sit than he saw a row of intense-faced young girls, and got up again, thinking, "You chicks musta been Lindy-hopping somewhere." He found a seat several rows ahead as the lights came on, and he saw the screen disappear behind a heavy red and gold curtain; then the curtain rising, and the man with the microphone and a uniformed attendant coming on the stage.

He felt for his bingo cards, smiling. The guy at the door wouldn't like it if he knew about his having *five* cards. Well, not everyone played the bingo game; and even with five cards he didn't have much of a chance. For Laura, though, he had to have faith. He studied the cards, each with its different numerals, punching the free center hole in each and spreading them neatly across his lap; and when the lights faded he sat slouched in his seat so that he could look from his cards to the bingo wheel with but a quick shifting of his eyes.

Ahead, at the end of the darkness, the man with the microphone was pressing a button attached to a long cord and spinning the bingo wheel and calling out the number each time the wheel came to rest. And each time the voice rang out his finger raced over the cards for the number. With five cards he had to move fast. He became nervous; there were too many cards, and the man went too fast with his grating voice. Perhaps he should just select one and throw the others away. But he was afraid. He became warm. Wonder how much Laura's doctor would cost? Damn that, watch the cards! And with despair he heard the man call three in a row which he missed on all five cards. This way he'd never win . . .

When he saw the row of holes punched across the third card, he sat paralyzed and heard the man call three more numbers before he stumbled forward, screaming.

"Bingo! Bingo!"

"Let that fool up there," someone called.

"Get up there, man!"

He stumbled down the aisle and up the steps to the stage into a light so sharp and bright that for a moment it blinded him, and he felt that he had moved into the spell of some strange, mysterious power. Yet it was as familiar as the sun, and he knew it was the perfectly familiar bingo.

The man with the microphone was saying something to the audience as he held out his card. A cold light flashed from the man's finger as the card left his hand. His knees trembled. The man stepped closer, checking the card against the numbers chalked on the board. Suppose he had made a mistake? The pomade on the man's hair made him feel faint, and he backed away. But the man was checking the card over the microphone now, and he had to stay. He stood tense, listening.

"Under the O, forty-four," the man chanted. "Under the I, seven. Under the G, three. Under the B, ninety-six. Under the N, thirteen!"

His breath came easier as the man smiled at the audience.

"Yessir, ladies and gentlemen, he's one of the chosen people!"

The audience rippled with laughter and applause.

"Step right up to the front of the stage."

He moved slowly forward, wishing that the light was not so bright.

"To win to-night's jackpot of $36.90 the wheel must stop between the double zero, understand?"

He nodded, knowing the ritual from the many days and nights he had watched the winners march across the stage to press the button that controlled the spinning wheel and receive the prizes. And now he followed the instructions as though he'd crossed the slippery stage a million prize-winning times.

The man was making some kind of a joke, and he nodded vacantly. So tense had he become that he felt a sudden desire to cry and shook it away. He felt vaguely that his whole life was determined by the bingo wheel; not only that which would happen now that he was at last before it, but all that had gone before, since his birth, and his mother's birth and the birth of his father. It had always been there, even though he had not been aware of it, handing out the unlucky cards and numbers of his days. The feeling persisted, and he started quickly away. I better get down from here before I make a fool of myself, he thought.

"Here, boy," the man called. "You haven't started yet."

Someone laughed as he went hesitantly back.

"Are you all reet?"

He grinned at the man's jive talk, but no words would come, and he knew it was not a convincing grin. For suddenly he knew that he stood on the slippery brink of some terrible embarrassment.

"Where are you from, boy?" the man asked.

"Down South."

"He's from down South, ladies and gentlemen," the man said. "Where from? Speak right into the mike."

"Rocky Mont," he said. "Rock' Mont, North Car'lina."

"So you decided to come down off that mountain to the U.S.," the man laughed. He felt that the man was making a fool of him, but then something cold was placed in his hand, and the lights were no longer behind him.

Standing before the wheel he felt alone, but that was somehow right, and he remembered his plan. He would give the wheel a short quick twirl. Just a touch of the button. He had watched it many times, and always it came close to double zero when it was short and quick. He steeled himself; the fear had left, and he felt a profound sense of promise, as though he were about to be repaid for all the things he'd suffered all his life. Trembling, he pressed the button. There was a whirl of lights, and in a second he realized with finality that though he wanted to, he could not stop. It was as though he held a high-powered line in his naked hand. His nerves tightened. As the wheel increased its speed it seemed to draw him more and more into its power, as though it held his fate; and with it came a deep need to submit, to whirl, to lose himself in its swirl of color. He could not stop it now. So let it be.

The button rested snugly in his palm where the man had placed it. And now he became aware of the man beside him, advising him through the microphone, while behind the shadowy audience hummed with noisy voices. He shifted his feet. There was still that feeling of helplessness within him, making part of him desire to turn back, even now that the jackpot was right in his hand. He squeezed the button until his fist ached. Then, like the sudden shriek of a subway whistle, a doubt tore through his head. Suppose he did not spin the wheel long enough? What could he do, and how could he tell? And then he knew, even as he wondered, that as long as he pressed the button, he could control the jackpot. He and only he could determine whether or not it was to be his. Not even the man with the microphone could do anything about it now. He felt drunk. Then, as though he had come down from a high hill into a valley of people, he heard the audience yelling.

"Come down from there, you jerk!"

"Let somebody else have a chance . . ."

"Ole Jack thinks he done found the end of the rainbow . . ."

The last voice was not unfriendly, and he turned and smiled dreamily into the yelling mouths. Then he turned his back squarely on them.

"Don't take too long, boy," a voice said.

He nodded. They were yelling behind him. Those folks did not understand what had happened to him. They had been playing the bingo game day in and night out for years, trying to win rent money or hamburger change. But not one of those wise guys had discovered this wonderful thing. He watched the wheel whirling past the numbers and experienced a burst of exaltation: This is God! This is the really truly God! He said it aloud, "This is God!"

He said it with such absolute conviction that he feared he would fall fainting into the footlights. But the crowd yelled so loud that they could not hear. Those fools, he thought. I'm here trying to tell them the most wonderful secret in the world, and they're yelling like they gone crazy. A hand fell upon his shoulder.

"You'll have to make a choice now, boy. You've taken too long."

He brushed the hand violently away.

"Leave me alone, man. I know what I'm doing!"

The man looked surprised and held on to the microphone for support. And because he did not wish to hurt the man's feelings he smiled, realizing with a sudden pang that there was no way of explaining to the man just why he had to stand there pressing the button forever.

"Come here," he called tiredly.

The man approached, rolling the heavy microphone across the stage.

"Anybody can play this bingo game, right?" he said.

"Sure, but . . ."

He smiled, feeling inclined to be patient with this slick looking white man with his blue shirt and his sharp gabardine suit.

"That's what I thought," he said. "Anybody can win the jackpot as long as they get the lucky number, right?"

"That's the rule, but after all . . ."

"That's what I thought," he said. "And the big prize goes to the man who knows how to win it?"

The man nodded speechlessly.

"Well then, go on over there and watch me win like I want to. I ain't going to hurt nobody," he said, "and I'll show you how to win. I mean to show the whole world how it's got to be done."

And because he understood, he smiled again to let the man know that he held nothing against him for being white and impatient. Then he refused to see the man any longer and stood pressing the button, the voices of the crowd reaching him like sounds in distant streets. Let them yell. All the Negroes down there were just ashamed because he was black like them. He smiled inwardly, knowing how it was. Most of the time he was ashamed of what Negroes did himself. Well, let them be ashamed for something this time. Like him. He was like a long thin black wire that was being stretched and wound upon the bingo wheel; wound until he wanted to scream; wound, but this time himself controlling the winding and the sadness and the shame, and because he did, Laura would be all right. Suddenly the lights flickered. He staggered backwards. Had something gone wrong? All this noise. Didn't they know that although he controlled the wheel, it also controlled him, and unless he pressed the button forever and forever and ever it would stop, leaving him high and dry, dry and high on this hard high slippery hill and Laura dead? There was only one chance; he had to do whatever the wheel demanded. And gripping the button in despair, he discovered with surprise that it imparted a nervous energy. His spine tingled. He felt a certain power.

Now he faced the raging crowd with defiance, its screams penetrating his eardrums like trumpets shrieking from a juke-box. The vague faces glowing in the bingo lights gave him a sense of himself that he had never known before. He was running the show, by God! They had to react to him, for he was their luck. This is *me*, he thought. Let the bastards yell. Then someone was laughing inside him, and he realized that somehow he had forgotten his own name. It was a sad, lost feeling to lose your name, and a crazy thing to do. That name had been given him by the white man who had owned his grandfather a long lost time ago down South. But maybe those wise guys knew his name.

"Who am I?" he screamed.

"Hurry up and bingo, you jerk!"

They didn't know either, he thought sadly. They didn't even know their own names, they were all poor nameless bastards. Well, he didn't need that old name; he was reborn. For as long as he pressed the button he was The-man-who-pressed-the-button-who-held-the-prize-who-was-the-King-of-Bingo. That was the way it was, and he'd have to press the button even if nobody understood, even though Laura did not understand.

"Live!" he shouted.

The audience quieted like the dying of a huge fan.

"Live, Laura, baby. I got holt of it now, sugar. Live!"

He screamed it, tears streaming down his face. "I got nobody but YOU!"

The screams tore from his very guts. He felt as though the rush of blood to his head would burst out in baseball seams of small red droplets, like a head beaten by police clubs. Bending over he saw a trickle of blood splashing the toe of his shoe. With his free hand he searched his head. It was his nose. God, suppose something has gone wrong? He felt that the whole audience had somehow entered him and was stamping its feet in his stomach and he was unable to throw them out. They wanted the prize, that was it. They wanted the secret for themselves. But they'd never get it; he would keep the bingo wheel whirling forever, and Laura would be safe in the wheel. But would she? It had to be, because if she were not safe the wheel would cease to turn; it could not go on. He had to get away, *vomit* all, and his mind formed an image of himself running with Laura in his arms down the tracks of the subway just ahead of an A train, running desperately *vomit* with people screaming for him to come out but knowing no way of leaving the tracks because to stop would bring the train crushing down upon him and to attempt to leave across the other tracks would mean to run into a hot third rail as high as his waist which threw blue sparks that blinded his eyes until he could hardly see.

He heard singing and the audience was clapping its hands.

Shoot the liquor to him, Jim, boy!
Clap-clap-clap
Well a-calla the cop
He's blowing his top!
Shoot the liquor to him, Jim, boy!

Bitter anger grew within him at the singing. They think I'm crazy. Well let 'em laugh. I'll do what I got to do.

He was standing in an attitude of intense listening when he saw that they were watching something on the stage behind him. He felt weak. But when he turned he saw no one. If only his thumb did not ache so. Now they were applauding. And for a moment he thought that the wheel had stopped. But that was impossible, his thumb still pressed the button. Then he saw them. Two men in uniform beckoned from the end of the stage. They were coming toward him, walking in step, slowly, like a tap-dance team returning for a third encore. But their shoulders shot forward, and he backed away, looking wildly about. There was nothing to fight them with. He had only the long black cord which led to a plug somewhere back stage, and he couldn't use that because it operated the bingo wheel. He backed slowly, fixing the men with his eyes as his lips stretched over his teeth in a tight, fixed grin; moved toward the end of the stage and realizing that he couldn't go much further, for suddenly the cord became taut and he couldn't afford to break the cord. But he had to do something. The audience was howling. Suddenly he stopped dead, seeing the men halt, their legs lifted as in an interrupted step of a slow-motion dance. There was nothing to do but run in the other direction and he dashed forward, slipping and sliding. The men fell back, surprised. He struck out violently going past.

"Grab him!"

He ran, but all too quickly the cord tightened, resistingly, and he turned and ran back again. This time he slipped them, and discovered by running in a circle before the wheel he could keep the cord from tightening. But this way he had to flail his arms to keep the men away. Why couldn't they leave a man alone? He ran, circling.

"Ring down the curtain," someone yelled. But they couldn't do that. If they did the wheel flashing from the projection room would be cut off. But they had him before he could tell them so, trying to pry open his fist, and he was wrestling and trying to bring his knees into the fight and holding on to the button, for it was his life. And now he was down, seeing a foot coming down, crushing his wrist cruelly, down, as he saw the wheel whirling serenely above.

"I can't give it up," he screamed. Then quietly, in a confidential tone, "Boys, I really can't give it up."

It landed hard against his head. And in the blank moment they had it away from him, completely now. He fought them trying to pull him up from the stage as he watched the wheel spin slowly to a stop. Without surprise he saw it rest at double-zero.

"You see," he pointed bitterly.

"Sure, boy, sure, it's O.K.," one of the men said smiling.

And seeing the man bow his head to someone he could not see, he felt very, very happy; he would receive what all the winners received.

But as he warmed in the justice of the man's tight smile he did not see the man's slow wink, nor see the bow-legged man behind him step clear of the swiftly descending curtain and set himself for a blow. He only felt the dull pain exploding in his skull, and he knew even as it slipped out of him that his luck had run out on the stage.

Fact Questions and Exercises

1. What is the central character doing as the story begins?
2. Identify Laura.
3. Describe the action of the movie that the central character watches just before the bingo game.
4. Where did the central character spend his boyhood?
5. At what number must the bingo wheel stop in order for the central character to win the $36.90 jackpot? Where does the wheel finally stop?
6. Of what is the central character speaking when he says "This is God!"?
7. The central character sees blood on his shoe. Where does the blood come from?

For Discussion and Writing

1. What themes or topics are introduced in the first paragraph? How are these themes and topics developed in the remainder of the story? What are some of the things learned about the central character in the first paragraph?
2. The central character, referring to the movie projector beam, says "Everything was fixed." In the story, does Ellison show that everything *is* fixed for the central character? How? Does the man have any control over his own life? Or is he at the mercy of forces over which he has no command?
3. Analyze the central character. Where is he from? What is known about his ancestors? To what race does he belong? Why is he so dependent on winning the bingo game?
4. The wheel of fortune used in the bingo game is perhaps the most obvious symbol Ellison uses. What are some others? How do these symbols help explain the meaning of the story?

irley Jackson [1919–1965]

in was born in San Francisco, California, but was reared in ...ochester, New York. She graduated from Syracuse University, where she founded the university's literary journal. Although she did write a number of novels and short stories, her reputation rests mainly on "The Lottery," a tale of human brutality in ritualistic, symbolic terms. Among her other works are *Life Among the Savages* (1945) and *The Hauntings of Hill House* (1959).

The Lottery

The morning of June 27th was clear and sunny, with the fresh warmth of a full-summer day; the flowers were blossoming profusely and the grass was richly green. The people of the village began to gather in the square, between the post office and the bank, around ten o'clock; in some towns there were so many people that the lottery took two days and had to be started on June 26th, but in this village, where there were only about three hundred people, the whole lottery took less than two hours, so it could begin at ten o'clock in the morning and still be through in time to allow the villagers to get home for noon dinner.

The children assembled first, of course. School was recently over for the summer, and the feeling of liberty sat uneasily on most of them; they tended to gather together quietly for a while before they broke into boisterous play, and their talk was still of the classroom and the teacher, of books and reprimands. Bobby Martin had already stuffed his pockets full of stones, and the other boys soon followed his example, selecting the smoothest and roundest stones; Bobby and Harry Jones and Dickie Delacroix—the villagers pronounced this name "Dellacroy"—eventually made a great pile of stones in one corner of the square and guarded it against the raids of the other boys. The girls stood aside, talking among themselves, looking over their shoulders at the boys, and the very small children rolled in the dust or clung to the hands of their older brothers or sisters.

Soon the men began to gather, surveying their own children, speaking of planting and rain, tractors and taxes. They stood together, away from the pile of stones in the corner, and their jokes were quiet and they smiled rather than laughed. The women, wearing faded house dresses and sweaters, came shortly after their menfolk. They greeted one another and exchanged bits of gossip as they went to join their husbands. Soon the women, standing by their husbands, began to call to their children, and the children came reluctantly, having to be called four or five times. Bobby Martin ducked under his mother's grasping hand and ran, laughing, back to the pile of stones. His father spoke up sharply, and Bobby came quickly and took his place between his father and his oldest brother.

The lottery was conducted—as were the square dances, the teenage club, the Halloween program—by Mr. Summers, who had time and energy to devote to civic activities. He was a round-faced, jovial man and he ran the coal business, and people were sorry for him, because he had no children and his wife was a scold. When he arrived in the square, carrying the black wooden box, there was a murmur of conversation among the villagers, and he waved and called, "Little late today, folks." The postmaster, Mr. Graves, followed him, carrying a three-legged stool, and the stool was put in the center of the square and Mr. Summers set the black box down on it. The villagers kept their distance, leaving a space between themselves and the stool, and when Mr. Summers said, "Some of you fellows want to give me a hand?" there was a hesitation before two men, Mr. Martin and his oldest son, Baxter, came forward to hold the box steady on the stool while Mr. Summers stirred up the papers inside it.

The original paraphernalia for the lottery had been lost long ago, and the black box now resting on the stool had been put into use even before Old Man Warner, the oldest man in town, was born. Mr Summers spoke frequently to the villagers about making a new box, but no one liked to upset even as much tradition as was represented by the black box. There was a story that the present box had been made with some pieces of the box that had preceded it, the one that had been constructed when the first people settled down to make a village here. Every year, after the lottery, Mr. Summers began talking again about a new box, but every year the subject was allowed to fade off without anything's being done. The black box grew shabbier each year; by now it was no longer completely black but splintered badly along one side to show the original wood color, and in some places faded or stained.

Mr. Martin and his oldest son, Baxter, held the black box securely on the stool until Mr. Summers had stirred the papers thoroughly with his hand. Because so much of the ritual had been forgotten or discarded, Mr. Summers had been successful in having slips of paper substituted for the chips of wood that had been used for generations. Chips of wood, Mr. Summers had argued, had been all very well when the village was tiny, but now that the population was more than three hundred and likely to keep on growing, it was necessary to use something that would fit more easily into the black box. The night before the lottery, Mr. Summers and Mr. Graves made up the slips of paper and put them in the box, and it was then taken to the safe of Mr. Summer's coal company and locked up until Mr. Summers was ready to take it to the square next morning. The rest of the year, the box was put away, sometimes one place, sometimes another; it had spent one year in Mr. Graves's barn and another year under foot in the post office, and sometimes it was set on a shelf in the Martin grocery and left there.

There was a great deal of fussing to be done before Mr. Summers declared the lottery open. There were the lists to make up—of heads of families, heads of households in each family, members of each household in each family. There was the proper swearing-in of Mr. Summers by the postmaster, as the official of the lottery; at one time, some people remembered, there had been a recital of some sort; performed by the official of the lottery, a perfunctory, tuneless chant that had been rattled off duly each year; some people believed that the official of the lottery used to stand just so when he said or sang it, others believed that he was supposed to walk among the people, but years and years ago this part of the ritual had been allowed to lapse. There had been, also, a ritual salute, which the official of the lottery had had to use in addressing each person who came up to draw from the box, but this also had changed with time, until now it was felt necessary only for the official to speak to each person approaching. Mr. Summers was very good at all this; in his clean white shirt and blue jeans, with one hand resting carelessly on the black box, he seemed very proper and important as he talked interminably to Mr. Graves and the Martins.

Just as Mr. Summers finally left off talking and turned to the assembled villagers, Mrs. Hutchinson came hurriedly along the path to the square, her sweater thrown over her shoulders, and slid into place in the back of the crowd. "Clean forgot what day it was," she said to Mrs. Delacroix, who stood next to her, and they both laughed softly. "Thought my old man was out back stacking wood." Mrs. Hutchinson went on, "and then I looked out the window and the kids was gone, and then I remembered it was the twenty-seventh and came a-running." She dried her hands on her apron, and Mrs. Delacroix said, "You're in time, though. They're still talking away up there."

Mrs. Hutchinson craned ner neck to see through the crowd and found her husband and children standing near the front. She tapped Mrs. Delacroix on the arm as a farewell and began to make her way through the crowd. The people separated good-humoredly to let her through; two or three people said, in voices just loud enough to be heard across the crowd, "Here comes your Missus, Hutchinson," and "Bill, she made it after all." Mrs. Hutchinson reached her husband, and Mr. Summers, who had been waiting, said cheerfully, "Thought we were going to have to get on without you, Tessie." Mrs. Hutchinson said, grinning, "Wouldn't have me leave m'dishes in the sink, now, would you, Joe?," and soft laughter ran through the crowd as the people stirred back into position after Mrs. Hutchinson's arrival.

"Well, now," Mr. Summers said soberly, "guess we better get started, get this over with, so's we can go back to work. Anybody ain't here?"

"Dunbar," several people said. "Dunbar, Dunbar."

Mr. Summers consulted his list. "Clyde Dunbar," he said. "That's right. He's broke his leg, hasn't he? Who's drawing for him?"

"Me, I guess," a woman said, and Mr. Summers turned to look at her. "Wife draws for her husband," Mr. Summers said. "Don't you have a grown boy to do it for you, Janey?" Although Mr. Summers and everyone else in the village knew the answer perfectly well, it was the business of the official of the lottery to ask such questions formally. Mr. Summers waited with an expression of polite interest while Mrs. Dunbar answered.

"Horace's not but sixteen yet," Mrs. Dunbar said regretfully. "Guess I gotta fill in for the old man this year."

"Right," Mr. Summers said. He made a note on the list he was holding. Then he asked, "Watson boy drawing this year?"

A tall boy in the crowd raised his hand. "Here," he said. "I'm drawing for m'mother and me." He blinked his eyes nervously and ducked his head as several voices in the crowd said things like "Good fellow, Jack," and "Glad to see your mother's got a man to do it."

"Well," Mr. Summers said, "guess that's everyone. Old Man Warner make it?"

"Here," a voice said, and Mr. Summers nodded.

A sudden hush fell on the crowd as Mr. Summers cleared his throat and looked at the list. "All ready?" he called. "Now, I'll read the names—heads of families first—and the men come up and take a paper out of the box. Keep the paper folded in your hand without looking at it until everyone has had a turn. Everything clear?"

The people had done it so many times that they only half listened to the directions; most of them were quiet, wetting their lips, not looking around. Then Mr. Summers raised one hand high and said, "Adams." A man disengaged himself from the crowd and came forward. "Hi, Steve," Mr. Summers said, and Mr. Adams said, "Hi, Joe." They grinned at one another humorlessly and nervously. Then Mr. Adams reached into the black box and took out a folded paper. He held it firmly by one corner as he turned and went hastily back to his place in the crowd, where he stood a little apart from his family not looking down at his hand.

"Allen," Mr. Summers said. "Anderson. . . . Bentham."

"Seems like there's no time at all between lotteries any more," Mrs. Delacroix said to Mrs. Graves in the back row. "Seems like we got through with the last one only last week."

"Time sure goes fast," Mrs. Graves said.

"Clark. . . . Delacroix."

"There goes my old man," Mrs. Delacroix said. She held her breath while her husband went forward.

"Dunbar," Mrs. Summers said, and Mrs. Dunbar went steadily to the box while one of the women said, "Go on, Janey," and another said, "There she goes."

"We're next," Mrs. Graves said. She watched while Mr. Graves came around from the side of the box, greeted Mr. Summers gravely, and selected a slip of paper from the box. By now, all through the crowd there were men holding the small folded papers in their large hands, turning them over and over nervously. Mrs. Dunbar and her two sons stood together, Mrs. Dunbar holding the slip of paper.

"Harburt. . . . Hutchinson."

"Get up there, Bill," Mrs. Hutchinson said, and the people near her laughed.

"Jones."

"They do say," Mr. Adams said to Old Man Warner, who stood next to him, "that over in the north village they're talking of giving up the lottery."

Old Man Warner snorted. "Pack of crazy fools," he said. "Listening to the young folks, nothing's good enough for *them*. Next thing you know, they'll be wanting to go back to living in caves, nobody work any more, live *that* way for a while. Used to be a saying about 'Lottery in June, corn be heavy soon.' First thing you know, we'd all be eating stewed chickweed and acorns. There's *always* been a lottery," he added petulantly. "Bad enough to see young Joe Summers up there joking with everybody."

"Some places have already quit lotteries," Mrs. Adams said.

"Nothing but trouble in *that*," Old Man Warner said stoutly. "Pack of young fools."

"Martin." And Bobby Martin watched his father go forward. "Overdyke. . . . Percy."

"I wish they'd hurry," Mrs. Dunbar said to her older son. "I wish they'd hurry."

"They're almost through," her son said.

"You get ready to run tell Dad," Mrs. Dunbar said.

Mr. Summers called his own name and then stepped forward precisely and selected a slip from the box. Then he called "Warner."

"Seventy-seventh year I been in the lottery," Old Man Warner said as he went through the crowd. "Seventy-seventh time."

"Watson." The tall boy came awkwardly through the crowd. Someone said, "Don't be nervous, Jack," and Mr. Summers said, "Take your time, son."

"Zanini."

After that, there was a long pause, a breathless pause, until Mr. Summers, holding his slip of paper in the air, said, "All right, fellows." For a minute, no one moved, and then all the slips of paper were opened. Suddenly, all the women began to speak at once, saying, "Who is it?," "Who's got it?," "Is it the Dunbars?," "Is it the Watsons?" Then the voices began to say, "It's Hutchinson. It's Bill," "Bill Hutchinson's got it."

"Go tell your father," Mrs. Dunbar said to her older son.

People began to look around to see the Hutchinsons. Bill Hutchinson was standing quiet staring down at the paper in his hand. Suddenly Tessie Hutchinson shouted to Mr. Summers, "You didn't give him time enough to take any paper he wanted. I saw you. It wasn't fair."

"Be a good sport, Tessie," Mrs. Delacroix called, and Mrs. Graves said, "All of us took the same chance."

"Shut up, Tessie," Bill Hutchinson said.

"Well, everyone," Mr. Summers said, "that was done pretty fast, and now we've got to be hurrying a little more to get done in time." He consulted his next list. "Bill," he said, "you draw for the Hutchinson family. You got any other households in the Hutchinsons?"

"There's Don and Eva," Mrs. Hutchinson yelled. "Make *them* take their chance!"

"Daughters draw with their husbands' families, Tessie," Mr. Summers said gently. "You know that as well as anyone else."

"It wasn't *fair*," Tessie said.

"I guess not, Joe," Bill Hutchinson said regretfully. "My daughter draws with her husband's family, that's only fair. And I've got no other family except the kids."

"Then, as far as drawing for families is concerned, it's you," Mr. Summers said in explanation, "and as far as drawing for households is concerned, that's you, too. Right?"

"Right," Bill Hutchinson said.

"How many kids, Bill?" Mr. Summers asked formally.

"Three," Bill Hutchinson said. "There's Bill, Jr., and Nancy, and little Dave. And Tessie and me."

"All right, then," Mr. Summers said. "Harry, you got their tickets back?"

Mr. Graves nodded and held up the slips of paper. "Put them in the box, then," Mr. Summers directed. "Take Bill's and put it in."

"I think we ought to start over," Mrs. Hutchinson said, as quietly as she could. "I tell you it wasn't *fair*. You didn't give him time enough to choose. *Everybody* saw that."

Mr. Graves had selected the five slips and put them in the box, and he dropped all the papers but those onto the ground, where the breeze caught them and lifted them off.

"Listen, everybody," Mrs. Hutchinson was saying to the people around her.

"Ready, Bill?" Mr. Summers asked, and Bill Hutchinson, with one quick glance around at his wife and children, nodded.

"Remember," Mr. Summers said, "take the slips and keep them folded until each person has taken one. Harry, you help little Dave." Mr. Graves took the hand of the little boy, who came willingly with him up to the box. "Take a paper out of the box, Davy," Mr. Summers said. Davy put his hand into the box and laughed. "Take just *one* paper," Mr. Summers said. "Harry, you hold it for him." Mr. Graves took the child's hand and removed the folded paper from the tight fist and held it while little Dave stood next to him and looked up at him wonderingly.

"Nancy next," Mr. Summers said. Nancy was twelve, and her school friends breathed heavily as she went forward, switching her skirt, and took a slip daintily from the box. "Bill, Jr.," Mr. Summers said, and Billy, his face red and his feet over-large, nearly knocked the box over as he got a paper out. "Tessie," Mr. Summers said. She hesitated for a minute, looking around defiantly, and then set her lips and went up to the box. She snatched a paper out and held it behind her.

"Bill," Mr. Summers said, and Bill Hutchinson reached into the box and felt around, bringing his hand out at last with the slip of paper in it.

The crowd was quiet. A girl whispered, "I hope it's not Nancy," and the sound of the whisper reached the edges of the crowd.

"It's not the way it used to be," Old Man Warner said clearly. "People ain't the way they used to be."

"All right," Mr. Summers said. "Open the papers. Harry, you open little Dave's."

Mr. Graves opened the slip of paper and there was a general sigh through the crowd as he held it up and everyone could see that it was blank. Nancy and Bill, Jr. opened theirs at the same time, and both beamed and laughed, turning around to the crowd and holding their slips of paper above their heads.

"Tessie," Mr. Summers said. There was a pause, and then Mr. Summers looked at Bill Hutchinson, and Bill unfolded his paper and showed it. It was blank.

"It's Tessie," Mr. Summers said, and his voice was hushed. "Show us her paper, Bill."

Bill Hutchinson went over to his wife and forced the slip of paper out of her hand. It had a black spot on it, the black spot Mr. Summers had made the night before with the heavy pencil in the coal-company office. Bill Hutchinson held it up, and there was a stir in the crowd.

"All right, folks," Mr. Summers said. "Let's finish quickly."

Although the villagers had forgotten the ritual and lost the original black box, they still remembered to use stones. The pile of stones the boys had made earlier was ready; there were stones on the ground with the blowing scraps of paper that had come out of the box. Mrs. Delacroix selected a stone so large she had to pick it up with both hands and turned to Mrs. Dunbar. "Come on," she said. "Hurry up."

Mrs. Dunbar had small stones in both hands, and she said, gasping for breath, "I can't run at all. You'll have to go ahead and I'll catch up with you."

The children had stones already, and someone gave little Davy Hutchinson a few pebbles.

Tessie Hutchinson was in the center of a cleared space by now, and she held her hands out desperately as the villagers moved in on her. "It isn't fair," she said. A stone hit her on the side of the head.

Old Man Warner was saying, "Come on, come on, everyone." Steve Adams was in the front of the crowd of villagers, with Mrs. Graves beside him.

"It isn't fair, it isn't right," Mrs. Hutchinson screamed, and then they were upon her.

Fact Questions and Exercises

1. During which month of the year does the lottery take place? *June*
2. What is the name of the man who conducts the lottery? *Joe Summers*
3. Identify the black wooden box.
4. How is the lottery conducted?
5. Who wins the lottery?
6. What happens to the person who draws the black spot?

For Discussion and Writing

1. Look at the second paragraph. How does it serve as an effective beginning for the story? Does it arouse interest and suspense? Does it foreshadow what follows?
2. How long has the lottery been a yearly practice? What purpose does it serve? Is it important that the lottery is conducted on June 27 and that the man who runs it is Mr. Summers? Why?
3. What seems to be the townspeople's attitude toward the lottery? Do they seem to enjoy it? If so, how is this enjoyment expressed? Does anyone want to abolish the lottery? Who speaks out in support of the lottery? What does Jackson seem to be saying about people in general?
4. Check the definition of "myth" in the Guide to Literary Terms. Suggest a myth that might serve as the background for this story. How does it add to the meaning of the story?

Ray Bradbury [1920–   ]

Bradbury was born in Waukegan, Illinois. As a child, he wrote and illustrated his own stories and, in high school, edited his own science-fiction magazine. He moved to Los Angeles in 1940, and sold newspapers while trying to establish himself as a writer. By 1945 he was regarded as one of America's best science-fiction writers. His stories are usually affirmative in outlook and highly unscientific, and marked by a prose style that is both poetic and colloquial. Among his best-known books are *The Illustrated Man* (1951), *Fahrenheit 451* (1953), and *I Sing the Body Electric* (1969).

August 2026:
There Will Come Soft Rains

In the living room the voice clock sang. *Tick-tock, seven o'clock, time to get up, time to get up, seven o'clock!* as if it were afraid that nobody would. The morning house lay empty. The clock ticked on, repeating and repeating its sounds into the emptiness. *Seven-nine, breakfast time, seven-nine!*

In the kitchen the breakfast stove gave a hissing sigh and ejected from its warm interior eight pieces of perfectly browned toast, eight eggs sunnyside up, sixteen slices of bacon, two coffees, and two cool glasses of milk.

"Today is August 4, 2026," said a second voice from the kitchen ceiling, "in the city of Allendale, California." It repeated the date three times for memory's sake. "Today is Mr. Featherstone's birthday. Today is the anniversary of Tilita's marriage. Insurance is payable, as are the water, gas and light bills."

Somewhere in the walls, relays clicked, memory tapes glided under electric eyes.

Eight-one, tick-tock, eight-one o'clock, off to school, off to work, run, run, eight-one! But no doors slammed, no carpets took the soft tread of rubber heels. It was raining outside. The weather box on the front door sang quietly: "Rain, rain, go away; rubbers, raincoats for today . . ." And the rain tapped on the empty house, echoing.

Outside, the garage chimed and lifted its door to reveal the waiting car. After a long wait the door swung down again.

At eight-thirty the eggs were shriveled and the toast was like stone. An aluminum wedge scraped them into the sink, where hot water whirled them down a metal throat which digested and flushed them away to the distant sea. The dirty dishes were dropped into a hot washer and emerged twinkling dry.

Nine-fifteen, sang the clock, *time to clean.*

Out of warrens in the wall, tiny robot mice darted. The rooms were acrawl with the small cleaning animals, all rubber and metal. They thudded against chairs, whirling their mustached runners, kneading the rug nap, sucking gently at hidden dust. Then, like mysterious invaders, they popped into their burrows. Their pink electric eyes faded. The house was clean.

Ten o'clock. The sun came out from behind the rain. The house stood alone in a city of rubble and ashes. This was the one house left standing. At night the ruined city gave off a radioactive glow which could be seen for miles.

Ten-fifteen. The garden sprinklers whirled up in golden founts, filling the soft morning air with scatterings of brightness. The water pelted windowpanes, running down the charred west side where the house had been burned evenly free of its white paint. The entire west face of the house was black, save for five places. Here the silhouette in paint of a man mowing a lawn. Here, as in a photograph, a woman bent to pick flowers. Still farther over, their images burned on wood in one titanic instant, a small boy, hands flung into the air; higher up, the image of a thrown ball, and opposite him a girl, hands raised to catch a ball which never came down.

The five spots of paint—the man, the woman, the children, the ball— remained. The rest was a thin charcoaled layer.

The gentle sprinkler rain filled the garden with falling light.

Until this day, how well the house had kept its peace. How carefully it had inquired, "Who goes there? What's the password?" and, getting no answer from lonely foxes and whining cats, it had shut up its windows and drawn shades in an oldmaidenly preoccupation with self-protection which bordered on a mechanical paranoia.

It quivered at each sound, the house did. If a sparrow brushed a window, the shade snapped up. The bird, startled, flew off! No, not even a bird must touch the house!

The house was an altar with ten thousand attendants, big, small, servicing, attending, in choirs. But the gods had gone away, and the ritual of the religion continued senselessly, uselessly.

Twelve noon.

A dog whined, shivering, on the front porch.

The front door recognized the dog voice and opened. The dog, once huge and fleshy, but now gone to bone and covered with sores, moved in and through the house, tracking mud. Behind it whirred angry mice, angry at having to pick up mud, angry at inconvenience.

For not a leaf fragment blew under the door but what the wall panels flipped open and the copper scrap rats flashed swiftly out. The offending dust, hair, or paper, seized in miniature steel jaws, was raced back to the burrows. There, down tubes which fed into the cellar, it was dropped into the sighing vent of an incinerator which sat like evil Baal in a dark corner.

The dog ran upstairs, hysterically yelping to each door, at last realizing, as the house realized, that only silence was here.

It sniffed the air and scratched the kitchen door. Behind the door, the stove was making pancakes which filled the house with a rich baked odor and the scent of maple syrup.

The dog frothed at the mouth, lying at the door, sniffing, its eyes turned to fire. It ran wildly in circles, biting at its tail, spun in a frenzy, and died. It lay in the parlor for an hour.

Two o'clock, sang a voice.

Delicately sensing decay at last, the regiments of mice hummed out as softly as blown gray leaves in an electrical wind.

Two-fifteen.

The dog was gone.

In the cellar, the incinerator glowed suddenly and a whirl of sparks leaped up the chimney.

Two thirty-five.

Bridge tables sprouted from patio walls. Playing cards fluttered onto pads in a shower of pips. Martinis manifested on an oaken bench with egg-salad sandwiches. Music played.

But the tables were silent and the cards untouched.

At four o'clock the tables folded like great butterflies back through the paneled walls.

Four-thirty.

The nursery walls glowed.

Animals took shape: yellow giraffes, blue lions, pink antelopes, lilac panthers cavorting in crystal substance. The walls were glass. They looked out upon color and fantasy. Hidden films clocked through well-oiled sprockets, and the walls lived. The nursery floor was woven to resemble a crisp, cereal meadow. Over this ran aluminum roaches and iron crickets, and in the hot still air butterflies of delicate red tissue wavered among the sharp aroma of animal spoors! There was the sound like a great matted yellow hive of bees within a dark bellows, the lazy bumble of a purring lion. And there was the patter of okapi feet and the murmur of a fresh jungle rain, like other hoofs, falling upon the summer-starched grass. Now the walls dissolved into distances of parched weed, mile on mile, and warm endless sky. The animals drew away into thorn brakes and water holes.

It was the children's hour.

Five o'clock. The bath filled with clear hot water.

Six, seven, eight o'clock. The dinner dishes manipulated like magic tricks, and in the study a *click.* In the metal stand opposite the hearth where a fire now blazed up warmly, a cigar popped out, half an inch of soft gray ash on it, smoking, waiting.

Nine o'clock. The beds warmed their hidden circuits, for nights were cool here.

Nine-five. A voice spoke from the study ceiling:

"Mrs. McClellan, which poem would you like this evening?"

The house was silent.

The voice said at last, "Since you express no preference, I shall select a poem at random." Quiet music rose to back the voice. "Sara Teasdale. As I recall, your favorite. . . .

"There will come soft rains and the smell of the ground,
And swallows circling with their shimmering sound;

And frogs in the pools singing at night,
And wild plum trees in tremulous white;

Robins will wear their feathery fire,
Whistling their whims on a low fence-wire;

And not one will know of the war, not one
Will care at last when it is done.

Not one would mind, neither bird nor tree,
If mankind perished utterly;

And Spring herself, when she woke at dawn
Would scarcely know that we were gone."

The fire burned on the stone hearth and the cigar fell away into a mound of quiet ash on its tray. The empty chairs faced each other between the silent walls, and the music played.

At ten o'clock the house began to die.

The wind blew. A falling tree bough crashed through the kitchen window. Cleaning solvent, bottled, shattered over the stove. The room was ablaze in an instant!

"Fire!" screamed a voice. The house lights flashed, water pumps shot water from the ceilings. But the solvent spread on the linoleum, licking, eating, under the kitchen door, while the voices took it up in chorus: "Fire, fire, fire!"

The house tried to save itself. Doors sprang tightly shut, but the windows were broken by the heat and the wind blew and sucked upon the fire.

The house gave ground as the fire in ten billion angry sparks moved with flaming ease from room to room and then up the stairs. While scurrying water rats squeaked from the walls, pistoled their water, and ran for more. And the wall sprays let down showers of mechanical rain.

But too late. Somewhere, sighing, a pump shrugged to a stop. The quenching rain ceased. The reserve water supply which had filled baths and washed dishes for many quiet days was gone.

The fire crackled up the stairs. It fed upon Picassos and Matisses in the upper halls, like delicacies, baking off the oily flesh, tenderly crisping the canvases into black shavings.

Now the fire lay in beds, stood in windows, changed the colors of drapes!

And then, reinforcements.

From attic trapdoors, blind robot faces peered down with faucet mouths gushing green chemical.

The fire backed off, as even an elephant must at the sight of a dead snake. Now there were twenty snakes whipping over the floor, killing the fire with a clear cold venom of green froth.

But the fire was clever. It had sent flames outside the house, up through the attic to the pumps there. An explosion! The attic brain which directed the pumps was shattered into bronze shrapnel on the beams.

The fire rushed back into every closet and felt of the clothes hung there.

The house shuddered, oak bone on bone, its bared skeleton cringing from the heat, its wire, its nerves revealed as if a surgeon had torn the skin off to let the red veins and capillaries quiver in the scalded air. Help, help! Fire! Run, run! Heat snapped mirrors like the brittle winter ice. And the voices wailed. Fire, fire, run, run, like a tragic nursery rhyme, a dozen voices, high, low, like children dying in a forest, alone, alone. And the voices fading as the wires popped their sheathings like hot chestnuts. One, two, three, four, five voices died.

In the nursery the jungle burned. Blue lions roared, purple giraffes bounded off. The panthers ran in circles, changing color, and ten million animals, running before the fire, vanished off toward a distant steaming river. . . .

Ten more voices died. In the last instant under the fire avalanche, other choruses, oblivious, could be heard announcing the time, playing music, cutting the lawn by remote-control mower, or setting an umbrella frantically out and in the slamming and opening front door, a thousand things happening, like a clock shop when each clock strikes the hour insanely before or after the other, a scene of maniac confusion, yet unity; singing, screaming, a few last cleaning mice darting bravely out to carry the horrid ashes away! And one voice, with sublime disregard for the situation, read poetry aloud in the fiery study, until all the film spools burned, until all the wires withered and the circuits cracked.

The fire burst the house and let it slam flat down, puffing out skirts of spark and smoke.

In the kitchen, an instant before the rain of fire and timber, the stove could be seen making breakfasts at a psychopathic rate, ten dozen eggs, six loaves of toast, twenty dozen bacon strips, which, eaten by fire, started the stove working again, hysterically hissing!

The crash. The attic smashing into kitchen and parlor. The parlor into cellar, cellar into sub-cellar. Deep freeze, armchair, film tapes, circuits, beds, and all like skeletons thrown in a cluttered mound deep under.

Smoke and silence. A great quantity of smoke.

Dawn showed faintly in the east. Among the ruins, one wall stood alone. Within the wall, a last voice said, over and over again and again, even as the sun rose to shine upon the heaped rubble and steam:

"Today is August 5, 2026, today is August 5, 2026, today is . . ."

Fact Questions and Exercises

1. Note the paragraph that begins *"Ten-fifteen."* on page 255. What has produced the silhouettes on the face of the house?
2. Why do only "lonely foxes and whining cats" visit the house?
3. Who or what are the "ten thousand attendants" of the house?
4. Define "Baal" as it appears on page 256.
5. What details indicate that the family led a relatively carefree and wealthy life?
6. What causes the house to catch fire?

For Discussion and Writing

1. August 5, 1945, (United States time) was the date when the first atomic bomb was dropped on Japan. Does this help explain the story in any way? Does Bradbury actually relate what has happened to all the people? How, then, does the reader know what the story is about?
2. Comment on the passage that begins "The house was an altar . . ." (page 256). To what was the house an altar? What religion did it serve? How does Baal fit into this altar-religion concept?
3. How does the poem by Sara Teasdale fit the theme of the story? For instance, do both the poem and the story imply that man is insignificant? Nature's wind helps destroy the house. Does this relate to the war and nature aspects of the Teasdale poem? What is the significance of the sun rising to shine over the rubble?

James Baldwin [1924–   ]

Baldwin was born in the Harlem section of New York City, the oldest of nine children. His father was a preacher, and Baldwin was himself, for a while, a boy-preacher. After graduating from high school, however, he abandoned both religion and family to devote himself to writing. He left the United States and settled in France. There he finished his first novel, *Go Tell It on the Mountain* (1953), a somewhat autobiographical book that makes use of Baldwin's early experiences in Harlem. Baldwin has since published a number of short stories, novels, plays, and essays, and is generally considered to be one of the finest writers now at work. Among his best-known books are *Giovanni's Room* (1956), *Nobody Knows My Name,* (1961), and *Another Country* (1962).

Sonny's Blues

I read about it in the paper, in the subway, on my way to work. I read it, and I couldn't believe it, and I read it again. Then perhaps I just stared at it, at the newsprint spelling out his name, spelling out the story. I stared at it in the swinging lights of the subway car, and in the faces and bodies of the people, and in my own face, trapped in the darkness which roared outside.

It was not to be believed and I kept telling myself that, as I walked from the subway station to the high school. And at the same time I couldn't doubt it. I was scared, scared for Sonny. He became real to me again. A great block of ice got settled in my belly and kept melting there slowly all day long, while I taught my classes algebra. It was a special kind of ice. It kept melting, sending trickles of ice water all up and down my veins, but it never got less. Sometimes it hardened and seemed to expand until I felt my guts were going to come spilling out or that I was going to choke or scream. This would always be at a moment when I was remembering some specific thing Sonny had once said or done.

When he was about as old as the boys in my classes his face had been bright and open, there was a lot of copper in it; and he'd had wonderfully direct brown eyes, and great gentleness and privacy. I wondered what he looked like now. He had been picked up, the evening before, in a raid on an apartment downtown, for peddling and using heroin.

I couldn't believe it: but what I mean by that is that I couldn't find any room for it anywhere inside me. I had kept it outside me for a long time. I hadn't wanted to know. I had had suspicions, but I didn't name them, I kept putting them away. I told myself that Sonny was wild, but he wasn't crazy. And he'd always been a good boy, he hadn't ever turned hard or evil or disrespectful, the way kids can, so quick, so quick, especially in Harlem. I didn't want to believe that I'd ever see my brother going down, coming to nothing, all that light in his face gone out, in the condition I'd already seen so many others. Yet it had happened and here I was, talking about algebra to a lot of boys who might, every one of them for all I knew, be popping off needles every time they went to the head. Maybe it did more for them than algebra could.

I was sure that the first time Sonny had ever had horse, he couldn't have been much older than these boys were now. These boys, now, were living as we'd been living then, they were growing up with a rush and their heads bumped abruptly against the low ceiling of their actual possibilities. They were filled with rage. All they really knew were two darknesses, the darkness of their lives, which was now closing in on them, and the darkness of the movies, which had blinded them to that other darkness, and in which they now, vindictively, dreamed, at once more together than they were at any other time, and more alone.

DESCRIPTION of SOCIETY

When the last bell rang, the last class ended, I let out my breath. It seemed I'd been holding it for all that time. My clothes were wet—I may have looked as though I'd been sitting in a steam bath, all dressed up, all afternoon. I sat alone in the classroom a long time. I listened to the boys outside, downstairs, shouting and cursing and laughing. Their laughter struck me for perhaps the first time. It was not the joyous laughter which—God knows why—one associates with children. It was mocking and insular, its intent was to denigrate. It was disenchanted, and in this, also, lay the authority of their curses. Perhaps I was listening to them because I was thinking about my brother and in them I heard my brother. And myself.

One boy was whistling a tune, at once very complicated, and very simple, it seemed to be pouring out of him as though he were a bird, and it sounded very cool and moving through all that harsh, bright air, only just holding its own through all those other sounds.

I stood up and walked over to the window and looked down into the courtyard. It was the beginning of the spring and the sap was rising in the boys. A teacher passed through them every now and again, quickly, as though he or she couldn't wait to get out of that courtyard, to get those boys out of their sight and off their minds. I started collecting my stuff. I thought I'd better get home and talk to Isabel.

Beg. of spring-time.

The courtyard was almost deserted by the time I got downstairs. I saw this boy standing in the shadow of a doorway, looking just like Sonny. I almost called his name. Then I saw that it wasn't Sonny, but somebody we used to know, a boy from around our block. He'd been Sonny's friend. He'd never been mine, having been too young for me, and, anyway, I'd never liked him. And now, even though he was a grown-up man, he still hung around that block, still spent hours on the street corners, was always high and raggy. I used to run into him from time to time and he'd often work around to asking me for a quarter or fifty cents. He always had some real good excuse, too, and I always gave it to him, I don't know why.

But now, abruptly, I hated him. I couldn't stand the way he looked at me, partly like a dog, partly like a cunning child. I wanted to ask him what the hell he was doing in the school courtyard.

He sort of shuffled over to me, and he said, "I see you got the papers. So you already know about it."

"You mean about Sonny? Yes, I already know about it. How come they didn't get you?"

He grinned. It made him repulsive and it also brought to mind what he'd looked like as a kid. "I wasn't there. I stay away from them people."

"Good for you." I offered him a cigarette and I watched him through the smoke. "You come all the way down here just to tell me about Sonny?"

"That's right." He was sort of shaking his head and his eyes looked strange, as though they were about to cross. The bright sun deadened his damp dark brown skin and it made his eyes look yellow and showed up the dirt in his kinked hair. He smelled funky. I moved a little away from him and I said, "Well, thanks. But I already know about it and I got to get home."

"I'll walk you a little ways," he said. We started walking. There were a couple of kids still loitering in the courtyard and one of them said goodnight to me and looked strangely at the boy beside me.

"What're you going to do?" he asked me. "I mean, about Sonny?"

"Look. I haven't seen Sonny for over a year. I'm not sure I'm going to do anything. Anyway, what the hell *can* I do?"

"That's right," he said quickly, "ain't nothing you can do. Can't much help old Sonny no more, I guess."

It was what I was thinking and so it seemed to me he had no right to say it.

"I'm surprised at Sonny, though," he went on—he had a funny way of talking, he looked straight ahead as though he were talking to himself—"I thought Sonny was a smart boy, I thought he was too smart to get hung."

"I guess he thought so too," I said sharply, "and that's how he got hung. And now about you? You're pretty goddamn smart, I bet."

Then he looked directly at me, just for a minute. "I ain't smart," he said. "If I was smart, I'd have reached for a pistol a long time ago."

"Look. Don't tell *me* your sad story, if it was up to me, I'd give you one." Then I felt guilty—guilty, probably, for never having supposed that the poor bastard *had* a story of his own, much less a sad one, and I asked, quickly, "What's going to happen to him now?"

He didn't answer this. He was off by himself some place. "Funny thing," he said, and from his tone we might have been discussing the quickest way to get to Brooklyn, "when I saw the papers this morning, the first thing I asked myself was if I had anything to do with it. I felt sort of responsible."

I began to listen more carefully. The subway station was on the corner, just before us, and I stopped. He stopped, too. We were in front of a bar and he ducked slightly, peering in, but whoever he was looking for didn't seem to be there. The juke box was blasting away with something black and bouncy and I half watched the barmaid as she danced her way from the juke box to her place behind the bar. And I watched her face as she laughingly responded to something someone said to her, still keeping time to the music. When she smiled one saw the little girl, one sensed the doomed, still-struggling woman beneath the battered face of the semi-whore.

"I never *give* Sonny nothing," the boy said finally, "but a long time ago I come to school high and Sonny asked me how it felt." He paused, I couldn't bear to watch him, I watched the barmaid, and I listened to the music which seemed to be causing the pavement to shake. "I told him it felt great." The music stopped, the barmaid paused and watched the juke box until the music began again. "It did."

All this was carrying me some place I didn't want to go. I certainly didn't want to know how it felt. It filled everything, the people, the houses, the music, the dark, quicksilver barmaid, with menace; and this menace was their reality.

"What's going to happen to him now?" I asked again.

"They'll send him away some place and they'll try to cure him." He shook his head. "Maybe he'll even think he's kicked the habit. Then they'll let him loose"—he gestured, throwing his cigarette into the gutter. "That's all."

"What do you mean, that's *all?*"

But I knew what he meant.

"I *mean,* that's *all.*" He turned his head and looked at me, pulling down the corners of his mouth. "Don't you know what I mean?" he asked, softly.

"How the hell *would* I know what you mean?" I almost whispered it, I don't know why.

"That's right," he said to the air, "how would *he* know what I mean?" He turned toward me again, patient and calm, and yet I somehow felt him shaking, shaking as though he were going to fall apart. I felt that ice in my guts again, the dread I'd felt all afternoon; and again I watched the barmaid, moving about the bar, washing glasses, and singing. "Listen. They'll let him out and then it'll just start all over again. That's what I mean."

"You mean—they'll let him out. And then he'll just start working his way back in again. You mean he'll never kick the habit. Is that what you mean?"

"That's right," he said, cheerfully. "*You* see what I mean."

"Tell me," I said at last, "why does he want to die? He must want to die, he's killing himself, why does he want to die?"

He looked at me in surprise. He licked his lips. "He don't want to die. He wants to live. Don't nobody want to die, ever."

Then I wanted to ask him—too many things. He could not have answered, or if he had, I could not have borne the answers. I started walking. "Well, I guess it's none of my business."

"It's going to be rough on old Sonny," he said. We reached the subway station. "This is your station?" he asked. I nodded. I took one step down. "Damn!" he said, suddenly. I looked up at him. He grinned again. "Damn it if I didn't leave all my money home. You ain't got a dollar on you, have you? Just for a couple of days, is all."

All at once something inside gave and threatened to come pouring out of me. I didn't hate him any more. I felt that in another moment I'd start crying like a child.

"Sure," I said. "Don't sweat." I looked in my wallet and didn't have a dollar, I only had a five. "Here," I said. "That hold you?"

He didn't look at it—he didn't want to look at it. A terrible, closed look came over his face, as though he were keeping the number on the bill a secret from him and me. "Thanks," he said, and now he was dying to see me go. "Don't worry about Sonny. Maybe I'll write him or something."

"Sure," I said. "You do that. So long."

"Be seeing you," he said. I went on down the steps.

And I didn't write Sonny or send him anything for a long time. When I finally did, it was just after my little girl died, he wrote me back a letter which made me feel like a bastard.

Here's what he said:

Dear brother,

You don't know how much I needed to hear from you. I wanted to write you many a time but I dug how much I must have hurt you and so I didn't write. But now I feel like a man who's been trying to climb up out of some deep, real deep, and funky hole and just saw the sun up there, outside. I got to get outside.

I can't tell you much about how I got here. I mean I don't know how to tell you. I guess I was afraid of something or I was trying to escape from something and you know I have never been very strong in the head (smile). I'm glad Mama and Daddy are dead and can't see what's happened to their son and I swear if I'd known what I was doing I would never have hurt you so, you and a lot of other fine people who were nice to me and who believed in me.

I don't want you to think it had anything to do with me being a musician. It's more than that. Or maybe less than that. I can't get anything straight in my head down here and I try not to think about what's going to happen to me when I get outside again. Sometime I think I'm going to flip and *never* get outside and sometime I think I'll come straight back. I tell you one thing, though, I'd rather blow my brains out than go through this again. But that's what they all say, so they tell me. If I tell you when I'm coming to New York and if you could meet me, I sure would appreciate it. Give my love to Isabel and the kids and I was sure sorry to hear about little Gracie. I wish I could be like Mama and say the Lord's will be done, but I don't know it seems to me that trouble is the one thing that never does get stopped and I don't know what good it does to blame it on the Lord. But maybe it does some good if you believe it.

Your brother,
Sonny

Then I kept in constant touch with him and I sent him whatever I could and I went to meet him when he came back to New York. When I saw him many things I thought I had forgotten came flooding back to me. This was because I had begun, finally, to wonder about Sonny, about the life that Sonny lived inside. This life, whatever it was, had made him older and thinner and it had deepened the distant stillness in which he had always moved. He looked very unlike my baby brother. Yet, when he smiled, when we shook hands, the baby brother I'd never known looked out from the depths of his private life, like an animal waiting to be coaxed into the light.

"How you been keeping?" he asked me.

"All right. And you?"

"Just fine." He was smiling all over his face. "It's good to see you again."

"It's good to see you."

The seven years' difference in our ages lay between us like a chasm: I wondered if these years would ever operate between us as a bridge. I was remembering, and it made it hard to catch my breath, that I had been there when he was born; and I had heard the first words he had ever spoken. When he started to walk, he walked from our mother straight to me. I caught him just before he fell when he took the first steps he ever took in this world.

"How's Isabel?"

"Just fine. She's dying to see you."

"And the boys?"

"They're fine, too. They're anxious to see their uncle."

"Oh, come on. You know they don't remember me."

"Are you kidding? Of course they remember you."

He grinned again. We got into a taxi. We had a lot to say to each other, far too much to know how to begin.

As the taxi began to move, I asked, "You still want to go to India?"

He laughed. "You still remember that. Hell, no. This place is Indian enough for me."

"It used to belong to them," I said.

And he laughed again. "They damn sure knew what they were doing when they got rid of it."

Years ago, when he was around fourteen, he'd been all hipped on the idea of going to India. He read books about people sitting on rocks, naked, in all kinds of weather, but mostly bad, naturally, and walking barefoot through hot coals and arriving at wisdom. I used to say that it sounded to me as though they were getting away from wisdom as fast as they could. I think he sort of looked down on me for that.

"Do you mind," he asked, "if we have the driver drive alongside the park? On the west side—I haven't seen the city in so long."

"Of course not," I said. I was afraid that I might sound as though I were humoring him, but I hoped he wouldn't take it that way.

So we drove along, between the green of the park and the stony, lifeless elegance of hotels and apartment buildings, toward the vivid, killing streets of our childhood. These streets hadn't changed, though housing projects jutted up out of them now like rocks in the middle of a boiling sea. Most of the houses in which we had grown up had vanished, as had the stores from which we had stolen, the basements in which we had first tried sex, the rooftops from which we had hurled tin cans and bricks. But houses exactly like the houses of our past yet dominated the landscape, boys exactly like the boys we once had been found themselves smothering in these houses, came down into the streets for light and air and found themselves encircled by disaster. Some escaped the trap, most didn't. Those who got out always left something of themselves behind, as some animals amputate a leg and leave it in the trap. It might be said, perhaps, that I had escaped, after all, I was a school teacher; or that Sonny had, he hadn't lived in Harlem for years. Yet, as the cab moved uptown through streets which seemed, with a rush, to darken with dark people, and as I covertly studied Sonny's face, it came to me that what we both were seeking through our separate cab windows was that part of ourselves which had been left behind. It's always at the hour of trouble and confrontation that the missing member aches.

We hit 110th Street and started rolling up Lenox Avenue. And I'd known this avenue all my life, but it seemed to me again, as it had seemed on the day I'd first heard about Sonny's trouble, filled with a hidden menace which was its very breath of life.

"We almost there," said Sonny.

"Almost." We were both too nervous to say anything more.

We live in a housing project. It hasn't been up long. A few days after it was up it seemed uninhabitably new, now, of course, it's already rundown. It looks like a parody of the good, clean, faceless life—God knows the people who live in it do their best to make it a parody. The beat-looking grass lying around isn't enough to make their lives green, the hedges will never hold out the streets, and they know it. The big windows fool no one, they aren't big enough to make space out of no space. They don't bother with the windows, they watch the TV screen instead. The playground is most popular with the children who don't play at jacks, or skip rope, or roller skate, or swing, and they can be found in it after dark. We moved in partly because it's not too far from where I teach, and partly for the kids; but it's really just like the houses in which Sonny and I grew up. The same things happen, they'll have the same things to remember. The moment Sonny and I started into the house I had the feeling that I was simply bringing him back into the danger he had almost died trying to escape.

Sonny has never been talkative. So I don't know why I was sure he'd be dying to talk to me when supper was over the first night. Everything went fine, the oldest boy remembered him, and the youngest boy liked him, and Sonny had remembered to bring something for each of them; and Isabel, who is really much nicer than I am, more open and giving, had gone to a lot of trouble about dinner and was genuinely glad to see him. And she's always been able to tease Sonny in a way that I haven't. It was nice to see her face so vivid again, and to hear her laugh and watch her make Sonny laugh. She wasn't, or, anyway, she didn't seem to be, at all uneasy or embarrassed. She chatted as though there were no subject which had to be avoided and she got Sonny past his first, faint stiffness. And thank God she was there, for I was filled with that icy dread again. Everything I did seemed awkward to me, and everything I said sounded freighted with hidden meaning. I was trying to remember everything I'd heard about dope addiction and I couldn't help watching Sonny for signs. I wasn't doing it out of malice. I was trying to find out something about my brother. I was dying to hear him tell me he was safe.

"Safe!" my father grunted, whenever Mama suggested trying to move to a neighborhood which might be safer for children. "Safe, hell! Ain't no place safe for kids, nor nobody."

He always went on like this, but he wasn't, ever, really as bad as he sounded, not even on weekends, when he got drunk. As a matter of fact, he was always on the lookout for "something a little better," but he died before he found it. He died suddenly, during a drunken weekend in the middle of the war, when Sonny was fifteen. He and Sonny hadn't even got on too well. And this was partly because Sonny was the apple of his father's eye. It was because he loved Sonny so much and was frightened for him, that he was always fighting with him. It doesn't do any good to fight with Sonny. Sonny just moves back, inside himself, where he can't be reached. But the principal reason that they never hit it off is that they were so much alike. Daddy was big and rough and loud-talking, just the opposite of Sonny, but they both had—that same privacy.

Mama tried to tell me something about this, just after Daddy died. I was home on leave from the army.

This was the last time I ever saw my mother alive. Just the same, this picture gets all mixed up in my mind with pictures I had of her when she was younger. The way I always see her is the way she used to be on a Sunday afternoon, say, when the old folks were talking after the big Sunday dinner. I always see her wearing pale blue. She'd be sitting on the sofa. And my father would be sitting in the easy chair, not far from her. And the living room would be full of church folks and relatives. There they sit, in chairs all around the living room, and the night is creeping up outside, but nobody knows it yet. You can see the darkness growing against the windowpanes and you hear the street noises every now and again, or maybe the jangling beat of a tambourine from one of the churches close by, but it's real quiet in the room. For a moment nobody's talking, but every face looks darkening, like the sky outside. And my mother rocks a little from the waist, and my father's eyes are closed. Everyone is looking at

[margin annotations: "Sonny's first nite Isabel", "Father", "Mother brings parallel between brother & Sonny: Narrator: Typical family afternoon"]

something a child can't see. For a minute they've forgotten the children. Maybe a kid is lying on the rug, half asleep. Maybe somebody's got a kid in his lap and is absent-mindedly stroking the kid's head. Maybe there's a kid, quiet and big-eyed, curled up in a big chair in the corner. The silence, the darkness coming, and the darkness in the faces frightens the child obscurely. He hopes that the hand which strokes his forehead will never stop—will never die. He hopes that there will never come a time when the old folks won't be sitting around the living room, talking about where they've come from, and what they've seen, and what's happened to them and their kinfolk.

But something deep and watchful in the child knows that this is bound to end, is already ending. In a moment someone will get up and turn on the light. Then the old folks will remember the children and they won't talk any more that day. And when light fills the room, the child is filled with darkness. He knows that every time this happens he's moved just a little closer to that darkness outside. The darkness outside is what the old folks have been talking about. It's what they've come from. It's what they endure. The child knows that they won't talk any more because if he knows too much about what's happened to *them*, he'll know too much too soon, about what's going to happen to *him*.

The last time I talked to my mother, I remember I was restless. I wanted to get out and see Isabel. We weren't married then and we had a lot to straighten out between us.

There Mama sat, in black, by the window. She was humming an old church song, *Lord, you brought me from a long ways off.* Sonny was out somewhere. Mama kept watching the streets.

"I don't know," she said, "if I'll ever see you again, after you go off from here. But I hope you'll remember the things I tried to teach you."

"Don't talk like that," I said, and smiled. "You'll be here a long time yet."

She smiled, too, but she said nothing. She was quiet for a long time. And I said, "Mama, don't you worry about nothing. I'll be writing all the time, and you be getting the checks. . . ."

"I want to talk to you about your brother," she said, suddenly. "If anything happens to me he ain't going to have nobody to look out for him."

"Mama," I said, "ain't nothing going to happen to you *or* Sonny. Sonny's all right. He's a good boy and he's got good sense."

"It ain't a question of his being a good boy," Mama said, "nor of his having good sense. It ain't only the bad ones, nor yet the dumb ones that gets sucked under." She stopped, looking at me. "Your Daddy once had a brother," she said, and she smiled in a way that made me feel she was in pain. "You didn't never know that, did you?"

"No," I said, "I never knew that," and I watched her face.

"Oh, yes," she said, "your Daddy had a brother." She looked out of the window again. "I know you never saw your Daddy cry. But *I* did—many a time, through all these years."

I asked her, "What happened to his brother? How come nobody's ever talked about him?"

This was the first time I ever saw my mother look old.

"His brother got killed," she said, "when he was just a little younger than you are now. I knew him. He was a fine boy. He was maybe a little full of the devil, but he didn't mean nobody no harm."

Revelation

Then she stopped and the room was silent, exactly as it had sometimes been on those Sunday afternoons. Mama kept looking out into the streets.

Father's Brother

"He used to have a job in the mill," she said, "and, like all young folks, he just liked to perform on Saturday nights. Saturday nights, him and your father would drift around to different places, go to dances and things like that, or just sit around with people they knew, and your father's brother would sing, he had a fine voice, and play along with himself on his guitar. Well, this particular Saturday night, him and your father was coming home from some place, and they were both a little drunk, and there was a moon that night, it was bright like day. Your father's brother was feeling kind of good, and he was whistling to himself, and he had his guitar slung over his shoulder. They was coming down a hill and beneath them was a road that turned off from the highway. Well, your father's brother, being always kind of frisky, decided to run down this hill, and he did, with that guitar banging and clanging behind him, and he ran across the road, and he was making water behind a tree. And your father was sort of amused at him and he was still coming down the hill, kind of slow. Then he heard a car motor and that same minute his brother stepped from behind the tree, into the road, in the moonlight. And he started to cross the road. And your father started to run down the hill, he says he don't know why. This car was full of white men. They was all drunk, and when they seen your father's brother they let out a great whoop and holler and they aimed the car straight at him. They was having fun, they just wanted to scare him, the way they do sometimes, you know. But they was drunk. And I guess the boy, being drunk, too, and scared, kind of lost his head. By the time he jumped it was too late. Your father says he heard his brother scream when the car rolled over him, and he heard the wood of that guitar when it give, and he heard them strings go flying, and he heard them white men shouting, and the car kept on a-going and it ain't stopped till this day. And, time your father got down the hill, his brother weren't nothing but blood and pulp."

Tears were gleaming on my mother's face. There wasn't anything I could say.

"He never mentioned it," she said, "because I never let him mention it before you children. Your Daddy was like a crazy man that night and for many a night thereafter. He says he never in his life seen anything as dark as that road after the lights of that car had gone away. Weren't nothing, weren't nobody on that road, just your Daddy and his brother and that busted guitar. Oh, yes. Your Daddy never did really get right again. Till the day he died he weren't sure but that every white man he saw was the man that killed his brother."

She stopped and took out her handkerchief and dried her eyes and looked at me.

"I ain't telling you all this," she said, "to make you scared or bitter or to make you hate nobody. I'm telling you this because you got a brother. And the world ain't changed."

I guess I didn't want to believe this. I guess she saw this in my face. She turned away from me, toward the window again, searching those streets.

"But I praise my Redeemer," she said at last, "that He called your Daddy home before me. I ain't saying it to throw no flowers at myself, but, I declare, it keeps me from feeling too cast down to know I helped your father get safely through this world. Your father always acted like he was the roughest, strongest man on earth. And everybody took him to be like that. But if he hadn't had *me* there—to see his tears!"

She was crying again. Still, I couldn't move. I said, "Lord, Lord, Mama. I didn't know it was like that."

"Oh, honey," she said, "there's a lot that you don't know. But you are going to find it out." She stood up from the window and came over to me. "You got to hold on to your brother," she said, "and don't let him fall, no matter what it looks like is happening to him and no matter how evil you gets with him. You going to be evil with him many a time. But don't you forget what I told you, you hear?"

"I won't forget," I said. "Don't you worry, I won't forget. I won't let nothing happen to Sonny."

My mother smiled as though she were amused at something she saw in my face. Then, "You may not be able to stop nothing from happening. But you got to let him know you's *there.*"

Two days later I was married, and then I was gone. And I had a lot of things on my mind and I pretty well forgot my promise to Mama until I got shipped home on a special furlough for her funeral.

And, after the funeral, with just Sonny and me alone in the empty kitchen, I tried to find out something about him.

"What do you want to do?" I asked him.

"I'm going to be a musician," he said.

For he had graduated, in the time I had been away, from dancing to the juke box to finding out who was playing what, and what they were doing with it, and he had bought himself a set of drums.

"You mean, you want to be a drummer?" I somehow had the feeling that being a drummer might be all right for other people but not for my brother Sonny.

"I don't think," he said, looking at me very gravely, "that I'll ever be a good drummer. But I think I can play a piano."

I frowned. I'd never played the role of the older brother quite so seriously before, had scarcely ever, in fact, *asked* Sonny a damn thing. I sensed myself in the presence of something I didn't really know how to handle, didn't understand. So I made my frown a little deeper as I asked: "What kind of musician do you want to be?"

He grinned. "How many kinds do you think there are?"

"Be *serious,*" I said.

He laughed, throwing his head back, and then looked at me. "I *am* serious."

"Well, then, for Christ's sake, stop kidding around and answer a serious question. I mean, do you want to be a concert pianist, you want to play classical music and all that, or—or what?" Long before I finished he was laughing again. "For Christ's *sake,* Sonny!"

He sobered, but with difficulty, "I'm sorry. But you sound so—*scared!*" and he was off again.

"Well, you may think it's funny now, baby, but it's not going to be so funny when you have to make your living at it, let me tell you *that.*" I was furious because I knew he was laughing at me and I didn't know why.

"No," he said, very sober now, and afraid, perhaps, that he'd hurt me. "I don't want to be a classical pianist. That isn't what interests me. I mean" —he paused, looking hard at me, as though his eyes would help me understand, and then gestured helplessly, as though perhaps his hand would help—"I mean, I'll have a lot of studying to do, and I'll have to study *everything*, but, I mean, I want to play *with*—jazz musicians." He stopped. "I want to play jazz," he said.

Well, the word had never before sounded as heavy, as real, as it sounded that afternoon in Sonny's mouth. I just looked at him and I was probably frowning a real frown by this time. I simply couldn't see why on earth he'd want to spend his time hanging around nightclubs, clowning around on bandstands, while people pushed each other around a dance floor. It seemed—beneath him, somehow. I had never thought about it before, had never been forced to, but I suppose I had always put jazz musicians in a class with what Daddy called "good-time people."

"Are you *serious*?"

"Hell, *yes*, I'm serious."

He looked more helpless than ever, and annoyed, and deeply hurt.

I suggested helpfully: "You mean—like Louis Armstrong?"

His face closed as though I'd struck him. "No, I'm not talking about none of that old-time, down home crap."

"Well, look, Sonny, I'm sorry, don't get mad. I just don't altogether get it, that's all. Name somebody—you know, a jazz musician you admire."

"Bird."

"Who?"

"Bird! Charlie Parker! Don't they teach you nothing in the goddamn army?"

I lit a cigarette. I was surprised and then a little amused to discover that I was trembling. "I've been out of touch," I said. "You'll have to be patient with me. Now. Who's this Parker character?"

"He's just one of the greatest jazz musicians alive," said Sonny, sullenly, his hands in his pockets, his back to me. "Maybe *the* greatest," he added, bitterly, "that's probably why *you* never heard of him."

"All right," I said, "I'm ignorant. I'm sorry. I'll go out and buy all the cat's records right away, all right?"

"It don't," said Sonny, with dignity, "make any difference to me. I don't care what you listen to. Don't do me no favors."

I was beginning to realize that I'd never seen him so upset before. With another part of my mind I was thinking that this would probably turn out to be one of those things kids go through and that I shouldn't make it seem important by pushing it too hard. Still, I didn't think it would do any harm to ask: "Doesn't all this take a lot of time? Can you make a living at it?"

He turned back to me and half leaned, half sat, on the kitchen table. "Everything takes time," he said, "and—well, yes, sure, I can make a living at it. But what I don't seem to be able to make you understand is that it's the only thing I want to do."

"Well, Sonny," I said, gently, "you know people can't always do exactly what they *want* to do—"

"*No*, I don't know that," said Sonny, surprising me. "I think people *ought* to do what they want to do, what else are they alive for?"

"You getting to be a big boy," I said desperately, "it's time you started thinking about your future."

"I'm thinking about my future," said Sonny, grimly. "I think about it all the time."

I gave up. I decided, if he didn't change his mind, that we could always talk about it later. "In the meantime," I said, "you got to finish school." We had already decided that he'd have to move in with Isabel and her folks. I knew this wasn't the ideal arrangement because Isabel's folks are inclined to be dicty and they hadn't especially wanted Isabel to marry me. But I didn't know what else to do. "And we have to get you fixed up at Isabel's."

There was a long silence. He moved from the kitchen table to the window. "That's a terrible idea. You know it yourself."

"Do you have a *better* idea?"

He just walked up and down the kitchen for a minute. He was as tall as I was. He had started to shave. I suddenly had the feeling that I didn't know him at all.

He stopped at the kitchen table and picked up my cigarettes. Looking at me with a kind of mocking, amused defiance, he put one between his lips. "You mind?"

"You smoking already?"

He lit the cigarette and nodded, watching me through the smoke. "I just wanted to see if I'd have the courage to smoke in front of you." He grinned and blew a great cloud of smoke to the ceiling. "It was easy." He looked at my face. "Come on, now. I bet you was smoking at my age, tell the truth."

I didn't say anything but the truth was on my face, and he laughed. But now there was something very strained in his laugh. "Sure. And I bet that ain't all you was doing."

He was frightening me a little. "Cut the crap," I said. "We already decided that you was going to go and live at Isabel's. Now what's got into you all of a sudden?"

"*You* decided it," he pointed out. "*I* didn't decide nothing." He stopped in front of me, leaning against the stove, arms loosely folded. "Look, brother. I don't want to stay in Harlem no more. I really don't." He was very earnest. He looked at me, then over toward the kitchen window. There was something in his eyes I'd never seen before, some thoughtfulness, some worry all his own. He rubbed the muscle of one arm. "It's time I was getting out of here."

"Where do you want to *go*, Sonny?"

"I want to join the army. Or the navy, I don't care. If I say I'm old enough, they'll believe me."

Then I got mad. It was because I was so scared. "You must be crazy. You goddamn fool, what the hell do you want to go and join the *army* for?"

"I just told you. To get out of Harlem."

"Sonny, you haven't even finished *school*. And if you really want to be a musician, how do you expect to study if you're in the *army*?"

He looked at me, trapped, and in anguish. "There's ways. I might be able to work out some kind of deal. Anyway, I'll have the G.I. Bill when I come out."

"*If* you come out." We stared at each other. "Sonny, please. Be reasonable. I know the setup is far from perfect. But we got to do the best we can."

"I ain't learning nothing in school," he said. "Even when I go." He turned away from me and opened the window and threw his cigarette out into the narrow alley. I watched his back. "At least, I ain't learning nothing you'd want me to learn." He slammed the window so hard I thought the glass would fly out, and turned back to me. "And I'm sick of the stink of these garbage cans!"

"Sonny," I said, "I know how you feel. But if you don't finish school now, you're going to be sorry later that you didn't." I grabbed him by the shoulders. "And you only got another year. It ain't so bad. And I'll come back and I swear I'll help you do *whatever* you want to do. Just try to put up with it till I come back. Will you please do that? For me?"

He didn't answer and he wouldn't look at me.

"Sonny. You hear me?"

He pulled away. "I hear you. But you never hear anything *I* say."

I didn't know what to say to that. He looked out of the window and then back at me. "OK," he said, and sighed. "I'll try."

Then I said, trying to cheer him up a little, "They got a piano at Isabel's. You can practice on it."

And as a matter of fact, it did cheer him up for a minute. "That's right," he said to himself. "I forgot that." His face relaxed a little. But the worry, the thoughtfulness, played on it still, the way shadows play on a face which is staring into the fire.

But I thought I'd never hear the end of that piano. At first, Isabel would write me, saying how nice it was that Sonny was so serious about his music and how, as soon as he came in from school, or wherever he had been when he was supposed to be at school, he went straight to that piano and stayed there until suppertime. And, after supper, he went back to that piano and stayed there until everybody went to bed. He was at the piano all day Saturday and all day Sunday. Then he bought a record player and started playing records. He'd play one record over and over again, all day long sometimes, and he'd improvise along with it on the piano. Or he'd play one section of the record, one chord, one change, one progression, then he'd do it on the piano. Then back to the record. Then back to the piano.

Well, I really don't know how they stood it. Isabel finally confessed that it wasn't like living with a person at all, it was like living with sound. And the sound didn't make sense to her, didn't make any sense to any of them—naturally. They began, in a way, to be afflicted by this presence that was living in their home. It was as though Sonny were some sort of god, or monster. He moved in an atmosphere which wasn't like theirs at all. They fed him and he ate, he washed himself, he walked in and out of their door; he certainly wasn't nasty or unpleasant or rude, Sonny isn't any of those things; but it was as though he were all wrapped up in some cloud, some fire, some vision all his own; and there wasn't any way to reach him.

At the same time, he wasn't really a man yet, he was still a child, and they had to watch out for him in all kinds of ways. They certainly couldn't throw him out. Neither did they dare to make a great scene about that piano because even they dimly sensed, as I sensed, from so many thousands of miles away, that Sonny was at that piano playing for his life.

But he hadn't been going to school. One day a letter came from the school board and Isabel's mother got it—there had, apparently, been other letters but

Sonny had torn them up. This day, when Sonny came in, Isabel's mother showed him the letter and asked where he'd been spending his time. And she finally got it out of him that he'd been down in Greenwich Village, with musicians and other characters, in a white girl's apartment. And this scared her and she started to scream at him and what came up, once she began—though she denies it to this day—was what sacrifices they were making to give Sonny a decent home and how little he appreciated it.

Sonny didn't play the piano that day. By evening, Isabel's mother had calmed down but then there was the old man to deal with, and Isabel herself. Isabel says she did her best to be calm but she broke down and started crying. She says she just watched Sonny's face. She could tell, by watching him, what was happening with him. And what was happening was that they penetrated his cloud, they had reached him. Even if their fingers had been a thousand times more gentle than human fingers ever are, he could hardly help feeling that they had stripped him naked and were spitting on that nakedness. For he also had to see that his presence, that music, which was life or death to him, had been torture for them and that they had endured it, not at all for his sake, but only for mine. And Sonny couldn't take that. He can take it a little better today than he could then but he's still not very good at it and, frankly, I don't know anybody who is.

The silence of the next few days must have been louder than the sound of all the music ever played since time began. One morning, before she went to work, Isabel was in his room for something and she suddenly realized that all of his records were gone. And she knew for certain that he was gone. And he was. He went as far as the navy would carry him. He finally sent me a postcard from some place in Greece and that was the first I knew that Sonny was still alive. I didn't see him any more until we were both back in New York and the war had long been over.

He was a man by then, of course, but I wasn't willing to see it. He came by the house from time to time, but we fought almost every time we met. I didn't like the way he carried himself, loose and dreamlike all the time, and I didn't like his friends, and his music seemed to be merely an excuse for the life he led. It sounded just that weird and disordered.

Then we had a fight, a pretty awful fight, and I didn't see him for months. By and by I looked him up, where he was living, in a furnished room in the Village, and I tried to make it up. But there were lots of other people in the room and Sonny just lay on his bed, and he wouldn't come downstairs with me, and he treated these other people as though they were his family and I weren't. So I got mad and then he got mad, and then I told him that he might just as well be dead as live the way he was living. Then he stood up and he told me not to worry about him any more in life, that he *was* dead as far as I was concerned. Then he pushed me to the door and the other people looked on as though nothing were happening, and he slammed the door behind me. I stood in the hallway, staring at the door. I heard somebody laugh in the room and then the tears came to my eyes. I started down the steps, whistling to keep from crying, I kept whistling to myself, *You going to need me, baby, one of these cold, rainy days.*

I read about Sonny's trouble in the spring. Little Grace died in the fall. She was a beautiful little girl. But she only lived a little over two years. She died of polio and she suffered. She had a slight fever for a couple of days, but it didn't

seem like anything and we just kept her in bed. And we would certainly have
called the doctor, but the fever dropped, she seemed to be all right. So we
thought it had just been a cold. Then, one day, she was up, playing, Isabel was in
the kitchen fixing lunch for the two boys when they'd come in from school, and
she heard Grace fall down in the living room. When you have a lot of children
you don't always start running when one of them falls, unless they start
screaming or something. And, this time, Grace was quiet. Yet, Isabel says that
when she heard that *thump* and then that silence, something happened to her to
make her afraid. And she ran to the living room and there was little Grace on the
floor, all twisted up, and the reason she hadn't screamed was that she couldn't
get her breath. And when she did scream, it was the worst sound, Isabel says,
that she'd ever heard in all her life, and she still hears it sometimes in her
dreams. Isabel will sometimes wake me up with a low, moaning, strangled sound
and I have to be quick to awaken her and hold her to me and where Isabel is
weeping against me seems a mortal wound.

I think I may have written Sonny the very day that little Grace was
buried. I was sitting in the living room in the dark, by myself, and I suddenly
thought of Sonny. My trouble made his real. common troubles brings there

One Saturday afternoon, when Sonny had been living with us, or, together
anyway, been in our house, for nearly two weeks, I found myself wandering
aimlessly about the living room, drinking from a can of beer, and trying to work
up the courage to search Sonny's room. He was out, he was usually out whenever
I was home, and Isabel had taken the children to see their grandparents.
Suddenly I was standing still in front of the living room window, watching
Seventh Avenue. The idea of searching Sonny's room made me still. I scarcely
dared to admit to myself what I'd be searching for. I didn't know what I'd do if I
found it. Or if I didn't.

On the sidewalk across from me, near the entrance to a barbecue joint,
some people were holding an old-fashioned revival meeting. The barbecue cook,
wearing a dirty white apron, his conked hair reddish and metallic in the pale sun,
and a cigarette between his lips, stood in the doorway, watching them. Kids and
older people paused in their errands and stood there, along with some older men
and a couple of very tough-looking women who watched everything that
happened on the avenue, as though they owned it, or were maybe owned by it.
Well, they were watching this, too. The revival was being carried on by three
sisters in black, and a brother. All they had were their voices and their Bibles and
a tambourine. The brother was testifying and while he testified two of the sisters
stood together, seeming to say, amen, and the third sister walked around with
the tambourine outstretched and a couple of people dropped coins into it. Then
the brother's testimony ended and the sister who had been taking up the
collection dumped the coins into her palm and transferred them to the pocket of
her long black robe. Then she raised both hands, striking the tambourine against
the air, and then against one hand, and she started to sing. And the two other
sisters and the brother joined in.

It was strange, suddenly, to watch, though I had been seeing these street
meetings all my life. So, of course, had everybody else down there. Yet, they
paused and watched and listened and I stood still at the window *"Tis the old ship
of Zion,"* they sang, and the sister with the tambourine kept a steady, jangling
beat, *"it has rescued many a thousand!"* Not a soul under the sound of their voices
was hearing this song for the first time, not one of them had been rescued. Nor

had they seen much in the way of rescue work being done around them. Neither did they especially believe in the holiness of the three sisters and the brother, they knew too much about them, knew where they lived, and how. The woman with the tambourine, whose voice dominated the air, whose face was bright with joy, was divided by very little from the women who stood watching her, a cigarette between her heavy chapped lips, her hair a cuckoo's nest, her face scarred and swollen from many beatings, and her black eyes glittering like coal. Perhaps they both knew this, which was why, when, as rarely, they addressed each other, they addressed each other as Sister. As the singing filled the air the watching, listening faces underwent a change, the eyes focusing on something within; the music seemed to soothe a poison out of them; and time seemed, nearly, to fall away from the sullen, belligerent, battered faces, as though they were fleeing back to their first condition, while dreaming of their last. The barbecue cook half shook his head and smiled, and dropped his cigarette and disappeared into his joint. A man fumbled in his pockets for change and stood holding it in his hand impatiently, as though he had just remembered a pressing appointment further up the avenue. He looked furious. Then I saw Sonny, standing on the edge of the crowd. He was carrying a wide, flat notebook with a green cover, and it made him look, from where I was standing, almost like a schoolboy. The coppery sun brought out the copper in his skin, he was very faintly smiling, standing very still. Then the singing stopped, the tambourine turned into a collection plate again. The furious man dropped in his coins and vanished, so did a couple of the women, and Sonny dropped some change in the plate, looking directly at the woman with a little smile. He started across the avenue, toward the house. He has a slow, loping walk, something like the way Harlem hipsters walk, only he's imposed on this his own half-beat. I had never really noticed it before.

I stayed at the window, both relieved and apprehensive. As Sonny disappeared from my sight, they began singing again. And they were still singing when his key turned in the lock.

"Hey," he said.

"Hey, yourself. You want some beer?"

"No. Well, maybe." But he came up to the window and stood beside me, looking out. "What a warm voice," he said.

They were singing *If I could only hear my mother pray again!*

"Yes," I said, "and she can sure beat that tambourine."

"But what a terrible song," he said, and laughed. He dropped his notebook on the sofa and disappeared into the kitchen. "Where's Isabel and the kids?"

"I think they went to see their grandparents. You hungry?"

"No." He came back into the living room with his can of beer. "You want to come some place with me tonight?"

I sensed, I don't know how, that I couldn't possibly say no. "Sure. Where?"

He sat down on the sofa and picked up his notebook and started leafing through it. "I'm going to sit in with some fellows in a joint in the Village."

"You mean, you're going to play, tonight?"

"That's right." He took a swallow of his beer and moved back to the window. He gave me a sidelong look. "If you can stand it."

"I'll try," I said.

Death of child brings narrator back to reality

He smiled to himself and we both watched as the meeting across the way broke up. The three sisters and the brother, heads bowed, were singing *God be with you till we meet again.* The faces around them were very quiet. Then the song ended. The small crowd dispersed. We watched the three women and the lone man walk slowly up the avenue.

"When she was singing before," said Sonny, abruptly, "her voice reminded me for a minute of what heroin feels like sometimes—when it's in your veins. It makes you feel sort of warm and cool at the same time. And distant. And—and sure." He sipped his beer, very deliberately not looking at me. I watched his face. "It makes you feel—in control. Sometimes you've got to have that feeling."

"Do you?" I sat down slowly in the easy chair.

"Sometimes." He went to the sofa and picked up his notebook again. "Some people do."

"In order," I asked, "to play?" And my voice was very ugly, full of contempt and anger.

"Well"—he looked at me with great, troubled eyes, as though, in fact, he hoped his eyes would tell me things he could never otherwise say—"They *think* so. And *if* they think so—!"

"And what do *you* think?" I asked.

He sat on the sofa and put his can of beer on the floor. "I don't know," he said, and I couldn't be sure if he were answering my question or pursuing his thoughts. He face didn't tell me. "It's not so much to *play*. It's to *stand* it, to be able to make it at all. On any level." He frowned and smiled: "In order to keep from shaking to pieces."

"But these friends of yours," I said, "they seem to shake themselves to pieces pretty goddamn fast."

"Maybe." He played with the notebook. And something told me that I should curb my tongue, that Sonny was doing his best to talk, that I should listen. "But of course you only know the ones that've gone to pieces. Some don't—or at least they haven't *yet* and that's just about all *any* of us can say." He paused. "And then there are some who just live, really, in hell, and they know it and they see what's happening and they go right on. I don't know." He sighed, dropped the notebook, folded his arms. "Some guys, you can tell from the way they play, they on something *all* the time. And you can see that, well, it makes something real for them. But of course," he picked up his beer from the floor and sipped it and put the can down again, "they *want* to, too, you've got to see that. Even some of them that say they don't—*some*, not all."

"And what about you?" I asked—I couldn't help it. "What about you? Do *you* want to?"

He stood up and walked to the window and remained silent for a long time. Then he sighed. "Me," he said. Then: "While I was downstairs before, on my way here, listening to that woman sing, it struck me all of a sudden how much suffering she must have had to go through—to sing like that. It's *repulsive* to think you have to suffer that much."

I said: "But there's no way not to suffer—is there, Sonny?"

"I believe not," he said and smiled, "but that's never stopped anyone from trying." He looked at me. "Has it?" I realized, with this mocking look, that there stood between us, forever, beyond the power of time or forgiveness, the fact that I had held silence—so long!—when he had needed human speech to help him. He turned back to the window. "No, there's no way not to suffer. But you try all kinds of ways to keep from drowning in it, to keep on top of it, and to make it seem—well, like *you*. Like you did something, all right, and now you're suffering for it. You know?" I said nothing. "Well, you know," he said, impatiently, "why *do* people suffer? Maybe it's better to do something to give it a reason, *any* reason."

"But we just agreed," I said, "that there's no way not to suffer. Isn't it better, then, just to—take it?"

"But nobody just takes it," Sonny cried, "that's what I'm telling you! *Everybody* tries not to. You're just hung up on the *way* some people try—it's not *your* way!"

The hair on my face began to itch, my face felt wet. "That's not true," I said, "that's not true. I don't give a damn what other people do, I don't even care how they suffer. I just care how *you* suffer." And he looked at me. "Please believe me," I said, "I don't want to see you—die—trying not to suffer."

"I won't," he said, flatly, "die trying not to suffer. At least, not any faster than anybody else."

"But there's no need," I said, trying to laugh, "is there? in killing yourself."

I wanted to say more, but I couldn't. I wanted to talk about will power and how life could be—well, beautiful. I wanted to say that it was all within; but was it? or, rather, wasn't that exactly the trouble? And I wanted to promise that I would never fail him again. But it would all have sounded—empty words and lies.

So I made the promise to myself and prayed that I would keep it.

"It's terrible sometimes, inside," he said, "that's what's the trouble. You walk these streets, black and funky and cold, and there's not really a living ass to talk to, and there's nothing shaking, and there's no way of getting it out—that storm inside. You can't talk it and you can't make love with it, and when you finally try to get with it and play it, you realize *nobody's* listening. So *you've* got to listen. You got to find a way to listen."

And then he walked away from the window and sat on the sofa again, as though all the wind had suddenly been knocked out of him. "Sometimes you'll do *anything* to play, even cut your mother's throat." He laughed and looked at me. "Or your brother's." Then he sobered. "Or your own." Then: "Don't worry. I'm all right now and I think I'll *be* all right. But I can't forget—where I've been. I don't mean just the physical place I've been, I mean where I've *been*. And *what* I've been."

"What have you been, Sonny?" I asked.

He smiled—but sat sideways on the sofa, his elbow resting on the back, his fingers playing with his mouth and chin, not looking at me. "I've been something I didn't recognize, didn't know I could be. Didn't know anybody could be." He stopped, looking inward, looking helplessly young, looking old. "I'm not talking about it now because I feel *guily* or anything like that—maybe it would be better if I did, I don't know. Anyway, I can't really talk about it. Not to you, not to anybody," and now he turned and faced me. "Sometimes, you know, and it was actually when I was most *out* of the world, I felt that I was in it, that I was *with* it, really, and I could play or I didn't really have to *play*, it just came out of me, it was there. And I don't know how I played, thinking about it now, but I

[handwritten margin note: Sonny tried to escape through drugs, didn't work, so he tried music]

know I did awful things, those times, sometimes, to people. Or it wasn't that I *did* anything to them—it was that they weren't real." He picked up the beer can; it was empty; he rolled it between his palms: "And other times—well, I needed a fix, I needed to find a place to lean, I needed to clear a space to *listen*—and I couldn't find it, and I—went crazy, I did terrible things to *me*, I was terrible *for* me." He began pressing the beer can between his hands, I watched the metal begin to give. It glittered, as he played with it, like a knife, and I was afraid he would cut himself, but I said nothing. "Oh well, I can never tell you. I was all by myself at the bottom of something, stinking and sweating and crying and shaking, and I smelled it, you know? *my* stink, and I thought I'd die if I couldn't get away from it and yet, all the same, I knew that everything I was doing was just locking me in with it. And I didn't know," he paused, still flattening the beer can, "I didn't know, I still *don't* know, something kept telling me that maybe it was good to smell your own stink, but I didn't think that *that* was what I'd been trying to do—and—who can stand it?" and he abruptly dropped the ruined beer can, looking at me with a small, still smile, and then rose, walking to the window as though it were the lodestone rock. I watched his face, he watched the avenue. "I couldn't tell you when Mama died—but the reason I wanted to leave Harlem so bad was to get away from drugs. And then, when I ran away, that's what I was running from—really. When I came back, nothing had changed, *I* hadn't changed. I was just—older." And he stopped, drumming with his fingers on the windowpane. The sun had vanished, soon darkness would fall. I watched his face. "It can come again," he said, almost as though speaking to himself. Then he turned to me. "It can come again," he repeated. "I just want you to know that."

"All right," I said, at last. "So it can come again. All right."

He smiled, but the smile was sorrowful. "I had to try to tell you," he said.

"Yes," I said. "I understand that."

"You're my brother," he said, looking straight at me, and not smiling at all.

"Yes," I repeated, "yes, I understand that."

He turned back to the window, looking out. "All that hatred down there," he said, "all that hatred and misery and love. It's a wonder it doesn't blow the avenue apart."

We went to the only nightclub on a short, dark street, downtown. We squeezed through the narrow, chattering, jam-packed bar to the entrance of the big room, where the bandstand was. And we stood there for a moment, for the lights were very dim in this room and we couldn't see. Then, "Hello, boy," said a voice and an enormous black man, much older than Sonny or myself, erupted out of all that atmospheric lighting and put an arm around Sonny's shoulder. "I been sitting right here," he said, "waiting for you."

He had a big voice, too, and heads in the darkness turned toward us.

Sonny grinned and pulled a little away, and said, "Creole, this is my brother. I told you about him."

Creole shook my hand. "I'm glad to meet you, son," he said, and it was clear that he was glad to meet me *there*, for Sonny's sake. And he smiled, "You got a real musician in *your* family," and he took his arm from Sonny's shoulder and slapped him, lightly, affectionately, with the back of his hand.

"Well. Now I've heard it all," said a voice behind us. This was another musician, and a friend of Sonny's, a coal-black, cheerful-looking man, built close to the ground. He immediately began confiding to me, at the top of his lungs, the most terrible things about Sonny, his teeth gleaming like a lighthouse and his laugh coming up out of him like the beginning of an earthquake. And it turned out that everyone at the bar knew Sonny, or almost everyone; some were musicians, working there, or nearby, or not working, some were simply hangers-on, and some were there to hear Sonny play. I was introduced to all of them and they were all very polite to me. Yet, it was clear that, for them, I was only Sonny's brother. Here, I was in Sonny's world. Or, rather: his kingdom. Here, it was not even a question that his veins bore royal blood.

They were going to play soon and Creole installed me, by myself, at a table in a dark corner. Then I watched them. Creole, and the little black man, and Sonny, and the others, while they horsed around, standing just below the bandstand. The light from the bandstand spilled just a little short of them and, watching them laughing and gesturing and moving about, I had the feeling that they, nevertheless, were being most careful not to step into that circle of light too suddenly, that if they moved into the light too suddenly, without thinking, they would perish in flame. Then, while I watched, one of them, the small black man, moved into the light and crossed the bandstand and started fooling around with his drums. Then—being funny and being, also, extremely ceremonious—Creole took Sonny by the arm and led him to the piano. A woman's voice called Sonny's name and a few hands started clapping. And Sonny, also being funny and being ceremonious, and so touched, I think, that he could have cried, but neither hiding it nor showing it, riding it like a man, grinned, and put both hands to his heart and bowed from the waist.

Creole then went to the bass fiddle and a lean, very bright-skinned brown man jumped up on the bandstand and picked up his horn. So there they were, and the atmosphere on the bandstand and in the room began to change and tighten. Someone stepped up to the microphone and announced them. Then there were all kinds of murmurs. Some people at the bar shushed others. The waitress ran around, frantically getting in the last orders, guys and chicks got closer to each other, and the lights on the bandstand, on the quartet, turned to a kind of indigo. Then they all looked different there. Creole looked about him for the last time, as though he were making certain that all his chickens were in the coop, and then he—jumped and struck the fiddle. And there they were.

All I know about music is that not many people ever really hear it. And even then, on the rare occasions when something opens within, and the music enters, what we mainly hear, or hear corroborated, are personal, private, vanishing evocations. But the man who creates the music is hearing something else, is dealing with the roar rising from the void and imposing order on it as it hits the air. What is evoked in him, then, is of another order, more terrible because it has no words, and triumphant, too, for that same reason. And his triumph, when he triumphs, is ours. I just watched Sonny's face. His face was troubled, he was working hard, but he wasn't with it. And I had the feeling that, in a way, everyone on the bandstand was waiting for him, both waiting for him and pushing him along. But as I began to watch Creole, I realized that it was Creole who held them all back. He had them on a short rein. Up there, keeping the beat with his whole body, wailing on the fiddle, with his eyes half closed, he was listening to everything, but he was listening to Sonny. He was having a dialogue with Sonny. He wanted Sonny to leave the shoreline and strike out for the deep water. He was Sonny's witness that deep water and drowning were not the same thing—he had been there, and he knew. And he wanted Sonny to know. He was waiting for Sonny to do the things on the keys which would let Creole know that Sonny was in the water.

And, while Creole listened, Sonny moved, deep within, exactly like someone in torment. I had never before thought of how awful the relationship must be between the musician and his instrument. He has to fill it, this instrument, with the breath of life, his own. He has to make it do what he wants it to do. And a piano is just a piano. It's made out of so much wood and wires and little hammers and big ones, and ivory. While there's only so much you can do with it, the only way to find this out is to try; to try and make it do everything.

And Sonny hadn't been near a piano for over a year. And he wasn't on much better terms with his life, not the life that stretched before him now. He and the piano stammered, started one way, got scared, stopped; started another way, panicked, marked time, started again; then seemed to have found a direction, panicked again, got stuck. And the face I saw on Sonny I'd never seen before. Everything had been burned out of it, and, at the same time, things usually hidden were being burned in, by the fire and fury of the battle which was occurring in him up there.

Yet, watching Creole's face as they neared the end of the first set, I had the feeling that something had happened, something I hadn't heard. Then they finished, there was scattered applause, and then, without an instant's warning, Creole started into something else, it was almost sardonic, it was *Am I Blue.* And, as though he commanded, Sonny began to play. Something began to happen. And Creole let out the reins. The dry, low, black man said something awful on the drums. Creole answered, and the drums talked back. Then the horn insisted, sweet and high, slightly detached perhaps, and Creole listened, commenting now and then, dry, and driving, beautiful and calm and old. Then they all came together again, and Sonny was part of the family again. I could tell this from his face. He seemed to have found, right there beneath his fingers, a damn brand-new piano. It seemed that he couldn't get over it. Then, for awhile, just being happy with Sonny, they seemed to be agreeing with him that brand-new pianos certainly were a gas.

Then Creole stepped forward to remind them that what they were playing was the blues. He hit something in all of them, he hit something in me, myself, and the music tightened and deepened, apprehension began to beat the air. Creole began to tell us what the blues were all about. They were not about anything very new. He and his boys up there were keeping it new, at the risk of ruin, destruction, madness, and death, in order to find new ways to make us listen. For, while the tale of how we suffer, and how we are delighted, and how we may triumph is never new, it always must be heard. There isn't any other tale to tell, it's the only light we've got in all this darkness.

And this tale, according to that face, that body, those strong hands on those strings, has another aspect in every country, and a new depth in every generation. Listen, Creole seemed to be saying, listen. Now these are Sonny's blues. He made the little black man on the drums know it, and the bright, brown man on the horn. Creole wasn't trying any longer to get Sonny in the water. He was wishing him Godspeed. Then he stepped back, very slowly, filling the air with the immense suggestion that Sonny speak for himself.

Then they all gathered around Sonny and Sonny played. Every now and again one of them seemed to say, amen. Sonny's fingers filled the air with life, his life. But that life contained so many others. And Sonny went all the way back, he really began with the spare, flat statement of the opening phrase of the song. Then he began to make it his. It was very beautiful because it wasn't hurried and it was no longer a lament. I seemed to hear with what burning he had made it his, with what burning we had yet to make it ours, how we could cease lamenting. Freedom lurked around us and I understood, at last, that he could help us to be free if we would listen, that he would never be free until we did. Yet, there was no battle in his face now. I heard what he had gone through, and would continue to go through until he came to rest in earth. He had made it his: that long line, of which we knew only Mama and Daddy. And he was giving it back, as everything must be given back, so that, passing through death, it can live forever. I saw my mother's face again, and felt, for the first time, how the stones of the road she had walked on must have bruised her feet. I saw the moonlit road where my father's brother died. And it brought something else back to me, and carried me past it, I saw my little girl again and felt Isabel's tears again, and I felt my own tears begin to rise. And I was yet aware that this was only a moment, that the world waited outside, as hungry as a tiger, and that trouble stretched above us, longer than the sky.

Then it was over. Creole and Sonny let out their breath, both soaking wet, and grinning. There was a lot of applause and some of it was real. In the dark, the girl came by and I asked her to take drinks to the bandstand. There was a long pause, while they talked up there in the indigo light and after awhile I saw the girl put a Scotch and milk on top of the piano for Sonny. He didn't seem to notice it, but just before they started playing again, he sipped from it and looked toward me, and nodded. Then he put it back on top of the piano. For me, then, as they began to play again, it glowed and shook above my brother's head like the very cup of trembling.

Fact Questions and Exercises

1. What does the narrator do for a living?
2. How is Sonny related to the narrator?
3. Why has Sonny been arrested?
4. What is the name of the district in which Sonny and the narrator grew up?
5. What happened to the narrator's uncle?
6. What kind of musician does Sonny want to be? Does he realize this ambition?
7. Who is Grace? What happens to her?
8. Identify Creole.
9. What kind of drink does the narrator send to Sonny?

For Discussion and Writing

1. Note the story that the narrator's mother tells about his father's brother. Does this episode parallel or foreshadow the narrator's relationship with Sonny? How? What message is Mama trying to convey by telling the story?

2. Compare the characters of Sonny and the narrator. How are they alike? How do they differ? Do they ever come to understand each other?
3. What symbols are used in the story? For instance, how does Baldwin use song titles? Personal names? What allusions does he make to the Bible or religion? How does he use light and darkness?
4. What part does music play in the story? Does it bring order to Sonny's life? Does the narrator come to appreciate Sonny's music? Consequently, how does he better understand both Sonny and himself? Are the narrator's final thoughts optimistic?

Flannery O'Connor [1925–1964]

O'Connor was born in Savannah, Georgia, and was educated in private Catholic schools and the Women's College of Georgia. During the last years of her life she was a semi-invalid, having inherited the incurable *Lupus* disease that had killed her father. She produced little fiction, but that which she did publish is marked by a fascinating collection of themes— among them violence and death, "black humor," Christian allegory, and Southern degeneration. She is noted mainly for her short stories, which are usually ironic or satirical and marked by their swift, straightforward style and violent climaxes. Among her best-known works are *A Good Man is Hard to Find* (1955), *The Violent Bear It Away* (1960), and *Everything That Rises Must Converge* (1965).

The Life You Save May Be Your Own

Omniscient Perspective

stronger

Pulled together

[The old woman and her daughter were sitting on their porch when Mr. Shiftlet came up their road for the first time.] The old woman slid to the edge of her chair and leaned forward, shading her eyes from the piercing sunset with her hand. The daughter could not see far in front of her and continued to play with her fingers. Although the old woman lived in this desolate spot with only her daughter and she had never seen Mr. Shiftlet before, she could tell, even from a distance, that he was a tramp and no one to be afraid of. His left coat sleeve was folded up to show there was only half an arm in it and his gaunt figure listed slightly to the side as if the breeze were pushing him. He had on a black town suit and a brown felt hat that was turned up in the front and down in the back and he carried a tin tool box by a handle. He came on, at an amble, up her road, his face turned toward the sun which appeared to be balancing itself on the peak of a small mountain.

The old woman didn't change her position until he was almost into her yard; then she rose with one hand fisted on her hip. The daughter, a large girl in a short blue organdy dress, saw him all at once and jumped up and began to stamp and point and make excited speechless sounds.

Mr. Shiftlet stopped just inside the yard and set his box on the ground and tipped his hat at her as if she were not in the least afflicted; then he turned toward the old woman and swung the hat all the way off. He had long black slick hair that hung flat from a part in the middle to beyond the tips of his ears on either side. His face descended in forehead for more than half its length and ended suddenly with his features just balanced over a jutting steel-trap jaw. He seemed to be a young man but he had a look of composed dissatisfaction as if he understood life thoroughly.

"Good evening," the old woman said. She was about the size of a cedar fence post and she had a man's gray hat pulled down low over her head.

The tramp stood looking at her and didn't answer. He turned his back and faced the sunset. He swung both his whole and his short arm up slowly so that they indicated an expanse of sky and his figure formed a crooked cross. The old woman watched him with her arms folded across her chest as if she were the owner of the sun, and the daughter watched, her head thrust forward and her fat helpless hands hanging at the wrists. She had long pink-gold hair and eyes as blue as a peacock's neck.

He held the pose for almost fifty seconds and then he picked up his box and came on to the porch and dropped down on the bottom step. "Lady," he said in a firm nasal voice, "I'd give a fortune to live where I could see me a sun do that every evening."

"Does it every evening," the old woman said and sat back down. The daughter sat down too and watched him with a cautious sly look as if he were a bird that had come up very close. He leaned to one side, rooting in his pants pocket, and in a second he brought out a package of chewing gum and offered her a piece. She took it and unpeeled it and began to chew without taking her eyes off him. He offered the old woman a piece but she only raised her upper lip to indicate she had no teeth.

Mr. Shiftlet's pale sharp glance had already passed over everything in the yard—the pump near the corner of the house and the big fig tree that three of four chickens were preparing to roost in—and had moved to a shed where he saw the square rusted back of an automobile. "You ladies drive?" he asked.

"That car ain't run in fifteen year," the old woman said. "The day my husband died, it quit running."

"Nothing is like it used to be, lady," he said. "The world is almost rotten."

"That's right," the old woman said. "You from around here?"

"Name Tom T. Shiftlet," he murmured, looking at the tires.

"I'm pleased to meet you," the old woman said. "Name Lucynell Crater and daughter Lucynell Crater. What you doing around here, Mr. Shiftlet?"

He judged the car to be about a 1928 or '29 Ford. "Lady," he said, and turned and gave her his full attention, "lemme tell you something. There's one of these doctors in Atlanta that's taken a knife and cut the human heart—the human heart," he repeated, leaning forward, "out of a man's chest and held it in his hand," and he held his hand out, palm up, as if it were slightly weighted with the human heart, "and studied it like it was a day-old chicken, and, lady," he said, allowing a long significant pause in which his head slid forward and his clay-colored eyes brightened, "he don't know no more about it than you or me."

"That's right," the old woman said.

"Why, if he was to take that knife and cut into every corner of it, he still wouldn't know no more than you or me. What you want to bet?"

"Nothing," the old woman said wisely. "Where you come from, Mr. Shiftlet?"

He didn't answer. He reached into his pocket and brought out a sack of tobacco and a package of cigarette papers and rolled himself a cigarette, expertly with one hand, and attached it in a hanging position to his upper lip. Then he took a box of wooden matches from his pocket and struck one on his shoe. He held the burning match as if he were studying the mystery of flame while it traveled dangerously toward his skin. The daughter began to make loud noises and to point to his hand and shake her finger at him, but when the flame was just before touching him, he leaned down with his hand cupped over it as if he were going to set fire to his nose and lit the cigarette.

He flipped away the dead match and blew a stream of gray into the evening. A sly look came over his face. "Lady," he said, "nowadays, people'll do anything anyways. I can tell you my name is Tom T. Shiftlet and I come from Tarwater, Tennessee, but you never have seen me before: how you know I ain't lying? How you know my name ain't Aaron Sparks, lady, and I come from Singleberry, Georgia, or how you know it's not George Speeds and I come from Lucy, Alabama, or how you know I ain't Thompson Bright from Toolafalls, Mississippi?"

"I don't know nothing about you," the old woman muttered, irked.

"Lady," he said, "people don't care how they lie. Maybe the best I can tell you is, I'm a man; but listen, lady," he said and paused and made his tone more ominous still, "what is a man?"

The old woman began to gum a seed. "What you carry in that tin box, Mr. Shiflet?" she asked.

"Tools," he said, put back. "I'm a carpenter."

"Well, if you come out here to work, I'll be able to feed you and give you a place to sleep but I can't pay. I'll tell you that before you begin," she said.

There was no answer at once and no particular expression on his face. He leaned back against the two-by-four that helped support the porch roof. "Lady," he said slowly, "there's some men that some things mean more to them than money." The old woman rocked without comment and the daughter watched the trigger that moved up and down in his neck. He told the old woman then that all most people were interested in was money, but he asked what a man was made for. He asked her if a man was made for money, or what. He asked her what she thought she was made for but she didn't answer, she only sat rocking and wondered if a one-armed man could put a new roof on her garden house. He asked a lot of questions that she didn't answer. He told her that he was twenty-eight years old and had lived a varied life. He had been a gospel singer, a foreman on the railroad, an assistant in an undertaking parlor, and he had come over the radio for three months with Uncle Roy and his Red Creek Wranglers. He said he had fought and bled in the Arm Service of his country and visited every foreign land and that everywhere he had seen people that didn't care if they did a thing one way or another. He said he hadn't been raised thataway.

A fat yellow moon appeared in the branches of the fig tree as if it were going to roost there with the chickens. He said that a man had to escape to the country to see the world whole and that he wished he lived in a desolate place like this where he could see the sun go down every evening like God made it to do. *identifies w/ God*

"Are you married or are you single?" the old woman asked.

There was a long silence. "Lady," he asked finally, "where would you find you an innocent woman today? I wouldn't have any of this trash I could just pick up."

The daughter was leaning very far down, hanging her head almost between her knees, watching him through a triangular door she had made in her overturned hair; and she suddenly fell in a heap on the floor and began to whimper. Mr. Shiftlet straightened her out and helped her get back in the chair. *daughter*

"Is she your baby girl?" he asked.

"My only," the old woman said, "and she's the sweetest girl in the world. I wouldn't give her up for nothing on earth. She's smart too. She can sweep the floor, cook, wash, feed the chickens, and hoe. I wouldn't give her up for a casket of jewels."

"No," he said kindly, "don't ever let any man take her away from you."

"Any man come after her," the old woman said, "'ll have to stay around the place."

Mr. Shiftlet's eye in the darkness was focused on a part of the automobile bumper that glittered in the distance. "Lady," he said, jerking his short arm up as if he could point with it to her house and yard and pump, "there ain't a broken thing on this plantation that I couldn't fix for you, one-arm jackleg or not. I'm a man," he said with a sullen dignity, "even if I ain't a whole one. I got," he said, tapping his knuckles on the floor to emphasize the immensity of what he was going to say, "a moral intelligence!" and his face pierced out of the darkness into a shaft of doorlight and he stared at her as if he were astonished himself at this impossible truth.

The old woman was not impressed with the phrase. "I told you you could hang around and work for food," she said, "if you don't mind sleeping in that car yonder."

"Why listen, Lady," he said with a grin of delight, "the monks of old slept in their coffins!"

"They wasn't as advanced as we are," the old woman said.

The next morning he began on the roof of the garden house while Lucynell, the daughter, sat on a rock and watched him work. He had not been around a week before the change he had made in the place was apparent. He had patched the front and back steps, built a new hog pen, restored a fence, and taught Lucynell, who was completely deaf and had never said a word in her life, to say the word "bird." The big rosy-faced girl followed him everywhere, saying "Burrttddt ddbirrrttdt," and clapping her hands. The old woman watched from a distance, secretly pleased. She was ravenous for a son-in-law.

Mr. Shiftlet slept on the hard narrow back seat of the car with his feet out the side window. He had his razor and a can of water on a crate that served him as a bedside table and he put up a piece of mirror against the back glass and kept his coat neatly on a hanger that he hung over one of the windows.

In the evenings he sat on the steps and talked while the old woman and Lucynell rocked violently in their chairs on either side of him. The old woman's three mountains were black against the dark blue sky and were visited off and on by various planets and by the moon after it had left the chickens. Mr. Shiftlet pointed out that the reason he had improved this plantation was because he had taken a personal interest in it. He said he was even going to make the automobile run.

He had raised the hood and studied the mechanism and he said he could tell that the car had been built in the days when cars were really built. You take now, he said, one man puts in one bolt and another man puts in another bolt and another man puts in another bolt so that it's a man for a bolt. That's why you have to pay so much for a car: you're paying all those men. Now if you didn't have to pay but one man, you could get you a cheaper car and one that had had a personal interest taken in it, and it would be a better car. The old woman agreed with him that this was so.

Mr. Shiftlet said that the trouble with the world was that nobody cared, or stopped and took any trouble. He said he never would have been able to teach Lucynell to say a word if he hadn't cared and stopped long enough.

"Teach her to say something else," the old woman said.

"What you want her to say next?" Mr. Shiftlet asked.

The old woman's smile was broad and toothless and suggestive. "Teach her to say, 'sugarpie,' " she said.

Mr. Shiftlet already knew what was on her mind.

The next day he began to tinker with the automobile and that evening he told her that if she would buy a fan belt, he would be able to make the car run.

The old woman said she would give him the money. "You see that girl yonder?" she asked, pointing to Lucynell who was sitting on the floor a foot away, watching him, her eyes blue even in the dark. "If it was ever a man wanted to take her away, I would say, 'No man on earth is going to take that sweet girl of mine away from me!' but if he was to say, 'Lady, I don't want to take her away. I want her right here,' I would say, 'Mister, I don't blame you none. I wouldn't pass up a chance to live in a permanent place and get the sweetest girl in the world myself. You ain't no fool,' I would say."

"How old is she?" Mr. Shiftlet asked casually.

"Fifteen, sixteen," the old woman said. The girl was nearly thirty but because of her innocence it was impossible to guess.

"It would be a good idea to paint it too," Mr. Shiftlet remarked. "You don't want it to rust out."

"We'll see about that later," the old woman said.

The next day he walked into town and returned with the parts he needed, and a can of gasoline. Late in the afternoon, terrible noises issued from the shed and the old woman rushed out of the house, thinking Lucynell was somewhere having a fit. Lucynell was sitting on a chicken crate, stamping her feet and screaming, "Burrddttt! bddurrddtttt!" but her fuss was drowned out by the car. With a volley of blasts it emerged from the shed, moving in a fierce and stately way. Mr. Shiftlet was in the driver's seat, sitting very erect. He had an expression of serious modesty on his face as if he had just raised the dead.

That night, rocking on the porch, the old woman began her business at once. "You want you an innocent woman, don't you?" she asked sympathetically. "You don't want none of this trash."

"No'm, I don't," Mr. Shiftlet said.

"One that can't talk," she continued, "can't sass you back or use foul language. That's the kind for you to have. Right there," and she pointed to Lucynell sitting cross-legged in her chair, holding both feet in her hands.

"That's right," he admitted. "She wouldn't give me any trouble."

"Saturday," the old woman said, "you and her and me can drive into town and get married."

Mr. Shiftlet eased his position on the steps.

"I can't get married right now," he said. "Everything you want to do takes money and I ain't got any."

"What you need with money?" she asked.

"It takes money," he said. "Some people'll do anything anyhow these days, but the way I think, I wouldn't marry no woman that I couldn't take on a trip like she was somebody. I mean take her to a hotel and treat her. I wouldn't marry the Duchesser Windsor," he said firmly, "unless I could take her to a hotel and give her something good to eat.

"I was raised thataway and there ain't a thing I can do about it. My old mother taught me how to do."

"Lucynell don't even know what a hotel is," the old woman muttered. "Listen here, Mr. Shiftlet," she said, sliding forward in her chair, "you'd be getting a permanent house and a deep well and the most innocent girl in the world. You don't need no money. Lemme tell you something: there ain't any place in the world for a poor disabled friendless drifting man."

The ugly words settled in Mr. Shiftlet's head like a group of buzzards in the top of a tree. He didn't answer at once. He rolled himself a cigarette and lit it and then he said in an even voice, "Lady, a man is divided into two parts, body and spirit."

The old woman clamped her gums together.

"A body and a spirit," he repeated. "The body, lady, is like a house: it don't go anywhere; but the spirit, lady, is like an automobile: always on the move, always . . ."

"Listen, Mr. Shiftlet," she said, "my well never goes dry and my house is always warm in the winter and there's no mortgage on a thing about this place. You can go to the courthouse and see for yourself. And yonder under that shed is a fine automobile." She laid the bait carefully. "You can have it painted by Saturday. I'll pay for the paint."

In the darkness, Mr. Shiftlet's smile stretched like a weary snake waking up by a fire. After a second he recalled himself and said, "I'm only saying a man's spirit means more to him than anything else. I would have to take my wife off for the week end without no regards at all for cost. I got to follow where my spirit says to go."

"I'll give you fifteen dollars for a week-end trip," the old woman said in a crabbed voice. "That's the best I can do."

"That wouldn't hardly pay for more than the gas and the hotel," he said, "It wouldn't feed her."

"Seventeen-fifty," the old woman said. "That's all I got so it isn't any use you trying to milk me. You can take a lunch."

Mr. Shiftlet was deeply hurt by the word "milk." He didn't doubt that she had more money sewed up in her mattress but he had already told her he was not interested in her money. "I'll make that do," he said, and rose and walked off without treating with her further.

On Saturday the three of them drove into town in the car that the paint had barely dried on and Mr. Shiftlet and Lucynell were married in the Ordinary's office while the old woman witnessed. As they came out of the courthouse, Mr. Shiftlet began twisting his neck in his collar. He looked morose and bitter as if he had been insulted while someone held him. "That didn't satisfy me none," he said. "That was just something a woman in an office did, nothing but paper work and blood tests. What do they know about my blood? If they was to take my heart and cut it out," he said, "they wouldn't know a thing about me. It didn't satisfy me at all."

"It satisfied the law," the old woman said sharply.

"The law," Mr. Shiftlet said, and spit, "It's the law that don't satisfy me."

He had painted the car dark green with a yellow band around it just under the windows. The three of them climbed in the front seat and the old woman said, "Don't Lucynell look pretty? Looks like a baby doll." Lucynell was dressed up in a white dress that her mother had uprooted from a trunk and there was a Panama hat on her head with a bunch of red wooden cherries on the brim. Every now and then her placid expression was changed by a sly isolated little thought like a shoot of green in the desert. "You got a prize!" the old woman said.

Mr. Shiftlet didn't even look at her.

They drove back to the house to let the old woman off and pick up the lunch. When they were ready to leave, she stood staring in the window of the car, with her fingers clenched around the glass. Tears began to seep sideways out of her eyes and run along dirty creases in her face. "I ain't ever been parted with her for two days before," she said.

Mr. Shiftlet started the motor.

"And I wouldn't let no man have her but you because I seen you would do right. Goodbye, Sugarbaby," she said, clutching at the sleeve of the white dress. Lucynell looked straight at her and didn't seem to see her there at all. Mr. Shiftlet eased the car forward so that she had to move her hands.

The early afternoon was clear and open and surrounded by pale blue sky. The hills flattened under the car one after another and the climb and dip and swerve went entirely to Mr. Shiftlet's head so that he forgot his morning bitterness. He had always wanted an automobile but he had never been able to afford one before. He drove very fast because he wanted to make Mobile by nightfall.

Occasionally he stopped his thoughts long enough to look at Lucynell in the seat beside him. She had eaten lunch as soon as they were out of the yard and now she was pulling the cherries off the hat one by one and throwing them out the window. He became depressed in spite of the car. He had driven about a hundred miles when he decided that she must be hungry again and at the next small town they came to, he stopped in front of an aluminum-painted eating place called The Hot Spot and took her in and ordered her a plate of ham and grits. The ride had made her sleepy and as soon as she got up on the stool, she rested her head on the counter and shut her eyes. There was no one in The Hot Spot but Mr. Shiftlet and the boy behind the counter, a pale youth with a greasy rag hung over his shoulder. Before he could dish up the food, she was snoring gently.

"Give it to her when she wakes up," Mr. Shiftlet said. "I'll pay for it now."

The boy bent over her and stared at the long pink-gold hair and the half-shut sleeping eyes. Then he looked up and stared at Mr. Shiftlet. "She looks like an angel of Gawd," he murmured.

"Hitch-hiker," Mr. Shiftlet explained. "I can't wait. I got to make Tuscaloosa."

The boy bent over again and very carefully touched his finger to a strand of the golden hair and Mr. Shiftlet left.

He was more depressed than ever as he drove on by himself. The late afternoon had grown hot and sultry and the country had flattened out. Deep in the sky a storm was preparing very slowly and without thunder as if it meant to drain every drop of air from the earth before it broke. There were times when Mr. Shiftlet preferred not to be alone. He felt too that a man with a car had a responsibility to others and he kept his eye out for a hitch-hiker. Occasionally he saw a sign that warned: "Drive carefully. The life you save may be your own."

The narrow road dropped off on either side into dry fields and here and there a shack of a filling station stood in a clearing. The sun began to set directly in front of the automobile. It was a reddening ball that through his windshield was slightly flat on the bottom and top. He saw a boy in overalls and a gray hat standing on the edge of the road and he slowed the car down and stopped in front of him. The boy didn't have his hand raised to thumb the ride, he was only standing there, but he had a small cardboard suitcase and his hat was set on his head in a way to indicate that he had left somewhere for good. "Son," Mr. Shiftlet said, "I see you want a ride."

The boy didn't say he did or he didn't but he opened the door of the car and got in, and Mr. Shiftlet started driving again. The child held the suitcase on his lap and folded his arms on top of it. He turned his head and looked out the window away from Mr. Shiftlet. Mr. Shiftlet felt oppressed. "Son," he said after a minute, "I got the best old mother in the world so I reckon you only got the second best."

The boy gave him a quick dark glance and then turned his face back out the window.

"It's nothing so sweet," Mr. Shiftlet continued, "as a boy's mother. She taught him his first prayers at her knee, she give him love when no other would, she told him what was right and what wasn't, and she seen that he done the right thing. Son," he said, "I never rued a day in my life like the one I rued when I left that old mother of mine."

The boy shifted in his seat but he didn't look at Mr. Shiftlet. He unfolded his arms and put one hand on the door handle.

"My mother was a angel of Gawd," Mr. Shiftlet said in a very strained voice. "He took her from heaven and giver to me and I left her." His eyes were instantly clouded over with a mist of tears. The car was barely moving.

The boy turned angrily in the seat. "You go to the devil!" he cried. "My old woman is a flea bag and yours is a stinking pole cat!" and with that he flung the door open and jumped out with his suitcase into the ditch.

Mr. Shiftlet was so shocked that for about a hundred feet he drove along slowly with the door still open. A cloud, the exact color of the boy's hat and shaped like a turnip, had descended over the sun, and another, worse looking, crouched behind the car. Mr. Shiftlet felt that the rottenness of the world was about to engulf him. He raised his arm and let it fall again to his breast. "Oh Lord!" he prayed, "Break forth and wash the slime from this earth!"

The turnip continued slowly to descend. After a few minutes there was a guffawing peal of thunder from behind and fantastic raindrops, like tin-can tops, crashed over the rear of Mr. Shiftlet's car. Very quickly he stepped on the gas and with his stump sticking out the window he raced the galloping shower into Mobile.

Fact Questions and Exercises

Tom T. Shiflet

1. What is the name of the stranger who visits the old woman and her daughter?
2. What is the stranger's physical disability? _one-armed_
3. What is the stranger's supposed profession? _carpenter_
4. What is the daughter's affliction? _deaf / dumb_
5. The mother owns something that the stranger wants. What is it? _Car_
6. What word does the stranger teach the daughter to say? _BIRD_
7. Ultimately, what does the stranger do with the daughter? _marries & leaves her_
8. What fact gives the story its title? _Road Sign_
9. At the end of the story, where is the stranger going? _Mobile_

For Discussion and Writing

Mother & Daughter
Lucynell Crater

1. What does Mr. Shiftlet's name suggest about his character? _a drifter, tramp_ How does his name relate to the kind of life he leads? How does it relate to the car he wants? Do the other names that he suggests for himself on page 284 have a similar meaning? If so, explain.
2. In the story, Mrs. Crater says she would not give up her daughter "for a casket of jewels." _No_ Is Mrs. Crater serious? _yes_ Is she establishing a basis for bargaining with Shiftlet? Does either Mrs. Crater or Mr. Shiftlet really care for the daughter? _No_ If not, what does each gain from their bargain?
3. Cite details in the story that suggest a mysterious quality about Mr. Shiftlet. Is he totally evil? _No_ Is anything he does good? _yes_
4. Mr. Shiftlet refers to his mother as "a angel of Gawd." The boy in the café uses the same phrase to describe the daughter. What is the significance of this?
5. What does the car symbolize? What other symbols does O'Connor use? How do they relate to the overall purpose of the story?

John Barth [1930–   ]

Barth was born in Cambridge, Maryland, and was educated at Johns Hopkins University. From 1953 to 1965 Barth taught at Pennsylvania State University. He is presently a professor of English at the State University of New York, Buffalo; he is married and has three children. His rather conventional academic and personal life contrasts with the sometimes grotesque and experimental qualities of his fiction. For instance, _The Floating Opera_ (1956) is the story of a lawyer who contemplates suicide on a showboat loaded with his townspeople; and _The End of the Road_ (1958) is the story of an adulterous wife who chokes to death while undergoing an abortion. *Lost in the Funhouse* (1968), from which the following selection is taken, is a collection of experimental stories—some of which are meant to be read aloud or read as if the reader were listening to a tape of the author's voice. Barth also demonstrates his mastery of satire in other of his works, among these *The Sot-Weed Factor* (1960).

Lost in the Funhouse

For whom is the funhouse fun? Perhaps for lovers. For Ambrose it is *a place of fear and confusion.* He has come to the seashore with his family for the holiday, *the occasion of their visit is Independence Day, the most important secular holiday of the United States of America.* A single straight underline is the manuscript mark for italic type, *which in turn* is the printed equivalent to oral emphasis of words and phrases as well as the customary type for titles of complete works, not to mention. Italics are also employed, in fiction stories especially, for "outside," intrusive, or artificial voices, such as radio announcements, the texts of telegrams and newspaper articles, et cetera. They should be used *sparingly.* If passages originally in roman type are italicized by someone repeating them, it's customary to acknowledge the fact. *Italics mine.*

Ambrose was "at that awkward age." His voice came out high-pitched as a child's if he let himself get carried away; to be on the safe side, therefore, he moved and spoke with *deliberate calm* and *adult gravity.* Talking soberly of unimportant or irrelevant matters and listening consciously to the sound of your own voice are useful habits for maintaining control in this difficult interval. *En route* to Ocean City he sat in the back seat of the family car with his brother Peter, age fifteen, and Magda G——, age fourteen, a pretty girl and exquisite young lady, who lived not far from them on B—— Street in the town of D——, Maryland. Initials, blanks, or both were often substituted for proper names in nineteenth-century fiction to enhance the illusion of reality. It is as if the author felt it necessary to delete the names for reasons of tact or legal liability. Interestingly, as with other aspects of realism, it is an *illusion* that is being enhanced, by purely artificial means. Is it likely, does it violate the principle of verisimilitude, that a thirteen-year-old boy could make such a sophisticated observation? A girl of fourteen is *the psychological coeval* of a boy of fifteen or sixteen; a thirteen-year-old boy, therefore, even one precocious in some other respects, might be three years *her emotional junior.*

Thrice a year—on Memorial, Independence, and Labor Days—the family visits Ocean City for the afternoon and evening. When Ambrose and Peter's father was their age, the excursion was made by train, as mentioned in the novel *The 42nd Parallel* by John Dos Passos. Many families from the same neighborhood used to travel together, with dependent relatives and often with Negro servants; schoolfuls of children swarmed through the railway cars; everyone shared everyone else's Maryland fried chicken, Virginia ham, deviled eggs, potato salad, beaten biscuits, iced tea. Nowadays (that is, in 19——, the year of our story) the journey is made by automobile—more comfortably and quickly though without the extra fun though without the *camaraderie* of a general excursion. It's all part of the deterioration of American life, their father declares; Uncle Karl supposes that when the boys take *their* families to Ocean City for the holidays they'll fly in Autogiros. Their mother, sitting in the middle of the front seat like Magda in the second, only with her arms on the seat-back behind the men's shoulders, wouldn't want the good old days back again, the steaming trains and stuffy long dresses; on the other hand she can do without Autogiros, too, if she has to become a grandmother to fly in them.

Description of physical appearance and mannerisms is one of several standard methods of characterization used by writers of fiction. It is also important to "keep the senses operating"; when a detail from one of the five senses, say visual, is "crossed" with a detail from another, say auditory, the reader's imagination is oriented to the scene, perhaps unconsciously. This procedure may be compared to the way surveyors and navigators determine their positions by two or more compass bearings, a process known as triangulation. The brown hair on Ambrose's mother's forearms gleamed in the sun like. Though right-handed, she took her left arm from the seat-back to press the dashboard cigar lighter for Uncle Karl. When the glass bead in its handle glowed red, the lighter was ready for use. The smell of Uncle Karl's cigar smoke reminded one of. The fragrance of the ocean came strong to the picnic ground where they always stopped for lunch, two miles inland from Ocean City. Having to pause for a full hour almost within sound of the breakers was difficult for Peter and Ambrose when they were younger; even at their present age it was not easy to keep their anticipation, *stimulated by the briny spume,* from turning into short temper. The Irish author James Joyce, in his unusual novel entitled *Ulysses,* now available in this country, uses the adjectives *snot-green* and *scrotum-tightening* to describe the sea. Visual, auditory, tactile, olfactory, gustatory. Peter and Ambrose's father, while steering their black 1936 LaSalle sedan with one hand, could with the other remove the first cigarette from a white pack of Lucky Strikes and, more remarkably, light it with a match forefingered from its book and thumbed against the flint paper without being detached. The matchbook cover merely advertised U.S. War Bonds and Stamps. A fine metaphor, simile, or other figure of speech, in addition to its obvious "first-order" relevance to the thing it describes, will be seen upon reflection to have a second order of significance: it may be drawn from the *milieu* of the action, for example, or be particularly appropriate to the sensibility of the narrator, even hinting to the reader things of which the narrator is unaware; or it may cast further and subtler lights upon the things it describes, sometimes ironically qualifying the more evident sense of the comparison.

To say that Ambrose's and Peter's mother was *pretty* is to accomplish nothing; the reader may acknowledge the proposition, but his imagination is not engaged. Besides, Magda was also pretty, yet in an altogether different way. Although she lived on B—— Street she had very good manners and did better than average in school. Her figure was very well developed for her age. Her right hand lay casually on the plush upholstery of the seat, very near Ambrose's left leg on which his own hand rested. The space between their legs, between her right and his left leg, was out of the line of sight of anyone sitting on the other side of Magda, as well as anyone glancing into the rear-view mirror. Uncle Karl's face resembled Peter's—rather, vice versa. Both had dark hair and eyes, short husky statures, deep voices. Magda's left hand was probably in a similar position on her left side. The boy's father is difficult to describe; no particular feature of his appearance or manner stood out. He wore glasses and was principal of a T—— County grade school. Uncle Karl was a masonry contractor.

Although Peter must have known as well as Ambrose that the latter, because of his position in the car, would be the first to see the electrical towers of the power plant at V——, the halfway point of their trip, he leaned forward and slightly toward the center of the car and pretended to be looking for them through the flat pinewoods and tuckahoe creeks along the highway. For as long as the boys could remember, "looking for the Towers" had been a feature of the first half of their excursions to Ocean City, "looking for the standpipe" of the second. Though the game was childish, their mother preserved the tradition of rewarding the first to see the Towers with a candy-bar or piece of fruit. She insisted now that Magda play the game; the prize, she said, was "something hard to get nowadays." Ambrose decided not to join in; he sat far back in his seat. Magda, like Peter, leaned forward. Two sets of straps were discernible through the shoulders of her sun dress; the inside right one, a brassiere-strap, was fastened or shortened with a small safety pin. The right armpit of her dress, presumably the left as well, was damp with perspiration. The simple strategy for being first to espy the Towers, which Ambrose had understood by the age of four, was to sit on the right-hand side of the car. Whoever sat there, however, had also to put up with the worst of the sun, and so Ambrose, without mentioning the matter, chose sometimes the one and sometimes the other. Not impossibly Peter had never caught on to the trick, or thought that his brother hadn't simply because Ambrose on occasion preferred shade to a Baby Ruth or tangerine.

The shade-sun situation didn't apply to the front seat, owing to the windshield; if anything the driver got more sun, since the person on the passenger side not only was shaded below by the door and dashboard but might swing down his sunvisor all the way too.

"Is that them?" Magda asked. Ambrose's mother teased the boys for letting Magda win, insinuating that "somebody [had] a girlfriend." Peter and Ambrose's father reached a long thin arm across their mother to butt his cigarette in the dashboard ashtray, under the lighter. The prize this time for seeing the Towers first was a banana. Their mother bestowed it after chiding their father for wasting a half-smoked cigarette when everything was so scarce. Magda, to take the prize, moved her hand from so near Ambrose's that he could have touched it as though accidentally. She offered to share the prize, things like that were so hard to find; but everyone insisted it was hers alone. Ambrose's mother sang an iambic trimeter couplet from a popular song, femininely rhymed:

> "What's good is in the Army;
> What's left will never harm me."

Uncle Karl tapped his cigar ash out the ventilator window; some particles were sucked by the slipstream back into the car through the rear window on the passenger side. Magda demonstrated her ability to hold a banana in one hand and peel it with her teeth. She still sat forward; Ambrose pushed his glasses back onto the bridge of his nose with his left hand, which he then negligently let fall to the seat cushion immediately behind her. He even permitted the single hair, gold, on the second joint of his thumb to brush the fabric of her skirt. Should she have sat back at that instant, his hand would have been caught under her.

Plush upholstery prickles uncomfortably through gabardine slacks in the July sun. The function of the *beginning* of a story is to introduce the principal characters, establish their initial relationships, set the scene for the main action, expose the background of the situation if necessary, plant motifs and foreshadowings where appropriate, and initiate the first complication or whatever of the "rising action." Actually, if one imagines a story called "The Funhouse," or "Lost in the Funhouse," the details of the drive to Ocean City don't seem especially relevant. The *beginning* should recount the events between Ambrose's first sight of the funhouse early in the afternoon and his entering it with Magda and Peter in the evening. The *middle* would narrate all relevant events from the time he goes in to the time he loses his way; middles have the double and contradictory function of delaying the climax while at the same time preparing the reader for it and fetching him to it. Then the *ending* would tell what Ambrose does while he's lost, how he finally finds his way out, and what everybody makes of the experience. So far there's been no real dialogue, very little sensory detail, and nothing in the way of a *theme.* And a long time has gone by already without anything happening; it makes a person wonder. We haven't even reached Ocean City yet: we will never get out of the funhouse.

The more closely an author identifies with the narrator, literally or metaphorically, the less advisable it is, as a rule, to use the first-person narrative viewpoint. Once three years previously the young people *aforementioned* played Niggers and Masters in the backyard; when it was Ambrose's turn to be Master and theirs to be Niggers Peter had to go serve his evening papers; Ambrose was afraid to punish Magda alone, but she led him to the whitewashed Torture Chamber between the woodshed and the privy in the Slaves Quarters; there she knelt sweating among bamboo rakes and dusty Mason jars, pleadingly embraced his knees, and while bees droned in the lattice as if on an ordinary summer afternoon, purchased clemency at a surprising price set by herself. Doubtless she remembered nothing of this event; Ambrose on the other hand seemed unable to forget the least detail of his life. He even recalled how, standing beside himself with awed impersonality in the reeky heat, he'd stared the while at an empty cigar box in which Uncle Karl kept stone-cutting chisels: beneath the words *El Producto* a laureled, loose-toga'd lady regarded the sea from a marble bench; beside her, forgotten or not yet turned to, was a five-stringed lyre. Her chin reposed on the back of her right hand; her left depended negligently from the bench-arm. The lower half of scene and lady was peeled away; the words EXAMINED BY —— were inked there into the wood. Nowadays cigar boxes are made of pasteboard. Ambrose wondered what Magda would have done, Ambrose wondered what Magda would do when she sat back on his hand as he resolved she should. Be angry. Make a teasing joke of it. Give no sign at all. For a long time she leaned forward, playing cowpoker with Peter against Uncle Karl and Mother and watching for the first sign of Ocean City. At nearly the same instant, picnic ground and Ocean City standpipe hove into view; an Amoco filling station on their side of the road cost Mother and Uncle Karl fifty cows and the game; Magda bounced back, clapping her right hand on Mother's right arm; Ambrose moved clear "in the nick of time."

At this rate our hero, at this rate our protagonist will remain in the funhouse forever. Narrative ordinarily consists of alternating dramatization and summarization. One symptom of nervous tension, paradoxically, is repeated and violent yawning; neither Peter nor Magda nor Uncle Karl nor Mother reacted in this manner. Although they were no longer small children, Peter and Ambrose were each given a dollar to spend on boardwalk amusements in addition to what money of their own they'd brought along. Magda too, though she protested she had ample spending money. The boys' mother made a little scene out of distributing the bills; she pretended that her sons and Magda were small children and cautioned them not to spend the sum too quickly or in one place. Magda promised with a merry laugh and, having both hands free, took the bill with her left. Peter laughed also and pledged in a falsetto to be a good boy. His imitation of a child was not clever. The boys' father was tall and thin, balding, fair-complexioned. Assertions of that sort are not effective; the reader may acknowledge the proposition, but. We should be much farther along than we are; something has gone wrong; not much of this preliminary rambling seems relevant. Yet everyone begins in the same place; how is it that most go along without difficulty but a few lose their way?

"Stay out from under the boardwalk," Uncle Karl growled from the side of his mouth. The boys' mother pushed his shoulder *in mock annoyance.* They were all standing before Fat May the Laughing Lady who advertised the funhouse. Larger than life, Fat May mechanically shook, rocked on her heels, slapped her thighs while recorded laughter—uproarious, female—came amplified from a hidden loudspeaker. It chuckled, wheezed, wept; tried in vain to catch its breath; tittered, groaned, exploded raucous and anew. You couldn't hear it without laughing yourself, no matter how you felt. Father came back from talking to a Coast-Guardsman on duty and reported that the surf was spoiled with crude oil from tankers recently torpedoed offshore. Lumps of it, difficult to remove, made tarry tidelines on the beach and stuck on swimmers. Many bathed in the surf nevertheless and came out speckled; other paid to use a municipal pool and only sunbathed on the beach. We would do the latter. We would do the latter. We would do the latter.

Under the boardwalk, matchbook covers, grainy other things. What is the story's theme? Ambrose is ill. He perspires in the dark passages; candied apples-on-a-stick, delicious looking, disappointing to eat. Funhouses need men's and ladies' rooms at intervals. Others perhaps have also vomited in corners and corridors; may even have had bowel movements liable to be stepped in in the dark. The word *fuck* suggests suction and/or and/or flatulence. Mother and Father; grandmothers and grandfathers on both sides; great-grandmothers and great-grandfathers on four sides, et cetera. Count a generation as thirty years; in approximately the year when Lord Baltimore was granted charter to the province of Maryland by Charles I, five hundred twelve women—English, Welsh, Bavarian, Swiss—of every class and character, received into themselves the penises the intromittent organs of five hundred twelve men, ditto, in every circumstance and posture, to conceive the five hundred twelve ancestors of the two hundred fifty-six ancestors of the et cetera et cetera et cetera et cetera et cetera et cetera et cetera et cetera of the author, of the narrator, of this story, *Lost in the Funhouse.* In alleyways, ditches, canopy beds, pinewoods, bridal suites, ship's cabins, coach-and-fours, coaches-and-four, sultry toolsheds; on the cold sand under boardwalks, littered with *El Producto* cigar butts, treasured with Lucky Strike cigarette stubs, Coca-Cola caps, gritty turds, cardboard lollipop sticks, matchbook covers warning that A Slip of the Lip Can Sink a Ship. The shluppish whisper, continuous as seawash round the globe, tidelike falls and rises with the circuit of dawn and dusk.

Magda's teeth. She *was* left-handed. Perspiration. They've gone all the way, through, Magda and Peter, they've been waiting for hours with Mother and Uncle Karl while Father searches for his lost son; they draw french-fried potatoes from a paper cup and shake their heads. They've named the children they'll one day have and bring to Ocean City on holidays. Can spermatozoa properly be thought of as male animalcules when there are no female spermatozoa? They grope through hot, dark windings, past Love's Tunnel's fearsome obstacles. Some perhaps lose their way.

Peter suggested then and there that they do the fun-house; he had been through it before, so had Magda, Ambrose hadn't and suggested, his voice cracking on account of Fat May's laughter, that they swim first. All were chuckling, couldn't help it; Ambrose's father, Ambrose's and Peter's father came up grinning like a lunatic with two boxes of syrup-coated popcorn, one for Mother, one for Magda; the men were to help themselves. Ambrose walked on Magda's right; being by nature left-handed, she carried the box in her left hand. Up front the situation was reversed.

"What are you limping for?" Magda inquired of Ambrose. He supposed in a husky tone that his foot had gone to sleep in the car. Her teeth flashed. "Pins and needles?" It was the honeysuckle on the lattice of the former privy that drew the bees. Imagine being stung there. How long is this going to take?

The adults decided to forgo the pool; but Uncle Karl insisted they change into swimsuits and do the beach. "He wants to watch the pretty girls," Peter teased, and ducked behind Magda from Uncle Karl's pretended wrath. "You've got all the pretty girls you need right here," Magda declared, and Mother said: "Now that's the gospel truth." Magda scolded Peter, who reached over her shoulder to sneak some popcorn. "Your brother and father aren't getting any." Uncle Karl wondered if they were going to have fireworks that night, what with the shortages. It wasn't the shortages, Mr. M—— replied; Ocean City had fireworks from pre-war. But it was too risky on account of the enemy submarines, some people thought.

"Don't seem like Fourth of July without fireworks," said Uncle Karl. The inverted tag in dialogue writing is still considered permissible with proper names or epithets, but sounds old-fashioned with personal pronouns. "We'll have 'em again soon enough," predicted the boys' father. Their mother declared she could do without fireworks: they reminded her too much of the real thing. Their father said all the more reason to shoot off a few now and again. Uncle Karl asked *rhetorically* who needed reminding, just look at people's hair and skin.

"The oil, yes," said Mrs. M——.

Ambrose had a pain in his stomach and so didn't swim but enjoyed watching the others. He and his father burned red easily. Magda's figure was exceedingly well developed for her age. She too declined to swim, and got mad, and became angry when Peter attempted to drag her into the pool. She always swam, he insisted; what did she mean not swim? Why did a person come to Ocean City?

"Maybe I want to lay here with Ambrose," Magda teased.

Nobody likes a pedant.

"Aha," said Mother. Peter grabbed Magda by one ankle and ordered Ambrose to grab the other. She squealed and rolled over on the beach blanket. Ambrose pretended to help hold her back. Her tan was darker than even Mother's and Peter's. "Help out, Uncle Karl!" Peter cried. Uncle Karl went to seize the other ankle. Inside the top of her swimsuit, however, you could see the line where the sunburn ended and, when she hunched her shoulders and squealed again, one nipple's auburn edge. Mother made them behave themselves. "*You* should certainly know," she said to Uncle Karl. Archly. "That when a lady says she doesn't feel like swimming, a gentleman doesn't ask questions." Uncle Karl said excuse *him*; Mother winked at Magda; Ambrose blushed; stupid Peter kept saying "Phooey on *feel like!*" and tugging at Magda's ankle; then even he got the point, and cannonballed with a holler into the pool.

"I swear," Magda said, in mock *in feigned* exasperation.

The diving would make a suitable literary symbol. To go off the high board you had to wait in a line along the poolside and up the ladder. Fellows tickled girls and goosed one another and shouted to the ones at the top to hurry up, or razzed them for bellyfloppers. Once on the springboard some took a great while posing or clowning or deciding on a dive or getting up their nerve; others ran right off. Especially among the younger fellows the idea was to strike the funniest pose or do the craziest stunt as you fell, a thing that got harder to do as you kept on and kept on. But whether you hollered *Geronimo!* or *Sieg heil!*, held your nose or "rode a bicycle," pretended to be shot or did a perfect jacknife or changed your mind halfway down and ended up with nothing, it was over in two seconds, after all that wait. Spring, pose, splash. Spring, neat-o, splash. Spring, aw fooey, splash.

The grown-ups had gone on; Ambrose wanted to converse with Magda; she was remarkably well developed for her age; it was said that that came from rubbing with a turkish towel, and there were other theories. Ambrose could think of nothing to say except how good a diver Peter was, who was showing off for her benefit. You could pretty well tell by looking at their bathing suits and arm muscles how far along the different fellows were. Ambrose was glad he hadn't gone in swimming, the cold water shrank you up so. Magda pretended to be uninterested in the diving; she probably weighed as much as he did. If you knew your way around in the funhouse like your own bedroom, you could wait until a girl came along and then slip away without ever getting caught, even if her boyfriend was right with her. She'd think *he* did it! It would be better to be the boyfriend, and act outraged, and tear the funhouse apart.

Not act; *be.*

"He's a master diver," Ambrose said. In feigned admiration. "You really have to slave away at it to get that good." What would it matter anyhow if he asked her right out whether she remembered, even teased her with it as Peter would have?

There's no point in going farther; this isn't getting anybody anywhere; they haven't even come to the funhouse yet. Ambrose is off the track, in some new or old part of the place that's not supposed to be used; he strayed into it by some one-in-a-million chance, like the time the roller-coaster car left the tracks in the nineteen-teens against all the laws of physics and sailed over the boardwalk in the dark. And they can't locate him because they don't know where to look. Even the designer and operator have forgotten this other part, that winds around on itself like a whelk shell. That winds around the right part like the snakes on Mercury's caduceus. Some people, perhaps, don't "hit their stride" until their twenties, when the growing-up business is over and women appreciate other things besides wisecracks and teasing and strutting. Peter didn't have one-tenth the imagination *he* had, not one-tenth. Peter did this naming-their-children thing as a joke, making up names like Aloysius and Murgatroyd, but Ambrose knew *exactly* how it would feel to be married and have children of your own, and be a loving husband and father, and go comfortably to work in the mornings and to bed with your wife at night, and wake up with her there. With a breeze coming through the sash and birds and mockingbirds singing in the Chinese-cigar trees. His eyes watered, there aren't enough ways to say that. He would be quite famous in his line of work. Whether Magda was his wife or not, one evening when he was wise-lined and gray at the temples he'd smile gravely, at a fashionable dinner party, and remind her of his youthful passion. The time they went with his family to Ocean City; the *erotic fantasies* he used to have about her. How long ago it seemed, and childish! Yet tender, too, *n'est-ce pas?* Would she have imagined that the world-famous whatever remembered how many strings were on the lyre on the bench beside the girl on the label of the cigar box he'd stared at in the toolshed at age ten while she, age eleven. Even then he had felt *wise beyond his years;* he'd stroked her hair and said in his deepest voice and correctest English, as to a dear child: "I shall never forget this moment."

But though he had breathed heavily, groaned as if ecstatic, what he'd really felt throughout was an odd detachment, as though some one else were Master. Strive as he might to be transported, he heard his mind take notes upon the scene: *This is what they call* passion. *I am experiencing it.* Many of the digger machines were out of order in the penny arcades and could not be repaired or replaced for the duration. Moreover the prizes, made now in USA, were less interesting than formerly, pasteboard items for the most part, and some of the machines wouldn't work on white pennies. The gypsy fortune-teller machine might have provided a foreshadowing of the climax of this story if Ambrose had operated it. It was even dilapidateder than most: the silver coating was worn off the brown metal handles, the glass windows around the dummy were cracked and taped, her kerchiefs and silks long-faded. If a man lived by himself, he could take a department-store mannequin with flexible joints and modify her in certain ways. *However:* by the time he was that old he'd have a real woman. There was a machine that stamped your name around a white-metal coin with a star in the middle: *A——.* His son would be the second, and when the lad reached thirteen or so he would put a strong arm around his shoulder and tell him calmly: "It is perfectly normal. We have all been through it. It will not last forever." Nobody knew how to be what they were right. He'd smoke a pipe, teach his son how to fish and softcrab, assure him he needn't worry about himself. Magda would certainly give, Magda would certainly yield a great deal of milk, although guilty of occasional solecisms. "It don't taste so bad. Suppose the lights came on now!"

The day wore on. You think you're yourself, but there are other persons in you. Ambrose gets hard when Ambrose doesn't want to, *and obversely.* Ambrose watches them disagree; Ambrose watches him watch. In the fun-house mirror-room you can't see yourself go on forever, because no matter how you stand, your head gets in the way. Even if you had a glass periscope, the image of your eye would cover up the thing you really wanted to see. The police will come; there'll be a story in the papers. That must be where it happened. Unless he can find a surprise exit, an unofficial backdoor or escape hatch opening on an alley, say, and then stroll up to the family in front of the funhouse and ask where everybody's been; *he's* been out of the place for ages. That's just where it happened, in that last lighted room: Peter and Magda found the right exit; he found one that you weren't supposed to find and strayed off into the works somewhere. In a perfect funhouse you'd be able to go only one way, like the divers off the highboard; getting lost would be impossible; the doors and halls would work like minnow traps or the valves in veins.

On account of German U-boats, Ocean City was "browned out": streetlights were shaded on the seaward side; shop-windows and boardwalk amusement places were kept dim, not to silhouette tankers and Liberty-ships for torpedoing. In a short story about Ocean City, Maryland, during World War II, the author could make use of the image of sailors on leave in the penny arcades and shooting galleries, sighting through the crosshairs of toy machine guns at swastika'd subs, while out in the black Atlantic a U-boat skipper squints through his periscope at real ships outlined by the glow of penny arcades. After dinner the family strolled back to the amusement end of the boardwalk. The boys' father had burnt red as always and was masked with Noxzema, a minstrel in reverse. The grownups stood at the end of the boardwalk where the Hurricane of '33 had cut an inlet from the ocean to Assawoman Bay.

"Pronounced with a long *o*," Uncle Karl reminded Magda with a wink. His shirt sleeves were rolled up; Mother punched his brown biceps with the arrowed heart on it and said his mind was naughty. Fat May's laugh came suddenly from the funhouse, as if she'd just got the joke; the family laughed too at the coincidence. Ambrose went under the boardwalk to search for out-of-town matchbook covers with the aid of his pocket flashlight; he looked out from the edge of the North American continent and wondered how far their laughter carried over the water. Spies in rubber rafts, survivors in lifeboats. If the joke had been beyond his understanding, he could have said: *"The laughter was over his head."* And let the reader see the serious wordplay on second reading.

He turned the flashlight on and then off at once even before the woman whooped. He sprang away, heart athud, dropping the light. What had the man grunted? Perspiration drenched and chilled him by the time he scrambled up to the family. "See anything?" his father asked. His voice wouldn't come; he shrugged and violently brushed sand from his pants legs.

"Let's ride the old flying horses!" Magda cried. I'll never be an author. It's been forever already, everybody's gone home, Ocean City's deserted, the ghost-crabs are tickling across the beach and down the littered cold streets. And the empty halls of clapboard hotels and abandoned funhouses. A tidal wave; an enemy air raid; a monster-crab swelling like an island from the sea. *The inhabitants fled in terror.* Magda clung to his trouser leg; he alone knew the maze's secret. "He gave his life that we might live," said Uncle Karl with a scowl of pain, as he. The fellow's hands had been tattooed; the woman's legs, the woman's fat white legs had. *An astonishing coincidence.* He yearned to tell Peter. He wanted to throw up for excitement. They hadn't even chased him. He wished he were dead.

One possible ending would be to have Ambrose come across another lost person in the dark. They'd match their wits together against the funhouse, struggle like Ulysses past obstacle after obstacle, help and encourage each other. Or a girl. By the time they found the exit they'd be closest friends, sweethearts if it were a girl; they'd know each other's inmost souls, be bound together *by the cement of shared adventure;* then they'd emerge into the light and it would turn out that his friend was a Negro. A blind girl. President Roosevelt's son. Ambrose's former archenemy.

Shortly after the mirror room he'd groped along a musty corridor, his heart already misgiving him at the absence of phosphorescent arrows and other signs. He'd found a crack of light—not a door, it turned out, but a seam between the plyboard wall panels—and squinting up to it, espied a small old man, *in appearance not unlike* the photographs at home of Ambrose's late grandfather, nodding upon a stool beneath a bare, speckled bulb. A crude panel of toggle- and knife-switches hung beside the open fuse box near his head; elsewhere in the little room were wooden levers and ropes belayed to boat cleats. At the time, Ambrose wasn't lost enough to rap or call; later he couldn't find that crack. Now it seemed to him that he'd possibly dozed off for a few minutes somewhere along the way; certainly he was exhausted from the afternoon's sunshine and the evening's problems; he couldn't be sure he hadn't dreamed part or all of the sight. Had an old black wall fan droned like bees and shimmied two flypaper streamers? Had the funhouse operator—gentle, somewhat sad and tired-appearing, in expression not unlike the photographs at home of Ambrose's late Uncle Konrad—murmured in his sleep? Is there really such a person as Ambrose, or is he a figment of the author's imagination? Was it Assawoman Bay or Sinepuxent? Are there other errors of fact in this fiction? Was there another sound besides the little slap slap of thigh on ham, like water sucking at the chine-boards of a skiff?

When you're lost, the smartest thing to do is stay put till you're found, hollering if necessary. But to holler guarantees humiliation as well as rescue; keeping silent permits some saving of face—you can act surprised at the fuss when your rescuers find you and swear you weren't lost, if they do. What's more you might find your own way yet, *however belatedly.*

"Don't tell me your foot's still asleep!" Magda exclaimed as the three young people walked from the inlet to the area set aside for ferris wheels, carrousels, and other carnival rides, they having decided in favor of the vast and ancient merry-go-round instead of the funhouse. What a sentence, everything was wrong from the outset. People don't know what to make of him, he doesn't know what to make of himself, he's only thirteen, *athletically and socially inept,* not astonishingly bright, but there are antennae; he has . . . some sort of receivers in his head; things speak to him, he understands more than he should, the world winks at him through its objects, grabs grinning at his coat. Everybody else is in on some secret he doesn't know; they've forgotten to tell him. Through simple *procrastination* his mother put off his baptism until this year. Everyone else had it done as a baby; he'd assumed the same of himself, as had his mother, so she claimed, until it was time for him to join Grace Methodist-Protestant and the oversight came out. He was mortified, but pitched sleepless through his private catechizing, intimidated by the ancient mysteries, a thirteen year old would never say that, resolved to experience conversion like St. Augustine. When the water touched his brow and Adam's sin left him, he contrived by a strain like defecation to bring tears into his eyes—but felt nothing. There was some simple, radical difference about him; he hoped it was genius, feared it was madness, devoted himself to amiability and inconspicuousness. Alone on the seawall near his house he was seized by the terrifying transports he'd thought to find in toolshed, in Communion-cup. The grass was alive! The town, the river, himself, were not imaginary; time roared in his ears like wind; the world was *going on!* This part ought to be dramatized. The Irish author James Joyce once wrote. Ambrose M——is going to scream.

There is no *texture of rendered sensory detail*, for one thing. The faded distorting mirrors beside Fat May; the impossibility of choosing a mount when one had but a single ride on the great carrousel; the *vertigo attendant on his recognition* that Ocean City was worn out, the place of fathers and grandfathers, straw-boatered men and parasoled ladies survived by their amusements. Money spent, the three paused at Peter's insistence beside Fat May to watch the girls get their skirts blown up. The object was to tease Magda, who said: "I swear, Peter M——, you've got a one-track mind! Amby and me aren't *interested* in such things." In the tumbling-barrel, too, just inside the Devil's-mouth entrance to the funhouse, the girls were upended and their boyfriends and others could see up their dresses if they cared to. Which was the whole point, Ambrose realized. Of the entire funhouse! If you looked around, you noticed that almost all the people on the boardwalk were paired off into couples except the small children; in a way, that was the whole point of Ocean City! If you had X-ray eyes and could see everything going on at that instant under the boardwalk and in all the hotel rooms and cars and alleyways, you'd realize that all that normally *showed,* like restaurants and dance halls and clothing and test-your-strength machines, was merely preparation and intermission. Fat May screamed.

Because he watched the goings-on from the corner of his eye, it was Ambrose who spied the half-dollar on the boardwalk near the tumbling-barrel. Losers weepers. The first time he'd heard some people moving through a corridor not far away, just after he'd lost sight of the crack of light, he'd decided not to call to them, for fear they'd guess he was scared and poke fun; it sounded like roughnecks; he'd hoped they'd come by and he could follow in the dark without their knowing. Another time he'd heard just one person, unless he imagined it, bumping along as if on the other side of the plywood; perhaps Peter coming back for him, or Father, or Magda lost too. Or the owner and operator of the funhouse. He'd called out once, as though merrily: "Anybody know where the heck we are?" But the query was too stiff, his voice cracked, when the sounds stopped he was terrified: maybe it was a queer who waited for fellows to get lost, or a longhaired filthy monster that lived in some cranny of the funhouse. He stood rigid for hours it seemed like, scarcely respiring. His future was shockingly clear, in outline. He tried holding his breath to the point of unconsciousness. There ought to be a button you could push to end your life absolutely without pain; disappear in a flick, like turning out a light. He would push it instantly! He despised Uncle Karl. But he despised his father too, for not being what he was supposed to be. Perhaps his father hated *his* father, and so on, and his son would hate him, and so on. Instantly!

Naturally he didn't have nerve enough to ask Magda to go through the funhouse with him. With incredible nerve and to everyone's surprise he invited Magda, quietly and politely, to go through the funhouse with him. "I warn you, I've never been through it before," he added, *laughing easily:* "but I reckon we can manage somehow. The important thing to remember, after all, is that it's meant to be a *fun*house; that is, a place of amusement. If people really got lost or injured or too badly frightened in it, the owner'd go out of business. There'd even be lawsuits. No character in a work of fiction can make a speech this long without interruption or acknowledgment from the other characters."

Mother teased Uncle Karl: "Three's a crowd, I always heard." But actually Ambrose was relieved that Peter now had a quarter too. Nothing was what it looked like. Every instant, under the surface of the Atlantic Ocean, millions of living animals devoured one another. Pilots were falling in flames over Europe; women were being forcibly raped in the South Pacific. His father should have taken him aside and said: "There is a simple secret to getting through the funhouse, as simple as being first to see the Towers. Here it is. Peter does not know it; neither does your Uncle Karl. You and I are different. Not surprisingly, you've often wished you weren't. Don't think I haven't noticed how unhappy your childhood has been! But you'll understand, when I tell you, why it had to be kept secret until now. And you won't regret not being like your brother and your uncle. *On the contrary*!" If you knew all the stories behind all the people on the boardwalk, you'd see that *nothing* was what it looked like. Husbands and wives often hated each other; parents didn't necessarily love their children; et cetera. A child took things for granted because he had nothing to compare his life to and everybody acted as if things were as they should be. Therefore each saw himself as the hero of the story, when the truth might turn out to be that he's the villain, or the coward. And there wasn't one thing you could do about it!

Hunchbacks, fat ladies, fools—that no one chose what he was was unbearable. In the movies he'd meet a beautiful young girl in the funhouse; they'd have hairs-breadth escapes from real dangers; he'd do and say the right things; she also; in the end they'd be lovers; their dialogue lines would match up; he'd be perfectly at ease; she'd not only like him well enough, she'd think he was *marvelous;* she'd lie awake thinking about *him,* instead of vice versa—the way *his* face looked in different lights and how he stood and exactly what he'd said—and yet that would be only one small episode in his wonderful life, among many many others. Not a *turning point* at all. What had happened in the toolshed was nothing. He hated, he loathed his parents! One reason for not writing a lost-in-the-funhouse story is that either everybody's felt what Ambrose feels, in which case it goes without saying, or else no normal person feels such things, in which case Ambrose is a freak. "Is anything more tiresome, in fiction, than the problems of sensitive adolescents?" And it's all too long and rambling, as if the author. For all a person knows the first time through, the end could be just around any corner; perhaps, *not impossibly* it's been within reach any number of times. On the other hand he may be scarcely past the start, with everything yet to get through, an intolerable idea.

Fill in: His father's raised eyebrows when he announced his decision to do the funhouse with Magda. Ambrose understands now, but didn't then, that

his father was wondering whether he knew what the funhouse was *for*—
especially since he didn't object, as he should have, when Peter decided to come
along too. The ticket-woman, witch-like, mortifying him when inadvertently he
gave her his name-coin instead of the half-dollar, then unkindly calling Magda's
attention to the birthmark on his temple: "Watch out for him, girlie, he's a
marked man!" She wasn't even cruel, he understood, only vulgar and insensi-
tive. Somewhere in the world there was a young woman with such splendid
understanding that she'd see him entire, like a poem or story, and find his words
so valuable after all that when he confessed his apprehensions she would explain
why they were in fact the very things that made him precious to her . . . and to
Western Civilization! There was no such girl, the simple truth being. Violent
yawns as they approached the mouth. Whispered advice from an old-timer on a
bench near the barrel: "Go crabwise and ye'll get an eyeful without upsetting!"
Composure vanished at the first pitch: Peter hollered joyously, Magda tumbled,
shrieked, clutched her skirt; Ambrose scrambled crabwise, tight-lipped with
terror, was soon out, watched his dropped name-coin slide among the couples.
Shamefaced he saw that to get through expeditiously was not the point; Peter
feigned assistance in order to trip Magda up, shouted "I see Christmas!" when
her legs went flying. The old man, his latest betrayer, cackled approval. A dim
hall then of black-thread cobwebs and recorded gibber; he took Magda's elbow to
steady her against revolving discs set in the slanted floor to throw your feet out
from under, and explained to her in a calm, deep voice his theory that each phase
of the funhouse was triggered either automatically, by a series of photo-electric
devices, or else manually by operators stationed at peepholes. But he lost his
voice thrice as the discs unbalanced him; Magda was anyhow squealing; but at
one point she clutched him about the waist to keep from falling, and her right
cheek pressed for a moment against his belt-buckle. Heroically he drew her up, it
was his chance to clutch her close as if for support and say: "I love you." He even
put an arm lightly about the small of her back before a sailor-and-girl pitched into
them from behind, sorely treading his left big toe and knocking Magda asprawl
with them. The sailor's girl was a string-haired hussy with a loud laugh and light
blue drawers; Ambrose realized that he wouldn't have said "I love you" anyhow,
and was smitten with self-contempt. How much better it would be to be that
common sailor! A wiry little Seaman 3rd, the fellow squeezed a girl to each side
and stumbled hilarious into the mirror room, closer to Magda in thirty seconds
than Ambrose had got in thirteen years. She giggled at something the fellow said
to Peter; she drew her hair from her eyes with a movement so womanly it struck
Ambrose's heart; Peter's smacking her backside then seemed particularly coarse.
But Magda made a pleased indignant face and cried, "All right for *you*, mister!"
and pursued Peter into the maze without a backward glance. The sailor followed
after, leisurely, drawing his girl against his hip; Ambrose understood not only
that they were all so relieved to be rid of his burdensome company that they
didn't even notice his absence, but that he himself shared their relief. Stepping
from the treacherous passage at last into the mirror-maze, he saw once again,
more clearly than ever, how readily he deceived himself into supposing he was a
person. He even foresaw, wincing at his dreadful self-knowledge, that he would
repeat the deception, at ever-rarer intervals, all his wretched life, so fearful were
the alternatives. Fame, madness, suicide; perhaps all three. It's not believable
that so young a boy could articulate that reflection, and in fiction the merely true

must always yield to the plausible. Moreover, the symbolism is in places heavy-footed. Yet Ambrose M—— understood, as few adults do, that the famous loneliness of the great was no popular myth but a general truth—furthermore, that it was as much cause as effect.

All the preceding except the last few sentences is exposition that should've been done earlier or interspersed with the present action instead of lumped together. No reader would put up with so much with such *prolixity*. It's interesting that Ambrose's father, though presumably an intelligent man (as indicated by his role as grade-school principal), neither encouraged nor discouraged his sons at all in any way—as if he either didn't care about them or cared all right but didn't know how to act. If this fact should contribute to one of them's becoming a celebrated but wretchedly unhappy scientist, was it a good thing or not? He too might someday face the question; it would be useful to know whether it had tortured his father for years, for example, or never once crossed his mind.

In the maze two important things happened. First, our hero found a name-coin someone else had lost or discarded: AMBROSE, suggestive of the famous lightship and of his late grandfather's favorite dessert, which his mother used to prepare on special occasions out of coconut, oranges, grapes, and what else. Second, as he wondered at the endless replication of his image in the mirrors, second, as he *lost himself in the reflection* that the necessity for an observer makes perfect observation impossible, better make him eighteen at least, yet that would render other things unlikely, he heard Peter and Magda chuckling somewhere together in the maze. "Here!" "No, here!" they shouted at each other; Peter said, "Where's Amby?" Magda murmured. "Amb?" Peter called. In a pleased, friendly voice. He didn't reply. The truth was, his brother was a *happy-go-lucky youngster* who'd've been better off with a regular brother of his own, but who seldom complained of his lot and was generally cordial. Ambrose's throat ached; there aren't enough different ways to say that. He stood quietly while the two young people giggled and thumped through the glittering maze, hurrah'd their discovery of its exit, cried out in joyful alarm at what next beset them. Then he set his mouth and followed after, as he supposed, took a wrong turn, strayed into the pass *wherein he lingers yet.*

The action of conventional dramatic narrative may be represented by a diagram called Freitag's Triangle:

or more accurately by a variant of that diagram:

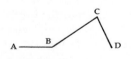

in which *AB* represents the exposition, *B* the introduction of conflict, *BC* the "rising action," complication, or development of the conflict, *C* the climax, or turn of the action, *CD* the dénouement, or resolution of the conflict. While there is no reason to regard this pattern as an absolute necessity, like many other conventions it became conventional because great numbers of people over many years learned by trial and error that it was effective; one ought not to forsake it, therefore, unless one wishes to forsake as well the effect of drama or has clear cause to feel that deliberate violation of the "normal" pattern can better can better effect that effect. This can't go on much longer; it can go on forever. He died telling stories to himself in the dark; years later, when that vast unsuspected area of the funhouse came to light, the first expedition found his skeleton in one of its labyrinthine corridors and mistook it for part of the entertainment. He died of starvation telling himself stories in the dark; but unbeknownst unbeknownst to him, an assistant operator of the funhouse, happening to overhear him, crouched just behind the plyboard partition and wrote down his every word. The operator's daughter, an exquisite young woman with a figure unusually well developed for her age, crouched just behind the partition and transcribed his every word. Though she had never laid eyes on him, she recognized that here was one of Western Culture's truly great imaginations, the eloquence of whose suffering would be an inspiration to unnumbered. And her heart was torn between her love for the misfortunate young man (yes, she loved him, though she had never laid though she knew him only—but how well!—through his words, and the deep, calm voice in which he spoke them) between her love et cetera and her womanly intuition that only in suffering and isolation could he give voice et cetera. Lone dark dying. Quietly she kissed the rough plyboard, and a tear fell upon the page. Where she had written in shorthand *Where she had written in shorthand* Where she had written in shorthand *Where she* et cetera. A long time ago we should have passed the apex of Freitag's Triangle and made brief work of the dénouement; the plot doesn't rise by meaningful steps but winds upon itself, digresses, retreats, hesitates, sighs, collapses, expires. The climax of the story must be its protagonist's discovery of a way to get through the funhouse. But he has found none, may have ceased to search.

What relevance does the war have to the story? Should there be fireworks outside or not?

Ambrose wandered, languished, dozed. Now and then he fell into his habit of rehearsing to himself the unadventurous story of his life, narrated from the third-person point of view, from his earliest memory parenthesis of maple leaves stirring in the summer breath of tidewater Maryland end of parenthesis to the present moment. Its principal events, on this telling, would appear to have been *A, B, C,* and *D.*

He imagined himself years hence, successful, married, at ease in the world, the trials of his adolescence far behind him. He has come to the seashore with his family for the holiday: how Ocean City has changed! But at one seldom at one ill-frequented end of the boardwalk a few derelict amusements survive from times gone by: the great carrousel from the turn of the century, with its monstrous griffins and mechanical concert band; the roller coaster rumored since 1916 to have been condemned; the mechanical shooting gallery in which only the image of our enemies changed. His own son laughs with Fat May and wants to know what a funhouse is; Ambrose hugs the sturdy lad close and smiles around his pipestem at his wife.

The family's going home. Mother sits between Father and Uncle Karl, who teases him good-naturedly who chuckles over the fact that the comrade with whom he'd fought his way shoulder to shoulder through the funhouse had turned out to be a blind Negro girl—to their mutual discomfort, as they'd opened their souls. But such are the walls of custom, which even. Whose arm is where? How must it feel. He dreams of a funhouse vaster by far than any yet constructed; but by then they may be out of fashion, like steamboats and excursion trains. Already quaint and seedy: the draperied ladies on the frieze of the carrousel are his father's father's mooncheeked dreams; if he thinks of it more he will vomit his apple-on-a-stick.

He wonders: will he become a regular person? Something has gone wrong; his vaccination didn't take; at the Boy-Scout initiation campfire he only pretended to be deeply moved, as he pretends to this hour that it is not so bad after all in the funhouse, and that he has a little limp. How long will it last? He envisions a truly astonishing funhouse, incredibly complex yet utterly controlled from a great central switchboard like the console of a pipe organ. Nobody had enough imagination. He could design such a place himself, wiring and all, and he's only thirteen years old. He would be its operator: panel lights would show what was up in every cranny of its cunning of its multifarious vastness; a switch-flick would ease this fellow's way, complicate that's, to balance things out; if anyone seemed lost or frightened, all the operator had to do was.

He wishes he had never entered the funhouse. But he has. Then he wishes he were dead. But he's not. Therefore he will construct funhouses for others and be their secret operator—though he would rather be among the lovers for whom funhouses are designed.

Fact Questions and Exercises

1. On what day do Ambrose and his family go to the seashore?
2. Who is the "Irish author" Barth refers to in describing the sea?
3. What is the reward for first spotting the "towers of the power plant"? Who wins?
4. What is the significance of the toolshed?
5. What is the setting? In what city does the story take place? In what year? What details support your answers?
6. Describe the scene under the boardwalk.
7. Which character in the story gets lost in the funhouse?
8. Barth uses a triangle as a diagram. What does the triangle represent?
9. At the end of the story, what does Ambrose dream of designing?

For Discussion and Writing

1. In this story, Barth uses an unusual technique—writing a story while at the same time commenting on how a writer creates such a story. What effect does this technique have? Is Barth ridiculing the writing of fiction? Is he being ironic?
2. Does Barth draw parallels between the funhouse and real life? That is, is the story in part a parable? If so, how are the funhouse and Ambrose's experiences like life in general? Comment on the mirrors, reflections, distortions, and illusions.
3. Barth asks: "What relevance does the war have to the story?" Can you answer

that question? Note the date of the trip to the beach and the many references to the war.

4. What actually happens in the story? For instance, what happens between Magda and Ambrose in the toolshed? What is the relationship between Magda and Peter? At the end of the story, is Ambrose going back home with his family or is he still lost in the funhouse? Is the author's vagueness intentional? What effect does it create?

John Updike [1932–   ]

Updike was born in Reading, Pennsylvania, but was reared on a farm near Shillington, Pennsylvania. He graduated from Harvard and studied at the Ruskin School of Drawing and Fine Art at Oxford University in England. Upon returning to America, he worked for the *New Yorker* magazine until 1957, at which time he quit to devote himself to writing. His fiction is marked by irony and technical expertise; he often takes an insignificant subject and creates from it a powerful statement about human conduct and motivation. His best-known works are *The Poorhouse Fair* (1959), *Rabbit, Run* (1960), *Pigeon Feathers and Other Stories* (1962), *Couples* (1968), and *Rabbit Redux* (1971).

A & P

In walks these three girls in nothing but bathing suits. I'm in the third checkout slot, with my back to the door, so I don't see them until they're over by the bread. The one that caught my eye first was the one in the plaid green two-piece. She was a chunky kid, with a good tan and a sweet broad soft-looking can with those two crescents of white just under it, where the sun never seems to hit, at the top of the backs of her legs. I stood there with my hand on a box of HiHo crackers trying to remember if I rang it up or not. I ring it up again and the customer starts giving me hell. She's one of these cash-register-watchers, a witch about fifty with rouge on her cheekbones and no eyebrows, and I know it made her day to trip me up. She'd been watching cash registers for fifty years and probably never seen a mistake before.

By the time I got her feathers smoothed and her goodies into a bag—she gives me a little snort in passing, if she'd been born at the right time they would have burned her over in Salem—by the time I get her on her way the girls had circled around the bread and were coming back, without a pushcart, back my way along the counters, in the aisle between the checkouts and the Special bins. They didn't even have shoes on. There was this chunky one, with the two-piece—it was bright green and the seams on the bra were still sharp and her belly was still pretty pale so I guessed she just got it (the suit)—there was this one, with one of those chubby berry-faces, the lips all bunched together under her nose, this one, and a tall one, with black hair that hadn't quite frizzed right, and one of those sunburns right across under the eyes, and a chin that was too long—you know, the kind of girl other girls think is very "striking" and "attractive" but never quite makes it, as they very well know, which is why they like her so much—and then the third one, that wasn't quite so tall. She was the queen. She kind of led them, the other two peeking around and making their shoulders round. She didn't look around, not this queen, she just walked straight on slowly, on these long white prima-donna legs. She came down a little hard on her heels, as if she didn't walk in her bare feet that much, putting down her heels and then letting the weight move along to her toes as if she was testing the floor with every step, putting a little deliberate extra action into it. You never know for sure how girls' minds work (do you really think it's a mind in there or just a little buzz like a bee in a glass jar?) but you got the idea she had talked the other two into coming in here with her, and now she was showing them how to do it, walk slow and hold yourself straight.

She had on a kind of dirty-pink—beige maybe, I don't know—bathing suit with a little nubble all over it and, what got me, the straps were down. They were off her shoulders looped loose around the cool tops of her arms, and I guess as a result the suit had slipped a little on her, so all around the top of the cloth there was this shining rim. If it hadn't been there you wouldn't have known there could have been anything whiter than those shoulders. With the straps pushed off, there was nothing between the top of the suit and the top of her head except just *her,* this clean bare plane of the top of her chest down from the shoulder bones like a dented sheet of metal tilted in the light. I mean, it was more than pretty.

She had sort of oaky hair that the sun and salt had bleached, done up in a bun that was unravelling, and a kind of prim face. Walking into the A & P with your straps down, I suppose it's the only kind of face you *can* have. She held her head so high her neck, coming up out of those white shoulders, looked kind of stretched, but I didn't mind. The longer her neck was, the more of her there was.

She must have felt in the corner of her eye me and over my shoulder Stokesie in the second slot watching, but she didn't tip. Not this queen. She kept her eyes moving across the racks, and stopped, and turned so slow it made my stomach rub the inside of my apron, and buzzed to the other two, who kind of huddled against her for relief, and then they all three of them went up the cat - and - dog - food - breakfast - cereal - macaroni - rice - raisins - seasonings - spreads - spaghetti - soft - drinks - crackers - and - cookies aisle. From the third slot I look straight up this aisle to the meat counter, and I watched them all the way. The fat one with the tan sort of fumbled with the cookies, but on second thought she put the package back. The sheep pushing their carts down the aisle—the girls were walking against the usual traffic (not that we have one-way signs or anything)—were pretty hilarious. You could see them, when Queenie's white shoulders dawned on them, kind of jerk, or hop, or hiccup, but their eyes snapped back to their own baskets and on they pushed. I bet you could set off dynamite in an A & P and the people would by and large keep reaching and checking oatmeal off their lists and muttering "Let me see, there was a third thing, began with A, asparagus, no, ah, yes, applesauce!" or whatever it is they do mutter. But there was no doubt, this jiggled them. A few houseslaves in pin curlers even looked around after pushing their carts past to make sure what they had seen was correct.

You know, it's one thing to have a girl in a bathing suit down on the beach, where what with the glare nobody can look at each other much anyway, and another thing in the cool of the A & P, under the fluorescent lights, against all those stacked packages, with her feet paddling along naked over our checkerboard green-and-cream rubber-tile floor.

["Oh Daddy" Stokesie said beside me. "I feel so faint."]

"Darling," I said, "Hold me tight." Stokesie's married, with two babies chalked up on his fuselage already, but as far as I can tell that's the only difference. He's twenty-two, and I was nineteen this April.

"Is it done?" he asks, the responsible married man finding his voice. I forgot to say he thinks he's going to be manager some sunny day, maybe in 1990 when it's called the Great Alexandrov and Petrooshki Tea Company or something.

What he meant was, our town is five miles from a beach, with a big *Location* summer colony out on the Point, but we're right in the middle of town, and the women generally put on a shirt or shorts or something before they get out of the car into the street. And anyway these are usually women with six children and varicose veins mapping their legs and nobody, including them, could care less. As I say, we're right in the middle of town, and if you stand at our front doors you can see two banks and the Congregational church and the newspaper store and three real-estate offices and about twenty-seven old freeloaders tearing up Central Street because the sewer broke again. It's not as if we're on the Cape; we're north of Boston and there's people in this town haven't seen the ocean for *Location* twenty years.

The girls had reached the meat counter and were asking McMahon something. He pointed, they pointed, and they shuffled out of sight behind a pyramid of Diet Delight peaches. All that was left for us to see was old McMahon patting his mouth and looking after them sizing up their joints. Poor kids, I began to feel sorry for them, they couldn't help it.

Now here comes the sad part of the story, at least my family says it's sad, but I don't think it's so sad myself. The store's pretty empty, it being Thursday afternoon, so there was nothing much to do except lean on the register and wait for the girls to show up again. The whole store was like a pinball machine and I didn't know which tunnel they'd come out of. After a while they came around out of the far aisle, around the light bulbs, records at discount of the Caribbean Six or Tony Martin Sings or some such gunk you wonder they waste the wax on, sixpacks of candy bars, and plastic toys done up in cellophane that fall apart when a kid looks at them anyway. Around they come, Queenie still leading the way, and holding a little gray jar in her hand. Slots Three through Seven are unmanned and I could see her wondering between Stokes and me, but Stokesie with his usual luck draws an old party in baggy gray pants who stumbles up with four giant cans of pineapple juice (what do these bums *do* with all the pineapple juice? I've often asked myself) so the girls come to me. Queenie puts down the jar and I take it into my fingers icy cold. Kingfish Fancy Herring Snacks in Pure Sour Cream: 49¢. Now her hands are empty, not a ring or a bracelet, bare as God made them, and I wonder where the money's coming from. Still with that prim look she lifts a folded dollar bill out of the hollow at the center of her nubbled pink top. The jar went heavy in my hand. Really, I thought that was so cute.

Then everybody's luck begins to run out. Lengel comes in from haggling with a truck full of cabbages on the lot and is about to scuttle into that door marked MANAGER behind which he hides all day when the girls touch his eye.

Lengel's pretty dreary, teaches Sunday school and the rest, but he doesn't miss that much. He comes over and says, "Girls, this isn't the beach."

Queenie blushes, though maybe it's just a brush of sunburn I was noticing for the first time, now that she was so close. "My mother asked me to pick up a jar of herring snacks." Her voice kind of startled me, the way voices do when you see the people first, coming out so flat and dumb yet kind of tony, too, the way it ticked over "pick up" and "snacks." All of a sudden I slid right down her voice into her living room. Her father and the other men were standing around in ice-cream coats and bow ties and the women were in sandals picking up herring snacks on toothpicks off a big glass plate and they were all holding drinks the color of water with olives and sprigs of mint in them. When my parents have somebody over they get lemonade and if it's a real racy affair Schlitz in tall glasses with "They'll Do It Every Time" cartoons stencilled on.

"That's all right," Lengel said, "But this isn't the beach." His repeating this struck me as funny, as if it had just occurred to him, and he had been thinking all these years the A & P was a great big dune and he was the head lifeguard. He didn't like my smiling—as I say he doesn't miss much—but he concentrates on giving the girls that sad Sunday-school-superintendent stare.

Queenie's blush is no sunburn now, and the plump one in plaid, that I liked better from the back—a really sweet can—pipes up, "We weren't doing any shopping. We just came in for the one thing."

"That makes no difference," Lengel tells her, and I could see from the way his eyes went that he hadn't noticed she was wearing a two-piece before. "We want you decently dressed when you come in here."

"We *are* decent," Queenie says suddenly, her lower lip pushing, getting sore now that she remembers her place, a place from which the crowd that runs the A & P must look pretty crummy. Fancy Herring Snacks flashed in her very blue eyes.

"Girls, I don't want to argue with you. After this come in here with your shoulders covered. It's our policy." He turns his back. That's policy for you. Policy is what the kingpins want. What the others want is juvenile delinquency.

All this while, the customers had been showing up with their carts but, you know, sheep, seeing a scene, they had all bunched up on Stokesie, who shook open a paper bag as gently as peeling a peach, not wanting to miss a word. I could feel in the silence everybody getting nervous, most of all Lengel, who asks me, "Sammy, have you rung up their purchase?"

I thought and said "No" but it wasn't about that I was thinking. I go through the punches, 4, 9, GROC, TOT—it's more complicated than you think, and after you do it often enough, it begins to make a little song, that you hear words to, in my case "Hello (*bing*) there, you (*gung*) hap-py *peepul* (*splat*)!"—the *splat* being the drawer flying out. I uncrease the bill, tenderly as you may imagine, it just having come from between the two smoothest scoops of vanilla I had ever known were there, and pass a half and a penny into her narrow pink palm, and nestle the herrings in a bag and twist its neck and hand it over, all the time thinking.

The girls, and who'd blame them, are in a hurry to get out, so I say, "I quit" to Lengel quick enough for them to hear, hoping they'll stop and watch me, their unsuspected hero. They keep right on going, into the electric eye; the door flies open and they flicker across the lot to their car, Queenie and Plaid and Big

Tall Goony-Goony (not that as raw material she was so bad), leaving me with Lengel and a kink in his eyebrow.

"Did you say something, Sammy?"

"I said I quit."

"I thought you did."

"You didn't have to embarrass them."

"It was they who were embarrassing us."

I started to say something that come out "Fiddle-de-doo." It's a saying of my grandmother's, and I know she would have been pleased.

"I don't think you know what you're saying," Lengel said.

"I know you don't," I said. "But I do." I pull the bow at the back of my apron and start shrugging it off my shoulders. A couple customers that had been heading for my slot begin to knock against each other, like scared pigs in a chute.

Lengel sighs and begins to look very patient and old and gray. He's been a friend of my parents for years. "Sammy, you don't want to do this to your Mom and Dad," he tells me. It's true, I don't. But it seems to me that once you begin a gesture it's fatal not to go through with it. I fold the apron, "Sammy" stitched in red on the pocket, and put in on the counter, and drop the bow tie on top of it. The bow tie is theirs, if you've ever wondered. "You'll feel this for the rest of your life," Lengel says, and I know that's true, too, but remembering how he made that pretty girl blush makes me so scrunchy inside I punch the No Sale tab and the machine whirs "pee-pul" and the drawer splats out. One advantage to this scene taking place in summer, I can follow this up with a clean exit, there's no fumbling around getting your coat and galoshes. I just saunter into the electric eye in my white shirt that my mother ironed the night before, and the door heaves itself open, and outside the sunshine is skating around on the asphalt.

[right margin, handwritten:] guilt trip

[right margin, handwritten:] summer time

I look around for my girls, but they're gone, of course. There wasn't anybody but some young married screaming with her children about some candy they didn't get by the door of a powder-blue Falcon station wagon. Looking back in the big windows, over the bags of peat moss and aluminum lawn furniture stacked on the pavement, I could see Lengel in my place in the slot, checking the sheep through. His face was dark gray and his back stiff, as if he'd just had an injection of iron, and my stomach kind of fell as I felt how hard the world was going to be to me hereafter.

Fact Questions and Exercises

1. What job does Sammy perform at the A & P? How old is he? *Check-out, 19*
2. Identify "the queen." *The leader of the 3 girls*
3. How are the girls dressed? *In swimsuits*
4. What is the first thing that Lengel says to the girls? *GIRLS, This IS NOT THE BEACH*
5. What does Sammy do to protest the girls' treatment? *Quits his job*

For Discussion and Writing

1. In the first paragraph Updike mentions a "witch about fifty." Later he comments that "they would have burned her over in Salem." To what event in American history is Updike alluding? Does this historical allusion help

explain the meaning of the story? How? Compare Updike's use of history with Hawthorne's use of the same general information.

2. Characterize Sammy. How old is he? Where does he live? To what social class does he seem to belong? What are his motivations for quitting his job? Why is a knowledge of the narrator important in understanding the story?

3. Why does Sammy conclude that the world was going to be hard on him from now on? What ideas and values has he revealed that lead him to this conclusion?

Joyce Carol Oates [1938–   ]

Oates was born in Lockport, New York, and was educated at Syracuse University and the University of Wisconsin. She presently teaches at the University of Windsor in Ontario, Canada. She is a prolific writer, and her best-known novel, *Them*, won the National Book Award in 1970. The theme of her fiction is often the violence of modern life. In her novel *The Assassins* (1975), for instance, Oates carefully explores the assassination ethic that has recently appeared in American society. Among her other works are *By the North Gate* (1963), *The Wheel of Love* (1970), and *Marriages and Infidelities* (1972).

Where Are You Going, Where Have You Been?

for Bob Dylan

Her name was Connie. She was fifteen and she had a quick nervous giggling habit of craning her neck to glance into mirrors, or checking other people's faces to make sure her own was all right. Her mother, who noticed everything and knew everything and who hadn't much reason any longer to look at her own face, always scolded Connie about it. "Stop gawking at yourself, who are you? You think you're so pretty?" she would say. Connie would raise her eyebrows at these familiar complaints and look right through her mother, into a shadowy vision of herself as she was right at that moment: she knew she was pretty and that was everything. Her mother had been pretty once too, if you could believe those old snapshots in the album, but now her looks were gone and that was why she was always after Connie.

"Why don't you keep your room clean like your sister? How've you got your hair fixed—what the hell stinks? Hair spray? You don't see your sister using that junk."

Her sister June was twenty-four and still lived at home. She was a secretary in the high school Connie attended, and if that wasn't bad enough—with her in the same building—she was so plain and chunky and steady that Connie had to hear her praised all the time by her mother and her mother's sisters. June did this, June did that, she saved money and helped clean the house and cooked and Connie couldn't do a thing, her mind was all filled with trashy daydreams. Their father was away at work most of the time and when he came home he wanted supper and he read the newspaper at supper and after supper he went to bed. He didn't bother talking much to them, but around his bent head Connie's mother kept picking at her until Connie wished her mother was dead and she herself was dead and it was all over. "She makes me want to throw up sometimes," she complained to her friends. She had a high, breathless, amused voice which made everything she said sound a little forced, whether it was sincere or not.

There was one good thing: June went places with girl friends of hers, girls who were just as plain and steady as she, and so when Connie wanted to do that her mother had no objections. The father of Connie's best girl friend drove the girls the three miles to town and left them off at a shopping plaza, so that they could walk through the stores or go to a movie, and when he came to pick them up again at eleven he never bothered to ask what they had done.

They must have been familiar sights, walking around that shopping plaza in their shorts and flat ballerina slippers that always scuffed the sidewalk, with charm bracelets jingling on their thin wrists; they would lean together to whisper and laugh secretly if someone passed by who amused or interested them. Connie had long dark blond hair that drew anyone's eye to it, and she wore part of it pulled up on her head and puffed out and the rest of it she let fall down her back. She wore a pull-over jersey blouse that looked one way when she was at home and another way when she was away from home. Everything about her had two sides to it, one for home and one for anywhere that was not home: her walk that could be childlike and bobbing, or languid enough to make anyone think she was hearing music in her head, her mouth which was pale and smirking most of the time, but bright and pink on these evenings out, her laugh which was cynical and drawling at home—"Ha, ha, very funny"—but high-pitched and nervous anywhere else, like the jingling of the charms on her bracelet.

Sometimes they did go shopping or to a movie, but sometimes they went across the highway, ducking fast across the busy road, to a drive-in restaurant where older kids hung out. The restaurant was shaped like a big bottle, though squatter than a real bottle, and on its cap was a revolving figure of a grinning boy who held a hamburger aloft. One night in mid-summer they ran across, breathless with daring, and right away someone leaned out a car window and invited them over, but it was just a boy from high school they didn't like. It made them feel good to be able to ignore him. They went up through the maze of parked and cruising cars to the bright-lit, fly-infested restaurant, their faces pleased and expectant as if they were entering a sacred building that loomed out of the night to give them what haven and what blessing they yearned for. They sat at the counter and crossed their legs at the ankles, their thin shoulders rigid with excitement, and listened to the music that made everything so good: the music was always in the background like music at a church service, it was something to depend on.

A boy named Eddie came in to talk with them. He sat backwards on his stool, turning himself jerkily around in semi-circles and then stopping and turning again, and after a while he asked Connie if she would like something to eat. She said she did and so she tapped her friend's arm on her way out—her friend pulled her face up into a brave droll look—and Connie said she would meet her at eleven, across the way. "I just hate to leave her like that," Connie said earnestly, but the boy said that she wouldn't be alone for long. So they went out to his car and on the way Connie couldn't help but let her eyes wander over the windshields and faces all around her, her face gleaming with a joy that had nothing to do with Eddie or even this place; it might have been the music. She drew her shoulders up and sucked in her breath with the pure pleasure of being alive, and just at that moment she happened to glance at a face just a few feet from hers. It was a boy with shaggy black hair, in a convertible jalopy painted gold. He stared at her and then his lips widened into a grin. Connie slit her eyes at him and turned away, but she couldn't help glancing back and there he was still watching her. He wagged a finger and laughed and said, "Gonna get you, baby," and Connie turned away again without Eddie noticing anything.

She spent three hours with him, at the restaurant where they ate hamburgers and drank Cokes in wax cups that were always sweating, and then down an alley a mile or so away, and when he left her off at five to eleven only the movie house was still open at the plaza. Her girl friend was there, talking with a boy. When Connie came up the two girls smiled at each other and Connie said, "How was the movie?" and the girl said, "*You* should know." They rode off with the girl's father, sleepy and pleased, and Connie couldn't help but look at the darkened shopping plaza with its big empty parking lot and its signs that were faded and ghostly now, and over at the drive-in restaurant where cars were still circling tirelessly. She couldn't hear the music at this distance.

Next morning June asked her how the movie was and Connie said, "So-so."

She and that girl and occasionally another girl went out several times a week that way, and the rest of the time Connie spent around the house—it was summer vacation—getting in her mother's way and thinking, dreaming, about the boys she met. But all the boys fell back and dissolved into a single face that was not even a face, but an idea, a feeling, mixed up with the urgent insistent pounding of the music and the humid night air of July. Connie's mother kept dragging her back to the daylight by finding things for her to do or saying, suddenly, "What's this about the Pettinger girl?"

And Connie would say nervously, "Oh, her. That dope." She always drew thick clear lines between herself and such girls, and her mother was simple and kindly enough to believe her. Her mother was so simple, Connie thought, that it was maybe cruel to fool her so much. Her mother went scuffling around the house in old bedroom slippers and complained over the telephone to one sister about the other, then the other called up and the two of them complained about the third one. If June's name was mentioned her mother's tone was approving, and if Connie's name was mentioned it was disapproving. This did not really mean she disliked Connie and actually Connie thought that her mother preferred her to June because she was prettier, but the two of them kept up a pretense of exasperation, a sense that they were tugging and struggling over something of little value to either of them. Sometimes, over coffee, they were almost friends, but something would come up—some vexation that was like a fly buzzing suddenly around their heads—and their faces went hard with contempt.

One Sunday Connie got up at eleven—none of them bothered with church—and washed her hair so that it could dry all day long, in the sun. Her parents and sisters were going to a barbecue at an aunt's house and Connie said no, she wasn't interested, rolling her eyes to let mother know just what she thought of it. "Stay home alone then," her mother said sharply. Connie sat out back in a lawn chair and watched them drive away, her father quiet and bald, hunched around so that he could back the car out, her mother with a look that was still angry and not at all softened through the windshield, and in the back seat poor old June all dressed up as if she didn't know what a barbecue was, with all the running yelling kids and the flies. Connie sat with her eyes closed in the sun, dreaming and dazed with the warmth about her as if this were a kind of love, the caresses of love, and her mind slipped over onto throughts of the boy she had been with the night before and how nice he had been, how sweet it always was, not the way someone like June would suppose but sweet, gentle, the way it was in movies and promised in songs; and when she opened her eyes she hardly knew where she was, the back yard ran off into weeds and a fence-line of trees and behind it the sky was perfectly blue and still. The asbestos "ranch house" that was now three years old startled her—it looked small. She shook her head as if to get awake.

It was too hot. She went inside the house and turned on the radio to drown out the quiet. She sat on the edge of her bed, barefoot, and listened for an hour and a half to a program called XYZ Sunday Jamboree, record after record of hard, fast, shrieking songs she sang along with, interspersed by exclamations from "Bobby King": "An' look here you girls at Napoleon's—Son and Charley want you to pay real close attention to this song coming up!"

And Connie paid close attention herself, bathed in a glow of slow-pulsed joy that seemd to rise mysteriously out of the music itself and lay languidly about the airless little room, breathed in and breathed out with each gentle rise and fall of her chest.

After a while she heard a car coming up the drive. She sat up at once, startled, because it couldn't be her father so soon. The gravel kept crunching all the way in from the road—the driveway was long—and Connie ran to the window. It was a car she didn't know. It was an open jalopy, painted a bright gold that caught the sunlight opaquely. Her heart began to pound and her fingers snatched at her hair, checking it, and she whispered "Christ. Christ," wondering how bad she looked. The car came to a stop at the side door and the horn sounded four short taps as if this were a signal Connie knew.

She went into the kitchen and approached the door slowly, then hung out the screen door, her bare toes curling down off the step. There were two boys in the car and now she recognized the driver: he had shaggy, shabby black hair that looked crazy as a wig and he was grinning at her.

"I ain't late, am I?" he said.

"Who the hell do you think you are?" Connie said.

"Toldja I'd be out, didn't I?"

"I don't even know who you are."

She spoke sullenly, careful to show no interest or pleasure, and he spoke in a fast bright monotone. Connie looked past him to the other boy, taking her time. He had fair brown hair, with a lock that fell onto his forehead. His sideburns gave him a fierce, embarrassed look, but so far he hadn't even bothered to glance at her. Both boys wore sunglasses. The driver's glasses were metallic and mirrored everything in miniature.

"You wanta come for a ride?" he said.

Connie smirked and let her hair fall loose over one shoulder.

"Don'tcha like my car? New paint job," he said. "Hey."

"What?"

"You're cute."

She pretended to fidget, chasing flies away from the door.

"Don'tcha believe me, or what?" he said.

"Look, I don't even know who you are," Connie said in disgust.

"Hey, Ellie's got a radio, see. Mine's broke down." He lifted his friend's arm and showed her the little transistor the boy was holding, and now Connie began to hear the music. It was the same program that was playing inside the house.

"Bobby King?" she said.

"I listen to him all the time. I think he's great."

"He's kind of great," Connie said reluctantly.

"Listen, that guy's *great*. He knows where the action is."

Connie blushed a little, because the glasses made it impossible for her to see just what this boy was looking at. She couldn't decide if she liked him or if he was just a jerk, and so she dawdled in the doorway and wouldn't come down or go back inside. She said, "What's all that stuff painted on your car?"

"Can'tcha read it?" He opened the door very carefully, as if he was afraid it might fall off. He slid out just as carefully, planting his feet firmly on the ground, the tiny metallic world in his glasses slowing down like gelatine hardening and in the midst of it Connie's bright green blouse. "This here is my name, to begin with," he said. ARNOLD FRIEND was written in tar-like black letters on the side, with a drawing of a round grinning face that reminded Connie of a pumpkin, except it wore sunglasses. "I wanta introduce myself, I'm Arnold Friend and that's my real name and I'm gonna be your friend, honey, and inside the car's Ellie Oscar, he's kinda shy." Ellie brought his transistor radio up to his shoulder and balanced it there. "Now these numbers are a secret code, honey," Arnold Friend explained. He read off the numbers 33, 19, 17 and raised his eyebrows at her to see what she thought of that, but she didn't think much of it. The left rear fender had been smashed and around it was written, on the gleaming gold background: DONE BY CRAZY WOMAN DRIVER. Connie had to laugh at that. Arnold Friend was pleased at her laughter and looked up at her. "Around the other side's a lot more—you wanta come and see them?"

"No."

"Why not?"

"Why should I?"

"Don'tcha wanta see what's on the car? Don'tcha wanta go for a ride?"

"I don't know."

"Why not?"

"I got things to do."

"Like what?"

"Things."

He laughed as if she had said something funny. He slapped his thighs. He was standing in a strange way, leaning back against the car as if he were balancing himself. He wasn't tall, only an inch or so taller than she would be if she came down to him. Connie liked the way he was dressed, which was the way all of them dressed: tight faded jeans stuffed into black, scuffed boots, a belt that pulled his waist in and showed how lean he was, and a white pull-over shirt that was a little soiled and showed the hard small muscles of his arms and shoulders. He looked as if he probably did hard work, lifting and carrying things. Even his neck looked muscular. And his face was a familiar face, somehow: the jaw and chin and cheeks slightly darkened, because he hadn't shaved for a day or two, and the nose long and hawk-like, sniffing as if she were a treat he was going to gobble up and it was all a joke.

"Connie, you ain't telling the truth. This is your day set aside for a ride with me and you know it," he said, still laughing. The way he straightened and recovered from his fit of laughing showed that it had been all fake.

"How do you know what my name is?" she said suspiciously.

"It's Connie."

"Maybe and maybe not."

"I know my Connie," he said, wagging his finger. Now she remembered him even better, back at the restaurant, and her cheeks warmed at the thought of how she sucked in her breath just at the moment she passed him—how she must have looked to him. And he had remembered her. "Ellie and I come out here especially for you," he said. "Ellie can sit in back. How about it?"

"Where?"

"Where what?"

"Where're we going?"

He looked at her. He took off the sunglasses and she saw how pale the skin around his eyes was, like holes that were not in shadow but instead in light. His eyes were like chips of broken glass that catch the light in an amiable way. He smiled. It was as if the idea of going for a ride somewhere, to some place, was a new idea to him.

"Just for a ride, Connie sweetheart."

"I never said my name was Connie," she said.

"But I know what it is. I know your name and all about you, lots of things," Arnold Friend said. He had not moved yet but stood still leaning back against the side of his jalopy. "I took a special interest in you, such a pretty girl, and found out all about you like I know your parents and sister are gone somewheres and I know where and how long they're going to be gone, and I know who you were with last night, and your best girl friend's name is Betty. Right?"

He spoke in a simple lilting voice, exactly as if he were reciting the words to a song. His smile assured her that everthing was fine. In the car Ellie turned up the volume on his radio and did not bother to look around at them.

"Ellie can sit in the back seat," Arnold Friend said. He indicated his friend with a casual jerk of his chin, as if Ellie did not count and she should not bother with him.

"How'd you find out all that stuff?" Connie said.

"Listen: Betty Schultz and Tony Fitch and Jimmy Pettinger and Nancy Pettinger," he said, in a chant. "Raymond Stanley and Bob Hutter—"

"Do you know all those kids?"

"I know everybody."

"Look, you're kidding. You're not from around here."

"Sure."

"But—how come we never saw you before?"

"Sure you saw me before," he said. He looked down at his boots, as if he were a little offended. "You just don't remember."

"I guess I'd remember you," Connie said.

"Yeah?" He looked up at this, beaming. He was pleased. He began to mark time with the music from Ellie's radio, tapping his fists lightly together.

Connie looked away from his smile to the car, which was painted so bright it almost hurt her eyes to look at it. She looked at that name, ARNOLD FRIEND. And up at the front fender was an expression that was familiar—MAN THE FLYING SAUCERS. It was an expression kids had used the year before, but didn't use this year. She looked at it for a while as if the words meant something to her that she did not yet know.

"What're you thinking about? Huh?" Arnold Friend demanded. "Not worried about your hair blowing around in the car, are you?"

"No."

"Think I maybe can't drive good?"

"How do I know?"

"You're a hard girl to handle. How come?" he said. "Don't you know I'm your friend? Didn't you see me put my sign in the air when you walked by?"

"What sign?"

"My sign." And he drew an X in the air, leaning out toward her. They were maybe ten feet apart. After his hand fell back to his side the X was still in the air, almost visible. Connie let the screen door close and stood perfectly still inside it, listening to the music from her radio and the boy's blend together. She stared at Arnold Friend. He stood there so stiffly relaxed, pretending to be relaxed, with one hand idly on the door handle as if he were keeping himself up that way and had no intention of ever moving again. She recognized most things about him, the tight jeans that showed his thighs and buttocks and the greasy leather boots and the tight shirt, and even that slippery friendly smile of his, that sleepy dreamy smile that all the boys used to get across ideas they didn't want to put into words. She recognized all this and also the singsong way he talked, slightly mocking, kidding, but serious and a little melancholy, and she recognized the way he tapped one fist against the other in homage to the perpetual music behind him. But all these things did not come together.

She said suddenly. "Hey, how old are you?"

His smile faded. She could see then that he wasn't a kid, he was much older—thirty, maybe more. At this knowledge her heart began to pound faster.

"That's a crazy thing to ask. Can'tcha see I'm your own age?"

"Like hell you are."

"Or maybe a coupla years older, I'm eighteen."

"Eighteen?" she said doubtfully.

He grinned to reassure her and lines appeared at the corners of his mouth. His teeth were big and white. He grinned so broadly his eyes became slits and she saw how thick the lashes were, thick and black as if painted with a black tar-like material. Then he seemed to become embarrassed, abruptly, and looked over his shoulder at Ellie. "*Him,* he's crazy," he said, "Ain't he a riot, he's a nut, a real character." Ellie was still listening to the music. His sunglasses told nothing about what he was thinking. He wore a bright orange shirt unbuttoned halfway to show his chest, which was a pale, bluish chest and not muscular like Arnold Friend's. His shirt collar was turned up all around and the very tips of the collar pointed out past his chin as if they were protecting him. He was pressing the transistor radio up against his ear and sat there in a kind of daze, right in the sun.

"He's kinda strange," Connie said.

"Hey, she says you're kinda strange! Kinda strange!" Arnold Friend cried. He pounded on the car to get Ellie's attention. Ellie turned for the first time and Connie saw with shock that he wasn't a kid either—he had a fair, hairless face, cheeks reddened slightly as if the veins grew too close to the surface of his skin, the face of a forty-year-old baby. Connie felt a wave of dizziness rise in her at this sight and she stared at him as if waiting for something to change the shock of the moment, make it all right again. Ellie's lips kept shaping words, mumbling along with the words blasting in his ear.

"Maybe you two better go away," Connie said faintly.

"What? How come?" Arnold Friend cried. "We come out here to take you for a ride. It's Sunday." He had the voice of the man on the radio now. It was the same voice, Connie thought. "Don'tcha know it's Sunday all day and honey, no matter who you were with last night today you're with Arnold Friend and don't you forget it!—Maybe you better step out here," he said, and this last was in a different voice. It was a little flatter, as if the heat was finally getting to him.

"No. I got things to do."

"Hey."

"You two better leave."

"We ain't leaving until you come with us."

"Like hell I am—"

"Connie, don't fool around with me. I mean, don't fool *around*," he said, shaking his head. He laughed incredulously. He placed his sunglasses on top of his head, carefully, as if he were indeed wearing a wig, and brought the stems down behind his ears. Connie stared at him, another wave of dizziness and fear rising in her so that for a moment he wasn't even in focus but was just a blur, standing there against his gold car, and she had the idea that he had driven up the driveway all right but had come from nowhere before that and belonged nowhere and that everything about him and even about the music that was so familiar to her was only half real.

"If my father comes and sees you—"

"He ain't coming. He's at a barbecue."

"How do you know that?"

"Aunt Tillie's. Right now they're—uh—they're drinking. Sitting around," he said vaguely, squinting as if he were staring all the way to town and over to Aunt Tillie's back yard. Then the vision seemed to get clear and he nodded energetically. "Yeah. Sitting around. There's your sister in a blue dress, huh? And high heels, the poor sad bitch—nothing like you, sweetheart! And your mother's helping some fat woman with the corn, they're cleaning the corn—husking the corn—"

"What fat woman?" Connie cried.

"How do I know what fat woman, I don't know every goddamn fat woman in the world!" Arnold Friend laughed.

"Oh, that's Mrs. Hornby. . . . Who invited her?" Connie said. She felt a little lightheaded. Her breath was coming quickly.

"She's too fat. I don't like them fat. I like them the way you are, honey," he said smiling sleepily at her. They stared at each other for a while, through the screen door. He said softly, "Now what you're going to do is this: you're going to come out that door. You're going to sit up front with me and Ellie's going to sit in the back, the hell with Ellie, right? This isn't Ellie's date. You're my date. I'm your lover, honey."

"What? You're crazy—"

"Yes, I'm your lover. You don't know what that is but you will," he said.

"I know that too. I know all about you. But look: it's real nice and you couldn't ask for nobody better than me, or more polite. I always keep my word. I'll tell you how it is, I'm always nice at first, the first time. I'll hold you so tight and you won't think you have to try to get away or pretend anything because you'll know you can't. And I'll come inside you where it's all secret and you'll give in to me and you'll love me—"

"Shut up! You're crazy!" Connie said. She backed away from the door. She put her hands against her ears as if she'd heard something terrible, something not meant for her. "People don't talk like that, you're crazy," she muttered. Her heart was almost too big now for her chest and its pumping made sweat break out all over her. She looked out to see Arnold Friend pause and then take a step toward the porch lurching. He almost fell. But, like a clever drunken man, he managed to catch his balance. He wobbled in his high boots and grabbed hold of one of the porch posts.

"Honey?" he said. "You still listening?"

"Get the hell out of here!"

"Be nice, honey. Listen."

"I'm going to call the police—"

He wobbled again and out of the side of his mouth came a fast spat curse, an aside not meant for her to hear. But even this "Christ!" sounded forced. Then he began to smile again. She watched this smile come, awkward as if he were smiling from inside a mask. His whole face was a mask, she thought wildly, tanned down onto his throat but then running out as if he had plastered make-up on his face but had forgotten about his throat.

"Honey—? Listen, here's how it is. I always tell the truth and I promise you this: I ain't coming in that house after you."

"You better not! I'm going to call the police if you—if you don't—"

"Honey," he said, talking right through her voice, "honey, I'm not coming in there but you are coming out here. You know why?"

She was panting. The kitchen looked like a place she had never seen before, some room she had run inside but which wasn't good enough, wasn't going to help her. The kitchen window had never had a curtain, after three years, and there were dishes in the sink for her to do—probably—and if you ran your hand across the table you'd probably feel something sticky there.

"You listening, honey? Hey?"

"—going to call the police—"

"Soon as you touch the phone I don't need to keep my promise and can come inside. You won't want that."

She rushed forward and tried to lock the door. Her fingers were shaking. "But why lock it," Arnold Friend said gently, talking right into her face. "It's just a screen door. It's just nothing." One of his boots was at a strange angle, as if his foot wasn't in it. It pointed out to the left, bent at the ankle. "I mean, anybody can break through a screen door and glass and wood and iron or anything else if he needs to, anybody at all and specially Arnold Friend. If the place got lit up with a fire honey you'd come running out into my arms, right into my arms and safe at home—like you knew I was your lover and'd stopped fooling around. I don't mind a nice shy girl but I don't like no fooling around." Part of those words were spoken with a slight rhythmic lilt, and Connie somehow recognized them—the echo of a song from last year, about a girl rushing into her boy friend's arms and coming home again—

Connie stood barefoot on the linoleum floor, staring at him. "What do you want?" she whispered.

"I want you," he said.

"What?"

"Seen you that night and thought, that's the one, yes sir. I never needed to look any more."

"But my father's coming back. He's coming to get me. I had to wash my hair first—" She spoke in a dry, rapid voice, hardly raising it for him to hear.

"No, your daddy is not coming and yes, you had to wash your hair and you washed it for me. It's nice and shining and all for me, I thank you, sweetheart," he said, with a mock bow, but again he almost lost his balance. He had to bend and adjust his boots. Evidently his feet did not go all the way down; the boots must have been stuffed with something so that he would seem taller. Connie stared out at him and behind him Ellie in the car, who seemed to be looking off toward Connie's right, into nothing. This Ellie said, pulling the words out of the air one after another as if he were just discovering them, "You want me to pull out the phone?"

"Shut your mouth and keep it shut," Arnold Friend said, his face red from bending over or maybe from embarrassment because Connie had seen his boots. "This ain't none of your business."

"What—what are you doing? What do you want?" Connie said. "If I call the police they'll get you, they'll arrest you—"

"Promise was not to come in unless you touch that phone, and I'll keep that promise," he said. He resumed his erect position and tried to force his shoulders back. He sounded like a hero in a movie, declaring something important. He spoke too loudly and it was as if he were speaking to someone behind Connie. "I ain't made plans for coming in that house where I don't belong but just for you to come out to me, the way you should. Don't you know who I am?"

"You're crazy," she whispered. She backed away from the door but did not want to go into another part of the house, as if this would give him permission to come through the door. "What do you. . . . You're crazy, you . . ."

"Huh? What're you saying, honey?"

Her eyes darted everywhere in the kitchen. She could not remember what it was, this room.

"This is how it is, honey: you come out and we'll drive away, have a nice ride. But if you don't come out we're gonna wait till your people come home and then they're all going to get it."

"You want that telephone pulled out?" Ellie said. He held the radio away from his ear and grimaced, as if without the radio the air was too much for him.

"I toldja shut up, Ellie," Arnold Friend said, "you're deaf, get a hearing aid, right? Fix yourself up. This little girl's no trouble and's gonna be nice to me, so Ellie keep to yourself, this ain't your date—right? Don't hem in on me. Don't hog. Don't crush. Don't bird dog. Don't trail me," he said in a rapid meaningless voice, as if he were running through all the expressions he'd learned but was no longer sure which one of them was in style, then rushing on to new ones, making them up with his eyes closed. "Don't crawl under my fence, don't squeeze in my chipmunk hole, don't sniff my glue, suck my popsicle, keep your own greasy fingers on yourself!" He shaded his eyes and peered at Connie, who was backed against the kitchen table. "Don't mind him honey he's just a creep. He's a dope. Right? I'm the boy for you and like I said you come out here nice like a lady and give me your hand, and nobody else gets hurt, I mean, your nice old bald-headed daddy and your mummy and your sister in her high heels. Because listen: why bring them in this?"

"Leave me alone," Connie whispered.

"Hey, you know that old woman down the road, the one with the chickens and stuff—you know her?"

"She's dead!"

"Dead? What? You know her?" Arnold Friend said.

"She's dead—"

"Don't you like her?"

"She's dead—she's—she isn't here any more—"

"But don't you like her, I mean, you got something against her? Some grudge or something?" Then his voice dipped as if he were conscious of a rudeness. He touched the sunglasses perched on top of his head as if to make sure they were still there. "Now you be a good girl."

"What are you going to do?"

"Just two things, or maybe three," Arnold Friend said. "But I promise it won't last long and you'll like me that way you get to like people you're close to. You will. It's all over for you here, so come on out. You don't want your people in any trouble, do you?"

She turned and bumped against a chair or something, hurting her leg, but she ran into the back room and picked up the telephone. Something roared in her ear, a tiny roaring and she was so sick with fear that she could do nothing but listen to it—the telephone was clammy and very heavy and her fingers groped down to the dial but were too weak to touch it. She began to scream into the phone, into the roaring. She cried out, she cried for her mother, she felt her breath start jerking back and forth in her lungs as if it were something Arnold Friend were stabbing her with again and again with no tenderness. A noisy sorrowful wailing rose all about her and she was locked inside it the way she was locked inside this house.

After a while she could hear again. She was sitting on the floor with her wet back against the wall.

Arnold Friend was saying from the door, "That's a good girl. Put the phone back."

She kicked the phone away from her.

"No, honey. Pick it up. Put it back right."

She picked it up and put it back. The dial tone stopped.

"That's a good girl. Now you come outside."

She was hollow with what had been fear, but what was now just an emptiness. All that screaming had blasted it out of her. She sat, one leg cramped under her, and deep inside her brain was something like a pinpoint of light that kept going and would not let her relax. She thought, I'm not going to see my mother again. She thought, I'm not going to sleep in my bed again. Her bright green blouse was all wet.

Arnold Friend said, in a gentle-loud voice that was like a stage voice, "The place where you came from ain't there any more, and where you had in mind to go is cancelled out. This place you are now—inside your daddy's house—is nothing but a cardboard box I can knock down any time. You know that and always did know it. You hear me?"

She thought, I have got to think. I have to know what to do.

"We'll go out to a nice field, out in the country here where it smells so nice and it's sunny," Arnold Friend said. "I'll have my arms tight around you so you won't need to try to get away and I'll show you what love is like, what it does. The hell with this house! It looks solid all right," he said. He ran a fingernail down the screen and the noise did not make Connie shiver, as it would have the day before. "Now put your hand on your heart, honey. Feel that? That feels solid too but we know better, be nice to me, be sweet like you can because what else is there for a girl like you but to be sweet and pretty and give in? —and get away before her people come back?"

She felt her pounding heart. Her hand seemed to enclose it. She thought for the first time in her life that it was nothing that was hers, that belonged to her, but just a pounding, living thing inside this body that wasn't really hers either.

"You don't want them to get hurt," Arnold Friend went on. "Now get up, honey. Get up all by yourself."

She stood.

"Now turn this way. That's right. Come over here to me—Ellie, put that away, didn't I tell you? You dope. You miserable creepy dope," Arnold Friend said. His words were not angry but only part of an incantation. The incantation was kindly. "Now come out through the kitchen to me honey and let's see a smile, try it, you're a brave sweet little girl and now they're eating corn and hotdogs cooked to bursting over an outdoor fire, and they don't know one thing about you and never did and honey you're better than them because not a one of them would have done this for you."

Connie felt the linoleum under her feet; it was cool. She brushed her hair back out of her eyes. Arnold Friend let go of the post tentatively and opened his arms for her, his elbows pointing in toward each other and his wrists limp, to show that this was an embarrassed embrace and a little mocking, he didn't want to make her self-conscious.

She put out her hand against the screen. She watched herself push the door slowly open as if she were safe back somewhere in the other doorway, watching this body and this head of long hair moving out into the sunlight where Arnold Friend waited.

"My sweet little blue-eyed girl," he said, in a half-sung sigh that had nothing to do with her brown eyes but was taken up just the same by the vast sunlit reaches of the land behind him and on all sides of him, so much land that Connie had never seen before and did not recognize except to know that she was going to it.

Fact Questions and Exercises

1. How old is Connie? How does she differ from her sister June?
2. What has Connie been doing just before Arnold arrives at her house?
3. Who is Arnold Friend? Describe him. Describe his car.
4. Where are Connie's parents and sister when Arnold comes to the house? Who accompanies Arnold to Connie's house?
5. Ultimately, does Connie leave with Arnold? Where does he want to take her?

For Discussion and Writing

1. Characterize Arnold Friend. How old is he? What does he look like? Why does he travel with Ellie? What powers does he claim to possess? Is his name important? Ironic?

2. Is Connie both attracted to and repelled by Arnold? Point out details to support your answer. Why does Connie react to Arnold in the way she does?

3. The story is dedicated to Bob Dylan. Joyce Carol Oates has said that she thought of Dylan's song "It's All Over Now, Baby Blue" in writing this story. Do you know the song? How does it help explain the story?

4. Symbolically, what does Arnold Friend represent? How does he control Connie? Is Connie sexually attracted to Arnold? To what "land" is Connie going? Compare this story with "Flowering Judas."

THE
NOVELLA

Franz Kafka [1883–1924]

Kafka was born in Prague, Czechoslovakia, the son of a successful and demanding Jewish merchant. In 1906 Kafka received a doctorate of jurisprudence, and thereafter worked several years for the Austrian government. Kafka was a solitary man who knew that he was dying of tuberculosis, and for whom writing was private therapy. None of his long novels was published during his lifetime; and in fact, he directed that all of his manuscripts be destroyed—a final wish that fortunately was not granted. Kafka's life was marked by his inability to live up to his father's expectations and by several unhappy love affairs. His works reflect the loneliness and frustration of people trapped by guilt and forces beyond their control or understanding. His best-known works include *The Trial* (1925), *The Castle* (1926), and *Amerika* (1927). *The Metamorphosis*, published in 1915, was one of the few of his stories published while Kafka was still living.

The Metamorphosis

I

As Gregor Samsa awoke one morning from uneasy dreams he found himself transformed in his bed into a gigantic insect. He was lying on his hard, as it were armor-plated, back and when he lifted his head a little he could see his dome-like brown belly divided into stiff arched segments on top of which the bed quilt could hardly keep in position and was about to slide off completely. His numerous legs, which were pitifully thin compared to the rest of his bulk, waved helplessly before his eyes.

What has happened to me? he thought. It was no dream. His room, a regular human bedroom, only rather too small, lay quiet between the four familiar walls. Above the table on which a collection of cloth samples was unpacked and spread out—Samsa was a commercial traveler—hung the picture which he had recently cut out of an illustrated magazine and put into a pretty gilt frame. It showed a lady, with a fur cap and a fur stole, sitting upright and holding out to the spectator a huge fur muff into which the whole of her forearm had vanished!

Gregor's eyes turned next to the window, and the overcast sky—one could hear rain drops beating on the window gutter—made him quite melancholy. What about sleeping a little longer and forgetting all this nonsense, he thought, but it could not be done, for he was accustomed to sleep on his right side and in his present condition, he could not turn himself over. However violently he forced himself towards his right side he always rolled on to his back again. He tried it at least a hundred times, shutting his eyes to keep from seeing his struggling legs, and only desisted when he began to feel in his side a faint dull ache he had never experienced before.

Oh God, he thought, what an exhausting job I've picked on! Traveling about day in, day out. It's much more irritating work than doing the actual business in the office, and on top of that there's the trouble of constant traveling, of worrying about train connections, the bed and irregular meals, casual acquaintances that are always new and never become intimate friends. The devil take it all! He felt a slight itching up on his belly; slowly pushed himself on his back nearer to the top of the bed so that he could lift his head more easily; identified the itching place which was surrounded by many small white spots the nature of which he could not understand and made to touch it with a leg, but drew the leg back immediately, for the contact made a cold shiver run through him.

He slid down again into his former position. This getting up early, he thought, makes one quite stupid. A man needs his sleep. Other commercials live like harem women. For instance, when I come back to the hotel of a morning to write up the orders I've got, these others are only sitting down to breakfast. Let me just try that with my chief; I'd be sacked on the spot. Anyhow, that might be quite a good thing for me, who can tell? If I didn't have to hold my hand because of my parents I'd have given notice long ago, I'd have gone to the chief and told him exactly what I think of him. That would knock him endways from his desk! It's a queer way of doing, too, this sitting on high at a desk and talking down to employees, especially when they have to come quite near because the chief is hard of hearing. Well, there's still hope; once I've saved enough money to pay back my parents' debts to him—that should take another five or six years—I'll do it without fail. I'll cut myself completely loose then. For the moment, though, I'd better get up, since my train goes at five.

He looked at the alarm clock ticking on the chest. Heavenly Father! he thought. It was half-past six o'clock and the hands were quietly moving on, it was even past the half-hour, it was getting on toward quarter to seven. Had the alarm clock not gone off? From the bed one could see that it had been properly set for four o'clock; of course it must have gone off. Yes, but was it possible to sleep quietly through the ear-splitting noise? Well, he had not slept quietly, yet apparently all the more soundly for that. But what was he to do now? The next train went at seven o'clock; to catch that he would need to hurry like mad and his samples weren't even packed up, and he himself wasn't feeling particularly fresh and active. And even if he did catch the train he wouldn't avoid a row with the chief, since the firm's porter would have been waiting for the five o'clock train and would have long since reported his failure to turn up. The porter was a creature of the chief's, spineless and stupid. Well, supposing he were to say he was sick? But that would be most unpleasant and would look suspicious, since during his five years' employment he had not been ill once. The chief himself would be sure to come with the sick-insurance doctor, would reproach his parents with their son's laziness and would cut all excuses short by referring to the insurance doctor, who of course regarded all mankind as perfectly healthy malingerers. And would he be so far wrong on this occasion? Gregor really felt quite well, apart from a drowsiness that was utterly superfluous after such a long sleep, and he was even unusually hungry.

As all this was running through his mind at top speed without his being able to decide to leave his bed—the alarm clock had just struck a quarter to seven—there came a cautious tap at the door behind the head of his bed. "Gregor," said a voice—it was his mother's—"it's a quarter to seven. Hadn't you a train to catch?" That gentle voice! Gregor had a shock as he heard his own voice answering hers, unmistakably his own voice, it was true, but with a persistent horrible twittering squeak behind it like an undertone, that left the words in their clear shape only for the first moment and then rose up reverberating round them to destroy their sense, so that one could not be sure one had heard them rightly. Gregor wanted to answer at length and explain everything, but in the circumstances he confined himself to saying: "Yes, yes, thank you, Mother, I'm getting up now." The wooden door between them must have kept the change in his voice from being noticeable outside, for his mother contented herself with this statement and shuffled away. Yet this brief exchange of words had made the other members of the family aware that Gregor was still in the house, as they had not expected, and at one of the side doors his father was already knocking, gently, yet with his fist. "Gregor, Gregor," he called, "what's the matter with you?" And after a while he called again in a deeper voice: "Gregor! Gregor!" At the other side door his sister was saying in a low, plaintive tone: "Gregor? Aren't you well? Are you needing anything?" He answered them both at once: "I'm just ready," and did his best to make his voice sound as normal as possible by enunciating the words very clearly and leaving long pauses between them. So his father went back to his breakfast, but his sister whispered: "Gregor, open the door, do." However, he was not thinking of opening the door, and felt thankful for the prudent habit he had acquired in traveling of locking all doors during the night, even at home.

His immediate intention was to get up quietly without being disturbed, to put on his clothes and above all eat his breakfast, and only then to consider what else was to be done, since in bed, he was well aware, his meditations would come to no sensible conclusion. He remembered that often enough in bed he had felt small aches and pains, probably caused by awkward postures, which had proved purely imaginary once he got up, and he looked forward eagerly to seeing this morning's delusions gradually fall away. That the change in his voice was nothing but the precursor of a severe chill, a standing ailment of commercial travelers, he had not the least possible doubt.

To get rid of the quilt was quite easy; he had only to inflate himself a little and it fell off by itself. But the next move was difficult, especially because he was so uncommonly broad. He would have needed arms and hands to hoist himself up; instead he had only the numerous little legs which never stopped waving in all directions and which he could not control in the least. When he tried to bend one of them it was the first to stretch itself straight; and did he succeed at last in making it do what he wanted, all the other legs meanwhile waved the more wildly in a high degree of unpleasant agitation. "But what's the use of lying idle in bed," said Gregor to himself.

He thought that he might get out of bed with the lower part of his body first, but this lower part, which he had not yet seen and of which he could form no clear conception, proved too difficult to move; it shifted so slowly; and when finally, almost wild with annoyance, he gathered his forces together and thrust out recklessly, he had miscalculated the direction and bumped heavily against the lower end of the bed, and the stinging pain he felt informed him that precisely this lower part of his body was at the moment probably the most sensitive.

So he tried to get the top part of himself out first, and cautiously moved his head towards the edge of the bed. That proved easy enough, and despite it's breadth the mass bulk of his body at last slowly followed the movement of his head. Still, when he finally got his head free over the edge of the bed he felt too scared to go on advancing, for after all if he let himself fall in this way it would take a miracle to keep his head from being injured. And at all costs he must not lose consciousness now, precisely now; he would rather stay in bed.

But when after a repetition of the same efforts he lay in his former position again, sighing, and watched his little legs struggling against each other more wildly than ever, if that were possible, and saw no way of bringing any order into this arbitrary confusion, he told himself again that it was impossible to stay in bed and that the most sensible course was to risk everything for the smallest hope of getting away from it. At the same time he did not forget meanwhile to remind himself that cool reflection, the coolest possible, was much better than desperate resolves. In such moments he focused his eyes as sharply as possible on the window, but, unfortunately, the prospect of the morning fog, which muffled even the other side of the narrow street, brought him little encouragement and comfort. "Seven o'clock already," he said to himself when the alarm clock chimed again, "seven o'clock already and still such a thick fog." And for a little while he lay quiet, breathing lightly, as if perhaps expecting such complete repose to restore all the things to their real and normal condition.

But then he said to himself: "Before it strikes a quarter past seven I must be quite out of this bed, without fail. Anyhow, by that time someone will have come from the office to ask for me, since it opens before seven." And he set himself to rocking his whole body at once in a regular rhythm, with the idea of swinging it out of the bed. If he tipped himself out in that way he could keep his head from injury by lifting it at an acute angle when he fell. His back seemed to be hard and was not likely to suffer from a fall on the carpet. His biggest worry was the loud crash he would not be able to help making, which would probably cause anxiety, if not terror, behind all the doors. Still, he must take the risk.

When he was already half out of the bed—the new method was more a game than an effort, for he needed only to hitch himself across by rocking to and fro—it struck him how simple it would be if he could get help. Two strong people—he thought of his father and the servant girl—would be amply sufficient; they would only have to thrust their arms under this convex back, lever him out of the bed, bend down with their burden and then be patient enough to let him turn himself right over on to the floor, where it was to be hoped his legs would then find their proper function. Well, ignoring the fact that the doors were all locked, ought he really to call for help? In spite of his misery he could not suppress a smile at the very idea of it.

He had got so far that he could barely keep his equilibrium when he rocked himself strongly, and he would have to nerve himself very soon for the final decision since in five minutes, time it would be a quarter past seven—when the front door bell rang. "That's someone from the office," he said to himself, and grew almost rigid, while his little legs only jigged about all the faster. For a moment everything stayed quiet. "They're not going to open the door," said Gregor to himself, catching at some kind of irrational hope. But then of course the servant girl went as usual to the door with her heavy tread and opened it. Gregor needed only to hear the first good morning of the visitor to know immediately who it was—the chief clerk himself. What a fate, to be condemned to work for a firm where the smallest omission at once gave rise to the gravest suspicion! Were all employees in a body nothing but scoundrels, was there not among them one single loyal devoted man who, had he wasted only an hour or so of the firm's time in a morning, was so tormented by conscience as to be driven out of his mind and actually incapable of leaving his bed? Wouldn't it really have been sufficient to send an apprentice to inquire—if any inquiry were necessary at all—did the chief clerk himself have to come and thus indicate to the entire family, an innocent family, that this suspicious circumstance could be investigated by no one less versed in affairs than himself? And more through the agitation caused by these reflections than through any act of will Gregor swung himself out of bed with all his strength. There was a loud thump, but it was not really a crash. His fall was broken to some extent by the carpet, his back, too, was less stiff than he thought, and so there was merely a dull thud, not so very startling. Only he had not lifted his head carefully enough and had hit it; he turned it and rubbed it on the carpet in pain and irritation.

"That was something falling down in there," said the chief clerk in the next room to the left. Gregor tried to suppose to himself that something like what had happened to him today might some day happen to the chief clerk; one really could not deny that it was possible. But as if in brusque reply to this supposition the chief clerk took a couple of firm steps in the next-door room and his patent leather boots creaked. From the right-hand room his sister was whispering to inform him of the situation: "Gregor, the chief clerk's here." "I know," muttered Gregor to himself; but he didn't dare to make his voice loud enough for his sister to hear it.

"Gregor," said his father now from the left-hand room, "the chief clerk has come and wants to know why you didn't catch the early train. We don't know what to say to him. Besides, he wants to talk to you in person. So open the door, please. He will be good enough to excuse the untidiness of your room." "Good morning, Mr. Samsa," the chief clerk was calling amiably meanwhile. "He's not well," said his mother to the visitor, while his father was still speaking through the door, "he's not well, sir, believe me. What else would make him miss a train! The boy thinks about nothing but his work. It makes me almost cross the way he never goes out in the evenings; he's been here the last eight days and has stayed at home every single evening. He just sits there quietly at the table reading a newspaper or looking through railway timetables. The only amusement he gets is doing fretwork. For instance, he spent two or three evenings cutting out a little picture frame; you would be surprised to see how pretty it is; it's hanging in his room; you'll see it in a minute when Gregor opens the door. I must say I'm glad you've come, sir; we should never have got him to unlock the door by ourselves; he's so obstinate; and I'm sure he's unwell, though he wouldn't have it to be so this morning." "I'm just coming," said Gregor slowly and carefully, not moving an inch for fear of losing one word of the conversation. "I can't think of any other explanation, madam," said the chief clerk, "I hope it's nothing serious. Although on the other hand I must say that we men of business—fortunately or unfortunately—very often simply have to ignore any slight indisposition, since business must be attended to." "Well, can the chief clerk come in now?" asked Gregor's father impatiently, again knocking on the door. "No," said Gregor. In the left-hand room a painful silence followed this refusal, in the right-hand room his sister began to sob.

Why didn't his sister join the others? She was probably newly out of bed and hadn't even begun to put on her clothes yet. Well, why was she crying? Because he wouldn't get up and let the chief clerk in, because he was in danger of losing his job, and because the chief would begin dunning his parents again for the old debts? Surely these were things one didn't need to worry about for the present. Gregor was still at home and not in the least thinking of deserting the family. At the moment, true, he was lying on the carpet and no one who knew the condition he was in could seriously expect him to admit the chief clerk. But for such a small discourtesy, which could plausibly be explained away somehow later on, Gregor could hardly be dismissed on the spot. And it seemed to Gregor that it would be much more sensible to leave him in peace for the present than to trouble him with tears and entreaties. Still, of course, their uncertainty bewildered them all and excused their behavior.

"Mr. Samsa," the chief clerk called now in a louder voice, "what's the matter with you? Here you are, barricading yourself in your room, giving only 'yes' and 'no' for answers, causing your parents a lot of unnecessary trouble and neglecting—I mention this only in passing—neglecting your business duties in an incredible fashion. I am speaking here in the name of your parents and of your chief, and I beg you quite seriously to give me an immediate and precise explanation. You amaze me, you amaze me. I thought you were a quiet, dependable person, and now all at once you seem bent on making a disgraceful exhibition of yourself. The chief did hint to me early this morning a possible explanation for your disappearance—with reference to the cash payments that were entrusted to you recently—but I almost pledged my solemn word of honor that this could not be so. But now that I see how incredibly obstinate you are, I no longer have the slightest desire to take your part at all. And your position in the firm is not so unassailable. I came with the intention of telling you all this in private, but since you are wasting my time so needlessly I don't see why your parents shouldn't hear it too. For some time past your work has been most unsatisfactory; this is not the season of the year for a business boom, of course, we admit that, but a season of the year for doing no business at all, that does not exist, Mr. Samsa, must not exist."

"But, sir," cried Gregor, beside himself and in his agitation forgetting everything else, "I'm just going to open the door this very minute. A slight illness, an attack of giddiness, has kept me from getting up. I'm still lying in bed. But I feel all right again. I'm getting out of bed now. Just give me a moment or two longer! I'm not quite so well as I thought. But I'm all right, really. How a thing like that can suddenly strike one down! Only last night I was quite well, my parents can tell you, or rather I did have a slight presentiment. I must have showed some sign of it. Why didn't I report it at the office! But one always think that an indisposition can be got over without staying in the house. Oh sir, do spare my parents! All that you're reproaching me with now has no foundation; no one has ever said a word to me about it. Perhaps you haven't looked at the last orders I sent in. Anyhow, I can still catch the eight o'clock train, I'm much the better for my few hours' rest. Don't let me detain you here, sir; I'll be attending to business very soon, and do be good enough to tell the chief so and to make my excuses to him!"

And while all this was tumbling out pell-mell and Gregor hardly knew what he was saying, he had reached the chest quite easily, perhaps because of the practice he had had in bed, and was now trying to lever himself upright by means of it. He meant actually to open the door, actually to show himself and speak to the chief clerk; he was eager to find out what the others, after all their insistence, would say at the sight of him. If they were horrified then the responsibility was no longer his and he could stay quiet. But if they took it calmly, then he had no reason either to be upset, and could really get to the station for the eight o'clock train if he hurried. At first he slipped down a few times from the polished surface of the chest, but at length with a last heave he stood upright; he paid no more attention to the pains in the lower part of his body, however they smarted. Then he let himself fall against the back of a near-by chair, and clung with his little legs to the edges of it. That brought him into control of himself again and he stopped speaking, for now he could listen to what the chief clerk was saying.

"Did you understand a word of it?" the chief clerk was asking; "surely he can't be trying to make fools of us?" "Oh dear," cried his mother, in tears, "perhaps he's terribly ill and we're tormenting him. Grete! Grete!" she called out then. "Yes Mother?" called his sister from the other side. They were calling to each other across Gregor's room. "You must go this minute for the doctor. Gregor is ill. Go for the doctor, quick. Did you hear how he was speaking?" "That was no human voice," said the chief clerk in a voice noticeably low beside the shrillness of the mother's. "Anna! Anna!" his father was calling through the hall to the kitchen, clapping his hands, "get a locksmith at once!" And the two girls were already running through the hall with a swish of skirts—how could his sister have got dressed so quickly?—and were tearing the front door open. There was no sound of its closing again; they had evidently left it open, as one does in houses where some great misfortune has happened.

But Gregor was now much calmer. The words he uttered were no longer understandable, apparently, although they seemed clear enough to him, even clearer than before, perhaps because his ear had grown accustomed to the sound of them. Yet at any rate people now believed that something was wrong with him, and were ready to help him. The positive certainty with which these first measures had been taken comforted him. He felt himself drawn once more into the human circle and hoped for great and remarkable results from both the doctor and the locksmith, without really distinguishing precisely between them. To make his voice as clear as possible for the decisive conversation that was now imminent he coughed a little, as quietly as he could, of course, since this noise too might not sound like a human cough for all he was able to judge. In the next room meanwhile there was complete silence. Perhaps his parents were sitting at the table with the chief clerk, whispering, perhaps they were all leaning against the door and listening.

Slowly Gregor pushed the chair towards the door, then let go of it, caught hold of the door for support—the soles at the end of his little legs were somewhat sticky—and rested against it for a moment after his efforts. Then he set himself to turning the key in the lock with his mouth. It seemed, unhappily, that he hadn't really any teeth—what could he grip the key with?—but on the other hand his jaws were certainly very strong; with their help he did manage to set the key in motion, heedless of the fact that he was undoubtedly damaging them somewhere, since a brown fluid issued from his mouth, flowed over the key and dripped on the floor. "Just listen to that," said the chief clerk next door; "he's turning the key." That was a great encouragement to Gregor; but they should all have shouted encouragement to him, his father and mother too: "Go on, Gregor," they should have called out, "keep going, hold on to that key!" And in the belief that they were all following his efforts intently, he clenched his jaws recklessly on the key with all the force at his command. As the turning of the key progressed he circled round the lock, holding on now only with his mouth, pushing on the key, as required, or pulling it down again with all the weight of his body. The louder click of the finally yielding lock literally quickened Gregor. With a deep breath of relief he said to himself: "So I didn't need the locksmith," and laid his head on the handle to open the door wide.

Since he had to pull the door towards him, he was still invisible when it was really wide open. He had to edge himself slowly round the near half of the double door, and to do it very carefully if he was not to fall plump upon his back just on the threshold. He was still carrying out this difficult manoeuvre, with no time to observe anything else, when he heard the chief clerk utter a loud "Oh!"—it sounded like a gust of wind—and now he could see the man, standing as he was nearest to the door, clapping one hand before his open mouth and slowly backing away as if driven by some invisible steady pressure. His mother—in spite of the chief clerk's being there her hair was still undone and sticking up in all directions—first clasped her hands and looked at his father, then took two steps towards Gregor and fell on the floor among her outspread skirts, her face quite hidden on her breast. His father knotted his fist with a fierce expression on his face as if he meant to knock Gregor back into his room, then looked uncertainly round the living room, covered his eyes with his hands and wept till his great chest heaved.

Gregor did not go now into the living room, but leaned against the inside of the firmly shut wing of the door, so that only half his body was visible and his head above it bending sideways to look at the others. The light had meanwhile strengthened; on the other side of the street one could see clearly a section of the endlessly long, dark gray building opposite—it was a hospital—abruptly punctuated by its row of regular windows; the rain was still falling, but only in large singly discernible and literally singly splashing drops. The breakfast dishes were set out on the table lavishly, for breakfast was the most important meal of the day to Gregor's father, who lingered it out for hours over various newspapers. Right opposite Gregor on the wall hung a photograph of himself on military service, as a lieutenant, hand on sword, a carefree smile on his face, inviting one to respect his uniform and military bearing. The door leading to the hall was open, and one could see that the front door stood open too, showing the landing beyond and the beginning of the stairs going down.

"Well," said Gregor, knowing perfectly that he was the only one who had retained any composure, "I'll put my clothes on at once, pack up my samples and start off. Will you only let me go? You see, sir, I'm not obstinate, and I'm willing to work; traveling is a hard life, but I couldn't live without it. Where are you going, sir? To the office? Yes? Will you give me a true account of all this? One can be temporarily incapacitated, but that's just the moment for remembering former services and bearing in mind that later on, when the incapacity has been got over, one will certainly work with all the more industry and concentration. I'm loyally bound to serve the chief, you know that very well. Besides, I have to provide for my parents and my sister. I'm in great difficulties, but I'll get out of them again. Don't make things any worse for me than they are. Stand up for me in the firm. Travelers are not popular there, I know. People think they earn sacks of money and just have a good time. A prejudice there's no particular reason for revising. But you, sir, have a more comprehensive view of affairs than the rest of the staff, yes, let me tell you in confidence, a more comprehensive view than the chief himself, who, being the owner, lets his judgment easily be swayed against one of his employees. And you know very well that the traveler, who is never seen in the office almost the whole year round, can so easily fall a victim to gossip and ill luck and unfounded complaints, which he mostly knows nothing about, except when he comes back exhausted from his rounds, and only then suffers in person from their evil consequences, which he can no longer trace back to the original causes. Sir, sir, don't go away without a word to me to show that you think me in the right at least to some extent!"

But at Gregor's very first words the chief clerk had already backed away and only stared at him with parted lips over one twitching shoulder. And while Gregor was speaking he did not stand still one moment but stole away towards the door, without taking his eyes off Gregor, yet only an inch at a time, as if obeying some secret injunction to leave the room. He was already at the hall, and the suddenness with which he took his last step out of the living room would have made one believe he had burned the sole of his foot. Once in the hall he stretched his right arm before him towards the staircase, as if some supernatural power were waiting there to deliver him.

Gregor perceived that the chief clerk must on no account be allowed to go away in this frame of mind if his position in the firm were not to be endangered to the utmost. His parents did not understand this so well; they had convinced themselves in the course of years that Gregor was settled for life in this firm, and besides they were so occupied with their immediate troubles that all foresight had forsaken them. Yet Gregor had this foresight. The chief clerk must be detained, soothed, persuaded and finally won over; the whole future of Gregor and his family depended on it! If only his sister had been there! She was intelligent; she had begun to cry while Gregor was still lying quietly on his back. And no doubt the chief clerk, so partial to ladies, would have been guided by her; she would have shut the door of the flat and in the hall talked him out of his horror. But she was not there, and Gregor would have to handle the situation himself. And without remembering that he was still unaware what powers of movement he possessed, without even remembering that his words in all possibility, indeed in all likelihood, would again be unintelligible, he let go the wing of the door, pushed himself through the opening, started to walk towards the chief clerk, who was already ridiculously clinging with both hands to the railing on the landing; but immediately, as he was feeling for a support, he fell down with a little cry upon all his numerous legs. Hardly was he down when he experienced for the first time this morning a sense of physical comfort; his legs had firm ground under them; they were completely obedient, as he noted with joy; they even strove to carry him forward in whatever direction he chose; and he was inclined to believe that a final relief from all his sufferings was at hand. But in the same moment as he found himself on the floor, rocking with suppressed eagerness to move, not far from his mother, indeed just in front of her, she, who had seemed so completely crushed, sprang all at once to her feet, her arms and fingers outspread, cried: "Help, for God's sake, help!" bent her head down as if to see Gregor better, yet on the contrary kept backing senselessly away; had quite forgotten that the laden table stood behind her; sat upon it hastily, as if in absence of mind, when she bumped into it; and seemed altogether unaware that the big coffee pot beside her was upset and pouring coffee in a flood over the carpet.

"Mother, Mother," said Gregor in a low voice, and looked up at her. The chief clerk, for the moment, had quite slipped from his mind; instead, he could not resist snapping his jaws together at the sight of the streaming coffee. That made his mother scream again, she fled from the table and fell into the arms of his father, who hastened to catch her. But Gregor had now no time to spare for his parents; the chief clerk was already on the stairs; with his chin on the banisters he was taking one last backward look. Gregor made a spring, to be as sure as possible of overtaking him; the chief clerk must have divined his intention, for he leaped down several steps and vanished; he was still yelling "Ugh!" and it echoed through the whole staircase.

Unfortunately, the flight of the chief clerk seemed completely to upset Gregor's father, who had remained relatively calm until now, for instead of running after the man himself, or at least not hindering Gregor in his pursuit, he seized in his right hand the walking stick which the chief clerk had left behind on a chair, together with a hat and greatcoat, snatched in his left hand a large newspaper from the table and began stamping his feet and flourishing the stick and the newspaper to drive Gregor back into his room. No entreaty of Gregor's availed, indeed no entreaty was even understood, however humbly he bent his head his father only stamped on the floor the more loudly. Behind his father his mother had torn open a window, despite the cold weather, and was leaning far out of it with her face in her hands. A strong draught set in from the street to the staircase, the window curtains blew in, the newspapers on the table fluttered, stray pages whisked over the floor. Pitilessly Gregor's father drove him back, hissing and crying "Shoo!" like a savage. But Gregor was quite unpracticed in walking backwards, it really was a slow business. If he only had a chance to turn round he could get back to his room at once, but he was afraid of exasperating his father by the slowness of such a rotation and at any moment the stick in his father's hand might hit him a fatal blow on the back or on the head. In the end, however, nothing else was left for him to do since to his horror he observed that in moving backwards he could not even control the direction he took; and so, keeping an anxious eye on his father all the time over his shoulder, he began to turn round as quickly as he could, which was in reality very slowly. Perhaps his father noted his good intentions, for he did not interfere except every now and then to help him in the manoeuvre from a distance with the point of the stick. If only he would have stopped making that unbearable hissing noise! It made Gregor quite lose his head. He had turned almost completely round when the hissing noise so distracted him that he even turned a little the wrong way again. But when at last his head was fortunately right in front of the doorway, it appeared that his body was too broad simply to get through the opening. His father, of course, in his present mood was far from thinking of such a thing as opening the other half of the door, to let Gregor have enough space. He had merely the fixed idea of driving Gregor back into his room as quickly as possible. He would never have suffered Gregor to make the circumstantial preparations for standing up on end and perhaps slipping his way through the door. Maybe he was now making more noise than ever to urge Gregor forward, as if no obstacle impeded him; to Gregor, anyhow, the noise in his rear sounded no longer like the voice of one single father; this was really no joke, and Gregor thrust himself—come what might—into the doorway. One side of his body rose up, he was tilted at an angle in the doorway, his flank was quite bruised, horrid blotches stained the white door, soon he was stuck fast and, left to himself, could not have moved at all, his legs on one side fluttered trembling in the air, those on the other were crushed painfully to the floor—when from behind his father gave him a strong push which was literally a deliverance and he flew far into the room, bleeding freely. The door was slammed behind him with the stick, and then at last there was silence.

II

Not until it was twilight did Gregor awake out of a deep sleep, more like a swoon than a sleep. He would certainly have waked up of his own accord not much later, for he felt himself sufficiently rested and well-slept, but it seemed to him as if a fleeting step and a cautious shutting of the door leading into the hall had aroused him. The electric lights in the street cast a pale sheen here and there on the ceiling and the upper surfaces of the furniture, but down below, where he lay, it was dark. Slowly, awkwardly trying out his feelers, which he now first learned to appreciate, he pushed his way to the door to see what had been happening there. His left side felt like one single long, unpleasantly tense scar, and he had actually to limp on his two rows of legs. One little leg, moreover, had been severely damaged in the course of that morning's events—it was almost a miracle that only one had been damaged—and trailed uselessly behind him.

He had reached the door before he discovered what had really drawn him to it; the smell of food. For there stood a basin filled with fresh milk in which floated little sops of white bread. He could almost have laughed with joy, since he was now still hungrier than in the morning, and he dipped his head almost over the eyes straight into the milk. But soon in disappointment he withdrew it again; not only did he find it difficult to feed because of his tender left side—and he could only feed with the palpitating collaboration of his whole body—he did not like the milk either, although milk had been his favorite drink and that was certainly why his sister had set it there for him, indeed it was almost with repulsion that he turned away from the basin and crawled back to the middle of the room.

He could see through the crack of the door that the gas was turned on in the living room, but while usually at this time his father made a habit of reading the afternoon newspaper in a loud voice to his mother and occasionally to his sister as well, not a sound was now to be heard. Well, perhaps his father had recently given up this habit of reading aloud, which his sister had mentioned so often in conversation and in her letters. But there was the same silence all around, although the flat was certainly not empty of occupants. "What a quiet life our family has been leading," said Gregor to himself, and as he sat there motionless staring into the darkness he felt great pride in the fact that he had been able to provide such a life for his parents and sister in such a fine flat. But what if all the quiet, the comfort, the contentment were now to end in horror? To keep himself from being lost in such thoughts Gregor took refuge in movement and crawled up and down the room.

Once during the long evening one of the side doors was opened a little and quickly shut again, later the other side door too; someone had apparently wanted to come in and then thought better of it. Gregor now stationed himself immediately before the living room door, determined to persuade any hesitating visitor to come in or at least to discover who it might be; but the door was not opened again and he waited in vain. In the early morning, when the doors were locked, they had all wanted to come in, now that he had opened one door and the other apparently had been opened during the day, no one came in and even the keys were on the other side of the doors.

It was late at night before the gas went out in the living room, and Gregor could easily tell that his parents and his sister had all stayed awake until then, for he could clearly hear the three of them stealing away on tiptoe. No one was likely to visit him, not until the morning, that was certain; so he had plenty of time to meditate at his leisure on how he was to arrange his life afresh. But the lofty, empty room in which he had to lie flat on the floor filled him with an apprehension he could not account for, since it had been his very own room for the past five years—and with a half-unconscious action, not without a slight feeling of shame, he scuttled under the sofa, where he felt comfortable at once, although his back was a little cramped and he could not lift his head up, and his only regret was that his body was too broad to get the whole of it under the sofa.

He stayed there all night, spending the time partly in a light slumber, from which his hunger kept waking him up with a start and partly in worrying and sketching vague hopes, which all led to the same conclusion, that he must lie low for the present and, by exercising patience and the utmost consideration, help the family to bear the inconvenience he was bound to cause them in his present condition.

Very early in the morning, it was still almost night, Gregor had the chance to test the strength of his new resolutions, for his sister, nearly fully dressed, opened the door from the hall and peered in. She did not see him at once, yet when she caught sight of him under the sofa—well, he had to be somewhere, he couldn't have flown away, could he?—she was so startled that without being able to help it she slammed the door shut again. But as if regretting her behavior she opened the door again immediately and came in on tiptoe, as if she were visiting an invalid or even a stranger. Gregor had pushed his head forward to the very edge of the sofa and watched her. Would she notice that he had left the milk standing, and not for lack of hunger, and would she bring in some other kind of food more to his taste? If she did not do it of her own accord, he would rather starve than draw her attention to the fact, although he felt a wild impulse to dart out from under the sofa, throw himself at her feet and beg for something to eat. But his sister at once noticed, with surprise, that the basin was still full, except for a little milk that had been spilt all around it, she lifted it immediately, not with her bare hands, true, but with a cloth and carried it away. Gregor was wildly curious to know what she would bring instead, and made various speculations about it. Yet what she actually did next, in the goodness of her heart, he could never have guessed at. To find out what he liked she brought him a whole selection of food, all set out on an old newspaper. There were old, half-decayed vegetables, bones from last night's supper covered with a white sauce that had thickened; some raisins and almonds; a piece of cheese that Gregor would have called uneatable two days ago; a dry roll of bread, a buttered roll, and a roll both buttered and salted. Besides all that, she set down the same basin, into which she had poured some water, and which was apparently to be reserved for his exclusive use. And, with fine tact, knowing that Gregor would not eat in her presence, she withdrew quickly and even turned the key, to let him understand that he could take his ease as much as he liked. Gregor's legs all whizzed towards the food. His wounds must have healed completely, moreover, for he felt no disability, which amazed him and made him reflect how more than a month ago he had cut one finger a little with a knife and had still suffered pain from the wound only a day before yesterday. Am I less sensitive now? he thought, and sucked greedily at the cheese, which above all the other edibles attracted him at once and strongly. One after another and with tears of satisfaction in his eyes he quickly devoured the cheese, the vegetables and the sauce; the fresh food, on the other hand, had no charms for him, he could not even stand the smell of it and actually dragged away to some little distance the things he could eat. He had long finished his meal and was only lying lazily on the same spot when his sister turned the key slowly as a sign for him to retreat. That roused him at once, although he was nearly asleep, and he hurried under the sofa again. But it took considerable self-control for him to stay under the sofa, even for the short time his sister was in the room, since the large meal had swollen his body somewhat and he was so cramped he could hardly breathe. Slight attacks of breathlessness afflicted him and his eyes were starting a little out of his head as he watched his unsuspecting sister sweeping together with a broom not only the remains of what he had eaten but the things he had not touched, as if these were now of no use to anyone, and hastily shoveling it all into a bucket, which she covered with a wooden lid and carried away. Hardly had she turned her back when Gregor came from under the sofa and stretched and puffed himself out.

In this manner Gregor was fed, once in the early morning while his parents and the servant girl were still asleep, and a second time after they had all had their midday dinner, for then his parents took a short nap and the servant girl could be sent out on some errand or other by his sister. Not that they would have wanted him to starve, of course, but perhaps they could not have borne to know more about his feeding than from hearsay, perhaps too his sister wanted to spare them such little anxieties wherever possible, since they had quite enough to bear as it was.

Under what pretext the doctor and the locksmith had been got rid of on that first morning Gregor could not discover, for since what he said was not understood by the others it never struck any of them, not even his sister, that he could understand what they said, and so whenever his sister came into his room he had to content himself with hearing her utter only a sigh now and then and an occasional appeal to the saints. Later on, when she had got a little used to the situation—of course she could never get completely used to it—she sometimes threw out a remark which was kindly meant or could be so interpreted. "Well, he liked his dinner today," she would say when Gregor had made a good clearance of his food; and when he had not eaten, which gradually happened more and more often, she would say almost sadly: "Everything's been left standing again."

But although Gregor could get no news directly, he overheard a lot from the neighboring rooms, and as soon as voices were audible, he would run to the door of the room concerned and press his whole body against it. In the first few days especially there was no conversation that did not refer to him somehow, even if only indirectly. For two whole days there were family consultations at every mealtime about what should be done; but also between meals the same subject was discussed, for there were always at least two members of the family at home, since no one wanted to be alone in the flat and to leave it quite empty was unthinkable. And on the very first of these days the household cook—it was not quite clear what and how much she knew of the situation—went down on her knees to his mother and begged leave to go, and when she departed, a quarter of an hour later, gave thanks for her dismissal with tears in her eyes as if for the greatest benefit that could have been conferred on her, and without any prompting swore a solemn oath that she would never say a single word to anyone about what had happened.

Now Gregor's sister had to cook too, helping her mother; true, the cooking did not amount to much, for they ate scarcely anything. Gregor was always hearing one of the family vainly urging another to eat and getting no answer but: "Thanks, I've had all I want," or something similar. Perhaps they drank nothing either. Time and again his sister kept asking his father if he wouldn't like some beer and offered kindly to go and fetch it herself, and when he made no answer suggested that she could ask the concierge to fetch it, so that he need feel no sense of obligation, but then a round "No" came from his father and no more was said about it.

In the course of that very first day Gregor's father explained the family's financial position and prospects to both his mother and his sister. Now and then he rose from the table to get some voucher or memorandum out of the small safe he had rescued from the collapse of his business five years earlier. One could hear him opening the complicated lock and rustling papers out and shutting it again. This statement made by his father was the first cheerful information Gregor had heard since his imprisonment. He had been of the opinion that nothing at all was left over from his father's business, at least his father had never said anything to the contrary, and of course he had not asked him directly. At that time Gregor's sole desire was to do his utmost to help the family to forget as soon as possible the catastrophe which had overwhelmed the business and thrown them all into a state of complete despair. And so he had set to work with unusual ardor and almost overnight had become a commercial traveler instead of a little clerk, with of course much greater chances of earning money, and his success was immediately translated into good round coin which he could lay on the table for his amazed and happy family. These had been fine times, and they had never recurred, at least not with the same sense of glory, although later on Gregor had earned so much money that he was able to meet the expenses of the whole household and did so. They had simply got used to it, both the family and Gregor; the money was gratefully accepted and gladly given, but there was no special uprush of warm feeling. With his sister alone had he remained intimate, and it was a secret plan of his that she, who loved music, unlike himself, and could play movingly on the violin, should be sent next year to study at the Conservatorium, despite the great expense that would entail, which must be made up in some other way. During his brief visits home the Conservatorium was often mentioned in the talks he had with his sister, but always merely as a beautiful dream which could never come true, and his parents discouraged even these innocent references to it; yet Gregor had made up his mind firmly about it and meant to announce the fact with due solemnity on Christmas Day.

Such were the thoughts, completely futile in his present condition, that went through his head as he stood clinging upright to the door and listening. Sometimes out of sheer weariness he had to give up listening and let his head fall negligently against the door, but he always had to pull himself together again at once, for even the slight sound his head made was audible next door and brought all conversation to a stop. "What can he be doing now?" his father would say after a while, obviously turning towards the door, and only then would the interrupted conversation gradually be set going again.

Gregor was now informed as amply as he could wish—for his father tended to repeat himself in his explanations, partly because it was a long time since he had handled such matters and partly because his mother could not always grasp things at once—that a certain amount of investments, a very small amount of it was true, had survived the wreck of their fortunes and had even increased a little because the dividends had not been touched meanwhile. And besides that, the money Gregor brought home every month—he had kept only a few dollars for himself—had never been quite used up and now amounted to a small capital sum. Behind the door Gregor nodded his head eagerly, rejoiced at this evidence of unexpected thrift and foresight. True, he could really have paid off some more of his father's debts to the chief with his extra money, and so brought much nearer the day on which he could quit his job, but doubtless it was better the way his father had arranged it.

Yet this capital was by no means sufficient to let the family live on the interest of it; for one year, perhaps, or at the most two, they could live on the principal, that was all. It was simply a sum that ought not to be touched and should be kept for a rainy day; money for living expenses would have to be earned. Now his father was still hale enough but an old man, and he had done no work for the past five years and could not be expected to do much; during these five years, the first years of leisure in his laborious though unsuccessful life, he had grown rather fat and become sluggish. And Gregor's old mother, how was she to earn a living with her asthma, which troubled her even when she walked through the flat and kept her lying on a sofa every other day panting for breath beside an open window? And was his sister to earn her bread, she who was still a child of seventeen and whose life hitherto had been so pleasant, consisting as it did in dressing herself nicely, sleeping long, helping in the housekeeping, going out to a few modest entertainments and above all playing the violin? At first whenever the need for earning money was mentioned Gregor let go his hold on the door and threw himself down on the cool leather sofa beside it, he felt so hot with shame and grief.

Often he just lay there the long nights through without sleeping at all, scrabbling for hours on the leather. Or he nerved himself to the great effort of pushing an armchair to the window, then crawled up over the window sill and, braced against the chair, leaned against the window panes, obviously in some recollection of the sense of freedom that looking out of a window always used to give him. For in reality day by day things that were even a little way off were growing dimmer to his sight; the hospital across the street, which he used to execrate for being all too often before his eyes, was now quite beyond his range of vision, and if he had not known that he lived in Charlotte Street, a quiet street but still a city street, he might have believed that his window gave on a desert waste where gray sky and gray land blended indistinguishably into each other. His quick-witted sister only needed to observe twice that the armchair stood by the window; after that whenever she had tidied the room she always pushed the chair back to the same place at the window and even left the inner casements open.

If he could have spoken to her and thanked her for all she had to do for him, he could have borne her ministrations better; as it was, they oppressed him.

She certainly tried to make as light as possible of whatever was disagreeable in her task, and as time went on she succeeded, of course, more and more, but time brought more enlightenment to Gregor too. The very way she came in distressed him. Hardly was she in the room when she rushed to the window, without even taking time to shut the door, careful as she was usually to shield the sight of Gregor's room from the others, and as if she were almost suffocating tore the casements open with hasty fingers, standing then in the open draught for a while even in the bitterest cold and drawing deep breaths. This noisy scurry of hers upset Gregor twice a day; he would crouch trembling under the sofa all the time, knowing quite well that she would certainly have spared him such a disturbance had she found it at all possible to stay in his presence without opening the window.

On one occasion, about a month after Gregor's metamorphosis, when there was surely no reason for her to be still startled at his appearance, she came a little earlier than usual and found him gazing out of the window, quite motionless, and thus well placed to look like a bogey. Gregor would not have been surprised had she not come in at all, for she could not immediately open the window while he was there, but not only did she retreat, she jumped back as if in alarm and banged the door shut; a stranger might well have thought that he had been lying in wait for her there meaning to bite her. Of course he hid himself under the sofa at once, but he had to wait until midday before she came again, and she seemed more ill at ease than usual. This made him realize how repulsive the sight of him still was to her, and that it was bound to go on being repulsive, and what an effort it must cost her not to run away even from the sight of the small portion of his body that stuck out from under the sofa. In order to spare her that, therefore, one day he carried a sheet on his back to the sofa—it cost him four hours' labor—and arranged it there in such a way as to hide him completely, so that even if she were to bend down she could not see him. Had she considered the sheet unnecessary, she would certainly have stripped it off the sofa again, for it was clear enough that this curtaining and confining of himself was not likely to conduce Gregor's comfort, but she left it where it was, and Gregor even fancied that he caught a thankful glance from her eye when he lifted the sheet carefully a very little with his head to see how she was taking the new arrangement.

For the first fortnight his parents could not bring themselves to the point of entering his room, and he often heard them expressing their appreciation of his sister's activities, whereas formerly they had frequently scolded her for being as they thought a somewhat useless daughter. But now, both of them often waited outside the door, his father and his mother, while his sister tidied his room, and as soon as she came out she had to tell them exactly how things were in the room, what Gregor had eaten, how he had conducted himself this time and whether there was not perhaps some slight improvement in his condition. His mother, moreover, began relatively soon to want to visit him, but his father and sister dissuaded her at first with arguments which Gregor listened to very attentively and altogether approved. Later, however, she had to be held back by main force, and when she cried out: "Do let me in to Gregor, he is my unfortunate son! Can't you understand that I must go to him?" Gregor thought that it might be well to have her come in, not every day, of course, but perhaps once a week; she understood things, after all, much better than his sister, who was only a child despite the efforts she was making and had perhaps taken on so difficult a task merely out of childish thoughtlessness.

Gregor's desire to see his mother was soon fulfilled. During the daytime he did not want to show himself at the window, out of consideration for his parents, but he could not crawl very far around the few square yards of floor space he had, nor could he bear lying quietly at rest all during the night, while he was fast losing any interest he had ever taken in food, so that for mere recreation he had formed the habit of crawling crisscross over the walls and ceiling. He especially enjoyed hanging suspended from the ceiling; it was much better than lying on the floor; one could breathe more freely; one's body swung and rocked lightly; and in the almost blissful absorption induced by this suspension it could happen to his own surprise that he let go and fell plump on the floor. Yet he now had his body much better under control than formerly, and even such a big fall did him no harm. His sister at once remarked the new distraction Gregor had found for himself—he left traces behind him of the sticky stuff on his soles wherever he crawled—and she got the idea in her head of giving him as wide a field as possible to crawl in and of removing the pieces of furniture that hindered him, above all the chest of drawers and the writing desk. But that was more than she could manage all by herself; she did not dare ask her father to help her; and as for the servant girl, a young creature of sixteen who had had the courage to stay on after the cook's departure, she could not be asked to help, for she had begged as an especial favor that she might keep the kitchen door locked and open it only on a definite summons; so there was nothing left but to apply to her mother at an hour when her father was out. And the old lady did come, with exclamations of joyful eagerness, which, however, died away at the door of Gregor's room. Gregor's sister, of course, went in first, to see that everything was in order before letting his mother enter. In great haste Gregor pulled the sheet lower and rucked it more in folds so that it really looked as if it had been thrown accidentally over the sofa. And this time he did not peer out from under it; he renounced the pleasure of seeing his mother on this occasion and was only glad that she had come at all. "Come in, he's out of sight," said his sister, obviously leading her mother in by the hand. Gregor could now hear the two women struggling to shift the heavy old chest from its place, and his sister claiming the greater part of the labor for herself, without listening to the admonitions of her mother who feared she might overstrain herself. It took a long time. After at least a quarter of an hour's tugging his mother objected that the chest had better be left where it was, for in the first place it was too heavy and could never be got out before his father came home, and standing in the middle of the room like that it would only hamper Gregor's movements, while in the second place it was not at all certain that removing the furniture would be doing a service to Gregor. She was inclined to think to the contrary; the sight of the naked walls made her own heart heavy, and why shouldn't Gregor have the same feeling, considering that he had been used to his furniture for so long and might feel forlorn without it. "And doesn't it look," she concluded in a low voice—in fact she had been almost whispering all the time as if to avoid letting Gregor, whose exact whereabouts she did not know, hear even the tones of her voice, for she was convinced that he could not understand her words— "doesn't it look as if we were showing him, by taking away his furniture, that we have given up hope of his ever getting better and are just leaving him coldly to himself? I think it would be best to keep his room exactly as it has always been, so that when he comes back to us he will find everything unchanged and be able all the more easily to forget what has happened in between."

On hearing these words from his mother Gregor realized that the lack of all direct human speech for the past two months together with the monotony of family life must have confused his mind, otherwise he could not account for the fact that he had quite earnestly looked forward to having his room emptied of furnishing. Did he really want his warm room, so comfortably fitted with old family furniture, to be turned into a naked den in which he would certainly be able to crawl unhampered in all directions but at the price of shedding simultaneously all recollection of his human background? He had indeed been so near the brink of forgetfulness that only the voice of his mother, which he had not heard for so long, had drawn him back from it. Nothing should be taken out of his room; everything must stay as it was; he could not dispense with the good influence of the furniture on his state of mind; and even if the furniture did hamper him in his senseless crawling round and round, that was no drawback but a great advantage.

Unfortunately his sister was of the contrary opinion; she had grown accustomed, and not without reason, to consider herself an expert in Gregor's affairs as against her parents, and so her mother's advice was now enough to make her determined on the removal not only of the chest and the writing desk, which had been her first intention, but of all the furniture except the indispensable sofa. This determination was not, of course, merely the outcome of childish recalcitrance and of the self-confidence she had recently developed so unexpectedly and at such cost; she had in fact perceived that Gregor needed a lot of space to crawl about in, while on the other hand he never used the furniture at all, so far as could be seen. Another factor might have been also the enthusiastic temperament of an adolescent girl, which seeks to indulge itself on every opportunity and which now tempted Grete to exaggerate the horror of her brother's circumstances in order that she might do all the more for him. In a room where Gregor lorded it all alone over empty walls no one save herself was likely ever to set foot.

And so she was not to be moved from her resolve by her mother who seemed moreover to be ill at ease in Gregor's room and therefore unsure of herself, was soon reduced to silence and helped her daughter as best she could to push the chest outside. Now, Gregor could do without the chest, if need be, but the writing desk he must retain. As soon as the two women had got the chest out of his room, groaning as they pushed it, Gregor stuck his head out from under the sofa to see how he might intervene as kindly and cautiously as possible. But as bad luck would have it, his mother was the first to return, leaving Grete clasping the chest in the room next door where she was trying to shift it all by herself, without of course moving it from the spot. His mother however was not accustomed to the sight of him, it might sicken her and so in alarm Gregor backed quickly to the other end of the sofa, yet could not prevent the sheet from swaying a little in front. That was enough to put her on the alert. She paused, stood still for a moment and then went back to Grete.

Although Gregor kept reassuring himself that nothing out of the way was happening, but only a few bits of furniture were being changed round, he soon had to admit that all this trotting to and fro of the two women, their little ejaculations and the scraping of furniture along the floor affected him like a vast disturbance coming from all sides at once, and however much he tucked in his head and legs and cowered to the very floor he was bound to confess that he would not be able to stand it for long. They were clearing his room out; taking away everything he loved; the chest in which he kept his fret saw and other tools was already dragged off; they were now loosening the writing desk which had almost sunk into the floor, the desk at which he had done all his homework when he was at the commercial academy, at the grammar school before that, and, yes, even at the primary school—he had no more time to waste in weighing the good intentions of the two women, whose existence he had by now almost forgotten, for they were so exhausted that they were laboring in silence and nothing could be heard but the heavy scuffing of their feet.

And so he rushed out—the women were just leaning against the writing desk in the next room to give themselves a breather—and four times changed his direction, since he really did not know what to rescue first, then on the wall opposite, which was already otherwise cleared, he was struck by the picture of the lady muffled in so much fur and quickly crawled up to it and pressed himself to the glass, which was a good surface to hold on to and comforted his hot belly. This picture at least, which was entirely hidden beneath him, was going to be removed by nobody. He turned his head towards the door of the living room so as to observe the women when they came back.

They had not allowed themselves much of a rest and were already coming; Grete had twined her arm round her mother and was almost supporting her. "Well, what shall we take now?" said Grete, looking round. Her eyes met Gregor's from the wall. She kept her composure, presumably because of her mother, bent her head down to her mother, to keep her from looking up, and said, although in a fluttering, unpremeditated voice: "Come, hadn't we better go back to the living room for a moment?" Her intentions were clear enough to Gregor, she wanted to bestow her mother in safety and then chase him down from the wall. Well, just let her try it! He clung to his picture and would not give it up. He would rather fly in Grete's face.

But Grete's words had succeeded in disquieting her mother, who took a step to one side, caught sight of the huge brown mass on the flowered wallpaper, and before she was really conscious that what she saw was Gregor screamed in a loud, hoarse voice: "Oh God, oh God!" fell with outspread arms over the sofa as if giving up and did not move. "Gregor!" cried his sister, shaking her fist and glaring at him. This was the first time she had directly addressed him since his metamorphosis. She ran into the next room for some aromatic essence with which to rouse her mother from her fainting fit. Gregor wanted to help too—there was still time to rescue the picture—but he was stuck fast to the glass and had to tear himself loose; he then ran after his sister into the next room as if he could advise her, as he used to do, but then had to stand helplessly behind her; she meanwhile searched among various small bottles and when she turned round started in alarm at the sight of him; one bottle fell on the floor and broke, a splinter of glass cut Gregor's face and some kind of corrosive medicine splashed him; without pausing a moment longer Grete gathered up all the bottles she could carry and ran to her mother with them; she banged the door shut with her foot. Gregor was now cut off from his mother, who was perhaps nearly dying because of him; he dared not open the door for fear of frightening away his sister, who had to stay with her mother; there was nothing he could do but wait; and harrassed by self-reproach and worry he began now to crawl to and fro, over everything, walls, furniture and ceiling, and finally in his despair, when the whole room seemed to be reeling round him, fell down on to the middle of the big table.

A little while elapsed, Gregor was still lying there feebly and all around was quiet, perhaps that was a good omen. Then the doorbell rang. The servant girl was of course locked in her kitchen, and Grete would have to open the door. It was his father. "What's been happening?" were his first words; Grete's face must have told him everything. Grete answered in a muffled voice, apparently hiding her head on his breast: "Mother has been fainting, but she's better now. Gregor's broken loose." "Just what I expected," said his father, "just what I've been telling you, but you women would never listen." It was clear to Gregor that his father had taken the worst interpretation of Grete's all too brief statement and was assuming that Gregor had been guilty of some violent act. Therefore Gregor must now try to propitiate his father, since he had neither time nor means for an explanation. And so he fled to the door of his own room and crouched against it, to let his father see as soon as he came in from the hall that his son had the good intention of getting back into his room immediately and that it was not necessary to drive him there, but that if only the door were opened he would disappear at once.

Yet his father was not in the mood to perceive such fine distinctions. "Ah!" he cried as soon as he appeared, in a tone which sounded at once angry and exultant. Gregor drew his head back from the door and lifted it to look at his father. Truly, this was not the father he had imagined to himself; admittedly he had been too absorbed of late in his new recreation of crawling over the ceiling to take the same interest as before in what was happening elsewhere in the flat, and he ought really to be prepared for some changes. And yet, and yet, could that be his father? The man who used to lie wearily sunk in bed whenever Gregor set out on a business journey; who welcomed him back of an evening lying in a long chair in a dressing gown; who could not really rise to his feet but only lifted his arms in greeting, and on the rare occasions when he did go out with his family, on one or two Sundays a year and on high holidays, walked between Gregor and his mother, who were slow walkers anyhow, even more slowly than they did, muffled in his old greatcoat, shuffling laboriously forward with the help of his crook-handled stick which he set down most cautiously at every step and, whenever he wanted to say anything, nearly always came to a full stop and gathered his escort around him? Now he was standing there in fine shape; dressed in a smart blue uniform with gold buttons, such as bank messengers wear; his strong double chin bulged over the stiff high collar of his jacket; from under his bushy eyebrows his black eyes darted fresh and penetrating glances; his onetime tangled white hair had been combed flat on either side of a shining and carefully exact parting. He pitched his cap, which bore a gold monogram, probably the badge of some bank, in a wide sweep across the whole room on to a sofa and with the tail-ends of his jacket thrown back, his hands in his trouser pockets, advanced with a grim visage towards Gregor. Likely enough he did not himself know what he meant to do; at any rate he lifted his feet uncommonly high, and Gregor was dumbfounded at the enormous size of his shoe soles. But Gregor could not risk standing up to him, aware as he had been from the very first day of his new life that his father believed only the severest measures suitable for dealing with him. And so he ran before his father, stopping when he stopped and scuttled forward again when his father made any kind of move. In this way they circled the room several times without anything decisive happening; indeed the whole operation did not even look like a pursuit because it was carried out so slowly. And so Gregor did not leave the floor, for he feared that his father might take as a piece of peculiar wickedness any excursion of his over the walls or the ceiling. All the same, he could not stay this course much longer, for while his father took one step he had to carry out a whole series of movements. He was already beginning to feel breathless, just as in his former life his lungs had not been very dependable. As he was staggering along, trying to concentrate his energy on running, hardly keeping his eyes open; in his dazed state never even thinking of any other escape than simply going forward; and having almost forgotten that the walls were free to him, which in this room were well provided with finely carved pieces of furniture full of knobs and crevices—suddenly something lightly flung landed close behind him and rolled before him. It was an apple; a second apple followed immediately; Gregor came to a stop in alarm; there was no point in running on, for his father was determined to bombard him. He had filled his pockets with fruit from the dish on the sideboard and was now shying apple after apple, without taking particularly good aim for the moment. The small red apples rolled about the floor as if magnetized and cannoned into each other. An apple thrown without much force grazed Gregor's back and glanced off harmlessly. But another following immediately landed right on his back and sank in; Gregor wanted to drag himself forward, as if this startling, incredible pain could be left behind him; but he felt as if nailed to the spot and flattened himself out in a complete derangement of all his senses. With his last conscious look he saw the door of his room being torn open and his mother rushing out ahead of his screaming sister, in her underbodice, for her daughter had loosened her clothing to let her breathe more freely and recover from her swoon, he saw his mother rushing towards his father, leaving one after another behind her on the floor her loosened petticoats, stumbling over her petticoats straight to his father and embracing him, in complete union with him—but here Gregor's sight began to fail—with her hands clasped round his father's neck as she begged for her son's life.

III

The serious injury done to Gregor, which disabled him for more than a month—the apple went on sticking in his body as a visible reminder, since no one ventured to remove it—seemed to have made even his father recollect that Gregor was a member of the family, despite his present unfortunate and repulsive shape, and ought not to be treated as an enemy, that, on the contrary, family duty required the suppression of disgust and the exercise of patience, nothing but patience.

And although his injury had impaired, probably for ever, his power of movement, and for the time being it took him long, long minutes to creep across his room like an old invalid—there was no question now of crawling up the wall—yet in his own opinion he was sufficiently compensated for this worsening of his condition by the fact that towards evening the living-room door, which he used to watch intently for an hour or two beforehand, was always thrown open, so that lying in the darkness of his room, invisible to the family, he could see them all at the lamp-lit table and listen to their talk, by general consent as it were, very different from his earlier eavesdropping.

True, their intercourse lacked the lively character of former times, which he had always called to mind with a certain wistfulness in the small hotel bedrooms where he had been wont to throw himself down, tired out, on damp bedding. They were now mostly very silent. Soon after supper his father would fall asleep in his armchair; his mother and sister would admonish each other to be silent; his mother, bending low over the lamp, stitched at fine sewing for an underwear firm; his sister, who had taken a job as a salesgirl, was learning shorthand and French in the evenings on the chance of bettering herself. Sometimes his father woke up, and as if quite unaware that he had been sleeping said to his mother: "What a lot of sewing you're doing today!" and at once fell asleep again, while the two women exchanged a tired smile.

With a kind of mulishness his father persisted in keeping his uniform on even in the house; his dressing gown hung uselessly on its peg and he slept fully dressed where he sat, as if he were ready for service at any moment and even here only at the beck and call of his superior. As a result, his uniform, which was not brand-new to start with, began to look dirty, despite all the loving care of the mother and sister to keep it clean, and Gregor often spent whole evenings gazing at the many greasy spots on the garment, gleaming with gold buttons always in a high state of polish, in which the old man sat sleeping in extreme discomfort and yet quite peacefully.

As soon as the clock struck ten his mother tried to rouse his father with gentle words and to persuade him after that to get into bed, for sitting there he could not have a proper sleep and that was what he needed most, since he had to go to duty at six. But with the mulishness that had obsessed him since he became a bank messenger he always insisted on staying longer at the table, although he regularly fell asleep again and in the end only with the greatest trouble could be got out of his armchair and into his bed. However insistently Gregor's mother and sister kept urging him with gentle reminders, he would go on slowly shaking his head for a quarter of an hour, keeping his eyes shut, and refuse to get to his feet. The mother plucked at his sleeve, whispering endearments in his ear, the sister left her lessons to come to her mother's help, but Gregor's father was not to be caught. He would only sink down deeper in his chair. Not until the two women hoisted him up by the armpits did he open his eyes and look at them both, one after the other, usually with the remark: "This is a life. This is the peace and quiet of my old age." And leaning on the two of them he would heave himself up, with difficulty, as if he were a great burden to himself, suffer them to lead him as far as the door and then wave them off and go on alone, while the mother abandoned her needlework and the sister her pen in order to run after him and help him farther.

Who could find time, in this overworked and tired-out family, to bother about Gregor more than was absolutely needful? The household was reduced more and more, the servant girl was turned off; a gigantic bony charwoman with white hair flying round her head came in morning and evening to do the rough work; everything else was done by Gregor's mother, as well as great piles of sewing. Even various family ornaments, which his mother and sister used to wear with pride at parties and celebrations, had to be sold, as Gregor discovered of an evening from hearing them all discuss the prices obtained. But what they lamented most was the fact that they could not leave the flat which was much too big for their present circumstances, because they could not think of any way to shift Gregor. Yet Gregor saw well enough that consideration for him was not the main difficulty preventing the removal, for they could have easily shifted him in some suitable box with a few air holes in it; what really kept them from moving into another flat was rather their own complete hopelessness and the belief that they had been singled out for a misfortune such as had never happened to any of their relations or acquaintances. They fulfilled to the uttermost all that the world demands of poor people, the father fetched breakfast for the small clerks in the bank, the mother devoted her energy to making underwear for strangers, the sister trotted to and fro behind the counter at the behest of customers, but more than this they had not the strength to do. And the wound in Gregor's back began to nag at him afresh when his mother and sister, after getting his father into bed, came back again, left their work lying, drew close to each other and sat cheek by cheek; when his mother, pointing towards his room, said: "Shut that door now, Grete," and he was left again in darkness, while next door the women mingled their tears or perhaps sat dry-eyed staring at the table.

Gregor hardly slept at all by night or by day. He was often haunted by the idea that next time the door opened he would take the family's affairs in hand again just as he used to do; once more, after this long interval, there appeared in his thoughts the figures of the chief and the chief clerk, the commercial travelers and the apprentices, the porter who was so dull-witted, two or three friends in other firms, a chambermaid in one of the rural hotels, a sweet and fleeting memory, a cashier in a milliner's shop, whom he had wooed earnestly but too slowly—they all appeared, together with strangers or people he had quite forgotten, but instead of helping him and his family they were one and all unapproachable and he was glad when they vanished. At other times he would not be in the mood to bother about his family, he was only filled with rage at the way they were neglecting him, and although he had no clear idea of what he might care to eat he would make plans for getting into the larder to take the food that was after all his due, even if he were not hungry. His sister no longer took thought to bring him what might especially please him, but in the morning and at noon before she went to business hurriedly pushed into his room with her foot any food that was available, and in the evening cleared it out again with one sweep of the broom, heedless of whether it had been merely tasted, or—as most frequently happened—left untouched. The cleaning of his room, which she now did always in the evenings, could not have been more hastily done. Streaks of dirt stretched along the walls, here and there lay balls of dust and filth. At first Gregor used to station himself in some particularly filthy corner when his sister arrived, in order to reproach her with it, so to speak. But he could have sat there for weeks without getting her to make any improvements; she could see the dirt as well as he did, but she had simply made up her mind to leave it alone. And yet, with a touchiness that was new to her, which seemed anyhow to have infected the whole family, she jealously guarded her claim to be the sole caretaker of Gregor's room. His mother once subjected his room to a thorough cleaning, which was achieved only by means of several buckets of water—all this dampness of course upset Gregor too and he lay widespread, sulky and motionless on the sofa—but she was well punished for it. Hardly had his sister noticed the changed aspect of his room that evening than she rushed in high dudgeon into the living room and, despite the imploringly raised hands of her mother, burst into a storm of weeping, while her parents—her father had of course been startled out of his chair—looked on at first in helpless amazement; then they too began to go into action; the father reproached the mother on his right for not having left the cleaning of Gregor's room to his sister; shrieked at the sister on his left that never again was she to be allowed to clean Gregor's room; while the mother tried to pull the father into his bedroom, since he was beyond himself with agitation; the sister, shaken with sobs, then beat upon the table with her small fists; and Gregor hissed loudly with rage because not one of them thought of shutting the door to spare him such a spectacle and so much noise.

Still, even if the sister, exhausted by her daily work, had grown tired of looking after Gregor as she did formerly, there was no need for his mother's intervention or for Gregor's being neglected at all. The charwoman was there. This old widow, whose strong bony frame had enabled her to survive the worst a long life could offer, by no means recoiled from Gregor. Without being in the least curious she had once by chance opened the door of his room and at the sight of Gregor, who, taken by surprise, began to rush to and fro although no one was chasing him, merely stood there with her arms folded. From that time she never failed to open his door a little for a moment, morning and evening, to have a look at him. At first she even used to call him to her, with words which apparently she took to be friendly, such as: "Come along, then, you old dung beetle!" or "Look at the old dung beetle, then!" To such allocutions Gregor made no answer, but stayed motionless where he was, as if the door had never opened. Instead of being allowed to disturb him so senselessly whenever the whim took her, she should rather have been ordered to clean out his room daily, that charwoman! Once, early in the morning—heavy rain was lashing on the windowpanes, perhaps a sign that spring was on the way—Gregor was so exasperated when she began addressing him again that he ran at her, as if to attack her, although slowly and feebly enough. But the charwoman instead of showing fright merely lifted high a chair that happened to be beside the door, and as she stood there with her mouth wide open it was clear that she meant to shut it only when she brought the chair down on Gregor's back. "So you're not coming any nearer?" she asked, as Gregor turned away again, and quietly put the chair back into the corner.

Gregor was now eating hardly anything. Only when he happened to pass the food laid out for him did he take a bit of something in his mouth as a pastime, kept it there for an hour at a time and usually spat it out again. At first he thought it was chagrin over the state of his room that prevented him from eating, yet he soon got used to the various changes in his room. It had become a habit in the family to push into his room things there was no room for elsewhere, and there were plenty of these now, since one of the rooms had been let to three lodgers. These serious gentlemen—all three of them with full beards, as Gregor once observed through a crack in the door—had a passion for order, not only in their own room but, since they were now members of the household, in all its arrangements, especially in the kitchen. Superfluous, not to say dirty, objects they could not bear. Besides, they had brought with them most of the furnishings they needed. For this reason many things could be dispensed with that it was no use trying to sell but that should not be thrown away either. All of them found their way into Gregor's room. The ash can likewise and the kitchen garbage can. Anything that was not needed for the moment was simply flung into Gregor's room by the charwoman, who did everything in a hurry; fortunately Gregor usually saw only the object, whatever it was, and the hand that held it. Perhaps she intended to take the things away again as time and opportunity offered, or to collect them until she could throw them all out in a heap, but in fact they just lay wherever she happened to throw them, except when Gregor pushed his way through the junk heap and shifted it somewhat, at first out of necessity, because he had not room enough to crawl, but later with increasing enjoyment, although after such excursions, being sad and weary to death, he would lie motionless for hours. And since the lodgers often ate their supper at home in the common living room, the living-room door stayed shut many an evening, yet Gregor reconciled himself quite easily to the shutting of the door, for often enough on evenings when it was opened he had disregarded it entirely and lain in the darkest corner of his room, quite unnoticed by the family. But on one occasion the charwoman left the door open a little and it stayed ajar even when the lodgers came in for supper and the lamp was lit. They set themselves at the top end of the table where formerly Gregor and his father and mother had eaten their meals, unfolded their napkins and took knife and fork in hand. At once his mother appeared in the other doorway with a dish of meat and close behind her his sister with a dish of potatoes piled high. The food steamed with a thick vapor. The lodgers bent over the food set before them as if to scrutinize it before eating, in fact the man in the middle, who seemed to pass for an authority with the other two, cut a piece of meat as it lay on the dish, obviously to discover if it were tender or should be sent back to the kitchen. He showed satisfaction, and Gregor's mother and sister, who had been watching anxiously, breathed freely and began to smile.

The family itself took its meals in the kitchen. None the less, Gregor's father came into the living room before going into the kitchen and with one prolonged bow, cap in hand, made a round of the table. The lodgers all stood up and murmured something in their beards. When they were alone again they ate their food in almost complete silence. It seemed remarkable to Gregor that among the various noises coming from the table he could always distinguish the sound of their masticating teeth, as if this were a sign to Gregor that one needed teeth in order to eat, and that with toothless jaws even of the finest make one could do nothing. "I'm hungry enough," said Gregor sadly to himself, "but not for that kind of food. How these lodgers are stuffing themselves, and here am I dying of starvation!"

On that very evening—during the whole of his time there Gregor could not remember ever having heard the violin—the sound of violin-playing came from the kitchen. The lodgers had already finished their supper, the one in the middle had brought out a newspaper and given the other two a page apiece, and now they were leaning back at ease reading and smoking. When the violin began to play they pricked up their ears, got to their feet, and went on tiptoe to the hall door where they stood huddled together. Their movements must have been heard in the kitchen, for Gregor's father called out: "Is the violin-playing disturbing you gentlemen? It can be stopped at once." "On the contrary," said the middle lodger, "could not Fräulein Samsa come and play in this room, beside us, where it is much more convenient and comfortable?" "Oh certainly," cried Gregor's father, as if he were the violin-player. The lodgers came back into the living room and waited. Presently Gregor's father arrived with the music stand, his mother carrying the music and his sister with the violin. His sister quietly made everything ready to start playing; his parents, who had never let rooms before and so had an exaggerated idea of the courtesy due to lodgers, did not venture to sit down on their own chairs; his father leaned against the door, the right hand thrust between two buttons of his livery coat, which was formally buttoned up; but his mother was offered a chair by one of the lodgers and, since she left the chair just where he had happened to put it, sat down in a corner to one side.

Gregor's sister began to play; the father and mother, from either side, intently watched the movements of her hands. Gregor, attracted by the playing ventured to move forward a little until his head was actually inside the living room. He felt hardly any surprise at his growing lack of consideration for the others; there had been a time when he prided himself on being considerate. And yet just on this occasion he had more reason than ever to hide himself, since owing to the amount of dust which lay thick in his room and rose into the air at the slightest movement, he too was covered with dust; fluff and hair and remnants of food trailed with him, caught on his back and along his sides; his indifference to everything was much too great for him to turn on his back and scrape himself clean on the carpet, as once he had done several times a day. And in spite of his condition, no shame deterred him from advancing a little over the spotless floor of the living room.

To be sure, no one was aware of him. The family was entirely absorbed in the violin-playing; the lodgers, however, who first of all had stationed themselves, hands in pockets, much too close behind the music stand so that they could all have read the music, which must have bothered his sister, had soon retreated to the window, half-whispering with downbent heads, and stayed there while his father turned an anxious eye on them. Indeed, they were making it more than obvious that they had been disappointed in their expectation of hearing good or enjoyable violin-playing, that they had had more than enough of the performance and only out of courtesy suffered a continued disturbance of their peace. From the way they all kept blowing the smoke of their cigars high in the air through nose and mouth one could divine their irritation. And yet Gregor's sister was playing so beautifully. Her face leaned sideways, intently and sadly her eyes followed the notes of music. Gregor crawled a little farther forward and lowered his head to the ground so that it might be possible for his eyes to meet hers. Was he an animal, that music had such an effect upon him? He felt as if the way were opening before him to the unknown nourishment he craved. He was determined to push forward till he reached his sister, to pull at her skirt and so let her know that she was to come into his room with her violin, for no one here appreciated her playing as he would appreciate it. He would never let her out of his room, at least, not so long as he lived; his frightful appearance would become, for the first time, useful to him; he would watch all the doors of his room at once and spit at intruders; but his sister should need no constraint, she should stay with him of her own free will; she should sit beside him on the sofa, bend down her ear to him and hear him confide that he had had the firm intention of sending her to the Conservatorium, and that, but for his mishap, last Christmas—surely Christmas was long past?—he would have announced it to everybody without allowing a single objection. After this confession his sister would be so touched that she would burst into tears, and Gregor would then raise himself to her shoulder and kiss her on the neck, which, now that she went to business, she kept free of any ribbon or collar.

"Mr. Samsa!" cried the middle lodger, to Gregor's father, and pointed, without wasting any more words, at Gregor, now working himself slowly forwards. The violin fell silent, the middle lodger first smiled to his friends with a shake of the head and then looked at Gregor again. Instead of driving Gregor out, his father seemed to think it more needful to begin by soothing down the lodgers, although they were not at all agitated and apparently found Gregor more entertaining than the violin-playing. He hurried towards them and, spreading out his arms, tried to urge them back into their own room and at the same time to block their view of Gregor. They now began to be really a little angry, one could not tell whether because of the old man's behavior or because it had just dawned on them that all unwittingly they had such a neighbor as Gregor next door. They demanded explanations of his father, they waved their arms like him, tugged uneasily at their beards, and only with reluctance backed towards their room. Meanwhile Gregor's sister, who stood there as if lost when her playing was so abruptly broken off, came to life again, pulled herself together all at once after standing for a while holding violin and bow in nervelessly hanging hands and staring at her music, pushed her violin into the lap of her mother, who was still sitting in her chair fighting asthmatically for breath, and ran into the lodgers' room to which they were now being shepherded by her father rather more quickly than before. One could see the pillows and blankets on the beds flying under her accustomed fingers and being laid in order. Before the lodgers had actually reached their room she had finished making the beds and slipped out.

The old man seemed once more to be so possessed by his mulish self-assertiveness that he was forgetting all the respect he should show to his lodgers. He kept driving them on and driving them on until in the very door of the bedroom the middle lodger stamped his foot loudly on the floor and so brought him to a halt. "I beg to announce," said the lodger, lifting one hand and looking also at Gregor's mother and sister, "that because of the disgusting conditions prevailing in this household and family"—here he spat on the floor with emphatic brevity—"I give you notice on the spot. Naturally I won't pay you a penny for the days I have lived here, on the contrary I shall consider bringing an action for damages against you, based on claims—believe me—that will be easily susceptible of proof." He ceased and stared straight in front of him, as if he expected something. In fact his two friends at once rushed into the breach with these words: "And we too give notice on the spot." On that he seized the door-handle and shut the door with a slam.

Gregor's father, groping with his hands, staggered forward and fell into his chair; it looked as if he were stretching himself there for his ordinary evening nap, but the marked jerkings of his head, which was as if uncontrollable, showed that he was far from asleep. Gregor had simply stayed quietly all the time on the spot where the lodgers had espied him. Disappointment at the failure of his plan, perhaps also the weakness arising from extreme hunger, made it impossible for him to move. He feared, with a fair degree of certainty, that at any moment the general tension would discharge itself in a combined attack upon him, and he lay waiting. He did not react even to the noise made by the violin as it fell off his mother's lap from under her trembling fingers and gave out a resonant note.

"My dear parents," said his sister, slapping her hand on the table by way of introduction, "things can't go on like this. Perhaps you don't realize that, but I do. I won't utter my brother's name in the presence of this creature, and so all I say is: we must try to get rid of it. We've tried to look after it and to put up with it as far as is humanly possible, and I don't think anyone could reproach us in the slightest."

"She is more than right," said Gregor's father to himself. His mother, who was still choking for lack of breath, began to cough hollowly into her hand with a wild look in her eyes.

His sister rushed over to her and held her forehead. His father's thoughts seemed to have lost their vagueness at Grete's words, he sat more upright, fingering his service cap that lay among the plates still lying on the table from the lodgers' supper, and from time to time looked at the still form of Gregor.

"We must try to get rid of it," his sister now said explicitly to her father, since her mother was coughing too much to hear a word, "it will be the death of both of you, I can see that coming. When one has to work as hard as we do, all of us, one can't stand this continual torment at home on top of it. At least I can't stand it any longer." And she burst into such a passion of sobbing that her tears dropped on her mother's face, where she wiped them off mechanically.

"My dear," said the old man sympathetically, and with evident understanding, "but what can we do?"

Gregor's sister merely shrugged her shoulders to indicate the feeling of helplessness that had now overmastered her during her weeping fit, in contrast to her former confidence.

"If he could understand us," said her father, half questioningly; Grete, still sobbing, vehemently waved a hand to show how unthinkable that was.

"If he could understand us," repeated the old man, shutting his eyes to consider his daughter's conviction that understanding was impossible, "then perhaps we might come to some agreement with him. But as it is—"

"He must go," cried Gregor's sister, "that's the only solution, Father. You must just try to get rid of the idea that this is Gregor. The fact that we've believed it for so long is the root of all our trouble. But how can it be Gregor? If this were Gregor, he would have realized long ago that human beings can't live with such a creature, and he'd have gone away on his own accord. Then we wouldn't have any brother, but we'd be able to go on living and keep his memory in honor. As it is, this creature persecutes us, drives away our lodgers, obviously wants the whole apartment to himself and would have us all sleep in the gutter. Just look, Father," she shrieked all at once, "he's at it again!" And in an excess of panic that was quite incomprehensible to Gregor, she even quitted her mother, literally thrusting the chair from her as if she would rather sacrifice her mother than stay so near to Gregor, and rushed behind her father, who also rose up, being simply upset by her agitation, and half-spread his arms out as if to protect her.

Yet Gregor had not the slightest intention of frightening anyone, far less his sister. He had only begun to turn round in order to crawl back to his room but it was certainly a startling operation to watch, since because of his disabled condition he could not execute the difficult turning movements except by lifting his head and then bracing it against the floor over and over again. He paused and looked round. His good intentions seemed to have been recognized; the alarm had only been momentary. Now they were all watching him in melancholy silence. His mother lay in her chair, her legs stiffly outstretched and pressed together, her eyes almost closing for sheer weariness; his father and his sister were sitting beside each other, his sister's arm around the old man's neck.

Perhaps I can go on turning round now, thought Gregor, and began his labors again. He could not stop himself from panting with the effort, and had to pause now and then to take breath. Nor did anyone harass him, he was left entirely to himself. When he had completed the turn-round he began at once to crawl straight back. He was amazed at the distance separating him from his room and could not understand how in his weak state he had managed to accomplish the same journey so recently, almost without remarking it. Intent on crawling as fast as possible, he barely noticed that not a single word, not an ejaculation from his family, interfered with his progress. Only when he was already in the doorway did he turn his head round, not completely, for his neck muscles were getting stiff, but enough to see that nothing had changed behind him except that his sister had risen to her feet. His last glance fell on his mother, who was not quite overcome by sleep.

Hardly was he well inside his room when the door was hastily pushed shut, bolted and locked. The sudden noise in his rear startled him so much that his little legs gave beneath him. It was his sister who had shown much haste. She had been standing ready waiting and had made a light spring forward. Gregor had not even heard her coming, and she cried "At last!" to her parents as she turned the key in the lock.

"And what now?" said Gregor to himself, looking round in the darkness. Soon he made the discovery that he was now unable to stir a limb. This did not surprise him, rather it seemed unnatural that he should ever actually have been able to move on these feeble little legs. Otherwise he felt relatively comfortable. True, his whole body was aching, but it seemed that the pain was gradually growing less and would finally pass away. The rotting apple in his back and the inflamed area around it, all covered with soft dust, already hardly troubled him. He thought of his family with tenderness and love. The decision that he must disappear was one that he held to even more strongly than his sister, if that were possible. In this state of vacant and peaceful meditation he remained until the tower clock struck three in the morning. The first broadening of light in the world outside the window entered his consciousness once more. Then his head sank to the floor of its own accord and from his nostrils came the last faint flicker of his breath.

When the charwoman arrived early in the morning—what between her strength and her impatience she slammed all the doors so loudly, never mind how often she had been begged not to do so, that no one in the whole apartment could enjoy any quiet sleep after her arrival—she noticed nothing unusual as she took her customary peep into Gregor's room. She thought he was lying motionless on purpose, pretending to be in the sulks; she credited him with every kind of intelligence. Since she happened to have the long-handled broom in her hand she tried to tickle him up with it from the doorway. When that too produced no reaction she felt provoked and poked at him a little harder, and only when she had pushed him along the floor without meeting any resistance was her attention aroused. It did not take her long to establish the truth of the matter, and her eyes widened, she let out a whistle, yet did not waste much time over it but tore open the door of the Samsas' bedroom and yelled into the darkness at the top of her voice: "Just look at this, it's dead; it's lying here dead and done for!"

Mr. and Mrs. Samsa started up in their double bed and before they realized the nature of the charwoman's announcement had some difficulty in overcoming the shock of it. But then they got out of bed quickly, one on either side. Mr. Samsa throwing a blanket over his shoulders, Mrs. Samsa in nothing but her nightgown; in this array they entered Gregor's room. Meanwhile the door of the living room opened, too, where Grete had been sleeping since the advent of the lodgers; she was completely dressed as if she had not been to bed, which seemed to be confirmed also by the paleness of her face. "Dead?" said Mrs. Samsa, looking questioningly at the charwoman, although she could have investigated for herself and the fact was obvious enough without investigation. "I should say so," said the charwoman, proving her words by pushing Gregor's corpse a long way to one side with her broomstick. Mrs. Samsa made a movement as if to stop her, but checked it. "Well," said Mr. Samsa, "now thanks be to God." He crossed himself, and the three women followed his example. Grete, whose eyes never left the corpse, said: "Just see how thin he was. It's such a long time since he's eaten anything. The food came out again just as it went in." Indeed, Gregor's body was completely flat and dry, as could only now be seen when it was no longer supported by the legs and nothing prevented one from looking closely at it.

"Come in beside us, Grete, for a little while," said Mrs. Samsa with a tremulous smile, and Grete, not without looking back at the corpse, followed her parents into their bedroom. The charwoman shut the door and opened the window wide. Although it was so early in the morning a certain softness was perceptible in the fresh air. After all, it was already the end of March.

The three lodgers emerged from their room and were surprised to see no breakfast; they had been forgotten. "Where's our breakfast?" said the middle lodger peevishly to the charwoman. But she put her finger to her lips and hastily, without a word, indicated by gestures that they should go into Gregor's room. They did so and stood, their hands in the pockets of their somewhat shabby coats, around Gregor's corpse in the room where it was now fully light.

At that the door of the Samsas' bedroom opened and Mr. Samsa appeared in his uniform, his wife on one arm, his daughter on the other. They all looked a little as if they had been crying; from time to time Grete hid her face on her father's arm.

"Leave my house at once!" said Mr. Samsa, and pointed to the door without disengaging himself from the women. "What do you mean by that?" said the middle lodger, taken somewhat aback, with a feeble smile. The two others put their hands behind them and kept rubbing them together, as if in gleeful expectation of a fine set-to in which they were bound to come off the winners. "I mean just what I say," answered Mr. Samsa, and advanced in a straight line with his two companions towards the lodger. He stood his ground at first quietly, looking at the floor as if his thoughts were taking a new pattern in his head. "Then let us go, by all means," he said, and looked up at Mr. Samsa as if in a sudden access of humility he were expecting some renewed sanction for this decision. Mr. Samsa merely nodded briefly once or twice with meaning eyes. Upon that the lodger really did go with long strides into the hall, his two friends had been listening and had quite stopped rubbing their hands for some moments and now went scuttling after him as if afraid that Mr. Samsa might get into the hall before them and cut them off from their leader. In the hall they all three took their hats from the rack, their sticks from the umbrella stand, bowed in silence and quitted the apartment. With a suspiciousness which proved quite unfounded Mr. Samsa and the two women followed them out to the landing; leaning over the banister they watched the three figures slowly but surely going down the long stairs, vanishing from sight at a certain turn of the staircase on every floor and coming into view again after a moment or so; the more they dwindled, the more the Samsa family's interest in them dwindled, and when a butcher's boy met them and passed them on the stairs coming up proudly with a tray on his head, Mr. Samsa and the two women soon left the landing and as if a burden had been lifted from them went back into their apartment.

They decided to spend this day in resting and going for a stroll; they had not only deserved such a respite from work, but absolutely needed it. And so they sat down at the table and wrote three notes of excuse, Mr. Samsa to his board of management, Mrs. Samsa to her employer and Grete to the head of her firm. While they were writing, the charwoman came in to say that she was going now, since her morning's work was finished. At first they only nodded without looking up, but as she kept hovering there they eyed her irritably. "Well?" said Mr. Samsa. The charwoman stood grinning in the doorway as if she had good news to impart to the family but meant not to say a word unless properly questioned. The small ostrich feather standing upright on her hat, which had annoyed Mr. Samsa ever since she was engaged, was waving gaily in all directions. "Well, what is it then?" asked Mrs. Samsa, who obtained more respect from the charwoman than the others. "Oh," said the charwoman, giggling so amiably that she could not at once continue, "just this, you don't need to bother about how to get rid of the thing next door. It's been seen to already." Mrs. Samsa and Grete bent over their letters again, as if preoccupied; Mr. Samsa, who perceived that she was eager to begin describing it all in detail, stopped her with a decisive hand. But since she was not allowed to tell her story, she remembered the great hurry she was in, being obviously deeply huffed; "Bye, everybody," she said, whirling off violently, and departed with a frightful slamming of doors.

"She'll be given notice tonight," said Mr. Samsa, but neither from his wife nor his daughter did he get any answer, for the charwoman seemed to have shattered again the composure they had barely achieved. They rose, went to the window and stayed there, clasping each other tight. Mr. Samsa turned in his chair to look at them and quietly observed them for a little. Then he called out: "Come along now, do. Let bygones be bygones. And you might have some consideration for me." The two of them complied at once, hastened to him, caressed him and quickly finished their letters.

Then they all three left the apartment together, which was more than they had done for months, and went by tram into the open country outside the town. The tram, in which they were the only passengers, was filled with warm sunshine. Leaning comfortably back in their seats they canvassed their prospects for the future, and it appeared on closer inspection that these were not at all bad, for the jobs they had got, which so far they had never really discussed with each other, were all three admirable and likely to lead to better things later on. The greatest immediate improvement in their condition would of course arise from moving to another house; they wanted to take a smaller and cheaper but also better situated and more easily run apartment than the one they had, which Gregor had selected. While they were thus conversing, it struck both Mr. and Mrs. Samsa, almost at the same moment, as they became aware of their daughter's increasing vivacity, that in spite of all the sorrow of recent times, which had made her cheeks pale, she had bloomed into a pretty girl with a good figure. They grew quieter and half unconsciously exchanged glances of complete agreement, having come to the conclusion that it would soon be time to find a good husband for her. And it was like a confirmation of their new dreams and excellent intentions that at the end of their journey their daughter sprang to her feet first and stretched her young body.

Fact Questions and Exercises

1. What was Gregor's profession before his metamorphosis?
2. In the early part of the story, what details indicate that Gregor has been a lonely and insecure person?
3. What details indicate that Gregor does not immediately accept the fact that he has become an insect?
4. With whom does Gregor live? Approximately how old do you think he is?
5. What is the first indication in the story that other people suspect Gregor is no longer human?
6. Who has supported the family? Which details reveal this information?
7. Which member of the family shows the most compassion for Gregor? Point out details to support your answer.
8. Does Gregor become an insect mentally as well as physically? Does he retain any of his powers of human thought and sensibilities? Give facts to support your answer.
9. Why doesn't Mrs. Samsa want to remove the furniture from Gregor's room?
10. Why does Gregor leave his room on the day the furniture is moved?
11. What changes in the living arrangements of the home cause Gregor's room to be used as a "junk" room?
12. What musical instrument does Grete begin to play? How does Gregor react to her playing?
13. What finally makes the family decide that it must get rid of Gregor?
14. Describe Mr. Samsa's attitude toward his insect son. What scenes help you determine this attitude?
15. Who is the first to discover that Gregor has died?

For Discussion and Writing

1. Check the definition of "climax" in the Guide to Literary Terms. Where is the climax in the story? Is it, as some critics claim, in the first sentence? If so, do you think the story would be improved if Kafka had waited to reveal Gregor's metamorphosis?
2. Characterize Gregor. How is his becoming an insect an extension of the person he was before?
3. Are there indications in the story that a desire for money has caused the family to lose sight of other values? Explain. Is this desire partially responsible for Gregor's change?
4. Do the other members of the family undergo a "metamorphosis" also? Discuss the theme of change as it appears at different levels in the story.

Consider, for instance, whether Gregor develops "manly" traits—traits he never had as a human being.

5. Gregor "starves" to death; what kind of starvation is Kafka talking about? Is it simply lack of food?

6. Consider the themes of isolation and failure of communication in *The Metamorphosis*. Does Kafka give any facts to support these themes? Does he present any hope that isolation can be avoided? Does Gregor's drastic change have any positive effects?

Philip Roth [1933–   ]

Roth was born in Newark, New Jersey, and was educated at Bucknell and the University of Chicago. He has taught at the University of Iowa, Princeton, and the Universities of Pennsylvania and Chicago; his first novel, *Letting Go* (1962), is a fictional account of his student and teacher experiences. His first collection of stories, *Goodbye, Columbus* (from which the following short novel is taken), brought Roth immediate fame when it was published in 1959. He has since published a number of acclaimed novels, including *Portnoy's Complaint* (1969), *Our Gang* (1971), and *My Life as a Man* (1974). Roth is considered to be one of America's most talented post-World War II writers. His works demonstrate an adept use of dialogue and sharp social satire, and a pervasive, if sometimes outrageous, sense of humor.

Goodbye, Columbus

"The heart is half a prophet."
YIDDISH PROVERB

The first time I saw Brenda she asked me to hold her glasses. Then she stepped out to the edge of the diving board and looked foggily into the pool; it could have been drained, myopic Brenda would never have known it. She dove beautifully, and a moment later she was swimming back to the side of the pool, her head of short-clipped auburn hair held up, straight ahead of her, as though it were a rose on a long stem. She glided to the edge and then was beside me. "Thank you," she said, her eyes watery though not from the water. She extended a hand for her glasses but did not put them on until she turned and headed away. I watched her move off. Her hands suddenly appeared behind her. She caught the bottom of her suit between thumb and index finger and flicked what flesh had been showing back where it belonged. My blood jumped.

That night, before dinner, I called her.

"Who are you calling?" my Aunt Gladys asked.

"Some girl I met today."

"Doris introduced you?"

"Doris wouldn't introduce me to the guy who drains the pool, Aunt Gladys."

"Don't criticize all the time. A cousin's a cousin. How did you meet her?"

"I didn't really meet her. I saw her."

"Who is she?"

"Her last name is Patimkin."

"Patimkin I don't know," Aunt Gladys said, as if she knew anybody who belonged to the Green Lane Country Club. "You're going to call her you don't know her?"

"Yes," I explained. "I'll introduce myself."

"Casanova," she said, and went back to preparing my uncle's dinner. None of us ate together: my Aunt Gladys ate at five o'clock, my cousin Susan at five-thirty, me at six, and my uncle at six-thirty. There is nothing to explain this beyond the fact that my aunt is crazy.

"Where's the suburban phone book?" I asked after pulling out all the books tucked under the telephone table.

"What?"

"The suburban phone book. I want to call Short Hills."

"That skinny book? What, I gotta clutter my house with that, I never use it?"

"Where is it?"

"Under the dresser where the leg came off."

"For God's sake," I said.

"Call information better. You'll go yanking around there, you'll mess up my drawers. Don't bother me, you see your uncle'll be home soon. I haven't even fed *you* yet."

"Aunt Gladys, suppose tonight we all eat together. It's hot, it'll be easier for you."

"Sure, I should serve four different meals at once. You eat pot roast, Susan with the cottage cheese, Max has steak. Friday night is his steak night, I wouldn't deny him. And I'm having a little cold chicken. I should jump up and down twenty different times? What am I, a workhorse?"

"Why don't we all have steak, or cold chicken—"

"Twenty years I'm running a house. Go call your girl friend."

But when I called, Brenda Patimkin wasn't home. She's having dinner at the club, a woman's voice told me. Will she be home after (my voice was two octaves higher than a choirboy's)? I don't know, the voice said, she may go driving golf balls. Who is this? I mumbled some words—nobody she wouldn't know I'll call back no message thank you sorry to bother . . . I hung up somewhere along in there. Then my aunt called me and I steeled myself for dinner.

She pushed the black whirring fan up to *High* and that way it managed to stir the cord that hung from the kitchen light.

"What kind of soda you want? I got ginger ale, plain seltzer, black raspberry, and bottle cream soda I could open up."

"None, thank you."

"You want water?"

"I don't drink with my meals. Aunt Gladys, I've told you that every day for a year already—"

"Max could drink a whole case with his chopped liver only. He works hard all day. If you worked hard you'd drink more."

At the stove she heaped up a plate with pot roast, gravy, boiled potatoes, and peas and carrots. She put it in front of me and I could feel the heat of the food in my face. Then she cut two pieces of rye bread and put that next to me, on the table.

I forked a potato in half and ate it, while Aunt Gladys, who had seated herself across from me, watched. "You don't want bread," she said, "I wouldn't cut it it should go stale."

"I *want* bread," I said.

"You don't like with seeds, do you?"

I tore a piece of bread in half and ate it.

"How's the meat?" she said.

"Okay. Good."

"You'll fill yourself with potatoes and bread, the meat you'll leave over I'll have to throw it out."

Suddenly she leaped up from the chair. "Salt!" When she returned to the table she plunked a salt shaker down in front of me—pepper wasn't served in her home: she'd heard on Galen Drake that it was not absorbed by the body, and it was disturbing to Aunt Gladys to think that anything she served might pass through a gullet, stomach, and bowel just for the pleasure of the trip.

"You're going to pick the peas out is all? You tell me that, I wouldn't buy with the carrots."

"I love carrots," I said, "I love them." And to prove it, I dumped half of them down my throat and the other half onto my trousers.

"Pig," she said.

Though I am very fond of desserts, especially fruit, I chose not to have any. I wanted, this hot night, to avoid the conversation that revolved around my choosing fresh fruit over canned fruit, or canned fruit over fresh fruit; whichever I preferred, Aunt Gladys always had an abundance of the other jamming her refrigerator like stolen diamonds. "He wants canned peaches, I have a refrigerator full of grapes I have to get rid of . . ." Life was a throwing off for poor Aunt Gladys, her greatest joys were taking out the garbage, emptying her pantry, and making threadbare bundles for what she still referred to as the Poor Jews in Palestine. I only hope she dies with an empty refrigerator, otherwise she'll ruin eternity for everyone else, what with her Velveeta turning green, and her naval oranges growing fuzzy jackets down below.

My Uncle Max came home and while I dialed Brenda's number once again, I could hear soda bottles being popped open in the kitchen. The voice that answered this time was high, curt, and tired. "Hullo."

I launched into my speech. "Hello-Brenda-Brenda-you-don't-know-me - that - is - you - don't - know - my - name - but - I - held - your - glasses - for - you - this - afternoon - at - the - club . . . You asked - me - to - I'm - not - a - member - my - cousin - Doris - is - Doris - Klugman - I - asked - who - you - were . . ." I breathed, gave her a chance to speak, and then went ahead and answered the silence on the other end. "Doris? She's the one who's always reading *War and Peace.* That's how I know it's the summer, when Doris is reading *War and Peace.*" Brenda didn't laugh; right from the start she was a practical girl.

"What's your name?" she said.

"Neil Klugman. I held your glasses at the board, remember?"

She answered me with a question of her own, one, I'm sure, that is an embarrassment to both the homely and the fair. "What do you look like?"

"I'm . . . dark."

"Are you a Negro?"

"No," I said.

"What *do* you look like?"

"May I come see you tonight and show you?"

"That's nice," she laughed. "I'm playing tennis tonight."

"I thought you were driving golf balls."

"I drove them already."

"How about after tennis?"

"I'll be sweaty after," Brenda said.

It was not to warn me to clothespin my nose and run in the opposite direction; it was a fact, it apparently didn't bother Brenda, but she wanted it recorded.

"I don't mind," I said, and hoped by my tone to earn a niche somewhere between the squeamish and the grubby. "Can I pick you up?"

She did not answer a minute; I heard her muttering, "Doris Klugman, Doris Klugman . . ." Then she said, "Yes, Briarpath Hills, eight-fifteen."

"I'll be driving a—" I hung back with the year, "a tan Plymouth. So you'll know me. How will I know you?" I said with a sly, awful laugh.

"I'll be sweating," she said and hung up.

Once I'd driven out of Newark, past Irvington and the packed-in tangle of railroad crossings, switchmen shacks, lumberyards, Dairy Queens, and used-car lots, the night grew cooler. It was, in fact, as though the hundred and eighty feet that the suburbs rose in altitude above Newark brought one closer to heaven, for the sun itself became bigger, lower, and rounder, and soon I was driving past long lawns which seemed to be twirling water on themselves, and past houses where no one sat on stoops, where lights were on but no windows open, for those inside, refusing to share the very texture of life with those of us outside, regulated with a dial the amounts of moisture that were allowed access to their skin. It was only eight o'clock, and I did not want to be early, so I drove up and down the streets whose names were those of eastern colleges, as though the township, years ago, when things were named, had planned the destinies of the sons of its citizens. I thought of my Aunt Gladys and Uncle Max sharing a Mounds bar in the cindery darkness of their alley, on beach chairs, each cool breeze sweet to them as the promise of afterlife, and after a while I rolled onto the gravel roads of the small park where Brenda was playing tennis. Inside my glove compartment it was as though the map of *The City Streets of Newark* had metamorphosed into crickets, for those mile-long tarry streets did not exist for me any longer, and the night noises sounded loud as the blood whacking at my temples.

I parked the car under the black-green canopy of three oaks, and walked towards the sound of the tennis balls. I heard an exasperated voice say, "Deuce *again.*" It was Brenda and she sounded as though she was sweating considerably. I crackled slowly up the gravel and heard Brenda once more. "My ad," and then just as I rounded the path, catching a cuff full of burrs, I heard, "Game!" Her racket went spinning up in the air and she caught it neatly as I came into sight.

"Hello," I called.

"Hello, Neil. One more game," she called. Brenda's words seemed to infuriate her opponent, a pretty brown-haired girl, not quite so tall as Brenda, who stopped searching for the ball that had been driven past her, and gave both Brenda and myself a dirty look. In a moment I learned the reason why: Brenda was ahead five games to four, and her cocksureness about there being just one game remaining aroused enough anger in her opponent for the two of us to share.

As it happened, Brenda finally won, though it took more games than she'd expected. The other girl, whose name sounded like Simp, seemed happy to end it at six all, but Brenda, shifting, running, up on her toes, would not stop, and finally all I could see moving in the darkness were her glasses, a glint of them, the clasp of her belt, her socks, her sneakers, and, on occasion, the ball. The darker it got the more savagely did Brenda rush the net, which seemed curious, for I had noticed that earlier, in the light, she had stayed back, and even when she had had to rush, after smashing back a lob, she didn't look entirely happy about being so close to her opponent's racket. Her passion for winning a point seemed outmatched by an even stronger passion for maintaining her beauty as it was. I suspected that the red print of a tennis ball on her cheek would pain her more than losing all the points in the world. Darkness pushed her in, however, and she stroked harder, and at last Simp seemed to be running on her ankles. When it was all over, Simp refused my offer of a ride home and indicated with a quality of speech borrowed from some old Katherine Hepburn movie that she could manage for herself; apparently her manor lay no further than the nearest briar patch. She did not like me and I her, though I worried it, I'm sure, more than she did.

"Who is *she?*"

"Laura Simpson Stolowitch."

"Why don't you call her Stolo?" I asked.

"Simp is her Bennington name. The ass."

"Is that where you go to school?" I asked.

She was pushing her shirt up against her skin to dry the perspiration. "No. I go to school in Boston."

I disliked her for the answer. Whenever anyone asks me where I went to school I come right out with it: Newark Colleges of Rutgers University. I may say it a bit too ringingly, too fast, too up-in-the-air, but I say it. For an instant Brenda reminded me of the pug-nosed little bastards from Montclair who come down to the library during vacations, and while I stamp out their books, they stand around tugging their elephantine scarves until they hang to their ankles, hinting all the while at "Boston" and "New Haven."

"Boston University?" I asked, looking off at the trees.

"Radcliffe."

We were still standing on the court, bounded on all sides by white lines. Around the bushes back of the court, fire-flies were cutting figure eights in the thorny-smelling air and then, as the night suddenly came all the way in, the leaves on the trees shone for an instant, as though they'd just been rained upon. Brenda walked off the court, with me a step behind her. Now I had grown accustomed to the dark, and as she ceased being merely a voice and turned into a sight again, some of my anger at her "Boston" remark floated off and I let myself appreciate her. Her hands did not twitch at her bottom, but the form revealed itself, covered or not, under the closeness of her kahki Bermudas. There were two wet triangles on the back of her tiny-collared white polo shirt, right where her wings would have been if she'd had a pair. She wore, to complete the picture, a tartan belt, white socks, and white tennis sneakers.

As she walked she zipped the cover on her racket.

"Are you anxious to get home?" I said.

"No."

"Let's sit here. It's pleasant."

"Okay."

We sat down on a bank of grass slanted enough for us to lean back without really leaning; from the angle it seemed as though we were preparing to watch some celestial event, the christening of a new star, the inflation to full size of a half-ballooned moon. Brenda zipped and unzipped the cover while she spoke; for the first time she seemed edgy. Her edginess coaxed mine back, and so we were ready now for what, magically, it seemed we might be able to get by without: a meeting.

"What does your cousin Doris look like?" she asked.

"She's dark—"

"Is she—"

"No," I said. "She has freckles and dark hair and she's very tall."

"Where does she go to school?"

"Northampton."

She did not answer and I don't know how much of what I meant she had understood.

"I guess I don't know her," she said after a moment. "Is she a new member?"

"I think so. They moved to Livingston only a couple of years ago."

"Oh."

No new star appeared, at least for the next five minutes.

"Did you remember me from holding your glasses?" I said.

"Now I do," she said. "Do you live in Livingston too?"

"No, Newark."

"We lived in Newark when I was a baby," she offered.

"Would you like to go home?" I was suddenly angry.

"No. Let's walk though."

Brenda kicked a stone and walked a step ahead of me.

"Why is it you rush the net only after dark?" I said.

She turned to me and smiled. "You noticed? Old Simp the Simpleton doesn't."

"Why do you?"

"I don't like to be up too close, unless I'm sure she won't return it."

"Why?"

"My nose."

"What?"

"I'm afraid of my nose. I had it bobbed."

"What?"

"I had my nose fixed."

"What was the matter with it?"

"It was bumpy."

"A lot?"

"No," she said, "I was pretty. Now I'm prettier. My brother's having his fixed in the fall."

"Does he want to be prettier?"

She didn't answer and walked ahead of me again.

"I don't mean to sound facetious. I mean why's he doing it?"

"He *wants* to . . . unless he becomes a gym teacher . . . but he won't," she said. "We all look like my father."

"Is he having his fixed?"

"Why are you so nasty?"

"I'm not. I'm sorry." My next question was prompted by a desire to sound interested and thereby regain civility; it didn't quite come out as I'd expected—I said it too loud. "How much does it cost?"

Brenda waited a moment but then she answered. "A thousand dollars. Unless you go to a butcher."

"Let me see if you got your money's worth."

She turned again; she stood next to a bench and put the racket down on it. "If I let you kiss me would you stop being nasty?"

We had to take about two too many steps to keep the approach from being awkward, but we pursued the impulse and kissed. I felt her hand on the back of my neck and so I tugged her towards me, too violently perhaps, and slid my own hands across the side of her body and around to her back. I felt the wet spots on her shoulder blades, and beneath them, I'm sure of it, a faint fluttering, as though something stirred so deep in her breasts, so far back it could make itself felt through her shirt. It was like the fluttering of wings, tiny wings no bigger than her breasts. The smallness of the wings did not bother me—it would not take an eagle to carry me up those lousy hundred and eighty feet that make summer nights so much cooler in Short Hills than they are in Newark.

2

The next day I held Brenda's glasses for her once again, this time not as momentary servant but as afternoon guest; or perhaps as both, which still was an improvement. She wore a black tank suit and went barefooted, and among the other women, with their Cuban heels and boned-up breasts, their knuckle-sized rings, their straw hats, which resembled immense wicker pizza plates and had been purchased, as I heard one deeply tanned woman rasp, "from the cutest little *shvartze* when we docked at Barbados," Brenda among them was elegantly simple, like a sailor's dream of a Polynesian maiden, albeit one with prescription sun glasses and the last name of Patimkin. She brought a little slurp of water with her when she crawled back towards the pool's edge, and at the edge she grabbed up with her hands and held my ankles, tightly and wet.

"Come in," she said up to me, squinting. "We'll play."

"Your glasses," I said.

"Oh break the goddamn things. I hate them."

"Why don't you have your eyes fixed?"

"There you go again."

"I'm sorry," I said. "I'll give them to Doris."

Doris, in the surprise of the summer, had gotten past Prince Andrey's departure from his wife, and now sat brooding, not, it turned out, over the lonely fate of poor Princess Liza, but at the skin which she had lately discovered to be peeling off her shoulders.

"Would you watch Brenda's glasses?" I said.

"Yes." She fluffed little scales of translucent flesh into the air. "Damn it."

I handed her the glasses.

"Well, for God's sake," she said, "I'm not going to hold them. Put them down. *I'm* not her slave."

"You're a pain in the ass, you know that, Doris?" Sitting there, she looked a little like Laura Simpson Stolowitch, who was, in fact, walking somewhere off at the far end of the pool, avoiding Brenda and me because (I liked to think) of the defeat Brenda had handed her the night before, or maybe (I didn't like to think) because of the strangeness of my presence. Regardless, Doris had to bear the weight of my indictment of both Simp and herself.

"Thank you," she said. "After I invite you up for the day."

"That was yesterday."

"What about last year?"

"That's right, your mother told you last year too—invite Esther's boy so when he writes his parents they won't complain we don't look after him. Every summer I get my day."

"You should have gone with them. That's not our fault. You're not our charge," and when she said it, I could just tell it was something she'd heard at home, or received in a letter one Monday mail, after she'd returned to Northampton from Stowe, or Dartmouth, or perhaps from that weekend when she'd taken a shower with her boyfriend in Lowell House.

"Tell your father not to worry. Uncle Aaron, the sport. I'll take care of myself," and I ran on back to the pool, ran into a dive, in fact, and came up like a dolphin beside Brenda, whose legs I slid upon with my own.

"How's Doris?" she said.

"Peeling," I said. "She's going to have her skin fixed."

"*Stop* it," she said, and dove down beneath us till I felt her clamping her hands on the soles of my feet. I pulled back and then down too, and then, at the bottom, no more than six inches above the wiggling black lines that divided the pool into lanes for races, we bubbled a kiss into each other's lips. She was smiling there, at *me,* down at the bottom of the swimming pool of the Green Lane Country Club. Way above us, legs shimmied in the water and a pair of fins skimmed greenly by: my cousin Doris could peel away to nothing for all I cared, my Aunt Gladys have twenty feedings every night, my father and mother could roast away their asthma down in the furnace of Arizona, those penniless deserters—I didn't care for anything but Brenda. I went to pull her towards me just as she started fluttering up; my hand hooked on to the front of her suit and the cloth pulled away from her. Her breasts swam towards me like two pink-nosed fish and she let me hold them. Then, in a moment, it was the sun who kissed us both, and we were out of the water, too pleased with each other to smile. Brenda shook the wetness of her hair onto my face and with the drops that touched me I felt she had made a promise to me about the summer, and, I hoped, beyond.

"Do you want your sun glasses?"

"You're close enough to see," she said. We were under a big blue umbrella, side-by-side on two chaise longues, whose plastic covers sizzled against our suits and flesh; I turned my head to look at Brenda and smelled that pleasant little burning odor in the skin of my shoulders. I turned back up to the sun, as did she, and as we talked, and it grew hotter and brighter, the colors splintered under my closed eyelids.

"This is all very fast," she said.

"Nothing's happened," I said softly.

"No. I guess not. I sort of feel something has."

"In eighteen hours?"

"Yes. I feel . . . pursued," she said after a moment.

"*You* invited *me*, Brenda."

"Why do you always sound a little nasty to me?"

"Did I sound nasty? I don't mean to. Truly."

"You do! *You* invited *me*, Brenda. So what?" she said. "That isn't what I mean anyway."

"I'm sorry."

"Stop apologizing. You're so automatic about it, you don't even mean it."

"Now you're being nasty to me," I said.

"No. Just stating the facts. Let's not argue. I like you." She turned her head and looked as though she too paused a second to smell the summer on her own flesh. "I like the way you look." She saved it from embarrassing me with that factual tone of hers.

"Why?" I said.

"Where did you get those fine shoulders? Do you play something?"

"No," I said. "I just grew up and they came with me."

"I like your body. It's fine."

"I'm glad," I said.

"You like mine, don't you?"

"No," I said.

"Then it's denied you," she said.

I brushed her hair flat against her ear with the back of my hand and then we were silent a while.

"Brenda," I said, "you haven't asked me anything about me."

"How you feel? Do you want me to ask you how you feel?"

"Yes," I said, accepting the back door she gave me, though probably not for the same reasons she had offered it.

"How *do* you feel?"

"I want to swim."

"Okay," she said.

We spent the rest of the afternoon in the water. There were eight of those long lines painted down the length of the pool and by the end of the day I think we had parked for a while in every lane, close enough to the dark stripes to reach out and touch them. We came back to the chairs now and then and sang hesitant, clever, nervous, gentle dithyrambs about how we were beginning to feel towards one another. Actually we did not have the feelings we said we had until we spoke them—at least I didn't; to phrase them was to invent them and own them. We whipped our strangeness and newness into a froth that resembled love, and we dared not play too long with it, talk too much of it, or it would flatten and fizzle away. So we moved back and forth from chairs to water, from talk to silence, and considering my unshakable edginess with Brenda, and the high walls of ego that rose, buttresses and all, between her and her knowledge of herself, we managed pretty well.

At about four o'clock, at the bottom of the pool, Brenda suddenly wrenched away from me and shot up to the surface. I shot up after her.

"What's the matter?" I said.

First she whipped the hair off her forehead. Then she pointed a hand down towards the base of the pool. "My brother," she said, coughing some water free inside her.

And suddenly, like a crew-cut Proteus rising from the sea, Ron Patimkin emerged from the lower depths we'd just inhabited and his immensity was before us.

"Hey, Bren," he said, and pushed a palm flat into the water so that a small hurricane beat up against Brenda and me.

"What are you so happy about?" she said.

"The Yankees took two."

"Are we going to have Mickey Mantle for dinner?" she said. "When the Yankees win," she said to me, treading so easily she seemed to have turned the chlorine to marble beneath her, "we set an extra place for Mickey Mantle."

"You want to race?" Ron asked.

"No, Ronald. Go race alone."

Nobody has as yet said a word about me. I treaded unobtrusively as I could, as a third party, unintroduced, will step back and say nothing, awaiting the amenities. I was tired, however, from the afternoon's sport, and wished to hell brother and sister would not tease and chat much longer. Fortunately Brenda introduced me. "Ronald, this is Neil Klugman. This is my brother, Ronald Patimkin."

Of all things there in the fifteen feet water, Ron reached out his hand to shake. I returned the shake, not quite as monumentally as he apparently expected; my chin slipped an inch into the water and all at once I was exhausted.

"Want to race?" Ron asked me good-naturedly.

"Go ahead, Neil, race with him. I want to call home and tell them you're coming to dinner."

"Am I? I'll have to call my aunt. You didn't say anything. My clothes—"

"We dine au naturel."

"What?" Ronald said.

"Swim, baby," Brenda said to him and it ached me some when she kissed him on the face.

I begged out of the race, saying I had to make a phone call myself, and once upon the tiled blue border of the pool, looked back to see Ron taking the length in sleek, immense strokes. He gave one the feeling that after swimming the length of the pool a half dozen times he would have earned the right to drink its contents; I imagined he had, like my Uncle Max, a colossal thirst and a gigantic bladder.

Aunt Gladys did not seem relieved when I told her she'd have only three feedings to prepare that night. "Fancy-shmancy" was all she said to me on the phone.

We did not eat in the kitchen; rather, the six of us—Brenda, myself, Ron, Mr. and Mrs. Patimkin, and Brenda's little sister, Julie—sat around the dining room table, while the maid, Carlota, a Navaho-faced Negro who had little holes in her ears but no earrings, served us the meal. I was seated next to Brenda, who was dressed in what was *au naturel* for her: Bermudas, the close ones, white polo shirt, tennis sneakers and white socks. Across from me was Julie, ten, round-faced, bright, who before dinner, while the other little girls on the street had been playing with jacks and boys and each other, had been on the back lawn putting golf balls with her father. Mr. Patimkin reminded me of my father, except that when he spoke he did not surround each syllable with a wheeze. He was tall, strong, ungrammatical, and a ferocious eater. When he attacked his salad—after drenching it in bottled French dressing—the veins swelled under the heavy skin of his forearm. He ate three helpings of salad, Ron had four, Brenda and Julie had two, and only Mrs. Patimkin and I had one each. I did not like Mrs. Patimkin, though she was certainly the handsomest of all of us at the table. She was disastrously polite to me, and with her purple eyes, her dark hair, and large, persuasive frame, she gave me the feeling of some captive beauty, some wild princess, who has been tamed and made the servant to the king's daughter—who was Brenda.

Outside, through the wide picture window, I could see the back lawn with its twin oak trees. I say oaks, though fancifully, one might call them sporting-goods trees. Beneath their branches, like fruit dropped from their limbs, were two irons, a golf ball, a tennis can, a baseball bat, basketball, a first-baseman's glove, and what was apparently a riding crop. Further back, near the scrubs that bounded the Patimkin property and in front of the small basketball court, a square red blanket, with a white O stitched in the center, looked to be on fire against the green grass. A breeze must have blown outside, for the net on the basket moved; inside we ate in the steady coolness of air by Westinghouse. It was a pleasure, except that eating among those Brobdingnags, I felt for quite a while as though four inches had been clipped from my shoulders, three inches from my height, and for good measure, someone had removed my ribs and my chest had settled meekly in towards my back.

There was not much dinner conversation; eating was heavy and methodical and serious, and it would be just as well to record all that was said in one swoop, rather than indicate the sentences lost in the passing of food, the words gurgled into mouthfuls, the syntax chopped and forgotten in heapings, spillings, and gorgings.

To Ron: When's Harriet calling?

Ron: Five o'clock.

Julie: It *was* five o'clock.

Ron: Their time.

Julie: Why is it that it's earlier in Milwaukee? Suppose you took a plane back and forth all day. You'd never get older.

Brenda: That's right, sweetheart.

Mrs. P.: What do you give the child misinformation for? Is that why she goes to school?

Brenda: I don't know why she goes to school.

Mr. P. (lovingly): College girl.

Ron: Where's Carlota? Carlota!

Mrs. P.: Carlota, give Ronald more.

Carlota (calling): More what?

Ron: Everything.

Mr. P.: Me too.

Mrs. P.: They'll have to *roll* you on the links.

Mr. P. (pulling his shirt up and slapping his black, curved belly): What are you talking about? Look at that?

Ron (yanking his T-shirt up): Look at *this.*

Brenda (to me): Would you care to bare your middle?

Me [the choir boy again]: No.

Mrs. P.: That's right, Neil.

Me: Yes. Thank you.

Carlota (over my shoulder, like an unsummoned spirit): Would *you* like more?

Me: No.

Mr. P.: He eats like a bird.

Julie: Certain birds eat a lot.

Brenda: Which ones?

Mrs. P.: Let's not talk about animals at the dinner table. Brenda, why do you encourage her?

Ron: Where's Carlota, I gotta play tonight.

Mr. P.: Tape your wrist, don't forget.

Mrs. P.: Where do you live, Bill?

Brenda: Neil.

Mrs. P.: Didn't I say Neil?

Julie: You said "Where do you live, *Bill?"*

Mrs. P.: I must have been thinking of something else.

Ron: I hate tape. How the hell can I play in tape?

Julie: Don't curse.

Mrs. P.: That's right.

Mr. P.: What is Mantle batting now?

Julie: Three twenty-eight.

Ron: Three twenty-five.

Julie: Eight!

Ron: Five, jerk! He got three for four in the second game.

Julie: *Four* for four.

Ron: That was an error, Minoso should have had it.

Julie: I didn't think so.

Brenda (to me): See?

Mrs. P.: See what?

Brenda: I was talking to Bill.

Julie: Neil.

Mr. P.: Shut up and eat.

Mrs. P.: A little less talking, young lady.

Julie: I didn't say anything.

Brenda: She was talking to me, sweetie.

Mr. P.: What's this *she* business. Is that how you call your mother? What's dessert?

The phone rings, and though we are awaiting dessert, the meal seems at a formal end, for Ron breaks for his room, Julie shouts "Harriet!" and Mr. Patimkin is not wholly successful in stifling a belch, though the failure even more than the effort ingratiates him to me. Mrs. Patimkin is directing Carlota not to mix the milk silverware and the meat silverware again, and Carlota is eating a peach while she listens; under the table I feel Brenda's fingers tease my calf. I am full.

We sat under the biggest of the oak trees while out on the basketball court Mr. Patimkin played five and two with Julie. In the driveway Ron was racing the motor of the Volkswagen. "Will somebody *please* move the Chrysler out from behind me?" he called angrily. "I'm late as it is."

"Excuse me," Brenda said, getting up.

"I think I'm behind the Chrysler," I said.

"Let's go," she said.

We backed the cars out so that Ron could hasten on to his game. Then we reparked them and went back to watching Mr. Patimkin and Julie.

"I like your sister," I said.

"So do I," she said. "I wonder what she'll turn out to be."

"Like you," I said.

"I don't know," she said. "Better probably." And then she added, "or maybe worse. How can you tell? My father's nice to her, but I'll give her another three years with my mother . . . Bill," she said, musingly.

"I didn't mind that," I said. "She's very beautiful, your mother."

"I can't even think of her as my mother. She hates me. Other girls, when they pack in September, at least their mothers help them. Not mine. She'll be busy sharpening pencils for Julie's pencil box while I'm carrying my trunk around upstairs. And it's so obvious why. It's practically a case study."

"Why?"

"She's jealous. It's so corny I'm ashamed to say it. Do you know my mother had the best back-hand in New Jersey? Really, she was the best tennis player in the state, man or woman. You ought to see the pictures of her when she was a girl. She was so healthy-looking. But not chubby or anything. She was soulful, truly. I love her in those pictures. Sometimes I say to her how beautiful the pictures are. I even asked to have one blown up so I could have it at school. 'We have other things to do with our money, young lady, than spend it on old photographs.' Money! My father's up to here with it, but whenever I buy a coat you should hear her. 'You don't have to go to Bonwit's, young lady, Ohrbach's has the strongest fabrics of any of them.' Who *wants* a strong fabric! Finally I get what I want, but not till she's had a chance to aggravate me. Money is a waste for her. She doesn't even know how to enjoy it. She still thinks we live in Newark."

"But you get what you want," I said.

"Yes. Him," and she pointed out to Mr. Patimkin who had just swished his third straight set shot through the basket to the disgruntlement, apparently, of Julie, who stamped so hard at the ground that she raised a little dust storm around her perfect young legs.

"He's not too smart but he's sweet at least. He doesn't treat my brother the way she treats me. Thank God, for that. Oh, I'm tired of talking about them. Since my freshman year I think every conversation I've ever had has always wound up about my parents and how awful it is. It's universal. The only trouble is they don't know it."

From the way Julie and Mr. Patimkin were laughing now, out on the court, no problem could ever have seemed less universal; but, of course, it was universal for Brenda, more than that, cosmic—it made every cashmere sweater a battle with her mother, and her life, which, I was certain, consisted to a large part of cornering the market on fabrics that felt soft to the skin, took on the quality of a Hundred Years' War . . .

I did not intend to allow myself such unfaithful thoughts, to line up with Mrs. Patimkin while I sat beside Brenda, but I could not shake from my elephants's brain that she-still-thinks-we-live-in-Newark remark. I did not speak, however, fearful that my tone would shatter our post-dinner ease and intimacy. It had been so simple to be intimate with water pounding and securing all our pores, and later, with the sun heating them and drugging our senses, but now, in the shade and the open, cool and clothed in her own grounds, I did not want to voice a word that would lift the cover and reveal that hideous emotion I always felt for her, and is the underside of love. It will not always *stay* the underside—but I am skipping ahead.

Suddenly, little Julie was upon us. "Want to play?" she said to me. "Daddy's tired."

"C'mon," Mr. Patimkin called. "Finish for me."

I hesitated—I hadn't held a basketball since high school—but Julie was dragging at my hand, and Brenda said, "Go ahead."

Mr. Patimkin tossed the ball towards me while I wasn't looking and it bounced off my chest, leaving a round dust spot, like the shadow of a moon, on my shirt. I laughed, insanely.

"Can't you catch?" Julie said.

Like her sister, she seemed to have a knack for asking practical, infuriating questions.

"Yes."

"Your turn," she said. "Daddy's behind forty-seven to thirty-nine. Two hundred wins."

For an instant, as I placed my toes in the little groove that over the years had been nicked into a foul line, I had one of those instantaneous waking dreams that plague me from time to time, and send, my friends tell me, deadly cataracts over my eyes: the sun had sunk, crickets had come and gone, the leaves had blackened, and still Julie and I stood alone on the lawn, tossing the ball at the basket; "Five hundred wins," she called, and then when she beat me to five hundred she called, "Now *you* have to reach it," and I did, and the night lengthened, and she called, "*Eight* hundred wins," and we played on and then it was eleven hundred that won and we played on and it never was morning.

"Shoot," Mr. Patimkin said. "You're me."

That puzzled me, but I took my set shot and, of course, missed. With the Lord's blessing and a soft breeze, I made the lay-up.

"You have forty-one. I go," Julie said.

Mr. Patimkin sat on the grass at the far end of the court. He took his shirt off, and in his undershirt, and his whole day's growth of beard, looked like a trucker. Brenda's old nose fitted him well. There was a bump in it, all right; up at the bridge it seemed as though a small eight-sided diamond had been squeezed in under the skin. I knew Mr. Patimkin would never bother to have that stone cut from his face, and yet, with joy and pride, no doubt, had paid to have Brenda's diamond removed and dropped down some toilet in Fifth Avenue Hospital.

Julie missed her set shot, and I admit to a slight, gay, flutter of heart.

"Put a little spin on it," Mr. Patimkin told her.

"Can I take it again?" Julie asked me.

"Yes." What with paternal directions from the sidelines and my own grudging graciousness on the court, there did not seem much of a chance for me to catch up. And I wanted to, suddenly, I wanted to win, to run little Julie into the ground. Brenda was back on one elbow, under the tree, chewing on a leaf, watching. And up in the house, at the kitchen window, I could see that the curtain had swished back—the sun too low now to glare off electrical appliances—and Mrs. Patimkin was looking steadily out at the game. And then Carlota appeared on the back steps, eating a peach and holding a pail of garbage in her free hand. She stopped to watch too.

It was my turn again. I missed the set shot and laughingly turned to Julie and said, "Can I take it again?"

"No!"

So I learned how the game was played. Over the years Mr. Patimkin had taught his daughters that free throws were theirs for the asking; he could afford to. However, with the strange eyes of Short Hills upon me, matrons, servants, and providers, I somehow felt I couldn't. But I had to and I did.

"Thanks a lot, Neil," Julie said when the game was ended—at 100—and the crickets had come.

"You're welcome."

Under the trees, Brenda smiled. "Did you let her win?"

"I think so," I said. "I'm not sure."

There was something in my voice that prompted Brenda to say, comfortingly, "Even Ron lets her win."

"It's all nice for Julie," I said.

3

The next morning I found a parking space on Washington Street directly across from the library. Since I was twenty minutes early I decided to stroll in the park rather than cross over to work; I didn't particularly care to join my colleagues, who I knew would be sipping early morning coffee in the binding room, smelling still of all the orange crush they'd drunk that weekend at Asbury Park. I sat on a bench and looked out towards Broad Street and the morning traffic. The Lackawanna commuter trains were rumbling in a few blocks to the north and I could hear them, I thought—the sunny green cars, old and clean, with windows that opened all the way. Some mornings, with time to kill before work, I would walk down to the tracks and watch the open windows roll in, on their sills the elbows of tropical suits and the edges of briefcases, the properties of businessmen arriving in town from Maplewood, the Oranges, and the suburbs beyond.

The park, bordered by Washington Street on the west and Broad on the east, was empty and shady and smelled of trees, night, and dog leavings; and there was a faint damp smell too, indicating that the huge rhino of a water cleaner had passed by already, soaking and whisking the downtown streets. Down Washington Street, behind me, was the Newark Museum—I could see it without even looking; two oriental vases in front like spittoons for a rajah, and next to it the little annex to which we had traveled on special buses as schoolchildren. The annex was a brick building, old and vine-covered, and always reminded me of New Jersey's link with the beginning of the country, with George Washington, who had trained his scrappy army—a little bronze tablet informed us children—in the very park where I now sat. At the far end of the park, beyond the Museum, was the bank building where I had gone to college. It had been converted some years before into an extension of Rutgers University; in fact, in what once had been the bank president's waiting room I had taken a course called Contemporary Moral Issues. Though it was summer now, and I was out of college three years, it was not hard for me to remember the other students, my friends, who had worked evenings in Bamberger's and Kresge's and had used the commissions they'd earned pushing ladies' out-of-season shoes to pay their laboratory fees. And then I looked out to Broad Street again. Jammed between a grimy-windowed bookstore and a cheesy luncheonette was the marquee of a tiny art theater—how many years had passed since I'd stood beneath that marquee, lying about the year of my birth so as to see Hedy Lamarr swim naked in *Ecstasy*; and then, having slipped the ticket taker an extra quarter, what disappointment I had felt at the frugality of her Slavic charm . . . Sitting there in the park, I felt a deep knowledge of Newark, an attachment so rooted that it could not help but branch out into affection.

Suddenly it was nine o'clock and everything was scurrying. Wobbly-heeled girls revolved through the doors of the telephone building across the way, traffic honked desperately, policemen barked, whistled, and waved motorists to and fro. Over at St. Vincent's Church the huge dark portals swung back and those bleary-eyes that had risen early for Mass now blinked at the light. Then the worshipers had stepped off the church steps and were racing down the streets towards desks, filing cabinets, secretaries, bosses, and—if the Lord had seen fit to remove a mite of harshness from their lives—to the comfort of air-conditioners pumping at their windows. I got up and crossed over to the library, wondering if Brenda was awake yet.

The pale cement lions stood unconvincing guard on the library steps, suffering their usual combination of elephantiasis and arteriosclerosis, and I was prepared to pay them as little attention as I had for the past eight months were it not for a small colored boy who stood in front of one of them. The lion had lost all of its toes the summer before to a safari of juvenile delinquents, and now a new tormentor stood before him, sagging a little in his knees, and growling. He would growl, low and long, drop back, wait, then growl again. Then he would straighten up, and, shaking his head, he would say to the lion, "Man, you's a coward . . ." Then, once again, he'd growl.

The day began the same as any other. From behind the desk on the main floor, I watched the hot high-breasted teen-age girls walk twitchingly up the wide flight of marble stairs that led to the main reading room. The stairs were an imitation of a staircase somewhere in Versailles, though in their toreador pants and sweaters these young daughters of Italian leatherworkers, Polish brewery hands, and Jewish furriers were hardly duchesses. They were not Brenda either, and any lust that sparked inside me through the dreary day was academic and time-passing. I looked at my watch occasionally, thought of Brenda, and waited for lunch and then for after lunch, when I would take over the Information Desk upstairs and John McKee, who was only twenty-one but wore elastic bands around his sleeves, would march starchily down the stairs to work assiduously at stamping books in and out. John McRubberbands was in his last year at Newark State Teachers College where he was studying at the Dewey Decimal System in preparation for his lifework. The library was not going to be my lifework, I knew it. Yet, there had been some talk—from Mr. Scapello, an old eunuch who had learned somehow to disguise his voice as a man's—that when I returned from my summer vacation I would be put in charge of the Reference Room, a position that had been empty ever since that morning when Martha Winney had fallen off a high stool in the Encyclopedia Room and shattered all those frail bones that come together to form what in a woman half her age we would call the hips.

I had strange fellows at the library and, in truth, there were many hours when I never quite knew how I'd gotten there or why I stayed. But I did stay and after a white waited patiently for that day when I would go into the men's room on the main floor for a cigarette and, studying myself as I expelled smoke into the mirror, would see that at some moment during the morning I had gone pale, and that under my skin, as under McKee's and Scapello's and Miss Winney's, there was a thin cushion of air separating the blood from the flesh. Someone had pumped it there while I was stamping out a book, and so life from now on would be not a throwing off, as it was for Aunt Gladys, and not a gathering in, as it was for Brenda, but a bouncing off, a numbness. I began to fear this, and yet, in my musclesless devotion to my work, seemed edging towards it, silently, as Miss Winney used to edge up to the *Britannica.* Her stool was empty now and awaited me.

Just before lunch the lion tamer came wide-eyed into the library. He stood still for a moment, only his fingers moving, as though he were counting the number of marble stairs before him. Then he walked creepily about on the marble floor, snickering at the clink of his taps and the way his little noise swelled up to the vaulted ceiling. Otto, the guard at the door, told him to make less noise with his shoes, but that did not seem to bother the little boy. He clacked on his tiptoes, high, secretively, delighted at the opportunity Otto had given him to practice this posture. He tiptoed up to me.

"Hey," he said, "where's the heart section?"

"The what?" I said.

"The heart section. Ain't you got no heart section?"

He had the thickest sort of southern Negro dialect and the only word that came clear to me was the one that sounded like heart.

"How do you spell it?" I said.

"*Heart.* Man, pictures. Drawing books. Where you got them?"

"You mean art books? Reproductions?"

He took my polysyllabic word for it. "Yea, they's them."

"In a couple places," I told him. "Which artist are you interested in?"

The boy's eyes narrowed so that his whole face seemed black. He started backing away, as he had from the lion. "All of them . . ." he mumbled.

"That's okay," I said. "You go look at whichever ones you want. The next flight up. Follow the arrow to where it says Stack Three. You remember that? Stack Three. Ask somebody upstairs."

He did not move; he seemed to be taking my curiosity about his taste as a kind of poll-tax investigation. "Go ahead," I said, slashing my face with a smile, "right up there . . ."

And like a shot he was scuffling and tapping up towards the heart section.

After lunch I came back to the in-and-out desk and there was John McKee, waiting, in his pale blue slacks, his black shoes, his barber-cloth shirt with the elastic bands, and a great knit tie, green, wrapped into a Windsor knot, that was huge and jumped when he talked. His breath smelled of hair oil and his hair of breath and when he spoke, spittle cobwebbed the corners of his mouth. I did not like him and at times had the urge to yank back on his armbands and slingshoot him out past Otto and the lions into the street.

"Has a little Negro boy passed the desk? With a thick accent? He's been hiding in the art books all morning. You know what those boys *do* in there."

"I saw him come in, John."

"So did I. Has he gone *out* though."

"I haven't noticed. I guess so."

"Those are *very* expensive books."

"Don't be so nervous, John. People are supposed to touch them."

"There is touching," John said sententiously, "and there is touching. Someone should check on him. I was afraid to leave the desk here. You know the way they treat the housing projects we give them."

"*You* give them?"

"The city. Have you seen what they do at Seth Boyden? They threw *beer* bottles, those big ones, on the *lawn.* They're taking over the city."

"Just the Negro sections."

"It's easy to laugh, you don't live near them. I'm going to call Mr. Scapello's office to check the Art Section. Where did he ever find out about art?"

"You'll give Mr. Scapello an ulcer, so soon after his egg-and-pepper sandwich. I'll check, I have to go upstairs anyway."

"You know what they do in there," John warned me.

"Don't worry, Johnny, *they're* the ones who'll get warts on their dirty little hands."

"Ha ha. Those books happen to cost—"

So that Mr. Scapello would not descend upon the boy with his chalky fingers, I walked up the three flights to Stack Three, past the receiving room where rheumy-eyed Jimmy Boylen, our fifty-one-year-old boy, unloaded books from a cart; past the reading room, where bums off Mulberry Street slept over *Popular Mechanics*; past the smoking corridor where damp-browed summer students from the law school relaxed, some smoking, others trying to rub the colored dye from their tort texts off their fingertips; and finally, past the periodical room, where a few ancient ladies who'd been motored down from Upper Montclair now huddled in their chairs, pince-nezing over yellowed, fraying society pages in old old copies of the Newark *News.* Up on Stack Three I found the boy. He was seated on the glass-brick floor holding an open book in his lap, a book, in fact, that was bigger than his lap and had to be propped up by his knees. By the light of the window behind him I could see the hundreds of spaces between the hundreds of tiny black corkscrews that were his hair. He was very black and shiny, and the flesh of his lips did not so much appear to be a different color as it looked to be unfinished and awaiting another coat. The lips were parted, the eyes wide, and even the ears seemed to have a heightened receptivity. He looked ecstatic—until he saw me, that is. For all he knew I was John McKee.

"That's okay," I said before he could even move, "I'm just passing through. You read."

"Ain't nothing to read. They's pictures."

"Fine." I fished around the lowest shelves a moment, playing at work.

"Hey, mister," the boy said after a minute, "where is this?"

"Where is what?"

"Where is these pictures? These people, man, they sure does look cool. They ain't no yelling or shouting here, you could just see it."

He lifted the book so I could see. It was an expensive large-sized edition of Gauguin reproductions. The page he had been looking at showed an $8^{1}/_{2} \times 11$ print, in color, of three native women standing knee-high in a rose-colored stream. It *was* a silent picture, he was right.

"That's Tahiti. That's an island in the Pacific Ocean."

"That ain't no place you could go, is it? Like a ree-*sort*?"

"You could go there, I suppose. It's very far. People live there . . ."

"Hey, *look,* look here at this one." He flipped back to a page where a young brown-skinned maid was leaning forward on her knees, as though to dry her hair. "Man," the boy said, "that's the fuckin life." The euphoria of his diction would have earned him eternal banishment from the Newark Public Library and its branches had John or Mr. Scapello—or, God forbid, the hospitalized Miss Winney—come to investigate.

"Who took these pictures?" he asked me.

"Gauguin. He didn't take them, he painted them. Paul Gauguin. He was a Frenchman."

"Is he a white man or a colored man?"

"He's white."

"Man," the boy smiled, chuckled almost, "I knew that. He don't *take* pictures like no colored men would. He's a good picture taker . . . Look, look, look here at this one. Ain't that the fuckin *life*?"

I agreed it was and left.

Later I sent Jimmy Boylen hopping down the stairs to tell McKee that everything was all right. The rest of the day was uneventful. I sat at the Information Desk thinking about Brenda and reminding myself that that evening I would have to get gas before I started up to Short Hills, which I could see now, in my mind's eye, at dusk, rose-colored, like a Gauguin stream.

When I pulled up to the Patimkin house that night, everybody but Julie was waiting for me on the front porch: Mr. and Mrs., Ron, and Brenda, wearing a dress. I had not seen her in a dress before and for an instant she did not look like the same girl. But that was only half the surprise. So many of those Lincolnesque college girls turn out to be limbed for shorts alone. Not Brenda. She looked, in a dress, as though she'd gone through life so attired, as though she'd never worn shorts, or bathing suits, or pajamas, or anything but that pale linen dress. I walked rather bouncingly up the lawn, past the huge weeping willow, towards the waiting Patimkins, wishing all the while that I'd had my car washed. Before I'd even reached them, Ron stepped forward and shook my hand, vigorously, as though he hadn't seen me since the Diaspora. Mrs. Patimkin smiled and Mr. Patimkin grunted something and continued twitching his wrists before him, then raising an imaginary golf club and driving a ghost of a golf ball up and away towards the Orange Mountains, that are called Orange, I'm convinced, because in that various suburban light that's the *only* color they do not come dressed in.

"We'll be right back," Brenda said to me. "You have to sit with Julie. Carlota's off."

"Okay," I said.

"We're taking Ron to the airport."

"Okay."

"Julie doesn't want to go. She says Ron pushed her in the pool this afternoon. We've been waiting for you, so we don't miss Ron's plane. Okay?"

"Okay."

Mr. and Mrs. Patimkin and Ron moved off, and I flashed Brenda just the hint of a glare. She reached out and took my hand a moment.

"How do you like me?" she said.

"You're great to baby-sit for. Am I allowed all the milk and cake I want?"

"Don't be angry, baby. We'll be right back." Then she waited a moment, and when I failed to deflate the pout from my mouth, she gave *me* a glare, no hints about it. "I *meant* how do you like me in a dress!" Then she ran off towards the Chrysler, trotting in her high heels like a colt.

When I walked into the house, I slammed the screen door behind me.

"Close the other door too," a little voice shouted. "The air-conditioning."

I closed the other door, obediently.

"Neil?" Julie called.

"Yes."

"Hi. Want to play five and two?"

"No."

"Why not?"

I did not answer.

"I'm in the television room," she called.

"Good."

"Are you supposed to stay with me?"

"Yes."

She appeared unexpectedly through the dining room. "Want to read a book report I wrote?"

"Not now."

"What do you want to do?" she said.

"Nothing, honey. Why don't you watch TV?"

"All right," she said disgustedly, and kicked her way back to the television room.

For a while I remained in the hall, bitten with the urge to slide quietly out of the house, into my car, and back to Newark, where I might even sit in the alley and break candy with my own. I felt like Carlota; no, not even as comfortable as that. At last I left the hall and began to stroll in and out of rooms on the first floor. Next to the living room was the study, a small knotty-pine room jammed with cater-cornered leather chairs and a complete set of *Information Please Almanacs*. On the wall hung three colored photo-paintings; they were the kind which, regardless of the subjects, be they vital or infirm, old or youthful, are characterized by bud-cheeks, wet lips, pearly teeth, and shiny, metallized hair. The subjects in this case were Ron, Brenda, and Julie at about ages fourteen, thirteen, and two. Brenda had long auburn hair, her diamond-studded nose, and no glasses; all combined to make her look a regal thirteen-year-old who'd just gotten smoke in her eyes. Ron was rounder and his hairline was lower, but that love of spherical objects and lined courts twinkled in his boyish eyes. Poor little Julie was lost in the photo-painter's Platonic idea of childhood; her tiny humanity was smothered somewhere back of gobs of pink and white.

There were other pictures about, smaller ones, taken with a Brownie Reflex before photo-paintings had become fashionable. There was a tiny picture of Brenda on a horse; another of Ron in bar mitzvah suit, *yamalkah*, and *tallas*; and two pictures framed together—one of a beautiful, faded woman, who must have been, from the eyes, Mrs. Patimkin's mother, and the other of Mrs. Patimkin herself, her hair in a halo, her eyes joyous and not those of a slowly aging mother with a quick and lovely daughter.

I walked through the archway into the dining room and stood a moment looking out at the sporting goods tree. From the television room that winged off the dining room, I could hear Julie listening to *This Is Your Life.* The kitchen, which winged off the other side, was empty, and apparently, with Carlota off, the Patimkins had had dinner at the club. Mr. and Mrs. Patimkin's bedroom was in the middle of the house, down the hall, next to Julie's, and for a moment I wanted to see what size bed those giants slept in—I imagined it wide and deep as a swimming pool—but I postponed my investigation while Julie was in the house, and instead opened the door in the kitchen that led down to the basement.

The basement had a different kind of coolness from the house, and it had a smell, which was something the upstairs was totally without. It felt cavernous down there, but in a comforting way, like the simulated caves children make for themselves on rainy days, in hall closets, under blankets, or in between the legs of dining room tables.I flipped on the light at the foot of the stairs and was not surprised at the pine paneling, the bamboo furniture, the ping-pong table, and the mirrored bar that was stocked with every kind and size of glass, ice bucket, decanter, mixer, swizzle stick, shot glass, pretzel bowl—all the bacchanalian paraphernalia, plentiful, orderly, and untouched, as it can be only in the bar of a wealthy man who never entertains drinking people, who himself does not drink, who, in fact, gets a fishy look from his wife when every several months he takes a shot of schnapps before dinner. I went behind the bar where there was an aluminum sink that had not seen a dirty glass, I'm sure, since Ron's bar mitzvah party, and would not see another, probably, until one of the Patimkin children was married or engaged. I would have poured myself a drink—just as a wicked wage for being forced into servantry—but I was uneasy about breaking the label on a bottle of whiskey. You had to break a label to get a drink. On the shelf back of the bar were two dozen bottles—twenty-three to be exact—of Jack Daniels, each with a little booklet tied to its collared neck informing patrons how patrician of them it was to drink the stuff. And over the Jack Daniels were more photos: there was a blown-up newspaper photo of Ron palming a basketball in one hand like a raisin; under the picture it said, "*Center,* Ronald Patimkin, Millburn High School, 6' 4", 217 pounds." And there was another picture of Brenda on a horse, and next to that, a velvet mounting board with ribbons and medals clipped to it: Essex County Horse Show 1949, Union County Horse Show 1950, Garden State Fair 1952, Morristown Horse Show 1953, and so on—all for Brenda, for jumping and running or galloping or whatever else young girls receive ribbons for. In the entire house I hadn't seen one picture of Mr. Patimkin.

The rest of the basement, back of the wide pine-paneled room, was gray cement walls and linoleum floor and contained innumerable electrical appliances, including a freezer big enough to house a family of Eskimos. Beside the freezer, incongruously, was a tall old refrigerator; its ancient presence was a reminder to me of the Patimkin roots in Newark. This same refrigerator had once stood in the kitchen of an apartment in some four-family house, probably in the same neighborhood where I had lived all my life, first with my parents and then, when the two of them went wheezing off to Arizona, with my aunt and uncle. After Pearl Harbor the refrigerator had made the move up to Short Hills; Patimkin Kitchen and Bathroom Sinks had gone to war: no new barracks was complete until it had a squad of Patimkin sinks lined up in its latrine.

I opened the door of the old refrigerator; it was not empty. No longer did it hold butter, eggs, herring in cream sauce, ginger ale, tuna fish salad, an occasional corsage—rather it was heaped with fruit, shelves swelled with it, every color, every texture, and hidden within, every kind of pit. There were greengage plums, black plums, red plums, apricots, nectarines, peaches, long horns of grapes, black, yellow, red, and cherries, cherries flowing out of boxes and staining everything scarlet. And there were melons—cantaloupes and honeydews—and on the top shelf, half of a huge watermelon, a thin sheet of wax paper clinging to its bare red face like a wet lip. Oh Patimkin! Fruit grew in their refrigerator and sporting goods dropped from their trees!

I grabbed a handful of cherries and then a nectarine, and I bit right down to its pit.

"You better wash that or you'll get diarrhea."

Julie was standing behind me in the pine-paneled room. She was wearing *her* Bermudas and *her* white polo shirt which was unlike Brenda's only in that it had a little dietary history of its own.

"What?" I said.

"They're not washed yet," Julie said, and in such a way that it seemed to place the refrigerator itself out-of-bounds, if only for me.

"That's all right," I said, and devoured the nectarine and put the pit in my pocket and stepped out of the refrigerator room, all in one second. I still didn't know what to do with the cherries. "I was just looking around," I said.

Julie didn't answer.

"Where's Ron going?" I asked, dropping the cherries into my pocket, among my keys and change.

"Milwaukee."

"For long?"

"To see Harriet. They're in love."

We looked at each other for longer than I could bear. "Harriet?" I asked.

"Yes."

Julie was looking at me as though she were trying to look behind me, and then I realized that I was standing with my hands out of sight. I brought them around to the front, and, I swear it, she did peek to see if they were empty.

We confronted one another again; she seemed to have a threat in her face.

Then she spoke. "Want to play ping-pong?"

"God, yes," I said, and made for the table with two long, bounding steps. "You can serve."

Julie smiled and we began to play.

I have no excuses to offer for what happened next. I began to win and I liked it.

"Can I take that one over?" Julie said. "I hurt my finger yesterday and it just hurt when I served."

"No."

I continued to win.

"That wasn't fair, Neil. My shoelace came untied. Can I take it—"

"No."

We played, I ferociously.

"Neil, you leaned over the table. That's illegal—"

"I didn't lean and it's not illegal."

I felt the cherries hopping among my nickels and pennies.

"Neil, you gypped me out of a point. You have nineteen and I have eleven—"

"Twenty and *ten*," I said. "Serve!"

She did and I smashed my return past her—it zoomed off the table and skittered into the refrigerator room.

"You're a cheater!" she screamed at me. "You cheat!" Her jaw was trembling as though she carried a weight on top of her pretty head. "I *hate* you!" And she threw her racket across the room and it clanged off the bar, just as, outside, I heard the Chrysler crushing gravel in the driveway.

"The game isn't over," I said to her.

"You cheat! And you were stealing fruit!" she said, and ran away before I had my chance to win.

Later that night, Brenda and I made love, our first time. We were sitting on the sofa in the television room and for some ten minutes had not spoken a word to each other. Julie had long since gone to a weepy bed, and though no one had said anything to me about her crying, I did not know if the child had mentioned my fistful of cherries, which, some time before, I had flushed down the toilet.

The television set was on and though the sound was off and the house quiet, the gray pictures still wiggled at the far end of the room. Brenda was quiet and her dress circled her legs, which were tucked back beneath her. We sat there for some while and did not speak. Then she went into the kitchen and when she came back she said that it sounded as though everyone was asleep. We sat a while longer, watching the soundless bodies on the screen eating a silent dinner in someone's silent restaurant. When I began to unbutton her dress she resisted me, and I like to think it was because she knew how lovely she looked in it. But she looked lovely, my Brenda, anyway, and we folded it carefully and held each other close and soon there we were, Brenda falling, slowly but with a smile, and me rising.

How can I describe loving Brenda? It was so sweet, as though I'd finally scored that twenty-first point.

When I got home I dialed Brenda's number, but not before my aunt heard and rose from her bed.

"Who are you calling at this hour? The doctor?"

"No."

"What kind phone calls, one o'clock at night?"

"Shhh!" I said.

"He tells *me* shhh. Phone calls one o'clock at night, we haven't got a big enough bill," and then she dragged herself back into the bed, where with a martyr's heart and bleary eyes she had resisted the downward tug of sleep until she'd heard my key in the door.

Brenda answered the phone.

"Neil?" she said.

"Yes," I whispered. "You didn't get out of bed, did you?"

"No," she said, "the phone is next to the bed."

"Good. How is it in bed?"

"Good. Are you in bed?"

"Yes," I lied, and tried to right myself by dragging the phone by its cord as close as I could to my bedroom.

"I'm in bed with you," she said.

"That's right," I said, "and I'm with you."

"I have the shades down, so it's dark and I don't see you."

"I don't see you either."

"That was so nice, Neil."

"Yes. Go to sleep, sweet, I'm here," and we hung up without goodbyes. In the morning, as planned, I called again, but I could hardly hear Brenda or myself for that matter, for Aunt Gladys and Uncle Max were going on a Workmen's Circle picnic in the afternoon, and there was some trouble about grape juice that had dripped all night from a jug in the refrigerator and by morning had leaked out onto the floor. Brenda was still in bed and so could play our game with some success, but I had to pull down all the shades of my senses to imagine myself beside her. I could only pray our nights and mornings would come, and soon enough they did.

4

Over the next week and a half there seemed to be only two people in my life: Brenda and the little colored kid who liked Gauguin. Every morning before the library opened, the boy was waiting; sometimes he seated himself on the lion's back, sometimes under his belly, sometimes he just stood around throwing pebbles at his mane. Then he would come inside, tap around the main floor until Otto stared him up on tiptoes, and finally headed up the long marble stairs that led to Tahiti. He did not always stay to lunch time, but one very hot day he was there when I arrived in the morning and went through the door behind me when I left at night. The next morning, it was, that he did not show up, and as though in his place, a very old man appeared, white, smelling of Life Savers, his nose and jowls showing erupted veins beneath them. "Could you tell me where I'd find the art section?"

"Stack Three," I said.

In a few minutes, he returned with a big brown-covered book in his hand. He placed it on my desk, withdrew his card from a long moneyless billfold and waited for me to stamp out the book.

"Do you want to take this book *out*?" I said.

He smiled.

I took his card and jammed the metal edge into the machine; but I did not stamp down. "Just a minute," I said. I took a clipboard from under the desk and flipped through a few pages, upon which were games of battleship and tick-tack-toe that I'd been playing through the week with myself. "I'm afraid there's a hold on this book."

"A what?"

"A hold. Someone's called up and asked that we hold it for them. Can I take your name and address and drop a card when it's free . . ."

And so I was able, not without flushing once or twice, to get the book back in the stacks. When the colored kid showed up later in the day, it was just where he'd left it the afternoon before.

As for Brenda, I saw her every evening and when there was not a night game that kept Mr. Patimkin awake and in the TV room, or a Hadassah card party that sent Mrs. Patimkin out of the house and brought her in at unpredictable hours, we made love before the silent screen. One muggy, low-skied night Brenda took me swimming at the club. We were the only ones in the pool, and all the chairs, the cabañas, the lights, the diving boards, the very water seemed to exist only for our pleasure. She wore a blue suit that looked purple in the lights and down beneath the water it flashed sometimes green, sometimes black. Late in the evening a breeze came up off the golf course and we wrapped ourselves in one huge towel, pulled two chaise longues together, and despite the bartender, who was doing considerable pacing back and forth by the bar window, which overlooked the pool, we rested side by side on the chairs. Finally the bar light itself flipped off, and then, in a snap, the lights around the pool went down and out. My heart must have beat faster, or something, for Brenda seemed to guess my sudden doubt—*we should go*, I thought.

She said: "That's okay."

It was very dark, the sky was low and starless, and it took a while for me to see, once again, the diving board a shade lighter than the night, and to distinguish the water from the chairs that surrounded the far side of the pool.

I pushed the straps of her bathing suit down but she said no and rolled an inch away from me, and for the first time in the two weeks I'd known her she asked me a question about me.

"Where are your parents?" she said.

"Tucson," I said. "Why?"

"My mother asked me."

I could see the life guard's chair now, white almost.

"Why are you still here? Why aren't you with them?" she asked.

"I'm not a child any more, Brenda," I said, more sharply than I'd intended. "I just can't go wherever my parents are."

"But then why do you stay with your aunt and uncle?"

"They're not my parents."

"They're better?"

"No. Worse. I don't *know* why I stay with them."

"Why?" she said.

"Why don't I know?"

"Why do you stay? You do know, don't you?"

"My job, I suppose. It's convenient from there, and it's cheap, and it pleases my parents. My aunt's all right really . . . Do I really have to explain to your mother why I live where I do?"

"It's not for my mother. I want to know. I wondered why you weren't with your parents, that's all."

"Are you cold?" I asked.

"No."

"Do you want to go home?"

"No, not unless you do. Don't you feel well, Neil?"

"I feel all right," and to let her know that I was still me, I held her to me, though that moment I was without desire.

"Neil?"

"What?"

"What about the library?"

"Who wants to know that?"

"My father," she laughed.

"And you?"

She did not answer a moment. "And me," she said finally.

"Well, what about it? Do I like it? It's okay. I sold shoes once and like the library better. After the Army they tried me for a couple months at Uncle Aaron's real estate company—Doris' father—and I like the library better than that . . ."

"How did you get a job *there*?"

"I worked there for a little while when I was in college, then when I quit Uncle Aaron's, oh, I don't know . . ."

"What did you take in college?"

"At Newark Colleges of Rutgers University I majored in philosophy. I am twenty-three years old. I—"

"Why do you sound nasty again?"

"Do I?"

"Yes."

I didn't say I was sorry.

"Are you planning on making a career of the library?"

"Bren, I'm not planning anything. I haven't planned a thing in three years. At least for the year I've been out of the Army. In the Army I used to plan to go away weekends. I'm—I'm not a planner." After all the truth I'd suddenly given her, I shouldn't have ruined it for myself with that final lie. I added, "I'm a liver."

"I'm a pancreas," she said.

"I'm a—"

And she kissed the absurd game away; she wanted to be serious.

"Do you love me, Neil?"

I did not answer.

"I'll sleep with you whether you do or not, so tell me the truth."

"That was pretty crude."

"Don't be prissy," she said.

"No. I mean a crude thing to say about me."

"I don't understand," she said, and she didn't, and that she didn't pained me; I allowed myself the minor subterfuge, however, of forgiving Brenda her obtuseness. "Do you?" she said.

"No."

"I want you to."

"What about the library?"

"What about it?" she said.

Was it obtuseness again? I thought not—and it wasn't, for Brenda said, "When you love me, there'll be nothing to worry about."

"Then of course I'll love you." I smiled.

"I know you will," she said. "Why don't you go in the water, and I'll wait for you and close my eyes, and when you come back you'll surprise me with the wet. Go ahead."

"You like games, don't you?"

"Go ahead. I'll close my eyes."

I walked down to the edge of the pool and dove in. The water felt colder than it had earlier, and when I broke through and was headed blindly down I felt a touch of panic. At the top again, I started to swim the length of the pool and then turned at the end and started back, but suddenly I was sure that when I left the water Brenda would be gone. I'd be alone in this damn place. I started for the side and pulled myself up and ran to the chairs and Brenda was there and I kissed her.

"God," she shivered, "you didn't stay long."

"I know."

"My turn," she said, and then she was up and a second later I heard a little crack of water and then nothing. Nothing for quite a while.

"Bren," I called softly, "are you all right?" but no one answered.

I found her glasses on the chair beside me and held them in my hands. "Brenda?"

Nothing.

"Brenda?"

"No fair calling," she said and gave me her drenched self. "Your turn," she said.

This time I stayed below the water for a long time and when I surfaced again my lungs were ready to pop. I threw my head back for air and above me saw the sky, low like a hand pushing down, and I began to swim as though to move out from under its pressure. I wanted to get back to Brenda, for I worried once again—and there was no evidence, was there?—that if I stayed away too long she would not be there when I returned. I wished that I had carried her glasses away with me, so she would have to wait for me to lead her back home. I was having crazy thoughts, I knew, and yet they did not seem uncalled for in the darkness and strangeness of that place. Oh how I wanted to call out to her from the pool, but I knew she would not answer and I forced myself to swim the length a third time, and then a fourth, but midway through the fifth I felt a weird fright again, had momentary thoughts of my own extinction, and that time when I came back I held her tighter than either of us expected.

"Let go, let go," she laughed, "my turn—"

"But Brenda—"

But Brenda was gone and this time it seemed as though she'd never come back. I settled back and waited for the sun to dawn over the ninth hole, prayed it would if only for the comfort of its light, and when Brenda finally returned to me I would not let her go, and her cold wetness crept into me somehow and made me shiver. "That's it, Brenda. Please, no more games," I said, and then when I spoke again I held her so tightly I almost dug my body into hers, "I love you," I said, "I do."

So the summer went on. I saw Brenda every evening; we went swimming, we went for walks, we went for rides, up through the mountains so far and so long that by the time we started back the fog had begun to emerge from the trees and push out into the road, and I would tighten my hands on the wheel and Brenda would put on her glasses and watch the white line for me. And we would eat—a few nights after my discovery of the fruit refrigerator Brenda led me to it herself. We would fill huge soup bowls with cherries, and in serving dishes for roast beef we would heap slices of watermelon. Then we would go up and out the back doorway of the basement and onto the back lawn and sit under the sporting-goods tree, the light from the TV room the only brightness we had out there. All we would hear for a while were just the two of us spitting pits. "I wish they would take root overnight and in the morning there'd just be watermelons and cherries."

"If they took root in this yard, sweetie, they'd grow refrigerators and Westinghouse Preferred. I'm not being nasty," I'd add quickly, and Brenda would laugh, and say she felt like a greengage plum, and I would disappear down into the basement and the cherry bowl would now be a greengage plum bowl, and then a nectarine bowl, and then a peach bowl, until, I have to admit it, I cracked my frail bowel, and would have to spend the following night, sadly, on the wagon. And then too we went out for corned beef sandwiches, pizza, beer and shrimp, ice cream sodas, and hamburgers. We went to the Lions Club Fair one night and Brenda won a Lions Club ashtray by shooting three baskets in a row. And when Ron came home from Milwaukee we went from time to time to see him play basketball in the semi-pro summer league, and it was those evenings that I felt a stranger with Brenda, for she knew all the players' names, and though for the most part they were gawky-limbed and dull, there was one named Luther Ferrari who was neither, and whom Brenda had dated for a whole year in high school. He was Ron's closest friend and I remembered his name from the Newark *News*; he was one of the great Ferrari brothers. All State all of them in at least two sports. It was Ferrari who called Brenda Buck, a nickname which apparently went back to her ribbon-winning days. Like Ron, Ferrari was exceedingly polite, as though it was some affliction of those over six feet three; he was gentlemanly towards me and gentle towards Brenda, and after a while I balked when the suggestion was made that we go to see Ron play. And then one night we discovered that at eleven o'clock the cashier of the Hilltop Theatre went home and the manager disappeared into his office, and so that summer we saw the last quarter of at least fifteen movies, and then when we were driving home—driving Brenda home, that is—we would try to reconstruct the beginnings of the films. Our favorite last quarter of a movie was *Ma and Pa Kettle in the City*, our favorite fruit, greengage plums, and our favorite, our only, people, each other. Of course we ran into others from time to time, some of Brenda's friends, and occasionally, one or two of mine. One night in August we even went to a bar out on Route 6 with Laura Simpson Stolowitch and her fiancé, but it was a dreary evening. Brenda and I seemed untrained in talking to others, and so we danced a great deal, which we realized was one thing we'd never done before. Laura's boyfriend drank stingers pompously and Simp—Brenda wanted me to call her Stolo but I didn't—Simp drank a tepid combination of something like ginger ale and soda. Whenever we returned to the table, Simp would be talking about "the dance" and her fiancé about "the film," until finally Brenda asked him "Which film?" and then we danced till closing time. And when we went back to Brenda's we filled a bowl with cherries which we carried into the TV room and ate sloppily for a while; and later, on the sofa, we loved each other and when I moved from the darkened room to the bathroom I could always feel cherry pits against my bare soles. At home, undressing for the second time that night, I would find red marks on the undersides of my feet.

And how did her parents take all of this? Mrs. Patimkin continued to smile at me and Mr. Patimkin continued to think I ate like a bird. When invited to dinner I would, for his benefit, eat twice what I wanted, but the truth seemed to be that after he'd characterized my appetite that first time, he never really bothered to look again. I might have eaten ten times my normal amount, have finally killed myself with food, he would still have considered me not a man but a sparrow. No one seemed distressed by my presence, though Julie had cooled considerably; consequently, when Brenda suggested to her father that at the end of August I spend a week of my vacation at the Patimkin house, he pondered a moment, decided on the five iron, made his approach shot, and said yes. And when she passed on to her mother the decision of Patimkin Sink, there wasn't much Mrs. Patimkin could do. So, through Brenda's craftiness, I was invited.

On that Friday morning that was to be my last day of work, my Aunt Gladys saw me packing my bag and she asked where I was going. I told her. She did not answer and I thought I saw awe in those red-rimmed hysterical eyes—I had come a long way since that day she'd said to me on the phone, "Fancy-schmancy."

"How long you going, I should know how to shop I wouldn't buy too much. You'll leave me with a refrigerator full of milk it'll go bad it'll stink up the refrigerator—"

"A week," I said.

"A *week*?" she said. "They got room for a week?"

"Aunt Gladys, they don't live over the store."

"I lived over a store I wasn't ashamed. Thank God we always had a roof. We never went begging in the streets," she told me as I packed the Bermudas I'd just bought, "and your cousin Susan we'll put through college, Uncle Max should live and be well. We didn't send her away to camp for August, she doesn't have shoes when she wants them, sweaters she doesn't have a drawerful—"

"I didn't say anything, Aunt Gladys."

"You don't get enough to eat here? You leave over sometimes I show your Uncle Max your plate it's a shame. A child in Europe could make a four-course meal from what you leave over."

"Aunt Gladys." I went over to her. "I get everything I want here. I'm just taking a vacation. Don't I deserve a vacation?"

She held herself to me and I could feel her trembling. "I told your mother I would take care of her Neil she shouldn't worry. And now you go running—"

I put my arms around her and kissed her on the top of her head." "C'mon," I said, "you're being silly. I'm not running away. I'm just going away for a week, on a vacation."

"You'll leave their telephone number God forbid you should get sick."

"Okay."

"Millburn they live?"

"Short Hills. I'll leave the number."

"Since when do Jewish people live in Short Hills? They couldn't be real Jews believe me."

"They're real Jews," I said.

"I'll see it I'll believe it." She wiped her eyes with the corner of her apron, just as I was zipping up the sides of the suitcase. "Don't close the bag yet. I'll make a little package with some fruit in it, you'll take with you."

"Okay, Aunt Gladys," and on the way to work that morning I ate the orange and the two peaches that she'd put in a bag for me.

A few hours later Mr. Scapello informed me that when I returned from my vacation after Labor Day, I would be hoisted up onto Martha Winney's stool. He himself, he said, had made the same move some twelve years ago, and so it appeared that if I could manage to maintain my balance I might someday be Mr. Scapello. I would also get an eight-dollar increase in salary which was five dollars more than the increase Mr. Scapello had received years before. He shook my hand and then started back up the long flight of marble stairs, his behind barging against his suit jacket like a hoop. No sooner had he left my side than I smelled spearmint and looked up to see the old man with veiny nose and jowls.

"Hello, young man," he said pleasantly. "Is the book back?"

"What book?"

"The Gauguin. I was shopping and I thought I'd stop by to ask. I haven't gotten the card yet. It's two weeks already."

"No," I said, and as I spoke I saw that Mr. Scapello had stopped midway up the stairs and turned as though he'd forgotten to tell me something. "Look," I said to the old man, "it should be back any day." I said it with a finality that bordered on rudeness, and I alarmed myself, for suddenly I saw what would happen: the old man making a fuss, Mr. Scapello gliding down the stairs, Mr. Scapello scampering up to the stacks, Scapello scandalized, Scapello profuse, Scapello presiding at the ascension of John McKee to Miss Winney's stool. I turned to the old man, "Why don't you leave your phone number and I'll try to get a hold of it this afternoon—" but my attempt at concern and courtesy came too late, and the man growled some words about public servants, a letter to the Mayor, snotty kids, and left the library, thank God, only a second before Mr. Scapello returned to my desk to remind me that everyone was chipping in for a present for Miss Winney and that if I liked I should leave a half dollar on his desk during the day.

After lunch the colored kid came in. When he headed past the desk for the stairs, I called over to him. "Come here," I said. "Where are you going?"

"The heart section."

"What book are you reading?"

"That Mr. Go-again's book. Look, man, I ain't doing nothing wrong. I didn't do *no* writing in *anything*. You could search me—"

"I know you didn't. Listen, if you like that book so much why don't you please take it home? Do you have a library card?"

"No, sir, I didn't take *nothing*."

"No, a library card is what we give to you so you can take books home. Then you won't have to come down here every day. Do you go to school?"

"Yes, sir. Miller Street School. But this here's summertime. It's okay I'm not in school. I ain't *supposed* to be in school."

"I know. As long as you go to school you can *have* a library card. You could take the book home."

"What you keep telling me take that book home for? At home somebody dee-*stroy* it."

"You could hide it someplace, in a desk—"

"Man," he said, squinting at me, "why don't you want me to come round here?"

"I didn't say you shouldn't."

"I *likes* to come here. I likes them stairs."

"I like them too," I said. "But the trouble is that someday somebody's going to take that book out."

He smiled. "Don't you worry," he said to me. "Ain't nobody done that yet," and he tapped off to the stairs and Stack Three.

Did I perspire that day! It was the coolest of the summer, but when I left work in the evening my shirt was sticking to my back. In the car I opened my bag, and while the rush-hour traffic flowed down Washington Street, I huddled in the back and changed into a clean shirt so that when I reached Short Hills I'd look as though I was deserving of an interlude in the suburbs. But driving up Central Avenue I could not keep my mind on my vacation, or for that matter on my driving: to the distress of pedestrians and motorists, I ground gears, overshot cross-walks, hesitated at green and red lights alike. I kept thinking that while I was on vacation that jowly bastard would return to the library, that the colored kid's book would disappear, that my new job would be taken away from me, that, in fact, my old job—but then why should I worry about all that: the library wasn't going to be *my* life.

5

"Ron's getting married!" Julie screamed at me when I came through the door. "Ron's getting married!"

"Now?" I said.

"Labor Day! He's marrying Harriet, he's marrying Harriet." She began to sing it like a jump-rope song, nasal and rhythmic. "I'm going to be a sister-in-law!"

"Hi," Brenda said, "I'm going to be a sister-in-law."

"So I hear. When did it happen?"

"This afternoon he told us. They spoke long distance for forty minutes last night. She's flying here next week, and there's going to be a *huge* wedding. My parents are flittering all over the place. They've got to arrange everything in about a day or two. And my father's taking Ron in the business—but he's going to have to start at two hundred a week and then work himself up. That'll take till October.

"I thought he was going to be a gym teacher."

"He was. But now he has responsibilities . . ."

And at dinner Ron expanded on the subject of responsibilities and the future.

"We're going to have a boy," he said, to his mother's delight, "and when he's about six months old I'm going to sit him down with a basketball in front of him, and a football, and a baseball, and then whichever one he reaches for, that's the one we're going to concentrate on."

"Suppose he doesn't reach for any of them," Brenda said.

"Don't be funny, young lady," Mrs. Patimkin said.

"I'm going to be an aunt," Julie sang, and she stuck her tongue out at Brenda.

"When is Harriet coming?" Mr. Patimkin breathed through a mouthful of potatoes.

"A week from yesterday."

"Can she sleep in my room?" Julie cried. "*Can* she?"

"No, the guest room—" Mrs. Patimkin began, but then she remembered me—with a crushing side glance from those purple eyes, and said, "Of course."

Well, I did eat like a bird. After dinner my bag was carried—by me—up to the guest room which was across from Ron's room and right down the hall from Brenda. Brenda came along to show me the way.

"Let me see your bed, Bren."

"Later," she said.

"Can we? Up here?"

"I think so," she said. "Ron sleeps like a log."

"Can I stay the night?"

"I don't know."

"I could get up early and come back in here. We'll set the alarm."

"It'll wake everybody up."

"I'll remember to get up. I can do it."

"I better not stay up here with you too long," she said. "My mother'll have a fit. I think she's nervous about your being here."

"So am I. I hardly know them. Do you think I should really stay a whole week?"

"A whole week? Once Harriet gets here it'll be so chaotic you can probably stay two months."

"You think so?"

"Yes."

"Do you want me to?"

"Yes," she said, and went down the stairs so as to ease her mother's conscience.

I unpacked my bag and dropped my clothes into a drawer that was empty except for a packet of dress shields and a high school yearbook. In the middle of my unpacking, Ron came clunking up the stairs.

"Hi," he called into my room.

"Congratulations," I called back. I should have realized that any word of ceremony would provoke a handshake from Ron; he interrupted whatever it was he was about to do in his room, and came into mine.

"Thanks." He pumped me. "Thanks."

Then he sat down on my bed and watched me as I finished unpacking. I have one shirt with a Brooks Brothers label and I let it linger on the bed a while; the Arrows I heaped in the drawer. Ron sat there rubbing his forearm and grinning. After a while I was thoroughly unsettled by the silence.

"Well," I said, "that's something."

He agreed, to *what* I don't know.

"How does it feel?" I asked, after another longer silence.

"Better. Ferrari smacked it under the boards."

"Oh. Good," I said. "How does getting married feel?"

"Ah, okay, I guess."

I leaned against the bureau and counted stitches in the carpet.

Ron finally risked a journey into language. "Do you know anything about music?" he asked.

"Something, yes."

"You can listen to my phonograph if you want."

"Thanks, Ron. I didn't know you were interested in music."

"Sure. I got all the Andre Kostelanetz records ever made. You like Mantovani? I got all of him too. I like semiclassical a lot. You can hear my Columbus record if you want . . ." he dwindled off. Finally he shook my hand and left.

Downstairs I could hear Julie singing. "I'm going to be an a-a-aunt," and Mrs. Patimkin saying to her, "No, honey, you're going to be a sister-in-law. Sing that, sweetheart," but Julie continued to sing, "I'm going to be an a-a-aunt," and then I heard Brenda's voice joining hers, singing, "We're going to be an a-a-aunt," and then Julie joined that, and finally Mrs. Patimkin called to Mr. Patimkin, "Will you make her stop encouraging her . . ." and soon the duet ended.

And then I heard Mrs. Patimkin again. I couldn't make out the words but Brenda answered her. Their voices grew louder; finally I could hear perfectly. "I need a houseful of company at a time like this?" It was Mrs. Patimkin. "I asked you, Mother." "You asked your father. I'm the one you should have asked first. He doesn't know how much extra work this is for me . . ." "My God, Mother, you'd think we didn't have Carlota and Jenny." "Carlota and Jenny can't do everything. This is not the Salvation Army!" "What the hell does that mean?" "Watch your tongue, young lady. That may be very well for your college friends." "Oh, stop it, Mother!" "Don't raise your voice to me. When's the last time you lifted a finger to help around here?" "I'm not a slave . . . I'm a daughter." "You ought to learn what a day's work means." "Why?" Brenda said. "Why?" "Because you're lazy," Mrs. Patimkin answered, "and you think the world owes you a living." "Whoever said that?" "You ought to earn some money and buy your own clothes." "Why? Good God, Mother, Daddy could live off the stocks alone, for God's sake. What are you complaining about?" "When's the last time you washed the dishes!" "Jesus Christ!" Brenda flared, "Carlota washes the dishes!" "Don't Jesus Christ me!" "Oh, Mother!" and Brenda was crying. "Why the hell are you like this!" "That's it," Mrs. Patimkin said "cry in front of your company . . ." "My company . . ." Brenda wept, "why don't you go yell at him too . . . why is everyone so nasty to me . . ."

From across the hall I heard Andre Kostelanetz let several thousand singing violins loose on "Night and Day." Ron's door was open and I saw he was stretched out, colossal, on his bed; he was singing along with the record. The words belonged to "Night and Day," but I didn't recognize Ron's tune. In a minute he picked up the phone and asked the operator for a Milwaukee number. While she connected him, he rolled over and turned up the volume on the record player, so that it would carry the nine hundred miles west.

I heard Julie downstairs. "Ha ha, Brenda's crying, ha ha, Brenda's crying."

And then Brenda was running up the stairs. "Your day'll come, you little bastard!" she called.

"*Brenda!*" Mrs. Patimkin called.

"*Mommy!*" Julie cried. "Brenda cursed at me!"

"What's going *on* here!" Mr. Patimkin shouted.

"You call *me*, Mrs. P?" Carlota shouted.

And Ron, in the other room, said, "Hello, Har, I told them . . ."

I sat down on my Brooks Brothers shirt and pronounced my own name out loud.

"Goddam her!" Brenda said to me as she paced up and down my room.

"Bren, do you think I should go—"

"Shhh . . ." She went to the door of my room and listened. "They're going visiting, thank God."

"Brenda—"

"Shhh . . . They've gone."

"Julie too?"

"Yes," she said. "Is Ron in his room? His door is closed."

"He went out."

"You can't hear anybody move around here. They all creep around in *sneakers*. Oh Neil."

"Bren, I asked you, maybe I should just stay through tomorrow and then go."

"Oh, it isn't you she's angry about."

"I'm not helping any."

"It's Ron, really. That he's getting married just has her flipped. And me. Now with that goody-good Harriet around she'll just forget I ever exist."

"Isn't that okay with you?"

She walked off to the window and looked outside. It was dark and cool; the trees rustled and flapped as though they were sheets that had been hung out to dry. Everything outside hinted at September, and for the first time I realized how close we were to Brenda's departure for school.

"Is it, Bren?" but she was not listening to me.

She walked across the room to a door at the far end of the room. She opened it.

"I thought that was a closet," I said.

"Come here."

She held the door back and we leaned into the darkness and could hear the strange wind hissing in the eaves of the house.

"What's in here?" I said.

"Money."

Brenda went into the room. When the puny sixty-watt bulb was twisted on, I saw that the place was full of old furniture—two wing chairs with hair-oil lines at the back, a sofa with a paunch in its middle, a bridge table, two bridge chairs with their stuffing showing, a mirror whose backing had peeled off, shadeless lamps, lampless shades, a coffee table with a cracked glass top, and a pile of rolled up shades.

"What is this?" I said.

"A storeroom. Our old furniture."

"How old?"

"From Newark," she said. "Come here." She was on her hands and knees in front of the sofa and was holding up its paunch to peek beneath.

"Brenda, what the hell are we doing here? You're getting filthy."

"It's not here."

"*What?*"

"The money. I told you."

I sat down on a wing chair, raising some dust. It had begun to rain outside, and we could smell the fall dampness coming through the vent that was outlined at the far end of the storeroom. Brenda got up from the floor and sat down on the sofa. Her knees and Bermudas were dirty and when she pushed her hair back she dirtied her forehead. There among the disarrangement and dirt I had the strange experience of seeing us, *both* of us, placed among disarrangement and dirt: we looked like a young couple who had just moved into a new apartment; we had suddenly taken stock of our furniture, finances, and future, and all we could feel any pleasure about was the clean smell of outside, which reminded us we were alive, but which, in a pinch, would not feed us.

"What money?" I said again.

"The hundred-dollar bills. From when I was a little girl . . ." and she breathed deeply. "When I was little and we'd just moved from Newark, my father took me up here one day. He took me into this room and told me that if anything should ever happen to him, he wanted me to know where there was some money that I should have. He said it wasn't for anybody else but me, and that I should never tell anyone about it, not even Ron. Or my mother."

"How much was it?"

"Three hundred-dollar bills. I'd never seen them before. I was nine, around Julie's age. I don't think we'd been living here a month. I remember I used to come up here about once a week, when no one was home but Carlota, and crawl under the sofa and make sure it was still here. And it always was. He never mentioned it once again. Never."

"Where is it? Maybe someone stole it."

"I don't know, Neil. I suppose he took it back."

"When it was gone," I said, "my God, didn't you tell him? Maybe Carlota—"

"I never knew it was gone, until just now. I guess I stopped looking at one time or another . . . And then I forgot about it. Or just didn't think about it. I mean I always had enough, I didn't need this. I guess one day *he* figured I wouldn't need it."

Brenda paced up to the narrow, dust-covered window and drew her initials on it.

"Why did you want it now?" I said.

"I don't know . . ." she said and went over and twisted the bulb off.

I didn't move from the chair and Brenda, in her tight shorts and shirt, seemed naked standing there a few feet away. Then I saw her shoulders shaking. "I wanted to find it and tear it up in little pieces and put the goddam pieces in her purse! If it was there, I swear it, I would have done it."

"I wouldn't have let you, Bren."

"Wouldn't you have?"

"No."

"Make love to me, Neil. Right now."

"Where?"

"Do it! *Here*. On this cruddy cruddy cruddy sofa."

And I obeyed her.

The next morning Brenda made breakfast for the two of us. Ron had gone off to his first day of work—I'd heard him singing in the shower only an hour after I'd returned to my own room; in fact, I had still been awake when the Chrysler had pulled out of the garage, carrying boss and son down to the Patimkin works in Newark. Mrs. Patimkin wasn't home either; she had taken her car and had gone off to the Temple to talk to Rabbi Kranitz about the wedding. Julie was on the back lawn playing at helping Carlota hang the clothes.

"You know what I want to do this morning?" Brenda said. We were eating a grapefruit, sharing it rather sloppily, for Brenda couldn't find a paring knife, and so we'd decided to peel it down like an orange and eat the segments separately.

"What?" I said.

"Run," she said. "Do you ever run?"

"You mean on a track? God, yes. In high school we had to run a mile every month. So we wouldn't be Momma's boys. I think the bigger your lungs get the more you're supposed to hate your mother."

"I want to run," she said, "and I want you to run. Okay?"

"Oh, Brenda . . ."

But an hour later, after a breakfast that consisted of another grapefruit, which apparently is all a runner is supposed to eat in the morning, we had driven the Volkswagen over to the high school, behind which was a quarter-mile track. Some kids were playing with a dog out in the grassy center of the track, and at the far end, near the woods, a figure in white shorts with slits in the side, and no shirt, was twirling, twirling, and then flinging a shot put as far as he could. After it left his hand he did a little eagle-eyed tap dance while he watched it arch and bend and land in the distance.

"You know," Brenda said, "you look like me. Except bigger."

We were dressed similarly, sneakers, sweat socks, khaki Bermudas, and sweat shirts, but I had the feeling that Brenda was not talking about the accidents of our dress—if they were accidents. She meant, I was sure, that I was somehow beginning to look the way she wanted me to. Like herself.

"Let's see who's faster," she said, and then we started along the track. Within the first eighth of a mile the three little boys and their dog were following us. As we passed the corner where the shot putter was, he waved at us; Brenda called "Hi!" and I smiled, which, as you may or may not know, makes one engaged in serious running feel inordinately silly. At the quarter mile the kids dropped off and retired to the grass, the dog turned and started the other way, and I had a tiny knife in my side. Still I was abreast of Brenda, who as we started on the second lap, called "Hi!" once again to the lucky shot putter, who was reclining on the grass now, watching us, and rubbing his shot like a crystal ball. Ah, I thought, there's the sport.

"How about us throwing the shot put?" I panted.

"After," she said, and I saw beads of sweat clinging to the last strands of hair that shagged off her ear. When we approached the half mile Brenda suddenly swerved off the track onto the grass and tumbled down; her departure surprised me and I was still running.

"Hey, Bob Mathias," she called, "let's lie in the sun . . ."

But I acted as though I didn't hear her and though my heart pounded in my throat and my mouth was dry as a drought, I made my legs move, and swore I would not stop until I'd finished one more lap. As I passed the shot putter for the third time, I called "Hi!"

She was excited when I finally pulled up alongside of her. "You're good," she said. My hands were on my hips and I was looking at the ground and sucking air—rather, air was sucking me, I didn't have much to say about it.

"Uh-huh," I breathed.

"Let's do this every morning," she said. "We'll get up and have two grapefruit, and then you'll come out here and run. I'll time you. In two weeks you'll break four minutes, won't you, sweetie? I'll get Ron's stop watch." She was so excited—she'd slid over on the grass and was pushing my socks up against my wet ankles and calves. She bit my kneecap.

"Okay," I said.

"Then we'll go back and have a real breakfast."

"Okay."

"You drive back," she said, and suddenly she was up and running ahead of me, and then we were headed back in the car.

And the next morning, my mouth still edgy from the grapefruit segments, we were at the track. We had Ron's stop watch and a towel for me, for when I was finished.

"My legs are a little sore," I said.

"Do some exercises," Brenda said. "I'll do them with you." She heaped the towel on the grass and together we did deep knee bends, and sit-ups, and push-ups, and some high-knee raising in place. I felt overwhelmingly happy.

"I'm just going to run a half today, Bren. We'll see what I do . . ." and I heard Brenda click the watch, and then when I was on the far side of the track, the clouds trailing above me like my own white, fleecy tail, I saw that Brenda was on the ground, hugging her knees, and alternately checking the watch and looking out at me. We were the only ones there, and it all reminded me of one of those scenes in race-horse movies, where an old trainer like Walter Brennan and a young handsome man clock the beautiful girl's horse in the early Kentucky morning, to see if it really is the fastest two-year-old alive. There were differences all right—one being simply that at the quarter mile Brenda shouted out to me, "A minute and fourteen seconds," but it was pleasant and exciting and clean and when I was finished Brenda was standing up and waiting for me. Instead of a tape to break I had Brenda's sweet flesh to meet, and I did, and it was the first time she said that she loved me.

We ran—I ran—every morning, and by the end of the week I was running a 7:02 mile, and always at the end there was the little click of the watch and Brenda's arms.

At night, I would read in my pajamas, while Brenda, in her room, read, and we would wait for Ron to go to sleep. Some nights we had to wait longer than others, and I would hear the leaves swishing outside, for it had grown cooler at the end of August, and the air-conditioning was turned off at night and we were all allowed to open our windows. Finally Ron would be ready for bed. He would stomp around his room and then he would come to the door in his shorts and T-shirt and go into the bathroom where he would urinate loudly and brush his teeth. After he brushed his teeth I would go in to brush mine. We would pass in the hall and I would give him a hearty and sincere "Goodnight." Once in the bathroom, I would spend a moment admiring my tan in the mirror; behind me I could see Ron's jock straps hanging out to dry on the Hot and Cold knobs of the shower. Nobody ever questioned their tastefulness as adornment, and after a few nights I didn't even notice them.

While Ron brushed his teeth and I waited in my bed for my turn, I could hear the record player going in his room. Generally, after coming in from basketball, he would call Harriet—who was now only a few days away from us—and then would lock himself up with *Sports Illustrated* and Mantovani; however, when he emerged from his room for his evening toilet, it was not a Mantovani record I would hear playing, but something else, apparently what he'd once referred to as his Columbus record. I *imagined* that was what I heard, for I could not tell much from the last moments of sound. All I heard were bells moaning evenly and soft patriotic music behind them, and riding over it all, a deep kind of Edward R. Murrow gloomy voice: "*And so goodbye, Columbus,*" the voice intoned, "*. . . goodbye, Columbus . . . goodbye . . .*" Then there would be silence and Ron would be back in his room; the light would switch off and in only a few mintues I would hear him rumbling down into that exhilarating, restorative, vitamin-packed sleep that I imagined athletes to enjoy.

One morning near sneaking-away time I had a dream and when I awakened from it, there was just enough dawn coming into the room for me to see the color of Brenda's hair. I touched her in her sleep, for the dream had unsettled me: it had taken place on a ship, an old sailing ship like those you see in pirate movies. With me on the ship was the little colored kid from the library—I was the captain and he my mate, and we were the only crew members. For a while it was a pleasant dream; we were anchored in the harbor of an island in the Pacific and it was very sunny. Up on the beach there were beautiful bare-skinned Negresses, and none of them moved; but suddenly *we* were moving, our ship, out of the harbor, and the Negresses moved slowly down to the shore and began to throw leis at us and say "Goodbye, Columbus . . . goodbye, Columbus . . . goodbye . . ." and though we did not want to go, the little boy and I, the boat was moving and there was nothing we could do about it, and he shouted at me that it was my fault and I shouted it was his for not having a library card, but we were wasting our breath, for we were further and further from the island, and soon the natives were nothing at all. Space was all out of proportion in the dream, and things were sized and squared in no way I'd ever seen before, and I think it was that more than anything else that steered me into consciousness. I did not want to leave Brenda's side that morning, and for a while I played with the little point at the nape of her neck, where she'd had her hair cut. I stayed longer than I should have, and when finally I returned to my room I almost ran into Ron who was preparing for his day at Patimkin Kitchen and Bathroom Sinks.

6

That morning was supposed to have been my last at the Patimkin house; however, when I began to throw my things into my bag late in the day, Brenda told me I could unpack—somehow she'd managed to inveigle another week out

of her parents, and I would be able to stay right through till Labor Day, when
Ron would be married; then, the following morning Brenda would be off to
school and I would go back to work. So we would be with each other until the
summer's last moment.

This should have made me overjoyed, but as Brenda trotted back down
the stairs to accompany her family to the airport—where they were to pick up
Harriet—I was not joyful but disturbed as I had been more and more with the
thought that when Brenda went back to Radcliffe, that would be the end for me. I
was convinced that even Miss Winney's stool was not high enough for me to see
clear up to Boston. Nevertheless, I tossed my clothing back into the drawer and
was able, finally, to tell myself that there'd been no hints of ending our affair
from Brenda, and any suspicions I had, any uneasiness, was spawned in my own
uncertain heart. Then I went into Ron's room to call my aunt.

"Hello?" she said.

"Aunt Gladys," I said, "how are you?"

"You're sick." ·

"No, I'm having a fine time. I wanted to call you. I'm going to stay
another week."

"Why?"

"I told you. I'm having a good time. Mrs. Patimkin asked me to stay until
Labor Day."

"You've got clean underwear?"

"I'm washing it at night. I'm okay, Aunt Gladys."

"By hand you can't get it clean."

"It's clean enough. Look, Aunt Gladys, I'm having a wonderful time."

"*Shmutz* he lives in and I shouldn't worry."

"How's Uncle Max?" I asked.

"What should he be? Uncle Max is Uncle Max. You, I don't like the way
your voice sounds."

"Why? Do I sound like I've got on dirty underwear?"

"Smart guy. Someday you'll learn."

"What?"

"What do you mean *what*? You'll find out. You'll stay there too long
you'll be too good for us."

"Never, sweetheart," I said.

"I'll see it I'll believe it."

"Is it cool in Newark, Aunt Gladys?"

"It's snowing," she said.

"Hasn't it been cool all week?"

"You sit around all day it's cool. For me it's not February, believe me."

"Okay, Aunt Gladys. Say hello to everybody."

"You got a letter from your mother."

"Good. I'll read it when I get home."

"You couldn't take a ride down you'll read it?"

"It'll wait. I'll drop them a note. Be a good girl," I said.

"What about your socks?"

"I go barefoot. Goodbye, honey." And I hung up.

Down in the kitchen Carlota was getting dinner ready. I was always
amazed at how Carlota's work never seemed to get in the way of her life. She

made household chores seem like illustrative gestures of whatever it was she was singing, even, if as now, it was "I Get a Kick out of You." She moved from the oven to the automatic dishwasher—she pushed buttons, turned dials, peeked in the glass-doored oven, and from time to time picked a big black grape out of a bunch that lay on the sink. She chewed and chewed, humming all the time, and then, with a deliberated casualness, shot the skin and the pit directly into the garbage disposal unit. I said hello to her as I went out the back door, and though she did not return the greeting, I felt a kinship with one who, like me, had been partially wooed and won on Patimkin fruit.

Out on the lawn I shot baskets for a while; then I picked up an iron and drove a cotton golf ball limply up into the sunlight; then I kicked a soccer ball towards the oak tree; then I tried shooting foul shots again. Nothing diverted me—I felt open-stomached, as though I hadn't eaten for months, and though I went back inside and came out with my own handful of grapes, the feeling continued, and I knew it had nothing to do with my caloric intake; it was only a rumor of the hollowness that would come when Brenda was away. The fact of her departure had, of course, been on my mind for a while, but overnight it had taken on a darker hue. Curiously, the darkness seemed to have something to do with Harriet, Ron's intended, and I thought for a time that it was simply the reality of Harriet's arrival that had dramatized the passing of time: we had been talking about it and now suddenly it was here—just as Brenda's departure would be here before we knew it.

But it was more than that: the union of Harriet and Ron reminded me that separation need not be a permanent state. People could marry each other, even if they were young! And yet Brenda and I had never mentioned marriage, except perhaps for that night at the pool when she'd said, "When you love me, everything will be all right." Well, I loved her, and she me, and things didn't seem all right at all. Or was I inventing troubles again? I supposed I should really have thought my lot improved considerably; yet, there on the lawn, the August sky seemed too beautiful and temporary to bear, and I wanted Brenda to marry me. Marriage, though, was not what I proposed to her when she drove the car up the driveway, alone, some fifteen minutes later. That proposal would have taken a kind of courage that I did not think I had. I did not feel myself prepared for any answer but "Hallelujah!" Any other kind of yes wouldn't have satisfied me, and any kind of no, even one masked behind the words, "Let's wait, sweetheart," would have been my end. So I imagine that's why I proposed the surrogate, which turned out finally to be far more daring than I knew it to be at the time.

"Harriet's plane is late, so I drove home," Brenda called.

"Where's everyone else?"

"They're going to wait for her and have dinner at the airport. I have to tell Carlota," and she went inside.

In a few minutes she appeared on the porch. She wore a yellow dress that cut a wide-bottomed U across her shoulders and neck, and showed where the tanned flesh began above her breasts. On the lawn she stepped out of her heels and walked barefoot over to where I was sitting under the oak tree.

"Women who wear high heels all the time get tipped ovaries," she said.

"Who told you that?"

"I don't remember. I like to think everything's ship-shape in there."

"Brenda, I want to ask you something . . ."

She yanked the blanket with the big O on it over to us and sat down.

"What?" she said.

"I know this is out of the blue, though really it's not . . . I want you to buy a diaphragm. To go to a doctor and get one."

She smiled. "Don't worry, sweetie, we're careful. Everything is okay."

"But that's the safest."

"We're safe. It'd be a waste."

"Why take chances?"

"But we *aren't*. How many things do you need."

"Honey, it isn't bulk I'm interested in. It's not even safety," I added.

"You just want me to own one, is that it? Like a walking stick, or a pith helmet—"

"Brenda, I want you to own one for . . . for the sake of pleasure."

"Pleasure? Whose? The doctor's?"

"Mine," I said.

She did not answer me, but rubbed her fingers along the ridge of her collarbone to wipe away the tiny globes of perspiration that had suddenly formed there.

"No, Neil, it's silly."

"Why?"

"Why? It just is."

"You know why it's silly, Brenda—because *I* asked you to do it?"

"That's sillier."

"If you asked *me* to buy a diaphragm we'd have to go straight to the Yellow Pages and find a gynecologist open on Saturday afternoon."

"I would never ask you to do that, baby."

"It's the truth," I said, though I was smiling. "It's the truth."

"It's not," she said, and got up and walked over to the basketball court, where she walked on the white lines that Mr. Patimkin had laid the day before.

"Come back here," I said.

"Neil, it's silly and I don't want to talk about it."

"Why are you being so selfish?"

"Selfish? You're the one who's being selfish. It's your pleasure . . ."

"That's right. My pleasure. Why not!"

"Don't raise your voice. Carlota."

"Then get the hell over here," I said.

She walked over to me, leaving white footprints on the grass. "I didn't think you were such a creature of the flesh," she said.

"Didn't you?" I said. "I'll tell you something that you ought to know. It's not even the pleasures of the flesh I'm talking about."

"Then frankly, I don't know *what* you're talking about. Why you're even bothering. Isn't what we use sufficient?"

"I'm bothering just because I want you to go to a doctor and get a diaphragm. That's all. No explanation. Just do it. Do it because I asked you to."

"You're not being reasonable—"

"Goddamit, Brenda!"

"Goddamit yourself!" she said and went up into the house.

I closed my eyes and leaned back and in fifteen minutes, or maybe less, I heard somebody stroking at the cotton golf ball. She had changed into shorts and a blouse and was still barefoot.

We didn't speak with each other, but I watched her bring the club back of her ear, and then swing through, her chin tilted up with the line of flight a regular golf ball would have taken.

"That's five hundred yards," I said.

She didn't answer but walked after the cotton ball and then readied for another swing.

"Brenda. Please come here."

She walked over, dragging the club over the grass.

"What?"

"I don't want to argue with you."

"Nor I with you," she said. "It was the first time."

"Was it such an awful thing for me to ask?"

She nodded.

"Bren, I know it was probably a surprise. It was for me. But we're not children."

"Neil, I just don't want to. It's not because you asked me to, either. I don't know where you get that from. That's not it."

"Then why is it?"

"Oh everything. I just don't feel *old* enough for all that equipment."

"What does age have to do with it?"

"I don't mean age. I just mean—well, *me.* I mean it's so conscious a thing to do."

"Of course it's conscious. That's exactly it. Don't you see? It would change us."

"It would change me."

"Us. Together."

"Neil, how do you think I'd feel lying to some doctor."

"You can go to Margaret Sanger, in New York. They don't ask any questions."

"You've done this before?"

"No," I said. "I just know. I read Mary McCarthy."

"That's exactly right. That's just what I'd feel like, somebody out of *her.*"

"Don't be dramatic," I said.

"You're the one who's being dramatic. You think there would be something affairish about it, then. Last summer I went with this whore who I sent out to buy—"

"Oh, Brenda, you're a selfish egotistical bitch! You're the one who's thinking about 'last summer,' about an end for us. In fact, that's the whole thing, isn't it—"

"That's right, I'm a bitch. I want this to end. That's why I ask you to stay another week, that's why I let you sleep with me in my own house. What's the *matter* with you! Why don't you and my mother take turns—one day she can plague me, the next you—"

"Stop it!"

"Go to hell, all of you!" Brenda said, and now she was crying and I knew when she ran off I would not see her, as I didn't, for the rest of the afternoon.

Harriet Ehrlich impressed me as a young lady singularly unconscious of a motive in others or herself. All was surfaces, and she seemed a perfect match for

Ron, and too for the Patimkins. Mrs. Patimkin, in fact, did just as Brenda prophesied: Harriet appeared, and Brenda's mother lifted one wing and pulled the girl in towards the warm underpart of her body, where Brenda herself would have liked to nestle. Harriet was built like Brenda, although a little chestier, and she nodded her head insistently whenever anyone spoke. Sometimes she would even say the last few words of your sentence with you, though that was infrequent; for the most part she nodded and kept her hands folded. All evening, as the Patimkins planned where the newlyweds should live, what furniture they should buy, how soon they should have a baby—all through this I kept thinking that Harriet was wearing white gloves, but she wasn't.

Brenda and I did not exchange a word or a glance; we sat, listening, Brenda somewhat more impatient than me. Near the end Harriet began calling Mrs. Patimkin "Mother," and once, "Mother Patimkin," and that was when Brenda went to sleep. I stayed behind, mesmerized almost by the dissection, analysis, reconsideration, and finally, the embracing of the trivial. At last Mr. and Mrs. Patimkin tumbled off to bed, and Julie, who had fallen asleep on her chair, was carried into her room by Ron. That left us two non-Patimkins together.

"Ron tells me you have a very interesting job."

"I work in the library."

"I've always liked reading."

"That'll be nice, married to Ron."

"Ron likes music."

"Yes," I said. What had I *said*?

"You must get first crack at the best-sellers," she said.

"Sometimes," I said.

"Well," she said, flapping her hands on her knees, "I'm sure we'll all have a good time together. Ron and I hope you and Brenda will double with us soon."

"Not tonight." I smiled. "Soon. Will you excuse me?"

"Good night. I like Brenda very much."

"Thank you," I said as I started up the stairs.

I knocked gently on Brenda's door.

"I'm sleeping."

"Can I come in?" I asked.

Her door opened an inch and she said, "Ron will be up soon."

"We'll leave the door open. I only want to talk."

She let me in and I sat in the chair that faced the bed.

"How do you like your sister-in-law?"

"I've met her before."

"Brenda, you don't have to sound so damn terse."

She didn't answer and I just sat there yanking the string on the shade up and down.

"Are you still angry?" I asked at last.

"Yes."

"Don't be," I said. "You can forget about my suggestion. It's not worth it if this is what's going to happen."

"What did you expect to happen?"

"Nothing. I didn't think it would be so horrendous."

"That's because you can't understand my side."

"Perhaps."

"No perhaps about it."

"*Okay*," I said. "I just wish you'd realize what it is you're getting angry about. It's not my suggestion, Brenda."

"No? What is it?"

"It's me."

"Oh don't start that again, will you? I can't win, no matter what I say."

"Yes, you can," I said. "You have."

I walked out of her room, closing the door behind me for the night.

When I got downstairs the following morning there was a great deal of activity. In the living room I heard Mrs. Patimkin reading a list to Harriet while Julie ran in and out of rooms in search of a skate key. Carlota was vacuuming the carpet; every appliance in the kitchen was bubbling, twisting, and shaking. Brenda greeted me with a perfectly pleasant smile and in the dining room, where I walked to look out at the back lawn and the weather, she kissed me on the shoulder.

"Hello," she said.

"Hello."

"I have to go with Harriet this morning," Brenda told me. "So we can't run. Unless you want to go alone."

"No. I'll read or something. Where are you going?"

"We're going to New York. Shopping. She's going to buy a wedding dress. For after the wedding. To go away in."

"What are *you* going to buy?"

"A dress to be maid of honor in. If I go with Harriet then I can go to Bergdorf's without all that Orhbach's business with my mother."

"Get me something, will you?" I said.

"Oh, Neil, are you going to bring that up again!"

"I was only *fooling*. I wasn't even thinking about that."

"Then why did you say it?"

"Oh Jesus!" I said, and went outside and drove my car down into Millburn Center where I had some eggs and coffee.

When I came back, Brenda was gone, and there were only Carlota, Mrs. Patimkin, and myself in the house. I tried to stay out of whichever rooms they were in, but finally Mrs. Patimkin and I wound up sitting opposite each other in the TV room. She was checking off names on a long sheet of paper she held; next to her, on the table, were two thin phone books which she consulted from time to time.

"No rest for the weary," she said to me.

I smiled hugely, embracing the proverb as though Mrs. Patimkin had just then coined it. "Yes. Of course," I said. "Would you like some help? Maybe I could help you check something."

"Oh, no," she said with a little head-shaking dismissal, "it's for Hadassah."

"Oh," I said.

I sat and watched her until she asked, "Is your mother in Hadassah?"

"I don't know if she is now. She was in Newark."

"Was she an active member?"

"I guess so, she was always planting trees in Israel for someone."

"Really?" Mrs. Patimkin said. "What's her name?"

"Esther Klugman. She's in Arizona now. Do they have Hadassah there?"

"Wherever there are Jewish women."

"Then I guess she is. She's with my father. They went there for their asthma. I'm staying with my aunt in Newark. She's not in Hadassah. My Aunt Sylvia is, though. Do you know her, Aaron Klugman and Sylvia? They belong to your club. They have a daughter, my cousin Doris—" I couldn't stop myself "—They live in Livingston. Maybe it isn't Hadassah my Aunt Sylvia belongs to. I think it's some TB organization. Or cancer. Muscular dystrophy, maybe. I know she's interested in *some* disease."

"That's very nice," Mrs. Patimkin said.

"Oh yes."

"They do very good work."

"I know."

Mrs. Patimkin, I thought, had begun to warm to me; she let the purple eyes stop peering and just look out at the world for a while without judging. "Are you interested in B'nai Brith?" she asked me. "Ron is joining, you know, as soon as he gets married."

"I think I'll wait till then," I said.

Petulantly, Mrs. Patimkin went back to her lists, and I realized it had been foolish of me to risk lightheartedness with her about Jewish affairs. "You're active in the Temple, aren't you?" I asked with all the interest I could muster.

"Yes," she said.

"What Temple do *you* belong to?" she asked in a moment.

"We used to belong to Hudson Street Synagogue. Since my parents left, I haven't had much contact."

I didn't know whether Mrs. Patimkin caught a false tone in my voice. Personally I thought I had managed my rueful confession pretty well, especially when I recalled the decade of paganism prior to my parents' departure. Regardless, Mrs. Patimkin asked immediately—and strategically it seemed— "We're all going to Temple Friday night. Why don't you come with us? I mean, are you orthodox or conservative?"

I considered. "Well, I haven't gone in a long time . . . I sort of switch . . ." I smiled. "I'm just Jewish," I said well-meaningly, but that too sent Mrs. Patimkin back to her Hadassah work. Desperately I tried to think of something that would convince her I wasn't an infidel. Finally I asked: "Do you know Martin Buber's work?"

"Buber . . . Buber," she said, looking at her Hadassah list. "Is he orthodox or conservative?" she asked.

". . . He's a philosopher."

"Is he *reformed*?" she asked, piqued either at my evasiveness or at the possibility that Buber attended Friday night services without a hat, and Mrs. Buber had only one set of dishes in her kitchen.

"Orthodox," I said faintly.

"That's very nice," she said.

"Yes."

"Isn't Hudson Street Synagogue orthodox?" she asked.

"I don't know."

"I thought you belonged."

"I was bar-mitzvahed there."

"And you don't know that it's orthodox?"

"Yes. I do. It is."

"Then *you* must be."

"Oh, yes, I am," I said. "What are you?" I popped, flushing.

"Orthodox. My husband is conservative," which meant, I took it, that he didn't care. "Brenda is nothing, as you probably know."

"Oh?" I said. "No, I didn't know that."

"She was the best Hebrew student I've ever seen," Mrs. Patimkin said, "but then, of course, she got too big for her britches."

Mrs. Patimkin looked at me, and I wondered whether courtesy demanded that I agree. "Oh, I don't know," I said at last, "I'd say Brenda is conservative. Maybe a little reformed . . ."

The phone rang, rescuing me, and I spoke a silent orthodox prayer to the Lord.

"Hello," Mrs. Patimkin said. ". . . no . . . I can *not*, I have all the Hadassah calls to make . . ."

I acted as though I were listening to the birds outside, though the closed windows let no natural noises in.

"Have Ronald drive them up . . . But we can't wait, not if we want it on time . . ."

Mrs. Patimkin glanced up at me; then she put one hand over the mouthpiece. "Would you ride down to Newark for me?"

I stood. "Yes. Surely."

"Dear?" she said back into the phone, "Neil will come for it . . . No, *Neil*, Brenda's friend . . . Yes . . . Goodbye.

"Mr. Patimkin has some silver patterns I have to see. Would you drive down to his place and pick them up?"

"Of course."

"Do you know where the shop is?"

"Yes."

"Here," she said, handing a key ring to me, "take the Volkswagen."

"My car is right outside."

"Take these," she said.

Patimkin Kitchen and Bathroom Sinks was in the heart of the Negro section of Newark. Years ago, at the time of the great immigration, it had been the Jewish section, and still one could see the little fish stores, the kosher delicatessens, the Turkish baths, where my grandparents had shopped and bathed at the beginning of the century. Even the smells had lingered: whitefish, corned beef, sour tomatoes—but now, on top of these, was the grander greasier smell of auto wrecking shops, the sour stink of a brewery, the burning odor from a leather factory; and on the streets, instead of Yiddish, one heard the shouts of Negro children playing at Willie Mays with a broom handle and half a rubber ball. The neighborhood had changed: the old Jews like my grandparents had struggled and died, and their offspring had struggled and prospered, and moved further and further west, towards the edge of Newark, then out of it, and up the slope of the Orange Mountains, until they had reached the crest and started down the other side, pouring into Gentile territory as the Scotch-Irish had poured through the Cumberland Gap. Now, in fact, the Negroes were making the same migration, following the steps of the Jews, and those who remained in the Third Ward lived the most squalid of lives and dreamed in their fetid mattresses of the piny smell of Georgia nights.

I wondered, for an instant only, if I would see the colored kid from the library on the streets here. I didn't, of course, though I was sure he lived in one of the scabby, peeling buildings out of which dogs, children, and aproned women moved continually. On the top floors, windows were open, and the very old, who could no longer creak down the long stairs to the street, sat where they had been put, in the screenless windows, their elbows resting on fluffless pillows, and their heads tipping forward on their necks, watching the push of the young and the pregnant and the unemployed. Who would come after the Negroes? Who was left? No one, I thought, and someday these streets, where my grandmother drank hot tea from an old *jahrzeit* glass, would be empty and we would all of us have moved to the crest of the Orange Mountains, and wouldn't the dead stop kicking at the slats in their coffins then?

I pulled the Volkswagen up in front of a huge garage door that said across the front of it:

PATIMKIN KITCHEN AND BATHROOM SINKS
"Any Size—Any Shape"

Inside I could see a glass-enclosed office; it was in the center of an immense warehouse. Two trucks were being loaded in the rear, and Mr. Patimkin, when I saw him, had a cigar in his mouth and was shouting at someone. It was Ron, who was wearing a white T-shirt that said Ohio State Athletic Association across the front. Though he was taller than Mr. Patimkin, and almost as stout, his hands hung weakly at his sides like a small boy's; Mr. Patimkin's cigar locomoted in his mouth. Six Negroes were loading one of the trucks feverishly, tossing—my stomach dropped—sink bowls at one another.

Ron left Mr. Patimkin's side and went back to directing the men. He thrashed his arms about a good deal, and though on the whole he seemed rather confused, he didn't appear to be at all concerned about anybody dropping a sink. Suddenly I could see myself directing the Negroes—I would have an ulcer in an hour. I could almost hear the enamel surfaces shattering on the floor. And I could hear myself: "Watch it, you guys. Be careful, will you? *Whoops!* Oh, please be—*watch* it! Watch! Oh!" Suppose Mr. Patimkin should come up to me and say, "Okay, boy, you want to marry my daughter, let's see what you can do." Well, he would see: in a moment that floor would be a shattered mosaic, a crunchy path of enamel. "Klugman, what kind of worker are you? You work like you eat!" "That's right, that's right, I'm a sparrow, let me go." "Don't you even know how to load and unload?" "Mr. Patimkin, even breathing gives me trouble, sleep tires me out, let me go, let me go . . ."

Mr. Patimkin was headed back to the fish bowl to answer a ringing phone, and I wrenched myself free of my reverie and headed towards the office too. When I entered, Mr. Patimkin looked up from the phone with his eyes; the sticky cigar was in his free hand—he moved it at me, a greeting. From outside I heard Ron call in a high voice, "You can't all go to lunch at the same time. We haven't got all day!"

"Sit down," Mr. Patimkin shot at me, though when he went back to his conversation I saw there was only one chair in the office, his. People did not sit at

Patimkin Sink—here you earned your money the hard way, standing up. I busied myself looking at the several calendars that hung from filing cabinets; they showed illustrations of women so dreamy, so fantastically thighed and uddered, that one could not think of them as pornographic. The artist who had drawn the calendar girls for "Lewis Construction Company," and "Earl's Truck and Auto Repair," and "Grossman and Son, Paper Box" had been painting some third sex I had never seen.

"Sure, sure, sure," Mr. Patimkin said into the phone. "Tomorrow, don't tell me tomorrow. Tomorrow the world could blow up."

At the other end someone spoke. Who was it? Lewis from the construction company? Earl from truck repair?

"I'm running a business, Grossman, not a charity."

So it was Grossman being browbeaten at the other end.

"Shit on that," Mr. Patimkin said. "You're not the only one in town, my good friend," and he winked at me.

Ah-ha, a conspiracy against Grossman. Me and Mr. Patimkin. I smiled as collusively as I knew how.

"All right then, we're here till five . . . No later."

He wrote something on a piece of paper. It was only a big X.

"My kid'll be here," he said. "Yea, he's in the business."

Whatever Grossman said on the other end, it made Mr. Patimkin laugh. Mr. Patimkin hung up without a goodbye.

He looked out the back to see how Ron was doing. "Four years in college he can't unload a truck."

I didn't know what to say but finally chose the truth. "I guess I couldn't either."

"You could learn. What am I, a genius? I learned. Hard work never killed anybody."

To that I agreed.

Mr. Patimkin looked at his cigar. "A man works hard he's got something. You don't get anywhere sitting on your behind, you know . . . The biggest men in the country worked hard, believe me. Even Rockefeller. Success don't come easy . . ." He did not say this so much as he mused it out while he surveyed his dominion. He was not a man enamored of words, and I had the feeling that what had tempted him into this barrage of universals was probably the combination of Ron's performance and my presence—me, the outsider who might one day be an insider. But did Mr. Patimkin ever consider that possibility? I did not know; I only knew that these few words he did speak could hardly transmit all the satisfaction and surprise he felt about the life he had managed to build for himself and his family.

He looked out at Ron again. "Look at him, if he played basketball like that they'd throw him the hell off the court." But he was smiling when he said it.

He walked over to the door. "Ronald, let them go to lunch."

Ron shouted back, "I thought I'd let some go now, and some later."

"Why?"

"Then somebody'll always be—"

"No fancy deals here," Mr. Patimkin shouted. "We all go to lunch at once."

Ron turned back. "All right, boys, lunch!"

His father smiled at me. "Smart boy? Huh?" He tapped his head. "That took brains, huh? He ain't got the stomach for business. He's an idealist," and then I think Mr. Patimkin suddenly realized who *I* was, and eagerly corrected himself so as not to offend. "That's all right, you know, if you're a schoolteacher, or like you, you know, a student or something like that. Here you need a little of the *gonif* in you. You know what that means? *Gonif*?"

"Thief," I said.

"You know more than my own kids. They're *goyim*, my kids, that's how much they understand." He watched the Negro loading gang walk past the office and shouted out to them, "You guys know how long an hour is? All right, you'll be back in an hour!"

Ron came into the office and of course shook my hand.

"Do you have that stuff for Mrs. Patimkin?" I asked.

"Ronald, get him the silver patterns." Ron turned away and Mr. Patimkin said, "When I got married we had forks and knives from the five and ten. This kid needs gold to eat off," but there was no anger; far from it.

I drove to the mountains in my own car that afternoon, and stood for a while at the wire fence watching the deer lightly prance, coyly feed, under the protection of signs that read DO NOT FEED THE DEER, *By Order of South Mountain Reservation.* Alongside me at the fence were dozens of kids; they giggled and screamed when the deer licked the popcorn from their hands, and then were sad when their own excitement sent the young loping away towards the far end of the field where their tawny-skinned mothers stood regally watching the traffic curl up the mountain road. Young white-skinned mothers, hardly older than I, and in many instances younger, chatted in their convertibles behind me, and looked down from time to time to see what their children were about. I had seen them before, when Brenda and I had gone out for a bite in the afternoon, or had driven up here for lunch: in clutches of three and four they sat in the rustic hamburger joints that dotted the Reservation area while their children gobbled hamburgers and malteds and were given dimes to feed the jukebox. Though none of the little ones were old enough to read the song titles, almost all of them could holler out the words, and they did, while the mothers, a few of whom I recognized as high school mates of mine, compared suntans, supermarkets, and vacations. They looked immortal sitting there. Their hair would always stay the color they desired, their clothes the right texture and shade; in their homes they would have simple Swedish modern when that was fashionable, and if huge, ugly baroque ever came back, out would go the long, midget-legged marble coffee table and in would come Louis Quatorze. These were the goddesses, and if I were Paris I could not have been able to choose among them, so microscopic were the differences. Their fates had collapsed them into one. Only Brenda shone. Money and comfort would not erase her singleness—they hadn't yet, or had they? What was I loving, I wondered, and since I am not one to stick scalpels into myself, I wiggled my hand in the fence and allowed a tiny-nosed buck to lick my thoughts away.

When I returned to the Patimkin house, Brenda was in the living room looking more beautiful than I had ever seen her. She was modeling her new dress for Harriet and her mother. Even Mrs. Patimkin seemed softened by the sight of her; it looked as though some sedative had been injected into her, and so relaxed the Brenda-hating muscles around her eyes and mouth.

Brenda, without glasses, modeled in place; when she looked at me it was a kind of groggy, half-waking look I got, and though others might have interpreted it as sleepiness it sounded in my veins as lust. Mrs. Patimkin told her finally that she'd bought a very nice dress and I told her she looked lovely and Harriet told her she was very beautiful and that *she* ought to be the bride, and then there was an uncomfortable silence while all of us wondered who ought to be the groom.

Then when Mrs. Patimkin had led Harriet out to the kitchen, Brenda came up to me and said, "I *ought* to be the bride."

"You ought, sweetheart." I kissed her, and suddenly she was crying.

"What is it, honey?" I said.

"Let's go outside."

On the lawn, Brenda was no longer crying but her voice sounded very tired.

"Neil, I called Margaret Sanger Clinic," she said. "When I was in New York."

I didn't answer.

"Neil, they *did* ask if I was married. God, the woman sounded like my mother . . ."

"What did you say?"

"I said *no*."

"What did she say?"

"I don't know. I hung up." She walked away and around the oak tree. When she appeared again she'd stepped out of her shoes and held one hand on the tree, as though it were a Maypole she were circling.

"You can call them back," I said.

She shook her head. "No, I can't. I don't even know why I called in the first place. We were shopping and I just walked away, looked up the number, and called."

"Then you can go to a doctor."

She shook again.

"Look, Bren," I said, rushing to her, "we'll go together, to a doctor. In New York—"

"I don't want to go to some dirty little office—"

"We won't. We'll go to the most posh gynecologist in New York. One who gets *Harper's Bazaar* for the reception room. How does that sound?"

She bit her lower lip.

"You'll come with me?" she asked.

"I'll come with you."

"To the office?"

"Sweetie, your husband wouldn't come to the office."

"No?"

"He'd be working."

"But you're not," she said.

"I'm on vacation," I said, but I had answered the wrong question. "Bren, I'll wait and when you're all done we'll buy a drink. We'll go out to dinner."

"Neil, I shouldn't have called Margaret Sanger—it's not right."

"It is, Brenda. It's the most right thing we can do." She walked away and I was exhausted from pleading. Somehow I felt I could have convinced her had I been a bit more crafty; and yet I did not want it to be craftiness that changed her mind. I was silent when she came back, and perhaps it was just that, my *not* saying anything, that prompted her finally to say, "I'll ask Mother Patimkin if she wants us to take Harriet too . . ."

7

I shall never forget the heat and mugginess of that afternoon we drove into New York. It was four days after the day she'd called Margaret Sanger—she put it off and put it off, but finally on Friday, three days before Ron's wedding and four before her departure, we were heading through the Lincoln Tunnel, which seemed longer and fumier than ever, like Hell with tiled walls. Finally we were in New York and smothered again by the thick day. I pulled around the policeman who directed traffic in his shirt sleeves and up onto the Port Authority roof to park the car.

"Do you have cab fare?" I said.

"Aren't you going to come with me?"

"I thought I'd wait in the bar. Here, downstairs."

"You can wait in Central Park. His office is right across the street."

"Bren, what's the diff—" But when I saw the look that invaded her eyes I gave up the air-conditioned bar to accompany her across the city. There was a sudden shower while our cab went cross-town, and when the rain stopped the streets were sticky and shiny, and below the pavement was the rumble of the subways, and in all it was like entering the ear of a lion.

The doctor's office was in the Squibb Building, which is across from Bergdorf Goodman's and so was a perfect place for Brenda to add to her wardrobe. For some reason we had never once considered her going to a doctor in Newark, perhaps because it was too close to home and might allow for possibilities of discovery. When Brenda got to the revolving door she looked back at me; her eyes were very watery, even with her glasses, and I did not say a word, afraid what a word, any word, might do. I kissed her hair and motioned that I would be across the street by the Plaza fountain, and then I watched her revolve through the doors. Out on the street the traffic moved slowly as though the humidity were a wall holding everything back. Even the fountain seemed to be bubbling boiling water on the people who sat at its edge, and in an instant I decided against crossing the street, and turned south on Fifth and began to walk the steaming pavement towards St. Patrick's. On the north steps a crowd was gathered; everyone was watching a model being photographed. She was wearing a lemon-colored dress and had her feet pointed like a ballerina, and as I passed into the church I heard some lady say, "If I ate cottage cheese *ten* times a day, I couldn't be that skinny."

It wasn't much cooler inside the church, though the stillness and the flicker of the candles made me think it was. I took a seat at the rear and while I couldn't bring myself to kneel, I did lean forward onto the back of the bench before me, and held my hands together and closed my eyes. I wondered if I looked like a Catholic, and in my wonderment I began to make a little speech to myself. Can I call the self-conscious words I spoke prayer? At any rate, I called my audience God. God, I said, I am twenty-three years old. I want to make the best of things. Now the doctor is about to wed Brenda to me, and I am not entirely certain this is all for the best. What is it I love, Lord? Why have I chosen? Who is Brenda? The race is to the swift. Should I have stopped to think?

I was getting no answers, but I went on. If we meet You at all, God, it's that we're carnal, and acquisitive, and thereby partake of You. I am carnal, and I know You approve, I just know it. But how carnal can I get? I am acquisitive. Where do I turn now in my acquisitiveness? Where do we meet? Which prize is You?

It was an ingenious meditation, and suddenly I felt ashamed. I got up and walked outside, and the noise of Fifth Avenue met me with an answer:

Which prize do you think, *schmuck*? Gold dinnerware, sporting-goods trees, nectarines, garbage disposals, bumpless noses, Patimkin Sink, Bonwit Teller—

But damn it, God, that *is* You!

And God only laughed, that clown.

On the steps around the fountain I sat in a small arc of a rainbow that the sun had shot through the spray of the water. And then I saw Brenda coming out of the Squibb Building. She carried nothing with her, like a woman who's only been window shopping, and for a moment I was glad that in the end she had disobeyed my desire.

As she crossed the street, though, that little levity passed, and then I was myself again.

She walked up before me and looked down at where I sat; when she inhaled she filled her entire body, and then let her breath out with a "*Whew*!"

"Where is it?" I said.

My answer, at first, was merely that victorious look of hers, the one she'd given Simp the night she'd beaten her, the one I'd gotten the morning I finished the third lap alone. At last she said, "I'm wearing it."

"Oh, Bren."

"He said shall I wrap it or will you take it with you?"

"Oh Brenda, I love you."

We slept together that night, and so nervous were we about our new toy that we performed like kindergartners, or (in the language of that country) like a lousy double-play combination. And then the next day we hardly saw one another at all, for with the last-minute wedding preparations came scurrying, telegramming, shouting, crying, rushing—in short, lunacy. Even the meals lost their Patimkin fullness, and were tortured out of Kraft cheese, stale onion rolls, dry salami, a little chopped liver, and fruit cocktail. It was hectic all weekend, and I tried as best I could to keep clear of the storm, at whose eye, Ron, clumsy and smiling, and Harriet, flittering and courteous, were being pulled closer and closer together. By Sunday night fatigue had arrested hysteria and all of the Patimkins, Brenda included, had gone off to an early sleep. When Ron went into the bathroom to brush his teeth I decided to go in and brush mine. While I stood over the sink he checked his supports for dampness; then he hung them on the shower knobs and asked me if I would like to listen to his records for a while. It was not out of boredom and loneliness that I accepted; rather a brief spark of lockerroom comradery had been struck there among the soap and the water and the tile, and I thought that perhaps Ron's invitation was prompted by a desire to spend his last moments as a Single Man with another Single Man. If I was right, then it was the first real attestation he'd given to my masculinity. How could I refuse?

I sat on the unused twin bed.

"You want to hear Mantovani?"

"Sure," I said.

"Who do you like better, him or Kostelanetz?"

"It's a toss-up."

Ron went to his cabinet. "Hey, how about the Columbus record? Brenda ever play it for you?"

"No. I don't think so."

He extracted a record from its case, and like a giant with a sea shell, placed it gingerly on the phonograph. Then he smiled at me and leaned back onto his bed. His arms were behind his head and his eyes fixed on the ceiling. "They give this to all the seniors. With the yearbook—" but he hushed as soon as the sound began. I watched Ron and listened to the record.

At first there was just a roll of drums, then silence, then another drum roll—and then softly, a marching song, the melody of which was very familiar. When the song ended, I heard the bells, soft, loud, then soft again. And finally there came a Voice, bowel-deep and historic, the kind one associates with documentaries about the rise of Fascism.

"The year, 1956. The season, fall. The place, Ohio State University . . ."

Blitzkrieg! Judgment Day! The Lord had lowered his baton, and the Ohio State Glee Club were lining out the Alma Mater as if their souls depended on it. After one desperate chorus, they fell, still screaming, into bottomless oblivion, and the Voice resumed:

"The leaves had begun to turn and redden on the trees. Smoky fires line Fraternity Row, as pledges rake the leaves and turn them to a misty haze. Old faces greet new ones, new faces meet old, and another year has begun . . ."

Music. Glee Club in great comeback. Then the Voice: "The place, the banks of the Olentangy. The event, Homecoming Game, 1956. The opponent, the ever dangerous Illini . . ."

Roar of crowd. New voice—Bill Stern: "Illini over the ball. The snap. Linday fading to pass, he finds a receiver, he passes long *long* down field—and IT'S INTERCEPTED BY NUMBER 43, HERB CLARK OF OHIO STATE! Clark evades one tackler, he evades another as he comes up to midfield. Now he's picking up blockers, he's down to the 45, the 40, the 35—"

And as Bill Stern egged on Clark, and Clark, Bill Stern, Ron, on his bed, with just a little body-english, eased Herb Clark over the goal.

"And it's the Buckeyes ahead now, 21 to 19. *What a game!*"

The Voice of History baritoned in again: "But the season was up and down, and by the time the first snow had covered the turf, it was the sound of dribbling and the cry *Up and In!* that echoed through the fieldhouse . . ."

Ron closed his eyes.

"The Minnesota game," a new, high voice announced, "and for some of our seniors, their last game for the red and white . . . The players are ready to come out on the floor and into the spotlight. There'll be a big hand of appreciation from this capacity crowd for some of the boys who won't be back next year. Here comes Larry Gardner, big Number 7, out onto the floor, Big Larry from Akron, Ohio . . ."

"Larry—" announced the P.A. system; "Larry," the crowd roared back.

"And here comes Ron Patimkin dribbling out. Ron, Number 11, from Short Hills, New Jersey. Big Ron's last game, and it'll be some time before Buckeye fans forget him . . ."

Big Ron tightened on his bed as the loudspeaker called his name; his ovation must have set the nets to trembling. Then the rest of the players were announced, and then basketball season was over, and it was Religious Emphasis Week, the Senior Prom (Billy May blaring at the gymnasium roof), Fraternity Skit Night, E.E. Cummings reading to students (verse, silence, applause); and then, finally, commencement:

"The campus is hushed this day of days. For several thousand young men and women it is a joyous yet a solemn occasion. And for their parents a day of laughter and a day of tears. It is a bright green day, it is June the seventh of the year one thousand nine hundred and fifty-seven and for these young Americans the most stirring day of their lives. For many this will be their last glimpse of the campus, of Columbus, for many many years. Life calls us, and anxiously if not nervously we walk out into the world and away from the pleasures of these ivied walls. But not from its memories. They will be the concomitant, if not the fundament, of our lives. We shall choose husbands and wives, we shall choose jobs and homes, we shall sire children and grandchildren, but we will not forget you, Ohio State. In the years ahead we will carry with us always memories of thee, Ohio State . . ."

Slowly, softly, the OSU band begins the Alma Mater, and then the bells chime that last hour. Soft, very soft, for it is spring.

There was goose flesh on Ron's veiny arms as the Voice continued. "We offer ourselves to you then, world, and come at you in search of Life. And to you, Ohio State, to you Columbus, we say thank you, thank you and goodbye. We will miss you, in the fall, in the winter, in the spring, but some day we shall return. Till then, goodbye, Ohio State, goodbye, red and white, goodbye, Columbus . . . goodbye, Columbus . . . goodbye . . ."

Ron's eyes were closed. The band was upending its last truckload of nostalgia, and I tiptoed from the room, in step with the 2163 members of the Class of '57.

I closed my door, but then opened it and looked back at Ron: he was still humming on his bed. Thee! I thought, my brother-in-law!

The wedding.

Let me begin with the relatives.

There was Mrs. Patimkin's side of the family: her sister Molly, a tiny buxom hen whose ankles swelled and ringed her shoes, and who would remember Ron's wedding if for no other reason than she'd martyred her feet in three-inch heels, and Molly's husband, the butter and egg man, Harry Grossbart, who had earned his fortune with barley and corn in the days of Prohibition. Now he was active in the Temple and whenever he saw Brenda he swatted her on the can; it was a kind of physical bootlegging that passed, I guess, for familial affection. Then there was Mrs. Patimkin's brother, Marty Kreiger, the Kosher

Hot-Dog King, an immense man, as many stomachs as he had chins, and already, at fifty-five, with as many heart attacks as chins and stomachs combined. He had just come back from a health cure in the Catskills, where he said he'd eaten nothing but All-Bran and had won $1500 at gin rummy. When the photographer came by to take pictures, Marty put his hand on his wife's pancake breasts and said, "Hey, how about a picture of this!" His wife, Sylvia, was a frail, spindly woman with bones like a bird's. She had cried throughout the ceremony, and sobbed openly, in fact, when the rabbi had pronounced Ron and Harriet "man and wife in the eyes of God and the State of New Jersey." Later, at dinner, she had hardened enough to slap her husband's hand as it reached out for a cigar. However, when he reached across to hold her breast she just looked aghast and said nothing.

Also there were Mrs. Patimkin's twin sisters, Rose and Pearl, who both had white hair, the color of Lincoln convertibles, and nasal voices, and husbands who followed after them but talked only to each other, as though, in fact, sister had married sister, and husband had married husband. The husbands, named Earl Klein and Manny Kartzman, sat next to each other during the ceremony, then at dinner, and once, in fact, while the band was playing between courses, they rose, Klein and Kartzman, as though to dance, but instead walked to the far end of the hall where together they paced off the width of the floor. Earl, I learned later, was in the carpet business, and apparently he was trying to figure how much money he would make if the Hotel Pierre favored him with a sale.

On Mr. Patimkin's side there was only Leo, his half-brother. Leo was married to a woman named Bea whom nobody seemed to talk to. Bea kept hopping up and down during the meal and running over to the kiddie table to see if her little girl, Sharon, was being taken care of. "I told her not to take the kid. Get a babysitter, I said." Leo told me this while Brenda danced with Ron's best man, Ferrari. "She says, what are we, millionaires? No, for Christ sake, but my brother's kids gets married, I can have a little celebration. No, we gotta *shlep* the kid with us. Aah, it gives her something to do! . . ." He looked around the hall. Up on the stage Harry Winters (né Weinberg) was leading his band in a medley from *My Fair Lady*; on the floor, all ages, all sizes, all shapes were dancing. Mr. Patimkin was dancing with Julie, whose dress had slipped down from her shoulders to reveal her soft small back, and long neck, like Brenda's. He danced in little squares and was making considerable effort not to step on Julie's toes. Harriet, who was, as everyone said, a beautiful bride, was dancing with her father. Ron danced with Harriet's mother, Brenda with Ferrari, and I had sat down for a while in the empty chair beside Leo so as not to get maneuvered into dancing with Mrs. Patimkin, which seemed to be the direction towards which things were moving.

"You're Brenda's boy friend? Huh?" Leo said.

I nodded—earlier in the evening I'd stopped giving blushing explanations. "You gotta deal there, boy," Leo said, "you don't louse it up."

"She's very beautiful," I said.

Leo poured himself a glass of champagne, and then waited as though he expected a head to form on it; when one didn't he filled the glass to the brim.

"Beautiful, not beautiful, what's the difference. I'm a practical man. I'm on the bottom, so I gotta be. You're Aly Khan you worry about marrying movie stars. I wasn't born yesterday . . . You know how old I was when I got married?

Thirty-five years old. I don't know what the hell kind of hurry I was in." He drained his glass and refilled it. "I'll tell you something, one good thing happened to me in my whole life. Two maybe. Before I came back from overseas I got a letter from my wife—she wasn't my wife then. My mother-in-law found an apartment for us in Queens. Sixty-two fifty a month it cost. That's the last good thing that happened."

"What was the first?"

"What first?"

"You said *two* things," I said.

"I don't remember. I say two because my wife tells me I'm sarcastic and a cynic. That way maybe she won't think I'm such a wise guy."

I saw Brenda and Ferrari separate, and so excused myself and started for Brenda, but just then Mr. Patimkin separated from Julie and it looked as though the two men were going to switch partners. Instead the four of them stood on the dance floor and when I reached them they were laughing and Julie was saying, "What's so funny!" Ferrari said "Hi" to me and whisked Julie away, which sent her into peals of laughter.

Mr. Patimkin had one hand on Brenda's back and suddenly the other one was on mine. "You kids having a good time?" he said.

We were sort of swaying, the three of us, to "Get Me to the Church on Time."

Brenda kissed her father. "Yes," she said. "I'm so drunk my head doesn't even need my neck."

"It's a fine wedding, Mr. Patimkin."

"You want anything just ask me . . ." he said, a little drunken himself. "You're two good kids . . . How do you like that brother of yours getting married? . . . Huh? . . . Is that a girl or is that a girl?"

Brenda smiled, and though she apparently throught her father had spoken of her, I was sure he'd been referring to Harriet.

"You like weddings, Daddy?" Brenda said.

"I like my kids' weddings . . ." He slapped me on the back. "You two kids, you want anything? Go have a good time. Remember," he said to Brenda, "you're my honey . . ." Then he looked at me. "Whatever my Buck wants is good enough for me. There's no business too big it can't use another head."

I smiled though not directly at him, and beyond I could see Leo sopping up champagne and watching the three of us; when he caught my eye he made a sign with his hand, a circle with his thumb and forefinger, indicating, "That a boy, that a boy!"

After Mr. Patimkin departed, Brenda and I danced closely, and we only sat down when the waiters began to circulate with the main course. The head table was noisy, particularly at our end where the men were almost all teammates of Ron's, in one sport or another; they ate a fantastic number of rolls. Tank Feldman, Ron's roommate, who had flown in from Toledo, kept sending the waiter back for rolls, for celery, for olives, and always to the squealing delight of Gloria Feldman, his wife, a nervous, undernourished girl who continually looked down the front of her gown as though there was some sort of construction project going on under her clothes. Gloria and Tank, in fact, seemed to be self-appointed precinct captains at our end. They proposed toasts, burst into wild song, and continually referred to Brenda and me as "love birds." Brenda smiled at this with her eyeteeth and I brought up a cheery look from some fraudulent auricle of my heart.

And the night continued: we ate, we drank, we danced—Rose and Pearl did the Charleston with one another (while their husbands examined woodwork and chandeliers), and then I did the Charleston with none other than Gloria Feldman, who made coy, hideous faces at me all the time we danced. Near the end of the evening, Brenda, who'd been drinking champagne like her Uncle Leo, did a Rita Hayworth tango with herself, and Julie fell asleep on some ferns she'd whisked off the head table and made into a mattress at the far end of the hall. I felt a numbness creep into my hard palate, and by three o'clock people were dancing in their coats, shoeless ladies were wrapping hunks of wedding cake in napkins for their children's lunch, and finally Gloria Feldman made her way over to our end of the table and said, freshly, "Well, our little Radcliffe smarty, what have you been doing all summer?"

"Growing a penis."

Gloria smiled and left as quickly as she'd come, and Brenda without another word headed shakily away for the ladies' room and the rewards of overindulgence. No sooner had she left than Leo was beside me, a glass in one hand, a new bottle of champagne in the other.

"No sign of the bride and groom?" he said, leering. He'd lost most of his consonants by this time and was doing the best he could with long, wet vowels. "Well, you're next, kid. I see it in the cards . . . You're nobody's sucker . . ." And he stabbled me in the side with the top of the bottle, spilling champagne onto the side of my rented tux. He straightened up, poured more onto his hand and glass, but then suddenly he stopped. He was looking into the lights which were hidden beneath a long bank of flowers that adorned the front of the table. He shook the bottle in his hand as though to make it fizz. "The son of a bitch who invented the fluorescent bulb should drop dead!" He set the bottle down and drank.

Up on the stage Harry Winters brought his musicians to a halt. The drummer stood up, stretched, and they all began to open up cases and put their instruments away. On the floor, relatives, friends, associates, were holding each other around the waists and the shoulders, and small children huddled around their parents' legs. A couple of kids ran in and out of the crowd, screaming at tag, until one was grabbed by an adult and slapped soundly on the behind. He began to cry, and couple by couple the floor emptied. Our table was a tangle of squashed everything; napkins, fruits, flowers; there were empty whisky bottles, droopy ferns, and dishes puddled with unfinished cherry jubilee, gone sticky with the hours. At the end of the table Mr. Patimkin was sitting next to his wife, holding her hand. Opposite them, on two bridge chairs that had been pulled up, sat Mr. and Mrs. Ehrlich. They spoke quietly and evenly, as though they had known each other for years and years. Everything had slowed down now, and from time to time people would come up to the Patimkins and Ehrlichs, wish them *mazel tov*, and then drag themselves and their families out into the September night, which was cool and windy, someone said, and reminded me that soon would come winter and snow.

"They never wear out, those things, you know that." Leo was pointing to the fluorescent lights that shone through the flowers. "They last for years. They could make a car like that if they wanted, that could never wear out. It would run on water in the summer and snow in the winter. But they wouldn't do it, the big boys . . . Look at me," Leo said, splashing his suit front with champagne, "I sell a good bulb. You can't get the kind of bulb I sell in the drugstores. It's a quality bulb. But I'm the little guy. I don't even own a car. His brother, and I don't even own an automobile. I take a train wherever I go. I'm the only guy I know who wears out three pairs of rubbers every winter. Most guys get new ones when they lose the old ones. I wear them out, like shoes. Look," he said, leaning into me. "I could sell a crappy bulb, it wouldn't break my heart. But it's not good business."

The Ehrlichs and Patimkins scraped back their chairs and headed away, all except Mr. Patimkin who came down the table towards Leo and me.

He slapped Leo on the back. "Well, how you doing, *shtarke?*"

"All right, Ben. All right . . ."

"You have a good time?"

"You had a nice affair, Ben, it must've cost a pretty penny, believe me . . ."

Mr. Patimkin laughed. "When I make out my income tax I go to see Leo. He knows just how much money I spent . . . You need a ride home?" he asked me.

"No, thanks. I'm waiting for Brenda. We have my car."

"Good night," Mr. Patimkin said.

I watched him step down off the platform that held the head table, and then start towards the exit. Now the only people in the hall—the shambles of a hall—were myself, Leo, and his wife and child who slept, both of them, with their heads pillowed on a crumpled tablecloth at a table down on the floor before us. Brenda still wasn't around.

"When you got it," Leo said, rubbing his fingers together, "you can afford to talk like a big shot. Who needs a guy like me any more. Salesmen, you spit on them. You can go to the supermarket and buy anything. Where my wife shops you can buy sheets and pillowcases. Imagine, a grocery store! Me, I sell to gas stations, factories, small businesses, all up and down the east coast. Sure, you can sell a guy in a gas station a crappy bulb that'll burn out in a week. For inside the pumps I'm talking, it takes a certain kind of bulb. A utility bulb. All right, so you sell him a crappy bulb, and then a week later he puts in a new one, and while he's screwing it in he still remembers your name. Not me. I sell a quality bulb. It lasts a month, five weeks, before it even flickers, then it gives you another couple days, dim maybe, but so you shouldn't go blind. It hangs on, it's a quality bulb. Before it even burns out you notice it's getting darker, so you put a new one in. What people don't like is when one minute it's sunlight and the next dark. Let it glimmer a few days and they don't feel so bad. Nobody ever throws out my bulb—they figure they'll save them, can always use them in a pinch. Sometimes I say to a guy, you ever throw out a bulb you bought from Leo Patimkin? You gotta use psychology. That's why I'm sending my kid to college. You don't know a little psychology these days, you're licked . . ."

He lifted an arm and pointed out to his wife; then he slumped down in his seat. "Aaach!" he said, and drank off half a glass of champagne. "I'll tell you, I go as far as New London, Connecticut. That's as far as I'll go, and when I come home at night I stop first for a couple drinks. Martinis. Two I have, sometimes three. That seems fair, don't it? But to her a little sip or a bathtubfull, it smells the same. She says it's bad for the kid if I come home smelling. The kid's a baby, for

God's sake, she thinks that's the way I'm *supposed* to smell. A forty-eight-year-old man with a three-year-old kid! She'll give me a thrombosis that kid. My wife, she wants me to come home early and play with the kid before she goes to bed. Come home, she says, and *I'll* make you a drink. Hah! I spend all day sniffing gas, leaning under hoods with a grimy *poilishehs* in New London, trying to force a lousy bulb into a socket—I'll screw it in myself, I tell them—and she thinks I want to come home and drink a martinti from a jelly glass! How long are you going to stay in bars, she says. Till a Jewish girl is Miss Rheingold!

"Look," he went on after another drink, "I love my kid like Ben loves his Brenda. It's not that I don't want to play with her. But if I play with the kid and then at night get into bed with my wife, then she can't expect fancy things from me. It's one or the other. I'm no movie star."

Leo looked at his empty glass and put it on the table; he tilted the bottle up and drank the champagne like soda water. "How much do you think I make a week?" he said.

"I don't know."

"Take a guess."

"A hundred dollars."

"Sure, and tomorrow they're gonna let the lions out of the cage in Central Park. What do you think I make?"

"I can't tell."

"A cabdriver makes more than me. That's a fact. My wife's brother is a cabdriver, *he* lives in Kew Gardens. And he don't take no crap, no sir, not those cabbies. Last week it was raining one night and I said the hell with it, I'm taking a cab. I'd been all day in Newton, Mass. I don't usually go so far, but on the train in the morning I said to myself, stay on, go further, it'll be a change. And I know all the time I'm kidding myself. I wouldn't even make up the extra fare it cost me. But I stay on. And at night I still had a couple boxes with me, so when the guy pulls up at Grand Central there's like a genie inside me says get in. I even threw the bulbs in, not even caring if they broke. And this cabbie says, Whatya want to do, buddy, rip the leather? Those are brand new seats I got. No, I said. Jesus Christ, he says, some goddam people. I get in and give him a Queens address which ought to shut him up, but no, all the way up the Drive he was Jesus Christing me. It's hot in the cab, so I open a window and *then* he turns around and says, Whatya want to do, give me a cold in the neck? I just got over a goddam cold . . ." Leo looked at me, bleary-eyed. "This city is crazy! If I had a little money I'd get out of here in a minute. I'd go to California. They don't need bulbs out there it's so light. I went to New Guinea during the war from San Francisco. *There*," he burst, "there is the other good thing that happened to me, that night in San Francisco with this Hannah Schreiber. That's the both of them, you asked me I'm telling you—the apartment my mother-in-law got us, and this Hannah Schreiber. One night was all. I went to a B'nai Brith dance for servicemen in the basement of some big temple, and I met her. I wasn't married then, so don't make faces."

"I'm not."

"She had a nice little room by herself. She was going to school to be a teacher. Already I knew something was up because she let me feel inside her slip in the cab. Listen to me, I sound like I'm always in cabs. Maybe two other times in my life. To tell the truth I don't even enjoy it. All the time I'm riding I'm watching the meter. Even the pleasures I can't enjoy!"

"What about Hannah Schreiber?"

He smiled, flashing some gold in his mouth. "How do you like that name? She was only a girl, but she had an old lady's name. In the room she says to me she believes in oral love. I can still hear her: Leo Patimkin, I believe in oral love. I don't know what the hell she means. I figure she was one of those Christian Scientists or some cult or something. So I said, But what about for soldiers, guys going overseas who may get killed, God forbid." He shrugged his shoulders. "The smartest guy in the world I wasn't. But that's twenty years almost, I was still wet behind the ears. I'll tell you, every once in a while my wife—you know, she does for me what Hannah Schreiber did. I don't like to force her, she works hard. That to her is like a cab to me. I wouldn't force her. I can remember every time, I'll bet. Once after a Seder, my mother was still living, she should rest in peace. My wife was up to here with Mogen David. In fact, *twice* after Seders. Aachhh! Everything good in my life I can count on my fingers! God forbid some one should leave me a million dollars, I wouldn't even have to take off my shoes. I got a whole other hand yet."

He pointed to the fluorescent bulbs with the nearly empty champagne bottle. "You call that a light? That's a light to *read* by? It's purple, for God's sake! Half the blind men in the world ruined themselves by those damn things. You know who's behind them? The optometrists! I'll tell you, if I could get a couple hundred for all my stock and the territory, I'd sell tomorrow. That's right, Leo A. Patimkin, one semester accounting, City College nights, will sell equipment, territory, good name. I'll buy two inches in the *Times.* The territory is from here to everywhere. I go where I want, my own boss, no one tells me what to do. You know the Bible? 'Let there be light—and there's Leo Patimkin!' That's my trademark, I'll sell that too. I tell them that slogan, the *poilishehs,* they think I'm making it up. What good is it to be smart unless you're in on the ground floor! I got more brains in my pinky than Ben got in his whole *head.* Why is it he's on top and I'm on the bottom! *Why!* Believe me, if you're born lucky, you're lucky!" And then he exploded into silence.

I had the feeling that he was going to cry, so I leaned over and whispered to him, "You better go home." He agreed, but I had to raise him out of his seat and steer him by one arm down to his wife and child. The little girl could not be awakened, and Leo and Bea asked me to watch her while they went out into the lobby to get their coats. When they returned, Leo seemed to have dragged himself back to the level of human communication. He shook my hand with real feeling. I was very touched.

"You'll go far," he said to me. "You're a smart boy, you'll play it safe. Don't louse things up."

"I won't."

"Next time we see you it'll be *your* wedding," and he winked at me. Bea stood alongside, muttering goodbye all the while he spoke. He shook my hand again and then picked the child out of her seat, and they turned towards the door. From the back, round-shouldered, burdened, child-carrying, they looked like people fleeing a captured city.

Brenda, I discovered, was asleep on a couch in the lobby. It was almost four o'clock and the two of us and the desk clerk were the only ones in the hotel lobby. At first I did not waken Brenda, for she was pale and wilted and I knew she had been sick. I sat beside her, smoothing her hair back off her ears. How would I ever come to know her, I wondered, for as she slept I felt I knew no more of her than what I could see in a photograph. I stirred her gently and in a half-sleep she walked beside me out to the car.

It was almost dawn when we came out of the Jersey side of the Lincoln Tunnel. I switched down to my parking lights, and drove on to the Turnpike, and there out before me I could see the swampy meadows that spread for miles and miles, watery, blotchy, smelly, like an oversight of God. I thought of that other oversight, Leo Patimkin, half-brother to Ben. In a few hours he would be on a train heading north, and as he passed Scarsdale and White Plains, he would belch and taste champagne and let the flavor linger in his mouth. Alongside him on the seat, like another passenger, would be cartons of bulbs. He would get off at New London, or maybe, inspired by the sight of his half-brother, he would stay on again, hoping for some new luck further north. For the world was Leo's territory, every city, every swamp, every road and highway. He could go on to Newfoundland if he wanted, Hudson Bay, and on up to Thule, and then slide down the other side of the globe and rap on frosted windows on the Russian steppes, if he wanted. But he wouldn't. Leo was forty-eight years old, and he had learned. He pursued discomfort and sorrow, all right, but if you had a heartful by the time you reached New London, what new awfulness could you look forward to in Vladivostok?

The next day the wind was blowing the fall in and the branches of the weeping willow were fingering at the Patimkin front lawn. I drove Brenda to the train at noon, and she left me.

8

Autumn came quickly. It was cold and in Jersey the leaves turned and fell overnight. The following Saturday I took a ride up to see the deer, and did not even get out of the car, for it was too brisk to be standing at the wire fence, and so I watched the animals walk and run in the dimness of the late afternoon, and after a while everything, even the objects of nature, the trees, the clouds, the grass, the weeds, reminded me of Brenda, and I drove back down to Newark. Already we had sent our first letters and I had called her late one night, but in the mail and on the phone we had some difficulty discovering one another; we had not the style yet. That night I tried her again, and someone on her floor said she was out and would not be in till late.

Upon my return to the library I was questioned by Mr. Scapello about the Gauguin book. The jowly gentleman *had* sent a nasty letter about my discourtesy, and I was only able to extricate myself by offering a confused story in an indignant tone. In fact, I even managed to turn it around so that Mr. Scapello was apologizing to me as he led me up to my new post, there among the encyclopedias, the bibliographies, the indexes and guides. My bullying surprised me, and I wondered if some of it had not been learned from Mr. Patimkin that morning I'd heard him giving Grossman an earful on the phone. Perhaps I was more of a businessman than I thought. Maybe I could learn to become a Patimkin with ease . . .

Days passed slowly; I never did see the colored kid again, and when, one noon, I looked in the stacks, Gauguin was gone, apparently charged out finally by the jowly man. I wondered what it had been like that day the colored kid had discovered the book was gone. Had he cried? For some reason I imagined that he had blamed it on me, but then I realized that I was confusing the dream I'd had with reality. Chances were he had discovered someone else, Van Gogh, Vermeer . . . But no, they were not his kind of artists. What had probably happened was that he'd given up on the library and gone back to playing Willie Mays in the streets. He was better off, I thought. No sense carrying dreams of Tahiti in your head, if you can't afford the fare.

Let's see, what else did I do? I ate, I slept, I went to the movies. I sent broken-spined books to the bindery—I did everything I'd ever done before, but now each activity was surrounded by a fence, existed alone, and my life consisted of jumping from one fence to the next. There was no flow, for that had been Brenda.

And then Brenda wrote saying that she could be coming in for the Jewish holidays which were only a week away. I was so overjoyed I wanted to call Mr. and Mrs. Patimkin, just to tell them of my pleasure. However, when I got to the phone and had actually dialed the first two letters, I knew that at the other end there would be silence; if there was anything said, it would only be Mrs. Patimkin asking, "What is it you want?" Mr. Patimkin had probably forgotten my name.

That night, after dinner, I gave Aunt Gladys a kiss and told her she shouldn't work so hard.

"In less than a week it's Rosh Hashana and he thinks I should take a vacation. Ten people I'm having. What do you think, a chicken cleans itself? Thank God, the holidays come once a year. I'd be an old woman before my time."

But then it was only nine people Aunt Gladys was having, for only two days after her letter Brenda called.

"Oy Gut!" Aunt Gladys called. "Long *distance!*"

"Hello?" I said.

"Hello, sweetie?"

"Yes." I said.

"What *is* it?" Aunt Gladys tugged at my shirt. "What is it?"

"It's for me."

"Who?" Aunt Gladys said, pointing into the receiver.

"Brenda," I said.

"Yes?" Brenda said.

"Brenda?" Aunt Gladys said. "What does she call long distance, I almost had a heart attack."

"Because she's in Boston," I said. "Please, Aunt Gladys . . ."

And Aunt Gladys walked off, mumbling, "These kids . . ."

"Hello," I said again into the phone.

"Neil, how are you?"

"I love you."

"Neil, I have bad news. I can't come in this week."

"But, honey, it's the Jewish holidays."

"Sweet*heart*," she laughed.

"Can't you say that, for an excuse?"

"I have a test Saturday, and a paper, and you know if I went home I wouldn't get anything done . . ."

"You would."

"Neil, I just *can't.* My Mother'd make me go to Temple, and I wouldn't even have enough time to see *you.*"

"Oh God, Brenda."

"Sweetie?"

"Yes?"

"Can't you come up here?" she asked.

"I'm working."

"The Jewish holidays," she said.

"Honey, I can't. Last year I didn't take them off, I can't all—"

"You can say you had a conversion."

"Besides, my aunt's having all the family for dinner, and you know what with my parents—"

"Come up, Neil."

"I can't just take two days off, Bren. I just got promoted and a raise—"

"The hell with the raise."

"Baby, it's my job."

"Forever?" she said.

"No."

"Then come. I've got a hotel room."

"For me?"

"For us."

"Can you do that?"

"No and yes. People do it."

"Brenda, you tempt me."

"Be tempted."

"I could take a train Wednesday right from work."

"You could stay till Sunday night."

"Bren, I can't. I still have to be back to work on Saturday."

"Don't you ever get a day *off*?" she said.

"Tuesdays," I said glumly.

"God."

"And Sunday," I added.

Brenda said something but I did not hear her, for Aunt Gladys called, "You talk all day long distance?"

"Quiet!" I shouted back to her.

"Neil, will you?"

"Damn it, yes," I said.

"Are you angry?"

"I don't think so. I'm going to come up."

"Till Sunday."

"We'll see."

"Don't feel upset, Neil. You sound upset. It is the Jewish holidays. I mean you *should* be off."

"That's right," I said. "I'm an orthodox Jew, for God's sake, I ought to take advantage of it."

"That's right," she said.

"Is there a train around six?"

"Every hour, I think."

"Then I'll be on the one that leaves at six."

"I'll be at the station," she said. "How will I know you?"

"I'll be disguised as an orthodox Jew."

"Me too," she said.

"Good night, love," I said.

Aunt Gladys cried when I told her I was going away for Rosh Hashana.

"And I was preparing a big meal," she said.

"And can still prepare it."

"What will I tell your mother?"

"I'll tell her, Aunt Gladys. Please. You have no right to get upset . . ."

"Someday you'll have a family you'll know what it's like."

"I have a family now."

"What's a matter," she said, blowing her nose, "That girl couldn't come home to see her family it's the holidays?"

"She's in school, she just can't—"

"If she loved her family she'd find time. We don't live six hundred years."

"She does love her family."

"Then one day a year you could break your heart and pay a visit."

"Aunt Gladys, you don't understand."

"Sure," she said, "when I'm twenty-three years old I'll understand everything."

I went to kiss her and she said, "Go away from me, go run to Boston . . ."

The next morning I discovered that Mr. Scapello didn't want me to leave on Rosh Hashana either, but I unnerved him, I think, by hinting that his coldness about my taking the two days off might just be so much veiled anti-Semitism, so on the whole he was easier to manage. At lunch time I took a walk down to Penn Station and picked up a train schedule to Boston. That was my bedtime reading for the next three nights.

She did not look like Brenda, at least for the first minute. And probably to her I did not look like me. But we kissed and held each other, and it was strange to feel the thickness of our coats between us.

"I'm letting my hair grow," she said in the cab, and that in fact was all she said. Not until I helped her out of the cab did I notice the thin gold band shining on her left hand.

She hung back, strolling casually about the lobby while I signed the register "Mr. and Mrs. Neil Klugman," and then in the room we kissed again.

"Your heart's pounding," I said to her.

"I know," she said.

"Are you nervous?"

"No."

"Have you done this before?" I said.

"I read Mary McCarthy."

She took off her coat and instead of putting it in the closet, she tossed it across the chair. I sat down on the bed; she didn't.

"What's the matter?"

Brenda took a deep breath and walked over to the window, and I thought that perhaps it would be best for me to ask nothing—for us to get used to each other's presence in quiet. I hung her coat and mine in the empty closet, and left the suitcase—mine and hers—standing by the bed.

Brenda was kneeling backwards in the chair, looking out the window as though out the window was where she'd rather be. I came up behind her and put my hands around her body and held her breasts, and when I felt the cool draft that swept under the sill, I realized how long it had been since that first warm night when I had put my arms around her and felt the tiny wings beating in her back. And then I realized why I'd really come to Boston—it had been long enough. It was time to stop kidding about marriage.

"Is something the matter?" I said.

"Yes."

It wasn't the answer I'd expected; I wanted no answer really, only to soothe her nervousness with my concern.

But I asked, "What is it? Why didn't you mention it on the phone?"

"It only happened today."

"School?"

"Home. They found out about us."

I turned her face up to mine. "That's okay. I told my aunt I was coming here too. What's the difference?"

"About the summer. About our sleeping together."

"Oh?"

"Yes."

". . . Ron?"

"No."

"That night, you mean, did Julie—"

"No," she said, "it wasn't *anybody*."

"I don't get it."

Brenda got up and walked over to the bed where she sat down on the edge. I sat in the chair.

"My mother found the thing."

"The diaphragm?"

She nodded.

"When?" I asked.

"The other day, I guess." She walked to the bureau and opened her purse. "Here, you can read them in the order I got them." She tossed an envelope at me; it was dirty-edged and crumpled, as though it had been in and out of her pockets a good many times. "I got this one this morning," she said. "Special delivery."

I took out the letter and read:

PATIMKIN KITCHEN AND BATHROOM SINKS
"Any Size—Any Shape"

Dear Brenda—

Don't pay any Attention to your Mother's letter when you get it. I love you honey if you want a coat I'll buy You a coat. You could always have anything you wanted. We have every faith in you so you won't be too upset by what your mother says in her Letter. Of course she is a little hystericall because of the shock and she has been Working so hard for Hadassah. She is a Woman and it is hard for her to understand some of the Shocks in life. Of course I can't say We weren't all surprised because from the beginning I was nice to him and Thought he would appreciate the nice vacation we supplied for him. Some People never turn out the way you hope and pray but I am willing to forgive and call Buy Gones, Buy Gones. You have always up till now been a good Buck and got good scholastic Grades and Ron has always been what we wanted a Good Boy, most important, and a Nice boy. This late in my life believe me I am not going to start hating my own flesh and blood. As for your mistake it takes Two to make a mistake and now that you will be away at school and from him and what you got involved in you will probably do all right I have every faith you will. You have to have faith in your children like in a Business or any serious undertaking and there is nothing that is so bad that we can't forgive especially when Our own flesh and blood is involved. We have a nice close nitt family and why not???? Have a nice Holiday and in Temple I will say a Prayer for you as I do every year. On Monday I want you to go into Boston and buy a coat. Whatever you need because I know how Cold it gets up where you are . . . Give my regards to Linda and remember to bring her home with you on Thanksgiving like last year. You two had such a nice time. I have always never said bad things about any of your friends or Rons and that this should happen is only the exception that proves the rule. Have a Happy Holiday.

Your Father

And then it was signed "Ben Patimkin", but that was crossed out and written beneath "Your Father" were again, like an echo, the words, "Your Father."

"Who's Linda?" I asked.

"My roommate, last year." She tossed another envelope to me. "Here. I got this one in the afternoon. Air Mail."

The letter was from Brenda's mother. I started to read it and then put it down a moment. "You got this *after*?"

"Yes," she said. "When I got his I didn't know what was happening. Read hers."

I began again.

Dear Brenda:
I don't even know how to begin. I have been crying all morning and have had to skip my board meeting this afternoon because my eyes are so red. I never thought this would happen to a daughter of mine. I wonder if you know what I mean, if it is at least on your conscience, so I won't have to degrade either of us with a description. All I can say is that this morning when I was cleaning out the drawers and putting away your summer clothing I came upon something in your bottom drawer, *under* some sweaters which you probably remember leaving there. I cried the minute I saw it and I haven't stopped crying yet. Your father called a while ago and now he is driving home because he heard how upset I was on the phone.

I don't know what we ever did that you should reward us this way. We gave you a nice home and all the love and respect a child needs. I always was proud when you were a little girl that you could take care of yourself so well. You took care of Julie so beautifully it was a treat to see, when you were only fourteen years old. But you drifted away from your family, even though we sent you to the best schools and gave you the best money could buy. Why you should reward us this way is a question I'll carry with me to the grave.

About your friend I have no words. He is his parents' responsibility and I cannot imagine what kind of home life he had that he could act that way. Certainly that was a fine way to repay us for the hospitality we were nice enough to show to him, a perfect stranger. That the two of you should be carrying on like that in our very house I will never in my life be able to understand. Times certainly have changed since I was a girl that this kind of thing could go on. I keep asking myself if at least you didn't think of us while you were doing that. If not for me, how could you do this to your father? God forbid Julie should ever learn of this.

God only knows what you have been doing all these years we put our trust in you.

You have broken your parents' hearts and you should know that. This is some thank you for all we gave you.

Mother

She only signed "Mother" once, and that was in an extraordinarily miniscule hand, like a whisper.

"Brenda," I said.

"What?"

"Are you starting to cry?"

"No. I cried already."

"Don't start again."

"I'm trying not to, for God's sake."

"Okay . . . Brenda, can I ask you one question?"

"What?"

"Why did you leave it home?"

"Because I didn't plan on using it here, that's why."

"Suppose I'd come up. I mean I have come up, what about that?"

"I thought I'd come down first."

"So then couldn't you have carried it down then? Like a toothbrush?"

"Are you trying to be funny?"

"No. I'm just asking you why you left it home."

"I told you," Brenda said, "I thought I'd come home."

"But, Brenda, that doesn't make any sense. Suppose you did come home, and then you came back again. Wouldn't you have taken it with you then?"

"I don't *know*."

"Don't get angry," I said.

"You're the one who's angry."

"I'm upset, I'm not angry."

"I'm upset then too."

I did not answer but walked to the window and looked out. The stars and moon were out, silver and hard, and from the window I could see over to the Harvard campus where lights burned and then seemed to flicker when the trees blew across them.

"Brenda . . ."

"What?"

"Knowing how your mother feels about you, wasn't it silly to leave it home? Risky?"

"What does how she feels about me have to do with it?"

"You can't trust her."

"Why can't I?"

"Don't you see. You *can't*."

"Neil, she was only cleaning out the drawers."

"Didn't you know she would?"

"She never did before. Or maybe she did. Neil, I couldn't think of everything. We slept together night after night and nobody heard or noticed—"

"Brenda, why the hell are you willfully confusing things?"

"I'm not!"

"Okay," I said softly. "All right."

"It's you who's confusing things," Brenda said. "You act as though I wanted her to find it."

I didn't answer.

"Do you believe *that*?" she said, after neither of us had spoken for a full minute.

"I don't know."

"Oh, Neil, you're *crazy*."

"What was crazier than leaving that damn thing around?"

"It was an oversight."

"Now it's an oversight, before it was deliberate."

"It was an oversight about the drawer. It wasn't an oversight about leaving it," she said.

"Brenda, sweetheart, wouldn't the safest, smartest, easiest, simplest thing have been to have taken it with you? Wouldn't it?"

"It didn't make any difference either way."

"Brenda, this is the most frustrating argument of my life!"

"You keep making it seem as though I *wanted* her to find it. Do you think I need this? Do you? I can't even go home any more."

"Is that so?"

"Yes!"

"No," I said. "You can go home—your father will be waiting with two coats and a half-dozen dresses."

"What about my mother?"

"It'll be the same with her."

"Don't be absurd. How can I face them!"

"Why can't you face them? Did you do anything wrong?"

"Neil, look at the reality of the thing, will you?"

"*Did* you do anything wrong?"

"Neil, *they* think it's wrong. They're my parents."

"But do you think it's wrong—"

"That doesn't *matter*."

"It does to me, Brenda . . ."

"Neil, why are *you* confusing things? You keep accusing me of things."

"Damn it, Brenda, you're guilty of some things."

"*What?*"

"Of leaving that damn diaphragm there. How can you call it an oversight!"

"Oh, Neil, don't start any of that psychoanalytic crap!"

"Then why else did you do it? You wanted her to find it!"

"Why?"

"I don't know, Brenda, *why?*"

"Oh!" she said, and she picked up the pillow and threw it back on to the bed.

"What happens now, Bren?" I said.

"What does that mean?"

"Just that. What happens now?"

She rolled over on to the bed and buried her head in it.

"Don't start crying," I said.

"I'm *not.*"

I was still holding the letters and took Mr. Patimkin's from its envelope.

"Why does your father capitalize all these letters?"

She didn't answer.

" 'As for your mistake,' " I read aloud to Brenda, " 'it takes Two to make a mistake and now that you will be away at school and from him and what you got involved in you will probably do all right I have every faith you will. Your Father. Your Father.' "

She turned and looked at me; but silently.

" 'I have always never said bad things about any of your friends or Rons and that this should happen is only the exception that proves the rule. Have a Happy Holiday.' " I stopped; in Brenda's face there was positively no threat of tears; she looked, suddenly, solid and decisive. "Well, what are you going to do?" I asked.

"Nothing."

"Who are you going to bring home Thanksgiving—Linda?" I said, "or me?"

"Who *can* I bring home, Neil?"

"I don't know, who can you?"

"Can I bring you home?"

"I don't know," I said, "can you?"

"Stop repeating the question!"

"I sure as hell can't give you the answer."

"Neil, be realistic. After this, can I bring you home? Can you see us all sitting around the table?"

"I can't if you can't, and I can if you can."

"Are you going to speak Zen, for God's sake!"

"Brenda, the choices aren't mine. You can bring Linda or me. You can go home or not go home. That's another choice. Then you don't even have to worry about choosing between me and Linda."

"Neil, you don't understand. They're still my parents. They did send me to the best schools, didn't they? They have given me everything I've wanted, haven't they?"

"Yes."

"Then how can I not go home? I *have* to go home."

"Why?"

"You don't understand. Your parents don't bother you any more. You're lucky."

"Oh, sure. I live with my crazy aunt, that's a real bargain."

"Families are different. You don't understand."

"Goddamit, I understand more than you think. I understand why the hell you left that thing lying around. Don't you? Can't you put two and two together?"

"Neil, what are you talking about! You're the one who doesn't understand. You're the one who from the very beginning was accusing me of things? Remember? Isn't it so? Why don't you have your eyes fixed? Why don't you have this fixed, that fixed? As if it were my fault that I *could* have them fixed. You kept acting as if I was going to run away from you every minute. And now you're doing it again, telling me I planted that thing on purpose."

"I loved you, Brenda, so I cared."

"I loved *you*. That's why I got that damn thing in the first place."

And then we heard the tense in which we'd spoken and we settled back into ourselves and silence.

A few minutes later I picked up my bag and put on my coat. I think Brenda was crying too when I went out the door.

Instead of grabbing a cab immediately, I walked down the street and out towards the Harvard Yard which I had never seen before. I entered one of the gates and then headed out along a path, under the tired autumn foliage and the dark sky. I wanted to be alone, in the dark; not because I wanted to think about anything, but rather because, for just a while, I wanted to think about nothing. I walked clear across the Yard and up a little hill and then I was standing in front of the Lamont Library, which, Brenda had once told me, had Patimkin Sinks in its rest rooms. From the light of the lamp on the path behind me I could see my reflection in the glass front of the building. Inside, it was dark and there were no students to be seen, no librarians. Suddenly, I wanted to set down my suitcase and pick up a rock and heave it right through the glass, but of course I didn't. I simply looked at myself in the mirror the light made of the window. I was only that substance, I thought, those limbs, that face that I saw in front of me. I looked, but the outside of me gave up little information about the inside of me. I wished I could scoot around to the other side of the window, faster than light or sound or Herb Clark on Homecoming Day, to get behind that image and catch whatever it was that looked through those eyes. What was it inside me that had turned pursuit and clutching into love, and then turned it inside out again? What was it that had turned winning into losing, and losing—who knows—into winning? I was sure I had loved Brenda, though standing there, I knew I couldn't any longer. And I knew it would be a long while before I made love to anyone the way I had made love to her. With anyone else, could I summon up such a passion? Whatever spawned my love for her, had that spawned such lust too? If she had only been slightly *not* Brenda . . . but then would I have loved her? I looked hard at the image of me, at that darkening of the glass, and then my gaze pushed through it, over the cool floor, to a broken wall of books, imperfectly shelved.

I did not look very much longer, but took a train that got me into Newark just as the sun was rising on the first day of the Jewish New Year. I was back in plenty of time for work.

Fact Questions and Exercises

1. In what city and state do the Patimkins live? (Is it helpful in understanding the story to know that this suburb is one of the wealthiest in America, and is inhabited primarily by non-Jewish families?)
2. What college did Neil attend?
3. What did Brenda have done to her nose? Why?
4. Point out the ways in which Roth emphasizes the Patimkins' competitive drive.
5. What word does the Negro boy use for "art"? How does his mispronunciation relate to the Yiddish proverb quoted at the beginning of the story? What artist does the boy admire?
6. Where are Neil's parents? With whom is he living?
7. What do the Patimkins keep in the room off the guest bedroom?
8. What fact or episode gives the novella its title?
9. What does Neil insist that Brenda purchase? Does she buy it?
10. In what religious faith have Neil and Brenda been reared? Do they still adhere to this religion?
11. What is the source of the Patimkin wealth?
12. In the novel, who sells light bulbs?
13. What discovery does Mrs. Patimkin make that leads, in part, to the end of Brenda and Neil's relationship?
14. How much time elapses between Neil's meeting Brenda and the end of the story?

For Discussion and Writing

1. Neil's last name, Klugman, has two possible meanings in Yiddish: clever fellow or sad fellow. Discuss the name and its meanings in relation to Neil's character and to the various themes in the story. Some of these themes are: wealth versus poverty, love versus sexuality, and art versus artistic insensitivity. You may, of course, discover others.
2. How does the episode of the boy and Gauguin parallel (or help explain) the relationship between Neil and Brenda?
3. Various symbols are used in the story—the town of Short Hills is one. Point out other symbolic usages, and discuss how they are applied to develop the various themes.
4. Characterize Brenda. Is she a likeable (even lovable) girl who is at the mercy of her heredity and environment? Or is she a calculating person who uses her sex and wealth selfishly, inflicting pain on others?
5. Beginning on page 409, Roth presents Neil's ideas about God. Could these ideas also reflect Neil's or the author's view of life in America? Explain.
6. Someone once observed that there are two tragedies in life—not getting what you want, and getting what you want. Does this comment apply to *Goodbye,*

Columbus? Consider the question not only in terms of Neil and Brenda, but also in terms of the Patimkins and American life.

7. There are many love relationships in this novella—Aunt Gladys and Uncle Max, Mr. and Mrs. Patimkin, Leo and Bea, Neil and Brenda, Ron and Harriet. Discuss the ways in which Roth presents these relationships. Why, for instance, is Brenda and Neil's relationship the only one that does not end in marriage?

Sophocles [496–406 B.C.] *5th century B.C.*

Sophocles was born at Kolonos, Greece. Very little is known about his life; we do know that he wrote well over one hundred plays, of which only seven remain. *Oedipus Rex* (429 B.C.) is the first of three plays that concern King Oedipus; the other two are *Oedipus at Colonus* and *Antigone*. Sophocles is noted as a theatrical innovator—he introduced painted scenery, increased the size of the chorus from twelve to fifteen members, and made the chorus an integral part of the dramatic action.

429 B.C.

Oedipus Rex

PERSONS REPRESENTED

OEDIPUS *King of Thebes*	MESSENGER
A PRIEST	SHEPHERD OF LAÏOS
CREON *Iocaste's Brother*	SECOND MESSENGER
TEIRESIAS	CHORUS OF THEBAN ELDERS
IOCASTE *Queen (wife & mother of Oedipus)*	

THE SCENE: *Before the palace of Oedipus, King of Thebes. A central door and two lateral doors open onto a platform which runs the length of the facade. On the platform, right and left, are altars; and three steps lead down into the "orchestra," or chorus-ground. At the beginning of the action these steps are crowded by* SUPPLIANTS *who have brought branches and chaplets of olive leaves and who lie in various attitudes of despair.* OEDIPUS *enters.*

PROLOGUE

OEDIPUS: My children, generations of the living
In the line of Kadmos, nursed at his ancient hearth:
Why have you strewn yourselves before these altars
In supplication, with your boughs and garlands?
The breath of incense rises from the city   5
With a sound of prayer and lamentation.
                     Children,
I would not have you speak through messengers,
And therefore I have come myself to hear you—
I, Oedipus, who bear the famous name.
(*To a* PRIEST.) You, there, since you are eldest in the company,
Speak for them all, tell me what preys upon you,   10
Whether you come in dread, or crave some blessing:

means swollen foot

Everybody is upset in the town

Tell me, and never doubt that I will help you
In every way I can; I should be heartless
Were I not moved to find you suppliant here.

PRIEST: Great Oedipus, O powerful King of Thebes!   15
You see how all the ages of our people
Cling to your altar steps: here are boys
Who can barely stand alone, and here are priests
By weight of age, as I am a priest of God,
And young men chosen from those yet unmarried;   20
As for the others, all that multitude,
They wait with olive chaplets in the squares,
At the two shrines of Pallas, and where Apollo
Speaks in the glowing embers.

               Your own eyes
Must tell you: Thebes is in her extremity   25
And can not lift her head from the surge of death.
A rust consumes the buds and fruits of the earth;
The herds are sick; children die unborn,
And labor is vain. The god of plague and pyre
Raids like detestable lightning through the city,   30
And all the house of Kadmos is laid waste,
All emptied, and all darkened: Death alone
Battens upon the misery of Thebes.

You are not one of the immortal gods, we know;
Yet we have come to you to make our prayer   35
As to the man of all men best in adversity
And wisest in the ways of God. You saved us
From the Sphinx, that flinty singer, and the tribute
We paid to her so long; yet you were never
Better informed than we, nor could we teach you: 40
It was some god breathed in you to set us free.

Therefore, O mighty King, we turn to you:
Find us our safety, find us a remedy,
Whether by counsel of the gods or men.
A king of wisdom tested in the past   45
Can act in a time of troubles, and act well.
Noblest of men, restore
Life to your city! Think how all men call you
Liberator for your triumph long ago;
Ah, when your years of kingship are remembered,   50
Let them not say *We rose, but later fell*—
Keep the State from going down in the storm!
Once, years ago, with happy augury,
You brought us fortune; be the same again!
No man questions your power to rule the land: 55
But rule over men, not over a dead city!
Ships are only hulls, citadels are nothing,
When no life moves in the empty passageways.

OEDIPUS: Poor children! You may be sure I know
        All that you longed for in your coming here.
        I know that you are deathly sick; and yet,   60
        Sick as you are, not one is as sick as I.
        Each of you suffers in himself alone
        His anguish, not another's; but my spirit
        Groans for the city, for myself, for you.   65

        I was not sleeping, you are not waking me.
        No, I have been in tears for a long while
        And in my restless thought walked many ways.
        In all my search, I found one helpful course,
        And that I have taken: I have sent Creon,   70
        Son of Menoikeus, brother of the Queen,
        To Delphi, Apollo's place of revelation,
        To learn there, if he can,
        What act or pledge of mine may save the city.
        I have counted the days, and now, this very day,   75
        I am troubled, for he has overstayed his time.
        What is he doing? He has been gone too long.
        Yet whenever he comes back, I should do ill
        To scant whatever hint the god may give.

PRIEST: It is a timely promise. At this instant   80
        They tell me Creon is here.

OEDIPUS: O Lord Apollo!
        May his news be fair as his face is radiant!

PRIEST: It could not be otherwise: he is crowned with bay,
        The chaplet is thick with berries.

OEDIPUS: We shall soon know;
        He is near enough to hear us now.

        (*Enter* CREON.)

                            O Prince: 85
        Brother: son of Menoikeus:
        What answer do you bring us from the god?

CREON: It is favorable. I can tell you, great afflictions
        Will turn out well, if they are taken well.

OEDIPUS: What was the oracle? These vague words   90
        Leave me still hanging between hope and fear.

CREON: Is it your pleasure to hear me with all these
        Gathered around us? I am prepared to speak,
        But should we not go in?

OEDIPUS: Let them all hear it.
        It is for them I suffer, more than for myself.   95

CREON: Then I will tell you what I heard at Delphi.

        In plain words
        The god commands us to expel from the land of Thebes
        An old defilement that it seems we shelter.

Justice is big issue

It is a deathly thing, beyond expiation.   100
We must not let it feed upon us longer.

OEDIPUS: What defilement? How shall we rid ourselves of it?

CREON: By exile or death, blood for blood. It was
Murder that brought the plague-wind on the city.

OEDIPUS: Murder of whom? Surely the god has named him?   105

CREON: My Lord: long ago Laïos was our king,
Before you came to govern us.

OEDIPUS: I know:
I learned of him from others; I never saw him.

CREON: He was murdered; and Apollo commands us now
to take revenge upon whoever killed him.   110

OEDIPUS: Upon whom? Where are they? Where shall we find a clue
To solve that crime, after so many years?

CREON: Here in this land, he said.
                                    If we make enquiry,
We may touch things that otherwise escape us.

OEDIPUS: Tell me: Was Laïos murdered in his house,   115
Or in the fields, or in some foreign country?

CREON: He said he planned to make a pilgrimage.
He did not come home again.

OEDIPUS: And was there no one,
No witness, no companion, to tell what happened?

CREON: They were all killed but one, and he got away   120
So frightened that he could remember one thing only.

OEDIPUS: What was that one thing? One may be the key
To everything, if we resolve to use it.

CREON: He said that a band of highwaymen attacked them,
Outnumbered them, and overwhelmed the King.   125

OEDIPUS: Strange, that a highwayman should be so daring—
Unless some faction here bribed him to do it.

CREON: We thought of that. But after Laïos' death
New troubles arose and we had no avenger.

OEDIPUS: What troubles could prevent your hunting down the killers? 130

CREON: The riddling Sphinx's song
Made us deaf to all mysteries but her own.

OEDIPUS: Then once more I must bring what is dark to light.
It is most fitting that Apollo shows,
As you do, this compunction for the dead.   135
You shall see how I stand by you, as I should,
To avenge the city and the city's god,
And not as though it were for some distant friend,
But for my own sake, to be rid of evil.
Whoever killed King Laïos might—who knows?—   140
Decide at any moment to kill me as well.
By avenging the murdered king I protect myself.

Come, then, my children: leave the altar steps,
Lift up your olive boughs!
                    One of you go
And summon the people of Kadmos to gather here.   145
I will do all that I can; you may tell them that.
         (*Exit a* PAGE.)

So, with the help of God,
We shall be saved—or else indeed we are lost.

PRIEST: Let us rise, children. It was for this we came,
And now the King has promised it himself.   150
Phoibos has sent us an oracle; may he descend
Himself to save us and drive out the plague.

         (*Exeunt* OEDIPUS *and* CREON *into the palace by the central
         door. The* PRIEST *and the* SUPPLIANTS *disperse R and L. After a
         short pause the* CHORUS *enters the orchestra.*)

PARODOS

[STROPHE ONE

CHORUS: What is God singing in his profound
         Delphi of gold and shadow?
         What oracle for Thebes, the sunwhipped city?
         Fear unjoints me, the roots of my heart tremble.
         Now I remember, O Healer, your power, and wonder;   5
         Will you send doom like a sudden cloud, or weave it
         Like nightfall of the past?
         Speak, speak to us, issue of holy sound:
         Dearest to our expectancy: be tender!

[ANTISTROPHE ONE

         Let me pray to Athenê, the immortal daughter of Zeus,   10
         And to Artemis her sister
         Who keeps her famous throne in the market ring,
         And to Apollo, bowman at the far butts of heaven—

         O gods, descend! Like three streams leap against
         The fires of our grief, the fires of darkness;   15
         Be swift to bring us rest!

         As in the old time from the brilliant house
         Of air you stepped to save us, come again!

[STROPHE TWO

Now our afflictions have no end,
Now all our stricken host lies down   20
And no man fights off death with his mind;
The noble plowland bears no grain,
And groaning mothers can not bear—

See, how our lives like birds take wing,
Like sparks that fly when a fire soars,   25
To the shore of the god of evening.

[ANTISTROPHE TWO

The plague burns on, it is pitiless,
Though pallid children laden with death
Lie unwept in the stony ways,

And old gray women by every path   30
Flock to the strand about the altars

There to strike their breasts and cry
Worship of Phoibos in wailing prayers:
Be kind, God's golden child!

[STROPHE THREE

There are no swords in this attack by fire,   35
No shields, but we are ringed with cries.
Send the besieger plunging from our homes
Into the vast sea-room of the Atlantic
Or into the waves that foam eastward of Thrace—
For the day ravages what the night spares—   40
Destroy our enemy, lord of the thunder!
Let him be riven by lightning from heaven!

[ANTISTROPHE THREE

Phoibos Apollo, stretch the sun's bowstring,
That golden cord, until it sing for us,
Flashing arrows in heaven!   45
                              Artemis, Huntress,
Race with flaring lights upon our mountains!

O scarlet god, O golden-banded brow,
O Theban Bacchos in a storm of Maenads,

(*Enter* OEDIPUS, *C.*)

Whirl upon Death, that all the Undying hate!
Come with blinding cressets, come in joy!   50

SCENE ONE

OEDIPUS: Is this your prayer? It may be answered. Come,
Listen to me, act as the crisis demands,
And you shall have relief from all these evils.
Until now I was a stranger to this tale,
As I had been a stranger to the crime.   5
Could I track down the murderer without a clue?
But now, friends,
As one who became a citizen after the murder,
I make this proclamation to all Thebans:
If any man knows by whose hand Laïos, son of Labdakos,   10
Met his death, I direct that man to tell me everything,
No matter what he fears for having so long withheld it.
Let it stand as promised that no further trouble
Will come to him, but he may leave the land in safety.

Moreover: If anyone knows the murderer to be foreign,   15
Let him not keep silent: he shall have his reward from me.
However, if he does conceal it; if any man
Fearing for his friend or for himself disobeys this edict,
Hear what I propose to do:

I solemnly forbid the people of this country,   20
Where power and throne are mine, ever to receive that man
Or speak to him, no matter who he is, or let him
Join in sacrifice, lustration, or in prayer.
I decree that he be driven from every house,
Being, as he is, corruption itself to us: the Delphic   25
Voice of Zeus has pronounced this revelation.
Thus I associate myself with the oracle
And take the side of the murdered King.

As for the criminal, I pray to God—
Whether it be a lurking thief, or one of a number—   30
I pray that the man's life be consumed in evil and wretchedness.
And as for me, this curse applies no less
If it should turn out that the culprit is my guest here,
Sharing my hearth.
                    You have heard the penalty.
I lay it on you now to attend to this   35
For my sake, for Apollo's, for the sick
Sterile city that heaven has abandoned.

Suppose the oracle had given you no command:
Should this defilement go uncleansed for ever?
You should have found the murderer: your king,   40
A noble king, had been destroyed!
                              Now I,
Having the power that he held before me,
Having his bed, begetting children there
Upon his wife, as he would have, had he lived—
Their son would have been my children's brother,   45
If Laïos had had luck in fatherhood!
(But surely ill luck rushed upon his reign)—
I say I take the son's part, just as though
I were his son, to press the fight for him
And see it won! I'll find the hand that brought   50
Death to Labdakos' and Polydoros' child,
Heir of Kadmos' and Agenor's line.
And as for those who fail me,
May the gods deny them the fruit of the earth,
Fruit of the womb, and may they rot utterly!   55
Let them be wretched as we are wretched, and worse!

For you, for loyal Thebans, and for all
Who find my actions right, I pray the favor
Of justice, and of all the immortal gods.

CHORAGOS: Since I am under oath, my lord, I swear   60
     I did not do the murder, I can not name
     The murderer. Might not the oracle
     That has ordained the search tell where to find him?
OEDIPUS: An honest question. But no man in the world
     Can make the gods do more than the gods will.   65
CHORAGOS: There is one last expedient—
OEDIPUS: Tell me what it is.
     Though it seem slight, you must not hold it back.
CHORAGOS: A lord clairvoyant to the lord Apollo,
     As we all know, is the skilled Teiresias.
     One might learn much about this from him, Oedipus.   70
OEDIPUS: I am not wasting time:
     Creon spoke of this, and I have sent for him—
     Twice, in fact; it is strange that he is not here.
CHORAGOS: The other matter—that old report—seems useless.
OEDIPUS: Tell me. I am interested in all reports.   75
CHORAGOS: The King was said to have been killed by highwaymen.
OEDIPUS: I know. But we have no witnesses to that.
CHORAGOS: If the killer can feel a particle of dread,
     Your curse will bring him out of hiding!
OEDIPUS: No.
     The man who dared that act will fear no curse.   80

(*Enter the blind seer* TEIRESIAS, *led by a* PAGE.)

CHORAGOS: But there is one man who may detect the criminal.
　　　　This is Teiresias, this is the holy prophet
　　　　In whom, alone of all men, truth was born.

OEDIPUS: Teiresias: seer: student of mysteries,
　　　　Of all that's taught and all that no man tells,　　　　　　　85
　　　　Secrets of Heaven and secrets of the earth:
　　　　Blind though you are, you know the city lies
　　　　Sick with plague; and from this plague, my lord,
　　　　We find that you alone can guard or save us.

　　　　Possibly you did not hear the messengers?　　　　　　　　90
　　　　Apollo, when we sent to him,
　　　　Sent us back word that this great pestilence
　　　　Would lift, but only if we established clearly
　　　　The identity of those who murdered Laïos.
　　　　They must be killed or exiled.　　　　　　　　　　　　95
　　　　　　　　　　　　　　　Can you use
　　　　Birdflight or any art of divination
　　　　To purify yourself, and Thebes, and me
　　　　From this contagion? We are in your hands.
　　　　There is no fairer duty
　　　　Than that of helping others in distress.　　　　　　　　100

TEIRESIAS: How dreadful knowledge of the truth can be
　　　　When there's no help in truth! I knew this well,
　　　　But did not act on it: else I should not have come.

OEDIPUS: What is troubling you? Why are your eyes so cold?

TEIRESIAS: Let me go home. Bear your own fate, and I'll　　　　105
　　　　Bear mine. It is better so: trust what I say.

OEDIPUS: What you say is ungracious and unhelpful
　　　　To your native country. Do not refuse to speak.

TEIRESIAS: When it comes to speech, your own is neither temperate
　　　　Nor opportune. I wish to be more prudent.　　　　　　110

OEDIPUS: In God's name, we all beg you—

TEIRESIAS:　　　　　　　　　　　　You are all ignorant.
　　　　No; I will never tell you what I know.
　　　　Now it is my misery; then, it would be yours.

OEDIPUS: What! You do know something, and will not tell us?
　　　　You would betray us all and wreck the State?　　　　　115

TEIRESIAS: I do not intend to torture myself, or you.
　　　　Why persist in asking? You will not persuade me.

OEDIPUS: What a wicked old man you are! You'd try a stone's
　　　　Patience! Out with it! Have you no feeling at all?

TEIRESIAS: You call me unfeeling. If you could only see　　　120
　　　　The nature of your own feelings . . .

OEDIPUS: Why,
  Who would not feel as I do? Who could endure
  Your arrogance toward the city?

TEIRESIAS: What does it matter!
  Whether I speak or not, it is bound to come.

OEDIPUS: Then, if "it" is bound to come, you are bound to tell me.   125

TEIRESIAS: No, I will not go on. Rage as you please.

OEDIPUS: Rage? Why not!
                          And I'll tell you what I think:
  You planned it, you had it done, you all but
  Killed him with your own hands: if you had eyes,
  I'd say the crime was yours, and yours alone.   130

TEIRESIAS: So? I charge you, then,
  Abide by the proclamation you have made:
  From this day forth
  Never speak again to these men or to me;
  You yourself are the pollution of this country.   135

OEDIPUS: You dare say that? Can you possibly think you have
  Some way of going free, after such insolence?

TEIRESIAS: I have gone free. It is the truth sustains me.

OEDIPUS: Who taught you shamelessness? It was not your craft.

TEIRESIAS: You did. You made me speak. I did not want to.   140

OEDIPUS: Speak what? Let me hear it again more clearly.

TEIRESIAS: Was it not clear before? Are you tempting me?

OEDIPUS: I did not understand it. Say it again.

TEIRESIAS: I say that you are the murderer whom you seek.

OEDIPUS: Now twice you have spat out infamy. You'll pay for it!

TEIRESIAS: Would you care for more? Do you wish to be really angry?   145

OEDIPUS: Say what you will. Whatever you say is worthless.

TEIRESIAS: I say you live in hideous shame with those
  Most dear to you. You can not see the evil.

OEDIPUS: It seems you can go on mouthing like this for ever.   150

TEIRESIAS: I can, if there is power in truth.

OEDIPUS: There is:
  But not for you, not for you,
  You sightless, witless, senseless, mad old man!

TEIRESIAS: You are the madman. There is no one here
  Who will not curse you soon, as you curse me.   155

OEDIPUS: You child of endless night! You can not hurt me
  Or any other man who sees the sun.

TEIRESIAS: True: it is not from me your fate will come.
  That lies within Apollo's competence,
  As it is his concern.   160

OEDIPUS: Tell me:
  Are you speaking for Creon, or for yourself?

[handwritten note: Contradiction (ll. 158, 9)]

TEIRESIAS: Creon is no threat. You weave your own doom.

OEDIPUS: Wealth, power, craft of statesmanship!
Kingly position, everywhere admired!
What savage envy is stored up against these,   165
If Creon, whom I trusted, Creon my friend,
For this great office which the city once
Put in my hands unsought—if for this power
Creon desires in secret to destroy me!

[handwritten note: short-tempered]
[handwritten note: sincere, well-intentioned; always wants to take everything into his own hands]

He has bought this decrepit fortune-teller, this
Collector of dirty pennies, this prophet fraud—   170
Why, he is no more clairvoyant than I am!
                                              Tell us:
Has your mystic mummery ever approached the truth?
When that hellcat the Sphinx was performing here,
What help were you to these people?   175
Her magic was not for the first man who came along:
It demanded a real exorcist. Your birds—
What good were they? or the gods, for the matter of that?
But I came by,
Oedipus, the simple man, who knows nothing—   180
I thought it out for myself, no birds helped me!
And this is the man you think you can destroy,
That you may be close to Creon when he's king!
Well you and your friend Creon, it seems to me,
Will suffer most. If you were not an old man,   185
You would have paid already for your plot.

[handwritten note: feels superior to others]

CHORAGOS: We can not see that his words or yours
Have been spoken except in anger, Oedipus,
And of anger we have no need. How can God's will
Be accomplished best? That is what most concerns us.   190

TEIRESIAS: You are a king. But where argument's concerned
I am your man, as much a king as you.
I am not your servant, but Apollo's.
I have no need of Creon to speak for me.

Listen to me. You mock my blindness, do you?   195
But I say that you, with both your eyes, are blind:
You can not see the wretchedness of your life,
Nor in whose house you live, no, nor with whom.
Who are your father and mother? Can you tell me?
You do not even know the blind wrongs   200
That you have done them, on earth and in the world below.
But the double lash of your parents' curse will whip you
Out of this land some day, with only night
Upon your precious eyes.
Your cries then—where will they not be heard?   205
What fastness of Kithairon will not echo them?

And that bridal-descant of yours—you'll know it then,
The song they sang when you came here to Thebes
And found your misguided berthing.
All this, and more, that you can not guess at now,   210
Will bring you to yourself among your children.

Be angry, then. Curse Creon. Curse my words.
I tell you, no man that walks upon the earth
Shall be rooted out more horribly than you.

OEDIPUS: Am I to bear this from him?—Damnation   215
Take you! Out of this place! Out of my sight!

Ironic → TEIRESIAS: I would not have come at all if you had not asked me.

OEDIPUS: Could I have told that you'd talk nonsense, that
You'd come here to make a fool of yourself, and of me?

TEIRESIAS: A fool? Your parents thought me sane enough.   220

OEDIPUS: My parents again!—Wait: who were my parents?

TEIRESIAS: This day will give you a father, and break your heart.

OEDIPUS: Your infantile riddles! Your damned abracadabra!

TEIRESIAS: You were a great man once at solving riddles.

OEDIPUS: Mock me with that if you like; you will find it true.   225

TEIRESIAS: It was true enough. It brought about your ruin.

OEDIPUS: But if it saved this town?

TEIRESIAS (*to the* PAGE):

                    Boy, give me your hand.

OEDIPUS: Yes, boy; lead him away.

                    —While you are here
We can do nothing. Go; leave us in peace.

TEIRESIAS: I will go when I have said what I have to say.   230
How can you hurt me? And I tell you again:
The man you have been looking for all this time,
The damned man, the murderer of Laïos,
That man is in Thebes. To your mind he is foreignborn,
But it will soon be shown that he is a Theban,   235
A revelation that will fail to please.

                    A blind man,
Who has his eyes now; a penniless man, who is rich now;
And he will go tapping the strange earth with his staff;
To the children with whom he lives now he will be
Brother and father—the very same; to her   240
Who bore him, son and husband—the very same
Who came to his father's bed, wet with his father's blood.

Enough. Go think that over.
If later you find error in what I have said,
You may say that I have no skill in prophecy.   245

(*Exit* TEIRESIAS, *led by his* PAGE. OEDIPUS *goes into the palace.*)

Specific Prophecy

never crosses Oedipus' mind that it may be him.

ODE ONE,

[STROPHE ONE

CHORUS: The Delphic stone of prophecies
        Remembers ancient regicide
        And a still bloody hand.
        That killer's hour of flight has come.
        He must be stronger than riderless   5
        Coursers of untiring wind,
        For the son of Zeus armed with his father's thunder
        Leaps in lightning after him;
        And the Furies follow him, the sad Furies.

Son of
APOLLOS

[ANTISTROPHE ONE

        Holy Parnassos' peak of snow   10
        Flashes and blinds that secret man,
        That all shall hunt him down:
        Though he may roam the forest shade
        Like a bull gone wild from pasture
        To rage through glooms of stone.
        Doom comes down on him; flight will not avail him;   15
        For the world's heart calls him desolate,
        And the immortal Furies follow, for ever follow.

[STROPHE TWO

        But now a wilder thing is heard
        From the old man skilled at hearing Fate in the wingbeat
                of a bird.
        Bewildered as a blown bird, my soul hovers and can not find   20
        Foothold in this debate, or any reason or rest of mind.
        But no man ever brought—none can bring
        Proof of strife between Thebes' royal house,
        Labdakos' line, and the son of Polybos;   25
        And never until now has any man brought word
        Of Laïos' dark death staining Oedipus the King.

[ANTISTROPHE TWO

        Divine Zeus and Apollo hold
        Perfect intelligence alone of all tales ever told;
        And well though this diviner works, he works in his own night;   30
        No man can judge that rough unknown or trust in second sight,

For wisdom changes hands among the wise.
Shall I believe my great lord criminal
At a raging word that a blind old man let fall?
I saw him, when the carrion woman faced him of old,   35
Prove his heroic mind! These evil words are lies.   *Take Oedipus' side*

SCENE TWO

CREON: Men of Thebes:
I am told that heavy accusations
Have been brought against me by King Oedipus.

I am not the kind of man to bear this tamely.

If in these present difficulties   5
He holds me accountable for any harm to him
Through anything I have said or done—why, then,
I do not value life in this dishonor.
It is not as though this rumor touched upon
Some private indiscretion. The matter is grave.   10
The fact is that I am being called disloyal
To the State, to my fellow citizens, to my friends.

CHORAGOS: He may have spoken in anger, not from his mind.

CREON: But did you not hear him say I was the one
Who seduced the old prophet into lying?   15

CHORAGOS: The thing was said; I do not know how seriously.

CREON: But you were watching him! Were his eyes steady?
Did he look like a man in his right mind?

CHORAGOS: I do not know.
I can not judge the behavior of great men.
But here is the King himself.   20

(*Enter* OEDIPUS.)

OEDIPUS: So you dared come back.
Why? How brazen of you to come to my house,
You murderer!
                Do you think I do not know
That you plotted to kill me, plotted to steal my throne?
Tell me, in God's name: am I coward, a fool,
That you should dream you could accomplish this?   25
A fool who could not see your slippery game?
A coward, not to fight back when I saw it?
You are the fool, Creon, are you not? hoping
Without support or friends to get a throne?
Thrones may be won or bought: you could do neither.   30

CREON: Now listen to me. You have talked; let me talk, too.
You can not judge unless you know the facts.

OEDIPUS: You speak well: there is one fact; but I find it hard
    To learn from the deadliest enemy I have.

CREON: That above all I must dispute with you.   35

OEDIPUS: That above all I will not hear you deny.

CREON: If you think there is anything good in being stubborn
    Against all reason, then I say you are wrong.

OEDIPUS: If you think a man can sin against his own kind
    And not be punished for it, I say you are mad.   40

CREON: I agree. But tell me: what have I done to you?

OEDIPUS: You advised me to send for that wizard, did you not?

CREON: I did. I should do it again.

OEDIPUS: Very well. Now tell me;
    How long has it been since Laïos—

CREON: What of Laïos?

OEDIPUS: Since he vanished in that onset by the road?   45

CREON: It was long ago, a long time.

OEDIPUS: And this prophet,
    Was he practicing here then?

CREON: He was; and with honor, as now.

OEDIPUS: Did he speak of me at that time?

CREON: He never did;
    At least, not when I was present.

OEDIPUS: But . . . the enquiry?
    I suppose you held one?   50

CREON: We did, but we learned nothing.

OEDIPUS: Why did the prophet not speak against me then?

CREON: I do not know; and I am the kind of man
    Who holds his tongue when he has no facts to go on.

OEDIPUS: There's one fact that you know, and you could tell it.

CREON: What fact is that? If I know it, you shall have it.   55

OEDIPUS: If he were not involved with you, he could not say
    That it was I who murdered Laïos.

CREON: If he says that, you are the one that knows it!—
    But now it is my turn to question you.

OEDIPUS: Put your questions. I am no murderer.   60

CREON: First, then: You married my sister?

OEDIPUS: I married your sister

CREON: And you rule the kingdom equally with her?

OEDIPUS: Everything that she wants she has from me.

CREON: And I am the third, equal to both of you?

OEDIPUS: That is why I call you a bad friend.   65

CREON: No. Reason it out, as I have done.
    Think of this first. Would any sane man prefer

Power, with all a king's anxieties,
To that same power and the grace of sleep?
Certainly not I.   70
I have never longed for the king's power—only his rights.
Would any wise man differ from me in this?
As matters stand, I have my way in everything
With your consent, and no responsibilities.
If I were king, I should be a slave to policy.   75

How could I desire a scepter more
That what is now mine—untroubled influence?
No, I have not gone mad; I need no honors,
Except those with the perquisites I have now.
I am welcome everywhere; every man salutes me,   80
And those who want your favor seek my ear,
Since I know how to manage what they ask.
Should I exchange this ease for that anxiety?
Besides, no sober mind is treasonable.
I hate anarchy   85
And never would deal with any man who likes it.

Test what I have said. Go to the priestess
At Delphi, ask if I quoted her correctly.
And as for this other thing: if I am found
Guilty of treason with Teiresias,   90
Then sentence me to death! You have my word
It is a sentence I should cast my vote for—
But not without evidence!
                              You do wrong
When you take good men for bad, bad men for good.
A true friend thrown aside—why, life itself   95
Is not more precious!
                        In time you will know this well:
For time, and time alone, will show the just man,
Though scoundrels are discovered in a day.
CHORAGOS: This is well said, and a prudent man would ponder it.
  Judgments too quickly formed are dangerous.   100
OEDIPUS: But is he not quick in his duplicity?
  And shall I not be quick to parry him?
  Would you have me stand still, hold my peace, and let
  This man win everything, through my inaction?
CREON: And you want—what is it, then? To banish me?   105
OEDIPUS: No, not exile. It is your death I want,
  So that all the world may see what treason means.
CREON: You will persist, then? You will not believe me?
OEDIPUS: How can I believe you?
CREON: Then you are a fool.

OEDIPUS: To save myself?   110
CREON: In justice, think of me.
OEDIPUS: You are evil incarnate.
CREON: But suppose that you are wrong?
OEDIPUS: Still I must rule.
CREON: But not if you rule badly.
OEDIPUS: O city, city!
CREON: It is my city, too!
CHORAGOS: Now, my lords, be still. I see the Queen,
    Iocaste, coming from her palace chambers;   115
    And it is time she came, for the sake of you both.
    This dreadful quarrel can be resolved through her.

      (*Enter* IOCASTE.)

IOCASTE: Poor foolish men, what wicked din is this?
    With Thebes sick to death, is it not shameful
    That you should rake some private quarrel up?   120
    (*To* OEDIPUS.) Come into the house.
                      —And you, Creon, go now:
    Let us have no more of this tumult over nothing.
CREON: Nothing? No, sister: what your husband plans for me
    Is one of two great evils: exile or death.
OEDIPUS: He is right.   125
           Why, woman I have caught him squarely
    Plotting against my life.
CREON: No! Let me die
    Accurst if ever I have wished you harm!
IOCASTE: Ah, believe it, Oedipus!
    In the name of the gods, respect this oath of his
    For my sake, for the sake of these people here!   130

      [STROPHE ONE

CHORAGOS: Open your mind to her, my lord. Be ruled by her, I beg you!
OEDIPUS: What would you have me do?
CHORAGOS: Respect Creon's word. He has never spoken like a fool,
    And now he has sworn an oath.
OEDIPUS: You know what you ask?
CHORAGOS: I do.
OEDIPUS: Speak on, then.
CHORAGOS: A friend so sworn should not be baited so,   135
    In blind malice, and without final proof.
OEDIPUS: You are aware, I hope, that what you say
    Means death for me, or exile at the least.

[STROPHE TWO

CHORAGOS: No, I swear by Helios, first in Heaven!
 May I die friendless and accurst,   140
 The worst of deaths, if ever I meant that!
  It is the withering fields
   That hurt my sick heart:
  Must we bear all these ills,
   And now your bad blood as well?   145

OEDIPUS: Then let him go. And let me die, if I must,
 Or be driven by him in shame from the land of Thebes.
 It is your unhappiness, and not his talk,
 That touches me.
     As for him—
 Wherever he is, I will hate him as long as I live.   150

CREON: Ugly in yielding, as you were ugly in rage!
 Natures like yours chiefly torment themselves.

OEDIPUS: Can you not go? Can you not leave me?

CREON: I can.
 You do not know me; but the city knows me,
 And in its eyes I am just, if not in yours.   155

   (*Exit* CREON.)

[ANTISTROPHE ONE

CHORAGOS: Lady Iocaste, did you not ask the King to go to his
    chambers?

IOCASTE: First tell me what has happened.

CHORAGOS: There was suspicion without evidence; yet it rankled
 As even false charges will.

IOCASTE: On both sides?

CHORAGOS: On both.

IOCASTE: But what was said?

CHORAGOS: Oh let it rest, let it be done with!   160
 Have we not suffered enough?

OEDIPUS: You see to what your decency has brought you:
 You have made difficulties where my heart saw none.

[ANTISTROPHE TWO

CHORAGOS: Oedipus, it is not once only I have told you—
 You must know I should count myself unwise   165
 To the point of madness, should I now forsake you—
  You, under whose hand,
   In the storm of another time,

Our dear land sailed out free.
But now stand fast at the helm!   170

IOCASTE: In God's name, Oedipus, inform your wife as well:
Why are you so set in this hard anger?

OEDIPUS: I will tell you, for none of these men deserves
My confidence as you do. It is Creon's work,
His treachery, his plotting against me.   175

IOCASTE: Go on, if you can make this clear to me.

OEDIPUS: He charges me with the murder of Laïos.

IOCASTE: Has he some knowledge? Or does he speak from hearsay?

OEDIPUS: He would not commit himself to such a charge,
But he has brought in that damnable soothsayer   180
To tell his story.

IOCASTE: Set your mind at rest.
If it is a question of soothsayers, I tell you
That you will find no man whose craft gives knowledge
Of the unknowable.

Here is my proof:

An oracle was reported to Laïos once   185
(I will not say from Phoibos himself, but from   *Apollo*
His appointed ministers, at any rate)
That his doom would be death at the hands of his own son—
His son, born of his flesh and of mine!

Now, you remember the story: Laïos was killed   190
By marauding strangers where three highways meet;
But his child had not been three days in this world
Before the King had pierced the baby's ankles
And left him to die on a lonely mountainside.
Thus, Apollo never caused that child   195
To kill his father, and it was not Laïos' fate
To die at the hands of his son, as he had feared.
This is what prophets and prophecies are worth!
Have no dread of them.
                         It is God himself
Who can show us what he wills, in his own way.   200

OEDIPUS: How strange a shadowy memory crossed my mind,
Just now while you were speaking; it chilled my heart.

IOCASTE: What do you mean? What memory do you speak of?

OEDIPUS: If I understand you, Laïos was killed
At a place where three roads meet.

IOCASTE: So it was said;   205
We have no later story.

OEDIPUS: Where did it happen?

IOCASTE: Phokis, it is called: at a place where the Theban Way
Divides into the roads towards Delphi and Daulia.

Contrast

where 3 highways meet!

OEDIPUS: When?

IOCASTE: We had the news not long before you came
And proved the right to your succession here.   210

OEDIPUS: Ah, what net has God been weaving for me?

IOCASTE: Oedipus! Why does this trouble you?

OEDIPUS: Do not ask me yet.
First, tell me how Laïos looked, and tell me
How old he was.

IOCASTE: He was tall, his hair just touched
With white; his form was not unlike your own.   215

OEDIPUS: I think that I myself may be accurst
By my own ignorant edict.

IOCASTE: You speak strangely.
It makes me tremble to look at you, my King.

OEDIPUS: I am not sure that the blind man can not see.
But I should know better if you were to tell me—   220

IOCASTE: Anything—though I dread to hear you ask it.

OEDIPUS: Was the King lightly escorted, or did he ride
With a large company, as a ruler should?

IOCASTE: There were five men with him in all: one was a herald;
And a single chariot, which he was driving.   225

OEDIPUS: Alas, that makes it plain enough!
                            But who—
Who told you how it happened?

IOCASTE: A household servant,
The only one to escape.

OEDIPUS: And is he still
A servant of ours?

IOCASTE: No; for when he came back at last
And found you enthroned in the place of the dead king,   230
He came to me, touched my hand with his, and begged
That I would send him away to the frontier district
Where only the shepherds go—
As far away from the city as I could send him.
I granted his prayer; for although the man was a slave,   235
He had earned more than this favor at my hands.

OEDIPUS: Can he be called back quickly?

IOCASTE: Easily.
But why?

OEDIPUS: I have taken too much upon myself
Without enquiry; therefore I wish to consult him.

IOCASTE: Then he shall come.   240
                    But am I not one also
To whom you might confide these fears of yours?

OEDIPUS: That is your right; it will not be denied you,
Now least of all; for I have reached a pitch

Of wild foreboding. Is there anyone
To whom I should sooner speak?   245
Polybos of Corinth is my father.
My mother is a Dorian: Meropê.
I grew up chief among the men of Corinth
Until a strange thing happened—
Not worth my passion, it may be, but strange.   250

At a feast, a drunken man maundering in his cups   *angry*
Cries out that I am not my father's son!

I contained myself that night, though I felt anger
And a sinking heart. The next day I visited
My father and mother, and questioned them. They stormed,   255
Calling it all the slanderous rant of a fool;
And this relieved me. Yet the suspicion
Remained always aching in my mind;
I knew there was talk; I could not rest;
And finally, saying nothing to my parents,   260
I went to the shrine at Delphi.
The god dismissed my question without reply;
He spoke of other things.
                              Some were clear,
Full of wretchedness, dreadful, unbearable:
As, that I should lie with my own mother, breed   265
Children from whom all men would turn their eyes;
And that I should be my father's murderer.

I heard all this, and fled. And from that day
Corinth to me was only in the stars
Descending in that quarter of the sky,   270
As I wandered farther and farther on my way
To a land where I should never see the evil
Sung by the oracle. And I came to this country
Where, so you say, King Laïos was killed.

I will tell you all that happened there, my lady.   275

There were three highways
Coming together at a place I passed;
And there a herald came towards me, and a chariot
Drawn by horses, with a man such as you describe
Seated in it. The groom leading the horses   280
Forced me off the road at his lord's command;
But as this charioteer lurched over towards me
I struck him in my rage. The old man saw me
And brought his double goad down upon my head
As I came abreast.
                    He was paid back, and more!   285
Swinging my club in this right hand I knocked him

*Oedipus tells story
Kills his
natural father,
King Laïos*

Before the shepherd appears, he
Oedipus thinks he
has found out all

Out of his car, and he rolled on the ground.

                                             I killed him.

I killed them all.
Now if that stranger and Laïos were—kin,
Where is a man more miserable than I?   290
More hated by the gods? Citizen and alien alike
Must never shelter me or speak to me—
I must be shunned by all.
                        And I myself
Pronounced this malediction upon myself!

Think of it: I have touched you with these hands,   295
These hands that killed your husband. What defilement!

Am I all evil, then? It must be so,
Since I must flee from Thebes, yet never again
See my own countrymen, my own country,
For fear of joining my mother in marriage   300
And killing Polybos, my father.
                                    Ah,
Denial
of fate's part
If I was created so, born to this fate,
Who could deny the savagery of God?

O holy majesty of heavenly powers!
May I never see that day! Never!   305
Rather let me vanish from the race of men
Than know the abomination destined me!

CHORAGOS: We too, my lord, have felt dismay at this.
        But there is hope: you have yet to hear the shepherd.

OEDIPUS: Indeed, I fear no other hope is left me.   310

IOCASTE: What do you hope from him when he comes?

OEDIPUS: This much:
        If his account of the murder tallies with yours,
        Then I am cleared.

IOCASTE: What was it that I said
        Of such importance?

OEDIPUS: Why, "marauders," you said,
        Killed the King, according to this man's story.   315
        If he maintains that still, if there were several,
        Clearly the guilt is not mine: I was alone.
        But if he says one man, singlehanded, did it,
        Then the evidence all points to me.

IOCASTE: You may be sure that he said there were several;   320
        And can he call back that story now? He can not.
        The whole city heard it as plainly as I.
        But suppose he alters some detail of it:
        He can not ever show that Laïos' death

Fulfilled the oracle: for Apollo said   325
My child was doomed to kill him; and my child—
Poor baby!—it was my child that died first.
No. From now on, where oracles are concerned,
I would not waste a second thought on any.

OEDIPUS: You may be right.   330
                              But come: let someone go
For the shepherd at once. This matter must be settled.

IOCASTE: I will send for him.
          I would not wish to cross you in anything,
          And surely not in this.—Let us go in.

          (*Exeunt into the palace.*)

ODE TWO

          [STROPHE ONE

CHORUS: Let me be reverent in the ways of right,
          Lowly the paths I journey on;
          Let all my words and actions keep
          The laws of the pure universe
          From highest Heaven handed down.   5
          For Heaven is their bright nurse,
          Those generations of the realms of light;
          Ah, never of mortal kind were they begot,
          Nor are they slaves of memory, lost in sleep:
          Their Father is greater than Time, and ages not.   10

          [ANTISTROPHE ONE

          The tyrant is a child of Pride
          Who drinks from his great sickening cup
          Recklessness and vanity,
          Until from his high crest headlong
          He plummets to the dust of hope.   15
          That strong man is not strong.
          But let no fair ambition be denied;
          May God protect the wrestler for the State
          In government, in comely policy,
          Who will fear God, and on His ordinance wait.   20

          [STROPHE TWO

          Haughtiness and the high hand of disdain
          Tempt and outrage God's holy law;

And any mortal who dares hold
No immortal Power in awe
Will be caught up in a net of pain: 25
The price for which his levity is sold.
Let each man take due earnings, then,
And keep his hands from holy things,
And from blasphemy stand apart—
Else the crackling blast of heaven   30
Blows on his head, and on his desperate heart;
Though fools will honor impious men,
In their cities no tragic poet sings.

[ANTISTROPHE TWO

Shall we lose faith in Delphi's obscurities,
We who have heard the world's core   35
Discredited, and the sacred wood
Of Zeus at Elis praised no more?
The deeds and the strange prophecies
Must make a pattern yet to be understood.
Zeus, if indeed you are lord of all,   40
Throned in light over night and day,
Mirror this in your endless mind:
Our masters call the oracle
Words on the wind, and the Delphic vision blind!
Their hearts no longer know Apollo,   45
And reverence for the gods has died away.

SCENE THREE

(*Enter* IOCASTE.)

IOCASTE: Prince of Thebes, it has occurred to me
To visit the altars of the gods, bearing
These branches as a suppliant, and this incense.
Our King is not himself: his noble soul
Is overwrought with fantasies of dread,   5
Else he would consider
The new prophecies in the light of the old.
He will listen to any voice that speaks disaster,
And my advice goes for nothing.

(*She approaches the altar, R.*)

To you, then, Apollo,
Lycean lord, since you are nearest, I turn in prayer.   10
Receive these offerings, and grant us deliverance
From defilement. Our hearts are heavy with fear

When we see our leader distracted, as helpless sailors
Are terrified by the confusion of their helmsman.

(*Enter* MESSENGER.)

MESSENGER: Friends, no doubt you can direct me: 15
    Where shall I find the house of Oedipus,
    Or, better still, where is the King himself?

CHORAGOS: It is this very place, stranger; he is inside.
    This is his wife and mother of his children.

MESSENGER: I wish her happiness in a happy house,   20
    Blest in all the fulfillment of her marriage.

IOCASTE: I wish as much for you: your courtesy
    Deserves a like good fortune. But now, tell me:
    Why have you come? What have you to say to us?

MESSENGER: Good news, my lady, for your house and your husband.   25

IOCASTE: What news? Who sent you here?

MESSENGER: I am from Corinth.
    The news I bring ought to mean joy for you,
    Though it may be you will find some grief in it.

IOCASTE: What is it? How can it touch us in both ways?

MESSENGER: The people of Corinth, they say,   30
    Intend to call Oedipus to be their king.

IOCASTE: But old Polybos—is he not reigning still?

MESSENGER: No. Death holds him in his sepulchre.

IOCASTE: What are you saying? Polybos is dead?

MESSENGER: If I am not telling the truth, may I die myself.   35

IOCASTE (*to a* MAIDSERVANT): Go in, go quickly; tell this to your master.

    O riddlers of God's will, where are you now!
    This was the man whom Oedipus, long ago,
    Feared so, fled so, in dread of destroying him—
    But it was another fate by which he died.   40

(*Enter* OEDIPUS, *C.*)

OEDIPUS: Dearest Iocaste, why have you sent for me?

IOCASTE: Listen to what this man says, and then tell me
    What has become of the solemn prophecies.

OEDIPUS: Who is this man? What is his news for me?

IOCASTE: He has come from Corinth to announce your father's death! 45

OEDIPUS: Is it true, stranger? Tell me in your own words.

MESSENGER: I can not say it more clearly: the King is dead.

OEDIPUS: Was it by treason? Or by an attack of illness?

MESSENGER: A little thing brings old men to their rest.

OEDIPUS: It was sickness, then?   50

MESSENGER: Yes, and his many years.

OEDIPUS: Ah!
Why should a man respect the Pythian hearth, or
Give heed to the birds that jangle above his head?
They prophesied that I should kill Polybos,
Kill my own father; but he is dead and buried,   55
And I am here—I never touched him, never,
Unless he died of grief for my departure,
And thus, in a sense, through me. No. Polybos
Has packed the oracles off with him underground.
They are empty words.   60

IOCASTE: Had I not told you so?

OEDIPUS: You had; it was my faint heart that betrayed me.

IOCASTE: From now on never think of those things again.

OEDIPUS: And yet—must I not fear my mother's bed?

IOCASTE: Why should anyone in this world be afraid,
Since Fate rules us and nothing can be foreseen?   65
A man should live only for the present day.

Have no more fear of sleeping with your mother:
How many men, in dreams, have lain with their mothers!
No reasonable man is troubled by such things.

OEDIPUS: That is true; only—   70
If only my mother were not still alive!
But she is alive. I can not help my dread.

IOCASTE: Yet this news of your father's death is wonderful.

OEDIPUS: Wonderful. But I fear the living woman.

MESSENGER: Tell me, who is this woman that you fear?   75

OEDIPUS: It is Meropê, man; the wife of King Polybos.

MESSENGER: Meropê? Why should you be afraid of her?

OEDIPUS: An oracle of the gods, a dreadful saying.

MESSENGER: Can you tell me about it or are you sworn to silence?

OEDIPUS: I can tell you, and I will.   80
Apollo said through his prophet that I was the man
Who should marry his own mother, shed his father's blood
With his own hands. And so, for all these years
I have kept clear of Corinth, and no harm has come—
Though it would have been sweet to see my parents again.   85

MESSENGER: And is this the fear that drove you out of Corinth?

OEDIPUS: Would you have me kill my father?

MESSENGER: As for that
You must be reassured by the news I gave you.

OEDIPUS: If you could reassure me, I would reward you.

MESSENGER: I had that in mind, I will confess: I thought   90
I could count on you when you returned to Corinth.

OEDIPUS: No: I will never go near my parents again.

MESSENGER: Ah, son, you still do not know what you are doing—

OEDIPUS: What do you mean? In the name of God tell me!

MESSENGER: If these are your reasons for not going home.   95

OEDIPUS: I tell you, I fear the oracle may come true.

MESSENGER: And guilt may come upon you through your parents?

OEDIPUS: That is the dread that is always in my heart.

MESSENGER: Can you not see that all your fears are groundless?

OEDIPUS: How can you say that? They are my parents, surely?   100

MESSENGER: Polybos was not your father.

OEDIPUS: Not my father?

MESSENGER: No more your father than the man speaking to you.

OEDIPUS: But you are nothing to me.

MESSENGER: Neither was he.

OEDIPUS: Then why did he call me son?

MESSENGER: I will tell you:
     Long ago he had you from my hands, as a gift.   105

OEDIPUS: Then how could he love me so, if I was not his?

MESSENGER: He had no children, and his heart turned to you.

OEDIPUS: What of you? Did you buy me? Did you find me by chance?

MESSENGER: I came upon you in the crooked pass of Kithairon.

OEDIPUS: And what were you doing there?   110

MESSENGER: Tending my flocks.

OEDIPUS: A wandering shepherd?

MESSENGER: But your savior, son, that day.

OEDIPUS: From what did you save me?

MESSENGER: Your ankles should tell you that.

OEDIPUS: Ah, stranger, why do you speak of that childhood pain?

MESSENGER: I cut the bonds that tied your ankles together.

OEDIPUS: I have had the mark as long as I can remember.   115

MESSENGER: That was why you were given the name you bear.

OEDIPUS: God! Was it my father or my mother who did it?
     Tell me!

MESSENGER: I do not know. The man who gave you to me
     Can tell you better than I.   120

OEDIPUS: It was not you that found me, but another?

MESSENGER: It was another shepherd gave you to me.

OEDIPUS: Who was he? Can you tell me who he was?

MESSENGER: I think he was said to be one of Laïos' people.

OEDIPUS: You mean the Laïos who was king here years ago?   125

MESSENGER: Yes; King Laïos; and the man was one of his herdsmen.

OEDIPUS: Is he still alive? Can I see him?

MESSENGER: These men here
    Know best about such things.

OEDIPUS: Does anyone here
    Know this shepherd that he is talking about?
    Have you seen him in the fields, or in the town?   130
    If you have, tell me. It is time things were made plain.

CHORAGOS: I think the man he means is that same shepherd
    You have already asked to see. Iocaste perhaps
    Could tell you something.

OEDIPUS: Do you know anything
    About him, Lady? Is he the man we have summoned?   135
    Is that the man this shepherd means?

IOCASTE: Why think of him?
    Forget this herdsman. Forget it all.
    This talk is a waste of time.

OEDIPUS: How can you say that,
    When the clues to my true birth are in my hands?

IOCASTE: For God's love, let us have no more questioning!   140
    Is your life nothing to you?
    My own is pain enough for me to bear.

OEDIPUS: You need not worry. Suppose my mother a slave,
    And born of slaves: no baseness can touch you.

IOCASTE: Listen to me, I beg you: do not do this thing!   145

OEDIPUS: I will not listen; the truth must be made known.

IOCASTE: Everything that I say is for your own good!

OEDIPUS: My own good
    Snaps my patience, then; I want none of it.

IOCASTE: You are fatally wrong! May you never learn who you are!

OEDIPUS: Go, one of you, and bring the shepherd here.   150
    Let us leave this woman to brag of her royal name.

IOCASTE: Ah, miserable!
    That is the only word I have for you now.
    That is the only word I can ever have.

                (Exit into the palace.)

CHORAGOS: Why has she left us, Oedipus? Why has she gone   155
    In such a passion of sorrow? I fear this silence:
    Something dreadful may come of it.

OEDIPUS: Let it come!
    However base my birth, I must know about it.
    The Queen, like a woman, is perhaps ashamed
    To think of my low origin. But I
    Am a child of Luck; I can not be dishonored.   160
    Luck is my mother; the passing months, my brothers,
    Have seen me rich and poor.

If this is so,
How could I wish that I were someone else?
How could I not be glad to know my birth?   165

ODE THREE

[STROPHE

CHORUS: If ever the coming time were known
         To my heart's pondering,
         Kithairon, now by Heaven I see the torches
         At the festival of the next full moon,
         And see the dance, and hear the choir sing   5
         A grace to your gentle shade:
         Mountain where Oedipus was found,
         O mountain guard of a noble race!
         May the god who heals us lend his aid,
         And let that glory come to pass   10
         For our king's cradling-ground.

         [ANTISTROPHE

Of the nymphs that flower beyond the years,
Who bore you, royal child,
To Pan of the hills or the timberline Apollo,
Cold in delight where the upland clears,   15
Or Hermês for whom Kyllenê's heights are piled?
Or flushed as evening cloud,
Great Dionysos, roamer of mountains,
He—was it he who found you there,
And caught you up in his own proud   20
Arms from the sweet god-ravisher
Who laughed by the Muses' fountains?

SCENE FOUR

OEDIPUS: Sirs: though I do not know the man,
          I think I see him coming, this shepherd we want:
          He is old, like our friend here, and the men
          Bringing him seem to be servants of my house.
          But you can tell, if you have ever seen him.   5

          (*Enter* SHEPHERD *escorted by servants.*)

CHORAGOS: I know him, he was Laïos' man. You can trust him.
OEDIPUS: Tell me first, you from Corinth: is this the shepherd
          We were discussing?
MESSENGER: This is the very man.

OEDIPUS (*to* SHEPHERD): Come here. No, look at me. You must answer
  Everything I ask.—You belonged to Laïos?   10

SHEPHERD: Yes, born his slave, brought up in his house.

OEDIPUS: Tell me: what kind of work did you do for him?

SHEPHERD: I was a shepherd of his most of my life.

OEDIPUS: Where mainly did you go for pasturage?

SHEPHERD: Sometimes Kithairon, sometimes the hills near-by.   15

OEDIPUS: Do you remember ever seeing this man out there?

SHEPHERD: What would he be doing there? This man?

OEDIPUS: This man standing here. Have you ever seen him before?

SHEPHERD: No. At least, not to my recollection.

MESSENGER: And that is not strange, my lord. But I'll refresh   20
  His memory: he must remember when we two
  Spent three whole seasons together, March to September,
  On Kithairon or thereabouts. He had two flocks;
  I had one. Each autumn I'd drive mine home
  And he would go back with his to Laïos' sheepfold.—   25
  Is this not true, just as I have described it?

SHEPHERD: True, yes; but it was all so long ago.

MESSENGER: Well, then: do you remember, back in those days
  That you gave me a baby boy to bring up as my own?

SHEPHERD: What if I did? What are you trying to say?   30

MESSENGER: King Oedipus was once that little child.

SHEPHERD: Damn you, hold your tongue!

OEDIPUS: No more of that!
  It is your tongue needs watching, not this man's.

SHEPHERD: My King, my Master, what is it I have done wrong?

OEDIPUS: You have not answered his question about the boy.   35

SHEPHERD: He does not know . . . He is only making trouble . . .

OEDIPUS: Come, speak plainly, or it will go hard with you.

SHEPHERD: In God's name, do not torture an old man!

OEDIPUS: Come here, one of you; bind his arms behind him.

SHEPHERD: Unhappy king! What more do you wish to learn?   40

OEDIPUS: Did you give this man the child he speaks of?

SHEPHERD: I did.
  And I would to God I had died that very day.

OEDIPUS: You will die now unless you speak the truth.

SHEPHERD: Yet if I speak the truth, I am worse than dead.

OEDIPUS: Very well; since you insist upon delaying—   45

SHEPHERD: No! I have told you already that I gave him the boy.

OEDIPUS: Where did you get him? From your house? From somewhere else?

SHEPHERD: Not from mine, no. A man gave him to me.

OEDIPUS: Is that man here? Do you know whose slave he was?

SHEPHERD: For God's love, my King, do not ask me any more!   50

OEDIPUS: <u>You are a dead man if I have to ask you again.</u>   *threatens to kill him if he doesn't tell him.*

SHEPHERD: Then . . . Then the child was from the palace of Laïos.

OEDIPUS: A slave child? or a child of his own line?

SHEPHERD: Ah, I am on the brink of dreadful speech!

OEDIPUS: And I of dreadful hearing. Yet I must hear.   55

SHEPHERD: If you must be told, then . . .

                  They said it was Laïos' child,
But it is your wife who can tell you about that.

OEDIPUS: My wife!—Did she give it to you?

SHEPHERD: My lord, she did.

OEDIPUS: Do you know why?

SHEPHERD: I was told to get rid of it.

OEDIPUS: An unspeakable mother!   60

SHEPHERD: There had been prophecies . . .

OEDIPUS: Tell me.

SHEPHERD: It was said that the boy would kill his own father.

OEDIPUS: Then why did you give him over to this old man?

SHEPHERD: I pitied the baby, my King,
And I thought that this man would take him far away
To his own country.   65

           He saved him—but for what a fate!
For if you are what this man says you are,
No man living is more wretched than Oedipus.

OEDIPUS: Ah God!
It was true!
        All the prophecies!
           —Now,
O Light, may I look on you for the last time!   70
I, Oedipus,
Oedipus, damned in his birth, in his marriage damned,
Damned in the blood he shed with his own hand!

    (*He rushes into the palace.*)

ODE FOUR

    [STROPHE ONE

CHORUS: Alas for the seed of men.

    What measure shall I give these generations
    That breathe on the void and are void
    And exist and do not exist?

    Who bears more weight of joy   5
    Than mass of sunlight shifting in images,

Or who shall make his thought stay on
That down time drifts away?

Your splendor is all fallen.

O naked brow of wrath and tears,   10
O change of Oedipus!
I who saw your days call no man blest—
Your great days like ghósts góne.

       [ANTISTROPHE ONE

That mind was a strong bow.
Deep, how deep you drew it then, hard archer,   15
At a dim fearful range,
And brought dear glory down!

You overcame the stranger—
The virgin with her hooking lion claws—
And though death sang, stood like a tower   20
To make pale Thebes take heart.

Fortress against our sorrow!

Divine king, giver of laws,
Majestic Oedipus!
No prince in Thebes had ever such renown,   25
No prince won such grace of power.

       [STROPHE TWO

And now of all men ever known
Most pitiful is this man's story:
His fortunes are most changed, his state
Fallen to a low slave's   30
Ground under bitter fate.

O Oedipus, most royal one!
The great door that expelled you to the light
Gave at night—ah, gave night to your glory:
As to the father, to the fathering son.   35

All understood too late.

How could that queen whom Laïos won,
The garden that he harrowed at his height,
Be silent when that act was done?

[ANTISTROPHE TWO

But all eyes fail before time's eye,   40
All actions come to justice there.
Though never willed, though far down the deep past,
Your bed, your dread sirings,
Are brought to book at last.
Child by Laïos doomed to die,   45
Then doomed to lose that fortunate little death,
Would God you never took breath in this air
That with my wailing lips I take to cry:

For I weep the world's outcast.

I was blind, and now I can tell why: 50
Asleep, for you had given ease of breath
To Thebes, while the false years went by.

EXODOS

(*Enter, from the palace,* SECOND MESSENGER.)

SECOND MESSENGER: Elders of Thebes, most honored in this land,
What horrors are yours to see and hear, what weight
Of sorrow to be endured, if, true to your birth,
You venerate the line of Labdakos!
I think neither Istros nor Phasis, those great rivers,   5
Could purify this place of the corruption
It shelters now, or soon must bring to light—
Evil not done unconsciously, but willed.

The greatest griefs are those we cause ourselves.

CHORAGOS: Surely, friend, we have grief enough already;   10
What new sorrow do you mean?
SECOND MESSENGER: The Queen is dead.
CHORAGOS: Iocaste? Dead? But at whose hand?
SECOND MESSENGER: Her own.
The full horror of what happened you can not know,
For you did not see it; but I, who did, will tell you
As clearly as I can how she met her death.   15

When she had left us,
In passionate silence, passing through the court,
She ran to her apartment in the house,
Her hair clutched by the fingers of both hands.
She closed the doors behind her; then, by that bed   20
Where long ago the fatal son was conceived—
That son who should bring about his father's death—

We heard her call upon Laïos, dead so many years,
And heard her wail for the double fruit of her marriage,
A husband by her husband, children by her child.   25

Exactly how she died I do not know:
For Oedipus burst in moaning and would not let us
Keep vigil to the end: it was by him
As he stormed about the room that our eyes were caught.
From one to another of us he went, begging a sword,   30
Cursing the wife who was not his wife, the mother
Whose womb had carried his own children and himself.
I do not know: it was none of us aided him,
But surely one of the gods was in control!
For with a dreadful cry   35
He hurled his weight, as though wrenched out of himself,
At the twin doors: the bolts gave, and he rushed in.
And there we saw her hanging, her body swaying
From the cruel cord she had noosed about her neck.
A great sob broke from him, heartbreaking to hear,   40
As he loosed the rope and lowered her to the ground.

I would blot out from my mind what happened next!
For the King ripped from her gown the golden brooches
That were her ornament, and raised them, and plunged them
                down
Straight into his own eyeballs, crying, "No more,   45
No more shall you look on the misery about me,
The horrors of my own doing! Too long you have known
The faces of those whom I should never have seen,
Too long been blind to those for whom I was searching!
From this hour, go in darkness!" And as he spoke,   50
He struck at his eyes—not once, but many times;
And the blood spattered his beard,
Bursting from his ruined sockets like red hail.

So from the unhappiness of two this evil has sprung,
A curse on the man and woman alike. The old   55
Happiness of the house of Labdakos
Was happiness enough: where is it today?
It is all wailing and ruin, disgrace, death—all
The misery of mankind that has a name—
And it is wholly and for ever theirs.   60

CHORAGOS: Is he in agony still? Is there no rest for him?

SECOND MESSENGER: He is calling for someone to lead him to the gates
So that all the children of Kadmos may look upon
His father's murderer, his mother's—no,
I can not say it!   65
                And then he will leave Thebes,
Self-exiled, in order that the curse

Which he himself pronounced may depart from the house.
He is weak, and there is none to lead him,
So terrible in his suffering.
                              But you will see:
Look, the doors are opening; in a moment   70
You will see a thing that would crush a heart of stone.

   (*The central door is opened*; OEDIPUS, *blinded, is led in.*)

CHORAGOS: Dreadful indeed for men to see.
   Never have my own eyes
   Looked on a sight so full of fear.

   Oedipus!   75
   What madness came upon you, what daemon
   Leaped on your life with heavier
   Punishment than a mortal man can bear?
   No: I can not even
   Look at you, poor ruined one.   80
   And I would speak, question, ponder,
   If I were able. No.
   You make me shudder.

OEDIPUS: God.   God.
   Is there a sorrow greater?
   Where shall I find harbor in this world?   85
   My voice is hurled far on a dark wind.
   What has God done to me?

CHORAGOS: Too terrible to think of, or to see.

Oedipus's first words after he blinds himself

                    [STROPHE ONE

OEDIPUS: O cloud of night,   90
   Never to be turned away: night coming on,
   I can not tell how: night like a shroud!

   My fair winds brought me here.
                              Oh God. Again
   The pain of the spikes where I had sight,
   The flooding pain   95
   Of memory, never to be gouged out.

CHORAGOS: This is not strange.
   You suffer it all twice over, remorse in pain,
   Pain in remorse.

                    [ANTISTROPHE ONE

OEDIPUS: Ah dear friend   100
   Are you faithful even yet, you alone?

Are you still standing near me, will you stay here,
Patient, to care for the blind?

                       The blind man!
Yet even blind I know who it is attends me,
By the voice's tone—   105
Though my darkness hide the comforter.

CHORAGOS: Oh fearful act!
What god was it drove you to rake black
Night across your eyes?

[STROPHE TWO

OEDIPUS: Apollo. Apollo. Dear   110
Children, the god was Apollo.
He brought my sick, sick fate upon me.
But the blinding hand was my own!
How could I bear to see
When all my sight was horror everywhere?   115

CHORAGOS: Everywhere; that is true.

OEDIPUS: And now what is left?
Images? Love? A greeting even,
Sweet to the senses? Is there anything?
Ah, no, friends: lead me away.   120
Lead me away from Thebes.

                       Lead the great wreck
And hell of Oedipus, whom the gods hate.

CHORAGOS: Your fate is clear, you are not blind to that.
Would God you had never found it out!

[ANTISTROPHE TWO

OEDIPUS: Death take the man who unbound   125
My feet on that hillside
And delivered me from death to life! What life?
If only I had died,
This weight of monstrous doom
Could not have dragged me and my darlings down.   130

CHORAGOS: I would have wished the same.

OEDIPUS: Oh never to have come here
With my father's blood upon me! Never
To have been the man they call his mother's husband!
Oh accurst! Oh child of evil,   135
To have entered that wretched bed—

                       the selfsame one!
More primal than sin itself, this fell to me.

CHORAGOS: I do not know how I can answer you.
You were better dead than alive and blind.

OEDIPUS: Do not counsel me any more. This punishment   140
    That I have laid upon myself is just.
    If I had eyes,
    I do not know how I could bear the sight
    Of my father, when I came to the house of Death,
    Or my mother: for I have sinned against them both   145
    So vilely that I could not make my peace
    By strangling my own life.
                  Or do you think my children,
    Born as they were born, would be sweet to my eyes?
    Ah never, never! Nor this town with its high walls,
    Nor the holy images of the gods.
               For I,   150
    Thrice miserable—Oedipus, noblest of all the line
    Of Kadmos, have condemned myself to enjoy
    These things no more, by my own malediction
    Expelling that man whom the gods declared
    To be a defilement in the house of Laïos.   155
    After exposing the rankness of my own guilt,
    How could I look men frankly in the eyes?
    No, I swear it,
    If I could have stifled my hearing at its source,
    I would have done it and made all this body   160
    A tight cell of misery, blank to light and sound:
    So I should have been safe in a dark agony
    Beyond all recollection.
              Ah Kithairon!
    Why did you shelter me? When I was cast upon you,
    Why did I not die? Then I should never   165
    Have shown the world my execrable birth.

    Ah Polybos! Corinth, city that I believed
    The ancient seat of my ancestors: how fair
    I seemed, your child! And all the while this evil
    Was cancerous within me!   170
             For I am sick
    In my daily life, sick in my origin.

    O three roads, dark ravine, woodland and way
    Where three roads met: you, drinking my father's blood,
    My own blood, spilled by my own hand: can you remember
    The unspeakable things I did there, and the things   175
    I went on from there to do?
              O marriage, marriage!
    The act that engendered me, and again the act
    Performed by the son in the same bed—
                 Ah, the net
    Of incest, mingling fathers, brothers, sons,
    With brides, wives, mothers: the last evil   180

That can be known by men: no tongue can say
How evil!
        No. For the love of God, conceal me
Somewhere far from Thebes; or kill me; or hurl me
Into the sea, away from men's eyes for ever.

Come, lead me. You need not fear to touch me.   185
Of all men, I alone can bear this guilt.

    (*Enter* CREON.)

CHORAGOS: We are not the ones to decide; but Creon here
    May fitly judge of what you ask. He only
    Is left to protect the city in your place.

OEDIPUS: Alas, how can I speak to him? What right have I   190
    To beg his courtesy whom I have deeply wronged?

CREON: I have not come to mock you, Oedipus,
    Or to reproach you, either.
    (*To* ATTENDANTS.)   —You, standing there:
    If you have lost all respect for man's dignity,
    At least respect the flame of Lord Helios: 195
    Do not allow this pollution to show itself
    Openly here, an affront to the earth
    And Heaven's rain and the light of day. No, take him
    Into the house as quickly as you can.
    For it is proper   200
    That only the close kindred see his grief.

OEDIPUS: I pray you in God's name, since your courtesy
    Ignores my dark expectation, visiting
    With mercy this man of all men most execrable:
    Give me what I ask—for your good, not for mine.   205

CREON: And what is it that you would have me do?

OEDIPUS: Drive me out of this country as quickly as may be
    To a place where no human voice can ever greet me.

CREON: I should have done that before now—only,
    God's will had not been wholly revealed to me.   210

OEDIPUS: But his command is plain: the parricide
    Must be destroyed. I am that evil man.

CREON: That is the sense of it, yes; but things are,
    We had best discover clearly what is to be done.

OEDIPUS: You would learn more about a man like me?   215

CREON: You are ready now to listen to the god.

OEDIPUS: I will listen. But it is to you
    That I must turn for help. I beg you, hear me.

The woman in there—
Give her whatever funeral you think proper: 220
She is your sister.

—But let me go, Creon!
Let me purge my father's Thebes of the pollution
Of my living here, and go out to the wild hills,
To Kithairon, that has won such fame with me,
The tomb my mother and father appointed for me,   225
And let me die there, as they willed I should.
And yet I know
Death will not ever come to me through sickness
Or in any natural way: I have been preserved
For some unthinkable fate. But let that be.   230
As for my sons, you need not care for them.
They are men, they will find some way to live.
But my poor daughters, who have shared my table,
Who never before have been parted from their father—
Take care of them, Creon; do this for me.   235
And will you let me touch them with my hands
A last time, and let us weep together?
Be kind, my lord,
Great prince, be kind!
                        Could I but touch them,
They would be mine again, as when I had my eyes.   240

      (*Enter* ANTIGONE *and* ISMENE, *attended.*)

Ah, God!
Is it my dearest children I hear weeping?
Has Creon pitied me and sent my daughters?
CREON: Yes, Oedipus: I knew that they were dear to you
In the old days, and know you must love them still.   245
OEDIPUS: May God bless you for this—and be a friendlier
Guardian to you than he has been to me!

Children, where are you?
Come quickly to my hands; they are your brother's—
Hands that have brought your father's once clear eyes   250
To this way of seeing—
                        Ah dearest ones,
I had neither sight nor knowledge then, your father
By the woman who was the source of his own life!
And I weep for you—having no strength to see you—,
I weep for you when I think of the bitterness   255
That men will visit upon you all your lives.
What homes, what festivals can you attend
Without being forced to depart again in tears?
And when you come to marriageable age,
Where is the man, my daughters, who would dare   260
Risk the bane that lies on all my children?
Is there any evil wanting? Your father killed
His father; sowed the womb of her who bore him;

Engendered you at the fount of his own existence!
That is what they will say of you.
                                        Then, whom   265
Can you ever marry? There are no bridegrooms for you,
And your lives must wither away in sterile dreaming.
O Creon, son of Menoikeus!
You are the only father my daughters have,
Since we, their parents, are both of us gone for ever.   270
They are your own blood: you will not let them
Fall into beggary and loneliness;
You will keep them from the miseries that are mine!
Take pity on them; see, they are only children,
Friendless except for you. Promise me this,   275
Great Prince, and give me your hand in token of it.

        (CREON *clasps his right hand.*)

Children:
I could say much, if you could understand me,
But as it is, I have only this prayer for you:
Live where you can, be as happy as you can—   280
Happier, please God, than God has made your father!

CREON: Enough. You have wept enough. Now go within.

OEDIPUS: I must, but it is hard.

CREON: Time eases all things.

OEDIPUS: But you must promise—

CREON: Say what you desire.

OEDIPUS: Send me from Thebes!

CREON: God grant that I may!   285

OEDIPUS: But since God hates me . . .

CREON: No, he will grant your wish.

OEDIPUS: You promise?

CREON: I can not speak beyond my knowledge.

OEDIPUS: Then lead me in.

CREON: Come now, and leave your children.

OEDIPUS: No! Do not take them from me!

CREON: Think no longer
That you are in command here, but rather think   290
How, when you were, you served your own destruction.

        (*Exeunt into the house all but the* CHORUS; *the* CHORAGOS
        chants directly to the audience.)

CHORAGOS: Men of Thebes: look upon Oedipus.

This is the king who solved the famous riddle
And towered up, most powerful of men.
No mortal eyes but looked on him with envy,   295

Yet in the end ruin swept over him.
*Let every man in mankind's frailty
Consider his last day; and let none
Presume on his good fortune until he find
Life, at his death, a memory without pain.   300

Summary
The lesson to be learned

Fact Questions and Exercises

1. Describe the condition of Thebes as the play opens, pointing out the specific lines that supply this information.
2. What does the priest mean when he says that Creon "is crowned with bay"?
3. Who is the one person who escaped when King Laïos was murdered?
4. Identify Teiresias. What is his affliction? How does he learn his information?
5. Why doesn't Creon want to be king?
6. Identify the Sphinx. What part has it played in Oedipus's life?
7. Why had Oedipus's father tried to kill his infant son? How did Oedipus escape death?
8. Who is Oedipus's wife?
9. What happens to Oedipus at the end of the play? What happens to Iocaste?
10. Who becomes king after Oedipus?

For Discussion and Writing

1. In the play, Oedipus becomes progressively aware of his sins. Does Sophocles imply that Oedipus would have been better off if he had remained ignorant of his deeds? What does this mean in terms of the value of human knowledge? What, for instance, does Iocaste mean when she says that "you will find no man whose craft gives knowledge / Of the unknowable"?
2. Fate is an important concept in the play; what does "fate" mean in *Oedipus Rex*? How does fate affect your characterization of Oedipus? Does Oedipus have any control over his actions? If not, can he be held accountable for what he does? Could he have altered any of the events that led to his fall. Ultimately, does his fall serve a good purpose? If so, in what ways?
3. How many different types of blindness are there in the play? For instance, how does Teiresias "see"? In what ways is Oedipus "blind"?
4. Hubris, or pride, is usually considered to be Oedipus's fatal flaw; do you agree? If so, how do you account for the fact that the gods have predetermined Oedipus's life?

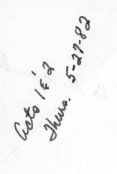

William Shakespeare [1564–1616]

Shakespeare was born in Stratford-on-Avon, England, and probably attended grammar school there. Few facts are known about his life: we do know that by 1592 he was established in London as a noted actor and playwright; by 1610 he had retired to Stratford, a wealthy and famous man. Since no collected edition was published before his death, there is some debate about the text of Shakespeare's poems and plays; the following text of *Hamlet*, for instance, is a combination of several extant versions. Despite the confusion that sometimes surrounds his life and work, there is no doubt that Shakespeare is among the greatest writers in world literature. No simple summation of Shakespeare's plays and sonnets can be offered; his works demonstrate too great diversity and complexity. He had a genius for lyrics, humor, psychological insights, and the creation of a lively array of characters.

The Tragedy of Hamlet, Prince of Denmark

[DRAMATIS PERSONAE

CLAUDIUS, *King of Denmark*
HAMLET, *son to the late King Hamlet, and nephew to the present King*
POLONIUS, *Lord Chamberlain*
HORATIO, *friend to Hamlet*
LAERTES, *son to Polonius*
VOLTEMAND
CORNELIUS
ROSENCRANTZ
GUILDENSTERN   } *courtiers*
OSRIC
GENTLEMAN
MARCELLUS } *officers*
BARNARDO

FRANCISCO, *a soldier*
REYNALDO, *servant to Polonius*
FORTINBRAS, *Prince of Norway*
NORWEGIAN CAPTAIN
DOCTOR OF DIVINITY
PLAYERS
Two CLOWNS, *grave-diggers*
ENGLISH AMBASSADORS
GERTRUDE, *Queen of Denmark, and mother to Hamlet*
OPHELIA, *daughter to Polonius*
GHOST *of Hamlet's Father*
LORDS, LADIES, OFFICERS, SOLDIERS, SAILORS, MESSENGERS, *and* ATTENDANTS

scene: *Denmark*]

ACT ONE, SCENE ONE

Enter BARNARDO *and* FRANCISCO, *two sentinels*, [*meeting*].

BARNARDO: Who's there?
FRANCISCO: Nay, answer me. Stand and unfold yourself.

BARNARDO: Long live the King!

FRANCISCO: Barnardo.

BARNARDO: He.   5

FRANCISCO: You come most carefully upon your hour.

BARNARDO: 'Tis now strook twelf. Get thee to bed, Francisco.

FRANCISCO: For this relief much thanks. 'Tis bitter cold,
    And I am sick at heart.

BARNARDO: Have you had quiet guard?

FRANCISCO: Not a mouse stirring.   10

BARNARDO: Well, good night.
    If you do meet Horatio and Marcellus,
    The rivals of my watch, bid them make haste.

        Enter HORATIO *and* MARCELLUS.

FRANCISCO: I think I hear them. Stand ho! Who is there?

HORATIO: Friends to this ground.

MARCELLUS: And liegemen to the Dane.   15

FRANCISCO: Give you good night.

MARCELLUS: O, farewell, honest [soldier].
    Who hath reliev'd you?

FRANCISCO: Barnardo hath my place.
    Give you good night.   (*Exit* FRANCISCO.)

MARCELLUS: Holla, Barnardo!

BARNARDO: Say—
    What, is Horatio there?

HORATIO: A piece of him.   19

BARNARDO: Welcome, Horatio, welcome, good Marcellus.

HORATIO: What, has this thing appear'd again to-night?

BARNARDO: I have seen nothing.

MARCELLUS: Horatio says 'tis but our fantasy,
    And will not let belief take hold of him
    Touching this dreaded sight twice seen of us;
    Therefore I have entreated him along,   25
    With us to watch the minutes of this night,
    That if again this apparition come,
    He may approve our eyes and speak to it.

(Handwritten margin note: Barnardo relieves Francisco)

(Handwritten margin note: Horatio does not believe Barnardo's and Marcellus' story)

Words and passages enclosed in square brackets in the text above are either emendations of the copy-text or additions to it.

I.i. Location: Elsinore. A guard-platform of the castle.
2. *answer me:* i.e. *you* answer *me.* Francisco is on watch; Barnardo has come to relieve him. *unfold yourself:* make known who you are. **3.** *Long . . . King.* Perhaps a password, perhaps simply an utterance to allow the voice to be recognized. **7.** *strook twelf:* struck twelve. **9.** *sick at heart:* in low spirits. **13.** *rivals:* partners. **15.** *liegemen . . . Dane:* loyal subjects to the King of Denmark. **16.** *Give:* God give. **23.** *fantasy:* imagination. **29.** *approve:* corroborate.

HORATIO: Tush, tush, 'twill not appear.

BARNARDO: Sit down a while,   30
And let us once again assail your ears,
That are so fortified against our story,
What we have two nights seen.

HORATIO: Well, sit we down,
And let us hear Barnardo speak of this.

BARNARDO: Last night of all,   35
When yond same star that's westward from the pole
Had made his course t' illume that part of heaven
Where now it burns, Marcellus and myself,
The bell then beating one—

Enter GHOST.

MARCELLUS: Peace, break thee off! Look where it comes again!

BARNARDO: In the same figure like the King that's dead.

MARCELLUS: Thou art a scholar, speak to it, Horatio.

BARNARDO: Looks 'a not like the King? Mark it, Horatio.

HORATIO: Most like; it [harrows] me with fear and wonder.

BARNARDO: It would be spoke to.

MARCELLUS: Speak to it, Horatio.

HORATIO: What art thou that usurp'st this time of night,
Together with that fair and warlike form   47
In which the majesty of buried Denmark
Did sometimes march? By heaven I charge thee speak!

MARCELLUS: It is offended.

BARNARDO: See, it stalks away!   50

HORATIO: Stay! Speak, speak, I charge thee speak!   (*Exit* GHOST.)

MARCELLUS: 'Tis gone, and will not answer.

BARNARDO: How now, Horatio? you tremble and look pale.
Is not this something more than fantasy?
What think you on't?   55

HORATIO: Before my God, I might not this believe
Without the sensible and true avouch
Of mine own eyes.

MARCELLUS: Is it not like the King?

HORATIO: As thou art to thyself.
Such was the very armor he had on
When he the ambitious Norway combated.   60
So frown'd he once when in an angry parle

36. *pole:* pole star. 37. *his:* its (the commonest form of the neuter possessive singular in Shakespeare's day). 41. *like:* in the likeness of. 42. *a scholar:* i.e. one who knows how best to address it. 43. *'a:* he. 45. *It . . . to:* A ghost had to be spoken to before it could speak. 46. *usurp'st:* The ghost, a supernatural being, has invaded the realm of nature. 48. *majesty . . . Denmark:* late King of Denmark. 49. *sometimes:* formerly. 57. *sensible:* relating to the senses. *avouch:* guarantee. 61. *Norway:* King of Norway. 62. *parle:* parley.

He smote the sledded [Polacks] on the ice.

sleds or sledges *Poles*

'Tis strange.

MARCELLUS: Thus twice before, and jump at this dead hour, *precisely* 65

With martial stalk hath he gone by our watch.

HORATIO: In what particular thought to work I know not,

But in the gross and scope of mine opinion, *wholeness; range*

This bodes some strange eruption to our state. *upheaval*

MARCELLUS: Good now, sit down, and tell me, he that knows, 70

Why this same strict and most observant watch

So nightly toils the subject of the land, *causes to work; subjects*

And [why] such daily [cast] of brazen cannon,

And foreign mart for implements of war, *foreign markets*

Why such impress of shipwrights, whose sore task *forced service*

Does not divide the Sunday from the week,

What might be toward, that this sweaty haste *in preparation*

Doth make the night joint-laborer with the day:

Who is't that can inform me?

HORATIO: That can I,

At least the whisper goes so: our last king, 80

Whose image even but now appear'd to us,

Was, as you know, by Fortinbras of Norway,

Thereto prick'd on by a most emulate pride, *rivalry*

Dar'd to the combat; in which our valiant Hamlet 84

(For so this side of our known world esteem'd him)

Did slay this Fortinbras, who, by a seal'd compact

Well ratified by law and heraldy, *governing combat; heraldry*

Did forfeit (with his life) all [those] his lands

Which he stood seiz'd of, to the conqueror; *possessed of*

Against the which a moi'ty competent *portion; equivalent* 90

Was gaged by our king, which had [return'd] *pledged* *would have*

To the inheritance of Fortinbras, *possession*

Had he been vanquisher; as by the same comart, *bargain*

And carriage of the article [design'd], *tenor; drawn up*

His fell to Hamlet. Now, sir, young Fortinbras, 95

Of unimproved mettle hot and full, *untried*

Hath in the skirts of Norway here and there *outlying territories*

Shark'd up a list of lawless resolutes *gathered up hastily*

For food and diet to some enterprise

That hath a stomach in't, which is no other, *relish of danger* / *demand for courage* 100

---

63. *sledded:* using sleds or sledges. *Polacks:* Poles. 65. *jump:* precisely. 67–68. *In . . . opinion:* while I have no precise theory about it, my general feeling is that. *Gross* = wholeness, totality; *scope* = range. 69. *eruption:* upheaval. 72. *toils:* causes to work. *subject:* subjects. 74. *foreign mart:* dealing with foreign markets. 75. *impress:* forced service. 77. *toward:* in preparation. 83. *emulate:* emulous, proceeding from rivalry. 87. *law and heraldy:* heraldic law (governing combat). *Heraldy* is a variant of *heraldry.* 89. *seiz'd of:* possessed of. 90. *moi'ty:* portion. *competent:* adequate, i.e. equivalent. 91. *gaged:* pledged. *had:* would have. 92. *inheritance:* possession. 93. *comart:* bargain. 94. *carriage:* tenor. *design'd:* drawn up. 96. *unimproved:* untried (?) or not directed to any useful end (?). 97. *skirts:* outlying territories. 98. *Shark'd up:* gathered up hastily and indiscriminately. 100. *stomach:* relish of danger (?) or demand for courage (?).

As it doth well appear unto our state,
But to recover of us, by strong hand
And terms compulsatory, those foresaid lands
So by his father lost; and this, I take it,
Is the main motive of our preparations,   105
The source of this our watch, and the chief head
Of this post-haste and romage in the land.

BARNARDO: I think it be no other but e'en so.
    Well may it sort that this portentous figure
    Comes armed through our watch so like the King   110
    That was and is the question of these wars.

HORATIO: A mote it is to trouble the mind's eye.
    In the most high and palmy state of Rome,
    A little ere the mightiest Julius fell,
    The graves stood [tenantless] and the sheeted dead   115
    Did squeak and gibber in the Roman streets.
    As stars with trains of fire, and dews of blood,
    Disasters in the sun; and the moist star
    Upon whose influence Neptune's empire stands
    Was sick almost to doomsday with eclipse.   120
    And even the like precurse of [fear'd] events,
    As harbingers preceding still the fates
    And prologue to the omen coming on,
    Have heaven and earth together demonstrated
    Unto our climatures and countrymen.   125

          Enter GHOST.

But soft, behold! lo where it comes again!   *It spreads his arms.*
I'll cross it though it blast me. Stay, illusion!
If thou hast any sound or use of voice,
Speak to me.
If there be any good thing to be done   130
That may to thee do ease, and grace to me,
Speak to me.
If thou art privy to thy country's fate,
Which happily foreknowing may avoid,
O speak!   135
Or if thou hast uphoarded in thy life
Extorted treasure in the womb of earth,

106. *head:* source. 107. *romage:* rummage, bustling activity. 109. *sort:* fit. *portentous:* ominous. 116. One or more lines may have been lost between this line and the next. 118. *Disasters:* ominous signs. *moist star:* moon. 119. *Neptune's empire stands:* the seas are dependent. 120. *sick . . . doomsday:* i.e. almost totally darkened. When the Day of Judgment is imminent, says Matthew 24:29, "the moon shall not give her light." *eclipse:* There were a solar and two total lunar eclipses visible in England in 1598; they caused gloomy speculation. 121. *precurse:* foreshadowing. 122. *harbingers:* advance messengers. *still:* always. 123. *omen:* i.e. the events portended. 125. *climatures:* regions. 126 s.d. *his:* its. 127. *cross it:* cross its path, confront it directly. *blast:* wither (by supernatural means). 134. *happily:* haply, perhaps.

For which, they say, your spirits oft walk in death,
Speak of it, stay and speak! (*The cock crows.*) Stop it,
    Marcellus.

MARCELLUS: Shall I strike it with my partisan? *spear*   140

HORATIO: Do, if it will not stand.

BARNARDO: 'Tis here!

HORATIO: 'Tis here!

MARCELLUS: 'Tis gone!   [*Exit* GHOST.]
    We do it wrong, being so majestical,
    To offer it the show of violence,
    For it is as the air, invulnerable,   145
    And our vain blows malicious mockery.

BARNARDO: It was about to speak when the cock crew.

HORATIO: And then it started like a guilty thing
    Upon a fearful summons. I have heard
    The cock, that is the trumpet to the morn,   150
    Doth with his lofty and shrill-sounding throat
    Awake the god of day, and at his warning,
    Whether in sea or fire, in earth or air,
    Th' extravagant and erring spirit hies
    To his confine; and of the truth herein   155
    This present object made probation.

MARCELLUS: It faded on the crowing of the cock.
    Some say that ever 'gainst that season comes
    Wherein our Saviour's birth is celebrated,
    This bird of dawning singeth all night long,   160
    And then they say no spirit dare stir abroad,
    The nights are wholesome, then no planets strike,
    No fairy takes, nor witch hath power to charm,
    So hallowed, and so gracious, is that time.

HORATIO: So have I heard and do in part believe it.   165
    But look, the morn in russet mantle clad
    Walks o'er the dew of yon high eastward hill.
    Break we our watch up, and by my advice
    Let us impart what we have seen to-night
    Unto young Hamlet, for, upon my life,   170
    This spirit, dumb to us, will speak to him.
    Do you consent we shall acquaint him with it,
    As needful in our loves, fitting our duty?

MARCELLUS: Let's do't, I pray, and I this morning know
    Where we shall find him most convenient.   *Exeunt.* 175

---

138. *your:* Colloquial and impersonal; cf. I.v.167, IV.iii.21, 23. Most editors adopt *you* from F1. **140.** *partisan:* long-handled spear. **146.** *malicious mockery:* mockery of malice, i.e. empty pretenses of harming it. **150.** *trumpet:* trumpeter. **154.** *extravagant:* wandering outside its proper bounds. *erring:* wandering abroad. *hies:* hastens. **156.** *object:* sight. *probation:* proof. **158.** *'gainst:* just before. **162.** *strike:* exert malevolent influence. **163.** *takes:* bewitches, charms. **164.** *gracious:* blessed. **166.** *russet:* coarse greyish-brown cloth.

SCENE TWO

> *Flourish. Enter* CLAUDIUS, KING OF DENMARK, GERTRUDE THE
> QUEEN; COUNCIL: *as* POLONIUS; *and his son* LAERTES, HAMLET,
> *cum aliis* [*including* VOLTEMAND *and* CORNELIUS].

KING: Though yet of Hamlet our dear brother's death
The memory be green, and that it us befitted
To bear our hearts in grief, and our whole kingdom
To be contracted in one brow of woe,
Yet so far hath discretion fought with nature   5
That we with wisest sorrow think on him
Together with remembrance of ourselves.
Therefore our sometime sister, now our queen,
Th' imperial jointress to this warlike state,
Have we, as 'twere with a defeated joy,   10
With an auspicious, and a dropping eye,
With mirth in funeral, and with dirge in marriage,
In equal scale weighing delight and dole,
Taken to wife; nor have we herein barr'd
Your better wisdoms, which have freely gone   15
With this affair along. For all, our thanks.
Now follows that you know young Fortinbras,
Holding a weak supposal of our worth,
Or thinking by our late dear brother's death
Our state to be disjoint and out of frame,   20
Co-leagued with this dream of his advantage,
He hath not fail'd to pester us with message
Importing the surrender of those lands
Lost by his father, with all bands of law,
To our most valiant brother. So much for him.   25
Now for ourself, and for this time of meeting,
Thus much the business is: we have here writ
To Norway, uncle of young Fortinbras—
Who, impotent and bedred, scarcely hears
Of this his nephew's purpose—to suppress   30
His further gait herein, in that the levies,
The lists, and full proportions are all made
Out of his subject; and we here dispatch
You, good Cornelius, and you, Voltemand,
For bearers of this greeting to old Norway,   35

I.ii. Location: The castle.
o.s.d. Flourish: trumpet fanfare. *cum aliis:* with others. **2.** *befitted:* would befit. **4.** *contracted in:* (1) reduced to; (2) knit or wrinkled in. *brow of woe:* mournful brow.
9. *jointress:* joint holder. **10.** *defeated:* impaired. **11.** *auspicious . . . dropping:* cheerful . . . weeping. **15.** *freely:* fully, without reservation. **17.** *know:* be informed, learn. **18.** *supposal:* conjecture, estimate. **21.** *Co-leagued:* joined. **22.** *pester . . . message:* trouble me with persistent messages (the original sense of *pester* is "overcrowd"). **23.** *Importing:* having as import. **24.** *bands:* bonds, binding terms. **29.** *impotent and bedred:* feeble and bedridden. **31.** *gait:* proceeding. **31–33.** *in . . . subject:* since the troops are all drawn from his subjects.

Giving to you no further personal power
To business with the King, more than the scope
Of these delated articles allow.   [*Giving a paper.*]
Farewell, and let your haste commend your duty.

CORNELIUS, VOLTEMAND: In that, and all things, will we show our duty.   40

KING: We doubt it nothing; heartily farewell.

                              [*Exeunt* VOLTEMAND *and* CORNELIUS.]
And now, Laertes, what's the news with you?
You told us of some suit, what is't, Laertes?
You cannot speak of reason to the Dane
And lose your voice. What wouldst thou beg, Laertes,
That shall not be my offer, not thy asking?   46
The head is not more native to the heart,
The hand more instrumental to the mouth,
Than is the throne of Denmark to thy father.
What wouldst thou have, Laertes?

LAERTES: My dread lord,
Your leave and favor to return to France,
From whence though willingly I came to Denmark
To show my duty in your coronation,
Yet now I must confess, that duty done,
My thoughts and wishes bend again toward France,   55
And bow them to your gracious leave and pardon.

KING: Have you your father's leave? What says Polonius?

POLONIUS: H'ath, my lord, wrung from me my slow leave
By laborsome petition, and at last
Upon his will I seal'd my hard consent.
I do beseech you give him leave to go.

KING: Take thy fair hour, Laertes, time be thine,
And thy best graces spend it at thy will!
But now, my cousin Hamlet, and my son—

HAMLET [*Aside.*]: A little more than kin, and less than kind.   65

KING: How is it that the clouds still hang on you?

HAMLET: Not so, my lord, I am too much in the sun.

QUEEN: Good Hamlet, cast thy nighted color off,
And let thine eye look like a friend on Denmark.
Do not for ever with thy vailed lids   70
Seek for thy noble father in the dust.
Thou know'st 'tis common, all that lives must die,
Passing through nature to eternity.

---

38. *delated:* extended, detailed (a variant of *dilated*).   **41.** *nothing:* not at all.   **45.** *lose:* waste.   **47.** *native:* closely related.   **48.** *instrumental:* serviceable.   **51.** *leave and favor:* gracious permission.   **56.** *pardon:* permission to depart.   **58.** *H'ath:* he hath.   **60.** *hard:* reluctant.   **64.** *cousin:* kinsman (used in familiar address to any collateral relative more distant than a brother or sister; here to a nephew).   **65.** *A little . . . kind:* closer than a nephew, since you are my mother's husband; yet more distant than a son, too (and not well disposed to you).   **67.** *sun:* With obvious quibble on *son.*   **70.** *vailed:* downcast. **72.** *common:* general, universal.

HAMLET: Ay, madam, it is common.

QUEEN: If it be,
Why seems it so particular with thee?   75

HAMLET: Seems, madam? nay, it is, I know not "seems."
'Tis not alone my inky cloak, [good] mother,
Nor customary suits of solemn black,
Nor windy suspiration of forc'd breath,   *sighing*
No, nor the fruitful river in the eye,   *crying*   80
Nor the dejected havior of the visage,
Together with all forms, moods, [shapes] of grief,
✳ That can [denote] me truly. These indeed seem,
For they are actions that a man might play,
But I have that within which passes show,   85
These but the trappings and the suits of woe. ✳

KING: 'Tis sweet and commendable in your nature, Hamlet,
To give these mourning duties to your father.
But you must know your father lost a father,
That father lost, lost his, and the survivor bound   90
In filial obligation for some term
To do obsequious sorrow. But to persever
In obstinate condolement is a course
Of impious stubbornness, 'tis unmanly grief,
It shows a will most incorrect to heaven,   95
A heart unfortified, or mind impatient,
An understanding simple and unschool'd:
For what we know must be, and is as common
As any the most vulgar thing to sense,
Why should we in our peevish opposition   100
Take it to heart? Fie, 'tis a fault to heaven,
A fault against the dead, a fault to nature,
To reason most absurd, whose common theme
Is death of fathers, and who still hath cried,
From the first corse till he that died to-day,   105
"This must be so." We pray you throw to earth
This unprevailing woe, and think of us
As of a father, for let the world take note
You are the most immediate to our throne,
And with no less nobility of love   110
Than that which dearest father bears his son
Do I impart toward you. For your intent
In going back to school in Wittenberg,
It is most retrograde to our desire,
And we beseech you bend you to remain   115

King Hamlet's death & Hamlet's reaction to it

Present King wants Hamlet to stay up/them.

---

75. *particular:* individual, personal.   80. *fruitful:* copious.   92. *obsequious:* proper to obsequies.   93. *condolement:* grief.   95. *incorrect:* unsubmissive.   99. *any . . . sense:* what is
perceived to be commonest.   101. *to:* against.   103. *absurd:* contrary.   107. *unprevailing:*
unavailing.   111. *dearest:* most loving.   112. *impart:* i.e. impart love.

Here in the cheer and comfort of our eye,
Our chiefest courtier, cousin, and our son.

QUEEN: Let not thy mother lose her prayers, Hamlet,
I pray thee stay with us, go not to Wittenberg.

HAMLET: I shall in all my best obey you, madam.

KING: Why, 'tis a loving and a fair reply.
Be as ourself in Denmark. Madam, come.
This gentle and unforc'd accord of Hamlet
Sits smiling to my heart, in grace whereof,
No jocund health that Denmark drinks to-day,   125
But the great cannon to the clouds shall tell,
And the King's rouse the heaven shall bruit again,
Respeaking earthly thunder. Come away.

Flourish. Exeunt all but HAMLET.

HAMLET: O that this too too sallied flesh would melt,   *Wants to die*
Thaw, and resolve itself into a dew!   130
Or that the Everlasting had not fix'd
His canon 'gainst [self-]slaughter! O God, God,
How [weary], stale, flat, and unprofitable
Seem to me all the uses of this world!
Fie on't, ah fie! 'tis an unweeded garden   135
That grows to seed, things rank and gross in nature
Possess it merely. That it should come [to this]!
But two months dead, nay, not so much, not two.
So excellent a king, that was to this
Hyperion to a satyr, so loving to my mother   140
That he might not beteem the winds of heaven
Visit her face too roughly. Heaven and earth,
Must I remember? Why, she should hang on him
As if increase of appetite had grown
By what it fed on, and yet, within a month—   145
Let me not think on't! Frailty, thy name is woman!—
A little month, or ere those shoes were old
With which she followed my poor father's body,
Like Niobe, all tears—why, she [even she]—
O God, a beast that wants discourse of reason   150
Would have mourn'd longer—married with my uncle,
My father's brother, but no more like my father
Than I to Hercules. Within a month,
Ere yet the salt of most unrighteous tears
Had left the flushing in her galled eyes,   155
She married—O most wicked speed: to post

Handwritten marginal notes:
mother asks to stay; Hamlet agrees
compares his mother's mourning to a beast
Compares his uncle's likeness to his father; as himself to Hercules

---

127. *rouse:* bumper, drink. *bruit:* loudly declare. **129.** *sallied:* sullied. Many editors prefer the F1 reading, *solid.* **132.** *canon:* law. **134.** *uses:* customs. **137.** *merely:* utterly. **139.** *to:* in comparison with. **140.** *Hyperion:* the sun-god. **141.** *beteem:* allow. **147.** *or ere:* before. **149.** *Niobe.* She wept endlessly for her children, whom Apollo and Artemis had killed. **150.** *wants . . . reason:* lacks the power of reason (which distinguishes men from beasts). **154.** *unrighteous:* i.e. hypocritical. **155.** *flushing:* redness. *galled:* inflamed.

With such dexterity to incestious sheets,
It is not, nor it cannot come to good,
But break my heart, for I must hold my tongue. ✳

Enter HORATIO, MARCELLUS, *and* BARNARDO.

HORATIO: Hail to your lordship!

HAMLET: I am glad to see you well.
　　　Horatio—or I do forget myself.   161

HORATIO: The same, my lord, and your poor servant ever.

HAMLET: Sir, my good friend—I'll change that name with you.
　　　And what make you from Wittenberg, Horatio?
　　　Marcellus.   165

MARCELLUS: My good lord.

HAMLET: I am very glad to see you. [*To* BARNARDO.]
　　　　　Good even, sir.—
　　　But what, in faith, make you from Wittenberg?

HORATIO: A truant disposition, good my lord.

HAMLET: I would not hear your enemy say so,   170
　　　Nor shall you do my ear that violence
　　　To make it truster of your own report
　　　Against yourself. I know you are no truant.
　　　But what is your affair in Elsinore?
　　　We'll teach you to drink [deep] ere you depart.   175

HORATIO: My lord, I came to see your father's funeral.

HAMLET: I prithee do not mock me, fellow student,
　　　I think it was to [see] my mother's wedding.

HORATIO: Indeed, my lord, it followed hard upon.

HAMLET: Thrift, thrift, Horatio, the funeral bak'd-meats
　　　Did coldly furnish forth the marriage tables.   180
　　　Would I had met my dearest foe in heaven
　　　Or ever I had seen that day, Horatio!
　　　My father—methinks I see my father.   184

HORATIO: Where, my lord?

HAMLET: In my mind's eye, Horatio.

HORATIO: I saw him once, 'a was a goodly king.

HAMLET: 'A was a man, take him for all in all,
　　　I shall not look upon his like again.

HORATIO: My lord, I think I saw him yesternight.

HAMLET: Saw, who?   190

HORATIO: My lord, the King your father.

HAMLET: The King my father?

---

157. *incestious:* incestuous. The marriage of a man to his brother's widow was so regarded until long after Shakespeare's day.　163. *change:* exchange.　164. *what . . . from:* what are you doing away from.　169. *truant disposition:* inclination to play truant.　177. *studient:* student.　181. *coldly:* when cold.　182. *dearest:* most intensely hated.　183. *Or:* ere, before.

HORATIO: Season your admiration for a while
    With an attent ear, till I may deliver,
    Upon the witness of these gentlemen,
    This marvel to you.

HAMLET: For God's love let me hear!   195

HORATIO: Two nights together had these gentlemen,
    Marcellus and Barnardo, on their watch,
    In the dead waste and middle of the night,
    Been thus encount'red: a figure like your father,
    Armed at point exactly, cap-a-pe,   200
    Appears before them, and with solemn march
    Goes slow and stately by them; thrice he walk'd
    By their oppress'd and fear-surprised eyes
    Within his truncheon's length, whilst they, distill'd
    Almost to jelly with the act of fear,   205
    Stand dumb and speak not to him. This to me
    In dreadful secrecy impart they did,
    And I with them the third night kept the watch,
    Where, as they had delivered, both in time,
    Form of the thing, each word made true and good,   210
    The apparition comes. I knew your father,
    These hands are not more like.

HAMLET: But where was this?

MARCELLUS: My lord, upon the platform where we watch.

HAMLET: Did you not speak to it?

HORATIO: My lord, I did,
    But answer made it none. Yet once methought   215
    It lifted up it head and did address
    Itself to motion like as it would speak;
    But even then the morning cock crew loud,
    And at the sound it shrunk in haste away
    And vanish'd from our sight.

HAMLET: 'Tis very strange.   220

HORATIO: As I do live, my honor'd lord, 'tis true,
    And we did think it writ down in our duty
    To let you know of it.

HAMLET: Indeed, [indeed,] sirs. But this troubles me.
    Hold you the watch to-night?

[MARCELLUS, BARNARDO:]   We do my lord.   225

HAMLET: Arm'd, say you?

[MARCELLUS, BARNARDO:] Arm'd, my lord.

---

192. *Season:* temper. *admiration:* wonder. 193. *deliver:* report. 198. *waste:* empty expanse. 200. *at point exactly:* in every particular. *cap-a-pe:* from head to foot.
203. *fear-surprised:* overwhelmed by fear. 204. *truncheon:* short staff carried as a symbol of military command. 205. *act:* action, operation. 207. *dreadful:* held in awe, i.e. solemnly sworn. 212. *are . . . like:* i.e. do not resemble each other more closely than the apparition resembled him. 216. *it:* its. 216–217. *address . . . motion:* begin to make a gesture.

HAMLET: From top to toe?

[MARCELLUS, BARNARDO:] My lord, from head to foot.

HAMLET: Then saw you not his face.

HORATIO: O yes, my lord, he wore his beaver up.   230

HAMLET: What, look'd he frowningly?

HORATIO: A countenance more
In sorrow than in anger.

HAMLET: Pale, or red?

HORATIO: Nay, very pale.

HAMLET: And fix'd his eyes upon you?

HORATIO: Most constantly.

HAMLET: I would I had been there.

HORATIO: It would have much amaz'd you.   235

HAMLET: Very like, [very like]. Stay'd it long?

HORATIO: While one with moderate haste might tell a hundreth.

BOTH [MARCELLUS, BARNARDO]: Longer, longer.

HORATIO: Not when I saw't.

HAMLET: His beard was grisl'd, no?

HORATIO: It was, as I have seen it in his life,   240
A sable silver'd.

HAMLET: I will watch to-night,
Perchance 'twill walk again.

HORATIO: I warr'nt it will.

HAMLET: If it assume my noble father's person,
I'll speak to it though hell itself should gape
And bid me hold my peace. I pray you all,   245
If you have hitherto conceal'd this sight,
Let it be tenable in your silence still,
And whatsomever else shall hap to-night,
Give it an understanding but no tongue.
I will requite your loves. So fare you well.   250
Upon the platform 'twixt aleven and twelf
I'll visit you.

ALL: Our duty to your honor.

HAMLET: Your loves, as mine to you; farewell.

                                        Exeunt [all but HAMLET].

My father's spirit—in arms! All is not well,   254
I doubt some foul play. Would the night were come!
Till then sit still, my soul. [Foul] deeds will rise,
Though all the earth o'erwhelm them, to men's eyes.

                                                        Exit.

---

230. *beaver:* visor.   237. *tell a hundreth:* count a hundred.   239. *grisl'd:* grizzled, mixed
with grey.   247. *tenable:* held close.   251. *aleven:* eleven.   255. *doubt:* suspect.

SCENE THREE

Enter LAERTES *and* OPHELIA, *his sister.*

LAERTES: My necessaries are inbark'd. Farewell.
    And, sister, as the winds give benefit
    And convey [is] assistant, do not sleep,
    But let me hear from you.

OPHELIA: Do you doubt that?

LAERTES: For Hamlet, and the trifling of his favor,   5
    Hold it a fashion and a toy in blood,
    A violet in the youth of primy nature,
    Forward, not permanent, sweet, not lasting,
    The perfume and suppliance of a minute—
    No more.

OPHELIA: No more but so?

LAERTES: Think it no more: 10
    For nature crescent does not grow alone
    In thews and [bulk], but as this temple waxes,
    The inward service of the mind and soul
    Grows wide withal. Perhaps he loves you now,
    And now no soil nor cautel doth besmirch   15
    The virtue of his will, but you must fear,
    His greatness weigh'd, his will is not his own,
    [For he himself is subject to his birth:]
    He may not, as unvalued persons do,
    Carve for himself, for on his choice depends   20
    The safety and health of this whole state,
    And therefore must his choice be circumscrib'd
    Unto the voice and yielding of that body
    Whereof he is the head. Then if he says he loves you,
    It fits your wisdom so far to believe it   25
    As he in his particular act and place
    May give his saying deed, which is no further
    Than the main voice of Denmark goes withal.
    Then weigh what loss your honor may sustain
    If with too credent ear you list his songs,   30
    Or lose your heart, or your chaste treasure open
    To his unmast'red importunity.

I.iii. Location: Polonius' quarters in the castle.
1. *inbark'd:* embarked, abroad. 3. *convey is assistant:* means of transport is available.
6. *a fashion:* i.e. standard behavior for a young man. *toy in blood:* idle fancy of youthful
passion. 7. *primy:* springlike. 8. *Forward:* early of growth. 9. *suppliance:* pastime.
11. *crescent:* growing, increasing. 12. *thews:* muscles, sinews. 12–14. *as . . . withal:* as
the body develops, the powers of mind and spirit grow along with it. 15. *soil:* stain.
cautel: deceit. 16. *will:* desire. 17. *His greatness weigh'd:* considering his princely status.
19. *unvalued:* of low rank. 20. *Carve for himself:* indulge his own wishes. 23. *voice:* vote,
approval. *yielding:* consent. *that body:* i.e. the state. 26. *in . . . place:* i.e. acting as he
must act in the position he occupies. 28. *main:* general. *goes withal:* accord with.
30. *credent:* credulous.

Fear it, Ophelia, fear it, my dear sister,
And keep you in the rear of your affection,
Out of the shot and danger of desire.   35
The chariest maid is prodigal enough
If she unmask her beauty to the moon.
Virtue itself scapes not calumnious strokes.
The canker galls the infants of the spring
Too oft before their buttons be disclos'd,   40
And in the morn and liquid dew of youth
Contagious blastments are most imminent.
Be wary then, best safety lies in fear:
Youth to itself rebels, though none else near.

OPHELIA: I shall the effect of this good lesson keep   45
As watchman to my heart. But, good my brother,
Do not, as some ungracious pastors do,
Show me the steep and thorny way to heaven,
Whiles, [like] a puff'd and reckless libertine,
Himself the primrose path of dalliance treads,   50
And reaks not his own rede.

LAERTES: O, fear me not.

Enter POLONIUS.

I stay too long—but here my father comes.
A double blessing is a double grace,
Occasion smiles upon a second leave.   54

POLONIUS: Yet here, Laertes? Aboard, aboard, for shame!
The wind sits in the shoulder of your sail,
And you are stay'd for. There—[*laying his hand on*
    LAERTES' *head*] my blessing with thee!
And these few precepts in thy memory
Look thou character. Give thy thoughts no tongue,
Nor any unproportion'd thought his act.   60
Be thou familiar, but by no means vulgar:
Those friends thou hast, and their adoption tried,
Grapple them unto thy soul with hoops of steel,
But do not dull thy palm with entertainment
Of each new-hatch'd, unfledg'd courage. Beware   65
Of entrance to a quarrel, but being in,
Bear't that th' opposed may beware of thee.
Give every man thy ear, but few thy voice,
Take each man's censure, but reserve thy judgment.

---

35. *shot:* range. **39.** *canker:* canker-worm. **40.** *buttons:* buds. *disclos'd:* opened.
42. *blastments:* withering blights. **44.** *to:* of. **47.** *ungracious:* graceless. **49.** *puff'd:*
bloated. **51.** *reaks:* recks, heeds. *rede:* advice. *fear me not:* don't worry about me.
54. *Occasion:* opportunity (here personified, as often). *smiles upon:* i.e. graciously bestows.
59. *character:* inscribe. **60.** *unproportion'd:* unfitting. **61.** *familiar:* affable, sociable.
vulgar: friendly with everybody. **62.** *their adoption tried:* their association with you tested
and proved. **65.** *courage:* spirited, young blood. **67.** *Bear't that:* manage it in such a way
that. **69.** *Take:* listen to. *censure:* opinion.

Costly thy habit as thy purse can buy,   70
But not express'd in fancy, rich, not gaudy,
For the apparel oft proclaims the man,
And they in France of the best rank and station
[Are] of a most select and generous chief in that.
Neither a borrower nor a lender [be],   75
For [loan] oft loses both itself and friend,
And borrowing dulleth [th'] edge of husbandry.
This above all: to thine own self be true,
And it must follow, as the night the day,
Thou canst not then be false to any man.   80
Farewell, my blessing season this in thee!

Polonius' famous speech

LAERTES: Most humbly do I take my leave, my lord.

POLONIUS: The time invests you, go, your servants tend.

LAERTES: Farewell, Ophelia, and remember well
　　What I have said to you.

OPHELIA:　　　　　　　　　'Tis in my memory lock'd,
　　And you yourself shall keep the key of it.   86

LAERTES: Farewell.   *Exit* LAERTES.

POLONIUS: What is't, Ophelia, he hath said to you?

OPHELIA: So please you, something touching the Lord Hamlet.

POLONIUS: Marry, well bethought.   90
　　'Tis told me, he hath very oft of late
　　Given private time to you, and you yourself
　　Have of your audience been most free and bounteous.
　　If it be so—as so 'tis put on me,
　　And that in way of caution—I must tell you,   95
　　You do not understand yourself so clearly
　　As it behooves my daughter and your honor.
　　What is between you? Give me up the truth.

OPHELIA: He hath, my lord, of late made many tenders
　　Of his affection to me.   100

POLONIUS: Affection, puh! You speak like a green girl,
　　Unsifted in such perilous circumstance.
　　Do you believe his tenders, as you call them?

OPHELIA: I do not know, my lord, what I should think.

POLONIUS: Marry, I will teach you: think yourself a baby   105
　　That you have ta'en these tenders for true pay,
　　Which are not sterling. Tender yourself more dearly,
　　Or (not to crack the wind of the poor phrase,
　　[Wringing] it thus) you'll tender me a fool.

Polonius tells Ophelia to watch her step w/ Hamlet or she will make a fool of her father

74. *generous:* noble. *chief:* eminence (?). But the line is probably corrupt. Perhaps *of a* is intrusive, in which case *chief* = chiefly. 77. *husbandry:* thrift. 81. *season:* preserve (?) or ripen, make fruitful (?). 83. *invests:* besieges. *tend:* wait. 90. *Marry:* indeed (originally the name of the Virgin Mary used as an oath). 94. *put on:* told to. 99. *tenders:* offers. 102. *Unsifted:* untried. 106. *tenders:* With play on the sense "money offered in payment" (as in *legal tender*). 107. *Tender:* hold, value. 109. *Wringing:* straining, forcing to the limit. *tender . . . fool:* (1) show me that you are a fool; (2) make me look like a fool; (3) present me with a (bastard) grandchild.

OPHELIA: My lord, he hath importun'd me with love
    In honorable fashion.   111

POLONIUS: Ay, fashion you may call it. Go to, go to.

OPHELIA: And hath given countenance to his speech, my lord,
    With almost all the holy vows of heaven.

POLONIUS: Ay, springes to catch woodcocks. I do know,
    When the blood burns, how prodigal the soul   116
    Lends the tongue vows. These blazes, daughter,
    Giving more light than heat, extinct in both
    Even in their promise, as it is a-making,
    You must not take for fire. From this time   120
    Be something scanter of your maiden presence,
    Set your entreatments at a higher rate
    Than a command to parle. For Lord Hamlet,
    Believe so much in him, that he is young,
    And with a larger teder may he walk   125
    Than may be given you. In few, Ophelia,
    Do not believe his vows, for they are brokers,
    Not of that dye which their investments show,
    But mere [implorators] of unholy suits,
    Breathing like sanctified and pious bonds,   130
    The better to [beguile]. This is for all:
    I would not, in plain terms, from this time forth
    Have you so slander any moment leisure
    As to give words or talk with the Lord Hamlet.
    Look to't, I charge you. Come your ways.   135

OPHELIA: I shall obey, my lord.   *Exeunt.*

Ophelia is not to see or talk to Hamlet

SCENE FOUR

Enter HAMLET, HORATIO, *and* MARCELLUS.

HAMLET: The air bites shrowdly, it is very cold.

HORATIO: It is [a] nipping and an eager air.

HAMLET: What hour now?

HORATIO: I think it lacks of twelf.

MARCELLUS: No, it is strook.

12:00 A.M.

112. *fashion.* See note on line 6.   113. *countenance:* authority.   115. *springes:* snares.
woodcocks. Proverbially gullible birds.   122–23. *Set . . . parle:* place a higher value on your
favors; do not grant interviews simply because he asks for them. Polonius uses a military
figure: *entreatments* = negotiations for surrender; *parle* = parley, discuss terms.   124. *so
. . . him:* no more than this with respect to him.   125. *larger teder:* longer tether.
127. *brokers:* procurers.   128. *Not . . . show:* not of the color of their garments (*investments*) exhibit, i.e. not what they seem.   129. *mere:* out-and-out.   130. *bonds:* (lover's)
vows or assurances. Many editors follow Theobald in reading *bawds*.   133. *slander:*
disgrace. *moment:* momentary.   135. *Come your ways:* come along.
I.iv. Location: The guard-platform of the castle.
1. *shrowdly:* shrewdly, wickedly.   2. *eager:* sharp.

HORATIO: Indeed? I heard it not. It then draws near the season   5
Wherein the spirit held his wont to walk.

A flourish of trumpets, and two pieces goes off [*within*].

What does this mean, my lord?
HAMLET: The King doth wake to-night and takes his rouse,
Keeps wassail, and the swagg'ring up-spring reels;
And as he drains his draughts of Rhenish down,   10
The kettle-drum and trumpet thus bray out
The triumph of his pledge.

HORATIO: Is it a custom?

HAMLET: Ay, marry, is't,
But to my mind, though I am native here
And to the manner born, it is a custom   15
More honor'd in the breach than the observance.
This heavy-headed revel east and west
Makes us traduc'd and tax'd of other nations.
They clip us drunkards, and with swinish phrase
Soil our addition, and indeed it takes   20
From our achievements, though perform'd at height,
The pith and marrow of our attribute.
So, oft it chances in particular men,
That for some vicious mole of nature in them,
As in their birth, wherein they are not guilty   25
(Since nature cannot choose his origin),
By their o'ergrowth of some complexion
Oft breaking down the pales and forts of reason,
Or by some habit, that too much o'er-leavens
The form of plausive manners—that these men,   30
Carrying, I say, the stamp of one defect,
Being nature's livery, or fortune's star,
His virtues else, be they as pure as grace,
As infinite as man may undergo,
Shall in the general censure take corruption   35
From that particular fault: the dram of [ev'l]

[Handwritten note in right margin: The present King is partying (drinking and dancing)]

6 s.d. *pieces:* canon. 8. *doth . . . rouse:* i.e. holds revels far into the night. 9. *wassail:* carousal. *up-spring:* wild dance. 10. *Rhenish:* Rhine wine. 12. *triumph . . . pledge:* accomplishment of his toast (by draining his cup at a single draught). 15. *manner:* custom (of carousing). 16. *more . . . observance:* which it is more honorable to break than to observe. 18. *tax'd of:* censured by. 19. *clip:* clepe, call. 20. *addition:* titles of honor. 21. *at height:* most excellently. 22. *attribute:* reputation. 23. *particular:* individual. 24. *vicious . . . nature:* small natural blemish. 26. *his:* its. 27. *By . . . complexion:* by the excess of some one of the humors (which were thought to govern the disposition). 28. *pales:* fences. 29. *o'er-leavens:* makes itself felt throughout (as leaven works in the whole mass of dough). 30. *plausive:* pleasing. 32. *Being . . . star:* i.e. whether they were born with it, or got it by misfortune. *Star* means "blemish." 34. *undergo:* carry the weight of, sustain. 35. *general censure:* popular opinion. 36. *dram:* minute amount. *ev'l:* evil,

Doth all the noble substance of a doubt
To his own scandal.

    Enter GHOST.

HORATIO: Look, my lord, it comes!

HAMLET: Angels and ministers of grace defend us!
    Be thou a spirit of health, or goblin damn'd,   40
    Bring with thee airs from heaven, or blasts from hell,
    By thy intents wicked, or charitable,
    Thou com'st in such a questionable shape
    That I will speak to thee. I'll call thee Hamlet,
    King, father, royal Dane. O, answer me!   45
    Let me not burst in ignorance, but tell
    Why thy canoniz'd bones, hearsed in death,
    Have burst their cerements; why the sepulchre,
    Wherein we saw thee quietly interr'd,
    Hath op'd his ponderous and marble jaws   50
    To cast thee up again. What may this mean,
    That thou, dead corse, again in complete steel
    Revisits thus the glimpses of the moon,
    Making night hideous, and we fools of nature
    So horridly to shake our disposition   55
    With thoughts beyond the reaches of our souls?
    Say why is this? wherefore? what should we do?
                     [GHOST] *beckons* [HAMLET].

HORATIO: It beckons you to go away with it,
    As if it some impartment did desire
    To you alone.

MARCELLUS: Look with what courteous action   60
    It waves you to a more removed ground,
    But do not go with it.

HORATIO: No, by no means.

HAMLET: It will not speak, then I will follow it.

HORATIO: Do not, my lord.

HAMLET: Why, what should be the fear?
    I do not set my life at a pin's fee,   65
    And for my soul, what can it do to that,
    Being a thing immortal as itself?
    It waves me forth again, I'll follow it.

HORATIO: What if it tempt you toward the flood, my lord,
    Or to the dreadful summit of the cliff   70

with a pun on *eale,* "yeast" (cf. *o'er-leavens* in line 29). **37.** *of a doubt.* A famous crux, for which many emendations have been suggested, the most widely accepted being Steevens' *often dout* (i.e. extinguish). **38.** *To . . . scandal:* i.e. so that it all shares in the disgrace. **40.** *of health:* wholesome, good. **43.** *questionable:* inviting talk. **47.** *canoniz'd:* buried with the prescribed rites. **48.** *cerements:* grave-clothes. **52.** *complete steel:* full armor. **53.** *Revisits.* The *-s* ending in the second person singular is common. **54.** *fools of nature:* the children (or the dupes) of a purely natural order, baffled by the supernatural. **55.** *disposition:* nature. **59.** *impartment:* communication. **65.** *fee:* worth.

That beetles o'er his base into the sea,
And there assume some other horrible form
Which might deprive your sovereignty of reason,
And draw you into madness? Think of it.
The very place puts toys of desperation,   75
Without more motive, into every brain
That looks so many fadoms to the sea
And hears it roar beneath.

HAMLET: It waves me still.—
Go on, I'll follow thee.

MARCELLUS: You shall not go, my lord.

HAMLET: Hold off your hands.   80

HORATIO: Be rul'd, you shall not go.

HAMLET: ✱ My fate cries out, ✱
And makes each petty artere in this body
As hardy as the Nemean lion's nerve.
Still am I call'd. Unhand me, gentlemen.
By heaven, I'll make a ghost of him that lets me!   85
I say away!—Go on, I'll follow thee.

                              Exeunt GHOST *and* HAMLET.

Hamlet threatens to kill Horatio & Marcellus if they don't let go of him

HORATIO: He waxes desperate with [imagination].   87

MARCELLUS: Let's follow. 'Tis not fit thus to obey him.

HORATIO: Have after. To what issue will this come?   89

✗ MARCELLUS: Something is rotten in the state of Denmark.   ✗

HORATIO: Heaven will direct it.

MARCELLUS: Nay, let's follow him.   *Exeunt.* 91

SCENE FIVE

        Enter GHOST *and* HAMLET.

HAMLET: Whither wilt thou lead me? Speak, I'll go no further.

GHOST: Mark me.

HAMLET: I will.

GHOST: My hour is almost come
When I to sulph'rous and tormenting flames   *Going to hell?*
Must render up myself.

HAMLET: Alas, poor ghost!

GHOST: Pity me not, but lend thy serious hearing   5
To what I shall unfold.

HAMLET: Speak, I am bound to hear.

73. *deprive . . . reason:* unseat reason from the rule of your mind. 75. *toys of desperation:*
fancies of desperate action, i.e. inclinations to jump off. 77. *fadoms:* fathoms. 82. *artere:*
variant spelling of *artery;* here, ligament, sinew. 83. *Nemean lion.* Slain by Hercules as
one of his twelve labors. *nerve.* sinew. 85. *lets:* hinders. 91. *it:* i.e. the issue.
I.v. Location: On the battlements of the castle.

GHOST: So art thou to revenge, when thou shalt hear.

HAMLET: What?

GHOST: I am thy father's spirit,
      Doom'd for a certain term to walk the night,   10
      And for the day confin'd to fast in fires,
      Till the foul crimes done in my days of nature
      Are burnt and purg'd away. But that I am forbid
      To tell the secrets of my prison-house,
      I could a tale unfold whose lightest word   15
      Would harrow up thy soul, freeze thy young blood,
      Make thy two eyes like stars start from their spheres,
      Thy knotted and combined locks to part,
      And each particular hair to stand an end,
      Like quills upon the fearful porpentine.   20
      But this eternal blazon must not be
      To ears of flesh and blood. List, list, O, list!
      If thou didst ever thy dear father love—

HAMLET: O God!

GHOST: Revenge his foul and most unnatural murther.   25

HAMLET: Murther!

GHOST: Murther most foul, as in the best it is,
      But this most foul, strange, and unnatural.

HAMLET: Haste me to know't, that I with wings as swift
      As meditation, or the thoughts of love,   30
      May sweep to my revenge.

GHOST: I find thee apt,
      And duller shouldst thou be than the fat weed
      That roots itself in ease on Lethe wharf,
      Wouldst thou not stir in this. Now, Hamlet, hear:
      'Tis given out that, sleeping in my orchard,   35
      A serpent stung me, so the whole ear of Denmark
      Is by a forged process of my death
      Rankly abus'd; but know, thou noble youth,
      The serpent that did sting thy father's life
      Now wears his crown.

HAMLET: O my prophetic soul!   40
      My uncle?

GHOST: Ay, that incestuous, that adulterate beast,
      With witchcraft of his wits, with traitorous gifts—
      O wicked wit and gifts that have the power
      So to seduce!—won to his shameful lust   45
      The will of my most seeming virtuous queen.

11. *fast:* do penance. 12. *crimes:* sins. 17. *spheres:* eye-sockets; with allusion to the revolving spheres in which, according to the Ptolemaic astronomy, the stars were fixed. 19. *an end:* on end. 20. *fearful porpentine:* frightened porcupine. 21. *eternal blazon:* revelation of eternal things. 30. *meditation:* thought. 33. *Lethe:* river of Hades, the water of which made the drinker forget the past. *wharf:* bank. 35. *orchard:* garden. 37. *forged process:* false account. 38. *abus'd:* deceived. 42. *adulterate:* adulterous.

O Hamlet, what [a] falling-off was there
From me, whose love was of that dignity
That it went hand in hand even with the vow
I made to her in marriage, and to decline   50
Upon a wretch whose natural gifts were poor
To those of mine!
But virtue, as it never will be moved,
Though lewdness court it in a shape of heaven,
So [lust], though to a radiant angel link'd,   55
Will [sate] itself in a celestial bed
And prey on garbage.
But soft, methinks I scent the morning air,
Brief let me be. Sleeping within my orchard,
My custom always of the afternoon,   60
Upon my secure hour thy uncle stole,
With juice of cursed hebona in a vial,
And in the porches of my ears did pour
The leprous distillment, whose effect
Holds such an enmity with blood of man   65
That swift as quicksilver it courses through
The natural gates and alleys of the body,
And with a sudden vigor it doth [posset]
And curd, like eager droppings into milk,
The thin and wholesome blood. So did it mine,   70
And a most instant tetter bark'd about,
Most lazar-like, with vile and loathsome crust
All my smooth body.
Thus was I, sleeping, by a brother's hand
Of life, of crown, of queen, at once dispatch'd,   75
Cut off even in the blossoms of my sin,
Unhous'led, disappointed, unanel'd,
No reck'ning made, but sent to my account
With all my imperfections on my head.
O, horrible, O, horrible, most horrible!   80
If thou hast nature in thee, bear it not,
Let not the royal bed of Denmark be
A couch for luxury and damned incest.
But howsomever thou pursues this act,
Taint not thy mind, nor let thy soul contrive   85
Against thy mother aught. Leave her to heaven,
And to those thorns that in her bosom lodge
To prick and sting her. Fare thee well at once!

54. *shape of heaven:* angelic form.   61. *secure:* carefree.   62. *hebona:* ebony (which Shakespeare, following a literary tradition, and perhaps also associating the word with *henbane,*
thought the name of a poison).   68. *posset:* curdle.   69. *eager:* sour.   71. *tetter:* scabby
eruption.   *bark'd:* formed a hard covering, like bark on a tree.   72. *lazar-like:* leper-
like.   75. *at once:* all at the same time.   *dispatch'd:* deprived.   77. *Unhous'led:* without the
Eucharist.   *disappointed:* without (spiritual) preparation.   *unanel'd:* unanointed, without
extreme unction.   81. *nature:* natural feeling.   83. *luxury:* lust.

The glow-worm shows the matin to be near,
And gins to pale his uneffectual fire.   90
Adieu, adieu, adieu! remember me.   [*Exit.*]

HAMLET: O all you host of heaven! O earth! What else?
And shall I couple hell? O fie, hold, hold, my heart,
And you, my sinows, grow not instant old,
But bear me [stiffly] up. Remember thee!   95
Ay, thou poor ghost, whiles memory holds a seat
In this distracted globe. Remember thee!
Yea, from the table of my memory
I'll wipe away all trivial fond records,
All saws of books, all forms, all pressures past   100
That youth and observation copied there,
And thy commandement all alone shall live
Within the book and volume of my brain,
Unmix'd with baser matter. Yes, by heaven!
O most pernicious woman!   105
O villain, villain, smiling, damned villian!
My tables—meet it is I set it down
That one may smile, and smile, and be a villain!
At least I am sure it may be so in Denmark.   [*He writes.*]
So, uncle, there you are. Now to my word: 110
It is "Adieu, adieu! remember me."
I have sworn't.

HORATIO [*Within.*]: My lord, my lord!

MARCELLUS [*Within.*]:   Lord Hamlet!

> *Enter* HORATIO *and* MARCELLUS.

HORATIO: Heavens secure him!

HAMLET: So be it!

MARCELLUS: Illo, ho, ho, my lord!   115

HAMLET: Hillo, ho, ho, boy! Come, [bird,] come.

MARCELLUS: How is't, my noble lord?

HORATIO: What news, my lord?

HAMLET: O, wonderful!

HORATIO: Good my lord, tell it.

HAMLET: No, you will reveal it.

HORATIO: Not I, my lord, by heaven.

MARCELLUS: Nor I, my lord.

HAMLET: How say you then, would heart of man once think it?—   121
But you'll be secret?

BOTH [HORATIO, MARCELLUS]: Ah, by heaven, [my lord].

---

89. *matin:* morning. **90.** *gins:* begins. **94.** *sinows:* sinews. **97.** *globe:* head. **98.** *table:*
writing tablet. **99.** *fond:* foolish. **100.** *saws:* wise sayings. *forms:* shapes, images.
pressures: impressions. **110.** *word:* i.e. word of command from the Ghost. **116.** *Hillo*
. . . *come.* Hamlet answers Marcellus' halloo with a falconer's cry.

[Handwritten margin note at lines 100–105:] Hamlet will forget all things ever he knew to think only of avenging his Father's death.

[Handwritten margin note at lines 116–121:] Horatio & Marcellus want to know what the ghost said to Hamlet

HAMLET: There's never a villain dwelling in all Denmark
    But he's an arrant knave.

HORATIO: There needs no ghost, my lord, come from the grave
    To tell us this.   125

HAMLET: Why, right, you are in the right,
    And so, without more circumstance at all,
    I hold it fit that we shake hands and part,
    You, as your business and desire shall point you,
    For every man hath business and desire,   130
    Such as it is, and for my own poor part,
    I will go pray.

HORATIO: These are but wild and whirling words, my lord.

HAMLET: I am sorry they offend you, heartily,
    Yes, faith, heartily.

HORATIO: There's no offense, my lord,   135

HAMLET: Yes, by Saint Patrick, but there is, Horatio,
    And much offense too. Touching this vision here,
    It is an honest ghost, that let me tell you.
    For your desire to know what is between us,
    O'ermaster't as you may. And now, good friends,
    As you are friends, scholars, and soldiers,   141
    Give me one poor request.

HORATIO: What is't, my lord, we will.

HAMLET: Never make known what you have seen to-night.

BOTH [HORATIO, MARCELLUS]: My lord, we will not.

HAMLET: Nay, but swear't.

HORATIO: In faith,
    My lord, not I.

MARCELLUS: Nor I, my lord, in faith.   146

HAMLET: Upon my sword.

MARCELLUS: We have sworn, my lord, already.

HAMLET: Indeed, upon my sword, indeed.

                     GHOST *cries under the stage.*

GHOST: Swear.

HAMLET: Ha, ha, boy, say'st thou so? Art thou there, truepenny?   150
    Come on, you hear this fellow in the cellarage,
    Consent to swear.

HORATIO: Propose the oath, my lord.

HAMLET: Never to speak of this that you have seen,
    Swear by my sword.

GHOST [*Beneath.*]: Swear.   155

HAMLET: *Hic et ubique?* Then we'll shift our ground.
    Come hither, gentlemen,

---

127. *circumstance:* ceremony. **138.** *honest:* true, genuine. **143.** *What is't:* whatever it is.
147. *Upon my sword:* i.e. on the cross formed by the hilt. **150.** *truepenny:* trusty fellow.

[handwritten marginal note: Hamlet will not tell them.]

And lay your hands again upon my sword.
Swear by my sword
Never to speak of this that you have heard.   160

GHOST [*Beneath.*]: Swear by his sword.

HAMLET: Well said, old mole, canst work i' th' earth so fast?
A worthy pioner! Once more remove, good friends.

HORATIO: O day and night, but this is wondrous strange!   164

HAMLET: And therefore as a stranger give it welcome.
There are more things in heaven and earth, Horatio,
Than are dreamt of in your philosophy.
But come—
Here, as before, never, so help you mercy,
How strange or odd some'er I bear myself—   170
As I perchance hereafter shall think meet
To put an antic disposition on—
That you, at such times seeing me, never shall,
With arms encumb'red thus, or this headshake,
Or by pronouncing of some doubtful phrase,   175
As "Well, well, we know," or "We could, and if we would,"
Or "If we list to speak," or "There be, and if they might,"
Or such ambiguous giving out, to note
That you know aught of me—this do swear,
So grace and mercy at your most need help you.   180

GHOST [*Beneath.*]: Swear.   [*They swear.*]

HAMLET: Rest, rest, perturbed spirit! So, gentlemen,
With all my love I do commend me to you,
And what so poor a man as Hamlet is
May do t' express his love and friending to you,   185
God willing, shall not lack. Let us go in together,
And still your fingers on your lips, I pray.
The time is out of joint—O cursed spite,
That ever I was born to set it right!
Nay, come, let's go together.   *Exeunt.*   190

ACT TWO, SCENE ONE

Enter old POLONIUS *with his man* [REYNALDO].

POLONIUS: Give him this money and these notes, Reynaldo.

REYNALDO: I will, my lord.

POLONIUS: You shall do marvell's wisely, good Reynaldo,

---

156. *Hic et ubique:* here and everywhere.   163. *pioner:* digger, miner (variant of *pioneer*).
165. *as . . . welcome:* give it the welcome due in courtesy to strangers.   167. *your.* See note
on I.i.138.   *philosophy:* i.e. natural philosophy, science.   172. *put . . . on:* behave in some
fantastic manner, act like a madman.   174. *encumb'red:* folded.   176. *and if:* if.   177. *list:*
cared, had a mind.   178. *note:* indicate.   187. *still:* always.   190. *Nay . . . together.* They
are holding back to let him go first.
II.i. Location: Polonius' quarters in the castle.

Before you visit him, to make inquire
Of his behavior.

REYNALDO: My lord, I did intend it.   5

POLONIUS: Marry, well said, very well said. Look you, sir,
Inquire me first what Danskers are in Paris,
And how, and who, what means, and where they keep,
What company, at what expense; and finding
By this encompassment and drift of question   10
That they do know my son, come you more nearer
Than your particular demands will touch it.
Take you as 'twere some distant knowledge of him,
As thus, "I know his father and his friends,
And in part him." Do you mark this, Reynaldo?   15

REYNALDO: Ay, very well, my lord.

POLONIUS: "And in part him—but," you may say, "not well.
But if't be he I mean, he's very wild,
Addicted so and so," and there put on him
What forgeries you please: marry, none so rank   20
As may dishonor him, take heed of that,
But, sir, such wanton, wild, and usual slips
As are companions noted and most known
To youth and liberty.

REYNALDO: As gaming, my lord.

POLONIUS: Ay, or drinking, fencing, swearing, quarrelling,   25
Drabbing—you may go so far.

REYNALDO: My lord, that would dishonor him.

POLONIUS: Faith, as you may season it in the charge:
You must not put another scandal on him,
That he is open to incontinency—   30
That's not my meaning. But breathe his faults so quaintly
That they may seem the taints of liberty,
The flash and outbreak of a fiery mind,
A savageness in unreclaimed blood,
Of general assault.

REYNALDO: But, my good lord—   35

POLONIUS: Wherefore should you do this?

REYNALDO: Ay, my lord,
I would know that.

POLONIUS: Marry, sir, here's my drift,
And I believe it is a fetch of wit:

---

3. *marvell's:* marvellous(ly).   7. *Danskers:* Danes.   8. *keep:* lodge.   10. *encompassment:*
circuitousness.   *drift of question:* directing of the conversation.   12. *particular demands:*
direct questions.   20. *forgeries:* invented charges.   22. *wanton:* sportive.   26. *Drabbing:*
whoring.   28. *Faith.* Most editors read *Faith, no,* following F1; this makes easier sense.
season: qualify, temper.   30. *open to incontinency:* habitually profligate.   31. *quaintly:*
artfully.   34. *unreclaimed:* untamed.   35. *Of general assault:* i.e. to which young men are
generally subject.   38. *fetch of wit:* ingenious device.

You laying these slight sallies on my son,
As 'twere a thing a little soil'd [wi' th'] working,   40
Mark you,
Your party in converse, him you would sound,
Having ever seen in the prenominate crimes
The youth you breathe of guilty, be assur'd
He closes with you in this consequence: 45
"Good sir," or so, or "friend," or "gentleman,"
According to the phrase or the addition
Of man and country.

REYNALDO: Very good, my lord.

POLONIUS: And then, sir, does 'a this—'a does—what was
            I about to say?
        By the mass, I was about to say something.   50
        Where did I leave?

REYNALDO: At "closes in the consequence."

POLONIUS: At "closes in consequence," ay, marry.
        He closes thus: "I know the gentleman.
        I saw him yesterday, or th' other day,
        Or then, or then, with such or such, and as you say,   55
        There was 'a gaming, there o'ertook in 's rouse,
        There falling out at tennis"; or, perchance,
        "I saw him enter such a house of sale,"
        Videlicet, a brothel, or so forth. See you now,
        Your bait of falsehood take this carp of truth,   60
        And thus do we of wisdom and of reach,
        With windlasses and with assays of bias,
        By indirections find directions out;
        So by my former lecture and advice
        Shall you my son. You have me, have you not?   65

REYNALDO: My lord, I have.

POLONIUS: God buy ye, fare ye well.

REYNALDO: Good my lord.

POLONIUS: Observe his inclination in yourself.

REYNALDO: I shall, my lord.

POLONIUS: And let him ply his music.

REYNALDO: Well, my lord.   70

POLONIUS: Farewell.   *Exit* REYNALDO.

---

39. *sallies:* sullies, blemishes. 40. *soil'd . . . working:* i.e. shopworn. 43. *Having:* if he
has. *prenominate crimes:* aforementioned faults. 45. *closes:* falls in. *in this consequence:*
as follows. 47. *addition:* style of address. 56. *o'ertook in 's rouse:* overcome by drink.
61. *reach:* capacity, understanding. 62. *windlasses:* roundabout methods. *assays of bias:*
indirect attempts (a figure from the game of bowls, in which the player must make
allowance for the curving course his bowl will take toward its mark). 63. *directions:* the
way things are going. 65. *have me:* understand me. 66. *God buy ye:* good-buy (a
contraction of *God be with you*). 68. *in:* by. Polonius asks him to observe Laertes directly,
as well as making inquiries. 70. *let him ply:* see that he goes on with.

Enter OPHELIA.

              How now, Ophelia, what's the matter?

OPHELIA: O my lord, my lord, I have been so affrighted!

POLONIUS: With what, i' th' name of God?

OPHELIA: My lord, as I was sewing in my closet,
    Lord Hamlet, with his doublet all unbrac'd,   75
    No hat upon his head, his stockins fouled,
    Ungart'red, and down-gyved to his ankle,
    Pale as his shirt, his knees knocking each other,
    And with a look so piteous in purport
    As if he had been loosed out of hell   80
    To speak of horrors—he comes before me.

POLONIUS: Mad for thy love?

OPHELIA: My lord, I do not know,
    But truly I do fear it.

POLONIUS: What said he?

OPHELIA: He took me by the wrist, and held me hard,
    Then goes he to the length of all his arm,   85
    And with his other hand thus o'er his brow,
    He falls to such perusal of my face
    As 'a would draw it. Long stay'd he so.
    At last, a little shaking of mine arm,
    And thrice his head thus waving up and down,   90
    He rais'd a sigh so piteous and profound
    As it did seem to shatter all his bulk
    And end his being. That done, he lets me go,
    And with his head over his shoulder turn'd,
    He seem'd to find his way without his eyes,   95
    For out a' doors he went without their helps,
    And to the last bended their light on me.

POLONIUS: Come, go with me. I will go seek the King.
    This is the very ecstasy of love,
    Whose violent property fordoes itself,   100
    And leads the will to desperate undertakings
    As oft as any passions under heaven
    That does afflict our natures. I am sorry—
    What, have you given him any hard words of late?

OPHELIA: No, my good lord, but as you did command
    I did repel his letters, and denied   106
    His access to me.

POLONIUS: That hath made him mad.
    I am sorry that with better heed and judgment
    I had not coted him. I fear'd he did but trifle

---

74. *closet:* private room. **75.** *unbrac'd:* unlaced. **76.** *stockins fouled:* stockings dirty.
77. *down-gyved:* hanging down like fetters on a prisoner's legs. **92.** *bulk:* body. **99.** *ecstasy:* madness. **100.** *property:* quality. *fordoes:* destroys. **109.** *coted:* observed.

And meant to wrack thee, but beshrow my jealousy!
By heaven, it is as proper to our age   111
To cast beyond ourselves in our opinions,
As it is common for the younger sort
To lack discretion. Come, go we to the King.
This must be known, which, being kept close, might move   115
More grief to hide, than hate to utter love.
Come.   *Exeunt.*

SCENE TWO

>   *Flourish. Enter* KING *and* QUEEN, ROSENCRANTZ *and* GUILDEN-
>   STERN [*cum aliis*].

KING: Welcome, dear Rosencrantz and Guildenstern!
 Moreover that we much did long to see you,
 The need we have to use you did provoke
 Our hasty sending. Something have you heard
 Of Hamlet's transformation; so call it,   5
 Sith nor th' exterior nor the inward man
 Resembles that it was. What it should be,
 More than his father's death, that thus hath put him
 So much from th' understanding of himself,
 I cannot dream of. I entreat you both   10
 That, being of so young days brought up with him,
 And sith so neighbored to his youth and havior,
 That you voutsafe your rest here in our court
 Some little time, so by your companies
 To draw him on to pleasures, and to gather   15
 So much as from occasion you may glean,
 Whether aught to us unknown afflicts him thus,
 That, open'd, lies within our remedy.
QUEEN: Good gentlemen, he hath much talk'd of you,
 And sure I am two men there is not living   20
 To whom he more adheres. If it will please you
 To show us so much gentry and good will
 As to expend your time with us a while
 For the supply and profit of our hope,
 Your visitation shall receive such thanks   25
 As fits a king's remembrance.

---

110. *beshrow:* beshrew, plague take. *jealousy:* suspicious mind. 111. *proper . . . age:*
characteristic of men of my age. 112. *cast beyond ourselves:* overshoot, go too far (by way
of caution). 115. *close:* secret. 115–16. *move . . . love:* cause more grievous consequences
by its concealment than we shall incur displeasure by making it known.
II.ii. Location: The castle.
2. *Moreover . . . you:* besides the fact that we wanted to see you for your own sakes.
6. *Sith:* since. 11. *of:* from. 13. *voutsafe your rest:* vouchsafe to remain. 21. *more ad-*
heres: is more attached. 22. *gentry:* courtesy. 24. *supply and profit:* support and advance-

ROSENCRANTZ: Both your Majesties
    Might, by the sovereign power you have of us,
    Put your dread pleasures more into command
    Than to entreaty.

GUILDENSTERN: But we both obey,
    And here give up ourselves, in the full bent,   30
    To lay our service freely at your feet,
    To be commanded.

KING: Thanks, Rosencrantz and gentle Guildenstern.

QUEEN. Thanks, Guildenstern and gentle Rosencrantz.
    And I beseech you instantly to visit   35
    My too much changed son. Go some of you
    And bring these gentlemen where Hamlet is.

GUILDENSTERN: Heavens make our presence and our practices
    Pleasant and helpful to him!

QUEEN: Ay, amen!
        Exeunt ROSENCRANTZ *and* GUILDENSTERN [*with some*
        ATTENDANTS].

     Enter POLONIUS.

POLONIUS: Th' embassadors from Norway, my good lord,
    Are joyfully return'd.   41

KING: Thou still hast been the father of good news.

POLONIUS: Have I, my lord? I assure my good liege
    I hold my duty as I hold my soul,
    Both to my God and to my gracious king;   45
    And I do think, or else this brain of mine
    Hunts not the trail of policy so sure
    As it hath us'd to do, that I have found
    The very cause of Hamlet's lunacy.

KING: O, speak of that, that do I long to hear.   50

POLONIUS: Give first admittance to th' embassadors;
    My news shall be the fruit to that great feast.

KING: Thyself do grace to them, and bring them in.   [*Exit* POLONIUS.]
    He tells me, my dear Gertrude, he hath found
    The head and source of all your son's distemper.   55

QUEEN: I doubt it is no other but the main,
    His father's death and our [o'erhasty] marriage.

     Enter [POLONIUS *with* VOLTEMAND *and* CORNELIUS,
     the] EMBASSADORS.

KING: Well, we shall sift him.—Welcome, my good friends!
    Say, Voltemand, what from our brother Norway?

---

ment.   **30.** *in . . . bent:* to our utmost.   **40.** *embassadors:* ambassadors.   **42.** *skill:* always.
43. *liege:* sovereign.   **47.** *policy:* statecraft.   **52.** *fruit:* dessert.   **55.** *head.* Synonymous with
source.   distemper: (mental) illness.   **56.** *doubt:* suspect.   *main:* main cause.

VOLTEMAND: Most fair return of greetings and desires.   60
    Upon our first, he sent out to suppress
    His nephew's levies, which to him appear'd
    To be a preparation 'gainst the Polack;
    But better look'd into, he truly found
    It was against your Highness. Whereat griev'd,   65
    That so his sickness, age, and impotence
    Was falsely borne in hand, sends out arrests
    On Fortinbras, which he, in brief, obeys,
    Receives rebuke from Norway, and in fine,
    Makes vow before his uncle never more   70
    To give th' assay of arms against your Majesty.
    Whereon old Norway, overcome with joy,
    Gives him threescore thousand crowns in annual fee,
    And his commission to employ those soldiers,
    So levied, as before, against the Polack,   75
    With an entreaty, herein further shown,   [*Giving a paper.*]
    That it might please you to give quiet pass
    Through your dominions for this enterprise.
    On such regards of safety and allowance
    As therein are set down.

KING: It likes us well,   80
    And at our more considered time we'll read,
    Answer, and think upon this business.
    Mean time, we thank you for your well-took labor.
    Go to your rest, at night we'll feast together.
    Most welcome home!

                    Exeunt EMBASSADORS [*and* ATTENDANTS].

POLONIUS: This business is well ended.   85
    My liege, and madam, to expostulate
    What majesty should be, what duty is,
    Why day is day, night night, and time is time,
    Were nothing but to waste night, day, and time;
    Therefore, [since] brevity is the soul of wit,   90
    And tediousness the limbs and outward flourishes,
    I will be brief. Your noble son is mad:
    Mad call I it, for to define true madness,
    What is't but to be nothing else but mad?
    But let that go.

QUEEN: More matter with less art.   95

POLONIUS: Madam, I swear I use no art at all.
    That he's mad, 'tis true, 'tis true 'tis pity,
    And pity 'tis 'tis true—a foolish figure,

[Handwritten margin note: Tells Polonius to say what's on his mind]

---

61. *Upon our first:* at our first representation.   **65.** *griev'd:* aggrieved, offended.   **67.** *borne in hand:* taken advantage of.   **69.** *in fine:* in the end.   **71.** *assay:* trial.   **79.** *On . . . allowance:* with such safeguards and provisos.   **80.** *likes:* pleases.   **81.** *consider'd:* suitable for consideration.   **86.** *expostulate:* expound.   **90.** *wit:* understanding, wisdom.   **95.** *art:* i.e. rhetorical art.   **98.** *figure:* figure of speech.

But farewell it, for I will use no art.
Mad let us grant him then, and now remains   100
That we find out the cause of this effect,
Or rather say, the cause of this defect,
For this effect defective comes by cause:
Thus it remains, and the remainder thus.
Perpend.   105
I have a daughter—have while she is mine—
Who in her duty and obedience, mark,
Hath given me this. Now gather, and surmise.
            [*Reads the salutation of the letter.*]
"To the celestial and my soul's idol, the most beautified   110
Ophelia"—
That's an ill phrase, a vile phrase, "beautified" is a vile
phrase. But you shall hear. Thus:
"In her excellent white bosom, these, etc."
QUEEN: Came this from Hamlet to her?
POLONIUS: Good madam, stay awhile. I will be faithful.
                              [*Reads the*] *letter.*
    "Doubt thou the stars are fire,   116
       Doubt that the sun doth move,
       Doubt truth to be a liar,
       But never doubt I love.
O dear Ophelia, I am ill at these numbers. I have not art
to reckon my groans, but that I love thee best, O most
best, believe it. Adieu.   122
       Thine evermore, most dear lady,
              whilst this machine is to him, Hamlet."
This in obedience hath my daughter shown me,   125
And more [above], hath his solicitings,
As they fell out by time, by means, and place,
All given to mine ear.
KING: But how hath she
Receiv'd his love?
POLONIUS: What do you think of me?
KING: As of a man faithful and honorable.   130
POLONIUS: I would fain prove so. But what might you think,
When I had seen this hot love on the wing—
As I perceiv'd it (I must tell you that)
Before my daughter told me—what might you,
Or my dear Majesty your queen here, think,   135
If I had play'd the desk or table-book,

Polonius reads Hamlet's letter to Ophelia before K & Q

---

103. *For . . . cause:* for this effect (which shows as a defect in Hamlet's reason) is not
merely accidental, and has a cause we may trace.   **105.** *Perpend:* consider.   **109.** *beautified:* beautiful (not an uncommon usage).   **118.** *Doubt:* suspect.   **120.** *ill . . . numbers:* bad
at versifying.   **121.** *reckon:* count (with a quibble on *numbers*).   **124.** *machine:* body.
126. *more above:* furthermore.   **131.** *fain:* willingly, gladly.   **136.** *play'd . . . table-book:* i.e.
noted the matter secretly.

Or given my heart a [winking,] mute and dumb,
Or look'd upon this love with idle sight,
What might you think? No, I went round to work,
And my young mistress thus I did bespeak: 140
"Lord Hamlet is a prince out of thy star;
This must not be"; and then I prescripts gave her,
That she should lock herself from [his] resort,
Admit no messengers, receive no tokens.
Which done, she took the fruits of my advice;   145
And he repell'd, a short tale to make,
Fell into a sadness, then into a fast,
Thence to a watch, thence into a weakness,
Thence to [a] lightness, and by this declension,
Into the madness wherein now he raves,   150
And all we mourn for.

KING: Do you think ['tis] this?

QUEEN: It may be, very like.

POLONIUS: Hath there been such a time—I would fain know that
That I have positively said, "'Tis so,"
When it prov'd otherwise?

KING: Not that I know.   155

POLONIUS [*Points to his head and shoulder.*]: Take this from
            this, if this be otherwise.
If circumstances lead me, I will find
Where truth is hid, though it were hid indeed
Within the centre.

KING: How may we try it further?

POLONIUS: You know sometimes he walks four hours together   160
Here in the lobby.

QUEEN: So he does indeed.

POLONIUS: At such a time I'll loose my daughter to him.
Be you and I behind an arras then,
Mark the encounter: if he love her not,
And be not from his reason fall'n thereon,   165
Let me be no assistant for a state,
But keep a farm and carters.

KING: We will try it.

                Enter HAMLET [*reading on a book*].

QUEEN: But look where sadly the poor wretch comes reading.

POLONIUS: Away, I do beseech you, both away.
I'll board him presently.   *Exeunt* KING *and* QUEEN.

137. *winking:* closing of the eyes. **138.** *idle sight:* noncomprehending eyes. **139.** *round:*
straightforwardly. **140.** *bespeak:* address. **141.** *star:* i.e. sphere, lot in life. **145.** *took
. . . of:* profited by, i.e. carried out. **146.** *repell'd:* repulsed. **148.** *watch:* sleeplessness,
149. *lightness:* lightheadedness. **159.** *centre:* i.e. of the earth (which in the Ptolemaic
system is also the centre of the universe). **163.** *arras:* hanging tapestry. **165.** *thereon:*
because of that.

O, give me leave,   170
How does my good Lord Hamlet?

HAMLET: Well, God-a-mercy.

POLONIUS: Do you know me, my lord?

HAMLET: Excellent well, you are a fishmonger.

POLONIUS: Not I, my lord.   175

HAMLET: Then I would you were so honest a man.

POLONIUS: Honest, my lord?

HAMLET: Ay, sir, to be honest, as this world goes, is to be one
man pick'd out of ten thousand.

POLONIUS: That's very true, my lord.   180

HAMLET: For if the sun breed maggots in a dead dog, being a
good kissing carrion—Have you a daughter?

POLONIUS: I have, my lord.

HAMLET: Let her not walk i' th' sun. Conception is a blessing,
but as your daughter may conceive, friend, look
to't.   186

POLONIUS [*Aside.*]: How say you by that? still harping on my
daughter. Yet he knew me not at first, 'a said I was a
fishmonger. 'A is far gone. And truly in my youth I
suff'red much extremity for love—very near this. I'll
speak to him again.—What do you read, my lord?   191

HAMLET: Words, words, words.

POLONIUS: What is the matter, my lord?

HAMLET: Between who?

POLONIUS: I mean, the matter that you read, my lord.   195

HAMLET: Slanders, sir; for the satirical rogue says here that old
men have grey beards, that their faces are wrinkled,
their eyes purging thick amber and plumtree gum, and
that they have a plentiful lack of wit, together with
most weak hams; all which, sir, though I most power-   200
fully and potently believe, yet I hold it not honesty to
have it thus set down, for yourself, sir, shall grow old as
I am, if like a crab you could go backward.

POLONIUS [*Aside.*]: Though this be madness, yet there is
method in't.—Will you walk out of the air, my lord?

HAMLET: Into my grave.   207

POLONIUS: Indeed that's out of the air. [*Aside.*] How pregnant
sometimes his replies are! a happiness that often

---

170. *board:* accost. *presently:* at once. **172.** *God-a-mercy:* thank you. **174.** *fishmonger.*
Usually explained as slang for "bawd," but no evidence has been produced for such a usage
in Shakespeare's day. **182.** *good kissing carrion:* flesh good enough for the sun to kiss.
184. *Conception:* understanding (with following play on the sense "conceiving a child").
193. *matter:* subject; but Hamlet replies as if he had understood Polonius to mean "cause
for a quarrel." **201.** *honesty:* a fitting thing. **206.** *method:* orderly arrangement, sequence
of ideas. *out . . . air.* Outdoor air was thought to be bad for invalids. **208.** *pregnant:* apt.

madness hits on, which reason and [sanity] could not   210
so prosperously be deliver'd of. I will leave him, [and
suddenly contrive the means of meeting between him]
and my daughter.—My lord, I will take my leave of
you.   214

HAMLET: You cannot take from me any thing that I will not
more willingly part withal—except my life, except my
life, except my life.

POLONIUS: Fare you well, my lord.

HAMLET: These tedious old fools!

Enter GUILDENSTERN *and* ROSENCRANTZ.

POLONIUS: You go to seek the Lord Hamlet, there he is.

ROSENCRANTZ [*To* POLONIUS]: God save you sir!   [*Exit* POLONIUS.]   221

GUILDENSTERN: My honor'd lord!

ROSENCRANTZ: My most dear lord!

HAMLET: My [excellent] good friends! How dost thou, Guildenstern? Ah, Rosencrantz! Good lads, how do you
both?   226

ROSENCRANTZ: As the indifferent children of the earth.

GUILDENSTERN: Happy, in that we are not [over-]happy, on
Fortune's [cap] we are not the very button.

HAMLET: Nor the soles of her shoe?   230

ROSENCRANTZ: Neither, my lord.

HAMLET: Then you live about her waist, or in the middle of her
favors?

GUILDENSTERN: Faith, her privates we.

HAMLET: In the secret parts of Fortune? O, most true, she is a
strumpet. What news?   236

ROSENCRANTZ: None, my lord, but the world's grown honest.

HAMLET: Then is doomsday near. But your news is not true.
[Let me question more in particular. What have you,
my good friends, deserv'd at the hands of Fortune, that
she sends you to prison hither?   241

GUILDENSTERN: Prison, my lord?

HAMLET: Denmark's a prison.

ROSENCRANTZ: Then is the world one.   244

HAMLET: A goodly one, in which there are many confines,
wards, and dungeons, Denmark being one o' th'
worst.

ROSENCRANTZ: We think not so, my lord.

HAMLET: Why then 'tis none to you; for there is nothing either

---

212. *suddenly:* at once. 227. *indifferent:* average. 234. *privates:* (1) intimate friends; (2) genitalia. 236. *strumpet.* A common epithet for Fortune, because she grants favors to all men. 246. *wards:* cells.

good or bad, but thinking makes it so. To me it is a
prison.   251

ROSENCRANTZ: Why then your ambition makes it one. 'Tis too
narrow for your mind.

HAMLET: O God, I could be bounded in a nutshell, and count
myself a king of infinite space—were it not that I have
bad dreams.   256

GUILDENSTERN: Which dreams indeed are ambition, for the
very substance of the ambitious is merely the shadow
of a dream.

HAMLET: A dream itself is but a shadow.   260

ROSENCRANTZ: Truly, and I hold ambition of so airy and light
a quality that it is but a shadow's shadow.

HAMLET: Then are our beggars bodies, and our monarchs and
outstretch'd heroes the beggars' shadows. Shall we to
th' court? for, by my fay, I cannot reason.

BOTH [ROSENCRANTZ, GUILDENSTERN]: We'll wait upon you.   266

HAMLET: No such matter. I will not sort you with the rest of my
servants; for to speak to you like an honest man, I am
most dreadfully attended.] But in the beaten way of
friendship, what make you at Elsinore?   270

ROSENCRANTZ: To visit you, my lord, no other occasion.

HAMLET: Beggar that I am, I am [even] poor in thanks —but I
thank you, and sure, dear friends, my thanks are too
dear a halfpenny. Were you not sent for? is it your own
inclining? is it a free visitation? Come, come, deal justly
with me. Come, come—nay, speak.

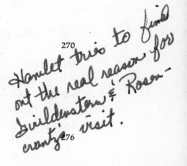

Hamlet tries to find out the real reason for Guildenstern & Rosencrantz' visit.

GUILDENSTERN: What should we say, my lord?

HAMLET: Any thing but to th' purpose. You were sent for, and
there is a kind of confession in your looks, which your
modesties have not craft enough to color. I know the
good King and Queen have sent for you.

ROSENCRANTZ: To what end, my lord?   282

HAMLET: That you must teach me. But let me conjure you,
by the rights of our fellowship, by the consonancy
of our youth, by the obligation of our ever-preserv'd
love, and by what more dear a better proposer can   286
charge you withal, be even and direct with me, whether
you were sent for or no!

---

263. *bodies:* i.e. not shadows (since they lack ambition).   264. *outstretch'd:* i.e. with their
ambition extended to the utmost (and hence producing stretched-out or elongaged shadows).   265. *fay:* faith.   266. *wait upon you:* attend you thither.   267. *sort:* associate.
269. *dreadfully:* execrably.   274. *too . . . halfpenny:* too expensive priced at a halfpenny,
i.e. not worth much.   275. *justly:* honestly.   278. *but.* Ordinarily punctuated with a comma
preceding, to give the sense "provided that it is"; but Q2 has no comma, and Hamlet may
intend, or include, the sense "except."   280. *modesties:* sense of shame.
284–85. *consonancy . . . youth:* similarity of our ages.   287. *charge:* urge, adjure.   *even:*
frank, honest (cf. modern "level with me").

Guildenstern tells Hamlet the two of them had been summoned

ROSENCRANTZ [*Aside to* GUILDENSTERN.]: What say you?

HAMLET [*Aside.*]: Nay then I have an eye of you!—If you love
    me, hold not off.   291

GUILDENSTERN: My lord, we were sent for.

HAMLET: I will tell you why, so shall my anticipation prevent
    your discovery, and your secrecy to the King and
    Queen moult no feather. I have of late—but wherefore   295
    I know not—lost all my mirth, forgone all custom of
    exercises; and indeed it goes so heavily with my
    disposition, that this goodly frame, the earth, seems to
    me a sterile promontory; this most excellent canopy,
    the air, look you, this brave o'erhanging firmament,   300
    this majestical roof fretted with golden fire, why, it
    appeareth nothing to me but a foul and pestilent
    congregation of vapors. What [a] piece of work is a
    man, how noble in reason, how infinite in faculties, in
    form and moving, how express and admirable in action,   305
    how like an angel in apprehension, how like a god! the
    beauty of the world; the paragon of animals; and yet to
    me what is this quintessence of dust? Man delights not
    me—nor women neither, though by your smiling you
    seem to say so.   310

ROSENCRANTZ: My lord, there was no such stuff in my
    thoughts.

HAMLET: Why did ye laugh then, when I said, "Man delights
    not me"?   314

ROSENCRANTZ: To think, my lord, if you delight not in man,
    what lenten entertainment the players shall receive
    from you. We coted them on the way, and hither are
    they coming to offer you service.

HAMLET: He that plays the king shall be welcome—his
    Majesty shall have tribute on me, the adventerous   320
    knight shall use his foil and target, the lover shall not
    sigh gratis, the humorous man shall end his part in
    peace, [the clown shall make those laugh whose lungs
    are [tickle] a' th' sere,] and the lady shall say her mind
    freely, or the [blank] verse shall halt for't. What players
    are they?   326

290. *of*: on. 293–294. *prevent your discovery*: forestall your disclosure (of what the King
and Queen have said to you in confidence). 295. *moult no feather*: not be impaired in
the least. 296–297. *custom of exercises*: my usual athletic activities. 300. *brave*: splendid.
301. *fretted*: ornamented as with fretwork. 303. *piece of work*: masterpiece. 305. *express*: exact. 308. *quintessence*: finest and purest extract. 316. *lenten entertainment*: meagre reception. 317. *coted*: outstripped. 320. *on*: of, from. 320–21. *adventerous*: adventurous, i.e. wandering in search of adventure. 321. *foil and target*: light fencing sword and
small shield. 322. *gratis*: without reward. *humorous*: dominated by some eccentric trait
(like the melancholy Jaques in *As You Like It*). 324. *tickle . . . sere*: i.e. easily made to
laugh (literally, describing a gun that goes off easily; *sere* = a catch in the gunlock; *tickle* =
easily affected, highly sensitive to stimulus). 325. *halt*: limp, come off lamely (the verse

ROSENCRANTZ: Even those you were wont to take such delight
in, the tragedians of the city.

HAMLET: How chances it they travel? Their residence,
both in reputation and profit, was better both
ways.   331

ROSENCRANTZ? I think their inhibition comes by the means of
the late innovation.

HAMLET: Do they hold the same estimation they did when I
was in the city? Are they so follow'd?   335

ROSENCRANTZ: No indeed are they not.

[HAMLET: How comes it? do they grow rusty?

ROSENCRANTZ: Nay, their endeavor keeps in the wonted pace;
but there is, sir, an aery of children, little eyases, that
cry out on the top of question, and are most tyrannically clapp'd for't. These are now the fashion, and so   341
[berattle] the common stages—so they call them—that
many wearing rapiers are afraid of goose-quills and
dare scarce come thither.   344

HAMLET: What, are they children? Who maintains 'em? How
are they escoted? Will they pursue the quality no longer
than they can sing? Will they not say afterwards, if
they should grow themselves to common players (as it
is [most like], if their means are [no] better), their
writers do them wrong, to make them exclaim against
their own succession?   351

ROSENCRANTZ: Faith, there has been much to do on both sides,
and the nation holds it no sin to tarre them to controversy. There was for a while no money bid for argument, unless the poet and the player went to cuffs in
the question.   356

HAMLET: Is't possible?

will not scan if she omits indecent words).   **332.** *inhibition:* hindrance (to playing in the
city). The word could be used of an official prohibition. See next note.   **333.** *innovation.*
Shakespeare elsewhere uses this word of a political uprising or revolt, and lines 332–33 are
often explained as meaning that the company had been forbidden to play in the city as the
result of some disturbance. It is commonly conjectured that the allusion is to the Essex
rebellion of 1601, but it is known that Shakespeare's company, though to some extent
involved on account of the special performance of *Richard II* they were commissioned to
give on the eve of the rising, were not in fact punished by inhibition. A second interpretation explains *innovation* as referring to the new theatrical vogue described in lines 339 ff.,
and conjectures that *inhibition* may allude to a Privy Council order of 1600 restricting the
number of London playhouses to two and the number of performances to two a
week.   **337–62.** *How . . . too.* This passage refers topically to the "War of the Theatres"
between the child actors and their poet Jonson on the one side, and on the other the
adults, with Dekker, Marston, and possibly Shakespeare as spokesmen, in 1600–
1601.   **339.** *aery:* nest.   *eyases:* unfledged hawks.   **340.** *cry . . . question:* cry shrilly above
others in controversy.   **340.** *tyrannically:* outrageously.   **342.** *berattle:* cry down, satirize.
common stages: public theatres (the children played at the Blackfriars, a private theatre).
343. *goose-quills:* pens (of satirical playwrights).   **346.** *escoted:* supported.   *quality:* profession (of acting).   **346–347.** *no . . . sing:* i.e. only until their voices change.   **351.** *succession:*
future.   **352.** *to do:* ado.   **353.** *tarre:* incite: **354.** *argument:* plot of a play.   **355–356.** *in the
question:* i.e. as part of the script.

GUILDENSTERN: O, there has been much throwing about of
    brains.

HAMLET: Do the boys carry it away?   360

ROSENCRANTZ: Ay, that they do, my lord—Hercules and his
    load too.]

HAMLET: It is not very strange, for my uncle is King of Den-
    mark, and those that would make mouths at him while
    my father liv'd, give twenty, forty, fifty, a hundred   365
    ducats a-piece for his picture in little. 'Sblood, there is
    something in this more than natural, if philoso-phy
    could find it out.   *A flourish [for the* PLAYERS].

GUILDENSTERN: There are the players.   369

HAMLET: Gentlemen, you are welcome to Elsinore. Your
    hands, come then: th' appurtenance of welcome is
    fashion and ceremony. Let me comply with you in this
    garb, [lest my] extent to the players, which, I tell you,
    must show fairly outwards, should more appear like
    entertainment than yours. You are welcome; but my
    uncle-father and aunt-mother are deceiv'd.   376

GUILDENSTERN: In what, my dear lord?

HAMLET: I am but mad north-north-west, When the wind is
    southerly I know a hawk from a hand-saw.

        Enter POLONIUS.

POLONIUS: Well be with you, gentlemen!   380

HAMLET [*Aside to them.*]: Hark you, Guildenstern, and you
    too—at each ear a hearer—that great baby you see
    there is not yet out of his swaddling-clouts.

ROSENCRANTZ: Happily he is the second time come to them, for
    they say an old man is twice a child.   385

HAMLET: I will prophesy, he comes to tell me of the players,
    mark it. [*Aloud.*] You say right, sir, a' Monday morn-
    ing, 'twas then indeed.

POLONIUS: My lord, I have news to tell you.

HAMLET: My lord, I have news to tell you. When Roscius was
    an actor in Rome—   391

POLONIUS: The actors are come hither, my lord.

---

360. *carry it away:* win.   361–62. *Hercules . . . too.* Hercules in the course of one of his
twelve labors supported the world for Atlas; the children do better, for they carry away the
world and Hercules as well. There is an allusion to the Globe playhouse, which reportedly
had for its sign the figure of Hercules upholding the world.   364. *mouths:* derisive faces.
366. *'Sblood:* by God's (Christ's) blood.   372. *comply:* observe the formalities.   373. *garb:*
fashion, manner.   *my extent:* i.e. the degree of courtesy I show.   374–75. *more . . . yours:*
seem to be a warmer reception than I have given you.   379. *hawk, hand-saw.* Both
cutting-tools; but also both birds, if *hand-saw* quibbles on *hernshaw,* "heron," a bird preyed
upon by the hawk.   383. *swaddling-clouts:* swaddling clothes.   384. *Happily:* haply, perhaps.   385. *twice:* i.e. for the second time.   390. *Roscius:* the most famous of Roman
actors (died 62 B.C.). News about him would be stale news indeed.

HAMLET: Buzz, buzz!

POLONIUS: Upon my honor—

HAMLET: "Then came each actor on his ass"—   395

POLONIUS: The best actors in the world, either for tragedy,
    comedy, history, pastoral, pastoral-comical, histori-
    cal-pastoral, [tragical-historical, tragical-comical- his-
    torical-pastoral,] scene individable, or poem unlimited;
    Seneca cannot be too heavy, nor Plautus too light,   400
    for the law of writ and the liberty: these are the
    only men.

HAMLET: O Jephthah, judge of Israel, what a treasure hadst
    thou!

POLONIUS: What a treasure had he, my lord?   405

HAMLET: Why—
        "One fair daughter, and no more,
            The which he loved passing well."

POLONIUS [Aside.]: Still on my daughter.

HAMLET: Am I not i' th' right, old Jephthah?   410

POLONIUS: If you call me Jephthah, my lord, I have a daughter
    that I love passing well.

HAMLET: Nay, that follows not.

POLONIUS: What follows then, my lord?

HAMLET: Why—   415
        "As by lot, God wot,"
    and then, you know,
        "It came to pass, as most like it was"—
    the first row of the pious chanson will show you more,
    for look where my abridgment comes.   420

            Enter the PLAYERS, [four or five].

You are welcome, masters, welcome all. I am glad to
see thee well. Welcome, good friends. O, old friend!
why, thy face is valanc'd since I saw thee last; com'st
thou to beard me in Denmark? What, my young lady
and mistress! by' lady, your ladyship is nearer to
heaven than when I saw you last, by the altitude of a   426
chopine. Pray God your voice, like a piece of uncurrent

393. *Buzz:* exclamation of impatience at someone who tells news already known.
399. *scene individable:* play observing the unity of place.   *poem unlimited:* play
ignoring rules such as the three unities.   **400.** *Seneca:* Roman writer of tragedies.
Plautus: Roman writer of comedies.   **401.** *for . . . liberty:* for strict observance of the rules,
or for freedom from them (with possible allusion to the location of playhouses, which were
not built in properties under city jurisdiction, but in the "liberties"—land once monastic and
now outside the jurisdiction of the city authorities).   **402.** *only:* very best (a frequent
use).   **403.** *Jephthah . . . Israel:* title of a ballad, from which Hamlet goes on to quote. For
the story of Jephthah and his daughter, see Judges 11.   **419.** *row:* stanza.   *chanson:* song,
ballad.   **420.** *abridgment:* (1) interruption; (2) pastime.   **423.** *valanc'd:* fringed, i.e. bearded.   **424.** *beard:* confront boldly (with obvious pun).   **425.** *by' lady:* by Our Lady.
427. *chopine:* thick-soled shoe.

gold, be not crack'd within the ring. Masters, you are all welcome. We'll e'en to't like [French] falc'ners—fly at any thing we see; we'll have a speech straight. Come give us a taste of your quality, come, a passionate speech.   432

[FIRST] PLAYER: What speech, my good lord?

HAMLET: I heard thee speak me a speech once, but it was never acted, or if it was, not above once; for the play, I remember, pleas'd not the million, 'twas caviary to the   436
general, but it was—as I receiv'd it, and others, whose judgments in such matters cried in the top of mine—an excellent play, well digested in the scenes, set down with as much modesty as cunning. I remember one said there were no sallets in the lines to make the matter   441
savory, nor no matter in the phrase that might indict the author of affection, but call'd it an honest method, as wholesome as sweet, and by very much more handsome than fine. One speech in't I chiefly lov'd, 'twas Aeneas' [tale] to Dido, and thereabout of it   446
especially when he speaks of Priam's slaughter. If it live in your memory, begin at this line—let me see, let me see:
"The rugged Pyrrhus, like th' Hyrcanian beast—"
'Tis not so, it begins with Pyrrhus: 451
"The rugged Pyrrhus, he whose sable arms,
Black as his purpose, did the night resemble
When he lay couched in th' ominous horse,
Hath now this dread and black complexion smear'd
With heraldy more dismal: head to foot   456
Now is he total gules, horridly trick'd
With blood of fathers, mothers, daughters, sons,
Bak'd and impasted with the parching streets,
That lend a tyrannous and a damned light   460
To their lord's murther. Roasted in wrath and fire,
And thus o'er-sized with coagulate gore,
With eyes like carbuncles, the hellish Pyrrhus

---

428. *crack'd . . . ring:* i.e. broken to the point where you can no longer play female roles. A coin with a crack extending far enough in from the edge to cross the circle surrounding the stamp of the sovereign's head was unacceptable in exchange (*uncurrent*).   **430.** *straight:* straightway.   **431.** *quality:* professional skill.   **436–437.** *caviary . . . general:* caviare to the common people, i.e. too choice for the multitude.   **438–39.** *cried . . . of:* were louder than, i.e. carried more authority than.   **441.** *sallets:* salads, i.e. spicy jokes.   **442.** *savory:* zesty.   **443.** *affection:* affectation.   **445.** *fine:* showily dressed (in language).   **448.** *Priam's slaughter:* the slaying of Priam (at the fall of Troy).   **450.** *Pyrrhus:* another name for Neoptolemus, Achilles' son.   *Hyrcanian beast.* Hyrcania in the Caucasus was notorious for his tigers.   **452.** *sable arms.* The Greeks within the Trojan horse had blackened their skin so as to be inconspicuous when they emerged at night.   **456.** *heraldy:* heraldry.   *dismal:* ill-boding.   **457.** *gules:* red (heraldic term).   *trick'd:* adorned.   **459.** *Bak'd:* caked.   *impasted:* crusted.   *with . . . streets:* i.e. by the heat from the burning streets.   **462.** *o'er-sized:* covered over as with a coat of sizing.   **463.** *carbuncles:* jewels believed to shine in the dark.

Old grandsire Priam seeks."
So proceed you.   465

POLONIUS: 'Fore God, my lord, well spoken, with good accent
and good discretion.

[FIRST] PLAYER: "Anon he finds him
Striking too short at Greeks. His antique sword,
Rebellious to his arm, lies where it falls,   470
Repugnant to command. Unequal match'd,
Pyrrhus at Priam drives, in rage strikes wide,
But with the whiff and wind of his fell sword
Th' unnerved father falls. [Then senseless Ilium,]
Seeming to feel this blow, with flaming top   475
Stoops to his base, and with a hideous crash
Takes prisoner Pyrrhus' ear; for lo his sword,
Which was declining on the milky head
Of reverent Priam, seem'd i' th' air to stick.
So as a painted tyrant Pyrrhus stood   480
[And,] like a neutral to his will and matter,
Did nothing.
But as we often see, against some storm,
A silence in the heavens, the rack stand still,
The bold winds speechless, and the orb below   485
As hush as death, anon the dreadful thunder
Doth rend the region; so after Pyrrhus' pause,
A roused vengeance sets him new a-work,
And never did the Cyclops' hammers fall
On Mars's armor forg'd for proof eterne   490
With less remorse than Pyrrhus' bleeding sword
Now falls on Priam.
Out, out, thou strumpet Fortune! All you gods,
In general synod take away her power!
Break all the spokes and [fellies] from her wheel,   495
And bowl the round nave down the hill of heaven
As low as to the fiends!"

POLONIUS: This is too long.

HAMLET: It shall to the barber's with your beard. Prithee say
on, he's for a jig or a tale of bawdry, or he sleeps. Say
on, come to Hecuba.   501

[FIRST] PLAYER: "But who, ah woe, had seen the mobled queen"—

HAMLET: "The mobled queen"?

POLONIUS: That's good, ["[mobled] queen" is good].

---

471. *Repugnant:* resistant, hostile. 473. *fell:* cruel. 474. *unnerved:* drained of strength.
senseless: insensible. *Ilium:* the citadel of Troy. 479. *reverent:* reverend, aged.
481. *like . . . matter:* i.e. poised midway between intention and performance. 483. *against:*
just before. 484. *rack:* cloud-mass. 487. *region:* i.e. air. 489. *Cyclops:* giants who
worked in Vulcan's smithy, where armor was made for the gods. 490. *proof eterne:* eternal
endurance. 491. *remorse:* pity. 495. *fellies:* rims. 496. *nave:* hub. 500. *jig:* song-and-
dance entertainment performed after the main play. 502. *mobled:* muffled.

[FIRST] PLAYER: "Run barefoot up and down, threat'ning the
    flames   505
    With bisson rheum, a clout upon that head
    Where late the diadem stood, and for a robe,
    About her lank and all o'er-teemed loins,
    A blanket, in the alarm of fear caught up—   509
    Who this had seen, with tongue in venom steep'd,
    'Gainst Fortune's state would treason have pronounc'd.
    But if the gods themselves did see her then,
    When she saw Pyrrhus make malicious sport
    In mincing with his sword her [husband's] limbs,
    The instant burst of clamor that she made,   515
    Unless things mortal move them not at all,
    Would have made milch the burning eyes of heaven,
    And passion in the gods."

POLONIUS: Look whe'er he has not turn'd his color and has
    tears in 's eyes. Prithee no more.   520

HAMLET: 'Tis well, I'll have thee speak out the rest of this soon.
    Good my lord, will you see the players well bestow'd?
    Do you hear, let them be well us'd, for they are the
    abstract and brief chronicles of the time. After your
    death you were better have a bad epitaph than their ill
    report while you live.   526

POLONIUS: My lord, I will use them according to their
    desert.

HAMLET: God's bodkin, man, much better: use every man
    after his desert, and who shall scape whipping? Use
    them after your own honor and dignity—the less
    they deserve, the more merit is in your bounty.
    Take them in.   533

POLONIUS: Come, sirs.   *[Exit.]*

HAMLET: Follow him, friends, we'll hear a play to-
    morrow.   *[Exeunt all the* PLAYERS *but the* FIRST.] 536
    Dost thou hear me, old friend? Can you play "The
    Murther of Gonzago"?

[FIRST PLAYER]: Ay, my lord.

HAMLET: We'll ha't to-morrow night. You could for need   540
    study a speech of some dozen lines, or sixteen lines,
    which I would set down and insert in't, could you
    not?

[FIRST] PLAYER: Ay, my lord.   544

---

506. *bisson rheum:* blinding tears. *clout:* cloth. **508.** *o'er-teemed:* worn out by childbear-
ing. **511.** *state:* rule, government. **517.** *milch:* moist (literally, milky). **518.** *passion:*
grief. **519.** *Look . . . not:* i.e. note how he has. **522.** *bestow'd:* lodged. **523.** *us'd:* treated.
529. *God's bodkin:* by God's (Christ's) little body. **540.** *for need:* if necessary.

HAMLET: Very well. Follow that lord, and look you mock him
    not. [*Exit* FIRST PLAYER.] My good friends, I'll leave you
    [till] night. You are welcome to Elsinore.
ROSENCRANTZ: Good my lord!
HAMLET: Ay so, God buy to you.

               Exeunt [ROSENCRANTZ *and* GUILDENSTERN].
               Now I am alone.

O, what a rogue and peasant slave am I!   550
Is it not monstrous that this player here,
But in a fiction, in a dream of passion,
Could force his soul so to his own conceit
That from her working all the visage wann'd,
Tears in his eyes, distraction in his aspect,   555
A broken voice, an' his whole function suiting
With forms to his conceit? And all for nothing,
For Hecuba!
What's Hecuba to him, or he to [Hecuba],
That he should weep for her? What would he do
Had he the motive and [the cue] for passion   561
That I have? He would drown the stage with tears,
And cleave the general ear with horrid speech,
Make mad the guilty, and appall the free,
Confound the ignorant, and amaze indeed   565
The very faculties of eyes and ears. Yet I,
A dull and muddy-mettled rascal, peak
Like John-a-dreams, unpregnant of my cause,
And can say nothing; no, not for a king,
Upon whose property and most dear life   570
A damn'd defeat was made. Am I a coward?
Who calls me villain, breaks my pate across,
Plucks off my beard and blows it in my face,
Tweaks me by the nose, gives me the lie i' th' throat
As deep as to the lungs? Who does me this?   575
Hah, 'swounds, I should take it; for it cannot be
But I am pigeon-liver'd, and lack gall
To make oppression bitter, or ere this
I should 'a' fatted all the region kites
With this slave's offal. Bloody, bawdy villain!   580
Remorseless, treacherous, lecherous, kindless villain!
Why, what an ass am I! This is most brave,
That I, the son of a dear [father] murthered,

553. *conceit:* imaginative conception. 556. *his whole function:* the operation of his whole body. 557. *forms:* actions, expressions. 564. *free:* innocent. 565. *amaze:* confound. 567. *muddy-mettled:* dull-spirited. *peak:* mope. 568. *John-a-dreams:* a sleepy fellow. *unpregnant of:* unquickened by. 571. *defeat:* destruction. 574–75. *gives . . . lungs:* calls me a liar in the extremest degree. 576. *'swounds:* by God's (Christ's) wounds. *should:* would certainly. 577. *am . . . gall:* i.e. am constitutionally incapable of resentment. That doves were mild because they had no gall was a popular belief. 579. *region kites:* kites of the air. 580. *offal:* entrails. 581. *kindless:* unnatural.

Prompted to my revenge by heaven and hell,
Must like a whore unpack my heart with words,
And fall a-cursing like a very drab,   586
A stallion. Fie upon't, foh!
About, my brains! Hum—I have heard
That guilty creatures sitting at a play
Have by the very cunning of the scene   590
Been strook so to the soul, that presently
They have proclaim'd their malefactions:
For murther, though it have no tongue, will speak
With most miraculous organ. I'll have these players
Play something like the murther of my father   595
Before mine uncle. I'll observe his looks,
I'll tent him to the quick. If 'a do blench,
I know my course. The spirit that I have seen
May be a [dev'l], and the [dev'l] hath power
T' assume a pleasing shape, yea, and perhaps,   600
Out of my weakness and my melancholy,
As he is very potent with such spirits,
Abuses me to damn me. I'll have grounds
More relative than this—the play's the thing   604
Wherein I'll catch the conscience of the King.   *Exit.*

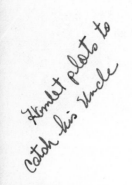

Hamlet plots to catch his uncle

ACT THREE, SCENE ONE

Enter KING, QUEEN, POLONIUS, OPHELIA, ROSENCRANTZ,
GUILDENSTERN, LORDS.

KING: An' can you by no drift of conference
        Get from him why he puts on this confusion,
        Grating so harshly all his days of quiet
        With turbulent and dangerous lunacy?

ROSENCRANTZ: He does confess he feels himself distracted,
        But from what cause 'a will by no means speak.

GUILDENSTERN: Nor do we find him forward to be sounded,
        But with a crafty madness keeps aloof
        When we would bring him on to some confession
        Of his true state.

QUEEN: Did he receive you well?   10

ROSENCRANTZ: Most like a gentleman.

587. *stallion:* male whore. Most editors adopt the F1 reading *scullion,* "kitchen menial."
588. *About:* to work. 591. *presently:* at once, then and there. 597. *tent:* probe. *blench:*
flinch. 602. *spirits:* states of temperament. 603. *Abuses:* deludes. 604. *relative:* closely
related (to fact), i.e. conclusive.
III.i. Location: The castle.
1. *An':* and. *drift of conference:* leading on of conversation. 7. *forward:* readily willing.
sounded: plumbed, probed. 8. *crafty madness:* i.e. mad craftiness, the shrewdness that
mad people sometimes exhibit.

GUILDENSTERN: But with much forcing of his disposition.

ROSENCRANTZ: Niggard of question, but of our demands
    Most free in his reply.

QUEEN: Did you assay him
    To any pastime?   15

ROSENCRANTZ: Madam, it so fell out that certain players
    We o'erraught on the way; of these we told him,
    And there did seem in him a kind of joy
    To hear of it. They are here about the court,
    And as I think, they have already order   20
    This night to play before him.

POLONIUS: 'Tis most true,
    And he beseech'd me to entreat your Majesties
    To hear and see the matter.

KING: With all my heart, and it doth much content me
    To hear him so inclin'd.   25
    Good gentlemen, give him a further edge,
    And drive his purpose into these delights.

ROSENCRANTZ: We shall, my lord.

                   Exeunt ROSENCRANTZ *and* GUILDENSTERN.

KING: Sweet Gertrude, leave us two,
    For we have closely sent for Hamlet hither,
    That he, as 'twere by accident, may here   30
    Affront Ophelia. Her father and myself,
    We'll so bestow ourselves that, seeing unseen,
    We may of their encounter frankly judge,
    And gather by him, as he is behav'd,
    If't be th' affliction of his love or no   35
    That thus he suffers for.

QUEEN: I shall obey you.
    And for your part, Ophelia, I do wish
    That your good beauties be the happy cause
    Of Hamlet's wildness. So shall I hope your virtues
    Will bring him to his wonted way again,   40
    To both your honors.

OPHELIA: Madam, I wish it may.   [*Exit* QUEEN.]

POLONIUS: Ophelia, walk you here.—Gracious, so please you,
    We will bestow ourselves. [*To* OPHELIA.] Read on this book,
    That show of such an exercise may color
    Your [loneliness]. We are oft to blame in this—   45
    'Tis too much prov'd—that with devotion's visage

---

12. *disposition:* inclination.   13. *question:* conversation.   *demands:* questions.   14. *assay:*
attempt to win.   17. *o'erraught:* passed (literally, overreached).   26. *edge:* stimulus.
27. *into:* on to.   29. *closely:* privately.   31. *Affront:* meet.   33. *frankly:* freely.   44. *exercise:* i.e. religious exercise (as the next sentence makes clear).   44–45. *color Your
loneliness:* make your solitude seem natural.   46. *too much prov'd:* too often proved true.

And pious action we do sugar o'er
The devil himself.

KING: [*Aside.*] O, 'tis too true!
How smart a lash that speech doth give my conscience!
The harlot's cheek, beautied with plast'ring art,   50
Is not more ugly to the thing that helps it
Than is my deed to my most painted word.
O heavy burthen!

POLONIUS: I hear him coming. Withdraw, my lord.

[*Exeunt* KING *and* POLONIUS.]

Enter HAMLET.

HAMLET: To be, or not to be, that is the question: 55
Whether 'tis nobler in the mind to suffer
The slings and arrows of outrageous fortune,
Or to take arms against a sea of troubles,
And by opposing, end them. To die, to sleep—
No more, and by a sleep to say we end   60
The heart-ache and the thousand natural shocks
That flesh is heir to; 'tis a consummation
Devoutly to be wish'd. To die, to sleep—
To sleep, perchance to dream—ay, there's the rub,
For in that sleep of death what dreams may come,   65
When we have shuffled off this mortal coil,
Must give us pause; there's the respect
That makes calamity of so long life:
For who would bear the whips and scorns of time,
Th' oppressor's wrong, the proud man's contumely,   70
The pangs of despis'd love, the law's delay,
The insolence of office, and the spurns
That patient merit of th' unworthy takes,
When he himself might his quietus make
With a bare bodkin; who would fardels bear,   75
To grunt and sweat under a weary life,
But that the dread of something after death,
The undiscover'd country, from whose bourn
No traveller returns, puzzles the will,
And makes us rather bear those ills we have   80
Than fly to others that we know not of?
Thus conscience does make cowards [of us all],

Should Hamlet commit suicide

47. *action:* demeanor. 51. *to . . . it:* in comparison with the paint that makes it look
beautiful. 56. *suffer:* submit to, endure patiently. 62. *consummation:* completion, end.
64. *rub:* obstacle (a term from the game of bowls). 66. *shuffled off:* freed ourselves
from. *this mortal coil:* the turmoil of this mortal life. 67. *respect:* consideration.
68. *of . . . life:* so long-lived. 69. *time:* the world. 74. *his quietus make:* write paid to his
account. 75. *bare bodkin:* mere dagger. *fardels:* burdens. 78. *undiscover'd:* not
disclosed to knowledge; about which men have no information. *bourn:* boundary, i.e.
region. 79. *puzzles:* paralyzes. 82. *conscience:* reflection (but with some of the modern
sense, too).

Hamlet's flaw

And thus the native hue of resolution
Is sicklied o'er with the pale cast of thought, *is this*
And enterprises of great pitch and moment   85
With this regard their currents turn awry,
And lose the name of action.—Soft you now,
The fair Ophelia. Nymph, in thy orisons
Be all my sins rememb'red.

OPHELIA: Good my lord,
How does your honor for this many a day?   90

HAMLET: I humbly thank you, well, [well, well].

OPHELIA: My lord, I have remembrances of yours
That I have longed long to redeliver.
I pray you now receive them.

HAMLET: No, not I,
I never gave you aught.   95

OPHELIA: My honor'd lord, you know right well you did,
And with them words of so sweet breath compos'd
As made these things more rich. Their perfume lost,
Take these again, for to the noble mind
Rich gifts wax poor when givers prove unkind.   100
There, my lord.

HAMLET: Ha, ha! are you honest?

OPHELIA: My lord?

HAMLET: Are you fair?

OPHELIA: What means your lordship?   105

HAMLET: That if you be honest and fair, [your honesty] should
admit no discourse to your beauty.

OPHELIA: Could beauty, my lord, have better commerce than
with honesty?   109

HAMLET: Ay, truly, for the power of beauty will sooner trans-
form honesty from what it is to a bawd than the force of
honesty can translate beauty into his likeness. This was
sometime a paradox, but now the time gives it proof. I
did love you once.   114

OPHELIA: Indeed, my lord, you made me believe so.

HAMLET: You should not have believ'd me, for virtue cannot so
[inoculate] our old stock but we shall relish of it. I lov'd
you not.

OPHELIA: I was the more deceiv'd.   119

HAMLET: Get thee [to] a nunn'ry, why wouldst thou be a
breeder of sinners? I am myself indifferent honest, but

83. *native hue:* natural (ruddy) complexion. 84. *pale cast:* pallor. *thought:* i.e. melancholy
thought, brooding. 85. *pitch:* loftiness (a term from falconry, signifying the highest point
of a hawk's flight). 88. *orisons:* prayers. 102. *honest:* chaste. 113. *sometime:* formerly.
paradox: tenet contrary to accepted belief. 116–17. *virtue . . . it:* virtue, engrafted on our
old stock (of viciousness), cannot so change the nature of the plant that no trace of the
original will remain. 121. *indifferent honest:* tolerably virtuous.

yet I could accuse me of such things that it were better
my mother had not borne me: I am very proud,
revengeful, ambitious, with more offenses at my beck
than I have thoughts to put them in, imagination to   125
give them shape, or time to act them in. What should
such fellows as I do crawling between earth and heav-
en? We are arrant knaves, believe none of us. Go thy
ways to a nunn'ry. Where's your father?   ✕

OPHELIA: At home, my lord.   130

HAMLET: Let the doors be shut upon him, that he may play the
fool no where but in 's own house. Farewell.

OPHELIA: O, help him, you sweet heavens!

HAMLET: If thou dost marry, I'll give thee this plague for thy
dowry: be thou as chaste as ice, as pure as snow,   135
thou shalt not escape calumny. Get thee to a nunn'ry,
farewell. Or if thou wilt needs marry, marry a fool,
for wise men know well enough what monsters you
make of them. To a nunn'ry, go, and quickly too.
Farewell.   140

OPHELIA: Heavenly powers, restore him!

HAMLET: I have heard of your paintings, well enough. God hath
given you one face, and you make yourselves another.
You jig and amble, and you [lisp,] you nickname God's
creatures and make your wantonness [your] ignorance.   145
Go to, I'll no more on't, it hath made me mad. I say we
will have no moe marriage. Those that are married
already (all but one) shall live, the rest shall keep as
they are. To a nunn'ry, go.   *Exit.*   149

OPHELIA: O, what a noble mind is here o'erthrown!
The courtier's, soldier's, scholar's, eye, tongue, sword,
Th' expectation and rose of the fair state,
The glass of fashion and the mould of form,
Th' observ'd of all observers, quite, quite down!
And I, of ladies most deject and wretched,   155
That suck'd the honey of his [music] vows,
Now see [that] noble and most sovereign reason
Like sweet bells jangled out of time, and harsh;
That unmatch'd form and stature of blown youth
Blasted with ecstasy. O, woe is me   160
T' have seen what I have seen, see what I see!
                                    [OPHELIA *withdraws.*]

138. *monsters.* Alluding to the notion that the husbands of unfaithful wives grew horns.
138. *you:* you women.   144–45. *You . . . creatures:* i.e. you walk and talk affectedly.
145. *make . . . ignorance:* excuse your affectation as ignorance.   147. *moe:* more.
152. *expectation:* hope. *rose:* ornament.   *fair.* Probably proleptic: "(the kingdom) made
fair by his presence."   153. *glass:* mirror.   *mould of form:* pattern of (courtly) behavior.
154. *observ'd . . . observers.* Shakespeare uses *observe* to mean not only "behold,
mark attentively" but also "pay honor to."   159. *blown:* in full bloom.   160. *Blasted:*
withered.   *ecstasy:* madness.

Enter KING *and* POLONIUS.

KING: Love? his affections do not that way tend,
Nor what he spake, though it lack'd form a little,
Was not like madness. There's something in his soul
O'er which his melancholy sits on brood,
And I do doubt that hatch and the disclose   165
Will be some danger; which for to prevent,
I have in quick determination
Thus set it down: he shall with speed to England
For the demand of our neglected tribute.
Haply the seas, and countries different,   170
With variable objects, shall expel
This something-settled matter in his heart,
Whereon his brains still beating puts him thus
From fashion of himself. What think you on't?   175

POLONIUS: It shall do well; but yet do I believe
The origin and commencement of his grief
Sprung from neglected love. [OPHELIA *comes forward.*]
          How now, Ophelia?
You need not tell us what Lord Hamlet said,
We heard it all. My lord, do as you please.   180
But if you hold it fit, after the play
Let his queen-mother all alone entreat him
To show his grief. Let her be round with him,
And I'll be plac'd (so please you) in the ear
Of all their conference. If she find him not,   185
To England send him, or confine him where
Your wisdom best shall think.

KING: It shall be so.
Madness in great ones must not [unwatch'd] go.

Exeunt.

The King wants to send Hamlet to England.

Polonius tells K. Claudius to get Gautrude alone w/ Hamlet to find out what she thinks is Hamlet's problem. Polonius' plans to listen to the conversation.

SCENE TWO

Enter HAMLET *and three of the* PLAYERS.

HAMLET: Speak the speech, I pray you, as I pronounc'd it to
you, trippingly on the tongue, but if you mouth it, as
many of our players do, I had as live the town-crier
spoke my lines. Nor do not saw the air too much with
your hand, thus, but use all gently, for in the very   5
torrent, tempest, and, as I may say, whirlwind of your
passion, you must acquire and beget a temperance that

---

162. *affections:* inclinations, feelings. 166. *doubt:* fear. *disclose.* Synonymous with
hatch; see also V.i.287. 178. *neglected:* unrequited. 183. *his grief:* what is troubling him.
round: blunt, outspoken. 185. *find him:* learn the truth about him.
III.ii. Location: The castle.
2. *mouth:* pronounce with exaggerated distinctness or declamatory effect. 3. *live:* lief,
willingly.

may give it smoothness. O, it offends me to the soul to hear a robustious periwig-pated fellow tear a passion to totters, to very rags, to spleet the ears of the groundlings, who for the most part are capable of nothing but inexplicable dumb shows and noise. I would have such a fellow whipt for o'erdoing Termagant, it out-Herods Herod, pray you avoid it.

[FIRST] PLAYER: I warrant your honor.

HAMLET: Be not too tame neither, but let your own discretion be your tutor. Suit the action to the word, the word to the action, with this special observance, that you o'erstep not the modesty of nature: for any thing so o'erdone is from the purpose of playing, whose end, both at the first and now, was and is, to hold as 'twere the mirror up to nature: to show virtue her feature, scorn her own image, and the very age and body of the time his form and pressure. Now this overdone, or come tardy off, though it makes the unskillful laugh, cannot but make the judicious grieve; the censure of which one must in your allowance o'erweigh a whole theatre of others. O, there be players that I have seen play—and heard others [praise], and that highly—not to speak it profanely, that, neither having th' accent of Christians nor the gait of Christian, pagan, nor man, have so strutted and bellow'd that I have thought some of Nature's journeymen had made men, and not made them well, they imitated humanity so abominably.

[FIRST] PLAYER: I hope we have reform'd that indifferently with us, [sir].

HAMLET: O, reform it altogether. And let those that play your clowns speak no more than is set down for them, for there be of them that will themselves laugh to set on some quantity of barren spectators to laugh too, though in the mean time some necessary question of the play be then to be consider'd. That's villainous, and shows a most pitiful ambition in the fool that uses it. Go make you ready.   [*Exeunt* PLAYERS.]

10

15

20

25

30

35

40

45

10. *totters:* tatters.   *spleet:* split.   10. *groundlings:* those who paid the lowest admission price and stood on the ground in the "yard" or pit of the theatre.   *capable of:* able to take in.   13. *Termagant:* a supposed god of the Saracens, whose role in medieval drama, like that of Herod (line 14), was noisy and violent.   19. *modesty:* moderation.   20. *from:* contrary to.   23. *scorn:* i.e. that which is worthy of scorn.   24. *pressure:* impression (as of a seal), exact image.   25. *tardy:* inadequately.   26. *censure:* judgment.   27. *which one:* (even) one of whom.   *allowance:* estimation.   30. *profanely:* irreverently.   33–35. *some . . . abominably:* i.e. they were so unlike men that it seemed Nature had not made them herself, but had delegated the task to mediocre assistants.   36. *indifferently:* pretty well.   40. *of them:* some of them.   44. *fool:* (1) stupid person; (2) actor playing a fool's role.

Enter POLONIUS, GUILDENSTERN, *and* ROSENCRANTZ.

How now, my lord? Will the King hear this piece of
work?

POLONIUS: And the Queen too, and that presently.

HAMLET: Bid the players make haste.   [*Exit* POLONIUS.]
Will you two help to hasten them?   50

ROSENCRANTZ: Ay, my lord.   *Exeunt they two.*

HAMLET: What ho, Horatio!

Enter HORATIO.

HORATIO: Here, sweet lord, at your service.

HAMLET: Horatio, thou art e'en as just a man
As e'er my conversation cop'd withal.   55

HORATIO: O my dear lord—

HAMLET: Nay, do not think I flatter,
For what advancement may I hope from thee
That no revenue hast but thy good spirits
To feed and clothe thee? Why should the poor be flatter'd?
No, let the candied tongue lick absurd pomp,   60
And crook the pregnant hinges of the knee
Where thrift may follow fawning. Dost thou hear?
Since my dear soul was mistress of her choice
And could of men distinguish her election,
Sh' hath seal'd thee for herself, for thou hast been   65
As one in suff'ring all that suffers nothing,
A man that Fortune's buffets and rewards
Hast ta'en with equal thanks; and blest are those
Whose blood and judgment are so well co-meddled,
That they are not a pipe for Fortune's finger   70
To sound what stop she please. Give me that man
That is not passion's slave, and I will wear him
In my heart's core, ay, in my heart of heart,
As I do thee. Something too much of this.
There is a play to-night before the King,   75
One scene of it comes near the circumstance
Which I have told thee of my father's death.
I prithee, when thou seest that act afoot,
Even with the very comment of thy soul
Observe my uncle. If his occulted guilt   80
Do not itself unkennel in one speech,

46–47. *piece of work:* masterpiece (said jocularly). **48.** *presently:* at once. **54.** *thou . . .
man:* i.e. you come as close to being what a man should be (*just* = exact, precise).
55. *my . . . withal:* my association with people has brought me into contact with.
60. *candied:* sugared, i.e. flattering. *absurd:* tasteless (Latin sense). **61.** *pregnant:* moving
readily. **62.** *thrift:* thriving, profit. **69.** *blood:* passions. *co-meddled:* mixed, blended.
73. *my heart of heart:* the heart of my heart. **79.** *very . . . soul:* your most intense critical
observation. **80.** *occulted:* hidden. **81.** *unkennel:* bring into the open.

It is a damned ghost that we have seen,
And my imaginations are as foul
As Vulcan's stithy. Give him heedful note,
For I mine eyes will rivet to his face,   85
And after we will both our judgments join
In censure of his seeming.

HORATIO: Well, my lord.
If 'a steal aught the whilst this play is playing,
And scape [detecting], I will pay the theft.

> [Sound a flourish. Danish march.] Enter Trumpets and
> Kettle-drums, KING, QUEEN, POLONIUS, OPHELIA, [ROSEN-
> CRANTZ, GUILDENSTERN, and other LORDS attendant, with his
> GUARD carrying torches].

HAMLET: They are coming to the play. I must be idle;   90
Get you a place.

KING: How fares our cousin Hamlet?

HAMLET: Excellent, i' faith, of the chameleon's dish: I
eat the air, promise-cramm'd—you cannot feed capons
so.   95

KING: I have nothing with this answer, Hamlet, these words
are not mine.

HAMLET: No, nor mine now. [To POLONIUS.] My lord, you
play'd once i' th' university, you say?

POLONIUS: That did I, my lord, and was accounted a good
actor.   101

HAMLET: What did you enact?

POLONIUS: I did enact Julius Caesar. I was kill'd i' th' Capitol;
Brutus kill'd me.

HAMLET: It was a brute part of him to kill so capital a calf there.
Be the players ready?   106

ROSENCRANTZ: Ay, my lord, they stay upon your patience.

QUEEN: Come hither, my dear Hamlet, sit by me.

HAMLET: No, good mother, here's metal more attrac-
tive.   [Lying down at OPHELIA's feet.]

POLONIUS [To the KING.]: O ho, do you mark that?   111

HAMLET: Lady, shall I lie in your lap?

OPHELIA: No, my lord.

[HAMLET: I mean, my head upon your lap?

OPHELIA: Ay, my lord.]   115

---

82. damned ghost: evil spirit, devil. 84. stithy: forge. 87. censure . . . seeming: reaching a
verdict on his behavior. 90. be idle: act foolish, pretend to be crazy. 92. fares. Hamlet
takes up this word in another sense. 93. chameleon's dish. Chameleons were thought to
feed on air. Hamlet says that he subsists on an equally nourishing diet, the promise of
succession. There is probably a pun on air/heir. 96. have nothing with: do not understand.
97. mine: i.e. an answer to my question. 105. part: action.

HAMLET: Do you think I meant country matters?

OPHELIA: I think nothing, my lord.

HAMLET: That's a fair thought to lie between maids' legs.

OPHELIA: What is, my lord?   120

HAMLET: Nothing.

OPHELIA: You are merry, my lord.

HAMLET: Who, I?

OPHELIA: Ay, my lord.   124

HAMLET: O God, your only jig-maker. What should a man do but be merry, for look you how cheerfully my mother looks, and my father died within 's two hours.

OPHELIA: Nay, 'tis twice two months, my lord.

HAMLET: So long? Nay then let the dev'l wear black, for I'll have a suit of sables. O heavens, die two months ago,   130 and not forgotten yet? Then there's hope a great man's memory may outlive his life half a year, but, by'r lady, 'a must build churches then, or else shall 'a suffer not thinking on, with the hobby-horse, whose epitaph is, "For O, for O, the hobby-horse is forgot."

> *The trumpets sounds. Dumb show follows.*
> *Enter a* KING *and a* QUEEN [*very lovingly*], *the* QUEEN *embracing him and he her.* [*She kneels and makes show of protestation unto him.*] *He takes her up and declines his head upon her neck. He lies him down upon a bank of flowers. She, seeing him asleep, leaves him. Anon come in another man, takes off his crown, kisses it, pours poison in the sleeper's ears, and leaves him. The* QUEEN *returns, finds the* KING *dead, makes passionate action. The pois'ner with some three or four* [*mutes*] *come in again, seem to condole with her. The dead body is carried away. The pois'ner woos the* QUEEN *with gifts; she seems harsh* [*and unwilling*] *awhile, but in the end accepts love.* [*Exeunt.*]

OPHELIA: What means this, my lord?   136

HAMLET: Marry, this' [miching] mallecho, it means mischief.

OPHELIA: Belike this show imports the argument of the play.   140

116. *country matters:* indecency.   125. *only:* very best.   *jig-maker:* one who composed or played in the farcical song-and-dance entertainments that followed plays.   127. *'s:* this.   129–30. *let . . . sables:* i.e. to the devil with my garments; after so long a time I am ready for the old man's garb of sables (fine fur).   133–134. *not thinking on:* not being thought of, i.e. being forgotten.   135. *For . . . forgot:* line from a popular ballad lamenting puritanical suppression of such country sports as the May-games, in which the hobby-horse, a character costumed to resemble a horse, traditionally appeared.   137. *this' miching mallecho:* this is sneaking mischief.   139. *argument:* subject, plot.

Enter PROLOGUE.

HAMLET: We shall know by this fellow. The players cannot
keep [counsel], they'll tell all.

OPHELIA: Will 'a tell us what this show meant?

HAMLET: Ay, or any show that you will show him. Be not you
asham'd to show, he'll not shame to tell you what it
means.   146

OPHELIA: You are naught, you are naught. I'll mark the
play.

PROLOGUE:

    For us, and for our tragedy,
    Here stooping to your clemency,   150
    We beg your hearing patiently.   [*Exit.*]

HAMLET: Is this a prologue, or the posy of a ring?

OPHELIA: 'Tis brief, my lord.

HAMLET: As woman's love.

Enter [*two Players,*] KING *and* QUEEN.

[PLAYER] KING: Full thirty times hath Phoebus' cart gone round   155
    Neptune's salt wash and Tellus' orbed ground,
    And thirty dozen moons with borrowed sheen
    About the world have times twelve thirties been,
    Since love our hearts and Hymen did our hands
    Unite comutual in most sacred bands.   160

[PLAYER] QUEEN: So many journeys may the sun and moon
    Make us again count o'er ere love be done!
    But woe is me, you are so sick of late,
    So far from cheer and from [your] former state,
    That I distrust you. Yet though I distrust,   165
    Discomfort you, my lord, it nothing must,
    [For] women's fear and love hold quantity,
    In neither aught, or in extremity.
    Now what my [love] is, proof hath made you know,
    And as my love is siz'd, my fear is so.   170
    Where love is great, the littlest doubts are fear;
    Where little fears grow great, great love grows there.

[PLAYER] KING: Faith, I must leave thee, love, and shortly too;
    My operant powers their functions leave to do,
    And thou shalt live in this fair world behind,   175
    Honor'd, belov'd, and haply one as kind
    For husband shalt thou—

---

142. *counsel:* secrets. 144. *Be not you:* if you are not. 147. *naught:* wicked. 152. *posy
. . . ring:* verse motto inscribed in a ring (necessarily short). 155. *Phoebus' cart:* the
sun-god's chariot. 156. *Tellus:* goddess of the earth. 159. *Hymen:* god of marriage.
160. *bands:* bonds. 165. *distrust:* fear for. 167. *hold quantity:* are related in direct proportion. 169. *proof:* experience. 174. *operant:* active, vital. *leave to do:* cease to perform.

[PLAYER] QUEEN: O, confound the rest!
    Such love must needs be treason in my breast.
    In second husband let me be accurs'd!
    None wed the second but who kill'd the first.   180

HAMLET [*Aside.*]: That's wormwood!

[PLAYER] QUEEN: The instances that second marriage move
    Are base respects of thrift, but none of love.
    A second time I kill my husband dead,
    When second husband kisses me in bed.   185

[PLAYER] KING: I do believe you think what now you speak,
    But what we do determine, oft we break.
    Purpose is but the slave to memory,
    Of violent birth, but poor validity,
    Which now, the fruit unripe, sticks on the tree,   190
    But fall unshaken when they mellow be.
    Most necessary 'tis that we forget
    To pay ourselves what to ourselves is debt.
    What to ourselves in passion we propose,
    The passion ending, doth the purpose lose.   195
    The violence of either grief or joy
    Their own enactures with themselves destroy.
    Where joy most revels, grief doth most lament;
    Grief [joys], joy grieves, on slender accident.
    This world is not for aye, nor 'tis not strange   200
    That even our loves should with our fortunes change:
    For 'tis a question left us yet to prove,
    Whether love lead fortune, or else fortune love.
    The great man down, you mark his favorite flies,
    The poor advanc'd makes friends of enemies.   205
    And hitherto doth love on fortune tend,
    For who not needs shall never lack a friend,
    And who in want a hollow friend doth try,
    Directly seasons him his enemy.
    But orderly to end where I begun,   210
    Our wills and fates do so contrary run
    That our devices still are overthrown,
    Our thoughts are ours, their ends none of our own:
    So think thou wilt no second husband wed,
    But die thy thoughts when thy first lord is dead.   215

[PLAYER] QUEEN: Nor earth to me give food, nor heaven light,
    Sport and repose lock from me day and night,

---

177. *confound the rest:* may destruction befall what you are about to speak of—a second marriage on my part.   182. *instances:* motives.   *move:* give rise to.   183. *respects of thrift:* considerations of advantage.   189. *validity:* strength, power to last.   192–93. *Most . . . debt:* i.e. such resolutions are debts we owe to ourselves, and it would be foolish to pay such debts.   194. *passion:* violent emotion.   196–97. *The violence . . . destroy:* i.e. both violent grief and violent joy fail of their intended acts because they destroy themselves by their very violence.   199. *slender accident:* slight occasion.   209. *seasons:* ripens, converts into.   212. *devices:* devisings, intentions.   *still:* always.

To desperation turn my trust and hope,
[An] anchor's cheer in prison be my scope!
Each opposite that blanks the face of joy   220
Meet what I would have well and it destroy!
Both here and hence pursue me lasting strife,
If once I be a widow, ever I be a wife!

HAMLET: If she should break it now!

[PLAYER] KING: 'Tis deeply sworn. Sweet, leave me here a while,   225
My spirits grow dull, and fain I would beguile
The tedious day with sleep.   [Sleeps.]

[PLAYER] QUEEN: Sleep rock thy brain,
And never come mischance between us twain!   Exit.

HAMLET: Madam, how like you this play?

QUEEN: The lady doth protest too much, methinks.

HAMLET: O but she'll keep her word.   231

KING: Have you heard the argument? is there no offense
in't?

HAMLET: No, no, they do but jest, poison in jest—no offense i'
the' world.   235

KING: What do you call the play?

HAMLET: "The Mouse-trap." Marry, how? tropically: this play
is the image of a murther done in Vienna; Gonzago is
the duke's name, his wife, Baptista. You shall see anon.
'Tis a knavish piece of work, but what of that? Your   240
Majesty, and we that have free souls, it touches us
not. Let the gall'd jade winch, our withers are unwrung.

                        Enter LUCIANUS.

This is one Lucianus, nephew to the king.

OPHELIA: You are as good as a chorus, my lord.   245

HAMLET: I could interpret between you and your love, if I could
see the puppets dallying.

OPHELIA: You are keen, my lord, you are keen.

HAMLET: It would cost you a groaning to take off mine
edge.   250

OPHELIA: Still better, and worse.

---

219. *anchor's cheer:* hermit's fare.   *my scope:* the extent of my comforts.   220. *blanks:*
blanches, makes pale (a symptom of grief).   233. *offense:* offensive matter (but Hamlet
quibbles on the sense "crime").   234. *jest:* i.e. pretend.   237. *tropically:* figuratively (with
play on *tropically*—which is the reading of Q1—and probably with allusion to the children's
saying *marry trap,* meaning "now you're caught").   238. *image:* representation.   241. *free
souls:* clear consciences.   242. *gall'd jade:* chafed horse.   *winch:* wince.   *withers:* ridge
between a horse's shoulders.   *unwrung:* not rubbed sore.   245. *chorus:* i.e. one who
explains the forthcoming action.   246–47. *I . . . dallying:* I could speak the dialogue between you and your lover like a puppet-master (with an indecent jest).   248. *keen:* bitter,
sharp.   251. *better, and worse:* i.e. more pointed and less decent.

HAMLET: So you mistake your husbands. Begin, murtherer,
leave thy damnable faces and begin. Come, the croaking raven doth bellow for revenge.

LUCIANUS: Thoughts black, hands apt, drugs fit, and time agreeing,   255
[Confederate] season, else no creature seeing,
Thou mixture rank, of midnight weeds collected,
With Hecat's ban thrice blasted, thrice [infected],
Thy natural magic and dire property
On wholesome life unsurps immediately.   260

[Pours the poison in his ears.]

HAMLET: 'A poisons him i' th' garden for his estate. His name's
Gonzago, the story is extant, and written in very choice
Italian. You shall see anon how the murtherer gets the
love of Gonzago's wife.

OPHELIA: The King rises.   265

[HAMLET: What, frighted with false fire?]

QUEEN: How fares my lord?

POLONIUS: Give o'er the play.

KING: Give me some light. Away!

POLONIUS: Lights, lights, lights!   270

Exeunt all but HAMLET *and* HORATIO.

HAMLET:

"Why, let the strooken deer go weep,
The hart ungalled play,
For some must watch while some must sleep,
Thus runs the world away."   274

Would not this, sir, and a forest of feathers—if the rest
of my fortunes turn Turk with me—with [two] Provincial roses on my raz'd shoes, get me a fellowship in a
cry of players?

HORATIO: Half a share.

HAMLET: A whole one, I.   280

"For thou dost know, O Damon dear,
This realm dismantled was
Of Jove himself, and now reigns here
A very, very"—pajock.

HORATIO: You might have rhym'd.   285

---

252. *So:* i.e. "for better, for worse," in the words of the marriage service. *mistake:* i.e. mis-take, take wrongfully. Their vows, Hamlet suggests, prove false. **253.** *faces:* facial expressions. **254.** *the croaking . . . revenge.* Misquoted from an old play, *The True Tragedy of Richard III.* **256.** *Confederate season:* the time being my ally. **258.** *Hecat's ban:* the curse of Hecate, goddess of witchcraft. **266.** *false fire:* i.e. a blank cartridge. **271.** *strooken:* struck, i.e. wounded. **272.** *ungalled:* unwounded. **273.** *watch:* stay awake. **275.** *feathers:* the plumes worn by tragic actors. **276.** *turn Turk:* i.e. go to the bad. **276–77.** *Provincial roses:* rosettes designed to look like a variety of French rose. **277.** *raz'd:* with decorating slashing. *fellowship:* partnership. **278.** *cry:* company. **282.** *dismantled:* divested, deprived. **284.** *pajock:* peacock (substituting for the rhyme-word *ass*). The natural history of the time attributed many vicious qualities to the peacock.

HAMLET: O good Horatio, I'll take the ghost's word for a thousand pound. Didst perceive?

HORATIO: Very well, my lord.

HAMLET: Upon the talk of the pois'ning?

HORATIO: I did very well note him.   290

HAMLET: Ah, ha! Come, some music! Come, the recorders!
        For if the King like not the comedy,
        Why then belike he likes it not, perdy.
Come, some music!   295

Enter ROSENCRANTZ *and* GUILDENSTERN.

GUILDENSTERN: Good my lord, voutsafe me a word with you.

HAMLET: Sir, a whole history.

GUILDENSTERN: The King, sir—

HAMLET: Ay, sir, what of him?   300

GUILDENSTERN: Is in his retirement marvellous distemp'red.

HAMLET: With drink, sir?

GUILDENSTERN: No, my lord, with choler.

HAMLET: Your wisdom should show itself more richer to signify this to the doctor, for for me to put him to his purgation would perhaps plunge him into more choler.   307

GUILDENSTERN: Good my lord, put your discourse into some frame, and [start] not so wildly from my affair.

HAMLET: I am tame, sir. Pronounce.   310

GUILDENSTERN: The Queen, your mother, in most great affliction of spirit, hath sent me to you.

HAMLET: You are welcome.

GUILDENSTERN: Nay, good my lord, this courtesy is not of the right breed. If it shall please you to make me a   315
wholesome answer, I will do your mother's commandement; if not, your pardon and my return shall be the end of [my] business.

HAMLET: Sir, I cannot.

ROSENCRANTZ: What, my lord?   320

HAMLET: Make you a wholesome answer—my wit's diseas'd. But, sir, such answer as I can make, you shall command, or rather, as you say, my mother. Therefore no more, but to the matter: my mother, you say—   325

---

294. *perdy:* assuredly (French *pardieu,* "by God"). **303.** *choler:* anger (but Hamlet willfully takes up the word in the sense "biliousness"). **305–6.** *put . . . purgation:* i.e. prescribe for what's wrong with him. **309.** *frame:* logical structure. **316.** *wholesome:* sensible, rational. **317.** *pardon:* permission for departure.

ROSENCRANTZ: Then thus she says: your behavior hath strook
 her into amazement and admiration.

HAMLET: O wonderful son, that can so stonish a mother! But is
 there no sequel at the heels of this mother's admira-
 tion? Impart.   330

ROSENCRANTZ: She desires to speak with you in her closet ere
 you go to bed.

HAMLET: We shall obey, were she ten times our mother. Have
 you any further trade with us.

ROSENCRANTZ: My lord, you once did love me.   335

HAMLET: And do still, by these pickers and stealers.

ROSENCRANTZ: Good my lord, what is your cause of distemper?
 You do surely bar the door upon your own liberty if you
 deny your griefs to your friend.

HAMLET: Sir, I lack advancement.   340

ROSENCRANTZ: How can that be, when you have the voice of
 the King himself for your succession in Denmark?

HAMLET: Ay, sir, but "While the grass grows"—the proverb is
 something musty.   344

   Enter the PLAYERS *with recorders.*

 O, the recorders! Let me see one.—To withdraw with
 you—why do you go about to recover the wind of me,
 as if you would drive me into a toil?

GUILDENSTERN: O my lord, if my duty be too bold, my love is
 too unmannerly.   349

HAMLET: I do not well understand that. Will you play upon this
 pipe?

GUILDENSTERN: My lord, I cannot.

HAMLET: I pray you.

GUILDENSTERN: Believe me, I cannot.

HAMLET: I do beseech you.   355

GUILDENSTERN: I know no touch of it, my lord.

HAMLET: It is as easy as lying. Govern these ventages with
 your fingers and [thumbs], give it breath with your
 mouth, and it will discourse most eloquent music. Look
 you, these are the stops.   360

GUILDENSTERN: But these cannot I command to any utt'rance
 of harmony. I have not the skill.

---

327. *amazement and admiration:* bewilderment and wonder. **328.** *stonish:* astound.
331. *closet:* private room. **336.** *pickers and stealers:* hands; which, as the Catechism says,
we must keep "from picking and stealing." **343.** *proverb:* i.e. "While the grass grows, the
steed starves." **344.** *something musty:* somewhat stale. **346.** *recover the wind:* get to
windward. **347.** *toil:* snare. **357.** *ventages:* stops.

HAMLET: Why, look you now, how unworthy a thing you make
of me! You would play upon me, you would seem to
know my stops, you would pluck out the heart of my   365
mystery, you would sound me from my lowest note to
[the top of] my compass; and there is much music,
excellent voice, in this little organ, yet cannot you make
it speak. 'Sblood, do you think I am easier to be play'd
on than a pipe? Call me what instrument you   370
will, though you fret me, [yet] you cannot play upon
me.

      Enter POLONIUS.

God bless you, sir.
POLONIUS: My lord, the Queen would speak with you, and
presently.   375
HAMLET: Do you see yonder cloud that's almost in shape of a
camel?
POLONIUS: By th' mass and 'tis, like a camel indeed.
HAMLET: Methinks it is like a weasel.
POLONIUS: It is back'd like a weasel.   380
HAMLET: Or like a whale.
POLONIUS: Very like a whale.
HAMLET: Then I will come to my mother by and by. [*Aside.*]
They fool me to the top of my bent.—I will come by
and by.   385
POLONIUS: I will say so.   [*Exit.*]
HAMLET: "By and by" is easily said. Leave me, friends.
                         [*Exeunt all but* HAMLET.]
'Tis now the very witching time of night,
When churchyards yawn and hell itself [breathes] out
Contagion to this world. Now could I drink hot blood,
And do such [bitter business as the] day   391
Would quake to look on. Soft, now to my mother.
O heart, lose not thy nature! let not ever
The soul of Nero enter this firm bosom,
Let me be cruel, not unnatural;   395
I will speak [daggers] to her, but use none.
My tongue and soul in this be hypocrites—
How in my words somever she be shent,
To give them seals never my soul consent!   *Exit.*

---

368. *organ:* instrument.   **371.** *fret:* (1) finger (an instrument); (2) vex.   **375.** *presently:* at
once.   **384.** *They . . . bent:* they make me play the fool to the limit of my ability.
384–85. *by and by:* at once.   **388.** *witching:* i.e. when the powers of evil are at large.
393. *nature:* natural affection, filial feeling.   **394.** *Nero.* Murderer of his mother.   **398.** *shent:*
rebuked.   **399.** *give them seals:* confirm them by deeds.

SCENE THREE

Enter KING, ROSENCRANTZ, *and* GUILDENSTERN.

KING: I like him not, nor stands it safe with us
To let his madness range. Therefore prepare you.
I your commission will forthwith dispatch,
And he to England shall along with you.
The terms of our estate may not endure
Hazard so near 's as doth hourly grow
Out of his brows.

GUILDENSTERN: We will ourselves provide.
Most holy and religious fear it is
To keep those many many bodies safe
That live and feed upon your Majesty.

ROSENCRANTZ: The single and peculiar life is bound
With all the strength and armor of the mind
To keep itself from noyance, but much more
That spirit upon whose weal depends and rests
The lives of many. The cess of majesty
Dies not alone, but like a gulf doth draw
What's near it with it. Or it is a massy wheel
Fix'd on the summit of the highest mount,
To whose [huge] spokes ten thousand lesser things
Are mortis'd and adjoin'd, which when it falls,
Each small annexment, petty consequence,
Attends the boist'rous [ruin]. Never alone
Did the King sigh, but [with] a general groan.

KING: Arm you, I pray you, to this speedy viage,
For we will fetters put about this fear,
Which now goes too free-footed.

ROSENCRANTZ: We will haste us.
Exeunt GENTLEMEN [ROSENCRANTZ *and* GUILDENSTERN].

Enter POLONIUS.

POLONIUS: My lord, he's going to his mother's closet.
Behind the arras I'll convey myself
To hear the process. I'll warrant she'll tax him home,
And as you said, and wisely was it said,
'Tis meet that some more audience than a mother,
Since nature makes them partial, should o'erhear

[margin, handwritten] King makes up his mind to definitely, to send Hamlet to England along w/ Guildenstern and Rosencrantz.

5

10

15

20

25

30

III.iii. Location: The castle.
1. *him:* i.e. his state of mind, his behavior.   3. *dispatch:* have drawn up.   5. *terms:*
conditions, nature.   *our estate:* my position (as king).   7. *his brows:* the madness visible in
his face (?).   8. *fear:* concern.   11. *single and peculiar:* individual and private.   13. *noyance:* injury.   15. *cess:* cessation, death.   16. *gulf:* whirlpool.   20. *mortis'd:* fixed.
22. *Attends:* accompanies.   *ruin:* fall.   24. *Arm:* prepare.   *viage:* voyage.   25. *fear:* object
of fear.   29. *process:* course of the talk.   *tax him home:* take him severely to task.

The speech, of vantage. Fare you well, my liege,
I'll call upon you ere you go to bed,
And tell you what I know.

KING: Thanks, dear my lord.   35

Exit [POLONIUS].

O, my offense is rank, it smells to heaven,
It hath the primal eldest curse upon't,
A brother's murther. Pray can I not,
Though inclination be as sharp as will.
My stronger guilt defeats my strong intent,   40
And, like a man to double business bound,
I stand in pause where I shall first begin,
And both neglect. What if this cursed hand
Were thicker than itself with brother's blood,
Is there not rain enough in the sweet heavens   45
To wash it white as snow? Whereto serves mercy
But to confront the visage of offense?
And what's in prayer but this twofold force,
To be forestalled ere we come to fall,
Or [pardon'd] being down? then I'll look up.   50
My fault is past, but, O, what form of prayer
Can serve my turn? "Forgive me my foul murther"?
That cannot be, since I am still possess'd
Of those effects for which I did the murther:
My crown, mine own ambition, and my queen.   55
May one be pardon'd and retain th' offense?
In the corrupted currents of this world
Offense's gilded hand may [shove] by justice,
And oft 'tis seen the wicked prize itself
Buys out the law, but 'tis not so above: 60
There is no shuffling, there the action lies
In his true nature, and we ourselves compell'd,
Even to the teeth and forehead of our faults,
To give in evidence. What then? What rests?
Try what repentance can. What can it not?   65
Yet what can it, when one can not repent?
O wretched state! O bosom black as death!
O limed soul, that struggling to be free
Art more engag'd! Help, angels! Make assay,
Bow, stubborn knees, and heart, with strings of steel,

---

33. *of vantage:* from an advantageous position (?) or in addition (?).   **37.** *primal eldest curse:* i.e. God's curse on Cain, who also slew his brother.   **39.** *Though . . . will:* though my desire is as strong as my resolve to do so.   **41.** *bound:* committed.   **43.** *neglect:* omit.   **46–47.** *Whereto . . . offense:* i.e. what function has mercy except when there has been sin.   **56.** *th' offense:* i.e. the "effects" or fruits of the offense.   **57.** *currents:* courses. **58.** *gilded:* i.e. bribing.   **59.** *wicked prize:* rewards of vice.   **61.** *shuffling:* evasion.   *the action lies:* the charge comes for legal consideration.   **63.** *Even . . . forehead:* i.e. fully recognizing their features, extenuating nothing.   **64.** *rests:* remains.   **68.** *limed:* caught (as in birdlime, a sticky substance used for catching birds).   **69.** *engag'd:* entangled.

Be soft as sinews of the new-born babe! 71
All may be well. *[He kneels.]*

Enter HAMLET.

HAMLET: Now might I do it [pat], now 'a is a-praying;
And now I'll do't—and so 'a goes to heaven,
And so am I [reveng'd]. That would be scann'd: 75
A villain kills my father, and for that
I, his sole son, do this same villain send
To heaven.
Why, this is [hire and salary], not revenge.
'A took my father grossly, full of bread, 80
With all his crimes broad blown, as flush as May,
And how his audit stands who knows save heaven?
But in our circumstance and course of thought
'Tis heavy with him. And am I then revenged,
To take him in the purging of his soul, 85
When he is fit and season'd for his passage?
No!
Up, sword, and know thou a more horrid hent:
When he is drunk asleep, or in his rage,
Or in th' incestious pleasure of his bed, 90
At game a-swearing, or about some act
That has no relish of salvation in't—
Then trip him, that his heels may kick at heaven,
And that his soul may be as damn'd and black
As hell, whereto it goes. My mother stays, 95
This physic but prolongs thy sickly days. *Exit.*

KING [*Rising.*]: My words fly up, my thoughts remain below:
Words without thoughts never to heaven go. *Exit.*

SCENE FOUR

Enter [QUEEN] GERTRUDE *and* POLONIUS.

POLONIUS: 'A will come straight. Look you lay home to him.
Tell him his pranks have been too broad to bear with,
And that your Grace hath screen'd and stood between
Much heat and him. I'll silence me even here;
Pray you be round [with him]. 5

QUEEN: I'll [warr'nt] you, fear me not. Withdraw,
I hear him coming. *[POLONIUS hides behind the arras.]*

75. *would be scann'd:* must be carefully considered. **80.** *grossly:* in a gross state; not spiritually prepared. **81.** *crimes:* sins. *broad blown:* in full bloom. *flush:* lusty, vigorous. **82.** *audit:* account. **83.** *in . . . thought:* i.e. to the best of our knowledge and belief. **88.** *Up:* into the sheath. *know . . . hent:* be grasped at a more dreadful time. **92.** *relish:* trace. **96.** *physic:* (attempted) remedy, i.e. prayer.
III.iv. Location: The Queen's closet in the castle.
1. *lay . . . him:* reprove him severely. **2.** *broad:* unrestrained. **5.** *round:* plain-spoken.
6. *fear me not:* have no fears about my handling of the situation.

Enter HAMLET.

HAMLET: Now, mother, what's the matter?

QUEEN: Hamlet, thou hast thy father much offended.

HAMLET: Mother, you have my father much offended.   10

QUEEN: Come, come, you answer with an idle tongue.

HAMLET: Go, go, you question with a wicked tongue.

QUEEN: Why, how now, Hamlet?

HAMLET: What's the matter now?

QUEEN: Have you forgot me?

HAMLET: No, by the rood, not so:
You are the Queen, your husband's brother's wife,
And would it were not so, you are my mother.   16

QUEEN: Nay, then I'll set those to you that can speak.

HAMLET: Come, come, and sit you down, you shall not boudge;
You go not till I set you up a glass
Where you may see the [inmost] part of you.   20

QUEEN: What wilt thou do? Thou wilt not murther me?
Help ho!

POLONIUS [*Behind.*]: What ho, help!

HAMLET [*Drawing.*]: How now? A rat? Dead, for a ducat, dead!
[*Kills* POLONIUS *through the arras.*]

POLONIUS [*Behind.*]: O, I am slain.

QUEEN: O me, what hast thou done?

HAMLET: Nay, I know not, is it the King?   26

QUEEN: O, what a rash and bloody deed is this!

HAMLET: A bloody deed! almost as bad, good mother,
As kill a king, and marry with his brother.

QUEEN: As kill a king!

HAMLET: Ay, lady, it was my word.
[*Parts the arras and discovers* POLONIUS.]
Thou wretched, rash, intruding fool, farewell!   31
I took thee for thy better. Take thy fortune;
Thou find'st to be too busy is some danger.—
Leave wringing of your hands. Peace, sit you down,
And let me wring your heart, for so I shall   35
If it be made of penetrable stuff,
If damned custom have not brass'd it so
That it be proof and bulwark against sense.

QUEEN: What have I done, that thou dar'st wag thy tongue
In noise so rude against me?

---

11. *idle:* foolish. 14. *rood:* cross. 18. *boudge:* budge. 24. *for a ducat:* I'll wager a
ducat. 33. *busy:* officious, meddlesome. 37. *damned custom:* i.e. the habit of ill-
doing. *brass'd:* hardened, literally, plated with brass. 38. *proof:* armor. *sense:* feeling.

HAMLET: Such an act   40
  That blurs the grace and blush of modesty,
  Calls virtue hypocrite, takes off the rose
  From the fair forehead of an innocent love
  And sets a blister there, makes marriage vows
  As false as dicers' oaths, O, such a deed   45
  As from the body of contraction plucks
  The very soul, and sweet religion makes
  A rhapsody of words. Heaven's face does glow
  O'er this solidity and compound mass
  With heated visage, as against the doom;   50
  Is thought-sick at the act.

QUEEN: Ay me, what act,
  That roars so loud and thunders in the index?

HAMLET: Look here upon this picture, and on this,
  The counterfeit presentment of two brothers.
  See what a grace was seated on this brow: 55
  Hyperion's curls, the front of Jove himself,
  An eye like Mars, to threaten and command,
  A station like the herald Mercury
  New lighted on a [heaven-]kissing hill,
  A combination and a form indeed,   60
  Where every god did seem to set his seal
  To give the world assurance of a man.
  This was your husband. Look you now what follows:
  Here is your husband, like a mildewed ear,
  Blasting his wholesome brother. Have you eyes?   65
  Could you on this fair mountain leave to feed,
  And batten on this moor? ha, have you eyes?
  You cannot call it love, for at your age
  The heyday in the blood is tame, it's humble,
  And waits upon the judgment, and what judgment   70
  Would step from this to this? Sense sure you have,
  Else could you not have motion, but sure that sense
  Is apoplex'd, for madness would not err,
  Nor sense to ecstasy was ne'er so thrall'd
  But it reserv'd some quantity of choice   75
  To serve in such a difference. What devil was't
  That thus hath cozen'd you at hoodman-blind?

---

44. *blister:* brand of shame.   **46.** *contraction:* the making of contracts, i.e. the assuming of solemn obligation.   **47.** *religion:* i.e. sacred vows.   **48.** *rhapsody:* miscellaneous collection, jumble.   *glow:* i.e. with anger.   **49.** *this . . . mass:* i.e. the earth. *Compound* = compounded of the four elements.   **50.** *as . . . doom:* as if for Judgment Day.   **52.** *index:* i.e. table of contents. The index was formerly placed at the beginning of a book.   **54.** *counterfeit presentment:* painted likenesses.   **56.** *Hyperion's:* the sun-god's.   *front:* forehead.   **58.** *station:* bearing.   **64.** *ear:* i.e. of grain.   **67.** *batten:* gorge.   **69.** *heyday:* excitement.
71. *Sense:* sense perception, the five senses.   **73.** *apoplex'd:* paralyzed.   **73–76.** *madness . . . difference:* i.e. madness itself could not go so far astray, nor were the senses ever so enslaved by lunacy that they did not retain the power to make so obvious a distinction.
77. *cozen'd:* cheated.   *hoodman-blind:* blindman's bluff.

Eyes without feeling, feeling without sight,
Ears without hands or eyes, smelling sans all,
Or but a sickly part of one true sense   80
Could not so mope. O shame, where is thy blush?
Rebellious hell,
If thou canst mutine in a matron's bones,
To flaming youth let virtue be as wax
And melt in her own fire. Proclaim no shame   85
When the compulsive ardure gives the charge,
Since frost itself as actively doth burn,
And reason [panders] will.
QUEEN: O Hamlet, speak no more!
Thou turn'st my [eyes into my very] soul,
And there I see such black and [grained] spots   90
As will [not] leave their tinct.
HAMLET: Nay, but to live
In the rank sweat of an enseamed bed,
Stew'd in corruption, honeying and making love
Over the nasty sty!
QUEEN: O, speak to me no more!
These words like daggers enter in my ears.   95
No more, sweet Hamlet!
HAMLET: A murtherer and a villain!
A slave that is not twentith part the [tithe]
Of your precedent lord, a Vice of kings,
A cutpurse of the empire and the rule,
That from a shelf the precious diadem stole,   100
And put it in his pocket—
QUEEN: No more!

Enter GHOST [*in his night-gown*].

HAMLET: A king of shreds and patches—
Save me, and hover o'er me with your wings,
You heavenly guards! What would your gracious figure?
QUEEN: Alas, he's mad!   105
HAMLET: Do you not come your tardy son to chide,
That, laps'd in time and passion, lets go by
Th' important acting of your dread command?
O, say!
GHOST: Do not forget! This visitation   110
Is but to whet thy almost blunted purpose

---

79. *sans:* without. 81. *mope:* be dazed. 83. *mutine:* rebel. 85–88. *Proclaim . . . will:* do not call it sin when the hot blood of youth is responsible for lechery, since here we see people of calmer age on fire for it; and reason acts as procurer for desire, instead of restraining it. *Ardure* = ardor. 90. *grained:* fast-dyed, indelible. 91. *leave their tinct:* lose their color. 92. *enseamed:* greasy. 97. *twentith:* twentieth. 98. *precedent:* former. *Vice:* buffoon (like the Vice of the morality plays). 101 s.d. *night-gown:* dressing gown. 102. *of . . . patches:* clownish (alluding to the motley worn by jesters) (?) or patched-up, beggarly (?). 107. *laps'd . . . passion:* "having suffered time to slip and passion to cool" (Johnson). 108. *important:* urgent.

But look amazement on thy mother sits,
O, step between her and her fighting soul.
Conceit in weakest bodies strongest works,
Speak to her, Hamlet.

HAMLET: How is it with you, lady?   115

QUEEN: Alas, how is't with you,
That you do bend your eye on vacancy,
And with th' incorporal air do hold discourse?
Forth at your eyes your spirits wildly peep,
And as the sleeping soldiers in th' alarm,   120
Your bedded hair, like life in excrements,
Start up and stand an end. O gentle son,
Upon the heat and flame of thy distemper
Sprinkle cool patience. Whereon do you look?

HAMLET: On him, on him! look you how pale he glares!   125
His form and cause conjoin'd, preaching to stones,
Would make them capable.—Do not look upon me,
Lest with this piteous action you convert
My stern effects, then what I have to do
Will want true color—tears perchance for blood.   130

QUEEN: To whom do you speak this?

HAMLET: Do you see nothing there?

QUEEN: Nothing at all, yet all that is I see.

HAMLET: Nor did you nothing hear?

QUEEN: No, nothing but ourselves.

HAMLET: Why, look you there, look how it steals away!
My father, in his habit as he lived!   135
Look where he goes, even now, out at the portal!

                                                              Exit GHOST.

QUEEN: This is the very coinage of your brain,
This bodiless creation ecstasy
Is very cunning in.

HAMLET: [Ecstasy?]
My pulse as yours doth temperately keep time,   140
And makes as healthful music. It is not madness
That I have utt'red. Bring me to the test,
And [I] the matter will reword, which madness
Would gambol from. Mother, for love of grace,
Lay not that flattering unction to your soul,   145
That not your trespass but my madness speaks;
It will but skin and film the ulcerous place,

---

112. *amazement:* utter bewilderment.   **114.** *Conceit:* imagination.   **120.** *in th' alarm:* when
the call to arms is sounded.   **121.** *excrements:* outgrowths, here, hair (also used of nails).
122. *an end:* on end.   **124.** *patience:* self-control.   **126.** *His . . . cause:* his appearance and
what he has to say.   **127.** *capable:* sensitive, receptive.   **128.** *convert:* alter.   **129.** *effects:*
(purposed) actions.   **130.** *want true color:* lack its proper appearance.   **135.** *habit:* dress.
138. *ecstasy:* madness.   **144.** *gambol:* start, jerk away.   **145.** *flattering unction:* soothing
ointment.

Whiles rank corruption, mining all within,
Infects unseen. Confess yourself to heaven,
Repent what's past, avoid what is to come,   150
And do not spread the compost on the weeds
To make them ranker. Forgive me this my virtue,
For in the fatness of these pursy times
Virtue itself of vice must pardon beg,
Yea, curb and woo for leave to do him good.   155

QUEEN: O Hamlet, thou hast cleft my heart in twain.

HAMLET: O, throw away the worser part of it,
And [live] the purer with the other half.
Good night, but go not to my uncle's bed—
Assume a virtue, if you have it not.   160
That monster custom, who all sense doth eat,
Of habits devil, is angel yet in this,
That to the use of actions fair and good
He likewise gives a frock or livery
That aptly is put on. Refrain [to-]night,   165
And that shall lend a kind of easiness
To the next abstinence, the next more easy;
For use almost can change the stamp of nature,
And either [. . . .] the devil or throw him out
With wondrous potency. Once more good night,
And when you are desirous to be blest,   171
I'll blessing beg of you. For this same lord,

                              [*Pointing to* POLONIUS.]

I do repent; but heaven hath pleas'd it so
To punish me with this, and this with me,
That I must be their scourge and minister.   175
I will bestow him, and will answer well
The death I gave him. So again good night.
I must be cruel only to be kind.
This bad begins and worse remains behind.
One word more, good lady.

QUEEN: What shall I do?   180

HAMLET: Not this, by no means, that I bid you do:
Let the bloat king tempt you again to bed,
Pinch wanton on your cheek, call you his mouse,
And let him, for a pair of reechy kisses,
Or paddling in your neck with his damn'd fingers,   185

---

151. *compost:* manure. 153. *pursy:* puffy, out of condition. 155. *curb and woo:* bow and
entreat. 161. *all . . . eat:* wears away all natural feeling. 162. *Of habits devil:* i.e. though
it acts like a devil in establishing bad habits. Most editors read (in lines 161–62) *eat / Of
habits evil,* following Theobald. 164–65. *frock . . . on:* i.e. a "habit" or customary garment, readily put on without need of any decision. 168. *use:* habit. 169. A word seems to
be wanting after *either.* 171. *desirous . . . blest:* i.e. repentant. 175. *scourge and minister:*
the agent of heavenly justice against human crime. *Scourge* suggests a permissive cruelty
(Tamburlaine was the "scourge of God"), but "woe to him by whom the offense cometh";
the scourge must suffer for the evil it performs. 176. *bestow:* dispose of. *answer:* answer
for. 179. *behind:* to come. 184. *reechy:* filthy.

Make you to ravel all this matter out,
That I essentially am not in madness,
But mad in craft. 'Twere good you let him know,
For who that's but a queen, fair, sober, wise,
Would from a paddock, from a bat, a gib,   190
Such dear concernings hide? Who would do so?
No, in despite of sense and secrecy,
Unpeg the basket on the house's top,
Let the birds fly, and like the famous ape,
To try conclusions in the basket creep,   195
And break your own neck down.

QUEEN: Be thou assur'd, if words be made of breath,
And breath of life, I have no life to breathe
What thou hast said to me.

HAMLET: I must to England, you know that?

QUEEN: Alack,   200
I had forgot. 'Tis so concluded on.

HAMLET: There's letters seal'd, and my two schoolfellows,
Whom I will trust as I will adders fang'd,
They bear the mandate, they must sweep my way
And marshal me to knavery. Let it work,   205
For 'tis the sport to have the enginer
Hoist with his own petar, an't shall go hard
But I will delve one yard below their mines,
And blow them at the moon. O, 'tis most sweet
When in one line two crafts directly meet.   210
This man shall set me packing;
I'll lug the guts into the neighbor room.
Mother, good night indeed. This counsellor
Is now most still, most secret, and most grave,
Who was in life a foolish prating knave.   215
Come, sir, to draw toward an end with you.
Good night, mother.
                    Exeunt [severally, HAMLET *tugging in* POLONIUS].

ACT FOUR, SCENE ONE

            Enter KING *and* QUEEN *with* ROSENCRANTZ *and* GUILDENSTERN.

KING: There's matter in these sighs, these profound heaves—
You must translate, 'tis fit we understand them.
Where is your son?

190. *paddock:* toad. *gib:* tom-cat. 191. *dear concernings:* matters of intense concern.
193. *Unpeg the basket:* open the door of the cage. 194. *famous ape.* The actual story has
been lost. 195. *conclusions:* experiments (to see whether he too can fly if he enters the
cage and then leaps out). 196. *down:* by the fall. 205. *knavery:* some knavish scheme
against me. 206. *enginer:* deviser of military "engines" or contrivances. 207. *Hoist with:*
blown up by. *petar:* petard, bomb. 210. *crafts:* plots. 211. *packing:* (1) taking on a load;
(2) leaving in a hurry. 216. *draw . . . end:* finish my conversation.
IV.i. Location: The castle.

QUEEN: Bestow this place on us a little while.

          [Exeunt ROSENCRANTZ *and* GUILDENSTERN.]

    Ah, mine own lord, what have I seen to-night!   5

KING: What, Gertrude? How does Hamlet?

QUEEN: Mad as the sea and wind when both contend
    Which is the mightier. In his lawless fit,
    Behind the arras hearing something stir,
    Whips out his rapier, cries, "A rat, a rat!"   10
    And in this brainish apprehension kills
    The unseen good old man.

KING: O heavy deed!
    It had been so with us had we been there.
    His liberty is full of threats to all,
    To you yourself, to us, to every one.   15
    Alas, how shall this bloody deed be answer'd?
    It will be laid to us, whose providence
    Should have kept short, restrain'd, and out of haunt
    This mad young man; but so much was our love,
    We would not understand what was most fit,   20
    But like the owner of a foul disease,
    To keep it from divulging, let it feed
    Even on the pith of life. Where is he gone?

QUEEN: To draw apart the body he hath kill'd,
    O'er whom his very madness, like some ore   25
    Among a mineral of metals base,
    Shows itself pure: 'a weeps for what is done.

KING: O Gertrude, come away!
    The sun no sooner shall the mountains touch,
    But we will ship him hence, and this vile deed   30
    We must with all our majesty and skill
    Both countenance and excuse. Ho, Guildenstern!

        Enter ROSENCRANTZ *and* GUILDENSTERN.

    Friends both, go join you with some further aid:
    Hamlet in madness hath Polonius slain,
    And from his mother's closet hath he dragg'd him.   35
    Go seek him out, speak fair, and bring the body
    Into the chapel. I pray you haste in this.

            [Exeunt ROSENCRANTZ *and* GUILDENSTERN.]

    Come, Gertrude, we'll call up our wisest friends
    And let them know both what we mean to do
    And what's untimely done, [. . . .]   40
    Whose whisper o'er the world's diameter,

---

11. *brainish apprehension:* crazy notion.   16. *answer'd:* i.e. satisfactorily accounted for to the public.   17. *providence:* foresight.   18. *short:* on a short leash.   *out of haunt:* away from other people.   22. *divulging:* being revealed.   25. *ore:* vein of gold.   26. *mineral:* mine.   40. Some words are wanting at the end of the line. Capell's conjecture, *so, haply, slander,* probably indicates the intended sense of the passage.

As level as the cannon to his blank,
Transports his pois'ned shot, may miss our name,
And hit the woundless air. O, come away!
My soul is full of discord and dismay.   *Exeunt.*   45

SCENE TWO

    Enter HAMLET.

HAMLET: Safely stow'd.

[GENTLEMEN (*Within.*): Hamlet! Lord Hamlet!]

[HAMLET:] But soft, what noise? Who calls on Hamlet? O,
    here they come.

    Enter ROSENCRANTZ *and* [GUILDENSTERN].

ROSENCRANTZ: What have you done, my lord, with the dead body?   5

HAMLET: [Compounded] it with dust, whereto 'tis kin.

ROSENCRANTZ: Tell us where 'tis, that we may take it thence,
    And bear it to the chapel.

HAMLET: Do not believe it.

ROSENCRANTZ: Believe what?   10

HAMLET: That I can keep your counsel and not mine own
    own. Besides, to be demanded of a spunge, what
    replication should be made by the son of a king?

ROSENCRANTZ: Take you me for a spunge, my lord?   14

HAMLET: Ay, sir, that soaks up the King's countenance, his
    rewards, his authorities. But such officers do the King
    best service in the end: he keeps them, like [an ape] an
    apple, in the corner of his jaw, first mouth'd, to be last
    swallow'd. When he needs what you have glean'd, it is
    but squeezing you, and, spunge, you shall be dry
    again.   21

ROSENCRANTZ: I understand you not, my lord.

HAMLET: I am glad of it, a knavish speech sleeps in a
    foolish ear.

ROSENCRANTZ: My lord, you must tell us where the body is,
    and go with us to the King.   26

HAMLET: The body is with the King, but the King is not
    with the body. The King is a thing—

GUILDENSTERN: A thing, my lord?

---

42. *As level:* with aim as good.   *blank:* target.   44. *woundless:* incapable of being hurt.
IV.ii. Location: The castle.
12. *demanded of:* questioned by.   *spunge:* sponge.   13. *replication:* reply.   15. *counte-*
nance: favor.   23. *sleeps:* is meaningless.   27–28. *The body . . . the body.* Possibly alluding
to the legal fiction that the king's dignity is separate from his mortal body.

HAMLET: Of nothing, bring me to him. [Hide fox, and all
    after.]   *Exeunt.*   31

SCENE THREE

Enter KING *and two or three.*

KING: I have sent to seek him, and to find the body.
    How dangerous is it that this man goes loose!
    Yet must not we put the strong law on him.
    He's lov'd of the distracted multitude,
    Who like not in their judgment, but their eyes,   5
    And where 'tis so th' offender's scourge is weigh'd,
    But never the offense. To bear all smooth and even,
    This sudden sending him away must seem
    Deliberate pause. Diseases desperate grown
    By desperate appliance are reliev'd,   10
    Or not at all.

Enter ROSENCRANTZ.

    How now, what hath befall'n?
ROSENCRANTZ: Where the dead body is bestow'd, my lord,
    We cannot get from him.
KING: But where is he?
ROSENCRANTZ: Without, my lord, guarded, to know your pleasure.
KING: Bring him before us.
ROSENCRANTZ: Ho, bring in the lord.   15

They [HAMLET *and* GUILDENSTERN] *enter.*

KING: Now, Hamlet, where's Polonius?
HAMLET: At supper.
KING: At supper? where?
HAMLET: Not where he eats, but where 'a is eaten; a cer-
    tain convocation of politic worms are e'en at him.   20
    Your worm is your only emperor for diet: we fat all
    creatures else to fat us, and we fat ourselves for
    maggots; your fat king and your lean beggar is but
    variable service, two dishes, but to one table—that's the
    end.   25
KING: Alas, alas!

---

30. *Of nothing:* of no account. Cf. "Man is like a thing of nought, his time passeth away
like a shadow" (Psalm 144:4 in the Prayer Book version). "Hamlet at once insults the King
and hints that his days are numbered" (Dover Wilson). **30–31.** *Hide . . . after.* Probably a
cry in some game resembling hide-and-seek.
IV.iii. Location: The castle.
4. *distracted:* unstable. **6.** *scourge:* i.e. punishment. **7.** *bear:* manage. **8–9.** *must . . .
pause:* i.e. must be represented as a maturely considered decision. **20.** *politic:* crafty,
prying; "such worms as might breed in a politician's corpse" (Dowden). *e'en:* even
now. **21.** *for diet:* with respect to what it eats. **24.** *variable service:* different courses of a
meal.

HAMLET: A man may fish with the worm that hath eat of a
    king, and eat of the fish that hath fed of that worm.

KING: What dost thou mean by this?

HAMLET: Nothing but to show you how a king may go a
    progress through the guts of a beggar.   31

KING: Where is Polonius?

HAMLET: In heaven, send thither to see; if your messenger
    find him not there, seek him i' th' other place
    yourself. But if indeed you find him not within this   35
    month, you shall nose him as you go up the stairs into
    the lobby.

KING [To ATTENDANTS.]: Go seek him there.

HAMLET: 'A will stay till you come.   [Exeunt ATTENDANTS.]

KING: Hamlet, this deed, for thine especial safety—   40
    Which we do tender, as we dearly grieve
    For that which thou hast done—must send thee hence
    [With fiery quickness]; therefore prepare thyself,
    The bark is ready, and the wind at help,
    Th' associates tend, and every thing is bent   45
    For England.

HAMLET: For England.

KING: Ay, Hamlet.

HAMLET: Good.

KING: So is it, if thou knew'st our purposes.

HAMLET: I see a cherub that sees them. But come, for England!
    Farewell, dear mother.

KING: Thy loving father, Hamlet.   50

HAMLET: My mother: father and mother is man and wife, man
    and wife is one flesh—so, my mother. Come, for
    England!   Exit.

KING: Follow him at foot, tempt him with speed aboard.
    Delay it not, I'll have him hence to-night.   55
    Away, for everything is seal'd and done
    That else leans on th' affair. Pray you make haste.
          [Exeunt ROSENCRANTZ and GUILDENSTERN.]
    And, England, if my love thou hold'st at aught—
    As my great power thereof may give thee sense,
    Since yet thy cicatrice looks raw and red   60
    After the Danish sword, and thy free awe
    Pays homage to us—thou mayst not coldly set

---

31. *progress:* royal journey of state.   **41.** *tender:* regard with tenderness, hold dear.
dearly: with intense feeling.   **44.** *at help:* a favorable.   **45.** *Th':* thy.   *tend:* await.   *bent:*
made ready.   **48.** *I . . . them:* i.e. heaven sees them.   **54.** *at foot:* at his heels, close
behind.   **57.** *leans on:* relates to.   **58.** *England:* King of England.   **60.** *cicatrice:* scar.
61–62. *thy . . . Pays:* your fear makes you pay voluntarily.   **62.** *coldly set:* undervalue,
disregard.

Our sovereign process, which imports at full,
By letters congruing to that effect,
The present death of Hamlet. Do it, England,   65
For like the hectic in my blood he rages,
And thou must cure me. Till I know 'tis done,
How e'er my haps, my joys [were] ne'er [begun].   *Exit.*

SCENE FOUR

Enter FORTINBRAS *with his army over the stage.*

FORTINBRAS: Go, captain, from me greet the Danish king.
Tell him that by his license Fortinbras
Craves the conveyance of a promis'd march
Over his kingdom. You know the rendezvous.
If that his Majesty would aught with us,   5
We shall express our duty in his eye,
And let him know so.
CAPTAIN: I will do't, my lord.
FORTINBRAS: Go softly on.   [*Exeunt all but the* CAPTAIN.]

Enter HAMLET, ROSENCRANTZ, [GUILDENSTERN,] *etc.*

HAMLET: Good sir, whose powers are these?
CAPTAIN: They are of Norway, sir.   10
HAMLET: How purpos'd, sir, I pray you?
CAPTAIN: Against some part of Poland.
HAMLET: Who commands them, sir?
CAPTAIN: The nephew to old Norway, Fortinbras.
HAMLET: Goes it against the main of Poland, sir,   15
Or for some frontier?
CAPTAIN: Truly to speak, and with no addition,
We go to gain a little patch of ground
That hath in it no profit but the name.
To pay five ducats, five, I would not farm it;   20
Nor will it yield to Norway or the Pole
A ranker rate, should it be sold in fee.
HAMLET: Why then the Polack never will defend it.
CAPTAIN: Yes, it is already garrison'd.
HAMLET: Two thousand souls and twenty thousand ducats   25
Will not debate the question of this straw.

---

63. *process:* command.   64. *congruing to:* in accord with.   65. *present:* immediate.
66. *hectic:* continuous fever.   68. *haps:* fortunes.
IV.iv. Location: The Danish coast, near the castle.
3. *conveyance of:* escort for.   6. *eye:* presence.   8. *softly:* slowly.   9. *powers:* forces.
15. *main:* main territory.   20. *To pay:* i.e. for an annual rent of.   *farm:* lease.   22. *ranker:*
higher.   *in fee:* outright.   26. *Will not debate:* i.e. will scarcely be enough to fight out.

This is th' imposthume of much wealth and peace,
That inward breaks, and shows no cause without
Why the man dies. I humbly thank you, sir.

CAPTAIN: God buy you, sir. [*Exit.*]

ROSENCRANTZ: Will't please you go, my lord? 30

HAMLET: I'll be with you straight—go a little before.

[*Exeunt all but* HAMLET.]

How all occasions do inform against me,
And spur my dull revenge! What is a man,
If his chief good and market of his time
Be but to sleep and feed? a beast, no more. 35
Sure He that made us with such large discourse,
Looking before and after, gave us not
That capability and godlike reason
To fust in us unus'd. Now whether it be
Bestial oblivion, or some craven scruple 40
Of thinking too precisely on th' event—
A thought which quarter'd hath but one part wisdom
And ever three parts coward—I do not know
Why yet I live to say, "This thing's to do,"
Sith I have cause, and will, and strength, and means 45
To do't. Examples gross as earth exhort me:
Witness this army of such mass and charge,
Led by a delicate and tender prince,
Whose spirit with divine ambition puff'd
Makes mouths at the invisible event, 50
Exposing what is mortal and unsure
To all that fortune, death, and danger dare,
Even for an egg-shell. Rightly to be great
Is not to stir without great argument,
But greatly to find quarrel in a straw 55
When honor's at the stake. How stand I then,
That have a father kill'd, a mother stain'd,
Excitements of my reason and my blood,
And let all sleep, while to my shame I see
The imminent death of twenty thousand men, 60
That for a fantasy and trick of fame
Go to their graves like beds, fight for a plot
Whereon the numbers cannot try the cause,
Which is not tomb enough and continent
To hide the slain? O, from this time forth, 65
My thoughts be bloody, or be nothing worth! *Exit.*

27. *imposthume:* abscess. 32. *inform against:* denounce, accuse. 34. *market:* purchase,
profit. 36. *discourse:* reasoning power. 39. *fust:* grow mouldy. 40. *oblivion:* forgetfulness. 41. *event:* outcome. 46. *gross:* large, obvious. 47. *mass and charge:* size and
expense. 50. *Makes mouths at:* treats scornfully. *invisible:* i.e. unforeseeable. 54. *Is
not to:* i.e. is *not* not to. *argument:* cause. 55. *greatly:* nobly. 58. *Excitements of:* urgings
by. 61. *fantasy:* caprice. *trick:* trifle. 63. *Whereon . . . cause:* which isn't large enough
to let the opposing armies engage upon it. 64. *continent:* container.

SCENE FIVE

Enter HORATIO, [QUEEN] GERTRUDE, *and a* GENTLEMAN.

QUEEN: I will not speak with her.

GENTLEMAN: She is importunate, indeed distract.
Her mood will needs be pitied.

QUEEN: What would she have?

GENTLEMAN: She speaks much of her father, says she hears
There's tricks i' th' world, and hems, and beats her heart,   5
Spurns enviously at straws, speaks things in doubt
That carry but half sense. Her speech is nothing,
Yet the unshaped use of it doth move
The hearers to collection; they yawn at it,
And botch the words up fit to their own thoughts,   10
Which as her winks and nods and gestures yield them,
Indeed would make one think there might be thought,
Though nothing sure, yet much unhappily.

HORATIO: 'Twere good she were spoken with, for she may strew
Dangerous conjectures in ill-breeding minds.   15

[QUEEN:] Let her come in.   [*Exit* GENTLEMAN.]
[*Aside.*] To my sick soul, as sin's true nature is,
Each toy seems prologue to some great amiss,
So full of artless jealousy is guilt,
It spills itself in fearing to be spilt.   20

Enter OPHELIA [*distracted, with her hair down, playing on a lute*].

OPHELIA: Where is the beauteous majesty of Denmark?

QUEEN: How now, Ophelia?

OPHELIA: "How should I your true-love know   *She sings.*
                From another one?
                By his cockle hat and staff,   25
                And his sandal shoon."

QUEEN: Alas, sweet lady, what imports this song?

OPHELIA: Say you? Nay, pray you mark.

IV.v. Location: The castle.
6. *Spurns . . . straws:* spitefully takes offense at trifles. *in doubt:* obscurely. 7. *Her speech:* what she says. 8. *unshaped use:* distracted manner. 9. *collection:* attempts to gather the meaning. *yawn at:* strive, as if open-mouthed, to grasp (?). Most editors adopt the F1 reading *aim at.* 10. *botch:* patch. 11. *Which:* i.e. the words. 12. *thought:* inferred, conjectured. 15. *ill-breeding:* conceiving ill thoughts, prone to think the worst. 18. *toy:* trifle. *amiss:* calamity. 19. *artless jealousy:* uncontrolled suspicion. 20. *spills:* destroys. 23–24. These lines resemble a passage in an earlier ballad beginning "As you came from the holy land / Of Walsingham." Probably all the song fragments sung by Ophelia were familiar to the Globe audience, but only one other line (187) is from a ballad still extant. 25. *cockle hat:* hat bearing a cockle shell, the badge of a pilgrim to the shrine of St. James of Compostela in Spain. *staff.* Another mark of a pilgrim. 26. *shoon:* shoes (already an archaic form in Shakespeare's day).

"He is dead and gone, lady, *Song.*
   He is dead and gone, 30
   At his head a grass-green turf,
   At his heels a stone."

  O ho!

QUEEN: Nay, but, Ophelia—

OPHELIA: Pray you mark. *[Sings.]* 35

    "White his shroud as the mountain snow"—

    Enter KING.

QUEEN: Alas, look here, my lord.

OPHELIA: "Larded all with sweet flowers, *Song.*
    Which bewept to the ground did not go
    With true-love showers." 40

KING: How do you, pretty lady?

OPHELIA: Well, God dild you! They say the owl was a baker's
daughter. Lord, we know what we are, but know not
what we may be. God be at your table!

KING: Conceit upon her father. 45

OPHELIA: Pray let's have no words of this, but when they ask
you what it means, say you this:

    "To-morrow is Saint Valentine's day *Song.*
    All in the morning betime,
    And I am maid at your window, 50
    To be your Valentine.

    "Then up he rose and donn'd his clo'es,
    And dupp'd the chamber-door,
    Let in the maid, that out a maid
    Never departed more." 55

KING: Pretty Ophelia!

OPHELIA: Indeed without an oath I'll make an end on't. *[Sings.]*

    "By Gis, and by Saint Charity,
    Alack, and fie for shame!
    Young men will do't if they come to't, 60
    By Cock, they are to blame.

    "Quoth she, 'Before you tumbled me,
    You promis'd me to wed.'"

---

38. *Larded:* adorned. **39.** *not.* Contrary to the expected sense, and unmetrical; explain
Ophelia's alteration of the line to accord with the facts of Polonius' burial (see line 84).
42. *dild:* yield, reward. *owl.* Alluding to the legend of a baker's daughter whom Jesus
turned into an owl because she did not respond generously to his request for bread.
45. *Conceit:* fanciful brooding. **53.** *dupp'd:* opened. **58.** *Gis:* contraction of *Jesus.*
61. *Cock:* corruption of *God.*

(He answers.)
    "'So would I 'a' done, by yonder sun,   65
     And thou hadst not come to my bed.'"

KING: How long hath she been thus?

OPHELIA: I hope all will be well. We must be patient, but I
  cannot choose but weep to think they would lay him i'
  th' cold ground. My brother shall know of it, and so I   70
  thank you for your good counsel. Come, my coach!
  Good night, ladies, good night. Sweet ladies, good
  night, good night.   [*Exit.*]

KING: Follow her close, give her good watch, I pray you. [*Exit* HORATIO.]
  O, this is the poison of deep grief, it springs   75
  All from her father's death—and now behold!
  O Gertrude, Gertrude,
  When sorrows come, they come not single spies,
  But in battalions: first, her father slain;
  Next, your son gone, and he most violent author   80
  Of his own just remove; the people muddied,
  Thick and unwholesome in [their] thoughts and whispers
  For good Polonius' death; and we have done but greenly
  In hugger-mugger to inter him; poor Ophelia
  Divided from herself and her fair judgment,   85
  Without the which we are pictures, or mere beasts;
  Last, and as much containing as all these,
  Her brother is in secret come from France,
  Feeds on this wonder, keeps himself in clouds,
  And wants not buzzers to infect his ear   90
  With pestilent speeches of his father's death,
  Wherein necessity, of matter beggar'd,
  Will nothing stick our person to arraign
  In ear and ear. O my dear Gertrude, this,
  Like to a murd'ring-piece, in many places   95
  Gives me superfluous death.   *A noise within.*

[QUEEN: Alack, what noise is this?]

KING: Attend!
  Where is my Swissers? Let them guard the door.

    Enter a MESSENGER.

  What is the matter?

MESSENGER: Save yourself, my lord!
  The ocean, overpeering of his list,   100
  Eats not the flats with more impiteous haste

---

66. *And:* if. **78.** *spies:* i.e. soldiers sent ahead of the main force to reconnoiter, scouts.
81. *muddied:* confused. **83.** *greenly:* unwisely. **84.** *In hugger-mugger:* secretly and hastily. **89.** *in clouds:* i.e. in cloudy surmise and suspicion (rather than the light of fact).
90. *wants:* lacks. *buzzers:* whispering informers. **92.** *of matter beggar'd:* destitute of
facts. **93.** *nothing . . . arraign:* scruple not at all to charge me with the crime.
95. *murd'ring-piece:* cannon firing a scattering charge. **98.** *Swissers:* Swiss guards.
100. *overpeering . . . list:* rising higher than its shores.

Than young Laertes, in a riotous head,
O'erbears your officers. The rabble call him lord,
And as the world were not but to begin,
Antiquity forgot, custom not known,   105
The ratifiers and props of every word,
[They] cry, "Choose we, Laertes shall be king!"
Caps, hands, and tongues applaud it to the clouds,
"Laertes shall be king, Laertes king!"   *A noise within.*

QUEEN: How cheerfully on the false trail they cry!
O, this is counter, you false Danish dogs!   111

Enter LAERTES *with others.*

KING: The doors are broke.

LAERTES: Where is this king? Sirs, stand you all without.

ALL: No, let 's come in.

LAERTES: I pray you give me leave.

ALL: We will, we will.   115

LAERTES: I thank you, keep the door. [*Exeunt* LAERTES'
followers.] O thou vile king,
Give me my father!

QUEEN: Calmly, good Laertes.

LAERTES: That drop of blood that's calm proclaims me bastard,
Cries cuckold to my father, brands the harlot
Even here between the chaste unsmirched brow   120
Of my true mother.

KING: What is the cause, Laertes,
That thy rebellion looks so giant-like?
Let him go, Gertrude, do not fear our person:
There's such divinity doth hedge a king
That treason can but peep to what it would,   125
Acts little of his will. Tell me, Laertes,
Why thou art thus incens'd. Let him go, Gertrude.
Speak, man.

LAERTES: Where is my father?

KING: Dead.

QUEEN: But not by him.

KING: Let him demand his fill.   130

LAERTES: How came he dead? I'll not be juggled with.
To hell, allegiance! vows, to the blackest devil!
Conscience and grace, to the profoundest pit!
I dare damnation. To this point I stand,
That both the worlds I give to negligence,   135

---

102. *in . . . head:* with a rebellious force.   104. *as:* as if.   106. *word:* pledge, promise.
111. *counter:* on the wrong scent (literally, following the scent backward).   123. *fear:* fear
for.   125. *would:* i.e. would like to do.   135. *both . . . negligence:* i.e. I don't care what the
consequences are in this world or in the next.

Let come what comes, only I'll be reveng'd
Most throughly for my father.

KING: Who shall stay you?

LAERTES: My will, not all the world's:
And for my means, I'll husband them so well,
They shall go far with little.

KING: Good Laertes,   140
If you desire to know the certainty
Of your dear father, is't writ in your revenge
That, swoopstake, you will draw both friend and foe,
Winner and loser?

LAERTES: None but his enemies.

KING: Will you know them then?   145

LAERTES: To his good friends thus wide I'll ope my arms
And like the king life-rend'ring pelican,
Repast them with my blood.

KING: Why, now you speak
Like a good child and a true gentleman.
That I am guiltless of your father's death,   150
And am most sensibly in grief for it,
It shall as level to your judgment 'pear
As day does to your eye.

                              A noise within: "Let her come in!"

LAERTES: How now, what noise is that?

                    Enter OPHELIA.

O heat, dry up my brains! tears seven times salt   155
Burn out the sense and virtue of mine eye!
By heaven, thy madness shall be paid with weight
[Till] our scale turn the beam. O rose of May!
Dear maid, kind sister, sweet Ophelia!
O heavens, is't possible a young maid's wits   160
Should be as mortal as [an old] man's life?
[Nature is fine in love, and where 'tis fine,
It sends some precious instance of itself
After the thing it loves.]

OPHELIA: "They bore him barefac'd on the bier   *Song*   165
              [Hey non nonny, nonny, hey nonny,]
              And in his grave rain'd many a tear"—

Fare you well, my dove!

---

137. *throughly:* thoroughly. 138. *world's:* i.e. world's will. 143. *swoopstake:* sweeping up
everything without discrimination (modern *sweepstake*). 147. *pelican.* The female pelican
was believed to draw blood from her own breast to nourish her young. 149. *good child:*
faithful son. 151. *sensibly:* feelingly. 152. *level:* plain. 156. *virtue:* faculty. 162. *fine in:*
refined or spiritualized by. 163. *instance:* proof, token. So delicate is Ophelia's love for her
father that her sanity has pursued him into the grave.

LAERTES: Hadst thou thy wits and didst persuade revenge,
It could not move thus.   170

OPHELIA: You must sing, "A-down, a-down," and you call him
a-down-a. O how the wheel becomes it! It is the false
steward, that stole his master's daughter.

LAERTES: This nothing's more than matter.   174

OPHELIA: There's rosemary, that's for remembrance; pray
you, love, remember. And there is pansies, that's for
thoughts.

LAERTES: A document in madness, thoughts and remembrance
fitted.   179

OPHELIA [*To* CLAUDIUS.]: There's fennel for you, and columbines. [*To* GERTRUDE.] There's rue for you, and here's
some for me; we may call it herb of grace a' Sundays.
You may wear your rue with a difference. There's a
daisy. I would give you some violets, but they wither'd
all when my father died. They say 'a made a good
end—   [*Sings.*]   186

"For bonny sweet Robin is all my joy."

LAERTES: Thought and afflictions, passion, hell itself,
She turns to favor and to prettiness.

OPHELIA: "And will 'a not come again?   *Song.*
And will 'a not come again?   191
No, no, he is dead,
Go to thy death-bed,
He never will come again.

"His beard was as white as snow,   195
[All] flaxen was his pole,
He is gone, he is gone,
And we cast away moan,
God 'a' mercy on his soul!"

And of all Christians' souls, [I pray God]. God buy
you.   [*Exit.*]

LAERTES: Do you [see] this, O God?   202

KING: Laertes, I must commune with your grief,
Or you deny me right. Go but apart,

---

169. *persuade:* argue logically for. **171–72.** *and . . . a-down-a:* "if he indeed agrees that
Polonius is 'a-down,' i.e fallen low" (Dover Wilson). **172.** *wheel:* refrain (?) or spinning-
wheel, at which women sang ballads (?). **174.** *matter:* lucid speech. **178.** *A document in
madness:* a lesson contained in mad talk. **180–181.** *fennel, columbines.* Symbols respectively of flattery and ingratitude. **181.** *rue.* Symbolic of sorrow and repentance. **183.** *with a
difference:* i.e. to represent a different cause of sorrow. *Difference* is a term from heraldry,
meaning a variation in a coat of arms made to distinguish different members of a family.
184. *daisy, violets.* Symbolic respectively of dissembling and faithfulness. It is not clear who
are the recipients of these. **188.** *Thought:* melancholy. **189.** *favor:* grace, charm.
196. *flaxen:* white. *pole:* poll, head.

Make choice of whom your wisest friends you will,
And they shall hear and judge 'twixt you and me.   206
If by direct or by collateral hand
They find us touch'd, we will our kingdom give,
Our crown, our life, and all that we call ours,
To you in satisfaction; but if not,   210
Be you content to lend your patience to us,
And we shall jointly labor with your soul
To give it due content.

LAERTES: Let this be so.
His means of death, his obscure funeral—
No trophy, sword, nor hatchment o'er his bones,   215
No noble rite nor formal ostentation—
Cry to be heard, as 'twere from heaven to earth,
That I must call't in question.

KING: So you shall,
And where th' offense is, let the great axe fall.   219
I pray you go with me.   *Exeunt.*

SCENE SIX

Enter HORATIO *and others.*

HORATIO: What are they that would speak with me?

GENTLEMAN: Sea-faring men, sir. They say they have letters
   for you.

HORATIO: Let them come in.   [*Exit* GENTLEMAN.]
   I do not know from what part of the world,   5
   I should be greeted, if not from Lord Hamlet.

   Enter SAILORS.

[FIRST] SAILOR: God bless you, sir.

HORATIO: Let him bless thee too.

[FIRST] SAILOR: 'A shall, sir, and['t] please him. There's a letter
   for you, sir—it came from th' embassador that was   10
   bound for England—if your name be Horatio, as I am
   let to know it is.

HORATIO [*Reads.*]: "Horatio, when thou shalt have overlook'd
   this, give these fellows some means to the King, they
   have letters for him. Ere we were two days old at sea, a   15
   pirate of very warlike appointment gave us chase.
   Finding ourselves too slow of sail, we put on a compell'd valor, and in the grapple I boarded them. On the

___

207. *collateral:* i.e. indirect.   208. *touch'd:* guilty.   215. *trophy:* memorial.   *hatchment:*
heraldic memorial tablet.   216. *formal ostentation:* fitting and customary ceremony.
218. *That:* so that.
IV.vi. Location: The castle.

instant they got clear of our ship, so I alone became
their prisoner. They have dealt with me like thieves of   20
mercy, but they knew what they did: I am to do a
[good] turn for them. Let the King have the letters I
have sent, and repair thou to me with as much speed as
thou wouldest fly death. I have words to speak in thine
ear will make thee dumb, yet are they much too light   25
for the [bore] of the matter. These good fellows will
bring thee where I am. Rosencrantz and Guildenstern
hold their course for England, of them I have much to
tell thee. Farewell.

> [He] that thou knowest thine,   30
> Hamlet."

Come, I will [give] you way for these your letters,
And do't the speedier that you may direct me
To him from whom you brought them.   *Exeunt.*

SCENE SEVEN

> *Enter* KING *and* LAERTES.

KING: Now must your conscience my acquittance seal,
And you must put me in your heart for friend,
Sith you have heard, and with a knowing ear,
That he which hath your noble father slain
Pursued my life.

LAERTES: It well appears. But tell me   5
Why you [proceeded] not against these feats
So criminal and so capital in nature,
As by your safety, greatness, wisdom, all things else
You mainly were stirr'd up.

KING: O, for two special reasons,
Which may to you perhaps seem much unsinow'd,   10
But yet to me th' are strong. The Queen his mother
Lives almost by his looks, and for myself—
My virtue or my plague, be it either which—
She is so [conjunctive] to my life and soul,
That, as the star moves not but in his sphere,   15
I could not but by her. The other motive,
Why to a public count I might not go,
Is the great love the general gender bear him,
Who, dipping all his faults in their affection,

20–21. *thieves of mercy;* merciful thieves.   26. *bore:* calibre, size (gunnery term).
IV,vii. Location: The castle.
1. *my acquittance seal:* ratify my acquittal, i.e. acknowledge my innocence in Polonius'
death.   6. *feats:* acts.   8. *safety:* i.e. regard for your own safety.   9. *mainly:* powerfully.
10. *unsinow'd:* unsinewed, i.e. weak.   13. *either which:* one or the other.   14. *conjunctive:*
closely joined.   15. *in his sphere:* by the movement of the sphere in which it is fixed (as
the Ptolemaic astronomy taught).   17. *count:* reckoning.   18. *the general gender:* everybody.

Work like the spring that turneth wood to stone,   20
Convert his gyves to graces, so that my arrows,
Too slightly timber'd for so [loud a wind],
Would have reverted to my bow again,
But not where I have aim'd them.

LAERTES: And so have I a noble father lost,   25
A sister driven into desp'rate terms,
Whose worth, if praises may go back again,
Stood challenger on mount of all the age
For her perfections—but my revenge will come.

KING: Break not your sleeps for that. You must not think   30
That we are made of stuff so flat and dull
That we can let our beard be shook with danger
And think it pastime. You shortly shall hear more.
I lov'd your father, and we love ourself,
And that, I hope, will teach you to imagine—   35

> *Enter a* MESSENGER *with letters.*

[How now? What news?

MESSENGER: Letters, my lord, from Hamlet:]
These to your Majesty, this to the Queen.

KING: From Hamlet? Who brought them?

MESSENGER: Sailors, my lord, they say, I saw them not.
They were given me by Claudio. He receiv'd them   40
Of him that brought them.

KING: Laertes, you shall hear them.
—Leave us.   [*Exit* MESSENGER.]
[*Reads.*] "High and mighty, You shall know I am set
naked on your kingdom. To-morrow shall I beg leave
to see your kingly eyes, when I shall, first asking you   45
pardon thereunto, recount the occasion of my sudden
[and more strange] return.
                        [Hamlet.]"
What should this mean? Are all the rest come back?
Or is it some abuse, and no such thing?   50

LAERTES: Know you the hand?

KING: 'Tis Hamlet's character. "Naked"!
And in a postscript here he says "alone."
Can you devise me?

LAERTES: I am lost in it, my lord. But let him come,
It warms the very sickness in my heart   55
That I [shall] live and tell him to his teeth,
"Thus didst thou."

---

21. *gyves:* fetters.   26. *terms:* condition.   27. *go back again:* i.e. refer to what she was
before she went mad.   28. *on mount:* pre-eminent.   30. *for that:* i.e. for fear of losing your
revenge.   31. *flat:* spiritless.   32. *let . . . shook.* To ruffle or tweak a man's beard was an
act of insolent defiance that he could not disregard without loss of honor. Cf. II.ii.573.
with: by   44. *naked:* destitute.   46. *pardon thereunto:* permission to do so.   50. *abuse:*
deceit.   51. *character:* handwriting.   53. *devise me:* explain it to me.

KING: If it be so, Laertes—
As how should it be so? how otherwise?—
Will you be rul'd by me?

LAERTES: Ay, my lord,
So you will not o'errule me to a peace.   60

KING: To thine own peace. If he be now returned
As [checking] at his voyage, and that he means
No more to undertake it, I will work him
To an exploit, now ripe in my device,
Under the which he shall not choose but fall;   65
And for his death no wind of blame shall breathe,
But even his mother shall uncharge the practice,
And call it accident.

LAERTES: My lord, I will be rul'd,
The rather if you could devise it so
That I might be the organ.

KING: It falls right.   70
You have been talk'd of since your travel much,
And that in Hamlet's hearing, for a quality
Wherein they say you shine. Your sum of parts
Did not together pluck such envy from him
As did that one, and that, in my regard,   75
Of the unworthiest siege.

LAERTES: What part is that, my lord?

KING: A very riband in the cap of youth,
Yet needful too, for youth no less becomes
The light and careless livery that it wears
Than settled age his sables and his weeds,   80
Importing health and graveness. Two months since
Here was a gentleman of Normandy:
I have seen myself, and serv'd against, the French,
And they can well on horseback, but this gallant
Had witchcraft in't, he grew unto his seat,   85
And to such wondrous doing brought his horse,
As had he been incorps'd and demi-natur'd
With the brave beast. So far he topp'd [my] thought,
That I in forgery of shapes and tricks
Come short of what he did.

LAERTES: A Norman was't?   90

KING: A Norman.

LAERTES: Upon my life, Lamord.

---

58. *As . . . otherwise:* How can he have come back? Yet he obviously has.   60. *So:* provided that.   62. *checking at:* turning from (like a falcon diverted from its quarry by other prey).   67. *uncharge the practice:* adjudge the plot no plot, i.e. fail to see the plot.   70. *organ:* instrument, agent.   72. *quality:* skill.   73. *Your . . . parts:* all your (other) accomplishments put together.   76. *unworthiest:* i.e. least important (with no implication of unsuitableness).   *siege:* status, position.   80. *weeds:* (characteristic) garb.   81. *Importing . . . graveness:* signifying prosperity and dignity.   84. *can . . . horseback:* are excellent riders.   87. *incorps'd:* made one body.   *demi-natur'd:* i.e. become half of a composite animal.   89. *forgery:* mere imagining.

KING: The very same.

LAERTES: I know him well. He is the brooch indeed
    And gem of all the nation.

KING: He made confession of you,   95
    And gave you such a masterly report
    For art and exercise in your defense,
    And for your rapier most especial,
    That he cried out 'twould be a sight indeed
    If one could match you. The scrimers of their nation
    He swore had neither motion, guard, nor eye,   101
    If you oppos'd them. Sir, this report of his
    Did Hamlet so envenom with his envy
    That he could nothing do but wish and beg
    Your sudden coming o'er to play with you.   105
    Now, out of this—

LAERTES: What out of this, my lord?

KING: Laertes, was your father dear to you?
    Or are you like the painting of a sorrow,
    A face without a heart?

LAERTES: Why ask you this?   109

KING: Not that I think you did not love your father,
    But that I know love is begun by time,
    And that I see, in passages of proof,
    Time qualifies the spark and fire of it.
    There lives within the very flame of love
    A kind of week or snuff that will abate it,   115
    And nothing is at a like goodness still,
    For goodness, growing to a plurisy,
    Dies in his own too much. That we would do,
    We should do when we would; for this "would" changes,
    And hath abatements and delays as many   120
    As there are tongues, are hands, are accidents,
    And then this "should" is like a spendthrift's sigh,
    That hurts by easing. But to the quick of th' ulcer:
    Hamlet comes back. What would you undertake
    To show yourself indeed your father's son   125
    More than in words?

LAERTES: To cut his throat i' th' church.

KING: No place indeed should murther sanctuarize,
    Revenge should have no bounds. But, good Laertes,
    Will you do this, keep close within your chamber.

---

93. *brooch*: ornament (worn in the hat).   95. *made . . . you*: acknowledged your excellence.   100. *scrimers*: fencers.   105. *sudden*: speedy.   111. *time*: i.e. a particular set of
circumstances.   112. *in . . . proof*: i.e. by the test of experience, by actual examples.
113. *qualifies*: moderates.   115. *week*: wick.   116. *nothing . . . still*: nothing remains forever at the same pitch of perfection.   117. *plurisy*: plethora (a variant spelling of *pleurisy*,
which was erroneously related to *plus*, stem *plur-*, "more, overmuch."   118. *too much*:
excess.   122. *spendthrift's sigh*. A sigh was supposed to draw blood from the heart.
123. *hurts by easing*: injures us at the same time that it gives us relief.   127. *sanctuarize*:
offer asylum to.   129. *Will . . . this*: if you want to undertake this.

Hamlet return'd shall know you are come home. 130
We'll put on those shall praise your excellence,
And set a double varnish on the fame
The Frenchman gave you, bring you in fine together,
And wager o'er your heads. He, being remiss,
Most generous, and free from all contriving, 135
Will not peruse the foils, so that with ease,
Or with a little shuffling, you may choose
A sword unbated, and in a [pass] of practice
Requite him for your father.

LAERTES: I will do't,
And for [that] purpose I'll anoint my sword. 140
I bought an unction of a mountebank,
So mortal that, but dip a knife in it,
Where it draws blood, no cataplasm so rare,
Collected from all simples that have virtue
Under the moon, can save the thing from death 145
That is but scratch'd withal. I'll touch my point
With this contagion, that if I gall him slightly,
It may be death.

KING: Let's further think of this,
Weigh what convenience both of time and means
May fit us to our shape. If this should fail, 150
And that our drift look through our bad performance,
'Twere better not assay'd; therefore this project
Should have a back or second, that might hold
If this did blast in proof. Soft, let me see.
We'll make a solemn wager on your cunnings— 155
I ha't!
When in your motion you are hot and dry—
As make your bouts more violent to that end—
And that he calls for drink, I'll have preferr'd him
A chalice for the nonce, whereon but sipping, 160
If he by chance escape your venom'd stuck,
Our purpose may hold there. But stay, what noise?

     Enter QUEEN.

QUEEN: One woe doth tread upon another's heel,
So fast they follow. Your sister's drown'd, Laertes.

LAERTES: Drown'd! O, where? 165

---

131. *put on those:* incite those who.   132. *double varnish:* second coat of varnish.   133. *in fine:* finally.   134. *remiss:* careless, overtrustful.   135. *generous:* noble-minded.   *free . . . contriving:* innocent of sharp practices.   136. *peruse:* examine.   137. *shuffling:* cunning exchange.   138. *unbated:* not blunted.   *pass of practice:* tricky thrust.   141. *unction:* ointment.   *mountebank:* travelling quack-doctor.   142. *mortal:* deadly.   143. *cataplasm:* poultice.   144. *simples:* medicinal herbs.   *virtue:* curative power.   147. *gall:* graze.
150. *fit . . . shape:* i.e. suit our purposes best.   151. *drift:* purpose.   *look through:* become visible, be detected.   153. *back or second:* i.e. a second plot in reserve for emergency.
154. *blast in proof:* blow up while being tried (an image from gunnery).   158. *As:* i.e. and you should.   159. *preferr'd:* offered to. Most editors adopt the F1 reading *prepar'd*.
160. *nonce:* occasion.   161. *stuck:* thrust (from *stoccado*, a fencing term).

QUEEN: There is a willow grows askaunt the brook,
That shows his hoary leaves in the glassy stream,
Therewith fantastic garlands did she make
Of crow-flowers, nettles, daisies, and long purples
That liberal shepherds give a grosser name,   170
But our cull-cold maids do dead men's fingers call them.
There on the pendant boughs her crownet weeds
Clamb'ring to hang, an envious sliver broke,
When down her weedy trophies and herself
Fell in the weeping brook. Her clothes spread wide,   174
And mermaid-like awhile they bore her up,
Which time she chaunted snatches of old lauds,
As one incapable of her own distress,
Or like a creature native and indued
Unto that element. But long it could not be   180
Till that her garments, heavy with their drink,
Pull'd the poor wretch from her melodious lay
To muddy death.

LAERTES: Alas, then she is drown'd?

QUEEN: Drown'd, drown'd.

LAERTES: Too much of water hast thou, poor Ophelia,
And therefore I forbid my tears; but yet   186
It is our trick. Nature her custom holds.
Let shame say what it will; when these are gone,
The woman will be out. Adieu, my lord,
I have a speech a' fire that fain would blaze,   190
But that this folly drowns it.   *Exit.*

KING: Let's follow, Gertrude.
How much I had to do to calm his rage!
Now fear I this will give it start again,
Therefore let's follow.   *Exeunt.*

ACT FIVE, SCENE ONE

Enter two CLOWNS [*with spades and mattocks*].

FIRST CLOWN: Is she to be buried in Christian burial when she
willfully seeks her own salvation?

SECOND CLOWN: I tell thee she is, therefore make her grave
straight. The crowner hath sate on her, and finds it
Christian burial.   5

---

166. *askaunt:* sideways over.   167. *hoary:* grey-white.   168. *Therewith:* i.e. with willow
branches.   169. *long purples:* wild orchids.   170. *liberal:* free-spoken.   171. *cull-cold:*
chaste.   172. *crownet:* made into coronets.   173. *envious sliver:* malicious branch.
177. *lauds:* hymns.   178. *incapable:* insensible.   179. *indued:* habituated.   187. *It:* i.e.
weeping.   *trick:* natural way.   188. *these:* these tears.   189. *The woman . . . out:* my wom-
anish traits will be gone for good.
V.i. Location: A churchyard.
o.s.d. *Clowns:* rustics.   4. *straight:* immediately.   *crowner:* coroner.

FIRST CLOWN: How can that be, unless she drown'd herself in her own defense?

SECOND CLOWN: Why, 'tis found so.

FIRST CLOWN: It must be [*se offendendo*], it cannot be else. For here lies the point: if I drown myself wittingly, it argues an act, and an act hath three branches—it is to act, to do, to perform; [*argal*], she drown'd herself wittingly.   10

SECOND CLOWN: Nay, but hear you, goodman delver—   14

FIRST CLOWN: Give me leave. Here lies the water; good. Here stands the man; good. If the man go to this water and drown himself, it is, will he, nill he, he goes, mark you that. But if the water come to him and drown him, he drowns not himself; argal, he that is not guilty of his own death shortens not his own life.   20

SECOND CLOWN: But is this law?

FIRST CLOWN: Ay, marry, is't—crowner's quest law.

SECOND CLOWN: Will you ha' the truth an't? If this had not been a gentlewoman, she should have been buried out a' Christian burial.   25

FIRST CLOWN: Why, there thou say'st, and the more pity that great folk should have count'nance in this world to drown or hang themselves, more than their even-Christen. Come, my spade. There is no ancient gentlemen but gard'ners, ditchers, and grave-makers; they hold up Adam's profession.   31

SECOND CLOWN: Was he a gentleman?

FIRST CLOWN: 'A was the first that ever bore arms.

[SECOND CLOWN; Why, he had none.

FIRST CLOWN: What, art a heathen? How dost thou under-   35
stand the Scripture? The Scripture says Adam digg'd; could he dig without arms?] I'll put another question to thee. If thou answerest me not to the purpose, confess thyself—

SECOND CLOWN: Go to.   40

FIRST CLOWN: What is he that builds stronger than either the mason, the shipwright, or the carpenter?

SECOND CLOWN: The gallows-maker, for that outlives a thousand tenants.   44

FIRST CLOWN: I like thy wit well, in good faith. The gallows does well; but how does it well? It does well to those

---

9. *se offendendo:* blunder for *se defendendo,* "in self-defense."   **12.** *argal:* blunder for *ergo,* "therefore."   **15–20.** *Here . . . life.* Alluding to a very famous suicide case, that of Sir James Hales, a judge who drowned himself in 1554; it was long cited in the courts. The clown gives a garbled account of the defense summing-up and the verdict.   **17.** *nill he:* will he not.   **22.** *quest:* inquest.   **28–29.** *even-Christen:* fellow-Christians.   **34.** *none:* i.e. no coat of arms.

that do ill. Now thou dost ill to say the gallows is built
stronger than the church; argal, the gallows may do
well to thee. To't again, come.

SECOND CLOWN: Who builds stronger than a mason, a ship-
wright, or a carpenter?   51

FIRST CLOWN: Ay, tell me that, and unyoke.

SECOND CLOWN: Marry, now I can tell.

FIRST CLOWN: To't.

SECOND CLOWN: Mass, I cannot tell.   55

Enter HAMLET *and* HORATIO [*afar off*].

FIRST CLOWN: Cudgel thy brains no more about it, for your dull
ass will not mend his pace with beating, and when you
are ask'd this question next, say "a gravemaker": the
houses he makes lasts till doomsday. Go get thee in,
and fetch me a sup of liquor.   60

[*Exit* SECOND CLOWN. FIRST CLOWN *digs.*]

"In youth when I did love, did love,   *Song.*
    Methought it was very sweet,
To contract—O—the time for—a—my behove,
    O, methought there—a—was nothing—a—meet."

HAMLET: Has this fellow no feeling of his business? 'a sings in
grave-making.   66

HORATIO: Custom hath made it in him a property of
easiness.

HAMLET: 'Tis e'en so, the hand of little employment hath the
daintier sense.   70

FIRST CLOWN: "But age with his stealing steps   *Song.*
    Hath clawed me in his clutch,
    And hath shipped me into the land,
    As if I had never been such."   74

[*Throws up a shovelful of earth with a skull in it.*]

HAMLET: That skull had a tongue in it, and could sing once.
How the knave jowls it to the ground, as if 'twere
Cain's jaw-bone, that did the first murder! This might
be the pate of a politician, which this ass now o'erreaches, one that would circumvent God, might it
not?   80

HORATIO: It might, my lord.

HAMLET: Or of a courtier, which could say, "Good morrow,
sweet lord! How dost thou, sweet lord?" This
might be my Lord Such-a-one, that prais'd my Lord

52. *unyoke:* i.e. cease to labor, call it a day.   **55.** *Mass:* by the mass.   **63.** *contract . . .*
behove: shorten, i.e. spend agreeably . . . advantage. The song, punctuated by the grunts
of the clown as he digs, is a garbled version of a poem by Thomas Lord Vaux,
entitled "The Aged Lover Renounceth Love."   **67.** *Custom:* habit.   **67–68.** *a property*
of easiness: i.e. a thing he can do with complete ease of mind.   **70.** *daintier sense:* more
delicate sensitivity.   **76.** *jowls:* dashes.   **78.** *politician:* schemer, intriguer.
78–79. *o'erreaches:* gets the better of (with play on the literal sense).   **79.** *circumvent*
God: bypass God's law.

Such-a-one's horse when 'a [meant] to beg it, might
it not?   86

HORATIO: Ay, my lord.

HAMLET: Why, e'en so, and now my Lady Worm's, chopless,
and knock'd about the [mazzard] with a sex-
ton's spade. Here's fine revolution, and we had the   90
trick to see't. Did these bones cost no more the breeding, but to play at loggats with them? Mine ache to
think on't.

FIRST CLOWN: "A pickaxe and a spade, a spade,   *Song.*
            For and a shrouding sheet: 95
            O, a pit of clay for to be made
            For such a guest is meet."

                            [*Throws up another skull.*]

HAMLET: There's another. Why may not that be the skull of
a lawyer? Where be his quiddities now, his quillities,
his cases, his tenures, and his tricks? Why does he   100
suffer this mad knave now to knock him about the
sconce with a dirty shovel, and will not tell him of his
action of battery? Hum! This fellow might be in 's time
a great buyer of land, with his statutes, his recognizances, his fines, his double vouchers, his recoveries. [Is   105
this the fine of his fines, and the recovery of his
recoveries,] to have his fine pate full of fine dirt? Will
[his] vouchers vouch him no more of his purchases,
and [double ones too], than the length and breadth of a
pair of indentures? The very conveyances of his lands   110
will scarcely lie in this box, and must th' inheritor
himself have no more, ha?

HORATIO: Not a jot more, my lord.

HAMLET: Is not parchment made of sheep-skins?

HORATIO: Ay, my lord, and of calves'-skins too.   115

HAMLET: They are sheep and calves which seek out assurance
in that. I will speak to this fellow. Whose grave's this,
sirrah?

FIRST CLOWN: Mine, sir.   [*Sings.*]

            "[O], a pit of clay for to be made   120
            [For such a guest is meet]."

---

88. *chopless:* lacking the lower jaw. **89.** *mazzard:* head. **90.** *revolution:* change. *and:* if.
91. *trick:* knack, ability. *Did . . . cost:* were . . . worth. **92.** *loggats:* a game in which
blocks of wood were thrown at a stake. **99.** *quiddities:* subtleties, quibbles. *quillities:*
fine distinctions. **100.** *tenures:* titles to real estate. **102.** *sconce:* head. **104, 105.** *statutes,*
recognizances: bonds securing debts by attaching land and property. **105, 106.** *fines,*
recoveries: procedures for converting an entailed estate to freehold. **105.** *double vouchers:*
documents guaranteeing title to real estate, signed by two persons. **106.** *fine:* end.
110. *pair of indentures:* legal document cut into two parts which fitted together on a
serrated edge. Perhaps Hamlet thus refers to the two rows of teeth in the skull, or to the
bone sutures. **110.** *conveyances:* documents relating to transfer of property. **111.** *this*
box: i.e. the skull itself. *inheritor:* owner. **118.** *sirrah:* term of address to inferiors.

HAMLET: I think it be thine indeed, for thou liest in't.

FIRST CLOWN: You lie out on't, sir, and therefore 'tis not yours; for my part, I do not lie in't, yet it is mine.   124

HAMLET: Thou dost lie in't, to be in't and say it is thine. 'Tis for the dead, not for the quick; therefore thou liest.

FIRST CLOWN: 'Tis a quick lie, sir, 'twill away again from me to you.

HAMLET: What man dost thou dig it for?   130

FIRST CLOWN: For no man, sir.

HAMLET: What woman then?

FIRST CLOWN: For none neither.

HAMLET: Who is to be buried in't?   134

FIRST CLOWN: One that was a woman, sir, but, rest her soul, she's dead.

HAMLET: How absolute the knave is! we must speak by the card, or equivocation will undo us. By the Lord, Horatio, this three years I have took note of it: the age is grown so pick'd that the toe of the peasant comes so   140
near the heel of the courtier, he galls his kibe. How long hast thou been grave-maker?

FIRST CLOWN: Of [all] the days i' th' year, I came to't that day that our last king Hamlet overcame Fortinbras.

HAMLET: How long is that since?   145

FIRST CLOWN: Cannot you tell that? Every fool can tell that. It was that very day that young Hamlet was born —he that is mad, and sent into England.

HAMLET: Ay, marry, why was he sent into England?

FIRST CLOWN: Why, because 'a was mad. 'A shall recover his wits there, or if 'a do not, 'tis no great matter there.   152

HAMLET: Why?

FIRST CLOWN: 'Twill not be seen in him there, there the men are as mad as he.

HAMLET: How came he mad?

FIRST CLOWN: Very strangely, they say.

HAMLET: How strangely?

FIRST CLOWN: Faith, e'en with losing his wits.

HAMLET: Upon what ground?   160

FIRST CLOWN: Why, here in Denmark. I have been sexton here, man and boy, thirty years.

---

137. *absolute:* positive.   137–138. *by the card:* by the compass, i.e. punctiliously.
138. *equivocation:* ambiguity.   140. *pick'd:* refined.   141. *galls his kibe:* rubs the courtier's chilblain.

HAMLET: How long will a man lie i' th' earth ere he rot?   164

FIRST CLOWN: Faith, if 'a be not rotten before 'a die—as we have many pocky corses, that will scarce hold the laying in—'a will last you some eight year or nine year. A tanner will last you nine year.

HAMLET: Why he more than another?   169

FIRST CLOWN: Why, sir, his hide is so tann'd with his trade that 'a will keep out water a great while, and your water is a sore decayer of your whoreson dead body. Here's a skull now hath lien you i' the' earth three and twenty years.

HAMLET: Whose was it?   175

FIRST CLOWN: A whoreson mad fellow's it was. Whose do you think it was?

HAMLET: Nay, I know not.

FIRST CLOWN: A pestilence on him for a mad rogue! 'a pour'd a flagon of Rhenish on my head once. This same skull, sir, was, sir, Yorick's skull, the King's jester.

HAMLET: This?   [*Takes the skull.*]   182

FIRST CLOWN: E'en that.

HAMLET: Alas, poor Yorick! I knew him, Horatio, a fellow of infinite jest, of most excellent fancy. He hath bore   185
me on his back a thousand times, and now how abhorr'd in my imagination it is! my gorge rises at it. Here hung those lips that I have kiss'd I know not how oft. Where be your gibes now, your gambols, your songs, your flashes of merriment, that were wont to set   190
the table on a roar? Not one now to mock your own grinning—quite chop-fall'n. Now get you to my lady's [chamber], and tell her, let her paint an inch thick, to this favor she must come; make her laugh at that. Prithee, Horatio, tell me one thing.   195

HORATIO: What's that, my lord?

HAMLET: Dost thou think Alexander look'd a' this fashion i' th' earth?

HORATIO: E'en so.

HAMLET: And smelt so? pah!   [*Puts down the skull.*]

HORATIO: E'en so, my lord.   201

HAMLET: To what base uses we may return, Horatio! Why may not imagination trace the noble dust of Alexander, till 'a find it stopping a bunghole?

---

166. *pocky:* rotten with venereal disease. **166–67.** *hold . . . in:* last out the burial.
192. *chop-fall'n:* (1) lacking the lower jaw; (2) downcast. **194.** *favor:* appearance.

HORATIO: 'Twere to consider too curiously, to consider
    so.   206

HAMLET: No, faith, not a jot, but to follow him thither with
    modesty enough and likelihood to lead it: Alexander
    died, Alexander was buried, Alexander returneth to
    dust, the dust is earth, of earth we make loam, and why   210
    of that loam whereto he was converted might they not
    stop a beer-barrel?
    Imperious Caesar, dead and turn'd to clay,
    Might stop a hole to keep the wind away.
    O that the earth which kept the world in awe   215
    Should patch a wall t' expel the [winter's] flaw!
    But soft, but soft awhile, here comes the King,

Enter KING, QUEEN, LAERTES, *and* [*a* DOCTOR OF DIVINITY,
following] *the corse,* [*with* LORDS *attendant*].

    The Queen, the courtiers. Who is this they follow?
    And with such maimed rites? This doth betoken
    The corse they follow did with desp'rate hand   220
    Foredo it own life. 'Twas of some estate.
    Couch we a while and mark.   [*Retiring with* HORATIO.]

LAERTES: What ceremony else?

HAMLET: That is Laertes, a very noble youth. Mark.

LAERTES: What ceremony else?   225

DOCTOR: Her obsequies have been as far enlarg'd
    As we have warranty. Her death was doubtful,
    And but that great command o'ersways the order,
    She should in ground unsanctified been lodg'd
    Till the last trumpet; for charitable prayers,   230
    [Shards,] flints, and pebbles should be thrown on her.
    Yet here she is allow'd her virgin crants,
    Her maiden strewments, and the bringing home
    Of bell and burial.

LAERTES: Must there no more be done?

DOCTOR: No more be done:
    We should profane the service of the dead   236
    To sing a requiem and such rest to her
    As to peace-parted souls.

LAERTES: Lay her i' th' earth,
    And from her fair and unpolluted flesh

---

205. *curiously:* closely, minutely.   208. *modesty:* moderation.   210. *loam:* a mixture of
moistened clay with sand, straw, etc.   213. *Imperious:* imperial.   216. *flaw:* gust.
219. *maimed rites:* lack of customary ceremony.   221. *Foredo:* fordo, destroy.   *it:* its.
estate: rank.   222. *Couch we:* let us conceal ourselves.   227. *doubtful:* i.e. the subject of an
"open verdict."   228. *order:* customary procedure.   229. *should:* would certainly.   230. *for:*
instead of.   232. *crants:* garland.   233. *maiden strewments:* flowers scattered on the grave
of an unmarried girl.   233–34. *bringing . . . burial:* i.e. burial in consecrated ground, with
the bell tolling.   237. *requiem:* dirge.

May violets spring! I tell thee, churlish priest,   240
A minist'ring angel shall my sister be
When thou liest howling.

HAMLET: What, the fair Ophelia!

QUEEN [*Scattering flowers.*]: Sweets to the sweet, farewell!
I hop'd thou shouldst have been my Hamlet's wife.
I thought thy bride-bed to have deck'd, sweet maid,
And not have strew'd thy grave.

LAERTES: O, treble woe   246
Fall ten times [treble] on that cursed head
Whose wicked deed thy most ingenious sense
Depriv'd thee of! Hold off the earth a while,
Till I have caught her once more in mine arms.   250
                              [*Leaps in the grave.*]
Now pile your dust upon the quick and dead,
Till of this flat a mountain you have made
T' o'ertop old Pelion, or the skyish head
Of blue Olympus.

HAMLET [*Coming forward.*]: What is he whose grief
Bears such an emphasis, whose phrase of sorrow   255
Conjures the wand'ring stars and makes them stand
Like wonder-wounded hearers? This is I,
Hamlet the Dane!   [HAMLET *leaps in after* LAERTES.]

LAERTES: The devil take thy soul!   [*Grappling with him.*]

HAMLET: Thou pray'st not well.
I prithee take thy fingers from my throat.   260
For though I am not splenitive [and] rash,
Yet have I in me something dangerous,
Which let thy wisdom fear. Hold off thy hand!

KING: Pluck them asunder.

QUEEN: Hamlet, Hamlet!

ALL: Gentlemen!

HORATIO: Good my lord, be quiet.   265
          [*The* ATTENDANTS *part them, and they come out of the
          grave.*]

HAMLET: Why, I will fight with him upon this theme
Until my eyelids will no longer wag.

QUEEN: O my son, what theme?

HAMLET: I lov'd Ophelia. Forty thousand brothers
Could not with all their quantity of love   270
Make up my sum. What wilt thou do for her?

KING: O, he is mad, Laertes.

---

243. *Sweets:* flowers.   248. *ingenious:* intelligent.   253, 254. *Pelion, Olympus:* mountains in
northeastern Greece.   255. *emphasis, phrase.* Rhetorical terms, here used in disparaging
reference to Laertes inflated language.   256. *Conjures:* puts a spell upon.   *wand'ring stars:*
planets.   258. *the Dane.* This title normally signifies the King.   261. *splenitive:* impetuous.

QUEEN: For love of God, forbear him.

HAMLET: 'Swounds, show me what thou't do.
Woo't weep, woo't fight, woo't fast, woo't tear thyself?   275
Woo't drink up eisel, eat a crocodile?
I'll do't. Dost [thou] come here to whine?
To outface me with leaping in her grave?
Be buried quick with her, and so will I.
And if thou prate of mountains, let them throw   280
Millions of acres on us, till our ground,
Singeing his pate against the burning zone,
Make Ossa like a wart! Nay, and thou'lt mouth,
I'll rant as well as thou.

QUEEN: This is mere madness,
And [thus] a while the fit will work on him;   285
Anon, as patient as the female dove,
When that her golden couplets are disclosed,
His silence will sit drooping.

HAMLET: Hear you, sir,
What is the reason that you use me thus?
I lov'd you ever. But it is no matter.   290
Let Hercules himself do what he may,
The cat will mew, and dog will have his day.   *Exit* HAMLET.

KING: I pray thee, good Horatio, wait upon him.   [*Exit*] HORATIO.
[*To* LAERTES.] Strengthen your patience in our last
     night's speech,
We'll put the matter to the present push.—   295
Good Gertrude, set some watch over your son.
This grave shall have a living monument.
An hour of quiet [shortly] shall we see,
Till then in patience our proceeding be.   *Exeunt.*

SCENE TWO

Enter HAMLET *and* HORATIO.

HAMLET: So much for this, sir, now shall you see the other—
You do remember all the circumstance?

HORATIO: Remember it, my lord!

HAMLET: Sir, in my heart there was a kind of fighting
That would not let me sleep. [Methought] I lay   5

274. *thou't:* thou wilt.   275. *Woo't:* wilt thou.   276. *eisel:* vinegar.   *crocodile:* crocodile.
280. *if . . . mountains.* Referring to lines 251–54.   282. *burning zone:* sphere of the sun.
283. *Ossa:* another mountain in Greece, near Pelion and Olympus.   *mouth:* talk bombast
(synonymous with *rant* in the next line).   284. *mere:* utter.   286. *patient:* calm.
287. *golden couplets:* pair of baby birds, covered with yellow down.   *disclosed:* hatched.
291–92. *Let . . . day:* i.e. nobody can prevent another from making the scenes he feels he
has a right to.   294. *in:* i.e. by recalling.   295. *present push:* immediate test.   297. *living:*
enduring (?) or in the form of a lifelike effigy (?).
V.ii. Location: The castle.
1. *see the other:* i.e. hear the other news I have to tell you (hinted at in the letter to
Horatio, IV.vi.24–25).

Worse than the mutines in the [bilboes]. Rashly—
And prais'd be rashness for it—let us know
Our indiscretion sometime serves us well
When our deep plots do pall, and that should learn us
There's a divinity that shapes our ends,   10
Rough-hew them how we will—

HORATIO: That is most certain.

HAMLET: Up from my cabin,
    My sea-gown scarf'd about me, in the dark
    Grop'd I to find out them, had my desire,
    Finger'd their packet, and in fine withdrew   15
    To mine own room again, making so bold,
    My fears forgetting manners, to [unseal]
    Their grand commission; where I found, Horatio—
    Ah, royal knavery!—an exact command,
    Larded with many several sorts of reasons,   20
    Importing Denmark's health and England's too,
    With, ho, such bugs and goblins in my life,
    That, on the supervise, no leisure bated,
    No, not to stay the grinding of the axe,
    My head should be strook off.

HORATIO: Is't possible?   25

HAMLET: Here's the commission, read it at more leisure.
    But wilt thou hear now how I did proceed?

HORATIO: I beseech you.

HAMLET: Being thus benetted round with [villainies],
    Or I could make a prologue to my brains,   30
    They had begun the play. I sat me down,
    Devis'd a new commission, wrote it fair.
    I once did hold it, as our statists do,
    A baseness to write fair, and labor'd much
    How to forget that learning, but, sir, now   35
    It did me yeman's service. Wilt thou know
    Th' effect of what I wrote?

HORATIO: Ay, good my lord.

HAMLET: An earnest conjuration from the King,
    As England was his faithful tributary,
    As love between them like the palm might flourish,   40
    As peace should still her wheaten garland wear

6. *mutines:* mutineers (but the term *mutiny* was in Shakespeare's day used of almost any
act of rebellion against authority). *bilboes:* fetters attached to a heavy iron bar. *Rashly:*
on impulse. 7. *know:* recognize, acknowledge. 9. *pall:* lose force, come to nothing.
learn: teach. 10. *shapes our ends:* gives final shape to our designs. 11. *Rough-hew them:*
block them out in initial form. 15. *Finger'd:* filched, "pinched." 20. *Larded:* garnished.
21. *Importing:* relating to. 22. *bugs . . . life:* terrifying things in prospect if I were permitted to remain alive. *Bugs* = bugaboos. 23. *supervise:* perusal. *bated:* deducted (from the
stipulated speediness). 24. *stay:* wait for. 30. *Or:* before. 32. *fair:* i.e. in a beautiful
hand (such as a professional scribe would use). 33. *statists:* statesmen, public officials.
34. *A baseness:* i.e. a skill befitting men of low rank. 36. *yeman's:* yeoman's, i.e. solid,
substantial. 37. *effect:* purport, gist.

And stand a comma 'tween their amities,
And many such-like [as's] of great charge,
That on the view and knowing of these contents,
Without debatement further, more or less,   45
He should those bearers put to sudden death,
Not shriving time allow'd.

HORATIO: How was this seal'd?

HAMLET: Why, even in that was heaven ordinant.
I had my father's signet in my purse,
Which was the model of that Danish seal;   50
Folded the writ up in the form of th' other,
[Subscrib'd] it, gave't th' impression, plac'd it safely,
The changeling never known. Now the next day
Was our sea-fight, and what to this was sequent
Thou knowest already.   55

HORATIO: So Guildenstern and Rosencrantz go to't.

HAMLET: [Why, man, they did make love to this employment,]
They are not near my conscience. Their defeat
Does by their own insinuation grow.
'Tis dangerous when the baser nature comes   60
Between the pass and fell incensed points
Of mighty opposites.

HORATIO: Why, what a king is this!

HAMLET: Does it not, think thee, stand me now upon—
He that hath kill'd my king and whor'd my mother,
Popp'd in between th' election and my hopes,   65
Thrown out his angle for my proper life,
And with such coz'nage—is't not perfect conscience
[To quit him with this arm? And is't not to be damn'd,
To let this canker of our nature come
In further evil?   70

HORATIO: It must be shortly known to him from England
What is the issue of the business there.

HAMLET: It will be short; the interim's mine,
And a man's life's no more than to say "one."
But I am very sorry, good Horatio,   75
That to Laertes I forgot myself,

42. *comma:* connective, link.   43. *as's . . . charge:* (1) weighty clauses
beginning with *as;* (2) asses with heavy loads.   47. *shriving time:* time for confession and absolution.   48. *ordinant:* in charge, guiding.   50. *model:* small copy.   52. *Sub-
scrib'd:* signed.   53. *changeling:* i.e. Hamlet's letter, substituted secretly for the genuine
letter, as fairies substituted their children for human children.   *never known:* never recognized as a substitution (unlike the fairies' changelings).   56. *go to't:* i.e. are going to their
death.   58. *defeat:* ruin, overthrow.   59. *insinuation:* winding their way into the affair.
60. *baser:* inferior.   61. *pass:* thrust.   *fell:* fierce.   63. *stand . . . upon:* i.e. rest upon me as
a duty.   65. *election:* i.e. as King of Denmark.   66. *angle:* hook and line.   *proper:* very.
67. *coz'nage:* trickery.   68. *quit him:* pay him back.   69. *canker:* cancerous sore.
69–70. *come In:* grow into.   74. *a man's . . . more:* i.e. to kill a man takes no more time.
say "one." Perhaps this is equivalent to "deliver one sword thrust"; see line 280 below,
where Hamlet says "One" as he makes the first hit.

For by the image of my cause I see
The portraiture of his. I'll [court] his favors.
But sure the bravery of his grief did put me
Into a tow'ring passion.

HORATIO: Peace, who comes here?]   80

Enter [young OSRIC,] *a courtier.*

OSRIC: Your lordship is right welcome back to Denmark.

HAMLET: I humbly thank you, sir.—Dost know this water-fly?

HORATIO: No, my good lord.

HAMLET: Thy state is the more gracious, for 'tis a vice to
know him. He hath much land, and fertile; let a   85
beast be lord of beasts, and his crib shall stand at the
King's mess. 'Tis a chough, but, as I say, spacious in
the possession of dirt.

OSRIC: Sweet lord, if your lordship were at leisure, I should
impart a thing to you from his Majesty.   90

HAMLET: I will receive it, sir, with all diligence of spirit.
[Put] your bonnet to his right use, 'tis for the
head.

OSRIC: I thank your lordship, it is very hot.

HAMLET: No, believe me, 'tis very cold, the wind is   95
northerly.

OSRIC: It is indifferent cold, my lord, indeed.

HAMLET: But yet methinks it is very [sultry] and hot [for] my
complexion.

OSRIC: Exceedingly, my lord, it is very sultry—as 'twere   100
—I cannot tell how. My lord, his Majesty bade me
signify to you that 'a has laid a great wager on your
head. Sir, this is the matter—

HAMLET: I beseech you remember.

[HAMLET *moves him to put on his hat.*]

OSRIC: Nay, good my lord, for my ease, in good faith.   105
Sir, here is newly come to court Laertes, believe me, an
absolute [gentleman], full of most excellent differences,
of very soft society, and great showing; indeed, to
speak sellingly of him, he is the card or calendar of

---

77. *image:* likeness.   79. *bravery:* ostentatious expression.   82. *water-fly:* i.e. tiny, vainly
agitated creature.   84. *gracious:* virtuous.   85–87. *let . . . mess:* i.e. if a beast owned as
many cattle as Osric, he could feast with the King.   87. *chough:* jackdaw, a bird that could
be taught to speak.   92. *bonnet:* hat.   97. *indifferent:* somewhat.   99. *complexion:* temperament.   105. *for my ease:* i.e. I am really more comfortable with my hat off (a polite
insistence on maintaining ceremony).   107. *absolute:* complete, possessing every quality a
gentleman should have.   *differences:* distinguishing characteristics, personal qualities.
108. *soft:* agreeable.   *great showing:* splendid appearance.   109. *sellingly:* i.e. like a seller
to a prospective buyer; in a fashion to do full justice. Most editors follow Q3 in reading
feelingly = with exactitude, as he deserves.   *card or calendar:* chart or register, i.e. com-
pendious guide.

gentry; for you shall find in him the continent of what   110
part a gentleman would see.

HAMLET: Sir, his definement suffers no perdition in you,
though I know to divide him inventorially would
dozy th' arithmetic of memory, and yet but yaw
neither in respect of his quick sail; but in the verity of   115
extolment, I take him to be a soul of great article,
and his infusion of such dearth and rareness as, to
make true diction of him, his semblable is his mirror,
and who else would trace him, his umbrage,
nothing more.   120

OSRIC: Your lordship speaks most infallibly of him.

HAMLET: The concernancy, sir? Why do we wrap the gentleman in our more rawer breath?

OSRIC: Sir?

HORATIO: Is't not possible to understand in another tongue?   125
You will to't, sir, really.

HAMLET: What imports the nomination of this gentleman?

OSRIC: Of Laertes?

HORATIO: His purse is empty already: all 's golden words   130
are spent.

HAMLET: Of him, sir.

OSRIC: I know you are not ignorant—

HAMLET: I would you did, sir, yet, in faith, if you did, it would
not much approve me. Well, sir?   135

OSRIC: You are not ignorant of what excellence Laertes
is—

HAMLET: I dare not confess that, lest I should compare with
him in excellence, but to know a man well were to
know himself.   140

OSRIC: I mean, sir, for [his] weapon, but in the impu-
tation laid on him by them, in his meed he's
unfellow'd.

HAMLET: What's his weapon?

OSRIC: Rapier and dagger.   145

---

110. *gentry:* gentlemanly behavior.   110–11. *the continent . . . part:* one who contains every quality.   112. *perdition:* loss.   114. *dozy:* make dizzy.   *yaw:* keep deviating erratically from its course (said of a ship).   115. *neither:* for all that.   *in respect of:* compared with.   115–16. *in . . . extolment:* to praise him truly.   116. *article:* scope (?) or importance (?).   117. *infusion:* essence, quality.   *dearth:* scarceness.   118. *make true diction:* speak truly.   *his semblable:* his only likeness or equal.   119. *who . . . him:* anyone else who tries to follow him.   119. *umbrage:* shadow.   122. *concernancy:* relevance.   123. *more rawer breath:* i.e. words too crude to describe him properly.   125. *in another tongue:* i.e. when someone else is the speaker.   126. *You . . . really:* i.e. you can do it if you try.   127. *nomination:* naming, mention.   135. *approve:* commend.   138–39. *compare . . . excellence:* i.e. seem to claim the same degree of excellence for myself.   139. *but.* The sense seems to require *for.*   140. *himself:* i.e. oneself.   141–42. *in . . . them:* i.e. in popular estimation.   142. *meed:* merit.

HAMLET: That's two of his weapons—but well.

OSRIC: The King, sir, hath wager'd with him six Barbary horses, against the which he has impawn'd, as I take it, six French rapiers and poniards, with their assigns, as girdle, [hangers], and so. Three of the carriages, in faith, are very dear to fancy, very responsive to the hilts, most delicate carriages, and of very liberal conceit.   150

HAMLET: What call you the carriages?

HORATIO: I knew you must be edified by the margent ere you had done.   155

OSRIC: The [carriages], sir, are the hangers.

HAMLET: The phrase would be more germane to the matter if we could carry a cannon by our sides; I would it [might be] hangers till then. But on: six Barb'ry horses against six French swords, their assigns, and three liberal-conceited carriages; that's the French bet against the Danish. Why is this all [impawn'd, as] you call it?   160

OSRIC: The King, sir, hath laid, sir, that in a dozen passes between yourself and him, he shall not exceed you three hits; he hath laid on twelve for nine; and it would come to immediate trial, if your lordship would vouchsafe the answer.   165

HAMLET: How if I answer no?   170

OSRIC: I mean, my lord, the opposition of your person in trial.

HAMLET: Sir, I will walk here in the hall. If it please his Majesty, it is the breathing time of day with me. Let the foils be brought, the gentleman willing, and the King hold his purpose, I will win for him and I can; if not, I will gain nothing but my shame and the odd hits.   175

OSRIC: Shall I deliver you so?

HAMLET: To this effect, sir—after what flourish your nature will.   180

OSRIC: I commend my duty to your lordship.

148. *impawn'd:* stake.   149. *assigns:* appurtenances.   150. *hangers:* straps on which the swords hang from the girdle.   *carriages:* properly, gun-carriages; here used affectedly in place of *hangers.*   151. *fancy:* taste.   151. *very responsive to:* matching well. 152–153. *liberal conceit:* elegant design.   155. *must . . . margent:* would require enlightenment from a marginal note.   165. *laid:* wagered.   166–67. *he . . . hits.* Laertes must win by at least eight to four (if none of the "passes" or bouts are draws), since at seven to five he would be only two up.   167. *he . . . nine.* Not satisfactorily explained despite much discussion. One suggestion is that Laertes has raised the odds against himself by wagering that out of twelve bouts he will win nine.   169. *answer:* encounter (as Hamlet's following quibble forces Osric to explain in his next speech).   174. *breathing . . . me:* my usual hour for exercise.   180. *after what flourish:* with whatever embellishment of language.   182. *commend my duty:* offer my dutiful respects (but Hamlet picks up the phrase in the sense "praise my manner of bowing").

HAMLET: Yours. [*Exit* OSRIC.] ['A] does well to commend it
himself, there are no tongues else for 's turn.

HORATIO: This lapwing runs away with the shell on his   185
head.

HAMLET: 'A did [comply], sir, with his dug before 'a suck'd
it. Thus has he, and many more of the same breed
that I know the drossy age dotes on, only got the
tune of the time, and out of an habit of encounter, a   190
kind of [yesty] collection, which carries them through
and through the most [profound] and [winnow'd]
opinions, and do but blow them to their trial, the
bubbles are out.

Enter a LORD.

LORD: My lord, his Majesty commended him to you by   195
young Osric, who brings back to him that you attend
him in the hall. He sends to know if your pleasure hold
to play with Laertes, or that you will take longer
time.

HAMLET: I am constant to my purposes, they follow the   200
King's pleasure. If his fitness speaks, mine is ready;
now or whensoever, provided I be so able as now.

LORD: The King and Queen and all are coming
down.

HAMLET: In happy time.   205

LORD: The Queen desires you to use some gentle entertainment to Laertes before you fall to play.

HAMLET: She well instructs me.   [*Exit* LORD.]

HORATIO: You will lose, my lord.

HAMLET: I do not think so; since he went into France I   210
have been in continual practice. I shall win at the odds.
Thou wouldst not think how ill all's here about my
heart—but it is no matter.

HORATIO: Nay, good my lord—

HAMLET: It is but foolery, but it is such a kind of [gain-]   215
giving, as would perhaps trouble a woman.

HORATIO: If your mind dislike any thing, obey it. I will forestall
their repair hither, and say you are not fit.

185. *lapwing:* a foolish bird which upon hatching was supposed to run with part of the
eggshell still over its head. (Osric has put his hat on at last.)   187. *comply . . . dug:* bow
politely to his mother's nipple.   189. *drossy:* i.e. worthless.   190. *tune . . . time:* i.e. fashionable ways of talk.   *habit of encounter:* mode of social intercourse.   191. *yesty:* yeasty,
frothy.   *collection:* i.e. anthology of fine phrases.   192. *winnow'd:* sifted, choice.
193. *opinions:* judgments.   *blow . . . trial:* test them by blowing on them, i.e. make
even the least demanding trial of them.   194. *out:* blown away (?) or at an end, done
for (?).   201. *If . . . ready:* i.e. if this is a good moment for him, it is for me also.
206–7. *gentle entertainment:* courteous greeting.   215–216. *gain-giving:* misgiving.

HAMLET: Not a whit, we defy augury. There is special provi-   577
    dence in the fall of a sparrow. If it be [now],'tis not to   220
    come; if it be not to come, it will be now; if it be not
    now, yet it [will] come—the readiness is all. Since no
    man, of aught he leaves, knows what is't to leave
    betimes, let be.

        A table prepar'd, [and flagons of wine on it. Enter] Trumpets,
        Drums, and Officers with cushions, foils, daggers; KING,
        QUEEN, LAERTES, [OSRIC,] *and all the State.*

KING: Come, Hamlet, come, and take this hand from me.   225
               [*The* KING *puts* LAERTES' *hand into* HAMLET'S.]

HAMLET: Give me your pardon, sir. I have done you wrong,
    But pardon't as you are a gentleman.
    This presence knows,
    And you must needs have heard, how I am punish'd
    With a sore distraction. What I have done   230
    That might your nature, honor, and exception
    Roughly awake, I here proclaim was madness.
    Was't Hamlet wrong'd Laertes? Never Hamlet!
    If Hamlet from himself be ta'en away,
    And when he's not himself does wrong Laertes,   235
    Then Hamlet does it not, Hamlet denies it.
    Who does it then? His madness. If't be so,
    Hamlet is of the faction that is wronged,
    His madness is poor Hamlet's enemy.
    [Sir, in this audience,]   240
    Let my disclaiming from a purpos'd evil
    Free me so far in your most generous thoughts,
    That I have shot my arrow o'er the house
    And hurt my brother.

LAERTES: I am satisfied in nature,
    Whose motive in this case should stir me most   245
    To my revenge, but in my terms of honor
    I stand aloof, and will no reconcilement
    Till by some elder masters of known honor
    I have a voice and president of peace
    To [keep] my name ungor'd. But [till] that time   250
    I do receive your offer'd love like love,
    And will not wrong it.

219–20. *special . . . sparrow.* See Matthew 10:29.   **223.** *of aught:* i.e.
whatever.   **223–24.** *knows . . . betimes:* knows what is the best time to leave it.
224 s.d. *State:* nobles.   **228.** *presence:* assembled court.   **229.** *punish'd:*
afflicted.   **231.** *exception:* objection.   **241.** *my . . . evil:* my declaration that I intended no
harm.   **242.** *Free:* absolve.   **244.** *in nature:* so far as my personal feelings are
concerned.   **246.** *in . . . honor:* i.e. as a man governed by an established code of
honor.   **249–50.** *have . . . ungor'd:* can secure an opinion backed by precedent that I can
make peace with you without injury to my reputation.

HAMLET: I embrace it freely,
And will this brothers' wager frankly play.
Give us the foils. [Come on.]

LAERTES: Come, one for me.

HAMLET: I'll be your foil, Laertes; in mine ignorance
Your skill shall like a star i' th' darkest night   256
Stick fiery off indeed.

LAERTES: You mock me, sir.

HAMLET: No, by this hand.

KING: Give them the foils, young Osric. Cousin Hamlet,
You know the wager?

HAMLET: Very well, my lord.   260
Your Grace has laid the odds a' th' weaker side.

KING: I do not fear it, I have seen you both;
But since he is [better'd], we have therefore odds.

LAERTES: This is too heavy; let me see another.

HAMLET: This likes me well. These foils have all a length?
                                        [Prepare to play.]

OSRIC: Ay, my good lord.   266

KING: Set me the stoups of wine upon that table.
If Hamlet gives the first or second hit,
Or quit in answer of the third exchange,
Let all the battlements their ord'nance fire.   270
The King shall drink to Hamlet's better breath,
And in the cup an [union] shall he throw,
Richer than that which four successive kings
In Denmark's crown have worn. Give me the cups,
And let the kettle to the trumpet speak.   275
The trumpet to the cannoneer without,
The cannons to the heavens, the heaven to earth,
"Now the King drinks to Hamlet." Come begin;
                                        Trumpets the while.
And you, the judges, bear a wary eye.

HAMLET: Come on sir.

LAERTES: Come, my lord.
                              [They play and HAMLET scores a hit.]

HAMLET: One.

LAERTES: No.

HAMLET: Judgment.   280

253. *brothers'*: i.e. amicable, as if between brothers. *frankly:* freely, without constraint. 255. *foil:* thin sheet of metal placed behind a jewel to set it off. 257. *Stick . . . off:* blaze out in contrast. 261. *laid the odds:* i.e. wagered a higher stake (horses to rapiers). 263. *is better'd:* has perfected his skill *odds:* i.e. the arrangement that Laertes must take more bouts than Hamlet to win. 265. *likes:* pleases. *a length:* the same length. 267. *stoups:* tankards. 269. *quit . . . exchange:* pays back wins by Laertes in the first and second bouts by taking the third. 272. *union:* an especially fine pearl. 275. *kettle:* kettle-drum.

OSRIC: A hit, a very palpable hit.

LAERTES: Well, again.

KING: Stay, give me drink. Hamlet, this pearl is thine,
Here's to thy health! Give him the cup.

> *Drums, trumpets [sound] flourish. A piece goes off [within].*

HAMLET: I'll play this bout first, set it by a while.   284
Come. [*They play again.*] Another hit; what say you?

LAERTES: [A touch, a touch,] I do confess't.

KING: Our son shall win.

QUEEN: He's fat, and scant of breath.
Here, Hamlet, take my napkin, rub thy brows.
The Queen carouses to thy fortune, Hamlet.

HAMLET: Good madam!

KING: Gertrude, do not drink.   290

QUEEN: I will, my lord, I pray you pardon me.

KING [*Aside.*]: It is the pois'ned cup, it is too late.

HAMLET: I dare not drink yet, madam; by and by.

QUEEN: Come, let me wipe thy face.

LAERTES: My lord, I'll hit him now.

KING: I do not think't.

LAERTES [*Aside.*]: And yet it is almost against my conscience.   296

HAMLET: Come, for the third, Laertes, you do but dally.
I pray you pass with your best violence;
I am sure you make a wanton of me.

LAERTES: Say you so? Come on.   [*They play.*]   300

OSRIC: Nothing, neither way.

LAERTES: Have at you now!

> [LAERTES *wounds* HAMLET; *then, in scuffling, they change rapiers.*]

KING: Part them, they are incens'd.

HAMLET: Nay, come again.   [HAMLET *wounds* LAERTES. *The* QUEEN *falls.*]

OSRIC: Look to the Queen there ho!

HORATIO: They bleed on both sides. How is it, my lord?

OSRIC: How is't, Laertes?   305

LAERTES: Why, as a woodcock to mine own springe, Osric:
I am justly kill'd with mine own treachery.

HAMLET: How does the Queen?

KING: She sounds to see them bleed.

---

287. *fat:* sweaty. **289.** *carouses:* drinks a toast. **299.** *make . . . me:* i.e. are holding back
in order to let me win, as one does with a spoiled child (*wanton*). **306.** *springe:* snare.
308. *sounds:* swoons.

QUEEN: No, no, the drink, the drink—O my dear Hamlet—
    The drink, the drink! I am pois'ned.   [*Dies.*]   310

HAMLET: O villainy! Ho, let the door be lock'd!
    Treachery! Seek it out.

LAERTES: It is here, Hamlet. [Hamlet,] thou art slain.
    No med'cine in the world can do thee good;
    In thee there is not half an hour's life.   315
    The treacherous instrument is in [thy] hand,
    Unbated and envenom'd. The foul practice
    Hath turn'd itself on me. Lo here I lie,
    Never to rise again. Thy mother's pois'ned.
    I can no more—the King, the King's to blame.   320

HAMLET: The point envenom'd too!
    Then, venom, to thy work.   [*Hurts the* KING.]

ALL: Treason! treason!

KING: O, yet defend me, friends, I am but hurt.

HAMLET: Here, thou incestious, [murd'rous], damned Dane,   325
    Drink [off] this potion! Is [thy union] here?
    Follow my mother!   [KING *dies.*]

LAERTES: He is justly served,
    It is a poison temper'd by himself.
    Exchange forgiveness with me, noble Hamlet.
    Mine and my father's death come not upon thee,   330
    Nor thine on me!   [*Dies.*]

HAMLET: Heaven make thee free of it! I follow thee.
    I am dead, Horatio. Wretched queen, adieu!
    You that look pale, and tremble at this chance,
    That are but mutes or audience to this act,   335
    Had I but time—as this fell sergeant, Death,
    Is strict in his arrest—O, I could tell you—
    But let it be. Horatio, I am dead,
    Thou livest. Report me and my cause aright
    To the unsatisfied.

HORATIO: Never believe it;   340
    I am more an antique Roman than a Dane.
    Here's yet some liquor left.

HAMLET: As th' art a man,
    Give me the cup. Let go! By heaven, I'll ha't!
    O God, Horatio, what a wounded name,   344
    Things standing thus unknown, shall I leave behind me!
    If thou didst ever hold me in thy heart,
    Absent thee from felicity a while,
    And in this harsh world draw thy breath in pain

---

317. *Unbated:* not blunted. *foul practice:* vile plot. **322 s.d.** *Hurts:* wounds. **328.** *temper'd:* mixed. **332.** *make thee free:* absolve you. **335.** *mutes or audience:* silent spectators. **336.** *fell:* cruel. *sergeant:* sheriff's officer. **341.** *antique Roman:* i.e. one who will commit suicide on such an occasion.

To tell my story.   *A march afar off* [*and a shot within*].
          What warlike noise is this?
                    [OSRIC *goes to the door and returns.*]

OSRIC: Young Fortinbras, with conquest come from Poland,   350
To th' embassadors of England gives
This warlike volley.

HAMLET: O, I die, Horatio,
The potent poison quite o'er-crows my spirit.
I cannot live to hear the news from England,
But I do prophesy th' election lights   355
On Fortinbras, he has my dying voice.
So tell him, with th' occurrents more and less
Which have solicited—the rest is silence.   [*Dies.*]

HORATIO: Now cracks a noble heart. Good night,
          sweet prince,
And flights of angels sing thee to thy rest!   [*March within.*]   360
Why does the drum come hither?

          Enter FORTINBRAS *with the* [ENGLISH] EMBASSADORS, [*with
          Drum, Colors, and Attendants*].

FORTINBRAS: Where is this sight?

HORATIO: What is it you would see?
If aught of woe or wonder, cease your search.

FORTINBRAS: This quarry cries on havoc. O proud death,
What feast is toward in thine eternal cell,   365
That thou so many princes at a shot
So bloodily hast strook?

[FIRST] EMBASSADOR: The sight is dismal,
And our affairs from England come too late.
The ears are senseless that should give us hearing,
To tell him his commandment is fulfill'd,   370
That Rosencrantz and Guildenstern are dead.
Where should we have our thanks?

HORATIO: Not from his mouth,
Had it th' ability of life to thank you.
He never gave commandement for their death.
But since so jump upon this bloody question,   375
You from the Polack wars, and you from England,
Are here arrived, give order that these bodies
High on a stage be placed to the view,
And let me speak to [th'] yet unknowing world
How these things came about. So shall you hear   380
Of carnal, bloody, and unnatural acts,

---

353. *o'er-crows:* triumphs over (a term derived from cockfighting).   *spirit:* vital energy.
356. *voice:* vote.   357. *occurrents:* occurrences.   358. *solicited:* instigated.   364. *This . . .
havoc:* this heap of corpses proclaims a massacre.   365. *toward:* in preparation.   372. *his:*
i.e. the King's.   375. *jump:* precisely, pat.   *question:* matter.   378. *stage:* platform.

Of accidental judgments, casual slaughters,
Of deaths put on by cunning and [forc'd] cause,
And in this upshot, purposes mistook
Fall'n on th' inventors' heads: all this can I   385
Truly deliver.

FORTINBRAS: Let us haste to hear it,
And call the noblest to the audience.
For me, with sorrow, I embrace my fortune.
I have some rights, of memory in this kingdom,
Which now to claim my vantage doth invite me.   390

HORATIO: Of that I shall have also cause to speak,
And from his mouth whose voice will draw [on] more.
But let this same be presently perform'd
Even while men's minds are wild, lest more mischance
On plots and errors happen.

FORTINBRAS: Let four captains   395
Bear Hamlet like a soldier to the stage,
For he was likely, had he been put on,
To have prov'd most royal; and for his passage,
The soldiers' music and the rite of war
Speak loudly for him.   400
Take up the bodies. Such a sight as this
Becomes the field, but here shows much amiss.
Go bid the soldiers shoot.

> *Exeunt* [*marching; after the which a peal of ordinance are shot off*].

382. *judgments:* retributions. *casual:* happening by chance. **383.** *put on:* instigated.
389. *of memory:* unforgotten. **390.** *my vantage:* i.e. my opportune presence at a moment
when the throne is empty. **392.** *his . . . more:* the mouth of one (Hamlet) whose vote will
induce others to support your claim. **393.** *presently:* at once. **394.** *wild:* distraught.
397. *put on:* put to the test (by becoming king). **398.** *passage:* death. **402.** *Becomes
. . . amiss:* befits the battlefield, but appears very much out of place here.

Fact Questions and Exercises

1. In Act 1, Scene 1, what "started like a guilty thing / Upon a fearful summons"?
2. How has old king Hamlet died? What duty does his death place on Hamlet?
3. Identify Rosencrantz and Guildenstern. What happens to them?
4. How does Hamlet treat Ophelia? Ultimately, what happens to her?
5. Describe the play that the strolling players present before King Claudius. What is the play's title? Why does Hamlet have this play performed?
6. Describe the circumstances of Polonius's death.
7. Why does Laertes want to kill Hamlet?

8. How are Claudius and Gertrude killed? Who becomes king after Claudius's death?
9. What is Hamlet's final request of Horatio?

For Discussion and Writing

1. Discuss Hamlet's "madness." Why does he pretend to be insane? Is he in any way truly insane? That is, does he fall prey to his own antics? How have outside forces helped make Hamlet "mad"?
2. Note the various crimes that are committed in the play. Which is the first committed that, in turn, leads to the other crimes? Who and what are corrupted by these crimes? Do innocent people suffer because of these crimes? Do these crimes leave the country vulnerable to opportunistic men—Fortinbras, for instance?
3. Does Hamlet want to assume the duty that his father's death places on him? Why does he fail to act immediately? Why does he treat various people as he does—Ophelia, for example? In the final scene, why does he want his name cleared?
4. Is *Hamlet* a tragedy? What is Hamlet's fatal flaw? Which of his traits contribute to his greatness or heroism? In what ways does *Hamlet* compare with *Oedipus Rex*? Discuss the conditions in Thebes and Denmark at the end of each of the plays.
5. In commenting on *Hamlet*, Samuel Taylor Coleridge says that "the contrast between the clowns and Hamlet [presents] two extremes." In what ways do Hamlet and the clowns contrast? Coleridge suggests that the clowns represent a "mockery of logic" and Hamlet, "logic." What facts support this idea? What other purposes do the clowns serve in the play?

Molière [1622–1673]

Jean Baptiste Poquelin (Molière) was born in Paris, France, and was educated at the Collège de Clermont, a Jesuit school. At twenty-one he decided to become an actor, a profession that in seventeenth-century France was regarded with scorn. He was, however, an accomplished performer who often acted in his own plays. By 1660 he had become a favorite of Louis XIV and was eventually given the honor of performing at the Théâtre du Palais Royal. As a playwright, he elevated comedy to a status equal with that of tragedy, using his scathing humor to expose human failings. *The Misanthrope* (1666), for instance, presents an individual trying to cope with society, while maintaining dignity and integrity in the face of almost certain defeat or humiliation. Though indeed a comedy, *The Misanthrope* is nevertheless a profound drama.

The Misanthrope

CHARACTERS

ALCESTE, *in love with Célimène*
PHILINTE, *Alceste's friend*
ORONTE, *in love with Célimène*
CELIMENE, *Alceste's beloved*
ELIANTE, *Célimène's cousin*
ARSINOE, *a friend of Célimène's*
ACASTE } *Marquesses*
CLITANDRE
BASQUE, *Célimène's servant*
A GUARD *of the Marshalsea*
DUBOIS, *Alceste's valet*

The Scene throughout is in Célimène's house at Paris.

ACT ONE, SCENE ONE

[PHILINTE, ALCESTE]

PHILINTE: Now, what's got into you?
ALCESTE [*seated*]:   Kindly leave me alone.
PHILINTE: Come, come, what is it? This lugubrious tone . . .
ALCESTE: Leave me, I said; you spoil my solitude.
PHILINTE: Oh, listen to me, now, and don't be rude.
ALCESTE: I choose to be rude, Sir, and to be hard of hearing.   5
PHILINTE: These ugly moods of yours are not endearing;
         Friends though we are, I really must insist . . .

ALCESTE [*abruptly rising*]: Friends? Friends, you say? Well, cross me off
        your list.
    I've been your friend till now, as you well know;
    But after what I saw a moment ago   10
    I tell you flatly that our ways must part.
    I wish no place in a dishonest heart.

PHILINTE: Why, what have I done, Alceste? Is this quite just?

ALCESTE: My God, you ought to die of self-disgust.
    I call your conduct inexcusable, Sir,   15
    And every man of honor will concur.
    I see you almost hug a man to death,
    Exclaim for joy until you're out of breath,
    And supplement these loving demonstrations
    With endless offers, vows, and protestations;   20
    Then when I ask you "Who was that?" I find
    That you can barely bring his name to mind!
    Once the man's back is turned, you cease to love him,
    And speak with absolute indifference of him!
    By God, I say it's base and scandalous   25
    To falsify the heart's affections thus;
    If I caught myself behaving in such a way,
    I'd hang myself for shame, without delay.

PHILINTE: It hardly seems a hanging matter to me;
    I hope that you will take it graciously   30
    If I extend myself a slight reprieve,
    And live a little longer, by your leave.

ALCESTE: How dare you joke about a crime so grave?

PHILINTE: What crime? How else are people to behave?

ALCESTE: I'd have them be sincere, and never part   35
    With any word that isn't from the heart.

PHILINTE: When someone greets us with a show of pleasure,
    It's but polite to give him equal measure,
    Return his love the best that we know how,
    And trade him offer for offer, vow for vow   40

ALCESTE: No, no, this formula you'd have me follow,
    However fashionable, is false and hollow,
    And I despise the frenzied operations
    Of all these barterers of protestations,
    These lavishers of meaningless embraces,   45
    These utterers of obliging commonplaces,
    Who court and flatter everyone on earth
    And praise the fool no less than the man of worth.
    Should you rejoice that someone fondles you,
    Offers his love and service, swears to be true,   50
    And fills your ears with praises of your name,
    When to the first damned fop he'll say the same?
    No, no: no self-respecting heart would dream

Of prizing so promiscuous an esteem;
However high the praise, there's nothing worse   55
Than sharing honors with the universe.
Esteem is founded on comparison:
To honor all men is to honor none.
Since you embrace this indiscriminate vice,
Your friendship comes at far too cheap a price;   60
I spurn the easy tribute of a heart
Which will not set the worthy man apart:
I choose, Sir, to be chosen; and in fine,
The friend of mankind is no friend of mine.

PHILINTE: But in polite society, custom decrees   65
    That we show certain outward courtesies. . . .

ALCESTE: Ah, no! we should condemn with all our force
    Such false and artificial intercourse.
    Let men behave like men; let them display
    Their inmost hearts in everything they say;   70
    Let the heart speak, and let our sentiments
    Not mask themselves in silly compliments.

PHILINTE: In certain cases it would be uncouth
    And most absurd to speak the naked truth;
    With all respect for your exalted notions,   75
    It's often best to veil one's true emotions.
    Wouldn't the social fabric come undone
    If we were wholly frank with everyone?
    Suppose you met with someone you couldn't bear;
    Would you inform him of it then and there?   80

ALCESTE: Yes.

PHILINTE: Then you'd tell old Emilie it's pathetic
    The way she daubs her features with cosmetic
    And plays the gay coquette at sixty-four?

ALCESTE: I would.

PHILINTE: And you'd call Dorilas a bore,
    And tell him every ear at court is lame   85
    From hearing him brag about his noble name?

ALCESTE: Precisely.

PHILINTE: Ah, you're joking.

ALCESTE: *Au contraire:*
    In this regard there's none I'd choose to spare.
    All are corrupt; there's nothing to be seen
    In court or town but aggravates my spleen.   90
    I fall into deep gloom and melancholy
    When I survey the scene of human folly,
    Finding on every hand base flattery,
    Injustice, fraud, self-interest, treachery. . . .
    Ah, it's too much; mankind has grown so base,   95
    I mean to break with the whole human race.

PHILINTE: This philosophic rage is a bit extreme;
    You've no idea how comical you seem;
    Indeed, we're like those brothers in the play
    Called *School for Husbands*, one of whom was prey . . .   100

ALCESTE: Enough, now! None of your stupid similes.

PHILINTE: Then let's have no more tirades, if you please.
    The world won't change, whatever you say or do;
    And since plain speaking means so much to you,
    I'll tell you plainly that by being frank   105
    You've earned the reputation of a crank,
    And that you're thought ridiculous when you rage
    And rant against the manners of the age.

ALCESTE: So much the better; just what I wish to hear.
    No news could be more grateful to my ear.   110
    All men are so detestable in my eyes,
    I should be sorry if they thought me wise.

PHILINTE: Your hatred's very sweeping, is it not?

ALCESTE: Quite right: I hate the whole degraded lot.

PHILINTE: Must all poor human creatures be embraced,   115
    Without distinction, by your vast distaste?
    Even in these bad times, there are surely a few . . .

ALCESTE: No, I include all men in one dim view:
    Some men I hate for being rogues: the others
    I hate because they treat the rogues like brothers,   120
    And, lacking a virtuous scorn for what is vile,
    Receive the villain with a complaisant smile.
    Notice how tolerant people choose to be
    Toward that bold rascal who's at law with me.
    His social polish can't conceal his nature;   125
    One sees at once that he's a treacherous creature;
    No one could possibly be taken in
    By those soft speeches and that sugary grin.
    The whole world knows the shady means by which
    The low-brow's grown so powerful and rich,   130
    And risen to a rank so bright and high
    That virtue can but blush, and merit sigh.
    Whenever his name comes up in conversation,
    None will defend his wretched reputation;
    Call him knave, liar, scoundrel, and all the rest,   135
    Each head will nod, and no one will protest.
    And yet his smirk is seen in every house,
    He's greeted everywhere with smiles and bows,
    And when there's any honor that can be got
    By pulling strings, he'll get it, like as not.   140
    My God! It chills my heart to see the ways
    Men come to terms with evil nowadays;
    Sometimes, I swear, I'm moved to flee and find
    Some desert land unfouled by humankind.

PHILINTE: Come, let's forget the follies of the times   145
          And pardon mankind for its petty crimes;
          Let's have an end of rantings and of railings,
          And show some leniency toward human failings.
          This world requires a pliant rectitude;
          Too stern a virtue makes one stiff and rude;   150
          Good sense views all extremes with detestation,
          And bids us to be noble in moderation.
          The rigid virtues of the ancient days
          Are not for us; they jar with all our ways
          And ask of us too lofty a perfection.   155
          Wise men accept their times without objection,
          And there's no greater folly, if you ask me,
          Than trying to reform society.
          Like you, I see each day a hundred and one
          Unhandsome deeds that might be better done,   160
          But still, for all the faults that meet my view,
          I'm never known to storm and rave like you.
          I take men as they are, or let them be,
          And teach my soul to bear their frailty;
          And whether in court or town, whatever the scene,   165
          My phlegm's as philosophic as your spleen.
ALCESTE: This phlegm which you so eloquently commend,
          Does nothing ever rile it up, my friend?
          Suppose some man you trust should treacherously
          Conspire to rob you of your property,   170
          And do his best to wreck your reputation?
          Wouldn't you feel a certain indignation?
PHILINTE: Why, no. These faults of which you so complain
          Are part of human nature, I maintain,
          And it's no more a matter for disgust   175
          That men are knavish, selfish and unjust,
          Than that the vulture dines upon the dead,
          And wolves are furious, and apes ill-bred.
ALCESTE: Shall I see myself betrayed, robbed, torn to bits,
          And not . . . Oh, let's be still and rest our wits.   180
          Enough of reasoning, now. I've had my fill.
PHILINTE: Indeed, you would do well, Sir, to be still.
          Rage less at your opponent, and give some thought
          To how you'll win this lawsuit that he's brought.
ALCESTE: I assure you I'll do nothing of the sort.   185
PHILINTE: Then who will plead your case before the court?
ALCESTE: Reason and right and justice will plead for me.
PHILINTE: Oh, Lord. What judges do you plan to see?
ALCESTE: Why, none. The justice of my cause is clear.
PHILINTE: Of course, man; but there's politics to fear. . . .   190

ALCESTE: No, I refuse to lift a hand. That's flat.
  I'm either right, or wrong.
PHILINTE: Don't count on that.
ALCESTE: No, I'll do nothing.
PHILINTE: Your enemy's influence
  Is great, you know . . .
ALCESTE: That makes no difference.
PHILINTE: It will; you'll see.
ALCESTE: Must honor bow to guile?   195
  If so, I shall be proud to lose the trial.
PHILINTE: Oh, really . . .
ALCESTE: I'll discover by this case
  Whether or not men are sufficiently base
  And impudent and villainous and perverse
  To do me wrong before the universe.   200
PHILINTE: What a man!
ALCESTE: Oh, I could wish, whatever the cost,
  Just for the beauty of it, that my trial were lost.
PHILINTE: If people heard you talking so, Alceste,
  They'd split their sides. Your name would be a jest.
ALCESTE: So much the worse for jesters.
PHILINTE: May I enquire   205
  Whether this rectitude you so admire,
  And these hard virtues you're enamored of
  Are qualities of the lady whom you love?
  It much suprises me that you, who seem
  To view mankind with furious disesteem,   210
  Have yet found something to enchant your eyes
  Amidst a species which you so despise.
  And what is more amazing, I'm afraid,
  Is the most curious choice your heart has made.
  The honest Éliante is fond of you,   215
  Arsinoé, the prude, admires you too;
  And yet your spirit's been perversely led
  To choose the flighty Célimène instead,
  Whose brittle malice and coquettish ways
  So typify the manners of our days.   220
  How is it that the traits you most abhor
  Are bearable in this lady you adore?
  Are you so blind with love that you can't find them?
  Or do you contrive, in her case, not to mind them?
ALCESTE: My love for that young widow's not the kind   225
  That can't perceive defects; no, I'm not blind.
  I see her faults, despite my ardent love,
  And all I see I fervently reprove.

And yet I'm weak; for all her falsity,
That woman knows the art of pleasing me,   230
And though I never cease complaining of her,
I swear I cannot manage not to love her.
Her charm outweighs her faults; I can but aim
To cleanse her spirit in my love's pure flame.

PHILINTE: That's no small task; I wish you all success.   235
    You think then that she loves you?

ALCESTE: Heavens, yes!
    I wouldn't love her did she not love me.

PHILINTE: Well, if her taste for you is plain to see,
    Why do these rivals cause you such despair?

ALCESTE: True love, Sir, is possessive, and cannot bear   240
    To share with all the world. I'm here today
    To tell her she must send that mob away.

PHILINTE: If I were you, and had your choice to make,
    Éliante, her cousin, would be the one I'd take;
    That honest heart, which cares for you alone,   245
    Would harmonize far better with your own.

ALCESTE: True, true: each day my reason tells me so;
    But reason doesn't rule in love, you know.

PHILINTE: I fear some bitter sorrow is in store;
    This love . . .

SCENE TWO

[ORONTE, ALCESTE, PHILINTE]

ORONTE [to ALCESTE]: The servants told me at the door   250
    That Éliante and Célimène were out,
    But when I heard, dear Sir, that you were about,
    I came to say, without exaggeration,
    That I hold you in the vastest admiration,
    And that it's always been my dearest desire   255
    To be the friend of one I so admire.
    I hope to see my love of merit requited,
    And you and I in friendship's bond united.
    I'm sure you won't refuse—if I may be frank—
    A friend of my devotedness—and rank.   260

    During this speech of ORONTE's, ALCESTE *is abstracted, and
    seems unaware that he is being spoken to. He only breaks off
    his reverie when* ORONTE *says:*

It was for you, if you please, that my words were intended.

ALCESTE: For me, Sir?

ORONTE: Yes, for you. You're not offended?

ALCESTE: By no means. But this much surprises me. . . .
    The honor comes most unexpectedly. . . .

ORONTE: My high regard should not astonish you;   265
    The whole world feels the same. It is your due.

ALCESTE: Sir . . .

ORONTE: Why, in all the State there isn't one
    Can match your merits; they shine, Sir, like the sun.

ALCESTE: Sir . . .

ORONTE: You are higher in my estimation
    Than all that's most illustrious in the nation.   270

ALCESTE: Sir . . .

ORONTE: If I lie, may heaven strike me dead!
    To show you that I mean what I have said,
    Permit me, Sir, to embrace you most sincerely,
    And swear that I will prize our friendship dearly.
    Give me your hand. And now, Sir, if you choose,   275
    We'll make our vows.

ALCESTE: Sir . . .

ORONTE: What! You refuse?

ALCESTE: Sir, it's a very great honor you extend:
    But friendship is a sacred thing, my friend;
    It would be profanation to bestow
    The name of friend on one you hardly know.   280
    All parts are better played when well-rehearsed;
    Let's put off friendship, and get acquainted first.
    We may discover it would be unwise
    To try to make our natures harmonize.

ORONTE: By heaven! You're sagacious to the core;   285
    This speech has made me admire you even more.
    Let time, then, bring us closer day by day;
    Meanwhile, I shall be yours in every way.
    If, for example, there should be anything
    You wish at court, I'll mention it to the King.   290
    I have his ear, of course; it's quite well known
    That I am much in favor with the throne.
    In short, I am your servant. And now, dear friend,
    Since you have such fine judgment, I intend
    To please you, if I can, with a small sonnet   295
    I wrote not long ago. Please comment on it,
    And tell me whether I ought to publish it.

ALCESTE: You must excuse me, Sir; I'm hardly fit
    To judge such matters.

ORONTE: Why not?

ALCESTE: I am, I fear,
    Inclined to be unfashionably sincere.   300

ORONTE: Just what I ask; I'd take no satisfaction
In anything but your sincere reaction.
I beg you not to dream of being kind.

ALCESTE: Since you desire it, Sir, I'll speak my mind.

ORONTE: *Sonnet.* It's a sonnet. . . . *Hope* . . . The poem's addressed   305
To a lady who wakened hopes within my breast.
Hope . . . this is not the pompous sort of thing,
Just modest little verses, with a tender ring.

ALCESTE: Well, we shall see.

ORONTE: *Hope* . . . I'm anxious to hear
Whether the style seems properly smooth and clear,   310
And whether the choice of words is good or bad.

ALCESTE: We'll see, we'll see.

ORONTE: Perhaps I ought to add
That it took me only a quarter-hour to write it.

ALCESTE: The time's irrelevant, Sir: kindly recite it.

ORONTE [*reading*]: Hope comforts us awhile, 'tis true,   315
Lulling our cares with careless laughter,
And yet such joy is full of rue,
My Phyllis, if nothing follows after.

PHILINTE: I'm charmed by this already; the style's delightful.

ALCESTE [*sotto voce, to* PHILINTE]: How can you say that? Why, the thing
is frightful.   320

ORONTE: Your fair face smiled on me awhile,
But was it kindness so to enchant me?
'Twould have been fairer not to smile,
If hope was all you meant to grant me.

PHILINTE: What a clever thought! How handsomely you phrase it!   325

ALCESTE [*sotto voce, to* PHILINTE]: You know the thing is trash. How dare
you praise it?

ORONTE: If it's to be my passion's fate
Thus everlastingly to wait,
Then death will come to set me free:
For death is fairer than the fair;   330
Phyllis, to hope is to despair
When one must hope eternally.

PHILINTE: The close is exquisite—full of feeling and grace.

ALCESTE [*sotto voce, aside*]: Oh, blast the close; you'd better close your
face
Before you send your lying soul to hell.   335

PHILINTE: I can't remember a poem I've liked so well.

ALCESTE [*sotto voce, aside*]: Good Lord!

ORONTE [*to* PHILINTE]:   I fear you're flattering me a bit.

PHILINTE: Oh, no!

ALCESTE [*sotto voce, aside*]: What else d'you call it, you hypocrite?

ORONTE [*to* ALCESTE]: But you, Sir, keep your promise now: don't shrink
　　From telling me sincerely what you think.　　　　　　　　340

ALCESTE: Sir, these are delicate matters; we all desire
　　To be told that we've the true poetic fire.
　　But once, to one whose name I shall not mention,
　　I said, regarding some verse of his invention,
　　That gentlemen should rigorously control　　　　　　　345
　　That itch to write which often afflicts the soul;
　　That one should curb the heady inclination
　　To publicize one's little avocation;
　　And that in showing off one's works of art
　　One often plays a very clownish part.　　　　　　　　350

ORONTE: Are you suggesting in a devious way
　　That I ought not . . .

ALCESTE:　　　　　　　　Oh, that I do not say.
　　Further, I told him that no fault is worse
　　Than that of writing frigid, lifeless verse,
　　And that the merest whisper of such a shame　　　　　355
　　Suffices to destroy a man's good name.

ORONTE: D'you mean to say my sonnet's dull and trite?

ALCESTE: I don't say that. But I went on to cite
　　Numerous cases of once-respected men
　　Who came to grief by taking up the pen.　　　　　　360

ORONTE: And am I like them? Do I write so poorly?

ALCESTE: I don't say that. But I told this person, "Surely
　　You're under no necessity to compose;
　　Why you should wish to publish, heaven knows.
　　There's no excuse for printing tedious rot　　　　　　365
　　Unless one writes for bread, as you do not.
　　Resist temptation, then, I beg of you;
　　Conceal your pastimes from the public view;
　　And don't give up, on any provocation,
　　Your present high and courtly reputation,　　　　　　370
　　To purchase at a greedy printer's shop
　　The name of silly author and scribbling fop."
　　These were the points I tried to make him see.

ORONTE: I sense that they are also aimed at me;
　　But now—about my sonnet—I'd like to be told . . .　　375

ALCESTE: Frankly, that sonnet should be pigeonholed.
　　You've chosen the worst models to imitate.
　　The style's unnatural. Let me illustrate:
　　　　For example, *Your fair face smiled on me awhile,*
　　　　Followed by, *'Twould have been fairer not to smile!*　　380
　　　　Or this: *such joy is full of rue;*
　　　　Or this: *For death is fairer than the fair;*

> Or, *Phyllis, to hope is to despair*
> *When one must hope eternally!*

This artificial style, that's all the fashion,   385
Has neither taste, nor honesty, nor passion;
It's nothing but a sort of wordy play,
And nature never spoke in such a way.
What, in this shallow age, is not debased?
Our fathers, though less refined, had better taste;   390
I'd barter all that men admire today
For one old love song I shall try to say:

> If the King had given me for my own
> Paris, his citadel
> And I for that must leave alone   395
> Her whom I love so well,
> I'd say then to the Crown,
> Take back your glittering town;
> My darling is more fair, I swear,
> My darling is more fair.   400

The rhyme's not rich, the style is rough and old,
But don't you see that it's the purest gold
Beside the tinsel nonsense now preferred,
And that there's passion in its every word?

> If the King had given me for my own   405
> Paris, his citadel
> And I for that must leave alone
> Her whom I love so well,
> I'd say then to the Crown,
> Take back your glittering town;   410
> My darling is more fair, I swear,
> My darling is more fair.

There speaks a loving heart. [*To* PHILINTE.] You're laughing, eh?
Laugh on, my precious wit. Whatever you say,
I hold that song's worth all the bibelots   415
That people hail today with ah's and oh's.

ORONTE: And I maintain my sonnet's very good.

ALCESTE: It's not at all surprising that you should.
  You have your reasons; permit me to have mine
  For thinking that you cannot write a line.   420

ORONTE: Others have praised my sonnet to the skies.

ALCESTE: I lack their art of telling pleasant lies.

ORONTE: You seem to think you've got no end of wit.

ALCESTE: To praise your verse, I'd need still more of it.

ORONTE: I'm not in need of your approval, Sir.   425

ALCESTE: That's good; you couldn't have it if you were.

ORONTE: Come now, I'll lend you the subject of my sonnet;
  I'd like to see you try to improve upon it.

ALCESTE: I might, by chance, write something just as shoddy;
  But then I wouldn't show it to everybody.

ORONTE: You're most opinionated and conceited.

ALCESTE: Go find your flatterers, and be better treated.

ORONTE: Look here, my little fellow, pray watch your tone.

ALCESTE: My great big fellow, you'd better watch your own.

PHILINTE [*stepping between them*]: Oh, please, please, gentlemen!
  This will never do.   435

ORONTE: The fault is mine, and I leave the field to you.
  I am your servant, Sir, in every way.

ALCESTE: And I, Sir, am your most abject valet.

SCENE THREE

[PHILINTE, ALCESTE]

PHILINTE: Well, as you see, sincerity in excess
  Can get you into a very pretty mess;   440
  Oronte was hungry for appreciation. . . .

ALCESTE: Don't speak to me.

PHILINTE: What?

ALCESTE: No more conversation.

PHILINTE: Really, now . . .

ALCESTE: Leave me alone.

PHILINTE: If I . . .

ALCESTE: Out of my sight!

PHILINTE: But what . . .

ALCESTE: I won't listen.

PHILINTE: But . . .

ALCESTE: Silence!

PHILINTE: Now, is it polite . . .

ALCESTE: By heaven, I've had enough. Don't follow me.   445

PHILINTE: Ah, you're just joking. I'll keep you company.

ACT TWO, SCENE ONE

[ALCESTE, CELIMENE]

ALCESTE: Shall I speak plainly, Madam? I confess
  Your conduct gives me infinite distress,
  And my resentment's grown too hot to smother.
  Soon, I foresee, we'll break with one another.
  If I said otherwise, I should deceive you;   5
  Sooner or later, I shall be forced to leave you,
  And if I swore that we shall never part,
  I should misread the omens of my heart.

CELIMENE: You kindly saw me home, it would appear,
    So as to pour invectives in my ear.   10

ALCESTE: I've no desire to quarrel. But I deplore
    Your inability to shut the door
    On all these suitors who beset you so.
    There's what annoys me, if you care to know.

CELIMENE: Is it my fault that all these men pursue me?   15
    Am I to blame if they're attracted to me?
    And when they gently beg an audience,
    Ought I to take a stick and drive them hence?

ALCESTE: Madam, there's no necessity for a stick;
    A less responsive heart would do the trick.   20
    Of your attractiveness I don't complain;
    But those your charms attract, you then detain
    By a most melting and receptive manner,
    And so enlist their hearts beneath your banner.
    It's the agreeable hopes which you excite   25
    That keep these lovers round you day and night;
    Were they less liberally smiled upon,
    That sighing troop would very soon be gone.
    But tell me, Madam, why it is that lately
    This man Clitandre interests you so greatly?   30
    Because of what high merits do you deem
    Him worthy of the honor of your esteem?
    Is it that your admiring glances linger
    On the splendidly long nail of his little finger?
    Or do you share the general deep respect   35
    For the blond wig he chooses to affect?
    Are you in love with his embroidered hose?
    Do you adore his ribbons and his bows?
    Or is it that this paragon bewitches
    Your tasteful eye with his vast German breeches?   40
    Perhaps his giggle, or his falsetto voice,
    Makes him the latest gallant of your choice?

CELIMENE: You're much mistaken to resent him so.
    Why I put up with him you surely know:
    My lawsuit's very shortly to be tried,   45
    And I must have his influence on my side.

ALCESTE: Then lose your lawsuit, Madam, or let it drop;
    Don't torture me by humoring such a fop.

CELIMENE: You're jealous of the whole world, Sir.

ALCESTE: That's true,
    Since the whole world is well-received by you.   50

CELIMENE: That my good nature is so unconfined
    Should serve to pacify your jealous mind;
    Were I to smile on one, and scorn the rest,
    Then you might have some cause to be distressed.

ALCESTE: Well, if I musn't be jealous, tell me, then,   55
    Just how I'm better treated than other men.

CELIMENE: You know you have my love. Will that not do?

ALCESTE: What proof have I that what you say is true?

CELIMENE: I would expect, Sir, that my having said it
    Might give the statement a sufficient credit.   60

ALCESTE: But how can I be sure that you don't tell
    The selfsame thing to other men as well?

CELIMENE: What a gallant speech! How flattering to me!
    What a sweet creature you make me out to be!
    Well then, to save you from the pangs of doubt,   65
    All that I've said I hereby cancel out;
    Now, none but yourself shall make a monkey of you:
    Are you content?

ALCESTE: Why, why am I doomed to love you?
    I swear that I shall bless the blissful hour
    When this poor heart's no longer in your power!   70
    I make no secret of it: I've done my best
    To exorcise this passion from my breast;
    But thus far all in vain; it will not go;
    It's for my sins that I must love you so.

CELIMENE: Your love for me is matchless, Sir; that's clear.   75

ALCESTE: Indeed, in all the world it has no peer;
    Words can't describe the nature of my passion,
    And no man ever loved in such a fashion.

CELIMENE: Yes, it's a brand-new fashion, I agree:
    You show your love by castigating me,   80
    And all your speeches are enraged and rude.
    I've never been so furiously wooed.

ALCESTE: Yet you could calm that fury, if you chose.
    Come, shall we bring our quarrels to a close?
    Let's speak with open hearts, then, and begin . . .   85

SCENE TWO

[CELIMENE, ALCESTE, BASQUE]

CELIMENE: What is it?

BASQUE: Acaste is here.

CELIMENE: Well, send him in.

SCENE THREE

[CELIMENE, ALCESTE]

ALCESTE: What! Shall we never be alone at all?
    You're always ready to receive a call,

And you can't bear, for ten ticks of the clock,
Not to keep open house for all who knock.   90
CELIMENE: I couldn't refuse him: he'd be most put out.
ALCESTE: Surely that's not worth worrying about.
CELIMENE: Acaste would never forgive me if he guessed
    That I consider him a dreadful pest.
ALCESTE: If he's a pest, why bother with him then?   95
CELIMENE: Heavens! One can't antagonize such men;
    Why, they're the chartered gossips of the court,
    And have a say in things of every sort.
    One must receive them, and be full of charm;
    They're no great help, but they can do you harm,   100
    And though your influence be ever so great,
    They're hardly the best people to alienate.
ALCESTE: I see, dear lady, that you could make a case
    For putting up with the whole human race;
    These friendships that you calculate so nicely . . .   105

SCENE FOUR

[ALCESTE, CELIMENE, BASQUE]

BASQUE: Madam, Clitandre is here as well.
ALCESTE: Precisely.
CELIMENE: Where are you going?
ALCESTE: Elsewhere.
CELIMENE: Stay.
ALCESTE: No, no.
CELIMENE: Stay, Sir.
ALCESTE: I can't.
CELIMENE: I wish it.
ALCESTE: No, I must go.
    I beg you, Madam, not to press the matter;
    You know I have no taste for idle chatter.   110
CELIMENE: Stay. I command you.
ALCESTE: No, I cannot stay.
CELIMENE: Very well; you have my leave to go away.

SCENE FIVE

[ELIANTE, PHILINTE, ACASTE, CLITANDRE, ALCESTE, CELIMENE, BASQUE]

ELIANTE [to CELIMENE]: The Marquesses have kindly come to call.
    Were they announced?

CELIMENE: Yes. Basque, bring chairs for all.

BASQUE *provides the chairs, and exits.*

[*To* ALCESTE.] You haven't gone?

ALCESTE: No; and I shan't depart   115
Till you decide who's foremost in your heart.

CELIMENE: Oh, hush.

ALCESTE: It's time to choose; take them, or me.

CELIMENE: You're mad.

ALCESTE: I'm not, as you shall shortly see.

CELIMENE: Oh?

ALCESTE: You'll decide.

CELIMENE: You're joking now, dear friend.

ALCESTE: No, no; you'll choose; my patience is at an end.   120

CLITANDRE: Madam, I come from court, where poor Cléonte
Behaved like a perfect fool, as is his wont.
Has he no friend to counsel him, I wonder,
And teach him less unerringly to blunder?

CELIMENE: It's true, the man's a most accomplished dunce;   125
His gauche behavior charms the eye at once;
And every time one sees him, on my word,
His manner's grown a trifle more absurd.

ACASTE: Speaking of dunces, I've just now conversed
With old Damon, who's one of the very worst;   130
I stood a lifetime in the broiling sun
Before his dreary monologue was done.

CELIMENE: Oh, he's a wondrous talker, and has the power
To tell you nothing hour after hour:
If, by mistake, he ever came to the point,   135
The shock would put his jawbone out of joint.

ELIANTE [*to* PHILINTE]: The conversation takes its usual turn,
And all our dear friends' ears will shortly burn.

CLITANDRE: Timante's a character, Madam.

CELIMENE: Isn't he, though?
A man of mystery from top to toe,   140
Who moves about in a romantic mist
On secret missions which do not exist.
His talk is full of eyebrows and grimaces;
How tired one gets of his momentous faces;
He's always whispering something confidential   145
Which turns out to be quite inconsequential;
Nothing's too slight for him to mystify;
He even whispers when he says "good-by."

ACASTE: Tell us about Géralde.

CELIMENE: That tiresome ass.
He mixes only with the titled class,   150

And fawns on dukes and princes, and is bored
With anyone who's not at least a lord.
The man's obsessed with rank, and his discourses
Are all of hounds and carriages and horses;
He uses Christian names with all the great,   155
And the word Milord, with him, is out of date.

CLITANDRE: He's very taken with Bélise, I hear.

CELIMENE: She is the dreariest company, poor dear.
Whenever she comes to call, I grope about
To find some topic which will draw her out,   160
But, owing to her dry and faint replies,
The conversation wilts, and droops, and dies.
In vain one hopes to animate her face
By mentioning the ultimate commonplace;
But sun or shower, even hail or frost   165
Are matters she can instantly exhaust.
Meanwhile her visit, painful though it is,
Drags on and on through mute eternities,
And though you ask the time, and yawn, and yawn,
She sits there like a stone and won't be gone.   170

ACASTE: Now for Adraste.

CELIMENE: O, that conceited elf
Has a gigantic passion for himself;
He rails against the court, and cannot bear it
That none will recognize his hidden merit;
All honors given to others give offense   175
To his imaginary excellence.

CLITANDRE: What about young Cléon? His house, they say,
Is full of the best society, night and day.

CELIMENE: His cook has made him popular, not he:
It's Cléon's table that people come to see.   180

ELIANTE: He gives a splendid dinner, you must admit.

CELIMENE: But must he serve himself along with it?
For my taste, he's a most insipid dish
Whose presence sours the wine and spoils the fish.

PHILINTE: Damis, his uncle, is admired no end.   185
What's your opinion, Madam?

CELIMENE: Why, he's my friend.

PHILINTE: He seems a decent fellow, and rather clever.

CELIMENE: He works too hard at cleverness, however.
I hate to see him sweat and struggle so
To fill his conversation with *bons mots*.   190
Since he's decided to become a wit
His taste's so pure that nothing pleases it;
He scolds at all the latest books and plays,
Thinking that wit must never stoop to praise,
That finding fault's a sign of intellect,   195

That all appreciation is abject,
And that by damning everything in sight
One shows oneself in a distinguished light.
He's scornful even of our conversations:
Their trivial nature sorely tries his patience;   200
He folds his arms, and stands above the battle,
And listens sadly to our childish prattle.

ACASTE: Wonderful, Madam! You've hit him off precisely.

CLITANDRE: No one can sketch a character so nicely.

ALCESTE: How bravely, Sirs, you cut and thrust at all   205
These absent fools, till one by one they fall:
But let one come in sight, and you'll at once
Embrace the man you lately called a dunce,
Telling him in a tone sincere and fervent
How proud you are to be his humble servant.   210

CLITANDRE: Why pick on us? *Madame's* been speaking, Sir.
And you should quarrel, if you must, with her.

ALCESTE: No, no, by God, the fault is yours, because
You lead her on with laughter and applause,
And make her think that she's the more delightful   215
The more her talk is scandalous and spiteful.
Oh, she would stoop to malice far, far less
If no such claque approved her cleverness.
It's flatterers like you whose foolish praise
Nourishes all the vices of these days.   220

PHILINTE: But why protest when someone ridicules
Those you'd condemn, yourself, as knaves or fools?

CELIMENE: Why, Sir? Because he loves to make a fuss.
You don't expect him to agree with us,
When there's an opportunity to express   225
His heaven-sent spirit of contrariness?
What other people think, he can't abide;
Whatever they say, he's on the other side;
He lives in deadly terror of agreeing;
'Twould make him seem an ordinary being.   230
Indeed, he's so in love with contradiction,
He'll turn against his most profound conviction
And with a furious eloquence deplore it,
If only someone else is speaking for it.

ALCESTE: Go on, dear lady, mock me as you please;   235
You have your audience in ecstasies.

PHILINTE: But what she says is true: you have a way
Of bridling at whatever people say;
Whether they praise or blame, your angry spirit
Is equally unsatisfied to hear it.   240

ALCESTE: Men, Sir, are always wrong, and that's the reason
That righteous anger's never out of season;

All that I hear in all their conversation
Is flattering praise or reckless condemnation.

CELIMENE: But . . .

ALCESTE: No, no Madam, I am forced to state   245
That you have pleasures which I deprecate,
And that these others, here, are much to blame
For nourishing the faults which are your shame.

CLITANDRE: I shan't defend myself, Sir; but I vow
I'd thought this lady faultless until now.   250

ACASTE: I see her charms and graces, which are many;
But as for faults, I've never noticed any.

ALCESTE: I see them, Sir; and rather than ignore them,
I strenuously criticize her for them.
The more one loves, the more one should object   255
To every blemish, every least defect.
Were I this lady, I would soon get rid
Of lovers who approved of all I did,
And by their slack indulgence and applause
Endorsed my follies and excused my flaws.   260

CELIMENE: If all hearts beat according to your measure,
The dawn of love would be the end of pleasure;
And love would find its perfect consummation
In ecstasies of rage and reprobation.

ELIANTE: Love, as a rule, affects men otherwise,   265
And lovers rarely love to criticize.
They see their lady as a charming blur,
And find all things commendable in her.
If she has any blemish, fault, or shame,
They will redeem it by a pleasing name.   270
The pale-faced lady's lily-white, perforce;
The swarthy one's a sweet brunette, of course;
The spindly lady has a slender grace;
The fat one has a most majestic pace;
The plain one, with her dress in disarray,   275
They classify as *beauté négligée;*
The hulking one's a goddess in their eyes,
The dwarf, a concentrate of Paradise;
The haughty lady has a noble mind;
The mean one's witty, and the dull one's kind;   280
The chatterbox has liveliness and verve,
The mute one has a virtuous reserve.
So lovers manage, in their passion's cause,
To love their ladies even for their flaws.

ALCESTE: But I still say . . .

CELIMENE: I think it would be nice   285
To stroll around the gallery once or twice.
What! You're not going, Sirs?

CLITANDRE *and* ACASTE: No, Madam, no.

ALCESTE: You seem to be in terror lest they go.
　　　　Do what you will, Sirs; leave, or linger on,
　　　　But I shan't go till after you are gone.   290

ACASTE: I'm free to linger, unless I should perceive
　　　　Madame is tired, and wishes me to leave.

CLITANDRE: And as for me, I needn't go today
　　　　Until the hour of the King's *coucher.*

CELIMENE [*to* ALCESTE]: You're joking, surely?

ALCESTE: Not in the least; we'll see   295
　　　　Whether you'd rather part with them, or me.

SCENE SIX

　　　　[ALCESTE, CELIMENE, ELIANTE, ACASTE, PHILINTE, CLITANDRE,
　　　　BASQUE]

BASQUE [*to* ALCESTE]: Sir, there's a fellow here who bids me state
　　　　That he must see you, and that it can't wait.

ALCESTE: Tell him that I have no such pressing affairs.

BASQUE: It's a long tailcoat that this fellow wears,   300
　　　　With gold all over.

CELIMENE [*to* ALCESTE]: You'd best go down and see.
　　　　Or—have him enter.

SCENE SEVEN

　　　　[ALCESTE, CELIMENE, ELIANTE, ACASTE, PHILINTE, CLITANDRE,
　　　　GUARD]

ALCESTE [*confronting the* GUARD]: Well, what do you want with me?
　　　　Come in Sir.

GUARD: I've a word, Sir, for your ear.

ALCEST: Speak it aloud, Sir; I shall strive to hear.

GUARD: The Marshals have instructed me to say   305
　　　　You must report to them without delay.

ALCESTE: Who? Me, Sir?

GUARD: Yes, Sir; you.

ALCESTE: But what do they want?

PHILINTE [*to* ALCESTE]: To scotch your silly quarrel with Oronte.

CELIMENE [*to* PHILINTE]: What quarrel?

PHILINTE: Oronte and he have fallen out
　　　　Over some verse he spoke his mind about;   310
　　　　The Marshals wish to arbitrate the matter.

ALCESTE: Never shall I equivocate or flatter!

PHILINTE: You'd best obey their summons; come, let's go.

ALCESTE: How can they mend our quarrel, I'd like to know?   315
  Am I to make a cowardly retraction,
  And praise those jingles to his satisfaction?
  I'll not recant; I've judged that sonnet rightly.
  It's bad.

PHILINTE: But you might say so more politely. . . .

ALCESTE: I'll not back down; his verses make me sick.

PHILINTE: If only you could be more politic!   320
  But come, let's go.

ALCESTE: I'll go, but I won't unsay
  A single word.

PHILINTE: Well, let's be on our way.

ALCESTE: Till I am ordered by my lord the King
  To praise that poem, I shall say the thing
  Is scandalous, by God, and that the poet   325
  Ought to be hanged for having the nerve to show it.

    To CLITANDRE *and* ACASTE, *who are laughing.*

  By heavens, Sirs, I really didn't know
  That I was being humorous.

CELIMENE: Go, Sir, go;
  Settle your business.

ALCESTE: I shall, and when I'm through,
  I shall return to settle things with you.   330

ACT THREE, SCENE ONE

[CLITANDRE, ACASTE]

CLITANDRE: Dear Marquess, how contented you appear;
  All things delight you, nothing mars your cheer.
  Can you, in perfect honesty, declare
  That you've a right to be so debonair?

ACASTE: By Jove, when I survey myself, I find   5
  No cause whatever for distress of mind.
  I'm young and rich; and I can in modesty
  Lay claim to an exalted pedigree;
  And owing to my name and my condition
  I shall not want for honors and position.   10
  Then as to courage, that most precious trait,
  I seem to have it, as was proved of late
  Upon the field of honor, where my bearing,
  They say, was very cool and rather daring.
  I've wit, of course; and taste in such perfection   15

That I can judge without the least reflection,
And at the theater, which is my delight,
Can make or break a play on opening night,
And lead the crowd in hisses or bravos,
And generally be known as one who knows.   20
I'm clever, handsome, gracefully polite;
My waist is small, my teeth are strong and white;
As for my dress, the world's astonished eyes
Assure me that I bear away the prize.
I find myself in favor everywhere,   25
Honored by men, and worshiped by the fair;
And since these things are so, it seems to me
I'm justified in my complacency.

CLITANDRE: Well, if so many ladies hold you dear,
Why do you press a hopeless courtship here?   30

ACASTE: Hopeless, you say? I'm not the sort of fool
That likes his ladies difficult and cool.
Men who are awkward, shy, and peasantish
May pine for heartless beauties, if they wish,
Grovel before them, bear their cruelties,   35
Woo them with tears and sighs and bended knees,
And hope by dogged faithfulness to gain
What their poor merits never could obtain.
For men like me, however, it makes no sense
To love on trust, and foot the whole expense.   40
Whatever any lady's merits be,
I think, thank God, that I'm as choice as she;
That if my heart is kind enough to burn
For her, she owes me something in return;
And that in any proper love affair   45
The partners must invest an equal share.

CLITANDRE: You think, then, that our hostess favors you?

ACASTE: I've reason to believe that that is true.

CLITANDRE: How did you come to such a mad conclusion?
You're blind, dear fellow. This is sheer delusion.   50

ACASTE: All right, then: I'm deluded and I'm blind.

CLITANDRE: Whatever put the notion in your mind?

ACASTE: Delusion.

CLITANDRE: What persuades you that you're right?

ACASTE: I'm blind.

CLITANDRE: But have you any proofs to cite?

ACASTE: I tell you I'm deluded.

CLITANDRE: Have you, then,   55
Received some secret pledge from Célimène?

ACASTE: Oh, no: she scorns me.

CLITANDRE: Tell me the truth, I beg.

ACASTE: She just can't bear me.

CLITANDRE: Ah, don't pull my leg.
          Tell me what hope she's given you, I pray.

ACASTE: I'm hopeless, and it's you who win the day.   60
          She hates me thoroughly, and I'm so vexed
          I mean to hang myself on Tuesday next.

CLITANDRE: Dear Marquess, let us have an armistice
          And make a treaty. What do you say to this?
          If ever one of us can plainly prove   65
          That Célimène encourages his love,
          The other must abandon hope, and yield,
          And leave him in possession of the field.

ACASTE: Now, there's a bargain that appeals to me;
          With all my heart, dear Marquess, I agree.   70
          But hush.

SCENE TWO

[CELIMENE, ACASTE, CLITANDRE]

CELIMENE: Still here?

CLITANDRE: 'Twas love that stayed our feet.

CELIMENE: I think I heard a carriage in the street.
          Whose is it? D'you know?

SCENE THREE

[CELIMENE, ACASTE, CLITANDRE, BASQUE]

BASQUE: Arsinoé is here,
          Madame.

CELIMENE: Arsinoé, you say? Oh, dear.

BASQUE: Éliante is entertaining her below.   75

CELIMENE: What brings the creature here, I'd like to know?

ACASTE: They say she's dreadfully prudish, but in fact
          I think her piety . . .

CELIMENE: It's all an act.
          At heart she's worldly, and her poor success
          In snaring men explains her prudishness.   80
          It breaks her heart to see the beaux and gallants
          Engrossed by other women's charms and talents,
          And so she's always in a jealous rage
          Against the faulty standards of the age.
          She lets the world believe that she's a prude   85
          To justify her loveless solitude,
          And strives to put a brand of moral shame
          On all the graces that she cannot claim.

But still she'd love a lover; and Alceste
Appears to be the one she'd love the best.   90
His visits here are poison to her pride;
She seems to think I've lured him from her side;
And everywhere, at court or in the town,
The spiteful, envious woman runs me down.
In short, she's just as stupid as can be,   95
Vicious and arrogant in the last degree,
And . . .

SCENE FOUR

[ARSINOE, CELIMENE, CLITANDRE, ACASTE]

CELIMENE: Ah! What happy chance has brought you here?
   I've thought about you ever so much, my dear.
ARSINOE: I've come to tell you something you should know.
CELIMENE: How good of you to think of doing so!   100

    CLITANDRE and ACASTE go out, laughing.

SCENE FIVE

[ARSINOE, CELIMENE]

ARSINOE: It's just as well those gentlemen didn't tarry.
CELIMENE: Shall we sit down?
ARSINOE: That won't be necessary.
   Madam, the flame of friendship ought to burn
   Brightest in matters of the most concern,
   And as there's nothing which concerns us more   105
   Than honor, I have hastened to your door
   To bring you, as your friend, some information
   About the status of your reputation.
   I visited last night, some virtuous folk,
   And, quite by chance, it was of you they spoke;   110
   There was, I fear, no tendency to praise
   Your light behavior and your dashing ways.
   The quantity of gentlemen you see
   And your by now notorious coquetry
   Were both so vehemently criticized   115
   By everyone, that I was much surprised.
   Of course, I needn't tell you where I stood;
   I came to your defense as best I could,
   Assured them you were harmless, and declared
   Your soul was absolutely unimpaired.   120
   But there are some things, you must realize,
   One can't excuse, however hard one tries,
   And I was forced at last into conceding

That your behavior, Madam, is misleading,
That makes a bad impression, giving rise   125
To ugly gossip and obscene surmise,
And that if you were more *overtly* good,
You wouldn't be so much misunderstood.
Not that I think you've been unchaste—no! no!
The saints preserve me from a thought so low!   130
But mere good conscience never did suffice:
One must avoid the outward show of vice.
Madam, you're too intelligent, I'm sure,
To think my motives anything but pure
In offering you this counsel—which I do   135
Out of a zealous interest in you.

CELIMENE: Madam, I haven't taken you amiss;
I'm very much obliged to you for this;
And I'll at once discharge the obligation
By telling you about *your* reputation.   140
You've been so friendly as to let me know
What certain people say of me, and so
I mean to follow your benign example
By offering you a somewhat similar sample.
The other day, I went to an affair   145
And found some most distinguished people there
Discussing piety, both false and true.
The conversation soon came round to you.
Alas! Your prudery and bustling zeal
Appeared to have a very slight appeal.   150
Your affectation of a grave demeanor,
Your endless talk of virtue and of honor,
The aptitude of your suspicious mind
For finding sin where there is none to find,
Your towering self-esteem, that pitying face   155
With which you contemplate the human race,
Your sermonizings and your sharp aspersions
On people's pure and innocent diversions—
All these were mentioned, Madam, and, in fact,
Were roundly and concertedly attacked.   160
"What good," they said, "are all these outward shows,
When everything belies her pious pose?
She prays incessantly; but then, they say,
She beats her maids and cheats them of their pay;
She shows her zeal in every holy place,   165
But still she's vain enough to paint her face;
She holds that naked statues are immoral,
But with a naked *man* she'd have no quarrel."
Of course, I said to everybody there
That they were being viciously unfair;   170
But still they were disposed to criticize you,
And all agreed that someone should advise you

To leave the morals of the world alone,
And worry rather more about your own.
They felt that one's self-knowledge should be great   175
Before one thinks of setting others straight;
That one should learn the art of living well
Before one threatens other men with hell,
And that the Church is best equipped, no doubt,
To guide our souls and root our vices out.   180
Madam, you're too intelligent, I'm sure,
To think my motives anything but pure
In offering you this counsel—which I do
Out of a zealous interest in you.

ARSINOE: I dared not hope for gratitude, but I   185
Did not expect so acid a reply;
I judge, since you've been so extremely tart,
That my good counsel pierced you to the heart.

CELIMENE: Far from it, Madam. Indeed, it seems to me
We ought to trade advice more frequently.   190
One's vision of oneself is so defective
That it would be an excellent corrective.
If you are willing, Madam, let's arrange
Shortly to have another frank exchange
In which we'll tell each other, *entre nous,*   195
What you've heard tell of me, and I of you.

ARSINOE: Oh, people never censure you, my dear;
It's me they criticize. Or so I hear.

CELIMENE: Madam, I think we either blame or praise
According to our taste and length of days.   200
There is a time of life for coquetry,
And there's a season, too, for prudery.
When all one's charms are gone, it is, I'm sure,
Good strategy to be devout and pure:
It makes one seem a little less forsaken.   205
Some day, perhaps, I'll take the road you've taken:
Time brings all things. But I have time aplenty,
And see no cause to be a prude at twenty.

ARSINOE: You give your age in such a gloating tone
That one would think I was an ancient crone;   210
We're not so far apart, in sober truth,
That you can mock me with a boast of youth!
Madam, you baffle me. I wish I knew
What moves you to provoke me as you do.

CELIMENE: For my part, Madam, I should like to know   215
Why you abuse me everywhere you go.
Is it my fault, dear lady, that your hand
Is not, alas, in very great demand?
If men admire me, if they pay me court
And daily make me offers of the sort   220

You'd dearly love to have them make to you,
How can I help it? What would you have me do?
If what you want is lovers, please feel free
To take as many as you can from me.

ARSINOE: Oh, come. D'you think the world is losing sleep   225
Over that flock of lovers which you keep,
Or that we find it difficult to guess
What price you pay for their devotedness?
Surely you don't expect us to suppose
Mere merit could attract so many beaux?   230
It's not your virtue that they're dazzled by;
Nor is it virtuous love for which they sigh.
You're fooling no one, Madam; the world's not blind;
There's many a lady heaven has designed
To call men's noblest, tenderest feelings out,   235
Who has no lovers dogging her about;
From which it's plain that lovers nowadays
Must be acquired in bold and shameless ways,
And only pay one court for such reward
As modesty and virtue can't afford.   240
Then don't be quite so puffed up, if you please,
About your tawdry little victories;
Try, if you can, to be a shade less vain,
And treat the world with somewhat less disdain.
If one were envious of your amours,   245
One soon could have a following like yours;
Lovers are no great trouble to collect
If one prefers them to one's self-respect.

CELIMENE: Collect them then, my dear; I'd love to see
You demonstrate that charming theory;   250
Who knows, you might . . .

ARSINOE: Now, Madam, that will do;
It's time to end this trying interview.
My coach is late in coming to your door,
Or I'd have taken leave of you before.

CELIMENE: Oh, please don't feel that you must rush away;   255
I'd be delighted, Madam, if you'd stay.
However, lest my conversation bore you,
Let me provide some better company for you;
This gentleman, who comes most apropos,
Will please you more than I could do, I know.   260

SCENE SIX

[ALCESTE, CELIMENE, ARSINOE]

CELIMENE: Alceste, I have a little note to write
Which simply must go out before tonight;

Please entertain *Madame;* I'm sure that she
Will overlook my incivility.

[ALCESTE, ARSINOE]

ARSINOE: Well, Sir, our hostess graciously contrives   265
    For us to chat until my coach arrives;
    And I shall be forever in her debt
    For granting me this little *tete-a-tete.*
    We women very rightly give our hearts
    To men of noble character and parts,   270
    And your especial merits, dear Alceste,
    Have roused the deepest sympathy in my breast.
    Oh, how I wish they had sufficient sense
    At court, to recognize your excellence!
    They wrong you greatly, Sir. How it must hurt you   275
    Never to be rewarded for your virtue!

ALCESTE: Why, Madam, what cause have I to feel aggrieved?
    What great and brilliant thing have I achieved?
    What service have I rendered to the King
    That I should look to him for anything?   280

ARSINOE: Not everyone who's honored by the State
    Has done great services. A man must wait
    Till time and fortune offer him the chance.
    Your merit, Sir, is obvious at a glance,
    And . . .

ALCESTE: Ah, forget my merit; I'm not neglected.   285
    The court, I think, can hardly be expected
    To mine men's souls for merit, and unearth
    Our hidden virtues and our secret worth.

ARSINOE: *Some* virtues, though, are far too bright to hide;
    Yours are acknowledged, Sir, on every side.   290
    Indeed, I've heard you warmly praised of late
    By persons of considerable weight.

ALCESTE: This fawning age has praise for everyone,
    And all distinctions, Madam, are undone.
    All things have equal honor nowadays,   295
    And no one should be gratified by praise.
    To be admired, one only need exist,
    And every lackey's on the honors list.

ARSINOE: I only wish, Sir, that you had your eye
    On some position at court, however high;   300
    You'd only have to hint at such a notion
    For me to set the proper wheels in motion;
    I've certain friendships I'd be glad to use
    To get you any office you might choose.

ALCESTE: Madam, I fear that any such ambition   305
    Is wholly foreign to my disposition.
    The soul God gave me isn't of the sort
    That prospers in the weather of a court.
    It's all too obvious that I don't possess
    The virtues necessary for success.   310
    My one great talent is for speaking plain;
    I've never learned to flatter or to feign;
    And anyone so stupidly sincere
    Had best not seek a courtier's career.
    Outside the court, I know, one must dispense   315
    With honors, privilege, and influence;
    But still one gains the right, foregoing these,
    Not to be tortured by the wish to please.
    One needn't live in dread of snubs and slights,
    Nor praise the verse that every idiot writes,   320
    Nor humor silly Marquesses, nor bestow
    Politic sighs on Madam So-and-So.

ARSINOE: Forget the court, then; let the matter rest.
    But I've another cause to be distressed
    About your present situation, Sir.   325
    It's to your love affair that I refer.
    She whom you love, and who pretends to love you,
    Is, I regret to say, unworthy of you.

ALCESTE: Why, Madam? Can you seriously intend
    To make so grave a charge against your friend?   330

ARSINOE: Alas, I must. I've stood aside too long
    And let that lady do you grievous wrong;
    But now my debt to conscience shall be paid:
    I tell you that your love has been betrayed.

ALCESTE: I thank you, Madam; you're extremely kind.   335
    Such words are soothing to a lover's mind.

ARSINOE: Yes, though she *is* my friend, I say again
    You're very much too good for Célimène.
    She's wantonly misled you from the start.

ALCESTE: You may be right; who knows another's heart?   340
    But ask yourself if it's the part of charity
    To shake my soul with doubts of her sincerity.

ARSINOE: Well, if you'd rather be a dupe than doubt her,
    That's your affair. I'll say no more about her.

ALCESTE: Madam, you know that doubt and vague suspicion   345
    Are painful to a man in my position;
    It's most unkind to worry me this way
    Unless you've some real proof of what you say.

ARSINOE: Sir, say no more: all doubts shall be removed,
    And all that I've been saying shall be proved.   350
    You've only to escort me home, and there
    We'll look into the heart of this affair.

I've ocular evidence which will persuade you
Beyond a doubt, that Célimène's betrayed you.
Then, if you're saddened by that revelation,   355
Perhaps I can provide some consolation.

ACT FOUR, SCENE ONE

[ELIANTE, PHILINTE]

PHILINTE: Madam, he acted like a stubborn child;
I thought they never would be reconciled;
In vain we reasoned, threatened, and appealed;
He stood his ground and simply would not yield.
The Marshals, I feel sure, have never heard   5
An argument so splendidly absurd.
"No, gentlemen," said he, "I'll not retract.
His verse is bad: extremely bad, in fact.
Surely it does the man no harm to know it.
Does it disgrace him, not to be a poet?   10
A gentleman may be respected still,
Whether he writes a sonnet well or ill.
That I dislike his verse should not offend him;
In all that touches honor, I commend him;
He's noble, brave, and virtuous—but I fear   15
He can't in truth be called a sonneteer.
I'll gladly praise his wardrobe; I'll endorse
His dancing, or the way he sits a horse;
But, gentlemen, I cannot praise his rhyme.
In fact, it ought to be a capital crime   20
For anyone so sadly unendowed
To write a sonnet, and read the thing aloud."
At length he fell into a gentler mood
And, striking a concessive attitude,
He paid Oronte the following courtesies: 25
"Sir, I regret that I'm so hard to please,
And I'm profoundly sorry that your lyric
Failed to provoke me to a panegyric."
After these curious words, the two embraced,
And then the hearing was adjourned—in haste.   30

ELIANTE: His conduct has been very singular lately;
Still, I confess that I respect him greatly.
The honesty in which he takes such pride
Has—to my mind—its noble, heroic side.
In this false age, such candor seems outrageous;   35
But I could wish that it were more contagious.

PHILINTE: What most intrigues me in our friend Alceste
Is the grand passion that rages in his breast.

The sullen humors he's compounded of
Should not, I think, dispose his heart to love;   40
But since they do, it puzzles me still more
That he should choose your cousin to adore.

ELIANTE: It does, indeed, belie the theory
That love is born of gentle sympathy,
And that the tender passion must be based   45
On sweet accords of temper and of taste.

PHILINTE: Does she return his love, do you suppose?

ELIANTE: Ah, that's a difficult question, Sir. Who knows?
How can we judge the truth of her devotion?
Her heart's a stranger to its own emotion.   50
Sometimes it thinks it loves, when no love's there;
At other times it loves quite unaware.

PHILINTE: I rather think Alceste is in for more
Distress and sorrow than he's bargained for;
Were he of my mind, Madam, his affection   55
Would turn in quite a different direction,
And we would see him more responsive to
The kind regard which he receives from you.

ELIANTE: Sir, I believe in frankness, and I'm inclined,
In matters of the heart, to speak my mind.   60
I don't oppose his love for her; indeed,
I hope with all my heart that he'll succeed,
And were it in my power, I'd rejoice
In giving him the lady of his choice.
But if, as happens frequently enough   65
In love affairs, he meets with a rebuff—
If Célimène should grant some rival's suit—
I'd gladly play the role of substitute;
Nor would his tender speeches please me less
Because they'd once been made without success.   70

PHILINTE: Well, Madam, as for me, I don't oppose
Your hopes in this affair; and heaven knows
That in my conversations with the man
I plead your cause as often as I can.
But if those two should marry, and so remove   75
All chance that he will offer you his love,
Then I'll declare my own, and hope to see
Your gracious favor pass from him to me.
In short, should you be cheated of Alceste,
I'd be most happy to be second best.   80

ELIANTE: Philinte, you're teasing.

PHILINTE: Ah, Madam, never fear;
No words of mine were ever so sincere,
And I shall live in fretful expectation
Till I can make a fuller declaration.

SCENE TWO

[ALCESTE, ELIANTE, PHILINTE]

ALCESTE: Avenge me, Madam! I must have satisfaction.   85
    Or this great wrong will drive me to distraction!

ELIANTE: Why, what's the matter? What's upset you so?

ALCESTE: Madam, I've had a mortal, mortal blow.
    If Chaos repossessed the universe,
    I swear I'd not be shaken any worse.   90
    I'm ruined. . . . I can say no more. . . . My soul . . .

ELIANTE: Do try, Sir, to regain your self-control.

ALCESTE: Just heaven! Why were so much beauty and grace
    Bestowed on one so vicious and so base?

ELIANTE: Once more, Sir, tell us. . . .

ALCESTE: My world has gone to wrack;   95
    I'm—I'm betrayed; she's stabbed me in the back:
    Yes, Célimène (who would have thought it of her?)
    Is false to me, and has another lover.

ELIANTE: Are you quite certain? Can you prove these things?

PHILINTE: Lovers are prey to wild imaginings   100
    And jealous fancies. No doubt there's some mistake. . . .

ALCESTE: Mind your own business, Sir, for heaven's sake.

    To ELIANTE.

    Madam, I have the proof that you demand
    Here in my pocket, penned by her own hand.
    Yes, all the shameful evidence one could want   105
    Lies in this letter written to Oronte—
    Oronte! whom I felt sure she couldn't love,
    And hardly bothered to be jealous of.

PHILINTE: Still, in a letter, appearances may deceive;
    This may not be so bad as you believe.   110

ALCESTE: Once more I beg you, Sir, to let me be;
    Tend to your own affairs; leave mine to me.

ELIANTE: Compose yourself; this anguish that you feel . . .

ALCESTE: Is something, Madam, you alone can heal.
    My outraged heart, beside itself with grief,   115
    Appeals to you for comfort and relief.
    Avenge me on your cousin, whose unjust
    And faithless nature has deceived my trust;
    Avenge a crime your pure soul must detest.

ELIANTE: But how, Sir?

ALCESTE: Madam, this heart within my breast   120
    Is yours; pray take it; redeem my heart from her,
    And so avenge me on my torturer.

Let her be punished by the fond emotion,
The ardent love, the bottomless devotion,
The faithful worship which this heart of mine   125
Will offer up to yours as to a shrine.

ELIANTE: You have my sympathy, Sir, in all you suffer;
Nor do I scorn the noble heart you offer;
But I suspect you'll soon be mollified,
And this desire for vengeance will subside.   130
When some beloved hand has done us wrong
We thirst for retribution—but not for long;
However dark the deed that she's committed,
A lovely culprit's very soon acquitted.
Nothing's so stormy as an injured lover,   135
And yet no storm so quickly passes over.

ALCESTE: No, Madam, no—this is no lovers' spat;
I'll not forgive her; it's gone too far for that;
My mind's made up; I'll kill myself before
I waste my hopes upon her any more.   140
Ah, here she is. My wrath intensifies.
I shall confront her with her tricks and lies,
And crush her utterly, and bring you then
A heart no longer slave to Célimène.

SCENE THREE

[CELIMENE, ALCESTE]

ALCESTE [aside]: Sweet heaven, help me to control my passion.   145
CELIMENE [aside]: Oh, Lord.

     To ALCESTE.

             Why stand there staring in that fashion?
And what d'you mean by those dramatic sighs,
And that malignant glitter in your eyes?

ALCESTE: I mean that sins which cause the blood to freeze
Look innocent beside your treacheries;   150
That nothing Hell's or Heaven's wrath could do
Ever produced so bad a thing as you.

CELIMENE: Your compliments were always sweet and pretty.

ALCESTE: Madam, it's not the moment to be witty.
No, blush and hang your head; you've ample reason,   155
Since I've the fullest evidence of your treason.
Ah, this is what my sad heart prophesied;
Now all my anxious fears are verified;
My dark suspicion and my gloomy doubt
Divined the truth, and now the truth is out.   160
For all your trickery, I was not deceived;

It was my bitter stars that I believed.
But don't imagine that you'll go scot-free;
You shan't misuse me with impunity.
I know that love's irrational and blind;   165
I know the heart's not subject to the mind,
And can't be reasoned into beating faster;
I know each soul is free to choose its master;
Therefore had you but spoken from the heart,
Rejecting my attentions from the start,   170
I'd have no grievance, or at any rate
I could complain of nothing but my fate.
Ah, but so falsely to encourage me—
That was a treason and a treachery
For which you cannot suffer too severely,   175
And you shall pay for that behavior dearly.
Yes, now I have no pity, not a shred;
My temper's out of hand; I've lost my head;
Shocked by the knowledge of your double-dealings,
My reason can't restrain my savage feelings;   180
A righteous wrath deprives me of my senses,
And I won't answer for the consequences.

CELIMENE: What does this outburst mean? Will you please explain?
Have you, by any chance, gone quite insane?

ALCESTE: Yes, yes, I went insane the day I fell   185
A victim to your black and fatal spell,
Thinking to meet with some sincerity
Among the treacherous charms that beckoned me.

CELIMENE: Pooh. Of what treachery can you complain?

ALCESTE: How sly you are, how cleverly you feign!   190
But you'll not victimize me any more.
Look: here's a document you've seen before.
This evidence, which I acquired today,
Leaves you, I think, without a thing to say.

CELIMENE: Is this what sent you into such a fit?   195

ALCESTE: You should be blushing at the sight of it.

CELIMENE: Ought I to blush? I truly don't see why.

ALCESTE: Ah, now you're being bold as well as sly;
Since there's no signature, perhaps you'll claim . . .

CELIMENE: I wrote it, whether or not it bears my name.   200

ALCESTE: And you can view with equanimity
This proof of your disloyalty to me!

CELIMENE: Oh, don't be so outrageous and extreme.

ALCESTE: You take this matter lightly, it would seem.
Was it no wrong to me, no shame to you,   205
That you should send Oronte this billet-doux?

CELIMENE: Oronte! Who said it was for him?

ALCESTE: Why, those
　　Who brought me this example of your prose.
　　But what's the difference? If you wrote the letter
　　To someone else, it pleases me no better.   210
　　My grievance and your guilt remain the same.

CELIMENE: But need you rage, and need I blush for shame;
　　If this was written to a *woman* friend?

ALCESTE: Ah! Most ingenious. I'm impressed no end;
　　And after that incredible evasion   215
　　Your guilt is clear. I need no more persuasion.
　　How dare you try so clumsy a deception?
　　D'you think I'm wholly wanting in perception?
　　Come, come, let's see how brazenly you'll try
　　To bolster up so palpable a lie: 220
　　Kindly construe this ardent closing section
　　As nothing more than sisterly affection!
　　Here, let me read it. Tell me, if you dare to,
　　That this is for a woman . . .

CELIMENE: I don't care to.
　　What right have you to badger and berate me,   225
　　And so highhandedly interrogate me?

ALCESTE: Now, don't be angry; all I ask of you
　　Is that you justify a phrase or two . . .

CELIMENE: No, I shall not. I utterly refuse,
　　And you may take those phrases as you choose.   230

ALCESTE: Just show me how this letter could be meant
　　For a woman's eyes, and I shall be content.

CELIMENE: No, no, it's for Oronte; you're perfectly right.
　　I welcome his attentions with delight,
　　I prize his character and his intellect,   235
　　And everything is just as you suspect.
　　Come, do your worst now; give your rage free rein;
　　But kindly cease to bicker and complain.

ALCESTE [*aside*]: Good God! Could anything be more inhuman?
　　Was ever a heart so mangled by a woman?   240
　　When I complain of how she has betrayed me,
　　She bridles, and commences to upbraid me!
　　She tries my tortured patience to the limit;
　　She won't deny her guilt; she glories in it!
　　And yet my heart's too faint and cowardly   245
　　To break these chains of passion, and be free,
　　To scorn her as it should, and rise above
　　This unrewarded, mad, and bitter love.

　　　　　　To CELIMENE.

　　Ah, traitress, in how confident a fashion
　　You take advantage of my helpless passion,
　　And use my weakness for your faithless charms

To make me once again throw down my arms!
But do at least deny this black transgression;
Take back that mocking and perverse confession;
Defend this letter and your innocence,   255
And I, poor fool, will aid in your defense.
Pretend, pretend, that you are just and true,
And I shall make myself believe in you.

CELIMENE: Oh, stop it. Don't be such a jealous dunce,
Or I shall leave off loving you at once.   260
Just why should I *pretend*? What could impel me
To stoop so low as that? And kindly tell me
Why, if I loved another, I shouldn't merely
Inform you of it, simply and sincerely!
I've told you where you stand, and that admission   265
Should altogether clear me of suspicion;
After so generous a guarantee,
What right have you to harbor doubts of me?
Since women are (from natural reticence)
Reluctant to declare their sentiments,   270
And since the honor of our sex requires
That we conceal our amorous desires,
Ought any man for whom such laws are broken
To question what the oracle has spoken?
Should he not rather feel an obligation   275
To trust that most obliging declaration?
Enough, now. Your suspicions quite disgust me;
Why should I love a man who doesn't trust me?
I cannot understand why I continue,
Fool that I am, to take an interest in you.   280
I ought to choose a man less prone to doubt,
And give you something to be vexed about.

ALCESTE: Ah, what a poor enchanted fool I am;
These gentle words, no doubt, were all a sham,
But destiny requires me to entrust   285
My happiness to you, and so I must.
I'll love you to the bitter end, and see
How false and treacherous you dare to be.

CELIMENE: No, you don't really love me as you ought.

ALCESTE: I love you more than can be said or thought;   290
Indeed, I wish you were in such distress
That I might show my deep devotedness.
Yes, I could wish that you were wretchedly poor,
Unloved, uncherished, utterly obscure;
That fate had set you down upon the earth   295
Without possessions, rank, or gentle birth;
Then, by the offer of my heart, I might
Repair the great injustice of your plight;
I'd raise you from the dust, and proudly prove
The purity and vastness of my love.   300

CELIMENE: This is a strange benevolence indeed!
    God grant that I may never be in need. . . .
    Ah, here's Monsier Dubois, in quaint disguise.

SCENE FOUR

[CELIMENE, ALCESTE, DUBOIS]

ALCESTE: Well, why this costume? Why those frightened eyes?
    What ails you?

DUBOIS: Well, Sir, things are most mysterious.   305

ALCESTE: What do you mean?

DUBOIS: I fear they're very serious.

ALCESTE: What?

DUBOIS: Shall I speak more loudly?

ALCESTE: Yes; speak out.

DUBOIS: Isn't there someone here, Sir?

ALCESTE: Speak, you lout!
    Stop wasting time.

DUBOIS: Sir, we must slip away.

ALCESTE: How's that?

DUBOIS: We must decamp without delay.   310

ALCESTE: Explain yourself.

DUBOIS: I tell you we must fly.

ALCESTE: What for?

DUBOIS: We mustn't pause to say good-by.

ALCESTE: Now what d'you mean by all of this, you clown?

DUBOIS: I mean, Sir, that we've got to leave this town.

ALCESTE: I'll tear you limb from limb and joint from joint   315
    If you don't come more quickly to the point.

DUBOIS: Well, Sir, today a man in a black suit,
    Who wore a black and ugly scowl to boot,
    Left us a document scrawled in such a hand
    As even Satan couldn't understand.   320
    It bears upon your lawsuit, I don't doubt;
    But all hell's devils couldn't make it out.

ALCESTE: Well, well, go on. What then? I fail to see
    How this event obliges us to flee.

DUBOIS: Well, Sir, an hour later, hardly more,   325
    A gentleman who's often called before
    Came looking for you in an anxious way.
    Not finding you, he asked me to convey
    (Knowing I could be trusted with the same)
    The following message. . . . Now, what *was* his name?   330

ALCESTE: Forget his name, you idiot. What did he say?

DUBOIS: Well, it was one of your friends, Sir, anyway.
    He warned you to begone, and he suggested
    That if you stay, you may well be arrested.

ALCESTE: What? Nothing more specific? Think, man, think!   335

DUBOIS: No, Sir. He had me bring him pen and ink,
    And dashed you off a letter which, I'm sure,
    Will render things distinctly less obscure.

ALCESTE: Well—let me have it!

CELIMENE: What *is* this all about?

ALCESTE: God knows; but I have hopes of finding out.   340
    How long am I to wait, you blitherer?

DUBOIS [*after a protracted search for the letter*]: I must have left it on
        your table, Sir.

ALCESTE: I ought to . . .

CELIMENE: No, no, keep your self-control;
    Go find out what's behind his rigmarole.

ALCESTE: It seems to me that fate, no matter what I do,   345
    Has sworn that I may not converse with you;
    But, Madam, pray permit your faithful lover
    To try once more before the day is over.

ACT FIVE, SCENE ONE

[ALCESTE, PHILINTE]

ALCESTE: No, it's too much. My mind's made up, I tell you.

PHILINTE: Why should this blow, however hard, compel you . . .

ALCESTE: No, no, don't waste your breath in argument;
    Nothing you say will alter my intent;
    This age is vile, and I've made up my mind   5
    To have no further commerce with mankind.
    Did not truth, honor, decency, and the laws
    Oppose my enemy and approve my cause?
    My claims were justified in all men's sight;
    I put my trust in equity and right;   10
    Yet, to my horror and the world's disgrace,
    Justice is mocked, and I have lost my case!
    A scoundrel whose dishonesty is notorious
    Emerges from another lie victorious!
    Honor and right condone his brazen fraud,   15
    While rectitude and decency applaud!
    Before his smirking face, the truth stands charmed,
    And virtue conquered, and the law disarmed!
    His crime is sanctioned by a court decree!
    And not content with what he's done to me,   20
    The dog now seeks to ruin me by stating
    That I composed a book now circulating,

A book so wholly criminal and vicious
That even to speak its title is seditious!
Meanwhile Oronte, my rival, lends his credit   25
To the same libelous tale, and helps to spread it!
Oronte! a man of honor and of rank,
With whom I've been entirely fair and frank;
Who sought me out and forced me, willy-nilly,
To judge some verse I found extremely silly;   30
And who, because I properly refused
To flatter him, or see the truth abused,
Abets my enemy in a rotten slander!
There's the reward of honesty and candor!
The man will hate me to the end of time   35
For failing to commend his wretched rhyme!
And not this man alone, but all humanity
Do what they do from interest and vanity;
They prate of honor, truth, and righteousness,
But lie, betray, and swindle nonetheless.   40
Come then: man's villainy is too much to bear;
Let's leave this jungle and this jackal's lair.
Yes! treacherous and savage race of men,
You shall not look upon my face again.

PHILINTE: Oh, don't rush into exile prematurely;   45
Things aren't as dreadful as you make them, surely.
It's rather obvious, since you're still at large,
That people don't believe your enemy's charge.
Indeed, his tale's so patently untrue
That it may do more harm to him than you.   50

ALCESTE: Nothing could do that scoundrel any harm:
His frank corruption is his greatest charm,
And, far from hurting him, a further shame
Would only serve to magnify his name.

PHILINTE: In any case, his bald prevarication   55
Has done no injury to your reputation,
And you may feel secure in that regard.
As for your lawsuit, it should not be hard
To have the case reopened, and contest
This judgment . . .

ALCESTE: No, no, let the verdict rest.   60
Whatever cruel penalty it may bring,
I wouldn't have it changed for anything.
It shows the times' injustice with such clarity
That I shall pass it down to our posterity
As a great proof and signal demonstration   65
Of the black wickedness of this generation.
It may cost twenty thousand francs; but I
Shall pay their twenty thousand, and gain thereby
The right to storm and rage at human evil,
And send the race of mankind to the devil.   70

PHILINTE: Listen to me . . .

ALCESTE: Why? What can you possibly say?
    Don't argue, Sir; your labor's thrown away.
    Do you propose to offer lame excuses
    For men's behavior and the times' abuses?

PHILINTE: No, all you say I'll readily concede: 75
    This is a low, conniving age indeed;
    Nothing but trickery prospers nowadays,
    And people ought to mend their shabby ways.
    Yes, man's a beastly creature; but must we then
    Abandon the society of men?   80
    Here in the world, each human frailty
    Provides occasion for philosophy,
    And that is virtue's noblest exercise;
    If honesty shone forth from all men's eyes,
    If every heart were frank and kind and just,   85
    What could our virtues do but gather dust
    (Since their employment is to help us bear
    The villainies of men without despair)?
    A heart well-armed with virtue can endure. . . .

ALCESTE: Sir, you're a matchless reasoner, to be sure;   90
    Your words are fine and full of cogency;
    But don't waste time and eloquence on me.
    My reason bids me go, for my own good.
    My tongue won't lie and flatter as it should;
    God knows what frankness it might next commit,   95
    And what I'd suffer on account of it.
    Pray let me wait for Célimène's return
    In peace and quiet. I shall shortly learn,
    By her response to what I have in view,
    Whether her love for me is feigned or true.   100

PHILINTE: Till then, let's visit Éliante upstairs.

ALCESTE: No, I am too weighed down with somber cares.
    Go to her, do; and leave me with my gloom
    Here in the darkened corner of this room.

PHILINTE: Why, that's no sort of company, my friend;   105
    I'll see if Éliante will not descend.

SCENE TWO

[CELIMENE, ORONTE, ALCESTE]

ORONTE: Yes, Madam, if you wish me to remain
    Your true and ardent lover, you must deign
    To give me some more positive assurance.
    All this suspense is quite beyond endurance.   110
    If your heart shares the sweet desires of mine,
    Show me as much by some convincing sign;

And here's the sign I urgently suggest:
That you no longer tolerate Alceste,
But sacrifice him to my love, and sever   115
All your relations with the man forever.

CELIMENE: Why do you suddenly dislike him so?
You praised him to the skies not long ago.

ORONTE: Madam, that's not the point. I'm here to find
Which way your tender feelings are inclined.   120
Choose, if you please, between Alceste and me,
And I shall stay or go accordingly.

ALCESTE [*emerging from the corner*]: Yes, Madam, choose; this
gentleman's demand
Is wholly just, and I support his stand.
I too am true and ardent; I too am here   125
To ask you that you make your feelings clear.
No more delays, now; no equivocation;
The time has come to make your declaration.

ORONTE: Sir, I've no wish in any way to be
An obstacle to your felicity.   130

ALCESTE: Sir, I've no wish to share her heart with you;
That may sound jealous, but at least it's true.

ORONTE: If, weighing us, she leans in your direction . . .

ALCESTE: If she regards you with the least affection . . .

ORONTE: I swear I'll yield her to you there and then.   135

ALCESTE: I swear I'll never see her face again.

ORONTE: Now, Madam, tell us what we've come to hear.

ALCESTE: Madam, speak openly and have no fear.

ORONTE: Just say which one is to remain your lover.

ALCESTE: Just name one name, and it will all be over.   140

ORONTE: What! Is it possible that you're undecided?

ALCESTE: What! Can your feelings possibly be divided?

CELIMENE: Enough: this inquisition's gone too far:
How utterly unreasonable you are!
Not that I couldn't make the choice with ease;   145
My heart has no conflicting sympathies;
I know full well which one of you I favor,
And you'd not see me hesitate or waver.
But how can you expect me to reveal
So cruelly and bluntly what I feel?   150
I think it altogether too unpleasant
To choose between two men when both are present;
One's heart has means more subtle and more kind
Of letting its affections be divined,
Nor need one be uncharitably plain   155
To let a lover know he loves in vain.

ORONTE: No, no, speak plainly; I for one can stand it.
I beg you to be frank.

ALCESTE: And I demand it.
    The simple truth is what I wish to know,
    And there's no need for softening the blow.   160
    You've made an art of pleasing everyone,
    But now your days of coquetry are done:
    You have no choice now, Madam, but to choose,
    For I'll know what to think if you refuse;
    I'll take your silence for a clear admission   165
    That I'm entitled to my worst suspicion.

ORONTE: I thank you for this ultimatum, Sir,
    And I may say I heartily concur.

CELIMENE: Really, this foolishness is very wearing:
    Must you be so unjust and overbearing?   170
    Haven't I told you why I must demur?
    Ah, here's Éliante; I'll put the case to her.

SCENE THREE

[ELIANTE, PHILINTE, CELIMENE, ORONTE, ALCESTE]

CELIMENE: Cousin, I'm being persecuted here
    By these two persons, who, it would appear,
    Will not be satisfied till I confess   175
    Which one I love the more, and which the less,
    And tell the latter to his face that he
    Is henceforth banished from my company.
    Tell me, has ever such a thing been done?

ELIANTE: You'd best not turn to me; I'm not the one   180
    To back you in a matter of this kind:
    I'm all for those who frankly speak their mind.

ORONTE: Madam, you'll search in vain for a defender.

ALCESTE: You're beaten, Madam, and may as well surrender.

ORONTE: Speak, speak, you must; and end this awful strain.   185

ALCESTE: Or don't, and your position will be plain.

ORONTE: A single word will close this painful scene.

ALCESTE: But if you're silent, I'll know what you mean.

SCENE FOUR

[ARSINOE, CELIMENE, ELIANTE, ALCESTE, PHILINTE, ACASTE,
CLITANDRE, ORONTE]

ACASTE [to CELIMENE]: Madam, with all due deference, we two
    Have come back to pick a little bone with you.   190

CLITANDRE [to ORONTE and ALCESTE]: I'm glad you're present, Sirs, as
            you'll soon learn,
    Our business here is also your concern.

ARSINOE [*to* CELIMENE]: Madam, I visit you so soon again
        Only because of these two gentlemen,
        Who came to me indignant and aggrieved   195
        About a crime too base to be believed.
        Knowing your virtue, having such confidence in it,
        I couldn't think you guilty for a minute,
        In spite of all their telling evidence;
        And, rising about our little difference,   200
        I've hastened here in friendship's name to see
        You clear yourself of this great calumny.

ACASTE: Yes, Madam, let us see with what composure
        You'll manage to respond to this disclosure.
        You lately sent Clitandre this tender note.   205

CLITANDRE: And this one, for Acaste, you also wrote.

ACASTE [*to* ORONTE *and* ALCESTE]: You'll recognize this writing, Sirs, I
                think;
        The lady is so free with pen and ink
        That you must know it all too well, I fear.
        But listen: this is something you should hear.   210

        "How absurd you are to condemn my lightheartedness in
society, and to accuse me of being happiest in the company of
others. Nothing could be more unjust; and if you do not come to me
instantly and beg pardon for saying such a thing, I shall never
forgive you as long as I live. Our big bumbling friend the Vis-   215
count . . ."
What a shame that he's not here.
        "Our big bumbling friend the Viscount, whose name stands
first in your complaint, is hardly a man to my taste; and ever since
the day I watched him spend three-quarters of an hour spitting into 220
a well, so as to make circles in the water, I have been unable to
think highly of him. As for the little Marquess . . ."
In all modesty, gentlemen, that is I.
        "As for the little Marquess, who sat squeezing my hand for
such a long while yesterday, I find in all respects the most trifling 225
creature alive; and the only things of value about him are his cape
and his sword. As for the man with the green ribbons . . ."
[*To* ALCESTE.] It's your turn now, Sir.
        "As for the man with the green ribbons, he amuses me now
and then with his bluntness and his bearish ill-humor; but there are 230
many times indeed when I think him the greatest bore in the world.
And as for the sonneteer . . ."
[*To* ORONTE.] Here's your helping.
        "And as for the sonneteer, who has taken it into his head to
be witty, and insists on being an author in the teeth of opinion, I 235
simply cannot be bothered to listen to him, and his prose wearies
me quite as much as his poetry. Be assured that I am not always so
well entertained as you suppose; that I long for your company,
more than I dare to say, at all these entertainments to which people

drag me; and that the presence of those one loves is the true and   240
perfect seasoning to all one's pleasures."

CLITANDRE: And now for me.

"Clitandre, whom you mention, and who so pesters me
with his saccharine speeches, is the last man on earth for whom I
could feel any affection. He is quite mad to suppose that I love him,   245
and so are you, to doubt that you are loved. Do come to your
senses; exchange your suppositions for his; and visit me as often as
possible, to help me bear the annoyance of his unwelcome attentions."

It's a sweet character that these letters show,   250
And what to call it, Madam, you well know.
Enough. We're off to make the world acquainted
With this sublime self-portrait that you've painted.

ACASTE: Madam, I'll make you no farewell oration;
No, you're not worthy of my indignation.   255
Far choicer hearts than yours, as you'll discover,
Would like this little Marquess for a lover.

SCENE FIVE

[CELIMENE, ELIANTE, ARSINOE, ALCESTE, ORONTE, PHILINTE]

ORONTE: So! After all those loving letters you wrote,
You turn on me like this, and cut my throat!
And your dissembling, faithless heart, I find,   260
Has pledged itself by turns to all mankind!
How blind I've been! But now I clearly see;
I thank you, Madam, for enlightening me.
My heart is mine once more, and I'm content;
The loss of it shall be your punishment.   265

To ALCESTE.

Sir, she is yours; I'll seek no more to stand
Between your wishes and this lady's hand.

SCENE SIX

[CELIMENE, ELIANTE, ARSINOE, ALCESTE, PHILINTE]

ARSINOE [to CELIMENE]: Madam, I'm forced to speak. I'm far too stirred
To keep my counsel, after what I've heard.
I'm shocked and staggered by your want of morals.   270
It's not my way to mix in others' quarrels;
But really, when this fine and noble spirit,
This man of honor and surpassing merit,
Laid down the offering of his heart before you,
How *could* you . . .

ALCESTE: Madam, permit me, I implore you,   275
    To represent myself in this debate.
    Don't bother, please, to be my advocate.
    My heart, in any case, could not afford
    To give your services their due reward;
    And if I chose, for consolation's sake,   280
    Some other lady, 'twould not be you I'd take.

ARSINOE: What makes you think you could, Sir? And how dare you
    Imply that I've been trying to ensnare you?
    If you can for a moment entertain
    Such flattering fancies, you're extremely vain.   285
    I'm not so interested as you suppose
    In Célimène's discarded gigolos.
    Get rid of that absurd illusion, do.
    Women like me are not for such as you.
    Stay with this creature, to whom you're so attached;   290
    I've never seen two people better matched.

SCENE SEVEN

[CELIMENE, ELIANTE, ALCESTE, PHILINTE]

ALCESTE [*to* CELIMENE]: Well, I've been still throughout this exposé,
    Till everyone but me has said his say.
    Come, have I shown sufficient self-restraint?
    And may I now . . .

CELIMENE: Yes, make your just complaint.   295
    Reproach me freely, call me what you will;
    You've every right to say I've used you ill.
    I've wronged you, I confess it; and in my shame
    I'll make no effort to escape the blame.
    The anger of those others I could despise;   300
    My guilt toward you I sadly recognize.
    Your wrath is wholly justified, I fear;
    I know how culpable I must appear,
    I know all things bespeak my treachery,
    And that, in short, you've grounds for hating me.   305
    Do so; I give you leave.

ALCESTE: Ah, traitress—how,
    How should I cease to love you, even now?
    Though mind and will were passionately bent
    On hating you, my heart would not consent.

    To ELIANTE *and* PHILINTE.

    Be witness to my madness, both of you;   310
    See what infatuation drives one to;
    But wait; my folly's only just begun,
    And I shall prove to you before I'm done
    How strange the human heart is, and how far
    From rational we sorry creatures are.   315

To CELIMENE.

Woman, I'm willing to forget your shame,
And clothe your treacheries in a sweeter name;
I'll call them youthful errors, instead of crimes,
And lay the blame on these corrupting times.
My one condition is that you agree   320
To share my chosen fate, and fly with me
To that wild, trackless, solitary place
In which I shall forget the human race.
Only by such a course can you atone
For those atrocious letters; by that alone   325
Can you remove my present horror of you,
And make it possible for me to love you.

CELIMENE: What! *I* renounce the world at my young age,
And die of boredom in some hermitage?

ALCESTE: Ah, if you really loved me as you ought,   330
You wouldn't give the world a moment's thought;
Must you have me, and all the world beside?

CELIMENE: Alas, at twenty one is terrified
Of solitude. I fear I lack the force
And depth of soul to take so stern a course.   335
But if my hand in marriage will content you,
Why, there's a plan which I might well consent to,
And . . .

ALCESTE: No, I detest you now. I could excuse
Everything else, but since you thus refuse
To love me wholly, as a wife should do,   340
And see the world in me, as I in you,
Go! I reject your hand, and disenthrall
My heart from your enchantments, once for all.

SCENE EIGHT

[ELIANTE, ALCESTE, PHILINTE]

ALCESTE [*to* ELIANTE]: Madam, your virtuous beauty has no peer;
Of all this world you only are sincere;   345
I've long esteemed you highly, as you know;
Permit me ever to esteem you so,
And if I do not now request your hand,
Forgive me, Madam, and try to understand.
I feel unworthy of it; I sense that fate   350
Does not intend me for the married state.
That I should do you wrong by offering you
My shattered heart's unhappy residue,
And that in short . . .

ELIANTE: Your argument's well taken:
Nor need you fear that I shall feel forsaken.   355

Were I to offer him this hand of mine,
Your friend Philinte, I think, would not decline.

PHILINTE: Ah, Madam, that's my heart's most cherished goal,
For which I'd gladly give my life and soul.

ALCESTE [*to* ELIANTE *and* PHILINTE]: May you be true to all you now
    profess,   360
And so deserve unending happiness.
Meanwhile, betrayed and wronged in everything,
I'll flee this bitter world where vice is king,
And seek some spot unpeopled and apart
Where I'll be free to have an honest heart.   365

PHILINTE: Come, Madam, let's do everything we can
To change the mind of this unhappy man.

Fact Questions and Exercises

1. What does "misanthrope" mean? In the play, who is a misanthrope?
2. Why, in the opening lines of the play, is Alceste angry at Philinte? That is, what is the "crime so grave" that Alceste mentions?
3. What is Philinte's defense against Alceste's accusations? Cite specific lines to support your answer.
4. How are Célimène and Éliante related? How, according to Philinte, do they differ in character?
5. At his first appearance in the play, what does Oronte recite to Philinte and Alceste? What is Alceste's reaction?
6. What is Acaste's evaluation of himself? Cite specific lines to support your answer.
7. What charge is brought against Alceste in Act 5 that makes him decide to go into exile?
8. Ultimately, does Célimène accept Alceste's proposal of marriage? What reasons does she give for her decision?

For Discussion and Writing

1. Which character in the play do you find most admirable? Least admirable? What are your reasons?
2. Check the Guide to Literary Terms for a definition of "comedy of manners." Is *The Misanthrope* a comedy of manners? What elements make the play "comic"? Are there facets of tragedy in the play? If so, what are they?
3. There is much ado about "love" in the play. What do Célimène and Alceste seem to mean by "love"? Can you explain how Alceste, Célimène, and the other characters turn their affections on and off so easily?
4. Characterize Alceste. What are his motivations? What are his faults? His virtues? Is he a hero? Or, is he as foolish as those he condemns?
5. What point is Molière trying to make? Does he advocate complete frankness? Or does Molière suggest a middle ground somewhere between Alceste's honesty and Célimène's hypocrisy?

Henrik Ibsen [1828–1906]

Ibsen was born in Skien, Norway, the son of a merchant who had fallen into poverty. Ibsen was educated sporadically in public schools. At the age of fifteen, he left home to become a druggist's apprentice, but his interests soon turned to drama. He was so successful that in 1851 he was made the official playwright of the Norwegian national theater. His fame was somewhat compromised by plays such as *A Doll's House* (1879) and *Ghosts* (1881)—realistic plays that were considered scandalous. Today, however, Ibsen is best remembered for these realistic dramas—plays that speak against social conventions, and advocate moral and personal liberation. In his day, his plays were considered revolutionary, but represented, in great part, the launching of modern drama. In his late plays, Ibsen refined his realism and wrote significant symbolic dramas, such as, *The Lady from the Sea* (1888) and *Hedda Gabler* (1890).

Ghosts

A Family Drama in Three Acts

Characters

MRS. HELEN ALVING, *widow of Captain Alving,*
     late Chamberlain to the King
OSWALD ALVING, *her son, a painter*
PASTOR MANDERS
JACOB ENGSTRAND, *a carpenter*
REGINA ENGSTRAND, *Mrs. Alving's maid*

> *The action takes place at Mrs. Alving's country house, beside one of the large fjords in Western Norway.*

ACT ONE

> (*A spacious garden-room, with one door to the left, and two doors to the right. In the middle of the room a round table, with chairs about it. On the table lie books, periodicals, and newspapers. In the foreground to the left a window, and by it a small sofa, with a work table in front of it. In the background, the room is continued into a somewhat narrower conservatory, the walls of which are formed by large panes of glass. In the right-hand wall of the conservatory is a door leading down into the garden. Through the glass wall a gloomy fjord-landscape is faintly visible, veiled by steady rain.*)
> (ENGSTRAND, *the carpenter, stands by the garden door. His left leg is somewhat bent; he has a clump of wood under the sole of*

his boot. REGINA, *with an empty garden syringe in her hand, hinders him from advancing.*)

REGINA (*in a low voice*): What do you want? Stop where you are. You're positively dripping.

ENGSTRAND: It's the Lord's own rain, my girl.

REGINA: It's the devil's rain, *I* say.

ENGSTRAND: Lord, how you talk, Regina. (*Limps a step or two forward into the room.*) It's just this as I wanted to say—

REGINA: Don't clatter so with that foot of yours, I tell you! The young master's asleep upstairs.

ENGSTRAND: Asleep? In the middle of the day?

REGINA: It's no business of yours.

ENGSTRAND: I was out on the loose last night—

REGINA: I can quite believe that.

ENGSTRAND: Yes, we're weak vessels, we poor mortals, my girl—

REGINA: So it seems.

ENGSTRAND: —and temptations are manifold in this world, you see. But all the same, I was hard at work, God knows, at half-past five this morning.

REGINA: Very well; only be off now. I won't stop here and have *rendezvous's* with you.

ENGSTRAND: What do you say you won't have?

REGINA: I won't have any one find you here; so just you go about your business.

ENGSTRAND (*advances a step or two*): Blest if I go before I've had a talk with you. This afternoon I shall have finished my work at the school-house, and then I shall take to-night's boat and be off home to the town.

REGINA (*mutters*): Pleasant journey to you!

ENGSTRAND: Thank you, my child. To-morrow the Orphanage is to be opened, and then there'll be fine doings, no doubt, and plenty of intoxicating drink going, you know. And nobody shall say of Jacob Engstrand that he can't keep out of temptation's way.

REGINA: Oh!

ENGSTRAND: You see, there's to be heaps of grand folks here to-morrow. Pastor Manders is expected from town, too.

REGINA: He's coming to-day.

ENGSTRAND: There, you see! And I should be cursedly sorry if he found out anything against me, don't you understand?

REGINA: Oho! is that your game?

ENGSTRAND: Is what my game?

REGINA (*looking hard at him*): What are you going to fool Pastor Manders into doing, this time?

ENGSTRAND: Sh! sh! Are you crazy? Do *I* want to fool Pastor Manders? Oh no! Pastor Manders has been far too good a friend to me for that. But I just wanted to say, you know—that I mean to be off home again to-night.

REGINA: The sooner the better, say I.

ENGSTRAND: Yes, but I want you with me, Regina.

REGINA (*open-mouthed*): You want me—? What are you talking about?

ENGSTRAND: I want you to come home with me, I say.

REGINA (*scornfully*): Never in this world shall you get me home with you.

ENGSTRAND: Oh, we'll see about that.

REGINA: Yes, you may be sure we'll see about it! Me, that have been brought up by a lady like Mrs. Alving! Me, that am treated almost as a daughter here! Is it me you want to go home with you?—to a house like yours? For shame?

ENGSTRAND: What the devil do you mean? Do you set yourself up against your father, you hussy?

REGINA (*mutters without looking at him*): You've said often enough I was no concern of yours.

ENGSTRAND: Pooh! Why should you bother about that—

REGINA: Haven't you many a time sworn at me and called me a—? *Fi donc!*

ENGSTRAND: Curse me, now, if ever I used such an ugly word.

REGINA: Oh, I remember very well what word you used.

ENGSTRAND: Well, but that was only when I was a bit on, don't you know? Temptations are manifold in this world, Regina.

REGINA: Ugh!

ENGSTRAND: And besides, it was when your mother was that aggravating—I had to find something to twit her with, my child. She was always setting up for a fine lady. (*Mimics.*) "Let me go, Engstrand; let me be. Remember I was three years in Chamberlain Alving's family at Rosenvold." (*Laughs.*) Mercy on us! She could never forget that the Captain was made a Chamberlain while she was in service here.

REGINA: Poor mother! you very soon tormented her into her grave.

ENGSTRAND (*with a twist of his shoulders*): Oh, of course! I'm to have the blame for everything.

REGINA (*turns away; half aloud*): Ugh—! And that leg, too!

ENGSTRAND: What do you say, my child?

REGINA: *Pied de mouton.*

ENGSTRAND: Is that English, eh?

REGINA: Yes.

ENGSTRAND: Ay, ay; you've picked up some learning out here; and that may come in useful now, Regina.

REGINA (*after a short silence*): What do you want with me in town?

ENGSTRAND: Can you ask what a father wants with his only child? A'n't I a lonely, forlorn widower?

REGINA: Oh, don't try on any nonsense like that with me! Why do you want me?

ENGSTRAND: Well, let me tell you, I've been thinking of setting up in a new line of business.

REGINA (*contemptuously*): You've tried that often enough, and much good you've done with it.

ENGSTRAND: Yes, but this time you shall see, Regina! Devil take me—

REGINA (*stamps*): Stop your swearing!

ENGSTRAND: Hush, hush; you're right enough there, my girl. What I wanted to say was just this—I've laid by a very tidy pile from this Orphanage job.

REGINA: Have you? That's a good thing for you.

ENGSTRAND: What can a man spend his ha'pence on here in this country hole?

REGINA: Well, what then?

ENGSTRAND: Why, you see, I thought of putting the money into some paying speculation. I thought of a sort of a sailor's tavern—

REGINA: Pah!

ENGSTRAND: A regular high-class affair, of course; not any sort of pig-sty for common sailors. No! damn it! it would be for captains and mates, and—and—regular swells, you know.

REGINA: And I was to—?

ENGSTRAND: You were to help, to be sure. Only for the look of the thing, you understand. Devil a bit of hard work shall you have, my girl. You shall do exactly what you like.

REGINA: Oh, indeed!

ENGSTRAND: But there must be a petticoat in the house; that's as clear as daylight. For I want to have it a bit lively-like in the evenings, with singing and dancing, and so on. You must remember they're weary wanderers on the ocean of life. (*Nearer.*) Now don't be a fool and stand in your own light, Regina. What's to become of you out here? Your mistress has given you a lot of learning; but what good is that to you? You're to look after the children at the new Orphanage, I hear. Is that the sort of thing for you, eh? Are you so dead set on wearing your life out for a pack of dirty brats?

REGINA: No; if things go as I want them to— Well there's no saying—there's no saying.

ENGSTRAND: What do you mean by "there's no saying"?

REGINA: Never you mind.—How much money have you saved?

ENGSTRAND: What with one thing and another, a matter of seven or eight hundred crowns.

REGINA: That's not so bad.

ENGSTRAND: It's enough to make a start with, my girl.

REGINA: Aren't you thinking of giving me any?

ENGSTRAND: No, I'm blest if I am!

REGINA: Not even of sending me a scrap of stuff for a new dress?

ENGSTRAND: Come to town with me, my lass, and you'll soon get dresses enough.

REGINA: Pooh! I can do that on my own account, if I want to.

ENGSTRAND: No, a father's guiding hand is what you want, Regina. Now, I've got my eye on a capital house in Little Harbour Street. They don't want much ready-money; and it could be a sort of a Sailors' Home, you know.

REGINA: But I will not live with you! I have nothing whatever to do with you. Be off!

ENGSTRAND: You wouldn't stop long with me, my girl. No such luck! If you knew how to play your cards, such a fine figure of a girl as you've grown in the last year or two—

REGINA: Well?

ENGSTRAND: You'd soon get hold of some mate—or maybe even a captain—

REGINA: I won't marry any one of that sort. Sailors have no *savoir vivre*.

ENGSTRAND: What's that they haven't got?

REGINA: I know what sailors are, I tell you. They're not the sort of people to marry.

ENGSTRAND: Then never mind about marrying them. You can make it pay all the same. (*More confidentially.*) He—the Englishman—the man with the yacht—he came down with three hundred dollars, he did; and she wasn't a bit handsomer than you.

REGINA (*making for him*): Out you go!

ENGSTRAND (*falling back*): Come, come! You're not going to hit me, I hope.

REGINA: Yes, if you begin talking about mother I shall hit you. Get away with you, I say! (*Drives him back towards the garden door.*) And don't slam the doors. Young Mr. Alving—

ENGSTRAND: He's asleep; I know. You're mighty taken up about young Mr. Alving— (*More softly.*) Oho! you don't mean to say it's him as—?

REGINA: Be off this minute! You're crazy, I tell you! No, not that way. There comes Pastor Manders. Down the kitchen stairs with you.

ENGSTRAND (*towards the right*): Yes, yes, I'm going. But just you talk to him as is coming there. He's the man to tell you what a child owes its father. For I am your father all the same, you know. I can prove it from the church register.

> (*He goes out through the second door to the right, which* REGINA *has opened, and closes again after him.* REGINA *glances hastily at herself in the mirror, dusts herself with her pocket handkerchief, and settles her necktie; then she busies herself with the flowers.*)
>
> (PASTOR MANDERS, *wearing an overcoat, carrying an umbrella, and with a small travelling-bag on a strap over his shoulder, comes through the garden door into the conservatory.*)

MANDERS: Good-morning, Miss Engstrand.

REGINA (*turning around, surprised and pleased*): No, really! Good-morning, Pastor Manders. Is the steamer in already?

MANDERS: It is just in. (*Enters the sitting-room.*) Terrible weather we have been having lately.

REGINA (*follows him*): It's such blessed weather for the country, sir.

MANDERS: No doubt; you are quite right. We townspeople give too little thought to that. (*He begins to take off his overcoat.*)

REGINA: Oh, mayn't I help you?—There! Why, how wet it is! I'll just hang it up in the hall. And your umbrella, too—I'll open it and let it dry.

(*She goes out with the things through the second door on the right.* PASTOR MANDERS *takes off his travelling-bag and lays it and his hat on a chair. Meanwhile* REGINA *comes in again.*)

MANDERS: Ah, it's a comfort to get safe under cover. I hope everything is going on well here?

REGINA: Yes, thank you, sir.

MANDERS: You have your hands full, I suppose, in preparation for to-morrow?

REGINA: Yes, there's plenty to do, of course.

MANDERS: And Mrs. Alving is at home, I trust?

REGINA: Oh dear, yes. She's just upstairs, looking after the young master's chocolate.

MANDERS: Yes, by-the-bye—I heard down at the pier that Oswald had arrived.

REGINA: Yes, he came the day before yesterday. We didn't expect him before to-day.

MANDERS: Quite strong and well, I hope?

REGINA: Yes, thank you, quite; but dreadfully tired with the journey. He has made one rush right through from Paris—the whole way in one train, I believe. He's sleeping a little now, I think; so perhaps we'd better talk a little quietly.

MANDERS: Sh!—as quietly as you please.

REGINA (*arranging an arm-chair beside the table*): Now, do sit down, Pastor Manders, and make yourself comfortable. (*He sits down; she places a footstool under his feet.*) There! Are you comfortable now, sir?

MANDERS: Thanks, thanks, extremely so. (*Looks at her.*) Do you know, Miss Engstrand, I positively believe you have grown since I last saw you.

REGINA: Do you think so, sir? Mrs. Alving says I've filled out too.

MANDERS: Filled out? Well, perhaps a little; just enough.

(*Short pause.*)

REGINA: Shall I tell Mrs. Alving you are here?

MANDERS: Thanks, thanks, there is no hurry, my dear child.—By-the-bye, Regina, my good girl, tell me: how is your father getting on out here?

REGINA: Oh, thank you, sir, he's getting on well enough.

MANDERS: He called upon me last time he was in town.

REGINA: Did he, indeed? He's always so glad of a chance of talking to you, sir.

MANDERS: And you often look in upon him at his work, I daresay?

REGINA: I? Oh, of course, when I have time, I—

MANDERS: Your father is not a man of strong character, Miss Engstrand. He stands terribly in need of a guiding hand.

REGINA: Oh, yes; I daresay he does.

MANDERS: He requires some one near him whom he cares for, and whose judgment he respects. He frankly admitted as much when he last came to see me.

REGINA: Yes, he mentioned something of the sort to me. But I don't know whether Mrs. Alving can spare me; especially now that we've got the new Orphanage to attend to. And then I should be so sorry to leave Mrs. Alving; she has always been so kind to me.

MANDERS: But a daughter's duty, my good girl— Of course, we should first have to get your mistress's consent.

REGINA: But I don't know whether it would be quite proper for me, at my age, to keep house for a single man.

MANDERS: What! My dear Miss Engstrand! When the man is your own father!

REGINA: Yes, that may be; but all the same— Now, if it were in a thoroughly nice house, and with a real gentleman—

MANDERS: Why, my dear Regina—

REGINA: —one I could love and respect, and be a daughter to—

MANDERS: Yes, but my dear, good child—

REGINA: Then I should be glad to go to town. It's very lonely out here; you know yourself, sir, what it is to be alone in the world. And I can assure you I'm both quick and willing. Don't you know of any such place for me, sir?

MANDERS: I? No, certainly not.

REGINA: But, dear, dear sir, do remember me if—

MANDERS (*rising*): Yes, yes, certainly, Miss Engstrand.

REGINA: For if I—

MANDERS: Will you be so good as to tell your mistress I am here?

REGINA: I will at once, sir. (*She goes out to the left.*)

MANDERS (*paces the room two or three times, stands a moment in the background with his hands behind his back, and looks out over the garden. Then he returns to the table, takes up a book, and looks at the title-page; starts, and looks at several books*): Ha—indeed!

> (MRS. ALVING *enters by the door on the left; she is followed by* REGINA, *who immediately goes out by the first door on the right.*)

MRS. ALVING (*holds out her hand*): Welcome, my dear Pastor.

MANDERS: How do you do, Mrs. Alving? Here I am as I promised.

MRS. ALVING: Always punctual to the minute.

MANDERS: You may believe it was not easy for me to get away. With all the Boards and Committees I belong to—

MRS. ALVING: That makes it all the kinder of you to come so early. Now we can get through our business before dinner. But where is your portmanteau?

MANDERS (*quickly*): I left it down at the inn. I shall sleep there to-night.

MRS. ALVING (*suppressing a smile*): Are you really not to be persuaded, even now, to pass the night under my roof?

MANDERS: No, no, Mrs. Alving; many thanks. I shall stay at the inn, as usual. It is so conveniently near the landing-stage.

MRS. ALVING: Well, you must have your own way. But I really should have thought we two old people—

MANDERS: Now you are making fun of me. Ah, you're naturally in great spirits to-day—what with to-morrow's festival and Oswald's return.

MRS. ALVING: Yes; you can think what a delight it is to me! It's more than two years since he was home last. And now he has promised to stay with me all the winter.

MANDERS: Has he really? That is very nice and dutiful of him. For I can well believe that life in Rome and Paris has very different attractions from any we can offer here.

MRS. ALVING: Ah, but here he has his mother, you see. My own darling boy—he hasn't forgotten his old mother!

MANDERS: It would be grievous indeed, if absence and absorption in art and that sort of thing were to blunt his natural feelings.

MRS. ALVING: Yes, you may well say so. But there's nothing of that sort to fear with him. I'm quite curious to see whether you know him again. He'll be down presently; he's upstairs just now, resting a little on the sofa. But do sit down, my dear Pastor.

MANDERS: Thank you. Are you quite at liberty—?

MRS. ALVING: Certainly. (*She sits by the table.*)

MANDERS: Very well. Then let me show you— (*He goes to the chair where his travelling-bag lies, takes out a packet of papers, sits down on the opposite side of the table, and tries to find a clear space for the papers.*) Now, to begin with, here is— (*Breaking off.*) Tell me, Mrs. Alving, how do these books come to be here?

MRS. ALVING: These books? They are books I am reading.

MANDERS: Do you read this sort of literature?

MRS. ALVING: Certainly I do.

MANDERS: Do you feel better or happier for such reading?

MRS. ALVING: I feel, so to speak, more secure.

MANDERS: That is strange. How do you mean?

MRS. ALVING: Well, I seem to find explanation and confirmation of all sorts of things I myself have been thinking. For that is the wonderful part of it, Pastor Manders—there is really nothing new in these books, nothing but what most people think and believe. Only most people either don't formulate it to themselves, or else keep quiet about it.

MANDERS: Great heavens! Do you really believe that most people—?

MRS. ALVING: I do, indeed.

MANDERS: But surely not in this country? Not here among us?

MRS. ALVING: Yes, certainly; here as elsewhere.

MANDERS: Well, I really must say—!

MRS. ALVING: For the rest, what do you object to in these books?

MANDERS: Object to in them? You surely do not suppose that I have nothing better to do than to study such publications as these?

MRS. ALVING: That is to say, you know nothing of what you are condemning?

MANDERS: I have read enough about these writings to disapprove of them.

MRS. ALVING: Yes; but your own judgment—

MANDERS: My dear Mrs. Alving, there are many occasions in life when one must rely upon others. Things are so ordered in this world; and it is well that they are. Otherwise, what would become of society?

MRS. ALVING: Well, well, I daresay you're right there.

MANDERS: Besides, I of course do not deny that there may be much that is attractive in such books. Nor can I blame you for wishing to keep up with the intellectual movements that are said to be going on in the great world—where you have let your son pass so much of his life. But—

MRS. ALVING: But?

MANDERS (*lowering his voice*): But one should not talk about it, Mrs. Alving. One is certainly not bound to account to everybody for what one reads and thinks within one's own four walls.

MRS. ALVING: Of course not; I quite agree with you.

MANDERS: Only think, now, how you are bound to consider the interests of this Orphanage, which you decided on founding at a time when—if I understand you rightly—you thought very differently on spiritual matters.

MRS. ALVING: Oh, yes; I quite admit that. But it was about the Orphanage—

MANDERS: It was about the Orphanage we were to speak; yes. All I say is: prudence, my dear lady! And now let us get to business. (*Opens the packet, and takes out a number of papers.*) Do you see these?

MRS. ALVING: The documents?

MANDERS: All—and in perfect order. I can tell you it was hard work to get them in time. I had to put on strong pressure. The authorities are almost morbidly scrupulous when there is any decisive step to be taken. But here they are at last. (*Looks through the bundle.*) See! here is the formal deed of gift of the parcel of ground known as Solvik in the Manor of Rosenvold, with all the newly constructed buildings, schoolrooms, master's house, and chapel. And here is the legal fiat for the endowment and for the Bye-laws of the Institution. Will you look at them? (*Reads.*) "Bye-laws for the Children's Home to be known as 'Captain Alving's Foundation.'"

MRS. ALVING (*looks long at the paper*): So there it is.

MANDERS: I have chosen the designation "Captain" rather than "Chamberlain." "Captain" looks less pretentious.

MRS. ALVING: Oh, yes; just as you think best.

MANDERS: And here you have the Bank Account of the capital lying at interest to cover the current expenses of the Orphanage.

MRS. ALVING: Thank you; but please keep it—it will be more convenient.

MANDERS: With pleasure. I think we will leave the money in the Bank for the present. The interest is certainly not what we could wish—four per cent and six months' notice of withdrawal. If a good mortgage could be found later on—of course it must be a first mortgage and an unimpeachable security—then we could consider the matter.

MRS. ALVING: Certainly, my dear Pastor Manders. You are the best judge in these things.

MANDERS: I will keep my eyes open at any rate.—But now there is one thing more which I have several times been intending to ask you.

MRS. ALVING: And what is that?

MANDERS: Shall the Orphanage buildings be insured or not?

MRS. ALVING: Of course they must be insured.

MANDERS: Well, wait a moment, Mrs. Alving. Let us look into the matter a little more closely.

MRS. ALVING: I have everything insured; buildings and movables and stock and crops.

MANDERS: Of course you have—on your own estate. And so have I—of course. But here, you see, it is quite another matter. The Orphanage is to be consecrated, as it were, to a higher purpose.

MRS. ALVING: Yes, but that's no reason—

MANDERS: For my own part, I should certainly not see the smallest impropriety in guarding against all contingencies—

MRS. ALVING: No, I should think not.

MANDERS: But what is the general feeling in the neighbourhood? You, of course, know better than I.

MRS. ALVING: Well—the general feeling—

MANDERS: Is there any considerable number of people—really responsible people—who might be scandalised?

MRS. ALVING: What do you mean by "really responsible people"?

MANDERS: Well, I mean people in such independent and influential positions that one cannot help attaching some weight to their opinions.

MRS. ALVING: There are several people of that sort here, who would very likely be shocked if—

MANDERS: There, you see! In town we have many such people. Think of all my colleague's adherents! People would be only too ready to interpret our action as a sign that neither you nor I had the right faith in a Higher Providence.

MRS. ALVING: But for your own part, my dear Pastor, you can at least tell yourself that—

MANDERS: Yes, I know—I know; my conscience would be quite easy, that is true enough. But nevertheless we should not escape grave misinterpretation; and that might very likely react unfavourably upon the Orphanage.

MRS. ALVING: Well, in that case—

MANDERS: Nor can I entirely lose sight of the difficult—may even say painful—position in which *I* might perhaps be placed. In the leading circles of the town, people take a lively interest in this Orphanage. It is, of course, founded partly for the benefit of the town, as well; and it is to be hoped it will, to a considerable extent, result in lightening our Poor Rates. Now, as I have been your adviser, and have had the business arrangements in my hands, I cannot but fear that I may have to bear the brunt of fanaticism—

MRS. ALVING: Oh, you mustn't run the risk of that.

MANDERS: To say nothing of the attacks that would assuredly be made upon me in certain papers and periodicals, which—

MRS. ALVING: Enough, my dear Pastor Manders. That consideration is quite decisive.

MANDERS: Then you do not wish the Orphanage to be insured?

MRS. ALVING: No. We will let it alone.

MANDERS (*leaning back in his chair*): But if, now, a disaster were to happen? One can never tell— Should you be able to make good the damage?

MRS. ALVING: No; I tell you plainly I should do nothing of the kind.

MANDERS: Then I must tell you, Mrs. Alving—we are taking no small responsibility upon ourselves.

MRS. ALVING: Do you think we can do otherwise?

MANDERS: No, that is just the point; we really cannot do otherwise. We ought not to expose ourselves to misinterpretation; and we have no right whatever to give offence to the weaker brethren.

MRS. ALVING: You, as a clergyman, certainly should not.

MANDERS: I really think, too, we may trust that such an institution has fortune on its side; in fact, that it stands under a special providence.

MRS. ALVING: Let us hope so, Pastor Manders.

MANDERS: Then we will let it take its chance?

MRS. ALVING: Yes, certainly.

MANDERS: Very well. So be it. (*Makes a note.*) Then—no insurance.

MRS. ALVING: It's odd that you should just happen to mention the matter to-day—

MANDERS: I have often thought of asking you about it—

MRS. ALVING: —for we very nearly had a fire down there yesterday.

MANDERS: You don't say so!

MRS. ALVING: Oh, it was a trifling matter. A heap of shavings had caught fire in the carpenter's workshop.

MANDERS: Where Engstrand works?

MRS. ALVING: Yes. They say he's often very careless with matches.

MANDERS: He has so much on his mind, that man—so many things to fight against. Thank God, he is now striving to lead a decent life, I hear.

MRS. ALVING: Indeed! Who says so?

MANDERS: He himself assures me of it. And he is certainly a capital workman.

MRS. ALVING: Oh, yes; so long as he's sober—

MANDERS: Ah, that melancholy weakness! But he is often driven to it by his injured leg, he says. Last time he was in town I was really touched by him. He came and thanked me so warmly for having got him work here, so that he might be near Regina.

MRS. ALVING: He doesn't see much of her.

MANDERS: Oh, yes; he has a talk with her every day. He told me so himself.

MRS. ALVING: Well, it may be so.

MANDERS: He feels so acutely that he needs some one to keep a firm hold on him when temptation comes. That is what I cannot help liking about Jacob Engstrand: he comes to you so helplessly, accusing himself and confessing his own weakness. The last time he was talking to me— Believe me,

Mrs. Alving, supposing it were a real necessity for him to have Regina home again—

MRS. ALVING (*rising hastily*): Regina!

MANDERS: —you must not set yourself against it.

MRS. ALVING: Indeed I shall set myself against it. And besides—Regina is to have a position in the Orphanage.

MANDERS: But, after all, remember he is her father—

MRS. ALVING: Oh, I know very well what sort of a father he has been to her. No! She shall never go to him with my goodwill.

MANDERS (*rising*): My dear lady, don't take the matter so warmly. You sadly misjudge poor Engstrand. You seem to be quite terrified—

MRS. ALVING (*more quietly*): It makes no difference. I have taken Regina into my house, and there she shall stay. (*Listens.*) Hush, my dear Mr. Manders; say no more about it. (*Her face lights up with gladness.*) Listen! there is Oswald coming downstairs. Now we'll think of no one but him.

(OSWALD ALVING, *in a light overcoat, hat in hand, and smoking a large meerschaum, enters by the door on the left; he stops in the doorway.*)

OSWALD: Oh, I beg your pardon; I thought you were in the study. (*Comes forward.*) Good-morning, Pastor Manders.

MANDERS (*staring*): Ah— How strange—!

MRS. ALVING: Well now, what do you think of him, Mr. Manders?

MANDERS: I—I—can it really be—?

OSWALD: Yes, it's really the Prodigal Son, sir.

MANDERS (*protesting*): My dear young friend—

OSWALD: Well, then, the Lost Sheep Found.

MRS. ALVING: Oswald is thinking of the time when you were so much opposed to his becoming a painter.

MANDERS: To our human eyes many a step seems dubious, which afterwards proves— (*Wrings his hand.*) But first of all, welcome, welcome home! Do not think, my dear Oswald—I suppose I may call you by your Christian name?

OSWALD: What else should you call me?

MANDERS: Very good. What I wanted to say was this, my dear Oswald—you must not think that I utterly condemn the artist's calling. I have no doubt there are many who can keep their inner self unharmed in that profession, as in any other.

OSWALD: Let us hope so.

MRS. ALVING (*beaming with delight*): I know one who has kept both his inner and his outer self unharmed. Just look at him, Mr. Manders.

OSWALD (*moves restlessly about the room*): Yes, yes, my dear mother; let's say no more about it.

MANDERS: Why, certainly—that is undeniable. And you have begun to make a name for yourself already. The newspapers have often spoken of you, most favourably. Just lately, by-the-bye, I fancy I haven't seen your name quite so often.

OSWALD (*up in the conservatory*): I haven't been able to paint so much lately.

MRS. ALVING: Even a painter needs a little rest now and then.

MANDERS: No doubt, no doubt. And meanwhile he can be preparing himself and mustering his forces for some great work.

OSWALD: Yes.—Mother, will dinner soon be ready?

MRS. ALVING: In less than half an hour. He has a capital appetite, thank God.

MANDERS: And a taste for tobacco, too.

OSWALD: I found my father's pipe in my room—

MANDERS: Aha—then that accounts for it!

MRS. ALVING: For what?

MANDERS: When Oswald appeared there in the doorway, with the pipe in his mouth, I could have sworn I saw his father, large as life.

OSWALD: No, really?

MRS. ALVING: Oh, how can you say so? Oswald takes after me.

MANDERS: Yes, but there is an expression about the corners of the mouth— something about the lips—that reminds one exactly of Alving: at any rate, now that he is smoking.

MRS. ALVING: Not in the least. Oswald has rather a clerical curve about his mouth, I think.

MANDERS: Yes, yes; some of my colleagues have much the same expression.

MRS. ALVING: But put your pipe away, my dear boy; I won't have smoking in here.

OSWALD (*does so*): By all means. I only wanted to try it; for I once smoked it when I was a child.

MRS. ALVING: You?

OSWALD: Yes. I was quite small at the time. I recollect I came up to father's room one evening when he was in great spirits.

MRS. ALVING: Oh, you can't recollect anything of those times.

OSWALD: Yes, I recollect it distinctly. He took me on his knee, and gave me the pipe. "Smoke, boy," he said; "smoke away, boy!" And I smoked as hard as I could, until I felt I was growing quite pale, and the perspiration stood in great drops on my forehead. Then he burst out laughing heartily—

MANDERS: That was most extraordinary.

MRS. ALVING: My dear friend, it's only something Oswald has dreamt.

OSWALD: No, mother, I assure you I didn't dream it. For—don't you remember this?—you came and carried me out into the nursery. Then I was sick. and I saw that you were crying.—Did father often play such practical jokes?

MANDERS: In his youth he overflowed with the joy of life—

OSWALD: And yet he managed to do so much in the world; so much that was good and useful; although he died so early.

MANDERS: Yes, you have inherited the name of an energetic and admirable man, my dear Oswald Alving. No doubt it will be an incentive to you—

OSWALD: It ought to, indeed.

MANDERS: It was good of you to come home for the ceremony in his honour.

OSWALD: I could do no less for my father.

MRS. ALVING: And I am to keep him so long! That is the best of all.

MANDERS: You are going to pass the winter at home, I hear.

OSWALD: My stay is indefinite, sir.—But, ah! it is good to be at home!

MRS. ALVING (*beaming*): Yes, isn't it, dear?

MANDERS (*looking sympathetically at him*): You went out into the world early, my dear Oswald.

OSWALD: I did. I sometimes wonder whether it wasn't too early.

MRS. ALVING: Oh, not at all. A healthy lad is all the better for it; especially when he's an only child. He oughtn't to hang on at home with his mother and father, and get spoilt.

MANDERS: That is a very disputable point, Mrs. Alving. A child's proper place is, and must be, the home of his fathers.

OSWALD: There I quite agree with you, Pastor Manders.

MANDERS: Only look at your own son—there is no reason why we should not say it in his presence—what has the consequence been for him? He is six or seven and twenty, and has never had the opportunity of learning what a well-ordered home really is.

OSWALD: I beg your pardon, Pastor; there you're quite mistaken.

MANDERS: Indeed? I thought you had lived almost exclusively in artistic circles.

OSWALD: So I have.

MANDERS: And chiefly among the younger artists?

OSWALD: Yes, certainly.

MANDERS: But I thought few of those young fellows could afford to set up house and support a family.

OSWALD: There are many who cannot afford to marry, sir.

MANDERS: Yes, that is just what I say.

OSWALD: But they may have a home for all that. And several of them have, as a matter of fact; and very pleasant, well-ordered homes they are, too.

(MRS. ALVING *follows with breathless interest; nods, but says nothing.*)

MANDERS: But I'm not talking of bachelors' quarters. By a "home" I understand the home of a family, where a man lives with his wife and children.

OSWALD: Yes; or with his children and his children's mother.

MANDERS (*starts; clasps his hands*): But, good heavens—

OSWALD: Well?

MANDERS: Lives with—his children's mother!

OSWALD: Yes. Would you have him turn his children's mother out of doors?

MANDERS: Then it is illicit relations you are talking of! Irregular marriages, as people call them!

OSWALD: I have never noticed anything particularly irregular about the life these people lead.

MANDERS: But how is it possible that a—a young man or young woman with any decency of feeling can endure to live in that way?—in the eyes of all the world!

OSWALD: What are they to do? A poor young artist—a poor girl—marriage costs a great deal. What are they to do?

MANDERS: What are they to do? Let me tell you, Mr. Alving, what they ought to do. They ought to exercise self-restraint from the first; that is what they ought to do.

OSWALD: That doctrine will scarcely go down with warm-blooded young people who love each other.

MRS. ALVING: No, scarcely!

MANDERS (*continuing*): How can the authorities tolerate such things! Allow them to go on in the light of day! (*Confronting* MRS. ALVING.) Had I not cause to be deeply concerned about your son? In circles where open immorality prevails, and has even a sort of recognised position—!

OSWALD: Let me tell you, sir, that I have been in the habit of spending nearly all my Sundays in one or two such irregular homes—

MANDERS: Sunday of all days!

OSWALD: Isn't that the day to enjoy one's self? Well, never have I heard an offensive word, and still less have I witnessed anything that could be called immoral. No; do you know when and where I have come across immorality in artistic circles?

MANDERS: No, thank heaven, I don't!

OSWALD: Well, then, allow me to inform you. I have met with it when one or other of our pattern husbands and fathers has come to Paris to have a look round on his own account, and has done the artists the honour of visiting their humble haunts. They knew what was what. These gentlemen could tell us all about places and things we had never dreamt of.

MANDERS: What! Do you mean to say that respectable men from home here would—?

OSWALD: Have you never heard these respectable men, when they got home again, talking about the way in which immorality runs rampant abroad?

MANDERS: Yes, no doubt—

MRS. ALVING: I have too.

OSWALD: Well, you may take their word for it. They know what they are talking about! (*Presses his hands to his head.*) Oh! that that great, free, glorious life out there should be defiled in such a way!

MRS. ALVING: You mustn't get excited, Oswald. It's not good for you.

OSWALD: Yes; you're quite right, mother. It's bad for me, I know. You see, I'm wretchedly worn out. I shall go for a little turn before dinner. Excuse me, Pastor: I know you can't take my point of view; but I couldn't help speaking out. (*He goes out by the second door to the right.*)

MRS. ALVING: My poor boy!

MANDERS: You may well say so. Then this is what he has come to!

(MRS. ALVING *looks at him silently.*)

MANDERS (*walking up and down*): He called himself the Prodigal Son. Alas! alas!

(MRS. ALVING *continues looking at him.*)

MANDERS: And what do you say to all this?

MRS. ALVING: I say that Oswald was right in every word.

MANDERS (*stands still*): Right? Right! In such principles?

MRS. ALVING: Here, in my loneliness, I have come to the same way of thinking, Pastor Manders. But I have never dared to say anything. Well! now my boy shall speak for me.

MANDERS: You are greatly to be pitied, Mrs. Alving. But now I must speak seriously to you. And now it is no longer your business manager and adviser, your own and your husband's early friend, who stands before you. It is the priest—the priest who stood before you in the moment of your life when you had gone farthest astray.

MRS. ALVING: And what has the priest to say to me?

MANDERS: I will first stir up your memory a little. The moment is well chosen. To-morrow will be the tenth anniversary of your husband's death. To-morrow the memorial in his honour will be unveiled. To-morrow I shall have to speak to the whole assembled multitude. But to-day I will speak to you alone.

MRS. ALVING: Very well, Pastor Manders. Speak.

MANDERS: Do you remember that after less than a year of married life you stood on the verge of an abyss? That you forsook your house and home? That you fled from your husband? Yes, Mrs. Alving—fled, fled, and refused to return to him, however much he begged and prayed you?

MRS. ALVING: Have you forgotten how infinitely miserable I was in that first year?

MANDERS: It is the very mark of the spirit of rebellion to crave for happiness in this life. What right have we human beings to happiness? We have simply to do our duty, Mrs. Alving! And your duty was to hold firmly to the man you had once chosen, and to whom you were bound by the holiest ties.

MRS. ALVING: You know very well what sort of life Alving was leading—what excesses he was guilty of.

MANDERS: I know very well what rumours there were about him; and I am the last to approve the life he led in his young days, if report did not wrong him. But a wife is not appointed to be her husband's judge. It was your duty to bear with humility the cross which a Higher Power had, in its widsom, laid upon you. But instead of that you rebelliously throw away the cross, desert the backslider whom you should have supported, go and risk your good name and reputation, and—nearly succeed in ruining other people's reputation into the bargain.

MRS. ALVING: Other people's? One other person's, you mean.

MANDERS: It was incredibly reckless of you to seek refuge with me.

MRS. ALVING: With our clergyman? With our intimate friend?

MANDERS: Just on that account. Yes, you may thank God that I possessed the necessary firmness; that I succeeded in dissuading you from your wild designs; and that it was vouchsafed me to lead you back to the path of duty, and home to your lawful husband.

MRS. ALVING: Yes, Pastor Manders, that was certainly your work.

MANDERS: I was but a poor instrument in a Higher Hand. And what a blessing has it not proved to you, all the days of your life, that I induced you to resume the yoke of duty and obedience! Did not everything happen as I foretold? Did not Alving turn his back on his errors, as a man should? Did he not live with you from that time, lovingly and blamelessly, all his days? Did he not become a benefactor to the whole district? And did he not help you to rise to his own level, so that you, little by little, became his assistant in all his undertakings? And a capital assistant, too—oh, I know, Mrs. Alving, that praise is due to you.—But now I come to the next great error in your life.

MRS. ALVING: What do you mean?

MANDERS: Just as you once disowned a wife's duty, so you have since disowned a mother's.

MRS. ALVING: Ah—!

MANDERS: You have been all your life under the dominion of a pestilent spirit of self-will. The whole bias of your mind has been towards insubordination and lawlessness. You have never known how to endure any bond. Everything that has weighed upon you in life you have cast away without care or conscience, like a burden you were free to throw off at will. It did not please you to be a wife any longer, and you left your husband. You found it troublesome to be a mother, and you sent your child forth among strangers.

MRS. ALVING: Yes, that is true. I did so.

MANDERS: And thus you have become a stranger to him.

MRS. ALVING: No! no! I am not.

MANDERS: Yes, you are; you must be. And in what state of mind has he returned to you? Bethink yourself well, Mrs. Alving. You sinned greatly against your husband;—that you recognise by raising yonder memorial to him. Recognise now, also, how you have sinned against your son—there may yet be time to lead him back from the paths of error. Turn back yourself, and save what may yet be saved in him. For (*with uplifted forefinger*) verily, Mrs. Alving, you are a guilt-laden mother!—This I have thought it my duty to say to you.

(*Silence.*)

MRS. ALVING (*slowly and with self-control*): You have now spoken out, Pastor Manders; and to-morrow you are to speak publicly in memory of my husband. I shall not speak to-morrow. But now I will speak frankly to you, as you have spoken to me.

MANDERS: To be sure; you will plead excuses for your conduct—

MRS. ALVING: No. I will only tell you a story.

MANDERS: Well—?

MRS. ALVING: All that you have just said about my husband and me, and our life after you had brought me back to the path of duty—as you called it—about all that you know nothing from personal observation. From that moment you, who had been our intimate friend, never set foot in our house again.

MANDERS: You and your husband left the town immediately after.

MRS. ALVING: Yes; and in my husband's lifetime you never came to see us. It was business that forced you to visit me when you undertook the affairs of the Orphanage.

MANDERS (*softly and hesitatingly*): Helen—if that is meant as a reproach, I would beg you to bear in mind—

MRS. ALVING: —the regard you owed to your position, yes; and that I was a runaway wife. One can never be too cautious with such unprincipled creatures.

MANDERS: My dear—Mrs. Alving, you know that is an absurd exaggeration—

MRS. ALVING: Well well, suppose it is. My point is that your judgment as to my married life is founded upon nothing but common knowledge and report.

MANDERS: I admit that. What then?

MRS. ALVING: Well, then, Pastor Manders—I will tell you the truth. I have sworn to myself that one day you should know it—you alone!

MANDERS: What is the truth, then?

MRS. ALVING: The truth is that my husband died just as dissolute as he had lived all his days.

MANDERS (*feeling after a chair*): What do you say?

MRS. ALVING: After nineteen years of marriage, as dissolute—in his desires at any rate—as he was before you married us.

MANDERS: And those—those wild oats—those irregularities—those excesses, if you like—you call "a dissolute life"?

MRS. ALVING: Our doctor used the expression.

MANDERS: I do not understand you.

MRS. ALVING: You need not.

MANDERS: It almost makes me dizzy. Your whole married life, the seeming union of all these years, was nothing more than a hidden abyss!

MRS. ALVING: Neither more nor less. Now you know it.

MANDERS: This is—this is inconceivable to me. I cannot grasp it! I cannot realise it! But how was it possible to—? How could such a state of things be kept secret?

MRS. ALVING: That has been my ceaseless struggle, day after day. After Oswald's birth, I thought Alving seemed to be a little better. But it did not last long. And then I had to struggle twice as hard, fighting as though for life or death, so that nobody should know what sort of man my child's father was. And you know what power Alving had of winning people's hearts. Nobody seemed able to believe anything but good of him. He was one of those people whose life does not bite upon their reputation. But at last, Mr. Manders—for you must know the whole story—the most repulsive thing of all happened.

MANDERS: More repulsive than what you have told me!

MRS. ALVING: I had gone on bearing with him, although I knew very well the secrets of his life out of doors. But when he brought the scandal within our own walls—

MANDERS: Impossible! Here!

MRS. ALVING: Yes; here in our own home. It was there (*pointing towards the first door on the right*), in the dining-room, that I first came to know of it. I was busy with something in there, and the door was standing ajar. I heard our housemaid come up from the garden, with water for those flowers.

MANDERS: Well—?

MRS. ALVING: Soon after, I heard Alving come in too. I heard him say something softly to her. And then I heard—(*with a short laugh*)—oh! it still sounds in my ears, so hateful and yet so ludicrous—I heard my own servant-maid whisper, "Let me go, Mr. Alving! Let me be!"

MANDERS: What unseemly levity on his part! But it cannot have been more than levity, Mrs. Alving; believe me, it cannot.

MRS. ALVING: I soon knew what to believe. Mr. Alving had his way with the girl; and that connection had consequences, Mr. Manders.

MANDERS (*as though petrified*): Such things in this house! in this house!

MRS. ALVING: I had borne a great deal in this house. To keep him at home in the evenings, and at night, I had to make myself his boon companion in his secret orgies up in his room. There I have had to sit alone with him, to clink glasses and drink with him, and to listen to his ribald, silly talk. I have had to fight with him to get him dragged to bed—

MANDERS (*moved*): And you were able to bear all this!

MRS. ALVING: I had to bear it for my little boy's sake. But when the last insult was added; when my own servant maid—; then I swore to myself: This shall come to an end! And so I took the reins into my own hand—the whole control—over him and everything else. For now I had a weapon against him, you see; he dared not oppose me. It was then I sent Oswald away from home. He was nearly seven years old, and was beginning to observe and ask questions, as children do. That I could not bear. It seemed to me the child must be poisoned by merely breathing the air of this polluted home. That was why I sent him away. And now you can see, too, why he was never allowed to set foot inside his home so long as his father lived. No one knows what that cost me.

MANDERS: You have indeed had a life of trial.

MRS. ALVING: I could never have borne it if I had not had my work. For I may truly say that I have worked! All the additions to the estate—all the improvements—all the labour-saving appliances, that Alving was so much praised for having introduced—do you suppose he had energy for anything of the sort?—he, who lay all day on the sofa, reading an old Court Guide! No; but I may tell you this too: when he had his better intervals, it was I who urged him on; it was I who had to drag the whole load when he relapsed into his evil ways, or sank into querulous wretchedness.

MANDERS: And it is to this man that you raise a memorial?

MRS. ALVING: There you see the power of an evil conscience.

MANDERS: Evil—? What do you mean?

MRS. ALVING: It always seemed to me impossible but that the truth must come out and be believed. So the Orphanage was to deaden all rumours and set every doubt at rest.

MANDERS: In that you have certainly not missed your aim, Mrs. Alving.

MRS. ALVING: And besides, I had one other reason. I was determined that Oswald, my own boy, should inherit nothing whatever from his father.

MANDERS: Then it is Alving's fortune that—?

MRS. ALVING: Yes. The sums I have spent upon the Orphanage, year by year, make up the amount—I have reckoned it up precisely—the amount which made Lieutenant Alving "a good match" in his day.

MANDERS: I don't understand—

MRS. ALVING: It was my purchase-money. I do not choose that that money should pass into Oswald's hands. My son shall have everything from me—everything.

(OSWALD ALVING *enters through the second door to the right; he has taken off his hat and overcoat in the hall.*)

MRS. ALVING (*going towards him*): Are you back again already? My dear, dear boy!

OSWALD: Yes. What can a fellow do out of doors in this eternal rain? But I hear dinner is ready. That's capital!

REGINA (*with a parcel, from the dining-room*): A parcel has come for you, Mrs. Alving. (*Hands it to her.*)

MRS. ALVING (*with a glance at* MR. MANDERS): No doubt copies of the ode for to-morrow's ceremony.

MANDERS: H'm—

REGINA: And dinner is ready.

MRS. ALVING: Very well. We will come directly. I will just— (*Begins to open the parcel.*)

REGINA (*to* OSWALD): Would Mr. Alving like red or white wine?

OSWALD: Both, if you please.

REGINA: *Bien.* Very well, sir. (*She goes into the dining-room.*)

OSWALD: I may as well help to uncork it. (*He also goes into the dining room, the door of which swings half open behind him.*)

MRS. ALVING (*who has opened the parcel*): Yes, I thought so. Here is the Ceremonial Ode, Pastor Manders.

MANDERS (*with folded hands*): With what countenance I am to deliver my discourse to-morrow—!

MRS. ALVING: Oh, you will get through it somehow.

MANDERS (*softly, so as not to be heard in the dining-room*): Yes; it would not do to provoke scandal.

MRS. ALVING (*under her breath, but firmly*): No. But then this long, hateful comedy will be ended. From the day after to-morrow, I shall act in every way as though he who is dead had never lived in this house. There shall be no one here but my boy and his mother.

> (*From the dining-room comes the noise of a chair overturned, and at the same moment is heard.*)

REGINA (*sharply, but in a whisper*): Oswald! take care! are you mad? Let me go!

MRS. ALVING (*starts in terror*): Ah—!

> (*She stares mildly towards the half-open door.* OSWALD *is heard laughing and humming. A bottle is uncorked.*)

MANDERS (*agitated*): What can be the matter? What is it, Mrs. Alving?

MRS. ALVING (*hoarsely*): Ghosts! The couple from the conservatory—risen again!

MANDERS: Is it possible! Regina—? Is she—?

MRS. ALVING: Yes. Come. Not a word—!

> (*She seizes* PASTOR MANDERS *by the arm, and walks unsteadily towards the dining-room.*)

ACT TWO

> (*The same room. The mist still lies heavy over the landscape.*)
> (MANDERS *and* MRS. ALVING *enter from the dining-room.*)

MRS. ALVING (*still in the doorway*): Velbekomme, Mr. Manders. (*Turns back towards the dining-room.*) Aren't you coming too, Oswald?

OSWALD (*from within*): No, thank you. I think I shall go out a little.

MRS. ALVING: Yes, do. The weather seems a little brighter now. (*She shuts the dining-room door, goes to the hall door, and calls:*) Regina!

REGINA (*outside*): Yes, Mrs. Alving?

MRS. ALVING: Go down to the laundry, and help with the garlands.

REGINA: Yes, Mrs. Alving.

> (MRS. ALVING *assures herself that* REGINA *goes; then shuts the door.*)

MANDERS: I suppose he cannot overhear us in there?

MRS. ALVING: Not when the door is shut. Besides, he's just going out.

MANDERS: I am still quite upset. I don't know how I could swallow a morsel of dinner.

MRS. ALVING (*controlling her nervousness, walks up and down*): Nor I. But what is to be done now?

MANDERS: Yes; what is to be done? I am really quite at a loss. I am so utterly without experience in matters of this sort.

MRS. ALVING: I feel sure that, so far, no mischief has been done.

MANDERS: No; heaven forbid! But it is an unseemly state of things, nevertheless.

MRS. ALVING: It is only an idle fancy on Oswald's part; you may be sure of that.

MANDERS: Well, as I say, I am not accustomed to affairs of the kind. But I should certainly think—

MRS. ALVING: Out of the house she must go, and that immediately. That is as clear as daylight—

MANDERS: Yes, of course she must.

MRS. ALVING: But where to? It would not be right to—

MANDERS: Where to? Home to her father, of course.

MRS. ALVING: To whom did you say?

MANDERS: To her— But then, Engstrand is not—? Good God, Mrs. Alving, it's impossible! You must be mistaken after all.

MRS. ALVING: Unfortunately there is no possibility of mistake, Johanna confessed everything to me; and Alving could not deny it. So there was nothing to be done but to get the matter hushed up.

MANDERS: No, you could do nothing else.

MRS. ALVING: The girl left our service at once, and got a good sum of money to hold her tongue for the time. The rest she managed for herself when she got to town. She renewed her old acquaintance with Engstrand, no doubt let him see that she had money in her purse, and told him some tale about a foreigner who put in here with a yacht that summer. So she and Engstrand got married in hot haste. Why, you married them yourself.

MANDERS: But then how to account for—? I recollect distinctly Engstrand coming to give notice of the marriage. He was quite overwhelmed with contrition, and bitterly reproached himself for the misbehaviour he and his sweetheart had been guilty of.

MRS. ALVING: Yes; of course he had to take the blame upon himself.

MANDERS: But such a piece of duplicity on his part! And toward me too! I never could have believed it of Jacob Engstrand. I shall not fail to take him seriously to task; he may be sure of that.—And then the immorality of such a connection! For money—! How much did the girl receive?

MRS. ALVING: Three hundred dollars.

MANDERS: Just think of it—for a miserable three hundred dollars, to go and marry a fallen woman!

MRS. ALVING: Then what have you to say of me? I went and married a fallen man.

MANDERS: Why—good heavens!—what are you talking about! A fallen man!

MRS. ALVING: Do you think Alving was any purer when I went with him to the altar than Johanna was when Engstrand married her?

MANDERS: Well, but there is a world of difference between the two cases—

MRS. ALVING: Not so much difference after all—except in the price:—a miserable three hundred dollars and a whole fortune.

MANDERS: How can you compare such absolutely dissimilar cases? You had taken counsel with your own heart and with your natural advisers.

MRS. ALVING (*without looking at him*): I thought you understood where what you call my heart had strayed to at the time.

MANDERS (*distantly*): Had I understood anything of the kind, I should not have been a daily guest in your husband's house.

MRS. ALVING: At any rate, the fact remains that with myself I took no counsel whatever.

MANDERS: Well then, with your nearest relatives—as your duty bade you—with your mother and your two aunts.

MRS. ALVING: Yes, that is true. Those three cast up the account for me. Oh, it's marvellous how clearly they made out that it would be downright madness to refuse such an offer. If mother could only see me now, and know what all that grandeur has come to!

MANDERS: Nobody can be held responsible for the result. This, at least, remains clear: your marriage was in full accordance with law and order.

MRS. ALVING (*at the window*): Oh, that perpetual law and order! I often think that is what does all the mischief in this world of ours.

MANDERS: Mrs. Alving, that is a sinful way of talking.

MRS. ALVING: Well, I can't help it; I must have done with all this constraint and insincerity. I can endure it no longer. I must work my way out to freedom.

MANDERS: What do you mean by that?

MRS. ALVING (*drumming on the window-frame*): I ought never to have concealed the facts of Alving's life. But at that time I dared not do anything else—I was afraid, partly on my own account. I was such a coward.

MANDERS: A coward?

MRS. ALVING: If people had come to know anything, they would have said—"Poor man! with a runaway wife, no wonder he kicks over the traces."

MANDERS: Such remarks might have been made with a certain show of right.

MRS. ALVING (*looking steadily at him*): If I were what I ought to be, I should go to Oswald and say, "Listen, my boy: your father led a vicious life—"

MANDERS: Merciful heavens—!

MRS. ALVING: —and then I should tell him all I have told you—every word of it.

MANDERS: You shock me unspeakably, Mrs. Alving.

MRS. ALVING: Yes; I know that. I know that very well. I myself am shocked at the idea. (*Goes away from the window.*) I am such a coward.

MANDERS: You call it "cowardice" to do your plain duty? Have you forgotten that a son ought to love and honour his father and mother?

MRS. ALVING: Do not let us talk in such general terms. Let us ask: Ought Oswald to love and honour Chamberlain Alving?

MANDERS: Is there no voice in your mother's heart that forbids you to destroy your son's ideals?

MRS. ALVING: But what about the truth?

MANDERS: But what about the ideals?

MRS. ALVING: Oh—ideals, ideals! If only I were not such a coward!

MANDERS: Do not despise ideals, Mrs. Alving; they will avenge themselves cruelly. Take Oswald's case: he, unfortunately, seems to have few enough ideals as it is; but I can see that his father stands before him as an ideal.

MRS. ALVING: Yes, that is true.

MANDERS: And this habit of mind you have yourself implanted and fostered by your letters.

MRS. ALVING: Yes; in my superstitious awe for duty and the proprieties, I lied to my boy, year after year. Oh, what a coward—what a coward I have been!

MANDERS: You have established a happy illusion in your son's heart, Mrs. Alving; and assuredly you ought not to undervalue it.

MRS. ALVING: H'm; who knows whether it is so happy after all—? But, at any rate, I will not have any tampering with Regina. He shall not go and wreck the poor girl's life.

MANDERS: No; good God—that would be terrible!

MRS. ALVING: If I knew he was in earnest, and that it would be for his happiness—

MANDERS: What? What then?

MRS. ALVING: But it couldn't be; for unfortunately Regina is not the right sort of woman.

MANDERS: Well, what then? What do you mean?

MRS. ALVING: If I weren't such a pitiful coward, I should say to him, "Marry her, or make what arrangement you please, only let us have nothing underhand about it."

MANDERS: Merciful heavens, would you let them marry! Anything so dreadful—! so unheard of—

MRS. ALVING: Do you really mean "unheard of"? Frankly, Pastor Manders, do you suppose that throughout the country there are not plenty of married couples as closely akin as they?

MANDERS: I don't in the least understand you.

MRS. ALVING: Oh yes, indeed you do.

MANDERS: Ah, you are thinking of the possibility that—Alas! yes, family life is certainly not always so pure as it ought to be. But in such a case as you point to, one can never know—at least with any certainty. Here, on the other hand—that you, a mother, can think of letting your son—!

MRS. ALVING: But I cannot—I wouldn't for anything in the world; that is precisely what I am saying.

MANDERS: No, because you are a "coward," as you put it. But if you were not a "coward," then—? Good God! a connection so shocking!

MRS. ALVING: So far as that goes, they say we are all sprung from connections of that sort. And who is it that arranged the world so, Pastor Manders?

MANDERS: Questions of that kind I must decline to discuss with you, Mrs. Alving; you are far from being in the right frame of mind for them. But that you dare to call your scruples "cowardly"—!

MRS. ALVING: Let me tell you what I mean. I am timid and faint-hearted because of the ghosts that hang about me, and that I can never quite shake off.

MANDERS: What do you say hangs about you?

MRS. ALVING: Ghosts! When I heard Regina and Oswald in there, it was as though ghosts rose up before me. But I almost think we are all of us ghosts, Pastor Manders. It is not only what we have inherited from our father and mother that "walks" in us. It is all sorts of dead ideas, and lifeless old beliefs, and so forth. They have no vitality, but they cling to us all the same, and we cannot shake them off. Whenever I take up a newspaper, I seem to see ghosts gliding between the lines. There must be ghosts all the country over, as thick as the sands of the sea. And then we are, one and all, so pitifully afraid of the light.

MANDERS: Aha—here we have the fruits of your reading. And pretty fruits they are upon my word! Oh, those horrible, revolutionary, freethinking books!

MRS. ALVING: You are mistaken, my dear Pastor. It was you yourself who set me thinking; and I thank you for it with all my heart.

MANDERS: I!

MRS. ALVING: Yes—when you forced me under the yoke of what you called duty and obligation; when you lauded as right and proper what my whole soul rebelled against as something loathsome. It was then that I began to look into the seams of your doctrines. I wanted only to pick at a single knot; but when I had got that undone, the whole thing ravelled out. And then I understood that it was all machine-sewn.

MANDERS (*softly, with emotion*): And was that the upshot of my life's hardest battle?

MRS. ALVING: Call it rather your most pitiful defeat.

MANDERS: It was my greatest victory, Helen—the victory over myself.

MRS. ALVING: It was a crime against us both.

MANDERS: When you went astray, and came to me crying, "Here I am; take me!" I commanded you, saying, "Woman, go home to your lawful husband." Was that a crime?

MRS. ALVING: Yes, I think so.

MANDERS: We two do not understand each other.

MRS. ALVING: Not now, at any rate.

MANDERS: Never—never in my most secret thoughts have I regarded you otherwise than as another's wife.

MRS. ALVING: Oh—indeed?

MANDERS: Helen—!

MRS. ALVING: People so easily forget their past selves.

MANDERS: I do not. I am what I always was.

MRS. ALVING (*changing the subject*): Well well well; don't let us talk of old times any longer. You are now over head and ears in Boards and Committees, and I am fighting my battle with ghosts, both within me and without.

MANDERS: Those without I shall help you to lay. After all the terrible things I have heard from you to-day, I cannot in conscience permit an unprotected girl to remain in your house.

MRS. ALVING: Don't you think the best plan would be to get her provided for?—I mean, by a good marriage.

MANDERS: No doubt. I think it would be desirable for her in every respect. Regina is now at the age when— Of course I don't know much about these things, but—

MRS. ALVING: Regina matured very early.

MANDERS: Yes, I thought so. I have an impression that she was remarkably well developed, physically, when I prepared her for confirmation. But in the meantime, she ought to be at home, under her father's eye— Ah! but Engstrand is not— That he—that he—could so hide the truth from me!

(*A knock at the door into the hall.*)

MRS. ALVING: Who can this be? Come in!

ENGSTRAND (*in his Sunday clothes, in the doorway*): I humbly beg your pardon, but—

MANDERS: Aha! H'm—

MRS. ALVING: Is that you, Engstrand?

ENGSTRAND: —there was none of the servants about, so I took the great liberty of just knocking.

MRS. ALVING: Oh, very well. Come in. Do you want to speak to me?

ENGSTRAND (*comes in*): No, I'm obliged to you, ma'am; it was with his Reverence I wanted to have a word or two.

MANDERS (*walking up and down the room*): Ah—indeed! You want to speak to me, do you?

ENGSTRAND: Yes, I'd like so terrible much to—

MANDERS (*stops in front of him*): Well; may I ask what you want?

ENGSTRAND: Well, it was just this, your Reverence: we've been paid off down yonder—my grateful thanks to you, ma'am,—and now everything's finished, I've been thinking it would be but right and proper if we, that have been working so honestly together all this time—well, I was thinking we ought to end up with a little prayer-meeting to-night.

MANDERS: A prayer-meeting? Down at the Orphanage?

ENGSTRAND: Oh, if your Reverence doesn't think it proper—

MANDERS: Oh yes, I do; but—h'm—

ENGSTRAND: I've been in the habit of offering up a little prayer in the evenings, myself—

MRS. ALVING: Have you?

ENGSTRAND: Yes, every now and then—just a little edification, in a manner of speaking. But I'm a poor, common man, and have little enough gift, God help me!—and so I thought, as the Reverend Mr. Manders happened to be here, I'd—

MANDERS: Well, you see, Engstrand, I have a question to put to you first. Are you in the right frame of mind for such a meeting! Do you feel your conscience clear and at ease?

ENGSTRAND: Oh, God help us, your Reverence! we'd better not talk about conscience.

MANDERS: Yes, that is just what we must talk about. What have you to answer?

ENGSTRAND: Why—a man's conscience—it can be bad enough now and then.

MANDERS: Ah, you admit that. Then perhaps you will make a clean breast of it, and tell me—the real truth about Regina?

MRS. ALVING (*quickly*): Mr. Manders!

MANDERS (*reassuringly*): Please allow me—

ENGSTRAND: About Regina! Lord, what a turn you gave me! (*Looks at* MRS. ALVING.) There's nothing wrong about Regina, is there?

MANDERS: We will hope not. But I mean, what is the truth about you and Regina? You pass for her father, eh!

ENGSTRAND (*uncertain*): Well—h'm—your Reverence knows all about me and poor Johanna.

MANDERS: Come now, no more prevarication! Your wife told Mrs. Alving the whole story before quitting her service.

ENGSTRAND: Well, then, may—! Now, did she really?

MANDERS: You see we know you now, Engstrand.

ENGSTRAND: And she swore and took her Bible oath—

MANDERS: Did she take her Bible oath?

ENGSTRAND: No; she only swore; but she did it that solemn-like.

MANDERS: And you have hidden the truth from me all these years? Hidden it from me, who have trusted you without reserve, in everything.

ENGSTRAND: Well, I can't deny it.

MANDERS: Have I deserved this of you, Engstrand? Have I not always been ready to help you in word and deed, so far as it lay in my power? Answer me. Have I not?

ENGSTRAND: It would have been a poor look-out for me many a time but for the Reverend Mr. Manders.

MANDERS: And this is how you reward me! You cause me to enter falsehoods in the Church Register, and you withhold from me, year after year, the explanations you owed alike to me and to the the truth. Your conduct has been wholly inexcusable, Engstrand; and from this time forward I have done with you!

ENGSTRAND (with a sigh): Yes! I suppose there's no help for it.

MANDERS: How can you possibly justify yourself?

ENGSTRAND: Who could ever have thought she'd have gone and made bad worse by talking about it? Will your Reverence just fancy yourself in the same trouble as poor Johanna—

MANDERS: I!

ENGSTRAND: Lord bless you, I don't mean just exactly the same. But I mean, if your Reverence had anything to be ashamed of in the eyes of the world, as the saying goes. We menfolk oughtn't to judge a poor woman too hardly, your Reverence.

MANDERS: I am not doing so. It is you I am reproaching.

ENGSTRAND: Might I make so bold as to ask your Reverence a bit of a question?

MANDERS: Yes, if you want to.

ENGSTRAND: Isn't it right and proper for a man to raise up the fallen?

MANDERS: Most certainly it is.

ENGSTRAND: And isn't a man bound to keep his sacred word?

MANDERS: Why, of course he is; but—

ENGSTRAND: When Johanna had got into trouble through that Englishman—or it might have been an American or a Russian, as they call them—well, you see, she came down into the town. Poor thing, she'd sent me about my business once or twice before: for she couldn't bear the sight of anything as wasn't handsome; and I'd got this damaged leg of mine. Your Reverence recollects how I ventured up into a dancing saloon, where seafaring men was carrying on with drink and devilry, as the saying goes. And then, when I was for giving them a bit of an admonition to lead a new life—

MRS. ALVING (*at the window*): H'm—

MANDERS: I know all about that, Engstrand; the ruffians threw you downstairs. You have told me of the affair already. Your infirmity is an honour to you.

ENGSTRAND: I'm not puffed up about it, your Reverence. But what I wanted to say was, that when she came and confessed all to me, with weeping and gnashing of teeth, I can tell your Reverence I was sore at heart to hear it.

MANDERS: Were you indeed, Engstrand? Well, go on.

ENGSTRAND: So I says to her, "The American, he's sailing about on the boundless sea. And as for you, Johanna," says I, "you've committed a grievous sin, and you're a fallen creature. But Jacob Engstrand," says I, "he's got two good legs to stand upon, he has—" You see, your Reverence, I was speaking figurative-like.

MANDERS: I understand quite well. Go on.

ENGSTRAND: Well, that was how I raised her up and made an honest woman of her, so as folks shouldn't get to know how as she'd gone astray with foreigners.

MANDERS: In all that you acted very well. Only I cannot approve of your stooping to take money—

ENGSTRAND: Money? I? Not a farthing!

MANDERS (*inquiringly to* MRS. ALVING): But—

ENGSTRAND: Oh, wait a minute!—now I recollect. Johanna did have a trifle of money. But I would have nothing to do with that. "No," says I, "that's mammon; that's the wages of sin. This dirty gold—or notes, or whatever it was—we'll just fling that back in the American's face," says I. But he was off and away, over the stormy sea, your Reverence.

MANDERS: Was he really, my good fellow?

ENGSTRAND: He was indeed, sir. So Johanna and I, we agreed that the money should go to the child's education; and so it did, and I can account for every blessed farthing of it.

MANDERS: Why, this alters the case considerably.

ENGSTRAND: That's just how it stands, your Reverence. And I make so bold as to say as I've been an honest father to Regina, so far as my poor strength went; for I'm but a weak vessel, worse luck!

MANDERS: Well, well, my good fellow—

ENGSTRAND: All the same, I bear myself witness as I've brought up the child, and lived kindly with poor Johanna, and ruled over my own house, as the Scripture has it. But it couldn't never enter my head to go to your Reverence and puff myself up and boast because even the likes of me had done some good in the world. No, sir; when anything of that sort happens to Jacob Engstrand, he holds his tongue about it. It don't happen so terrible often, I daresay. And when I do come to see your Reverence, I find a mortal deal that's wicked and weak to talk about. For I said it before, and I says it again—a man's conscience isn't always as clean as it might be.

MANDERS: Give me your hand, Jacob Engstrand.

ENGSTRAND: Oh, Lord! your Reverence—

MANDERS: Come, no nonsense. (*Wrings his hand.*) There we are!

ENGSTRAND: And if I might humbly beg your Reverence's pardon—

MANDERS: You? On the contrary, it is I who ought to beg your pardon—

ENGSTRAND: Lord, no, sir!

MANDERS: Yes, assuredly. And I do it with all my heart. Forgive me for misunderstanding you. I only wish I could give you some proof of my hearty regret, and of my good-will towards you—

ENGSTRAND: Would your Reverence do it?

MANDERS: With the greatest pleasure.

ENGSTRAND: Well then, here's the very chance. With the bit of money I've saved here, I was thinking I might set up a Sailors' Home down in the town.

MRS. ALVING: You?

ENGSTRAND: Yes; it might be a sort of Orphanage, too, in a manner of speaking. There's such a many temptations for seafaring folk ashore. But in this Home of mine, a man might feel like as he was under a father's eye, I was thinking.

MANDERS: What do you say to this, Mrs. Alving?

ENGSTRAND: It isn't much as I've got to start with, Lord help me! But if I could only find a helping hand, why—

MANDERS: Yes, yes; we will look into the matter more closely. I entirely approve of your plan. But now, go before me and make everything ready, and get the candles lighted, so as to give the place an air of festivity. And then we will pass an edifying hour together, my good fellow; for now I quite believe you are in the right frame of mind.

ENGSTRAND: Yes, I trust I am. And so I'll say good-bye, ma'am, and thank you kindly; and take good care of Regina for me—(*wipes a tear from his eye*)—poor Johanna's child. Well, it's a queer thing, now; but it's just like as if she'd growd into the very apple of my eye. It is, indeed. (*He bows and goes out through the hall.*)

MANDERS: Well, what do you say of that man now, Mrs. Alving? That was a very different account of matters, was it not?

MRS. ALVING: Yes, it certainly was.

MANDERS: It only shows how excessively careful one ought to be in judging one's fellow creatures. But what a heartfelt joy it is to ascertain that one has been mistaken! Don't you think so?

MRS. ALVING: I think you are, and will always be, a great baby, Manders.

MANDERS: I?

MRS. ALVING (*laying her two hands upon his shoulders*): And I say that I have half a mind to put my arms round your neck, and kiss you.

MANDERS (*stepping hastily back*): No, no! God bless me! What an idea!

MRS. ALVING (*with a smile*): Oh, you needn't be afraid of me.

MANDERS (*by the table*): You have sometimes such an exaggerated way of expressing yourself. Now, let me just collect all the documents, and put them in my bag. (*He does so.*) There, that's all right. And now, good-bye for the present. Keep your eyes open when Oswald comes back. I shall look in again later. (*He takes his hat and goes out through the hall door.*)

MRS. ALVING (*sighs, looks for a moment out of the window, sets the room in order a little, and is about to go into the dining-room, but stops at the door with a half-suppressed cry*): Oswald, are you still at table?

OSWALD (*in the dining-room*): I'm only finishing my cigar.

MRS. ALVING: I thought you had gone for a little walk.

OSWALD: In such weather as this?

(*A glass clinks.* MRS. ALVING *leaves the door open, and sits down with her knitting on the sofa by the window.*)

OSWALD: Wasn't that Pastor Manders that went out just now?

MRS. ALVING: Yes; he went down to the Orphanage.

OSWALD: H'm. (*The glass and decanter clink again.*)

MRS. ALVING (*with a troubled glance*): Dear Oswald, you should take care of that liqueur. It is strong.

OSWALD: It keeps out the damp.

MRS. ALVING: Wouldn't you rather come in here, to me?

OSWALD: I mayn't smoke in there.

MRS. ALVING: You know quite well you may smoke cigars.

OSWALD: Oh, all right then; I'll come in. Just a tiny drop more first.—There! (*He comes into the room with his cigar, and shuts the door after him. A short silence.*) Where has the pastor gone to?

MRS. ALVING: I have just told you; he went down to the Orphanage.

OSWALD: Oh, yes; so you did.

MRS. ALVING: You shouldn't sit so long at table, Oswald.

OSWALD (*holding his cigar behind him*): But I find it so pleasant mother. (*Strokes and caresses her.*) Just think what it is for me to come home and sit at mother's own table, in mother's room, and eat mother's delicious dishes.

MRS. ALVING: My dear, dear boy!

OSWALD (*somewhat impatiently, walks about and smokes*): And what else can I do with myself here? I can't set to work at anything.

MRS. ALVING: Why can't you?

OSWALD: In such weather as this? Without a single ray of sunshine the whole day? (*Walks up the room.*) Oh, not to be able to work—!

MRS. ALVING: Perhaps it was not quite wise of you to come home?

OSWALD: Oh, yes, mother; I had to.

MRS. ALVING: You know I would ten times rather forgo the joy of having you here, than let you—

OSWALD (*stops beside the table*): Now just tell me, mother: does it really make you so very happy to have me home again?

MRS. ALVING: Does it make me happy!

OSWALD (*crumpling up a newspaper*): I should have thought it must be pretty much the same to you whether I was in existence or not.

MRS. ALVING: Have you the heart to say that to your mother, Oswald?

OSWALD: But you've got on very well without me all this time.

MRS. ALVING: Yes; I have got on without you. That is true.

(*A silence. Twilight slowly begins to fall.* OSWALD *paces to and fro across the room. He has laid his cigar down.*)

OSWALD (*stops beside* MRS. ALVING): Mother, may I sit on the sofa beside you?

MRS. ALVING (*makes room for him*): Yes, do, my dear boy.

OSWALD (*sits down*): There is something I must tell you, mother.

MRS. ALVING (*anxiously*): Well?

OSWALD (*looks fixedly before him*): For I can't go on hiding it any longer.

MRS. ALVING: Hiding what? What is it?

OSWALD (*as before*): I could never bring myself to write to you about it; and since I've come home—

MRS. ALVING (*seizes him by the arm*): Oswald, what is the matter?

OSWALD: Both yesterday and to-day I have tried to put the thoughts away from me—to cast them off; but it's no use.

MRS. ALVING (*rising*): Now you must tell me everything, Oswald!

OSWALD (*draws her down to the sofa again*): Sit still; and then I will try to tell you.—I complained of fatigue after my journey—

MRS. ALVING: Well? What then?

OSWALD: But it isn't that that is the matter with me; not any ordinary fatigue—

MRS. ALVING (*tries to jump up*): You are not ill, Oswald?

OSWALD (*draws her down again*): Sit still, mother. Do take it quietly. I'm not downright ill, either; not what is commonly called "ill." (*Clasps his hands above his head.*) Mother, my mind is broken down—ruined—I shall never be able to work again! (*With his hands before his face, he buries his head in her lap, and breaks into bitter sobbing.*)

MRS. ALVING (*white and trembling*): Oswald! Look at me! No, no; it's not true.

OSWALD (*looks up with despair in his eyes*): Never to be able to work again! Never!—never! A living death! Mother, can you imagine anyting so horrible?

MRS. ALVING: My poor boy! How has this horrible thing come upon you?

OSWALD (*sitting upright again*): That's just what I cannot possibly grasp or understand. I have never led a dissipated life—never, in any respect. You mustn't believe that of me, mother! I've never done that.

MRS. ALVING: I am sure you haven't, Oswald.

OSWALD: And yet this has come upon me just the same—this awful misfortune!

MRS. ALVING: Oh, but it will pass over, my dear, blessed boy. It's nothing but over-work. Trust me, I am right.

OSWALD (*sadly*): I thought so too, at first; but it isn't so.

MRS. ALVING: Tell me everything, from beginning to end.

OSWALD: Yes, I will.

MRS. ALVING: When did you first notice it?

OSWALD: It was directly after I had been home last time, and had got back to Paris again. I began to feel the most violent pains in my head—chiefly in the back of my head, they seemed to come. It was as though a tight iron ring was being screwed round my neck and upwards.

MRS. ALVING: Well, and then?

OSWALD: At first I thought it was nothing but the ordinary headache I had been so plagued with while I was growing up—

MRS. ALVING: Yes, yes—

OSWALD: But it wasn't that. I soon found that out. I couldn't work any more. I wanted to begin upon a big new picture, but my powers seemed to fail me; all my strength was crippled; I could form no definite images; everything swam before me—whirling round and round. Oh, it was an awful state! At last I sent for a doctor—and from him I learned the truth.

MRS. ALVING: How do you mean?

OSWALD: He was one of the first doctors in Paris. I told him my symptoms; and then he set to work asking me a string of questions which I thought had nothing to do with the matter. I couldn't imagine what the man was after—

MRS. ALVING: Well?

OSWALD: At last he said: "There has been something worm-eaten in you from your birth." He used that very word—*vermoulu.*

MRS. ALVING (*breathlessly*): What did he mean by that?

OSWALD: I didn't understand either, and begged him to explain himself more clearly. And then the old cynic said—(*Clenching his fist.*) Oh—!

MRS. ALVING: What did he say?

OSWALD: He said, "The sins of the fathers are visited upon the children."

MRS. ALVING (*rising slowly*): The sins of the fathers—!

OSWALD: I very nearly struck him in the face—

MRS. ALVING (*walks away across the room*): The sins of the fathers—

OSWALD (*smiles sadly*): Yes; what do you think of that? Of course I assured him that such a thing was out of the question. But do you think he gave in? No, he stuck to it; and it was only when I produced your letters and translated the passages relating to father—

MRS. ALVING: But then—?

OSWALD: Then of course he had to admit that he was on the wrong track; and so I learned the truth—the incomprehensible truth! I ought not to have taken part with my comrades in that lighthearted, glorious life of theirs. It had been too much for my strength. So I had brought it upon myself!

MRS. ALVING: Oswald! No, no; do not believe it!

OSWALD: No other explanation was possible, he said. That's the awful part of it. Incurably ruined for life—by my own heedlessness! All that I meant to have done in the world—I never dare think of it again—I'm not able to think of it. Oh! if I could only live over again, and undo all I have done! (*He buries his face in the sofa.*)

MRS. ALVING (*wrings her hands and walks, in silent struggle, backwards and forwards.*)

OSWALD (*after a while, looks up and remains resting upon his elbow*): If it had only been something inherited—something one wasn't responsible for! But this! To have thrown away so shamefully, thoughtlessly, recklessly, one's own happiness, one's own health, everything in the world—one's future, one's very life—!

MRS. ALVING: No, no, my dear, darling boy; this is impossible! (*Bends over him.*) Things are not so desperate as you think.

OSWALD: Oh, you don't know—(*Springs up.*) And then, mother, to cause you all this sorrow! Many a time I have almost wished and hoped that at bottom you didn't care so very much about me.

MRS. ALVING: I, Oswald? My only boy! You are all I have in the world! The only thing I care about!

OSWALD (*seizes both her hands and kisses them*): Yes, yes, I see it. When I'm at home, I see it, of course; and that's almost the hardest part for me.—But now you know the whole story; and now we won't talk any more about it to-day. I daren't think of it for long together. (*Goes up the room.*) Get me something to drink, mother.

MRS. ALVING: To drink? What do you want to drink now?

OSWALD: Oh, anything you like. You have some cold punch in the house.

MRS. ALVING: Yes, but my dear Oswald—

OSWALD: Don't refuse me, mother. Do be kind, now! I must have something to wash down all these gnawing thoughts. (*Goes into the conservatory.*) And then —it's so dark here! (MRS. ALVING *pulls a bell-rope on the right.*) And this ceaseless rain! It may go on week after week, for months together. Never to get a glimpse of the sun! I can't recollect ever having seen the sun shine all the times I've been at home.

MRS. ALVING: Oswald—you are thinking of going away from me.

OSWALD: H'm—(*Drawing a heavy breath.*)—I'm not thinking of anything. I cannot think of anything. (*In a low voice.*) I let thinking alone.

REGINA (*from the dining-room*): Did you ring, ma'am?

MRS. ALVING: Yes; let us have the lamp in.

REGINA: Yes, ma'am. It's ready lighted. (*Goes out.*)

MRS. ALVING (*goes across to* OSWALD): Oswald, be frank with me.

OSWALD: Well, so I am, mother. (*Goes to the table.*) I think I have told you enough.

(REGINA *brings the lamp and sets it upon the table.*)

MRS. ALVING: Regina, you may bring us a small bottle of champagne.

REGINA: Very well, ma'am. (*Goes out.*)

OSWALD (*puts his arm around* MRS. ALVING's *neck*): That's just what I wanted. I knew mother wouldn't let her boy go thirsty.

MRS. ALVING: My own, poor, darling Oswald; how could I deny you anything now?

OSWALD (*eagerly*): Is that true, mother? Do you mean it?

MRS. ALVING: How? what?

OSWALD: That you couldn't deny me anything.

MRS. ALVING: My dear Oswald—

OSWALD: Hush!

REGINA (*brings a tray with a half-bottle of champagne and two glasses, which she sets on the table*): Shall I open it?

OSWALD: No, thanks, I will do it myself.

(REGINA *goes out again.*)

MRS. ALVING (*sits down by the table*): What was it you meant—that I mustn't deny you?

OSWALD (*busy opening the bottle*): First let us have a glass—or two. (*The cork pops; he pours the wine into one glass, and is about to pour it into the other.*)

MRS. ALVING (*holding her hand over it*): Thanks; not for me.

OSWALD: Oh! won't you? Then I will! (*He empties the glass, fills, and empties it again; then he sits down by the table.*)

MRS. ALVING (*in expectancy*): Well?

OSWALD (*without looking at her*): Tell me—I thought you and Pastor Manders seemed so odd—so quiet—at dinner to-day.

MRS. ALVING: Did you notice it?

OSWALD: Yes. H'm— (*After a short silence.*) Tell me: what do you think of Regina?

MRS. ALVING: What do I think?

OSWALD: Yes; isn't she splendid?

MRS. ALVING: My dear Oswald, you don't know her as I do—

OSWALD: Well?

MRS. ALVING: Regina, unfortunately, was allowed to stay at home too long. I ought to have taken her earlier into my house.

OSWALD: Yes, but isn't she splendid to look at, mother? (*He fills his glass.*)

MRS. ALVING: Regina has many serious faults—

OSWALD: Oh, what does that matter? (*He drinks again.*)

MRS. ALVING: But I am fond of her, nevertheless, and I am responsible for her. I wouldn't for all the world have any harm happen to her.

OSWALD (*springs up*): Mother, Regina is my only salvation!

MRS. ALVING (*rising*): What do you mean by that?

OSWALD: I cannot go on bearing all this anguish of soul alone.

MRS. ALVING: Have you not your mother to share it with you?

OSWALD: Yes; that's what I thought; and so I came home to you. But that will not do. I see it won't do. I cannot endure my life here.

MRS. ALVING: Oswald!

OSWALD: I must live differently, mother. That is why I must leave you. I will not have you looking on at it.

MRS. ALVING: My unhappy boy! But, Oswald, while you are so ill as this—

OSWALD: If it were only the illness, I should stay with you, mother, you may be sure; for you are the best friend I have in the world.

MRS. ALVING: Yes, indeed I am, Oswald; am I not?

OSWALD (*wanders restlessly about*): But it's all the torment, the gnawing remorse—and then, the great, killing dread. Oh—that awful dread!

MRS. ALVING (*walking after him*): Dread? What dread? What do you mean?

OSWALD: Oh, you mustn't ask me any more. I don't know. I can't describe it.

MRS. ALVING (*goes over to the right and pulls the bell.*)

OSWALD: What is it you want?

MRS. ALVING: I want my boy to be happy—that is what I want. He sha'n't go on brooding over things. (*To* REGINA, *who appears at the door:*) More champagne—a large bottle.

(REGINA *goes.*)

OSWALD: Mother!

MRS. ALVING: Do you think we don't know how to live here at home?

OSWALD: Isn't she splended to look at? How beautifully she's built! And so thoroughly healthy!

MRS. ALVING (*sits by the table*): Sit down, Oswald; let us talk quietly together.

OSWALD (*sits*): I daresay you don't know, mother, that I owe Regina some reparation.

MRS. ALVING: You!

OSWALD: For a bit of thoughtlessness, or whatever you like to call it—very innocent, at any rate. When I was home last time—

MRS. ALVING: Well?

OSWALD: She used often to ask me about Paris, and I used to tell her one thing and another. Then I recollect I happened to say to her one day, "Shouldn't you like to go there yourself?"

MRS. ALVING: Well?

OSWALD: I saw her face flush, and then she said, "Yes, I should like it of all things." "Ah, well," I replied, "it might perhaps be managed"—or something like that.

MRS. ALVING: And then?

OSWALD: Of course I had forgotten all about it; but the day before yesterday I happened to ask her whether she was glad I was to stay at home so long—

MRS. ALVING: Yes?

OSWALD: And then she gave me such a strange look, and asked, "But what's to become of my trip to Paris?"

MRS. ALVING: Her trip!

OSWALD: And so it came out that she had taken the thing seriously; that she had been thinking of me the whole time, and had set to work to learn French—

MRS. ALVING: So that was why—!

OSWALD: Mother—when I saw that fresh, lovely, splendid girl standing there, before me—till then I had hardly noticed her—but when she stood there, as though with open arms ready to receive me—

MRS. ALVING: Oswald!

OSWALD: —then it flashed upon me that in her lay my salvation; for I saw that she was full of the joy of life.

MRS. ALVING (*starts*): The joy of life—? Can there be salvation in that?

REGINA (*from the dining-room, with a bottle of champagne*): I'm sorry to have been so long, but I had to go to the cellar. (*Places the bottle on the table.*)

OSWALD: And now bring another glass.

REGINA (*looks at him in surprise*): There is Mrs. Alving's glass, Mr. Alving.

OSWALD: Yes, but bring one for yourself, Regina. (REGINA *starts and gives a lightning-like side glance at* MRS. ALVING). Why do you wait?

REGINA (*softly and hesitatingly*): Is it Mrs. Alving's wish?

MRS. ALVING: Bring the glass, Regina. (REGINA *goes out into the dining-room.*)

OSWALD (*follows her with his eyes*): Have you noticed how she walks?—so firmly and lightly!

MRS. ALVING: This can never be, Oswald!

OSWALD: It's a settled thing. Can't you see that? It's no use saying anything against it.

(REGINA *enters with an empty glass, which she keeps in her hand.*)

OSWALD: Sit down, Regina.

(REGINA *looks inquiringly at* MRS. ALVING.)

MRS. ALVING: Sit down. (REGINA *sits on a chair by the dining-room door, still holding the empty glass in her hand.*) Oswald—what were you saying about the joy of life?

OSWALD: Ah, the joy of life, mother—that's a thing you don't know much about in these parts. I have never felt it here.

MRS. ALVING: Not when you are with me?

OSWALD: Not when I'm at home. But you don't understand that.

MRS. ALVING: Yes, yes; I think I almost understand it—now.

OSWALD: And then, too, the joy of work! At bottom, it's the same thing. But that, too, you know nothing about.

MRS. ALVING: Perhaps you are right. Tell me more about it, Oswald.

OSWALD: I only mean that here people are brought up to believe that work is a curse and a punishment for sin, and that life is something miserable, something it would be best to have done with, the sooner the better.

MRS. ALVING: "A vale of tears," yes; and we certainly do our best to make it one.

OSWALD: But in the great world people won't hear of such things. There, nobody really believes such doctrines any longer. There, you feel it a positive bliss and ecstasy merely to draw the breath of life. Mother, have you noticed that everything I have painted has turned upon the joy of life?—always, always upon the joy of life?—light and sunshine and glorious air—and faces radiant with happiness. That is why I'm afraid of remaining at home with you.

MRS. ALVING: Afraid? What are you afraid of here, with me?

OSWALD: I'm afraid lest all my instincts should be warped into ugliness.

MRS. ALVING (looks steadily at him): Do you think that is what would happen?

OSWALD: I know it. You may live the same life here as there, and yet it won't be the same life.

MRS. ALVING (who has been listening eagerly, rises, her eyes big with thought, and says): Now I see the sequence of things.

OSWALD: What is it you see?

MRS. ALVING: I see it now for the first time. And now I can speak.

OSWALD (rising): Mother, I don't understand you.

REGINA (who has also risen): Perhaps I ought to go?

MRS. ALVING: No. Stay here. Now I can speak. Now, my boy, you shall know the whole truth. And then you can choose. Oswald! Regina!

OSWALD: Hush! The Pastor——

MANDERS (enters by the hall door): There! We have had a most edifying time down there.

OSWALD: So have we.

MANDERS: We must stand by Engstrand and his Sailors' Home. Regina must go to him and help him—

REGINA: No thank you, sir.

MANDERS (noticing her for the first time): What—? You here? And with a glass in your hand!

REGINA (hastily putting the glass down): Pardon!

OSWALD: Regina is going with me, Mr. Manders.

MANDERS: Going! With you!

OSWALD: Yes; as my wife—if she wishes it.

MANDERS: But, merciful God—!

REGINA: I can't help it, sir.

OSWALD: Or she'll stay here, if I stay.

REGINA (involuntarily): Here!

MANDERS: I am thunderstruck at your conduct, Mrs. Alving.

MRS. ALVING: They will do neither one thing nor the other; for now I can speak out plainly.

MANDERS: You surely will not do that! No, no, no!

MRS. ALVING: Yes, I can speak and I will. And no ideals shall suffer after all.

OSWALD: Mother—what is it you are hiding from me?

REGINA (*listening*): Oh, ma'am, listen! Don't you hear shouts outside. (*She goes into the conservatory and looks out.*)

OSWALD (*at the window on the left*): What's going on? Where does that light come from?

REGINA (*cries out*): The Orphanage is on fire!

MRS. ALVING (*rushing to the window*): On fire!

MANDERS: On fire! Impossible! I've just come from there.

OSWALD: Where's my hat? Oh, never mind it—Father's Orphanage—! (*He rushes out through the garden door.*)

MRS. ALVING: My shawl, Regina! The whole place is in a blaze!

MANDERS: Terrible! Mrs. Alving, it is a judgment upon this abode of lawlessness.

MRS. ALVING: Yes, of course. Come, Regina.

> (*She and* REGINA *hasten out through the hall.*)

MANDERS (*clasps his hands together*): And we left it uninsured! (*He goes out the same way.*)

ACT THREE

> (*The room as before. All the doors stand open. The lamp is still burning on the table. It is dark out of doors; there is only a faint glow from the conflagration in the background to the left.*)
>
> (MRS. ALVING, *with a shawl over her head, stands in the conservatory, looking out.* REGINA, *also with a shawl on, stands a little behind her.*)

MRS. ALVING: The whole thing burnt!—burnt to the ground!

REGINA: The basement is still burning.

MRS. ALVING: How is it Oswald doesn't come home? There's nothing to be saved.

REGINA: Should you like me to take down his hat to him?

MRS. ALVING: Has he not even got his hat on?

REGINA (*pointing to the hall*): No; there it hangs.

MRS. ALVING: Let it be. He must come up now. I shall go and look for him myself.
(*She goes out through the garden door.*)

MANDERS (*comes in from the hall*): Is not Mrs. Alving here?

REGINA: She has just gone down the garden.

MANDERS: This is the most terrible night I ever went through.

REGINA: Yes; isn't it a dreadful misfortune, sir?

MANDERS: Oh, don't talk about it! I can hardly bear to think of it.

REGINA: How can it have happened—?

MANDERS: Don't ask me, Miss Engstrand! How should *I* know? Do you, too—? Is it not enough that your father—?

REGINA: What about him?

MANDERS: Oh, he has driven me distracted.

ENGSTRAND (*enters through the hall*): Your Reverence—

MANDERS (*turns round in terror*): Are you after me here, too?

ENGSTRAND: Yes, strike me dead, but I must—! Oh, Lord! what am I saying? But this is a terrible ugly business, your Reverence.

MANDERS (*walks to and fro*): Alas! alas!

REGINA: What's the matter?

ENGSTRAND: Why, it all came of this here prayer-meeting, you see. (*Softly.*) The bird's limed, my girl. (*Aloud.*) And to think it should be my doing that such a thing should be his Reverence's doing!

MANDERS: But I assure you, Engstrand—

ENGSTRAND: There wasn't another soul except your Reverence as ever laid a finger on the candles down there.

MANDERS (*stops*): So you declare. But I certainly cannot recollect that I ever had a candle in my hand.

ENGSTRAND: And I saw as clear as daylight how your Reverence took the candle and snuffed it with your fingers, and threw away the snuff among the shavings.

MANDERS: And you stood and looked on?

ENGSTRAND: Yes; I saw it as plain as a pike-staff, I did.

MANDERS: It's quite beyond my comprehension. Besides, it has never been my habit to snuff candles with my fingers.

ENGSTRAND: And terrible risky it looked, too, that it did! But is there such a deal of harm done after all, your Reverence?

MANDERS (*walks restlessly to and fro*): Oh, don't ask me!

ENGSTRAND (*walks with him*): And your Reverence hadn't insured it, neither?

MANDERS (*continuing to walk up and down*): No, no, no; I have told you so.

ENGSTRAND (*following him*): Not insured! And then to go straight away down and set light to the whole thing! Lord, Lord, what a misfortune!

MANDERS (*wipes the sweat from his forehead*): Ay, you may well say that, Engstrand.

ENGSTRAND: And to think that such a thing should happen to a benevolent Institution, that was to have been a blessing both to town and country, as the saying goes! The newspapers won't be for handling your Reverence very gently, I expect.

MANDERS: No; that is just what I am thinking of. That is almost the worst of the whole matter. All the malignant attacks and imputations—! Oh, it makes me shudder to think of it!

MRS. ALVING (*comes in from the garden*): He is not to be persuaded to leave the fire.

MANDERS: Ah, there you are, Mrs. Alving.

MRS. ALVING: So you have escaped your Inaugural Address, Pastor Manders.

MANDERS: Oh, I should so gladly—

MRS. ALVING (*in an undertone*): It is all for the best. That Orphanage would have done no one any good.

MANDERS: Do you think not?

MRS. ALVING: Do you think it would?

MANDERS: It is a terrible misfortune, all the same.

MRS. ALVING: Let us speak of it plainly, as a matter of business—Are you waiting for Mr. Manders, Engstrand?

ENGSTRAND (*at the hall door*): That's just what I'm a-doing of, ma'am.

MRS. ALVING: Then sit down meanwhile.

ENGSTRAND: Thank you, ma'am; I'd as soon stand.

MRS. ALVING (*to* MANDERS): I suppose you are going by the steamer?

MANDERS: Yes; it starts in an hour.

MRS. ALVING: Then be so good as to take all the papers with you. I won't hear another word about this affair. I have other things to think of—

MANDERS: Mrs. Alving—

MRS. ALVING: Later on I shall send you a Power of Attorney to settle everything as you please.

MANDERS: That I will very readily undertake. The original destination of the endowment must now be completely changed, alas!

MRS. ALVING: Of course it must.

MANDERS: I think, first of all, I shall arrange that the Solvik property shall pass to the parish. The land is by no means without value. It can always be turned to account for some purpose or other. And the interest of the money in the Bank I could, perhaps, best apply for the benefit of some undertaking of acknowledged value to the town.

MRS. ALVING: Do just as you please. The whole matter is now completely indifferent to me.

ENGSTRAND: Give a thought to my Sailors' Home, your Reverence.

MANDERS: Upon my word, that is not a bad suggestion. That must be considered.

ENGSTRAND: Oh, devil take considering—Lord forgive me!

MANDERS (*with a sigh*): And unfortunately I cannot tell how long I shall be able to retain control of these things—whether public opinion may not compel me to retire. It entirely depends upon the result of the official inquiry into the fire—

MRS. ALVING: What are you talking about?

MANDERS: And the result can by no means be foretold.

ENGSTRAND (*comes close to him*): Ay, but it can though. For here stands old Jacob Engstrand.

MANDERS: Well well, but—?

ENGSTRAND (*more softly*): And Jacob Engstrand isn't the man to desert a noble benefactor in the hour of need, as the saying goes.

MANDERS: Yes, but my good fellow—how—?

ENGSTRAND: Jacob Engstrand may be likened to a sort of a guardian angel, he may, your Reverence.

MANDERS: No, no; I really cannot accept that.

ENGSTRAND: Oh, that'll be the way of it, all the same. I know a man as has taken others' sins upon himself before now, I do.

MANDERS: Jacob! (*Wrings his hand.*) Yours is a rare nature. Well, you shall be helped with your Sailors' Home. That you may rely upon.

(ENGSTRAND *tries to thank him, but cannot for emotion.*)

MANDERS (*hangs his travelling-bag over his shoulders*): And now let us set out. We two will go together.

ENGSTRAND (*at the dining-room door, softly to* REGINA): You come along too, my lass. You shall live as snug as the yolk in an egg.

REGINA (*tosses her head*): *Merci!*

(*She goes out into the hall and fetches* MANDERS' *overcoat.*)

MANDERS: Good-bye, Mrs. Alving! and may the spirit of Law and Order descend upon this house, and that quickly.

MRS. ALVING: Good-bye, Pastor Manders. (*She goes up towards the conservatory, as she sees* OSWALD *coming in through the garden door.*)

ENGSTRAND (*while he and* REGINA *help* MANDERS *to get his coat on*): Good-bye, my child. And if any trouble should come to you, you know where Jacob Engstrand is to be found. (*Softly.*) Little Harbour Street, h'm—! (*To* MRS. ALVING *and* OSWALD.) And the refuge for wandering mariners shall be called "Chamberlain Alving's Home," that it shall! And if so be as I'm spared to carry on that house in my own way, I make so bold as to promise that it shall be worthy of the Chamberlain's memory.

MANDERS (*in the doorway*): H'm—h'm!—Come along, my dear Engstrand. Good-bye! Good-bye! (*He and* ENGSTRAND *go out through the hall.*)

OSWALD (*goes towards the table*): What house was he talking about?

MRS. ALVING: Oh, a kind of Home that he and Pastor Manders want to set up.

OSWALD: It will burn down like the other.

MRS. ALVING: What makes you think so?

OSWALD: Everything will burn. All that recalls father's memory is doomed. Here am I, too, burning down.

(REGINA *starts and looks at him.*)

MRS. ALVING: Oswald! You oughtn't to have remained so long down there, my poor boy.

OSWALD (*sits down by the table*): I almost think you are right.

MRS. ALVING: Let me dry your face, Oswald; you are quite wet. (*She dries his face with her pocket-handkerchief.*)

OSWALD (*stares indifferently in front of him*): Thanks, mother.

MRS. ALVING: Are you not tired, Oswald? Should you like to sleep?

OSWALD (*nervously*): No, no—not to sleep! I never sleep. I only pretend to. (*Sadly.*) That will come soon enough.

MRS. ALVING (*looking sorrowfully at him*): Yes, you really are ill, my blessed boy.

REGINA (*eagerly*): Is Mr. Alving ill?

OSWALD (*impatiently*): Oh, do shut all the doors! This killing dread—

MRS. ALVING: Close the doors, Regina.

> (REGINA *shuts them and remains standing by the hall door.* MRS. ALVING *takes her shawl off.* REGINA *does the same.* MRS. ALVING *draws a chair across to* OSWALD'S, *and sits by him.*)

MRS. ALVING: There now! I am going to sit beside you—

OSWALD: Yes, do. And Regina shall stay here too. Regina shall be with me always. You will come to the rescue, Regina, won't you?

REGINA: I don't understand—

MRS. ALVING: To the rescue?

OSWALD: Yes—when the need comes.

MRS. ALVING: Oswald, have you not your mother to come to the rescue?

OSWALD: You? (*Smiles.*) No, mother; that rescue you will never bring me. (*Laughs sadly.*) You! ha ha! (*Looks earnestly at her.*) Though, after all, who ought to do it if not you? (*Impetuously.*) Why can't you say "thou" to me, Regina? Why don't you call me "Oswald"?

REGINA (*softly*): I don't think Mrs. Alving would like it.

MRS. ALVING: You shall have leave to, presently. And meanwhile sit over here beside us.

> (REGINA *seats herself demurely and hesitatingly at the other side of the table.*)

MRS. ALVING: And now, my poor suffering boy, I am going to take the burden off your mind—

OSWALD: You, mother?

MRS. ALVING: —all the gnawing remorse and self-reproach you speak of.

OSWALD: And you think you can do that?

MRS. ALVING: Yes, now I can, Oswald. A little while ago you spoke of the joy of life; and at that word a new light burst for me over my life and everything connected with it.

OSWALD (*shakes his head*): I don't understand you.

MRS. ALVING: You ought to have known your father when he was a young lieutenant. He was brimming over with the joy of life!

OSWALD: Yes, I know he was.

MRS. ALVING: It was like a breezy day only to look at him. And what exuberant strength and vitality there was in him!

OSWALD: Well—?

MRS. ALVING: Well then, child of joy as he was—for he was like a child in those days—he had to live at home here in a half-grown town, which had no joys to offer him—only dissipations. He had no object in life—only an official position. He had no work into which he could throw himself heart and soul; he had only business. He had not a single comrade that could realise what the joy of life meant—only loungers and boon-companions—

OSWALD: Mother—!

MRS. ALVING: So the inevitable happened.

OSWALD: The inevitable?

MRS. ALVING: You told me yourself, this evening, what would become of you if you stayed at home.

OSWALD: Do you mean to say that father—?

MRS. ALVING: Your poor father found no outlet for the overpowering joy of life that was in him. And I brought no brightness into his home.

OSWALD: Not even you?

MRS. ALVING: They had taught me a great deal about duties and so forth, which I went on obstinately believing in. Everything was marked out into duties—into my duties, and his duties, and—I am afraid I made his home intolerable for your poor father, Oswald.

OSWALD: Why have you never spoken of this in writing to me?

MRS. ALVING: I have never before seen it in such a light that I could speak of it to you, his son.

OSWALD: In what light did you see it, then?

MRS. ALVING (slowly): I saw only this one thing: that your father was a broken-down man before you were born.

OSWALD (softly): Ah—! (He rises and walks away to the window.)

MRS. ALVING: And then, day after day, I dwelt on the one thought that by rights Regina should be at home in this house—just like my own boy.

OSWALD (turning round quickly): Regina—!

REGINA (springs up and asks, with bated breath): I—?

MRS. ALVING: Yes, now you know it, both of you.

OSWALD: Regina!

REGINA (to herself): So mother was that kind of woman.

MRS. ALVING: Your mother had many good qualities, Regina.

REGINA: Yes, but she was one of that sort, all the same. Oh, I've often suspected it; but— And now, if you please, ma'am, may I be allowed to go away at once?

MRS. ALVING: Do you really wish it, Regina?

REGINA: Yes, indeed I do.

MRS. ALVING: Of course you can do as you like; but—

OSWALD (goes toward REGINA): Go away now? Your place is here.

REGINA: Merci, Mr. Alving!—or now, I suppose, I may say Oswald. But I can tell you this wasn't at all what I expected.

MRS. ALVING: Regina, I have not been frank with you—

REGINA: No, that you haven't indeed. If I'd known that Oswald was an invalid, why— And now, too, that it can never come to anything serious between us— I really can't stop out here in the country and wear myself out nursing sick people.

OSWALD: Not even one who is so near to you?

REGINA: No, that I can't. A poor girl must make the best of her young days, or she'll be left out in the cold before she knows where she is. And I, too, have the joy of life in me, Mrs. Alving!

MRS. ALVING: Unfortunately, you have. But don't throw yourself away, Regina.

REGINA: Oh, what must be, must be. If Oswald takes after his father, I take after my mother, I dare say.—May I ask, ma'am, if Pastor Manders knows all this about me?

MRS. ALVING: Pastor Manders knows all about it.

REGINA (*busied in putting on her shawl*): Well then, I'd better make haste and get away by this steamer. The Pastor is such a nice man to deal with; and I certainly think I've as much right to a little of that money as he has—that brute of a carpenter.

MRS. ALVING: You are heartily welcome to it, Regina.

REGINA (*looks hard at her*): I think you might have brought me up as a gentleman's daughter, ma'am; it would have suited me better. (*Tosses her head.*) But pooh—what does it matter! (*With a bitter side glance at the corked bottle.*) I may come to drink champagne with gentlefolks yet.

MRS. ALVING: And if you ever need a home, Regina, come to me.

REGINA: No, thank you, ma'am. Pastor Manders will look after me, I know. And if the worst comes to the worst, I know of one house where I've every right to a place.

MRS. ALVING: Where is that?

REGINA: "Chamberlain Alving's Home."

MRS. ALVING: Regina—now I see it—you are going to your ruin.

REGINA: Oh, stuff! Good-bye. (*She nods and goes out through the hall.*)

OSWALD (*stands at the window and looks out*): Is she gone?

MRS. ALVING: Yes.

OSWALD (*murmuring aside to himself*): I think it was a mistake, this.

MRS. ALVING (*goes up behind him and lays her hands on his shoulders*): Oswald, my dear boy—has it shaken you very much?

OSWALD (*turns his face towards her*): All that about father, do you mean?

MRS. ALVING: Yes, about your unhappy father. I am so afraid it may have been too much for you.

OSWALD: Why should you fancy that? Of course it came upon me as a great surprise; but it can make no real difference to me.

MRS. ALVING (*draws her hands away*): No difference! That your father was so infinitely unhappy!

OSWALD: Of course I can pity him, as I would anybody else; but—

MRS. ALVING: Nothing more! Your own father!

OSWALD (*impatiently*): Oh, "father,"—"father"! I never knew anything of father. I remember nothing about him, except that he once made me sick.

MRS. ALVING: This is terrible to think of! Ought not a son to love his father, whatever happens?

OSWALD: When a son has nothing to thank his father for? has never known him? Do you really cling to that old superstition?—you who are so enlightened in other ways?

MRS. ALVING: Can it be only a superstition—?

OSWALD: Yes; surely you can see that, mother. It's one of those notions that are current in the world, and so—

MRS. ALVING (*deeply moved*): Ghosts!

OSWALD (*crossing the room*): Yes; you may call them ghosts.

MRS. ALVING (wildly): Oswald—then you don't love me, either!

OSWALD: You I know, at any rate—

MRS. ALVING: Yes, you know me; but is that all!

OSWALD: And, of course, I know how fond you are of me, and can't but be grateful to you. And then you can be so useful to me, now that I am ill.

MRS. ALVING: Yes, cannot I, Oswald? Oh, I could almost bless the illness that has driven you home to me. For I see very plainly that you are not mine: I have to win you.

OSWALD (*impatiently*): Yes yes yes; all these are just so many phrases. You must remember that I am a sick man, mother. I can't be much taken up with other people; I have enough to do thinking about myself.

MRS. ALVING (*in a low voice*): I shall be patient and easily satisfied.

OSWALD: And cheerful too, mother!

MRS. ALVING: Yes, my dear boy, you are quite right. (*Goes towards him.*) Have I relieved you of all remorse and self-reproach now?

OSWALD: Yes, you have. But now who will relieve me of the dread?

MRS. ALVING: The dread?

OSWALD (*walks across the room*): Regina could have been got to do it.

MRS. ALVING: I don't understand you. What is this about dread—and Regina?

OSWALD: Is it very late, mother?

MRS. ALVING: It is early morning. (*She looks out through the conservatory.*) The day is dawning over the mountains. And the weather is clearing, Oswald. In a little while you shall see the sun.

OSWALD: I'm glad of that. Oh, I may still have much to rejoice in and live for—

MRS. ALVING: I should think so, indeed!

OSWALD: Even if I can't work—

MRS. ALVING: Oh, you'll soon be able to work again, my dear boy—now that you haven't got all those gnawing and depressing thoughts to brood over any longer.

OSWALD: Yes, I'm glad you were able to rid me of all those fancies. And when I've got over this one thing more—(*Sits on the sofa.*) Now we will have a little talk, mother—

MRS. ALVING: Yes, let us. (*She pushes an arm-chair towards the sofa, and sits down close to him.*)

OSWALD: And meantime the sun will be rising. And then you will know all. And then I shall not feel this dread any longer.

MRS. ALVING: What is it that I am to know?

OSWALD (*not listening to her*): Mother, did you not say a little while ago, that there was nothing in the world you would not do for me, if I asked you?

MRS. ALVING: Yes, indeed I said so!

OSWALD: And you'll stick to it, mother?

MRS. ALVING: You may rely on that, my dear and only boy! I have nothing in the world to live for but you alone.

OSWALD: Very well, then; now you shall hear—Mother, you have a strong, steadfast mind, I know. Now you're to sit quite still when you hear it.

MRS. ALVING: What dreadful thing can it be—?

OSWALD: You're not to scream out. Do you hear? Do you promise me that? We will sit and talk about it quietly. Do you promise me, mother?

MRS. ALVING: Yes, yes; I promise. Only speak!

OSWALD: Well, you must know that all this fatigue—and my inability to think of work—all that is not the illness itself—

MRS. ALVING: Then what is the illness itself?

OSWALD: The disease I have as my birthright—(*he points to his forehead and adds very softly*)—is seated here.

MRS. ALVING (*almost voiceless*): Oswald! No—no!

OSWALD: Don't scream. I can't bear it. Yes, mother, it is seated here—waiting. And it may break out any day—at any moment.

MRS. ALVING: Oh, what horror—!

OSWALD: Now, quiet, quiet. That is how it stands with me—

MRS. ALVING (*springs up*): It's not true, Oswald! It's impossible! It cannot be so!

OSWALD: I have had one attack down there already. It was soon over. But when I came to know the state I had been in, then the dread descended upon me, raging and ravening; and so I sent off home to you as fast as I could.

MRS. ALVING: Then this is the dread—!

OSWALD: Yes—it's so indescribably loathsome, you know. Oh, if it had only been an ordinary mortal disease—! For I'm not so afraid of death— though I should like to live as long as I can.

MRS. ALVING: Yes, yes, Oswald, you must!

OSWALD: But this is so unutterably loathsome. To become a little baby again! To have to be fed! To have to—Oh, it's not to be spoken of!

MRS. ALVING: The child has his mother to nurse him.

OSWALD (*springs up*): No, never that! That is just what I will not have. I can't endure to think that perhaps I should lie in that state for many years—and get old and grey. And in the meantime you might die and leave me. (*Sits in* MRS. ALVING'S *chair.*) For the doctor said it wouldn't necessarily prove fatal at once. He called it a sort of softening of the brain—or something like that. (*Smiles sadly.*) I think that expression sounds so nice. It always sets me thinking of cherry-coloured velvet— something soft and delicate to stroke.

MRS. ALVING (*shrieks*): Oswald!

OSWALD (*springs up and paces the room*): And now you have taken Regina from me. If I could only have had her! She would have come to the rescue, I know.

MRS. ALVING (*goes to him*): What do you mean by that, my darling boy? Is there any help in the world that I would not give you?

OSWALD: When I got over my attack in Paris, the doctor told me that when it comes again—and it will come—there will be no more hope.

MRS. ALVING: He was heartless enough to—

OSWALD: I demanded it of him. I told him I had preparations to make—(*He smiles cunningly.*) And so I had. (*He takes a little box from his inner breast pocket and opens it.*) Mother, do you see this?

MRS. ALVING: What is it?

OSWALD: Morphia.

MRS. ALVING (*looks at him horror-struck*): Oswald—my boy.

OSWALD: I've scraped together twelve pilules—

MRS. ALVING (*snatches at it*): Give me the box, Oswald.

OSWALD: Not yet, mother. (*He hides the box again in his pocket.*)

MRS. ALVING: I shall never survive this!

OSWALD: It must be survived. Now if I'd had Regina here, I should have told her how things stood with me—and begged her to come to the rescue at the last. She would have done it. I know she would.

MRS. ALVING: Never!

OSWALD: When the horror had come upon me, and she saw me lying there helpless, like a little new-born baby, impotent, lost, hopeless—past all saving—

MRS. ALVING: Never in all the world would Regina have done this!

OSWALD: Regina would have done it. Regina was so splendidly light-hearted. And she would soon have wearied of nursing an invalid like me.

MRS. ALVING: Then heaven be praised that Regina is not here.

OSWALD: Well then, it is you that must come to the rescue, mother.

MRS. ALVING (*shrieks aloud*): I!

OSWALD: Who should do it if not you?

MRS. ALVING: I! your mother!

OSWALD: For that very reason.

MRS. ALVING: I, who gave you life!

OSWALD: I never asked you for life. And what sort of a life have you given me? I will not have it! You shall take it back again!

MRS. ALVING: Help! Help! (*She runs out into the hall.*)

OSWALD (*going after her*): Do not leave me! Where are you going?

MRS. ALVING (*in the hall*): To fetch the doctor, Oswald! Let me pass!

OSWALD (*also outside*): You shall not go out. And no one shall come in. (*The locking of a door is heard.*)

MRS. ALVING (*comes in again*): Oswald! Oswald—my child!

OSWALD (*follows her*): Have you a mother's heart for me—and yet can see me suffer from this unutterable dread?

MRS. ALVING (*after a moment's silence, commands herself, and says*): Here is my hand upon it.

OSWALD: Will you—?

MRS. ALVING: If it should ever be necessary. But it will never be necessary. No, no; it is impossible.

OSWALD: Well, let us hope so. And let us live together as long as we can. Thank you, mother. (*He seats himself in the arm-chair which* MRS. ALVING *has moved to the sofa. Day is breaking. The lamp is still burning on the table.*)

MRS. ALVING (*drawing near cautiously*): Do you feel calm now?

OSWALD: Yes.

MRS. ALVING (*bending over him*): It has been a dreadful fancy of yours, Oswald—nothing but a fancy. All this excitement has been too much for you. But now you shall have a long rest; at home with your mother, my own blessed boy. Everything you point to you shall have, just as when you were a little child.—There now. The crisis is over. You see how easily it passed! Oh, I was sure it would.—And do you see, Oswald, what a lovely day we are going to have? Brilliant sunshine! Now you can really see your home. (*She goes to the table and puts out the lamp. Sunrise. The glacier and the snow-peaks in the background glow in the morning light.*)

OSWALD (*sits in the arm-chair with his back towards the landscape, without moving. Suddenly he says*): Mother, give me the sun.

MRS. ALVING (*by the table, starts and looks at him*): What do you say?

OSWALD (*repeats, in a dull, toneless voice*): The sun. The sun.

MRS. ALVING (*goes to him*): Oswald, what is the matter with you?

(OSWALD *seems to shrink together in the chair; all his muscles relax; his face is expressionless, his eyes have a glassy stare.*)

MRS. ALVING (*quivering with terror*): What is this? (*Shrieks.*) Oswald! what is the matter with you? (*Falls on her knees beside him and shakes him.*) Oswald! Oswald! look at me! Don't you know me?

OSWALD (*tonelessly as before*): The sun.—The sun.

MRS. ALVING (*springs up in despair, entwines her hands in her hair and shrieks*): I cannot bear it! (*Whispers, as though petrified.*) I cannot bear it! Never! (*Suddenly.*) Where has he got them? (*Fumbles hastily in his breast.*) Here! (*Shrinks back a few steps and screams:*) No; no; no!—Yes!—No; no! (*She stands a few steps away from him with her hands twisted in her hair, and stares at him in speechless horror.*)

OSWALD (*sits motionless as before and says*): The sun.—The sun.

Fact Questions and Exercises

1. In the first few lines of Act 1, Engstrand mentions an orphanage: What part does this orphanage play in *Ghosts*? What happens to it?

2. Why does Pastor Manders refuse to "pass the night" in the Alving house?
3. During their first year of marriage, Mrs. Alving "fled" from her husband. Why? Who convinced her to return?
4. Why did Mrs. Alving send Oswald away when he was seven years old?
5. Who or what are the "ghosts"?
6. Jacob Engstrand is Regina's legal father. Who is her actual father? Why did Engstrand marry Regina's mother?
7. What did the doctor mean when he told Oswald that "the sins of the fathers are visited upon the children"?
8. How does Engstrand convince Pastor Manders that the pastor caused the fire? How does Engstrand use the pastor's guilt to Engstrand's benefit?
9. Whom does Oswald wish to marry? Aside from the fact of Oswald's illness, why can't they marry?
10. What happens to Oswald at the end of the play? What final decision must Mrs. Alving make concerning Oswald?

For Discussing and Writing

1. Mrs. Alving had taken Pastor Manders's advice and returned to her husband; in short, she did her "duty." What results from her conforming to social or conventional morality? Is she happy? What are her "rewards" for doing her duty?
2. *Ghosts* is considered a classic example of naturalism in drama. How does Ibsen express this naturalism? Are the characters controlled completely by forces of heredity, society, and chance? Do they have any degree of free will or self-determination? How does Ibsen present scientific knowledge in the play? Is it a beneficial or detrimental force?
3. Characterize Pastor Manders. What values or codes of conduct does he advocate? Does he, himself, abide by these values? Is there any indication that Manders is gullible and susceptible to the forces of "evil"? Explain.
4. Characterize Mrs. Alving. What are her motivations? Does Ibsen imply that she should have followed her natural instincts? If so, how do you account for what happened to her husband, a man who did follow his natural instincts?
5. In what ways is *Ghosts* a tragedy? That is, which specific aspects of the play produce tragic overtones or implications? For instance, what are Oswald's chances for recovery and happiness? What are Mrs. Alving's options regarding her ultimate decision? Can any decision she makes lead to a resolution of her problems?

Bernard Shaw [1856–1950]

Shaw was born in Dublin, Ireland. He quit school when he was fourteen; worked for a number of years in a land agent's office; and then moved to London in 1876, where he was active in politics and music. Partially because of the influence of Henrik Ibsen, whom Shaw admired, Shaw became interested in drama. Shaw's early plays reflect his devotion to socialism: he uses the drama to shock society into reexamining its conventional behavior. One of his typical ploys was to reverse the roles of the usual hero and villain, and then to show that the usual hero is, after all, the real hero—but for reasons at first unsuspected by the audience; this reversal can be seen in *Major Barbara* (1907). Most of his plays were accompanied by a long preface in which Shaw not only explained the play's purpose but held forth on a variety of other topics as well. Many of Shaw's works are considered to be better social commentaries than good drama, but in general, Shaw combines entertainment with provocative social examination. Shaw was also interested in a number of other projects, including spelling reform. In his work, he insisted that some of his spelling simplifications be retained—particularly the omission of apostrophes in contractions, and the wide spacing of letters to indicate italics or emphasis; he uses both simplifications in *Major Barbara*. Some of his better-known plays are *Man and Superman* (1904), *Pygmalion* (1912), and *Back to Methuselah* (1921).

    For anyone who wants to study the play seriously, it is essential to read Bernard Shaw's Preface to *Major Barbara*.

Major Barbara

CHARACTERS

ANDREW UNDERSHAFT, *a munitions manufacturer*
LADY BRITOMART, *his wife, from whom he lives apart*
STEPHEN ⎫
BARBARA ⎬ *their children*
SARAH ⎭
ADOLPHUS CUSINS, *a Professor of Greek, in love with Barbara*
CHARLES LOMAX, *a scion of the upper classes, in love with Sarah*
MORRISON, *Lady Britomart's butler*
ROMOLA (RUMMY) MITCHENS *and* BRONTERRE O'BRIEN (SNOBBY) PRICE *habitués of the West Ham Shelter of the Salvation Army*
JENNY HILL, *a young Salvation Army girl*
PETER SHIRLEY, *an older man who has lost his job*
BILL WALKER, *an intruder at the Shelter*
MRS. BAINES, *a senior officer in the Salvation Army*
BILTON, *a foreman at Undershaft's munitions works*

ACT ONE

It is after dinner in January 1906, in the library in LADY BRITOMART
UNDERSHAFT'S *house in Wilton Crescent. A large and comfortable
settee is in the middle of the room, upholstered in dark leather. A
person sitting on it (it is vacant at present) would have, on his right,*
LADY BRITOMART'S *writing table, with the lady herself busy at it; a
smaller writing table behind him on his left; the door behind him on*
LADY BRITOMART'S *side; and a window with a window seat directly
on his left. Near the window is an armchair.*

    LADY BRITOMART *is a woman of fifty or thereabouts, well
dressed and yet careless of her dress, well bred and quite reckless of
her breeding, well mannered and yet appallingly outspoken and
indifferent to the opinion of her interlocutors, amiable and yet
peremptory, arbitrary, and high-tempered to the last bearable
degree, and withal a very typical managing matron of the upper
class, treated as a naughty child until she grew into a scolding
mother, and finally settling down with plenty of practical ability and
worldly experience, limited in the oddest way with domestic and
class limitations, conceiving the universe exactly as if it were a large
house in Wilton Crescent, though handling her corner of it very
effectively on that assumption, and being quite enlightened and
liberal as to the books in the library, the pictures on the walls, the
music in the portfolios, and the articles in the papers.*

    Her son, STEPHEN, *comes in. He is a gravely correct young
man under 25, taking himself very seriously, but still in some awe of
his mother, from childish habit and bachelor shyness rather than
from any weakness of character.*

STEPHEN: Whats the matter?

LADY BRITOMART: Presently, Stephen.

    STEPHEN *submissively walks to the settee and sits down. He takes up
a Liberal weekly called The Speaker.*

LADY BRITOMART: Dont begin to read, Stephen. I shall require all your attention.

STEPHEN: It was only while I was waiting—

LADY BRITOMART: Dont make excuses, Stephen. [*He puts down The Speaker.*]
Now! [*She finishes her writing; rises; and comes to the settee.*] I have not
kept you waiting v e r y long, I think.

STEPHEN: Not at all, mother.

LADY BRITOMART: Bring me my cushion. [*He takes the cushion from the chair at
the desk and arranges it for her as she sits down on the settee.*] Sit down.
[*He sits down and fingers his tie nervously.*] Dont fiddle with your tie,
Stephen: there is nothing the matter with it.

STEPHEN: I beg your pardon. [*He fiddles with his watch chain instead.*]

LADY BRITOMART: Now are you attending to me, Stephen?

STEPHEN: Of course, mother.

LADY BRITOMART: No: it's n o t of course. I want something much more than your everyday matter-of-course attention. I am going to speak to you very seriously, Stephen. I wish you would let that chain alone.

STEPHEN [*hastily relinquishing the chain*]: Have I done anything to annoy you, mother? If so, it was quite unintentional.

LADY BRITOMART [*astonished*]: Nonsense! [*With some remorse.*] My poor boy, did you think I was angry with you?

STEPHEN: What is it, then, mother? You are making me very uneasy.

LADY BRITOMART [*squaring herself at him rather aggressively*]: Stephen: may I ask how soon you intend to realize that you are a grown-up man, and that I am only a woman?

STEPHEN [*amazed*]: Only a—

LADY BRITOMART: Dont repeat my words, please: it is a most aggravating habit. You must learn to face life seriously, Stephen. I really cannot bear the whole burden of our family affairs any longer. You must advise me; you must assume the responsibility.

STEPHEN: I!

LADY BRITOMART: Yes, you, of course. You were 24 last June. Youve been at Harrow and Cambridge. Youve been to India and Japan. You must know a lot of things, now; unless you have wasted your time most scandalous-ly. Well, a d v i s e me.

STEPHEN [*much perplexed*]: You know I have never interfered in the household—

LADY BRITOMART: No: I should think not. I dont want you to order the dinner.

STEPHEN: I mean in our family affairs.

LADY BRITOMART: Well, you must interfere now; for they are getting quite beyond me.

STEPHEN [*troubled*]: I have thought sometimes that perhaps I ought; but really, mother, I know so little about them; and what I do know is so painful! it is so impossible to mention some things to you—[*He stops, ashamed.*]

LADY BRITOMART: I suppose you mean your father.

STEPHEN [*almost inaudibly*]: Yes.

LADY BRITOMART: My dear: we cant go on all our lives not mentioning him. Of course you were quite right not to open the subject until I asked you to; but you are old enough now to be taken into my confidence, and to help me to deal with him about the girls.

STEPHEN: But the girls are all right. They are engaged.

LADY BRITOMART [*complacently*]: Yes: I have made a very good match for Sarah. Charles Lomax will be a millionaire at 35. But that is ten years ahead; and in the meantime his trustees cannot under the terms of his father's will allow him more than £800 a year.

STEPHEN: But the will says also that if he increases his income by his own exertions, they may double the increase.

LADY BRITOMART: Charles Lomax's exertions are much more likely to decrease his income than to increase it. Sarah will have to find at least another £800 a year for the next ten years; and even then they will be as poor as church mice. And what about Barbara? I thought Barbara was going to make the most brilliant career of all of you. And what does she do? Joins the Salvation Army; discharges her maid; lives on a pound a week; and walks in one evening with a professor of Greek whom she has picked up in the street, and who pretends to be a Salvationist, and actually plays the big drum for her in public because he has fallen head over ears in love with her.

STEPHEN: I was certainly rather taken aback when I heard they were engaged. Cusins is a very nice fellow, certainly: nobody would ever guess that he was born in Australia; but—

LADY BRITOMART: Oh, Adolphus Cusins will make a very good husband. After all, nobody can say a word against Greek: it stamps a man at once as an educated gentleman. And my family, thank Heaven, is not a pig-headed Tory one. We are Whigs, and believe in liberty. Let snobbish people say what they please: Barbara shall marry, not the man they like, but the man *I* like.

STEPHEN: Of course I was thinking only of his income. However, he is not likely to be extravagant.

LADY BRITOMART: Dont be too sure of that, Stephen. I know your quiet, simple, refined, poetic people like Adolphus: quite content with the best of everything! They cost more than your extravagant people, who are always as mean as they are second rate. No: Barbara will need at least £2000 a year. You see it means two additional households. Besides, my dear, y o u must marry soon. I dont approve of the present fashion of philandering bachelors and late marriages; and I am trying to arrange something for you.

STEPHEN: It's very good of you, mother; but perhaps I had better arrange that for myself.

LADY BRITOMART: Nonsense! you are much too young to begin matchmaking: you would be taken in by some pretty little nobody. Of course I dont mean that you are not to be consulted: you know that as well as I do. [STEPHEN *closes his lips and is silent.*] Now dont sulk, Stephen.

STEPHEN: I am not sulking, mother. What has all this got to do with—with—with my father?

LADY BRITOMART: My dear Stephen: where is the money to come from? It is easy enough for you and the other children to live on my income as long as we are in the same house; but I cant keep four families in four separate houses. You know how poor my father is: he has barely seven thousand a year now; and really, if he were not the Earl of Stevenage, he would have to give up society. He can do nothing for us. He says, naturally enough, that it is absurd that he should be asked to provide for the children of a man who is rolling in money. You see, Stephen, your father must be fabulously wealthy, because there is always a war going on somewhere.

STEPHEN: You need not remind me of that, mother. I have hardly ever opened a newspaper in my life without seeing our name in it. The Undershaft torpedo! The Undershaft quick firers! The Undershaft ten inch! The Undershaft disappearing rampart gun! The Undershaft submarine! and now the Undershaft aerial battleship! At Harrow they call me the Woolwich Infant. At Cambridge it was the same. A little brute at King's who was always trying to get up revivals, spoilt my Bible—your first birthday present to me—by writing under my name, "Son and heir to Undershaft and Lazarus, Death and Destruction Dealers: address, Christendom and Judea." But that was not so bad as the way I was kowtowed to everywhere because my father was making millions by selling cannons.

LADY BRITOMART: It is not only the cannons, but the war loans that Lazarus arranges under cover of giving credit for the cannons. You know, Stephen, it's perfectly scandalous. Those two men, Andrew Undershaft and Lazarus, positively have Europe under their thumbs. That is why your father is able to behave as he does. He is above the law. Do you think Bismarck or Gladstone or Disraeli could have openly defied every social and moral obligation all their lives as your father has? They simply wouldnt have dared. I asked Gladstone to take it up. I asked The Times to take it up. I asked the Lord Chamberlain to take it up. But it was just like asking them to declare war on the Sultan. They w o u l d n t. They said they couldnt touch him. I believe they were afraid.

STEPHEN: What could they do? He does not actually break the law.

LADY BRITOMART: Not break the law! He is always breaking the law. He broke the law when he was born: his parents were not married.

STEPHEN: Mother! Is that true?

LADY BRITOMART: Of course it's true: that was why we separated.

STEPHEN: He married without letting you know this!

LADY BRITOMART [rather taken aback by this inference]: Oh no. To do Andrew justice, that was not the sort of thing he did. Besides, you know the Undershaft motto: Unashamed. Everybody knew.

STEPHEN: But you said that was why you separated.

LADY BRITOMART: Yes, because he was not content with being a foundling himself: he wanted to disinherit you for another foundling. That was what I couldnt stand.

STEPHEN [ashamed]: Do you mean for—for—for—

LADY BRITOMART: Dont stammer, Stephen. Speak distinctly.

STEPHEN: But this is so frightful to me, mother. To have to speak to you about such things!

LADY BRITOMART: It's not pleasant for me, either, especially if you are still so childish that you must make it worse by a display of embarrassment. It is only in the middle classes, Stephen, that people get into a state of dumb helpless horror when they find that there are wicked people in the world. In our class, we have to decide what is to be done with wicked people; and nothing should disturb our self-possession. Now ask your question properly.

STEPHEN: Mother: have you no consideration for me? For Heaven's sake either treat me as a child, as you always do, and tell me nothing at all; or tell me everything and let me take it as best I can.

LADY BRITOMART: Treat you as a child! What do you mean? It is most unkind and ungrateful of you to say such a thing. You know I have never treated any of you as children. I have always made you my companions and friends, and allowed you perfect freedom to do and say whatever you liked, so long as you liked what I could approve of.

STEPHEN [*desperately*]: I daresay we have been the very imperfect children of a very perfect mother; but I do beg you to let me alone for once, and tell me about this horrible business of my father wanting to set me aside for another son.

LADY BRITOMART [*amazed*]: Another son! I never said anything of the kind. I never dreamt of such a thing. This is what comes of interrupting me.

STEPHEN: But you said—

LADY BRITOMART [*cutting him short*]: Now be a good boy, Stephen, and listen to me patiently. The Undershafts are descended from a foundling in the parish of St Andrew Undershaft in the city. That was long ago, in the reign of James the First. Well, this foundling was adopted by an armorer and gun-maker. In the course of time the foundling succeeded to the business; and from some notion of gratitude, or some vow or something, he adopted another foundling, and left the business to him. And that foundling did the same. Ever since that, the cannon business has always been left to an adopted foundling named Andrew Undershaft.

STEPHEN: But did they never marry? Were there no legitimate sons?

LADY BRITOMART: Oh yes: they married just as your father did; and they were rich enough to buy land for their own children and leave them well provided for. But they always adopted and trained some foundling to succeed them in the business; and of course they always quarrelled with their wives furiously over it. Your father was adopted in that way; and he pretends to consider himself bound to keep up the tradition and adopt somebody to leave the business to. Of course I was not going to stand that. There may have been some reason for it when the Undershafts could only marry women in their own class, whose sons were not fit to govern great estates. But there could be no excuse for passing over m y son.

STEPHEN [*dubiously*]: I am afraid I should make a poor hand of managing a cannon foundry.

LADY BRITOMART: Nonsense! you could easily get a manager and pay him a salary.

STEPHEN: My father evidently had no great opinion of my capacity.

LADY BRITOMART: Stuff, child! you were only a baby: it had nothing to do with your capacity. Andrew did it on principle, just as he did every perverse and wicked thing on principle. When my father remonstrated, Andrew actually told him to his face that history tells us of only two successful institutions: one the Undershaft firm, and the other the Roman Empire under the Antonines.[1] That was because the Antonine emperors all adopted their successors. Such rubbish! The Stevenages are as good as

1. A name applied to the "Five Good Emperors" who ruled Rome between 96 and 180 A.D.

the Antonines, I hope; and you are a Stevenage. But that was Andrew all over. There you have the man! Always clever and unanswerable when he was defending nonsense and wickedness: always awkward and sullen when he had to behave sensibly and decently!

STEPHEN: Then it was on my account that your home life was broken up, mother. I am sorry.

LADY BRITOMART: Well, dear, there were other differences. I really cannot bear an immoral man. I am not a Pharisee, I hope; and I should not have minded his merely d o i n g wrong things: we are none of us perfect. But your father didnt exactly d o wrong things: he said them and thought them: that was what was so dreadful. He really had a sort of religion of wrongness. Just as one doesnt mind men practising immorality so long as they own that they are in the wrong by preaching morality; so I couldnt forgive Andrew for preaching immorality while he practised morality. You would all have grown up without principles, without any knowledge of right and wrong, if he had been in the house. You know, my dear, your father was a very attractive man in some ways. Children did not dislike him; and he took advantage of it to put the wickedest ideas into their heads, and make them quite unmanageable. I did not dislike him myself: very far from it; but nothing can bridge over moral disagreement.

STEPHEN: All this simply bewilders me, mother. People may differ about matters of opinion, or even about religion; but how can they differ about right and wrong? Right is right; and wrong is wrong; and if a man cannot distinguish them properly, he is either a fool or a rascal: thats all.

LADY BRITOMART [touched]: Thats my own boy! [She pats his cheek.] Your father never could answer that: he used to laugh and get out of it under cover of some affectionate nonsense. And now that you understand the situation, what do you advise me to do?

STEPHEN: Well, what c a n you do?

LADY BRITOMART: I must get the money somehow.

STEPHEN: We cannot take money from him. I had rather go and live in some cheap place like Bedford Square or even Hampstead than take a farthing of his money.

LADY BRITOMART: But after all, Stephen, our present income comes from Andrew.

STEPHEN [shocked]: I never knew that.

LADY BRITOMART: Well, you surely didnt suppose your grandfather had anything to give me. The Stevenages could not do everything for you. We gave you social position. Andrew had to contribute s o m e t h i n g. He had a very good bargain, I think.

STEPHEN [bitterly]: We are utterly dependent on him and his cannons, then?

LADY BRITOMART: Certainly not: the money is settled. But he provided it. So you see it is not a question of taking money from him or not: it is simply a question of how much. I dont want any more for myself.

STEPHEN: Nor do I.

LADY BRITOMART: But Sarah does; and Barbara does. That is, Charles Lomax and

Adolphus Cusins will cost them more. So I must put my pride in my pocket and ask for it, I suppose. That is your advice, Stephen, is it not?

STEPHEN: No.

LADY BRITOMART [*sharply*]: Stephen!

STEPHEN: Of course if you are determined—

LADY BRITOMART: I am not determined: I ask your advice; and I am waiting for it. I will not have all the responsibility thrown on my shoulders.

STEPHEN [*obstinately*]: I would die sooner than ask him for another penny.

LADY BRITOMART [*resignedly*]: You mean that *I* must ask him. Very well, Stephen: it shall be as you wish. You will be glad to know that your grandfather concurs. But he thinks I ought to ask Andrew to come here and see the girls. After all, he must have some natural affection for them.

STEPHEN: Ask him here!!!

LADY BRITOMART: Do n o t repeat my words, Stephen. Where else can I ask him?

STEPHEN: I never expected you to ask him at all.

LADY BRITOMART: Now dont tease, Stephen. Come! you see that it is necessary that he should pay us a visit, dont you?

STEPHEN [*reluctantly*]: I suppose so, if the girls cannot do without his money.

LADY BRITOMART: Thank you, Stephen: I knew you would give me the right advice when it was properly explained to you. I have asked your father to come this evening. [STEPHEN *bounds from his seat.*] Dont jump, Stephen: it fidgets me.

STEPHEN [*in utter consternation*]: Do you mean to say that my father is coming here tonight—that he may be here at any moment?

LADY BRITOMART [*looking at her watch*]: I said nine. [*He gasps. She rises.*] Ring the bell, please. [STEPHEN *goes to the smaller writing table; presses a button on it; and sits at it with his elbows on the table and his head in his hands, outwitted and overwhelmed.*] It is ten minutes to nine yet; and I have to prepare the girls. I asked Charles Lomax and Adolphus to dinner on purpose that they might be here. Andrew had better see them in case he should cherish any delusions as to their being capable of supporting their wives. [*The butler enters:* LADY BRITOMART *goes behind the settee to speak to him.*] Morrison: go up to the drawing room and tell everybody to come down here at once. [MORRISON *withdraws.* LADY BRITOMART *turns to* STEPHEN.] Now remember, Stephen: I shall need all your countenance and authority. [*He rises and tries to recover some vestige of these attributes.*] Give me a chair, dear. [*He pushes a chair forward from the wall to where she stands, near the smaller writing table. She sits down; and he goes to the armchair, into which he throws himself.*] I dont know how Barbara will take it. Ever since they made her a major in the Salvation Army she has developed a propensity to have her own way and order people about which quite cows me sometimes. It's not ladylike: I'm sure I dont know where she picked it up. Anyhow, Barbara shant bully m e; but still it's just as well that your father should be here before she has time to refuse to meet him or make a fuss. Dont look nervous, Stephen: it will only encourage Barbara to make difficulties. *I* am nervous enough, goodness knows; but I dont shew it.

SARAH *and* BARBARA *come in with their respective young men,* CHARLES LOMAX *and* ADOLPHUS CUSINS. SARAH *is slender, bored, and mundane.* BARBARA *is robuster, jollier, much more energetic.* SARAH *is fashionably dressed:* BARBARA *is in Salvation Army uniform.* LOMAX, *a young man about town, is like many other young men about town. He is afflicted with a frivolous sense of humor which plunges him at the most inopportune moments into paroxysms of imperfectly suppressed laughter.* CUSINS *is a spectacled student, slight, thin haired, and sweet voiced, with a more complex form of* LOMAX's *complaint. His sense of humor is intellectual and subtle, and is complicated by an appalling temper. The lifelong struggle of a benevolent temperament and a high conscience against impulses of inhuman ridicule and fierce impatience has set up a chronic strain which has visibly wrecked his constitution. He is a most implacable, determined, tenacious, intolerant person who by mere force of character presents himself as—and indeed actually is—considerate, gentle, explanatory, even mild and apologetic, capable possibly of murder, but not of cruelty or coarseness. By the operation of some instinct which is not merciful enough to blind him with the illusions of love, he is obstinately bent on marrying* BARBARA. LOMAX *likes* SARAH *and thinks it will be rather a lark to marry her. Consequently, he has not attempted to resist* LADY BRITOMART's *arrangements to that end.*

All four look as if they had been having a good deal of fun in the drawing room. The girls enter first, leaving the swains outside. SARAH *comes to the settee.* BARBARA *comes in after her and stops at the door.*

BARBARA: Are Cholly and Dolly to come in?

LADY BRITOMART [*forcibly*]: Barbara: I will not have Charles called Cholly: the vulgarity of it positively makes me ill.

BARBARA: It's all right, mother: Cholly is quite correct nowadays. Are they to come in?

LADY BRITOMART: Yes, if they will behave themselves.

BARBARA [*through the door*]: Come in, Dolly; and behave yourself.

BARBARA *comes to her mother's writing table.* CUSINS *enters smiling, and wanders towards* LADY BRITOMART.

SARAH [*calling*]: Come in, Cholly. [LOMAX *enters, controlling his features very imperfectly, and places himself vaguely between* SARAH *and* BARBARA.]

LADY BRITOMART [*peremptorily*]: Sit down, all of you. [*They sit.* CUSINS *crosses to the window and seats himself there.* LOMAX *takes a chair.* BARBARA *sits at the writing table and* SARAH *on the settee.*] I dont in the least know what you are laughing at, Adolphus. I am surprised at you, though I expected nothing better from Charles Lomax.

CUSINS [*in a remarkably gentle voice*]: Barbara has been trying to teach me the West Ham Salvation March.

LADY BRITOMART: I see nothing to laugh at in that; nor should you if you are really converted.

CUSINS [*sweetly*]: You were not present. It was really funny, I believe.

LOMAX: Ripping.

LADY BRITOMART: Be quiet, Charles. Now listen to me, children. Your father is coming here this evening.

> *General stupefaction.* LOMAX, SARAH, *and* BARBARA *rise:* SARAH *scared, and* BARBARA *amused and expectant.*

LOMAX [*remonstrating*]: Oh I say!

LADY BRITOMART: You are not called on to say anything, Charles.

SARAH: Are you serious, mother?

LADY BRITOMART: Of course I am serious. It is on your account, Sarah, and also on Charles's. [*Silence.* SARAH *sits, with a shrug.* CHARLES *looks painfully unworthy.*] I hope you are not going to object, Barbara.

BARBARA: I! why should I? My father has a soul to be saved like anybody else. He's quite welcome as far as I am concerned. [*She sits on the table, and softly whistles 'Onward, Christian Soldiers.'*]

LOMAX [*still remonstrant*]: But really, dont you know! Oh I say!

LADY BRITOMART [*frigidly*]: What do you wish to convey, Charles?

LOMAX: Well, you must admit that this is a bit thick.

LADY BRITOMART [*turning with ominous suavity to* CUSINS]: Adolphus: you are a professor of Greek. Can you translate Charles Lomax's remarks into reputable English for us?

CUSINS [*cautiously*]: If I may say so, Lady Brit, I think Charles has rather happily expressed what we all feel. Homer, speaking of Autolycus, uses the same phrase. πυκινὸν δόμον ἐλθεῖν means a bit thick.

LOMAX [*handsomely*]: Not that I mind, you know, if Sarah dont. [*He sits.*]

LADY BRITOMART [*crushingly*]: Thank you. Have I y o u r permission, Adolphus, to invite my own husband to my own house?

CUSINS [*gallantly*]: You have my unhesitating support in everything you do.

LADY BRITOMART: Tush! Sarah: have you nothing to say?

SARAH: Do you mean that he is coming regularly to live here?

LADY BRITOMART: Certainly not. The spare room is ready for him if he likes to stay for a day or two and see a little more of you; but there are limits.

SARAH: Well, he cant eat us, I suppose. *I* dont mind.

LOMAX [*chuckling*]: I wonder how the old man will take it.

LADY BRITOMART: Much as the old woman will, no doubt, Charles.

LOMAX [*abashed*]: I didnt mean—at least—

LADY BRITOMART: You didnt t h i n k, Charles. You never do; and the result is, you never mean anything. And now please attend to me, children. Your father will be quite a stranger to us.

LOMAX: I suppose he hasnt seen Sarah since she was a little kid.

LADY BRITOMART: Not since she was a little kid, Charles, as you express it with that elegance of diction and refinement of thought that seem never to desert you. Accordingly—er— [*Impatiently.*] Now I have forgotten what I was going to say. That comes of your provoking me to be sarcastic, Charles. Adolphus: will you kindly tell me where I was.

CUSINS [*sweetly*]: You were saying that as Mr Undershaft has not seen his children since they were babies, he will form his opinion of the way you have brought them up from their behavior tonight, and that therefore you wish us all to be particularly careful to conduct ourselves well, especially Charles.

LADY BRITOMART [*with emphatic approval*]: Precisely.

LOMAX: Look here, Dolly: Lady Brit didnt say that.

LADY BRITOMART [*vehemently*]: I did, Charles. Adolphus's recollection is perfectly correct. It is most important that you should be good; and I do beg you for once not to pair off into opposite corners and giggle and whisper while I am speaking to your father.

BARBARA: All right, mother. We'll do you credit. [*She comes off the table, and sits in her chair with ladylike elegance.*]

LADY BRITOMART: Remember, Charles, that Sarah will want to feel proud of you instead of ashamed of you.

LOMAX: Oh I say! theres nothing to be exactly proud of, dont you know.

LADY BRITOMART: Well, try and look as if there was.

> MORRISON, *pale and dismayed, breaks into the room in unconcealed disorder.*

MORRISON: Might I speak a word to you, my lady?

LADY BRITOMART: Nonsense! Shew him up.

MORRISON: Yes, my lady. [*He goes.*]

LOMAX: Does Morrison know who it is?

LADY BRITOMART: Of course. Morrison has always been with us.

LOMAX: It must be a regular corker for him, dont you know.

LADY BRITOMART: Is this a moment to get on my nerves, Charles, with your outrageous expressions?

LOMAX: But this is something out of the ordinary, really—

MORRISON [*at the door*]: The—er—Mr Undershaft. [*He retreats in confusion.*]

> ANDREW UNDERSHAFT *comes in. All rise.* LADY BRITOMART *meets him in the middle of the room behind the settee.*
>
> ANDREW *is, on the surface, a stoutish, easygoing elderly man, with kindly patient manners, and an engaging simplicity of character. But he has a watchful, deliberate, waiting, listening face, and formidable reserves of power, both bodily and mental, in his capacious chest and long head. His gentleness is partly that of a strong man who has learnt by experience that his natural grip hurts ordinary people unless he handles them very carefully, and partly the mellowness of age and success. He is also a little shy in his present very delicate situation.*

LADY BRITOMART: Good evening, Andrew.

UNDERSHAFT: How d'ye do, my dear.

LADY BRITOMART: You look a good deal older.

UNDERSHAFT [*apologetically*]: I a m somewhat older. [*Taking her hand with a touch of courtship.*] Time has stood still with you.

LADY BRITOMART [*throwing away his hand*]: Rubbish! This is your family.

UNDERSHAFT [*surprised*]: Is it so large? I am sorry to say my memory is failing very badly in some things. [*He offers his hand with paternal kindness to* LOMAX.]

LOMAX [*jerkily shaking his hand*]: Ahdedoo.

UNDERSHAFT: I can see you are my eldest. I am very glad to meet you again, my boy.

LOMAX [*remonstrating*]: No, but look here dont you know—[*Overcome.*] Oh I say!

LADY BRITOMART [*recovering from momentary speechlessness*]: Andrew: do you mean to say that you dont remember how many children you have?

UNDERSHAFT: Well, I am afraid I— They have grown so much—er. Am I making any ridiculous mistake? I may as well confess: I recollect only one son. But so many things have happened since, of course—er—

LADY BRITOMART [*decisively*]: Andrew: you are talking nonsense. Of course you have only one son.

UNDERSHAFT: Perhaps you will be good enough to introduce me, my dear.

LADY BRITOMART: That is Charles Lomax, who is engaged to Sarah.

UNDERSHAFT: My dear sir, I beg your pardon.

LOMAX: Notatall. Delighted, I assure you.

LADY BRITOMART: This is Stephen.

UNDERSHAFT [*bowing*]: Happy to make your acquaintance, Mr Stephen. Then [*going to* CUSINS] y o u must be my son. [*Taking* CUSINS' *hand in his.*] How are you, my young friend? [*To* LADY BRITOMART.] He is very like you, my love.

CUSINS: You flatter me, Mr Undershaft. My name is Cusins: engaged to Barbara. [*Very explicitly.*] That is Major Barbara Undershaft, of the Salvation Army. That is Sarah, your second daughter. This is Stephen Undershaft, your son.

UNDERSHAFT: My dear Stephen, I b e g your pardon.

STEPHEN: Not at all.

UNDERSHAFT: Mr Cusins: I am much indebted to you for explaining so precisely. [*Turning to* SARAH.] Barbara, my dear—

SARAH [*prompting him*]: Sarah.

UNDERSHAFT: Sarah, of course. [*They shake hands. He goes over to* BARBARA.] Barbara—I am right this time, I hope?

BARBARA: Quite right. [*They shake hands.*]

LADY BRITOMART [*resuming command*]: Sit down, all of you. Sit down, Andrew. [*She comes forward and sits on the settee.* CUSINS *also brings his chair forward on her left.* BARBARA *and* STEPHEN *resume their seats.* LOMAX *gives his chair to* SARAH *and goes for another.*]

UNDERSHAFT: Thank you, my love.

LOMAX [*conversationally, as he brings a chair forward between the writing table and the settee, and offers it to* UNDERSHAFT]: Takes you some time to find out exactly where you are, dont it?

UNDERSHAFT [*accepting the chair, but remaining standing*]: That is not what embarrasses me, Mr Lomax. My difficulty is that if I play the part of a father, I shall produce the effect of an intrusive stranger; and if I play the part of a discreet stranger, I may appear a callous father.

LADY BRITOMART: There is no need for you to play any part at all, Andrew. You had much better be sincere and natural.

UNDERSHAFT [*submissively*]: Yes, my dear: I daresay that will be best. [*He sits down comfortably.*] Well, here I am. Now what can I do for you all?

LADY BRITOMART: You need not do anything, Andrew. You are one of the family. You can sit with us and enjoy yourself.

> *A painfully conscious pause.* BARBARA *makes a face at* LOMAX, *whose too long suppressed mirth immediately explodes in agonized neighings.*

LADY BRITOMART [*outraged*]: Charles Lomax: if you can behave yourself, behave yourself. If not, leave the room.

LOMAX: I'm awfully sorry, Lady Brit; but really you know, upon my soul! [*He sits on the settee between* LADY BRITOMART *and* UNDERSHAFT, *quite overcome.*]

BARBARA: Why dont you laugh if you want to, Cholly? It's good for your inside.

LADY BRITOMART: Barbara: you have had the education of a lady. Please let your father see that; and dont talk like a street girl.

UNDERSHAFT: Never mind me, my dear. As you know, I am not a gentleman; and I was never educated.

LOMAX [*encouragingly*]: Nobody'd know it, I assure you. You look all right, you know.

CUSINS: Let me advise you to study Greek, Mr Undershaft. Greek scholars are privileged men. Few of them know Greek; and none of them know anything else; but their position is unchallengeable. Other languages are the qualifications of waiters and commercial travellers: Greek is to a man of position what the hallmark is to silver.

BARBARA: Dolly: dont be insincere. Cholly: fetch your concertina and play something for us.

LOMAX [*jumps up eagerly, but checks himself to remark doubtfully to* UNDERSHAFT]: Perhaps that sort of thing isnt in your line, eh?

UNDERSHAFT: I am particularly fond of music.

LOMAX [*delighted*]: Are you? Then I'll get it. [*He goes upstairs for the instrument.*]

UNDERSHAFT: Do you play, Barbara?

BARBARA: Only the tambourine. But Cholly's teaching me the concertina.

UNDERSHAFT: Is Cholly also a member of the Salvation Army?

BARBARA: No: he says it's bad form to be a dissenter. But I dont despair of Cholly. I made him come yesterday to a meeting at the dock gates, and take the collection in his hat.

UNDERSHAFT [*looks whimsically at his wife*]:!!

LADY BRITOMART: It is not my doing, Andrew. Barbara is old enough to take her own way. She has no father to advise her.

BARBARA: Oh yes she has. There are no orphans in the Salvation Army.

UNDERSHAFT: Your father there has a great many children and plenty of experience, eh?

BARBARA [*looking at him with quick interest and nodding*]: Just so. How did y o u come to understand that? [LOMAX *is heard at the door trying the concertina.*]

LADY BRITOMART: Come in, Charles. Play us something at once.

LOMAX: Righto! [*He sits down in his former place, and preludes.*]

UNDERSHAFT: One moment, Mr Lomax. I am rather interested in the Salvation Army. Its motto might be my own: Blood and Fire.

LOMAX [*shocked*]: But not your sort of blood and fire, you know.

UNDERSHAFT: My sort of blood cleanses: my sort of fire purifies.

BARBARA: So do ours. Come down tomorrow to my shelter—the West Ham shelter—and see what we're doing. We're going to march to a great meeting in the Assembly Hall at Mile End. Come and see the shelter and then march with us: it will do you a lot of good. Can you play anything?

UNDERSHAFT: In my youth I earned pennies, and even shillings occasionally, in the streets and in public house parlors by my natural talent for step-dancing. Later on, I became a member of the Undershaft orchestral society, and performed passably on the tenor trombone.

LOMAX [*scandalized—putting down the concertina*]: Oh I say!

BARBARA: Many a sinner has played himself into heaven on the trombone, thanks to the Army.

LOMAX [*to* BARBARA, *still rather shocked*]: Yes; but what about the cannon business, dont you know? [*To* UNDERSHAFT.] Getting into heaven is not exactly in your line, is it?

LADY BRITOMART: Charles!!!

LOMAX: Well; but it stands to reason, dont it? The cannon business may be necessary and all that: we cant get on without cannons; but it isnt right, you know. On the other hand, there may be a certain amount of tosh about the Salvation Army—I belong to the Established Church myself—but still you cant deny that it's religion; and you cant go against religion, can you? At least unless youre downright immoral, dont you know.

UNDERSHAFT: You hardly appreciate my position, Mr Lomax—

LOMAX [*hastily*]: I'm not saying anything against you personally—

UNDERSHAFT: Quite so, quite so. But consider for a moment. Here I am, a profiteer in mutilation and murder. I find myself in a specially amiable humor just now because, this morning, down at the foundry, we blew twenty-seven dummy soldiers into fragments with a gun which formerly destroyed only thirteen.

LOMAX [*leniently*]: Well, the more destructive war becomes, the sooner it will be abolished, eh?

UNDERSHAFT: Not at all. The more destructive war becomes the more fascinating we find it. No, Mr Lomax: I am obliged to you for making the usual excuse for my trade; but I am not ashamed of it. I am not one of those men who keep their morals and their business in water-tight compartments. All the spare money my trade rivals spend on hospitals, cathedrals, and other receptacles for conscience money, I devote to experiments and researches in improved methods of destroying life and property. I have always done so; and I always shall. Therefore your Christmas card moralities of peace on earth and good-will among men are of no use to me. Your Christianity, which enjoins you to resist not evil, and to turn the other cheek, would make me a bankrupt. M y morality— m y religion—must have a place for cannons and torpedoes in it.

STEPHEN [coldly—almost sullenly]: You speak as if there were half a dozen moralities and religions to choose from, instead of one true morality and one true religion.

UNDERSHAFT: For me there is only one true morality; but it might not fit you, as you do not manufacture aerial battleships. There is only one true morality for every man; but every man has not the same true morality.

LOMAX [overtaxed]: Would you mind saying that again? I didnt quite follow it.

CUSINS: It's quite simple. As Euripides says, one man's meat is another man's poison morally as well as physically.

UNDERSHAFT: Precisely.

LOMAX: Oh, t h a t! Yes, yes, yes. True. True.

STEPHEN: In other words, some men are honest and some are scoundrels.

BARBARA: Bosh! There are no scoundrels.

UNDERSHAFT: Indeed? Are there any good men?

BARBARA: No. Not one. There are neither good men nor scoundrels: there are just children of one Father; and the sooner they stop calling one another names the better. You neednt talk to me: I know them. Ive had scores of them through my hands: scoundrels, criminals, infidels, philanthropists, missionaries, county councillors, all sorts. Theyre all just the same sort of sinner; and theres the same salvation ready for them all.

UNDERSHAFT: May I ask have you ever saved a maker of cannons?

BARBARA: No. Will you let me try?

UNDERSHAFT: Well, I will make a bargain with you. If I go to see you tomorrow in your Salvation Shelter, will you come the day after to see me in my cannon works?

BARBARA: Take care. It may end in your giving up the cannons for the sake of the Salvation Army.

UNDERSHAFT: Are you sure it will not end in your giving up the Salvation Army for the sake of the cannons?

BARBARA: I will take my chance of that.

UNDERSHAFT: And I will take my chance of the other. [They shake hands on it.] Where is your shelter?

BARBARA: In West Ham. At the sign of the cross. Ask anybody in Canning Town. Where are your works?

UNDERSHAFT: In Perivale St Andrews. At the sign of the sword. Ask anybody in Europe.

LOMAX: Hadnt I better play something?

BARBARA: Yes. Give us Onward, Christian Soldiers.

LOMAX: Well, thats rather a strong order to begin with, dont you know. Suppose I sing Thourt passing hence, my brother. It's much the same tune.

BARBARA: It's too melancholy. You get saved, Cholly; and youll pass hence, my brother, without making such a fuss about it.

LADY BRITOMART: Really, Barbara, you go on as if religion were a pleasant subject. Do have some sense of propriety.

UNDERSHAFT: I do not find it an unpleasant subject, my dear. It is the only one that capable people really care for.

LADY BRITOMART [*looking at her watch*]: Well, if you are determined to have it, I insist on having it in a proper and respectable way. Charles: ring for prayers.

> *General amazement.* STEPHEN *rises in dismay.*

LOMAX [*rising*]: Oh I say!

UNDERSHAFT [*rising*]: I am afraid I must be going.

LADY BRITOMART: You cannot go now, Andrew: it would be most improper. Sit down. What will the servants think?

UNDERSHAFT: My dear: I have conscientious scruples. May I suggest a compromise? If Barbara will conduct a little service in the drawing room, with Mr Lomax as organist, I will attend it willingly. I will even take part, if a trombone can be procured.

LADY BRITOMART: Dont mock, Andrew.

UNDERSHAFT [*shocked—to* BARBARA]: You dont think I am mocking, my love, I hope.

BARBARA: No, of course not; and it wouldnt matter if you were: half the Army came to their first meeting for a lark. [*Rising.*] Come along. [*She throws her arm round her father and sweeps him out, calling to the others from the threshold.*] Come, Dolly. Come, Cholly.

> CUSINS *rises.*

LADY BRITOMART: I will not be disobeyed by everybody. Adolphus: sit down. [*He does not.*] Charles: you may go. You are not fit for prayers: you cannot keep your countenance.

LOMAX: Oh I say! [*He goes out.*]

LADY BRITOMART [*continuing*]: But you, Adolphus, can behave yourself if you choose to. I insist on your staying.

CUSINS: My dear Lady Brit: there are things in the family prayer book that I couldnt bear to hear you say.

LADY BRITOMART: What things, pray?

CUSINS: Well, you would have to say before all the servants that we have done things we ought not to have done, and left undone things we ought to have done, and that there is no health in us. I cannot bear to hear you doing yourself such an injustice, and Barbara such an injustice. As for myself, I flatly deny it: I have done my best. I shouldnt dare to marry Barbara—I couldnt look you in the face—if it were true. So I must go to the drawing room.

LADY BRITOMART [*offended*]: Well, go. [*He starts for the door.*] And remember this, Adolphus: [*He turns to listen.*] I have a very strong suspicion that you went to the Salvation Army to worship Barbara and nothing else. And I quite appreciate the very clever way in which you systematically humbug me. I have found you out. Take care Barbara doesnt. Thats all.

CUSINS [*with unruffled sweetness*]: Dont tell on me. [*He steals out.*]

LADY BRITOMART: Sarah: if you want to go, go. Anything's better than to sit there as if you wished you were a thousand miles away.

SARAH [*languidly*]: Very well, mamma. [*She goes.*]

> LADY BRITOMART, *with a sudden flounce, gives way to a little gust of tears.*

STEPHEN [*going to her*]: Mother: whats the matter?

LADY BRITOMART [*swishing away her tears with a handkerchief*]: Nothing. Foolishness. You can go with him, too, if you like, and leave me with the servants.

STEPHEN: Oh, you mustnt think that, mother. I—I dont like him.

LADY BRITOMART: The others do. That is the injustice of a woman's lot. A woman has to bring up her children; and that means to restrain them, to deny them things they want, to set them tasks, to punish them when they do wrong, to do all the unpleasant things. And then the father, who has nothing to do but pet them and spoil them, comes in when all her work is done and steals their affection from her.

STEPHEN: He has not stolen our affection from you. It is only curiosity.

LADY BRITOMART [*violently*]: I wont be consoled, Stephen. There is nothing the matter with me. [*She rises and goes towards the door.*]

STEPHEN: Where are you going, mother?

LADY BRITOMART: To the drawing room, of course. [*She goes out. Onward, Christian Soldiers, on the concertina, with tambourine accompaniment, is heard when the door opens.*] Are you coming, Stephen?

STEPHEN: No. Certainly not. [*She goes. He sits down on the settee, with compressed lips and an expression of strong dislike.*]

ACT TWO

> *The yard of the West Ham shelter of the Salvation Army is a cold place on a January morning. The building itself, an old warehouse, is newly whitewashed. Its gabled end projects into the yard in the middle, with a door on the ground floor, and another in the loft above it without any balcony or ladder, but with a pulley rigged over it for hoisting sacks. Those who come from this central gable end into the yard have the gateway leading to the street on their left, with*

a stone horse-trough just beyond it, and, on the right, a penthouse shielding a table from the weather. There are forms at the table; and on them are seated a man and a woman, both much down on their luck, finishing a meal of bread (one thick slice each, with margarine and golden syrup) and diluted milk.

The man, a workman out of employment, is young, agile, a talker, a poser, sharp enough to be capable of anything in reason except honesty or altruistic considerations of any kind. The woman is a commonplace old bundle of poverty and hard-worn humanity. She looks sixty and probably is forty-five. If they were rich people, gloved and muffed and well wrapped up in furs and overcoats, they would be numbed and miserable; for it is a grindingly cold raw January day; and a glance at the background of grimy warehouses and leaden sky visible over the whitewashed walls of the yard would drive any idle rich person straight to the Mediterranean. But these two, being no more troubled with visions of the Mediterranean than of the moon, and being compelled to keep more of their clothes in the pawnshop, and less on their persons, in winter than in summer, are not depressed by the cold: rather are they stung into vivacity, to which their meal has just now given an almost jolly turn. The man takes a pull at his mug, and then gets up and moves about the yard with his hands deep in his pockets, occasionally breaking into a stepdance.

THE WOMAN: Feel better arter your meal, sir?

THE MAN: No. Call that a meal! Good enough for you, praps; but wot is it to me, an intelligent workin man.

THE WOMAN: Workin man! Wot are you?

THE MAN: Painter.

THE WOMAN [*sceptically*]: Yus, I dessay.

THE MAN: Yus, you dessay! I know. Every loafer that cant do nothink calls isself a painter. Well, I'm a real painter: grainer,[2] finisher, thirty-eight bob a week when I can get it.

THE WOMAN: Then why dont you go and get it?

THE MAN: I'll tell you why. Fust: I'm intelligent—fffff! it's rotten cold here [*he dances a step or two*]—yes: intelligent beyond the station o life into which it has pleased the capitalists to call me; and they dont like a man that sees through em. Second, an intelligent bein needs a doo share of appiness; so I drink somethink cruel when I get the chawnce. Third, I stand by my class and do as little as I can so's to leave arf the job for me fellow workers. Fourth, I'm fly[3] enough to know wots inside the law and wots outside it; and inside it I do as the capitalists do: pinch wot I can lay me ands on. In a proper state of society I am sober, industrious and honest: in Rome, so to speak, I do as the Romans do. Wots the consequence? When trade is bad—and it's rotten bad just now—and the employers az to sack arf their men, they generally start on me.

2. A person who paints imitation grain on wood or marble.
3. "Fly" means smart or knowing.

THE WOMAN: Whats your name?

THE MAN: Price. Bronterre O'Brien Price. Usually called Snobby Price, for short.

THE WOMAN: Snobby's a carpenter, aint it? You said you was a painter.

PRICE: Not that kind of snob, but the genteel sort. I'm too uppish, owing to my intelligence, and my father being a Chartist and a reading, thinking man: a stationer, too. I'm none of your common hewers of wood and drawers of water; and dont you forget it. [*He returns to his seat at the table, and takes up his mug.*] Wots y o u r name?

THE WOMAN: Rummy Mitchens, sir.

PRICE [*quaffing the remains of his milk to her*]: Your elth, Miss Mitchens.

RUMMY [*correcting him*]: Missis Mitchens.

PRICE: Wot! Oh Rummy, Rummy! Respectable married woman, Rummy, gittin rescued by the Salvation Army by pretendin to be a bad un. Same old game!

RUMMY: What am I to do? I cant starve. Them Salvation lasses is dear good girls; but the better you are, the worse they likes to think you were before they rescued you. Why shouldnt they av a bit o credit, poor loves? theyre worn to rags by their work. And where would they get the money to rescue us if we was to let on we're no worse than other people? You know what ladies and gentlemen are.

PRICE: Thievin swine! Wish I ad their job, Rummy, all the same. Wot does Rummy stand for? Pet name praps?

RUMMY: Short for Romola.

PRICE: For wot!?

RUMMY: Romola. It was out of a new book. Somebody me mother wanted me to grow up like.

PRICE: We're companions in misfortune, Rummy. Both on us got names that nobody cawnt pronounce. Consequently I'm Snobby and youre Rummy because Bill and Sally wasnt good enough for our parents. Such is life!

RUMMY: Who saved you, Mr Price? Was it Major Barbara?

PRICE: No: I come here on my own. I'm goin to be Bronterre O'Brien Price, the converted painter. I know wot they like. I'll tell em how I blasphemed and gambled and wopped my poor old mother—

RUMMY [*shocked*]: Used you to beat your mother?

PRICE: Not likely. She used to beat me. No matter: you come and listen to the converted painter, and youll hear how she was a pious woman that taught me me prayers at er knee, an how I used to come home drunk and drag her out o bed be er snow white airs, an lam into er with the poker.

RUMMY: That whats so unfair to us women. Your confessions is just as big lies as ours: you dont tell what you really done no more than us; but you men can tell your lies right out at the meetins and be made much of for it; while the sort o confessions we az to make az to be wispered to one lady at a time. It aint right, spite of all their piety.

PRICE: Right! Do you spose the Army'd be allowed if it went and did right? Not much. It combs our air and makes us good little blokes to be robbed and put upon. But I'll play the game as good as any of em. I'll see somebody struck by lightnin, or hear a voice sayin "Snobby Price: where will you spend eternity?" I'll av a time of it, I tell you.

RUMMY: You wont be let drink, though.

PRICE: I'll take it out in gorspellin, then. I dont want to drink if I can get fun enough any other way.

> JENNY HILL, *a pale, overwrought, pretty Salvation lass of 18, comes in through the yard gate, leading* PETER SHIRLEY, *a half hardened, half worn-out elderly man, weak with hunger.*

JENNY [*supporting him*]: Come! pluck up. I'll get you something to eat. Youll be all right then.

PRICE [*rising and hurrying officiously to take the old man off* JENNY's *hands*]: Poor old man! Cheer up, brother: youll find rest and peace and appiness ere. Hurry up with the food, miss: e's fair done. [JENNY *hurries into the shelter.*] Ere, buck up, daddy! shes fetchin y'a thick slice o breadn treacle, and a mug o skyblue.[4] [*He seats him at the corner of the table.*]

RUMMY [*gaily*]: Keep up your old art! Never say die!

SHIRLEY: I'm not an old man. I'm only 46. I'm as good as ever I was. The grey patch come in my hair before I was thirty. All it wants is three pennorth o hair dye: am I to be turned on the streets to starve for it? Holy God! Ive worked ten to twelve hours a day since I was thirteen, and paid my way all through; and now am I to be thrown into the gutter and my job given to a young man that can do it no better than me because Ive black hair that goes white at the first change?

PRICE [*cheerfully*]: No good jawrin about it. Youre ony a jumped-up, jerked-off, orspittle-turned-out incurable of an ole workin man: who cares about you? Eh? Make the thievin swine give you a meal: theyve stole many a one from you. Get a bit o your own back. [JENNY *returns with the usual meal.*] There you are, brother. Awsk a blessin an tuck that into you.

SHIRLEY [*looking at it ravenously but not touching it, and crying like a child*]: I never took anything before.

JENNY [*petting him*]: Come, come! the Lord sends it to you: he wasnt above taking bread from his friends; and why should you be? Besides, when we find you a job you can pay us for it if you like.

SHIRLEY [*eagerly*]: Yes, yes: thats true. I can pay you back: its only a loan. [*Shivering.*] Oh Lord! oh Lord! [*He turns to the table and attacks the meal ravenously.*]

JENNY: Well, Rummy, are you more comfortable now?

RUMMY: God bless you, lovey! youve fed my body and saved my soul, havnt you? [JENNY, *touched, kisses her.*] Sit down and rest a bit: you must be ready to drop.

JENNY: Ive been going hard since morning. But theres more work than we can do. I mustnt stop.

RUMMY: Try a prayer for just two minutes. Youll work all the better after.

4. Cheap, watery milk.

JENNY [*her eyes lighting up*]: Oh isnt it wonderful how a few minutes prayer revives you! I was quite lightheaded at twelve o'clock, I was so tired; but Major Barbara just sent me to pray for five minutes; and I was able to go on as if I had only just begun. [*To* PRICE.] Did you have a piece of bread?

PRICE [*with unction*]: Yes, miss; but Ive got the piece that I value more; and thats the peace that passeth hall hannerstennin.

RUMMY [*fervently*]: Glory Hallelujah!

> BILL WALKER, *a rough customer of about 25, appears at the yard gate and looks malevolently at* JENNY.

JENNY: That makes me so happy. When you say that, I feel wicked for loitering here. I must get to work again.

> *She is hurrying to the shelter, when the new-comer moves quickly up to the door and intercepts her. His manner is so threatening that she retreats as he comes at her truculently, driving her down the yard.*

BILL: Aw knaow you. Youre the one that took awy maw girl. Youre the one that set er agen me. Well, I'm gowin to ev er aht. Not that Aw care a carse for er or you: see? Bat Aw'll let er knaow; and Aw'll let y o u knaow. Aw'm gowing to give her a doin thatll teach er to cat awy from me. Nah in wiv you and tell er to cam aht afore Aw cam in and kick er aht. Tell er Bill Walker wants er. She'll knaow wot thet means; and if she keeps me witin itll be worse. You stop to jawr bect at me; and Aw'll stawt on you: d'ye eah? Theres your wy. In you gow. [*He takes her by the arm and slings her towards the door of the shelter. She falls on her hand and knee.* RUMMY *helps her up again.*]

PRICE [*rising, and venturing irresolutely towards* BILL]: Easy there, mate. She aint doin you no arm.

BILL: Oo are you callin mite? [*Standing over him threateningly.*] Youre gowin to stend ap for er, aw yer? Put ap your ends.

RUMMY [*running indignantly to him to scold him*]: Oh, you great brute—[*He instantly swings his left hand back against her face. She screams and reels back to the trough, where she sits down, covering her bruised face with her hands and rocking herself and moaning with pain.*]

JENNY [*going to her*]: Oh, God forgive you! How could you strike an old woman like that?

BILL [*seizing her by the hair so violently that she also screams, and tearing her away from the old woman*]: You Gawd forgimme again an Aw'll Gawd forgive you one on the jawr thetll stop you pryin for a week. [*Holding her and turning fiercely on* PRICE.] Ev you ennything to sy agen it?

PRICE [*intimidated*]: No, matey: she aint anything to do with me.

BILL: Good job for you! Aw'd pat two meals into you and fawt you with one finger arter, you stawved cur. [*To* JENNY.] Nah are you gowin to fetch aht Mog Ebbijem, or em Aw to knock your fice off you and fetch her meself?

JENNY [*writhing in his grasp*]: Oh please someone go in and tell Major Barbara—[*She screams again as he wrenches her head down; and* PRICE *and* RUMMY *flee into the shelter.*]

BILL: You want to gow in and tell your Mijor of me, do you?

JENNY: Oh please dont drag my hair. Let me go.

BILL: Do you or downt you? [*She stifles a scream.*] Yus or nao?

JENNY: God give me strength—

BILL [*striking her with his fist in the face*]: Gow an shaow her thet, and tell her if she wants one lawk it to cam and interfere with me. [JENNY, *crying with pain, goes into the shed. He goes to the form and addresses the old man.*] Eah: finish your mess; and git aht o maw wy.

SHIRLEY [*springing up and facing him fiercely, with the mug in his hand*]: You take a liberty with me, and I'll smash you over the face with the mug and cut your eye out. Aint you satisfied—young whelps like you—with takin the bread out o the mouths of your elders that have brought you up and slaved for you, but you must come shovin and cheekin and bullyin in here, where the bread o charity is sickenin in our stummicks?

BILL [*contemptuously, but backing a little*]: Wot good are you, you aold palsy mag? Wot good are you?

SHIRLEY: As good as you and better. I'll do a day's work agen you or any fat young soaker of your age. Go and take my job at Horrockses, where I worked for ten year. They want young men there: they cant afford to keep men over forty-five. Theyre very sorry—give you a character and happy to help you to get anything suited to your years—sure a steady man wont be long out of a job. Well, let em try y o u. Theyll find the differ. What do y o u know? Not as much as how to beeyave yourself—laying your dirty fist across the mouth of a respectable woman!

BILL: Downt provowk me to ly it acrost yours: d'ye eah?

SHIRLEY [*with blighting contempt*]: Yes: you like an old man to hit, dont you, when youve finished with the women. I aint seen you hit a young one yet.

BILL [*stung*]: You loy, you aold soupkitchener, you. There was a yang menn eah. Did Aw offer to itt him or did Aw not?

SHIRLEY: Was he starvin or was he not? Was he a man or only a crosseyed thief an a loafer? Would you hit my sin-in-law's brother?

BILL: Oo's ee?

SHIRLEY: Todger Fairmile o Balls Pond. Him that won £20 off the Japanese wrastler at the music hall by standin out 17 minutes 4 seconds agen him.

BILL [*sullenly*]: Aw'm nao music awl wrastler. Ken he box?

SHIRLEY: Yes: an you cant.

BILL: Wot! Aw cawnt, cawnt Aw? Wots thet you sy? [*Threatening him.*]

SHIRLEY [*not budging an inch*]: Will you box Todger Fairmile if I put him on to you? Say the word.

BILL [*subsiding with a slouch*]: Aw'll stend ap to enny menn alawv, if he was ten Todger Fairmawls. But Aw dont set ap to be a perfeshnal.

SHIRLEY [*looking down on him with unfathomable disdain*]: Y o u box! Slap an old woman with the back o your hand! You hadnt even the sense to hit her where a magistrate couldnt see the mark of it, you silly young lump of conceit and ignorance. Hit a girl in the jaw and only make her cry! If Todger Fairmile'd done it, she wouldnt a got up inside o ten minutes, no more than you would if he got on to you. Yah! I'd set about you myself if I had a week's feeding in me instead o two months' starvation. [*He turns his back on him and sits down moodily at the table.*]

BILL [*following him and stooping over him to drive the taunt in*]: You loy! youve the bread and treacle in you that you cam eah to beg.

SHIRLEY [*bursting into tears*]: Oh God! it's true: I'm only an old pauper on the scrap heap. [*Furiously.*] But youll come to it yourself; and then youll know. Youll come to it sooner than a teetotaller like me, fillin yourself with gin at this hour o the mornin!

BILL: Aw'm nao gin drinker, you oald lawr; bat wen Aw want to give my girl a bloomin good awdin Aw lawk to ev a bit o devil in me: see? An eah Aw emm, talkin to a rotten aold blawter like you sted o givin her wot for. [*Working himself into a rage.*] Aw'm gowin in there to fetch her aht. [*He makes vengefully for the shelter door.*]

SHIRLEY: Youre goin to the station on a stretcher, more likely; and theyll take the gin and the devil out of you there when they get you inside. You mind what youre about: the major here is the Earl o Stevenage's grand-daughter.

BILL [*checked*]: Garn![5]

SHIRLEY: Youll see.

BILL [*his resolution oozing*]: Well, Aw aint dan nathin to er.

SHIRLEY: Spose she said you did! who'd believe you?

BILL [*very uneasy, skulking back to the corner of the penthouse*]: Gawd! theres no jastice in this cantry. To think wot them people can do! Aw'm as good as er.

SHIRLEY: Tell her so. It's just what a fool like you would do.

> BARBARA, *brisk and businesslike, comes from the shelter with a note book, and addresses herself to* SHIRLEY. BILL, *cowed, sits down in the corner on a form, and turns his back on them.*

BARBARA: Good morning.

SHIRLEY [*standing up and taking off his hat*]: Good morning, miss.

BARBARA: Sit down: make yourself at home. [*He hesitates; but she puts a friendly hand on his shoulder and makes him obey.*] Now then! since youve made friends with us, we want to know all about you. Names and addresses and trades.

SHIRLEY: Peter Shirley. Fitter. Chucked out two months ago because I was too old.

BARBARA [*not at all surprised*]: Youd pass still. Why didnt you dye your hair?

---

5. "Go on" or "get away."

SHIRLEY: I did. Me age come out at a coroner's inquest on me daughter.

BARBARA: Steady?

SHIRLEY: Teetotaller. Never out of a job before. Good worker. And sent to the knackers like an old horse!

BARBARA: No matter: if you did your part God will do his.

SHIRLEY [*suddenly stubborn*]: My religion's no concern of anybody but myself.

BARBARA [*guessing*]: I know. Secularist?

SHIRLEY [*hotly*]: Did I offer to deny it?

BARBARA: Why should you? My own father's a Secularist, I think. Our Father— yours and mine—fulfils himself in many ways; and I daresay he knew what he was about when he made a Secularist of you. So buck up, Peter! we can always find a job for a steady man like you. [SHIRLEY *disarmed and a little bewildered, touches his hat. She turns from him to* BILL.] Whats y o u r name?

BILL [*insolently*]: Wots thet to you?

BARBARA [*calmly making a note*]: Afraid to give his name. Any trade?

BILL: Oo's afride to give is nime? [*Doggedly, with a sense of heroically defying the House of Lords in the person of Lord Stevenage.*] If you want to bring a chawge agen me, bring it. [*She waits, unruffled.*] Moy nime's Bill Walker.

BARBARA [*as if the name were familiar: trying to remember how*]: Bill Walker? [*Recollecting.*] Oh, I know: youre the man that Jenny Hill was praying for inside just now. [*She enters his name in her note book.*]

BILL: Oo's Jenny Ill? And wot call as she to pry for me?

BARBARA: I dont know. Perhaps it was you that cut her lip.

BILL [*defiantly*]: Yus, it w a s me that cat her lip. Aw aint afride o y o u.

BARBARA: How could you be, since youre not afraid of God? Youre a brave man, Mr Walker. It takes some pluck to do o u r work here; but none of us dare lift our hand against a girl like that, for fear of her father in heaven.

BILL [*sullenly*]: I want nan o your kentin jawr. I spowse you think Aw cam eah to beg from you, like this demmiged lot eah. Not me. Aw downt want your bread and scripe and ketlep.[6] Aw dont blieve in your Gawd, no more than you do yourself.

BARBARA [*sunnily apologetic and ladylike, as on a new footing with him*]: Oh, I beg your pardon for putting your name down, Mr Walker. I didnt understand. I'll strike it out.

BILL [*taking this as a slight, and deeply wounded by it*]: Eah! you let maw nime alown. Aint it good enaff to be in your book?

BARBARA [*considering*]: Well, you see, theres no use putting down your name unless I can do something for you, is there? Whats your trade?

BILL [*still smarting*]: Thets nao concern o yours.

BARBARA: Just so. [*Very businesslike.*] I'll put you down as [*writing*] the man who—struck—poor little Jenny Hill—in the mouth.

BILL [*rising threateningly*]: See eah. Awve ed enaff o this.

6. "Scripe" is a cheap, butterlike spread. "Ketlep" is a weak tea.

BARBARA [*quite sunny and fearless*]: What did you come to us for?

BILL: Aw cam for maw gel, see? Aw cam to tike her aht o this and to brike er jawr for er.

BARBARA [*complacently*]: You see I was right about your trade. [BILL, *on the point of retorting furiously, finds himself, to his great shame and terror, in danger of crying instead. He sits down again suddenly.*] Whats her name?

BILL [*dogged*]: Er nime's Mog Ebbijem: thets wot her nime is.

BARBARA: Mog Habbijam! Oh, she's gone to Canning Town, to our barracks there.

BILL [*fortified by his resentment of Mog's perfidy*]: Is she? [*Vindictively.*] Then Aw'm gowin to Kennintahn arter her. [*He crosses to the gate; hesitates; finally comes back at* BARBARA.] Are you loyin to me to git shat o me?

BARBARA: I dont want to get shut of you. I want to keep you here and save your soul. Youd better stay: youre going to have a bad time today, Bill.

BILL: Oo's gowin to give it to me? Y o u, preps?

BARBARA: Someone you dont believe in. But youll be glad afterwards.

BILL [*slinking off*]: Aw'll gow to Kennintahn to be aht o reach o your tangue. [*Suddenly turning on her with intense malice.*] And if Aw downt fawnd Mog there, Aw'll cam beck and do two years for you, selp me Gawd if Aw downt!

BARBARA [*a shade kindlier, if possible*]: It's no use, Bill. She's got another bloke.

BILL: Wot!

BARBARA: One of her own converts. He fell in love with her when he saw her with her soul saved, and her face clean, and her hair washed.

BILL [*surprised*]: Wottud she wash it for, the carroty slat? It's red.

BARBARA: It's quite lovely now, because she wears a new look in her eyes with it. It's a pity youre too late. The new bloke has put your nose out of joint, Bill.

BILL: Aw'll put his nowse aht o joint for him. Not that Aw care a carse for er, mawnd thet. But Aw'll teach her to drop me as if Aw was dirt. And Aw'll teach him to meddle with maw judy. Wots iz bleedin nime?

BARBARA: Sergeant Todger Fairmile.

SHIRLEY [*rising with grim joy*]: I'll go with him, miss. I want to see them two meet. I'll take him to the infirmary when it's over.

BILL [*to* SHIRLEY, *with undissembled misgiving*]: Is thet im you was speakin on?

SHIRLEY: Thats him.

BILL: Im that wrastled in the music awl?

SHIRLEY: The competitions at the National Sportin Club was worth nigh a hundred a year to him. He's gev em up now for religion; so he's a bit fresh for want of the exercise he was accustomed to. He'll be glad to see you. Come along.

BILL: Wots is wight?

SHIRLEY: Thirteen four.[7] [BILL's *last hope expires.*]

---

7. English equivalent of 186 pounds.

BARBARA: Go and talk to him, Bill. He'll convert you.

SHIRLEY: He'll convert your head into a mashed potato.

BILL [*sullenly*]: Aw aint afride of im. Aw aint afride of ennybody. Bat e can lick me. She's dan me. [*He sits down moodily on the edge of the horse-trough.*]

SHIRLEY: You aint goin. I thought not. [*He resumes his seat.*]

BARBARA [*calling*]: Jenny!

JENNY [*appearing at the shelter door with a plaster on the corner of her mouth*]: Yes, Major.

BARBARA: Send Rummy Mitchens out to clear away here.

JENNY: I think she's afraid.

BARBARA [*her resemblance to her mother flashing out for a moment*]: Nonsense! she must do as she's told.

JENNY [*calling into the shelter*]: Rummy: the Major says you must come.

> JENNY *comes to* BARBARA, *purposely keeping on the side next* BILL, *lest he should suppose that she shrank from him or bore malice.*

BARBARA: Poor little Jenny! Are you tired? [*Looking at the wounded cheek.*] Does it hurt?

JENNY: No: it's all right now. It was nothing.

BARBARA [*critically*]: It was as hard as he could hit, I expect. Poor Bill! You dont feel angry with him, do you?

JENNY: Oh no, no, no: indeed I dont, Major, bless his poor heart!

> BARBARA *kisses her; and she runs away merrily into the shelter.* BILL *writhes with an agonizing return of his new and alarming symptoms, but says nothing.* RUMMY MITCHENS *comes from the shelter.*

BARBARA [*going to meet* RUMMY]: Now Rummy, bustle. Take in those mugs and plates to be washed; and throw the crumbs about for the birds.

> RUMMY *takes the three plates and mugs; but* SHIRLEY *takes back his mug from her, as there is still some milk left in it.*

RUMMY: There aint any crumbs. This aint a time to waste good bread on birds.

PRICE [*appearing at the shelter door*]: Gentleman come to see the shelter, Major. Says he's your father.

BARBARA: All right. Coming. [SNOBBY *goes back into the shelter, followed by* BARBARA.]

RUMMY [*stealing across to* BILL *and addressing him in a subdued voice, but with intense conviction*]: I'd av the lor of you, you flat eared pignosed potwalloper,[8] if she'd let me. Youre no gentleman, to hit a lady in the face. [BILL, *with greater things moving in him, takes no notice.*]

SHIRLEY [*following her*]: Here! in with you and dont get yourself into more trouble by talking.

RUMMY [*with hauteur*]: I aint ad the pleasure o being introduced to you, as I can remember. [*She goes into the shelter with the plates.*]

---

8. One who owns a house and can vote.

SHIRLEY: Thats the—

BILL [*savagely*]: Downt you talk to me, d'ye eah? You lea me alown, or Aw'll do you a mischief. Aw'm not dirt under y o u r feet, ennywy.

SHIRLEY [*calmly*]: Dont you be afeerd. You aint such prime company that you need expect to be sought after. [*He is about to go into the shelter when* BARBARA *comes out, with* UNDERSHAFT *on her right.*]

BARBARA: Oh, there you are, Mr Shirley! [*Between them.*] This is my father: I told you he was a Secularist, didnt I? Perhaps youll be able to comfort one another.

UNDERSHAFT [*startled*]: A Secularist! Not the least in the world: on the contrary, a confirmed mystic.

BARBARA: Sorry, I'm sure. By the way, papa, what i s your religion? in case I have to introduce you again.

UNDERSHAFT: My religion? Well, my dear, I am a Millionaire. That is my religion.

BARBARA: Then I'm afraid you and Mr Shirley wont be able to comfort one another after all. Youre not a Millionaire, are you, Peter?

SHIRLEY: No; and proud of it.

UNDERSHAFT [*gravely*]: Poverty, my friend, is not a thing to be proud of.

SHIRLEY [*angrily*]: Who made your millions for you? Me and my like. Whats kep us poor? Keepin you rich. I wouldnt have your conscience, not for all your income.

UNDERSHAFT: I wouldnt have your income, not for all your conscience, Mr Shirley. [*He goes to the penthouse and sits down on a form.*]

BARBARA [*stopping* SHIRLEY *adroitly as he is about to retort*]: You wouldnt think he was my father, would you, Peter? Will you go into the shelter and lend the lasses a hand for a while: we're worked off our feet.

SHIRLEY [*bitterly*]: Yes: I'm in their debt for a meal, aint I?

BARBARA: Oh, not because youre in their debt, but for love of them, Peter, for love of them. [*He cannot understand, and is rather scandalized.*] There! dont stare at me. In with you; and give that conscience of yours a holiday. [*Bustling him into the shelter.*]

SHIRLEY [*as he goes in*]: Ah! it's a pity you never was trained to use your reason, miss. Youd have been a very taking lecturer on Secularism.

BARBARA *turns to her father.*

UNDERSHAFT: Never mind me, my dear. Go about your work; and let me watch it for a while.

BARBARA: All right.

UNDERSHAFT: For instance, whats the matter with that out-patient over there?

BARBARA [*looking at* BILL, *whose attitude has never changed, and whose expression of brooding wrath has deepened*]: Oh, we shall cure him in no time. Just watch. [*She goes over to* BILL *and waits. He glances up at her and casts his eyes down again, uneasy, but grimmer than ever.*] It w o u l d be nice to just stamp on Mog Habbijam's face, wouldnt it, Bill?

BILL [*starting up from the trough in consternation*]: It's a loy: Aw never said so. [*She shakes her head.*] Oo taold you wot was in moy mawnd?

BARBARA: Only your new friend.

BILL: Wot new friend?

BARBARA: The devil, Bill. When he gets round people they get miserable, just like you.

BILL [*with a heartbreaking attempt at devil-may-care cheerfulness*]: Aw aint miserable. [*He sits down again, and stretches his legs in an attempt to seem indifferent.*]

BARBARA: Well, if youre happy, why dont you look happy, as we do?

BILL [*his legs curling back in spite of him*]: Aw'm eppy enaff, Aw tell you. Woy cawnt you lea me alown? Wot ev I dan to y o u? Aw aint smashed y o u r fice, ev Aw?

BARBARA [*softly: wooing his soul*]: It's not me thats getting at you, Bill.

BILL: Oo else is it?

BARBARA: Somebody that doesn't intend you to smash women's faces, I suppose. Somebody or something that wants to make a man of you.

BILL [*blustering*]: Mike a menn o m e! Aint Aw a menn? eh? Oo sez Aw'm not a menn?

BARBARA: Theres a man in you somewhere, I suppose. But why did he let you hit poor little Jenny Hill? That wasnt very manly of him, was it?

BILL [*tormented*]: Ev dan wiv it, Aw tell you. Chack it. Aw'm sick o your Jenny Ill and er silly little fice.

BARBARA: Then why do you keep thinking about it? Why does it keep coming up against you in your mind? Youre not getting converted, are you?

BILL [*with conviction*]: Not ME. Not lawkly.

BARBARA: Thats right, Bill. Hold out against it. Put out your strength. Dont lets get you cheap. Todger Fairmile said he wrestled for three nights against his salvation harder than he ever wrestled with the Jap at the music hall. He gave in to the Jap when his arm was going to break. But he didnt give in to his salvation until his heart was going to break. Perhaps youll escape that. You havnt any heart, have you?

BILL: Wot d'ye mean? Woy aint Aw got a awt the sime as ennybody else?

BARBARA: A man with a heart wouldnt have bashed poor little Jenny's face, would he?

BILL [*almost crying*]: Ow, w i l l you lea me alown? Ev Aw ever offered to meddle with y o u, that you cam neggin and provowkin me lawk this? [*He writhes convulsively from his eyes to his toes.*]

BARBARA [*with a steady soothing hand on his arm and a gentle voice that never lets him go*]: It's your soul thats hurting you, Bill, and not me. Weve been through it all ourselves. Come with us, Bill. [*He looks wildly round.*] To brave manhood on earth and eternal glory in heaven. [*He is on the point of breaking down.*] Come. [*A drum is heard in the shelter; and* BILL, *with a gasp, escapes from the spell as* BARBARA *turns quickly.* ADOLPHUS *enters from the shelter with a big drum.*] Oh! there you are, Dolly. Let me introduce a new friend of mine, Mr Bill Walker. This is my bloke, Bill: Mr Cusins. [CUSINS *salutes with his drumstick.*]

BILL: Gowin to merry im?

BARBARA: Yes.

BILL [*fervently*]: Gawd elp im! Gaw-aw-aw-awd elp im!

BARBARA: Why? Do you think he wont be happy with me?

BILL: Awve aony ed to stend it for a mawnin: e'll ev to stand it for a lawftawm.

CUSINS: That is a frightful reflection, Mr Walker. But I cant tear myself away from her.

BILL: Well, Aw ken. [*To* BARBARA.] Eah! do you knaow where Aw'm gowin to, and wot Aw'm gowin to do?

BARBARA: Yes: youre going to heaven; and youre coming back here before the week's out to tell me so.

BILL: You loy. Aw'm gowin to Kennintahn, to spit in Todger Fairmawl's eye. Aw beshed Jenny Ill's fice; an nar Aw'll git me aown fice beshed and cam beck and shaow it to er. Ee'll itt me ardern Aw itt er. Thatll mike us square. [*To* ADOLPHUS.] Is thet fair or is it not? Youre a genlmn: you oughter knaow.

BARBARA: Two black eyes wont make one white one, Bill.

BILL: Aw didnt awst y o u. Cawnt you never keep your mahth shat? Oy awst the genlmn.

CUSINS [*reflectively*]: Yes: I think youre right, Mr Walker. Yes: I should do it. It's curious: it's exactly what an ancient Greek would have done.

BARBARA: But what good will it do?

CUSINS: Well, it will give Mr Fairmile some exercise; and it will satisfy Mr Walker's soul.

BILL: Rot! there aint nao sach a thing as a saoul. Ah kin you tell wevver Awve a saoul or not? You never seen it.

BARBARA: Ive seen it hurting you when you went against it.

BILL [*with compressed aggravation*]: If you was maw gel and took the word aht o me mahth lawk thet, Aw'd give you sathink youd feel urtin, Aw would. [*To* ADOLPHUS.] You tike maw tip, mite. Stop er jawr, or youll doy afoah your tawn. [*With intense expression.*] Wore aht: thets wot youll be: wore aht. [*He goes away through the gate.*]

CUSINS [*looking after him*]: I wonder!

BARBARA: Dolly! [*Indignant, in her mother's manner.*]

CUSINS: Yes, my dear, it's very wearing to be in love with you. If it lasts, I quite think I shall die young.

BARBARA: Should you mind?

CUSINS: Not at all. [*He is suddenly softened, and kisses her over the drum, evidently not for the first time, as people cannot kiss over a big drum without practice.* UNDERSHAFT *coughs.*]

BARBARA: It's all right, papa, weve not forgotten you. Dolly: explain the place to papa: I havnt time. [*She goes busily into the shelter.*]

UNDERSHAFT *and* ADOLPHUS *now have the yard to themselves.*
UNDERSHAFT, *seated on a form, and still keenly attentive, looks hard
at* ADOLPHUS. ADOLPHUS *looks hard at him.*

UNDERSHAFT: I fancy you guess something of what is in my mind, Mr Cusins.
[CUSINS *flourishes his drumsticks as if in the act of beating a lively rataplan,
but makes no sound.*] Exactly so. But suppose Barbara finds you out!

CUSINS: You know, I do not admit that I am imposing on Barbara. I am quite
genuinely interested in the views of the Salvation Army. The fact is, I am
a sort of collector of religions; and the curious thing is that I find I can
believe them all. By the way, have you any religion?

UNDERSHAFT: Yes.

CUSINS: Anything out of the common?

UNDERSHAFT: Only that there are two things necessary to Salvation.

CUSINS [*disappointed, but polite*]: Ah, the Church Catechism. Charles Lomax
also belongs to the Established Church.

UNDERSHAFT: The two things are—

CUSINS: Baptism and—

UNDERSHAFT: No. Money and gunpowder.

CUSINS [*surprised, but interested*]: That is the general opinion of our governing
classes. The novelty is in hearing any man confess it.

UNDERSHAFT: Just so.

CUSINS: Excuse me: is there any place in your religion for honor, justice, truth,
love, mercy and so forth?

UNDERSHAFT: Yes: they are the graces and luxuries of a rich, strong, and safe life.

CUSINS: Suppose one is forced to choose between them and money or gunpowder?

UNDERSHAFT: Choose money a n d gunpowder; for without enough of both you
cannot afford the others.

CUSINS: That is your religion?

UNDERSHAFT: Yes.

The cadence of this reply makes a full close in the conversation.
CUSINS *twists his face dubiously and contemplates* UNDERSHAFT.
UNDERSHAFT *contemplates him.*

CUSINS: Barbara wont stand that. You will have to choose between your religion
and Barbara.

UNDERSHAFT: So will you, my friend. She will find out that that drum of yours is
hollow.

CUSINS: Father Undershaft: you are mistaken: I am a sincere Salvationist. You
do not understand the Salvation Army. It is the army of joy, of love, of
courage: it has banished the fear and remorse and despair of the old
hell-ridden evangelical sects: it marches to fight the devil with trumpet
and drum, with music and dancing, with banner and palm, as becomes a
sally from heaven by its happy garrison. It picks the waster out of the

public house and makes a man of him: it finds a worm wriggling in a back kitchen, and lo! a woman! Men and women of rank too, sons and daughters of the Highest. It takes the poor professor of Greek, the most artificial and self-suppressed of human creatures, from his meal of roots, and lets loose the rhapsodist in him; reveals the true worship of Dionysos to him; sends him down the public street drumming dithyrambs. [*He plays a thundering flourish on the drum.*]

UNDERSHAFT: You will alarm the shelter.

CUSINS: Oh, they are accustomed to these sudden ecstasies. However, if the drum worries you—[*He pockets the drumsticks; unhooks the drum; and stands it on the ground opposite the gateway.*]

UNDERSHAFT: Thank you.

CUSINS: You remember what Euripides says about your money and gunpowder?

UNDERSHAFT: No.

CUSINS [*declaiming*]:

> One and another
> In money and guns may outpass his brother;
> And men in their millions float and flow
> And seethe with a million hopes as leaven;
> And they win their will; or they miss their will;
> And their hopes are dead or are pined for still;
> But whoe'er can know
> As the long days go
> That to live is happy, has found h i s heaven.

My translation: what do you think of it?

UNDERSHAFT: I think, my friend, that if you wish to know, as the long days go, that to live is happy, you must first acquire money enough for a decent life, and power enough to be your own master.

CUSINS: You are damnably discouraging. [*He resumes his declamation.*]

> Is it so hard a thing to see
> That the spirit of God—whate'er it be—
> The law that abides and changes not, ages long,
> The Eternal and Nature-born: t h e s e things be strong?
> What else is Wisdom? What of Man's endeavor,
> Or God's high grace so lovely and so great?
> To stand from fear set free? to breathe and wait?
> To hold a hand uplifted over Fate?
> And shall not Barbara be loved for ever?

UNDERSHAFT: Euripides mentions Barbara, does he?

CUSINS: It is a fair translation. The word means Loveliness.

UNDERSHAFT: May I ask—as Barbara's father—how much a year she is to be loved for ever on?

CUSINS: As Barbara's father, that is more your affair than mine. I can feed her by teaching Greek: that is about all.

UNDERSHAFT: Do you consider it a good match for her?

CUSINS [*with polite obstinacy*]: Mr Undershaft: I am in many ways a weak, timid, ineffectual person; and my health is far from satisfactory. But whenever I feel that I must have anything, I get it, sooner or later. I feel that way about Barbara. I dont like marriage: I feel intensely afraid of it; and I dont know what I shall do with Barbara or what she will do with me. But I feel that I and nobody else must marry her. Please regard that as settled.—Not that I wish to be arbitrary; but why should I waste your time in discussing what is inevitable?

UNDERSHAFT: You mean that you will stick at nothing: not even the conversion of the Salvation Army to the worship of Dionysos.[9]

CUSINS: The business of the Salvation Army is to save, not to wrangle about the name of the pathfinder. Dionysos or another: what does it matter?

UNDERSHAFT [*rising and approaching him*]: Professor Cusins: you are a young man after my own heart.

CUSINS: Mr Undershaft: you are, as far as I am able to gather, a most infernal old rascal; but you appeal very strongly to my sense of ironic humor.

UNDERSHAFT *mutely offers his hand. They shake.*

UNDERSHAFT [*suddenly concentrating himself*]: And now to business.

CUSINS: Pardon me. We are discussing religion. Why go back to such an uninteresting and unimportant subject as business?

UNDERSHAFT: Religion is our business at present, because it is through religion alone that we can win Barbara.

CUSINS: Have you, too, fallen in love with Barbara?

UNDERSHAFT: Yes, with a father's love.

CUSINS: A father's love for a grown-up daughter is the most dangerous of all infatuations. I apologize for mentioning my own pale, coy, mistrustful fancy in the same breath with it.

UNDERSHAFT: Keep to the point. We have to win her; and we are neither of us Methodists.

CUSINS: That doesnt matter. The power Barbara wields here—the power that wields Barbara herself—is not Calvinism, not Presbyterianism, not Methodism—

UNDERSHAFT: Not Greek Paganism either, eh?

CUSINS: I admit that. Barbara is quite original in her religion.

UNDERSHAFT [*triumphantly*]: Aha! Barbara Undershaft would be. Her inspiration comes from within herself.

CUSINS: How do you suppose it got there?

UNDERSHAFT [*in towering excitement*]: It is the Undershaft inheritance. I shall hand on my torch to my daughter. She shall make my converts and preach my gospel—

9. The Greek god of wine.

CUSINS: What! Money and gunpowder!

UNDERSHAFT: Yes, money and gunpowder. Freedom and power. Command of life and command of death.

CUSINS [*urbanely: trying to bring him down to earth*]: This is extremely interesting, Mr Undershaft. Of course you know that you are mad.

UNDERSHAFT [*with redoubled force*]: And you?

CUSINS: Oh, mad as a hatter. You are welcome to my secret since I have discovered yours. But I am astonished. Can a madman make cannons?

UNDERSHAFT: Would anyone else than a madman make them? And now [*with surging energy*] question for question. Can a sane man translate Euripides?

CUSINS: No.

UNDERSHAFT [*seizing him by the shoulder*]: Can a sane woman make a man of a waster or a woman of a worm?

CUSINS [*reeling before the storm*]: Father Colossus—Mammoth Millionaire—

UNDERSHAFT [*pressing him*]: Are there two mad people or three in this Salvation shelter today?

CUSINS: You mean Barbara is as mad as we are?

UNDERSHAFT [*pushing him lightly off and resuming his equanimity suddenly and completely*]: Pooh, Professor! let us call things by their proper names. I am a millionaire; you are a poet; Barbara is a savior of souls. What have we three to do with the common mob of slaves and idolaters? [*He sits down again with a shrug of contempt for the mob.*]

CUSINS: Take care! Barbara is in love with the common people. So am I. Have you never felt the romance of that love?

UNDERSHAFT [*cold and sardonic*]: Have you ever been in love with Poverty, like St Francis? Have you ever been in love with Dirt, like St Simeon! Have you ever been in love with disease and suffering, like our nurses and philanthropists? Such passions are not virtues, but the most unnatural of all the vices. This love of the common people may please an earl's granddaughter and a university professor; but I have been a common man and a poor man; and it has no romance for me. Leave it to the poor to pretend that poverty is a blessing: leave it to the coward to make a religion of his cowardice by preaching humility: we know better than that. We three must stand together above the common people: how else can we help their children to climb up beside us? Barbara must belong to us, not to the Salvation Army.

CUSINS: Well, I can only say that if you think you will get her away from the Salvation Army by talking to her as you have been talking to me, you dont know Barbara.

UNDERSHAFT: My friend: I never ask for what I can buy.

CUSINS [*in a white fury*]: Do I understand you to imply that you can buy Barbara?

UNDERSHAFT: No; but I can buy the Salvation Army.

CUSINS: Quite impossible.

UNDERSHAFT: You shall see. All religious organizations exist by selling themselves to the rich.

CUSINS: Not the Army. That is the Church of the poor.

UNDERSHAFT: All the more reason for buying it.

CUSINS: I dont think you quite know what the Army does for the poor.

UNDERSHAFT: Oh yes I do. It draws their teeth: that is enough for me as a man of business.

CUSINS: Nonsense! It makes them sober—

UNDERSHAFT: I prefer sober workmen. The profits are larger.

CUSINS: —honest—

UNDERSHAFT: Honest workmen are the most economical.

CUSINS: —attached to their homes—

UNDERSHAFT: So much the better: they will put up with anything sooner than change their shop.

CUSINS: —happy—

UNDERSHAFT: An invaluable safeguard against revolution.

CUSINS: —unselfish—

UNDERSHAFT: Indifferent to their own interests, which suits me exactly.

CUSINS: —with their thoughts on heavenly things—

UNDERSHAFT [*rising*]: And not on Trade Unionism nor Socialism. Excellent.

CUSINS [*revolted*]: You really are an infernal old rascal.

UNDERSHAFT [*indicating* PETER SHIRLEY, *who has just come from the shelter and strolled dejectedly down the yard between them*]: And this is an honest man!

SHIRLEY: Yes; and what av I got by it? [*He passes on bitterly and sits on the form, in the corner of the penthouse.*]

> SNOBBY PRICE, *beaming sanctimoniously, and* JENNY HILL *with a tambourine full of coppers, come from the shelter and go to the drum, on which* JENNY *begins to count the money.*

UNDERSHAFT [*replying to* SHIRLEY]: Oh, your employers must have got a good deal by it from first to last. [*He sits on the table, with one foot on the side form.* CUSINS, *overwhelmed, sits down on the same form nearer the shelter.* BARBARA *comes from the shelter to the middle of the yard. She is excited and a little overwrought.*]

BARBARA: Weve just had a splendid experience meeting at the other gate in Cripps's Lane. Ive hardly ever seen them so much moved as they were by your confession, Mr Price.

PRICE: I could almost be glad of my past wickedness if I could believe that it would elp to keep hathers stright.

BARBARA: So it will, Snobby. How much, Jenny?

JENNY: Four and tenpence, Major.

BARBARA: Oh Snobby, if you had given your poor mother just one more kick, we should have got the whole five shillings!

PRICE: If she heard you say that, miss, she'd be sorry I didnt. But I'm glad. Oh what a joy it will be to her when she hears I'm saved!

UNDERSHAFT: Shall I contribute the odd twopence, Barbara? The millionaire's mite, eh? [*He takes a couple of pennies from his pocket.*]

BARBARA: How did you make that twopence?

UNDERSHAFT: As usual. By selling cannons, torpedoes, submarines, and my new patent Grand Duke hand grenade.

BARBARA: Put it back in your pocket. You cant buy your salvation here for two pence: you must work it out.

UNDERSHAFT: Is twopence not enough? I can afford a little more, if you press me.

BARBARA: Two million millions would not be enough. There is bad blood on your hands; and nothing but good blood can cleanse them. Money is no use. Take it away. [*She turns to* CUSINS.] Dolly: you must write another letter for me to the papers. [*He makes a wry face.*] Yes: I know you dont like it; but it must be done. The starvation this winter is beating us: everybody is unemployed. The General says we must close this shelter if we cant get more money. I force the collections at the meetings until I am ashamed: dont I, Snobby?

PRICE: It's a fair treat to see you work it, miss. The way you got them up from three-and-six to four-and-ten with that hymn, penny by penny and verse by verse, was a caution. Not a Cheap Jack[10] on Mile End Waste could touch you at it.

BARBARA: Yes; but I wish we could do without it. I am getting at last to think more of the collection than of the people's souls. And what are those hatfuls of pence and halfpence? We want thousands! tens of thousands! hundreds of thousands! I want to convert people, not to be always begging for the Army in a way I'd die sooner than beg for myself.

UNDERSHAFT [*in profound irony*]: Genuine unselfishness is capable of anything, my dear.

BARBARA [*unsuspectingly, as she turns away to take the money from the drum and put it in a bag she carries*]: Yes, isnt it? [UNDERSHAFT *looks sardonically at* CUSINS.]

CUSINS [*aside to* UNDERSHAFT]: Mephistopheles! Machiavelli!

BARBARA [*tears coming into her eyes as she ties the bag and pockets it*]: How are we to feed them? I cant talk religion to a man with bodily hunger in his eyes. [*Almost breaking down.*] It's frightful.

JENNY [*running to her*]: Major, dear—

BARBARA [*rebounding*]: No: dont comfort me. It will be all right. We shall get the money.

UNDERSHAFT: How?

JENNY: By praying for it, of course. Mrs Baines says she prayed for it last night; and she has never prayed for it in vain: never once. [*She goes to the gate and looks out into the street.*]

10. A street vendor.

BARBARA [*who has dried her eyes and regained her composure*]: By the way, dad, Mrs Baines has come to march with us to our big meeting this afternoon; and she is very anxious to meet you, for some reason or other. Perhaps she'll convert you.

UNDERSHAFT: I shall be delighted, my dear.

JENNY [*at the gate: excitedly*]: Major! Major! heres that man back again.

BARBARA: What man?

JENNY: The man that hit me. Oh, I hope he's coming back to join us.

> BILL WALKER, *with frost on his jacket, comes through the gate, his hands deep in his pockets and his chin sunk between his shoulders, like a cleaned-out gambler. He halts between* BARBARA *and the drum.*

BARBARA: Hullo, Bill! Back already!

BILL [*nagging at her*]: Bin talkin ever sence, ev you?

BARBARA: Pretty nearly. Well, has Todger paid you out for poor Jenny's jaw?

BILL: Nao e aint.

BARBARA: I thought your jacket looked a bit snowy.

BILL: Sao it is snaowy. You want to knaow where the snaow cam from, downt you?

BARBARA: Yes.

BILL: Well, it cam from orf the grahnd in Pawkinses Corner in Kenintahn. It got rabbed orf be maw shaoulders: see?

BARBARA: Pity you didnt rub some off with your knees. Bill! That would have done you a lot of good.

BILL [*with sour mirthless humor*]: Aw was sivin anather menn's knees at the tawm. E was kneelin on moy ed, e was.

JENNY: Who was kneeling on your head?

BILL: Todger was. E was prying for me: prying camfortable wiv me as a cawpet. Sow was Mog. Sao was the aol bloomin meetin. Mog she says "Ow Lawd brike his stabborn sperrit; bat downt urt is dear art." Thet was wot she said. "Downt urt is dear art"! An er blowk—thirteen stun four!—kneelin wiv all is wight on me. Fanny, aint it?

JENNY: Oh no. We're so sorry, Mr Walker.

BARBARA [*enjoying it frankly*]: Nonsense! of course it's funny. Served you right, Bill! You must have done something to him first.

BILL [*doggedly*]: Aw did wot Aw said Aw'd do. Aw spit in is eye. E looks up at the skoy and sez, "Ow that Aw should be fahnd worthy to be spit upon for the gospel's sike!" e sez; an Mog sez "Glaory Allelloolier!"; an then e called me Braddher, an dahned me as if Aw was a kid and e was me mather worshin me a Setterda nawt. Aw ednt jast nao shaow wiv im at all. Arf the street pryed; an the tather arf larfed fit to split theirselves. [*To* BARBARA.] There! are you settisfawd nah?

BARBARA [*her eyes dancing*]: Wish I'd been there, Bill.

BILL: Yus: youd a got in a hextra bit o talk on me, wouldnt you?

JENNY: I'm so sorry, Mr Walker.

BILL [*fiercely*]: Downt you gow bein sorry for me: youve no call. Listen eah. Aw browk your jawr.

JENNY: No, it didnt hurt me: indeed it didnt, except for a moment. It was only that I was frightened.

BILL: Aw downt want to be forgive be you, or be ennybody. Wot Aw did Aw'll py for. Aw trawd to gat me aown jar browk to settisfaw you—

JENNY [*distressed*]: Oh no—

BILL [*impatiently*]: Tell y' Aw did: cawnt you listen to wots bein taold you? All Aw got be it was bein mide a sawt of in the pablic street for me pines. Well, if Aw cawnt settisfaw you one wy, Aw ken anather. Listen eah! Aw ed two quid sived agen the frost; and Awve a pahnd of it left. A mite o mawn last week ed words with the judy e's gowin to merry. E give er wot-for; and e's bin fawnd fifteen bob. E ed a rawt to itt er cause they was gowin to be merrid; but Aw ednt nao rawt to itt you; sao put anather fawv bob on an call it a pahnd's worth. [*He produces a sovereign.*] Eahs the manney. Tike it; and lets ev no more o your forgivin an pryin and your Mijor jawrin me. Let wot Aw dan be dan an pide for; and let there be a end of it.

JENNY: Oh, I couldnt take it, Mr Walker. But if you would give a shilling or two to poor Rummy Mitchens! you really did hurt her; and she's old.

BILL [*contemptuously*]: Not lawkly. Aw'd give her anather as soon as look at er. Let her ev the lawr o me as she threatened! S h e aint forgiven me: not mach. Wot Aw dan to er is not on me mawnd—wot she [*indicating* BARBARA] mawt call on me conscience—no more than stickin a pig. It's this Christian gime o yours that Aw wownt ev plyed agen me: this bloomin forgivin an neggin an jawrin that mikes a menn thet sore that iz lawf's a burdn to im. Aw wownt ev it, Aw tell you; sao tike your manney and stop thraowin your silly beshed fice hap agen me.

JENNY: Major: may I take a little of it for the Army?

BARBARA: No: the Army is not to be bought. We want your soul, Bill; and we'll take nothing less.

BILL [*bitterly*]: Aw knaow. Me an maw few shillins is not good enaff for you. Youre a earl's grendorter, you are. Nathink less than a anderd pahnd for you.

UNDERSHAFT: Come, Barbara! you could do a great deal of good with a hundred pounds. If you will set this gentleman's mind at ease by taking his pound, I will give the other ninety-nine.

BILL, *dazed by such opulence, instinctively touches his cap.*

BARBARA: Oh, youre too extravagant, papa. Bill offers twenty pieces of silver. All you need offer is the other ten. That will make the standard price to buy anybody who's for sale. I'm not; and the Army's not. [*To* BILL.] Youll never have another quiet moment, Bill, until you come round to us. You cant stand out against your salvation.

BILL [*sullenly*]: Aw cawnt stend aht agen music awl wrastlers and awtful tangued women. Awve offered to py. Aw can do no more. Tike it or leave it. There it is. [*He throws the sovereign on the drum, and sits down on the horse-trough. The coin facinates* SNOBBY PRICE, *who takes an early opportunity of dropping his cap on it.*]

> MRS BAINES *comes from the shelter. She is dressed as a Salvation Army Commissioner. She is an earnest looking woman of about 40, with a caressing, urgent voice, and an appealing manner.*

BARBARA: This is my father, Mrs Baines. [UNDERSHAFT *comes from the table, taking his hat off with marked civility.*] Try what you can do with him. He wont listen to me, because he remembers what a fool I was when I was a baby. [*She leaves them together and chats with* JENNY.]

MRS BAINES: Have you been shewn over the shelter, Mr Undershaft? You know the work we're doing, of course.

UNDERSHAFT [*very civilly*]: The whole nation knows it, Mrs Baines.

MRS BAINES: No, sir: the whole nation does not know it, or we should not be crippled as we are for want of money to carry our work through the length and breadth of the land. Let me tell you that there would have been rioting this winter in London but for us.

UNDERSHAFT: You really think so?

MRS BAINES: I know it. I remember 1886, when you rich gentlemen hardened your hearts against the cry of the poor. They broke the windows of your clubs in Pall Mall.

UNDERSHAFT [*gleaming with approval of their method*]: And the Mansion House Fund went up next day from thirty thousand pounds to seventy-nine thousand! I remember quite well.

MRS BAINES: Well, wont you help me to get at the people? They wont break windows then. Come here, Price. Let me shew you to this gentleman. [PRICE *comes to be inspected.*] Do you remember the window breaking?

PRICE: My ole father thought it was the revolution, maam.

MRS BAINES: Would you break windows now?

PRICE: Oh no, maam. The windows of eaven av bin opened to me. I know now that the rich man is a sinner like myself.

RUMMY [*appearing above at the loft door*]: Snobby Price!

PRICE: Wot is it?

RUMMY: Your mother's askin for you at the other gate in Cripps's Lane. She's heard about your confession. [PRICE *turns pale.*]

MRS BAINES: Go, Mr Price; and pray with her.

JENNY: You can go through the shelter, Snobby.

PRICE [*to* MRS BAINES]: I couldnt face her now, maam, with all the weight of my sins fresh on me. Tell her she'll find her son at ome, waiting for her in prayer. [*He skulks off through the gate, incidentally stealing the sovereign on his way out by picking up his cap from the drum.*]

MRS BAINES [*with swimming eyes*]: You see how we take the anger and the bitterness against you out of their hearts, Mr Undershaft.

UNDERSHAFT: It is certainly most convenient and gratifying to all large employers of labor, Mrs Baines.

MRS BAINES: Barbara: Jenny: I have good news: most wonderful news. [JENNY *runs to her.*] My prayers have been answered. I told you they would, Jenny, didnt I?

JENNY: Yes, yes.

BARBARA [*moving nearer to the drum*]: Have we got money enough to keep the shelter open?

MRS BAINES: I hope we shall have enough to keep all the shelters open. Lord Saxmundham has promised us five thousand pounds—

BARBARA: Horray!

JENNY: Glory!

MRS BAINES: —if—

BARBARA: "If!" If what?

MRS BAINES: —if five other gentlemen will give a thousand each to make it up to ten thousand.

BARBARA: Who is Lord Saxmundham? I never heard of him.

UNDERSHAFT [*who has pricked up his ears at the peer's name, and is now watching* BARBARA *curiously*]: A new creation, my dear. You have heard of Sir Horace Bodger?

BARBARA: Bodger! Do you mean the distiller? Bodger's whisky!

UNDERSHAFT: That is the man. He is one of the greatest of our public benefactors. He restored the cathedral at Hakington. They made him a baronet for that. He gave half a million to the funds of his party: they made him a baron for that.

SHIRLEY: What will they give him for the five thousand?

UNDERSHAFT: There is nothing left to give him. So the five thousand, I should think, is to save his soul.

MRS BAINES: Heaven grant it may! Oh Mr Undershaft, you have some very rich friends. Cant you help us towards the other five thousand? We are going to hold a great meeting this afternoon at the Assembly Hall in the Mile End Road. If I could only announce that one gentleman had come forward to support Lord Saxmundham, others would follow. Dont you know somebody? couldnt you? wouldnt you? [*Her eyes fill with tears.*] Oh, think of those poor people, Mr Undershaft: think of how much it means to them, and how little to a great man like you.

UNDERSHAFT [*sardonically gallant*]: Mrs Baines: you are irresistible. I cant disappoint you; and I cant deny myself the satisfaction of making Bodger pay up. You shall have your five thousand pounds.

MRS BAINES: Thank God!

UNDERSHAFT: You dont thank m e?

MRS BAINES: Oh sir, dont try to be cynical: dont be ashamed of being a good man. The Lord will bless you abundantly; and our prayers will be like a strong fortification round you all the days of your life. [*With a touch of caution.*] You will let me have the cheque to shew at the meeting, wont you? Jenny: go in and fetch a pen and ink. [JENNY *runs to the shelter door.*]

UNDERSHAFT: Do not disturb Miss Hill: I have a fountain pen. [JENNY *halts. He sits at the table and writes the cheque.* CUSINS *rises to make room for him. They all watch him silently.*]

BILL [*cynically, aside to* BARBARA, *his voice and accent horribly debased*]: Wot prawce selvytion nah?

BARBARA: Stop. [UNDERSHAFT *stops writing: they all turn to her in surprise.*] Mrs Baines: are you really going to take this money?

MRS BAINES [*astonished*]: Why not, dear?

BARBARA: Why not! Do you know what my father is? Have you forgotten that Lord Saxmundham is Bodger the whisky man? Do you remember how we implored the County Council to stop him from writing Bodger's Whisky in letters of fire against the sky; so that the poor drink-ruined creatures on the Embankment could not wake up from their snatches of sleep without being reminded of their deadly thirst by that wicked sky sign? Do you know that the worst thing I have had to fight here is not the devil, but Bodger, Bodger, Bodger, with his whisky, his distilleries, and his tied houses? Are you going to make our shelter another tied house for him, and ask me to keep it?

BILL: Rotten dranken whisky it is too.

MRS BAINES: Dear Barbara: Lord Saxmundham has a soul to be saved like any of us. If heaven has found the way to make a good use of his money, are we to set ourselves up against the answer to our prayers?

BARBARA: I know he has a soul to be saved. Let him come down here; and I'll do my best to help him to his salvation. But he wants to send his cheque down to buy us, and go on being as wicked as ever.

UNDERSHAFT [*with a reasonableness which* CUSINS *alone perceives to be ironical*]: My dear Barbara: alcohol is a very necessary article. It heals the sick—

BARBARA: It does nothing of the sort.

UNDERSHAFT: Well, it assists the doctor: that is perhaps a less questionable way of putting it. It makes life bearable to millions of people who could not endure their existence if they were quite sober. It enables Parliament to do things at eleven at night that no sane person would do at eleven in the morning. Is it Bodger's fault that this inestimable gift is deplorably abused by less than one per cent of the poor? [*He turns again to the table; signs the cheque; and crosses it.*]

MRS BAINES: Barbara: will there be less drinking or more if all those poor souls we are saving come tomorrow and find the doors of our shelters shut in their faces? Lord Saxmundham gives us the money to stop drinking—to take his own business from him.

CUSINS [*impishly*]: Pure self-sacrifice on Bodger's part, clearly! Bless dear Bodger! [BARBARA *almost breaks down as* ADOLPHUS, *too, fails her.*]

UNDERSHAFT [*tearing out the cheque and pocketing the book as he rises and goes past* CUSINS *to* MRS BAINES]: I also, Mrs Baines, may claim a little disinterestedness. Think of my business! think of the widows and orphans! the men and lads torn to pieces with shrapnel and poisoned with lyddite! [MRS BAINES *shrinks; but he goes on remorselessly*] the oceans of blood, not one drop of which is shed in a really just cause! the ravaged crops! the peaceful peasant forced, women and men, to till their fields, under the fire of opposing armies on pain of starvation! the bad blood of the fierce little cowards at home who egg on others to fight for the gratification of their national vanity! All this makes money for me: I am never richer, never busier than when the papers are full of it. Well, it is your work to preach peace on earth and goodwill to men. [MRS BAINES's *face lights up again.*] Every convert you make is a vote against war. [*Her lips move in prayer.*] Yet I give you this money to help you to hasten my own commercial ruin. [*He gives her the cheque.*]

CUSINS [*mounting the form in an ecstasy of mischief*]: The millennium will be inaugurated by the unselfishness of Undershaft and Bodger. Oh be joyful! [*He takes the drum-sticks from his pocket and flourishes them.*]

MRS BAINES [*taking the cheque*]: The longer I live the more proof I see that there is an Infinite Goodness that turns everything to the work of salvation sooner or later. Who would have thought that any good could have come out of war and drink? And yet their profits are brought today to the feet of salvation to do its blessed work. [*She is affected to tears.*]

JENNY [*running to MRS BAINES and throwing her arms around her*]: Oh dear! how blessed, how glorious it all is!

CUSINS [*in a convulsion of irony*]: Let us seize this unspeakable moment. Let us march to the great meeting at once. Excuse me just an instant. [*He rushes into the shelter.* JENNY *takes her tambourine from the drum head.*]

MRS BAINES: Mr Undershaft: have you ever seen a thousand people fall on their knees with one impulse and pray? Come with us to the meeting. Barbara shall tell them that the Army is saved, and saved through you.

CUSINS [*returning impetuously from the shelter with a flag and a trombone, and coming between MRS BAINES and UNDERSHAFT*]: You shall carry the flag down the first street, Mrs Baines. [*He gives her the flag.*] Mr Undershaft is a gifted trombonist: he shall intone an Olympian diapason to the West Ham Salvation March. [*Aside to UNDERSHAFT, as he forces the trombone on him.*] Blow, Machiavelli, blow.

UNDERSHAFT [*aside to him, as he takes the trombone*]: The trumpet in Zion! [CUSINS *rushes to the drum which he takes up and puts on.* UNDERSHAFT *continues, aloud.*] I will do my best. I could vamp a bass if I knew the tune.

CUSINS: It is a wedding chorus from one of Donizetti's operas; but we have converted it. We convert everything to good here, including Bodger. You remember the chorus. "For thee immense rejoicing—immenso giubilo— immenso giubilo." [*With drum obbligato.*] Rum tum ti tum, tum tum ti ta—

BARBARA: Dolly: you are breaking my heart.

CUSINS: What is a broken heart more or less here? Dionysos Undershaft has descended. I am possessed.

MRS BAINES: Come, Barbara: I must have my dear Major to carry the flag with me.

JENNY: Yes, yes, Major darling.

CUSINS *snatches the tambourine out of* JENNY's *hand and mutely offers it to* BARBARA.

BARBARA [*coming forward a little as she puts the offer behind her with a shudder, whilst* CUSINS *recklessly tosses the tambourine back to* JENNY *and goes to the gate*]: I cant come.

JENNY: Not come!

MRS BAINES [*with tears in her eyes*]: Barbara: do you think I am wrong to take the money?

BARBARA [*impulsively going to her and kissing her*]: No, no: God help you, dear, you must: you are saving the Army. Go; and may you have a great meeting!

JENNY: But arnt you coming?

BARBARA: No. [*She begins taking off the silver S brooch from her collar.*]

MRS BAINES: Barbara: what are you doing?

JENNY: Why are you taking your badge off? You cant be going to leave us, Major.

BARBARA [*quietly*]: Father: come here.

UNDERSHAFT [*coming to her*]: My dear! [*Seeing that she is going to pin the badge on his collar, he retreats to the penthouse in some alarm.*]

BARBARA [*following him*]: Dont be frightened. [*She pins the badge on and steps back towards the table, shewing him to the others.*] There! It's not much for £5000, is it?

MRS BAINES: Barbara: if you wont come and pray w i t h us, promise me you will pray f o r us.

BARBARA: I cant pray now. Perhaps I shall never pray again.

MRS BAINES: Barbara!

JENNY: Major!

BARBARA [*almost delirious*]: I cant bear any more. Quick march!

CUSINS [*calling to the procession in the street outside*]: Off we go. Play up, there! I m m e n s o g i u b i l o. [*He gives the time with his drum; and the band strikes up the march, which rapidly becomes more distant as the procession moves briskly away.*]

MRS BAINES: I must go, dear. Youre overworked: you will be all right tomorrow. We'll never lose you. Now Jenny: step out with the old flag. Blood and Fire! [*She marches out through the gate with her flag.*]

JENNY: Glory Hallelujah! [*Flourishing her tambourine and marching.*]

UNDERSHAFT [*to* CUSINS, *as he marches out past him easing the slide of his trombone*]: "My ducats and my daughter"!

CUSINS [*following him out*]: Money and gunpowder!

BARBARA: Drunkenness and Murder! My God: why hast thou forsaken me?

She sinks on the form with her face buried in her hands. The march passes away into silence. BILL WALKER *steals across to her.*

BILL [*taunting*]: Wot prawce selvytion nah?

SHIRLEY: Dont you hit her when she's down.

BILL: She itt me wen aw wiz dahn. Waw shouldnt Aw git a bit o me aown beck?

BARBARA [*raising her head*]: I didnt take y o u r money, Bill. [*She crosses the yard to the gate and turns her back on the two men to hide her face from them.*]

BILL [*sneering after her*]: Naow, it warnt enaff for you. [*Turning to the drum, he misses the money.*] Ellow! If you aint took it sammun else ez. Weres it gorn? Bly me if Jenny Ill didnt tike it arter all!

RUMMY [*screaming at him from the loft*]: You lie, you dirty blackguard! Snobby Price pinched it off the drum when he took up his cap. I was up here all the time an see im do it.

BILL: Wot! Stowl maw manney! Waw didnt you call thief on him, you silly aold macker you?

RUMMY: To serve you aht for ittin me acrost the fice. It's cost y'pahnd, that az. [*Raising a paean of squalid triumph.*] I done you. I'm even with you. Ive ad it aht o y— [BILL *snatches up* SHIRLEY'S *mug and hurls it at her. She slams the loft door and vanishes. The mug smashes against the door and falls in fragments.*]

BILL [*beginning to chuckle*]: Tell us, aol menn, wot o'clock this mawnin was it wen im as they call Snobby Prawce was sived?

BARBARA [*turning to him more composedly, and with unspoiled sweetness*]: About half past twelve, Bill. And he pinched your pound at a quarter to two. *I* know. Well, you cant afford to lose it. I'll send it to you.

BILL [*his voice and accent suddenly improving*]: Not if Aw wiz to stawve for it. Aw aint to be bought.

SHIRLEY: Aint you? Youd sell yourself to the devil for a pint o beer; ony there aint no devil to make the offer.

BILL [*unshamed*]: Sao Aw would, mite, and often ev, cheerful. But she cawnt baw me. [*Approaching* BARBARA.] You wanted maw saoul, did you? Well, you aint got it.

BARBARA: I nearly got it, Bill. But weve sold it back to you for ten thousand pounds.

SHIRLEY: And dear at the money!

BARBARA: No, Peter: it was worth more than money.

BILL [*salvationproof*]: It's nao good: you cawnt get rahnd me nah. Aw downt blieve in it; and Awve seen tody that Aw was rawt. [*Going.*] Sao long, aol soupkitchener! Ta, ta, Mijor Earl's Grendorter! [*Turning at the gate.*] Wot prawce selvytion nah? Snobby Prawce! Ha! ha!

BARBARA [*offering her hand*]: Goodbye, Bill.

BILL [*taken aback, half plucks his cap off; then shoves it on again defiantly*]: Git aht. [BARBARA *drops her hand, discouraged. He has a twinge of remorse.*] But thets aw rawt, you knaow. Nathink pasnl. Naow mellice. Sao long, Judy. [*He goes.*]

BARBARA: No malice. So long, Bill.

SHIRLEY [*shaking his head*]: You make too much of him, miss, in your innocence.

BARBARA [*going to him*]: Peter: I'm like you now. Cleaned out, and lost my job.

SHIRLEY: Youve youth and hope. Thats two better than me.

BARBARA: I'll get you a job, Peter. Thats hope for you: the youth will have to be enough for me. [*She counts her money.*] I have just enough left for two teas at Lockharts, a Rowton doss[11] for you, and my tram and bus home. [*He frowns and rises with offended pride. She takes his arm.*] Dont be proud, Peter: it's sharing between friends. And promise me youll talk to me and not let me cry. [*She draws him towards the gate.*]

SHIRLEY: Well, I'm not accustomed to talk to the like of you—

BARBARA [*urgently*]: Yes, yes: you must talk to me. Tell me about Tom Paine's books and Bradlaugh's lectures. Come along.

SHIRLEY: Ah, if you would only read Tom Paine in the proper spirit, miss! [*They go out through the gate together.*]

ACT THREE

> *Next day after lunch* LADY BRITOMART *is writing in the library in Wilton Crescent.* SARAH *is reading in the armchair near the window.* BARBARA, *in ordinary fashionable dress, pale and brooding, is on the settee.* CHARLES LOMAX *enters. He starts on seeing* BARBARA *fashionably attired and in low spirits.*

LOMAX: Youve left off your uniform!

> BARBARA *says nothing; but an expression of pain passes over her face.*

LADY BRITOMART [*warning him in low tones to be careful*]: Charles!

LOMAX [*much concerned, coming behind the settee and bending sympathetically over* BARBARA]: I'm awfully sorry, Barbara. You know I helped you all I could with the concertina and so forth. [*Momentously.*] Still, I have never shut my eyes to the fact that there is a certain amount of tosh about the Salvation Army. Now the claims of the Church of England—

LADY BRITOMART: Thats enough, Charles. Speak of something suited to your mental capacity.

LOMAX: But surely the Church of England is suited to all our capacities.

BARBARA [*pressing his hand*]: Thank you for your sympathy, Cholly. Now go and spoon with Sarah.

LOMAX [*dragging a chair from the writing table and seating himself affectionately by* SARAH'*s side*]: How is my ownest today?

SARAH: I wish you wouldnt tell Cholly to do things, Barbara. He always comes straight and does them. Cholly: we're going to the works this afternoon.

LOMAX: What works?

SARAH: The cannon works.

LOMAX: What? your governor's shop!

SARAH: Yes.

LOMAX: Oh I say!

11. A cheap boarding house.

CUSINS enters in poor condition. He also starts visibly when he sees BARBARA *without her uniform.*

BARBARA: I expected you this morning, Dolly. Didnt you guess that?

CUSINS [*sitting down beside her*]: I'm sorry. I have only just breakfasted.

SARAH: But weve just finished lunch.

BARBARA: Have you had one of your bad nights?

CUSINS: No: I had rather a good night: in fact, one of the most remarkable nights I have ever passed.

BARBARA: The meeting?

CUSINS: No: after the meeting.

LADY BRITOMART: You should have gone to bed after the meeting. What were you doing?

CUSINS: Drinking.

LADY BRITOMART:	Adolphus!
SARAH:	Dolly!
BARBARA:	Dolly!
LOMAX:	Oh I say!

LADY BRITOMART: What were you drinking, may I ask?

CUSINS: A most devilish kind of Spanish burgundy, warranted free from added alcohol: a Temperance burgundy in fact. Its richness in natural alcohol made any addition superfluous.

BARBARA: Are you joking, Dolly?

CUSINS [*patiently*]: No. I have been making a night of it with the nominal head of this household: that is all.

LADY BRITOMART: Andrew made you drunk!

CUSINS: No: he only provided the wine. I think it was Dionysos who made me drunk. [*To* BARBARA.] I told you I was possessed.

LADY BRITOMART: Youre not sober yet. Go home to bed at once.

CUSINS: I have never before ventured to reproach you, Lady Brit; but how could you marry the Prince of Darkness?

LADY BRITOMART: It was much more excusable to marry him than to get drunk with him. That is a new accomplishment of Andrew's, by the way. He usent to drink.

CUSINS: He doesnt now. He only sat there and completed the wreck of my moral basis, the rout of my convictions, the purchase of my soul. He cares for you, Barbara. That is what makes him so dangerous to me.

BARBARA: That has nothing to do with it, Dolly. There are larger loves and diviner dreams than the fireside ones. You know that, dont you?

CUSINS: Yes: that is our understanding. I know it. I hold to it. Unless he can win me on that holier ground he may amuse me for a while; but he can get no deeper hold, strong as he is.

BARBARA: Keep to that; and the end will be right. Now tell me what happened at the meeting?

CUSINS: It was an amazing meeting. Mrs Baines almost died of emotion. Jenny Hill simply gibbered with hysteria. The Prince of Darkness played his trombone like a madman: its brazen roarings were like the laughter of the damned. 117 conversions took place then and there. They prayed with the most touching sincerity and gratitude for Bodger, and for the anonymous donor of the £5000. Your father would not let his name be given.

LOMAX: That was rather fine of the old man, you know. Most chaps would have wanted the advertisement.

CUSINS: He said all the charitable institutions would be down on him like kites on a battle-field if he gave his name.

LADY BRITOMART: Thats Andrew all over. He never does a proper thing without giving an improper reason for it.

CUSINS: He convinced me that I have all my life been doing improper things for proper reasons.

LADY BRITOMART: Adolphus: now that Barbara has left the Salvation Army, you had better leave it too. I will not have you playing that drum in the streets.

CUSINS: Your orders are already obeyed, Lady Brit.

BARBARA: Dolly: were you ever really in earnest about it? Would you have joined if you had never seen me?

CUSINS [disingenuously]: Well—er—well, possibly, as a collector of religions—

LOMAX [cunningly]: Not as a drummer, though, you know. You are a very clearheaded brainy chap, Dolly; and it must have been apparent to you that there is a certain amount of tosh about—

LADY BRITOMART: Charles: if you must drivel, drivel like a grown-up man and not like a schoolboy.

LOMAX [out of countenance]: Well, drivel is drivel, dont you know, whatever a man's age.

LADY BRITOMART: In good society in England, Charles, men drivel at all ages by repeating silly formulas with an air of wisdom. Schoolboys make their own formulas out of slang, like you. When they reach your age, and get political private secretaryships and things of that sort, they drop slang and get their formulas out of The Spectator or The Times. Y o u had better confine yourself to The Times. You will find that there is a certain amount of tosh about The Times; but at least its language is reputable.

LOMAX [overwhelmed]: You are so awfully strong-minded, Lady Brit—

LADY BRITOMART: Rubbish! [MORRISON comes in.] What is it?

MORRISON: If you please, my lady, Mr Undershaft has just drove up to the door.

LADY BRITOMART: Well, let him in. [MORRISON hesitates.] Whats the matter with you?

MORRISON: Shall I announce him, my lady; or is he at home here, so to speak, my lady?

LADY BRITOMART: Announce him.

MORRISON: Thank you, my lady. You wont mind my asking, I hope. The occasion is in a manner of speaking new to me.

LADY BRITOMART: Quite right. Go and let him in.

MORRISON: Thank you, my lady. [*He withdraws.*]

LADY BRITOMART: Children: go and get ready. [SARAH *and* BARBARA *go upstairs for their out-of-door wraps.*] Charles: go and tell Stephen to come down here in five minutes: you will find him in the drawing room. [CHARLES *goes.*] Adolphus: tell them to send round the carriage in about fifteen minutes. [ADOLPHUS *goes.*]

MORRISON [*at the door*]: Mr Undershaft.

UNDERSHAFT *comes in.* MORRISON *goes out.*

UNDERSHAFT: Alone! How fortunate!

LADY BRITOMART [*rising*]: Dont be sentimental, Andrew. Sit down. [*She sits on the settee: he sits beside her, on her left. She comes to the point before he has time to breathe.*] Sarah must have £800 a year until Charles Lomax comes into his property. Barbara will need more, and need it permanently, because Adolphus hasnt any property.

UNDERSHAFT [*resignedly*]: Yes, my dear: I will see to it. Anything else? for yourself, for instance?

LADY BRITOMART: I want to talk to you about Stephen.

UNDERSHAFT [*rather wearily*]: Dont, my dear. Stephen doesnt interest me.

LADY BRITOMART: He does interest me. He is our son.

UNDERSHAFT: Do you really think so? He has induced us to bring him into the world; but he chose his parents very incongruously, I think. I see nothing of myself in him, and less of you.

LADY BRITOMART: Andrew: Stephen is an excellent son, and a most steady, capable, highminded young man. You are simply trying to find an excuse for disinheriting him.

UNDERSHAFT: My dear Biddy: the Undershaft tradition disinherits him. It would be dishonest of me to leave the cannon foundry to my son.

LADY BRITOMART: It would be most unnatural and improper of you to leave it to anyone else, Andrew. Do you suppose this wicked and immoral tradition can be kept up for ever? Do you pretend that Stephen could not carry on the foundry just as well as all the other sons of the big business houses?

UNDERSHAFT: Yes: he could learn the office routine without understanding the business, like all the other sons; and the firm would go on by its own momentum until the real Undershaft—probably an Italian or a German—would invent a new method and cut him out.

LADY BRITOMART: There is nothing that any Italian or German could do that Stephen could not do. And Stephen at least has breeding.

UNDERSHAFT: The son of a foundling! Nonsense!

LADY BRITOMART: My son, Andrew! And even you may have good blood in your veins for all you know.

UNDERSHAFT: True. Probably I have. That is another argument in favor of a foundling.

LADY BRITOMART: Andrew: dont be aggravating. And dont be wicked. At present you are both.

UNDERSHAFT: This conversation is part of the Undershaft tradition, Biddy. Every Undershaft's wife has treated him to it ever since the house was founded. It is mere waste of breath. If the tradition be ever broken it will be for an abler man than Stephen.

LADY BRITOMART [*pouting*]: Then go away.

UNDERSHAFT [*deprecatory*]: Go away!

LADY BRITOMART: Yes: go away. If you will do nothing for Stephen, you are not wanted here. Go to your foundling, whoever he is; and look after h i m.

UNDERSHAFT: The fact is, Biddy—

LADY BRITOMART: Dont call me Biddy. I dont call you Andy.

UNDERSHAFT: I will not call my wife Britomart: it is not good sense. Seriously, my love, the Undershaft tradition has landed me in a difficulty, I am getting on in years; and my partner Lazarus has at last made a stand and insisted that the succession must be settled one way or the other; and of course he is quite right. You see, I havnt found a fit successor yet.

LADY BRITOMART [*obstinately*]: There is Stephen.

UNDERSHAFT: Thats just it: all the foundlings I can find are exactly like Stephen.

LADY BRITOMART: Andrew!!

UNDERSHAFT: I want a man with no relations and no schooling: that is, a man who would be out of the running altogether if he were not a strong man. And I cant find him. Every blessed foundling nowadays is snapped up in his infancy by Barnardo homes, or School Board officers, or Boards of Guardians; and if he shews the least ability he is fastened on by schoolmasters; trained to win scholarships like a racehorse; crammed with secondhand ideas; drilled and disciplined in docility and what they call good taste; and lamed for life so that he is fit for nothing but teaching. If you want to keep the foundry in the family, you had better find an eligible foundling and marry him to Barbara.

LADY BRITOMART: Ah! Barbara! Your pet! You would sacrifice Stephen to Barbara.

UNDERSHAFT: Cheerfully. And you, my dear, would boil Barbara to make soup for Stephen.

LADY BRITOMART: Andrew: this is not a question of our likings and dislikings: it is a question of duty. It is your duty to make Stephen your successor.

UNDERSHAFT: Just as much as it is your duty to submit to your husband. Come, Biddy! these tricks of the governing class are of no use with me. I am one of the governing class myself; and it is a waste of time giving tracts to a missionary. I have the power in this matter; and I am not to be humbugged into using it for your purposes.

LADY BRITOMART: Andrew: you can talk my head off; but you cant change wrong into right. And your tie is all on one side. Put it straight.

UNDERSHAFT [*disconcerted*]: It wont stay unless it's pinned— [*He fumbles at it with childish grimaces.*]

STEPHEN *comes in.*

STEPHEN [*at the door*]: I beg your pardon. [*About to retire.*]

LADY BRITOMART: No: come in, Stephen. [STEPHEN *comes forward to his mother's writing table.*]

UNDERSHAFT [*not very cordially*]: Good afternoon.

STEPHEN [*coldly*]: Good afternoon.

UNDERSHAFT [*to* LADY BRITOMART]: He knows all about the tradition, I suppose?

LADY BRITOMART: Yes. [*To* STEPHEN.] It is what I told you last night, Stephen.

UNDERSHAFT [*sulkily*]: I understand you want to come into the cannon business.

STEPHEN: *I* go into trade! Certainly not.

UNDERSHAFT [*opening his eyes, greatly eased in mind and manner*]: Oh! in that case—

LADY BRITOMART: Cannons are not trade, Stephen. They are enterprise.

STEPHEN: I have no intention of becoming a man of business in any sense. I have no capacity for business and no taste for it. I intend to devote myself to politics.

UNDERSHAFT [*rising*]: My dear boy: this is an immense relief to me. And I trust it may prove an equally good thing for the country. I was afraid you would consider yourself disparaged and slighted. [*He moves toward* STEPHEN *as if to shake hands with him.*]

LADY BRITOMART [*rising and interposing*]: Stephen: I cannot allow you to throw away an enormous property like this.

STEPHEN [*stiffly*]: Mother: there must be an end of treating me as a child, if you please. [LADY BRITOMART *recoils, deeply wounded by his tone.*] Until last night I did not take your attitude seriously, because I did not think you meant it seriously. But I find now that you left me in the dark as to matters which you should have explained to me years ago. I am extremely hurt and offended. Any further discussion of my intentions had better take place with my father, as between one man and another.

LADY BRITOMART: Stephen! [*She sits down again, her eyes filling with tears.*]

UNDERSHAFT [*with grave compassion*]: You see, my dear, it is only the big men who can be treated as children.

STEPHEN: I am sorry, mother, that you have forced me—

UNDERSHAFT [*stopping him*]: Yes, yes, yes, yes: thats all right, Stephen. She wont interfere with you any more: your independence is achieved: you have won your latchkey. Dont rub it in; and above all, dont apologize. [*He resumes his seat.*] Now what about your future, as between one man and another—I beg your pardon, Biddy: as between two men and a woman.

LADY BRITOMART [*who has pulled herself together strongly*]: I quite understand, Stephen. By all means go your own way if you feel strong enough. [STEPHEN *sits down magisterially in the chair at the writing table with an air of affirming his majority.*]

UNDERSHAFT: It is settled that you do not ask for the succession to the cannon business.

STEPHEN: I hope it is settled that I repudiate the cannon business.

UNDERSHAFT: Come, come! dont be so devilishly sulky: it's boyish. Freedom should be generous. Besides, I owe you a fair start in life in exchange for disinheriting you. You cant become prime minister all at once. Havnt you a turn for something? What about literature, art, and so forth?

STEPHEN: I have nothing of the artist about me, either in faculty or character, thank Heaven!

UNDERSHAFT: A philosopher, perhaps? Eh?

STEPHEN: I make no such ridiculous pretension.

UNDERSHAFT: Just so. Well, there is the army, the navy, the Church, the Bar. The Bar requires some ability. What about the Bar?

STEPHEN: I have not studied law. And I am afraid I have not the necessary push—I believe that is the name barristers give to their vulgarity—for success in pleading.

UNDERSHAFT: Rather a difficult case, Stephen. Hardly anything left but the stage, is there? [STEPHEN *makes an impatient movement.*] Well, come! is there a n y t h i n g you know or care for?

STEPHEN [*rising and looking at him steadily*]: I know the difference between right and wrong.

UNDERSHAFT [*hugely tickled*]: You dont say so! What! no capacity for business, no knowledge of law, no sympathy with art, no pretension to philosophy; only a simple knowledge of the secret that has puzzled all the philosophers, baffled all the lawyers, muddled all the men of business, and ruined most of the artists: the secret of right and wrong. Why man, youre a genius, a master of masters, a god! At twentyfour, too!

STEPHEN [*keeping his temper with difficulty*]: You are pleased to be facetious. I pretend to nothing more than any honorable English gentleman claims as his birthright. [*He sits down angrily.*]

UNDERSHAFT: Oh, thats everybody's birthright. Look at poor little Jenny Hill, the Salvation lassie! she would think you were laughing at her if you asked her to stand up in the street and teach grammar or geography or mathematics or even drawing room dancing; but it never occurs to her to doubt that she can teach morals and religion. You are all alike, you respectable people. You cant tell me the bursting strain of a ten-inch gun, which is a very simple matter; but you all think you can tell me the bursting strain of a man under temptation. You darent handle high explosives; but youre all ready to handle honesty and truth and justice and the whole duty of man, and kill one another at that game. What a country! What a world!

LADY BRITOMART [*uneasily*]: What do you think he had better do, Andrew?

UNDERSHAFT: Oh, just what he wants to do. He knows nothing and he thinks he knows everything. That points clearly to a political career. Get him a private secretaryship to someone who can get him an Under Secretaryship; and then leave him alone. He will find his natural and proper place in the end on the Treasury Bench.

STEPHEN [*springing up again*]: I am sorry, sir, that you force me to forget the respect due to you as my father. I am an Englishman and I will not hear the Government of my country insulted. [*He thrusts his hands in his pockets, and walks angrily across to the window.*]

UNDERSHAFT [*with a touch of brutality*]: The government of your country! *I* am the government of your country: I, and Lazarus. Do you suppose that you and half a dozen amateurs like you, sitting in a row in that foolish gabble shop, can govern Undershaft and Lazarus? No, my friend: you will do what pays u s. You will make war when it suits us, and keep peace when it doesnt. You will find out that trade requires certain measures when we have decided on those measures. When I want anything to keep my dividends up, you will discover that my want is a national need. When other people want something to keep my dividends down, you will call out the police and military. And in return you shall have the support and applause of my newspapers, and the delight of imagining that you are a great statesman. Government of your country! Be off with you, my boy, and play with your caucuses and leading articles and historic parties and great leaders and burning questions and the rest of your toys. *I* am going back to my counting-house to pay the piper and call the tune.

STEPHEN [*actually smiling, and putting his hand on his father's shoulder with indulgent patronage*]: Really, my dear father, it is impossible to be angry with you. You dont know how absurd all this sounds to m e. You are very properly proud of having been industrious enough to make money; and it is greatly to your credit that you have made so much of it. But it has kept you in circles where you are valued for your money and deferred to for it, instead of in the doubtless very old-fashioned and behind-the-times public school and university where I formed my habits of mind. It is natural for you to think that money governs England; but you must allow me to think I know better.

UNDERSHAFT: And what d o e s govern England, pray?

STEPHEN: Character, father, character.

UNDERSHAFT: Whose character? Yours or mine?

STEPHEN: Neither yours nor mine, father, but the best elements in the English national character.

UNDERSHAFT: Stephen: Ive found your profession for you. Youre a born journalist. I'll start you with a high-toned weekly review. There!

> Before STEPHEN *can reply* SARAH, BARBARA, LOMAX, *and* CUSINS *come in ready for walking.* BARBARA *crosses the room to the window and looks out.* CUSINS *drifts amiably to the armchair.* LOMAX *remains near the door, whilst* SARAH *comes to her mother.*
>
> STEPHEN *goes to the smaller writing table and busies himself with his letters.*

SARAH: Go and get ready, mama: the carriage is waiting. [LADY BRITOMART *leaves the room.*]

UNDERSHAFT [*to* SARAH]: Good day, my dear. Good afternoon, Mr Lomax.

LOMAX [*vaguely*]: Ahdedoo.

UNDERSHAFT [*to* CUSINS]: Quite well after last night, Euripides, eh?

CUSINS: As well as can be expected.

UNDERSHAFT: Thats right. [*To* BARBARA.] So you are coming to see my death and devastation factory, Barbara?

BARBARA [*at the window*]: You came yesterday to see my salvation factory. I promised you a return visit.

LOMAX [*coming forward between* SARAH *and* UNDERSHAFT]: Youll find it awfully interesting. Ive been through the Woolwich Arsenal; and it gives you a ripping feeling of security, you know, to think of the lot of beggars we could kill if it came to fighting. [*To* UNDERSHAFT, *with sudden solemnity.*] Still, it must be rather an awful reflection for you, from the religious point of view as it were. Youre getting on, you know, and all that.

SARAH: You dont mind Cholly's imbecility, papa, do you?

LOMAX [*much taken aback*]: Oh I say!

UNDERSHAFT: Mr Lomax looks at the matter in a very proper spirit, my dear.

LOMAX: Just so. Thats all I meant, I assure you.

SARAH: Are you coming, Stephen?

STEPHEN: Well, I am rather busy—er— [*Magnanimously.*] Oh well, yes: I'll come. That is, if there is room for me.

UNDERSHAFT: I can take two with me in a little motor I am experimenting with for field use. You wont mind its being rather unfashionable. It's not painted yet; but it's bullet proof.

LOMAX [*appalled at the prospect of confronting Wilton Crescent in an unpainted motor*]: Oh I s a y!

SARAH: The carriage for me, thank you. Barbara doesnt mind what she's seen in.

LOMAX: I say, Dolly, old chap: do you really mind the car being a guy? Because of course if you do I'll go in it. Still—

CUSINS: I prefer it.

LOMAX: Thanks awfully, old man. Come, my ownest. [*He hurries out to secure his seat in the carriage.* SARAH *follows him.*]

CUSINS [*moodily walking across to* LADY BRITOMART's *writing table*]: Why are we two coming to this Works Department of Hell? that is what I ask myself.

BARBARA: I have always thought of it as a sort of pit where lost creatures with blackened faces stirred up smoky fires and were driven and tormented by my father? Is it like that, dad?

UNDERSHAFT [*scandalized*]: My dear! It is a spotlessly clean and beautiful hillside town.

CUSINS: With a Methodist chapel? Oh d o say theres a Methodist chapel.

UNDERSHAFT: There are two: a Primitive one and a sophisticated one. There is even an Ethical Society; but it is not much patronized, as my men are all strongly religious. In the High Explosives Sheds they object to the presence of Agnostics as unsafe.

CUSINS: And yet they dont object to you!

BARBARA: Do they obey all your orders?

UNDERSHAFT: I never give them any orders. When I speak to one of them it is "Well, Jones, is the baby doing well? and has Mrs Jones made a good recovery?" "Nicely, thank you, sir." And thats all.

CUSINS: But Jones has to be kept in order. How do you maintain discipline among your men?

UNDERSHAFT: I dont. They do. You see, the one thing Jones wont stand is any rebellion from the man under him, or any assertion of social equality between the wife of the man with 4 shillings a week less than himself, and Mrs Jones! Of course they all rebel against me, theoretically. Practically, every man of them keeps the man just below him in his place. I never meddle with them. I never bully them. I dont even bully Lazarus. I say that certain things are to be done; but I dont order anybody to do them. I dont say, mind you, that there is no ordering about and snubbing and even bullying. The men snub the boys and order them about; the carmen snub the sweepers; the artisans snub the unskilled laborers; the foremen drive and bully both the laborers and artisans; the assistant engineers find fault with the foremen; the chief engineers drop on the assistants; the departmental managers worry the chiefs; and the clerks have tall hats and hymnbooks and keep up the social tone by refusing to associate on equal terms with anybody. The result is a colossal profit, which comes to me.

CUSINS [*revolted*]: You really are a—well, what I was saying yesterday.

BARBARA: What was he saying yesterday?

UNDERSHAFT: Never mind, my dear. He thinks I have made you unhappy. Have I?

BARBARA: Do you think I can be happy in this vulgar silly dress? I! who have worn the uniform. Do you understand what you have done to me? Yesterday I had a man's soul in my hand. I set him in the way of life with his face to salvation. But when we took your money he turned back to drunkenness and derision. [*With intense conviction.*] I will never forgive you that. If I had a child, and you destroyed its body with your explosives—if you murdered Dolly with your horrible guns—I could forgive you if my forgiveness would open the gates of heaven to you. But to take a human soul from me, and turn it into the soul of a wolf! that is worse than any murder.

UNDERSHAFT: Does my daughter despair so easily? Can you strike a man to the heart and leave no mark on him?

BARBARA [*her face lighting up*]: Oh, you are right: he can never be lost now: where was my faith?

CUSINS: Oh, clever clever devil!

BARBARA: You may be a devil; but God speaks through you sometimes. [*She takes her father's hands and kisses them.*] You have given me back my happiness: I feel it deep down now, though my spirit is troubled.

UNDERSHAFT: You have learnt something. That always feels at first as if you had lost something.

BARBARA: Well, take me to the factory of death; and let me learn something more. There must be some truth or other behind all this frightful irony. Come, Dolly. [*She goes out.*]

CUSINS: My guardian angel! [*To* UNDERSHAFT.] Avaunt! [*He follows* BARBARA.]

STEPHENS [*quietly, at the writing table*]: You must not mind Cusins, father. He is a very amiable good fellow; but he is a Greek scholar and naturally a little eccentric.

UNDERSHAFT: Ah, quite so. Thank you, Stephen. Thank you. [*He goes out.*]

> STEPHEN *smiles patronizingly; buttons his coat responsibly; and crosses the room to the door.* LADY BRITOMART, *dressed for out-of-doors, opens it before he reaches it. She looks round for the others; looks at* STEPHEN; *and turns to go without a word.*

STEPHEN [*embarrassed*]: Mother—

LADY BRITOMART: Dont be apologetic, Stephen. And dont forget that you have outgrown your mother. [*She goes out.*]

> *Perivale St Andrews lies between two Middlesex hills, half climbing the northern one. It is an almost smokeless town of white walls, roofs of narrow green slates or red tiles, tall trees, domes, campaniles, and slender chimney shafts, beautifully situated and beautiful in itself. The best view of it is obtained from the crest of a slope about half a mile to the east, where the high explosives are dealt with. The foundry lies hidden in the depths between, the tops of its chimneys sprouting like huge skittles into the middle distance. Across the crest runs an emplacement of concrete, with a firestep, and a parapet which suggests a fortification, because there is a huge cannon of the obsolete Woolwich Infant pattern peering across it at the town. The cannon is mounted on an experimental gun carriage: possibly the original model of the Undershaft disappearing rampart gun alluded to by* STEPHEN. *The firestep, being a convenient place to sit, is furnished here and there with straw disc cushions; and at one place there is the additional luxury of a fur rug.*
>
> BARBARA *is standing on the firestep, looking over the parapet towards the town. On her right is the cannon; on her left the end of a shed raised on piles, with a ladder of three or four steps up to the door, which opens outwards and has a little wooden landing at the threshold, with a fire bucket in the corner of the landing. Several dummy soldiers more or less mutilated, with straw protruding from their gashes, have been shoved out of the way under the landing. A few others are nearly upright against the shed; and one has fallen forward and lies, like a grotesque corpse, on the emplacement. The parapet stops short of the shed, leaving a gap which is the beginning of the path down the hill through the foundry to the town. The rug is on the firestep near this gap. Down on the emplacement behind the cannon is a trolley carrying a huge conical bombshell with a red band painted on it. Further to the right is the door of an office, which, like the sheds, is of the lightest possible construction.*
>
> CUSINS *arrives by the path from the town.*

BARBARA: Well?

CUSINS: Not a ray of hope. Everything perfect! wonderful! real! It only needs a cathedral to be a heavenly city instead of a hellish one.

BARBARA: Have you found out whether they have done anything for old Peter Shirley?

CUSINS: They have found him a job as gatekeeper and timekeeper. He's frightfully miserable. He calls the time-keeping brainwork, and says he isnt used to it; and his gate lodge is so splendid that he's ashamed to use the rooms, and skulks in the scullery.

BARBARA: Poor Peter!

STEPHEN *arrives from the town. He carries a fieldglass.*

STEPHEN [*enthusiastically*]: Have you two seen the place? Why did you leave us?

CUSINS: I wanted to see everything I was not intended to see; and Barbara wanted to make the men talk.

STEPHEN: Have you found anything discreditable?

CUSINS: No. They call him Dandy Andy and are proud of his being a cunning old rascal; but it's all horribly, frightfully, immorally, unanswerably perfect.

SARAH *arrives.*

SARAH: Heavens! what a place! [*She crosses to the trolley.*] Did you see the nursing home!? [*She sits down on the shell.*]

STEPHEN: Did you see the libraries and schools!?

SARAH: Did you see the ball room and the banqueting chamber in the Town Hall!?

STEPHEN: Have you gone into the insurance fund, the pension fund, the building society, the various applications of cooperation!?

UNDERSHAFT *comes from the office, with a sheaf of telegrams in his hand.*

UNDERSHAFT: Well, have you seen everything? I'm sorry I was called away. [*Indicating the telegrams.*] Good news from Manchuria.

STEPHEN: Another Japanese victory?

UNDERSHAFT: Oh, I dont know. Which side wins does not concern us here. No: the good news is that the aerial battleship is a tremendous success. At the first trial it has wiped out a fort with three hundred soldiers in it.

CUSINS [*from the platform*]: Dummy soldiers?

UNDERSHAFT [*striding across to* STEPHEN *and kicking the prostrate dummy brutally out of his way*]: No: the real thing.

CUSINS *and* BARBARA *exchange glances. Then* CUSINS *sits on the step and buries his face in his hands.* BARBARA *gravely lays her hand on his shoulder. He looks up at her in whimsical desperation.*

UNDERSHAFT: Well, Stephen, what do you think of the place?

STEPHEN: Oh, magnificent. A perfect triumph of modern industry. Frankly, my dear father, I have been a fool: I had no idea of what it all meant: of all the wonderful forethought, the power of organization, the administrative capacity, the financial genius, the colossal capital it represents. I have been repeating to myself as I came through your streets "Peace hath her victories no less renowned than War." I have only one misgiving about it all.

UNDERSHAFT: Out with it.

STEPHEN: Well, I cannot help thinking that all this provision for every want of your workmen may sap their independence and weaken their sense of responsibility. And greatly as we enjoyed our tea at that splendid restaurant—how they gave us all that luxury and cake and jam and cream for threepence I really cannot imagine!—still you must remember that restaurants break up home life. Look at the continent, for instance! Are you sure so much pampering is really good for the men's characters?

UNDERSHAFT: Well you see, my dear boy, when you are organizing civilization you have to make up your mind whether trouble and anxiety are good things or not. If you decide that they are, then, I take it, you simply dont organize civilization; and there you are, with trouble and anxiety to make us all angels! But if you decide the other way, you may as well go through with it. However, Stephen, our characters are safe here. A sufficient dose of anxiety is always provided by the fact that we may be blown to smithereens at any moment.

SARAH: By the way, papa, where do you make the explosives?

UNDERSHAFT: In separate little sheds, like that one. When one of them blows up, it costs very little; and only the people quite close to it are killed.

> STEPHEN, *who is quite close to it, looks at it rather scaredly, and moves away quickly to the cannon. At the same moment the door of the shed is thrown abruptly open; and a foreman in overalls and list slippers comes out on the little landing and holds the door for* LOMAX, *who appears in the doorway.*

LOMAX [*with studied coolness*]: My good fellow: you neednt get into a state of nerves. Nothing's going to happen to you; and I suppose it wouldnt be the end of the world if anything did. A little bit of British pluck is what y o u want, old chap. [*He descends and strolls across to* SARAH.]

UNDERSHAFT [*to the foreman*]: Anything wrong, Bilton?

BILTON [*with ironic calm*]: Gentleman walked into the high explosives shed and lit a cigaret, sir: thats all.

UNDERSHAFT: Ah, quite so. [*Going over to* LOMAX.] Do you happen to remember what you did with the match?

LOMAX: Oh come! I'm not a fool. I took jolly good care to blow it out before I chucked it away.

BILTON: The top of it was red hot inside, sir.

LOMAX: Well, suppose it was! I didn't chuck it into any of y o u r messes.

UNDERSHAFT: Think no more of it, Mr Lomax. By the way, would you mind lending me your matches.

LOMAX [*offering his box*]: Certainly.

UNDERSHAFT: Thanks. [*He pockets the matches.*]

LOMAX [*lecturing to the company generally*]: You know, these high explosives dont go off like gunpowder, except when theyre in a gun. When theyre spread loose, you can put a match to them without the least risk: they just burn quietly like a bit of paper. [*Warming to the scientific interest of the subject.*] Did you know that, Undershaft? Have you ever tried?

UNDERSHAFT: Not on a large scale, Mr Lomax. Bilton will give you a sample of gun cotton when you are leaving if you ask him. You can experiment with it at home. [BILTON *looks puzzled.*]

SARAH: Bilton will do nothing of the sort, papa. I suppose it's your business to blow up the Russians and Japs; but you might really stop short of blowing up poor Cholly. [BILTON *gives it up and retires into the shed.*]

LOMAX: My ownest, there is no danger. [*He sits beside her on the shell.*]

LADY BRITOMART *arrives from the town with a bouquet.*

LADY BRITOMART [*impetuously*]: Andrew: you shouldnt have let me see this place.

UNDERSHAFT: Why, my dear?

LADY BRITOMART: Never mind why: you shouldnt have: thats all. To think of all that [*indicating the town*] being yours! and that you have kept it to yourself all these years!

UNDERSHAFT: It does not belong to me. I belong to it. It is the Undershaft inheritance.

LADY BRITOMART: It is not. Your ridiculous cannons and that noisy banging foundry may be the Undershaft inheritance; but all that plate and linen, all that furniture and those houses and orchards and gardens belong to us. They belong to m e: they are not a man's business. I wont give them up. You must be out of your senses to throw them all away; and if you persist in such folly, I will call in a doctor.

UNDERSHAFT [*stooping to smell the bouquet*]: Where did you get the flowers, my dear?

LADY BRITOMART: Your men presented them to me in your William Morris Labor Church.

CUSINS: Oh! It needed only that. A Labor Church! [*He mounts the firestep distractedly, and leans with his elbows on the parapet, turning his back to them.*]

LADY BRITOMART: Yes, with Morris's words in mosaic letters ten feet high round the dome. NO MAN IS GOOD ENOUGH TO BE ANOTHER MAN'S MASTER. The cynicism of it!

UNDERSHAFT: It shocked the men at first, I am afraid. But now they take no more notice of it than of the ten commandments in church.

LADY BRITOMART: Andrew: you are trying to put me off the subject of the inheritance by profane jokes. Well, you shant. I dont ask it any longer for Stephen: he has inherited far too much of your perversity to be fit for it. But Barbara has rights as well as Stephen. Why should not Adolphus succeed to the inheritance? I could manage the town for him; and he can look after the cannons, if they are really necessary.

UNDERSHAFT: I should ask nothing better if Adolphus were a foundling. He is exactly the sort of new blood that is wanted in English business. But he's not a foundling; and theres an end of it. [*He makes for the office door.*]

CUSINS [*turning to them*]: Not quite. [*They all turn and stare at him.*] I think—Mind! I am not committing myself in any way as to my future course—but I t h i n k the foundling difficulty can be got over. [*He jumps down to the emplacement.*]

UNDERSHAFT [*coming back to him*]: What do you mean?

CUSINS: Well, I have something to say which is in the nature of a confession.

SARAH:

LADY BRITOMART: } Confession!

BARBARA:

STEPHEN:

LOMAX: Oh I s a y!

CUSINS: Yes, a confession. Listen, all. Until I met Barbara I thought myself in the main an honorable, truthful man, because I wanted the approval of my conscience more than I wanted anything else. But the moment I saw Barbara, I wanted her far more than the approval of my conscience.

LADY BRITOMART: Adolphus!

CUSINS: It is true. You accused me yourself, Lady Brit, of joining the Army to worship Barbara; and so I did. She bought my soul like a flower at a street corner; but she bought it for herself.

UNDERSHAFT: What! Not for Dionysos or another?

CUSINS: Dionysos and all the others are in herself. I adored what was divine in her, and was therefore a true worshipper. But I was romantic about her too. I thought she was a woman of the people, and that a marriage with a professor of Greek would be far beyond the wildest social ambitions of her rank.

LADY BRITOMART: Adolphus!!

LOMAX: Oh I say!!!

CUSINS: When I learnt the horrible truth—

LADY BRITOMART: What do you mean by the horrible truth, pray?

CUSINS: That she was enormously rich; that her grandfather was an earl; that her father was the Prince of Darkness—

UNDERSHAFT: Chut!

CUSINS: —and that I was only an adventurer trying to catch a rich wife, then I stooped to deceive her about my birth.

BARBARA [*rising*]: Dolly!

LADY BRITOMART: Your birth! Now Adolphus, dont dare to make up a wicked story for the sake of these wretched cannons. Remember: I have seen photographs of your parents; and the Agent General for South Western Australia knows them personally and has assured me that they are most respectable married people.

CUSINS: So they are in Australia; but here they are outcasts. Their marriage is legal in Australia, but not in England. My mother is my father's deceased wife's sister; and in this island I am consequently a foundling. [*Sensation.*]

BARBARA: Silly! [*She climbs to the cannon, and leans, listening, in the angle it makes with the parapet.*]

CUSINS: Is the subterfuge good enough, Machiavelli?

UNDERSHAFT [*thoughtfully*]: Biddy: this may be a way out of the difficulty.

LADY BRITOMART: Stuff! A man cant make cannons any the better for being his own cousin instead of his proper self. [*She sits down on the rug with a bounce that expresses her downright contempt for their casuistry.*]

UNDERSHAFT [*to* CUSINS]: You are an educated man. That is against the tradition.

CUSINS: Once in ten thousand times it happens that the schoolboy is a born master of what they try to teach him. Greek has not destroyed my mind: it has nourished it. Besides, I did not learn it at an English public school.

UNDERSHAFT: Hm! Well, I cannot afford to be too particular: you have cornered the foundling market. Let it pass. You are eligible, Euripides: you are eligible.

BARBARA: Dolly: yesterday morning, when Stephen told us all about the tradition, you became very silent; and you have been strange and excited ever since. Were you thinking of your birth then?

CUSINS: When the finger of Destiny suddenly points at a man in the middle of his breakfast, it makes him thoughtful.

UNDERSHAFT: Aha! You have had your eye on the business, my young friend, have you?

CUSINS: Take care! There is an abyss of moral horror between me and your accursed aerial battleships.

UNDERSHAFT: Never mind the abyss for the present. Let us settle the practical details and leave your final decision open. You know that you will have to change your name. Do you object to that?

CUSINS: Would any man named Adolphus—any man called Dolly!—object to be called something else?

UNDERSHAFT: Good. Now, as to money! I propose to treat you handsomely from the beginning. You shall start at a thousand a year.

CUSINS [*with sudden heat, his spectacles twinkling with mischief*]: A thousand! You dare offer a miserable thousand to the son-in-law of a millionaire!

No, by Heavens, Machiavelli! you shall not cheat m e. You cannot do without m e; and I can do without you. I must have two thousand five hundred a year for two years. At the end of that time, if I am a failure, I go. But if I am a success, and stay on, you must give me the other five thousand.

UNDERSHAFT: What other five thousand?

CUSINS: To make the two years up to five thousand a year. The two thousand five hundred is only half pay in case I should turn out a failure. The third year I must have ten per cent on the profits.

UNDERSHAFT [*taken aback*]: Ten per cent! Why, man, do you know what my profits are?

CUSINS: Enormous, I hope: otherwise I shall require twentyfive per cent.

UNDERSHAFT: But, Mr Cusins, this is a serious matter of business. You are not bringing any capital into the concern.

CUSINS: What! no capital! Is my mastery of Greek no capital? Is my access to the subtlest thought, the loftiest poetry yet attained by humanity, no capital?

My character! my intellect! my life! my career! what Barbara calls my soul! are these no capital? Say another word; and I double my salary.

UNDERSHAFT: Be reasonable—

CUSINS [*peremptorily*]: Mr Undershaft: you have my terms. Take them or leave them.

UNDERSHAFT [*recovering himself*]: Very well. I note your terms; and I offer you half.

CUSINS [*disgusted*]: Half!

UNDERSHAFT [*firmly*]: Half.

CUSINS: You call yourself a gentleman; and you offer me half!!

UNDERSHAFT: I do not call myself a gentleman; but I offer you half.

CUSINS: This to your future partner! your successor! your son-in-law!

BARBARA: You are selling your own soul, Dolly, not mine. Leave me out of the bargain, please.

UNDERSHAFT: Come! I will go a step further for Barbara's sake. I will give you three fifths; but that is my last word.

CUSINS: Done!

LOMAX: Done in the eye! Why, *I* get only eight hundred, you know.

CUSINS: By the way, Mac, I am a classical scholar, not an arithmetical one. Is three fifths more than half or less?

UNDERSHAFT: More, of course.

CUSINS: I would have taken two hundred and fifty. How you can succeed in business when you are willing to pay all that money to a University don who is obviously not worth a junior clerk's wages!—well! What will Lazarus say?

UNDERSHAFT: Lazarus is a gentle romantic Jew who cares for nothing but string quartets and stalls at fashionable theatres. He will be blamed for your rapacity in money matters, poor fellow! as he has hitherto been blamed for mine. You are a shark of the first order, Euripides. So much the better for the firm!

BARBARA: Is the bargain closed, Dolly? Does your soul belong to him now?

CUSINS: No: the price is settled: that is all. The real tug of war is still to come. What about the moral question?

LADY BRITOMART: There is no moral question in the matter at all, Adolphus. You must simply sell cannons and weapons to people whose cause is right and just, and refuse them to foreigners and criminals.

UNDERSHAFT [*determinedly*]: No: none of that. You must keep the true faith of an Armorer, or you dont come in here.

CUSINS: What on earth is the true faith of an Armorer?

UNDERSHAFT: To give arms to all men who offer an honest price for them, without respect of persons or principles: to aristocrat and republican, to Nihilist and Tsar, to Capitalist and Socialist, to Protestant and Catholic, to burglar and policeman, to black man, white man and yellow man, to all sorts and conditions, all nationalities, all faiths, all follies, all causes and all crimes. The first Undershaft wrote up in his shop IF GOD GAVE THE

HAND, LET NOT MAN WITHHOLD THE SWORD. The second wrote up ALL HAVE THE RIGHT TO FIGHT: NONE HAVE THE RIGHT TO JUDGE. The third wrote up TO MAN THE WEAPON: TO HEAVEN THE VICTORY. The fourth had no literary turn; so he did not write up anything; but he sold cannons to Napoleon under the nose of George the Third. The fifth wrote up PEACE SHALL NOT PREVAIL SAVE WITH A SWORD IN HER HAND. The sixth, my master, was the best of all. He wrote up NOTHING IS EVER DONE IN THIS WORLD UNTIL MEN ARE PREPARED TO KILL ONE ANOTHER IF IT IS NOT DONE. After that, there was nothing left for the seventh to say. So he wrote up, simply, UNASHAMED.

CUSINS: My good Machiavelli, I shall certainly write something up on the wall; only, as I shall write it in Greek, you wont be able to read it. But as to your Armorer's faith, if I take my neck out of the noose of my own morality I am not going to put it into the noose of yours. I shall sell cannons to whom I please and refuse them to whom I please. So there!

UNDERSHAFT: From the moment when you become Andrew Undershaft, you will never do as you please again. Dont come here lusting for power, young man.

CUSINS: If power were my aim I should not come here for it. Y o u have no power.

UNDERSHAFT: None of my own, certainly.

CUSINS: I have more power than you, more will. You do not drive this place: it drives you. And what drives the place?

UNDERSHAFT [enigmatically]: A will of which I am a part.

BARBARA [startled]: Father! Do you know what you are saying; or are you laying a snare for my soul?

CUSINS: Dont listen to his metaphysics, Barbara. The place is driven by the most rascally part of society, the money hunters, the pleasure hunters, the military promotion hunters; and he is their slave.

UNDERSHAFT: Not necessarily. Remember the Armorer's Faith. I will take an order from a good man as cheerfully as from a bad one. If you good people prefer preaching and shirking to buying my weapons and fighting the rascals, dont blame me. I can make cannons: I cannot make courage and conviction. Bah! you tire me, Euripides, with your morality monger-ing. Ask Barbara: s h e understands. [He suddenly reaches up and takes BARBARA's hands, looking powerfully into her eyes.] Tell him, my love, what power really means.

BARBARA [hypnotized]: Before I joined the Salvation Army, I was in my own power; and the consequence was that I never knew what to do with myself. When I joined it, I had not time enough for all the things I had to do.

UNDERSHAFT [approvingly]: Just so. And why was that, do you suppose?

BARBARA: Yesterday I should have said, because I was in the power of God. [She resumes her self-possession, withdrawing her hands from his with a power equal to his own.] But you came and shewed me that I was in the power of Bodger and Undershaft. Today I feel—oh! how can I put it into words? Sarah: do you remember the earthquake at Cannes, when we were little children?—how little the surprise of the first shock mattered compared to the dread and horror of waiting for the second? That is how I feel in this place today. I stood on the rock I thought eternal; and without a word of warning it reeled and crumbled under me. I was safe with an infinite wisdom watching me, an army marching to Salvation with me; and in a moment, at a stroke of your pen in a cheque book, I stood alone; and the heavens were empty. That was the first shock of the earthquake: I am waiting for the second.

UNDERSHAFT: Come, come, my daughter! dont make too much of your little tinpot tragedy. What do we do here when we spend years of work and thought and thousands of pounds of solid cash on a new gun or an aerial battleship that turns out just a hairsbreadth wrong after all? Scrap it. Scrap it without wasting another hour or another pound on it. Well, you have made for yourself something that you call a morality or a religion or what not. It doesnt fit the facts. Well, scrap it. Scrap it and get one that does fit. That is what is wrong with the world at present. It scraps its obsolete steam engines and dynamos; but it wont scrap its old prejudices and its old moralities and its old religions and its old political constitutions. Whats the result? In machinery it does very well; but in morals and religion and politics it is working at a loss that brings it nearer bankruptcy every year. Dont persist in that folly. If your old religion broke down yesterday, get a newer and a better one for tomorrow.

BARBARA: Oh how gladly I would take a better one to my soul! But you offer me a worse one. [*Turning on him with sudden vehemence.*] Justify yourself: shew me some light through the darkness of this dreadful place, with its beautifully clean workshops, and respectable workmen, and model homes.

UNDERSHAFT: Cleanliness and respectability do not need justification, Barbara: they justify themselves. I see no darkness here, no dreadfulness. In your Salvation shelter I saw poverty, misery, cold and hunger. You gave them bread and treacle and dreams of heaven. I give from thirty shillings a week to twelve thousand a year. They find their own dreams; but I look after the drainage.

BARBARA: And their souls?

UNDERSHAFT: I saved their souls just as I saved yours.

BARBARA [*revolted*]: Y o u saved my soul! What do you mean?

UNDERSHAFT: I fed you and clothed you and housed you. I took care that you should have money enough to live handsomely—more than enough; so that you could be wasteful, careless, generous. That saved your soul from the seven deadly sins.

BARBARA [*bewildered*]: The seven deadly sins!

UNDERSHAFT: Yes, the deadly seven. [*Counting on his fingers.*] Food, clothing, firing, rent, taxes, respectability and children. Nothing can lift those seven millstones from Man's neck but money; and the spirit cannot soar until the millstones are lifted. I lifted them from your spirit. I enabled Barbara to become Major Barbara; and I saved her from the crime of poverty.

CUSINS: Do you call poverty a crime?

UNDERSHAFT: The worst of crimes. All the other crimes are virtues beside it: all the other dishonors are chivalry itself by comparison. Poverty blights whole cities; spreads horrible pestilences; strikes dead the very souls of all who come within sight, sound, or smell of it. What you call crime is nothing: a murder here and a theft there, a blow now and a curse then: what do they matter? they are only the accidents and illnesses of life: there are not fifty genuine professional criminals in London. But there are millions of poor people, abject people, dirty people, ill fed, ill clothed people. They poison us morally and physically: they kill the happiness of society: they force us to do away with our own liberties and to organize unnatural cruelties for fear they should rise against us and drag us down into their abyss. Only fools fear crime: we all fear poverty. Pah! [*turning on* BARBARA] you talk of your half-saved ruffian in West Ham: you accuse me of dragging his soul back to perdition. Well, bring him to me here; and I will drag his soul back again to salvation for you. Not by words and dreams; but by thirtyeight shillings a week, a sound house in a handsome street, and a permanent job. In three weeks he will have a fancy waistcoat; in three months a tall hat and a chapel sitting; before the end of the year he will shake hands with a duchess at a Primrose League meeting, and join the Conservative Party.

BARBARA: And will he be the better for that?

UNDERSHAFT: You know he will. Dont be a hypocrite, Barbara. He will be better fed, better housed, better clothed, better behaved; and his children will be pounds heavier and bigger. That will be better than an American cloth mattress in a shelter, chopping firewood, eating bread and treacle, and being forced to kneel down from time to time to thank heaven for it: knee drill, I think you call it. It is cheap work converting starving men with a Bible in one hand and a slice of bread in the other. I will undertake to convert West Ham to Mahometanism on the same terms. Try your hand on m y men: their souls are hungry because their bodies are full.

BARBARA: And leave the east end to starve?

UNDERSHAFT [*his energetic tone dropping into one of bitter and brooding remembrance*]: *I* was an east ender. I moralized and starved until one day I swore that I would be a full-fed free man at all costs; that nothing should stop me except a bullet, neither reason nor morals nor the lives of other men. I said "Thou shalt starve ere I starve"; and with that word I became free and great. I was a dangerous man until I had my will: now I am a useful, beneficent, kindly person. That is the history of most self-made millionaires, I fancy. When it is the history of every Englishman we shall have an England worth living in.

LADY BRITOMART: Stop making speeches, Andrew. This is not the place for them.

UNDERSHAFT [*punctured*]: My dear: I have no other means of conveying my ideas.

LADY BRITOMART: Your ideas are nonsense. You got on because you were selfish and unscrupulous.

UNDERSHAFT: Not at all. I had the strongest scruples about poverty and starvation. Your moralists are quite unscrupulous about both: they make virtues of them. I had rather be a thief than a pauper. I had rather be a murderer than a slave. I dont want to be either; but if you force the alternative on me, then, by Heaven, I'll choose the braver and more moral one. I hate poverty and slavery worse than any other crimes whatsoever. And let me tell you this. Poverty and slavery have stood up for centuries to your sermons and leading articles: they will not stand up to my machine guns. Dont preach at them: dont reason with them. Kill them.

BARBARA: Killing. Is that your remedy for everything?

UNDERSHAFT: It is the final test of conviction, the only lever strong enough to overturn a social system, the only way of saying Must. Let six hundred and seventy fools loose in the streets; and three policemen can scatter them. But huddle them together in a certain house in Westminister; and let them go through certain ceremonies and call themselves certain names until at last they get the courage to kill; and your six hundred and seventy fools become a government. Your pious mob fills up ballot papers and imagines it is governing its masters; but the ballot paper that really governs is the paper that has a bullet wrapped up in it.

CUSINS: That is perhaps why, like most intelligent people, I never vote.

UNDERSHAFT: Vote! Bah! When you vote, you only change the names of the cabinet. When you shoot, you pull down governments, inaugurate new epochs, abolish old orders and set up new. Is that historically true, Mr Learned Man, or is it not?

CUSINS: It is historically true. I loathe having to admit it. I repudiate your sentiments. I abhor your nature. I defy you in every possible way. Still, it is true. But it ought not to be true.

UNDERSHAFT: Ought! ought! ought! ought! ought! Are you going to spend your life saying ought, like the rest of our moralists? Turn your oughts into shalls, man. Come and make explosives with me. Whatever can blow men up can blow society up. The history of the world is the history of those who had courage enough to embrace this truth. Have you the courage to embrace it, Barbara?

LADY BRITOMART: Barbara: I positively forbid you to listen to your father's abominable wickedness. And you, Adolphus, ought to know better than to go about saying that wrong things are true. What does it matter whether they are true if they are wrong?

UNDERSHAFT: What does it matter whether they are wrong if they are true?

LADY BRITOMART [rising]: Children: come home instantly. Andrew: I am exceedingly sorry I allowed you to call on us. You are wickeder than ever. Come at once.

BARBARA [shaking her head]: It's no use running away from wicked people, mamma.

LADY BRITOMART: It is every use. It shews your disapprobation of them.

BARBARA: It does not save them.

LADY BRITOMART: I can see that you are going to disobey me. Sarah: are you coming home or are you not?

SARAH: I daresay it's very wicked of papa to make cannons; but I dont think I shall cut him on that account.

LOMAX [*pouring oil on the troubled waters*]: The fact is, you know, there is a certain amount of tosh about this notion of wickedness. It doesnt work. You must look at facts. Not that I would say a word in favor of anything wrong; but then, you see, all sorts of chaps are always doing all sorts of things; and we have to fit them in somehow, dont you know. What I mean is that you cant go cutting everybody; and thats about what it comes to. [*Their rapt attention to his eloquence makes him nervous.*] Perhaps I dont make myself clear.

LADY BRITOMART: You are lucidity itself, Charles. Because Andrew is successful and has plenty of money to give to Sarah, you will flatter him and encourage him in his wickedness.

LOMAX [*unruffled*]: Well, where the carcase is, there will the eagles be gathered, dont you know. [*To* UNDERSHAFT.] Eh? What?

UNDERSHAFT: Precisely. By the way, m a y I call you Charles?

LOMAX: Delighted. Cholly is the usual ticket.

UNDERSHAFT [*to* LADY BRITOMART]: Biddy—

LADY BRITOMART [*violently*]: Dont dare call me Biddy. Charles Lomax: you are a fool. Adolphus Cusins: you are a Jesuit. Stephen: you are a prig. Barbara: you are a lunatic. Andrew: you are a vulgar tradesman. Now you all know my opinion; and m y conscience is clear, at all events. [*She sits down with a vehemence that the rug fortunately softens.*]

UNDERSHAFT: My dear: you are the incarnation of morality. [*She snorts.*] Your conscience is clear and your duty done when you have called everybody names. Come, Euripides! it is getting late; and we all want to go home. Make up your mind.

CUSINS: Understand this, you old demon—

LADY BRITOMART: Adolphus!

UNDERSHAFT: Let him alone, Biddy. Proceed, Euripides.

CUSINS: You have me in a horrible dilemma. I want Barbara.

UNDERSHAFT: Like all young men, you greatly exaggerate the difference between one young woman and another.

BARBARA: Quite true, Dolly.

CUSINS: I also want to avoid being a rascal.

UNDERSHAFT [*with biting contempt*]: You lust for personal righteousness, for self-approval, for what you call a good conscience, for what Barbara calls salvation, for what I call patronizing people who are not so lucky as yourself.

CUSINS: I do not: all the poet in me recoils from being a good man. But there are things in me that I must reckon with. Pity—

UNDERSHAFT: Pity! The scavenger of misery.

CUSINS: Well, love.

UNDERSHAFT: I know. You love the needy and the outcast: you love the oppressed races, the negro, the Indian ryot,[12] the underdog everywhere.

12. Peasant.

Do you love the Japanese? Do you love the French? Do you love the English?

CUSINS: No. Every true Englishman detests the English. We are the wickedest nation on earth; and our success is a moral horror.

UNDERSHAFT: That is what comes of your gospel of love, is it?

CUSINS: May I not love even my father-in-law?

UNDERSHAFT: Who wants your love, man? By what right do you take the liberty of offering it to me? I will have your due heed and respect, or I will kill you. But your love! Damn your impertinence!

CUSINS [*grinning*]: I may not be able to control my affections, Mac.

UNDERSHAFT: You are fencing, Euripides. You are weakening: your grip is slipping. Come! try your last weapon. Pity and love have broken in your hand: forgiveness is still left.

CUSINS: No: forgiveness is a beggar's refuge. I am with you there: we must pay our debts.

UNDERSHAFT: Well said. Come! you will suit me. Remember the words of Plato.

CUSINS [*starting*]: Plato! Y o u dare quote Plato to m e!

UNDERSHAFT: Plato says, my friend, that society cannot be saved until either the Professors of Greek take to making gunpowder, or else the makers of gunpowder become Professors of Greek.

CUSINS: Oh, tempter, cunning tempter!

UNDERSHAFT: Come! choose, man, choose.

CUSINS: But perhaps Barbara will not marry me if I make the wrong choice.

BARBARA: Perhaps not.

CUSINS [*desperately perplexed*]: You hear!

BARBARA: Father: do you love nobody?

UNDERSHAFT: I love my best friend.

LADY BRITOMART: And who is that, pray?

UNDERSHAFT: My bravest enemy. That is the man who keeps me up to the mark.

CUSINS: You know, the creature is really a sort of poet in his way. Suppose he is a great man, after all!

UNDERSHAFT: Suppose you stop talking and make up your mind, my young friend.

CUSINS: But you are driving me against my nature. I hate war.

UNDERSHAFT: Hatred is the coward's revenge for being intimidated. Dare you make war on war? Here are the means: my friend Mr Lomax is sitting on them.

LOMAX [*springing up*]: Oh I say! You dont mean that this thing is loaded, do you? My ownest: come off it.

SARAH [*sitting placidly on the shell*]: If I am to be blown up, the more thoroughly it is done the better. Dont fuss, Cholly.

LOMAX [*to* UNDERSHAFT, *strongly remonstrant*]: Your own daughter, you know!

UNDERSHAFT: So I see. [*To* CUSINS.] Well, my friend, may we expect you here at six tomorrow morning?

CUSINS [*firmly*]: Not on any account. I will see the whole establishment blown up with its own dynamite before I will get up at five. My hours are healthy, rational hours: eleven to five.

UNDERSHAFT: Come when you please: before a week you will come at six and stay until I turn you out for the sake of your health. [*Calling.*] Bilton! [*He turns to* LADY BRITOMART, *who rises.*] My dear: let us leave these two young people to themselves for a moment. [BILTON *comes from the shed.*] I am going to take you through the gun cotton shed.

BILTON [*barring the way*]: You cant take anything explosive in here, sir.

LADY BRITOMART: What do you mean? Are you alluding to me?

BILTON [*unmoved*]: No, maam. Mr Undershaft has the other gentleman's matches in his pocket.

LADY BRITOMART [*abruptly*]: Oh! I beg your pardon. [*She goes into the shed.*]

UNDERSHAFT: Quite right, Bilton, quite right: here you are. [*He gives* BILTON *the box of matches.*] Come, Stephen. Come, Charles. Bring Sarah. [*He passes into the shed.*]

> BILTON *opens the box and deliberately drops the matches into the fire-bucket.*

LOMAX: Oh! I say. [BILTON *stolidly hands him the empty box.*] Infernal nonsense! Pure scientific ignorance! [*He goes in.*]

SARAH: Am I all right, Bilton?

BILTON: Youll have to put on list slippers, miss: thats all. Weve got em inside. [*She goes in.*]

STEPHEN [*very seriously to* CUSINS]: Dolly, old fellow, think. Think before you decide. Do you feel that you are a sufficiently practical man? It is a huge undertaking, an enormous responsibility. All this mass of business will be Greek to you.

CUSINS: Oh, I think it will be much less difficult than Greek.

STEPHEN: Well, I just want to say this before I leave you to yourselves. Dont let anything I have said about right and wrong prejudice you against this great chance in life. I have satisfied myself that the business is one of the highest character and a credit to our country. [*Emotionally.*] I am very proud of my father. I—[*Unable to proceed, he presses* CUSINS' *hand and goes hastily into the shed, followed by* BILTON.]

> BARBARA *and* CUSINS, *left alone together, look at one another silently.*

CUSINS: Barbara: I am going to accept this offer.

BARBARA: I thought you would.

CUSINS: You understand, dont you, that I had to decide without consulting you. If I had thrown the burden of the choice on you, you would sooner or later have despised me for it.

BARBARA: Yes: I did not want you to sell your soul for me any more than for this inheritance.

CUSINS: It is not the sale of my soul that troubles me: I have sold it too often to care about that. I have sold it for a professorship. I have sold it for an income. I have sold it to escape being imprisoned for refusing to pay taxes for hangmen's ropes and unjust wars and things that I abhor. What is all human conduct but the daily and hourly sale of our souls for trifles? What I am now selling it for is neither money nor position nor comfort, but for reality and for power.

BARBARA: You know that you will have no power, and that he has none.

CUSINS: I know. It is not for myself alone. I want to make power for the world.

BARBARA: I want to make power for the world too; but it must be spiritual power.

CUSINS: I think all power is spiritual: these cannons will not go off by themselves. I have tried to make spiritual power by teaching Greek. But the world can never be really touched by a dead language and a dead civilization. The people must have power; and the people cannot have Greek. Now the power that is made here can be wielded by all men.

BARBARA: Power to burn women's houses down and kill their sons and tear their husbands to pieces.

CUSINS: You cannot have power for good without having power for evil too. Even mother's milk nourishes murderers as well as heroes. This power which only tears men's bodies to pieces has never been so horribly abused as the intellectual power, the imaginative power, the poetic, religious power that can enslave men's souls. As a teacher of Greek I gave the intellectual man weapons against the common man. I now want to give the common man weapons against the intellectual man. I love the common people. I want to arm them against the lawyers, the doctors, the priests, the literary men, the professors, the artists, and the politicians, who, once in authority, are more disastrous and tyrannical than all the fools, rascals, and impostors. I want a power simple enough for common men to use, yet strong enough to force the intellectual oligarchy to use its genius for the general good.

BARBARA: Is there no higher power than that? [*Pointing to the shell.*]

CUSINS: Yes; but that power can destroy the higher powers just as a tiger can destroy a man: therefore Man must master that power first. I admitted this when the Turks and Greeks were last at war. My best pupil went out to fight for Hellas. My parting gift to him was not a copy of Plato's Republic, but a revolver and a hundred Undershaft cartridges. The blood of every Turk he shot—if he shot any—is on my head as well as on Undershaft's. That act committed me to this place for ever. Your father's challenge has beaten me. Dare I make war on war? I dare. I must. I will. And now, is it all over between us?

BARBARA [*touched by his evident dread of her answer*]: Silly baby Dolly! How could it be!

CUSINS [*overjoyed*]: Then you—you—you— Oh for my drum! [*He flourishes imaginary drumsticks.*]

BARBARA [*angered by his levity*]: Take care, Dolly, take care. Oh, if only I could get away from you and from father and from it all! if I could have the wings of a dove and fly away to heaven!

CUSINS: And leave m e!

BARBARA: Yes, you, and all the other naughty mischievous children of men. But I cant. I was happy in the Salvation Army for a moment. I escaped from the world into a paradise of enthusiasm and prayer and soul saving; but the moment our money ran short, it all came back to Bodger: it was he who saved our people: he, and the Prince of Darkness, my papa. Undershaft and Bodger: their hands stretch everywhere: when we feed a starving fellow creature, it is with their bread, because there is no other bread; when we tend the sick, it is in the hospitals they endow; if we turn from the churches they build, we must kneel on the stones of the streets they pave. As long as that lasts, there is no getting away from them. Turning our backs on Bodger and Undershaft is turning our backs on life.

CUSINS: I thought you were determined to turn your back on the wicked side of life.

BARBARA: There is no wicked side: life is all one. And I never wanted to shirk my share in whatever evil must be endured, whether it be sin or suffering. I wish I could cure you of middle-class ideas, Dolly.

CUSINS [gasping]: Middle cl—! A snub! A social snub to m e! from the daughter of a foundling!

BARBARA: That is why I have no class, Dolly: I come straight out of the heart of the whole people. If I were middle-class I should turn my back on my father's business; and we should both live in an artistic drawing room, with you reading the reviews in one corner, and I in the other at the piano, playing Schumann: both very superior persons, and neither of us a bit of use. Sooner than that, I would sweep out the guncotton shed, or be one of Bodger's barmaids. Do you know what would have happened if you had refused papa's offer?

CUSINS: I wonder!

BARBARA: I should have given you up and married the man who accepted it. After all, my dear old mother has more sense than any of you. I felt like her when I saw this place—felt that I must have it—that never, never, never could I let it go; only she thought it was the houses and the kitchen ranges and the linen and china, when it was really all the human souls to be saved: not weak souls in starved bodies, sobbing with gratitude for a scrap of bread and treacle, but fullfed, quarrelsome, snobbish, uppish creatures, all standing on their little rights and dignities, and thinking that my father ought to be greatly obliged to them for making so much money for him—and so he ought. That is where salvation is really wanted. My father shall never throw it in my teeth again that my converts were bribed with bread. [She is transfigured.] I have got rid of the bribe of bread. I have got rid of the bribe of heaven. Let God's work be done for its own sake: the work he had to create us to do because it cannot be done except by living men and women. When I die, let him be in my debt, not I in his; and let me forgive him as becomes a woman of my rank.

CUSINS: Then the way of life lies through the factory of death?

BARBARA: Yes, through the raising of hell to heaven and of man to God, through the unveiling of an eternal light in the Valley of The Shadow. [Seizing him *with both hands.*] Oh, did you think my courage would never come back? did you believe that I was a deserter? that I, who have stood in the streets, and taken my people to my heart, and talked of the holiest and greatest things with them, could ever turn back and chatter foolishly to fashionable people about nothing in a drawing room? Never, never, never, never: Major Barbara will die with the colors. Oh! and I have my dear little Dolly boy still; and he has found me my place and my work. Glory Hallelujah! [*She kisses him.*]

CUSINS: My dearest: consider my delicate health. I cannot stand as much happiness as you can.

BARBARA: Yes: it is not easy work being in love with me, is it? But it's good for you. [*She runs to the shed, and calls, childlike.*] Mamma! Mamma! [BILTON *comes out of the shed, followed by* UNDERSHAFT.] I want Mamma.

UNDERSHAFT: She is taking off her list slippers, dear. [*He passes on to* CUSINS.] Well? What does she say?

CUSINS: She has gone right up into the skies.

LADY BRITOMART [*coming from the shed and stopping on the steps, obstructing* SARAH, *who follows with* LOMAX. BARBARA *clutches like a baby at her mother's skirt.*]: Barbara: when will you learn to be independent and to act and think for yourself? I know as well as possible what that cry of "Mamma, Mamma," means. Always running to me!

SARAH [*touching* LADY BRITOMART's *ribs with her finger tips and imitating a bicycle horn*]: Pip! pip!

LADY BRITOMART [*highly indignant*]: How dare you say Pip! pip! to me, Sarah? You are both very naughty children. What do you want, Barbara?

BARBARA: I want a house in the village to live in with Dolly. [*Dragging at the skirt.*] Come and tell me which one to take.

UNDERSHAFT [*to* CUSINS]: Six o'clock tomorrow morning, Euripides.

Fact Questions and Exercises

1. How has Andrew Undershaft made his fortune?
2. What reason does Lady Britomart give Stephen for having "separated" from her husband?
3. In which scene does the reader learn that Undershaft has not maintained close ties with his family during his separation from Lady Britomart?
4. Identify Barbara's fiancé. What is his attitude toward marriage?
5. How does Undershaft "buy" the Salvation Army?
6. Point out some of the characterizing techniques that Shaw uses to distinguish the lower class, such as Rummy, from the aristocracy, as represented by the Undershafts.
7. Why doesn't Stephen want to take over his father's business? What profession does Stephen prefer?
8. Identify Perivale St. Andrews.
9. According to Undershaft, what are the "seven deadly sins"?
10. Ultimately, who agrees to take over Undershaft's business?

For Discussion and Writing

1. In his preface to *Major Barbara*, Shaw says that Undershaft is "a man who . . . knows that poverty is a crime" and that society has forced Undershaft to decide on a career of "energetic enterprise." Shaw also says that "if a man cannot look evil in the face without illusion, he will never know what it really is, or combat it effectually." In light of these observations, discuss Shaw's conception of Undershaft as a "hero" of modern society. How, for instance, does he compare Undershaft with Peter Shirley? What personal characteristics does Shaw seem to admire? Which ones does he seem to disparage? Do you agree that Undershaft is an admirable individual?

2. Characterize Barbara. What are her motivations? Why does she join the Salvation Army? Is this in reaction to her family? What values does she represent? Does she become disillusioned with these values? If so, why? How does she compare with her sister Sarah?

3. Shaw uses two types of "armies" to represent various and often conflicting social forces; discuss these armies. What forces or values do the armies signify? How do these values conflict? Does Shaw seem to view one set of values as preferable to the other? If so, what argument does he use to support his viewpoint?

4. Discuss Shaw's use of language. What, for example, does Cusins say about the English language? How does Shaw use language as a mark of social standing? How does the language of the younger generation in *Major Barbara* differ from that of the older generation? Which conventions of English usage does Shaw ignore?

Eugene O'Neill [1888–1953]

O'Neill was born in New York City, the son of a well-known actor and a drug-addicted mother. He attended Princeton briefly; was expelled; and then held a variety of jobs, among them searching for gold in Honduras. Eventually, he joined his father's acting company, but soon tired of that and shipped as a common seaman. In 1921 he spent six months in a sanatorium, seeking a cure for tuberculosis. Following this stay, he began to write the plays that would eventually make him America's leading dramatist. His plays are naturalistic and Freudian, and rely upon classical and biblical themes. *Long Day's Journey Into Night* (1956) is a drama based on O'Neill's own tragic life. Among his other plays are *Anna Christie* (1921), *Strange Interlude* (1928), and *Mourning Becomes Electra* (1931); *Desire Under the Elms* (1924) is perhaps the best-known and most representative of his plays. O'Neill was awarded the Nobel Prize in 1936.

Desire Under the Elms

A Play in Three Parts

CHARACTERS

EPHRAIM CABOT

SIMEON ⎫
PETER ⎬ *his sons*
EBEN ⎭

ABBIE PUTNAM

YOUNG GIRL, TWO FARMERS, THE FIDDLER, A SHERIFF, *and other folk from the neighboring farms*

The action of the entire play takes place in, and immediately outside of, the Cabot farmhouse in New England, in the year 1850. The south end of the house faces front to a stone wall with a wooden gate at center opening on a country road. The house is in good condition but in need of paint. Its walls are a sickly grayish, the green of the shutters faded. Two enormous elms are on each side of the house. They bend their trailing branches down over the roof. They appear to protect and at the same time subdue. There is a sinister maternity in their aspect, a crushing, jealous absorption. They have developed from their intimate contact with the life of man in the house an appalling humaneness. They brood oppressively over the house. They are like exhausted women resting their sagging breasts and hands and hair on its roof, and when it rains their tears trickle down monotonously and rot on the shingles.

There is a path running from the gate around the right corner of the house to the front door. A narrow porch is on this side. The end wall facing us has two windows in its upper story, two larger ones on the floor below.

The two upper are those of the father's bedroom and that of the brothers. On the left, ground floor, is the kitchen—on the right, the parlor, the shades of which are always drawn down.

PART ONE, SCENE ONE

(*Exterior of the Farmhouse. It is sunset of a day at the beginning of summer in the year 1850. There is no wind and everything is still. The sky above the roof is suffused with deep colors, the green of the elms glows, but the house is in shadow, seeming pale and washed out by contrast.*

A door opens and EBEN CABOT *comes to the end of the porch and stands looking down the road to the right. He has a large bell in his hand and this he swings mechanically, awakening a deafening clangor. Then he puts his hands on his hips and stares up at the sky. He sighs with a puzzled awe and blurts out with halting appreciation.*)

EBEN: God! Purty! (*His eyes fall and he stares about him frowningly. He is twenty-five, tall and sinewy. His face is well-formed, good-looking, but its expression is resentful and defensive. His defiant, dark eyes remind one of a wild animal's in captivity. Each day is a cage in which he finds himself trapped but inwardly unsubdued. There is a fierce repressed vitality about him. He has black hair, mustache, a thin curly trace of beard. He is dressed in rough farm clothes.*)

(*He spits on the ground with intense disgust, turns and goes back into the house.*)

(SIMEON *and* PETER *come in from their work in the fields. They are tall men, much older than their half-brother—*SIMEON *is thirty-nine and* PETER *thirty-seven—, built on a squarer, simpler model, fleshier in body, more bovine and homelier in face, shrewder and more practical. Their shoulders stoop a bit from years of farm work. They clump heavily along in their clumsy thick-soled boots caked with earth. Their clothes, their faces, hands, bare arms and throats are earth-stained. They smell of earth. They stand together for a moment in front of the house and, as if with the one impulse, stare dumbly up at the sky, leaning on their hoes. Their faces have a compressed, unresigned expression. As they look upward, this softens.*)

SIMEON (*grudgingly*): Purty.

PETER: Ay-eh.

SIMEON (*suddenly*): Eighteen year ago.

PETER: What?

SIMEON: Jenn. My woman. She died.

PETER: I'd fergot.

SIMEON: I rec'lect—now an' agin. Makes it lonesome. She'd hair long's a hoss' tail—an' yaller like gold!

PETER: Waal—she's gone. (*This with indifferent finality—then after a pause.*) They's gold in the West, Sim.

SIMEON (*still under the influence of sunset—vaguely*): In the sky?

PETER: Waal—in a manner o' speakin'—thar's the promise. (*Growing excited.*) Gold in the sky—in the West—Golden Gate—Californi-a!—Goldest West!—fields o' gold!

SIMEON (*excited in his turn*): Fortunes layin' just atop o' the ground waitin' t' be picked! Solomon's mines, they says! (*For a moment they continue looking up at the sky—then their eyes drop.*)

PETER (*with sardonic bitterness*): Here—it's stones atop o' the ground—stones atop o' stones—makin' stone walls—year atop o' year—him 'n' yew 'n' me 'n' then Eben—makin' stone walls fur him to fence us in!

SIMEON: We've wuked. Give our strength. Give our years. Plowed 'em under in the ground—(*he stamps rebelliously*)—rottin'—makin' soil for his crops! (*A pause.*) Waal—the farm pays good for hereabouts.

PETER: If we plowed in Californi-a, they'd be lumps o' gold in the furrow!

SIMEON: Californi-a's t'other side o' earth, a'most. We got t' calc'late—

PETER (*after a pause*): 'Twould be hard fur me, too, to give up what we've 'arned here by our sweat. (*A pause.* EBEN *sticks his head out of the dining-room window, listening.*)

SIMEON: Ay-eh. (*A pause.*) Mebbe—he'll die soon.

PETER (*doubtfully*): Mebbe.

SIMEON: Mebbe—fur all we knows—he's dead now.

PETER: Ye'd need proof.

SIMEON: He's been gone two months—with no word.

PETER: Left us in the fields an evenin' like this. Hitched up an' druv off into the West. That's plumb onnateral. He hain't never been off this farm 'ceptin' t' the village in thirty year or more, not since he married Eben's maw. (*A pause. Shrewdly.*) I calc'late we might git him declared crazy by the court.

SIMEON: He skinned 'em too slick. He got the best o' all on 'em. They'd never b'lieve him crazy. (*A pause.*) We got t' wait—till he's under ground.

EBEN (*with a sardonic chuckle*): Honor thy father! (*They turn, startled, and stare at him. He grins, then scowls.*) I pray he's died. (*They stare at him. He continues matter-of-factly.*) Supper's ready.

SIMEON AND PETER (*together*): Ay-eh.

EBEN (*gazing up at the sky*): Sun's downin' purty.

SIMEON AND PETER (*together*): Ay-eh. They's gold in the West.

EBEN: Ay-eh. (*Pointing.*) Yonder atop o' the hill pasture, ye mean?

SIMEON AND PETER (*together*): In Californi-a!

EBEN: Hunh? (*Stares at them indifferently for a second, then drawls.*) Waal— supper's gittin' cold. (*He turns back into kitchen.*)

SIMEON (*startled—smacks his lips*): I air hungry!

PETER (*sniffing*): I smells bacon!

SIMEON (*with hungry appreciation*): Bacon's good!

PETER (*in same tone*): Bacon's bacon! (*They turn, shouldering each other, their bodies bumping and rubbing together as they hurry clumsily to their food, like to friendly oxen toward their evening meal. They disappear around the right corner of house and can be heard entering the door.*)

(*The curtain falls.*)

SCENE TWO

(*The color fades from the sky. Twilight begins. The interior of the kitchen is now visible. A pine table is at center, a cookstove in the right rear corner, four rough wooden chairs, a tallow candle on the table. In the middle of the rear wall is fastened a big advertising poster with a ship in full sail and the word "California" in big letters. Kitchen utensils hang from nails. Everything is neat and in order but the atmosphere is of a men's camp kitchen rather than that of a home.*)

(*Places for three are laid.* EBEN *takes boiled potatoes and bacon from the stove and puts them on the table, also a loaf of bread and a crock of water.* SIMEON *and* PETER *shoulder in, slump down in their chairs without a word.* EBEN *joins them. The three eat in silence for a moment, the two elder as naturally unrestrained as beasts of the field,* EBEN *picking at his food without appetite, glancing at them with a tolerant dislike.*)

SIMEON (*suddenly turns to* EBEN): Looky here! Ye'd oughtn't t' said that, Eben.

PETER: 'Twa'n't righteous.

EBEN: What?

SIMEON: Ye prayed he'd died.

EBEN: Waal—don't yew pray it? (*A pause.*)

PETER: He's our Paw.

EBEN (*violently*): Not mine!

SIMEON (*dryly*): Ye'd not let no one else say that about yer Maw! Ha! (*He gives one abrupt sardonic guffaw.* PETER *grins.*)

EBEN (*very pale*): I meant—I hain't his'n—I hain't like him—he hain't me!

PETER (*dryly*): Wait till ye've growed his age!

EBEN (*intensely*): I'm Maw—every drop o' blood! (*A pause. They stare at him with indifferent curiosity.*)

PETER (*reminiscently*): She was good t' Sim 'n' me. A good Step-maw's scurse.

SIMEON: She was good t' everyone.

EBEN (*greatly moved, gets to his feet and makes an awkward bow to each of them—stammering*): I be thankful t' ye. I'm her—her heir. (*He sits down in confusion.*)

PETER (*after a pause—judicially*): She was good even t' him.

EBEN (*fiercely*): An' fur thanks he killed her!

SIMEON (*after a pause*): No one never kills nobody. It's allus somethin'. That's the murderer.

EBEN: Didn't he slave Maw t' death?

PETER: He's slaved himself t' death. He's slaved Sim 'n' me 'n' yew t' death— on'y none o' us hain't died—yit.

SIMEON: It's something'—drivin' him—t' drive us!

EBEN (*vengefully*): Waal—I hold him t' jedgment! (*Then scornfully.*) Somethin'! What's somethin'?

SIMEON: Dunno.

EBEN (*sardonically*): What's drivin' yew to Californi-a, mebbe? (*They look at him in surprise.*) Oh, I've heerd ye! (*Then, after a pause.*) But ye'll never go t' the gold fields!

PETER (*assertively*): Mebbe!

EBEN: Whar'll ye git the money?

PETER: We kin walk. It's an a'mighty ways—Californi-a—but if yew was t' put all the steps we've walked on this farm end t' end we'd be in the moon!

EBEN: The Injuns'll skulp ye on the plains.

SIMEON (*with grim humor*): We'll mebee make 'em pay a hair fur a hair!

EBEN (*decisively*): But t'ain't that. Ye won't never go because ye'll wait here for yer share o' the farm, thinkin allus he'll die soon.

SIMEON (*after a pause*): We've a right.

PETER: Two-thirds belongs t'us.

EBEN (*jumping to his feet*): Ye've no right! She wa'n't yewr Maw! It was her farm! Didn't he steal it from her? She's dead. It's my farm.

SIMEON (*sardonically*): Tell that t' Paw—when he comes! I'll bet ye a dollar he'll laugh—fur once in his life. Ha! (*He laughs himself in one single mirthless bark.*)

PETER (*amused in turn, echoes his brother*): Ha!

SIMEON (*after a pause*): What've ye got held agin us, Eben? Year arter year it's skulked in yer eye—somethin'.

PETER: Ay-eh.

EBEN: Ay-eh. They's somethin'. (*Suddenly exploding.*) Why didn't ye never stand between him 'n' my Maw when he was slavin' her to her grave—t' pay her back fur the kindness she done t' yew? (*There is a long pause. They stare at him in surprise.*)

SIMEON: Waal—the stock'd got t' be watered.

PETER: 'R they was woodin' t' do.

SIMEON: 'R plowin'.

PETER: 'R hayin'.

SIMEON: 'R spreadin' manure.

PETER: 'R weedin'.

SIMEON: 'R prunin'.

PETER: 'R milkin'.

EBEN (*breaking in harshly*): An' makin' walls—stone atop o' stone—makin' walls till yer heart's a stone ye heft up out o' the way o' growth onto a stone wall t' wall in yer heart!

SIMEON (*matter-of-factly*): We never had no time t' meddle.

PETER (*to* EBEN): Yew was fifteen afore yer Maw died—an' big fur yer age. Why didn't ye never do nothin'?

EBEN (*harshly*): They was chores t' do, wa'n't they? (*A pause—then slowly.*) It was on'y arter she died I come to think o' it. Me cookin'—doin' her work—that made me know her, suffer her sufferin'—she'd come back t' help—come back t' bile potatoes—come back t' fry bacon—come back t' bake biscuits—come back all cramped up t' shake the fire, an' carry ashes, her eyes weepin' an' bloody with smoke an' cinders same's they used t' be. She still comes back—stands by the stove thar in the evenin'—she can't find it nateral sleepin' an' restin' in peace. She can't git used t' bein' free—even in her grave.

SIMEON: She never complained none.

EBEN: She'd got too tired. She'd got too used t' bein' too tired. That was what he done. (*With vengeful passion.*) An' sooner'r later, I'll meddle. I'll say the thin's I didn't say then t' him! I'll yell 'em at the top o' my lungs. I'll see t' it my Maw gits some rest an' sleep in her grave! (*He sits down again, relapsing into a brooding silence. They look at him with a queer indifferent curiosity.*)

PETER (*after a pause*): Whar in tarnation d'ye s'pose he went, Sim?

SIMEON: Dunno. He druv off in the buggy, all spick an' span, with the mare all breshed an' shiny, druv off clackin' his tongue an' wavin' his whip. I remember it right well. I was finishin' plowin', it was spring an' May an' sunset, an' gold in the West, an' he druv off into it. I yells "Whar ye goin', Paw?" an' he hauls up by the stone wall a jiffy. His old snake's eyes was glitterin' in the sun like he'd been drinkin' a jugful an' he says with a mule's grin: "Don't ye run away till I come back!"

PETER: Wonder if he knowed we was wantin' fur Californi-a?

SIMEON: Mebbe. I didn't say nothin' and he says, lookin' kinder queer an' sick: "I been hearin' the hens cluckin' an' the roosters crowin' all the durn day. I been listen' t' the cows lowin' an' everythin' else kickin' up till I can't stand it no more. It's spring an' I'm feelin' damned," he says. "Damned like an old bare hickory tree fit on'y fur burnin'," he says. An' then I calc'late I must've looked a mite hopeful, fur he adds real spry and vicious: "But don't git no fool idee I'm dead. I've sworn t' live a hundred an' I'll do it, if on'y t' spite yer sinful greed! An' now I'm ridin' out t' learn God's message t' me in the spring, like the prophets done. An' yew git back t' yer plowin'," he says. An' he druv off singin' a hymn. I thought he was drunk—'r I'd stopped him goin'.

EBEN (*scornfully*): No, ye wouldn't! Ye're scared o' him. He's stronger—inside—than both o' ye put together!

PETER (*sardonically*): An' yew—be yew Samson?

EBEN: I'm gittin' stronger. I kin feel it growin' in me—growin' an' growin'—till it'll bust out—! (*He gets up and puts on his coat and a hat. They watch him, gradually breaking into grins.* EBEN *avoids their eyes sheepishly.*) I'm goin' out fur a spell—up the road.

PETER: T' the village?

SIMEON: T' see Minnie?

EBEN (*defiantly*): Ay-eh!

PETER (*jeeringly*): The Scarlet Woman!

SIMEON: Lust—that's what's growin' in ye!

EBEN: Waal—she's purty!

PETER: She's been purty for twenty year!

SIMEON: A new coat o' paint'll make a heifer out of forty.

EBEN: She hain't forty!

PETER: If she hain't. she's teeterin' on the edge.

EBEN (*desperately*): What d'yew know—

PETER: All they is . . . Sim knew her—an' then me arter—

SIMEON: An' Paw kin tell yew somethin' too! He was fust!

EBEN: D'ye mean t'say he . . . ?

SIMEON (*with a grin*): Ay-eh! We air his heirs in everythin'!

EBEN (*intensely*): That's more to it! That grows on it! It'll bust soon! (*Then violently.*) I'll go smash my fist in her face! (*He pulls open the door in rear violently.*)

SIMEON (*with a wink at* PETER—*drawlingly*): Mebbe—but the night's wa'm— purty—by the time ye git thar mebbe ye'll kiss her instead!

PETER: Sart'n he will! (*They both roar with coarse laughter.* EBEN *rushes out and slams the door—then the outside front door—comes around the corner of the house and stands still by the gate, staring up at the sky.*)

SIMEON (*looking after him*): Like his Paw.

PETER: Dead spit an' image!

SIMEON: Dog'll eat dog!

PETER: Ay-eh. (*Pause. With yearning.*) Mebbe a year from now we'll be in Californi-a.

SIMEON: Ay-eh. (*A pause. Both yawn*). Let's git t'bed. (*He blows out the candle. They go out door in rear.* EBEN *stretches his arms up to the sky— rebelliously.*)

EBEN: Waal—thar's a star, an' somewhar's they's him, an' here's me, an' thar's Min up the road—in the same night. What if I does kiss her? She's like t'night. she's soft 'n' wa'm, her eyes kin wink like a star, her mouth's wa'm, her arms're wa'm, she smells like a wa'm plowed field, she's purty . . . Ay-eh! By God A'mighty she's purty, an' I don't give a damn how many sins she's sinned afore mine or who she's sinned 'em with, my sin's as purty as any one on 'em! (*He strides off down the road to the left.*)

SCENE THREE

> (*It is the pitch darkness just before dawn.* EBEN *comes in from the left and goes around to the porch, feeling his way, chuckling bitterly and cursing half-aloud to himself.*)

EBEN: The cussed old miser! (*He can be heard going in the front door. There is a pause as he goes upstairs, then a loud knock on the bedroom door of the brothers.*) Wake up!

SIMEON (*startedly*): Who's thar?

EBEN (*pushing open the door and coming in, a lighted candle in his hand. The bedroom of the brothers is revealed. Its ceiling is the sloping roof. They can stand upright only close to the center dividing wall of the upstairs.* SIMEON *and* PETER *are in a double bed, front.* EBEN's *cot is to the rear.* EBEN *has a mixture of silly grin and vicious scowl on his face*): I be!

PETER (*angrily*): What in hell's-fire . . . ?

EBEN: I got news fur ye! Ha! (*He gives one abrupt sardonic guffaw.*)

SIMEON (*angrily*): Couldn't ye hold it 'til we'd got our sleep?

EBEN: It's nigh sunup. (*Then explosively.*) He's gone an' married agen!

SIMEON AND PETER (*explosively*): Paw?

EBEN: Got himself hitched to a female 'bout thirty-five—an' purty, they says . . .

SIMEON (*aghast*): It's a durn lie!

PETER: Who says?

SIMEON: They been stringin' ye!

EBEN: Think I'm a dunce, do ye? The hull village says. The preacher from New Dover, he brung the news—told it t'our preacher—New Dover, that's whar the old loon got himself hitched—that's whar the woman lived—

PETER (*no longer doubting—stunned*): Waal . . . !

SIMEON (*the same*): Waal . . . !

EBEN (*sitting down on a bed—with vicious hatred*): Ain't he a devil out o' hell? It's jest t' spite us—the damned old mule!

PETER (*after a pause*): Everythin'll go t' her now.

SIMEON: Ay-eh. (*A pause—dully.*) Waal—if it's done—

PETER: It's done us. (*Pause—then persuasively.*) They's gold in the fields o' Californi-a, Sim. No good a-stayin' here now.

SIMEON: Jest what I was a-thinkin'. (*Then with decision.*) S'well fust's last! Let's light out and git this mornin'.

PETER: Suits me.

EBEN: Ye must like walkin'.

SIMEON (*sardonically*): If ye'd grow wings on us we'd fly thar!

EBEN: Ye'd like ridin' better—on a boat, wouldn't ye? (*Fumbles in his pocket and takes out a crumpled sheet of foolscap.*) Waal, if ye sign this ye kin ride on a boat. I've had it writ out an' ready in case ye'd ever go. It says fur three hundred dollars t' each ye agree yewr shares o' the farm is sold t' me. (*They look suspiciously at the paper. A pause.*)

SIMEON (*wonderingly*): But if he's hitched agen—

PETER: An' whar'd yew git that sum o' money, anyways?

EBEN (*cunningly*): I know whar it's hid. I been waitin'—Maw told me. She knew whar it lay fur years, but she was waitin' . . . It's her'n—the money he hoarded from her farm an' hid from Maw. It's my money by rights now.

PETER: Whar's it hid?

EBEN (*cunningly*): Whar yew won't never find it without me. Maw spied on him—'r she'd never knowed. (*A pause. They look at him suspiciously, and he at them.*) Waal, is it fa'r trade?

SIMEON: Dunno.

PETER: Dunno.

SIMEON (*looking at window*): Sky's grayin'.

PETER: Ye better start the fire, Eben.

SIMEON: An' fix some vittles.

EBEN: Ay-eh. (*Then with a forced jocular heartiness.*) I'll git ye a good one. If ye're startin' t' hoof it t' Californi-a ye'll need somethin' that'll stick t' yer ribs. (*He turns to the door, adding meaningly.*) But ye kin ride on a boat if ye'll swap. (*He stops at the door and pauses. They stare at him.*)

SIMEON (*suspiciously*): Whar was ye all night?

EBEN (*defiantly*): Up t' Min's. (*Then slowly.*) Walkin' thar, fust I felt 's if I'd kiss her; then I got a-thinkin' o' what ye'd said o' him an' her an' I says, I'll bust her nose fur that! Then I got t' the village an' heerd the news an' I got madder'n hell an' run all the way t' Min's not knowin' what I'd do—(*He pauses—then sheepishly but more defiantly.*) Waal—when I seen her, I didn't hit her—nor I didn't kiss her nuther—I began t' beller like a calf an' cuss at the same time, I was so durn mad—an' she got scared—an' I jest grabbed holt an' tuk her! (*Proudly.*) Yes, siree! I tuk her. She may've been his'n—an' you'n, too—but she's mine now!

SIMEON (*dryly*): In love, air yew?

EBEN (*with lofty scorn*): Love! I don't take no stock in sech slop!

PETER (*winking at* SIMEON): Mebbe Eben's aimin' t' marry, too.

SIMEON: Min'd make a true faithful he'pmeet! (*They snicker.*)

EBEN: What do I care fur her—'ceptin' she's round an' wa'm? The p'int is she was his'n—an' now she b'longs t' me! (*He goes to the door—then turns—rebelliously.*) An' Min hain't sech a bad un. They's worse'n Min in the world, I'll bet ye! Wait'll we see this cow the Old Man's hitched t'! She'll beat Min, I got a notion! (*He starts to go out.*)

SIMEON (*suddenly*): Mebbe ye'll try t' make her your'n, too?

PETER: Ha! (*He gives a sardonic laugh of relish at this idea.*)

EBEN (*spitting with disgust*): Her—here—sleepin' with him—stealin' my Maw's farm! I'd as soon pet a skunk 'r kiss a snake! (*He goes out. The two stare after him suspiciously. A pause. They listen to his steps receding.*)

PETER: He's startin' the fire.

SIMEON: I'd like t' ride t' Californi-a—but—

PETER: Min might o' put some scheme in his head.

SIMEON: Mebbe it's all a lie 'bout Paw marryin'. We'd best wait an' see the bride.

PETER: An' don't sign nothin' till we does!

SIMEON: Nor till we've tested it's good money! (*Then with a grin.*) But if Paw's hitched we'd be sellin' Eben somethin' we'd never git nohow!

PETER: We'll wait an' see. (*Then with sudden vindictive anger.*) An' till he comes, let's yew 'n' me not wuk a lick, let Eben tend to thin's if he's a mind t', let's us just sleep an' eat an' drink likker, an' let the hull damned farm go t' blazes!

SIMEON (*excitedly*): By God, we've 'arned a rest! We'll play rich fur a change. I hain't a-going to stir outa bed till breakfast's ready.

PETER: An' on the table!

SIMEON (*after a pause—thoughtfully*): What d'ye calc'late she'll be like—our new Maw? Like Eben thinks?

PETER: More'n' likely.

SIMEON (*vindictively*): Waal—I hope she's a she-devil that'll make him wish he was dead an' livin' in the pit o' hell fur comfort!

PETER (*fervently*): Amen!

SIMEON (*imitating his father's voice*): "I'm ridin' out t' learn God's message t' me in the spring like the prophets done," he says. I'll bet right then an' thar he knew plumb well he was goin' whorin', the stinkin' old hypocrite!

SCENE FOUR

(*Same as Scene 2—shows the interior of the kitchen with a lighted candle on table. It is gray dawn outside.* SIMEON *and* PETER *are just finishing their breakfast.* EBEN *sits before his plate of untouched food, brooding frowningly.*)

PETER (*glancing at him rather irritably*): Lookin' glum don't help none.

SIMEON (*sarcastically*): Sorrowin' over his lust o' the flesh!

PETER (*with a grin*): Was she yer fust?

EBEN (*angrily*): None o' yer business. (*A pause.*) I was thinkin' o' him. I got a notion he's gittin' near—I kin feel him comin' on like yew kin feel malaria chill afore it takes ye.

PETER: It's too early yet.

SIMEON: Dunno. He'd like t' catch us nappin'—jest t' have somethin' t' hoss us 'round over.

PETER (*mechanically gets to his feet.* SIMEON *does the same*): Waal—let's git t' wuk. (*They both plod mechanically toward the door before they realize. Then they stop short.*)

SIMEON (*grinning*): Ye're a cussed fool, Pete—and I be wuss! Let him see we hain't wukin'! We don't give a durn!

PETER (*as they go back to the table*): Not a damned durn! It'll serve t' show him we're done with him. (*They sit down again.* EBEN *stares from one to the other with surprise.*)

SIMEON (*grins at him*): We're aimin' t' start bein' lilies o' the field.

PETER: Nary a toil 'r spin 'r lick o' wuk do we put in!

SIMEON: Ye're sole owner—till he comes—that's what ye wanted. Waal, ye got t' be sole hand, too.

PETER: The cows air bellerin'. Ye better hustle at the milkin'.

EBEN (*with excited joy*): Ye mean ye'll sign the paper?

SIMEON (*dryly*): Mebbe.

PETER: Mebbe.

SIMEON: We're considerin'. (*Peremptorily.*) Ye better git t' wuk.

EBEN (*with queer excitement*): It's Maw's farm agen! It's my farm! Them's my cows! I'll milk my durn fingers off fur cows o' mine! (*He goes out door in rear, they stare after him indifferently.*)

SIMEON: Like his Paw.

PETER: Dead spit 'n' image!

SIMEON: Waal—let dog eat dog! (EBEN *comes out of front door and around the corner of the house. The sky is beginning to grow flushed with sunrise.* EBEN *stops by the gate and stares around him with glowing, possessive eyes. He takes in the whole farm with his embracing glance of desire.*)

EBEN: It's purty! It's damned purty! It's mine! (*He suddenly throws his head back boldly and glares with hard, defiant eyes at the sky.*) Mine, d'ye hear? Mine! (*He turns and walks quickly off left, rear, toward the barn. The two brothers light their pipes.*)

SIMEON (*putting his muddy boots up on the table, tilting back his chair, and puffing defiantly*): Waal—this air solid comfort—fur once.

PETER: Ay-eh. (*He follows suit. A pause. Unconsciously they both sigh.*)

SIMEON (*suddenly*): He never was much o' a hand at milkin', Eben wa'n't.

PETER (*with a snort*): His hands air like hoofs! (*A pause.*)

SIMEON: Reach down the jug thar! Let's take a swaller. I'm feelin' kind o' low.

PETER: Good idee! (*He does so—gets two glasses—they pour out drinks of whisky.*) Here's t' the gold in Californi-a!

SIMEON: An' luck t' find it! (*They drink—puff resolutely—sigh—take their feet down from the table.*)

PETER: Likker don't pear t' sot right.

SIMEON: We hain't used t' it this early. (*A pause. They become very restless.*)

PETER: Gittin' close in this kitchen.

SIMEON (*with immense relief*): Let's git a breath o' air. (*They arise briskly and go out rear—appear around house and stop by the gate. They stare up at the sky with a numbed appreciation.*)

PETER: Purty!

SIMEON: Ay-eh. Gold's t' the East now.

PETER: Sun's startin' with us fur the Golden West.

SIMEON (*staring around the farm, his compressed face tightened, unable to conceal his emotion*): Waal—it's our last mornin'—mebbe.

PETER (*the same*): Ay-eh.

SIMEON (*stamps his foot on the earth and addresses it desperately*): Waal—ye've thirty year o' me buried in ye—spread out over ye—blood an' bone an' sweat—rotted away—fertilizin' ye—richin' yer soul—prime manure, by God, that's what I been t' ye!

PETER: Ay-eh! An' me!

SIMEON: An' yew, Peter. (*He sighs—then spits.*) Waal—no use'n cryin' over spilt milk.

PETER: They's gold in the West—an' freedom, mebbe. We been slaves t' stone walls here.

SIMEON (*defiantly*): We hain't nobody's slaves from this out—nor no thin's slaves nuther. (*A pause—restlessly.*) Speakin' o' milk, wonder how Eben's managin'?

PETER: I s'pose he's managin'.

SIMEON: Mebbe we'd ought t' help—this once.

PETER: Mebbe. The cows knows us.

SIMEON: An' likes us. They don't know him much.

PETER: An' the hosses, an' pigs, an' chickens. They don't know him much.

SIMEON: They knows us like brothers—an' likes us! (*Proudly.*) Hain't we raised 'em t' be fust-rate, number one prize stock?

PETER: We hain't—not no more.

SIMEON (*dully*): I was fergittin'. (*Then resignedly.*) Waal, let's go help Eben a spell an' git waked up.

PETER: Suits me. (*They are starting off down left, rear, for the barn when* EBEN *appears from there hurrying toward them, his face excited.*)

EBEN (*breathlessly*): Waal—har they be! The old mule an' the bride! I seen 'em from the barn down below at the turnin'.

PETER: How could ye tell that far?

EBEN: Hain't I as far-sight as he's near-sight? Don't I know the mare 'n' buggy, an' two people settin' in it? Who else. . . ? An' I tell ye I kin feel 'em a-comin' too! (*He squirms as if he had the itch.*)

PETER (*beginning to be angry*): Waal—let him do his own unhitchin'!

SIMEON (*angry in his turn*): Let's hustle in an' git our bundles an' be a-goin' as he's a-comin'. I don't want never t' step inside the door agen arter he's back. (*They both start back around the corner of the house.* EBEN *follows them.*)

EBEN (*anxiously*): Will ye sign it afore ye go?

PETER: Let's see the color o' the old skinflint's money an' we'll sign. (*They disappear left. The two brothers clump upstairs to get their bundles.* EBEN *appears in the kitchen, runs to window, peers out, comes back and pulls up a strip of flooring in under stove, takes out a canvas bag and puts it on table, then sets the floorboard back in place. The two brothers appear a moment after. They carry old carpet bags.*)

EBEN (*puts his hand on bag guardingly*): Have ye signed?

SIMEON (*shows paper in his hand*): Ay-eh. (*Greedily.*) Be that the money?

EBEN (*opens bags and pours out pile of twenty-dollar gold pieces*): Twenty-dollar pieces—thirty on 'em. Count 'em. (PETER *does so, arranging them in stacks of five, biting one or two to test them.*)

PETER: Six hundred. (*He puts them in bag and puts it inside his shirt carefully.*)

SIMEON (*handing paper to* EBEN): Har ye be.

EBEN (*after a glance, folds it carefully and hides it under his shirt—gratefully*): Thank yew.

PETER: Thank yew fur the ride.

SIMEON: We'll send ye a lump o' gold fur Christmas. (*A pause.* EBEN *stares at them and they at him.*)

PETER (*awkwardly*): Waal—we're a-goin'.

SIMEON: Comin' out t' the yard?

EBEN: No. I'm waitin' in here a spell. (*Another silence. The brothers edge awkwardly to door in rear—then turn and stand.*)

SIMEON: Waal—good-by.

PETER: Good-by.

EBEN: Good-by. (*They go out. He sits down at the table, faces the stove and pulls out the paper. He looks from it to the stove. His face, lighted up by the shaft of sunlight from the window, has an expression of trance. His lips move. The two brothers come out to the gate.*)

PETER (*looking off toward barn*): Thar he be—unhitchin'.

SIMEON (*with a chuckle*): I'll bet ye he's riled!

PETER: An' thar she be.

SIMEON: Let's wait 'n' see what our new Maw looks like.

PETER (*with a grin*): An' give him our partin' cuss!

SIMEON (*grinning*): I feel like raisin' fun. I feel light in my head an' feet.

PETER: Me, too. I feel like laffin' till I'd split up the middle.

SIMEON: Reckon it's the likker?

PETER: No. My feet feel itchin' t' walk an' walk—an' jump high over thin's—an'. . . .

SIMEON: Dance? (*A pause.*)

PETER (*puzzled*): It's plumb onnateral.

SIMEON (*a light coming over his face*): I calc'late it's 'cause school's out. It's holiday. Fur once we're free!

PETER (*dazedly*): Free?

SIMEON: The halter's broke—the harness is busted—the fence bars is down—the stone walls air crumblin' an' tumblin'! We'll be kickin' up an' tearin' away down the road!

PETER (*drawing a deep breath—oratorically*): Anybody that wants this stinkin' old rock-pile of a farm kin hev it. T'ain't our'n, no siree!

SIMEON (*takes the gate off its hinges and puts it under his arm*): We harby 'bolishes shet gates, an' open gates, an' all gates, by thunder!

PETER: We'll take it with us fur luck an' let 'er sail free down some river.

SIMEON (*as a sound of voices comes from left, rear*): Har they comes! (*The two brothers congeal into two stiff, grim-visaged statues.* EPHRAIM CABOT *and* ABBIE PUTNAM *come in.* CABOT *is seventy-five, tall and gaunt, with great, wiry, concentrated power, but stoop-shouldered from toil. His face is as hard as if it were hewn out of a boulder, yet there is a weakness in it, a petty pride in its own narrow strength. His eyes are small, close together, and extremely nearsighted, blinking continually in the effort to focus on objects, their stare having a straining, ingrowing quality. He is dressed in his dismal black Sunday suit.* ABBIE *is thirty-five, buxom, full of vitality. Her round face is pretty but marred by its rather gross sensuality. There is strength and obstinacy in her jaw, a hard determination in her eyes, and about her whole personality the same unsettled, untamed, desperate quality which is so apparent in* EBEN.)

CABOT (*as they enter—a queer strangled emotion in his dry cracking voice*): Har we be t' hum, Abbie.

ABBIE (*with lust for the word*): Hum! (*Her eyes gloating on the house without seeming to see the two stiff figures at the gate.*) It's purty—purty! I can't b'lieve it's r'ally mine.

CABOT (*sharply*): Yewr'n? Mine! (*He stares at her penetratingly. She stares back. He adds relentingly.*) Our'n—mebbe! It was lonesome too long. I was growin' old in the spring. A hum's got t' hev a woman.

ABBIE (*her voice taking possession*): A woman's got t' hev a hum!

CABOT (*nodding uncertainly*): Ay-eh. (*Then irritably.*) Whar be they? Ain't thar nobody about—'r wukin'—r' nothin'?

ABBIE (*sees the brothers. She returns their stare of cold appraising contempt with interest—slowly*): Thar's two men loafin' at the gate an' starin' at me like a couple o' strayed hogs.

CABOT (*straining his eyes*): I kin see 'em—but I can't make out. . . .

SIMEON: It's Simeon.

PETER: It's Peter.

CABOT (*exploding*): Why hain't ye wukin'?

SIMEON (*dryly*): We're waitin' t' welcome ye hum—yew an' the bride!

CABOT (*confusedly*): Huh? Waal—this be yer new Maw, boys. (*She stares at them and they at her.*)

SIMEON (*turns away and spits contemptuously*): I see her!

PETER (*spits also*): An' I see her!

ABBIE (*with the conqueror's conscious superiority*): I'll go in an' look at *my* house. (*She goes slowly around to porch.*)

SIMEON (*with a snort*): Her house!

PETER (*calls after her*): Ye'll find Eben inside. Ye better not tell him it's *yewr* house.

ABBIE (*mouthing the name*): Eben. (*Then quietly.*) I'll tell Eben.

CABOT (*with a contemptuous sneer*): Ye needn't heed Eben. Eben's a dumb fool—like his Maw—soft an' simple!

SIMEON (*with his sardonic burst of laughter*): Ha! Eben's a chip o' yew—spit 'n' image—hard 'n' bitter's a hickory tree! Dog'll eat dog. He'll eat ye yet, old man!

CABOT (*commandingly*): Ye git t' wuk!

SIMEON (*as* ABBIE *disappears in house—winks at* PETER *and says tauntingly*): So that thar's our new Maw, be it? Whar in hell did ye dig her up? (*He and* PETER *laugh.*)

PETER: Ha! Ye'd better turn her in the pen with the other sows. (*They laugh uproariously, slapping their thighs.*)

CABOT (*so amazed at their effrontery that he stutters in confusion*): Simeon! Peter! What's come over ye? Air ye drunk?

SIMEON: We're free, old man—free o' yew an' the hull damned farm! (*They grow more and more hilarious and excited.*)

PETER: An' we're startin' out fur the gold fields o' Californi-a!

SIMEON: Ye kin take this place an' burn it!

PETER: An' bury it—fur all we cares!

SIMEON: We're free, old man! (*He cuts a caper.*)

PETER: Free! (*He gives a kick in the air.*)

SIMEON (*in a frenzy*): Whoop!

PETER: Whoop! (*They do an absurd Indian war dance about the old man who is petrified between rage and the fear that they are insane.*)

SIMEON: We're free as Injuns! Lucky we don't skulp ye!

PETER: An' burn yer barn an' kill the stock!

SIMEON: An' rape yer new woman! Whoop! (*He and* PETER *stop their dance, holding their sides, rocking with wild laughter.*)

CABOT (*edging away*): Lust fur gold—fur the sinful, easy gold o' Californi-a! It's made ye mad!

SIMEON (*tauntingly*): Wouldn't ye like us to send ye back some sinful gold, ye old sinner?

PETER: They's gold besides what's in Californi-a! (*He retreats back beyond the vision of the old man and takes the bag of money and flaunts it in the air above his head, laughing.*)

SIMEON: And sinfuller, too!

PETER: We'll be voyagin' on the sea! Whoop! (*He leaps up and down.*)

SIMEON: Livin' free! Whoop! (*He leaps in turn.*)

CABOT (*suddenly roaring with rage*): My cuss on ye!

SIMEON: Take our'n in trade fur it! Whoop!

CABOT: I'll hev ye both chained up in the asylum!

PETER: Ye old skinflint! Good-by!

SIMEON: Ye old blood sucker! Good-by!

CABOT: Go afore I . . . !

PETER: Whoop! (*He picks a stone from the road.* SIMEON *does the same.*)

SIMEON: Maw'll be in the parlor.

PETER: Ay-eh! One! Two!

CABOT (*frightened*): What air ye. . . . ?

PETER: Three! (*They both throw, the stones hitting the parlor window with a crash of glass, tearing the shade.*)

SIMEON: Whoop!

PETER: Whoop!

CABOT (*in a fury now, rushing toward them*): If I kin lay hands on ye—I'll break yer bones fur ye! (*But they beat a capering retreat before him, SIMEON with the gate still under his arm. CABOT comes back, panting with impotent rage. Their voices as they go off take up the song of the gold-seekers to the old tune of "Oh, Susannah!"*)

> I jumped aboard the Liza ship,
> And traveled on the sea,
> And every time I thought of home
> I wished it wasn't me!
> Oh! Californi-a,
> That's the land fur me!
> I'm off to Californi-a!
> With my wash bowl on my knee.

(*In the meantime, the window of the upper bedroom on right is raised and ABBIE sticks her head out. She looks down at CABOT— with a sigh of relief.*)

ABBIE: Waal—that's the last o' them two, hain't it? (*He doesn't answer. Then in possessive tones.*) This here's a nice bedroom, Ephraim. It's a r'al nice bed. Is it my room, Ephraim?

CABOT (*grimly—without looking up*): Our'n! (*She cannot control a grimace of aversion and pulls back her head slowly and shuts the window. A sudden horrible thought seems to enter CABOT's head.*) They been up to somethin'! Mebbe—mebbe they've pizened the stock—'r somethin'! (*He almost runs off down toward the barn. A moment later the kitchen door is slowly pushed open and ABBIE enters. For a moment she stands looking at EBEN. He does not notice her at first. Her eyes take him in penetratingly with a calculating appraisal of his strength as against hers. But under this her desire is dimly awakened by his youth and good looks. Suddenly he becomes conscious of her presence and looks up. Their eyes meet. He leaps to his feet, glowering at her speechlessly.*)

ABBIE (*in her most seductive tones which she uses all through this scene*): Be you—Eben? I'm Abbie— (*She laughs.*) I mean, I'm yer new Maw.

EBEN (*viciously*): No, damn ye!

ABBIE (*as if she hadn't heard—with a queer smile*): Yer Paw's spoke a lot o' yew. . . .

EBEN: Ha!

ABBIE: Ye mustn't mind him. He's an old man. (*A long pause. They stare at each other.*) I don't want t' pretend playin' Maw t' ye, Eben. (*Admiringly.*) Ye're too big an' too strong fur that. I want t' be frens with ye. Mebbe with me fur a fren ye'd find ye'd like livin' here better. I kin make it easy fur ye with him, mebbe. (*With a scornful sense of power.*) I calc'late I kin git him t' do most anythin' fur me.

EBEN (*with bitter scorn*): Ha! (*They stare again,* EBEN *obscurely moved, physically attracted to her—in forced stilted tones.*) Yew kin go t' the devil!

ABBIE (*calmly*): If cussin' me does ye good, cuss all ye've a mind t'. I'm all prepared t' have ye agin me—at fust. I don't blame ye nuther. I'd feel the same at any stranger comin' t' take my Maw's place. (*He shudders. She is watching him carefully.*) Yew must've cared a lot fur yewr Maw, didn't ye? My Maw died afore I'd growed. I don't remember her none. (*A pause.*) But yew won't hate me long, Eben. I'm not the wust in the world—an' yew an' me've got a lot in common. I kin tell that by lookin' at ye. Waal—I've had a hard life, too—oceans o' trouble an' nuthin' but wuk fur reward. I was an orphan early an' had t' wuk fur others in other folks' hums. Then I married an' he turned out a drunken spreer an' so he had to wuk fur others an' me too agen in other folks' hums, an' the baby died, an' my husband got sick an' died too, an' I was glad sayin' now I'm free fur once, on'y I diskivered right away all I was free fur was t' wuk agen in other folks' hums, doin' other folks' wuk till I'd most give up hope o' ever doin' my own wuk in my own hum, an' then your Paw come. . . . (CABOT *appears returning from the barn. He comes to the gate and looks down the road the brothers have gone. A faint strain of their retreating voices is heard: "Oh, Californi-a! That's the place for me." He stands glowering, his fist clenched, his face grim with rage.*)

EBEN (*fighting against his growing attraction and sympathy—harshly*): An' bought yew—like a harlot! (*She is stung and flushes angrily. She has been sincerely moved by the recital of her troubles. He adds furiously.*) An' the price he's payin' ye—this farm—was my Maw's, damn ye!—an' mine now!

ABBIE (*with a cool laugh of confidence*): Yewr'n? We'll see 'bout that! (*Then strongly.*) Waal—what if I did need a hum? What else'd I marry an old man like him fur?

EBEN (*maliciously*): I'll tell him ye said that!

ABBIE (*smiling*): I'll say ye're lyin' a-purpose—an' he'll drive ye off the place!

EBEN: Ye devil!

ABBIE (*defying him*): This be my farm—this be my hum—this be my kitchen—!

EBEN (*furiously, as if he were going to attack her*): Shut up, damn ye!

ABBIE (*walks up to him—a queer coarse expression of desire in her face and body—slowly*): An' upstairs—that be my bedroom—an' my bed! (*He stares into her eyes, terribly confused and torn. She adds softly.*) I hain't bad nor mean—'ceptin' fur an enemy—but I got t' fight fur what's due me out o' life, if I ever 'spect t' git it. (*Then puttin her hand on his arm—seductively.*) Let's yew 'n' me be frens, Eben.

EBEN (*stupidly—as if hypnotized*): Ay-eh. (*Then furiously flinging off her arm.*) No, ye durned old witch! I hate ye! (*He rushes out the door.*)

ABBIE (*looks after him smiling satisfiedly—then half to herself, mouthing the word*): Eben's nice. (*She looks at the table, proudly.*) I'll wash up *my* dishes now. (EBEN *appears outside, slamming the door behind him. He comes around corner, stops on seeing his father, and stands staring at him with hate.*)

CABOT (*raising his arms to heaven in the fury he can no longer control*): Lord God o' Hosts, smite the undutiful sons with Thy wust cuss!

EBEN (*breaking in violently*): Yew 'n' yewr God! Allus cussin' folks—allus naggin' em!

CABOT (*oblivious to him—summoningly*): God o' the old! God o' the lonesome!

EBEN (*mockingly*): Naggin' His sheep t' sin! T' hell with yewr God! (CABOT *turns. He and* EBEN *glower at each other.*)

CABOT (*harshly*): So it's yew. I might've knowed it. (*Shaking his finger threateningly at him.*) Blasphemin' fool! (*Then quickly.*) Why hain't ye t' wuk?

EBEN: Why hain't yew? They've went. I can't wuk it all alone.

CABOT (*contemptuously*): Nor noways! I'm wuth ten o' ye yit, old's I be! Ye'll never be more'n half a man! (*Then, matter-of-factly.*) Waal—let's git t' the barn. (*They go. A last faint note of the "Californi-a" song is heard from the distance.* ABBIE *is washing her dishes.*)

(*The curtain falls.*)

PART TWO, SCENE ONE

(*The exterior of the farmhouse, as in Part I—a hot Sunday afternoon two months later.* ABBIE, *dressed in her best, is discovered sitting in a rocker at the end of the porch. She rocks listlessly, enervated by the heat, staring in front of her with bored, half-closed eyes.*)

(EBEN *sticks his head out of his bedroom window. He looks around furtively and tries to see—or hear—if anyone is on the porch, but although he has been careful to make no noise,* ABBIE *has sensed his movement. She stops rocking, her face grows animated and eager, she waits attentively.* EBEN *seems to feel her presence, he scowls back his thoughts of her and spits with exaggerated disdain—then withdraws back into the room.* ABBIE *waits, holding her breath as she listens with passionate eagerness for every sound within the house.*)

(EBEN *comes out. Their eyes meet. His falter, he is confused, he turns away and slams the door resentfully. At this gesture,* ABBIE *laughs tantalizingly, amused but at the same time piqued and irritated. He scowls, strides off the porch to the path and starts to walk past her to the road with a grand swagger of ignoring her existence. He is dressed in his store suit, spruced up, his face shines from soap and water.* ABBIE *leans forward on her chair, her eyes hard and angry now, and, as he passes her, gives a sneering, taunting chuckle.*)

EBEN (*stung—turns on her furiously*): What air yew cacklin' 'bout?

ABBIE (*triumphant*): Yew!

EBEN: What about me?

ABBIE: Ye look all slicked up like a prize bull.

EBEN (*with a sneer*): Waal—ye hain't so durned purty yerself, be ye? (*They stare into each other's eyes, his held by hers in spite of himself, hers glowingly possessive. Their physical attraction becomes a palpable force quivering in the hot air.*)

ABBIE (*softly*): Ye don't mean that, Eben. Ye may think ye mean it, mebbe, but ye don't. Ye can't. It's agin nature, Eben. Ye been fightin' yer nature ever since the day I come—tryin' t' tell yerself I hain't purty t'ye. (*She laughs a low humid laugh without taking her eyes from his. A pause—her body squirms desirously—she murmurs languorously.*) Hain't the sun strong an' hot? Ye kin feel it burnin' into the earth—Nature—makin' thin's grow—bigger 'n' bigger—burnin' inside ye—making' ye want t' grow—into somethin' else—till ye're jined with it—an' it's your'n—but it owns ye, too—an' makes ye grow bigger—like a tree—like them elums— (*She laughs again softly, holding his eyes. He takes a step toward her, compelled against his will.*) Nature'll beat ye, Eben. Ye might's well own up t' it fust 's last.

EBEN (*trying to break from her spell—confusedly*): If Paw'd hear ye goin' on. . . . (*Resentfully.*) But ye've made such a damned idjit out o' the old devil. . . ! (ABBIE *laughs.*)

ABBIE: Waal—hain't it easier fur yew with him changed softer?

EBEN (*defiantly*): No. I'm fightin' him—fightin' yew—fightin' fur Maw's rights t' her hum! (*This breaks her spell for him. He glowers at her.*) An' I'm onto ye. Ye hain't foolin' me a mite. Ye're aimin' t' swaller up everythin' an' make it your'n. Waal, you'll find I'm a heap sight bigger hunk nor yew kin chew! (*He turns from her with a sneer.*)

ABBIE (*trying to regain her ascendancy—seductively*): Eben!

EBEN: Leave me be! (*He starts to walk away.*)

ABBIE (*more commandingly*): Eben!

EBEN (*stops—resentfully*): What d'ye want?

ABBIE (*trying to conceal a growing excitement*): Whar air ye goin'?

EBEN (*with malicious nonchalance*): Oh—up the road a spell.

ABBIE: T' the village?

EBEN (*airly*): Mebbe.

ABBIE (*excitedly*): T' see that Min, I s'pose?

EBEN: Mebbe.

ABBIE (*weakly*): What d'ye want t' waste time on her fur?

EBEN (*revenging himself now—grinning at her*): Ye can't beat Nature, didn't ye say? (*He laughs and again starts to walk away.*)

ABBIE (*bursting out*): An ugly old hake!

EBEN (*with a tantalizing sneer*): She's purtier'n yew be!

ABBIE: That every wuthless drunk in the country has. . . .

EBEN (*tauntingly*): Mebbe—but she's better'n yew. She owns up fa'r 'n' squar' t' her doin's.

ABBIE (*furiously*): Don't ye dare compare. . . .

EBEN: She don't go sneakin' an' stealin'—what's mine.

ABBIE (*savagely seizing on his weak point*): Your'n? Yew mean—my farm?

EBEN: I mean the farm yew sold yerself fur like any other old whore—my farm!

ABBIE (*stung—fiercely*): Ye'll never live t' see the day when even a stinkin' weed on it 'll belong t' ye! (*Then in a scream.*) Git out o' my sight! Go on t' yer slut—disgracin' yer Paw 'n' me! I'll git yer Paw t' horsewhip ye off the place if I want t'! Ye're only livin' here 'cause I tolerate ye! Git along! I hate the sight o' ye! (*She stops, panting and glaring at him.*)

EBEN (*returning her glance in kind*): An' I hate the sight o' yew! (*He turns and strides off up the road. She follows his retreating figure with concentrated hate. Old* CABOT *appears coming up from the barn. The hard, grim expression of his face has changed. He seems in some queer way softened, mellowed. His eyes have taken on a strange, incongruous dreamy quality. Yet there is no hint of physical weakness about him—rather he looks more robust and younger.* ABBIE *sees him and turns away quickly with unconcealed aversion. He comes slowly up to her.*)

CABOT (*mildly*): War yew an' Eben quarrelin' agen?

ABBIE (*shortly*): No.

CABOT: Ye was talkin' a'mighty loud. (*He sits down on the edge of porch*).

ABBIE (*snappishly*): If ye heerd us they hain't no need askin' questions.

CABOT: I didn't hear what ye said.

ABBIE (*relieved*): Waal—it wa'n't nothin' t' speak on.

CABOT (*after a pause*): Eben's queer.

ABBIE (*bitterly*): He's the dead spit 'n' image o' yew!

CABOT (*queerly interested*): D'ye think so, Abbie? (*After a pause, ruminatingly.*) Me 'n' Eben's allus fit 'n' fit. I never could b'ar him noways. He's so thunderin' soft—like his Maw.

ABBIE (*scornfully*): Ay-eh! 'Bout as soft as yew be!

CABOT (*as if he hadn't heard*): Mebbe I been too hard on him.

ABBIE (*jeeringly*): Waal—ye're gittin' soft now—soft as slop! That's what Eben was sayin'.

CABOT (*his face instantly grim and ominous*): Eben was sayin'? Waal, he'd best not do nothin' t' try me 'r he'll soon diskiver. . . . (*A pause. She keeps her face turned away. His gradually softens. He stares up at the sky.*) Purty, hain't it?

ABBIE (*crossly*): I don't see nothin' purty.

CABOT: The sky. Feels like a wa'm field up thar.

ABBIE (*sarcastically*): Air yew aimin' t' buy up over the farm too? (*She snickers contemptuously.*)

CABOT (*strangely*): I'd like t' own my place up thar. (*A pause.*) I'm gittin' old, Abbie. I'm gittin' ripe on the bough. (*A pause. She stares at him mystified. He goes on.*) It's allus lonesome cold in the house—even when it's bilin' hot outside. Hain't yew noticed?

ABBIE: No.

CABOT: It's wa'm down t' the barn—nice smellin' an warm—with the cows. (*A pause.*) Cows is queer.

ABBIE: Like yew?

CABOT: Like Eben. (*A pause.*) I'm gittin' t' feel resigned t' Eben—jest as I got t' feel 'bout his Maw. I'm gittin' t' learn to b'ar his softness—jest like her'n. I calc'late I c'd a'most take t' him—if he wa'n't sech a dumb fool! (*A pause.*) I s'pose it's old age a-creepin' in my bones.

ABBIE (*indifferently*): Waal—ye hain't dead yet.

CABOT (*roused*): No, I hain't, yew bet—not by a hell of a sight—I'm sound 'n' tough as hickory! (*Then moodily.*) But arter three score and ten the Lord warns ye t' prepare. (*A pause.*) That's why Eben's come in my head. Now that his cussed sinful brothers is gone their path t' hell, they's no one left but Eben.

ABBIE (*resentfully*): They's me, hain't they? (*Agitatedly.*) What's all this sudden likin' ye've tuk to Eben? Why don't ye saying nothin' 'bout me? Hain't I yer lawful wife?

CABOT (*simply*): Ay-eh. Ye be. (*A pause—he stares at her desirously—his eyes grow avid—then with a sudden movement he seizes her hands and squeezes them, declaiming in a queer camp meeting preacher's tempo.*) Yew air my Rose o' Sharon! Behold, yew air fair; yer eyes air doves; yer lips air like scarlet; yer two breasts air like two fawns; yer navel be like a round goblet; yer belly be like a heap o' wheat. . . . (*He covers her hands with kisses. She does not seem to notice. She stares before her with hard angry eyes.*)

ABBIE (*jerking her hands away—harshly*): So ye're plannin' t' leave the farm t' Eben, air ye?

CABOT (*dazedly*): Leave. . . ? (*Then with resentful obstinacy.*) I hain't a-givin' it t' no one!

ABBIE (*remorselessly*): Ye can't take it with ye.

CABOT (*thinks a moment—then reluctantly*): No, I calc'late not. (*After a pause—with a strange passion.*) But if I could, I would, by the Etarnal! 'R if I could, in my dyin' hour, I'd set it afire an' watch it burn—this house an' every ear o' corn an' every tree down t' the last blade o' hay! I'd sit an' know it was all a-dying with me an' no one else'd ever own what was mine, what I'd made out o' nothin' with my own sweat 'n' blood! (*A pause—then he adds with a queer affection.*) 'Ceptin' the cows. Them I'd turn free.

ABBIE (*harshly*): An' me?

CABOT (*with a queer smile*): Ye'd be turned free, too.

ABBIE (*furiously*): So that's the thanks I git fur marryin' ye—t' have ye change kind to Eben who hates ye, an' talk o' turnin' me out in the road.

CABOT (*hastily*): Abbie! Ye know I wa'n't. . . .

ABBIE (*vengefully*): Just let me tell ye a thing or two 'bout Eben! Whar's he gone? T' see that harlot, Min! I tried fur t' stop him. Disgracin' yew an' me—on the Sabbath, too!

CABOT (*rather guiltily*): He's a sinner—nateral-born. It's lust eatin' his heart.

ABBIE (*enraged beyond endurance—wildly vindictive*): An' his lust fur me! Kin ye find excuses fur that?

CABOT (*stares at her—after a dead pause*): Lust—fur yew?

ABBIE (*defiantly*): He was tryin' t' make love t' me—when ye heerd us quarrelin'.

CABOT (*stares at her—then a terrible expression of rage comes over his face—he springs to his feet shaking all over*): By the A'mighty God—I'll end him!

ABBIE (*frightened now for* EBEN): No! Don't ye!

CABOT (*violently*): I'll git the shotgun an' blow his soft brains t' the top o' them elums!

ABBIE (*throwing her arms around him*): No, Ephraim!

CABOT (*pushing her away violently*): I will, by God!

ABBIE (*in a quieting tone*): Listen, Ephraim. 'Twa'n't nothin' bad—on'y a boy's foolin'—'twa'n't meant serious—jest jokin' an' teasin'. . . .

CABOT: Then why did ye say—lust?

ABBIE: It must hev sounded wusser'n I meant. An' I was mad at thinkin'—ye'd leave him the farm.

CABOT (*quieter but still grim and cruel*): Waal then, I'll horsewhip him off the place if that much'll content ye.

ABBIE (*reaching out and taking his hand*): No. Don't think o' me! Ye mustn't drive him off. 'Tain't sensible. Who'll ye get to help ye on the farm? They's no one hereabouts.

CABOT (*considers this—then nodding his appreciation*): Ye got a head on ye. (*Then irritably.*) Waal, let him stay. (*He sits down on the edge of the porch. She sits beside him. He murmurs contemptuously.*) I oughtn't t' git riled so—at that 'ere fool calf. (*A pause.*) But har's the p'int. What son o' mine'll keep on here t' the farm—when the Lord does call me? Simeon an' Peter air gone t' hell—an' Eben's follerin' 'em.

ABBIE: They's me.

CABOT: Ye're on'y a woman.

ABBIE: I'm yewr wife.

CABOT: That hain't me. A son is me—my blood—mine. Mine ought t' git mine. An' then it's still mine—even though I be six foot under. D'ye see?

ABBIE (*giving him a look of hatred*): Ay-eh. I see. (*She becomes very thoughtful, her face growing shrewd, her eyes studying* CABOT *craftily.*)

CABOT: I'm gittin' old—ripe on the bough. (*Then with a sudden forced reassurance.*) Not but what I hain't a hard nut t' crack even yet—an' fur many a year t' come! By the Etarnal, I kin break most o' the young fellers' backs at any kind o' work any day o' the year!

ABBIE (*suddenly*): Mebbe the Lord'll give *us* a son.

CABOT (*turns and stares at her eagerly*): Ye mean—a son—t' me 'n' yew?

ABBIE (*with a cajoling smile*): Ye're a strong man yet, hain't ye? 'Tain't noways impossible, be it? We know that. Why d'ye stare so? Hain't ye never thought o' that afore? I been thinkin' o' it all along. Ay-eh—an' I been prayin' it'd happen, too.

CABOT (*his face growing full of joyous pride and a sort of religious ecstasy*): Ye been prayin', Abbie?—fur a son?—t' us?

ABBIE: Ay-eh. (*With a grim resolution.*) I want a son now.

CABOT (*excitedly clutching both of her hands in his*): It'd be the blessin' o' God, Abbie—the blessin' o' God A'mighty on me—in my old age—in my lonesomeness! They hain't nothin' I wouldn't do fur ye then, Abbie. Ye'd hev on'y t' ask it—anythin' ye'd a mind t'!

ABBIE (*interrupting*): Would ye will the farm t' me then—t' me an' it. . . ?

CABOT (*vehemently*): I'd do anythin' ye axed, I tell ye! I swar it! May I be everlastin' damned t' hell if I wouldn't! (*He sinks to his knees pulling her down with him. He trembles all over with the fervor of his hopes.*) Pray t' the Lord agen, Abbie. It's the Sabbath! I'll jine ye! Two prayers air better nor one. "An' God hearkened unto Rachel"! An' God hearkened unto Abbie! Pray, Abbie! Pray fur him to hearken! (*He bows his head, mumbling. She pretends to do likewise but gives him a side glance of scorn and triumph.*)

SCENE TWO

> (*About eight in the evening. The interior of the two bedrooms on the top floor is shown.* EBEN *is sitting on the side of his bed in the room on the left. On account of the heat he has taken off everything but his undershirt and pants. His feet are bare. He faces front, brooding moodily, his chin propped on his hands, a desperate expression on his face.*)
>
> (*In the other room* CABOT *and* ABBIE *are sitting side by side on the edge of their bed, an old-four-poster with feather mattress. He is in his night shirt, she in her nightdress. He is still in the queer, excited mood into which the notion of a son has thrown him. Both rooms are lighted dimly and flickering by tallow candles.*)

CABOT: The farm needs a son.

ABBIE: I need a son.

CABOT: Ay-eh. Sometimes ye air the farm an' sometimes the farm be yew. That's why I clove t' ye in my lonesomeness. (*A pause. He pounds his knee with his fist.*) Me an' the farm has got t' beget a son!

ABBIE: Ye'd best go t' sleep. Ye're gittin' thin's all mixed.

CABOT (*with an impatient gesture*): No, I hain't. My mind's clear's a well. Ye don't know me, that's it. (*He stares hopelessly at the floor.*)

ABBIE (*indifferently*): Mebbe. (*In the next room* EBEN *gets up and paces up and down distractedly.* ABBIE *hears him. Her eyes fasten on the intervening wall with concentrated attention.* EBEN *stops and stares. Their hot glances seem to meet through the wall. Unconsciously he stretches out his arms for her and she half rises. Then aware, he mutters a curse at himself and flings himself face downward on the bed, his clenched fists above his head, his face buried in the pillow.* ABBIE *relaxes with a faint sigh but her eyes remain fixed on the wall; she listens with all her attention for some movement from* EBEN.)

CABOT (*suddenly raises his head and looks at her—scornfully*): Will ye ever know me—'r will any man 'r woman? (*Shaking his head.*) No. I calc'late 't wa'n't t' be. (*He turns away.* ABBIE *looks at the wall. Then, evidently unable to keep silent about his thoughts, without looking at his wife, he puts out his hand and clutches her knee. She starts violently, looks at him, sees he is not watching her, concentrates again on the wall and pays no attention to what he says.*) Listen, Abbie. When I come here fifty odd year ago—I was jest twenty an' the strongest an' hardest ye ever seen—ten times as strong an' fifty times as hard as Eben. Waal—this place was nothin' but fields o' stones. Folks laughed when I tuk it. They couldn't know what I knowed. When ye kin make corn sprout out o' stones, God's livin' in yew! They wa'n't strong enuf fur that! They reckoned God was easy. They laughed. They don't laugh no more. Some died hereabouts. Some went West an' died. They're all under ground—fur follerin' arter an easy God. God hain't easy. (*He shakes his head slowly.*) An' I growed hard. Folks kept allus sayin' he's a hard man like 'twas sinful t' be hard, so's at last I said back at 'em: Waal then, by thunder, ye'll git me hard an' see how ye like it! (*Then suddenly.*) But I give in t' weakness once. 'Twas arter I'd been here two year. I got weak—despairful—they was so many stones. They was a party leavin', givin' up, goin' West. I jined 'em. We tracked on 'n' on. We come t' broad medders, plains, whar the soil was black an' rich as gold. Nary a stone. Easy. Ye'd on'y to plow an' sow an' then set an' smoke yer pipe an' watch thin's grow. I could o' been a rich man—but somethin' in me fit me an' fit me—the voice o' God sayin': "This hain't wuth nothin' t' Me. Git ye back t' hum!" I got afeerd o' that voice an' I lit out back t' hum here, leavin' my claim an' crops t' whoever'd a mind t' take 'em. Ay-eh. I actoolly give up what was rightful mine! God's hard, not easy! God's in the stones! Build my church on a rock—out o' stones an' I'll be in them! That's what He meant t' Peter! (*He sighs heavily—a pause.*) Stones. I picked 'em up an' piled 'em into walls. Ye kin read the years o' my life in them walls, every day a hefted stone, climbin' over the hills up and down, fencin' in the fields that was mine, whar I'd made thin's grow out o' nothin'—like the will o' God, like the servant o' His hand. It wa'n't easy. It was hard an' He made me hard fur it. (*He pauses.*) All the time I kept gittin' lonesomer. I tuk a wife. She bore Simeon an' Peter. She was a good woman. She wuked hard. We was married twenty year. She never knowed me. She helped but she never knowed what she was helpin'. I was allus lonesome. She died. After that it wa'n't so lonesome fur a spell. (*A pause.*) I lost count o' the years. I had no time t' fool away countin' 'em. Sim an' Peter helped. The farm growed. It was all mine! When I thought o' that I didn't feel lonesome. (*A pause.*) But ye can't hitch yer mind t' one thin' day an' night. I tuk another wife—Eben's Maw. Her folks was contestin' me at law over my deeds t' the farm—my farm! That's why Eben keeps a-talkin' his fool talk o' this bein' his Maw's farm. She bore Eben. She was purty—but soft. She tried t' be hard. She couldn't. She never knowed me nor nothin'. It was lonesomer 'n hell with her. After a matter o' sixteen odd years, she died. (*A pause.*) I lived with the boys. They hated me 'cause I was hard. I hated them 'cause they was soft. They coveted the farm without knowin' what it meant. It made me bitter 'n wormwood. It aged me—them coveting what I'd made fur mine. Then this spring the call come—the voice o' God cryin' in my wilderness, in my lonesomeness—t' go out an' seek an' find! (*Turning to her with strange passion.*) I sought ye an' I found ye! Yew air my Rose o' Sharon! Yer eyes air like. . . . (*She has turned a blank face, resentful eyes to his. He stares at her for a moment—then harshly.*) Air ye any the wiser fur all I've told ye?

ABBIE (*confusedly*): Mebbe.

CABOT (*pushing her away from him—angrily*): Ye don't know nothin'—nor never will. If ye don't hev a son t' redeem ye. . . . (*This in a tone of cold threat.*)

ABBIE (*resentfully*): I've prayed, hain't I?

CABOT (*bitterly*): Pray agen—fur understandin'!

ABBIE (*a veiled threat in her tone*): Ye'll have a son out o' me, I promise ye.

CABOT: How kin ye promise?

ABBIE: I got second-sight, mebbe. I kin foretell. (*She gives a queer smile.*)

CABOT: I believe ye have. Ye give me the chills sometimes. (*He shivers.*) It's cold in this house. It's oneasy. They's thin's pokin' about in the dark—in the corners. (*He pulls on his trousers, tucking in his night shirt, and pulls on his boots.*)

ABBIE (*surprised*): Whar air ye goin'?

CABOT (*queerly*): Down whar it's restful—whar it's warm—down t' the barn. (*Bitterly.*) I kin talk t' the cows. They know. They know the farm an' me. They'll give me peace. (*He turns to go out the door.*)

ABBIE (*a bit frightenedly*): Air ye ailin' tonight, Ephraim?

CABOT: Growin'. Growin' ripe on the bough. (*He turns and goes, his boots clumping down the stairs. EBEN sits up with a start, listening. ABBIE is conscious of his movement and stares at the wall. CABOT comes out of the house around the corner and stands by the gate, blinking at the sky. He stretches up his hands in a tortured gesture.*) God A'mighty, call from the dark! (*He listens as if expecting an answer. Then his arms drop, he shakes his head and plods off toward the barn. EBEN and ABBIE stare at each other through the wall. EBEN sighs heavily and ABBIE echoes it. Both become terribly nervous, uneasy. Finally ABBIE gets up and listens, her ear to the wall. He acts as if he saw every move she was making, he becomes resolutely still. She seems driven into a decision—goes out the door in rear determinedly. His eyes follow her. Then as the door of his room is opened softly, he turns away, waits in an attitude of strained fixity. ABBIE stands for a second staring at him, her eyes burning with desire. Then with a little cry she runs over and throws her arms about his neck, she pulls his head back and covers his mouth with kisses. At first, he submits dumbly; then he puts his arms about her neck and returns her kisses, but finally, suddenly aware of his hatred, he hurls her away from him, springing to his feet. They stand speechless and breathless, panting like two animals.*)

ABBIE (*at last—painfully*): Ye shouldn't, Eben—ye shouldn't—I'd make ye happy!

EBEN (*harshly*): I don't want t' be happy—from yew!

ABBIE (*helplessly*): Ye do, Eben! Ye do! Why d'ye lie?

EBEN (*viciously*): I don't take t'ye, I tell ye! I hate the sight o' ye!

ABBIE (*with an uncertain troubled laugh*): Waal, I kissed ye anyways—an' ye kissed back—yer lips was burnin'—ye can't lie 'bout that! (*Intensely.*) If ye don't care, why did ye kiss me back—why was yer lips burnin'?

EBEN (*wiping his mouth*): It was like pizen on 'em. (*Then tauntingly.*) When I kissed ye back, mebbe I thought 'twas someone else.

ABBIE (*wildly*): Min?

EBEN: Mebbe.

ABBIE (*torturedly*): Did ye go t' see her? Did ye r'ally go? I thought ye mightn't. Is that why ye throwed me off jest now?

EBEN (*sneeringly*): What if it be?

ABBIE (*raging*): Then ye're a dog, Eben Cabot!

EBEN (*threateningly*): Ye can't talk that way t' me!

ABBIE (*with a shrill laugh*): Can't I? Did ye think I was in love with ye—a weak thin' like yew! Not much! I on'y wanted ye fur a purpose o' my own—an' I'll hev ye fur it yet 'cause I'm stronger'n yew be!

EBEN (*resentfully*): I knowed well it was on'y part o' yer plan t' swaller everythin'!

ABBIE (*tauntingly*): Mebbe!

EBEN (*furious*): Git out o' my room!

ABBIE: This air my room an' ye're on'y hired help!

EBEN (*threateningly*): Git out afore I murder ye!

ABBIE (*quite confident now*): I hain't a mite afeered. Ye want me, don't ye? Yes, ye do! An yer Paw's son'll never kill what he wants! Look at yer eyes! They's lust fur me in 'em, burning' 'em up! Look at yer lips now! They're tremblin' an' longin' t' kiss me, an' yer teeth t' bite! (*He is watching her now with a horrible fascination. She laughs a crazy triumphant laugh.*) I'm a-goin' t' make all o' this hum my hum! They's one room hain't mine yet, but it's a-goin' t' be tonight. I'm a-goin' down now an' light up! (*She makes him a mocking bow.*) Won't ye come courtin' me in the best parlor, Mister Cabot?

EBEN (*staring at her—horribly confused—dully*): Don't ye dare! It hain't been opened since Maw died an' was laid out thar! Don't ye. . . ! (*But her eyes are fixed on his so burningly that his will seems to wither before hers. He stands swaying toward her helplessly.*)

ABBIE (*holding his eyes and putting all her will into her words as she backs out the door*): I'll expect ye afore long, Eben.

EBEN (*stares after her for a while, walking toward the door. A light appears in the parlor window. He murmurs*): In the parlor? (*This seems to arouse connotations for he comes back and puts on his white shirt, collar, half ties the tie mechanically, puts on coat, takes his hat, stands barefooted looking about him in bewilderment, mutters wonderingly.*) Maw! Whar air yew? (*Then goes slowly toward the door in rear.*)

SCENE THREE

(*A few minutes later. The interior of the parlor is shown. A grim, repressed room like a tomb in which the family has been interred alive.* ABBIE *sits on the edge of the horsehair sofa. She has lighted all the candles and the room is revealed in all its preserved ugliness. A change has come over the woman. She looks awed and frightened now, ready to run away.*)

(*The door is opened and* EBEN *appears. His face wears an expression of obsessed confusion. He stands staring up at her, his arms hanging disjointedly from his shoulders, his feet bare, his hat in his hand.*)

ABBIE (*after a pause—with a nervous, formal politeness*): Won't ye set?

EBEN (*dully*): Ay-eh. (*Mechanically he places his hat carefully on the floor near the door and sits stiffly beside her on the edge of the sofa. A pause. They both remain rigid, looking straight ahead with eyes full of fear.*)

ABBIE: When I fust come in—in the dark—they seemed somethin' here.

EBEN (*simply*): Maw.

ABBIE: I kin still feel—somethin'. . . .

EBEN: It's Maw.

ABBIE: At first I was feered o' it. I wanted t' yell an' run. Now—since yew come—seems like it's growin' soft an' kind t' me. (*Addressing the air—queerly.*) Thank yew.

EBEN: Maw allus loved me.

ABBIE: Mebbe it knows I love yew, too. Mebbe that makes it kind t' me.

EBEN (*dully*): I dunno. I should think she'd hate ye.

ABBIE (*with certainty*): No. I kin feel it don't—not no more.

EBEN: Hate ye fur stealin' her place—here in her hum—settin' in her parlor whar she was laid— (*He suddenly stops, staring stupidly before him.*)

ABBIE: What is it, Eben?

EBEN (*in a whisper*): Seems like Maw didn't want me t' remind ye.

ABBIE (*excitedly*): I knowed, Eben! It's kind t' me! It don't b'ar me no grudges fur what I never knowed an' couldn't help!

EBEN: Maw b'ars him a grudge.

ABBIE: Waal, so does all o' us.

EBEN: Ay-eh. (*With passion.*) I does, by God!

ABBIE (*taking one of his hands in hers and patting it*): Thar! Don't git riled thinkin' o' him. Think o' yer Maw who's kind t' us. Tell me about yer Maw, Eben.

EBEN: They hain't nothin' much. She was kind. She was good.

ABBIE (*putting one arm over his shoulder. He does not seem to notice— passionately*): I'll be kind an' good t' ye!

EBEN: Sometimes she used t' sing fur me.

ABBIE: I'll sing fur ye!

EBEN: This was her hum. This was her farm.

ABBIE: This is my hum! This is my farm!

EBEN: He married her t' steal 'em. She was soft an' easy. He couldn't 'preciate her.

ABBIE: He can't 'preciate me!

EBEN: He murdered her with his hardness.

ABBIE: He's murderin' me!

EBEN: She died. (*A pause.*) Sometimes she used to sing fur me. (*He bursts into a fit of sobbing.*)

ABBIE (*both her arms around him—with wild passion*): I'll sing fur ye! I'll die fur ye! (*In spite of her overwhelming desire for him, there is a sincere maternal love in her manner and voice—a horribly frank mixture of lust and mother love.*) Don't cry, Eben! I'll take yer Maw's place! I'll be everythin' she was t' ye! Let me kiss ye, Eben! (*She pulls his head around. He makes a bewildered pretense of resistance. She is tender.*) Don't be afeered! I'll kiss ye pure, Eben—same 's if I was a Maw t' ye—an' ye kin kiss me back 's if yew was my son—my boy—sayin' good-night t' me! Kiss me, Eben. (*They kiss in restrained fashion. Then suddenly wild passion overcomes her. She kisses him lustfully again and again and he flings his arms about her and returns her kisses. Suddenly, as in the bedroom, he frees himself from her violently and springs to his feet. He is trembling all over, in a strange state of terror.* ABBIE *strains her arms toward him with fierce pleading.*) Don't ye leave me, Eben! Can't ye see it hain't enuf—lovin' ye like a Maw—can't ye see it's got t' be that an' more—much more—a hundred times more—fur me t' be happy—fur yew t' be happy?

EBEN (*to the presence he feels in the room*): Maw! Maw! What d'ye want? What air ye tellin' me?

ABBIE: She's tellin ye t' love me. She knows I love ye an' I'll be good t' ye. Can't ye feel it? Don't ye know? She's tellin' ye t' love me, Eben!

EBEN: Ay-eh. I feel—mebbe she—but—I can't figger out—why—when ye've stole her place—here in her hum—in the parlor whar she was—

ABBIE (*fiercely*): She knows I love ye!

EBEN (*his face suddenly lighting up with a fierce, triumphant grin*): I see it! I sees why. It's her vengeance on him—so's she kin rest quiet in her grave!

ABBIE (*wildly*): Vengeance o' God on the hull o' us! What d'we give a durn? I love ye, Eben! God knows I love ye! (*She stretches out her arms for him.*)

EBEN (*throws himself on his knees beside the sofa and grabs her in his arms—releasing all his pent-up passion*): An' I love yew, Abbie!—now I kin say it! I been dyin' fur want o' ye—every hour since ye come! I love ye! (*Their lips meet in a fierce, bruising kiss.*)

SCENE FOUR

> (*Exterior of the farmhouse. It is just dawn. The front door at right is opened and* EBEN *comes out and walks around to the gate. He is*

dressed in his working clothes. He seems changed. His face wears a bold and confident expression, he is grinning to himself with evident satisfaction. As he gets near the gate, the window of the parlor is heard opening and the shutters are flung back and ABBIE *sticks her head out. Her hair tumbles over her shoulders in disarray, her face is flushed, she looks at* EBEN *with tender, languorous eyes and calls softly.)*

ABBIE: Eben. (*As he turns—playfully.*) Jest one more kiss afore ye go. I'm goin' t' miss ye fearful all day.

EBEN: An me yew, ye kin bet! (*He goes to her. They kiss several times. He draws away, laughingly.*) Thar. That's enuf, hain't it? Ye won't hev none left fur next time.

ABBIE: I got a million o' 'em left fur yew! (*Then a bit anxiously.*) D'ye r'ally love me, Eben?

EBEN (*emphatically*): I like ye better'n any gal I ever knowed! That's gospel!

ABBIE: Likin hain't lovin'.

EBEN: Waal then—I love ye. Now air yew satisfied?

ABBIE: Ay-eh, I be. (*She smiles at him adoringly.*)

EBEN: I better git t' the barn. The old critter's liable t' suspicion an' come sneakin' up.

ABBIE (*with a confident laugh*): Let him! I kin allus pull the wool over his eyes. I'm goin' t' leave the shutters open and let in the sun 'n' air. This room's been dead long enuf. Now it's goin' t' be my room!

EBEN (*frowning*): Ay-eh.

ABBIE (*hastily*): I meant—our room.

EBEN: Ay-eh.

ABBIE: We made it our'n last night, didn't we? We give it life—our lovin' did. (*A pause.*)

EBEN (*with a strange look*): Maw's gone back t' her grave. She kin sleep now.

ABBIE: May she rest in peace! (*Then tenderly rebuking.*) Ye oughtn't t' talk o' sad thin's—this mornin'.

EBEN: It jest come up in my mind o' itself.

ABBIE: Don't let it. (*He doesn't answer. She yawns.*) Waal, I'm a-goin' t' steal a wink o' sleep. I'll tell the Old Man I hain't feelin' pert. Let him git his own vittles.

EBEN: I see him comin' from the barn. Ye better look smart an' git upstairs.

ABBIE: Ay-eh. Good-by. Don't ferget me. (*She throws him a kiss. He grins—then squares his shoulders and awaits his father confidently.* CABOT *walks slowly up from the left, staring up at the sky with a vague face.*)

EBEN (JOVIALLY): Mornin', Paw. Stargazin' in daylight?

CABOT: Purty, hain't it?

EBEN (*looking around him possessively*): It's a durned purty farm.

CABOT: I mean the sky.

EBEN (*grinning*): How d'ye know? Them eyes o' your'n can't see that fur. (*This tickles his humor and he slaps his thigh and laughs.*) Ho-ho! That's a good un!

CABOT (*grimly sarcastic*): Ye're feelin' right chipper, hain't ye? Whar'd ye steal the likker?

EBEN (*good-naturedly*): 'Tain't likker. Jest life. (*Suddenly holding out his hand— soberly.*) Yew 'n' me is quits. Let's shakes hands.

CABOT (*suspiciously*): What's come over ye?

EBEN: Then don't. Mebbe it's jest as well. (*A moment's pause.*) What's come over me? (*Queerly.*) Didn't ye feel her passin'—goin' back t' her grave?

CABOT (*dully*): Who?

EBEN: Maw. She kin rest now an' sleep content. She's quits with ye.

CABOT (*confusedly*): I rested. I slept good—down with the cows. They know how t' sleep. They're teachin' me.

EBEN (*suddenly jovial again*): Good fur the cows! Waal—ye better git t' work.

CABOT (*grimly amused*): Air yew bossin' me, ye calf?

EBEN (*beginning to laugh*): Ay-eh! I'm bossin' yew! Ha-ha-ha! See how ye like it! Ha-ha-ha! I'm the prize rooster o' this roost. Ha-ha-ha! (*He goes oft toward the barn laughing.*)

CABOT (*looks after him with scornful pity*): Soft-headed. Like his Maw. Dead spit 'n' image. No hope in him! (*He spits with contemptuous disgust.*) A born fool! (*Then matter-of-factly.*) Waal—I'm gittin' peckish. (*He goes toward door.*)

(*The curtain falls.*)

PART THREE, SCENE ONE

(*A night in late spring the following year. The kitchen and the two bedrooms upstairs are shown. The two bedrooms are dimly lighted by a tallow candle in each. EBEN is sitting on the side of the bed in his room, his chin propped on his fists, his face a study of the struggle he is making to understand his conflicting emotions. The noisy laughter and music from below where a kitchen dance is in progress annoy and distract him. He scowls at the floor.*)

(*In the next room a cradle stands beside the double bed.*)

(*In the kitchen all is festivity. The stove has been taken down to give more room to the dancers. The chairs, with wooden benches added, have been pushed back against the walls. On these are seated, squeezed in tight against one another, farmers and their wives and their young folks of both sexes from the neighboring farms. They are all chattering and laughing loudly. They evidently have some secret joke in common. There is no end of winking, of nudging, of meaning nods of the head toward CABOT who, in a state of extreme hilarious excitement increased by the amount he has drunk, is standing near the rear door where there is a small keg of whisky and serving drinks to all the men. In the left corner, front,*) *dividing the attention with her husband,* ABBIE *is sitting in a rocking chair, a shawl wrapped about her shoulders. She is very pale, her face is thin and drawn, her eyes are fixed anxiously on the open door in rear as if waiting for someone.)*

(*The* MUSICIAN *is tuning up his fiddle, seated in the far right corner. He is a lanky young fellow with a long, weak face. His pale eyes blink incessantly and he grins about him slyly with a greedy malice.)*

ABBIE (*suddenly turning to a* YOUNG GIRL *on her right*): Whar's Eben?

YOUNG GIRL (*eyeing her scornfully*): I dunno, Mrs. Cabot. I hain't seen Eben in ages. (*Meaningly.*) Seems like he's spent most o' his time t' hum since yew come.

ABBIE (*vaguely*): I tuk his Maw's place.

YOUNG GIRL: Ay-eh. So I've heerd. (*She turns away to retail this bit of gossip to her mother sitting next to her.* ABBIE *turns to her left to a big stoutish middle-aged* MAN *whose flushed face and starting eyes show the amount of "likker" he has consumed.*)

ABBIE: Ye hain't seen Eben, hev ye?

MAN: No, I hain't. (*Then he adds with a wink.*) If yew hain't, who would?

ABBIE: He's the best dancer in the county. He'd ought t' come an' dance.

MAN (*with a wink*): Mebbe he's doin' the dutiful an' walkin' the kid t' sleep. It's a boy, hain't it?

ABBIE (*nodding vaguely*): Ay-eh—born two weeks back—purty's a picter.

MAN: They all is—t' their Maws. (*Then in a whisper, with a nudge and a leer.*) Listen, Abbie—if ye ever git tired o' Eben, remember me! Don't fergit now! (*He looks at her uncomprehending face for a second—then grunts disgustedly.*) Waal—guess I'll likker agin. (*He goes over and joins* CABOT *who is arguing noisily with an old farmer over cows. They all drink.*)

ABBIE (*this time appealing to nobody in particular*): Wonder what Eben's a-doin'? (*Her remark is repeated down the line with many a guffaw and titter until it reaches the* FIDDLER. *He fastens his blinking eyes on* ABBIE.)

FIDDLER (*raisin his voice*): Bet I kin tell ye, Abbie, what Eben's doin'! He's down t' the church offerin' up prayers o' thanksgivin'. (*They all titter expectantly.*)

A MAN: What fur? (*Another titter.*)

FIDDLER: 'Cause unto him a—(*he hesitates just long enough*) brother is born! (*A roar of laughter. They all look from* ABBIE *to* CABOT. *She is oblivious, staring at the door.* CABOT, *although he hasn't heard the words, is irritated by the laughter, and steps forward, glaring about him. There is an immediate silence.*)

CABOT: What're ye all bleatin' about—like a flock o' goats? Why don't ye dance, damn ye? I axed ye here t' dance—t' eat, drink an' be merry—an' thar ye set cacklin' like a lot o' wet hens with the pip! Ye've swilled my likker an' guzzled my vittles like hogs, hain't ye? Then dance fur me, can't ye? That's fa'r an' squar', hain't it? (*A grumble of resentment goes around but they are all evidently in too much awe of him to express it openly.*)

FIDDLER (*slyly*): We're waitin' fur Eben. (*A suppressed laugh.*)

CABOT (*with a fierce exultation*): T'hell with Eben! Eben's done fur now! I got a new son! (*His mood switching with drunken suddenness.*) But ye needn't t' laugh at Eben, none o' ye! He's my blood, if he be a dumb fool. He's better nor any o' yew! He kin do a day's work a'most up t' what I kin—an' that'd put any o' yew pore critters t' shame!

FIDDLER: An' he kin do a good night's work, too! (*A roar of laughter.*)

CABOT: Laugh, ye damn fools! Ye're right jist the same, Fiddler. He kin work day an' night too, like I kin, if need be!

OLD FARMER (*from behind the keg where he is weaving drunkenly back and forth—with great simplicity*): They hain't many t' touch ye, Ephraim—a son at seventy-six. That's a hard man fur ye! I be on'y sixty-eight an' I couldn't do it. (*A roar of laughter in which* CABOT *joins uproariously.*)

CABOT (*slapping him on the back*): I'm sorry fur ye, Hi. I'd never suspicion sech weakness from a boy like yew!

OLD FARMER: An' I never reckoned yew had it in ye nuther, Ephraim. (*There is another laugh.*)

CABOT (*suddenly grim*): I got a lot in me—a hell of a lot—folks don't know on. (*Turning to the* FIDDLER.) Fiddle 'er up, durn ye! Give 'em somethin' t' dance t'! What air ye, an ornament? Hain't this a celebration? Then grease yer elbow an' go it!

FIDDLER (*seizes a drink which the* OLD FARMER *holds out to him and downs it*): Here goes! (*He starts to fiddle "Lady of the Lake." Four young fellows and four girls form in two lines and dance a square dance. The* FIDDLER *shouts directions for the different movements, keeping his words in the rhythm of the music and interspersing them with jocular personal remarks to the dancers themselves. The people seated along the walls stamp their feet and clap their hands in unison.* CABOT *is especially active in this respect. Only* ABBIE *remains apathetic, staring at the door as if she were alone in a silent room.*)

FIDDLER: Swing your partner t' the right! That's it, Jim! Give her a b'ar hug! Her Maw hain't lookin'. (*Laughter.*) Change partners! That suits ye, don't it, Essie, now ye got Reub afore ye? Look at her redden up, will ye? Waal, life is short an' so's love, as the feller says. (*Laughter.*)

CABOT (*excitedly, stamping his foot*): Go it, boys! Go it, gals!

FIDDLER (*with a wink at the others*): Ye're the spryest seventy-six ever I sees, Ephraim! Now if ye'd on'y good eyesight . . . ! (*Suppressed laughter. He gives* CABOT *no chance to retort but roars.*) Promenade! Ye're walkin' like a bride down the aisle, Sarah! Waal, while they's life they's allus hope, I've heerd tell. Swing your partner to the left! Gosh A'mighty, look at Johnny Cook highsteppin'! They hain't goin' t'be much strength left fur howin' in the corn lot t'morrow. (*Laughter.*)

CABOT: Go it! Go it! (*Then suddenly, unable to restrain himself any longer, he prances into the midst of the dancers, scattering them, waving his arms about wildly.*) Ye're all hoofs! Git out o' my road! Give me room! I'll show ye dancin'. Ye're all too soft! (*He pushes them roughly away. They crowd back toward the walls, muttering, looking at him resentfully.*)

FIDDLER (*jeeringly*): Go it, Ephraim! Go it! (*He starts "Pop, Goes the Weasel," increasing the tempo with every verse until at the end he is fiddling crazily as fast as he can go.*)

CABOT (*starts to dance, which he does very well and with tremendous vigor. Then he begins to improvise, cuts incredibly grotesque capers, leaping up and cracking his heels together, prancing around in a circle with body bent in an Indian war dance, then suddenly straightening up and kicking as high as he can with both legs. He is like a monkey on a string. And all the while he intersperses his antics with shouts and derisive comments*): Whoop! Here's dancin' fur ye! Whoop! See that! Seventy-six, if I'm a day! Hard as iron yet! Beatin' the young 'uns like I allus done! Look at me! I'd invite ye t' dance on my hundredth birthday on'y ye'll all be dead by then. Ye're a sickly generation! Yer hearts air pink, not red! Yer veins is full o' mud an' water! I be the on'y man in the county! Whoop! See that! I'm a Injun! I've killed Injuns in the West afore ye was born—an' skulped 'em too! They's a arrer wound on my backside I c'd show ye! The hull tribe chased me. I outrun 'em all—with the arrer stuck in me! An' I tuk vengeance on 'em. Ten eyes fur an eye, that was my motter! Whoop! Look at me! I kin kick the ceilin' off the room! Whoop!

FIDDLER (*stops playing—exhaustedly*): God A'mighty, I got enuf. Ye got the devil's strength in ye.

CABOT (*delightedly*): Did I beat yew, too? Waal, ye played smart. Hev a swig. (*He pours whisky for himself and* FIDDLER. *They drink. The others watch* CABOT *silently with cold, hostile eyes. There is a dead pause. The* FIDDLER *rests.* CABOT *leans against the keg, panting, glaring around him confusedly. In the room above,* EBEN *gets to his feet and tiptoes out the door in rear, appearing a moment later in the other bedroom. He moves silently, even frightenedly, toward the cradle and stands there looking down at the baby. His face is as vague as his reactions are confused, but there is a trace of tenderness, of interested discovery. At the same moment that he reaches the cradle,* ABBIE *seems to sense something. She gets up weakly and goes to* CABOT.)

ABBIE: I'm goin' up t' the baby.

CABOT (*with real solicitation*): Air ye able fur the stairs? D'ye want me t' help ye, Abbie?

ABBIE: No. I'm able. I'll be down agen soon.

CABOT: Don't ye git wore out! He needs ye, remember—our son does! (*He grins affectionately, patting her on the back. She shrinks from his touch.*)

ABBIE (*dully*): Don't tech me. I'm goin'—up. (*She goes.* CABOT *looks after her. A whisper goes around the room.* CABOT *turns. It ceases. He wipes his forehead streaming with sweat. He is breathing pantingly.*)

CABOT: I'm a-goin' out t' git fresh air. I'm feelin' a mite dizzy. Fiddle up thar! Dance, all o' ye! Here's likker fur them as wants it. Enjoy yerselves. I'll be back. (*He goes, closing the door behind him.*)

FIDDLER (*sarcastically*): Don't hurry none on our account! (*A suppressed laugh. He imitates* ABBIE.) Whar's Eben? (*More laughter.*)

A WOMAN (*loudly*): What's happened in this house is plain as the nose on yer face! (ABBIE *appears in the doorway upstairs and stands looking in surprise and adoration at* EBEN *who does not see her.*)

A MAN: Ssshh! He's li'ble t' be listenin' at the door. That'd be like him. (*Their voices die to an intensive whispering. Their faces are concentrated on this gossip. A noise as of dead leaves in the wind comes from the room.* CABOT *has come out from the porch and stands by the gate, leaning on it, staring at the sky blinkingly.* ABBIE *comes across the room silently.* EBEN *does not notice her until quite near.*)

EBEN (*starting*): Abbie!

ABBIE: Ssshh! (*She throws her arms around him. They kiss—then bend over the cradle together.*) Ain't he purty?—dead spit 'n' image o' yew!

EBEN (*pleased*): Air he? I can't tell none.

ABBIE: E-zactly like!

EBEN (*frowningly*): I don't like this. I don't like lettin' on what's mine's his'n. I been doin' that all my life. I'm gittin' t' the end o' b'airin' it!

ABBIE (*putting her finger on his lips*): We're doin' the best we kin. We got t' wait. Somethin's bound t' happen. (*She puts her arms around him.*) I got t' go back.

EBEN: I'm goin' out. I can't b'ar it with the fiddle playin' an' the laughin'.

ABBIE: Don't git feelin' low. I love ye, Eben. Kiss me. (*He kisses her. They remain in each other's arms.*)

CABOT (*at the gate, confusedly*): Even the music can't drive it out—somethin'. Ye kin feel it droppin' off the elums, climbin' up the roof, sneakin' down the chimney, pokin' in the corners! They's no peace in houses, they's no rest livin' with folks. Somethin's always livin' with ye. (*With a deep sigh.*) I'll go t' the barn an' rest a spell. (*He goes wearily toward the barn.*)

FIDDLER (*tuning up*): Let's celebrate the old skunk gittin' fooled! We kin have some fun now he's went. (*He starts to fiddle "Turkey in the Straw." There is real merriment now. The young folks get up to dance.*)

SCENE TWO

(*A half hour later—Exterior—*EBEN *is standing by the gate looking up at the sky, an expression of dumb pain bewildered by itself on his face.* CABOT *appears, returning from the barn, walking wearily, his eyes on the ground. He sees* EBEN *and his whole mood immediately changes. He becomes excited, a cruel, triumphant grin comes to his lips, he strides up and slaps* EBEN *on the back. From within comes the whining of the fiddle and the noise of stamping feet and laughing voices.*)

CABOT: So har ye be!

EBEN (*startled, stares at him, with a hatred for a moment—then dully*): Ay-eh.

CABOT (*surveying him jeeringly*): Why hain't ye been in t' dance? They was all axin' fur ye.

EBEN: Let 'em ax!

CABOT: They's a hull passel o' purty gals.

EBEN: T' hell with 'em!

CABOT: Ye'd ought t' be marryin' one o' 'em soon.

EBEN: I hain't marryin' no one.

CABOT: Ye might 'arn a share o' a farm that way.

EBEN (*with a sneer*): Like yew did, ye mean? I hain't that kind.

CABOT (*stung*): Ye lie! 'Twas yer Maw's folks aimed t' steal my farm from me.

EBEN: Other folks don't say so. (*After a pause—defiantly.*) An' I got a farm, anyways!

CABOT (*derisively*): Whar?

EBEN (*stamps a foot on the ground*): Har!

CABOT (*throws his head back and laughs coarsely*): Ho-ho! Ye hev, hev ye? Waal, that's a good un!

EBEN (*controlling himself—grimly*): Ye'll see!

CABOT (*stares at him suspiciously, trying to make him out—a pause—then with scornful confidence*): Ay-eh. I'll see. So'll ye. It's ye that's blind—blind as a mole underground. (EBEN *suddenly laughs, one short sardonic bark:* "Ha." *A pause.* CABOT *peers at him with renewed suspicion.*) What air ye hawin' 'bout? (EBEN *turns away without answering.* CABOT *grows angry.*) God A'mighty, yew air a dumb dunce! They's nothin' in that thick skull o' your'n but noise—like an empty keg it be! (EBEN *doesn't seem to hear.* CABOT's *rage grows.*) Yewr farm! God A'mighty! If ye wa'n't a born donkey ye'd know ye'll never own stick nor stone on it, specially now arter him bein' born. It's his'n, I tell ye—his'n arter I die—but I'll live a hundred jest t' fool ye all—an' he'll be growed then—yewr age a'most! (EBEN *laughs again his sardonic* "Ha." *This drives* CABOT *into a fury.*) Ha? Ye think ye kin git 'round that someways, do ye? Waal, it'll be her'n, too—Abbie's—ye won't git 'round her—she knows yer tricks—she'll be too much fur ye—she wants the farm her'n—she was afeerd o' ye—she told me ye was sneakin' 'round trying' t' make love t' her t' git her on yer side . . . ye . . . ye mad fool, ye! (*He raises his clenched fists threateningly.*)

EBEN (*is confronting him, choking with rage*): Ye lie, ye old skunk! Abbie never said no sech thing!

CABOT (*suddenly triumphant when he sees how shaken* EBEN *is*): She did. An' I says, I'll blow his brains t' the top o' them elums—an' she says no, that hain't sense, who'll ye git t'help ye on the farm in his place—an' then she says yew'n me ought t' have a son—I know we kin, she says—an' I says, if we do, ye kin have anythin' I've got ye've a mind t'. An' she says, I wants Eben cut off so's this farm'll be mine when ye die! (*With terrible gloating.*) An' that's what's happened, hain't it? An' the farm's her'n! An' the dust o' the road—that's you'rn! Ha! Now who's hawin'?

EBEN (*has been listening, petrified with grief and rage—suddenly laughs wildly and brokenly*): Ha-ha-ha! So that's her sneakin' game—all along!—like I suspicioned at fust—t' swaller it all—an' me, too . . ! (*Madly.*) I'll murder her! (*He springs toward the porch but* CABOT *is quicker and gets in between.*)

CABOT: No, ye don't!

EBEN: Git out o' my road! (*He tries to throw* CABOT *aside. They grapple in what becomes immediately a murderous struggle. The old man's concentrated strength is too much for* EBEN. CABOT *gets one hand on his throat and presses him back across the stone wall. At the same moment,* ABBIE *comes out on the porch. With a stifled cry she runs toward them.*)

ABBIE: Eben! Ephraim! (*She tugs at the hand on* EBEN's *throat.*) Let go, Ephraim! Ye're chokin' him!

CABOT (*removes his hand and flings* EBEN *sideways full length of the grass, gasping and choking. With a cry,* ABBIE *kneels beside him, trying to take his head on her lap, but he pushes her away.* CABOT *stands looking down with fierce triumph*): Ye needn't t've fret, Abbie, I wa'n't aimin' t' kill him. He hain't wuth hangin' fur—not by a hell of a sight! (*More and more triumphantly.*) Seventy-six an' him not thirty yit—an' look whar he be fur thinkin' his Paw was easy! No, by God, I hain't easy! An' him upstairs, I'll raise him t' be like me! (*He turns to leave them.*) I'm goin' in an' dance!—sing an' celebrate! (*He walks to the porch—then turns with a great grin.*) I don't calc'late it's left in him, but if he gits pesky, Abbie, ye jest sing out. I'll come a-runnin' an' by the Etarnal, I'll put him across my knee an' birch him! Ha-ha-ha! (*He goes into the house laughing. A moment later his loud "whoop" is heard.*)

ABBIE (*tenderly*): Eben. Air ye hurt? (*She tries to kiss him but he pushes her violently away and struggles to a sitting position.*)

EBEN (*gaspingly*): T'hell—with ye!

ABBIE (*not believing her ears*): It's me, Eben—Abbie—don't ye know me?

EBEN (*glowering at her with hatred*): Ay-eh—I know ye—now! (*He suddenly breaks down, sobbing weakly.*)

ABBIE (*fearfully*): Eben—what's happened t' ye—why did ye look at me 's if ye hated me?

EBEN (*violently, between sobs and gasps*): I do hate ye! Ye're a whore—a damn trickin' whore!

ABBIE (*shrinking back horrified*): Eben! Ye don't know what ye're sayin'!

EBEN (*scrambling to his feet and following her—accusingly*): Ye're nothin' but a stinkin' passel o' lies! Ye've been lyin' t' me every word ye spoke, day an' night, since we fust—done it. Ye've kept sayin' ye loved me. . . .

ABBIE (*frantically*): I do love ye! (*She takes his hand but he flings hers away.*)

EBEN (*unheeding*): Ye've made a fool o' me—a sick, dumb fool—a-purpose! Ye've been on'y playin' yer sneakin', stealin' game all along—gittin' me t' lie with ye so's ye'd hev a son he'd think was his'n, an' makin' him promise he'd give ye the farm and let me eat dust, if ye did git him a son! (*Staring at her with anguished, bewildered eyes.*) They must be a devil livin' in ye! T'ain't human t' be as bad as that be!

ABBIE (*stunned—dully*): He told yew. . . ?

EBEN: Hain't it true? It hain't no good in yew lyin'.

ABBIE (*pleadingly*): Eben, listen—ye must listen—it was long ago—afore we done nothin'—yew was scornin' me—goin' t' see Min—when I was lovin' ye—an' I said it t' him t' git vengeance on ye!

EBEN (*unheedingly. With tortured passion*): I wish ye was dead! I wish I was dead along with ye afore this come! (*Ragingly.*) But I'll git my vengeance too! I'll pray Maw t' come back t' help me—t' put her cuss on yew an' him!

ABBIE (*brokenly*): Don't ye, Eben! Don't ye! (*She throws herself on her knees before him, weeping.*) I didn't mean t' do bad t'ye! Fergive me, won't ye?

EBEN (*not seeming to hear her—fiercely*): I'll git squar' with the old skunk—an' yew! I'll tell him the truth 'bout the son he's so proud o'! Then I'll leave ye here t' pizen each other—with Maw comin' out o' her grave at nights—an' I'll go t' the gold fields o' Californi-a whar Sim an' Peter be!

ABBIE (*terrified*): Ye won't—leave me? Ye can't!

EBEN (*with fierce determination*): I'm a goin', I tell ye! I'll git rich thar an' come back and fight him fur the farm he stole—an' I'll kick ye both out in the road—t' beg an' sleep in the woods—an' yer son along with ye—t' starve an' die! (*He is hysterical at the end.*)

ABBIE (*with a shudder—humbly*): He's yewr son, too, Eben.

EBEN (*torturedly*): I wish he never was born! I wish he'd die this minit! I wish I'd never sot eyes on him! It's him—yew havin' him—a-purpose t' steal—that's changed everythin'!

ABBIE (*gently*): Did ye believe I loved ye—afore he come?

EBEN: Ay-eh—like a dumb ox!

ABBIE: An' ye don't believe no more?

EBEN: B'lieve a lyin' thief! Ha!

ABBIE (*shudders—then humbly*): An' did ye r'ally love me afore?

EBEN (*brokenly*): Ay-eh—an' ye was trickin' me!

ABBIE: An' ye don't love me now!

EBEN (*violently*): I hate ye, I tell ye!

ABBIE: An' ye're truly goin' West—goin' t' leave me—all account o' him being born?

EBEN: I'm a-goin' in the mornin'—or may God strike me t' hell!

ABBIE (*after a pause—with a dreadful cold intensity—slowly*): If that's what his comin' done t' me—killin' yewr love—takin' yew away—my on'y joy—the on'y joy I ever knowed—like heaven t' me—purtier'n heaven—then I hate him, too, even if I be his Maw!

EBEN (*bitterly*): Lies! Ye love him! He'll steal the farm fur ye! (*Brokenly.*) But t'ain't the farm so much—not no more—it's yew foolin' me—gettin' me t' love ye—lyin' yew loved me—jest t' git a son t' steal!

ABBIE (*distractedly*): He won't steal! I'd kill him fust! I do love ye! I'll prove t' ye. . . !

EBEN (*harshly*): T'ain't no use lyin' no more. I'm deaf t' ye! (*He turns away.*) I hain't seein' ye agen. Good-by!

ABBIE (*pale with anguish*): Hain't ye even goin' t' kiss me—not once—arter all we loved?

EBEN (*in a hard voice*): I hain't wantin' t' kiss ye never agen! I'm wantin' t' forgit I ever sot eyes on ye!

ABBIE: Eben!—ye mustn't—wait a spell—I want t' tell ye. . . .

EBEN: I'm a-goin' in t' git drunk. I'm a-goin' t' dance.

ABBIE (*clinging to his arm—with passionate earnestness*): If I could make it—'s if he'd never come up between us—if I could prove t' ye I wa'n't schemin' t' steal from ye—so's everythin' could be jest the same with us, lovin' each other jest the same, kissin' an' happy the same's we've been happy afore he come—if I could do it—ye'd love me agen, wouldn't ye? Ye'd kiss me agen? Ye wouldn't never leave me, would ye?

EBEN (*moved*): I calc'late not. (*Then shaking her hand off his arm—with a bitter smile.*) But ye hain't God, be ye?

ABBIE (*exultantly*): Remember ye've promised! (*Then with strange intensity.*) Mebbe I kin take back one thin' God does!

EBEN (*peering at her*): Ye're gittin cracked, hain't ye? (*Then going towards door.*) I'm a-goin' t' dance.

ABBIE (*calls after him intensely*): I'll prove t' ye! I'll prove I love ye better'n. . . . (*He goes in the door, not seeming to hear. She remains standing where she is, looking after him—then she finishes desperately.*) Bettern' everythin' else in the world!

SCENE THREE

(*Just before dawn in the morning—shows the kitchen and CABOT's bedroom. In the kitchen, by the light of a tallow candle on the table, EBEN is sitting, his chin propped on his hands, his drawn face blank and expressionless. His carpetbag is on the floor beside him. In the bedroom, dimly lighted by a small whale-oil lamp, CABOT lies asleep. ABBIE is bending over the cradle, listening, her face full of terror yet with an undercurrent of desperate triumph. Suddenly, she breaks down and sobs, appears about to throw herself on her knees beside the cradle; but the old man turns restlessly, groaning in his sleep, and she controls herself, and, shrinking away from the cradle with a gesture of horror, backs swiftly toward the door in rear and goes out. A moment later she comes into the kitchen and, running to EBEN, flings her arms about his neck and kisses him wildly. He hardens himself, he remains unmoved and cold, he keeps his eyes straight ahead.*)

ABBIE (*hysterically*): I done it, Eben! I told ye I'd do it! I've proved I love ye—better'n everythin'—so's ye can't never doubt me no more!

EBEN (*dully*): Whatever ye done, it hain't no good now.

ABBIE (*wildly*): Don't ye say that! Kiss me, Eben, won't ye? I need ye t' kiss me arter what I done! I need ye t' say ye love me!

EBEN (*kisses her without emotion—dully*): That's fur good-by. I'm a-goin' soon.

ABBIE: No! No! Ye won't go—not now!

EBEN (*going on with his own thoughts*): I been a-thinkin'—an' I hain't goin' t' tell Paw nothin'. I'll leave Maw t' take vengeance on ye. If I told him, the old skunk'd jest be stinkin' mean enuf to take it out on that baby. (*His voice showing emotion in spite of him.*) An' I don't want nothin' bad t' happen t' him. He hain't t' blame fur yew. (*He adds with a certain queer pride.*) An' he looks like me! An' by God, he's mine! An' some day I'll be a-comin' back an' . . . !

ABBIE (*too absorbed in her own thoughts to listen to him—pleadingly*): They's no cause fur ye t' go now—they's no sense—it's all the same's it was—they's nothin' come b'tween us now—arter what I done!

EBEN (*something in her voice arouses him. He stares at her a bit frightenedly*): Ye look mad, Abbie. What did ye do?

ABBIE: I—I killed him, Eben.

EBEN (*amazed*): Ye killed him?

ABBIE (*dully*): Ay-eh.

EBEN (*recovering from his astonishment—savagely*): An' serves him right! But we got t' do somethin' quick t' make it look s'if the old skunk'd killed himself when he was drunk. We kin prove by 'em all how drunk he got.

ABBIE (*wildly*): No! No! Not him! (*Laughing distractedly.*) But that's what I ought t' done, hain't it? I oughter killed him instead! Why didn't ye tell me?

EBEN (*appalled*): Instead? What d'ye mean?

ABBIE: Not him.

EBEN (*his face grown ghastly*): Not—not the baby!

ABBIE (*dully*): Ay-eh!

EBEN (*falls to his knees as if he'd been struck—his voice trembling with horror*): Oh God A'mighty! A'mighty God! Maw, whar was ye, why didn't ye stop her?

ABBIE (*simply*): She went back t' her grave that night we fust done it, remember? I hain't felt her about since. (*A pause.* EBEN *hides his head in his hands, trembling all over as if he had the ague. She goes on dully.*) I left the piller over his little face. Then he killed himself. He stopped breathin'. (*She begins to weep softly.*)

EBEN (*rage beginning to mingle with grief*): He looked like me. He was mine, damn ye!

ABBIE (*slowly and brokenly*): I didn't want t' do it. I hated myself fur doin' it. I loved him. He was so purty—dead spit 'n' image o' yew. But I loved yew more—an' yew was goin' away—far off whar I'd never see ye agen, never kiss ye, never feel ye pressed agin me agen—an' ye said ye hated me fur havin' him—ye said ye hated him an' wished he was dead—ye said if it hadn't been fur him comin' it'd be the same's afore between us.

EBEN (*unable to endure this, springs to his feet in a fury, threatening her, his twitching fingers seeming to reach out for her throat*): Ye lie! I never said—I never dreamed ye'd—I'd cut off my head afore I'd hurt his finger!

ABBIE (*piteously, sinking on her knees*): Eben, don't ye look at me like that—hatin' me—not after what I done fur ye—fur us—so's we could be happy agen—

EBEN (*furiously now*): Shut up, or I'll kill ye! I see yer game now—the same old sneakin' trick—ye're aimin' t' blame me fur the murder ye done!

ABBIE (*moaning—putting her hands over her ears*): Don't ye, Eben! Don't ye! (*She grasps his legs.*)

EBEN (*his mood suddenly changing to horror, shrinks away from her*): Don't ye tech me! Ye're pizen! How could ye—t' murder a pore little critter— Ye must've swapped yer soul t' hell! (*Suddenly raging.*) Ha! I kin see why ye done it! Not the lies ye just told—but 'cause ye wanted t' steal agen—steal the last thin' ye'd left me—my part o' him—no, the hull o' him—ye saw he looked like me—ye knowed he was all mine—an' ye couldn't b'ar it—I know ye! Ye killed him fur bein' mine! (*All this has driven him almost insane. He makes a rush past her for the door—then turns—shaking both fists at her, violently.*) But I'll take vengeance now! I'll git the Sheriff! I'll tell him everythin'! Then I'll sing "I'm off to Californi-a!" an' go— gold—Golden Gate—gold sun—fields o' gold in the West! (*This last he half shouts, half croons incoherently, suddenly breaking off pasionately.*) I'm a-goin' fur the Sheriff t' come an' git ye! I want ye tuk away, locked up from me! I can't stand t' luk at ye! Murderer an' thief 'r not, ye still tempt me! I'll give ye up t' the Sheriff! (*He turns and runs out, around the corner of house, panting and sobbing, and breaks into a swerving sprint down the road.*)

ABBIE (*struggling to her feet, runs to the door calling after him*): I love ye, Eben! I love ye! (*She stops at the door weakly, swaying, about to fall.*) I don't care what ye do—if ye'll on'y love me agen— (*She falls limply to the floor in a faint.*)

SCENE FOUR

(*About an hour later. Same as Scene 3. Shows the kitchen and CABOT's bedroom. It is after dawn. The sky is brilliant with the sunrise. In the kitchen, ABBIE sits at the table, her body limp and exhausted, her head bowed down over her arms, her face hidden. Upstairs, CABOT is still asleep but awakens with a start. He looks toward the window and gives a snort of surprise and irritation— throws back the covers and begins hurriedly pulling on his clothes. Without looking behind him, he begins talking to ABBIE whom he supposes beside him.*)

CABOT: Thunder 'n' lightin', Abbie! I hain't slept this late in fifty year! Looks 's if the sun was full riz a'most. Must've been the dancin' an' likker. Must be gittin' old. I hope Eben's t' wuk. Ye might've tuk the trouble t' rouse me, Abbie. (*He turns—sees no one there—surprised.*) Waal—whar air she? Gittin' vittles, I calc'late. (*He tiptoes to the cradle and peers down— proudly.*) Mornin', sonny. Purty's a picter! Sleepin' sound. He don't beller all night like most o' 'em. (*He goes quietly out the door in rear—a few moments later enters kitchen—sees ABBIE—with satisfaction.*) So thar ye be. Ye got any vittles cooked?

ABBIE (*without moving*): No.

CABOT (*coming to her, almost sympathetically*): Ye feelin' sick?

ABBIE: No.

CABOT (*pats her on shoulder. She shudders*): Ye'd best lie down a spell. (*Half jocularly.*) Yer son'll be needin' ye soon. He'd ought t' wake up with a gnashin' appetite, the sound way he's sleepin'.

ABBIE (*shudders—then in a dead voice*): He hain't never goin' t' wake up.

CABOT (*jokingly*): Takes after me this mornin'. I hain't slept so late in. . . .

ABBIE: He's dead.

CABOT (*stares at her—bewilderedly*): What. . . .

ABBIE: I killed him.

CABOT (*stepping back from her—aghast*): Air ye drunk—'r crazy—'r. . . !

ABBIE (*suddenly lifts her head and turns on him—wildly*): I killed him, I tell ye! I smothered him. Go up an' see if ye don't b'lieve me! (CABOT *stares at her a second, then bolts out the rear door, can be heard bounding up the stairs, and rushes into the bedroom and over to the cradle.* ABBIE *has sunk back lifelessly into her former position.* CABOT *puts his hand down on the body in the crib. An expression of fear and horror comes over his face.*)

CABOT (*shrinking away—trembling*): God A'mighty! God A'mighty. (*He stumbles out the door—in a short while returns to the kitchen—comes to* ABBIE, *the stunned expression still on his face—hoarsely.*) Why did ye do it? Why? (*As she doesn't answer, he grabs her violently by the shoulder and shakes her.*) I ax ye why ye done it! Ye'd better tell me 'r . . . !

ABBIE (*gives him a furious push which sends him staggering back and springs to her feet—with wild rage and hatred*): Don't ye dare tech me! What right hev ye t' question me 'bout him? He wa'n't yewr son! Think I'd have a son by yew? I'd die fust! I hate the sight o' ye an' allus did! It's yew I should've murdered, if I'd had good sense! I hate ye! I love Eben. I did from the fust. An' he was Eben's son—mine an' Eben's—not your'n!

CABOT (*stands looking at her dazedly—a pause—finding his words with an effort—dully*): That was it—what I felt—pokin' round the corners—while ye lied—holdin' yerself from me—sayin' ye'd a'ready conceived—. (*He lapses into crushed silence—then with a strange emotion.*) He's dead, sart'n. I felt his heart. Poor little critter! (*He blinks back one tear, wiping his sleeve across his nose.*)

ABBIE (*hysterically*): Don't ye! Don't ye! (*She sobs unrestrainedly.*)

CABOT (*with a concentrated effort that stiffens his body into a rigid line and hardens his face into a stony mask—through his teeth to himself*): I got t' be—like a stone—a rock o' jedgment! (*A pause. He gets complete control over himself—harshly.*) If he was Eben's, I be glad he air gone! An' mebbe I suspicioned it all along. I felt they was somethin' onnateral—somewhars—the house got so lonesome—an' cold—drivin' me down t' the barn—t' the beasts o' the field. . . . Ay-eh. I must've suspicioned—somethin'. Ye didn't fool me—not altogether, leastways—I'm too old a bird—growin' ripe on the bough. . . . (*He becomes aware he is wandering, straightens again, looks at* ABBIE *with a cruel grin.*) So ye'd liked t' hev murdered me 'stead o' him, would ye? Waal, I'll live to a hundred! I'll live t' see ye hung! I'll deliver ye up t' the jedgment o' God an' the law! I'll git the Sheriff now. (*Starts for the door.*)

ABBIE (*dully*): Ye needn't. Eben's gone fur him.

CABOT (*amazed*): Eben—gone fur the Sheriff?

ABBIE: Ay-eh.

CABOT: T' inform agen ye?

ABBIE: Ay-eh.

CABOT (*considers this—a pause—then in a hard voice*): Waal, I'm thankful fur him savin' me the trouble. I'll git t' wuk. (*He goes to the door—then turns—in a voice full of strange emotion.*) He'd ought t' been my son, Abbie. Ye'd ought t' loved me. I'm a man. If ye'd loved me, I'd never told no Sheriff on ye no matter what ye did, if they was t' brile me alive!

ABBIE (*defensively*): They's more to it nor yew know, makes him tell.

CABOT (*dryly*): Fur yewr sake, I hope they be. (*He goes out—comes around to the gate—stares up at the sky. His control relaxes. For a moment he is old and weary. He murmurs despairingly.*) God A'mighty, I be lonesomer'n ever! (*He hears running footsteps from the left, immediately is himself again.* EBEN *runs in, panting exhaustedly, wild-eyed and mad looking. He lurches through the gate.* CABOT *grabs him by the shoulder.* EBEN *stares at him dumbly.*) Did ye tell the Sheriff?

EBEN (*nodding stupidly*): Ay-eh.

CABOT (*gives him a push away that sends him sprawling—laughing with withering contempt*): Good fur ye! A prime chip o' yer Maw ye be! (*He goes toward the barn, laughing harshly.* EBEN *scrambles to his feet. Suddenly* CABOT *turns—grimly threatening.*) Git off this farm when the Sheriff takes her—or, by God, he'l have t' come back an' git me fur murder, too! (*He stalks off.* EBEN *does not appear to have heard him. He runs to the door and comes into the kitchen.* ABBIE *looks up with a cry of anguished joy.* EBEN *stumbles over and throws himself on his knees beside her—sobbing brokenly.*)

EBEN: Fergive me!

ABBIE (*happily*): Eben! (*She kisses him and pulls his head over against her breast.*)

EBEN: I love ye! Fergive me!

ABBIE (*ecstatically*): I'd fergive ye all the sins in hell fur sayin' that! (*She kisses his head, pressing it to her with a fierce passion of possession.*)

EBEN (*brokenly*): But I told the Sheriff. He's comin' fur ye!

ABBIE: I kin b'ar what happens t' me—now!

EBEN: I woke him up. I told him. He says, wait 'till I git dressed. I was waiting. I got to thinkin' o' yew. I got to thinkin' how I'd loved ye. It hurt like somethin' was bustin' in my chest an' head. I got t' cryin'. I knowed sudden I loved ye yet, an' allus would love ye!

ABBIE (*caressing his hair—tenderly*): My boy, hain't ye?

EBEN: I begun t' run back. I cut across the fields an' through the woods. I thought ye might have time t' run away—with me—an'. . . .

ABBIE (*shaking her head*): I got t' take my punishment—t' pay fur my sin.

EBEN: Then I want t' share it with ye.

ABBIE: Ye didn't do nothin'.

EBEN: I put it in yer head. I wisht he was dead! I as much as urged ye t' do it!

ABBIE: No. It was me alone!

EBEN: I'm as guilty as yew be! He was the child o' our sin.

ABBIE (*lifting her head as if defying God*): I don't repent that sin! I hain't askin' God t' fergive that!

EBEN: Nor me—but it led up t' the other—an' the murder ye did, ye did 'count 'o me—an' it's my murder, too, I'll tell the Sheriff—an' if ye deny it, I'll say we planned it t'gether—an' they'll all b'lieve me, fur they suspicion everythin' we've done, an' it'll seem likely an' true to 'em. An' it is true—way down. I did help ye—somehow.

ABBIE (*laying her head on his—sobbing*): No! I don't want yew t' suffer!

EBEN: I got t' pay fur my part o' the sin! An' I'd suffer wuss leavin' ye, goin' West, thinkin' o' ye day an' night, bein' out when yew was in— (*Lowering his voice.*) 'r bein' alive when yew was dead. (*A pause.*) I want t' share with ye, Abbie —prison 'r death 'r hell 'r anythin'! (*He looks into her eyes and forces a trembling smile.*) If I'm sharin' with ye, I won't feel lonesome, leastways.

ABBIE (*weakly*): Eben! I won't let ye! I can't let ye!

EBEN (*kissing her—tenderly*): Ye can't he'p yerself. I got ye beat fur once!

ABBIE (*forcing a smile—adoringly*): I hain't beat—s'long's I got ye!

EBEN (*hears the sound of feet outside*): Ssshh! Listen! They've come t' take us!

ABBIE: No, it's him. Don't give him no chance to fight ye, Eben. Don't say nothin'—no matter what he says. An' I won't, neither. (*It is* CABOT. *He comes up from the barn in a great state of excitement and strides into the house and then into the kitchen.* EBEN *is kneeling beside* ABBIE, *his arm around her, hers around him. They stare straight ahead.*)

CABOT (*stares at them, his face hard. A long pause—vindictively*): Ye make a slick pair o' murderin' turtle doves! Ye'd ought t' be both hung on the same limb an' left thar t' swing in the breeze an' rot—a warnin' t' old fools like me t' b'ar their lonesomeness alone—an fur young folks like ye t' hobble their lust. (*A pause. The excitement returns to his face, his eyes snap, he looks a bit crazy.*) I couldn't work today. I couldn't take no interest. T' hell with the farm! I'm leavin' it! I've turned the cows an' other stock loose! I've druv 'em into the woods whar they kin be free! By freein' 'em, I'm freein' myself! I'm quittin' here today! I'll set fire t' house an' barn an' watch 'em burn, and I'll leave yer Maw t' haunt the ashes, an' I'll will the fields back t' God, so that nothin' human kin never touch 'em! I'll be a-goin' to Californi-a—t' jine Simeon an' Peter—true sons o' mine if they be dumb fools—an' the Cabots'll find Solomon's Mines t'gether! (*He suddenly cuts a mad caper.*) Whoop! What was the song they sung? "Oh, Californi-a! That's the land fur me." (*He sings this—then gets on his knees by the floorboard under which the money was hid.*) An' I'll sail thar on one o' the finest clippers I kin find! I've got the money! Pity ye didn't know whar this was hidden so's ye could steal. . . . (*He has pulled up the board. He stares—feels—stares again. A pause of dead silence. He slowly turns, slumping into a sitting position on the floor, his eyes like those of a dead fish, his face the sickly green of an attack of nausea. He swallows painfully several times—forces a weak smile at last.*) So—ye did steal it!

EBEN (*emotionlessly*): I swapped it t' Sim an' Peter fur their share o' the farm—t' pay their passage t' Californi-a.

CABOT (*with one sardonic "Ha!" He begins to recover. Gets slowly to his feet —strangely.*) I calc'late God give it to 'em—not yew! God's hard, not easy! Mebbe they's easy gold in the West but it hain't God's gold. It hain't fur me. I kin hear His voice warnin' me agen t' be hard an' stay on my farm. I kin see his hand usin' Eben t' steal t' keep me from weakness. I kin feel I be in the palm o' His hand. His fingers guidin' me. (*A pause—then he mutters sadly.*) It's a-goin't be lonesomer now than ever it war afore—an' I'm gittin' old, Lord—ripe on the bough. . . . (*Then stiffening.*) Waal—what d'ye want? God's lonesome, hain't He? God's hard an' lonesome! (*A pause,* THE SHERIFF *with two men comes up the road from the left. They move cautiously to the door.* THE SHERIFF *knocks on it with the butt of his pistol.*)

SHERIFF: Open in the name o' the law! (*They start.*)

CABOT: They've come fur ye. (*He goes to the rear door.*) Come in, Jim! (*The three men enter.* CABOT *meets them in doorway.*) Jest a minit, Jim. I got 'em safe here. (THE SHERIFF *nods. He and his companions remain in the doorway.*)

EBEN (*suddenly calls*): I lied this mornin', Jim. I helped her do it. Ye kin take me, too.

ABBIE (*brokenly*): No!

CABOT: Take 'em both. (*He comes forward—stares at* EBEN *with a trace of grudging admiration.*) Purty good—fur yew! Waal, I got t' round up the stock. Good-by.

EBEN: Good-by.

ABBIE: Good-by. (CABOT *turns and strides past the men—comes out and around the corner of the house, his shoulders squared, his face stony, and stalks grimly toward the barn. In the meantime* THE SHERIFF *and men have come into the room.*)

SHERIFF (*embarrassedly*): Waal—we'd best start.

ABBIE: Wait. (*Turns to* EBEN.) I love ye, Eben.

EBEN: I love ye, Abbie. (*They kiss. The three men grin and shuffle embarrassedly.* EBEN *takes* ABBIE'S *hand. They go out the door in rear, the men following, and come from the house, walking hand in hand to the gate.* EBEN *stops there and points to the sunrise sky.*) Sun's a-rizin'. Purty, hain't it?

ABBIE: Ay-eh. (*They both stand for a moment looking up raptly in attitudes strangely aloof and devout.*)

SHERIFF (*looking around at the farm enviously—to his companion*): It's a jim-dandy farm, no denyin'. Wished I owned it!

(*The curtain falls.*)

Fact Questions and Exercises

1. During what year does the play take place? How does this time setting help determine the actions of Simeon and Peter? What is the geographical setting?
2. Explain the title of the play. What fact determines this title?
3. In the opening of the play Ephraim has "been gone two months." Why has he gone? What does he bring back with him?
4. How is Eben related to Simeon and Peter? How is he related to Abbie?
5. Identify Minnie.
6. How does Eben obtain Simeon and Peter's rights to the farm?
7. How does Abbie turn Ephraim against Eben? Why does she do this?
8. Why has the parlor of the house been closed for a number of years? Who reopens it?
9. Who is the father of Abbie's son? What happens to the child?
10. What happens to Eben and Abbie at the end of the play? What happens to Ephraim?

For Discussing and Writing

1. Fate or predetermination is an important factor in the play; discuss how O'Neill demonstrates and uses the idea of fate. How, for instance, is Eben affected by his dead mother? How does the geographical setting affect the characters? What roles does Abbie play in the "fatalism"?
2. In Part 1, Scene 2 these lines appear: "An' makin' walls—stone atop o' stone—makin' walls till yer heart's a stone ye heft up out o' the way o' growth onto a stone wall t' wall in yer heart!" Is the walled-in heart a theme in the drama? How? Are the characters isolated within themselves? Is this why their love is so destructive?
3. Is there a hero in the play? If so, who is it? What is the hero's fatal flaw? Is there, for instance, any similarity between *Desire Under the Elms* and *Oedipus Rex*? Explain.
4. There are some definite Biblical aspects to the play. Can you point them out? For instance, what is the importance of Ephraim's saying that God is hard? In general, how does O'Neill use Biblical allusions to develop the play?

Bertolt Brecht [1898–1956]

Brecht was born in Germany, but was forced to leave in 1933, with the rise
of Hitler. He spent many years in exile, including a period from 1941 to
1947, when he resided in the United States; he returned to East Germany
in 1948. His early plays reflect his disillusionment with the social
disintegration in Germany caused by the two world wars. In seeking to
re-establish order, Brecht committed himself to Marxism, a philosophy
evident in his plays, such as *The Caucasian Chalk Circle* (1948). The term
Brecht used to describe such plays is "epic"—suggesting a focus not on
one character, but on general human types. Thus, the audience can view
the play with detachment, grasping the "social truth" that the play
advocates.

The Caucasian Chalk Circle

CHARACTERS

OLD MAN *on the right*
PEASANT WOMAN *on the right*
YOUNG PEASANT
A VERY YOUNG WORKER
OLD MAN *on the left*
PEASANT WOMAN *on the left*
AGRICULTURIST KATO
GIRL TRACTORIST
WOUNDED SOLDIER
THE DELEGATE *from the capital*
THE SINGER
GEORGI ABASHWILI, *the Governor*
NATELLA, *the Governor's wife*
MICHAEL, *their son*
SHALVA, *an adjutant*
ARSEN KAZBEKI, *a fat prince*
MESSENGER *from the capital*
NIKO MIKADZE and MIKA LOLADZE,
    doctors
SIMON SHASHAVA, *a soldier*
GRUSHA VASHNADZE, *a kitchen maid*
OLD PEASANT *with the milk*
CORPORAL *and* PRIVATE
PEASANT *and his wife*
LAVRENTI VASHNADZE, *Grusha's
    brother*

ANIKO, *his wife*
PEASANT WOMAN, *for a while
    Grusha's mother-in-law*
JUSSUP, *her son*
MONK
AZDAK, *village recorder*
SHAUWA, *a policeman*
GRAND DUKE
DOCTOR
INVALID
LIMPING MAN
BLACKMAILER
LUDOVICA
INNKEEPER, *her father-in-law*
STABLEBOY
POOR OLD PEASANT WOMAN
IRAKLI, *her brother-in-law, a
    bandit*
THREE WEALTHY FARMERS
ILLO SHUBOLADZE *and* SANDRO
    OBOLADZE, *lawyers*
OLD MARRIED COUPLE
SOLDIERS, SERVANTS, PEASANTS,
BEGGARS, MUSICIANS, MERCHANTS,
NOBLES, ARCHITECTS

The time and the place: After a prologue, set in 1945, we move back perhaps 1000 years.

The action of The Caucasian Chalk Circle *centers on Nuka (or Nukha), a town in Azerbaijan. However, the capital referred to in the prologue is not Baku (capital of Soviet Azerbaijan) but Tiflis (or Tbilisi), capital of Georgia. When Azdak, later, refers to "the capital" he means Nuka itself, though whether Nuka was ever capital of Georgia I do not know: in what reading I have done on the subject I have only found Nuka to be the capital of a Nuka Khanate.*

The word "Georgia" has not been used in this English version because of its American associations; instead, the alternative name "Grusinia" (in Russian, Gruziya) has been used.

The reasons for resettling the old Chinese story in Transcaucasia are not far to seek. The play was written when the Soviet chief of state, Joseph Stalin, was a Georgian, as was his favorite poet, cited in the Prologue, Mayakovsky. And surely there is a point in having this story acted out at the place where Europe and Asia meet, a place incomparably rich in legend and history. Here Jason found the Golden Fleece. Here Noah's Ark touched ground. Here the armies of both Genghis Khan and Tamerlane wrought havoc.

—Eric Bentley, trans.

PROLOGUE

Summer, 1945.

Among the ruins of a war-ravaged Caucasian village the members of two Kolkhoz villages, mostly WOMEN *and* OLDER MEN*, are sitting in a circle, smoking and drinking wine. With them is a* DELEGATE *of the State Reconstruction Commission from Nuka.*

PEASANT WOMAN (*left, pointing*): In those hills over there we stopped three Nazi tanks, but the apple orchard was already destroyed.

OLD MAN (*right*): Our beautiful dairy farm: a ruin.

GIRL TRACTORIST: I laid the fire, Comrade.

(*Pause.*)

DELEGATE: Nuka, Azerbaijan S.S.R. Delegation received from the goat-breeding Kolkhoz "Rosa Luxemburg." This is a collective farm which moved eastwards on orders from the authorities at the approach of Hitler's armies. They are now planning to return. Their delegates have looked at the village and the land and found a lot of destruction. (DELEGATES *on the right nod.*) But the neighboring fruit farm—Kolkhoz (*to the left*) "Galinsk"—proposes to use the former grazing land of Kolkhoz "Rosa Luxemburg" for orchards and vineyards. This land lies in a valley where grass doesn't grow very well. As a delegate of the Reconstruction Commission in Nuka I request that the two Kolkhoz villages decide between themselves whether Kolkhoz "Rosa Luxemburg" shall return or not.

OLD MAN (*right*): First of all, I want to protest against the time limit on discussion. We of Kolkhoz "Rosa Luxemburg" have spent three days and three nights getting here. And now discussion is limited to half a day.

WOUNDED SOLDIER (*left*): Comrade, we haven't as many villages as we used to have. We haven't as many hands. We haven't as much time.

GIRL TRACTORIST: All pleasures have to be rationed. Tobacco is rationed, and wine. Discussion should be rationed.

OLD MAN (*right, sighing*): Death to the fascists! But I will come to the point and explain why we want our valley back. There are a great many reasons, but I'll begin with one of the simplest. Makinä Abakidze, unpack the goat cheese. (*A* PEASANT WOMAN *from right takes from a basket an enormous cheese wrapped in a cloth. Applause and laughter.*) Help yourselves, Comrades, start in!

OLD MAN (*left, suspiciously*): Is this a way of influencing us?

OLD MAN (*right, amid laughter*): How could it be a way of influencing you, Surab, you valley-thief? Everyone knows you'll take the cheese and the valley, too. (*Laughter.*) All I expect from you is an honest answer. Do you like the cheese?

OLD MAN (*left*): The answer is: yes.

OLD MAN (*right*): Really. (*Bitterly.*) I ought to have known you know nothing about cheese.

OLD MAN (*left*): Why not? When I tell you I like it?

OLD MAN (*right*): Because you can't like it. Because it's not what it was in the old days. And why not? Because our goats don't like the new grass as they did the old. Cheese is not cheese because grass is not grass, that's the thing. Please put that in your report.

OLD MAN (*left*): But your cheese is excellent.

OLD MAN (*right*): It isn't excellent. It's just passable. The new grazing land is no good, whatever the young people may say. One can't live there. It doesn't even smell of morning in the morning. (*Several people laugh.*)

DELEGATE: Don't mind their laughing: they understand you. Comrades, why does one love one's country? Because the bread tastes better there, the air smells better, voices sound stronger, the sky is higher, the ground is easier to walk on. Isn't that so?

OLD MAN (*right*): The valley has belonged to us from all eternity.

SOLDIER (*left*): What does *that* mean—from all eternity? Nothing belongs to anyone from all eternity. When you were young you didn't even belong to yourself. You belonged to the Kazbeki princes.

OLD MAN (*right*): Doesn't it make a difference, though, what kind of trees stand next to the house you are born in? Or what kind of neighbors you have? Doesn't that make a difference? We want to go back just to have you as our neighbors, valley-thieves! Now you can all laugh again.

OLD MAN (*left, laughing*): Then why don't you listen to what your neighbor, Kato Wachtang, our agriculturist, has to say about the valley?

PEASANT WOMAN (*right*): We've not said all we have to say about our valley. By no means. Not all the houses are destroyed. As for the dairy farm, at the least the foundation wall is still standing.

DELEGATE: You can claim State support—here and there—you know that. I have suggestions here in my pocket.

PEASANT WOMAN (*right*): Comrade Specialist, we haven't come here to haggle. I can't take your cap and hand you another, and say "This one's better." The other one might *be* better, but you *like* yours better.

GIRL TRACTORIST: A piece of land is not a cap—not in our country, Comrade.

DELEGATE: Don't get mad. It's true we have to consider a piece of land as a tool to produce something useful, but it's also true that we must recognize love for a particular piece of land. As far as I'm concerned, I'd like to find out more exactly what you (*to those on the left*) want to do with the valley.

OTHERS: Yes, let Kato speak.

KATO (*rising; she's in military uniform*): Comrades, last winter, while we were fighting in these hills here as Partisans, we discussed how, once the Germans were expelled, we could build up our fruit culture to ten times its original size. I've prepared a plan for an irrigation project. By means of a cofferdam on our mountain lake, 300 hectares of unfertile land can be irrigated. Our Kolkhoz could not only cultivate more fruit, but also have vineyards. The project, however, would pay only if the disputed valley of Kolkhoz "Rosa Luxemburg" were also included. Here are the calculations. (*She hands* DELEGATE *a briefcase.*)

OLD MAN (*right*): Write into the report that our Kolkhoz plans to start a new stud farm.

GIRL TRACTORIST: Comrades, the project was conceived during days and nights when we had to take cover in the mountains. We were often without ammunition for our half-dozen rifles. Even finding a pencil was difficult. (*Applause from both sides.*)

OLD MAN (*right*): Our thanks to the Comrades of Kolkhoz "Galinsk" and all those who've defended our country!

(*They shake hands and embrace.*)

PEASANT WOMAN (*left*): In doing this our thought was that our soldiers—both your men and our men—should return to a still more productive homeland.

GIRL TRACTORIST: As the poet Mayakovsky said: "The home of the Soviet people shall also be the home of Reason"!

(*The* DELEGATES *excluding the* OLD MAN *have got up, and with the* DELEGATE *specified proceed to study the Agriculturist's drawings. Exclamations such as:*)

"Why is the altitude of fall 22 meters?"—"This rock will have to be blown up"—"Actually, all they need is cement and dynamite"—"They force the water to come down here, that's clever!"

A VERY YOUNG WORKER (*right, to* OLD MAN, *right*): They're going to irrigate all the fields between the hills, look at that, Aleko!

OLD MAN (*right*): I'm not going to look. I knew the project would be good. I won't have a pistol pointed at me!

DELEGATE: But they only want to point a pencil at you!

(*Laughter.*)

OLD MAN (*right, gets up gloomily, and walks over to look at the drawings*): These valley-thieves know only too well that we in this country are suckers for machines and projects.

PEASANT WOMAN (*right*): Aleko Bereshwili, you have a weakness for new projects. That's well known.

DELEGATE: What about my report? May I write that you will all support the cession of your old valley in the interests of this project when you get back to your Kolkhoz?

PEASANT WOMAN (*right*): I will. What about you, Aleko?

OLD MAN (*right, bent over drawings*): I suggest that you give us copies of the drawings to take along.

PEASANT WOMAN (*right*): Then we can sit down and eat. Once he has the drawings and he's ready to discuss them, the matter is settled. I know him. And it will be the same with the rest of us.

(DELEGATES *laughingly embrace again.*)

OLD MAN (*left*): Long live the Kolkhoz "Rosa Luxemburg" and much luck to your horse-breeding project!

PEASANT WOMAN (*left*): In honor of the visit of the delegates from Kolkhoz "Rosa Luxemburg" and of the Specialist, the plan is that we all hear a presentation of the Singer Arkadi Tscheidse.

(*Applause.* GIRL TRACTORIST *has gone off to bring the* SINGER.)

PEASANT WOMAN (*right*): Comrades, your entertainment had better be good. It's going to cost us a valley.

PEASANT WOMAN (*left*): Arkadi Tscheidse knows about our discussion. He's promised to perform something that has a bearing on the problem.

KATO: We wired Tiflis three times. The whole thing nearly fell through at the last minute because his driver had a cold.

PEASANT WOMAN (*left*): Arkadi Tscheidse knows 21,000 lines of verse.

OLD MAN (*left*): He's hard to get. You and the Planning Commission should persuade him to come north more often, Comrade.

DELEGATE: We are more interested in economics, I'm afraid.

OLD MAN (*left, smiling*): You arrange the redistribution of vines and tractors, why not songs?

> (*Enter the* SINGER *Arkadi Tscheidse, led by* GIRL TRACTORIST. *He is a well-built man of simple manners, accompanied by* FOUR MUSICIANS *with their instruments. The artists are greeted with applause.*)

GIRL TRACTORIST: This is the Comrade Specialist, Arkadi.

(*The* SINGER *greets them all.*)

DELEGATE: Honored to make your acquaintance. I heard about your songs when I was a boy at school. Will it be one of the old legends?

SINGER: A very old one. It's called "The Chalk Circle" and comes from the Chinese. But we'll do it, of course, in a changed version. Comrades, it's an honor for me to entertain you after a difficult debate. We hope you will find that the voice of the old poet also sounds well in the shadow of Soviet tractors. It may be a mistake to mix different wines, but old and new wisdom mix admirably. Now I hope we'll get something to eat before the performance begins—it would certainly help.

VOICES: Surely. Everyone into the Club House!

(*While everyone begins to move,* DELEGATE *turns to* GIRL TRACTOR-IST.)

DELEGATE: I hope it won't take long. I've got to get back tonight.

GIRL TRACTORIST: How long will it last, Arkadi? The Comrade Specialist must get back to Tiflis tonight.

SINGER (*casually*): It's actually two stories. An hour or two.

GIRL TRACTORIST (*confidentially*): Couldn't you make it shorter?

SINGER: No.

VOICE: Arkadi Tscheidse's performance will take place here in the square after the meal.

(*And they all go happily to eat.*)

ONE. THE NOBLE CHILD

As the lights go up, the SINGER *is seen sitting on the floor, a black sheepskin cloak round his shoulders, and a little, well-thumbed notebook in his hand. A small group of listeners—the* CHORUS—*sits with him. The manner of his recitation makes it clear that he has told his story over and over again. He mechanically fingers the pages, seldom looking at them. With appropriate gestures, he gives the signal for each scene to begin.*

SINGER: In olden times, in a bloody time,
There ruled in a Caucasian city—
Men called it City of the Damned—
A Governor.
His name was Georgi Abashwili.
He was rich as Croesus
He had a beautiful wife
He had a healthy baby.
No other governor in Grusinia
Had so many horses in his stable
So many beggars on his doorstep
So many soldiers in his service
So many petitioners in his courtyard.
Georgi Abashwili—how shall I describe him to you?
He enjoyed his life.
On the morning of Easter Sunday
The Governor and his family went to church.

(*At the left a large doorway, at the right an even larger gateway.* BEGGARS *and* PETITIONERS *pour from the gateway, holding up thin* CHILDREN, *crutches, and petitions. They are followed by* IRON-SHIRTS, *and then, expensively dressed, the* GOVERNOR'S FAMILY.)

BEGGARS AND PETITIONERS: —Mercy! Mercy, Your Grace! The taxes are too high.
—I lost my leg in the Persian War, where can I get . . .
—My brother is innocent, Your Grace, a misunderstanding . . .
—The child is starving in my arms!
—Our petition is for our son's discharge from the army, our last remaining son!
—Please, Your Grace, the water inspector takes bribes.

(*One* SERVANT *collects the petitions. Another distributes coins from a purse.* SOLDIERS *push the crowd back, lashing at them with thick leather whips.*)

SOLDIER: Get back! Clear the church door!

(*Behind the* GOVERNOR, *his* WIFE, *and the* ADJUTANT, *the* GOVERNOR'S CHILD *is brought through the gateway in an ornate carriage.*)

CROWD: —The baby!
—I can't see it, don't shove so hard!
—God bless the child, Your Grace!

SINGER (*while the* CROWD *is driven back with whips*): For the first time on that Easter Sunday, the people saw the Governor's heir.
Two doctors never moved from the noble child, apple of the Governor's eye.
Even the mighty Prince Kazbeki bows before him at the church door.

(*The* FAT PRINCE *steps forwards and greets the* FAMILY.)

FAT PRINCE: Happy Easter, Natella Abashwili! What a day! When it was raining last night, I thought to myself, gloomy holidays! But this morning the sky was gay. I love a gay sky, a simple heart, Natella Abashwili. And little Michael is a governor from head to foot! Tititi! (*He tickles the* CHILD.)

GOVERNOR'S WIFE: What do you think, Arsen, at last Georgi has decided to start building the east wing. All those wretched slums are to be torn down to make room for the garden.

FAT PRINCE: Good news after so much bad! What's the latest on the war, Brother Georgi? (*The* GOVERNOR *indicates a lack of interest.*) Strategical retreat, I hear. Well, minor reverses are to be expected. Sometimes things go well, sometimes not. Such is war. Doesn't mean a thing, does it?

GOVERNOR'S WIFE: He's coughing, Georgi, did you hear? (*She speaks sharply to the* DOCTORS, *two dignified men standing close to the little carriage.*) He's coughing!

FIRST DOCTOR (*to the* SECOND): May I remind you, Niko Mikadze, that I was against the lukewarm bath? (*To the* GOVERNOR'S WIFE.) There's been a little error over warming the bath water, Your Grace.

SECOND DOCTOR (*equally polite*): Mika Loladze, I'm afraid I can't agree with you. The temperature of the bath water was exactly what our great, beloved Mishiko Oboladze prescribed. More likely a slight draft during the night, Your Grace.

GOVERNOR'S WIFE: But do pay more attention to him. He looks feverish, Georgi.

FIRST DOCTOR (*bending over the* CHILD): No cause for alarm, Your Grace. The bath water will be warmer. It won't occur again.

SECOND DOCTOR (*with a venomous glance at the* FIRST): I won't forget that, my dear Mika Loladze. No cause for concern, Your Grace.

FAT PRINCE: Well, well, well! I always say: "A pain in my liver? Then the doctor gets fifty strokes on the soles of his feet." We live in a decadent age. In the old days one said: "Off with his head!"

GOVERNOR'S WIFE: Let's go into church. Very likely it's the draft here.

>(*The procession of* FAMILY *and* SERVANTS *turns into the doorway. The* FAT PRINCE *follows, but the* GOVERNOR *is kept back by the* ADJUTANT, *a handsome young man. When the crowd of* PETITIONERS *has been driven off, a young dust-stained* RIDER, *his arm in a sling, remains behind.*)

ADJUTANT (*pointing at the* RIDER, *who steps forward*): Won't you hear the messenger from the capital, Your Excellency? He arrived this morning. With confidential papers.

GOVERNOR: Not before Service, Shalva. But did you hear Brother Kazbeki wish me a happy Easter? Which is all very well, but I don't believe it did rain last night.

ADJUTANT (*nodding*): We must investigate.

GOVERNOR: Yes, at once. Tomorrow.

>(*They pass through the doorway. The* RIDER, *who has waited in vain for an audience, turns sharply round and, muttering a curse, goes off. Only one of the palace guards—*SIMON SHASHAVA—*remains at the door.*)

SINGER: The city is still.
>Pigeons strut in the church square.
>A soldier of the Palace Guard
>Is joking with a kitchen maid
>As she comes up from the river with a bundle.

>(*A girl—*GRUSHA VASHNADZE—*comes through the gateway with a bundle made of large green leaves under her arm.*)

SIMON: What, the young lady is not in church? Shirking?

GRUSHA: I was dressed to go. But they needed another goose for the banquet. And they asked me to get it. I know about geese.

SIMON: A goose? (*He feigns suspicion.*) I'd like to see that goose. (GRUSHA *does not understand.*) One must be on one's guard with women. "I only went for a fish," they tell you, but it turns out to be something else.

GRUSHA (*walking resolutely toward him and showing him the goose*): There! If it isn't a fifteen-pound goose stuffed full of corn, I'll eat the feathers.

SIMON: A queen of a goose! The Governor himself will eat it. So the young lady has been down to the river again?

GRUSH: Yes, at the poultry farm.

SIMON: Really? At the poultry farm, down by the river . . . not higher up maybe? Near those willows?

GRUSHA: I only go to the willows to wash the linen.

SIMON (*insinuatingly*): Exactly.

GRUSHA: Exactly what?

SIMON (*winking*): Exactly that.

GRUSHA: Why shouldn't I wash the linen by the willows?

SIMON (*with exaggerated laughter*): "Why shouldn't I wash the linen by the willows!" That's good, really good!

GRUSHA: I don't understand the soldier. What's so good about it?

SIMON (*slyly*): "If something I know someone learns, she'll grow hot and cold by turns!"

GRUSHA: I don't know what I could learn about those willows.

SIMON: Not even if there was a bush opposite? That one could see everything from? Everything that goes on there when a certain person is—"washing linen"?

GRUSHA: What does go on? Won't the soldier say what he means and have done?

SIMON: Something goes on. Something can be seen.

GRUSHA: Could the soldier mean I dip my toes in the water when it's hot? There's nothing else.

SIMON: There's more. Your toes. And more.

GRUSHA: More what? At most my foot.

SIMON: Your foot. And a little more. (*He laughs heartily.*)

GRUSHA (*angrily*): Simon Shashava, you ought to be ashamed of yourself! To sit in a bush on a hot day and wait till a girl comes and dips her legs in the river! And I bet you bring a friend along too! (*She runs off.*)

SIMON (*shouting after her*): I didn't bring any friend along!

(*As the* SINGER *resumes his tale, the* SOLDIER *steps into the doorway as though to listen to the service.*)

SINGER: The city lies still
But why are there armed men?
The Governor's palace is at peace
But why is it a fortress?
And the Governor returned to his palace
And the fortress was a trap
And the goose was plucked and roasted
But the goose was not eaten this time
And noon was no longer the hour to eat:
Noon was the hour to die.

(*From the doorway at the left, the* FAT PRINCE *quickly appears, stands still, looks around. Before the gateway at the right two* IRONSHIRTS *are squatting and playing dice. The* FAT PRINCE *sees them, walks slowly past, making a sign to them. They rise: one goes through the gates and the other goes off at the right. Muffled voices are heard from various directions in the rear: "To your posts!" The palace is surrounded. The* FAT PRINCE *quickly goes off. Church bells in the distance. Enter, through the doorway, the* GOVERNOR'S FAMILY *and procession, returning from church.*)

GOVERNOR'S WIFE (*passing the* ADJUTANT): It's impossible to live in such a slum. But Georgi, of course, will only build for his little Michael. Never for me! Michael is all! All for Michael!

(*The procession turns into the gateway. Again the* ADJUTANT *lingers behind. He waits. Enter the wounded* RIDER *from the doorway. Two* IRONSHIRTS *of the Palace Guard have taken up positions by the gateway.*)

ADJUTANT (*to the* RIDER): The Governor does not wish to receive military news before dinner—especially if it's depressing, as I assume. In the afternoon His Excellency will confer with prominent architects. They're coming to dinner too. And here they are! (*Enter three* GENTLEMEN *through the doorway.*) Go to the kitchen and eat, my friend. (*As the* RIDER *goes, the* ADJUTANT *greets the* ARCHITECTS.) Gentlemen, His Excellency expects you at dinner. He will devote all his time to you and your great new plans. Come!

ONE OF THE ARCHITECTS: We marvel that His Excellency intends to build. There are disquieting rumors that the war in Persia has taken a turn for the worse.

ADJUTANT: All the more reason to build! There's nothing to those rumors anyway. Persia is a long way off, and the garrison here would let itself be hacked to bits for its Governor. (*Noise from the palace. The shrill scream of a woman. Someone is shouting orders. Dumbfounded, the* ADJUTANT *moves toward the gateway. An* IRONSHIRT *steps out, points his lance at him.*) What's this? Put down that lance, you dog.

ONE OF THE ARCHITECTS: It's the Princes! Don't you know the Princes met last night in the capital? And they're against the Grand Duke and his Governors? Gentlemen, we'd better make ourselves scarce. (*They rush off. The* ADJUTANT *remains helplessly behind.*)

ADJUTANT (*furiously to the Palace Guard*): Down with those lances! Don't you see the Governor's life is threatened?

(*The* IRONSHIRTS *of the Palace Guard refuse to obey. They stare coldly and indifferently at the* ADJUTANT *and follow the next events without interest.*)

SINGER: O blindness of the great!
    They go their way like gods,
    Great over bent backs,
    Sure of hired fists,

Trusting in the power
Which has lasted so long.
But long is not forever.
O change from age to age!
Thou hope of the people!

(*Enter the* GOVERNOR, *through the gateway, between two* SOLDIERS *armed to the teeth. He is in chains. His face is gray.*)

Up, great sir, deign to walk upright!
From your palace the eyes of many foes follow you!
And now you don't need an architect, a carpenter will do.
You won't be moving into a new palace
But into a little hole in the ground.
Look about you once more, blind man!

(*The arrested man looks round.*)

Does all you had please you?
Between the Easter Mass and the Easter meal
You are walking to a place whence no one returns.

(*The* GOVERNOR *is led off. A horn sounds an alarm. Noise behind the gateway.*)

When the house of a great one collapses
Many little ones are slain.
Those who had no share in the *good* fortunes of the mighty
Often have a share in their *mis*fortunes.
The plunging wagon
Drags the sweating oxen down with it
Into the abyss.

(*The* SERVANTS *come rushing through the gateway in panic.*)

SERVANTS (*among themselves*): —The baskets!
—Take them all into the third courtyard! Food for five days!
—The mistress has fainted! Someone must carry her down.
—She must get away.
—What about us? We'll be slaughtered like chickens, as always.
—Goodness, what'll happen? There's bloodshed already in the city, they say.
—Nonsense, the Governor has just been asked to appear at a Princes' meeting. All very correct. Everything'll be ironed out. I heard this on the best authority . . .

(*The two* DOCTORS *rush into the courtyard.*)

FIRST DOCTOR (*trying to restrain the other*): Niko Mikadze, it is your duty as a doctor to attend Natella Abashwili.

SECOND DOCTOR: My duty! It's yours!

FIRST DOCTOR: Whose turn is it to look after the child today, Niko Mikadze, yours or mine?

SECOND DOCTOR: Do you really think, Mika Loladze, I'm going to stay a minute longer in this accursed house on that little brat's account? (*They start fighting. All one hears is:* "You neglect your duty!" *and* "Duty, my foot!" *Then the* SECOND DOCTOR *knocks the* FIRST *down.*) Go to hell! (*Exit.*)

(*Enter the soldier,* SIMON SHASHAVA. *He searches in the crowd for* GRUSHA.)

SIMON: Grusha! There you are at last! What are you going to do?

GRUSHA: Nothing. If worst comes to worst, I've a brother in the mountains. How about you?

SIMON: Forget about me. (*Formally again.*) Grusha Vashnadze, your wish to know my plans fills me with satisfaction. I've been ordered to accompany Madam Abashwili as her guard.

GRUSHA: But hasn't the Palace Guard mutinied?

SIMON (*seriously*): That's a fact.

GRUSHA: Isn't it dangerous to go with her?

SIMON: In Tiflis, they say: Isn't the stabbing dangerous for the knife?

GRUSHA: You're not a knife, you're a man, Simon Shashava, what has that woman to do with you?

SIMON: That woman has nothing to do with me. I have my orders, and I go.

GRUSHA: The soldier is pigheaded: he is running into danger for nothing— nothing at all. I must get into the third courtyard, I'm in a hurry.

SIMON: Since we're both in a hurry we shouldn't quarrel. You need time for a good quarrel. May I ask if the young lady still has parents?

GRUSHA: No, just a brother.

SIMON: As time is short—my second question is this: Is the young lady as healthy as a fish in water?

GRUSHA: I may have a pain in the right shoulder once in a while. Otherwise I'm strong enough for my job. No one has complained. So far.

SIMON: That's well known. When it's Easter Sunday, and the question arises who'll run for the goose all the same, she'll be the one. My third question is this: Is the young lady impatient? Does she want apples in winter?

GRUSHA: Impatient? No. But if a man goes to war without any reason and then no message comes—that's bad.

SIMON: A message will come. And now my final question . . .

GRUSHA: Simon Shashava, I must get to the third courtyard at once. My answer is yes.

SIMON (*very embarrassed*): Haste, they say, is the wind that blows down the scaffolding. But they also say: The rich don't know what haste is. I'm from . . .

GRUSHA: Kutsk . . .

SIMON: The young lady has been inquiring about me? I'm healthy, I have no dependents, I make ten piasters a month, as paymaster twenty piasters, and I'm asking—very sincerely—for your hand.

GRUSHA: Simon Shashava, it suits me well.

SIMON (*taking from his neck a thin chain with a little cross on it*): My mother gave me this cross, Grusha Vashnadze. The chain is silver. Please wear it.

GRUSHA: Many thanks, Simon.

SIMON (*hangs it round her neck*): It would be better to go to the third courtyard now. Or there'll be difficulties. Anyway, I must harness the horses. The young lady will understand?

GRUSHA: Yes, Simon.

> (*They stand undecided.*)

SIMON: I'll just take the mistress to the troops that have stayed loyal. When the war's over, I'll be back. In two weeks. Or three. I hope my intended won't get tired, awaiting my return.

GRUSHA: Simon Shashava, I shall wait for you.
Go calmly into battle, soldier
The bloody battle, the bitter battle
From which not everyone returns:
When you return I shall be there.
I shall be waiting for you under the green elm
I shall be waiting for you under the bare elm
I shall wait until the last soldier has returned
And longer
When you come back from the battle
No boots will stand at my door
The pillow beside mine will be empty
And my mouth will be unkissed.
When you return, when you return
You will be able to say: It is just as it was.

SIMON: I thank you, Grusha Vashnadze. And good-bye!

> (*He bows low before her. She does the same before him. Then she runs quickly off without looking round. Enter the* ADJUTANT *from the gateway.*)

ADJUTANT (*harshly*): Harness the horses to the carriage! Don't stand there doing nothing, scum!

> (SIMON SHASHAVA *stands to attention and goes off. Two* SERVANTS *crowd from the gateway, bent low under huge trunks. Behind them, supported by her women, stumbles* NATELLA ABASHWILI. *She is followed by a* WOMAN *carrying the* CHILD.)

GOVERNOR'S WIFE: I hardly know if my head's still on. Where's Michael? Don't hold him so clumsily. Pile the trunks onto the carriage. No news from the city, Shalva?

ADJUTANT: None. All's quiet so far, but there's not a minute to lose. No room for all those trunks in the carriage. Pick out what you need. (*Exit quickly.*)

GOVERNOR'S WIFE: Only essentials! Quick, open the trunks! I'll tell you what I need. (*The trunks are lowered and opened. She points at some brocade dresses.*) The green one! And, of course, the one with the fur trimming. Where are Niko Mikadze and Mika Loladze? I've suddenly got the most terrible migraine again. It always starts in the temples. (*Enter* GRUSHA.) Taking your time, eh? Go and get the hot water bottles this minute! (GRUSHA *runs off, returns later with hot water bottles; the* GOVERNOR'S WIFE *orders her about by signs.*) Don't tear the sleeves.

A YOUNG WOMAN: Pardon, madam, no harm has come to the dress.

GOVERNOR'S WIFE: Because I stopped you. I've been watching you for a long time. Nothing in your head but making eyes at Shalva Tzereteli. I'll kill you, you bitch! (*She beats the* YOUNG WOMAN.)

ADJUTANT (*appearing in the gateway*): Please make haste, Natella Abashwili. Firing has broken out in the city. (*Exit.*)

GOVERNOR'S WIFE (*letting go of the* YOUNG WOMAN): Oh dear, do you think they'll lay hands on us? Why should they? Why? (*She herself begins to rummage in the trunks.*) How's Michael? Asleep?

WOMAN WITH THE CHILD: Yes, madam.

GOVERNOR'S WIFE: Then put him down a moment and get my little saffron-colored boots from the bedroom. I need them for the green dress. (*The* WOMAN *puts down the* CHILD *and goes off.*) Just look how these things have been packed! No love! No understanding! If you don't give them every order yourself . . . At such moments you realize what kind of servants you have! They gorge themselves at your expense, and never a word of gratitude! I'll remember this.

ADJUTANT (*entering, very excited*): Natella, you must leave at once!

GOVERNOR'S WIFE: Why? I've got to take this silver dress—it cost a thousand piasters. And that one there, and where's the wine-colored one?

ADJUTANT (*trying to pull her away*): Riots have broken out! We must leave at once. Where's the baby?

GOVERNOR'S WIFE (*calling to the* YOUNG WOMAN *who was holding the baby*): Maro, get the baby ready! Where on earth are you?

ADJUTANT (*leaving*): We'll probably have to leave the carriage behind and go ahead on horseback.

(*The* GOVERNOR'S WIFE *rummages again among her dresses, throws some onto the heap of chosen clothes, then takes them off again. Noises, drums are heard. The* YOUNG WOMAN *who was beaten creeps away. The sky begins to grow red.*)

GOVERNOR'S WIFE (*rummaging desperately*): I simply cannot find the wine-colored dress. Take the whole pile to the carriage. Where's Asja? And why hasn't Maro come back? Have you all gone crazy?

ADJUTANT (*returning*): Quick! Quick!

GOVERNOR'S WIFE (*to the* FIRST WOMAN): Run! Just throw them into the carriage!

ADJUTANT: We're not taking the carriage. And if you don't come now, I'll ride off on my own.

GOVERNOR'S WIFE (*as the* FIRST WOMAN *can't carry everything*): Where's that bitch Asja? (*The* ADJUTANT *pulls her away.*) Maro, bring the baby! (*To the* FIRST WOMAN.) Go and look for Masha. No, first take the dresses to the carriage. Such nonsense! I wouldn't dream of going on horseback!

(*Turning round, she sees the red sky, and starts back rigid. The fire burns. She is pulled out by the* ADJUTANT. *Shaking, the* FIRST WOMAN *follows with the dresses.*)

MARO (*from the doorway with the boots*): Madam! (*She sees the trunks and dresses and runs toward the* CHILD, *picks it up, and holds it a moment.*) They left it behind, the beasts. (*She hands it to* GRUSHA.) Hold it a moment. (*She runs off, following the* GOVERNOR'S WIFE.)

(*Enter* SERVANTS *from the gateway.*)

COOK: Well, so they've actually gone. Without the food wagons, and not a minute too early. It's time for us to clear out.

GROOM: This'll be an unhealthy neighborhood for quite a while. (*To one of the* WOMEN.) Suliko, take a few blankets and wait for me in the foal stables.

GRUSHA: What have they done with the Governor?

GROOM (*gesturing throat cutting*): Ffffft.

A FAT WOMAN (*seeing the gesture and becoming hysterical*): Oh dear, oh dear, oh dear, oh dear! Our master Georgi Abashwili! A picture of health he was, at the morning Mass—and now! Oh, take me away, we're all lost, we must die in sin like our master, Georgi Abashwili!

OTHER WOMAN (*soothing her*): Calm down, Nina! You'll be taken to safety. You've never hurt a fly.

FAT WOMAN (*being led out*): Oh dear, oh dear, oh dear! Quick! Let's all get out before they come, before they come!

A YOUNG WOMAN: Nine takes it more to heart than the mistress, that's a fact. They even have to have their weeping done for them.

COOK: We'd better get out, all of us.

ANOTHER WOMAN (*glancing back*): That must be the East Gate burning.

YOUNG WOMAN (*seeing the* CHILD *in* GRUSHA's *arms*): The baby! What are you doing with it?

GRUSHA: It got left behind.

YOUNG WOMAN: She simply left it there. Michael, who was kept out of all the drafts!

(*The* SERVANTS *gather round the* CHILD.)

GRUSHA: He's waking up.

GROOM: Better put him down, I tell you. I'd rather not think what'd happen to anybody who was found with that baby.

COOK: That's right. Once they get started, they'll kill each other off, whole families at a time. Let's go.

(*Exeunt all but* GRUSHA, *with the* CHILD *on her arm, and* TWO WOMEN.)

TWO WOMEN: Didn't you hear? Better put him down.

GRUSHA: The nurse asked me to hold him a moment.

OLDER WOMAN: She's not coming back, you simpleton.

YOUNGER WOMAN: Keep your hands off it.

OLDER WOMAN (*amiably*): Grusha, you're a good soul, but you're not very bright, and you know it. I tell you, if he had the plague he couldn't be more dangerous.

GRUSHA (*stubbornly*): He hasn't got the plague. He looks at me! He's human!

OLDER WOMAN: Don't look at *him*. You're a fool—the kind that always gets put upon. A person need only say, "Run for the salad, you have the longest legs," and you run. My husband has an ox cart—you can come with us if you hurry! Lord, by now the whole neighborhood must be in flames.

> (*Both* WOMEN *leave, sighing. After some hesitation,* GRUSHA *puts the sleeping* CHILD *down, looks at it for a moment, then takes a brocade blanket from the heap of clothes and covers it. Then both* WOMEN *return, dragging bundles.* GRUSHA *starts guiltily away from the* CHILD *and walks a few steps to one side.*)

YOUNGER WOMAN: Haven't you packed anything yet? There isn't much time, you know. The Ironshirts will be here from the barracks.

GRUSHA: Coming!

> (*She runs through the doorway. Both* WOMEN *go to the gateway and wait. The sound of horses is heard. They flee, screaming. Enter the* FAT PRINCE *with drunken* IRONSHIRTS. *One of them carries the* GOVERNOR's *head on a lance.*)

FAT PRINCE: Here! In the middle! (*One* SOLDIER *climbs onto the other's back, takes the head, holds it tentatively over the door.*) That's not the middle. Farther to the right. That's it. What I do, my friends, I do well. (*While with the hammer and nail, the* SOLDIER *fastens the head to the wall by its hair:*) This morning at the church door I said to Georgi Abashwili: "I love a gay sky." Actually, I prefer the lightning that comes out of a gay sky. Yes, indeed. It's a pity they took the brat along, though, I need him, urgently.

> (*Exit with* IRONSHIRTS *through the gateway. Trampling of horses again. Enter* GRUSHA *through the doorway looking cautiously about her. Clearly she has waited for the* IRONSHIRTS *to go. Carrying a bundle, she walks toward the gateway. At the last moment, she turns to see if the* CHILD *is still there. Catching sight of the head over the doorway, she screams. Horrified, she picks up her bundle again, and is about to leave when the* SINGER *starts to speak. She stands rooted to the spot.*)

SINGER: As she was standing between courtyard and gate,
She heard or she thought she heard a low voice calling.
The child called to her,
Not whining, but calling quite sensibly,
Or so it seemed to her.
"Woman," it said, "help me."
And it went on, not whining, but saying quite sensibly:
"Know, woman, he who hears not a cry for help

But passes by with troubled ears will never hear
The gentle call of a lover nor the blackbird at dawn
Nor the happy sigh of the tired grape-picker as the Angelus rings."

    (*She walks a few steps toward the* CHILD *and bends over it.*)

Hearing this she went back for one more look at the child:
Only to sit with him for a moment or two,
Only till someone should come,
His mother, or anyone.

    (*Leaning on a trunk, she sits facing the* CHILD.)

Only till she would have to leave, for the danger was too great,
The city was full of flame and crying.

    (*The light grows dimmer, as though evening and night were coming on.*)

Fearful is the seductive power of goodness!

    (GRUSHA *now settles down to watch over the* CHILD *through the night. Once, she lights a small lamp to look at it. Once, she tucks it in with a coat. From time to time she listens and looks to see whether someone is coming.*)

And she sat with the child a long time,
Till evening came, till night came, till dawn came.
She sat too long, too long she saw
The soft breathing, the small clenched fists,
Till toward morning the seduction was complete
And she rose, and bent down and, sighing, took the child
And carried it away.

    (*She does what the* SINGER *says as he describes it.*)

As if it was stolen goods she picked it up.
As if she was a thief she crept away.

TWO. THE FLIGHT INTO THE NORTHERN MOUNTAINS

SINGER: When Grusha Vashnadze left the city
    On the Grusinian highway
    On the way to the Northern Mountains
    She sang a song, she bought some milk.

CHORUS: How will this human child escape
    The bloodhounds, the trap-setters?
    Into the deserted mountains she journeyed
    Along the Grusinian highway she journeyed
    She sang a song, she bought some milk.

    (GRUSHA VASHNADZE *walks on. On her back she carries the* CHILD *in a sack, in one hand is a large stick, in the other a bundle. She sings.*)

The Song of the Four Generals

Four generals
Set out for Iran.
With the first one, war did not agree.
The second never won a victory.
For the third the weather never was right.
For the fourth the men would never fight.
Four generals
And not a single man!

Sosso Robakidse
Went march to Iran
With him the war did so agree
He soon had won a victory.
For him the weather was always right.
For him the men would always fight.
Sosso Robakidse,
He is our man!

(*A peasant's cottage appears.*)

GRUSHA (*to the* CHILD): Noontime is meal time. Now we'll sit hopefully in the grass, while the good Grusha goes and buys a little pitcher of milk. (*She lays the* CHILD *down and knocks at the cottage door. An* OLD MAN *opens it.*) Grandfather, could I have a little pitcher of milk? And a corn cake, maybe?

OLD MAN: Milk? We have no milk. The soldiers from the city have our goats. Go to the soldiers if you want milk.

GRUSHA: But grandfather, you must have a little pitcher of milk for a baby?

OLD MAN: And for a God-bless-you, eh?

GRUSHA: Who said anything about a God-bless-you? (*She shows her purse.*) We'll pay like princes. "Head in the clouds, backside in the water." (*The* PEASANT *goes off, grumbling, for milk.*) How much for the milk?

OLD MAN: Three piasters. Milk has gone up.

GRUSHA: Three piasters for this little drop? (*Without a word the* OLD MAN *shuts the door in her face.*) Michael, did you hear that? Three piasters! We can't afford it! (*She goes back, sits down again, and gives the* CHILD *her breast.*) Suck. Think of the three piasters. There's nothing there, but you *think* you're drinking, and that's something. (*Shaking her head, she sees that the* CHILD *isn't sucking any more. She gets up, walks back to the door, and knocks again.*) Open, grandfather, we'll pay. (*Softly.*) May lightning strike you! (*When the* OLD MAN *appears.*) I thought it would be half a piaster. But the baby must be fed. How about one piaster for that little drop?

OLD MAN: Two.

GRUSHA: Don't shut the door again. (*She fishes a long time in her bag.*) Here are two piasters. The milk better be good. I still have two days' journey ahead of me. It's a murderous business you have here—and sinful, too!

OLD MAN: Kill the soldiers if you want milk.

GRUSHA (*giving the* CHILD *some milk*): This is an expensive joke. Take a sip, Michael, it's a week's pay. Around here they think we earned our money just sitting on our behinds. Oh, Michael, Michael, you're a nice little load for a girl to take on! (*Uneasy, she gets up, puts the* CHILD *on her back, and walks on. The* OLD MAN, *grumbling, picks up the pitcher and looks after her unmoved.*)

SINGER: As Grusha Vashnadze went northward
The Princes' Ironshirts went after her.

CHORUS: How will the barefoot girl escape the Ironshirts,
The bloodhounds, the trap-setters?
They hunt even by night.
Pursuers never tire.
Butchers sleep little.

(*Two* IRONSHIRTS *are trudging along the highway.*)

CORPORAL: You'll never amount to anything, blockhead, your heart's not in it. Your senior officer sees this in little things. Yesterday, when I made the fat gal, yes, you grabbed her husband as I commanded, and you did kick him in the belly, at my request, but did you *enjoy* it, like a loyal Private, or were you just doing your duty? I've kept an eye on you, blockhead, you're a hollow reed and a tinkling cymbal, you won't get promoted. (*They walk a while in silence.*) Don't think I've forgotten how insubordinate you are, either. Stop limping! I forbid you to limp! You limp because I sold the horses, and I sold the horses because I'd never have got that price again. You limp to show me you don't like marching. I know you. It won't help. You wait. Sing!

TWO IRONSHIRTS (*singing*): Sadly to war I went my way
Leaving my loved one at her door.
My friends will keep her honor safe
Till from the war I'm back once more.

CORPORAL: Louder!

TWO IRONSHIRTS (*singing*): When 'neath a headstone I shall be
My love a little earth will bring:
"Here rest the feet that oft would run to me
And here the arms that oft to me would cling."

(*They begin to walk again in silence.*)

CORPORAL: A good soldier has his heart and soul in it. When he receives an order, he gets a hard-on, and when he drives his lance into the enemy's guts, he comes. (*He shouts for joy.*) He lets himself be torn to bits for his superior officer, and as he lies dying he takes note that his corporal is nodding approval, and that is reward enough, it's his dearest wish. *You* won't get any nod of approval, but you'll croak all right. Christ, how'm I to get my hands on the Governor's bastard with the help of a fool like you! (*They stay on stage behind.*)

SINGER: When Grusha Vashnadze came to the River Sirra
   Flight grew too much for her, the helpless child too heavy.
   In the cornfields the rosy dawn
   Is cold to the sleepless one, only cold.
   The gay clatter of the milk cans in the farmyard where the
         smoke rises
   Is only a threat to the fugitive.
   She who carries the child feels its weight and little more.

> (GRUSHA *stops in front of a farm. A fat* PEASANT WOMAN *is carrying a milk can through the door.* GRUSHA *waits until she has gone in, then approaches the house cautiously.*)

GRUSHA (*to the* CHILD): Now you've wet yourself again, and you know I've no linen. Michael, this is where we part company. It's far enough from the city. They wouldn't want you *so* much that they'd follow you all *this* way, little good-for-nothing. The peasant woman is kind, and can't you just smell the milk? (*She bends down to lay the* CHILD *on the threshold.*) So farewell, Michael, I'll forget how you kicked me in the back all night to make me walk faster. And you can forget the meager fare—it was meant well. I'd like to have kept you—your nose is so tiny—but it can't be. I'd have shown you your first rabbit, I'd have trained you to keep dry, but now I must turn around. My sweetheart the soldier might be back soon, and suppose he didn't find me? You can't ask that, can you? (*She creeps up to the door and lays the* CHILD *on the threshold. Then, hiding behind a tree, she waits until the* PEASANT WOMAN *opens the door and sees the bundle.*)

PEASANT WOMAN: Good heavens, what's this? Husband!

PEASANT: What is it? Let me finish my soup.

PEASANT WOMAN (*to the* CHILD): Where's your mother, then? Haven't you got one? It's a boy. Fine linen. He's from a good family, you can see that. And they just leave him on our doorstep. Oh, these are times!

PEASANT: If they think we're going to feed it, they're wrong. You can take it to the priest in the village. That's the best we can do.

PEASANT WOMAN: What'll the priest do with him? He needs a mother. There, he's waking up. Don't you think we could keep him, though?

PEASANT (*shouting*): No!

PEASANT WOMAN: I could lay him in the corner by the armchair. All I need is a crib. I can take him into the fields with me. See him laughing? Husband, we have a roof over our heads. We can do it. Not another word out of you!

> (*She carries the* CHILD *into the house. The* PEASANT *follows protesting.* GRUSHA *steps out from behind the tree, laughs, and hurries off in the opposite direction.*)

SINGER: Why so cheerful, making for home?

CHORUS: Because the child has won new parents with a laugh,
   Because I'm rid of the little one, I'm cheerful.

SINGER: And why so sad?

CHORUS: Because I'm single and free, I'm sad
Like someone who's been robbed
Someone who's newly poor.

(*She walks for a short time, then meets the two* IRONSHIRTS *who point their lances at her.*)

CORPORAL: Lady, you are running straight into the arms of the Armed Forces. Where are you coming from? And when? Are you having illicit relations with the enemy? Where is he hiding? What movements is he making in your rear? How about the hills? How about the valleys? How are your stockings held in position? (GRUSHA *stands there frightened.*) Don't be scared, we always withdraw, if necessary . . . what, blockhead? I always withdraw. In that respect at least, I can be relied on. Why are you staring like that at my lance? In the field no soldier drops his lance, that's a rule. Learn it by heart, blockhead. Now, lady, where are you headed?

GRUSHA: To meet my intended, one Simon Shashava, of the Palace Guard in Nuka.

CORPORAL: Simon Shashava? Sure, I know him. He gave me the key so I could look you up once in a while. Blockhead, we are getting to be unpopular. We must make her realize we have honorable intentions. Lady, behind apparent frivolity I conceal a serious nature, so let me tell you officially: I want a child from you. (GRUSHA *utters a little scream.*) Blockhead, she understands me. Uh-huh, isn't it a sweet shock? "Then first I must take the noodles out of the oven, Officer. Then first I must change my torn shirt, Colonel." But away with jokes, away with my lance! We are looking for a baby. A baby from a good family. Have you heard of such a baby, from the city, dressed in fine linen, and suddenly turning up here?

GRUSHA: No, I haven't heard a thing. (*Suddenly she turns around and runs back, panic-stricken. The* IRONSHIRTS *glance at each other, then follow her, cursing.*)

SINGER: Run, kind girl! The killers are coming!
Help the helpless babe, helpless girl!
And so she runs!

CHORUS: In the bloodiest times
There are kind people.

(*As* GRUSHA *rushes into the cottage, the* PEASANT WOMAN *is bending over the* CHILD's *crib.*)

GRUSHA: Hide him. Quick! The Ironshirts are coming! I laid him on your doorstep. But he isn't mine. He's from a good family.

PEASANT WOMAN: Who's coming? What Ironshirts?

GRUSHA: Don't ask questions. The Ironshirts that are looking for it.

PEASANT WOMAN: They've no business in my house. But I must have a little talk with you, it seems.

GRUSHA: Take off the fine linen. It'll give us away.

PEASANT WOMAN: Linen, my foot! In this house I make the decisions! "*You* can't vomit in *my* room!" Why did you abandon it? It's a sin.

GRUSHA (*looking out of the window*): Look, they're coming out from behind those trees! I shouldn't have run away, it made them angry. Oh, what shall I do?

PEASANT WOMAN (*looking out of the window and suddenly starting with fear*): Gracious! Ironshirts!

GRUSHA: They're after the baby.

PEASANT WOMAN: Suppose they come in!

GRUSHA: You mustn't give him to them. Say he's yours.

PEASANT WOMAN: Yes.

GRUSHA: They'll run him through if you hand him over.

PEASANT WOMAN: But suppose they ask for it? The silver for the harvest is in the house.

GRUSHA: If you let them have him, they'll run him through, right here in this room! You've got to say he's yours!

PEASANT WOMAN: Yes. But what if they don't believe me?

GRUSHA: You must be firm.

PEASANT WOMAN: They'll burn the roof over our heads.

GRUSHA: That's why you must say he's yours. His name's Michael. But I shouldn't have told you. (*The* PEASANT WOMAN *nods.*) Don't nod like that. And don't tremble—they'll notice.

PEASANT WOMAN: Yes.

GRUSHA: And stop saying yes, I can't stand it. (*She shakes the* WOMAN.) Don't you have any children?

PEASANT WOMAN (*muttering*): He's in the war.

GRUSHA: Then maybe *he's* an Ironshirt? Do you want *him* to run children through with a lance? You'd bawl him out. "No fooling with lances in my house!" you'd shout, "is that what I've reared you for? Wash your neck before you speak to your mother!"

PEASANT WOMAN: That's true, he couldn't get away with anything around here!

GRUSHA: So you'll say he's yours?

PEASANT WOMAN: Yes.

GRUSHA: Look! They're coming!

(*There is a knocking at the door. The* WOMEN *don't answer. Enter* IRONSHIRTS. *The* PEASANT WOMAN *bows low.*)

CORPORAL: Well, here she is. What did I tell you? What a nose I have! I *smelt* her. Lady, I have a question for you. Why did you run away? What did you think I would do to you? I'll bet it was something unchaste. Confess!

GRUSHA (*while the* PEASANT WOMAN *bows again and again*): I'd left some milk on the stove, and I suddenly remembered it.

CORPORAL: Or maybe you imagined I looked at you unchastely? Like there could be something between us? A carnal glance, know what I mean?

GRUSHA: I didn't see it.

CORPORAL: But it's possible, huh? You admit that much. After all, I might be a pig. I'll be frank with you: I could think of all sorts of things if we were alone. (*To the* PEASANT WOMAN.) Shouldn't you be busy in the yard? Feeding the hens?

PEASANT WOMAN (*falling suddenly to her knees*): Soldier, I didn't know a thing about it. Please don't burn the roof over our heads.

CORPORAL: What are you talking about?

PEASANT WOMAN: I had nothing to do with it. She left it on my doorstep, I swear it!

CORPORAL (*suddenly seeing the* CHILD *and whistling*): Ah, so there's a little something in the crib! Blockhead, I smell a thousand piasters. Take the old girl outside and hold on to her. It looks like I have a little cross-examining to do. (*The* PEASANT WOMAN *lets herself be led out by the* PRIVATE, *without a word.*) So, you've got the child I wanted from you! (*He walks toward the crib.*)

GRUSHA: Officer, he's mine. He's not the one you're after.

CORPORAL: I'll just take a look. (*He bends over the crib.*)

> (GRUSHA *looks round in despair.*)

GRUSHA: He's mine! He's mine!

CORPORAL: Fine linen!

> (Grusha *dashes at him to pull him away. He throws her off and again bends over the crib. Again looking round in despair, she sees a log of wood, seizes it, and hits the* CORPORAL *over the head from behind. The* CORPORAL *collapses. She quickly picks up the* CHILD *and rushes off.*)

SINGER: And in her flight from the Ironshirts
> After twenty-two days of journeying
> At the foot of the Janga-Tu Glacier
> Grusha Vashnadze decided to adopt the child.

CHORUS: The helpless girl adopted the helpless child.

> (GRUSHA *squats over a half-frozen stream to get the* CHILD *water in the hollow of her hand.*)

GRUSHA: Since no one else will take you, son,
> I must take you.
> Since no one else will take you, son,
> You must take me.
> O black day in a lean, lean year,
> The trip was long, the milk was dear,
> My legs are tired, my feet are sore:
> But I wouldn't be without you any more.
> I'll throw your silken shirt away
> And wrap you in rags and tatters.
> I'll wash you, son, and christen you in glacier water.
> We'll see it through together.

> (*She has taken off the* CHILD's *fine linen and wrapped it in a rag.*)

SINGER: When Grusha Vashnadze
      Pursued by the Ironshirts
      Came to the bridge on the glacier
      Leading to the villages of the Eastern Slope
      She sang the Song of the Rotten Bridge
      And risked two lives.

> (*A wind has risen. The bridge on the glacier is visible in the dark. One rope is broken and half the bridge is hanging down the abyss.* MERCHANTS, *two men and a woman, stand undecided before the bridge as* GRUSHA *and the* CHILD *arrive. One man is trying to catch the hanging rope with a stick.*)

FIRST MAN: Take your time, young woman. You won't get across here anyway.

GRUSHA: But I *have* to get the baby to the east side. To my brother's place.

MERCHANT WOMAN: Have to? How d'you mean, "have to"? I have to get there, too—because I have to buy carpets in Atum—carpets a woman had to sell because her husband had to die. But can *I* do what I have to? Can she? Andrei's been fishing for that rope for hours. And I ask you, how are we going to fasten it, even if he gets it up?

FIRST MAN (*listening*): Hush, I think I hear something.

GRUSHA: The bridge isn't quite rotted through. I think I'll try it.

MERCHANT WOMAN: *I* wouldn't—if the devil himself were after me. It's suicide.

FIRST MAN (*shouting*): Hi!

GRUSHA: Don't shout! (*To the* MERCHANT WOMAN.) Tell him not to shout.

FIRST MAN: But there's someone down there calling. Maybe they've lost their way.

MERCHANT WOMAN: Why shouldn't he shout? Is there something funny about you? Are they after you?

GRUSHA: All right, I'll tell. The Ironshirts are after me. I knocked one down.

SECOND MAN: Hide our merchandise!

> (*The* WOMAN *hides a sack behind a rock.*)

FIRST MAN: Why didn't you say so right away? (*To the others.*) If they catch her they'll make mincemeat out of her!

GRUSHA: Get out of my way. I've got to cross that bridge.

SECOND MAN: You can't. The precipice is two thousand feet deep.

FIRST MAN: Even with the rope it'd be no use. We could hold it up with our hands. But then we'd have to do the same for the Ironshirts.

GRUSHA: Go away.

> (*There are calls from the distance:* "Hi, up there!")

MERCHANT WOMAN: They're getting near. But you can't take the child on that bridge. It's sure to break. And look!

> (GRUSHA *looks down into the abyss. The* IRONSHIRTS *are heard calling again from below.*)

SECOND MAN: Two thousand feet!

GRUSHA: But those men are worse.

FIRST MAN: You can't do it. Think of the baby. Risk your life but not a child's.

SECOND MAN: With the child she's that much heavier!

MERCHANT WOMAN: Maybe she's *really* got to get across. Give *me* the baby. I'll hide it. Cross the bridge alone!

GRUSHA: I won't. We belong together. (*To the* CHILD.) "Live together, die together." (*She sings.*)

The Song of the Rotten Bridge

Deep is the abyss, son,
I see the weak bridge sway
But it's not for us, son,
To choose the way.

The way I know
Is the one you must tread,
And all you will eat
Is my bit of bread.

Of every four pieces
You shall have three.
Would that I knew
How big they will be!

Get out of my way, I'll try it without the rope.

MERCHANT WOMAN: You are tempting God!

(*There are shouts from below.*)

GRUSHA: Please, throw that stick away, or they'll get the rope and follow me. (*Pressing the* CHILD *to her, she steps onto the swaying bridge. The* MERCHANT WOMAN *screams when it looks as though the bridge is about to collapse. But* GRUSHA *walks on and reaches the far side.*)

FIRST MAN: She made it!

MERCHANT WOMAN (*who has fallen on her knees and begun to pray, angrily*): I still think it was a sin.

(*The* IRONSHIRTS *appear; the* CORPORAL's *head is bandaged.*)

CORPORAL: Seen a woman with a child?

FIRST MAN (*while the* SECOND MAN *throws the stick into the abyss*): Yes, there! But the bridge won't carry you!

CORPORAL: You'll pay for this, blockhead!

(GRUSHA, *from the far bank, laughs and shows the* CHILD *to the* IRONSHIRTS. *She walks on. The wind blows.*)

GRUSHA (*turning to the* CHILD): You mustn't be afraid of the wind. He's a poor thing too. He has to push the clouds along and he gets quite cold doing it. (*Snow starts falling.*) And the snow isn't so bad, either, Michael. It covers the little fir trees so they won't die in winter. Let me sing you a little song. (*She sings.*)

The Song of the Child

Your father is a bandit
A harlot the mother who bore you.
Yet honorable men
Shall kneel down before you.
Food to the baby horses
The tiger's son will take.
The mothers will get milk
From the son of the snake.

THREE. IN THE NORTHERN MOUNTAINS

SINGER: Seven days the sister, Grusha Vashnadze,
Journeyed across the glacier
And down the slopes she journeyed.
"When I enter my brother's house," she thought,
"He will rise and embrace me."
"Is that you, sister?" he will say,
"I have long expected you.
This is my dear wife,
And this is my farm, come to me by marriage,
With eleven horses and thirty-one cows. Sit down.
Sit down with your child at our table and eat."
The brother's house was in a lovely valley.
When the sister came to the brother,
She was ill from walking.
The brother rose from the table.

(*A fat peasant couple rise from the table.* LAVRENTI VASHNADZE *still has a napkin round his neck, as* GRUSHA, *pale and supported by a* SERVANT, *enters with the* CHILD.)

LAVRENTI: Where've *you* come from, Grusha?

GRUSHA (*feebly*): Across the Janga-Tu Pass, Lavrenti.

SERVANT: I found her in front of the hay barn. She has a baby with her.

SISTER-IN-LAW: Go and groom the mare.

(*Exit the* SERVANT.)

LAVRENTI: This is my wife Aniko.

SISTER-IN-LAW: I thought you were in service in Nuka.

GRUSHA (*barely able to stand*): Yes, I was.

SISTER-IN-LAW: Wasn't it a good job? We were told it was.

GRUSHA: The Governor got killed.

LAVRENTI: Yes, we heard there were riots. Your aunt told us. Remember, Aniko?

SISTER-IN-LAW: Here with us, it's very quiet. City people always want something going on. (*She walks toward the door, calling.*) Sosso, Sosso, don't take the cake out of the oven yet, d'you hear? Where on earth are you? (*Exit, calling.*)

LAVRENTI (*quietly, quickly*): Is there a father? (*As she shakes her head.*) I thought not. We must think up something. She's religious.

SISTER-IN-LAW (*returning*): Those servants! (*To* GRUSHA.) You have a child.

GRUSHA: It's mine. (*She collapses.* LAVRENTI *rushes to her assistance.*)

SISTER-IN-LAW: Heavens, she's ill—what are we going to do?

LAVRENTI (*escorting her to a bench near the stove*): Sit down, sit. I think it's just weakness, Aniko.

SISTER-IN-LAW: As long as it's not scarlet fever!

LAVRENTI: She'd have spots if it was. It's only weakness. Don't worry, Aniko. (*To* GRUSHA.) Better, sitting down?

SISTER-IN-LAW: Is the child hers?

GRUSHA: Yes, mine.

LAVRENTI: She's on her way to her husband.

SISTER-IN-LAW: I see. Your meat's getting cold. (LAVRENTI *sits down and begins to eat.*) Cold food's not food for you, the fat mustn't get cold, you know your stomach's your weak spot. (*To* GRUSHA.) If your husband's not in the city, where is he?

LAVRENTI: She got married on the other side of the mountain, she says.

SISTER-IN-LAW: On the other side of the mountain. I see. (*She also sits down to eat.*)

GRUSHA: I think I should lie down somewhere, Lavrenti.

SISTER-IN-LAW: If it's consumption we'll all get it. (*She goes on cross-examining her.*) Has your husband got a farm?

GRUSHA: He's a soldier.

LAVRENTI: But he's coming into a farm—a small one—from his father.

SISTER-IN-LAW: Isn't he in the war? Why not?

GRUSHA (*with effort*): Yes, he's in the war.

SISTER-IN-LAW: Then why d'you want to go to the farm?

LAVRENTI: When he comes back from the war, he'll return to his farm.

SISTER-IN-LAW: But you're going there now?

LAVRENTI: Yes, to wait for him.

SISTER-IN-LAW (*calling shrilly*): Sosso, the cake!

GRUSHA (*murmuring feverishly*): A farm—a soldier—waiting—sit down, eat.

SISTER-IN-LAW: It's scarlet fever.

GRUSHA (*starting up*): Yes, he's got a farm!

LAVRENTI: I think it's just weakness, Aniko. Would you look after the cake yourself, dear?

SISTER-IN-LAW: But when will he come back if war's broken out again as people say? (*She waddles off, shouting.*) Sosso! Where on earth are you? Sosso!

LAVRENTI (*getting up quickly and going to* GRUSHA): You'll get a bed in a minute. She has a good heart. But wait till after supper.

GRUSHA (*holding out the* CHILD *to him*): Take him.

LAVRENTI (*taking it and looking around*): But you can't stay here long with the child. She's religious, you see.

(GRUSHA *collapses.* LAVRENTI *catches her.*)

SINGER: The sister was so ill,
The cowardly brother had to give her shelter.
Summer departed, winter came.
The winter was long, the winter was short.
People mustn't know anything.
Rats mustn't bite.
Spring mustn't come.

(GRUSHA *sits over the weaving loom in a workroom. She and the* CHILD, *who is squatting on the floor, are wrapped in blankets. She sings.*)

The Song of the Center

And the lover started to leave
And his betrothed ran pleading after him
Pleading and weeping, weeping and teaching:
"Dearest mine, dearest mine
When you go to war as now you do
When you fight the foe as soon you will
Don't lead with the front line
And don't push with the rear line
At the front is red fire
In the rear is red smoke
Stay in the war's center
Stay near the standard bearer
The first always die
The last are also hit
Those in the center come home."

Michael, we must be clever. If we make ourselves as small as cockroaches, the sister-in-law will forget we're in the house, and then we can stay till the snow melts.

(*Enter* LAVRENTI. *He sits down beside his sister.*)

LAVRENTI: Why are you sitting there muffled up like coachmen, you two? Is it too cold in the room?

GRUSHA (*hastily removing one shawl*): It's not too cold, Lavrenti.

LAVRENTI: If it's too cold, you shouldn't be sitting here with the child. Aniko would never forgive herself! (*Pause.*) I hope our priest didn't question you about the child?

GRUSHA: He did, but I didn't tell him anything.

LAVRENTI: That's good. I wanted to speak to you about Aniko. She has a good heart but she's very, very sensitive. People need only mention our farm and she's worried. She takes everything hard, you see. One time our milkmaid went to church with a hole in her stocking. Ever since, Aniko has worn two pairs of stockings in church. It's the old family in her. (*He listens.*) Are you sure there are no rats around? If there are rats, you couldn't live here. (*There are sounds as of dripping from the roof.*) What's that dripping?

GRUSHA: It must be a barrel leaking.

LAVRENTI: Yes, it must be a barrel. You've been here six months, haven't you? Was I talking about Aniko? (*They listen again to the snow melting.*) You can't imagine how worried she gets about your soldier-husband. "Suppose he comes back and can't find her!" she says and lies awake. "He can't come before the spring," I tell her. The dear woman! (*The drops begin to fall faster.*) When d'you think he'll come? What do *you* think? (GRUSHA *is silent.*) Not before the spring, you agree? (GRUSHA *is silent.*) You don't believe he'll come at all? (GRUSHA *is silent.*) But when the spring comes and the snow melts here and on the passes, you can't stay on. They may come and look for you. There's already talk of an illegitimate child. (*The "glockenspiel" of the falling drops has grown faster and steadier.*) Grusha, the snow is melting on the roof. Spring is here.

GRUSHA: Yes.

LAVRENTI (*eagerly*): I'll tell you what we'll do. You need a place to go, and, because of the child (*he sighs*), you have to have a husband, so people won't talk. Now I've made cautious inquiries to see if we can find you a husband. Grusha, I *have* one. I talked to a peasant woman who has a son. Just the other side of the mountain. A small farm. And she's willing.

GRUSHA: But I *can't* marry! I must wait for Simon Shashava.

LAVRENTI: Of course. That's all been taken care of. You don't need a man in bed—you need a man on paper. And I've found you one. The son of this peasant woman is going to die. Isn't that wonderful? He's at his last gasp. And all in line with our story—a husband from the other side of the mountain! And when you met him he was at the last gasp. So you're a widow. What do you say?

GRUSHA: It's true I could use a document with stamps on it for Michael.

LAVRENTI: Stamps make all the difference. Without something in writing the Shah couldn't prove he's a Shah. And you'll have a place to live.

GRUSHA: How much does the peasant woman want?

LAVRENTI: Four hundred piasters.

GRUSHA: Where will you find it?

LAVRENTI (*guiltily*): Aniko's milk money.

GRUSHA: No one would know us there. I'll do it.

LAVRENTI (*getting up*): I'll let the peasant woman know. (*Quick exit.*)

GRUSHA: Michael, you make a lot of work. I came by you as the pear tree comes by sparrows. And because a Christian bends down and picks up a crust of bread so nothing will go to waste. Michael, it would have been better had I walked quickly away on that Easter Sunday in Nuka in the second courtyard. Now I *am* a fool.

SINGER: The bridegroom was on his deathbed when the bride arrived.
The bridegroom's mother was waiting at the door, telling her to hurry.
The bride brought a child along.
The witness hid it during the wedding.

> (*On one side the bed. Under the mosquito net lies a very* SICK MAN. GRUSHA *is pulled in at a run by her future mother-in-law. They are followed by* LAVRENTI *and the* CHILD.)

MOTHER-IN-LAW: Quick! Quick! Or he'll die on us before the wedding. (*To* LAVRENTI.) I was never told she had a child already.

LAVRENTI: What difference does it make? (*Pointing toward the* DYING MAN.) It can't matter to him—in his condition.

MOTHER-IN-LAW: To him? But I'll never survive the shame! We are honest people. (*She begins to weep.*) My Jussup doesn't have to marry a girl with a child!

LAVRENTI: All right, make it another two hundred piasters. You'll have it in writing that the farm will go to you: but she'll have the right to live here for two years.

MOTHER-IN-LAW (*drying her tears*): It'll hardly cover the funeral expenses. I hope she'll really lend a hand with the work. And what's happened to the monk? He must have slipped out through the kitchen window. We'll have the whole village on our necks when they hear Jussup's end is come! Oh dear! I'll go get the monk. But he mustn't see the child!

LAVRENTI: I'll take care he doesn't. But why only a monk? Why not a priest?

MOTHER-IN-LAW: Oh, he's just as good. I only made one mistake: I paid half his fee in advance. Enough to send him to the tavern. I only hope . . . (*She runs off.*)

LAVRENTI: She saved on the priest, the wretch! Hired a cheap monk.

GRUSHA: You *will* send Simon Shashava to see me if he turns up after all?

LAVRENTI: Yes. (*Pointing at the* SICK PEASANT.) Won't you take a look at him? (GRUSHA, *taking* MICHAEL *to her, shakes her head.*) He's not moving an eyelid. I hope we aren't too late.

> (*They listen. On the opposite side enter* NEIGHBORS *who look around and take up positions against the walls, thus forming another wall near the bed, yet leaving an opening so that the bed can be seen. They start murmuring prayers. Enter the* MOTHER-IN-LAW *with a* MONK. *Showing some annoyance and surprise, she bows to the guests.*)

MOTHER-IN-LAW: I hope you won't mind waiting a few moments? My son's bride has just arrived from the city. An emergency wedding is about to be celebrated. (*To the* MONK *in the bedroom.*) I might have known you couldn't keep your trap shut. (*To* GRUSHA.) The wedding can take place at once. Here's the license. Me and the bride's brother (LAVRENTI *tries to hide in the background, after having quietly taken* MICHAEL *back from* GRUSHA. *The* MOTHER-IN-LAW *waves him away.*) are the witnesses.

> (GRUSHA *has bowed to the* MONK. *They go to the bed. The* MOTHER-IN-LAW *lifts the mosquito net. The* MONK *starts reeling off the marriage ceremony in Latin. Meanwhile the* MOTHER-IN-LAW *beckons to* LAVRENTI *to get rid of the* CHILD, *but fearing that it will cry he draws its attention to the ceremony,* GRUSHA *glances once at the* CHILD, *and* LAVRENTI *waves the* CHILD's *hand in a greeting.*)

MONK: Are you prepared to be a faithful, obedient, and good wife to this man, and to cleave to him until death you do part?

GRUSHA (*looking at the* CHILD): I am.

MONK (*to the* SICK PEASANT): Are you prepared to be a good and loving husband to your wife until death you do part? (*As the* SICK PEASANT *does not answer, the* MONK *looks inquiringly around.*)

MOTHER-IN-LAW: Of course he is! Didn't you hear him say yes?

MONK: All right. We declare the marriage contracted! How about extreme unction?

MOTHER-IN-LAW: Nothing doing! The wedding cost quite enough. Now I must take care of the mourners. (*To* LAVRENTI.) Did we say seven hundred?

LAVRENTI: Six hundred. (*He pays.*) Now I don't want to sit with the guests and get to know people. So farewell, Grusha, and if my widowed sister comes to visit me, she'll get a welcome from my wife, or I'll show my teeth. (*Nods, gives the* CHILD *to* GRUSHA, *and leaves. The* MOURNERS *glance after him without interest.*)

MONK: May one ask where this child comes from?

MOTHER-IN-LAW: Is there a child? I don't see a child. And you don't see a child either—you understand? Or it may turn out I saw all sorts of things in the tavern! Now come on.

> (*After* GRUSHA *has put the* CHILD *down and told him to be quiet, they move over left,* GRUSHA *is introduced to the neighbors.*)

This is my daughter-in-law. She arrived just in time to find dear Jussup still alive.

ONE WOMAN: He's been ill now a whole year, hasn't he? When our Vassili was drafted he was there to say good-bye.

ANOTHER WOMAN: Such things are terrible for a farm. The corn all ripe and the farmer in bed! It'll really be a blessing if he doesn't suffer too long, I say.

FIRST WOMAN (*confidentially*): You know why we thought he'd taken to his bed? Because of the draft! And now his end is come!

MOTHER-IN-LAW: Sit yourselves down, please! And have some cakes!

> (*She beckons to* GRUSHA *and both women go into the bedroom, where they pick up the cake pans off the floor. The* GUESTS, *among them the* MONK, *sit on the floor and begin conversing in subdued voices.*)

ONE PEASANT (*to whom the* MONK *has handed the bottle which he has taken from his soutane*): There's a child, you say! How can that have happened to Jussup?

A WOMAN: She was certainly lucky to get herself married, with him so sick!

MOTHER-IN-LAW: They're gossiping already. And wolfing down the funeral cakes at the same time! If he doesn't die today, I'll have to bake some more tomorrow!

GRUSHA: I'll bake them for you.

MOTHER-IN-LAW: Yesterday some horsemen rode by, and I went out to see who it was. When I came in again he was lying there like a corpse! So I sent for you. It can't take much longer. (*She listens.*)

MONK: Dear wedding and funeral guests! Deeply touched, we stand before a bed of death and marriage. The bride gets a veil; the groom, a shroud: how varied, my children, are the fates of men! Alas! One man dies and has a roof over his head, and the other is married and the flesh turns to dust from which it was made. Amen.

MOTHER-IN-LAW: He's getting his own back. I shouldn't have hired such a cheap one. It's what you'd expect. A more expensive monk would behave himself. In Sura there's one with a real air of sanctity about him, but of course he charges a fortune. A fifty piaster monk like that has no dignity, and as for piety, just fifty piasters' worth and no more! When I came to get him in the tavern he'd just made a speech, and he was shouting: "The war is over, beware of the peace!" We must go in.

GRUSHA (*giving* MICHAEL *a cake*): Eat this cake, and keep nice and still, Michael.

> (*The two women offer cakes to the guests. The* DYING MAN *sits up in bed. He puts his head out from under the mosquito net, stares at the two women, then sinks back again. The* MONK *takes two bottles from his soutane and offers them to the* PEASANT *beside him. Enter three* MUSICIANS *who are greeted with a sly wink by the* MONK.)

MOTHER-IN-LAW (*to the* MUSICIANS): What are you doing here? With instruments?

ONE MUSICIAN: Brother Anastasius here (*pointing at the* MONK) told us there was a wedding on.

MOTHER-IN-LAW: What? You brought them? Three more on my neck! Don't you know there's a dying man in the next room.

MONK: A very tempting assignment for a musician: something that could be either a subdued Wedding March or a spirited Funeral Dance.

MOTHER-IN-LAW: Well, you might as well play. Nobody can stop you eating in any case.

> (*The* MUSICIANS *play a potpourri. The women serve cakes.*)

MONK: The trumpet sounds like a whining baby. And you, little drum, what have you got to tell the world?

DRUNKEN PEASANT (*beside the* MONK, *sings*): There was a young woman who said:

I thought I'd be happier, wed.
But my husband is old
And remarkably cold
So I sleep with a candle instead.

> (*The* MOTHER-IN-LAW *throws the* DRUNKEN PEASANT *out. The music stops. The* GUESTS *are embarrassed.*)

GUESTS (*loudly*): —Have you heard? The Grand Duke is back! But the Princes are against him.
—They say the Shah of Persia has lent him a great army to restore order in Grusinia.
—But how is that possible? The Shah of Persia is the enemy . . .
—The enemy of Grusinia, you donkey, not the enemy of the Grand Duke!
—In any case, the war's over, so our soldiers are coming back.

> (GRUSHA *drops a cake pan.* GUESTS *help her pick up the cake.*)

AN OLD WOMAN (*to* GRUSHA): Are you feeling bad? It's just excitement about dear Jussup. Sit down and rest a while, my dear. (GRUSHA *staggers.*)

GUESTS: Now everything'll be the way it was. Only the taxes'll go up because now we'll have to pay for the war.

GRUSHA (*weakly*): Did someone say the soldiers are back?

A MAN: I did.

GRUSHA: It can't be true.

FIRST MAN (*to a* WOMAN): Show her the shawl. We bought it from a soldier. It's from Persia.

GRUSHA (*looking at the shawl*): They are here. (*She gets up, takes a step, kneels down in prayer, takes the silver cross and chain out of her blouse, and kisses it.*)

MOTHER-IN-LAW (*while the guests silently watch* GRUSHA): What's the matter with you? Aren't you going to look after our guests? What's all this city nonsense got to do with us?

GUESTS (*resuming conversation while* GRUSHA *remains in prayer*): —You can buy Persian saddles from the soldiers too. Though many want crutches in exchange for them.
—The leaders on one side can win a war, the soldiers on both sides lose it.
—Anyway, the war's over. It's something they can't draft you any more.

> (*The* DYING MAN *sits bolt upright in bed. He listens.*)

—What we need is two weeks of good weather.
—Our pear trees are hardly bearing a thing this year.

MOTHER-IN-LAW (*offering cakes*): Have some more cakes and welcome! There are more!

> (*The* MOTHER-IN-LAW *goes to the bedroom with the empty cake pans. Unaware of the* DYING MAN, *she is bending down to pick up another tray when he begins to talk in a hoarse voice.*)

PEASANT: How many more cakes are you going to stuff down their throats? D'you think I can shit money?

> (*The* MOTHER-IN-LAW *starts, stares at him aghast, while he climbs out from behind the mosquito net.*)

FIRST WOMAN (*talking kindly to* GRUSHA *in the next room*): Has the young wife got someone at the front?

A MAN: It's good news that they're on their way home, huh?

PEASANT: Don't stare at me like that! Where's this wife you've saddled me with?

> (*Receiving no answer, he climbs out of bed and in his nightshirt staggers into the other room. Trembling, she follows him with the cake pan.*)

GUESTS (*seeing him and shrieking*): Good God! Jussup!

> (*Everyone leaps up in alarm. The* WOMEN *rush to the door.* GRUSHA, *still on her knees, turns round and stares at the* MAN.)

PEASANT: A funeral supper! You'd enjoy that, wouldn't you? Get out before I throw you out! (*As the* GUESTS *stampede from the house, gloomily to* GRUSHA.) I've upset the apple cart, huh? (*Receiving no answer, he turns round and takes a cake from the pan which his mother is holding.*)

SINGER: O confusion! The wife discovers she has a husband.
By day there's the child, by night there's the husband.
The lover is on his way both day and night.
Husband and wife look at each other.
The bedroom is small.

> (*Near the bed the* PEASANT *is sitting in a high wooden bathtub, naked, the* MOTHER-IN-LAW *is pouring water from a pitcher. Opposite* GRUSHA *cowers with* MICHAEL, *who is playing at mending straw mats.*)

PEASANT (*to his* MOTHER): That's her work, not yours. Where's she hiding out now?

MOTHER-IN-LAW (*calling*): Grusha! The peasant wants you!

GRUSHA (*to* MICHAEL): There are still two holes to mend.

PEASANT (*when* GRUSHA *approaches*): Scrub my back!

GRUSHA: Can't the peasant do it himself?

PEASANT: "Can't the peasant do it himself?" Get the brush! To hell with you! Are you the wife here? Or are you a visitor? (*To the* MOTHER-IN-LAW.) It's too cold!

MOTHER-IN-LAW: I'll run for hot water.

GRUSHA: Let me go.

PEASANT: You stay here. (*The* MOTHER-IN-LAW *exits.*) Rub harder. And no shirking. You've seen a naked fellow before. That child didn't come out of thin air.

GRUSHA: The child was not conceived in joy, if that's what the peasant means.

PEASANT (*turning and grinning*): You don't look the type. (GRUSHA *stops scrubbing him, starts back. Enter the* MOTHER-IN-LAW.)

PEASANT: A nice thing you've saddled me with! A simpleton for a wife!

MOTHER-IN-LAW: She just isn't cooperative.

PEASANT: Pour—but go easy! Ow! Go easy, I said. (*To* GRUSHA.) Maybe you did something wrong in the city . . . I wouldn't be surprised. Why else should you be here? But I won't talk about that. I've not said a word about the illegitimate object you brought into my house either. But my patience has limits! It's against nature. (*To the* MOTHER-IN-LAW.) More! (*To* GRUSHA.) And even if your soldier does come back, you're married.

GRUSHA: Yes.

PEASANT: But your soldier won't come back. Don't you believe it.

GRUSHA: No.

PEASANT: You're cheating me. You're my wife and you're not my wife. Where you lie, nothing lies, and yet no other woman can lie there. When I go to work in the morning I'm tired—when I lie down at night I'm awake as the devil. God has given you sex—and what d'you do? I don't have ten piasters to buy myself a woman in the city. Besides, it's a long way. Woman weeds the fields and opens up her legs, that's what our calendar says. D'you hear?

GRUSHA (*quietly*): Yes. I didn't mean to cheat you out of it.

PEASANT: She didn't mean to cheat me out of it! Pour some more water! (*The* MOTHER-IN-LAW *pours.*) Ow!

SINGER: As she sat by the stream to wash the linen
She saw his image in the water
And his face grew dimmer with the passing moons.
As she raised herself to wring the linen
She heard his voice from the murmuring maple
And his voice grew fainter with the passing moons.
Evasions and sighs grew more numerous,
Tears and sweat flowed.
With the passing moons the child grew up.

> (GRUSHA *sits by a stream, dipping linen into the water. In the rear, a few* CHILDREN *are standing.*)

GRUSHA (*to* MICHAEL): You can play with them, Michael, but don't let them boss you around just because you're the littlest. (MICHAEL *nods and joins the* CHILDREN. *They start playing.*)

BIGGEST BOY: Today it's the Heads-Off Game. (*To a* FAT BOY.) You're the Prince and you laugh. (*To* MICHAEL.) You're the Governor. (*To a* GIRL.) You're the Governor's wife and you cry when his head's cut off. And I do the cutting. (*He shows his wooden sword.*) With this. First, they lead the Governor into the yard. The Prince walks in front. The Governor's wife comes last.

> (*They form a procession. The* FAT BOY *is first and laughs. Then comes* MICHAEL, *then the* BIGGEST BOY, *and then the* GIRL, *who weeps.*)

MICHAEL (*standing still*): Me cut off head!

BIGGEST BOY: That's my job. You're the littlest. The Governor's the easy part. All you do is kneel down and get your head cut off—simple.

MICHAEL: Me want sword!

BIGGEST BOY: It's mine! (*He gives* MICHAEL *a kick.*)

GIRL (*shouting to* GRUSHA): He won't play his part!

GRUSHA (*laughing*): Even the little duck is a swimmer, they say.

BIGGEST BOY: You can be the Prince if you can laugh. (MICHAEL *shakes his head.*)

FAT BOY: I laugh best. Let him cut off the head just once. Then you do it, then me.

> (*Reluctantly, the* BIGGEST BOY *hands* MICHAEL *the wooden sword and kneels down. The* FAT BOY *sits down, slaps his thigh, and laughs with all his might. The* GIRL *weeps loudly.* MICHAEL *swings the big sword and "cuts off" the head. In doing so, he topples over.*)

BIGGEST BOY: Hey! I'll show you how to cut heads off!

> (MICHAEL *runs away. The* CHILDREN *run after him.* GRUSHA *laughs, following them with her eyes. On looking back, she sees* SIMON SHASHAVA *standing on the opposite bank. He wears a shabby uniform.*)

GRUSHA: Simon!

SIMON: Is that Grusha Vashnadze?

GRUSHA: Simon!

SIMON (*formally*): A good morning to the young lady. I hope she is well.

GRUSHA (*getting up gaily and bowing low*): A good morning to the soldier. God be thanked he has returned in good health.

SIMON: They found better fish, so they didn't eat me, said the haddock.

GRUSHA: Courage, said the kitchen boy. Good luck, said the hero.

SIMON: How are things here? Was the winter bearable? The neighbor considerate?

GRUSHA: The winter was a trifle rough, the neighbor as usual, Simon.

SIMON: May one ask if a certain person still dips her toes in the water when rinsing the linen?

GRUSHA: The answer is no. Because of the eyes in the bushes.

SIMON: The young lady is speaking of soldiers. Here stands a paymaster.

GRUSHA: A job worth twenty piasters?

SIMON: And lodgings.

GRUSHA (*with tears in her eyes*): Behind the barracks under the date trees.

SIMON: Yes, there. A certain person has kept her eyes open.

GRUSHA: She has, Simon.

SIMON: And has not forgotten? (GRUSHA *shakes her head.*) So the door is still on its hinges as they say? (GRUSHA *looks at him in silence and shakes her head again.*) What's this? Is anything not as it should be?

GRUSHA: Simon Shashava, I can never return to Nuka. Something has happened.

SIMON: What can have happened?

GRUSHA: For one thing, I knocked an Ironshirt down.

SIMON: Grusha Vashnadze must have had her reasons for that.

GRUSHA: Simon Shashava, I am no longer called what I used to be called.

SIMON (*after a pause*): I do not understand.

GRUSHA: When do women change their names, Simon? Let me explain. Nothing stands between us. Everything is just as it was. You must believe that.

SIMON: Nothing stands between us and yet there's something?

GRUSHA: How can I explain it so fast and with the stream between us? Couldn't you cross the bridge there?

SIMON: Maybe it's no longer necessary.

GRUSHA: It is very necessary. Come over on this side, Simon. Quick!

SIMON: Does the young lady wish to say someone has come too late?

> (GRUSHA *looks up at him in despair, her face streaming with tears.* SIMON *stares before him. He picks up a piece of wood and starts cutting it.*)

SINGER: So many words are said, so many left unsaid.
The soldier has come.
Where he comes from, he does not say.
Hear what he thought and did not say:
"The battle began, gray at dawn, grew bloody at noon.
The first man fell in front of me, the second behind me, the third
    at my side.
I trod on the first, left the second behind, the third was run
    through by the captain.
One of my brothers died by steel, the other by smoke.
My neck caught fire, my hands froze in my gloves, my toes in
    my socks.
I fed on aspen buds, I drank maple juice, I slept on stone, in water."

SIMON: I see a cap in the grass. Is there a little one already?

GRUSHA: There is, Simon. There's no keeping *that* from you. But please don't worry, it is not mine.

SIMON: When the wind once starts to blow, they say, it blows through every cranny. The wife need say no more. (GRUSHA *looks into her lap and is silent.*)

SINGER: There was yearning but there was no waiting.
The oath is broken. Neither could say why.
Hear what she thought but did not say:
"While you fought in the battle, soldier,
The bloody battle, the bitter battle
I found a helpless infant
I had not the heart to destroy him
I had to care for a creature that was lost
I had to stoop for breadcrumbs on the floor

I had to break myself for that which was not mine
That which was other people's.
Someone must help!
For the little tree needs water
The lamb loses its way when the shepherd is asleep
And its cry is unheard!"

SIMON: Give me back the cross I gave you. Better still, throw it in the stream. (*He turns to go.*)

GRUSHA (*getting up*): Simon Shashava, don't go away! He isn't mine! He isn't mine! (*She hears the children calling.*) What's the matter, children?

VOICES: Soldiers! And they're taking Michael away!

> (GRUSHA *stands aghast as two* IRONSHIRTS, *with* MICHAEL *between them, come toward her.*)

ONE OF THE IRONSHIRTS: Are you Grusha? (*She nods.*) Is this your child?

GRUSHA: Yes. (SIMON *goes.*) Simon!

IRONSHIRT: We have orders, in the name of the law, to take this child, found in your custody, back to the city. It is suspected that the child is Michael Abashwili, son and heir of the late Governor Georgi Abashwili, and his wife, Natella Abashwili. Here is the document and the seal. (*They lead the* CHILD *away.*)

GRUSHA (*running after them, shouting*): Leave him here. Please! He's mine!

SINGER: The Ironshirts took the child, the beloved child.
The unhappy girl followed them to the city, the dreaded city.
She who had borne him demanded the child.
She who had raised him faced trial.
Who will decide the case?
To whom will the child be assigned?
Who will the judge be? A good judge? A bad?
The city was in flames.
In the judge's seat sat Azdak.[1]

FOUR. THE STORY OF THE JUDGE

SINGER: Hear the story of the judge
How he turned judge, how he passed judgment, what kind of
        judge he was.
On that Easter Sunday of the great revolt, when the Grank Duke
        was overthrown
And his Governor Abashwili, father of our child, lost his head
The Village Scrivener Azdak found a fugitive in the woods and
        hid him in his hut.

> (AZDAK, *in rags and slightly drunk, is helping an* OLD BEGGAR *into his cottage.*)

---

1. "The name Azdak should be accented on the second syllable." [Bentley's note.]

AZDAK: Stop snorting, you're not a horse. And it won't do you any good with the police to run like a snotty nose in April. Stand still, I say. (*He catches the* OLD MAN, *who has marched into the cottage as if he'd like to go through the walls.*) Sit down. Feed. Here's a hunk of cheese. (*From under some rags, in a chest, he fishes out some cheese, and the* OLD MAN *greedily begins to eat.*) Haven't eaten in a long time, huh? (*The* OLD MAN *growls.*) Why were you running like that, asshole? The cop wouldn't even have seen you.

OLD MAN: Had to! Had to!

AZDAK: Blue funk? (THE OLD MAN *stares, uncomprehending.*) Cold feet? Panic? Don't lick your chops like a Grand Duke. Or an old sow. I can't stand it. We have to accept respectable stinkers as God made them, but not you! I once heard of a senior judge who farted at a public dinner to show an independent spirit! Watching you eat like that gives me the most awful ideas. Why don't you say something? (*Sharply.*) Show me your hand. Can't you hear? (*The* OLD MAN *slowly puts out his hand.*) White! So you're not a beggar at all! A fraud, a walking swindle! And I'm hiding you from the cops like you were an honest man! Why were you running like that if you're a landowner? For that's what you are. Don't deny it! I see it in your guilty face! (*He gets up.*) Get out! (*The* OLD MAN *looks at him uncertainly.*) What are you waiting for, peasant-flogger?

OLD MAN: Pursued. Need undivided attention. Make proposition . . .

AZDAK: Make what? A proposition? Well, if that isn't the height of insolence. He's making me a proposition! The bitten man scratches his fingers bloody, and the leech that's biting him makes him a proposition! Get out, I tell you!

OLD MAN: Understand point of view! Persuasion! Pay hundred thousand piasters one night! Yes?

AZDAK: What, you think you can buy me? For a hundred thousand piasters? Let's say a hundred and fifty thousand. Where are they?

OLD MAN: Have not them here. Of course. Will be sent. Hope do not doubt.

AZDAK: Doubt very much. Get out!

> (*The* OLD MAN *gets up, waddles to the door. A* VOICE *is heard offstage.*)

VOICE: Azdak!

> (*The* OLD MAN *turns, waddles to the opposite corner, stands still.*)

AZDAK (*calling out*): I'm not in! (*He walks to door.*) So *you're* sniffing around here again, Shauwa?

SHAUWA (*reproachfully*): You caught another rabbit, Azdak. And you'd promised me it wouldn't happen again!

AZDAK (*severely*): Shauwa, don't talk about things you don't understand. The rabbit is a dangerous and destructive beast. It feeds on plants, especially on the species of plants known as weeds. It must therefore be exterminated.

SHAUWA: Azdak, don't be so hard on me. I'll lose my job if I don't arrest you. I know you have a good heart.

AZDAK: I do not have a good heart! How often must I tell you I'm a man of intellect?

SHAUWA (*slyly*): I know, Azdak. You're a superior person. You say so yourself. I'm just a Christian and an ignoramus. So I ask you: When one of the Prince's rabbits is stolen, and I'm a policeman, what should I do with the offending party?

AZDAK: Shauwa, Shauwa, shame on you. You stand and ask me a question, than which nothing could be more seductive. It's like you were a woman—let's say that bad girl Nunowna, and you showed me your thigh—Nunowna's thigh, that would be—and asked me: "What shall I do with my thigh, it itches?" Is she as innocent as she pretends? Of course not. I catch a rabbit, but you catch a man. Man is made in God's image. Not so a rabbit, you know that. I'm a rabbit-eater, but you're a man-eater, Shauwa. And God will pass judgment on you. Shauwa, go home and repent. No, stop, there's something . . . (*He looks at the* OLD MAN *who stands trembling in the corner.*) No, it's nothing. Go home and repent. (*He slams the door behind* SHAUWA.) Now you're surprised, huh? Surprised I didn't hand you over? I couldn't hand over a bedbug to that animal. It goes against the grain. Now don't tremble because of a cop! So old and still so scared? Finish your cheese, but eat it like a poor man, or else they'll still catch you. Must I even explain how a poor man behaves? (*He pushes him down, and then gives him back the cheese.*) That box is the table. Lay your elbows on the table. Now, encircle the cheese on the plate like it might be snatched from you at any moment—what right have you to be safe, huh?—now, hold your knife like an undersized sickle, and give your cheese a troubled look because, like all beautiful things, it's already fading away. (AZDAK *watches him.*) They're after you, which speaks in your favor, but how can we be sure they're not mistaken about you? In Tiflis one time they hanged a landowner, a Turk, who could prove he quartered his peasants instead of merely cutting them in half, as is the custom, and he squeezed twice the usual amount of taxes out of them, his zeal was above suspicion. And yet they hanged him like a common criminal— because he was a Turk—a thing he couldn't do much about. What injustice! He got onto the gallows by a sheer fluke. In short, I don't trust you.

SINGER: Thus Azdak gave the old beggar a bed,
And learned that old beggar was the old butcher, the Grand
    Duke himself,
And was ashamed.
He denounced himself and ordered the policemen to take him to
    Nuka, to court, to be judged.

    (*In the court of justice three* IRONSHIRTS *sit drinking. From a beam hangs a man in judge's robes. Enter* AZDAK, *in chains, dragging* SHAUWA *behind him.*)

AZDAK (*shouting*): I've helped the Grand Duke, the Grand Thief, the Grand Butcher, to escape! In the name of justice I ask to be severely judged in public trial!

FIRST IRONSHIRT: Who's this queer bird?

SHAUWA: That's our Village Scrivener, Azdak.

AZDAK: I am contemptible! I am a traitor! A branded criminal! Tell them, flatfoot, how I insisted on being tied up and brought to the capital. Because I sheltered the Grand Duke, the Grand Swindler, by mistake. And how I found out afterwards. See the marked man denounce himself! Tell them how I forced you to walk half the night with me to clear the whole thing up.

SHAUWA: And all by threats. That wasn't nice of you, Azdak.

AZDAK: Shut your mouth, Shauwa. You don't understand. A new age is upon us! It'll go thundering over you. You're finished. The police will be wiped out—poof! Everything will be gone into, everything will be brought into the open. The guilty will give themselves up. Why? They couldn't escape the people in any case. (*To* SHAUWA.) Tell them how I shouted all along Shoemaker Street (*with big gestures, looking at the* IRONSHIRTS) "In my ignorance I let the Grand Swindler escape! So tear me to pieces, brothers!" I wanted to get it in first.

FIRST IRONSHIRT: And what did your brothers answer?

SHAUWA: They comforted him in Butcher Street, and they laughed themselves sick in Shoemaker Street. That's all.

AZDAK: But with you it's different. I can see you're men of iron. Brothers, where's the judge? I must be tried.

FIRST IRONSHIRT (*pointing at the hanged man*): There's the judge. And please stop "brothering" us. It's rather a sore spot this evening.

AZDAK: "There's the judge." An answer never heard in Grusinia before. Townsman, where's His Excellency the Governor? (*Pointing to the ground.*) There's His Excellency, stranger. Where's the Chief Tax Collector? Where's the official Recruiting Officer? The Patriarch? The Chief of Police? There, there, there—all there. Brothers, I expected no less of you.

SECOND IRONSHIRT: What? *What* was it you expected, funny man?

AZDAK: What happened in Persia, brother, what happened in Persia?

SECOND IRONSHIRT: What did happen in Persia?

AZDAK: Everybody was hanged. Viziers, tax collectors. Everybody. Forty years ago now. My grandfather, a remarkable man by the way, saw it all. For three whole days. Everywhere.

SECOND IRONSHIRT: And who ruled when the Vizier was hanged?

AZDAK: A peasant ruled when the Vizier was hanged.

SECOND IRONSHIRT: And who commanded the army?

AZDAK: A soldier, a soldier.

SECOND IRONSHIRT: And who paid the wages?

AZDAK: A dyer. A dyer paid the wages.

SECOND IRONSHIRT: Wasn't it a weaver, maybe?

FIRST IRONSHIRT: And why did all this happen, Persian?

AZDAK: Why did all this happen? Must there be a special reason? Why do you scratch yourself, brother? War! Too long a war! And no justice! My grandfather brought back a song that tells how it was. I will sing it for you. With my friend the policeman. (*To* SHAUWA.) And hold the rope tight. It's very suitable. (*He sings, with* SHAUWA *holding the rope tight around him.*)

The Song of Injustice in Persia

Why don't our sons bleed any more? Why don't our daughters
    weep?
Why do only the slaughterhouse cattle have blood in their veins?
Why do only the willows shed tears on Lake Urmia?
The king must have a new province, the peasant must give up his
    savings.
That the roof of the world might be conquered, the roof of the
    cottage is torn down.
Our men are carried to the ends of the earth, so that great ones
    can eat at home.
The soldiers kill each other, the marshals salute each other.
They bite the widow's tax money to see if it's good, their swords
    break
The battle was lost, the helmets were paid for.
Refrain: Is it so? Is it so?

SHAUWA (*refrain*):

    Yes, yes, yes, yes, yes it's so.

AZDAK: Want to hear the rest of it? (*The* FIRST IRONSHIRT *nods.*)
SECOND IRONSHIRT (*to* SHAUWA): Did he teach you that song?
SHAUWA: Yes, only my voice isn't very good.
SECOND IRONSHIRT: No. (*To* AZDAK.) Go on singing.
AZDAK: The second verse is about the peace. (*He sings.*)

    The offices are packed, the streets overflow with officials.
    The rivers jump their banks and ravage the fields.
    Those who cannot let down their own trousers rule countries.
    They can't count up to four, but they devour eight courses.
    The corn farmers, looking round for buyers, see only the starving.
    The weavers go home from their looms in rags.
    Refrain: Is it so? Is it so?

SHAUWA (*refrain*):

    Yes, yes, yes, yes, yes it's so.

AZDAK:

    That's why our sons don't bleed any more, that's why our
      daughters don't weep,

That's why only the slaughterhouse cattle have blood in
   their veins,
And only the willows shed tears by Lake Urmia toward
   morning.

FIRST IRONSHIRT: Are you going to sing that song here in town?

AZDAK: Sure. What's wrong with it?

FIRST IRONSHIRT: Have you noticed that the sky's getting red? (*Turning round,*
   AZDAK *sees the sky red with fire.*) It's the people's quarters on the outskirts
   of town. The carpet weavers have caught the "Persian Sickness," too.
   And they've been asking if Prince Kazbeki isn't eating too many courses.
   This morning they strung up the city judge. As for us we beat them to
   pulp. We were paid one hundred piasters per man, you understand?

AZDAK (*after a pause*): I understand. (*He glances shyly round and, creeping away,
   sits down in a corner, his head in his hands.*)

IRONSHIRTS (*to each other*): If there ever was a troublemaker it's him.
   —He must've come to the capital to fish in the troubled waters.

SHAUWA: Oh, I don't think he's a really bad character, gentlemen. Steals a few
   chickens here and there. And maybe a rabbit.

SECOND IRONSHIRT (*approaching* AZDAK): Came to fish in the troubled waters,
   huh?

AZDAK (*looking up*): I don't know why I came.

SECOND IRONSHIRT: Are you in with the carpet weavers maybe? (AZDAK *shakes his
   head.*) How about that song?

AZDAK: From my grandfather. A silly and ignorant man.

SECOND IRONSHIRT: Right. And how about the dyer who paid the wages?

AZDAK (*muttering*): That was in Persia.

FIRST IRONSHIRT: And this denouncing of yourself? Because you didn't hang
   the Grand Duke with your own hands?

AZDAK: Didn't I tell you I let him run? (*He creeps farther away and sits on the
   floor.*)

SHAUWA: I can swear to that: he let him run.

> (*The* IRONSHIRTS *burst out laughing and slap* SHAUWA *on the back.*
> AZDAK *laughs loudest. They slap* AZDAK *too, and unchain him. They
> all start drinking as the* FAT PRINCE *enters with a* YOUNG MAN.)

FIRST IRONSHIRT (*to* AZDAK, *pointing at the* FAT PRINCE): There's your "new age"
   for you! (*More laughter.*)

FAT PRINCE: Well, my friends, what is there to laugh about? Permit me a serious
   word. Yesterday morning the Princes of Grusinia overthrew the warmon-
   gering government of the Grand Duke and did away with his Governors.
   Unfortunately the Grand Duke himself escaped. In this fateful hour our
   carpet weavers, those eternal troublemakers, had the effrontery to stir up
   a rebellion and hang the universally loved city judge, our dear Illo
   Orbeliani. Ts—ts—ts. My friends, we need peace, peace, peace in
   Grusinia! And justice! So I've brought along my dear nephew Bizergan

Kazbeki. He'll be the new judge, hm? A very gifted fellow. What do you say? I want your opinion. Let the people decide!

SECOND IRONSHIRT: Does this mean *we* elect the judge?

FAT PRINCE: Precisely. Let the people propose some very gifted fellow! Confer among yourselves, my friends. (*The* IRONSHIRTS *confer.*) Don't worry, my little fox. The job's yours. And when we catch the Grand Duke we won't have to kiss this rabble's ass any longer.

IRONSHIRTS (*among themselves*):—Very funny: they're wetting their pants because they haven't caught the Grand Duke.

—When the outlook isn't so bright, they say: "My friends!" and "Let the people decide!"

—Now he even wants justice for Grusinia! But fun is fun as long as it lasts! (*Pointing at* AZDAK.) *He* knows all about justice. Hey, rascal, would you like this nephew fellow to be the judge?

AZDAK: Are you asking me? You're not asking *me*?!

FIRST IRONSHIRT: Why not? Anything for a laugh!

AZDAK: You'd like to test him to the marrow, correct? Have you a criminal on hand? An experienced one? So the candidate can show what he knows?

SECOND IRONSHIRT: Let's see. We do have a couple of doctors downstairs. Let's use them.

AZDAK: Oh, no, that's no good, we can't take real criminals till we're sure the judge will be appointed. He may be dumb, but he must be appointed, or the law is violated. And the law is a sensitive organ. It's like the spleen, you mustn't hit it—that would be fatal. Of course you can hang those two without violating the law, because there was no judge in the vicinity. But judgment, when pronounced, must be pronounced with absolute gravity—it's all such nonsense. Suppose, for instance, a judge jails a woman—let's say she's stolen a corn cake to feed her child—and this judge isn't wearing his robes—or maybe he's scratching himself while passing sentence and half is body is uncovered—a man's thigh *will* itch once in a while—the sentence this judge passes is a disgrace and the law is violated. In short it would be easier for a judge's robe and a judge's hat to pass judgment than for a man with no robe and no hat. If you don't treat it with respect, the law just disappears on you. Now you don't try out a bottle of wine by offering it to a dog; you'd only lose your wine.

FIRST IRONSHIRT: Then what do you suggest, hairsplitter?

AZDAK: I'll be the defendant.

FIRST IRONSHIRT: You? (*He bursts out laughing.*)

FAT PRINCE: What have you decided?

FIRST IRONSHIRT: We've decided to stage a rehearsal. Our friend here will be the defendant. Let the candidate be the judge and sit there.

FAT PRINCE: It isn't customary, but why not? (*To the* NEPHEW.) A mere formality, my little fox. What have I taught you? Who got there first—the slow runner or the fast?

NEPHEW: The silent runner, Uncle Arsen.

(*The* NEPHEW *takes the chair. The* IRONSHIRTS *and the* FAT PRINCE *sit on the steps. Enter* AZDAK, *mimicking the gait of the Grand Duke.*)

AZDAK (*in the Grand Duke's accent*): Is any here knows me? Am Grand Duke.

IRONSHIRTS: —*What* is he?

—The Grand Duke. He knows him, too.

—Fine. So get on with the trial.

AZDAK: Listen! Am accused instigating war? Ridiculous! Am saying ridiculous! That enough? If not, have brought lawyers. Believe five hundred. (*He points behind him, pretending to be surrounded by lawyers.*) Requisition all available seats for lawyers! (*The* IRONSHIRTS *laugh; the fat prince joins in.*)

NEPHEW (*to the* IRONSHIRTS): You really wish me to try this case? I find it rather unusual. From the taste angle, I mean.

FIRST IRONSHIRT: Let's go!

FAT PRINCE (*smiling*): Let him have it, my little fox!

NEPHEW: All right. People of Grusinia versus Grande Duke. Defendant, what have you got to say for yourself?

AZDAK: Plenty. Naturally, have read war lost. Only started on the advice of patriots. Like Uncle Arsen Kazbeki. Call Uncle Arsen as witness.

FAT PRINCE (*to the* IRONSHIRTS, *delightedly*): What a madcap!

NEPHEW: Motion rejected. One cannot be arraigned for declaring a war, which every ruler has to do once in a while, but only for running a war badly.

AZDAK: Rubbish! Did not run it at all! Had it run! Had it run by Princes! Naturally, they messed it up.

NEPHEW: Do you by any chance deny having been commander-in-chief?

AZDAK: Not at all! Always *was* commander-in-chief. At birth shouted at wet nurse. Was trained drop turds in toilet, grew accustomed to command. Always commanded officials rob my cash box. Officers flog soldiers only on command. Landowners sleep with peasants' wives only on strictest command. Uncle Arsen here grew his belly at *my* command!

IRONSHIRTS (*clapping*): He's good! Long live the Grand Duke!

FAT PRINCE: Answer him, my little fox: I'm with you.

NEPHEW: I shall answer him according to the dignity of the law. Defendant, preserve the dignity of the law!

AZDAK: Agreed. Command you proceed with trial!

NEPHEW: It is not your place to command me. You claim that the Princes forced you to declare war. How can you claim, then, that they—er—"messed it up"?

AZDAK: Did not send enough people. Embezzled funds. Sent sick horses. During attack, drinking in whorehouse. Call Uncle Arsen as witness.

NEPHEW: Are you making the outrageous suggestion that the Princes of this country did not fight?

AZDAK: No. Princes fought. Fought for war contracts.

FAT PRINCE (*jumping up*): That's too much! This man talks like a carpet weaver!

AZDAK: Really? Told nothing but truth.

FAT PRINCE: Hang him! Hang him!

FIRST IRONSHIRT (*pulling the* PRINCE *down*): Keep quiet! Go on, Excellency!

NEPHEW: Quiet! I now render a verdict: You must be hanged! By the neck! Having lost war!

AZDAK: Young man, seriously advise not fall publicly into jerky clipped speech. Cannot be watchdog if howl like wolf. Got it? If people realize Princes speak same language as Grand Duke, may hang Grand Duke *and Princes,* huh? By the way, must overrule verdict. Reason? War lost, but not for Princes. Princes won their war. Got 3,863,000 piasters for horses not delivered, 8,240,000 piasters for food supplies not produced. Are therefore victors. War lost only for Grusinia, which is not present in this court.

FAT PRINCE: I think that will do, my friends. (*To* AZDAK.) You can withdraw, funny man. (*To the* IRONSHIRTS.) You may now ratify the new judge's appointment, my friends.

FIRST IRONSHIRT: Yes, we can. Take down the judge's gown. (*One* IRONSHIRT *climbs on the back of the other, pulls the gown off the hanged man.*) (*To the* NEPHEW.) Now you run away so the right ass can get on the right chair. (*To* AZDAK.) Step forward! Go to the judge's seat! Now sit in it! (AZDAK *steps up, bows, and sits down.*) The judge was always a rascal! Now the rascal shall be a judge! (*The judge's gown is placed round his shoulders, the hat on his head.*) And what a judge!

SINGER: And there was civil war in the land.
The mighty were not safe.
And Azdak was made a judge by the Ironshirts.
And Azdak remained a judge for two years.

SINGER AND CHORUS: When the towns were set afire
And rivers of blood rose higher and higher,
Cockroaches crawled out of every crack.
And the court was full of schemers
And the church of foul blasphemers.
In the judge's cassock sat Azdak.

> (AZDAK *sits in the judge's chair, peeling an apple.* SHAUWA *is sweeping out the hall. On one side an* INVALID *in a wheelchair. Opposite, a* YOUNG MAN *accused of blackmail. An* IRONSHIRT *stands guard, holding the Ironshirts' banner.*)

AZDAK: In consideration of the large number of cases, the Court today will hear two cases at a time. Before I open the proceedings, a short announcement—I accept. (*He stretches out his hand. The* BLACKMAILER *is the only one to produce any money. He hands it to* AZDAK.) I reserve the right to punish one of the parties for contempt of court. (*He glances at the* INVALID.) You (*to the* DOCTOR) are a doctor, and you (*to the* INVALID) are bringing a complaint against him. Is the doctor responsible for your condition?

INVALID: Yes. I had a stroke on his account.

AZDAK: That would be professional negligence.

INVALID: Worse than negligence. I gave this man money for his studies. So far, he hasn't paid me back a cent. It was when I heard he was treating a patient free that I had my stroke.

AZDAK: Rightly. (*To a* LIMPING MAN.) And what are *you* doing here?

LIMPING MAN: I'm the patient, Your Honor.

AZDAK: He treated your leg for nothing?

LIMPING MAN: The wrong leg! My rheumatism was in the left leg, he operated on the right. That's why I limp.

AZDAK: And you were treated free?

INVALID: A five-hundred-piaster operation free! For nothing! For a God-bless-you! And I paid for this man's studies! (*To the* DOCTOR.) Did they teach you to operate free?

DOCTOR: Your Honor, it is the custom to demand the fee before the operation, as the patient is more willing to pay before an operation than after. Which is only human. In the case in question I was convinced, when I started the operation, that my servant had already received the fee. In this I was mistaken.

INVALID: He was mistaken! A good doctor doesn't make mistakes! He examines before he operates!

AZDAK: That's right. (*To* SHAUWA.) Public Prosecutor, what's the other case about?

SHAUWA (*busily sweeping*): Blackmail.

BLACKMAILER: High Court of Justice, I'm innocent. I only wanted to find out from the landowner concerned if he really *had* raped his niece. He informed me very politely that this was not the case, and gave me the money only so I could pay for my uncle's studies.

AZDAK: Hm. (*To the* DOCTOR.) You, on the other hand, can cite no extenuating circumstances for your offense, huh?

DOCTOR: Except that to err is human.

AZDAK: And you are aware that in money matters a good doctor is a highly responsible person? I once heard of a doctor who got a thousand piasters for a sprained finger by remarking that sprains have something to do with blood circulation, which after all a less good doctor might have over-looked, and who, on another occasion made a real gold mine out of a somewhat disordered gall bladder, he treated it with such loving care. You have no excuse, Doctor. The corn merchant Uxu had his son study medicine to get some knowledge of trade, our medical schools are so good. (*To the* BLACKMAILER.) What's the landowner's name?

SHAUWA: He doesn't want it mentioned.

AZDAK: In that case I will pass judgment. The Court considers the blackmail proved. And you (*to the* INVALID) are sentenced to a fine of one thousand piasters. If you have a second stroke, the doctor will have to treat you free. Even if he has to amputate. (*To the* LIMPING MAN.) As compensation, you will receive a bottle of rubbing alcohol. (*To the* BLACKMAILER.) You are sentenced to hand over half the proceeds of your deal to the Public Prosecutor to keep the landowner's name secret. You are advised, moreover, to study medicine—you seem well suited to that calling. (*To the* DOCTOR.) You have perpetrated an unpardonable error in the practice of your profession: you are acquitted. Next cases!

SINGER AND CHORUS: Men won't do much for a shilling.
    For a pound they may be willing.
    For twenty pounds the verdict's in the sack.
    As for the many, all too many,
    Those who've only got a penny—
    They've one single, sole recourse: Azdak.

(Enter AZDAK *from the caravansary on the highroad, followed by an old bearded* INNKEEPER. *The judge's chair is carried by a stableman and* SHAUWA. *An* IRONSHIRT, *with a banner, takes up his position.)*

AZDAK: Put me down. Then we'll get some air, maybe even a good stiff breeze from the lemon grove there. It does justice good to be done in the open: the wind blows her skirts up and you can see what she's got. Shauwa, we've been eating too much. These official journeys are exhausting. (*To the* INNKEEPER.) It's a question of your daughter-in-law?

INNKEEPER: Your Worship, it's a question of the family honor. I wish to bring an action on behalf of my son, who's away on business on the other side of the mountain. This is the offending stableman, and here's my daughter-in-law.

(Enter the DAUGHTER-IN-LAW, *a voluptuous wench. She is veiled.)*

AZDAK (*sitting down*): I accept. (*Sighing, the* INNKEEPER *hands him some money.*) Good. Now the formalities are disposed of. This is a case of rape?

INNKEEPER: Your Honor, I caught the fellow in the act. Ludovica was in the straw on the stable floor.

AZDAK: Quite right, the stable. Lovely horses! I specially liked the little roan.

INNKEEPER: The first thing I did, of course, was to question Ludovica. On my son's behalf.

AZDAK (*seriously*): I said I specially liked the little roan.

INNKEEPER (*coldly*): Really? Ludovica confessed the stableman took her against her will.

AZDAK: Take your veil off, Ludovica. (*She does so.*) Ludovica, you please the Court. Tell us how it happened.

LUDOVICA (*well schooled*): When I entered the stable to see the new foal the stableman said to me on his own accord: "It's hot today!" and laid his hand on my left breast. I said to him: "Don't do that!" But he continued to handle me indecently, which provoked my anger. Before I realized his sinful intentions, he got much closer. It was all over when my father-in-law entered and accidentally trod on me.

INNKEEPER (*explaining*): On my son's behalf.

AZDAK (*to the* STABLEMAN): You admit you started it?

STABLEMAN: Yes.

AZDAK: Ludovica, you like to eat sweet things?

LUDOVICA: Yes, sunflower seeds!

AZDAK: You like to lie a long time in the bathtub?

LUDOVICA: Half an hour or so.

AZDAK: Public Prosecutor, drop your knife—there on the ground. (SHAUWA *does so.*) Ludovica, pick up that knife. (LUDOVICA, *swaying her hips, does so.*) See that? (*He points at her.*) The way it moves? The rape is now proven. By eating too much—sweet things, especially—by lying too long in warm water, by laziness and too soft a skin, you have raped that unfortunate man. Think you can run around with a behind like that and get away with it in court? This is a case of intentional assault with a dangerous weapon! You are sentenced to hand over to the Court the little roan which your father liked to ride "on his son's behalf." And now, come with me to the stables, so the Court can inspect the scene of the crime, Ludovica.

SINGER AND CHORUS: When the sharks the sharks devour
Little fishes have their hour.
For a while the load is off their back.
On Grusinia's highways faring
Fixed-up scales of justice bearing
Strode the poor man's magistrate: Azdak.

And he gave to the forsaken
All that from the rich he'd taken.
And a bodyguard of roughnecks was Azdak's.
And our good and evil man, he
Smiled upon Grusinia's Granny.
His emblem was a tear in sealing wax.

All mankind should love each other
But when visiting your brother
Take an ax along and hold it fast.
Not in theory but in practice
Miracles are wrought with axes
And the age of miracles is not past.

> (AZDAK's *judge's chair is in a tavern. Three rich* FARMERS *stand before* AZDAK. SHAUWA *brings him wine. In a corner stands an* OLD PEASANT WOMAN. *In the doorway, and outside, stand villagers looking on. An* IRONSHIRT *stands guard with a banner.*)

AZDAK: The Public Prosecutor has the floor.

SHAUWA: It concerns a cow. For five weeks, the defendant has had a cow in her stable, the property of the farmer Suru. She was also found to be in possession of a stolen ham, and a number of cows belonging to Shutoff were killed after he asked the defendant to pay the rent on a piece of land.

FARMERS: —It's a matter of my ham, Your Honor.
        —It's a matter of my cow, Your Honor.
        —It's a matter of my land, Your Honor.

AZDAK: Well, Granny, what have *you* got to say to all this?

OLD WOMAN: Your Honor, one night toward morning, five weeks ago, there was a knock at my door, and outside stood a bearded man with a cow. "My dear woman," he said, "I am the miracle-working Saint Banditus and because your son has been killed in the war, I bring you this cow as a souvenir. Take good care of it.''

FARMERS: —The robber, Irakli, Your Honor!
—Her brother-in-law, Your Honor!
—The cow-thief!
—The incendiary!
—He must be beheaded!

(*Outside, a woman screams. The crowd grows restless, retreats. Enter the* BANDIT *Irakli with a huge ax.*)

BANDIT: A very good evening, dear friends! A glass of vodka!

FARMERS (*crossing themselves*): Irakli!

AZDAK: Public Prosecutor, a glass of vodka for our guest. And who are you?

BANDIT: I'm a wandering hermit, Your Honor. Thanks for the gracious gift. (*He empties the glass which* SHAUWA *has brought.*) Another!

AZDAK: I am Azdak. (*He gets up and bows. The* BANDIT *also bows.*) The Court welcomes the foreign hermit. Go on with your story, Granny.

OLD WOMAN: Your Honor, that first night I didn't yet know Saint Banditus could work miracles, it was only the cow. But one night, a few days later, the farmer's servants came to take the cow away again. Then they turned round in front of my door and went off without the cow. And bumps as big as a fist sprouted on their heads. So I knew that Saint Banditus had changed their hearts and turned them into friendly people.

(*The* BANDIT *roars with laughter.*)

FIRST FARMER: I know what changed them.

AZDAK: That's fine. You can tell us later. Continue.

OLD WOMAN: Your Honor, the next one to become a good man was the farmer Shutoff—a devil, as everyone knows. But Saint Banditus arranged it so he let me off the rent on the little piece of land.

SECOND FARMER: Because my cows were killed in the field.

(*The* BANDIT *laughs.*)

OLD WOMAN (*answering* AZDAK's *sign to continue*): Then one morning the ham came flying in at my window. It hit me in the small of the back. I'm still lame, Your Honor, look. (*She limps a few steps. The* BANDIT *laughs.*) Your Honor, was there ever a time when a poor old woman could get a ham *without* a miracle?

(*The* BANDIT *starts sobbing.*)

AZDAK (*rising from his chair*): Granny, that's a question that strikes against at the Court's heart. Be so kind as to sit here. (*The* OLD WOMAN, *hesitating, sits in the judge's chair.*)

AZDAK (*sits on the floor, glass in hand, reciting*): Granny
We could almost call you Granny Grusinia
The Woebegone
The Bereaved Mother

Whose sons have gone to war.
Receiving the present of a cow
She bursts out crying.
When she is beaten
She remains hopeful.
When she's not beaten
She's surprised.
On us
Who are already damned
May you render a merciful verdict
Granny Grusinia!

(*Bellowing at the* FARMERS.) Admit you don't believe in miracles, you atheists! Each of you is sentenced to pay five hundred piasters! For godlessness! Get out! (*The* FARMERS *slink out.*) And you Granny, and you (*to the* BANDIT) pious man, empty a pitcher of wine with the Public Prosecutor and Azdak!

SINGER AND CHORUS: And he broke the rules to save them.
Broken law like bread he gave them,
Brought them to shore upon his crooked back.
At long last the poor and lowly
Had someone who was not too holy
To be bribed by empty hands: Azdak.

For two years it was his pleasure
To give the beasts of prey short measure:
He became a wolf to fight the pack.
From All Hallows to All Hallows
On his chair beside the gallows
Dispensing justice in his fashion sat Azdak.

SINGER: But the era of disorder came to an end.
The Grand Duke returned.
The Governor's wife returned.
A trial was held.
Many died.
The people's quarters burned anew.
And fear seized Azdak.

> (AZDAK's *judge's chair stands again in the court of justice.* AZDAK *sits on the floor, shaving and talking to* SHAUWA. *Noises outside. In the rear the* FAT PRINCE's *head is carried by on a lance.*)

AZDAK: Shauwa, the days of your slavery are numbered, maybe even the minutes. For a long time now I have held you in the iron curb of reason, and it has torn your mouth till it bleeds. I have lashed you with reasonable arguments, I have manhandled you with logic. You are by nature a weak man, and if one slyly throws an argument in your path, you *have* to snap it up, you can't resist. It is your nature to lick the hand of some superior being. But superior beings can be of very different kinds. And now, with your liberation, you will soon be able to follow your natural inclinations, which are low. You will be able to follow your infallible instinct, which teaches you to plant your fat heel on the faces of men. Gone is the era of confusion and disorder, which I find described in the Song of Chaos. Let us now sing that song together in memory of those terrible days. Sit down and don't do violence to the music. Don't be afraid. It sounds all right. And it has a fine refrain. (*He sings.*)

The Song of Chaos

Sister, hide your face! Brother, take your knife!
The times are out of joint!
Big men are full of complaint
And small men full of joy.
The city says:
"Let us drive the mighty from our midst!"
Offices are raided. Lists of serfs are destroyed.
They have set Master's nose to the grindstone.
They who lived in the dark have seen the light.
The ebony poor box is broken.
Sesnem² wood is sawed up for beds.
Who had no bread have full barns.
Who begged for alms of corn now mete it out.

SHAUWA (*refrain*):

Oh, oh, oh, oh.

AZDAK (*refrain*):

Where are you, General, where are you?
Please, please, please, restore order!

The nobleman's son can no longer be recognized;
The lady's child becomes the son of her slave-girl
The councilors meet in a shed.
Once, this man was barely allowed to sleep on the wall;
Now, he stretches him limbs in a bed.
Once, this man rowed a boat; now, he owns ships.
Their owner looks for them, but they're his no longer.
Five men are sent on a journey by their master.
"Go yourself," they say, "we have arrived."

SHAUWA (*refrain*):

Oh, oh, oh, oh.

2. "I do not know what kind of wood this is, so I have left the word exactly as it stands in the German original. The song is based on an Egyptian papyrus which Brecht cites as such in his essay, "Five Difficulties in the Writing of the Truth." I should think he must have come across it in Adolf Erman's *Die Literatur der Aegypter*, 1923, pp. 130 ff. Erman too gives the word as Sesnem. The same papyrus is quoted in Karl Jaspers' *Man in the Modern Age* (Anchor edition, pp. 18–19) but without the sentence about the Sesnem wood." [Bentley's note.]

AZDAK (*refrain*):

> Where are you, General, where are you?
> Please, please, please, restore order!

Yes, so it might have been, had order been neglected much longer. But now the Grand Duke has returned to the capital, and the Persians have lent him an army to restore order with. The people's quarters are already aflame. Go and get me the big book I always sit on. (SHAUWA *brings the big book from the judge's chair.* AZDAK *opens it.*) This is the Statute Book and I've always used it, as you can testify. Now I'd better look in this book and see what they can do to me. I've let the down-and-outs get away with murder, and I'll have to pay for it. I helped poverty onto its skinny legs, so they'll hang me for drunkenness. I peeped into the rich man's pocket, which is bad taste. And I can't hide anywhere—everybody knows me because I've helped everybody.

SHAUWA: Someone's coming!

AZDAK (*in panic, he walks trembling to the chair*): It's the end. And now they'd enjoy seeing what a Great Man I am. I'll deprive them of that pleasure. I'll beg on my knees for mercy. Spittle will slobber down my chin. The fear of death is in me.

> (*Enter* NATELLA ABASHWILI, *the* GOVERNOR'S WIFE, *followed by the* ADJUTANT *and an* IRONSHIRT.)

GOVERNOR'S WIFE: What sort of a creature is that, Shalva?

AZDAK: A willing one, Your Highness, a man ready to oblige.

ADJUTANT: Natella Abashwili, wife of the late Governor, has just returned. She is looking for her two-year-old son, Michael. She has been informed that the child was carried off to the mountains by a former servant.

AZDAK: The child will be brought back, Your Highness, at your service.

ADJUTANT: They say that the person in question is passing it off as her own.

AZDAK: She will be beheaded, Your Highness, at your service.

ADJUTANT: That is all.

GOVERNOR'S WIFE (*leaving*): I don't like that man.

AZDAK (*following her to door, bowing*): At your service, Your Highness, it will all be arranged.

FIVE. THE CHALK CIRCLE

SINGER: Hear now the story of the trial
Concerning Governor Abashwili's child
And the determination of the true mother
By the famous test of the Chalk Circle.

> (*Law court in Nuka.* IRONSHIRTS *lead* MICHAEL *across stage and out at the back.* IRONSHIRTS *hold* GRUSHA *back with their lances under the gateway until the* CHILD *has been led through. Then she is*

admitted. She is accompanied by the former GOVERNOR'S COOK. *Distant noises and a fire-red sky.*)

GRUSHA (*trying to hide*): He's brave, he can wash himself now.

COOK: You're lucky. It's not a real judge. It's Azdak, a drunk who doesn't know what he's doing. The biggest thieves have got by through him. Because he gets everything mixed up and the rich never offer him big enough bribes, the like of us sometimes do pretty well.

GRUSHA: I *need* luck right now.

COOK: Touch wood. (*She crosses herself.*) I'd better offer up another prayer that the judge may be drunk. (*She prays with motionless lips, while* GRUSHA *looks around, in vain, for the* CHILD.) Why must you hold on to it at any price if it isn't yours? In days like these?

GRUSHA: He's mine. I brought him up.

COOK: Have you ever thought what'd happen when she came back?

GRUSHA: At first I thought I'd give him to her. Then I thought she wouldn't come back.

COOK: And even a borrowed coat keeps a man warm, hm? (GRUSHA *nods.*) I'll swear to anything for you. You're a decent girl. (*She sees the soldier* SIMON SHASHAVA *approaching.*) You've done wrong by Simon, though. I've been talking with him. He just can't understand.

GRUSHA (*unaware of* SIMON'S *presence*): Right now I can't be bothered whether he understands or not!

COOK: He knows the child isn't yours, but you married and not free "till death do you part"—he can't understand *that.*

(GRUSHA *sees* SIMON *and greets him.*)

SIMON (*gloomily*): I wish the lady to know I will swear I am the father of the child.

GRUSHA (*low*): Thank you, Simon.

SIMON: At the same time I wish the lady to know my hands are not tied—nor are hers.

COOK: You needn't have said that. You know she's married.

SIMON: And it needs no rubbing in.

(*Enter an* IRONSHIRT.)

IRONSHIRT: Where's the judge? Has anyone seen the judge?

ANOTHER IRONSHIRT (*stepping forward*): The judge isn't here yet. Nothing but a bed and a pitcher in the whole house!

(*Exeunt* IRONSHIRTS.)

COOK: I hope nothing has happened to him. With any other judge you'd have as much chance as a chicken has teeth.

GRUSHA (*who has turned away and covered her face*): Stand in front of me. I shouldn't have come to Nuka. If I run into the Ironshirt, the one I hit over the head . . .

(*She screams. An* IRONSHIRT *had stopped and, turning his back, had been listening to her. He now wheels around. It is the* CORPORAL, *and he has a huge scar across is face.*)

IRONSHIRT (*in the gateway*): What's the matter, Shotta? Do you know her?

CORPORAL (*after staring for some time*): No.

IRONSHIRT: She's the one who stole the Abashwili child, or so they say. If you know anything about it you can make some money, Shotta.

(*Exit the* CORPORAL, *cursing.*)

COOK: Was it him? (GRUSHA *nods.*) I think he'll keep his mouth shut, or he'd be admitting he was after the child.

GRUSHA: I'd almost forgotten him.

(*Enter the* GOVERNOR'S WIFE, *followed by the* ADJUTANT *and two* LAWYERS.)

GOVERNOR'S WIFE: At least there are no common people here, thank God. I can't stand their smell. It always gives me migraine.

FIRST LAWYER: Madam, I must ask you to be careful what you say until we have another judge.

GOVERNOR'S WIFE: But I didn't say anything, Illo Shuboladze. I love the people with their simple straightforward minds. It's only that their smell brings on my migraine.

SECOND LAWYER: There won't be many spectators. The whole population is sitting at home behind locked doors because of the riots in the people's quarters.

GOVERNOR'S WIFE (*looking at* GRUSHA): Is that the creature?

FIRST LAWYER: Please, most gracious Natella Abashwili, abstain from invective until it is certain the Grand Duke has appointed a new judge and we're rid of the present one, who's about the lowest fellow ever seen in judge's gown. Things are all set to move, you see.

(*Enter* IRONSHIRTS *from the courtyard.*)

COOK: Her Grace would pull your hair out on the spot if she didn't know Azdak is for the poor. He goes by the face.

(IRONSHIRTS *begin fastening a rope to a beam.* AZDAK, *in chains, is led in, followed by* SHAUWA, *also in chains. The three* FARMERS *bring up the rear.*)

AN IRONSHIRT: Trying to run away, were you? (*He strikes* AZDAK.)

ONE FARMER: Off with his judge's gown before we string him up!

(IRONSHIRTS *and* FARMERS *tear off* AZDAK'*s gown. His torn underwear is visible. Then someone kicks him.*)

AN IRONSHIRT (*pushing him into someone else*): What a load of justice? Here it is!

(*Accompanied by shouts of* "You take it!" *and* "Let me have him, Brother!" *they throw* AZDAK *back and forth until he collapses. Then he is lifted up and dragged under the noose.*)

GOVERNOR'S WIFE (*who, during this "ballgame," has clapped her hands hysterically*): I disliked that man from the moment I first saw him.

AZDAK (*covered with blood, panting*): I can't see. Give me a rag.

AN IRONSHIRT: What is it you want to see?

AZDAK: You, you dogs! (*He wipes the blood out of his eyes with his shirt.*) Good morning, dogs! How goes it, dogs! How's the dog world? Does it smell good? Got another boot for me to lick? Are you back at each other's throats, dogs?

> (*Accompanied by a* CORPORAL, *a dust-covered* RIDER *enters. He takes some documents from a leather case, looks at them, then interrupts.*)

RIDER: Stop! I bring a dispatch from the Grand Duke, containing the latest appointments.

CORPORAL (*bellowing*): Atten—shun!

RIDER: Of the new judge it says: "We appoint a man whom we have to thank for saving a life indispensable to the country's welfare—a certain Azdak of Nuka." Which is he?

SHAUWA (*pointing*): That's him, Your Excellency.

CORPORAL (*bellowing*): What's going on here?

AN IRONSHIRT: I beg to report that His Honor Azdak was already His Honor Azdak, but on these farmers' denunciation was pronounced the Grand Duke's enemy.

CORPORAL (*pointing at the* FARMERS): March them off! (*They are marched off. They bow all the time.*) See to it that His Honor Azdak is exposed to no more violence.

> (*Exeunt* RIDER *and* CORPORAL.)

COOK (*to* SHAUWA): She clapped her hands! I hope he saw it!

FIRST LAWYER: It's a catastrophe.

> (AZDAK *has fainted. Coming to, he is dressed again in judge's robes. He walks, swaying, toward the* IRONSHIRTS.)

AN IRONSHIRT: What does Your Honor desire?

AZDAK: Nothing, fellow dogs, or just an occasional boot to lick. (*To* SHAUWA.) I pardon you. (*He is unchained.*) Get me some red wine, the sweet kind. (SHAUWA *stumbles off.*) Get out of here, I've got to judge a case. (*Exeunt* IRONSHIRTS. SHAUWA *returns with a pitcher of wine.* AZDAK *gulps it down.*) Something for my backside. (SHAUWA *brings the Statute Book, puts it on the judge's chair.* AZDAK *sits on it.*) I accept.

> (*The* PROSECUTORS, *among whom a worried council has been held, smile with relief. They whisper.*)

COOK: Oh dear!

SIMON: A well can't be filled with dew, they say.

LAWYERS (*approaching* AZDAK, *who stands up, expectantly*): A quite ridiculous case, Your Honor. The accused has abducted a child and refuses to hand it over.

AZDAK (*stretching out his hand, glancing at* GRUSHA): A most attractive person. (*He fingers the money, then sits down, satisfied.*) I declare the proceedings open and demand the whole truth. (*To* GRUSHA.) Especially from you.

FIRST LAWYER: High Court of Justice! Blood, as the popular saying goes, is thicker than water. This old adage . . .

AZDAK (*interrupting*): The Court wants to know the lawyers' fee.

FIRST LAWYER (*surprised*): I beg your pardon? (AZDAK, *smiling, rubs his thumb and index finger.*) Oh, I see. Five hundred piasters, Your Honor, to answer the Court's somewhat unusual question.

AZDAK: Did you hear? The question is unusual. I ask it because I listen in quite a different way when I know you're good.

FIRST LAWYER (*bowing*): Thank you, Your Honor. High Court of Justice, of all ties the ties of blood are strongest. Mother and child—is there a more intimate relationship. Can one tear a child from its mother? High Court of Justice, she has conceived it in the holy ecstasies of love. She has carried it in her womb. She has fed it with her blood. She has borne it with pain. High Court of Justice, it has been observed that the wild tigress, robbed of her young, roams restless through the mountains, shrunk to a shadow. Nature herself . . .

AZDAK (*interrupting, to* GRUSHA): What's your answer to all this and anything else that lawyer might have to say?

GRUSHA: He's mine.

AZDAK: Is that all? I hope you can prove it. Why should I assign the child to you in any case?

GRUSHA: I brought him up like the priest says "according to my best knowledge and conscience." I always found him something to eat. Most of the time he had a roof over his head. And I went to such trouble for him. I had expenses too. I didn't look out for my own comfort. I brought the child up to be friendly with everyone, and from the beginning taught him to work. As well as he could, that is. He's still very little.

FIRST LAWYER: Your Honor, it is significant that the girl herself doesn't claim any tie of blood between her and the child.

AZDAK: The Court takes note of that.

FIRST LAWYER: Thank you, Your Honor. And now permit a woman bowed in sorrow—who has already lost her husband and now has also to fear the loss of her child—to address a few words to you. The gracious Natella Abashwili is . . .

GOVERNOR'S WIFE (*quietly*): A more cruel fate, sir, forces me to describe to you the tortures of a bereaved mother's soul, the anxiety, the sleepless nights, the . . .

SECOND LAWYER (*bursting out*): It's outrageous the way this woman is being treated! Her husband's palace is closed to her! The revenue of her estates is blocked, and she is cold-bloodedly told that it's tied to the heir. She can't do a thing without that child. She can't even pay her lawyers!! (*To the* FIRST LAWYER, *who, desperate about this outburst, makes frantic gestures to keep him from speaking.*) Dear Illo Shuboladze, surely it can be divulged now that the Abashwili estates are at stake?

FIRST LAWYER: Please, Honored Sandro Oboladze! We agreed . . . (*To* AZDAK.) Of course it is correct that the trial will also decide if our noble client can take over the Abashwili estates, which are rather extensive. I say "also" advisedly, for in the foreground stands the human tragedy of a mother, as Natella Abashwili very properly explained in the first words of her moving statement. Even if Michael Abashwili were not heir to the estates, he would still be the dearly beloved child of my client.

AZDAK: Stop! The Court is touched by the mention of estates. It's a proof of human feeling.

SECOND LAWYER: Thanks, Your Honor. Dear Illo Shuboladze, we can prove in any case that the woman who took the child is not the child's mother. Permit me to lay before the Court the bare facts. High Court of Justice, by an unfortunate chain of circumstances, Michael Abashwili was left behind on that Easter Sunday while his mother was making her escape. Grusha, a palace kitchen maid, was seen with the baby . . .

COOK: All her mistress was thinking of was what dresses she'd take along!

SECOND LAWYER (*unmoved*): Nearly a year later Grusha turned up in a mountain village with a baby and there entered into the state of matrimony with . . .

AZDAK: How'd you get to that mountain village?

GRUSHA: On foot, Your Honor. And he was mine.

SIMON: I'm the father, Your Honor.

COOK: I used to look after it for them, Your Honor. For five piasters.

SECOND LAWYER: This man is engaged to Grusha, High Court of Justice: his testimony is suspect.

AZDAK: Are you the man she married in the mountain village?

AZDAK (*to* GRUSHA): Why? (*Pointing at* SIMON.) Is he no good in bed? Tell the truth.

GRUSHA: We didn't get that far. I married because of the baby. So he'd have a roof over his head. (*Pointing at* SIMON.) He was in the war, Your Honor.

AZDAK: And now he wants you back again, huh?

SIMON: I wish to state in evidence . . .

GRUSHA (*angrily*): I am no longer free, Your Honor.

AZDAK: And the child, you claim, comes from whoring? (GRUSHA *doesn't answer.*) I'm going to ask you a question: What kind of child is he? A ragged little bastard? Or from a good family?

GRUSHA (*angrily*): He's an ordinary child.

AZDAK: I mean—did he have refined features from the beginning?

GRUSHA: He had a nose on his face.

AZDAK: A very significant comment! It has been said of me that I went out one time and sniffed at a rosebush before rendering a verdict—tricks like that are needed nowadays. Well, I'll make it short, and not listen to any more lies. (*To* GRUSHA.) Especially not yours. (*To all the accused.*) I can imagine what you've cooked up to cheat me! I know you people. You're swindlers.

GRUSHA (*suddenly*): I can understand you wanting to cut it short, now I've seen what you accepted!

AZDAK: Shut up! Did I accept anything from you?

GRUSHA (*while the* COOK *tries to restrain her*): I haven't got anything.

AZDAK: True. Quite true. From starvelings I never get a thing. I might just as well starve, myself. You want justice, but do you want to pay for it, hm? When you go to a butcher you know you have to pay, but you people go to a judge as if you were off to a funeral supper.

SIMON (*loudly*): When the horse was shod, the horsefly held out its leg, as the saying is.

AZDAK (*eagerly accepting the challenge*): Better a treasure in manure than a stone in a mountain stream.

SIMON: A fine day. Let's go fishing, said the angler to the worm.

AZDAK: I'm my own master, said the servant, and cut off his foot.

SIMON: I love you as a father, said the Czar to the peasants, and had the Czarevitch's head chopped off.

AZDAK: A fool's worst enemy is himself.

SIMON: However, a fart has no nose.

AZDAK: Fined ten piasters for indecent language in court! That'll teach you what justice is.

GRUSHA (*furiously*): A fine kind of justice! You play fast and loose with us because we don't talk as refined as that crowd with their lawyers.

AZDAK: That's true. You people are too dumb. It's only right you should get it in the neck.

GRUSHA: You want to hand the child over to her, and she wouldn't even know how to keep it dry, she's so "refined"! You know about as much about justice as I do!

AZDAK: There's something in that. I'm an ignorant man. Haven't even a decent pair of pants on under this gown. Look! With me, everything goes on food and drink—I was educated in a convent. Incidentally, I'll fine you ten piasters for contempt of court. And you're a very silly girl, to turn me against you, instead of making eyes at me and wiggling your backside a little to keep me in a good temper. Twenty piasters!

GRUSHA: Even if it was thirty, I'd tell you what I think of your justice, you drunken onion! (*Incoherently.*) How dare you talk to me like the cracked Isaiah on the church window? As if you were somebody? For you weren't born to this. You weren't born to rap your own mother on the knuckles if she swipes a little bowl of salt someplace. Aren't you ashamed of yourself when you see how I tremble before you? You've made yourself their servant so no one will take their houses from them—houses they had stolen! Since when have houses belonged to the bedbugs? But you're on the watch, or they couldn't drag our men into their wars! You bribetaker!

> (AZDAK *half gets up, starts beaming. With his little hammer he half-heartedly knocks on the table as if to get silence. As* GRUSHA's *scolding continues, he only beats time with his hammer.*)

I've no respect for you. No more than for a thief or a bandit with a knife! You can do what you want. You can take the child away from me, a hundred against one, but I tell you one thing: only extortioners should be chosen for a profession like yours, and men who rape children! As punishment! Yes, let *them* sit in judgment on their fellow creatures. It is worse than to hang from the gallows.

AZDAK (*sitting down*): Now it'll be thirty! And I won't go on squabbling with you—we're not in a tavern. What'd happen to my dignity as a judge? Anyway, I've lost interest in your case. Where's the couple who wanted a divorce? (*To* SHAUWA.) Bring 'em in. This case is adjourned for fifteen minutes.

FIRST LAWYER (*to the* GOVERNOR'S WIFE): Even without using the rest of the evidence, Madam, we have the verdict in the bag.

COOK (*to* GRUSHA): You've gone and spoiled your chances with him. You won't get the child now.

GOVERNOR'S WIFE: Shalva, my smelling salts!

(*Enter a very* OLD COUPLE.)

AZDAK: I accept. (*The* OLD COUPLE *don't understand.*) I hear you want to be divorced. How long have you been together?

OLD WOMAN: Forty years, Your Honor.

AZDAK: And why do you want a divorce?

OLD MAN: We don't like each other, Your Honor.

AZDAK: Since when?

OLD WOMAN: Oh, from the very beginning, Your Honor.

AZDAK: I'll think about your request and render my verdict when I'm through with the other case. (SHAUWA *leads them back.*) I need the child. (*He beckons* GRUSHA *to him and bends* GRUSHA *to him and bends not unkindly toward her.*) I've noticed you have a soft spot for justice. I don't believe he's your child, but if he *were* yours, woman, wouldn't you want him to be rich? You'd only have to say he wasn't yours, and he'd have a palace and many horses in his stable and many beggars on his doorstep and many soldiers in his service and many petitioners in his courtyard, wouldn't he? What do you say—don't you want him to be rich?

(GRUSHA *is silent.*)

SINGER: Hear now what the angry girl thought but did not say:

Had he golden shoes to wear
He'd be cruel as a bear
Evil would his life disgrace.
He'd laugh in my face.

Carrying a heart of flint
Is too troublesome a stint.
Being powerful and bad
Is hard on a lad.

Then let hunger be his foe!
Hungry men and women, no.

Let him fear the darksome night
But not daylight!

AZDAK: I think I understand you, woman.

GRUSHA (*suddenly and loudly*): I won't give him up. I've raised him, and he knows me.

(*Enter* SHAUWA *with the* CHILD.)

GOVERNOR'S WIFE: He's in rags!

GRUSHA: That's not true. But I wasn't given time to put his good shirt on.

GOVERNOR'S WIFE: He must have been in a pigsty.

GRUSHA (*furiously*): I'm not a pig, but there are some who are! Where did you leave your baby?

GOVERNOR'S WIFE: I'll show you, you vulgar creature! (*She is about to throw herself on* GRUSHA, *but is restrained by her lawyers.*) She's a criminal, she must be whipped. Immediately!

SECOND LAWYER (*holding his hand over her mouth*): Natella Abashwili, you promised . . . Your Honor, the plaintiff's nerves . . .

AZDAK: Plaintiff and defendant! The Court has listened to your case, and has come to no decision as to who the real mother is; therefore, I, the judge, am obliged to *choose* a mother for the child. I'll make a test. Shauwa, get a piece of chalk and draw a circle on the floor. (SHAUWA *does so.*) Now place the child in the center. (SHAUWA *puts* MICHAEL, *who smiles at* GRUSHA, *in the center of the circle.*) Stand near the circle, both of you. (*The* GOVERNOR'S WIFE *and* GRUSHA *step up to the circle.*) Now each of you take the child by one hand. (*They do so.*) The true mother is she who can pull the child out of the circle.

SECOND LAWYER (*quickly*): High Court of Justice, I object! The fate of the great Abashwili estates, which are tied to the child, as the heir, should not be made dependent on such a doubtful duel. In addition, my client does not command the strength of this person, who is accustomed to physical work.

AZDAK: She looks pretty well fed to me. Pull! (*The* GOVERNOR'S WIFE *pulls the* CHILD *out of the circle on her side;* GRUSHA *has let go and stands aghast.*) What's the matter with you? You didn't pull.

GRUSHA: I didn't hold on to him.

FIRST LAWYER (*congratulating the* GOVERNOR'S WIFE): What did I say! The ties of blood!

GRUSHA (*running to* AZDAK): Your Honor, I take back everything I said against you. I ask your forgiveness. But could I keep him till he can speak all the words? He knows a few.

AZDAK: Don't influence the Court. I bet you only know about twenty words yourself. All right, I'll make the test once more, just to be certain. (*The two women take up their positions again.*) Pull! (*Again* GRUSHA *lets go of the* CHILD.)

GRUSHA (*in despair*): I brought him up! Shall I also tear him to bits? I can't!

AZDAK (*rising*): And in this manner the Court has determined the true mother. (*To* GRUSHA.) Take your child and be off. I advise you not to stay in the city with him. (*To the* GOVERNOR'S WIFE.) And you disappear before I fine you for fraud. Your estates fall to the city. They'll be converted into a playground for the children. They need one, and I've decided it'll be called after me: Azdak's Garden.

> (*The* GOVERNOR'S WIFE *has fainted and is carried out by the* LAWYERS *and the* ADJUTANT. GRUSHA *stands motionless.* SHAUWA *leads the* CHILD *toward her.*)

Now I'll take off this judge's gown—it's got too hot for me. I'm not cut out for a hero. In token of farewell I invite you all to a little dance in the meadow outside. Oh, I'd almost forgotten something in my excitement . . . to sign the divorce decree. (*Using the judge's chair as a table, he writes something on a piece of paper, and prepares to leave. Dance music has started.*)

SHAUWA (*having read what is on the paper*): But that's not right. You've not divorced the old people. You've divorced Grusha!

AZDAK: Divorced the wrong couple? What a pity! And I never retract! If I did, how could we keep order in the land? (*To the* OLD COUPLE.) I'll invite you to my party instead. You don't mind dancing with each other, do you? (*To* GRUSHA *and* SIMON.) I've got forty piasters coming from you.

SIMON (*pulling out his purse*): Cheap at the price, Your Honor. And many thanks.

AZDAK (*pocketing the cash*): I'll be needing this.

GRUSHA (*to* MICHAEL): So we'd better leave the city tonight, Michael? (*To* SIMON.) You like him?

SIMON: With my respects, I like him.

GRUSHA: Now I can tell you: I took him because on that Easter Sunday I got engaged to you. So he's a child of love. Michael, let's dance.

> (*She dances with* MICHAEL, SIMON *dances with the* COOK, *the* OLD COUPLE *with each other.* AZDAK *stands lost in thought. The* DANCERS *soon hide from view. Occasionally he is seen, but less and less as more couples join the dance.*)

SINGER: And after that evening Azdak vanished and was never seen again.
The people of Grusinia did not forget him but long remembered
The period of his judging as a brief golden age,
Almost an age of justice.

> (*All the* COUPLES *dance off.* AZDAK *has disappeared.*)

But you, you who have listened to the Story of the Chalk Circle,
Take note what men of old concluded:
That what there is shall go to those who are good for it,
Children to the motherly, that they prosper,
Carts to good drivers, that they be driven well,
The valley to the waterers, that it yield fruit.

Fact Questions and Exercises

1. Describe the action in the Prologue. What is the setting?
2. Identify Michael. Who is his real mother?
3. What happens to the Governor, Georgi Abashwili?
4. Why does Grusha have to run away from the "Caucasian city"?
5. Describe the "Rotten Bridge" episode.
6. Why won't Grusha's brother and sister-in-law let Grusha stay with them?
7. Identify Azdak. What is his original profession? What does he become?
8. How does Azdak determine which woman will keep Michael?
9. Grusha has had to marry the peasant Jussup; how does she get out of this marriage in order to marry Simon?

For Discussing and Writing

1. Characterize Azdak. What kind of judge is he? Does he conform to the usual image of a judge? What does he mean when he says "I'm a rabbit-eater, but you're a maneater"? Azdak uses King Solomon's wisdom in the mother-child argument; does this help to explain his character and motivations?
2. Does Brecht imply that the desire for land and goods corrupts people? If this desire is not the corrupting factor, what is? Does Brecht present any characters who are both corrupt and moral? Does Brecht imply that poor people are kinder in proportion to how poor they are? If so, point out ways in which he makes this idea known. How often, for instance, is Grusha betrayed as she runs away from the Ironshirts?
3. Discuss the form of the play. How effective is the play-within-a-play technique? How does this play differ from most plays insofar as scenes and acts are concerned? How does the Singer serve as a unifying device?
4. Brecht has called this play a parable. In what ways is it a parable? Does Brecht make Biblical allusions? What is the moral? How does the parable (Azdak's and Grusha's story) relate to the situation set forth in the Prologue?
5. Is the play a comedy or a tragedy? If a comedy, how does it compare with *The Misanthrope* or *Major Barbara*? What elements of the play are comic? Are there any tragic elements in the play? If so, what are they? Could you, for instance, compare Azdak to Alceste?

Tennessee Williams [1911–   ]

Thomas Lanier Williams was born in Columbus, Mississippi, but moved to St. Louis, Missouri, when he was seven. He was educated at the University of Missouri, Washington University, and the University of Iowa. His early life, though secure, was marked by numerous family problems: including the mental deterioration of his sister Rose—who serves as the model for Laura in *The Glass Menagerie* (1945). Also, to help support his family, Williams was forced to work for three years in a shoe factory. Although Williams had written several earlier stories and plays, he was not recognized as a playwright until *The Glass Menagerie* was produced. Since then he has generally been considered a dominant figure in American drama. Most of his works have enjoyed great popular and critical success. His plays are marked by their use of symbols, characters who are powerful but distorted, and an often intensely poetic language. Among his best-known plays are *A Streetcar Named Desire* (1947), *The Rose Tattoo* (1951), and *The Night of the Iguana* (1961).

The Glass Menagerie

CHARACTERS

AMANDA WINGFIELD, *the mother, a little woman of great but confused vitality clinging frantically to another time and place. Her character- ization must be carefully created, not copied from type. She is not paranoiac, but her life is paranoia. There is much to admire in Amanda, and as much to love and pity as there is to laugh at. Certainly she has endurance and a* kind of heroism*, and though her foolishness makes her unwittingly cruel at times, there is tenderness in her slight person.*

LAURA WINGFIELD, *her daughter. Amanda, having failed to establish contact with reality, continues to live vitally in her illusions, but Laura's situation is even graver. A childhood illness* has left her crippled*, one leg slightly shorter than the other, and held in a brace. This defect need not be more than suggested on the stage. Stemming from this, Laura's separation increases till she is like a piece of her own glass collection,* too exquisitely fragile to move from the shelf.

TOM WINGFIELD, *her son and the narrator of the play. A poet with a job in a warehouse. His nature is not remorseless, but to escape from a trap he has to act without pity.*

JIM O'CONNOR, *the gentleman caller, a nice, ordinary, young man.*

SCENE: *An alley in St. Louis.*

Part I. *Preparation for a gentleman caller.*

Part II. *The gentleman calls.*

Time: *Now and the Past.*

SCENE ONE

The Wingfield apartment is in the rear of the building, one of those vast hive-like conglomerations of cellular living-units that flower as warty growths in overcrowded urban centers of lower middle-class population and are symptomatic of the impulse of this largest and fundamentally enslaved section of American society to avoid fluidity and differentiation and to exist and function as one interfused mass of automatism.

The apartment faces an alley and is entered by a fire-escape, a structure whose name is a touch of accidental poetic truth, for all of these huge buildings are always burning with the slow and implacable fires of human desperation. The fire-escape is included in the set—that is, the landing of it and steps descending from it.

The scene is memory and is therefore nonrealistic. Memory takes a lot of poetic license. It omits some details; others are exaggerated, according to the emotional value of the articles it touches, for memory is seated predominantly in the heart. The interior is therefore rather dim and poetic.

At the rise of the curtain, the audience is faced with the dark, grim rear wall of the Wingfield tenement. This building, which runs parallel to the footlights, is flanked on both sides by dark, narrow alleys which run into murky canyons of tangled clotheslines, garbage cans and the sinister latticework of neighboring fire-escapes. It is up and down these side alleys that exterior entrances and exits are made, during the play. At the end of TOM's *opening commentary, the dark tenement wall slowly reveals (by means of a transparency) the interior of the ground floor Wingfield apartment.*

Downstage is the living room, which also serves as a sleeping room for LAURA, *the sofa unfolding to make her bed. Upstage, center, and divided by a wide arch or second proscenium with transparent faded portieres (or second curtain), is the dining room. In an old-fashioned what-not in the living room are seen scores of transparent glass animals. A blown-up photograph of the father hangs on the wall of the living room, facing the audience, to the left of the archway. It is the face of a very handsome young man in a doughboy's First World War cap. He is gallantly smiling, ineluctably smiling, as if to say, "I will be smiling forever."*

The audience hears and sees the opening scenes in the dining room through both the transparent fourth wall of the building and the transparent gauze portieres of the dining-room arch. It is during this revealing scene that the fourth wall slowly ascends, out of sight. This transparent exterior wall is not brought down again until the very end of the play, during TOM's *final speech.*

The narrator is an undisguised convention of the play. He takes whatever license with dramatic convention as is convenient to his purposes.

TOM *enters dressed as a merchant sailor from alley, stage*

left, and strolls across the front of the stage to the fire-escape. There
he stops and lights a cigarette. He addresses the audience.

TOM: Yes, I have tricks in my pocket, I have things up my sleeve. But I am the
opposite of a stage magician. He gives you illusion that has the appearance of truth. I give you truth in the pleasant disguise of illusion.

To begin with, I turn back time. I reverse it to that quaint period,
the thirties, when the huge middle class of America was matriculating in a
school for the blind. Their eyes had failed them, or they had failed their
eyes, and so they were having their fingers pressed forcibly down on the
fiery Braille alphabet of a dissolving economy.

In Spain there was revolution. Here there was only shouting and
confusion.

In Spain there was Guernica. Here there were disturbances of
labor, sometimes pretty violent, in otherwise peaceful cities such as
Chicago, Cleveland, Saint Louis . . .

This is the social background of the play. (*Music.*)

The play is memory.

Being a memory play, it is dimly lighted, it is sentimental, it is not
realistic.

In memory everything seems to happen to music. That explains
the fiddle in the wings.

I am the narrator of the play, and also a character in it.

The other characters are my mother, Amanda, my sister, Laura,
and a gentleman caller who appears in the final scenes.

He is the most realistic character in the play, being an emissary
from a world of reality that we were somehow set apart from.

But since I have a poet's weakness for symbols, I am using this
character also as a symbol; he is the long delayed but always expected
something that we live for.

There is a fifth character in the play who doesn't appear except in
this larger-than-life-size photograph over the mantel.

This is our father who left us a long time ago.

He was a telephone man who fell in love with long distances; he
gave up his job with the telephone company and skipped the light
fantastic out of town . . .

The last we heard of him was a picture post-card from Mazatlan,
on the Pacific coast of Mexico, containing a message of two words—

"Hello—Good-bye!" and no address.

I think the rest of the play will explain itself . . .

(AMANDA's *voice becomes audible through the portieres. He divides*
the portieres and enters the upstage area. AMANDA *and* LAURA *are*
seated at a drop-leaf table. Eating is indicated by gestures without
food or utensils. AMANDA *faces the audience.* TOM *and* LAURA *are*
seated in profile.

(*The interior has lit up softly and through the scrim we see*
AMANDA *and* LAURA *seated at the table in the upstage area.*)

AMANDA (*calling*): Tom?

TOM: Yes, Mother.

AMANDA: We can't say grace until you come to the table!

TOM: Coming, Mother. (*He bows slightly and withdraws, reappearing a few moments later in his place at the table.*)

AMANDA (*to her son*): Honey, don't *push* with your *fingers*. If you have to push with something, the thing to push with is a crust of bread. And chew—chew! Animals have sections in their stomachs which enable them to digest food without mastication, but human beings are supposed to chew their food before they swallow it down. Eat food leisurely, son, and really enjoy it. A well-cooked meal has lots of delicate flavors that have to be held in the mouth for appreciation. So chew your food and give your salivary glands a chance to function!

> (TOM *deliberately lays his imaginary fork down and pushes his chair back from the table.*)

TOM: I haven't enjoyed one bite of this dinner because of your constant directions on how to eat it. It's you that make me rush through meals with your hawk-like attention to every bite I take. Sickening—spoils my appetite—all this discussion of—animals' secretion—salivary glands—mastication!

AMANDA (*lightly*): Temperament like a Metropolitan star! (*He rises and crosses downstage.*) You're not excused from the table.

TOM: I'm getting a cigarette.

AMANDA: You smoke too much.

> (LAURA *rises.*)

LAURA: I'll bring in the blanc mange.

> (*He remains standing with his cigarette by the portieres during the following.*)

AMANDA (*rising*): No, sister, no, sister—you be the lady this time and I'll be the darky.

LAURA: I'm already up.

AMANDA: Resume your seat, little sister—I want you to stay fresh and pretty—for gentlemen callers!

LAURA: I'm not expecting any gentlemen callers.

AMANDA (*crossing out to kitchenette. Airily*): Sometimes they come when they are least expected! Why, I remember one Sunday afternoon in Blue Mountain—(*enters kitchenette*).

TOM: I know what's coming!

LAURA: Yes. But let her tell it.

TOM: Again?

LAURA: She loves to tell it.

> (AMANDA *returns with bowl of dessert.*)

AMANDA: One Sunday afternoon in Blue Mountain—your mother received—

seventeen!—gentlemen callers! Why, sometimes there weren't chairs enough to accommodate them all. We had to send the nigger over to bring in folding chairs from the parish house.

TOM (*remaining at portieres*): How did you entertain those gentlemen callers?

AMANDA: I understood the art of conversation!

TOM: I bet you could talk.

AMANDA: Girls in those days *knew* how to talk, I can tell you.

TOM: Yes?

AMANDA: They knew how to entertain their gentlemen callers. It wasn't enough for a girl to be possessed of a pretty face and a graceful figure—although I wasn't slighted in either respect. She also needed to have a nimble wit and a tongue to meet all occasions.

TOM: What did you talk about?

AMANDA: Things of importance going on in the world! Never anything coarse or common or vulgar. (*She addresses* TOM *as though he were seated in the vacant chair at the table though he remains by portieres. He plays this scene as though he held the book.*) My callers were gentlemen—all! Among my callers were some of the most prominent young planters of the Mississippi Delta—planters and sons of planters!

> (TOM *motions for music and a spot of light on* AMANDA. *Her eyes lift, her face glows, her voice becomes rich and elegiac.*)

> There was young Champ Laughlin who later became vice-president of the Delta Planters Bank.

> Hadley Stevenson who was drowned in Moon Lake and left his widow one hundred and fifty thousand in Government bonds.

> There were the Cutrere brothers, Wesley and Bates. Bates was one of my bright particular beaux! He got in a quarrel with that wild Wainwright boy. They shot it out on the floor of Moon Lake Casino. Bates was shot through the stomach. Died in the ambulance on his way to Memphis. His widow was also well-provided for, came into eight or ten thousand acres, that's all. She married him on the rebound—never loved her—carried my picture on him the night he died!

> And there was that boy that every girl in the Delta had set her cap for! That beautiful, brilliant young Fitzhugh boy from Greene County!

TOM: What did he leave his widow?

AMANDA: He never married! Gracious, you talk as though all of my old admirers had turned up their toes to the daisies!

TOM: Isn't this the first you've mentioned that still survives?

AMANDA: That Fitzhugh boy went North and made a fortune—came to be known as the Wolf of Wall Street! He had the Midas touch, whatever he touched turned to gold!

> And I could have been Mrs. Duncan J. Fitzhugh, mind you! But—I picked your *father!*

LAURA (*rising*): Mother, let me clear the table.

AMANDA: No, dear, you go in the front and study your typewriter chart. Or practice your shorthand a little. Stay fresh and pretty!—It's almost time for our gentlemen callers to start arriving. (*She flounces girlishly toward the kitchenette.*) How many do you suppose we're going to entertain this afternoon?

(TOM *throws down the paper and jumps up with a groan.*)

LAURA (*alone in the dining room*): I don't believe we're going to receive any, Mother.

AMANDA (*reappearing, airily*): What? No one—not one? You must be joking! (LAURA *nervously echoes her laugh. She slips in a fugitive manner through the half-open portieres and draws them gently behind her. A shaft of very clear light is thrown on her face against the faded tapestry of the curtains. Music: "The Glass Menagerie" under faintly. Lightly*) Not one gentleman caller? It can't be true! There must be a flood, there must have been a tornado!

LAURA: It isn't a flood, it's not a tornado, Mother. I'm just not popular like you were in Blue Mountain . . . (TOM *utters another groan.* LAURA *glances at him with a faint, apologetic smile. Her voice catching a little.*) Mother's afraid I'm going to be an old maid.

(*The scene dims out with "Glass Menagerie" music.*)

SCENE TWO

On the dark stage the screen is lighted with the image of blue roses.

Gradually LAURA'S *figure becomes apparent and the screen goes out.*

The music subsides.

LAURA *is seated in the delicate ivory chair at the small claw-foot table.*

She wears a dress of soft violet material for a kimono—her hair tied back from her forehead with a ribbon.

She is washing and polishing her collection of glass.

AMANDA *appears on the fire-escape steps. At the sound of her ascent,* LAURA *catches her breath, thrusts the bowl of ornaments away and seats herself stiffly before the diagram of the typewriter keyboard as though it held her spellbound.*

Something has happened to AMANDA. *It is written in her face as she climbs to the landing: a look that is grim and hopeless and a little absurd.*

She has on one of those cheap or imitation velvety-looking cloth coats with imitation fur collar. Her hat is five or six years old, one of those dreadful cloche hats that were worn in the late twenties, and she is clasping an enormous black patent-leater pocketbook with nickel clamps and initials. This is her full-dress outfit, the one she usually wears to the D.A.R.

Before entering she looks through the door.

> *She purses her lips, opens her eyes very wide, rolls them upward and shakes her head.*
>
> *Then she slowly lets herself in the door. Seeing her mother's expression* LAURA *touches her lips with a nervous gesture.*

LAURA: Hello, Mother, I was—

> (*She makes a nervous gesture toward the chart on the wall.* AMANDA *leans against the shut door and stares at* LAURA *with a martyred look.*)

AMANDA: Deception? Deception? (*She slowly removes her hat and gloves, continuing the sweet suffering stare. She lets the hat and gloves fall on the floor—a bit of acting.*)

LAURA (*shakily*): How was the D.A.R. meeting? (AMANDA *slowly opens her purse and removes a dainty white handkerchief which she shakes out delicately and delicately touches to her lips and nostrils.*) Didn't you go to the D.A.R. meeting, Mother?

AMANDA (*faintly, almost inaudibly*): —No.—No. (*Then more forcibly*) I did not have the strength—to go to the D.A.R. In fact, I did not have the courage! I wanted to find a hole in the ground and hide myself in it forever! (*She crosses slowly to the wall and removes the diagram of the typewriter keyboard. She holds it in front of her for a second, staring at it sweetly and sorrowfully—then bites her lips and tears it into two pieces.*)

LAURA (*faintly*): Why did you do that, Mother? (AMANDA *repeats the same procedure with the chart of the Gregg Alphabet.*) Why are you—

AMANDA: Why? Why? How old are you, Laura?

LAURA: Mother, you know my age.

AMANDA: I thought that you were an adult; it seems that I was mistaken. (*She crosses slowly to the sofa and sinks down and stares at* LAURA.)

LAURA: Please don't stare at me, Mother.

> (AMANDA *closes her eyes and lowers her head. Count ten.*)

AMANDA: What are we going to do, what is going to become of us, what is the future?

> (*Count ten.*)

LAURA: Has something happened, Mother? (AMANDA *draws a long breath and takes out the handkerchief again. Dabbing process.*) Mother, has—something happened?

AMANDA: I'll be all right in a minute, I'm just bewildered—(*Count five*)—by life . . .

LAURA: Mother, I wish that you would tell me what's happened!

AMANDA: As you know, I was supposed to be inducted into my office at the D.A.R. this afternoon. But I stopped off at Rubicam's Business College to speak to your teachers about your having a cold and ask them what progress they thought you were making down there.

LAURA: Oh . . .

AMANDA: I went to the typing instructor and introduced myself as your mother. She didn't know who you were. Wingfield, she said. We don't have any such student enrolled at the school!

I assured her she did, that you had been going to classes since early in January.

"I wonder," she said, "if you could be talking about that terribly shy little girl who dropped out of school after only a few days' attendance?"

"No," I said, "Laura, my daughter, has been going to school every day for the past six weeks!"

"Excuse me," she said. She took the attendance book out and there was your name, unmistakably printed, and all the dates you were absent until they decided that you had dropped out of school.

I still said, "No, there must have been some mistake! There must have been some mix-up in the records!"

And she said, "No—I remember her perfectly now. Her hands shook so that she couldn't hit the right keys! The first time we gave a speed-test, she broke down completely—was sick at the stomach and almost had to be carried into the wash-room! After that morning she never showed up any more. We phoned the house but never got any answer"—while I was working at Famous and Barr, I suppose, demonstrating those—Oh!

I felt so weak I could barely keep on my feet!

I had to sit down while they got me a glass of water!

Fifty dollars' tuition, all of our plans—my hopes and ambitions for you—just gone up the spout, just gone up the spout like that.

(LAURA *draws a long breath and gets awkwardly to her feet. She crosses to the victrola and winds it up.*)

What are you doing?

LAURA: Oh! (*She releases the handle and returns to her seat.*)

AMANDA: Laura, where have you been going when you've gone out pretending that you were going to business college?

LAURA: I've just been going out walking.

AMANDA: That's not true.

LAURA: It is. I just went walking.

AMANDA: Walking? Walking? In winter? Deliberately courting pneumonia in that light coat? Where did you walk to, Laura?

LAURA: All sorts of places—mostly in the park.

AMANDA: Even after you'd started catching that cold?

LAURA: It was the lesser of two evils, Mother. I couldn't go back up. I—threw up—on the floor!

AMANDA: From half past seven till after five every day you mean to tell me you walked around the park, because you wanted to make me think that you were still going to Rubicam's Business College?

LAURA: It wasn't as bad as it sounds. I went inside places to get warmed up.

AMANDA: Inside where?

LAURA: I went in the art museum and the bird-houses at the Zoo. I visited the penguins every day! Sometimes I did without lunch and went to the movies. Lately I've been spending most of my afternoons in the Jewel-box, that big glass house where they raise the tropical flowers.

AMANDA: You did all this to deceive me, just for deception? (LAURA *looks down.*) Why?

LAURA: Mother, when you're disappointed, you get that awful suffering look on your face, like the picture of Jesus' mother in the museum!

AMANDA: Hush!

LAURA: I couldn't face it.

(*Pause. A whisper of strings.*)

AMANDA (*hopelessly fingering the huge pocketbook*): So what are we going to do the rest of our lives? Stay home and watch the parades go by? Amuse ourselves with the glass menagerie, darling? Eternally play those worn-out phonograph records your father left as a painful reminder of him?

We won't have a business career—we've given that up because it gave us nervous indigestion! (*Laughs wearily*) What is there left but dependency all our lives? I know so well what becomes of unmarried women who aren't prepared to occupy a position. I've seen such pitiful cases in the South—barely tolerated spinsters living upon the grudging patronage of sister's husband or brother's wife!—stuck away in some little mouse-trap of a room—encouraged by one in-law to visit another—little birdlike women without any nest—eating the crust of humility all their life!

Is that the future that we've mapped out for ourselves?

I swear it's the only alternative I can think of!

It isn't a very pleasant alternative, is it?

Of course—some girls *do marry.*

(LAURA *twists her hands nervously.*)

Haven't you ever liked some boy?

LAURA: Yes. I liked one once. (*Rises*) I came across his picture a while ago.

AMANDA (*with some interest*): He gave you his picture?

LAURA: No, it's in the year-book.

AMANDA (*disappointed*): Oh—a high-school boy.

LAURA: Yes. His name was Jim. (LAURA *lifts the heavy annual from the claw-foot table.*) Here he is in *The Pirates of Penzance.*

AMANDA (*absently*): The what?

LAURA: The operetta the senior class put on. He had a wonderful voice and we sat across the aisle from each other Mondays, Wednesdays and Fridays in the Aud. Here he is with the silver cup for debating! See his grin?

AMANDA (*absently*): He must have had a jolly disposition.

LAURA: He used to call me—Blue Roses.

AMANDA: Why did he call you such a name as that?

Blue roses – symbol of strange, Laura

6 yrs. after high school

LAURA: When I had that attack of pleurosis—he asked me what was the matter when I came back. I said pleurosis—he thought that I said Blue Roses! So that's what he always called me after that. Whenever he saw me, he'd holler, "Hello, Blue Roses!" I didn't care for the girl that he went out with. Emily Meisenbach. Emily was the best-dressed girl at Soldan. She never struck me, though, as being sincere . . . It says in the Personal Section—they're engaged. That's—six years ago! They must be married by now.

AMANDA: Girls that aren't cut out for business careers usually wind up married to some nice man. (*Gets up with a spark of revival.*) Sister, that's what you'll do!

> (LAURA *utters a startled, doubtful laugh. She reaches quickly for a piece of glass.*)

LAURA: But, Mother—

AMANDA: Yes? (*Crossing to photograph.*)

LAURA (*in a tone of frightened apology*): I'm—crippled!

AMANDA: Nonsense! Laura, I've told you never, never to use that word. Why, you're not crippled, you just have a little defect—hardly noticeable, even! When people have some slight disadvantage like that, they cultivate other things to make up for it—develop charm—and vivacity—and—*charm!* That's all you have to do! (*She turns again to the photograph.*) One thing your father had *plenty of*—was *charm!*

> (TOM *motions to the fiddle in the wings. The scene fades out with music.*)

SCENE THREE

> TOM *speaks from the fire-escape landing.*

TOM: After the fiasco at Rubicam's Business College, the idea of getting a gentleman caller for Laura began to play a more and more important part in Mother's calculations.

It became an obsession. Like some archetype of the universal unconscious, the image of the gentleman caller haunted our small apartment . . .

An evening at home rarely passed without some allusion to this image, this spectre, this hope . . .

Even when he wasn't mentioned, his presence hung in Mother's preoccupied look and in my sister's frightened, apologetic manner—hung like a sentence passed upon the Wingfields!

Mother was a woman of action as well as words.

She began to take logical steps in the planned direction.

Late that winter and in the early spring—realizing that extra money would be needed to properly feather the nest and plume the bird—she conducted a vigorous campaign on the telephone, roping in subscribers to one of those magazines for matrons called *The Home-maker's Companion*, the type of journal that features the serialized sublimations of ladies of letters who think in terms of delicate cup-like breasts, slim, tapering waists, rich, creamy thighs, eyes like wood-smoke in autumn, fingers that soothe and caress like strains of music, bodies as powerful as Etruscan sculpture.

> (AMANDA *enters with phone on long extension cord. She is spotted in the dim stage.*)

AMANDA: Ida Scott? This is Amanda <u>Wingfield</u>!

We *missed* you at the D.A.R. last Monday!

I said to myself: She's probably suffering with that sinus condition! How is that sinus condition?

Horrors! Heaven have mercy!—You're a Christian martyr, yes, that's what you are, a Christian martyr!

Well, I just now happened to notice that your subscription to the *Companion's* about to expire! Yes, it expires with the next issue, honey!—just when that wonderful new serial by Bessie Mae Hopper is getting off to such an exciting start. Oh, honey, it's something that you can't miss! You remember how *Gone With the Wind* took everybody by storm? You simply couldn't go out if you hadn't read it. All everybody *talked* was Scarlett O'Hara. Well, this is a book that critics already compare to *Gone With the Wind*. It's the *Gone With the Wind* of the post-World War generation!—What?—Burning?—Oh, honey, don't let them burn, go take a look in the oven and I'll hold the wire! Heavens—I think she's hung up!

> (*Before the stage is lighted, the violent voices of* TOM *and* AMANDA *are heard.*
>
> (*They are quarreling behind the portieres. In front of them stands* LAURA *with clenched hands and panicky expression.*
>
> (*A clear pool of light on her figure throughout this scene.*)

TOM: What in Christ's name am I—

AMANDA (*shrilly*): Don't you use that—

TOM: Supposed to do!

AMANDA: Expression! Not in my—

TOM: Ohhh!

AMANDA: Presence! Have you gone out of your senses?

TOM: I have, that's true, *driven* out!

AMANDA: What is the matter with you, you—big—big—IDIOT!

TOM: Look!—I've got *no thing*, no single thing—

AMANDA: Lower your voice!

TOM: In my life here that I can call my own! Everything is—

AMANDA: Stop that shouting!

TOM: Yesterday you confiscated my books! You had the nerve to—

AMANDA: I took that horrible novel back to the library—yes! That hideous book by that insane Mr. Lawrence. (TOM *laughs wildly.*) I cannot control the output of diseased minds or people who cater to them—(TOM *laughs still more wildly*) BUT I WON'T ALLOW SUCH FILTH BROUGHT INTO MY HOUSE! No, no, no, no, no!

TOM: House, house! Who pays rent on it, who makes a slave of himself to—

AMANDA (*fairly screeching*): Don't you DARE to—

TOM: No, no, *I* mustn't say things! *I've* got to just—

AMANDA: Let me tell you—

TOM: I don't want to hear any more!

> (*He tears the portieres open. The upstage area is lit with a turgid smoky red glow.*
>
> > (AMANDA'*s hair is in metal curlers and she wears a very old bathrobe, much too large for her slight figure, a relic of the faithless Mr. Wingfield.*
> >
> > (*An upright typewriter and a wild disarray of manuscripts is on the drop-leaf table. The quarrel was probably precipitated by* AMANDA'*s interruption of his creative labor. A chair lying overthrown on the floor.*
> > > (*Their gesticulating shadows are cast on the ceiling by the fiery glow.*)

AMANDA: You *will* hear more, you—

TOM: No, I won't hear more, I'm going out!

AMANDA: You come right back in—

TOM: Out, out, out! Because I'm—

AMANDA: Come back here, Tom Wingfield! I'm not through talking to you!

TOM: Oh, go—

LAURA (*desperately*): —Tom!

AMANDA: You're going to listen, and no more insolence from you! I'm at the end of my patience!

> (*He comes back toward her.*)

TOM: What do you think I'm at? Aren't I supposed to have any patience to reach the end of, Mother? I know, I know. It seems unimportant to you, what I'm *doing*—what I *want* to do—having a little *difference* between them! You don't think that—

AMANDA: I think you've been doing things that you're ashamed of. That's why you act like this. I don't believe that you go every night to the movies. Nobody goes to the movies night after night. Nobody in the right minds goes to the movies as often as you pretend to. People don't go to the movies at nearly midnight, and movies don't let out at two A.M. Come in stumbling. Muttering to yourself like a maniac! You get three hours' sleep and then go to work. Oh, I can picture the way you're doing down there. Moping, doping, because you're in no condition.

TOM (*wildly*): No, I'm in no condition!

AMANDA: What right have you got to jeopardize your job? Jeopardize the security of us all? How do you think we'd manage if you were—

TOM: Listen! You think I'm crazy *about* the *warehouse*? (*He bends fiercely toward her slight figure.*) You think I'm in love with the Continental Shoemakers? You think I want to spend fifty-five *years* down there in that—*celotex interior!* with—*fluorescent—tubes!* Look! I'd rather somebody picked up a crowbar and battered out my brains—than go back mornings! I *go!* Every time you come in yelling that God damn *"Rise and Shine!" "Rise and Shine!"* I say to myself, "How *lucky dead* people are!" But I get up. I *go!* For sixty-five dollars a month I give up all that I dream of doing and being *ever!* And you say self—*self's* all I ever think of. Why, listen, if self is what I thought of, Mother, I'd be where he is—GONE! (*Pointing to father's picture*) As far as the system of transportation reaches! (*He starts past her. She grabs his arm.*) Don't grab at me, Mother!

AMANDA: Where are you going?

TOM: I'm going to the *movies!*

AMANDA: I don't believe that lie!

TOM (*crouching toward her, overtowering her tiny figure. She backs away, gasping*): I'm going to opium dens! Yes, opium dens, dens of vice and criminals' hang-outs, Mother. I've joined the Hogan gang, I'm a hired assassin, I carry a tommy-gun in a violin case! I run a string of cat-houses in the Valley! They call me Killer, Killer Wingfield, I'm leading a double-life, a simple, honest warehouse worker by day, by night a dynamic *czar* of the *underworld, Mother.* I go to gambling casinos, I spin away fortunes on the roulette table! I wear a patch over one eye and a false mustache, sometimes I put on green whiskers. On those occasions they call me—*El Diablo!* Oh, I could tell you things to make you sleepless! My enemies plan to dynamite this place. They're going to blow us all sky-high some night! I'll be glad, very happy, and so will you! You'll go up, up on a broomstick, over Blue Mountain with seventeen gentlemen callers! You ugly—babbling old—*witch* . . .

> (*He goes through a series of violent, clumsy movements, seizing his overcoat, lunging to the door, pulling it fiercely open. The women watch him, aghast. His arm catches in the sleeve of the coat as he struggles to pull it on. For a moment is is pinioned by the bulky garment. With an outraged groan he tears the coat off again, splitting the shoulder of it, and hurls it across the room. It strikes against the shelf of LAURA's glass collection, there is a tinkle of shattering glass. LAURA cries out as if wounded. Music: "The Glass Menagerie."*)

LAURA (*shrilly*): *My glass!*—menagerie . . . (*She covers her face and turns away.*)

> (*But AMANDA is still stunned and stupefied by the "ugly witch" so that she barely notices this occurrence. Now she recovers her speech.*)

AMANDA (*in an awful voice*): I won't speak to you—until you apologize!

> (*She crosses through portieres and draws them together behind her. TOM is left with LAURA. LAURA clings weakly to the mantel with her face averted. TOM stares at her stupidly for a moment. Then he crosses to shelf. Drops awkwardly on his knees to collect the fallen glass, glancing at LAURA as if he would speak but couldn't. "The Glass Menagerie" steals in as the scene dims out.*)

SCENE FOUR

> *The interior is dark. Faint light in the alley.*
>
> *A deep-voiced bell in a church is tolling the hour of five as the scene commences.*
>
> TOM *appears at the top of the alley. After each solemn boom of the bell in the tower, he shakes a little noise-maker or rattle as if to express the tiny spasm of man in contrast to the sustained power and dignity of the Almighty. This and the unsteadiness of his advance make it evident that he has been drinking.*
>
> *As he climbs the few steps to the fire-escape landing, light steals up inside.* LAURA *appears in night-dress, observing* TOM'S *empty bed in the front room.*
>
> TOM *fishes in his pockets for door-key, removing a motley assortment of articles in the search, including a perfect shower of movie-ticket stubs and an empty bottle. At last he finds the key, but just as he is about to insert it, it slips from his fingers. He strikes a match and crouches below the door.*

TOM (*bitterly*): One crack—and it falls through!

> (LAURA *opens the door.*)

LAURA: Tom! Tom, what are you doing?

TOM: Looking for a door-key.

LAURA: Where have you been all this time?

TOM: I have been to the movies.

LAURA: All this time at the movies?

TOM: There was a very long program. There was a Garbo picture and a Mickey Mouse and a travelogue and a newsreel and a preview of coming attractions. And there was an organ solo and a collection for the milk-fund—simultaneously—which ended up in a terrible fight between a fat lady and an usher!

LAURA (*innocently*): Did you have to stay through everything?

TOM: Of course! And, oh, I forgot! There was a big stage show! The headliner on this stage show was Malvolio the Magician. He performed wonderful tricks, many of them, such as pouring water back and forth between pitchers. First it turned to wine and then it turned to beer and then it turned to whiskey. I know it was whiskey it finally turned into because he needed somebody to come up out of the audience to help him, and I came up—both shows! It was Kentucky Straight Bourbon. A very generous fellow, he gave souvenirs. (*He pulls from his back pocket a shimmering rainbow-colored scarf.*) He gave me this. This is his magic scarf. You can have it, Laura. You wave it over a canary cage and you get a bowl of goldfish. You wave it over the gold-fish bowl and they fly away canaries . . . But the wonderfullest trick of all was the coffin trick. We nailed him into a coffin and he got out of the coffin without removing one nail. (*He has come inside.*) There is a trick that would come in handy for me—get me out of this 2 by 4 situation! (*Flops onto bed and starts removing shoes.*)

LAURA: Tom—Shhh!

TOM: What're you shushing me for?

LAURA: You'll wake up Mother.

TOM: Goody, goody! Pay 'er back for all those "Rise an' Shines." (*Lies down, groaning*) You know it don't take much intelligence to get yourself into a nailed-up coffin, Laura. But who in hell ever got himself out of one without removing one nail?

> (*As if in answer, the father's grinning photograph lights up. Scene dims out.*
>> (*Immediately following: The church bell is heard striking six. At the sixth stroke the alarm clock goes off in* AMANDA's *room, and after a few moments we hear her calling: "Rise and Shine! Rise and Shine! Laura, go tell your brother to rise and shine!"*)

TOM (*sitting up slowly*): I'll rise—but I won't shine.

> (*The light increases.*)

AMANDA: Laura, tell your brother his coffee is ready.

> (LAURA *slips into front room.*)

LAURA: Tom!—It's nearly seven. Don't make Mother nervous. (*He stares at her stupidly. Beseechingly*) Tom, speak to Mother this morning. Make up with her, apologize, speak to her!

TOM: She won't to me. It's her that started not speaking.

LAURA: If you just say you're sorry she'll start speaking.

TOM: Her not speaking—is that such a tragedy?

LAURA: Please—please!

AMANDA (*calling from kitchenette*): Laura, are you going to do what I asked you to do, or do I have to get dressed and go out myself?

LAURA: Going, going—soon as I get on my coat! (*She pulls on a shapeless felt hat with nervous, jerky movement, pleadingly glancing at* TOM. *Rushes awkwardly for coat. The coat is one of* AMANDA's, *inaccurately made-over, the sleeves too short for* LAURA.) Butter and what else?

AMANDA (*entering upstage*): Just butter. Tell them to charge it.

LAURA: Mother, they make such faces when I do that.

AMANDA: Sticks and stones can break our bones, but the expression on Mr. Garfinkel's face won't harm us! Tell your brother his coffee is getting cold.

LAURA (*at door*): Do what I asked you, will you, will you, Tom?

> (*He looks sullenly away.*)

AMANDA: Laura, go now or just don't go at all!

LAURA (*rushing out*): Going—going!

> (*A second later she cries out.* TOM *springs up and crosses to door.* AMANDA *rushes anxiously in.* TOM *opens the door.*)

TOM: Laura?

LAURA: I'm all right. I slipped, but I'm all right.

AMANDA (*peering anxiously after her*): If anyone breaks a leg on those fire-escape steps, the landlord ought to be sued for every cent he possesses! (*She shuts door. Remembers she isn't speaking and returns to other room.*)

> (*As* TOM *enters listlessly for his coffee, she turns her back to him and stands rigidly facing the window on the gloomy gray vault of the areaway. Its light on her face with its aged but childish features is cruelly sharp, satirical as a Daumier print.*
> (*Music under: "Ave Maria."*
> (TOM *glances sheepishly but sullenly at her averted figure and slumps at the table. The coffee is scalding hot; he sips it and gasps and spits it back in the cup. At his gasp,* AMANDA *catches her breath and half turns. Then catches herself and turns back to window.*
> (TOM *blows on his coffee, glancing sidewise at his mother. She clears her throat.* TOM *clears his. He starts to rise. Sinks back down again, scratches his head, clears his throat again.* AMANDA *coughs.* TOM *raises his cup in both hands to blow on it, his eyes staring over the rim of it at his mother for several moments. Then he slowly sets the cup down and awkwardly and hesitantly rises from the chair.*)

TOM (*hoarsely*): Mother. I—I apologize, Mother. (AMANDA *draws a quick, shuddering breath. Her face works grotesquely. She breaks into childlike tears.*) I'm sorry for what I said, for everything that I said, I didn't mean it.

AMANDA (*sobbingly*): My devotion has made me a witch and so I make myself hateful to my children!

TOM: *No, you don't.*

AMANDA: I worry so much, don't sleep, it makes me nervous!

TOM (*gently*): I understand that.

AMANDA: I've had to put up a solitary battle all these years. But you're my right-hand bower! Don't fall down, don't fail!

TOM (*gently*): I try, Mother.

AMANDA (*with great enthusiasm*): Try and you will SUCCEED! (*The notion makes her breathless.*) Why, you—you're just *full* of natural endowments! Both of my children—they're *unusual* children! Don't you think I know it? I'm so—*proud!* Happy and—feel I've—so much to be thankful for but— Promise me one thing, Son!

TOM: What, Mother?

AMANDA: Promise, son, you'll—never be a drunkard!

TOM (*turns to her grinning*): I will never be a drunkard, Mother.

AMANDA: That's what frightened me so, that you'd be drinking! Eat a bowl of Purina!

TOM: Just coffee, Mother.

AMANDA: Shredded wheat biscuit?

TOM: No. No, Mother, just coffee.

AMANDA: You can't put in a day's work on an empty stomach. You've got ten minutes—don't gulp! Drinking too-hot liquids makes cancer of the stomach . . . Put cream in.

TOM: No, thank you.

AMANDA: To cool it.

TOM: No! No, thank you, I want it black.

AMANDA: I know, but it's not good for you. We have to do all that we can to build ourselves up. In these trying times we live in, all that we have to cling to is—each other . . . That's why it's so important to—Tom, I—I sent out your sister so I could discuss something with you. If you hadn't spoken I would have spoken to you. (*Sits down.*)

TOM (*gently*): What is it, Mother, that you want to discuss?

AMANDA: *Laura!*

> (TOM *puts his cup down slowly.*
> (*Music: "The Glass Menagerie."*)

TOM: —Oh.—Laura . . .

AMANDA (*touching his sleeve*): You know how Laura is. So quiet but—still water runs deep! She notices things and I think she—broods about them. (TOM *looks up.*) A few days ago I came in and she was crying.

TOM: What about?

AMANDA: You.

TOM: Me?

AMANDA: She has an idea that you're not happy here.

TOM: What gave her that idea?

AMANDA: What gives her any idea? However, you do act strangely. I—I'm not criticizing, understand *that!* I know your ambitions do not lie in the warehouse, that like everybody in the whole wide world—you've had to—make sacrifices, but—Tom—Tom—life's not easy, it calls for—Spartan endurance! There's so many things in my heart that I cannot describe to you! I never told you but I—*loved* your father . . .

TOM (*gently*): I know that, Mother.

AMANDA: And you—when I see you taking after his ways! Staying out late—and—well, you *had* been drinking the night you were in that—terrifying condition! Laura says that you hate the apartment and that you go out nights to get away from it! Is that true, Tom?

TOM: No. You say there's so much in your heart that you can't describe to me. That's true of me, too. There's so much in my heart that I can't describe to *you!* So let's respect each other's—

AMANDA: But, why—*why,* Tom—are you always so *restless?* Where do you *go* to, nights?

TOM: I—go to the movies.

AMANDA: Why do you go to the movies so much, Tom?

TOM: I go to the movies because—I like adventure. Adventure is something I don't have much of at work, so I go to the movies.

AMANDA: But, Tom, you go to the movies *entirely* too *much!*

TOM: I like a lot of adventure.

> (AMANDA *looks baffled, then hurt. As the familiar inquisition resumes he becomes hard and impatient again.* AMANDA *slips back into her querulous attitude toward him.*)

AMANDA: Most young men find adventure in their careers.

TOM: Then most young men are not employed in a warehouse.

AMANDA: The world is full of young men employed in warehouses and offices and factories.

TOM: Do all of them find adventure in their careers?

AMANDA: They do or they do without it! Not everybody has a craze for adventure.

TOM: Man is by instinct a lover, a hunter, a fighter, and none of those instincts are given much play at the warehouse!

AMANDA: Man is by instinct! Don't quote instinct to me! Instinct is something that people have got away from! It belongs to animals! Christian adults don't want it!

TOM: What do Christian adults want, then, Mother?

AMANDA: Superior things! Things of the mind and the spirit! Only animals have to satisfy instincts! Surely your aims are somewhat higher than theirs! Than monkeys—pigs—

TOM: I reckon they're not.

AMANDA: You're joking. However, that isn't what I wanted to discuss.

TOM (*rising*): I haven't much time.

AMANDA (*pushing his shoulders*): Sit down.

TOM: You want me to punch in red at the warehouse, Mother?

AMANDA: You have five minutes. I want to talk about Laura.

TOM: All right! What about Laura?

AMANDA: We have to be making some plans and provisions for her. She's older than you, two years, and nothing has happened. She just drifts along doing nothing. It frightens me terribly how she just drifts along.

TOM: I guess she's the type that people call home girls.

AMANDA: There's no such type, and if there is, it's a pity! That is unless the home is hers, with a husband!

TOM: What?

AMANDA: Oh, I can see the handwriting on the wall as plain as I see the nose in front of my face! It's terrifying!

> More and more you remind me of your father! He was out all hours without explanation!—Then *left! Good-bye!*
>
> And me with the bag to hold. I saw the letter you got from the Merchant Marine. I know what you're dreaming of. I'm not standing here blindfolded.
>
> Very well, then. Then *do* it!
>
> But not till there's somebody to take your place.

TOM: What do you mean?

AMANDA: I mean that as soon as Laura has got somebody to take care of her, married, a home of her own, independent—why, then you'll be free to go wherever you please, on land, on sea, whichever way the wind blows you!

But until that time you've got to look out for your sister. I don't say me because I'm old and don't matter! I say for your sister because she's young and dependent.

I put her in business college—a dismal failure! Frightened her so it made her sick at the stomach.

I took her over to the Young People's League at the church. Another fiasco. She spoke to nobody, nobody spoke to her. Now all she does is fool with those pieces of glass and play those worn-our records. What kind of a life is that for a girl to lead?

TOM: What can I do about it?

AMANDA: Overcome selfishness!

Self, self, self is all that you ever think of!

(TOM *springs up and crosses to get his coat. It is ugly and bulky. He pulls on a cap with earmuffs.*)

Where is your muffler? Put your wool muffler on!

(*He snatches it angrily from the closet and tosses it around his neck and pulls both ends tight.*)

Tom! I haven't said what I had in mind to ask you.

TOM: I'm too late to—

AMANDA (*catching his arm—very importunately. Then shyly*): Down at the warehouse, aren't there some—nice young men?

TOM: No!

AMANDA: There *must* be—*some* . . .

TOM: Mother—(*Gesture.*)

AMANDA: Find out one that's clean-living—doesn't drink and—ask him out for sister!

TOM: What?

AMANDA: For *sister!* To *meet!* Get *acquainted!*

TOM (*stamping to door*): Oh, my *go-osh!*

AMANDA: Will you? (*He opens door. Imploringly*) Will you? (*He starts down.*) Will you? *Will* you, dear?

TOM (*calling back*): YES!

(AMANDA *closes the door hesitantly and with a troubled but faintly hopeful expression.*
(*Spot* AMANDA *at phone.*)

AMANDA: Ella Cartwright? This is Amanda Wingfield!
How are you honey?
How is that kidney condition? (*Count five.*)
Horrors! (*Count five.*)

You're a Christian martyr, yes, honey, that's what you are, a Christian martyr!

Well, I just now happened to notice in my little red book that your subscription to the *Companion* has just run out! I knew that you wouldn't want to miss out on the wonderful serial starting in this new issue. It's by Bessie Mae Hopper, the first thing she's written since *Honeymoon for Three.*

Wasn't that a strange and interesting story? Well, this one is even lovelier, I believe. It has a sophisticated, society background. It's all about the horsey set on Long Island!

SCENE FIVE

> *It is early dusk of a spring evening. Supper has just been finished in the Wingfield apartment.* AMANDA *and* LAURA *in light-colored dresses are removing dishes from the table, in the upstage area, which is shadowy, their movements formalized almost as a dance or ritual, their moving forms as pale and silent as moths.*
>
> TOM, *in white shirt and trousers, rises from the table and crosses toward the fire-escape.*

AMANDA (*as he passes her*): Son, will you do me a favor?

TOM: What?

AMANDA: Comb your hair! You look so pretty when your hair is combed! (TOM *slouches on the sofa with evening paper. Enormous caption "Franco Triumphs."*) There is only one respect in which I would like you to emulate your father.

TOM: What respect is that?

AMANDA: The care he always took of his appearance. He never allowed himself to look untidy. (*He throws down the paper and crosses to fire-escape.*) Where are you going?

TOM: I'm going out to smoke.

AMANDA: You smoke too much. A pack a day at fifteen cents a pack. How much would that amount to in a month? Thirty times fifteen is how much, Tom? Figure it out and you will be astounded at what you could save. Enough to give you a night-school course in accounting at Washington U! Just think what a wonderful thing that would be for you, Son!

TOM: I'd rather smoke. (*He steps out on landing, letting the screen door slam.*)

AMANDA (*sharply*): I know! That's the tragedy of it . . . (*Alone, she turns to look at her husband's picture.*)

(*Dance music: "All the World Is Waiting for the Sunrise!"*)

TOM (*to the audience*): Across the alley from us was the Paradise Dance Hall. On evenings in spring the windows and doors were open and the music came outdoors. Sometimes the lights were turned out except for a large glass sphere that hung from the ceiling. It would turn slowly about and filter the dusk with delicate rainbow colors. Then the orchestra played a waltz or a tango, something that had a slow and sensuous rhythm. Couples would come outside, to the relative privacy of the alley. You could see them kissing behind ash-pits and telephone poles.

This was the compensation for lives that passed like mine, without any change or adventure.

Adventure and change were imminent in this year. They were waiting around the corner for all these kids.

Suspended in the mist over Berchtesgaden, caught in the folds of Chamberlain's umbrella—

In Spain there was Guernica!

But here there was only hot swing music and liquor, dance halls, bars, and movies, and sex that hung in the gloom like a chandelier and flooded the world with brief, deceptive rainbows . . .

All the world was waiting for bombardments!

(AMANDA *turns from the picture and comes outside.*)

AMANDA (*sighing*): A fire-escape landing's a poor excuse for a porch. (*She spreads a newspaper on a step and sits down, gracefully and demurely as if she were settling into a swing on a Mississippi veranda.*) What are you looking at?

TOM: The moon.

AMANDA: Is there a moon this evening?

TOM: It's rising over Garfinkel's Delicatessen.

AMANDA: So it is! A little silver slipper of a moon. Have you made a wish on it yet?

TOM: Um-hum.

AMANDA: What did you wish for?

TOM: That's a secret.

AMANDA: A secret, huh? Well, I won't tell mine either. I will be just as mysterious as you.

TOM: I bet I can guess what yours is.

AMANDA: Is my head so transparent?

TOM: You're not a sphinx.

AMANDA: No, I don't have secrets. I'll tell you what I wished for on the moon. Success and happiness for my precious children! I wish for that whenever there's a moon, and when there isn't a moon, I wish for it, too.

TOM: I thought perhaps you wished for a gentleman caller.

AMANDA: Why do you say that?

TOM: Don't you remember asking me to fetch one?

AMANDA: I remember suggesting that it would be nice for your sister if you brought home some nice young man from the warehouse. I think that I've made that suggestion more than once.

TOM: Yes, you have made it repeatedly.

AMANDA: Well?

TOM: We are going to have one.

AMANDA: *What?*

TOM: A gentleman caller!

(The annunciation is celebrated with music. AMANDA rises.)

AMANDA: You mean you have asked some nice young man to come over?

TOM: Yep. I've asked him to dinner.

AMANDA: You really did?

TOM: I did!

AMANDA: You did, and did he—*accept?*

TOM: He did!

AMANDA: Well, well—well, well! That's—lovely!

TOM: I thought that you would be pleased.

AMANDA: It's definite, then?

TOM: Very definite.

AMANDA: Soon?

TOM: Very soon.

AMANDA: For heaven's sake, stop putting on and tell me some things, will you?

TOM: What things do you want me to tell you?

AMANDA: *Naturally* I would like to know when he's *coming!*

TOM: He's coming tomorrow.

AMANDA: *Tomorrow?*

TOM: Yep. Tomorrow.

AMANDA: But, Tom!

TOM: Yes, Mother?

AMANDA: Tomorrow gives me no time!

TOM: Time for what?

AMANDA: Preparations! Why didn't you phone me at once, as soon as you asked him, the minute that he accepted? Then, don't you see, I could have been getting ready!

TOM: You don't have to make any fuss.

AMANDA: Oh, Tom, Tom, Tom, of course I have to make a fuss! I want things nice, not sloppy! Not thrown together. I'll certainly have to do some fast thinking, won't I?

TOM: I don't see why you have to think at all.

AMANDA: You just don't know. We can't have a gentleman caller in a pig-sty! All my wedding silver has to be polished, the monogrammed table linen ought to be laundered! The windows have to be washed and fresh curtains put up. And how about clothes? We have to *wear* something, don't we?

TOM: Mother, this boy is no one to make a fuss over!

AMANDA: Do you realize he's the first young man we've introduced to your sister?

It's terrible, dreadful, disgraceful that poor little sister has never received a single gentleman caller! Tom, come inside! (*She opens the screen door.*)

TOM: What for?

AMANDA: I want to ask you some things.

TOM: If you're going to make such a fuss, I'll call it off, I'll tell him not to come!

AMANDA: You certainly won't do anything of the kind. Nothing offends people worse than broken engagements. It simply means I'll have to work like a Turk! We won't be brilliant, but we will pass inspection. Come on inside. (TOM *follows, groaning.*) Sit down.

TOM: Any particular place you would like me to sit?

AMANDA: Thank heaven's I've got that new sofa! I'm also making payments on a floor lamp I'll have sent out! And put the chintz covers on, they'll brighten things up! Of course I'd hoped to have these walls repapered . . . What is the young man's name?

TOM: His name is O'Connor.

AMANDA: That, of course, means fish—tomorrow is Friday! I'll have that salmon loaf—with Durkee's dressing! What does he do? He works at the warehouse?

TOM: Of course! How else would I—

AMANDA: Tom, he—doesn't drink?

TOM: Why do you ask me that?

AMANDA: Your father *did!*

TOM: Don't get started on that!

AMANDA: He *does* drink, then?

TOM: Not that I know of!

AMANDA: Make sure, be certain! The last thing I want for my daughter's a boy who drinks!

TOM: Aren't you being a little bit premature? Mr. O'Connor has not yet appeared on the scene!

AMANDA: But will tomorrow. To meet your sister, and what do I know about his character? Nothing! Old maids are better off than wives of drunkards!

TOM: Oh, my God!

AMANDA: Be still!

TOM (*leaning forward to whisper*): Lots of fellows meet girls whom they don't marry!

AMANDA: Oh, talk sensibly, Tom—and don't be sarcastic! (*She has gotten a hairbrush.*)

TOM: What are you doing?

AMANDA: I'm brushing that cow-lick down!
What is this young man's position at the warehouse?

TOM (*submitting grimly to the brush and the interrogation*): This young man's position is that of a shipping clerk, Mother.

AMANDA: Sounds to me like a fairly responsible job, the sort of a job *you* would be in if you had more *get-up.*
What is his salary? Have you any idea?

TOM: I would judge it to be approximately eighty-five dollars a month.

AMANDA: Well—not princely, but—

TOM: Twenty more than I make.

AMANDA: Yes, how well I know! But for a family man, eighty-five dollars a month is not much more than you can just get by on . . .

TOM: Yes, but Mr. O'Connor is not a family man.

AMANDA: He might be, mightn't he? Some time in the future?

TOM: I see. Plans and provisions.

AMANDA: You are the only young man that I know of who ignores the fact that the future becomes the present, the present the past, and the past turns into everlasting regret if you don't plan for it!

TOM: I will think that over and see what I can make of it.

AMANDA: Don't be supercilious with your mother! Tell me some more about this—what do you call him?

TOM: James D. O'Connor. The D. is for Delaney.

AMANDA: Irish on *both* sides! *Gracious!* And doesn't drink?

TOM: Shall I call him up and ask him right this minute?

AMANDA: The only way to find out about those things is to make discreet inquiries at the proper moment. When I was a girl in Blue Mountain and it was suspected that a young man drank, the girl whose attentions he had been receiving, if any girl *was*, would sometimes speak to the minister of his church, or rather her father would if her father was living, and sort of feel him out on the young man's character. That is the way such things are discreetly handled to keep a young woman from making a tragic mistake!

TOM: Then how did you happen to make a tragic mistake?

AMANDA: That innocent look of your father's had everyone fooled!
    He *smiled*—the world was *enchanted!*
    No girl can do worse than put herself at the mercy of a handsome appearance!
    I hope that Mr. O'Connor is not too good-looking.

TOM: No, he's not too good-looking. He's covered with freckles and hasn't too much of a nose.

AMANDA: He's not right-down homely, though?

TOM: Not right-down homely. Just medium homely, I'd say.

AMANDA: Character's what to look for in a man.

TOM: That's what I've always said, Mother.

AMANDA: You've never said anything of the kind and I suspect you would never give it a thought.

TOM: Don't be so suspicious of me.

AMANDA: At least I hope he's the type that's up and coming.

TOM: I think he really goes in for self-improvement.

AMANDA: What reason have you to think so?

TOM: He goes to night school.

AMANDA (*beaming*): Splendid! What does he do, I mean study?

TOM: Radio engineering and public speaking!

AMANDA: Then he has visions of being advanced in the world!

Any young man who studies public speaking is aiming to have an executive job some day!

And radio engineering? A thing for the future!

Both of these facts are very illuminating. Those are the sort of things that a mother should know concerning any young man who comes to call on her daughter. Seriously or—not.

TOM: One little warning. He doesn't know about Laura. I didn't let on that we had dark ulterior motives. I just said, why don't you come and have dinner with us? He said okay and that was the whole conversation.

AMANDA: I bet it was! You're eloquent as an oyster.

However, he'll know about Laura when he gets here. When he sees how lovely and sweet and pretty she is, he'll thank his lucky stars he was asked to dinner.

TOM: Mother, you mustn't expect too much of Laura.

AMANDA: What do you mean?

TOM: Laura seems all those things to you and me because she's ours and we love her. We don't even notice she's crippled any more.

AMANDA: Don't say crippled! You know that I never allow that word to be used!

TOM: But face facts, Mother. She is and—that's not all—

AMANDA: What do you mean "not all"?

TOM: Laura is very different from other girls.

AMANDA: I think the difference is all to her advantage.

TOM: Not quite all—in the eyes of others—strangers—she's terribly shy and lives in a world of her own and those things make her seem a little peculiar to people outside the house.

AMANDA: Don't say peculiar.

TOM: Face the facts. She is.

(*The dance-hall music changes to a tango that has a minor and somewhat ominous tone.*)

AMANDA: In what way is she peculiar—may I ask?

TOM (*gently*): She lives in a world of her own—a world of—little glass ornaments, Mother . . . (*Gets up.* AMANDA *remains holding brush, looking at him, troubled.*) She plays old phonograph records and—that's about all—(*He glances at himself in the mirror and crosses to door.*)

AMANDA (*sharply*): Where are you going?

TOM: I'm going to the movies. (*Out screen door.*)

AMANDA: Not to the movies, every night to the movies! (*Follows quickly to screen door*) I don't believe you always go to the movies! (*He is gone.* AMANDA *looks worriedly after him for a moment. Then vitality and optimism return and she turns from the door. Crossing to portieres*) Laura! Laura!

(LAURA *answers from kitchenette.*)

LAURA: Yes, Mother.

AMANDA: Let those dishes go and come in front! (LAURA *appears with dish towel. Gaily*) Laura, come here and make a wish on the moon!

LAURA (*entering*): Moon—moon?

AMANDA: A little silver slipper of a moon.
　　　　Look over your left shoulder, Laura, and make a wish!

　　　　(LAURA *looks faintly puzzled as if called out of sleep.* AMANDA *seizes her shoulders and turns her at an angle by the door.*)

　　　　Now!
　　　　Now, darling, *wish!*

LAURA: What shall I wish for, Mother?

AMANDA (*her voice trembling and her eyes suddenly filling with tears*): Happiness! Good fortune!

　　　　(*The violin rises and the stage dims out.*)

SCENE SIX

TOM: And so the following evening I brought Jim home to dinner. I had known Jim slightly in high school. In high school Jim was a hero. He had a tremendous Irish good nature and vitality with the scrubbed and polished look of white chinaware. He seemed to move in a continual spotlight. He was a star in basketball, captain of the debating club, president of the senior class and the glee club and he sang the male lead in the annual light operas. He was always running or bounding, never just walking. He seemed always at the point of defeating the law of gravity. He was shooting with such velocity through his adolescence that you would logically expect him to arrive at nothing short of the White House by the time he was thirty. But Jim apparently ran into more interference after his graduation from Soldan. His speed has definitely slowed. Six years after he left high school he was holding a job that wasn't much better than mine.

He was the only one at the warehouse with whom I was on friendly terms. I was valuable to him as someone who could remember his former glory, who had seen him win basketball games and the silver cup in debating. He knew of my secret practice of retiring to a cabinet of the washroom to work on poems when business was slack in the warehouse. He called me Shakespeare. And while the other boys in the warehouse regarded me with suspicious hostility, Jim took a humorous attitude toward me. Gradually his attitude affected others, their hostility wore off and they also began to smile at me as people smile at an oddly fashioned dog who trots across their path at some distance.

I knew that Jim and Laura had known each other at Soldan, and I had heard Laura speak admiringly of his voice. I didn't know if Jim remembered her or not. In high school Laura had been as unobtrusive as Jim had been astonishing. If he did remember Laura, it was not as my sister, for when I asked him to dinner, he grinned and said, "You know, Shakespeare, I never thought of you as having folks!"

He was about to discover that I did . . .

(*Light up stage.*

(*Friday evening. It is about five-o'clock of a late spring evening which comes "scattering poems in the sky."*

(*A delicate lemony light is in the Wingfield apartment.*

(AMANDA *has worked like a Turk in preparation for the gentleman caller. The results are astonishing. The new floor lamp with its rose-silk shade is in place, a colored paper lantern conceals the broken light fixture in the ceiling, new billowing white curtains are at the windows, chintz covers are on chairs and sofa, a pair of new sofa pillows make their initial appearance.*

(*Open boxes and tissue paper are scattered on the floor.*

(LAURA *stands in the middle with lifted arms while* AMANDA *crouches before her, adjusting the hem of the new dress, devout and ritualistic. The dress is colored and designed by memory. The arrangement of* LAURA's *hair is changed; it is softer and more becoming. A fragile, unearthly prettiness has come out in* LAURA: *she is like a piece of translucent glass touched by light, given a momentary radiance, not actual, not lasting.*)

AMANDA (*impatiently*): Why are you trembling?

LAURA: Mother, you've made me so nervous!

AMANDA: How have I made you nervous?

LAURA: By all this fuss! You make it seem so important!

AMANDA: I don't understand you, Laura. You couldn't be satisfied with just sitting home, and yet whenever I try to arrange something for you, you seem to resist it. (*She gets up.*)

Now take a look at yourself.

No, wait! Wait just a moment—I have an idea!

LAURA: What is it now?

(AMANDA *produces two powder puffs which she wraps in handkerchiefs and stuffs in* LAURA's *bosom.*)

LAURA: Mother, what are you doing?

AMANDA: They call them "Gay Deceivers"!

LAURA: I won't wear them!

AMANDA: You will!

LAURA: Why should I?

AMANDA: Because, to be painfully honest, your chest is flat.

LAURA: You make it seem like we were setting a trap.

AMANDA: All pretty girls are a trap, a pretty trap, and men expect them to be.

Now look at yourself, young lady. This is the prettiest you will ever be!

I've got to fix myself now! You're going to be surprised by your mother's appearance! (*She crosses through portieres, humming gaily.*)

(LAURA *moves slowly to the long mirror and stares solemnly at herself.*

(*A wind blows the white curtains inward in a slow, graceful motion and with a faint, sorrowful sighing.*)

AMANDA (*off stage*): It isn't dark enough yet. (*She turns slowly before the mirror with a troubled look.*)

AMANDA (*laughing, off*): I'm going to show you something. I'm going to make a spectacular appearance!

LAURA: What is it, Mother?

AMANDA: Possess your soul in patience—you will see!

Something I've resurrected from that old trunk! Styles haven't changed so terribly much after all . . . (*She parts the portieres.*)

Now just look at your mother! (*She wears a girlish frock of yellowed voile with a blue silk sash. She carries a bunch of jonquils—the legend of her youth is nearly revived. Feverishly*) This is the dress in which I led the cotillion. Won the cakewalk twice at Sunset Hill, wore one spring to the Governor's ball in Jackson!

See how I sashayed around the ballroom, Laura? (*She raises her skirt and does a mincing step around the room.*)

I wore it on Sundays for my gentlemen callers! I had it on the day I met your father—

I had malaria fever all that spring. The change of climate from East Tennessee to the Delta—weakened resistance—I had a little temperature all the time—not enough to be serious—just enough to make me restless and giddy!—Invitations poured in—parties all over the Delta!—"Stay in bed," said Mother, "you have fever!"—but I just wouldn't.—I took quinine but kept on going, going!—Evenings, dances!—Afternoons, long, long rides! Picnics—lovely!—So lovely, that country in May.—All lacy with dogwood, literally flooded with jonquils!—That was the spring I had the craze for jonquils. Jonquils became an absolute obsession. Mother said, "Honey, there's no more room for jonquils." And still I kept on bringing in more jonquils. Whenever, wherever I saw them, I'd say, "Stop! Stop! I see jonquils!" I made the young men help me gather the jonquils! It was a joke, Amanda and her jonquils! Finally there were no more vases to hold them, every available space was filled with jonquils. No vases to hold them? All right, I'll hold them myself! And then I—(*She stops in front of the picture. Music.*) met your father! Malaria fever and jonquils and then—this—boy . . . (*She switches on the rose-colored lamp.*)

I hope they get here before it starts to rain. (*She crosses upstage and places the jonquils in bowl on table.*)

I gave your brother a little extra change so he and Mr. O'Connor could take the service car home.

LAURA (*with altered look*): What did you say his name was?

AMANDA: O'Connor.

LAURA: What is his first name?

AMANDA: I don't remember. Oh, yes, I do. It was—Jim!

(LAURA *sways slightly and catches hold of a chair.*)

LAURA (*faintly*): Not—Jim!

AMANDA: Yes, that was it, it was Jim! I've never known a Jim that wasn't nice!

(*Music: ominous.*)

LAURA: Are you sure his name is Jim O'Connor?

AMANDA: Yes. Why?

LAURA: Is he the one that Tom used to know in high school?

AMANDA: He didn't say so. I think he got to know him at the warehouse.

LAURA: There was a Jim O'Connor we both knew in high school—(*Then, with effort*) If that is the one that Tom is bringing to dinner—you'll have to excuse me, I won't come to the table.

AMANDA: What sort of nonsense is this?

LAURA: You asked me once if I'd ever liked a boy. Don't you remember I showed you this boy's picture?

AMANDA: You mean the boy you showed me in the year book?

LAURA: Yes, that boy.

AMANDA: Laura, Laura, were you in love with that boy?

LAURA: I don't know, Mother. All I know is I couldn't sit at the table if it was him!

AMANDA: It won't be him! It isn't the least bit likely. But whether it is or not, you will come to the table. You will not be excused.

LAURA: I'll have to be, Mother.

AMANDA: I don't intend to humor your silliness, Laura. I've had too much from you and your brother, both!

So just sit down and compose yourself till they come. Tom has forgotten his key so you'll have to let them in, when they arrive.

LAURA (*panicky*): Oh, Mother—*you* answer the door!

AMANDA (*lightly*): I'll be in the kitchen—busy!

LAURA: Oh, Mother, please answer the door, don't make me do it!

AMANDA (*crossing into kitchenette*): I've got to fix the dressing for the salmon. Fuss, fuss—silliness!—over a gentleman caller!

(*Door swings shut.* LAURA *is left alone.*

(*She utters a low moan and turns off the lamp—sits stiffly on the edge of the sofa, knotting her fingers together.*

(TOM *and* JIM *appear on the fire-escape steps and climb to landing. Hearing their approach,* LAURA *rises with a panicky gesture. She retreats to the portieres.*

(*The doorbell.* LAURA *catches her breath and touches her throat. Low drums.*)

AMANDA (*calling*): Laura, sweetheart! The door!

(LAURA *stares at it without moving.*)

JIM: I think we just beat the rain.

TOM: Uh-huh. (*He rings again, nervously.* JIM *whistles and fishes for a cigarette.*)

AMANDA (*very, very gaily*): Laura, that is your brother and Mr. O'Connor! Will you let them in, darling?

(LAURA *crosses toward kitchenette door.*)

LAURA (*breathlessly*): Mother—you go to the door!

(AMANDA *steps out of the kitchenette and stares furiously at* LAURA. *She points imperiously at the door.*)

LAURA: Please, please!

AMANDA (*in a fierce whisper*): What is the matter with you, you silly thing?

LAURA (*desperately*): Please, you answer it, *please!*

AMANDA: I told you I wasn't going to humor you, Laura. Why have you chosen this moment to lose your mind?

LAURA: Please, please, please, you go!

AMANDA: You'll have to go to the door because I can't!

LAURA (*despairingly*): I can't either!

AMANDA: *Why?*

LAURA: I'm *sick!*

AMANDA: I'm sick, too—of your nonsense! Why can't you and your brother be normal people? Fantastic whims and behavior!

(TOM *gives a long ring.*)

Preposterous goings on! Can you give me one reason—(*Calls out lyrically*) COMING! JUST ONE SECOND!—why you should be afraid to open a door? Now you answer it, Laura!

LAURA: Oh, oh, oh . . . (*She returns through the portieres. Darts to the victrola and winds it frantically and turns it on.*)

AMANDA: Laura Wingfield, you march right to that door!

LAURA: Yes—yes, Mother!

(*A faraway, scratchy rendition of "Dardanella" softens the air and gives her strength to move through it. She slips to the door and draws it cautiously open.*
(TOM *enters with the caller,* JIM O'CONNOR.)

TOM: Laura, this is Jim. Jim, this is my sister, Laura.

JIM (*stepping inside*): I didn't know that Shakespeare had a sister!

LAURA (*retreating stiff and trembling from the door*): How—how do you do?

JIM (*heartily extending his hand*): Okay!

(LAURA *touches it hesitantly with hers.*)

JIM: Your hand's *cold*, Laura!

LAURA: Yes, well—I've been playing the victrola . . .

JIM: Must have been playing classical music on it! You ought to play a little hot swing music to warm you up!

LAURA: Excuse me—I haven't finished playing the victrola . . . (*She turns awkwardly and hurries into the front room. She pauses a second by the victrola. Then catches her breath and darts through the portieres like a frightened deer.)*

JIM (*grinning*): What was the matter?

TOM: Oh—with Laura? Laura is—terribly shy.

JIM: Shy, huh? It's unusual to meet a shy girl nowadays. I don't believe you ever mentioned you had a sister.

TOM: Well, now you know. I have one. Here is the *Post Dispatch.* You want a piece of it?

JIM: Uh-huh.

TOM: What piece? The comics?

JIM: Sports! (*Glances at it*) Ole Dizzy Dean is on his bad behavior.

TOM (*disinterest*): Yeah? (*Lights cigarette and crosses back to fire-escape door.*)

JIM: Where are *you* going?

TOM: I'm going out on the terrace.

JIM (*goes after him*): You know, Shakespeare—I'm going to sell you a bill of goods!

TOM: What goods?

JIM: The course I'm taking.

TOM: Huh?

JIM: In public speaking! You and me, we're not the warehouse type.

TOM: Thanks—that's good news.
But what has public speaking got to do with it?

JIM: It fits you for—executive positions!

TOM: Awww.

JIM: I tell you it's done a helluva lot for me.

TOM: In what respect?

JIM: In every! Ask yourself what is the difference between you an' me and men in the office down front? Brains?—No!—Ability?—No! Then what? Just one little thing—

TOM: What is that one little thing?

JIM: Primarily it amounts to—social poise! Being able to square up to people and hold your own on any social level!

AMANDA (*off stage*): Tom?

TOM: Yes, Mother?

AMANDA: Is that you and Mr. O'Connor?

TOM: Yes, Mother.

AMANDA: Well, you just make yourselves comfortable in there.

TOM: Yes, Mother.

AMANDA: Ask Mr. O'Connor if he would like to wash his hands.

JIM: Aw, no—no—thank you—I took care of that at the warehouse. Tom—

TOM: Yes?

JIM: Mr. Mendoza was speaking to me about you.

TOM: Favorably?

JIM: What do you think?

TOM: Well—

JIM: You're going to be out of a job if you don't wake up.

TOM: I am waking up—

JIM: You show no signs.

TOM: The signs are interior.

I'm planning to change. (*He leans over the rail speaking with quiet exhilaration. The incandescent marquees and signs of the first-run movie houses light his face from across the alley. He looks like a voyager.*) I'm right at the point of committing myself to a future that doesn't include the warehouse and Mr. Mendoza or even a night-school course in public speaking.

JIM: What are you gassing about?

TOM: I'm tired of the movies.

JIM: Movies!

TOM: Yes, movies! Look at them—(*A wave toward the marvels of Grand Avenue*) All of those glamorous people—having adventures—hogging it all, gobbling the whole thing up! You know what happens? People go to the *movies* instead of *moving!* Hollywood characters are supposed to have all the adventures for everybody in America, while everybody in America sits in a dark room and watches them have them! Yes, until there's a war. That's when adventure becomes available to the masses! *Everyone's* dish, not only Gable's! Then the people in the dark room come out of the dark room to have some adventures themselves—Goody, goody!—It's our turn now, to go to the South Sea Island—to make a safari—to be exotic, far-off!—But I'm not patient. I don't want to wait till then. I'm tired of the *movies* and I am *about to move!*

JIM (*incredulously*): Move?

TOM: Yes.

JIM: When?

TOM: Soon!

JIM: Where? Where?

(*Theme three music seems to answer the question, while* TOM *thinks it over. He searches among his pockets.*)

TOM: I'm starting to boil inside. I know I seem dreamy, but inside—well, I'm boiling!—Whenever I pick up a shoe, I shudder a little thinking how short life is and what I am doing!—Whatever that means, I know it doesn't mean shoes—except as something to wear on a traveler's feet! (*Finds paper*) Look—

JIM: What?

TOM: I'm a member.

JIM (*reading*): The Union of Merchant Seamen.

TOM: I paid my dues this month, instead of the light bill.

JIM: You will regret it when they turn the lights off.

TOM: I won't be here.

JIM: How about your mother?

TOM: I'm like my father. The bastard son of a bastard! See how he grins? And he's been absent going on sixteen years!

JIM: You're just talking, you drip. How does your mother feel about it?

TOM: Shhh!—Here comes Mother! Mother is not acquainted with my plans!

AMANDA (*enters portieres*): Where are you all?

TOM: On the terrace, Mother.

> (*They start inside. She advances to them.* TOM *is distinctly shocked at her appearance. Even* JIM *blinks a little. He is making his first contact with girlish Southern vivacity and in spite of the night-school course in public speaking is somewhat thrown off the beam by the unexpected outlay of social charm.*
>
> (*Certain responses are attempted by* JIM *but are swept aside by* AMANDA's *gay laughter and chatter.* TOM *is embarrassed but after the first shock* JIM *reacts very warmly. Grins and chuckles, is altogether won over.*)

AMANDA (*coyly smiling, shaking her girlish ringlets*): Well, well, well, so this is Mr. O'Connor. Introductions entirely unnecessary. I've heard so much about you from my boy. I finally said to him, Tom—good gracious!—why don't you bring this paragon to supper? I'd like to meet this nice young man at the warehouse!—Instead of just hearing him sing your praises so much!

I don't know why my son is so stand-offish—that's not Southern behavior!

Let's sit down and—I think we could stand a little more air in here! Tom, leave the door open. I felt a nice fresh breeze a moment ago. Where has it gone to?

Mmm, so warm already! And not quite summer, even. We're going to burn up when summer really gets started.

However, we're having—we're having a very light supper. I think light things are better fo' this time of year. The same as light clothes are. Light clothes an' light food are what warm weather calls fo'. You know our blood gets so thick during th' winter—it takes a while fo' us to *adjust* ou'selves!—when the season changes . . .

It's come so quick this year. I wasn't prepared. All of a sudden—heavens! Already summer!—I ran to the trunk an' pulled out this light dress—Terribly old! Historical almost! But feels so good—so good an' co-ol, y' know . . .

TOM: Mother—

AMANDA: Yes, honey?

TOM: How about—supper?

AMANDA: Honey, you go ask Sister if supper is ready! You know that Sister is in full charge of supper!

Tell her you hungry boys are waiting for it.
(*To* JIM) Have you met Laura?

JIM: She—

AMANDA: Let you in? Oh, good, you've met already! It's rare for a girl as sweet an' pretty as Laura to be domestic! But Laura is, thank heavens, not only pretty but also very domestic. I'm not at all. I never was a bit. I never could make a thing but angel-food cake. Well, in the South we had so many servants. Gone, gone, gone. All vestige of gracious living! Gone completely! I wasn't prepared for what the future brought me. All of my gentlemen callers were sons of planters and so of course I assumed that I would be married to one and raise my family on a large piece of land with plenty of servants. But man proposes—and woman accepts the proposal!—To vary that old, old saying a little bit—I married no planter! I married a man who worked for the telephone company!—That gallantly smiling gentleman over there! (*Points to the picture*) A telephone man who—fell in love with long-distance!—Now he travels and I don't even know where!—But what am I going on for about my—tribulations?
Tell me yours—I hope you don't have any!
Tom?

TOM (*returning*): Yes, Mother?

AMANDA: Is supper nearly ready?

TOM: It looks to me like supper is on the table.

AMANDA: Let me look—(*She rises prettily and looks through portieres.*) Oh, lovely!—But where is Sister?

TOM: Laura is not feeling well and she says that she thinks she'd better not come to the table.

AMANDA: What?—Nonsense!—Laura? Oh, Laura!

LAURA (*off stage, faintly*): Yes, Mother.

AMANDA: You really must come to the table. We won't be seated until you come to the table!
Come in, Mr. O'Connor. You sit over there, and I'll—
Laura? Laura Wingfield!
You're keeping us waiting, honey! We can't say grace until you come to the table!

(*The back door is pushed weakly open and* LAURA *comes in. She is obviously quite faint, her lips trembling, her eyes wide and staring. She moves unsteadily toward the table.*
(*Outside a summer storm is coming abruptly. The white curtains billow inward at the windows and there is a sorrowful murmur and deep blue dusk.*
(LAURA *suddenly stumbles—she catches at a chair with a faint moan.*)

TOM: Laura!

AMANDA: Laura!

(*There is a clap of thunder.*)

(*Despairingly*) Why, Laura, you *are* sick, darling! Tom, help your sister into the living room, dear!

Sit in the living room, Laura—rest on the sofa.

Well!

(*To the gentleman caller*) Standing over the hot stove made her ill!—I told her that it was just too warm this evening, but—

(TOM *comes back in.* LAURA *is on the sofa.*)

Is Laura all right now?

TOM: Yes.

AMANDA: What *is* that? Rain? A nice cool rain has come up! (*She gives the gentleman caller a frightened look.*) I think we may—have grace— now . . .

(TOM *looks at her stupidly.*)

Tom, honey—you say grace!

TOM: Oh . . .

"For these and all thy mercies—"

(*They bow their heads,* AMANDA *stealing a nervous glance at* JIM. *In the living room* LAURA, *stretched on the sofa, clenches her hand to her lips, to hold back a shuddering sob.*)

God's Holy Name be praised—

(*The scene dims out.*)

SCENE SEVEN, A SOUVENIR

(*Half an hour later. Dinner is just being finished in the upstage area which is concealed by the drawn portierers.*

(*As the curtain rises* LAURA *is still huddled upon the sofa, her feet drawn under her, her head resting on a pale blue pillow, her eyes wide and mysteriously watchful. The new floor lamp with its shade of rose-colored silk gives a soft, becoming light to her face, bringing out the fragile, unearthly prettiness which usually escapes attention. There is a steady murmur of rain, but it is slackening and stops soon after the scene begins; the air outside becomes pale and luminous as the moon breaks out.*

(*A moment after the curtain rises, the lights in both rooms flicker and go out.*)

JIM: Hey, there, Mr. Light Bulb!

(AMANDA *laughs nervously.*)

AMANDA: Where was Moses when the lights went out? Ha-ha. Do you know the answer to that one, Mr. O'Connor?

JIM: No, Ma'am, what's the answer?

AMANDA: In the dark!

(JIM *laughs appreciatively.*)

Everybody sit still. I'll light the candles. Isn't it lucky we have them on the table? Where's a match? Which of you gentlemen can provide a match?

JIM: Here.

AMANDA: Thank you, sir.

JIM: Not at all, Ma'am!

AMANDA: I guess the fuse has burnt out. Mr. O'Connor, can you tell a burnt-out fuse? I know I can't and Tom is a total loss when it comes to mechanics.

(*Sound: getting up: voices recede a little to kitchenette.*)

Oh, be careful you don't bump into something. We don't want our gentleman caller to break his neck. Now wouldn't that be a fine howdy-do?

JIM: Ha-ha!

Where is the fuse-box?

AMANDA: Right here next to the stove. Can you see anything?

JIM: Just a minute.

AMANDA: Isn't electricity a mysterious thing?

Wasn't it Benjamin Franklin who tied a key to a kite?

We live in such a mysterious universe, don't we? Some people say that science clears up all the mysteries for us. In my opinion it only creates more!

Have you found it yet?

JIM: No, Ma'am. All these fuses look okay to me.

AMANDA: Tom!

TOM: Yes, Mother?

AMANDA: That light bill I gave you several days ago. The one I told you we got the notices about?

TOM: Oh.—Yeah.

AMANDA: You didn't neglect to pay it by any chance?

TOM: Why, I—

AMANDA: Didn't! I might have known it!

JIM: Shakespeare probably wrote a poem on that light bill, Mrs. Wingfield.

AMANDA: I might have known better than to trust him with it! There's such a high price for negligence in this world!

JIM: Maybe the poem will win a ten-dollar prize.

AMANDA: We'll just have to spend the remainder of the evening in the nineteenth century, before Mr. Edison made the Mazda lamp!

JIM: Candlelight is my favorite kind of light.

AMANDA: That shows you're romantic! But that's no excuse for Tom.

Well, we got through dinner. Very considerate of them to let us get through dinner before they plunged us into everlasting darkness, wasn't it, Mr. O'Connor?

JIM: Ha-ha!

AMANDA: Tom, as a penalty for your carelessness you can help me with the dishes.

JIM: Let me give you a hand.

AMANDA: Indeed you will not!

JIM: I ought to be good for something.

AMANDA: Good for something? (*Her tone is rhapsodic.*)
You? Why, Mr. O'Connor, nobody, *nobody's* given me this much entertainment in years—as you have!

JIM: Aw, now, Mrs. Wingfield!

AMANDA: I'm not exaggerating, not one bit! But Sister is all by her lonesome. You go keep her company in the parlor!
I'll give you this lovely old candelabrum that used to be on the altar at the church of the Heavenly Rest. It was melted a little out of shape when the church burnt down. Lightning struck it one spring. Gypsy Jones was holding a revival at the time and he intimated that the church was destroyed because the Episcopalians gave card parties.

JIM: Ha-ha.

AMANDA: And how about your coaxing Sister to drink a little wine? I think it would be good for her! Can you carry both at once?

JIM: Sure. I'm Superman!

AMANDA: Now, Thomas, get into this apron!

> (*The door of kitchenette swings closed on* AMANDA'S *gay laughter; the flickering light approaches the portieres.*
>
> (LAURA *sits up nervously as he enters. Her speech at first is low and breathless from the almost intolerable strain of being alone with a stranger.*
>
> (*In her first speeches in the scene, before* JIM'S *warmth overcomes her paralyzing shyness,* LAURA'S *voice is thin and breathless as though she has just run up a steep flight of stairs.*
>
> (JIM'S *attitude is gently humorous. In playing this scene it should be stressed that while the incident is apparently unimportant, it is to* LAURA *the climax of her secret life.*)

JIM: Hello, there, Laura.

LAURA (*faintly*): Hello. (*She clears her throat.*)

JIM: How are you feeling now? Better?

LAURA: Yes. Yes, thank you.

JIM: This is for you. A little dandelion wine. (*He extends it toward her with extravagant gallantry.*)

LAURA: Thank you.

JIM: Drink it—but don't get drunk!

> (*He laughs heartily.* LAURA *takes the glass uncertainly; laughs shyly.*)

Where shall I set the candles?

LAURA: Oh—oh, anywhere . . .

JIM: How about here on the floor? Any objections?

LAURA: No.

JIM: I'll spread a newspaper under to catch the drippings. I like to sit on the floor. Mind if I do?

LAURA: Oh, no.

JIM: Give me a pillow?

LAURA: What?

JIM: A pillow!

LAURA: Oh . . . (*Hands him one quickly.*)

JIM: How about you? Don't you like to sit on the floor?

LAURA: Oh—yes.

JIM: Why don't you, then?

LAURA: I—will.

JIM: Take a pillow!

> (LAURA *does. Sits on the other side of the candelabrum.* JIM *crosses his legs and smiles engagingly at her.*)

> I can't hardly see you sitting way over there.

LAURA: I can—see you.

JIM: I know, but that's not fair, I'm in the limelight.

> (LAURA *moves her pillow closer.*)

> Good! Now I can see you! Comfortable?

LAURA: Yes.

JIM: So am I. Comfortable as a cow! Will you have some gum?

LAURA: No, thank you.

JIM: I think that I will indulge, with your permission. (*Musingly unwraps it and holds it up*) Think of the fortune made by the guy that invented the first piece of chewing gum. Amazing, huh? The Wrigley Building is one of the sights of Chicago.—I saw it summer before last when I went up to the Century of Progress. Did you take in the Century of Progress?

LAURA: No, I didn't.

JIM: Well, it was quite a wonderful exposition. What impressed me most was the Hall of Science. Gives you an idea of what the future will be in America, even more wonderful than the present time is! (*Pause. Smiling at her*) Your brother tells me you're shy. Is that right, Laura?

LAURA: I—don't know.

JIM: I judge you to be an old-fashioned type of girl. Well, I think that's a pretty good type to be. Hope you don't think I'm being too personal—do you?

LAURA (*hastily, out of embarrassment*): I believe I *will* take a piece of gum, if you—don't mind. (*Clearing her throat*) Mr. O'Connor, have you—kept up with your singing?

JIM: Singing? Me?

LAURA: Yes. I remember what a beautiful voice you had.

JIM: When did you hear me sing?

> (*Voice off stage in the pause*
>
>> O blow, ye winds, heigh-ho,
>> A-roving I will go!
>> I'm off to my love
>> With a boxing glove—
>> Ten thousand miles away!)

JIM: You say you've heard me sing?

LAURA: Oh, yes! Yes, very often . . . I—don't suppose—you remember me—at all?

JIM (*smiling doubtfully*): You know I have an idea I've seen you before. I had that idea soon as you opened the door. It seemed almost like I was about to remember your name. But the name that I started to call you—wasn't a name! And so I stopped myself before I said it.

LAURA: Wasn't it—Blue Roses?

JIM (*springs up. Grinning*): Blue Roses!—My gosh yes—Blue Roses!
    That's what I had on my tongue when you opened the door!
    Isn't it funny what tricks your memory plays? I didn't connect you with high school somehow or other.
    But that's where it was; it was high school. I didn't even know you were Shakespeare's sister!
    Gosh, I'm sorry.

LAURA: I didn't expect you to. You—barely knew me!

JIM: But we did have a speaking acquaintance, huh?

LAURA: Yes, we—spoke to each other.

JIM: When did you recognize me?

LAURA: Oh, right away!

JIM: Soon as I came in the door?

LAURA: When I heard your name I thought it was probably you. I knew that Tom used to know you a little in high school. So when you came in the door—
    Well, then I was—sure.

JIM: Why didn't you *say* something, then?

LAURA (*breathlessly*): I didn't know what to say, I was—too surprised!

JIM: For goodness' sakes! You know, this sure is funny!

LAURA: Yes! Yes, isn't it, though . . .

JIM: Didn't we have a class in something together?

LAURA: Yes, we did.

JIM: What class was that?

LAURA: It was—singing—Chorus!

JIM: Aw!

LAURA: I sat across the aisle from you in the Aud.

JIM: Aw.

LAURA: Mondays, Wednesdays and Fridays.

JIM: Now I remember—you always came in late.

LAURA: Yes, it was so hard for me, getting upstairs. I had that brace on my leg—it clumped so loud!

JIM: I never heard any clumping.

LAURA (*wincing at the recollection*): To me it sounded like—thunder!

JIM: Well, well, well, I never even noticed.

LAURA: And everybody was seated before I came in. I had to walk in front of all those people. My seat was in the back row. I had to go clumping all the way up the aisle with everyone watching!

JIM: You shouldn't have been self-conscious.

LAURA: I know, but I was. It was always such a relief when the singing started.

JIM: Aw, yes, I've placed you now! I used to call you Blue Roses. How was it that I got started calling you that?

LAURA: I was out of school a little while with pleurosis. When I came back you asked me what was the matter. I said I had pleurosis—you thought I said Blue Roses. That's what you always called me after that!

JIM: I hope you didn't mind.

LAURA: Oh, no—I liked it. You see, I wasn't acquainted with many—people . . .

JIM: As I remember you sort of stuck by yourself.

LAURA: I—I—never have had much luck at—making friends.

JIM: I don't see why you wouldn't.

LAURA: Well, I—started out badly.

JIM: You mean being—

LAURA: Yes, it sort of—stood between me—

JIM: You shouldn't have let it!

LAURA: I know, but it did, and—

JIM: You were shy with people!

LAURA: I tried not to be but never could—

JIM: Overcome it?

LAURA: No, I—I never could!

JIM: I guess being shy is something you have to work out of kind of gradually.

LAURA (*sorrowfully*): Yes—I guess it—

JIM: Takes time!

LAURA: Yes—

JIM: People are not so dreadful when you know them. That's what you have to remember! And everybody has problems, not just you, but practically everybody has got some problems.

You think of yourself as having the only problems, as being the only one who is disappointed. But just look around you and you will see lots of people as disappointed as you are. For instance, I hoped when I was going to high school that I would be further along at this time, six years later, than I am now— You remember that wonderful write-up I had in *The Torch*?

LAURA: Yes! (*She rises and crosses to table.*)

JIM: It said I was bound to succeed in anything I went into! (LAURA *returns with the annual.*) Holy Jeez! *The Torch!*

> (*He accepts it reverently. They smile across it with mutual wonder.* LAURA *crouches beside him and they begin to turn through it.* LAURA's *shyness is dissolving in his warmth.*)

LAURA: Here you are in *The Pirates of Penzance!*

JIM (*wistfully*): I sang the baritone lead in that operetta.

LAURA (*raptly*): So—beautifully!

JIM (*protesting*): Aw—

LAURA: Yes, yes—beautifully—beautifully!

JIM: You heard me?

LAURA: All three times!

JIM: No!

LAURA: Yes!

JIM: All three performances?

LAURA (*looking down*): Yes.

JIM: Why?

LAURA: I—wanted to ask you to—autograph my program.

JIM: Why didn't you ask me to?

LAURA: You were always surrounded by your own friends so much that I never had a chance to.

JIM: You should have just—

LAURA: Well, I—thought you might think I was—

JIM: Thought I might think you was—what?

LAURA: Oh—

JIM (*with reflective relish*): I was beleaguered by females in those days.

LAURA: You were terribly popular!

JIM: Yeah—

LAURA: You had such a—friendly way—

JIM: I was spoiled in high school.

LAURA: Everybody—liked you!

JIM: Including you?

LAURA: I—yes, I—I did, too—(*She gently closes the book in her lap.*)

JIM: Well, well, well!—Give me that program, Laura. (*She hands it to him. He signs it with a flourish.*) There you are—better late than never!

LAURA: Oh, I—what a—surprise!

JIM: My signature isn't worth very much right now.
> But some day—maybe—it will increase in value!
> Being disappointed is one thing and being discouraged is something else. I am disappointed but I am not discouraged.
> I'm twenty-three years old.
> How old are you?

LAURA: I'll be twenty-four in June.

JIM: That's not old age!

LAURA: No, but—

JIM: You finished high school?

LAURA (*with difficulty*): I didn't go back.

JIM: You mean you dropped out?

LAURA: I made bad grades in my final examinations. (*She rises and replaces the book and the program. Her voice strained*) How is—Emily Meisenbach getting along?

JIM: Oh, that kraut-head!

LAURA: Why do you call her that?

JIM: That's what she was.

LAURA: You're not still—going with her?

JIM: I never see her.

LAURA: It said in the Personal Section that you were—engaged!

JIM: I know, but I wasn't impressed by that—propaganda!

LAURA: It wasn't—the truth?

JIM: Only in Emily's optimistic opinion!

LAURA: Oh—

> (JIM *lights a cigarette and leans indolently back on his elbows smiling at* LAURA *with a warmth and charm which lights her inwardly with altar candles. She remains by the table and turns in her hands a piece of glass to cover her tumult.*)

JIM (*after several reflective puffs on a cigarette*): What have you done since high school? (*She seems not to hear him.*) Huh? (LAURA *looks up.*) I said what have you done since high school, Laura?

LAURA: Nothing much.

JIM: You must have been doing something these six long years.

LAURA: Yes.

JIM: Well, then, such as what?

LAURA: I took a business course at business college—

JIM: How did that work out?

LAURA: Well, not very—well—I had to drop out, it gave me—indigestion—

> (JIM *laughs gently.*)

JIM: What are you doing now?

LAURA: I don't do anything—much. Oh, please don't think I sit around doing nothing! My glass collection takes up a good deal of time. Glass is something you have to take good care of.

JIM: What did you say—about glass?

LAURA: Collection I said—I have one—(*She clears her throat and turns away again, acutely shy.*)

JIM (*abruptly*): You know what I judge to be the trouble with you?

Inferiority complex! Know what that is? That's what they call it when someone low-rates himself!

I understand it because I had it, too. Although my case was not so aggravated as yours seems to be. I had it until I took up public speaking, developed my voice, and learned that I had an aptitude for science. Before that time I never thought of myself as being outstanding in any way whatsoever!

Now I've never made a regular study of it, but I have a friend who says I can analyze people better than doctors that make a profession of it. I don't claim that to be necessarily true, but I can sure guess a person's psychology, Laura! (*Takes out his gum*) Excuse me, Laura. I always take it out when the flavor is gone. I'll use this scrap of paper to wrap it in. I know how it is to get it stuck on a shoe.

Yep—that's what I judge to be your principal trouble. A lack of confidence in yourself as a person. You don't have the proper amount of faith in yourself. I'm basing that fact on a number of your remarks and also on certain observations I've made. For instance that clumping you thought was so awful in high school. You say that you even dreaded to walk into class. You see what you did? You dropped out of school, you gave up an education because of a clump, which as far as I know was practically non-existent! A little physical defect is what you have. Hardly noticeable even! Magnified thousands of times by imagination!

You know what my strong advice to you is? Think of yourself as *superior* in some way!

LAURA: In what way would I think?

JIM: Why, man alive, Laura! Just look about you a little. What do you see? A world full of common people! All of 'em born and all of 'em going to die!

Which of them has one-tenth of your good points! Or mine! Or anyone else's, as far as that goes—Gosh!

Everybody excels in some one thing. Some in many! (*Unconsciously glances at himself in the mirror.*)

All you've got to do is discover in *what!*

Take me, for instance. (*He adjusts his tie at the mirror.*)

My interest happens to lie in electro-dynamics. I'm taking a course in radio engineering at night school, Laura, on top of a fairly responsible job at the warehouse. I'm taking that course and studying public speaking.

LAURA: Ohhhh.

JIM: Because I believe in the future of television! (*Turning back to her.*)

I wish to be ready to go up right along with it. Therefore I'm planning to get in on the ground floor. In fact I've already made the right connections and all that remains is for the industry itself to get under way! Full steam—(*His eyes are starry.*)

Knowledge—Zzzzzp! Money—Zzzzzzp!—Power!

That's the cycle democracy is built on! (*His attitude is convincingly dynamic.* LAURA *stares at him, even her shyness eclipsed in her absolute wonder. He suddenly grins.*)

I guess you think I think a lot of myself!

LAURA: No—o-o-o, I—

JIM: Now how about you? Isn't there something you take more interest in than anything else?

LAURA: Well, I do—as I said—have my—glass collection—

(*A peal of girlish laughter from the kitchen.*)

JIM: I'm not right sure I know what you're talking about.
What kind of glass is it?

LAURA: Little articles of it, they're ornaments mostly!
Most of them are little animals made out of glass, the tiniest little animals in the world. Mother calls them a glass menagerie!
Here's an example of one, if you'd like to see it!
This one is one of the oldest. It's nearly thirteen.

(*Music: "The Glass Menagerie."*
(*He stretches out his hand.*)

Oh, be careful—if you breathe, it breaks!

JIM: I'd better not take it. I'm pretty clumsy with things.

LAURA: Go on, I trust you with him! (*Places it in his palm.*)
There now—you're holding him gently!
Hold him over the light, he loves the light! You see how the light shines through him?

JIM: It sure does shine!

LAURA: I shouldn't be partial, but he is my favorite one.

JIM: What kind of a thing is this one supposed to be?

LAURA: Haven't you noticed the single horn on his forehead?

JIM: A unicorn, huh?

LAURA: Mmm-hmmm!

JIM: Unicorns, aren't they extinct in the modern world?

LAURA: I know!

JIM: Poor little fellow, he must feel sort of lonesome.

LAURA (*smiling*): Well, if he does he doesn't complain about it. He stays on a shelf with some horses that don't have horns and all of them seem to get along nicely together.

JIM: How do you know?

LAURA (*lightly*): I haven't heard any arguments among them!

JIM (*grinning*): No arguments, huh? Well, that's a pretty good sign! Where shall I set him?

LAURA: Put him on the table. They all like a change of scenery once in a while!

JIM (*stretching*): Well, well, well, well—
Look how big my shadow is when I stretch!

LAURA: Oh, oh, yes—it stretches across the ceiling!

JIM (*crossing to door*): I think it's stopped raining. (*Opens fire-escape door.*)
Where does the music come from?

LAURA: From the Paradise Dance Hall across the alley.

JIM: How about cutting the rug a little, Miss Wingfield?

LAURA: Oh, I—

JIM: Or is your program filled up? Let me have a look at it. (*Grasps imaginary card*) Why, every dance is taken! I'll just have to scratch some out. (*Waltz music: "La Golondrina."*) Ahhh, a waltz! (*He executes some sweeping turns by himself then holds his arms toward* LAURA.)

LAURA (*breathlessly*): I—can't dance!

JIM: There you go, that inferiority stuff!

LAURA: I've never danced in my life!

JIM: Come on, try!

LAURA: Oh, but I'd step on you!

JIM: I'm not made out of glass.

LAURA: How—how—how do we start?

JIM: Just leave it to me. You hold your arms out a little.

LAURA: Like this?

JIM: A little bit higher. Right. Now don't tighten up, that's the main thing about it—relax.

LAURA (*laughing breathlessly*): It's hard not to.

JIM: Okay.

LAURA: I'm afraid you can't budge me.

JIM: What do you bet I can't? (*He swings her into motion.*)

LAURA: Goodness, yes, you can!

JIM: Let yourself go, now, Laura, just let yourself go.

LAURA: I'm—

JIM: Come on!

LAURA: Trying!

JIM: Not so stiff—Easy does it!

LAURA: I know but I'm—

JIM: Loosen th' backbone! There now, that's a lot better.

LAURA: Am I?

JIM: Lots, lots better! (*He moves her about the room in a clumsy waltz.*)

LAURA: Oh, my!

JIM: Ha-ha!

LAURA: Oh, my goodness!

JIM: Ha-ha-ha! (*They suddenly bump into the table.* JIM *stops.*) What did we hit on?

LAURA: Table.

JIM: Did something fall off it? I think—

LAURA: Yes.

JIM: I hope that it wasn't the little glass horse with the horn!

LAURA: Yes.

JIM: Aw, aw, aw. Is it broken?

LAURA: Now it is just like all the other horses.

JIM: It's lost its—

LAURA: Horn!

It doesn't matter. Maybe it's a blessing in disguise.

JIM: You'll never forgive me. I bet that was your favorite piece of glass.

LAURA: I don't have favorites much. It's no tragedy, Freckles. Glass breaks so easily. No matter how careful you are. The traffic jars the shelves and things fall off them.

JIM: Still I'm awfully sorry that I was the cause.

LAURA (*smiling*): I'll just imagine he had an operation.

The horn was removed to make him feel less—freakish! (*They both laugh.*)

Now he will feel more at home with the other horses, the ones that don't have horns . . .

JIM: Ha-ha, that's very funny! (*Suddenly serious.*)

I'm glad to see that you have a sense of humor.

You know—you're—well—very different!

Surprisingly different from anyone else I know! (*His voice becomes soft and hesitant with a genuine feeling.*)

Do you mind me telling you that?

(LAURA *is abashed beyond speech.*)

I mean it in a nice way . . .

(LAURA *nods shyly, looking away.*)

You make me feel sort of—I don't know how to put it!

I'm usually pretty good at expressing things, but—

This is something that I don't know how to say!

(LAURA *touches her throat and clears it—turns the broken unicorn in her hands.*)

(*Even softer*) Has anyone ever told you that you were pretty?

(*Pause: music.* LAURA *looks up slowly, with wonder, and shakes her head.*)

Well, you are! In a very different way from anyone else.

And all the nicer because of the difference, too. (*His voice becomes low and husky.* LAURA *turns away, nearly faint with the novelty of her emotions.*)

I wish that you were my sister. I'd teach you to have some confidence in yourself. The different people are not like other people, but being different is nothing to be ashamed of. Because other people are not such wonderful people. They're one hundred times one thousand. You're one times one! They walk all over the earth. You just stay here. They're common as—weeds, but—you—well, you're—*Blue Roses!*

(*Music changes.*)

LAURA: But blue is wrong for—roses . . .

JIM: It's right for you!—You're—pretty!

LAURA: In what respect am I pretty?

JIM: In all respects—believe me! Your eyes—your hair—are pretty! Your hands are pretty! (*He catches hold of her hand.*)

You think I'm making this up because I'm invited to dinner and have to be nice. Oh, I could do that! I could put on an act for you, Laura, and say lots of things without being very sincere. But this time I am. I'm talking to you sincerely. I happened to notice you had this inferiority complex that keeps you from feeling comfortable with people. Somebody needs to build your confidence up and make you proud instead of shy and turning away and—blushing—

Somebody—ought to—

Ought to—*kiss* you, Laura! (*His hand slips slowly up her arm to her shoulder. Music swells tumultuously. He suddenly turns her about and kisses her on the lips. When he releases her,* LAURA *sinks on the sofa with a bright, dazed look.* JIM *backs away and fishes in his pocket for a cigarette.*)

Stumble-john!

(*He lights the cigarette, avoiding her look.*

(*There is a peal of girlish laughter from* AMANDA *in the kitchen.*

(LAURA *slowly raises and opens her hand. It still contains the little broken glass animal. She looks at it with a tender, bewildered expression.*)

Stumble-john!

I shouldn't have done that—That was way off the beam.

You don't smoke, do you?

(*She looks up, smiling, not hearing the question.*

(*He sits beside her a little gingerly. She looks at him speechlessly—waiting.*

(*He coughs decorously and moves a little farther aside as he considers the situation and senses her feelings, dimly, with perturbation.*)

(*Gently*) Would you—care for a—mint?

(*She doesn't seem to hear him but her look grows brighter even.*)

Peppermint—Life-Saver?

My pocket's a regular drug store—wherever I go . . . (*He pops a mint in his mouth. Then gulps and decides to make a clean breast of it. He speaks slowly and gingerly.*)

Laura, you know, if I had a sister like you, I'd do the same thing as Tom. I'd bring out fellows and—introduce her to them. The right type of boys of a type to—appreciate her.

Only—well—he made a mistake about me.

Maybe I've got no call to be saying this. That may not have been the idea in having me over. But what if it was?

There's nothing wrong about that. The only trouble is that in my case—I'm not in a situation to—do the right thing.

I can't take down your number and say I'll phone.

I can't call up next week and—ask for a date.

I thought I had better explain the situation in case you—misunderstood it and—hurt your feelings . . .

(*Pause.*)

(*Slowly, very slowly,* LAURA's *look changes, her eyes returning slowly from his to the ornament in her palm.*

(AMANDA *utters another gay laugh in the kitchen.*)

LAURA (*faintly*): You—won't—call again?

JIM: No, Laura, I can't. (*He rises from the sofa.*)

As I was just explaining, I've—got strings on me.

Laura, I've—been going steady!

I go out all of the time with a girl named Betty. She's a home-girl like you, and Catholic, and Irish, and in a great many ways we—get along fine.

I met her last summer on a moonlight boat trip up the river to Alton, on the *Majestic*.

Well—right away from the start it was—love!

(LAURA *sways slightly forward and grips the arm of the sofa. He fails to notice, now enrapt in his own comfortable being.*)

Being in love has made a new man of me!

(*Leaning stiffly forward, clutching the arm of the sofa,* LAURA *struggles visibly with her storm. But* JIM *is oblivious, she is a long way off.*)

The power of love is really pretty tremendous!

Love is something that—changes the whole world, Laura!

(*The storm abates a little and* LAURA *leans back. He notices her again.*)

It happened that Betty's aunt took sick, she got a wire and had to go to Centralia. So Tom—when he asked me to dinner—I naturally just accepted the invitation, not knowing that you—that he—that I—(*He stops awkwardly.*)

Huh—I'm a stumble-john!

(*He flops back on the sofa.*

(*The holy candles in the altar of* LAURA's *face have been snuffed out. There is a look of almost infinite desolation.*

(JIM *glances at her uneasily.*)

I wish that you would—say something.

(*She bites her lip which was trembling and then bravely smiles. She opens her hand again on the broken glass ornament. Then she gently takes his hand and raises it level with her own. She carefully places the unicorn in the palm of his hand, then pushes his fingers closed upon it.*)

What are you—doing that for? You want me to have him?—
Laura? (*She nods.*) What for?

LAURA: A—souvenir . . . (*She rises unsteadily and crouches beside the victrola to
wind it up.*)

      (*At this moment* AMANDA *rushes brightly back in the front room.
She bears a pitcher of fruit punch in an old-fashioned cut-glass
pitcher and a plate of macaroons. The plate has a gold border and
poppies painted on it.*)

AMANDA: Well, well, well! Isn't the air delightful after the shower?
      I've made you children a little liquid refreshment.
      (*Turns gaily to the gentleman caller*) Jim, do you know that song
about lemonade?

      "Lemonade, lemonade
      Made in the shade and stirred with a spade—
      Good enough for any old maid!"

JIM (*uneasily*): Ha-ha! No—I never heard it.

AMANDA: Why, Laura! You look so serious!

JIM: We were having a serious conversation.

AMANDA: Good! Now you're better acquainted!

JIM (*uncertainly*): Ha-ha! Yes.

AMANDA: You modern young people are much more serious-minded than my
      generation. I was so gay as a girl!

JIM: You haven't changed, Mrs. Wingfield.

AMANDA: Tonight I'm rejuvenated! The gaiety of the occasion, Mr. O'Connor!
      (*She tosses her head with a peal of laughter. Spills lemonade.*)
      Oooo! I'm baptizing myself!

JIM: Here—let me—

AMANDA (*setting the pitcher down*): There now, I discovered we had some
      maraschino cherries. I dumped them in, juice and all!

JIM: You shouldn't have gone to that trouble, Mrs. Wingfield.

AMANDA: Trouble, trouble? Why, it was loads of fun!
      Didn't you hear me cutting up in the kitchen? I bet your ears were
      burning! I told Tom how outdone with him I was for keeping you to
      himself so long a time! He should have brought you over much, much
      sooner! Well, now that you've found your way, I want you to be a very
      frequent caller! Not just occasional but all the time.
      Oh, we're going to have a lot of gay times together! I see them
      coming!
      Mmm, just breathe that air! So fresh, and the moon's so pretty!
      I'll slip back out—I know where my place is when young folks are
      having a—serious conversation!

JIM: Oh, don't go out, Mrs. Wingfield. The fact of the matter is I've got to
    be going.

AMANDA: Going, now? You're joking! Why, it's only the shank of the evening, Mr. O'Connor!

JIM: Well, you know how it is.

AMANDA: You mean you're a young workingman and have to keep working-men's hours. We'll let you off early tonight. But only on the condition that next time you stay later.

What's the best night for you? Isn't Saturday night the best night for you workingmen?

JIM: I have a couple of time-clocks to punch, Mrs. Wingfield. One at morning, another one at night!

AMANDA: My, but you *are* ambitious! You work at night, too?

JIM: No, Ma'am, not work but—Betty! (*He crosses deliberately to pick up his hat. The band at the Paradise Dance Hall goes into a tender waltz.*)

AMANDA: Betty? Betty? Who's—Betty!

(*There is an ominous cracking sound in the sky.*)

JIM: Oh, just a girl. The girl I go steady with! (*He smiles charmingly. The sky falls.*)

AMANDA (*a long-drawn exhalation*): Ohhhh . . . Is it a serious romance, Mr. O'Connor?

JIM: We're going to be married the second Sunday in June.

AMANDA: Ohhhh—how nice!

Tom didn't mention that you were engaged to be married.

JIM: The cat's not out of the bag at the warehouse yet.

You know how they are. They call you Romeo and stuff like that. (*He stops at the oval mirror to put on his hat. He carefully shapes the brim and the crown to give a discreetly dashing effect.*)

It's been a wonderful evening, Mrs. Wingfield. I guess this is what they mean by Southern hospitality.

AMANDA: It really wasn't anything at all.

JIM: I hope it don't seem like I'm rushing off. But I promised Betty I'd pick her up at the Wabash depot, an' by the time I get my jalopy down there her train'll be in. Some women are pretty upset if you keep 'em waiting.

AMANDA: Yes, I know—The tyranny of women!

(*Extends her hand*) Good-bye, Mr. O'Connor.

I wish you luck—and happiness—and success! All three of them, and so does Laura!—Don't you, Laura?

LAURA: Yes!

JIM (*taking her hand*): Good-bye, Laura. I'm certainly going to treasure that souvenir. And don't you forget the good advice I gave you.

(*Raises his voice to a cheery shout*) So long, Shakespeare!

Thanks again, ladies—Good night! (*He grins and ducks jauntily out.*)

(*Still bravely grimacing, AMANDA closes the door on the gentleman caller. Then she turns back to the room with a puzzled expression. She and LAURA don't dare to face each other. LAURA crouches beside the victrola to wind it.*)

AMANDA (*faintly*): Things have a way of turning out so badly.
> I don't believe that I would play the victrola.
> Well, well—well—
> Our gentleman caller was engaged to be married!
> Tom!

TOM (*from back*): Yes, Mother?

AMANDA: Come in here a minute. I want to tell you something awfully funny.

TOM (*enters with macaroon and a glass of the lemonade*): Has the gentleman caller gotten away already?

AMANDA: The gentleman caller has made an early departure.
> What a wonderful joke you played on us!

TOM: How do you mean?

AMANDA: You didn't mention that he was engaged to be married.

TOM: Jim? Engaged?

AMANDA: That's what he just informed us.

TOM: I'll be jiggered! I didn't know about that.

AMANDA: That seems very peculiar.

TOM: What's peculiar about it?

AMANDA: Didn't you call him your best friend down at the warehouse?

TOM: He is, but how did I know?

AMANDA: It seems extremely peculiar that you wouldn't know your best friend was going to be married!

TOM: The warehouse is where I work, not where I know things about people!

AMANDA: You don't know things anywhere! You live in a dream; you manufacture illusions!

(*He crosses to door.*)

> Where are you going?

TOM: I'm going to the movies.

AMANDA: That's right, now that you've had us make such fools of ourselves. The effort, the preparations, all the expense! The new floor lamp, the rug, the clothes for Laura! All for what? To entertain some other girl's fiancé!
> Go to the movies, go! Don't think about us, a mother deserted, an unmarried sister who's crippled and has no job! Don't let anything interfere with your selfish pleasure!
> Just go, go, go—to the movies!

TOM: All right, I will! The more you shout about my selfishness to me the quicker I'll go, and I won't go to the movies!

AMANDA: Go, then! Then go to the moon—you selfish dreamer!

(TOM *smashes his glass on the floor. He plunges out on the fire-escape, slamming the door.* LAURA *screams.*
> (*Dance-hall music up.* TOM *goes to the rail and grips it desperately, lifting his face in the chill white moon light penetrating the narrow abyss of the alley.*

(TOM's *closing speech is timed with the interior pantomime. The interior scene is played as though viewed through soundproof glass.* AMANDA *appears to be making a comforting speech to* LAURA *who is huddled upon the sofa. Now that we cannot hear the mother's speech, her silliness is gone and she has dignity and tragic beauty.* LAURA's *dark hair hides her face until at the end of the speech she lifts it to smile at her mother.* AMANDA's *gestures are slow and graceful, almost dance-like, as she comforts the daughter. At the end of her speech she glances a moment at the father's picture—then withdraws through the portieres. At close of* TOM's *speech,* LAURA *blows out the candles, ending the play.*)

TOM: I didn't go to the moon, I went much further—for time is the longest distance between two places—

Not long after that I was fired for writing a poem on the lid of a shoe-box.

I left Saint Louis. I descended the steps of this fire-escape for a last time and followed, from then on, in my father's footsteps, attempting to find in motion what was lost in space—

I traveled around a great deal. The cities swept about me like dead leaves, leaves that were brightly colored but torn away from the branches.

I would have stopped, but I was pursued by something.

It always came upon me unawares, taking me altogether by surprise. Perhaps it was a familiar bit of music. Perhaps it was only a piece of transparent glass—

Perhaps I am walking along a street at night, in some strange city, before I have found companions. I pass the lighted window of a shop where perfume is sold. The window is filled with pieces of colored glass, tiny transparent bottles in delicate colors, like bits of a shattered rainbow.

Then all at once my sister touches my shoulder. I turn around and look into her eyes . . .

Oh, Laura, Laura, I tried to leave you behind me, but I am more faithful than I intended to be!

I reach for a cigarette, I cross the street, I run into the movies or a bar, I buy a drink, I speak to the nearest stranger—anything that can blow your candles out!

(LAURA *bends over the candles.*)

—for nowadays the world is lit by lightning! Blow out your candles, Laura—and so good-bye . . .

(*She blows the candles out.*)

Fact Questions and Exercises

1. Tom narrates the play from the "present"; but to what period does he "turn back time"? In what city is the play set?
2. Identify Blue Mountain. What is its importance in relation to Amanda?

3. Describe the circumstances surrounding Laura's enrollment in Rubicam's Business College.
4. What is Laura's physical handicap? *polio crippled*
5. Identify the glass menagerie.
6. Who is the Gentleman Caller? Where has Laura met him before his visit? Why does he call her "Blue Roses"? *cont. Shoemakers*
7. Where does Tom work while he is living with his mother and sister? Why is he called "Shakespeare"?
8. Who is the telephone man who "fell in love with long distance"? How does this person "appear" in the play?
9. Why is Tom fired from his job? What does he do after he is fired? *He left St. Louis*
10. Describe the final scene in which Laura appears.

For Discussion and Writing

1. Characterize Amanda. What kind of mother is she? What are her motivations? Why, for instance, does she insist on Laura's having gentlemen callers? In what ways does she use people?
2. Discuss Williams's use of symbols. What are some of the most apparent symbols? Note, for example, the glass unicorn. How do these symbols help clarify the play's meaning? Are the personalities of the characters in part revealed by the symbols that Williams uses?
3. The theme of escape is important in the play. How does Amanda escape? Laura? Tom? What are they escaping from? Are they successful?
4. Characterize Jim O'Connor. What are his values? How does he differ from Tom or Laura? How does Williams reveal Jim's character? What forces or conditions does Jim represent to the Wingfield family?
5. Note the various devices that Williams uses in staging the play. How do these help explain the action of the play? Do they add to the mood of the play—a play that Tom says is "memory"? Which of the devices do you think is most effective?

Edward Albee [1928–   ]

Albee, abandoned as an infant, was adopted by Reed Albee, a wealthy New York theater owner. Albee attended a series of private schools and spent two years at Trinity College in Pennsylvania. At twenty, he severed his relations with his adopted parents and began a bohemian life in Greenwich Village. His first play, *The Zoo Story*, was produced in 1960; a number of short plays immediately followed, establishing Albee's reputation as one of America's leading dramatists. Albee is commonly regarded as an absurdist, a label he has denied; yet most of his plays do attempt to lay bare the illusions by which people live, revealing the sometimes horrible and shocking cruelty that lies beneath social convention. His most famous play, *Who's Afraid of Virginia Woolf* (1962), is a funny, violent exposé of the private horrors of two faculty couples at an Ivy League school. The play won the Drama Circle Critics Award and was made into a successful movie.

The American Dream

THE PLAYERS

MOMMY
DADDY
GRANDMA
MRS. BARKER
YOUNG MAN

THE SCENE: *A living room. Two armchairs, one toward either side of the stage, facing each other diagonally out toward the audience. Against the rear wall, a sofa. A door, leading out from the apartment, in the rear wall, far stage-right. An archway, leading to other rooms, in the side wall, stage-left.*

> *At the beginning,* MOMMY *and* DADDY *are seated in the armchairs,* DADDY *in the armchair stage-left,* MOMMY *in the other.*
> *Curtain up. A silence. Then:*

MOMMY: I don't know what can be keeping them.

DADDY: They're late, naturally.

MOMMY: Of course, they're late; it never fails.

DADDY: That's the way things are today, and there's nothing you can do about it.

MOMMY: You're quite right.

DADDY: When we took this apartment, they were quick enough to have me sign the lease; they were quick enough to take my check for two months' rent in advance . . .

MOMMY: And one month's security . . .

DADDY: . . . and one month's security. They were quick enough to check my references; they were quick enough about all that. But now! But now, try to get the icebox fixed, try to get the doorbell fixed, try to get the leak in the johnny fixed! Just try it . . . they aren't so quick about *that.*

MOMMY: Of course not; it never fails. People think they can get away with anything these days . . . and, of course they can. I went to buy a new hat yesterday. (*Pause.*) I said, I went to buy a new hat yesterday.

DADDY: Oh! Yes . . . yes.

MOMMY: Pay attention.

DADDY: I *am* paying attention, Mommy.

MOMMY: Well, be sure you do.

DADDY: Oh, I am.

MOMMY: All right, Daddy; now listen.

DADDY: I'm listening, Mommy.

MOMMY: You're sure!

DADDY: Yes . . . yes, I'm sure, I'm all ears.

MOMMY (*giggles at the thought; then*): All right, now. I went to buy a new hat yesterday and I said, "I'd like a new hat, please." And so, they showed me a few hats, green ones and blue ones, and I didn't like any of them, not one bit. What did I say? What did I just say?

DADDY: You didn't like any of them, not one bit.

MOMMY: That's right; you just keep paying attention. And then they showed me one that I did like. It was a lovely little hat, and I said, "Oh, this is a lovely little hat; I'll take this hat; oh my, it's lovely. What color is it?" And they said, "Why, this is beige; isn't it a lovely little beige hat?" And I said, "Oh, it's just lovely." And so, I bought it. (*Stops, looks at* DADDY.)

DADDY (*to show he is paying attention*): And so you bought it.

MOMMY: And so I bought it, and I walked out of the store with the hat right on my head, and I ran spang into the chairman of our woman's club, and she said, "Oh, my dear, isn't that a lovely little hat? Where did you get that lovely little hat? It's the loveliest little hat; I've always wanted a wheat-colored hat *myself.*" And, I said, "Why, no, my dear; this hat is beige; beige." And she laughed and said, "Why no, my dear, that's a wheat-colored hat . . . wheat. I know beige from wheat." And I said, "Well, my dear, I know beige from wheat, too." What did I say? What did I just say?

DADDY (*tonelessly*): Well, my dear, I know beige from wheat, too.

MOMMY: That's right. And she laughed, and she said, "Well, my dear, they certainly put one over on you. That's wheat if I ever saw wheat. But it's lovely, just the same." And then she walked off. She's a dreadful woman, you don't know her; she has dreadful taste, two dreadful children, a dreadful house, and an absolutely adorable husband who sits in a wheel chair all the time. You don't know him. You don't know anybody, do you? She's just a dreadful woman, but she *is* chairman of our woman's club, so naturally I'm terribly fond of her. So, I went right back into the hat shop, and I said, "Look here; what do you mean selling me a hat that you say is beige, when it's wheat all the time . . . wheat! I can tell beige from wheat any day in the week, but not in this artificial light of yours." They have artificial lights, Daddy.

DADDY: Have they!

MOMMY: And I said, "The minute I got outside I could tell that it wasn't a beige hat at all; it was a wheat hat." And they said to me, "How could you tell that when you had the hat on the top of your head?" Well, that made me angry, and so I made a scene right there; I screamed as hard as I could; I took my hat off and I threw it down on the counter, and oh, I made a terrible scene. I said, I made a terrible scene.

DADDY (*snapping to*): Yes . . . yes . . . good for you!

MOMMY: And I made an absolutely terrible scene; and they became frightened, and they said, "Oh, madam; oh, madam." But I kept right on, and finally they admitted that they might have made a mistake; so they took my hat into the back, and then they came out again with a hat that looked exactly like it. I took one look at it, and I said, "This hat is wheat-colored; wheat." Well, of course, they said, "Oh, no, madam, this hat is beige; you go outside and see." So, I went outside, and lo and behold, it *was* beige. So I bought it.

DADDY (*clearing his throat*): I would imagine that it was the same hat they tried to sell you before.

MOMMY (*with a little laugh*): Well, of course it was!

DADDY: That's the way things are today; you just can't get satisfaction; you just try.

MOMMY: Well, *I* got satisfaction.

DADDY: That's right, Mommy. *You did* get satisfaction, didn't you?

MOMMY: Why are they so late? I don't know what can be keeping them.

DADDY: I've been trying for two weeks to have the leak in the johnny fixed.

MOMMY: You can't get satisfaction; just try. *I* can get satisfaction, but you can't.

DADDY: I've been trying for two weeks and it isn't so much for my sake; I can always go to the club.

MOMMY: It isn't so much for my sake, either; I can always go shopping.

DADDY: It's really for Grandma's sake.

MOMMY: Of course it's for Grandma's sake. Grandma cries every time she goes to the johnny as it is; but now that it doesn't work it's even worse, it makes Grandma think she's getting feeble-headed.

DADDY: Grandma *is* getting feeble-headed.

MOMMY: Of course Grandma is getting feeble-headed, but not about her johnny-do's.

DADDY: No; that's true. I must have it fixed.

MOMMY: WHY are they so late? I don't know what can be keeping them.

DADDY: When they came here the first time, they were ten minutes early; they were quick enough about it then.

(*Enter* GRANDMA *from the archway, stage-left. She is loaded down with boxes, large and small, neatly wrapped and tied.*)

MOMMY: Why Grandma, look at you! What *is* all that you're carrying?

GRANDMA: They're boxes. What do they look like?

MOMMY: Daddy! Look at Grandma; look at all the boxes she's carrying!

DADDY: My goodness, Grandma; look at all those boxes.

GRANDMA: Where'll I put them?

MOMMY: Heavens! I don't know. Whatever are they for?

GRANDMA: That's nobody's damn business.

MOMMY: Well, in that case, put them down next to Daddy; there.

GRANDMA (*dumping the boxes down, on and around* DADDY'S *feet*): I sure wish you'd get the john fixed.

DADDY: Oh, I do wish they'd come and fix it. We hear you . . . for hours . . . whimpering away. . . .

MOMMY: Daddy! What a terrible thing to say to Grandma!

GRANDMA: Yeah. For shame, talking to me that way.

DADDY: I'm sorry, Grandma.

MOMMY: Daddy's sorry, Grandma.

GRANDMA: Well, all right. In that case I'll go get the rest of the boxes. I suppose I deserve being talked to that way. I've gotten so old. Most people think that when you get so old, you either freeze to death, or you burn up. But you don't. When you get so old, all that happens is that people talk to you that way.

DADDY (*contrite*): I said I'm sorry, Grandma.

MOMMY: Daddy said he was sorry.

GRANDMA: Well, that's all that counts. People being sorry. Makes you feel better; gives you a sense of dignity, and that's all that's important . . . a sense of dignity. And it doesn't matter if you don't care, or not, either. You got to have a sense of dignity, even if you don't care, 'cause, if you don't have that, civilization's doomed.

MOMMY: You've been reading my book club selections again!

DADDY: How dare you read Mommy's book club selections, Grandma!

GRANDMA: Because I'm old! When you're old you gotta do something. When you get old, you can't talk to people because people snap at you. When you get so old, people talk to you that way. That's why you become deaf, so you won't be able to hear people talking to you that way. And that's why you go and hide under the covers in the big soft bed, so you won't feel the house shaking from people talking to you that way. That's why old people die, eventually. People talk to them that way. I've got to go and get the rest of the boxes. (GRANDMA *exits.*)

DADDY: Poor Grandma, I didn't mean to hurt her.

MOMMY: Don't you worry about it; Grandma doesn't know what she means.

DADDY: She knows what she says, though.

MOMMY: Don't you worry about it; she won't know that soon. I love Grandma.

DADDY: I love her, too. Look how nicely she wrapped these boxes.

MOMMY: Grandma has always wrapped boxes nicely. When I was a little girl, I was very poor, and Grandma was very poor, too, because Grandpa was in heaven. And every day, when I went to school, Grandma used to wrap a box for me, and I used to take it with me to school; and when it was lunchtime, all the little boys and girls used to take out their boxes of lunch, and they weren't wrapped nicely at all, and they used to open them and eat their chicken legs and chocolate cakes; and I used to say, "Oh, look at my lovely lunch box; it's so nicely wrapped it would break my heart to open it." And so, I wouldn't open it.

DADDY: Because it was empty.

MOMMY: Oh no. Grandma always filled it up, because she never ate the dinner she cooked the evening before; she gave me all her food for my lunch box the next day. After school, I'd take the box back to Grandma, and she'd open it and eat the chicken legs and chocolate cake that was inside. Grandma used to say, "I love day-old cake." That's where the expression day-old cake came from. Grandma always ate everything a day late. I used to eat all the other little boys' and girls' food at school, because they thought my lunch box was empty. They thought my lunch box was empty, and that's why I wouldn't open it. They thought I suffered from the sin of pride, and since that made them better than me, they were very generous.

DADDY: You were a very deceitful little girl.

MOMMY: We were very poor! But then I married you, Daddy, and now we're very rich.

DADDY: Grandma isn't rich.

MOMMY: No, but you've been so good to Grandma she feels rich. She doesn't know you'd like to put her in a nursing home.

DADDY: I wouldn't!

MOMMY: Well, heaven knows, *I* would! I can't stand it, watching her do the cooking and the housework, polishing the silver, moving the furniture. . . .

DADDY: She likes to do that. She says it's the least she can do to earn her keep.

MOMMY: Well, she's right. You can't live off people. I can live off you, because I married you. And aren't you lucky all I brought with me was Grandma. A lot of women I know would have brought their whole families to live off you. All I brought was Grandma. Grandma is all the family I have.

DADDY: I feel very fortunate.

MOMMY: You should. I have a right to live off of you because I married you, and because I used to let you get on top of me and bump your uglies; and I have a right to all your money when you die. And when you do, Grandma and I can live by ourselves . . . if she's still here. Unless you have her put away in a nursing home.

DADDY: I have no intention of putting her in a nursing home.

MOMMY: Well, I wish somebody would do something with her!

DADDY: At any rate, you're very well provided for.

MOMMY: You're my sweet Daddy; that's very nice.

DADDY: I love my Mommy.

(*Enter* GRANDMA *again, laden with more boxes.*)

GRANDMA (*dumping the boxes on and around* DADDY'S *feet*): There; that's the lot of them.

DADDY: They're wrapped so nicely.

GRANDMA (*to* DADDY): You won't get on my sweet side that way . . .

MOMMY: Grandma.

GRANDMA: . . . telling me how nicely I wrap boxes. Not after what you said: how I whimpered for hours. . . .

MOMMY: Grandma!

GRANDMA (*to* MOMMY): Shut up! (*To* DADDY.) You don't have any feelings, that's what's wrong with you. Old people make all sorts of noises, half of them they can't help. Old people whimper, and cry, and belch, and make great hollow rumbling sounds at the table; old people wake up in the middle of the night screaming, and find out they haven't even been asleep; and when old people *are* asleep, they try to wake up, and they can't . . . not for the longest time.

MOMMY: Homilies, homilies!

GRANDMA: And there's more, too.

DADDY: I'm really very sorry, Grandma.

GRANDMA: I know you are, Daddy; it's Mommy over there makes all the trouble. If you'd listened to me, you wouldn't have married her in the first place. She was a tramp and a trollop and a trull to boot, and she's no better now.

MOMMY: Grandma!

GRANDMA (*to* MOMMY): Shut up! (*To* DADDY.) When she was no more than eight years old she used to climb up on my lap and say, in a sickening little voice, "When I gwo up, I'm going to mahwy a wich old man; I'm going to set my wittle were end right down in a tub o' butter, that's what I'm going to do." And I warned you, Daddy; I told you to stay away from her type. I told you to. I did.

MOMMY: You stop that! You're my mother, not his!

GRANDMA: I am?

DADDY: That's right, Grandma. Mommy's right.

GRANDMA: Well, how would you expect somebody as old as I am to remember a thing like that? You don't make allowances for people. I want an allowance. I want an allowance!

DADDY: All right, Grandma; I'll see to it.

MOMMY: Grandma! I'm ashamed of you.

GRANDMA: Humf! It's a fine time to say that. You should have gotten rid of me a long time ago if that's the way you feel. You should have had Daddy set me up in business somewhere . . . I could have gone into the fur business, or I could have been a singer. But no; not you. You wanted me around so you could sleep in my room when Daddy got fresh. But now it isn't important, because Daddy doesn't want to get fresh with you any more, and I don't blame him. You'd rather sleep with me, wouldn't you, Daddy?

MOMMY: Daddy doesn't want to sleep with anyone. Daddy's been sick.

DADDY: I've been sick. I don't even want to sleep in the apartment.

MOMMY: You see? I told you.

DADDY: I just want to get everything over with.

MOMMY: That's right. Why are they so late? Why can't they get here on time?

GRANDMA (*an owl*): Who? Who? . . . Who? Who?

MOMMY: You know, Grandma.

GRANDMA: No, I don't.

MOMMY: Well, it doesn't really matter whether you do or not.

DADDY: Is that true?

MOMMY: Oh, more or less. Look how pretty Grandma wrapped these boxes.

GRANDMA: I didn't really like wrapping them; it hurt my fingers, and it frightened me. But it had to be done.

MOMMY: Why, Grandma?

GRANDMA: None of your damn business.

MOMMY: Go to bed.

GRANDMA: I don't want to go to bed. I just got up. I want to stay here and watch. Besides . . .

MOMMY: Go to bed.

DADDY: Let her stay up, Mommy; it isn't noon yet.

GRANDMA: I want to watch; besides . . .

DADDY: Let her watch, Mommy.

MOMMY: Well, all right, you can watch; but don't you dare say a word.

GRANDMA: Old people are very good at listening; old people don't like to talk; old people have colitis and lavender perfume. Now I'm going to be quiet.

DADDY: She never mentioned she wanted to be a singer.

MOMMY: Oh, I forgot to tell you, but it was ages ago. (*The doorbell rings.*) Oh, goodness! Here they are!

GRANDMA: Who? Who?

MOMMY: Oh, just some people.

GRANDMA: The van people? Is it the van people? Have you finally done it? Have you called the van people to come and take me away?

DADDY: Of course not, Grandma!

GRANDMA: Oh, don't be too sure. She'd have you carted off too, if she thought she could get away with it.

MOMMY: Pay no attention to her, Daddy. (*An aside to* GRANDMA.) My God, you're ungrateful! (*The doorbell rings again.*)

DADDY (*wringing his hands*): Oh dear; oh dear.

MOMMY (*still to* GRANDMA): Just you wait; I'll fix your wagon. (*Now to* DADDY.) Well, go let them in, Daddy. What are you waiting for?

DADDY: I think we should talk about it some more. Maybe we've been hasty
. . . a little hasty, perhaps. (*Doorbell rings again.*) I'd like to talk about it
some more.

MOMMY: There's no need. You made up your mind; you were firm; you were
masculine and decisive.

DADDY: We might consider the pros and the . . .

MOMMY: I won't argue with you; it has to be done; you were right. Open the
door.

DADDY: But I'm not sure that . . .

MOMMY: Open the door.

DADDY: Was I firm about it?

MOMMY: Oh, so firm; so firm.

DADDY: And was I decisive?

MOMMY: SO decisive! Oh, I shivered.

DADDY: And masculine? Was I really masculine?

MOMMY: Oh, Daddy, you were so masculine; I shivered and fainted.

GRANDMA: Shivered and fainted, did she? Humf!

MOMMY: You be quiet.

GRANDMA: Old people have a right to talk to themselves; it doesn't hurt the
gums, and it's comforting. (*Doorbell rings again.*)

DADDY: I shall now open the door.

MOMMY: WHAT a masculine Daddy! Isn't he a masculine Daddy?

GRANDMA: Don't expect me to say anything. Old people are obscene.

MOMMY: Some of your opinions aren't so bad. You know that?

DADDY (*backing off from the door*): Maybe we can send them away.

MOMMY: Oh, look at you! You're turning into jelly; you're indecisive; you're a
woman.

DADDY: All right. Watch me now; I'm going to open the door. Watch. Watch!

MOMMY: We're watching; we're watching.

GRANDMA: *I'm* not.

DADDY: Watch now; it's opening. (*He opens the door.*) It's open! (MRS. BARKER
steps into the room.) Here they are!

MOMMY: Here they are!

GRANDMA: Where?

DADDY: Come in. You're late. But, of course, we expected you to be late; we were
saying that we expected you to be late.

MOMMY: Daddy, don't be rude! We were saying that you just can't get satisfaction these days, and we were talking about you, of course. Won't you
come in?

MRS. BARKER: Thank you. I don't mind if I do.

MOMMY: We're very glad that you're here, late as you are. You do remember us,
don't you? You were here once before. I'm Mommy, and this is Daddy,
and that's Grandma, doddering there in the corner.

MRS. BARKER: Hello, Mommy; hello, Daddy; and hello there, Grandma.

DADDY: Now that you're here, I don't suppose you could go away and maybe come back some other time.

MRS. BARKER: Oh no; we're much too efficient for that. I said, hello there, Grandma.

MOMMY: Speak to them, Grandma.

GRANDMA: I don't see them.

DADDY: For shame, Grandma; they're here.

MRS. BARKER: Yes, we're here, Grandma. I'm Mrs. Barker. I remember you; don't you remember me?

GRANDMA: I don't recall. Maybe you were younger, or something.

MOMMY: Grandma! What a terrible thing to say!

MRS. BARKER: Oh now, don't scold her, Mommy; for all she knows she may be right.

DADDY: Uh . . . Mrs. Barker, is it? Won't you sit down?

MRS. BARKER: I don't mind if I do.

MOMMY: Would you like a cigarette, and a drink, and would you like to cross your legs?

MRS. BARKER: You forget yourself, Mommy; I'm a professional woman. But I will cross my legs.

DADDY: Yes, make yourself comfortable.

MRS. BARKER: I don't mind if I do.

GRANDMA: Are they still here?

MOMMY: Be quiet, Grandma.

MRS. BARKER: Oh, we're still here. My, what an unattractive apartment you have!

MOMMY: Yes, but you don't know what a trouble it is. Let me tell you . . .

DADDY: I was saying to Mommy . . .

MRS. BARKER: Yes, I know. I was listening outside.

DADDY: About the icebox, and . . . the doorbell . . . and the . . .

MRS. BARKER: . . . and the johnny. Yes, we're very efficient; we have to know everything in our work.

DADDY: Exactly what do you do?

MOMMY: Yes, what is your work?

MRS. BARKER: Well, my dear, for one thing, I'm chairman of your woman's club.

MOMMY: Don't be ridiculous. I was talking to the chairman of my woman's club just yester—Why, so you are. You remember, Daddy, the lady I was telling you about? The lady with the husband who sits in the *swing?* Don't you remember?

DADDY: No . . . no. . . .

MOMMY: Of course you do. I'm so sorry, Mrs. Barker. I would have known you anywhere, except in this artificial light. And look! You have a hat just like the one I bought yesterday.

MRS. BARKER (*with a little laugh*): No, not really; this hat is cream.

MOMMY: Well, my dear, that may look like a cream hat to you, but I can . . .

MRS. BARKER: No, now; you seem to forget who I am.

MOMMY: Yes, I do, don't I? Are you sure you're comfortable? Won't you take off your dress?

MRS. BARKER: I don't mind if I do. (*She removes her dress.*)

MOMMY: There. You must feel a great deal more comfortable.

MRS. BARKER: Well, I certainly *look* a great deal more comfortable.

DADDY: I'm going to blush and giggle.

MOMMY: Daddy's going to blush and giggle.

MRS. BARKER (*pulling the hem of her slip above her knees*): You're lucky to have such a man for a husband.

MOMMY: Oh, don't I know it!

DADDY: I just blushed and giggled and went sticky wet.

MOMMY: Isn't Daddy a caution, Mrs. Barker?

MRS. BARKER: Maybe if I smoked . . . ?

MOMMY: Oh, that isn't necessary.

MRS. BARKER: I don't mind if I do.

MOMMY: No; no, don't. Really.

MRS. BARKER: I don't mind . . .

MOMMY: I won't have you smoking in my house, and that's that! You're a professional woman.

DADDY: Grandma drinks AND smokes; don't you, Grandma?

GRANDMA: No.

MOMMY: Well, now, Mrs. Barker; suppose you tell us why you're here.

GRANDMA (*as* MOMMY *walks through the boxes*): The boxes . . . the boxes . . .

MOMMY: Be quiet, Grandma.

DADDY: What did you say, Grandma?

GRANDMA (*as* MOMMY *steps on several of the boxes*): The boxes, damn it!

MRS. BARKER: Boxes; she said boxes. She mentioned the boxes.

DADDY: What about the boxes, Grandma? Maybe Mrs. Barker is here because of the boxes. Is that what you meant, Grandma?

GRANDMA: I don't know if that's what I meant or not. It's certainly not what I *thought* I meant.

DADDY: Grandma is of the opinion that . . .

MRS. BARKER: Can we assume that the boxes are for us? I mean, can we assume that you had us come here for the boxes?

MOMMY: Are you in the habit of receiving boxes?

DADDY: A very good question.

MRS. BARKER: Well, that would depend on the reason we're here. I've got my fingers in so many little pies, you know. Now, I can think of one of my little activities in which we are in the habit of receiving *baskets*; but more in a literary sense than really. We *might* receive boxes, though, under very special circumstances. I'm afraid that's the best answer I can give you.

DADDY: It's a very interesting answer.

MRS. BARKER: *I* thought so. But, does it help?

MOMMY: No; I'm afraid not.

DADDY: I wonder if it might help us any if I said I feel misgivings, that I have definite qualms.

MOMMY: Where, Daddy?

DADDY: Well, mostly right here, right around where the stitches were.

MOMMY: Daddy had an operation, you know.

MRS. BARKER: Oh, you poor Daddy! I didn't know; but then, how could I?

GRANDMA: You might have asked; it wouldn't have hurt you.

MOMMY: Dry up, Grandma.

GRANDMA: There you go. Letting your true feelings come out. Old people aren't dry enough, I suppose. My sacks are empty, the fluid in my eyeballs is all caked on the inside edges, my spine is made of sugar candy, I breathe ice; but you don't hear me complain. Nobody hears old people complain because people think that's all old people do. And *that's* because old people are gnarled and sagged and twisted into the shape of a complaint. (*Signs off.*) That's all.

MRS. BARKER: What was wrong, Daddy?

DADDY: Well, you know how it is: the doctors took out something that was there and put in something that wasn't there. An operation.

MRS. BARKER: You're very fortunate, I should say.

MOMMY: Oh, he is; he is. All his life, Daddy has wanted to be a United States Senator, but now . . . why now he's changed his mind, and for the rest of his life he's going to want to be Governor . . . it would be nearer the apartment, you know.

MRS. BARKER: You *are* fortunate, Daddy.

DADDY: Yes, indeed; except that I get these qualms now and then, definite ones.

MRS. BARKER: Well, it's just a matter of things settling; you're like an old house.

MOMMY: Why Daddy, thank Mrs. Barker.

DADDY: Thank you.

MRS. BARKER: Ambition! That's the ticket. I have a brother who's very much like you, Daddy . . . ambitious. Of course, he's a great deal younger than you; he's even younger than I am . . . if such a thing is possible. He runs a little newspaper. Just a little newspaper . . . but he runs it. He's chief cook and bottle washer of that little newspaper, which he calls *The Village Idiot*. He has such a sense of humor; he's so self-deprecating, so modest. And he'd never admit it himself, but he *is the* Village Idiot.

MOMMY: Oh, I think that's just grand. Don't you think so, Daddy?

DADDY: Yes, just grand.

MRS. BARKER: My brother's a dear man, and he has a dear little wife, whom he loves, dearly. He loves her so much he just can't get a sentence out without mentioning her. He wants everybody to know he's married. He's really a stickler on that point; he can't be introduced to anybody and say hello without adding, ''Of course, I'm married.'' As far as I'm concerned, he's the chief exponent of Woman Love in this whole country; he's even been written up in psychiatric journals because of it.

DADDY: Indeed!

MOMMY: Isn't that lovely.

MRS. BARKER: Oh, I think so. There's too much woman hatred in this country, and that's a fact.

GRANDMA: Oh, I don't know.

MOMMY: Oh, I think that's just grand. Don't you think so, Daddy?

DADDY: Yes, just grand.

GRANDMA: In case anybody's interested . . .

MOMMY: Be quiet, Grandma.

GRANDMA: Nuts!

MOMMY: Oh, Mrs. Barker, you *must* forgive Grandma. She's rural.

MRS. BARKER: I don't mind if I do.

DADDY: Maybe Grandma has something to say.

MOMMY: Nonsense. Old people have nothing to say; and if old people *did* have something to say, nobody would listen to them. (*To* GRANDMA.) You see? I can pull that stuff just as easy as you can.

GRANDMA: Well, you got the rhythm, but you don't really have the quality. Besides, you're middle-aged.

MOMMY: I'm proud of it!

GRANDMA: Look. I'll show you how it's really done. Middle-aged people think they can do anything, but the truth is that middle-aged people can't do most things as well as they used to. Middle-aged people think they're special because they're like everybody else. We live in the age of deformity. You see? Rhythm *and* content. You'll learn.

DADDY: I do wish I weren't surrounded by women; I'd like some men around here.

MRS. BARKER: You can say that again!

GRANDMA: I don't hardly count as a woman, so can I say my piece?

MOMMY: Go on. Jabber away.

GRANDMA: It's very simple; the fact is, these boxes don't have anything to do with why this good lady is come to call. Now, if you're interested in knowing why these boxes *are* here . . .

DADDY: I'm sure that must be all very true, Grandma, but what does it have to do with why . . . pardon me, what is that name again?

MRS. BARKER: Mrs. Barker.

DADDY: Exactly. What does it have to do with why . . . that name again?

MRS. BARKER: Mrs. Barker.

DADDY: Precisely. What does it have to do with why what's-her-name is here?

MOMMY: They're here because we asked them.

MRS. BARKER: Yes. That's why.

GRANDMA: Now if you're interested in knowing why these boxes *are* here . . .

MOMMY: Well, nobody *is* interested!

GRANDMA: You can be as snippety as you like for all the good it'll do you.

DADDY: You two will have to stop arguing.

MOMMY: I don't argue with her.

DADDY: It will just have to stop.

MOMMY: Well, why don't you call a van and have her taken away?

GRANDMA: Don't bother; there's no need.

DADDY: No, now, perhaps I can go away myself. . . .

MOMMY: Well, one or the other; the way things are now it's impossible. In the first place, it's too crowded in this apartment. (*To* GRANDMA.) And it's you that takes up all the space, with your enema bottles, and your Pekinese, and God-only-knows-what-else . . . and now all these boxes. . . .

GRANDMA: These boxes are . . .

MRS. BARKER: I've never heard of enema *bottles*. . . .

GRANDMA: She means enema bags, but she doesn't know the difference. Mommy comes from extremely bad stock. And besides, when Mommy was born . . . well, it was a difficult delivery, and she had a head shaped like a banana.

MOMMY: You ungrateful—Daddy? Daddy, you see how ungrateful she is after all these years, after all the things we've done for her? (*To* GRANDMA.) One of these days you're going away in a van; that's what's going to happen to you!

GRANDMA: Do tell!

MRS. BARKER: Like a banana?

GRANDMA: Yup, just like a banana.

MRS. BARKER: My word!

MOMMY: You stop listening to her; she'll say anything. Just the other night she called Daddy a hedgehog.

MRS. BARKER: She didn't!

GRANDMA: That's right, baby; you stick up for me.

MOMMY: I don't know where she gets the words; on the television, maybe.

MRS. BARKER: Did you really call him a hedgehog?

GRANDMA: Oh look; what difference does it make whether I did or not?

DADDY: Grandma's right. Leave Grandma alone.

MOMMY (*to* DADDY): How dare you!

GRANDMA: Oh, leave her alone, Daddy; the kid's all mixed up.

MOMMY: You see? I told you. It's all those television shows. Daddy, you go right into Grandma's room and take her television and shake all the tubes loose.

DADDY: Don't mention tubes to me.

MOMMY: Oh! Mommy forgot! (*To* MRS. BARKER.) Daddy has tubes now, where he used to have tracts.

MRS. BARKER: Is that a fact!

GRANDMA: I know why this dear lady is here.

MOMMY: You be still.

MRS. BARKER: Oh, I do wish you'd tell me.

MOMMY: No! No! That wouldn't be fair at all.

DADDY: Besides, she knows why she's here; she's here because we called them.

MRS. BARKER: La! But that still leaves me puzzled. I know I'm here because you called us, but I'm such a busy girl, with this committee and that committee, and the Responsible Citizens Activities I indulge in.

MOMMY: Oh my; busy, busy.

MRS. BARKER: Yes, indeed. So I'm afraid you'll have to give me some help.

MOMMY: Oh, no. No, you must be mistaken. I can't believe we asked you here to give you any help. With the way taxes are these days, and the way you can't get satisfaction in ANYTHING . . . no, I don't believe so.

DADDY: And if you need help . . . why, I should think you'd apply for a Fulbright Scholarship. . . .

MOMMY: And if not that . . . why, then a Guggenheim Fellowship. . . .

GRANDMA: Oh, come on; why not shoot the works and try for the Prix de Rome. (*Under her breath to* MOMMY AND DADDY.) Beasts!

MRS. BARKER: Oh, what a jolly family. But let me think. I'm knee-deep in work these days; there's the Ladies' Auxiliary Air Raid Committee, for one thing; how do you feel about air raids?

MOMMY: Oh, I'd say we're hostile.

DADDY: Yes, definitely; we're hostile.

MRS. BARKER: Then, you'll be no help there. There's too much hostility in the world these days as it is; but I'll not badger you! There's a surfeit of badgers as well.

GRANDMA: While we're at it, there's been a run on old people, too. The Department of Agriculture, or maybe it wasn't the Department of Agriculture—anyway, it was some department that's run by a girl—put out figures showing that ninety per cent of the adult population of the country is over eighty years old . . . or eighty per cent is over ninety years old . . .

MOMMY: You're such a liar! You just finished saying that everyone is middle-aged.

GRANDMA: I'm just telling you what the government says . . . that doesn't have anything to do with what . . .

MOMMY: It's that television! Daddy, go break her television.

GRANDMA: You won't find it.

DADDY (*wearily getting up*): If I must . . . I must.

MOMMY: And don't step on the Pekinese; it's blind.

DADDY: It may be blind, but Daddy isn't. (*He exits, through the archway, stage-left.*)

GRANDMA: You won't find *it,* either.

MOMMY: Oh, I'm so fortunate to have such a husband. Just think; I could have a husband who was poor, or argumentative, or a husband who sat in a wheel chair all day . . . OOOOHHHH! *What* have I said? What *have* I said?

GRANDMA: You said you could have a husband who sat in a wheel . . .

MOMMY: I'm mortified! I could die! I could cut my tongue out! I could . . .

MRS. BARKER (*forcing a smile*): Oh, now . . . now . . . don't think about it . . .

MOMMY: I could . . . why, I could . . .

MRS. BARKER: . . . don't think about it . . . really. . . .

MOMMY: You're quite right. I won't think about it, and that way I'll forget that I ever said it, and that way it will be all right. (*Pause.*) There . . . I've forgotten. Well, now, now that Daddy is out of the room we can have some girl talk.

MRS. BARKER: I'm not sure that I . . .

MOMMY: You *do* want to have some girl talk, don't you?

MRS. BARKER: I was going to say I'm not sure that I wouldn't care for a glass of water. I feel a little faint.

MOMMY: Grandma, go get Mrs. Barker a glass of water.

GRANDMA: Go get it yourself. I quit.

MOMMY: Grandma loves to do little things around the house; it gives her a false sense of security.

GRANDMA: I quit! I'm through!

MOMMY: Now, you be a good Grandma, or you know what will happen to you. You'll be taken away in a van.

GRANDMA: You don't frighten me. I'm too old to be frightened. Besides . . .

MOMMY: WELL! I'll tend to you later. I'll hide your teeth . . . I'll . . .

GRANDMA: Everything's hidden.

MRS. BARKER: I *am* going to faint. I *am*.

MOMMY: Good heavens! I'll go myself. (*As she exits, through the archway, stage-left.*) I'll fix you, Grandma. I'll take care of you later. (*She exits.*)

GRANDMA: Oh, go soak your head. (*To* MRS. BARKER.) Well, dearie, how do you feel?

MRS. BARKER: A little better, I think. Yes, much better, thank you, Grandma.

GRANDMA: That's good.

MRS. BARKER: But . . . I feel so lost . . . not knowing why I'm here . . . and, on top of it, they say I was here before.

GRANDMA: Well, you were. You weren't *here*, exactly, because we've moved around a lot, from one apartment to another, up and down the social ladder like mice, if you like similes.

MRS. BARKER: I don't . . . particularly.

GRANDMA: Well, then, I'm sorry.

MRS. BARKER (*suddenly*): Grandma, I feel I can trust you.

GRANDMA: Don't be too sure; it's every man for himself around this place. . . .

MRS. BARKER: Oh . . . is it? Nonetheless, I really do feel that I can trust you. *Please* tell me why they called and asked us to come. I implore you!

GRANDMA: Oh my; that feels good. It's been so long since anybody implored me. Do it again. Implore me some more.

MRS. BARKER: You're your daughter's mother, all right!

GRANDMA: Oh, I don't mean to be hard. If you won't implore me, then beg me, or ask me, or entreat me . . . just anything like that.

MRS. BARKER: You're a dreadful old woman!

GRANDMA: You'll understand some day. Please!

MRS. BARKER: Oh, for heaven's sake! . . . I implore you . . . I beg you . . . I beseech you!

GRANDMA: Beseech! Oh, that's the nicest word I've heard in ages. You're a dear, sweet woman. . . . You . . . beseech . . . me. I can't resist that.

MRS. BARKER: Well, then . . . please tell me why they asked us to come.

GRANDMA: Well, I'll give you a hint. That's the best I can do, because I'm a muddleheaded old woman. Now listen, because it's important. Once upon a time, not too very long ago, but a long enough time ago . . . oh, about twenty years ago . . . there was a man very much like Daddy, and a woman very much like Mommy, who were married to each other, very much like Mommy and Daddy are married to each other; and they lived in an apartment very much like one that's very much like this one, and they lived there with an old woman who was very much like yours truly, only younger, because it was some time ago; in fact, they were all somewhat younger.

MRS. BARKER: How fascinating!

GRANDMA: Now, at the same time, there was a dear lady very much like you, only younger then, who did all sorts of Good Works. . . . And one of the Good Works this dear lady did was in something very much like a volunteer capacity for an organization very much like the Bye-Bye Adoption Service, which is nearby and which was run by a terribly deaf old lady very much like the Miss Bye-Bye who runs the Bye-Bye Adoption Service nearby.

MRS. BARKER: How enthralling!

GRANDMA: Well, be that as it may. Nonetheless, one afternoon this man, who was very much like Daddy, and this woman who was very much like Mommy came to see this dear lady who did all the Good Works, who was very much like you, dear, and they were very sad and very hopeful, and they cried and smiled and bit their fingers, and they said all the most intimate things.

MRS. BARKER: How spellbinding! What did they say?

GRANDMA: Well, it was very sweet. The woman, who was very much like Mommy, said that she and the man who was very much like Daddy had never been blessed with anything very much like a bumble of joy.

MRS. BARKER: A what?

GRANDMA: A bumble; a bumble of joy.

MRS. BARKER: Oh, like bundle.

GRANDMA: Well, yes; very much like it. Bundle, bumble; who cares? At any rate, the woman, who was very much like Mommy, said that they wanted a bumble of their own, but that the man, who was very much like Daddy, couldn't have a bumble; and the man, who was very much like Daddy, said that yes, they had wanted a bumble of their own, but that the woman, who was very much like Mommy, couldn't have one, and that now they wanted to buy something very much like a bumble.

MRS. BARKER: How engrossing!

GRANDMA: Yes. And the dear lady, who was very much like you, said something that was very much like, "Oh, what a shame; but take heart . . . I think we have just the bumble *for* you." And, well, the lady, who was very much like Mommy, and the man, who was very much like Daddy, cried and smiled and bit their fingers, and said some more intimate things, which were totally irrelevant but which were pretty hot stuff, and so the dear lady, who was very much like you, and who had something very much like a penchant for pornography, listened with something very much like enthusiasm. "Whee," she said. "Whoooopeeeeee!" But that's beside the point.

MRS. BARKER: I suppose *so*. But how gripping!

GRANDMA: Anyway . . . they *bought* something very much like a bumble, and they took it away with them. But . . . things didn't work out very well.

MRS. BARKER: You mean there was trouble?

GRANDMA: You got it. (*With a glance through the archway.*) But, I'm going to have to speed up now because I think I'm leaving soon.

MRS. BARKER: Oh. Are you really?

GRANDMA: Yup.

MRS. BARKER: But old people don't go anywhere; they're either taken places, or put places.

GRANDMA: Well, this old person is different. Anyway . . . things started going badly.

MRS. BARKER: Oh yes. Yes.

GRANDMA: Weeeeellll . . . in the first place, it turned out the bumble didn't look like either one of its parents. That was enough of a blow, but things got worse. One night, it cried its heart out, if you can imagine such a thing.

MRS. BARKER: Cried its heart out! Well!

GRANDMA: But that was only the beginning. Then it turned out it only had eyes for its Daddy.

MRS. BARKER: For its Daddy! Why, any self-respecting woman would have gouged those eyes right out of its head.

GRANDMA: Well, she did. That's exactly what she did. But then, it kept its nose up in the air.

MRS. BARKER: Ufggh! How disgusting!

GRANDMA: That's what they thought. But *then*, it began to develop an interest in its you-know-what.

MRS. BARKER: In its you-know-what! Well! I hope they cut its hands off at the wrists!

GRANDMA: Well, yes, they did that eventually. But first, they cut off its you-know-what.

MRS. BARKER: A much better idea!

GRANDMA: That's what they thought. But after they cut off its you-know-what, it *still* puts its hands under the covers, *looking* for its you-know-what. So, finally, they *had* to cut off its hands at the wrists.

MRS. BARKER: Naturally!

GRANDMA: And it was such a resentful bumble. Why, one day it called its Mommy a dirty name.

MRS. BARKER: Well, I hope they cut its tongue out!

GRANDMA: Of course. And then, as it got bigger, they found out all sorts of terrible things about it, like: it didn't have a head on its shoulders, it had no guts, it was spineless, its feet were made of clay . . . just dreadful things.

MRS. BARKER: Dreadful!

GRANDMA: So you can understand how they became discouraged.

MRS. BARKER: I certainly can! And what did they do?

GRANDMA: What did they do? Well, for the last straw, it finally up and died; and you can imagine how *that* made them feel, their having paid for it, and all. So, they called up the lady who sold them the bumble in the first place and told her to come right over to their apartment. They wanted satisfaction; they wanted their money back. That's what they wanted.

MRS. BARKER: My, my, my.

GRANDMA: How do you like *them* apples?

MRS. BARKER: My, my, my.

DADDY (*off stage*): Mommy! I can't find Grandma's television, and I can't find the Pekinese, either.

MOMMY (*off stage*): Isn't that funny! And I can't find the water.

GRANDMA: Heh, heh, heh. I told them everything was hidden.

MRS. BARKER: Did you hide the water, too?

GRANDMA (*puzzled*): No. No, I didn't do *that.*

DADDY (*off stage*): The truth of the matter is, I can't even find Grandma's room.

GRANDMA: Heh, heh, heh.

MRS. BARKER: My! You certainly did hide things, didn't you?

GRANDMA: Sure, kid, sure.

MOMMY (*sticking her head in the room*): Did you ever hear of such a thing, Grandma? Daddy can't find your television, and he can't find the Pekinese, and the truth of the matter is he can't even find your room.

GRANDMA: I told you. I hid everything.

MOMMY: Nonsense, Grandma! Just wait until I get my hands on you. You're a troublemaker . . . that's what you are.

GRANDMA: Well, I'll be out of here pretty soon, baby.

MOMMY: Oh, you don't know how right you are! Daddy's been wanting to send you away for a long time now, but I've been restraining him. I'll tell you one thing, though . . . I'm getting sick and tired of this fighting, and I might just let him have his way. Then you'll see what'll happen. Away you'll go; in a van, too. I'll let Daddy call the van man.

GRANDMA: I'm way ahead of you.

MOMMY: How can you be so old and so smug at the same time? You have no sense of proportion.

GRANDMA: You just answered your own question.

MOMMY: Mrs. Barker, I'd much rather you came into the kitchen for that glass of water, what with Grandma out here, and all.

MRS. BARKER: I don't see what Grandma has to do with it; and besides, I don't think you're very polite.

MOMMY: You seem to forget that you're a guest in this house . . .

GRANDMA: Apartment!

MOMMY: Apartment! And that you're a professional woman. So, if you'll be so good as to come into the kitchen, I'll be more than happy to show you where the water is, and where the glass is, and then you can put two and two together, if you're clever enough. (*She vanishes.*)

MRS. BARKER (*after a moment's consideration*): I suppose she's right.

GRANDMA: Well, that's how it is when people call you up and ask you over to do something for them.

MRS. BARKER: I suppose you're right, too. Well, Grandma, it's been very nice talking to you.

GRANDMA: And I've enjoyed listening. Say, don't tell Mommy or Daddy that I gave you that hint, will you?

MRS. BARKER: Oh, dear me, the hint! I'd forgotten about it, if you can imagine such a thing. No, I won't breathe a word of it to them.

GRANDMA: I don't know if it helped you any . . .

MRS. BARKER: I can't tell, yet. I'll have to . . . what *is* the word I want? . . . I'll have to relate it . . . that's it . . . I'll have to relate it to certain things that I *know,* and . . . draw . . . conclusions. . . . What I'll really have to do is to see if it applies to anything. I mean, after all, I *do* do volunteer work for an adoption service, but it isn't very much *like* the Bye-Bye Adoption Service . . . it *is* the Bye-Bye Adoption Service . . . and while I can remember Mommy and Daddy coming to see me, oh, about twenty years ago, about buying a bumble, I can't quite remember anyone very much *like* Mommy and Daddy coming to see me about buying a bumble. Don't you see? It really presents quite a problem. . . . I'll have to think about it . . . mull it . . . but at any rate, it was truly first-class of you to try to help me. Oh, will you still be here after I've had my drink of water?

GRANDMA: Probably . . . I'm not as spry as I used to be.

MRS. BARKER: Oh. Well, I won't say good-by then.

GRANDMA: No. Don't. (MRS. BARKER *exits through the archway.*) People don't say good-by to old people because they think they'll frighten them. Lordy! If they only knew how awful "hello" and "my, you're looking chipper" sounded, they wouldn't say those things either. The truth is, there isn't much you *can* say to old people that doesn't sound just terrible. (*The doorbell rings.*) Come on in! (*The* YOUNG MAN *enters.* GRANDMA *looks him over.*) Well, now, aren't you a breath of fresh air!

YOUNG MAN: Hello there.

GRANDMA: My, my, my. Are you the van man?

YOUNG MAN: The what?

GRANDMA: The van man. The van man. Are you come to take me away?

YOUNG MAN: I don't know what you're talking about.

GRANDMA: Oh. (*Pause.*) Well, (*Pause.*) My, my, aren't you something!

YOUNG MAN: Hm?

GRANDMA: I said, my, my, aren't you something.

YOUNG MAN: Oh. Thank you.

GRANDMA: You don't sound very enthusiastic.

YOUNG MAN: Oh, I'm . . . I'm used to it.

GRANDMA: Yup . . . yup. You know, if I were about a hundred and fifty years younger I could go for you.

YOUNG MAN: Yes, I imagine so.

GRANDMA: Unh-hunh . . . will you look at those muscles!

YOUNG MAN (*flexing his muscles*): Yes, they're quite good, aren't they?

GRANDMA: Boy, they sure are. They natural?

YOUNG MAN: Well, the basic structure was there, but I've done some work, too . . . you know, in a gym.

GRANDMA: I'll bet you have. You ought to be in the movies, boy.

YOUNG MAN: I know.

GRANDMA: Yup! Right up there on the old silver screen. But I suppose you've heard that before.

YOUNG MAN: Yes, I have.

GRANDMA: You ought to try out for them . . . the movies.

YOUNG MAN: Well, actually, I may have a career there yet. I've lived out on the West Coast almost all my life . . . and I've met a few people who . . . might be able to help me. I'm not in too much of a hurry, though. I'm almost as young as I look.

GRANDMA: Oh, that's nice. And will you look at that face!

YOUNG MAN: Yes, it's quite good, isn't it? Clean-cut, midwest farm boy type, almost insultingly good-looking in a typically American way. Good profile, straight nose, honest eyes, wonderful smile . . .

GRANDMA: Yup. Boy, you know what you are, don't you? You're the American Dream, that's what you are. All those other people, they don't know what they're talking about. You . . . *you* are the American Dream.

YOUNG MAN: Thanks.

MOMMY (*off stage*): Who rang the doorbell?

GRANDMA (*shouting off stage*): The American Dream!

MOMMY (*off stage*): What? What was that, Grandma?

GRANDMA (*shouting*): The American Dream! The American Dream! Damn it!

DADDY (*off stage*): How's that, Mommy?

MOMMY (*off stage*): Oh, some gibberish; pay no attention. Did you find Grandma's room?

DADDY (*off stage*): No. I can't even find Mrs. Barker.

YOUNG MAN: What was all that?

GRANDMA: Oh, that was just the folks, but let's not talk about them, honey; let's talk about you.

YOUNG MAN: All right.

GRANDMA: Well, let's see. If you're not the van man, what are you doing here?

YOUNG MAN: I'm looking for work.

GRANDMA: Are you! Well, what kind of work?

YOUNG MAN: Oh, almost anything . . . almost anything that pays. I'll do almost anything for money.

GRANDMA: Will you . . . will you? Hmmmm. I wonder if there's anything you could do around here?

YOUNG MAN: There might be. It looked to be a likely building.

GRANDMA: It's always looked to be a rather unlikely building to me, but I suppose you'd know better than I.

YOUNG MAN: I can sense these things.

GRANDMA: There *might* be something you could do around here. Stay there! Don't come any closer.

YOUNG MAN: Sorry.

GRANDMA: I don't mean I'd *mind.* I don't know whether I'd mind, or not . . . But it wouldn't look well; it would look just *awful.*

YOUNG MAN: Yes; I suppose so.

GRANDMA: Now, stay there, let me concentrate. What could you do? The folks have been in something of a quandary around here today, sort of a dilemma, and I wonder if you mightn't be some help.

YOUNG MAN: I hope so . . . if there's money in it. Do you have any money?

GRANDMA: Money! Oh, there's more money around here than you'd know what to do with.

YOUNG MAN: I'm not so sure.

GRANDMA: Well, maybe not. Besides, I've got money of my own.

YOUNG MAN: You have?

GRANDMA: Sure. Old people quite often have lots of money; more often than most people expect. Come here, so I can whisper to you . . . not too close. I might faint.

YOUNG MAN: Oh, I'm sorry.

GRANDMA: It's all right, dear. Anyway . . . have you ever heard of that big baking contest they run? The one where all the ladies get together in a big barn and bake away?

YOUNG MAN: I'm . . . not . . . sure. . . .

GRANDMA: Not so close. Well, it doesn't matter whether you've heard of it or not. The important thing is—and I don't want anybody to hear this . . . the folks think I haven't been out of the house in eight years—the important thing is that I won first prize in that baking contest this year. Oh, it was in all the papers; not under my own name, though. I used a *nom de boulangère;* I called myself Uncle Henry.

YOUNG MAN: Did you?

GRANDMA: Why not? I didn't see any reason not to. I look just as much like an old man as I do like an old woman. And you know what I called it . . . what I won for?

YOUNG MAN: No. What did you call it?

GRANDMA: I called it Uncle Henry's Day-Old Cake.

YOUNG MAN: That's a very nice name.

GRANDMA: And it wasn't any trouble, either. All I did was go out and get a store-bought cake, and keep it around for a while, and then slip it in, unbeknownst to anybody. Simple.

YOUNG MAN: You're a very resourceful person.

GRANDMA: Pioneer stock.

YOUNG MAN: Is all this true? Do you want me to believe all this?

GRANDMA: Well, you can believe it or not . . . it doesn't make any difference to me. All *I* know is, Uncle Henry's Day-Old Cake won me twenty-five thousand smackerolas.

YOUNG MAN: Twenty-five thou—

GRANDMA: Right on the old loggerhead. Now . . . how do you like them apples?

YOUNG MAN: Love 'em.

GRANDMA: I thought you'd be impressed.

YOUNG MAN: Money talks.

GRANDMA: Hey! You look familiar.

YOUNG MAN: Hm? Pardon?

GRANDMA: I said, you look familiar.

YOUNG MAN: Well, I've done some modeling.

GRANDMA: No . . . no. I don't mean that. You look familiar.

YOUNG MAN: Well, I'm a type.

GRANDMA: Yup; you sure are. Why do you say you'd do anything for money . . . if you don't mind my being nosy?

YOUNG MAN: No, no. It's part of the interviews. I'll be happy to tell you. It's that I have no talents at all, except what you see . . . my person; my body, my face. In every other way I am incomplete, and I must therefore . . . compensate.

GRANDMA: What do you mean, incomplete? You look pretty complete to me.

YOUNG MAN: I think I can explain it to you, partially because you're very old, and very old people have perceptions they keep to themselves, because if they expose them to other people . . . well, you know what ridicule and neglect are.

GRANDMA: I do, child, I do.

YOUNG MAN: Then listen. My mother died the night that I was born, and I never knew my father; I doubt my mother did. But, I wasn't alone, because lying with me . . . in the placenta . . . there was someone else . . . my brother . . . my twin.

GRANDMA: Oh, my child.

YOUNG MAN: We were identical twins . . . he and I . . . not fraternal . . . identical; we were derived from the same ovum; and in *this,* in that we were twins not from separate ova but from the same one, we had a kinship such as you cannot imagine. We . . . we felt each other breathe . . . his heartbeats thundered in my temples . . . mine in his . . . our stomachs ached and we cried for feeding at the same time . . . are you old enough to understand?

GRANDMA: I think so, child; I think I'm nearly old enough.

YOUNG MAN: I hope so. But we were separated when we were still very young, my brother, my twin and I . . . inasmuch as you can separate one being. We were torn apart . . . thrown to opposite ends of the continent. I don't know what became of my brother . . . to the rest of myself . . . except that, from time to time, in the years that have passed, I have suffered losses . . . that I can't explain. A fall from grace . . . a departure of innocence . . . loss . . . loss. How can I put it to you? All right; like this: Once . . . it was as if all at once my heart . . . became numb . . . almost as though I . . . almost as though . . . just like that . . . it had been wrenched from my body . . . and from that time I have been unable to love. Once . . . I was asleep at the time . . . I awoke, and my eyes were burning. And since that time I have been unable to see anything, *anything*, with pity, with affection . . . with anything but . . . cool disinterest. And my groin . . . even there . . . since one time . . . one specific agony . . . since then I have not been able to *love* anyone with my body. And even my hands . . . I cannot touch another person and feel love. And there is more . . . there are more losses, but it all comes down to this: I no longer have the capacity to feel anything. I have no emotions. I have been drained, torn asunder . . . disemboweled. I have, now, only my person . . . my body, my face. I use what I have . . . I let people love me . . . I accept the syntax around me, for while I know I cannot relate . . . I know I must be related *to*. I let people love me . . . I let people touch me . . . I let them draw pleasure from my groin . . . from my presence . . . from the fact of me . . . but, that is all it comes to. As I told you, I am incomplete . . . I can feel nothing. I can feel nothing. And so . . . here I am . . . as you see me. I am . . . but this . . . what you see. And it will always be thus.

GRANDMA: Oh, my child; my child. (*Long pause; then:*) I was mistaken . . . before. I don't know you from somewhere, but I knew . . . once . . . someone very much like you . . . or, very much as perhaps you were.

YOUNG MAN: Be careful; be very careful. What I have told you may not be true. In my profession . . .

GRANDMA: Shhhhhh. (*The* YOUNG MAN *bows his head, in acquiescence.*) Someone . . . to be more precise . . . who might have turned out to be very much like you might have turned out to be. And . . . unless I'm terribly mistaken . . . you've found yourself a job.

YOUNG MAN: What are my duties?

MRS. BARKER (*off stage*): Yoo-hoo! Yoo-hoo!

GRANDMA: Oh-oh. You'll . . . you'll have to play it by ear, my dear . . . unless I get a chance to talk to you again. I've got to go into my act, now.

YOUNG MAN: But, I . . .

GRANDMA: Yoo-hoo!

MRS. BARKER (*coming through archway*): Yoo-hoo . . . oh, there you are, Grandma. I'm glad to see somebody. I can't find Mommy or Daddy. (*Double takes.*) Well . . . who's this?

GRANDMA: This? Well . . . un . . . oh, this is the . . . un . . . the van man. That's who it is . . . the van man.

MRS. BARKER: So! It's true! They *did* call the van man. They *are* having you carted away.

GRANDMA (*shrugging*): Well, you know. It figures.

MRS. BARKER (*to* YOUNG MAN): How dare you cart this poor old woman away!

YOUNG MAN (*after a quick look at* GRANDMA, *who nods*): I do what I'm paid to do. I don't ask any questions.

MRS. BARKER (*after a brief pause*): Oh. (*Pause.*) Well, you're quite right, of course, and I shouldn't meddle.

GRANDMA (*to* YOUNG MAN): Dear, will you take my things out to the van? (*She points to the boxes.*)

YOUNG MAN (*after only the briefest hesitation*): Why certainly.

GRANDMA (*as the* YOUNG MAN *takes up half the boxes, exits by the front door*): Isn't that a nice young van man?

MRS. BARKER (*shaking her head in disbelief, watching the* YOUNG MAN *exit*): Unh-hunh . . . some things have changed for the better. I remember when I had *my* mother carted off . . . the van man who came for her wasn't anything near as nice as this one.

GRANDMA: Oh, did you have your mother carted off, too?

MRS. BARKER (*cheerfully*): Why certainly! Didn't you?

GRANDMA (*puzzling*): No . . . no, I didn't. At least, I can't remember. Listen dear; I got to talk to you for a second.

MRS. BARKER: Why certainly, Grandma.

GRANDMA: Now, listen.

MRS. BARKER: Yes, Grandma. Yes.

GRANDMA: Now listen carefully. You got this dilemma here with Mommy and Daddy . . .

MRS. BARKER: Yes! I wonder where they've gone to?

GRANDMA: They'll be back in. Now, LISTEN!

MRS. BARKER: Oh, I'm sorry.

GRANDMA: Now, you got this dilemma here with Mommy and Daddy, and I think I got the way out for you. (*The* YOUNG MAN *re-enters through the front door.*) Will you take the rest of my things out now, dear? (*To* MRS. BARKER, *while the* YOUNG MAN *takes the rest of the boxes, exits again by the front door.*) Fine. Now listen, dear. (*She begins to whisper in* MRS. BARKER'S *ear.*)

MRS. BARKER: Oh! Oh! Oh! I don't think I could . . . do you really think I could? Well, why not? What a wonderful idea . . . what an absolutely wonderful idea!

GRANDMA: Well, yes, I thought it was.

MRS. BARKER: And you so old!

GRANDMA: Heh, heh, heh.

MRS. BARKER: Well, I think it's absolutely marvelous, anyway. I'm going to find Mommy and Daddy right now.

GRANDMA: Good. You do that.

MRS. BARKER: Well, now. I think I will say good-by. I can't thank you enough. (*She starts to exit through the archway.*)

GRANDMA: You're welcome. Say it!

MRS. BARKER: Huh? What?

GRANDMA: Say good-by.

MRS. BARKER: Oh. Good-by. (*She exits.*) Mommy! I say, Mommy! Daddy!

GRANDMA: Good-by. (*By herself now, she looks about.*) Ah me. (*Shakes her head.*) Ah me. (*Takes in the room.*) Good-by. (*The* YOUNG MAN *re-enters.*)

GRANDMA: Oh, hello, there.

YOUNG MAN: All the boxes are outside.

GRANDMA (*a little sadly*): I don't know why I bother to take them with me. They don't have much in them . . . some old letters, a couple of regrets . . . Pekinese . . . blind at that . . . the television . . . my Sunday teeth . . . eighty-six years of living . . . some sounds . . . a few images, a little garbled by now . . . and, well . . . (*She shrugs.*) . . . you know . . . the things one accumulates.

YOUNG MAN: Can I get you . . . a cab, or something?

GRANDMA: Oh no, dear . . . thank you just the same. I'll take it from here.

YOUNG MAN: And what shall I do now?

GRANDMA: Oh, you stay here, dear. It will all become clear to you. It will be explained. You'll understand.

YOUNG MAN: Very well.

GRANDMA (*after one more look about*): Well . . .

YOUNG MAN: Let me see you to the elevator.

GRANDMA: Oh . . . that *would* be nice, dear.

(*They both exit by the front door, slowly.*)

(*Enter* MRS. BARKER, *followed by* MOMMY *and* DADDY.)

MRS. BARKER: . . . and I'm happy to tell you that the whole thing's settled. Just like that.

MOMMY: Oh, we're so glad. We were afraid there might be a problem, what with delays, and all.

DADDY: Yes, we're very relieved.

MRS. BARKER: Well, now; that's what professional women are for.

MOMMY: Why . . . where's Grandma? Grandma's not here! Where's Grandma? And look! The boxes are gone, too. Grandma's gone, and so are the boxes. She's taken off, and she's stolen something! Daddy!

MRS. BARKER: Why, Mommy, the van man was here.

MOMMY (*startled*): The what?

MRS. BARKER: The van man. The van man was here.

(*The lights might dim a little, suddenly.*)

MOMMY (*shakes her head*): No, that's impossible.

MRS. BARKER: Why, I saw him with my own two eyes.

MOMMY (*near tears*): No, no, that's impossible. No. There's no such thing as the van man. There is no van man. We . . . we made him up. Grandma? Grandma?

DADDY (*moving to* MOMMY): There, there, now.

MOMMY: Oh Daddy . . . where's Grandma?

DADDY: There, there, now.

(*While* DADDY *is comforting* MOMMY, GRANDMA *comes out, stage-right, near the footlights.*)

GRANDMA (*to the audience*): Shhhhhh! I want to watch this.

(*She motions to* MRS. BARKER *who, with a secret smile, tiptoes to the front door and opens it. The* YOUNG MAN *is framed therein. Lights up full again as he steps into the room.*)

MRS. BARKER: Surprise! Surprise! Here we are!

MOMMY: What? What?

DADDY: Hm? What?

MOMMY (*her tears merely sniffles now*): What surprise?

MRS. BARKER: Why, I told you. The surprise I told you about.

DADDY: You . . . you know, Mommy.

MOMMY: Sur . . . prise?

DADDY (*urging her to cheerfulness*): You remember, Mommy; why we asked . . . uh . . . what's-her-name to come here?

MRS. BARKER: Mrs. Barker, if you don't mind.

DADDY: Yes. Mommy? You remember now? About the bumble . . . about wanting satisfaction?

MOMMY (*her sorrow turning into delight*): Yes. Why yes! Of course! Yes! Oh, how wonderful!

MRS. BARKER (*to the* YOUNG MAN): This is Mommy.

YOUNG MAN: How . . . how do you do?

MRS. BARKER (*stage whisper*): Her name's Mommy.

YOUNG MAN: How . . . how do you do, Mommy?

MOMMY: Well! Hello there!

MRS. BARKER (*to the* YOUNG MAN): And that is Daddy.

YOUNG MAN: How do you do, sir?

DADDY: How do you do?

MOMMY (*herself again, circling the* YOUNG MAN, *feeling his arm, poking him*): Yes, sir! Yes, sirree! Now this is more like it. Now this is a great deal more like it! Daddy! Come see. Come see if this isn't a great deal more like it.

DADDY: I . . . I can see from here, Mommy. It does look a great deal more like it.

MOMMY: Yes, sir. Yes sirree! Mrs. Barker, I don't know *how* to thank you.

MRS. BARKER: Oh, don't worry about that. I'll send you a bill in the mail.

MOMMY: What this really calls for is a celebration. It calls for a drink.

MRS. BARKER: Oh, what a nice idea.

MOMMY: There's some sauterne in the kitchen.

YOUNG MAN: I'll go.

MOMMY: Will you? Oh, how nice. The kitchen's through the archway there. (*As the* YOUNG MAN *exits: to* MRS. BARKER.) He's very nice. Really top notch; much better than the other one.

MRS. BARKER: I'm glad you're pleased. And I'm glad everything's all straightened out.

MOMMY: Well, at least we know why we sent for you. We're glad that's cleared up. By the way, what's his name?

MRS. BARKER: Ha! Call him whatever you like. He's yours. Call him what you called the other one.

MOMMY: Daddy? What did we call the other one?

DADDY (*puzzles*): Why . . .

YOUNG MAN (*re-entering with a tray on which are a bottle of sauterne and five glasses*): Here we are!

MOMMY: Hooray! Hooray!

MRS. BARKER: Oh, good!

MOMMY (*moving to the tray*): So, let's—Five glasses? Why five? There are only four of us. Why five?

YOUNG MAN (*catches* GRANDMA'S *eye;* GRANDMA *indicates she is not there*): Oh, I'm sorry.

MOMMY: You must learn to count. We're a wealthy family, and you must learn to count.

YOUNG MAN: I will.

MOMMY: Well, everybody take a glass. (*They do.*) And we'll drink to celebrate. To satisfaction! Who says you can't get satisfaction these days!

MRS. BARKER: What dreadful sauterne!

MOMMY: Yes, isn't it? (*To* YOUNG MAN, *her voice already a little fuzzy from the wine.*) You don't know how happy I am to see you! Yes sirree. Listen, that time we had with . . . with the other one. I'll tell you about it some time. (*Indicates* MRS. BARKER.) After she's gone. She was responsible for all the trouble in the first place. I'll tell you all about it. (*Sidles up to him a little.*) Maybe . . . maybe later tonight.

YOUNG MAN (*not moving away*): Why yes. That would be very nice.

MOMMY (*puzzles*): Something familiar about you . . . you know that? I can't quite place it. . . .

GRANDMA (*interrupting . . . to audience*): Well, I guess that just about wraps it up. I mean, for better or worse, this is a comedy, and I don't think we'd better go any further. No, definitely not. So, let's leave things as they are right now . . . while everybody's happy . . . while everybody's got what he wants . . . or everybody's got what he thinks he wants. Good night, dears.

Fact Questions and Exercises

1. Describe the tantrum that Mommy throws about the wheat-colored hat.
2. Whose mother is Grandma? What does Grandma collect?
3. According to Mommy, why does she "have a right to live off of" Daddy?
4. Identify Mrs. Barker. What does she do that makes Daddy "blush and giggle"?
5. What did Mommy and Daddy do to the first son they adopted?
6. Who or what in the play is the American Dream?
7. Identify the "van man." Whose twin is he?
8. How has Grandma won "twenty-five thousand smackerolas"?
9. To whom is Grandma speaking in the final lines of the play?

For Discussion and Writing

1. Note the language of the play; how do Mommy and Daddy talk? Do they use conventional adult language? How does language act as a factor in characterizing Mommy and Daddy? Does Grandma use the same type of speech?
2. The play is a satire. How does Albee accomplish this? Note, for instance, the inversion of conventional or stereotyped characters. Does Grandma act the way most grandmothers are thought to act? Do Mommy and Daddy treat their child the way most parents would treat a child? What is Albee criticizing in his satire? What values does he imply are missing from American family life?
3. Discuss Albee's use of symbols. For instance, what does Grandma's box collection symbolize? What do the two adopted sons represent? Are Mommy and Daddy themselves symbols? If so, what do they symbolize?

Ed Bullins [1935–   ]

Bullins was born in Philadelphia, Pennsylvania. He has served as the director of the New Lafayette Theater in Harlem, and has worked in San Francisco and other American cities to establish theater groups. Bullins's plays are noted for their combination of the black experience with traditional theatrical and dramatic forms. In addition to his work as a writer and director of plays, Bullins has also published one novel, *The Reluctant Rapist* (1973). Among his better-known plays are *Clara's Old Man* (1965), *The Electronic Nigger* (1968), and *House Party* (1973).

A Son, Come Home

CHARACTERS

MOTHER, *early 50s*
SON, *30 years old*
THE GIRL
THE BOY

The BOY *and the* GIRL *wear black tights and shirts. They move the action of the play and express the* MOTHER'S *and the* SON'S *moods and tensions. They become various embodiments recalled from memory and history: they enact a number of personalities and move from mood to mood. The players are Black.*

At rise: Scene: Bare stage but for two chairs positioned so as not to interfere with the actions of the BOY *and the* GIRL. *The* MOTHER *enters, sits in chair and begins to use imaginary iron and board. She hums a spiritual as she works.*

MOTHER: You came three times . . . Michael? It took you three times to find me at home?

> *The* GIRL *enters, turns and peers through the cracked, imaginary door.*

SON'S VOICE [*offstage*]: Is Mrs. Brown home?

GIRL [*an old woman*]: What?

MOTHER: It shouldn't have taken you three times. I told you that I would be here by two and you should wait, Michael.

> *The* SON *enters, passes the* GIRL *and takes his seat upon the other chair. The* BOY *enters, stops on other side of the imaginary door and looks through at the* GIRL.

BOY: Is Mrs. Brown in?

GIRL: Miss Brown ain't come in yet. Come back later . . . She'll be in before dark.

MOTHER: It shouldn't have taken you three times . . . You should listen to me, Michael. Standin' all that time in the cold.

SON: It wasn't cold, Mother.

MOTHER: I told you that I would be here by two and you should wait, Michael.

BOY: Please tell Mrs. Brown that her son's in town to visit her.

GIRL: You little Miss Brown's son? Well, bless the Lord.

> *Calls over her shoulder.*

Hey, Mandy, do you hear that? Little Miss Brown upstairs got a son . . . a great big boy . . . He's come to visit her.

BOY: You'll tell her, won't you?

GIRL: Sure, I'll tell her.

> *Grins and shows gums.*

I'll tell her soon as she gets in.

MOTHER: Did you get cold, Michael?

SON: No, Mother. I walked around some . . . sightseeing.

BOY: I walked up Twenty-third Street toward South. I had phoned that I was coming.

MOTHER: Sightseeing? But this is your home, Michael . . . always has been.

BOY: Just before I left New York I phoned that I was taking the bus. Two hours by bus, that's all. That's all it takes. Two hours.

SON: This town seems so strange. Different than how I remember it.

MOTHER: Yes, you have been away for a good while . . . How long has it been, Michael?

BOY: Two hours down the Jersey Turnpike, the trip beginning at the New York Port Authority Terminal . . .

SON: . . . and then straight down through New Jersey to Philadelphia . . .

GIRL: . . . and home . . . Just imagine . . . little Miss Brown's got a son who's come home.

SON: Yes, home . . . an anachronism.

MOTHER: What did you say, Michael?

BOY: He said . . .

GIRL [*late teens*]: What's an anachronism, Mike?

SON: Anachronism: 1: an error in chronology; *esp:* a chronological misplacing of persons, events, objects, or customs in regard to each other; 2: a person or a thing that is chronologically out of place—anachronistic/ *also* anachronic/ *or* anachronous—anachronistically/ *also* anachronously.

MOTHER: I was so glad to hear you were going to school in California.

BOY: College.

GIRL: Yes, I understand.

MOTHER: How long have you been gone, Michael?

SON: Nine years.

BOY: Nine years it's been. I wonder if she'll know me . . .

MOTHER: You've put on so much weight, son. You know that's not healthy.

GIRL [*20 years old*]: And that silly beard . . . how . . .

SON: Oh . . . I'll take it off. I'm going on a diet tomorrow.

BOY: I wonder if I'll know her.

SON: You've put on some yourself, Mother.

MOTHER: Yes, the years pass. Thank the Lord.

BOY: I wonder if we've changed much.

GIRL: Yes, thank the Lord.

SON: The streets here seem so small.

MOTHER: Yes, it seems like that when you spend a little time in Los Angeles.

GIRL: I spent eighteen months there with your aunt when she was sick. She had nobody else to help her . . . she was so lonely. And you were in the service . . . away. You've always been away.

BOY: In Los Angeles the boulevards, the avenues, the streets . . .

SON: . . . are wide. Yes, they have some wide ones out West. Here, they're so small and narrow. I wonder how cars get through on both sides.

MOTHER: Why, you know how . . . we lived on Derby Street for over ten years, didn't we?

SON: Yeah, that was almost an alley.

MOTHER: Did you see much of your aunt before you left Los Angeles?

SON: What?

GIRL [*middle-aged woman to* BOY]: Have you found a job yet, Michael?

MOTHER: Your aunt. My sister.

BOY: Nawh, not yet . . . Today I just walked downtown . . . quite a ways . . . this place is plenty big, ain't it?

SON: I don't see too much of Aunt Sophie.

MOTHER: But you're so much alike.

GIRL: Well, your bags are packed and are sitting outside the door.

BOY: My bags?

MOTHER: You shouldn't be that way, Michael. You shouldn't get too far away from your family.

SON: Yes, Mother.

BOY: But I don't have any money. I had to walk downtown today. That's how much money I have. I've only been here a week.

GIRL: I packed your bags, Michael.

MOTHER: You never can tell when you'll need or want your family, Michael.

SON: That's right, Mother.

MOTHER: You and she are so much alike.

BOY: Well, goodbye, Aunt Sophie.

GIRL [*silence*]:

MOTHER: All that time in California and you hardly saw your aunt. My baby sister.

BOY: Tsk tsk tsk.

SON: I'm sorry, Mother.

MOTHER: In the letters I'd get from both of you there'd be no mention of the other. All these years. Did you see her again?

SON: Yes.

GIRL [on telephone]: Michael? Michael who? . . . Ohhh . . . Bernice's boy.

MOTHER: You didn't tell me about this, did you?

SON: No, I didn't.

BOY: Hello, Aunt Sophie. How are you?

GIRL: I'm fine, Michael. How are you? You're looking well.

BOY: I'm getting on okay.

MOTHER: I prayed for you.

SON: Thank you.

MOTHER: Thank the Lord, Michael.

BOY: Got me a job working for the city.

GIRL: You did now.

BOY: Yes, I've brought you something.

GIRL: What's this, Michael . . . ohhh . . . it's money.

BOY: It's for the week I stayed with you.

GIRL: Fifty dollars. But, Michael, you didn't have to.

MOTHER: Are you still writing that radical stuff, Michael?

SON: Radical?

MOTHER: Yes . . . that stuff you write and send me all the time in those little books.

SON: My poetry, Mother?

MOTHER: Yes, that's what I'm talking about.

SON: No.

MOTHER: Praise the Lord, son. Praise the Lord. Didn't seem like anything I had read in school.

BOY [on telephone]: Aunt Sophie? . . . Aunt Sophie? . . . It's me, Michael . . .

GIRL: Michael?

BOY: Yes . . . Michael . . .

GIRL: Oh . . . Michael . . . yes . . .

BOY: I'm in jail, Aunt Sophie . . . I got picked up for drunk driving.

GIRL: You did . . . how awful . . .

MOTHER: When you going to get your hair cut, Michael?

BOY: Aunt Sophie . . . will you please come down and sign my bail. I've got the money . . . I just got paid yesterday . . . They're holding more than enough for me . . . but the law says that someone has to sign for it.

MOTHER: You look almost like a hoodlum, Michael.

BOY: All you need to do is come down and sign . . . and I can get out.

MOTHER: What you tryin' to be . . . a savage or something? Are you keeping out of trouble, Michael?

GIRL: Ohhh . . . Michael . . . I'm sorry but I can't do nothin' like that . . .

BOY: But all you have to do is sign . . . I've got the money and everything.

GIRL: I'm sorry . . . I can't stick my neck out.

BOY: But, Aunt Sophie . . . if I don't get back to work I'll lose my job and everything . . . please . . .

GIRL: I'm sorry, Michael . . . I can't stick my neck out . . . I have to go now . . . Is there anyone I can call?

BOY: No.

GIRL: I could call your mother. She wouldn't mind if I reversed the charges on her, would she? I don't like to run my bills up.

BOY: No, thanks.

MOTHER: You and your aunt are so much alike.

SON: Yes, Mother. Our birthdays are in the same month.

MOTHER: Yes, that year was so hot . . . so hot and I was carrying you . . .

> *As the* MOTHER *speaks the* BOY *comes over and takes her by the hand and leads her from the chair, and they stroll around the stage, arm in arm. The* GIRL *accompanies them and she and the* BOY *enact scenes from the* MOTHER's *mind.*

. . . carrying you, Michael . . . and you were such a big baby . . . kicked all the time. But I was happy. Happy that I was having a baby of my own . . . I worked as long I could and bought you everything you might need . . . diapers . . . and bottles . . . and your own spoon . . . and even toys . . . and even books . . . And it was so hot in Philadelphia that year . . . Your Aunt Sophie used to come over and we'd go for walks . . . sometimes up on the avenue . . . I was living in West Philly then . . . in that old terrible section they called "The Bottom." That's where I met your father.

GIRL: You're such a fool, Bernice. No nigger . . . man or boy's . . . ever going to do a thing to me like that.

MOTHER: Everything's going to be all right, Sophia.

GIRL: But what is he going to do? How are you going to take care of a baby by yourself?

MOTHER: Everything's going to be all right, Sophia. I'll manage.

GIRL: You'll manage? How? Have you talked about marriage?

MOTHER: Oh, please, Sophia!

GIRL: What do you mean "please"? Have you?

MOTHER: I just can't. He might think . . .

GIRL: Think! That dirty nigger better think. He better think before he really messes up. And you better too. You got this baby comin' on. What are you going to do?

MOTHER: I don't know . . . I don't know what I can do.

GIRL: Is he still tellin' you those lies about . . .

MOTHER: They're not lies.

GIRL: Haaaa . . .

MOTHER: They're not.

GIRL: Some smooth-talkin' nigger comes up from Georgia and tell you he escaped from the chain gang and had to change his name so he can't get married 'cause they might find out . . . What kinda shit is that, Bernice?

MOTHER: Please, Sophia. Try and understand. He loves me. I can't hurt him.

GIRL: Loves you . . . and puts you through this?

MOTHER: Please . . . I'll talk to him . . . Give me a chance.

GIRL: It's just a good thing you got a family, Bernice. It's just a good thing. You know that, don't cha?

MOTHER: Yes . . . yes, I do . . . but please don't say anything to him.

SON: I've only seen my father about a half dozen times that I remember, Mother. What was he like?

MOTHER: Down in The Bottom . . . that's where I met your father. I was young and hinkty then. He had pretty brown legs and a small waist. Everybody used to call me Bernie . . . and me and my sister would go to Atlantic City on the weekends and work as waitresses in the evenings, and sit all afternoon on the black part of the beach at Boardwalk and Atlantic . . . getting blacker . . . and having the times of our lives. Your father probably still lives down in The Bottom . . . perched over some bar down there . . . drunk to the world . . . I can see him now . . . He had good white teeth then . . . not how they turned later when he started in drinkin' that wine and wouldn't stop . . . he was so nice then.

BOY: Awwww, listen, kid. I got my problems too.

GIRL: But Andy . . . I'm six months gone . . . and you ain't done nothin'.

BOY: Well, what can I do?

GIRL: Don't talk like that . . . What can you do? . . . You know what you can do.

BOY: You mean marry you? Now lissen, sweetheart . . .

GIRL: But what about our baby?

BOY: Your baby.

GIRL: Don't talk like that! It took more than me to get him.

BOY: Well . . . look . . . I'll talk to you later, kid. I got to go to work now.

GIRL: That's what I got to talk to you about too, Andy. I need some money.

BOY: Money! Is somethin' wrong with your head, woman? I ain't got no money.

GIRL: But I can't work much longer, Andy. You got to give me some money. Andy . . . you just gotta.

BOY: Woman . . . all I got to *ever* do is die and go to hell.

GIRL: Well, you gonna do that, Andy. You sho are . . . you know that, don't you? . . . You know that.

MOTHER: . . . Yes, you are, man. Praise the Lord. We all are . . . All of us . . . even though he ain't come for you yet to make you pay. Maybe he's waitin' for us to go together so I can be a witness to the retribution that's handed down. A witness to all that He'll bestow upon your sinner's head . . . A witness! . . . That's what I am, Andy! Do you hear me? . . . A witness!

SON: Mother . . . what's wrong? What's the matter?

MOTHER: Thank the Lord that I am not blinded and will see the fulfillment of divine . . .

SON: Mother!

MOTHER: Oh . . . is something wrong, Michael?

SON: You're shouting and walking around . . .

MOTHER: Oh . . . it's nothing, son. I'm just feeling the power of the Lord.

SON: Oh . . . is there anything I can get you, Mother?

MOTHER: No, nothing at all.

She sits again and irons.

SON: Where's your kitchen? . . . I'll get you some coffee . . . the way you like it. I bet I still remember how to fix it.

MOTHER: Michael . . . I don't drink anything like that no more.

SON: No?

MOTHER: Not since I joined the service of the Lord.

SON: Yeah? . . . Well, do you mind if I get myself a cup?

MOTHER: Why, I don't have a kitchen. All my meals are prepared for me.

SON: Oh . . . I thought I was having dinner with you.

MOTHER: No. There's nothing like that here.

SON: Well, could I take you out to a restaurant? . . . Remember how we used to go out all the time and eat? I've never lost my habit of liking to eat out. Remember . . . we used to come down to this part of town and go to restaurants. They used to call it home cooking then . . . now, at least where I been out West and up in Harlem . . . we call it soul food. I bet we could find a nice little restaurant not four blocks from here, Mother. Remember that old man's place we used to go to on Nineteenth and South? I bet he's dead now . . . but . . .

MOTHER: I don't even eat out no more, Michael.

SON: No?

MOTHER: Sometimes I take a piece of holy bread to work . . . or some fruit . . . if it's been blessed by my Spiritual Mother.

SON: I see.

MOTHER: Besides . . . we have a prayer meeting tonight.

SON: On Friday?

MOTHER: Every night. You'll have to be going soon.

SON: Oh.

MOTHER: You're looking well.

SON: Thank you.

MOTHER: But you look tired.

SON: Do I?

MOTHER: Yes, those rings around your eyes might never leave. Your father had them.

SON: Did he?

MOTHER: Yes . . . and cowlicks . . . deep cowlicks on each side of his head.

SON: Yes . . . I remember.

MOTHER: Do you?

The BOY *and the* GIRL *take crouching positions behind and in front of them. They are in a streetcar. The* BOY *behind the* MOTHER *and* SON, *the* GIRL *across the aisle, a passenger.*

MOTHER [*young woman to the* BOY]: Keep your damn hands off him, Andy!

BOY [*chuckles*]: Awww, c'mon . . . Bernie. I ain't seen him since he was in the crib.

MOTHER: And you wouldn't have seen neither of us . . . if I had anything to do with it . . . Ohhh . . . why did I get on this trolley?

BOY: C'mon . . . Bernie . . . don't be so stuckup.

MOTHER: Don't even talk to us . . . and stop reaching after him.

BOY: Awww . . . c'mon . . . Bernie. Let me look at him.

MOTHER: Leave us alone. Look . . . people are looking at us.

The GIRL *across the aisle has been peeking at the trio but looks toward front at the mention of herself.*

BOY: Hey, big boy . . . do you know who I am?

MOTHER: Stop it, Andy! Stop it, I say . . . Mikie . . . don't pay any attention to him . . . you hear?

BOY: Hey, big boy . . . know who I am? . . . I'm your daddy. Hey, there . . .

MOTHER: Shut up . . . shut up, Andy . . . you nothin to us.

BOY: Where you livin' at . . . Bernie? Let me come on by and see the little guy, huh?

MOTHER: No! You're not comin' near us . . . ever . . . you hear?

BOY: But I'm his father . . . look . . . Bernie . . . I've been an ass the way I've acted but . . .

MOTHER: He ain't got no father.

BOY: Oh, come off that nonsense, woman.

MOTHER: Mikie ain't got no father . . . his father's dead . . . you hear?

BOY: Dead?

MOTHER: Yes, dead. My son's father's dead.

BOY: What you talkin about? . . . He's the spittin' image of me.

MOTHER: Go away . . . leave us alone, Andrew.

BOY: See there . . . he's got the same name as me. His first name is Michael after your father . . . and Andrew after me.

MOTHER: No, stop that, you hear?

BOY: Michael Andrew . . .

MOTHER: You never gave him no name . . . his name is Brown . . . Brown. The same as mine . . . and my sister's . . . and my daddy . . . You never gave him nothin' . . . and you're dead . . . go away and get buried.

BOY: You know that trouble I'm in . . . I got a wife down there, Bernie. I don't care about her . . . what could I do?

MOTHER [*rises, pulling up the* SON]: We're leavin' . . . don't you try and follow us . . . you hear, Andy? C'mon . . . Mikie . . . watch your step now.

BOY: Well . . . bring him around my job . . . you know where I work. That's all . . . bring him around on payday.

MOTHER [*leaving*]: We don't need anything from you . . . I'm working . . . just leave us alone.

The BOY *turns to the* GIRL.

BOY [*shrugs*]: That's the way it goes . . . I guess. Ships passing on the trolley car . . . Hey . . . don't I know you from up around 40th and Market?

The GIRL *turns away.*

SON: Yeah . . . I remember him. He always had liquor on his breath.

MOTHER: Yes . . . he did. I'm glad that stuff ain't got me no more . . . Thank the Lord.

GIRL [*35 years old*]: You want to pour me another drink, Michael?

BOY [*15 years old*]: You drink too much, Mother.

GIRL: Not as much as some other people I know.

BOY: Well, me and the guys just get short snorts, Mother. But you really hide some port.

GIRL: Don't forget you talkin' to your mother. You gettin' more like your father every day.

BOY: Is that why you like me so much?

GIRL [*grins drunkenly*]: Oh, hush up now, boy . . . and pour me a drink.

BOY: There's enough here for me, too.

GIRL: That's okay . . . when Will comes in he'll bring something.

SON: How is Will, Mother?

MOTHER: I don't know . . . haven't seen Will in years.

SON: Mother.

MOTHER: Yes, Michael.

SON: Why you and Will never got married? . . . You stayed together for over ten years.

MOTHER: Oh, don't ask me questions like that, Michael.

SON: But why not?

MOTHER: It's just none of your business.

SON: But you could be married now . . . not alone in this room . . .

MOTHER: Will had a wife and child in Chester . . . you know that.

SON: He could have gotten a divorce, Mother . . . Why . . .

MOTHER: Because he just didn't . . . that's why.

SON: You never hear from him?

MOTHER: Last I heard . . . Will had cancer.

SON: Oh, he did.

MOTHER: Yes.

SON: Why didn't you tell me? . . . You could have written.

MOTHER: Why?

SON: So I could have known.

MOTHER: So you could have known? Why?

SON: Because Will was like a father to me . . . the only one I've really known.

MOTHER: A father? And you chased him away as soon as you got big enough.

SON: Don't say that, Mother.

MOTHER: You made me choose between you and Will.

SON: Mother.

MOTHER: The quarrels you had with him . . . the mean tricks you used to play . . . the lies you told to your friends about Will . . . He wasn't much . . . when I thought I had a sense of humor I us'ta call him just plain Will. But we was his family.

SON: Mother, listen.

MOTHER: And you drove him away . . . and he didn't lift a hand to stop you.

SON: Listen, Mother.

MOTHER: As soon as you were big enough you did all that you could to get me and Will separated.

SON: Listen.

MOTHER: All right, Michael . . . I'm listening.

> *Pause.*

SON: Nothing.

> *Pause. Lifts an imaginary object.*

Is this your tambourine?

MOTHER: Yes.

SON: Do you play it?

MOTHER: Yes.

SON: Well?

MOTHER: Everything I do in the service of the Lord I do as well as He allows.

SON: You play it at your meetings.

MOTHER: Yes, I do. We celebrate the life He has bestowed upon us.

SON: I guess that's where I get it from.

MOTHER: Did you say something, Michael?

SON: Yes. My musical ability.

MOTHER: Oh . . . you've begun taking your piano lessons again?

SON: No . . . I was never any good at that.

MOTHER: Yes, three different teachers and you never got past the tenth lesson.

SON: You have a good memory, Mother.

MOTHER: Sometimes, son. Sometimes.

SON: I play an electric guitar in a combo.

MOTHER: You do? That's nice.

SON: That's why I'm in New York. We got a good break and came East.

MOTHER: That's nice, Michael.

SON: I was thinking that Sunday I could rent a car and come down to get you and drive you up to see our show. You'll get back in plenty of time to rest for work Monday.

MOTHER: No, I'm sorry. I can't do that.

SON: But you would like it, Mother. We could have dinner up in Harlem, then go down and . . .

MOTHER: I don't do anything like that any more, Michael.

SON: You mean you wouldn't come to see me play even if I were appearing here in Philly?

MOTHER: That's right, Michael. I wouldn't come. I'm past all that.

SON: Oh, I see.

MOTHER: Yes, thank the Lord.

SON: But it's my life, Mother.

MOTHER: Good . . . then you have something to live for.

SON: Yes.

MOTHER: Well, you're a man now, Michael . . . I can no longer live it for you. Do the best with what you have.

SON: Yes . . . Yes, I will, Mother.

GIRL'S VOICE [offstage]: Sister Brown . . . Sister Brown . . . hello.

MOTHER [uneasy; peers at watch]: Oh . . . it's Mother Ellen . . . I didn't know it was so late.

GIRL [enters]: Sister Brown . . . how are you this evening?

MOTHER: Oh, just fine, Mother.

GIRL: Good. It's nearly time for dinner.

MOTHER: Oh, yes, I know.

GIRL: We don't want to keep the others waiting at meeting . . . do we?

MOTHER: No, we don't.

GIRL [self-assured]: Hello, son.

SON: Hello.

MOTHER: Oh, Mother . . . Mother . . .

GIRL: Yes, Sister Brown, what is it?

MOTHER: Mother . . . Mother . . . this is . . . this is . . .

>   *Pause.*

   . . . this is . . .

SON: Hello, I'm Michael. How are you?

MOTHER [*relieved*]: Yes, Mother . . . This is Michael . . . my son.

GIRL: Why, hello, Michael. I've heard so much about you from your mother. She prays for you daily.

SON [*embarrassed*]: Oh . . . good.

GIRL [*briskly*]: Well . . . I have to be off to see about the others.

MOTHER: Yes, Mother Ellen.

GIRL [*as she exits; chuckles*]: Have to tell everyone that you won't be keeping us waiting, Bernice.

>   *Silence.*

SON: Well, I guess I better be going, Mother.

MOTHER: Yes.

SON: I'll write.

MOTHER: Please do.

SON: I will.

MOTHER: You're looking well . . . Thank the Lord.

SON: Thank you, so are you, Mother.

>   *He moves toward her and hesitates.*

MOTHER: You're so much like your aunt. Give her my best . . . won't you?

SON: Yes, I will, Mother.

MOTHER: Take care of yourself, son.

SON: Yes, Mother. I will.

>   *The SON exits. The MOTHER stands looking after him as the lights go slowly down to . . .*

>   BLACKNESS

Fact Questions and Exercises

1. Describe the stage setting used in *A Son, Come Home.*
2. Identify Aunt Sophie. Where does she live?
3. What is "that radical stuff" the mother questions Michael about?
4. Why doesn't Aunt Sophie sign the bail for Michael?
5. Where did his mother live when Michael was born?
6. Identify Andy.
7. Why was Bernie never able to marry Will?
8. What kind of meeting is the mother going to as the play ends?
9. Who is a member of the combo that is performing in New York?

For Discussion and Writing

1. How does Bullins indicate past and present events in the play? By simultaneously presenting the past and present, what does Bullins imply about the characters' future?

2. Discuss the theme of isolation as it appears in the play. How does Bullins indicate the lack of human contact? For example, the mother goes into the "Lord's service." Is this a sincere religious move, or is it a way of compensating for her alienation from her son? Does the Lord's service further isolate her from her son? In what ways does this play compare to *The American Dream*? Do the plays share any similar themes?

THE POEM

Ballads

Ballads are popular narrative songs that have been passed down from generation to generation. Little is known about the origin of folk ballads, other than that they were probably composed between the thirteenth and seventeenth centuries, and that they have gone through a continual process of change. Few ballads were collected in print until the eighteenth century; their simplicity and power is directly attributable to the fact that they originated as oral songs, preserved in the memories of the people that transmitted them. The ballads presented here follow the text of F. J. Child's *The English and Scottish Popular Ballads* (1882), with the exception of several spelling modernizations.

Lord Randal

1
"Oh where ha' you been, Lord Randal, my son?
And where ha' you been, my handsome young man?"
"I ha' been at the greenwood; mother, mak my bed soon,
For I'm wearied wi' huntin', and fain wad[1] lie down."

2
"And wha met ye there, Lord Randal, my son?   5
And wha met you there, my handsome young man?"
"Oh I met wi' my true-love; mother, mak my bed soon,
For I'm wearied wi' huntin', and fain wad lie down."

3
"And what did she give you, Lord Randal, my son?
And what did she give you, my handsome young man?"   10
"Eels fried in a pan; mother, mak my bed soon,
For I'm wearied wi' huntin', and fain wad lie down."

4
"And wha gat your leavin's, Lord Randal, my son?
And wha gat your leavin's, my handsome young man?"
"My hawks and my hounds; mother, mak my bed soon,   15
For I'm wearied wi' huntin', and fain wad lie down."

5
"And what becam of them, Lord Randal, my son?
And what becam of them, my handsome young man?"
"They stretched their legs out and died; mother, mak my bed
                soon,
For I'm wearied wi' huntin', and fain wad lie down."   20

1. Would.

6

"O I fear you are poisoned, Lord Randal, my son!
I fear you are poisoned, my handsome young man!"
"O yes, I am poisoned; mother, mak my bed soon,
For I'm sick at the heart, and I fain wad lie down."

7

"What d' ye leave to your mother, Lord Randal, my son?   25
What d'ye leave to your mother, my handsome young man?"
"Four and twenty milk kye;[2] mother, mak my bed soon,
For I'm sick at the heart, and I fain wad lie down."

8

"What d' ye leave to your sister, Lord Randal, my son?
What d' ye leave to your sister, my handsome young man?"   30
"My gold and my silver; mother, mak my bed soon,
For I'm sick at the heart, and I fain wad lie down."

9

"What d' ye leave to your brother, Lord Randal, my son?
What d' ye leave to your brother, my handsome young man?"
"My houses and my lands; mother, mak my bed soon,   35
For I'm sick at the heart, and I fain wad lie down."

10

"What d' ye leave to your true-love, Lord Randal, my son?
What d' ye leave to your true-love, my handsome young man?"
"I leave her hell and fire; mother, mak my bed soon,
For I'm sick at the heart, and I fain wad lie down."   40

Sir Patrick Spens

1

The king sits in Dumferling town,
    Drinking the blude-reid wine:
"O whar will I get guid sailor,
    To sail this ship of mine?"

2

Up and spak an eldern knicht,   5
    Sat at the king's richt knee:
"Sir Patrick Spens is the best sailor
    That sails upon the sea."

2. Cows.

3

The king has written a braid letter
    And signed it wi' his hand,   10
And sent it to Sir Patrick Spens,
    Was walking on the sand.

4

The first line that Sir Patrick read,
    A loud lauch lauched he;
The next line that Sir Patrick read,   15
    The tear blinded his ee.

5

"O wha is this has done this deed,
    This ill deed done to me,
To send me out this time o' the year,
    To sail upon the sea?   20

6

"Mak haste, mak haste, my mirry men all,
    Our guid ship sails the morn."
"O say na sae,[3] my master dear,
    For I fear a deadly storm.

7

"Late, late yestre'en I saw the new moon   25
    Wi' the auld moon in hir arm,
And I fear, I fear, my dear master,
    That we will come to harm."

8

O our Scots nobles were richt laith[4]
    To weet their cork-heeled shoon,[5]   30
But lang or a' the play were played
    Their hats they swam aboon.[6]

9

O lang, lang may their ladies sit,
    Wi' their fans into their hand,
Or ere they see Sir Patrick Spens   35
    Come sailing to the land.

10

O lang, lang may the ladies stand
    Wi' their gold kems in their hair,
Waiting for their ain dear lords,
    For they'll see them na mair.   40

3. O say it isn't so.   4. Right loath.   5. Shoes.   6. The hats swam above; that is, the men drowned.

11

Half o'er, half o'er to Aberdour
    It's fifty fadom deep,
And there lies guid Sir Patrick Spens
    Wi' the Scots lords at his feet.

Bonny Barbara Allan

1

It was in and about the Martinmas[7] time,
    When the green leaves were a falling,
That Sir John Græme, in the West Country,
    Fell in love with Barbara Allan.

2

He sent his man down through the town,   5
    To the place where she was dwelling:
"O haste and come to my master dear,
    Gin ye be Barbara Allan."

3

O hooly, hooly[8] rose she up,
    To the place where he was lying,   10
And when she drew the curtain by:
    "Young man, I think you're dying."

4

"O it's I'm sick, and very, very sick,
    And 'tis a' for Barbara Allan."
"O the better for me ye s' never be,   15
    Though your heart's blood were a-spilling.

5

"O dinna ye mind, young man," said she,
    "When ye was in the tavern a drinking,
That ye made the healths gae round and round,
    And slighted Barbara Allan?"[9]   20

6

He turned his face unto the wall,
    And death was with him dealing:
"Adieu, adieu, my dear friends all,
    And be kind to Barbara Allan."

7. November 11. 8. Slowly. 9. That is, Sir John failed to toast Barbara Allan while drinking.

7

And slowly, slowly raise she up,   25
    And slowly, slowly left him,
And sighing said, she could not stay,
    Since death of life had reft him.

8

She had not gane a mile but twa,
    When she heard the dead-bell ringing,   30
And every jow[10] that the dead-bell geid,
    It cried, "Woe to Barbara Allan!"

9

"O mother, mother, make my bed!
    O make it saft and narrow!
Since my love died for me to-day,   35
    I'll die for him to-morrow."

The Wife of Usher's Well

1

There lived a wife at Usher's Well,
    And a wealthy wife was she;
She had three stout and stalwart sons,
    And sent them o'er the sea.

2

They hadna been a week from her   5
    A week but barely ane,
Whan word came to the carlin[11] wife
    That her three sons were gane.

3

They hadna been a week from her,
    A week but barely three,   10
Whan word came to the carlin wife
    That her sons she'd never see.

4

"I wish the wind may never cease,
    Nor fashes in the flood,
Till my three sons come hame to me,   15
    In earthly flesh and blood."

10. Stroke.   11. Poor, peasant.

5

It fell about the Martinmass,
    When nights are lang and mirk,
The carlin wife's three sons came hame,
    And their hats were o' the birk.[12]   20

6

It neither grew in syke[13] nor ditch,
    Nor yet in any sheugh;[14]
But at the gates o' Paradise,
    That birk grew fair eneugh.

7

"Blow up the fire, my maidens,   25
    Bring water from the well;
For a' my house shall feast this night,
    Since my three sons are well."

8

And she has made to them a bed,
    She's made it large and wide,   30
And she's ta'en her mantle her about,
    Sat down at the bed-side.

9

Up then crew the red, red cock,
    And up and crew the gray;
The eldest to the youngest said,   35
    "'T is time we were away."

10

The cock he hadna crawed but once,
    And clapped his wings at a',
When the youngest to the eldest said,
    "Brother, we must awa'.   40

11

"The cock doth craw, the day doth daw,
    The channerin' worm doth chide;
Gin[15] we be missed out o' our place,
    A sair[16] pain we maun bide.

12

"Fare ye weel, my mother dear!   45
    Fareweel to barn and byre!
And fare ye weel, the bonny lass,
    That kindles my mother's fire!"

12. Birch. 13. Trench. 14. Furrow. 15. If. 16. Sore.

Fact Questions and Exercises

1. In "Lord Randal," what has happened to the hawks and hounds?
2. What does Lord Randal leave to his "true-love"?
3. How does Sir Patrick Spens react to the order to sail at "this time o' the year"? Who orders him to sail?
4. What happens to Sir Patrick?
5. What does Barbara Allan tell Sir John when "she drew the curtain by"? What reason does she give for planning to die "tomorrow"?
6. How many sons does the Wife of Usher's Well have? What happens to her sons?

For Discussion and Writing

1. What similar themes or ideas appear in all these ballads? Discuss how these themes are presented in each poem.
2. Are there facts that are not explained in the ballads? For instance, why was Lord Randal poisoned? How do these "mysterious" elements affect your appreciation of the poems?
3. Discuss the form of the ballads. Is there a definite pattern? Are similar devices used, such as repetition? Does the fact that ballads were originally oral songs affect their form? If so, how?

Sir Thomas Wyatt the Elder [1503–1542]

Wyatt was born in Kent, England, and was educated at Cambridge. He spent most of his life as a diplomat, but he was banished from Court in 1536 and imprisoned for treason in 1541. "Mine Own John Poins" was probably composed during his banishment. Wyatt's poetry was written for private circulation— very little of it was published during his life. Although he wrote in a variety of forms, he is best remembered for introducing the sonnet into English. "Mine Own John Poins," however, reflects his ability with other poetic forms, as well as his disenchantment with English courtly life.

They Flee from Me

They flee from me, that sometime did me seek,
With naked foot stalking in my chamber.
I have seen them, gentle, tame, and meek,
That now are wild, and do not remember
That sometime they put themselves in danger   5
To take bread at my hand; and now they range,
Busily seeking with a continual change.

Thanked be Fortune it hath been otherwise,
Twenty times better; but once in special,
In thin array, after a pleasant guise,   10
When her loose gown from her shoulders did fall,
And she me caught in her arms long and small,
And therewith all sweetly did me kiss
And softly said, "Dear heart, how like you this?"

It was no dream, I lay broad waking.   15
But all is turned, thorough my gentleness,
Into a strange fashion of forsaking;
And I have leave to go, of her goodness,
And she also to use newfangleness.
But since that I so kindely[1] am served,   20
I fain would know what she hath deserved.

And Wilt Thou Leave Me Thus?

And wilt thou leave me thus?
    Say nay, say nay, for shame,
    To save thee from the blame
    Of all my grief and grame.
And wilt thou leave me thus?   5
    Say nay, say nay!

And wilt thou leave me thus,
    That hath loved thee so long,
    In wealth and woe among?
    And is thy heart so strong   10
As for to leave me thus?
    Say nay, say nay!

And wilt thou leave me thus,
    That hath given thee my heart,
    Never for to depart,   15
    Neither for pain nor smart;
And wilt thou leave me thus?
    Say nay, say nay!

And wilt thou leave me thus
    And have no more pity   20
    Of him that loveth thee?
    Alas, thy cruelty!
And wilt thou leave me thus?
    Say nay, say nay!

1. It means "Naturally," but "kindly" is also implied.

Mine Own John Poins

Mine own John Poins,[2] since ye delight to know
The cause why that homeward I me draw,
And flee the press of courts, whereso they go,
Rather than to live thrall, under the awe
Of lordly looks, wrapped within my cloak,   5
To will and lust learning to set a law;
It is not for because I scorn and mock
The power of them to whom Fortune hath lent
Charge over us, of right to strike the stroke.
But true it is that I have always meant   10
Less to esteem them than the common sort,
Of outward things that judge in their intent
Without regard what doth inward resort.
I grant sometime that of glory the fire
Doth touch my heart; me list not to report   15
Blame by honor, and honor to desire.
But how may I this honor now attain
That cannot dye the color black a liar?
My Poins, I cannot frame me tune to feign,
To cloak the truth, for praise without desert,   20
Of them that list all vice to retain.
I cannot honor them that sets their part
With Venus and Bacchus all their life long;
Nor hold my peace of them, although I smart.
I cannot crouch nor kneel to do so great a wrong,   25
To worship them like God on earth alone,
That are as wolves these sely[3] lambs among.
I cannot with my words complain and moan
Nor suffer naught, nor smart without complaint,
Nor turn the word that from my mouth is gone;   30
I cannot speak and look like a saint,
Use wiles for wit, or make deceit a pleasure;
And call craft counsel, for profit still to paint;
I cannot wrest the law to fill the coffer,
With innocent blood to feed myself fat,   35
And do most hurt where most help I offer.
I am not he that can allow the state
Of high Caesar, and damn Cato to die,
That with his death did 'scape out of the gate
From Caesar's hands,[4] if Livy do not lie,   40
And would not live where liberty was lost,
So did his heart the common weal apply.
I am not he, such eloquence to boast
To make the crow in singing as the swan,
Nor call the lion of coward beasts the most,   45

2. Wyatt's friend.   3. Innocent.   4. Cato committed suicide to "escape" Caesar.

That cannot take a mouse as the cat can;
And he that dieth of hunger of the gold,
Call him Alexander,[5] and say that Pan
Passeth Apollo in music manifold;
Praise Sir Thopas for a noble tale,   50
And scorn the story that the Knight told,[6]
Praise him for counsel that is drunk of ale;
Grin when he laugheth that beareth all the sway,
Frown when he frowneth, and groan when he is pale;
On others' lust to hang both night and day—   55
None of these points would ever frame in me;
My wit is naught: I cannot learn the way;
And much the less of things that greater be
That asken help of colors of device
To join the mean with each extremity.   60
With nearest virtue to cloak alway the vice,
And as to purpose, likewise it shall fall
To press the virtue that it may not rise;
As drunkenness good fellowship to call;
The friendly foe, with his double face,   65
Say he is gentle and courteous therewithal;
And say that favel[7] hath a goodly grace
In eloquence; and cruelty to name
Zeal of justice, and change in time and place;
And he that suff'reth offense without blame,   70
Call him pitiful, and him true and plain
That raileth reckless to every man's shame,
Say he is rude that cannot lie and feign,
The lecher a lover, and tyranny
To be the right of a prince's reign.   75
I cannot, I: no, no, it will not be.
This is the cause that I could never yet
Hang on their sleeves, that weigh, as thou mayst see,
A chip of chance more than a pound of wit.
This maketh me at home to hunt and hawk,   80
And in foul weather at my book to sit,
In frost and snow then with my bow to stalk.
No man doth mark whereso I ride or go.
In lusty leas at liberty I walk,
And of these news I feel nor weal nor woe,   85
Save that a clog doth hang yet at my heel.
No force for that, for it is ordered so
That I may leap both hedge and dike full well;
I am not now in France, to judge the wine,
With sav'ry sauce those delicates to feel;   90
Nor yet in Spain, where one must him incline,

5. Alexander the Great wanted to control the world.   6. Both Sir Thopas and the Knight
are characters in Chaucer's *Canterbury Tales*.   7. Flattery.

Rather than to be, outwardly to seem.
I meddle not with wits that be so fine;
Nor Flanders' cheer letteth[8] not my sight to deem
Of black and white, nor taketh my wit away   95
With beastliness, they beasts do so esteem.
Nor am I not where Christ is given in prey
For money, poison, and treason—at Rome
A common practice, used night and day.
But here I am in Kent and Christendom,   100
Among the Muses, where I read and rhyme;
Where, if thou list, my Poins, for to come,
Thou shalt be judge how I do spend my time.

8. Prevent.

Fact Questions and Exercises

1. To whom is Wyatt referring in "They Flee from Me" when he says that they are "gentle, tame, and meek"?
2. What is the refrain in "And Wilt Thou Leave Me Thus?"
3. What theme or "complaint" is found in both poems?
4. In "My Own John Poins," what are Wyatt's reasons for being drawn "homeward"? What has Wyatt been doing since he left the court?

For Discussion and Writing

1. In "They Flee from Me" and "And Wilt Thou Leave Me Thus?" what seems to be the speaker's attitude toward women—or, more specifically, toward his lovers? Why have they left him? Does he understand their actions?
2. In "My Own John Poins," what failings of courtly life does Wyatt point out? Does he condemn these shortcomings? What, if anything, does he suggest would improve or eliminate the court's problems?

Henry Howard, Earl of Surrey [1517–1547]

Surrey was born in England, the oldest son of the Duke of Norfolk. A descendent of kings, Surrey was apparently a wild youth, known for his carousing and general mischief. He later directed his energies to the military, and became a valiant soldier. Surrey's poetry, like that of Wyatt, was written for private circulation; little of it was printed before his death. He is noted for continuing the sonnet and developing the sonnet variation later used by Shakespeare (the Shakespearean or English sonnet).

The Soote Season

The soote[1] season, that bud and bloom forth brings,
With green hath clad the hill and eke the vale;
The nightingale with feathers new she sings;
The turtle[2] to her make[3] hath told her tale.
Summer is come, for every spray now springs;   5
The hart[4] hath hung his old head on the pale;
The buck in brake his winter coat he flings,
The fishes float with new repairéd scale;
The adder all her slough away she slings,
The swift swallow pursueth the flies small;   10
The busy bee her honey now she mings.[5]
Winter is worn, that was the flowers' bale.[6]
And thus I see among these pleasant things,
Each care decays, and yet my sorrow springs.

Love, That Doth Reign and Live Within My Thought

Love, that doth reign and live within my thought,
And built his seat within my captive breast,
Clad in the arms wherein with me he fought,
Oft in my face he doth his banner rest.
But she that taught me love and suffer pain,   5
My doubtful hope and eke my hot desire
With shamefast look to shadow and refrain,
Her smiling grace converteth straight to ire.
And coward Love, then, to the heart apace
Taketh his flight, where he doth lurk and plain,   10
His purpose lost, and dare not show his face.

1. Sweet. 2. Dove. 3. Mate. 4. Deer. 5. Remembers. 6. Harm.

For my lord's guilt thus faultless bide I pain,
Yet from my lord shall not my foot remove:
Sweet is the death that taketh end by love.

Wyatt Resteth Here

Wyatt resteth here, that quick[7] could never rest;
Whose heavenly gifts increased by disdain,
And virtue sank the deeper in his breast;
Such profit he of envy could obtain.
A head where wisdom mysteries did frame,   5
Whose hammers beat still in that lively brain
As on a stithy,[8] where some work of fame
Was daily wrought, to turn to Britain's gain.
A visage stern and mild, where both did grow,
Vice to contemn, in virtues to rejoice,   10
Amid great storms, whom grace assuréd so,
To live upright, and smile at fortune's choice.
A hand that taught what might be said in rhyme;
That reft Chaucer the glory of his wit;
A mark, the which—unperfited, for time—   15
Some may approach, but never none shall hit.
A tongue that served in foreign realms his king;
Whose courteous talk to virtue did enflame
Each noble heart; a worthy guide to bring
Our English youth, by travail, unto fame.   20
An eye whose judgment no affect could blind,
Friends to allure, and foes to reconcile;
Whose piercing look did represent a mind
With virtue fraught, reposéd, void of guile.
A heart where dread yet never so impressed   25
To hide the thought that might the truth advance;
In neither fortune lost, nor so repressed,
To swell in wealth, nor yield unto mischance.
A valiant corps,[9] where force and beauty met,
Happy, alas! too happy, but for foes,   30
Livéd, and ran the race that nature set;
Of manhood's shape, where she the mold did lose.
But to the heavens that simple soul is fled,
Which left with such as covet Christ to know
Witness of faith that never shall be dead,   35
Sent for our health, but not receivéd so.
Thus, for our guilt, this jewel have we lost;
The earth his bones, the heavens possess his ghost.

7. Alive. 8. Anvil. 9. Body.

Fact Questions and Exercises

1. What does this line from "The Soote Season" mean: "The hart hath hung his old head on the pale"?
2. Has the season eased the speaker's sorrow? Which lines support your answer?
3. In "Love, That Doth Reign," to whom or what does "he" in line 4 refer? To what does "she" in line 5 refer?
4. What is Surrey's evaluation of Wyatt as a poet?
5. Which of these poems are sonnets? (Check the Guide to Literary Terms for a definition of "sonnet.")

For Discussion and Writing

1. Compare "Wyatt Resteth Here" to Wyatt's "Mine Own John Poins." Does Wyatt's poem indicate that Surrey is correct in referring to Wyatt as a "worthy guide" for English youth? Are there other points in "Mine Own John Poins" that Surrey uses in his own poem?
2. Discuss the figurative language Surrey uses, particularly in the sonnets. Is it used effectively? Explain.

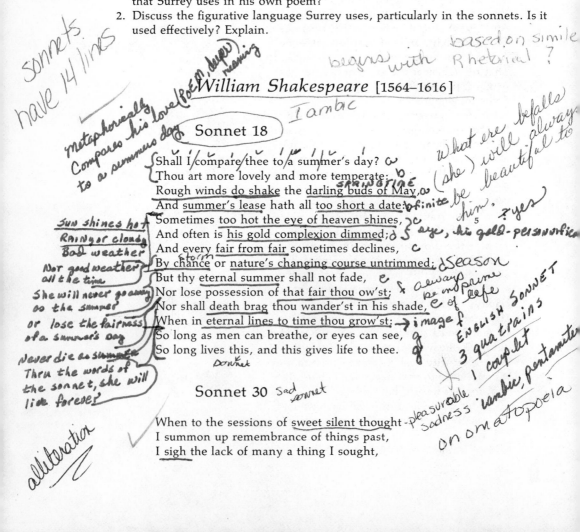

William Shakespeare [1564–1616]

Sonnet 18

Shall I compare thee to a summer's day?
Thou art more lovely and more temperate:
Rough winds do shake the darling buds of May,
And summer's lease hath all too short a date:
Sometimes too hot the eye of heaven shines,   5
And often is his gold complexion dimmed;
And every fair from fair sometimes declines,
By chance or nature's changing course untrimmed;
But thy eternal summer shall not fade,
Nor lose possession of that fair thou ow'st;
Nor shall death brag thou wander'st in his shade,
When in eternal lines to time thou grow'st:
So long as men can breathe, or eyes can see,
So long lives this, and this gives life to thee.

Sonnet 30

When to the sessions of sweet silent thought
I summon up remembrance of things past,
I sigh the lack of many a thing I sought,

(handwritten annotation: alliteration)

(handwritten annotation: hyperbole)

And with old woes new wail my dear time's waste:
Then can I drown an eye, unused to flow,
For precious friends hid in death's dateless night,   *(handwritten: euphemism)*   5
And weep afresh love's long since canceled woe,   *(handwritten: cries about lost loves)*
And moan the expense of many a vanished sight: *(handwritten: things seen he'll never see again)*

(handwritten annotation: melancholy)

Then can I grieve at grievances foregone,
And heavily from woe to woe tell o'er   *(handwritten: I'll relive again and grieve again)*
The sad account of fore-bemoanéd moan,   10
Which I new pay as if not paid before.
But if the while I think on thee, dear friend,   *(handwritten: but when I think of you, everything is ok; happy ending)*
All losses are restored and sorrows end.

Sonnet 55

Not marble, nor the gilded monuments
Of princes, shall outlive this powerful rhyme;
But you shall shine more bright in these contents
Than unswept stone, besmeared with sluttish time.
When wasteful war shall statues overturn,   5
And broils root out the work of masonry,
Nor Mars his sword nor war's quick fire shall burn
The living record of your memory.
'Gainst death and all-oblivious enmity
Shall you pace forth; your praise shall still find room   10
Even in the eyes of all posterity
That wear this world out to the ending doom.
So, till the judgment that yourself arise,
You live in this, and dwell in lovers' eyes.

Sonnet 71

No longer mourn for me when I am dead
Than you shall hear the surly sullen bell
Give warning to the world that I am fled
From this vile world, with vilest worms to dwell:
Nay, if you read this line, remember not   5
The hand that writ it; for I love you so,
That I in your sweet thoughts would be forgot,
If thinking on me then should make you woe.
Oh, if, I say, you look upon this verse
When I perhaps compounded am with clay,   10
Do not so much as my poor name rehearse,
But let your love even with my life decay;
Lest the wise world should look into your moan,
And mock you with me after I am gone.

Sonnet 73

Annotations (left margin):
See in him, the fall/winter time of year

Lines 1 & 2 metaphor - he + time of year

yellow leaves - symbol for autumn

Annotations (top): English Sonnet 3 quatrains couplet iambic, pentameter

That time of year thou mayst in me behold   a   *The time of life (old age) before death*
When yellow leaves, or none, or few, do hang   b   *AUTUMN*
Upon those boughs which shake against the cold,   a
Bare ruined choirs, where late the sweet birds sang.   b
In me thou see'st the twilight of such day   c   *NEXT TO DEATH*   5
As after sunset fadeth in the west;   d   *refer to gray light*
Which by and by black night doth take away,   c
Death's second self, that seals up all in rest.   d
In me thou see'st the glowing of such fire,   e   *symbolic*
That on the ashes of his youth doth lie,   f   10
As the deathbed whereon it must expire,   e
Consumed with that which it was nourished by.   f   *paradox*
This thou perceiv'st, which makes thy love more strong,   g
To love that well which thou must leave ere long.   g

Sonnet 97

Annotation (left): English Sonnet 3 quatrains 2 couplets

Annotation (right): Compares his feelings for his love w/ summer and winter

How like a winter hath my absence been   a
From thee, the pleasure of the fleeting year!   b
What freezings have I felt, what dark days seen!   a
What old December's bareness everywhere!   b
And yet this time removed was summer's time,   c   *Remembering how it is when they are together.*
The teeming autumn big with rich increase,   d
Bearing the wanton burthen of the prime,   c
Like widowed wombs after their lords' decease;   d
Yet this abundant issue seemed to me   e
But hope of orphans and unfathered fruit;   f
For summer and his pleasures wait on thee,   e   10   *When this (his love) is away, everything is dull, drear*
And, thou away, the very birds are mute;   f
Or, if they sing, 'tis with so dull a cheer   g
That leaves look pale, dreading the winter's near.   g

Sonnet 116

Annotations (left): speaking to his love   Personification →

true love doesn't change   constant

Annotation (top): nothing can change marriage of true minds

Annotation (right): Makes a profound statement concerning love's ability to w/stand any and all   5   And, if it doesn't, then it isn't love.

Let me not to the marriage of true minds
Admit impediments. Love is not love
Which alters when it alteration finds,
Or bends with the remover to remove:
Oh, no! it is an ever-fixèd mark,
That looks on tempests and is never shaken;
It is the star to every wandering bark(ship)
(star is constant)
ship is guided by stars

Whose worth's unknown, although his height be taken.[1]

metaphor Love's not Time's fool, though rosy lips and cheeks ⟶ *features change, love*
personification Within his bending sickle's compass come; *is still there*
Love alters not with his brief hours and weeks,
But bears it out even to the edge of doom.
If this be error and upon me proved,
I never writ, nor no man ever loved.

Sonnet 130

My mistress' eyes are nothing like the sun;   *a*
Coral is far more red than her lips' red;   *b*
If snow be white, why then her breasts are dun; *a*
If hairs be wires, black wires grow on her head. *b*
I have seen roses damasked, red and white,   *c*   5
But no such roses see I in her cheeks;   *d*
And in some perfumes is there more delight   *c*
Than in the breath that from my mistress reeks. *d*
I love to hear her speak, yet well I know   *e*
That music hath a far more pleasing sound;   *f*   10
I grant I never saw a goddess go;   *e*
My mistress, when she walks, treads on the ground. *f*
And yet, by heaven, I think my love as rare   *g*
As any she belied with false compare.   *g*

Sonnet 144

Two loves I have of comfort and despair,
Which like two spirits do suggest me still:
The better angel is a man right fair,
The worser spirit a woman, colored ill.
To win me soon to hell, my female evil   5
Tempteth my better angel from my side,
And would corrupt my saint to be a devil,
Wooing his purity with her foul pride.
And whether that my angel be turned fiend
Suspect I may, yet not directly tell;   10
But being both from me, both to each friend,
I guess one angel in another's hell.
Yet this shall I ne'er know, but live in doubt,
Till my bad angel fire my good one out.

---

1. Altitude; that is, the star's height can be measured by navigational instruments, but its intrinsic value remains unknown.

Sonnet 146

Poor soul, the center of my sinful earth,
Lord of these rebel powers that thee array,
Why dost thou pine within and suffer dearth,
Painting thy outward walls so costly gay?
Why so large cost, having so short a lease,   5
Dost thou upon thy fading mansion spend?
Shall worms, inheritors of this excess,
Eat up thy charge? Is this thy body's end?
Then, soul, live thou upon thy servant's loss,
And let that pine to aggravate thy store;   10
Buy terms divine in selling hours of dross;
Within be fed, without be rich no more.
So shalt thou feed on death, that feeds on men,
And death once dead, there's no more dying then.

Fact Questions and Exercises

1. In Sonnet 18, to what does "this" in line 14 refer?
2. In Sonnet 30, what does the phrase "drown an eye" mean? What restores the speaker's losses?
3. In Sonnet 55, what is more enduring than "gilded monuments" and "masonry"?
4. In Sonnet 71, what is the speaker's message to his love?
5. In Sonnet 73, the speaker compares himself to three different things; what are they? What is the moral of the poem?
6. In Sonnet 130, what is the speaker's mistress *not* like?
7. Who are the "two loves" in Sonnet 144?
8. In Sonnet 146, what different meanings does Shakespeare give to the word "pine" (lines 3 and 10)?

For Discussion and Writing

1. Do the sonnets present any similar themes? What, for instance, seem to be the speakers' attitudes toward the persons addressed? How does love in the sonnets compare to temporal things? In general, does the concept of time play a significant part in the sonnets?
2. Which of Shakespeare's sonnets do you prefer? What elements determine your choice? Write an analysis of the sonnet you have chosen.

John Donne [1572–1631]

Donne was born in England, the son of an old Roman Catholic family. He studied at Cambridge and Oxford, but took degrees from neither. Anti-Catholic sentiment was very strong in England, and, as a result, Donne was unable to practice law, his first

interest. In the 1590s he gave up his religion and became an
Anglican. His life is usually divided into two stages: the early
years, when he was a romantic young lover; and the later years,
when he was devoted to religion and the Anglican Church.
Perhaps too simply, his poetry is also usually divided between the
early poems, characterized by cynicism and bawdiness, and the
later devotional, or religious, poems. During the twentieth century, Donne's poetic reputation has greatly increased, partly as a
result of T. S. Eliot's admiration of his poems.

The Sun Rising

Busy old fool, unruly Sun,
Why dost thou thus,

Through windows, and through curtains, call on us?
Must to thy motions lovers' seasons run?

Saucy pedantic wretch, go chide   5
Late school-boys and sour prentices,

Go tell court-huntsmen that the king will ride,
Call country ants to harvest offices.
Love, all alike, no season knows nor clime,
Nor hours, days, months, which are the rags of time.   10

Thy beams so reverend and strong
Why shouldst thou think?

I could eclipse and cloud them with a wink,
But that I would not lose her sight so long.

If her eyes have not blinded thine,   15
Look, and tomorrow late tell me,

Whether both the Indias of spice and mine[1]
Be where thou left'st them, or lie here with me.
Ask for those kings whom thou saw'st yesterday,
And thou shalt hear, "All here in one bed lay."   20

She's all states, and all princes I;
Nothing else is.

Princes do but play us; compared to this,
All honour's mimic, all wealth alchemy.

Thou, Sun, art half as happy as we,   25
In that the world's contracted thus;
Thine age asks ease, and since thy duties be
To warm the world, that's done in warming us.

Shine here to us, and thou art everywhere;
This bed thy centre is, these walls thy sphere.   30

---

1. The East Indies was famous for its spices; the West Indies was famous for its metals,
or mines.

The Canonization

For God's sake hold your tongue, and let me love,
 Or chide my palsy, or my gout,
My five gray hairs, or ruined fortune, flout,
  With wealth your state, your mind with arts improve.
   Take you a course, get you a place,   5
   Observe His Honor, or His Grace,
Or the King's real, or his stamped face[2]
  Contemplate; what you will, approve,
  So you will let me love.

Alas, alas, who's injured by my love?   10
  What merchant's ships have my sighs drowned?
Who says my tears have overflowed his ground?
  When did my colds a forward spring remove?
   When did the heats which my veins fill
   Add one more to the plaguy bill?[3]   15
Soldiers find wars, and lawyers find out still
  Litigious men, which quarrels move,
  Though she and I do love.

Call us what you will, we are made such by love;
  Call her one, me another fly,   20
We're tapers too, and at our own cost die,
  And we in us find the eagle and the dove.
   The phoenix[4] riddle hath more wit
   By us: we two being one, are it.
So, to one neutral thing both sexes fit.   25
  We die and rise the same, and prove
  Mysterious by this love.

We can die by it, if not live by love,
  And if unfit for tombs and hearse
Our legend be, it will be fit for verse;   30
  And if no piece of chronicle we prove,
   We'll build in sonnets pretty rooms;
   As well as well-wrought urn becomes
The greatest ashes, as half-acre tombs,
  And by these hymns, all shall approve 35
  Us canonized for love.

And thus invoke us: You whom reverend love
  Made one another's hermitage;
You, to whom love was peace, that now is rage;

---

2. The king's face was stamped on coins. 3. Death by plague was so common that a list or "bill" was kept, giving the names of the dead. 4. A mythological bird that when burned in the funeral fire rises from its own ashes; Donne's "fire" is the fire of passion.

Who did the whole world's soul contract, and drove   40
      Into the glasses of your eyes
      (So made such mirrors, and such spies,
That they did all to you epitomize)
      Countries, towns, courts: Beg from above
      A pattern of your love!

Air and Angels

Twice or thrice had I loved thee,
Before I knew thy face or name;
So in a voice, so in a shapeless flame,
Angels affect us oft, and worshiped be;
      Still when, to where thou wert, I came,   5
Some lovely glorious nothing I did see.
      But since my soul, whose child love is,
Takes limbs of flesh, and else could nothing do,
      More subtle than the parent is
Love must not be, but take a body too;   10
      And therefore what thou wert, and who,
          I bid love ask, and now
That it assume thy body I allow,
And fix itself in thy lip, eye, and brow.

Whilst thus to ballast love I thought,   15
And so more steadily to have gone,
With wares which would sink admiration,
I saw I had love's pinnace[5] overfraught;
      Every thy hair for love to work upon
Is much too much, some fitter must be sought;   20
      For, nor in nothing, nor in things
Extreme and scatt'ring bright, can love inhere.
      Then as an angel, face and wings
Of air, not pure as it, yet pure doth wear,
      So thy love may be my love's sphere.   25
          Just such disparity
As is 'twixt air and angels' purity,
'Twixt women's love and men's will ever be.

The Relic

When my grave is broke up again
Some second guest to entertain

5. A small boat; also a woman.

(For graves have learned that woman-head
  To be to more than one a bed),
    And he that digs it, spies   5
A bracelet of bright hair about the bone,
    Will he not let'us alone,
And think that there a loving couple lies,
Who thought that this device might be some way
To make their souls, at the last busy day,   10
Meet at this grave, and make a little stay?

  If this fall in a time, or land,
  Where mis-devotion doth command,
  Then, he that digs us up, will bring
  Us to the bishop, and the king,   15
    To make us relics; then
Thou shalt be a Mary Magdalen, and I
    A something else thereby;
All women shall adore us, and some men;
And since at such time, miracles are sought, 20
I would have that age by this paper taught
What miracles we harmless lovers wrought.

  First, we loved well and faithfully,
  Yet knew not what we loved, nor why,
  Difference of sex no more we knew,   25
  Than our Guardian Angels do;
    Coming and going, we
Perchance might kiss, but not between those meals;
    Our hands ne'er touched the seals,
Which nature, injured by late law, sets free: 30
These miracles we did; but now alas,
All measure, and all language, I should pass,
Should I tell what a miracle she was.

The Flea

Mark but this flea, and mark in this,
How little that which thou deniest me is;
Me it sucked first, and now sucks thee,
And in this flea our two bloods mingled be;
Thou know'st that this cannot be said   5
A sin, or shame, or loss of maidenhead,
  Yet this enjoys before it woo,
  And pampered swells with one blood made of two,[6]
  And this, alas, is more than we would do.

6. A common seventeenth-century belief was that the blood of lovers actually intermixed during sexual intercourse.

Oh stay, three lives in one flea spare,   10
Where we almost, nay more than married, are.
This flea is you and I, and this
Our marriage bed and marriage temple is;
Though parents grudge, and you, we are met,
And cloistered in these living walls of jet,   15
          Though use make you apt to kill me
          Let not to that, self-murder added be,
          And sacrilege, three sins in killing three.

Cruel and sudden, hast thou since
Purpled thy nail, in blood of innocence?   20
Wherein could this flea guilty be,
Except in that drop which it sucked from thee?
Yet thou triumph'st, and say'st that thou
Find'st not thy self nor me the weaker now;
          'Tis true, then learn how false tears be;   25
          Just so much honor, when thou yield'st to me,
          Will waste, as this flea's death took life from thee.

The Good-Morrow

          I wonder, by my troth, what thou and I
                    Did, till we loved? were we not weaned till then?
          But sucked on country pleasures, childishly?
                    Or snorted we in the Seven Sleepers' den?[7]
          'Twas so; but this, all pleasures fancies be.   5
          If ever any beauty I did see,
Which I desired, and got, 'twas but a dream of thee.

          And now good-morrow to our waking souls,
                    Which watch not one another out of fear;
          For love, all love of other sights controls,   10
                    And makes one little room an everywhere.
          Let sea-discoverers to new worlds have gone,
          Let maps to other, worlds on worlds have shown,
Let us possess one world, each hath one, and is one.
          My face in thine eye, thine in mine appears,   15
                    And true plain hearts do in the faces rest;
          Where can we find two better hemispheres,
                    Without sharp north, without declining west?
          Whatever dies was not mixed equally,[8]
          If our two loves be one, or, thou and I   20

Love so alike that none do slacken, none can die.

7. According to legend, seven Christian youths slept for two centuries in a cave to avoid
Roman persecution.   8. At that time it was believed that if a thing was not made up of equal
and similar elements, it would decay.

Break of Day

'Tis true, 'tis day; what though it be?
O wilt thou therefore rise from me?[9]
Why should we rise, because 'tis light?
Did we lie down, because 'twas night?
Love, which in spite of darkness brought us hither,   5
Should in despite of light keep us together.

Light hath no tongue, but is all eye;
If it could speak as well as spy,
This were the worst that it could say,
That being well, I fain would stay,   10
And that I loved my heart and honor so,
That I would not from him, that had them, go.

Must business thee from hence remove?
O, that's the worst disease of love.
The poor, the foul, the false, love can   15
Admit, but not the busied man.
He which hath business, and makes love, doth do
Such wrong, as when a married man doth woo.

A Valediction: Forbidding Mourning

As virtuous men pass mildly'away,
    And whisper to their souls to go,
Whilst some of their sad friends do say
    The breath goes now, and some say, No;

So let us melt, and make no noise,   5
    No tear-floods, nor sigh-tempests move,
'Twere profanation of our joys
    To tell the laity our love.

Moving of th' earth brings harms and fears,
    Men reckon what it did and meant;   10
But trepidation of the spheres,
    Though greater far, is innocent.

Dull sublunary lovers' love
    (Whose soul is sense) cannot admit
Absence, because it doth remove   15
    Those things which elemented it.

9. The speaker is a woman.

But we by'a love so much refined
     That our selves know not what it is,
Inter-assuréd of the mind,
     Care less, eyes, lips, and hands to miss.   20

Our two souls therefore, which are one,
     Though I must go,[10] endure not yet
A breach, but an expansion,
     Like gold to airy thinness beat.

If they be two, they are two so   25
     As stiff twin compasses are two;
Thy soul, the fixed foot, makes no show
     To move, but doth, if th' other do.

And though it in the center sit,
     Yet when the other far doth roam,   30
It leans and hearkens after it,
     And grows erect, as that comes home.

Such wilt thou be to me, who must
     Like th' other foot, obliquely run;
Thy firmness makes my circle just,   35
     And makes me end where I begun.

The Ecstasy

Where, like a pillow on a bed,
     A pregnant bank swelled up to rest
The violet's reclining head,
     Sat we two, one another's best.
Our hands were firmly cemented   5
     With a fast balm, which thence did spring.
Our eye-beams twisted, and did thread
     Our eyes upon one double string;[11]
So to intergraft our hands, as yet
     Was all our means to make us one;   10
And pictures in our eyes to get
     Was all our propagation.
As 'twixt two equal armies, Fate
     Suspends uncertain victory,
Our souls (which to advance their state,   15
     Were gone out) hung 'twixt her and me.

10. Donne probably wrote this poem for his wife, before leaving for France in 1612. His wife was expecting a child, and Donne had misgivings about the trip; during his absence, the child was stillborn. **11.** At that time, people believed the eyes sent out beams that carried the image.

And whilst our souls negotiate there,
    We like sepulchral statues lay;
All day the same our postures were,
    And we said nothing all the day.   20
If any, so by love refined
    That he soul's language understood,
And by good love were grown all mind,
    Within convenient distance stood,
He (though he know not which soul spake,   25
    Because both meant, both spake the same)
Might thence a new concoction[12] take,
    And part far purer than he came.
This ecstasy doth unperplex,
    We said, and tell us what we love;   30
We see by this it was not sex;
    We see we saw not what did move;
But as all several souls contain
    Mixture of things, they know not what,
Love these mixed souls doth mix again,   35
    And makes both one, each this and that.
A single violet transplant,
    The strength, the color, and the size
(All which before was poor, and scant)
    Redoubles still, and multiplies.   40
When love, with one another so
    Interinanimates two souls,
That abler soul, which thence doth flow,
    Defects of loneliness controls.
We then, who are this new soul, know,   45
    Of what we are composed, and made,
For, th' atomies[13] of which we grow,
    Are souls, whom no change can invade.
But O alas, so long, so far
    Our bodies why do we forbear?   50
They are ours, though they are not we; we are
    The intelligences, they the sphere.
We owe them thanks because they thus,
    Did us to us at first convey,
Yielded their forces, sense, to us,   55
    Nor are dross to us, but allay.[14]
On man heaven's influence works not so
    But that it first imprints the air,[15]
So soul into the soul may flow,
    Though it to body first repair.   60
As our blood labors to beget
    Spirits as like souls as it can,

---

12. Perfected state.   13. Atoms.   14. Alloy.   15. According to astrologers, the stars affected the air and, therefore, affected people.

Because such fingers need to knit
    That subtle knot which makes us man:
So must pure lovers' souls descend   65
    T' affections, and to faculties
Which sense may reach and apprehend;
    Else a great Prince in prison lies.
To our bodies turn we then, that so
    Weak men on love revealed may look;   70
Love's mysteries in souls do grow,
    But yet the body is his book.
And if some lover, such as we,
    Have heard this dialogue of one,
Let him still mark us; he shall see   75
    Small change when we are to bodies gone.

Holy Sonnet 5

I am a little world made cunningly
Of elements, and an angelic sprite;[16]
But black sin hath betrayed to endless night
My world's both parts, and O, both parts must die.
You which beyond that heaven which was most high   5
Have found new spheres, and of new lands can write,
Pour new seas in mine eyes, that so I might
Drown my world with my weeping earnestly,
Or wash it if it must be drowned no more.
But O, it must be burnt! Alas, the fire[17]   10
Of lust and envy have burnt it heretofore,
And made it fouler; let their flames retire,
And burn me, O Lord, with a fiery zeal
Of Thee and Thy house, which doth in eating heal.

Holy Sonnet 10

Death be not proud, though some have called thee
Mighty and dreadful, for thou art not so.
For those whom thou think'st thou dost overthrow
Die not, poor Death, nor yet canst thou kill me.
From rest and sleep, which but thy pictures be,   5
Much pleasure, then from thee much more must flow;
And soonest our best men with thee do go—
Rest of their bones and souls' delivery!
Thou'rt slave to fate, kings and desperate men,
And dost with poison, war, and sickness dwell,   10

16. Spirit.   17. "Drowned" and "burnt" (lines 9 and 10) refer to God's promise not to flood the earth again and the belief that the world would next be destroyed by fire.

And poppy or charms can make us sleep as well,
And better than thy stroke; why swell'st thou then?
One short sleep past, we wake eternally,
And death shall be no more. Death, thou shalt die.

Holy Sonnet 14

Batter my heart, three-personed God; for You
As yet but knock, breathe, shine, and seek to mend;
That I may rise and stand, o'erthrow me, and bend
Your force to break, blow, burn, and make me new.
I, like an usurped town, to another due,
Labor to admit You, but O, to no end;
Reason, Your viceroy in me, me should defend,
But is captived, and proves weak or untrue.
Yet dearly I love You, and would be loved fain,
But am betrothed unto Your enemy.   10
Divorce me, untie or break that knot again;
Take me to You, imprison me, for I,
Except You enthrall me, never shall be free,
Nor ever chaste, except You ravish me.

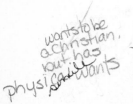

Holy Sonnet 19

Oh, to vex me, contraries meet in one;
Inconstancy unnaturally hath begot
A constant habit; that when I would not
I change in vows and in devotion.
As humorous is my contrition   5
As my profane love, and as soon forgot:
As riddlingly distempered, cold and hot;
As praying, as mute; as infinite, as none.
I durst not view heaven yesterday; and today
In prayers and flattering speeches I court God;   10
Tomorrow I quake with true fear of His rod.
So my devout fits come and go away
Like a fantastic ague: save that here
Those are my best days when I shake with fear.

Fact Questions and Exercises

1. In "The Sun Rising," why does the speaker choose not to "eclipse and cloud"
the sun's beams? According to the speaker, how can the sun "warm the
world"?

2. In "The Canonization," what does "litigious" mean (line 17)? What does "canonization" mean? Is this poem a dramatic monologue? If so, whom is the speaker addressing?
3. What is the "disparity" that exists between women's and men's love, according to "Air and Angels"?
4. What is the conceit that begins in line 25 of "A Valediction: Forbidding Mourning"? (See the Guide to Literary Terms for a definition of "conceit.")
5. In Holy Sonnet 10, why isn't death "mighty and dreadful"? Which line in the poem specifically indicates the speaker's belief in an afterlife?
6. In Holy Sonnet 14, who is asked to "o'erthrow me"? Why does the speaker ask this?
7. What are the "contraries" that vex the speaker in Holy Sonnet 19?

For Discussion and Writing

1. In the seventeenth century, the word "die," in addition to its ordinary meaning, referred to the consummation of the sexual act. How does Donne develop this double meaning in "The Canonization"? Does a knowledge of this double meaning enhance your understanding of the poem? Does Donne use it in other poems?
2. Donne's poems are usually divided into love poems and religious poems. What value does Donne advocate or show in the love poems? What values appear in the religious poems? Is there any similar use of metaphor and other figurative language in both types of poem? Is the speaker in the religious poems completely free of the values that are indicated in the love poems?

Robert Herrick [1591–1674]

Herrick was born in London, England. Against his wishes, he took orders in the church and moved to Devonshire, then considered the "country." He was ousted from his church post when the Puritans came to power; he was returned in 1660, when King Charles was restored to the throne. Herrick remained a bachelor; he lived a quiet, secluded life, his interests as much secular as clerical. The lovely females in his poems were Herrick's imaginary companions in his placid life.

Delight in Disorder

A sweet disorder in the dress
Kindles in clothes a wantonness.
A lawn about the shoulders thrown
Into a fine distraction;
An erring lace, which here and there   5
Enthralls the crimson stomacher;
A cuff neglectful, and thereby
Ribbons to flow confusedly;
A winning wave, deserving note,
In the tempestuous petticoat;   10
A careless shoestring, in whose tie
I see a wild civility;
Do more bewitch me than when art
Is too precise in every part.

Corinna's Going A-Maying

Get up, get up for shame! The blooming morn
Upon her wings presents the god unshorn.
See how Aurora[1] throws her fair
Fresh-quilted colours through the air:
    Get up, sweet slug-a-bed, and see   5
    The dew bespangling herb and tree!
Each flower has wept and bowed toward the east
Above an hour since, yet you not drest;
    Nay! not so much as out of bed?
    When all the birds have matins said   10
    And sung their thankful hymns: 'tis sin,
    Nay, profanation, to keep in,

---

1. Goddess of dawn.

Whenas a thousand virgins on this day
Spring sooner than the lark, to fetch in May.[2]

Rise and put on your foliage, and be seen   15
To come forth, like the spring-time, fresh and green,
    And sweet as Flora.[3] Take no care
    For jewels for your gown or hair:
Fear not; the leaves will strew
    Gems in abundance upon you: 20
Besides, the childhood of the day has kept,
Against you come, some orient pearls unwept.
    Come, and receive them while the light
    Hangs on the dew-locks of the night:
    And Titan[4] on the eastern hill   25
    Retires himself, or else stands still
Till you come forth! Wash, dress, be brief in praying:
Few beads are best when once we go a-Maying.

Come, my Corinna, come; and coming, mark
How each field turns a street, each street a park,   30
    Made green and trimmed with trees! see how
    Devotion gives each house a bough
    Or branch! each porch, each door, ere this,
    An ark, a tabernacle is,
Made up of white-thorn neatly interwove,   35
As if here were those cooler shades of love.
    Can such delights be in the street
    And open fields, and we not see't?
    Come, we'll abroad; and let's obey
    The proclamation made for May.   40
And sin no more, as we have done, by staying;
But, my Corinna, come, let's go a-Maying.

There's not a budding boy or girl this day
But is got up and gone to bring in May.
    A deal of youth ere this is come   45
    Back, and with white-thorn laden home.
    Some have dispatched their cakes and cream,
    Before that we have left to dream:
And some have wept, and wooed, and plighted troth,
And chose their priest, ere we can cast off sloth: 50
    Many a green-gown has been given,
    Many a kiss, both odd and even:
    Many a glance too has been sent
    From out the eye, love's firmament:
Many a jest told of the keys betraying   55
This night, and locks picked; yet we're not a-Maying!

2. It was the custom on May Day to gather blossoms and decorate the house with them.
3. Goddess of flowers. 4. The sun.

Come, let us go, while we are in our prime,
And take the harmless folly of the time!
    We shall grow old apace, and die
    Before we know our liberty.   60
    Our life is short, and our days run
    As fast away as does the sun.
And, as a vapour or a drop of rain,
Once lost, can ne'er be found again,
    So when or you or I are made   65
    A fable, song, or fleeting shade,
    All love, all liking, all delight
    Lies drowned with us in endless night.
Then, while time serves, and we are but decaying,
Come, my Corinna, come, let's go a-Maying.   70

To the Virgins, to Make Much of Time

Gather ye rosebuds while ye may,
    Old time is still a-flying;
And this same flower that smiles today
    Tomorrow will be dying.

The glorious lamp of heaven, the sun,   5
    The higher he's a-getting,
The sooner will his race be run,
    And nearer he's to setting.

That age is best which is the first,
    When youth and blood are warmer;   10
But being spent, the worse, and worst
    Times still succeed the former.

Then be not coy, but use your time,
    And, while ye may, go marry;
For, having lost but once your prime,   15
    You may forever tarry.

Fact Questions and Exercises

1. In "Delight in Disorder," to what kind of disorder is the speaker referring?
2. What arguments are used to convince Corinna that she should go "a-Maying"? What does the word "maying" mean? What time of year is the poem about?

For Discussion and Writing

1. Check the Guide to Literary Terms for a definition of "carpe diem"; discuss Herrick's poems as carpe diem statements. Point out specific lines in "Corinna's Going A-Maying" and "To the Virgins" that convey this philosophy. What values does this philosophy support? In general, what values contrast with the carpe diem philosophy? For instance, what values does Donne imply or express in the Holy Sonnets that are neither implied nor expressed by Herrick?

Form - pattern (figurative language) element
Content - body, what author is saying.

John Milton [1608–1674]

Milton was born in Cheapside, England. Though educated at Cambridge for the ministry, he chose to devote himself to literature. By his twenty-fifth year he had supposedly read everything written in English, Latin, Greek, and Italian. Milton's career was tumultuous: he had radical ideas about divorce, and most of his life was unsettled and controversial. After 1651 he was totally blind, impoverished, lost in obscurity, and occasionally imprisoned; still, under these circumstances he completed his masterpiece, *Paradise Lost* (1667)—a long, complex poem that seeks to justify "the ways of God to man." Without doubt, it is one of the greatest poems in literature.

How Soon Hath Time

Frustration
An identity crisis

How soon hath Time, the subtle thief of youth,   a
Stoln on his wing my three and twentieth year!   b
My hasting days fly on with full career,   b
But my late spring no bud or blossom shew'th.[1]   a
Perhaps my semblance might deceive the truth,   a
That I to manhood am arrived so near,   b
And inward ripeness doth much less appear,   b
That some more timely-happy spirits endu'th.[2]   a
Yet be it less or more, or soon or slow,   c
It shall be still in strictest measure even   d
To that same lot, however mean or high,   e
Toward which Time leads me, and the will of Heaven;   d
All is, if I have grace to use it so,   c
As ever in my great Taskmaster's eye.   e

youth stolen by time
going too fast
The death of a 23 yr. old man
Life goes on, but w/out the joy?
5 Appear to be a a man

3 contrast, less or more, soon or slow, mean or high

10

3 contrast

Personification metaphorical symbol
God

Italian Sonnet
2 quatrains/octave
2 tercets/sestet

iambic pentameter

1. Shows. 2. Endows.

When I Consider How My Light Is Spent

When I consider how my light[3] is spent
Ere half my days, in this dark world and wide,
And that one talent which is death to hide[4]
Lodged with me useless, though my soul more bent
To serve therewith my Maker, and present
My true account, lest he returning chide;
("Doth God exact day-labor, light denied?")
I fondly ask; but Patience to prevent
That murmur, soon replies, "God doth not need
Either man's work or his own gifts; who best   10
Bear his mild yoke, they serve him best. His state
Is kingly. Thousands at his bidding speed
And post o'er land and ocean without rest:
They also serve who only stand and wait."

Methought I Saw

Methought I saw my late espoused saint[5]
Brought to me like Alcestis[6] from the grave,
Whom Jove's great son to her glad husband gave,
Rescued from Death by force, though pale and faint.
Mine, as whom washed from spot of child-bed taint   5
Purification in the Old Law did save,
And such, as yet once more I trust to have
Full sight of her in heaven without restraint,
Came vested all in white, pure as her mind.
Her face was veiled; yet to my fancied sight   10
Love, sweetness, goodness, in her person shined
So clear as in no face with more delight.
But O, as to embrace me she inclined,
I waked, she fled, and day brought back my night.

On the Late Massacre in Piedmont

Avenge, O Lord, thy slaughtered saints,[7] whose bones
Lie scattered on the Alpine mountains cold,
Even them who kept thy truth so pure of old

3. Milton's eyesight; he was blind when this poem was written (ca.1652). 4. See Matt.
25:14-30. 5. Milton's second wife, Katherine Woodcock. 6. Hercules returned Alcestis,
wife of Admetus, from the dead. 7. On Easter Day, 1655, the Duke of Savoy killed seventeen
hundred members of a Protestant sect, in the Piedmont section of Italy.

When all our fathers worshiped stocks and stones,
Forget not: in thy book record their groans   5
  Who were thy sheep and in their ancient fold
  Slain by the bloody Piemontese that rolled
  Mother with infant down the rocks. Their moans
  The vales redoubled to the hills, and they
  To Heaven. Their martyred blood and ashes sow   10
  O'er all th' Italian fields where still doth sway
The triple tyrant:[8] that from these may grow
  A hundredfold, who having learnt thy way
  Early may fly the Babylonian woe.[9]

8. The Pope. **9.** See Rev. 14:8, 17:5, 18:10. Many Protestants viewed God's destruction of Babylon as symbolic of what was going to happen to the Roman Catholic Church.

Fact Questions and Exercises

1. How old is the speaker in "How Soon Hath Time"?
2. In "When I Consider How My Light Is Spent," what question is asked of God? What is Patience's reply?
3. Who does the speaker think he has seen in "Methought I Saw"? What line lets the reader know that the speaker has been dreaming?

For Discussion and Writing

1. In the poems, what does Milton seem to value? For instance, does he have a carpe diem philosophy? What values does he praise? Do these values allow an individual to overcome hardship or despair? Explain.
2. What is the speaker's mood in the sonnets? Gay? Unconcerned? Perplexed? Dreary? Explain your conclusions.

Andrew Marvell [1621–1678]

Marvell was born in Yorkshire, England, and was educated at Cambridge. Little is known about his early life, but as of 1650 he was an assistant to John Milton, then the Latin Secretary of the Commonwealth. Marvell was instrumental in saving Milton from execution when Charles II was restored. Marvell also served well, but without distinction, as a member of Parliament. During his lifetime he was not noted as a poet—today he is appreciated as a witty, thought-provoking writer.

To His Coy Mistress

Had we but world enough, and time,
This coyness, lady, were no crime.
We would sit down, and think which way
To walk, and pass our long love's day.
Thou by the Indian Ganges' side   5
Shoudst rubies find: I by the tide
of Humber[1] would complain. I would
Love you ten years before the flood,
And you should, if you please, refuse
Till the conversion of the Jews.[2]   10
My vegetable love should grow
Vaster than empires and more slow;
An hundred years should go to praise
Thine eyes, and on thy forehead gaze;
Two hundred to adore each breast,   15
But thirty thousand to the rest;
An age at least to every part,
And the last age should show your heart.
For, lady, you deserve this state,
Nor would I love at lower rate.   20
    But at my back I always hear
Time's wingéd chariot hurrying near;
And yonder all before us lie
Deserts of vast eternity.
Thy beauty shall no more be found;   25
Nor, in thy marble vault, shall sound
My echoing song; then worms shall try
That long-preserved virginity,
And your quaint honor turn to dust,
And into ashes all my lust: 30

1. A small English river.   2. Traditionally, the Jews will not be converted until Judgment Day.

The grave's a fine and private place,
But none, I think, do there embrace.
      Now therefore, while the youthful hue
Sits on thy skin like morning dew, *simile*
And while thy willing soul transpires   35
At every pore with instant fires,
Now let us sport us while we may,
And now, like amorous birds of prey, *simile*
Rather at once our time devour
Than languish in his slow-chapped³ power.   40
Let us roll all our strength and all
Our sweetness up into one ball,
And tear our pleasures with rough strife
Thorough the iron gates of life:
Thus, though we cannot make our sun   45
Stand still, yet we will make him run.

Let us enjoy every moment while we can

The Garden

How vainly men themselves amaze
To win the palm, the oak, or bays;⁴
And their incessant labors see
Crowned from some single herb, or tree,
Whose short and narrow-vergéd shade   5
Does prudently their toils upbraid;
While all flowers and all trees do close
To weave the garlands of repose!

Fair Quiet, have I found thee here,
And Innocence, thy sister dear?   10
Mistaken long, I sought you then
In busy companies of men.
Your sacred plants, if here below,
Only among the plants will grow;
Society is all but rude   15
To this delicious solitude.

No white nor red was ever seen
So amorous as this lovely green.
Fond lovers, cruel as their flame,
Cut in these trees their mistress' name: 20
Little, alas! they know or heed
How far these beauties hers exceed!
Fair trees! wheres'e'er your barks I wound
No name shall but your own be found.

3. Slow-jawed. **4** Victory wreaths.

When we have run our passion's heat,   25
Love hither makes his best retreat.
The gods, that mortal beauty chase,
Still in a tree did end their race;
Apollo hunted Daphne so,
Only that she might laurel grow;[5]   30
And Pan did after Syrinx speed,[6]
Not as a nymph, but for a reed.

What wondrous life is this I lead!
Ripe apples drop about my head;
The luscious clusters of the vine   35
Upon my mouth do crush their wine;
The nectarine, and curious peach,
Into my hands themselves do reach;
Stumbling on melons, as I pass,
Ensnared with flowers, I fall on grass.   40

Meanwhile, the mind, from pleasure less,
Withdraws into its happiness:
The mind, that ocean where each kind
Does straight its own resemblance find;[7]
Yet it creates, transcending these,   45
Far other worlds, and other seas;
Annihilating all that's made
To a green thought in a green shade.

Here at the fountain's sliding foot,
Or at some fruit-tree's mossy root,   50
Casting the body's vest aside,
My soul into the boughs does glide:
There like a bird it sits, and sings,
Then whets and combs its silver wings;
And, till prepared for longer flight,   55
Waves in its plumes the various light.

Such was that happy garden-state,
While man there walked without a mate:
After a place so pure and sweet,
What other help could yet be meet?   60
But 'twas beyond a mortal's share
To wander solitary there:
Two paradises 'twere in one,
To live in paradise alone.

---

5. In mythology, Daphne changed into a laurel after being pursued by Apollo.   **6.** Pan pursued Syrinx until she changed into a reed.   **7.** It was believed that each creature on land had a twin in the ocean.

How well the skillful gardener drew   65
Of flowers, and herbs, this dial new;
Where, from above, the milder sun
Does through a fragrant zodiac run;
And, as it works, the industrious bee
Computes its time as well as we.   70
How could such sweet and wholesome hours
Be reckoned but with herbs and flowers!

Fact Questions and Exercises

1. Why, according to the speaker in "To His Coy Mistress," should the lady stop preserving her "quaint honor"? What is described as "a fine and private place"?
2. How does Marvell use the word "coy" in this poem? What is its connotation and denotation?
3. In "The Garden," how does society compare to the "delicious solitude"? What color is praised?
4. What allusions does Marvell make to the Garden of Eden? Point out specific lines.

For Discussion and Writing

1. In "To His Coy Mistress," what is the speaker's attitude toward his "mistress"? What is he trying to convince her to do? Does he seem to respect her and her wishes? Is his argument convincing? Does it seem to respect the woman's intellect?
2. Do you see any one theme throughout Marvell's poems? They both concern "love," but do the poems present the same attitude toward love? How, for instance, does the attitude presented in "The Garden" differ from that in "To His Coy Mistress"? How does the speaker of the poems move from seduction to solitude?
3. Discuss the theme of time as it appears in "To His Coy Mistress." What are the various symbols used that relate to time? How does time motivate the speaker? Are there implications that the mistress does not share the speaker's view of time?

Alexander Pope [1688–1744]

Pope was born in London, England, but grew up in the country at
Binfield. Because he was a Roman Catholic, Pope could not attend
a university, receive patronage, or vote. In a sense, writing was
the only profession open to him; consequently, he was one of the
first Englishmen to support himself solely by writing. Pope was
physically deformed and beset by a number of illnesses; nevertheless, he managed to become a successful and famous poet,
best-known for his satires, such as "The Rape of the Lock"
(1712–1714). Although Pope's satires were of specific people and
evils in his generation, they also dealt with universal types and
problems, and can still be appreciated by today's reader.

The Rape of the Lock

An Heroi-comical Poem

Nolueram, Belinda, tuos violare capillos;
sed juvat hoc precibus me tribuisse tuis.[1]
—MARTIAL

CANTO I

What dire offense from amorous causes springs,
What mighty contests rise from trivial things,
I sing—This verse to Caryll, Muse! is due:
This, even Belinda may vouchsafe to view:
Slight is the subject, but not so the praise,   5
If she inspire, and he approve my lays.
        Say what strange motive, Goddess! could compel
A well-bred lord to assault a gentle belle?
Oh, say what stranger cause, yet unexplored,
Could make a gentle belle reject a lord?   10
In tasks so bold can little men engage,
And in soft bosoms dwells such mighty rage?
        Sol through white curtains shot a timorous ray,
And oped those eyes that must eclipse the day.
Now lapdogs give themselves the rousing shake,   15
And sleepless lovers just at twelve awake:
Thrice rung the bell, the slipper knocked the ground,
And the pressed watch returned a silver sound.
Belinda still her downy pillow pressed,
Her guardian Sylph prolonged the balmy rest: 20
'Twas he had summoned to her silent bed

---

1. "I did not wish to ravage your locks, Belinda; but I am happy to have given this tribute to
your wishes."

The morning dream that hovered o'er her head.
A youth more glittering than a birthnight beau
(That even in slumber caused her cheek to glow)
Seemed to her ear his winning lips to lay,   25
And thus in whispers said, or seemed to say:
     "Fairest of mortals, thou distinguished care
Of thousand bright inhabitants of air!
If e'er one vision touched thy infant thought,
Of all the nurse and all the priest have taught,   30
Of airy elves by moonlight shadows seen,
The silver token, and the circled green,
Or virgins visited by angel powers,
With golden crowns and wreaths of heavenly flowers,
Hear and believe! thy own importance know,   35
Nor bound thy narrow veins to things below.
Some secret truths, from learned pride concealed,
To maids alone and children are revealed:
What though no credit doubting wits may give?
The fair and innocent shall still believe.   40
Know, then, unnumbered spirits round thee fly,
The light militia of the lower sky:
These, though unseen, are ever on the wing,
Hang o'er the box, and hover round the Ring.[2]
Think what an equipage thou hast in air,   45
And view with scorn two pages and a chair.
As now your own, our beings were of old,
And once enclosed in woman's beauteous mold;
Thence, by a soft transition, we repair
From earthly vehicles to these of air.   50
Think not, when woman's transient breath is fled,
That all her vanities at once are dead:
Succeeding vanities she still regards,
And though she plays no more, o'erlooks the cards.
Her joy in gilded chariots, when alive,   55
And love of ombre,[3] after death survive.
For when the Fair in all their pride expire,
To their first elements their souls retire:
The sprites of fiery termagants in flame
Mount up, and take a Salamander's name.   60
Soft yielding minds to water glide away,
And sip, with Nymphs, their elemental tea.
The graver prude sinks downward to a Gnome,
In search of mischief still on earth to roam.
The light coquettes in Sylphs aloft repair,   65
And sport and flutter in the fields of air.
     "Know further yet; whoever fair and chaste

---

2. A theater box and the Hyde Park "ring" where carriages drove.   3. A popular card game
similar to bridge.

Rejects mankind, is by some Sylph embraced:
For spirits, freed from mortal laws, with ease
Assume what sexes and what shapes they please.   70
What guards the purity of melting maids,
In courtly balls, and midnight masquerades,
Safe from the treacherous friend, the daring spark,
The glance by day, the whisper in the dark,
When kind occasion prompts their warm desires,   75
When music softens, and when dancing fires?
'Tis but their Sylph, the wise Celestials know,
Though Honor is the word with men below.
        "Some nymphs there are, too conscious of their face,
For life predestined to the Gnomes' embrace.   80
These swell their prospects and exalt their pride,
When offers are disdained, and love denied:
Then gay ideas crowd the vacant brain,
While peers, and dukes, and all their sweeping train,
And garters, stars, and coronets appear,   85
And in soft sounds, 'your Grace' salutes their ear.
'Tis these that early taint the female soul,
Instruct the eyes of young coquettes to roll,
Teach infant cheeks a bidden blush to know,
And little hearts to flutter at a beau.   90
        "Oft, when the world imagine women stray,
The Sylphs through mystic mazes guide their way,
Through all the giddy circle they pursue,
And old impertinence expel by new.
What tender maid but must a victim fall   95
To one man's treat, but for another's ball?
When Florio speaks what virgin could withstand,
If gentle Damon did not squeeze her hand?
With varying vanities, from every part,
They shift the moving toyshop of their heart;   100
Where wigs with wigs, with sword-knots sword-knots strive,
Beaux banish beaux, and coaches coaches drive.
This erring mortals levity may call;
Oh, blind to truth! the Sylphs contrive it all.
        "Of these am I, who thy protection claim,   105
A watchful sprite, and Ariel is my name.
Late, as I ranged the crystal wilds of air,
In the clear mirror of thy ruling star
I saw, alas! some dread event impend,
Ere to the main this morning sun descend,   110
But Heaven reveals not what, or how, or where:
Warned by the Sylph, O pious maid, beware!
This to disclose is all thy guardian can:
Beware of all, but most beware of Man!"   115
        He said; when Shock,[4] who thought she slept too long,

4. Common name for small dogs.

Leaped up, and waked his mistress with his tongue.
'Twas then, Belinda, it report say true,
Thy eyes first opened on a billet-doux;
Wounds, charms, and ardors were no sooner read,
But all the vision vanished from thy head.   120
　　　And now, unveiled, the toilet stands displayed,
Each silver vase in mystic order laid.
First, robed in white, the nymph intent adores,
With head uncovered, the cosmetic powers.
A heavenly image in the glass appears;   125
To that she bends, to that her eyes she rears.
The inferior priestess, at her altar's side,
Trembling begins the sacred rites of pride.
Unnumbered treasures ope at once, and here
The various offerings of the world appear;   130
From each she nicely culls with curious toil,
And decks the goddess with the glittering spoil.
This casket India's glowing gems unlocks,
And all Arabia breathes from yonder box.
The tortoise here and elephant unite,   135
Transformed to combs, the speckled and the white.
Here files of pins extend their shining rows,
Puffs, powders, patches, Bibles, billet-doux.
Now awful Beauty put on all its arms;
The fair each moment rises in her charms,   140
Repairs her smiles, awakens every grace,
And calls forth all the wonders of her face;
Sees by degrees a purer blush arise,
And keener lightnings quicken in her eyes.
The busy Sylphs surround their darling care,   145
These set the head, and those divide the hair,
Some fold the sleeve, whilst others plait the gown;
And Betty's praised for labors not her own.

CANTO II

　　　Not with more glories, in the ethereal plain,
The sun first rises o'er the purpled main,
Than, issuing forth, the rival of his beams
Launched on the bosom of the silver Thames.
Fair nymphs and well-dressed youths around her shone,   5
But every eye was fixed on her alone.
On her white breast a sparkling cross she wore,
Which Jews might kiss, and infidels adore.
Her lively looks a sprightly mind disclose,
Quick as her eyes, and as unfixed as those: 10
Favors to none, to all she smiles extends;
Oft she rejects, but never once offends.
Bright as the sun, her eyes the gazers strike,
And, like the sun, they shine on all alike.

Yet graceful ease, and sweetness void of pride,   15
Might hide her faults, if belles had faults to hide:
If to her share some female errors fall,
Look on her face, and you'll forget 'em all.
    This nymph, to the destruction of mankind,
Nourished two locks which graceful hung behind   20
In equal curls, and well conspired to deck
With shining ringlets the smooth ivory neck.
Love in these labyrinths his slaves detains,
And mighty hearts are held in slender chains.
With hairy springes we the birds betray,   25
Slight lines of hair surprise the finny prey,
Fair tresses man's imperial race ensnare,
And beauty draws us with a single hair.
    The adventurous Baron the bright locks admired,
He saw, he wished, and to the prize aspired.   30
Resolved to win, he meditates the way,
By force to ravish, or by fraud betray;
For when success a lover's toil attends,
Few ask if fraud or force attained his ends.
    For this, ere Phoebus rose, he had implored   35
Propitious Heaven, and every power adored,
But chiefly Love—to Love an altar built,
Of twelve vast French romances, neatly gilt.
There lay three garters, half a pair of gloves,
And all the trophies of his former loves.   40
With tender billet-doux he lights the pyre,
And breathes three amorous sighs to raise the fire.
Then prostrate falls, and begs with ardent eyes
Soon to obtain, and long possess the prize:
The powers gave ear, and granted half his prayer,   45
The rest the winds dispersed in empty air.
    But now secure the painted vessel glides,
The sunbeams trembling on the floating tides,
While melting music steals upon the sky,
And softened sounds along the waters die.   50
Smooth flow the waves, the zephyrs gentle play,
Belinda smiled, and all the world was gay.
All but the Sylph—with careful thoughts oppressed,
The impending woe sat heavy on his breast.
He summons straight his denizens of air;   55
The lucid squadrons round the sails repair:
Soft o'er the shrouds aërial whispers breathe
That seemed but zephyrs to the train beneath.
Some to the sun their insect-wings unfold,
Waft on the breeze, or sink in clouds of gold.   60
Transparent forms too find for mortal sight,
Their fluid bodies half dissolved in light,
Loose to the wind their airy garments flew,

Thin glittering textures of the filmy dew,
Dipped in the richest tincture of the skies,   65
Where light disports in ever-mingling dyes,
While every beam new transient colors flings,
Colors that change whene'er they wave their wings.
Amid the circle, on the gilded mast,
Superior by the head was Ariel placed;   70
His purple pinions opening to the sun,
He raised his azure wand, and thus begun:
          "Ye Sylphs and Sylphids, to your chief give ear!
Fays, Fairies, Genii, Elves, and Daemons, hear!
Ye know the spheres and various tasks assigned   75
By laws eternal to the aërial kind.
Some in the fields of purest ether play,
And bask and whiten in the blaze of day.
Some guide the course of wandering orbs on high,
Or roll the planets through the boundless sky.   80
Some less refined, beneath the moon's pale light
Pursue the stars that shoot athwart the night,
Or suck the mists in grosser air below,
Or dip their pinions in the painted bow,
Or brew fierce tempests on the wintry main,   85
Or o'er the glebe distill the kindly rain.
Others on earth o'er human race preside,
Watch all their ways, and all their actions guide:
Of these the chief the care of nations own,
And guard with arms divine the British Throne.   90
          "Our humbler province is to tend the Fair,
Not a less pleasing, though less glorious care:
To save the powder from too rude a gale,
Nor let the imprisoned essences exhale;
To draw fresh colors from the vernal flowers;   95
To steal from rainbows e'er they drop in showers
A brighter wash; to curl their waving hairs,
Assist their blushes, and inspire their airs;
Nay oft, in dreams invention we bestow,
To change a flounce, or add a furbelow.   100
          "This day black omens threat the brightest fair,
That e'er deserved a watchful spirit's care;
Some dire disaster, or by force or slight,
But what, or where, the Fates have wrapped in night:
Whether the nymph shall break Diana's law,[5]   105
Or some frail china jar receive a flaw,
Or stain her honor or her new brocade,
Forget her prayers, or miss a masquerade,
Or lose her heart, or necklace, at a ball;
Or whether Heaven has doomed that Shock must fall.   110

5. Chastity.

Haste, then, ye spirits! to your charge repair:
The fluttering fan be Zephyretta's care;
The drops to thee, Brillante, we consign;
And, Momentilla, let the watch be thine;
Do thou, Crispissa, tend her favorite Lock;   115
Ariel himself shall be the guard of Shock.
　　　"To fifty chosen Sylphs, of special note,
We trust the important charge, the petticoat;
Oft have we known that sevenfold fence to fail,
Though stiff with hoops, and armed with ribs of whale.   120
Form a strong line about the silver bound,
And guard the wide circumference around.
　　　"Whatever spirit, careless of his charge,
His post neglects, or leaves the fair at large,
Shall feel sharp vengeance soon o'ertake his sins,   125
Be stopped in vials, or transfixed with pins,
Or plunged in lakes of bitter washes lie,
Or wedged whole ages in a bodkin's eye;
Gums and pomatums shall his flight restrain,
While clogged he beats his silken wings in vain,   130
Or alum styptics with contracting power
Shrink his thin essence like a riveled flower:
Or, as Ixion fixed, the wretch shall feel
The giddy motion of the whirling mill,[6]
In fumes of burning chocolate shall glow,   135
And tremble at the sea that froths below!"
　　　He spoke; the spirits from the sails descend;
Some, orb in orb, around the nymph extend;
Some thread the mazy ringlets of her hair;
Some hang upon the pendants of her ear: 140
With beating hearts the dire event they wait,
Anxious, and trembling for the birth of Fate.

CANTO III

　　　Close by those meads, forever crowned with flowers,
Where Thames with pride surveys his rising towers,
There stands a structure of majestic frame,
Which from the neighboring Hampton takes its name.
Here Britain's statesmen oft the fall foredoom   5
Of foreign tyrants and of nymphs at home;
Here thou, great Anna! whom three realms obey,
Dost sometimes counsel take—and sometimes tea.
　　　Hither the heroes and the nymphs resort,
To taste awhile the pleasures of a court;   10
In various talk the instructive hours they passed,
Who gave the ball, or paid the visit last;

6. Ixion was tied to a turning wheel for insulting Juno.

One speaks the glory of the British Queen,
And one describes a charming Indian screen;
A third interprets motions, looks, and eyes;   15
At every word a reputation dies.
Snuff, or the fan, supply each pause of chat,
With singing, laughing, ogling, and all that.
            Meanwhile, declining from the noon of day,
The sun obliquely shoots his burning ray;   20
The hungry judges soon the sentence sign,
And wretches hang that jurymen may dine;
The merchant from the Exchange returns in peace,
And the long labors of the toilet cease.
Belinda now, whom thirst of fame invites,   25
Burns to encounter two adventurous knights,
At ombre singly to decide their doom,
And swells her breast with conquests yet to come.
Straight the three bands prepare in arms to join,
Each band the number of the sacred nine.
Soon as she spreads her hand, the aërial guard   30
Descend, and sit on each important card:
First Ariel perched upon a Matadore,
Then each according to the rank they bore;
For Sylphs, yet mindful of their ancient race,
Are, as when women, wondrous fond of place.   35
            Behold, four Kings in majesty revered,
With hoary whiskers and a forky beard;
And four fair Queens whose hands sustain a flower,
The expressive emblem of their softer power;
Four Knaves in garbs succinct, a trusty band,   40
Caps on their heads, and halberts in their hand;
And parti-colored troops, a shining train,
Draw forth to combat on the velvet plain.[7]
            The skillful nymph reviews her force with care;   45
"Let Spades be trumphs!" she said, and trumps they were.
            Now move to war her sable Matadores,
In show like leaders of the swarthy Moors.
Spadillio first, unconquerable lord!
Led off two captive trumps, and swept the board.   50
As many more Manillio forced to yield,
And marched a victor from the verdant field.
Him Basto followed, but his fate more hard
Gained but one trump and one plebeian card.
With his broad saber next, a chief in years,   55
The hoary Majesty of Spades appears,
Puts forth one manly leg, to sight revealed,
The rest his many-colored robe concealed.
The rebel Knave, who dares his prince engage,

7. The green cloth on which the card game is being played.

Proves the just victim of his royal rage.   60
Even mighty Pam, that kings and queens o'erthrew
And mowed down armies in the fights of loo,
Sad chance of war! now distitute of aid,
Falls undistinguished by the victor Spade.
        Thus far both armies to Belinda yield;   65
Now to the Baron fate inclines the field.
His warlike amazon her host invades,
The imperial consort of the crown of Spades.
The Club's black tyrant first her victim died,
Spite of his haughty mien and barbarous pride.   70
What boots the regal circle on his head,
His giant limbs, in state unwieldy spread?
That long behind he trails his pompous robe,
And of all monarchs only grasps the globe?
        The Baron now his Diamonds pours apace;   75
The embroidered King who shows but half his face,
And his refulgent Queen, with powers combined
Of broken troops an easy conquest find.
Clubs, Diamonds, Hearts, in wild disorder seen,
With throngs promiscuous strew the level green.   80
Thus when dispersed a routed army runs,
Of Asia's troops, and Afric's sable sons,
With like confusion different nations fly,
Of various habit, and of various dye,
The pierced battalions disunited fall   85
In heaps on heaps; one fate o'erwhelms them all.
        The Knave of Diamonds tries his wily arts,
And wins (oh, shameful chance!) the Queen of Hearts.
At this, the blood the virgin's cheek forsook,
A livid paleness spreads o'er all her look;   90
She sees, and trembles at the approaching ill,
Just in the jaws of ruin, and Codille,
And now (as oft in some distempered state)
On one nice trick depends the general fate.
An Ace of Hearts steps forth: the King unseen   95
Lurked in her hand, and mourned his captive Queen.
He springs to vengeance with an eager pace,
And falls like thunder on the prostrate Ace.
The nymph exulting fills with shouts the sky,
The walls, the woods, and long canals reply.   100
        O thoughtless mortals! ever blind to fate,
Too soon dejected, and too soon elate:
Sudden these honors shall be snatched away,
And cursed forever this victorious day.
        For lo! the board with cups and spoons is crowned,   105
The berries crackel, and the mill turns round;
On shining altars of Japan they raise
The silver lamp; the fiery spirits blaze:

From silver spouts the grateful liquors glide,
While China's earth receives the smoking tide, 110
At once they gratify their scent and taste,
And frequent cups prolong the rich repast.
Straight hover round the fair her airy band;
Some, as she sipped, the fuming liquor fanned,
Some o'er her lap their careful plumes displayed, 115
Trembling, and conscious of the rich brocade.
Coffee (which makes the politician wise,
And see through all things with his half-shut eyes)
Sent up in vapors to the Baron's brain
New stratagems, the radiant Lock to gain. 120
Ah, cease, rash youth! desist ere 'tis too late,
Fear the just Gods, and think of Scylla's fate!
Changed to a bird, and sent to flit in air,
She dearly pays for Nisus' injured hair![8]
    But when to mischief mortals bend their will, 125
How soon they find fit instruments of ill!
Just then, Clarissa drew with tempting grace
A two-edged weapon from her shining case:
So ladies in romance assist their knight,
Present the spear, and arm him for the fight. 130
He takes the gift with reverence, and extends
The little engine on his fingers' ends;
This just behind Belinda's neck he spread,
As o'er the fragrant steams she bends her head.
Swift to the Lock a thousand sprites repair, 135
A thousand wings, by turns, blow back the hair,
And thrice they twitched the diamond in her ear,
Thrice she looked back, and thrice the foe drew near.
Just in that instant, anxious Ariel sought
The close recesses of the virgin's thought; 140
As on the nosegay in her breast reclined,
He watched the ideas rising in her mind,
Sudden he viewed, in spite of all her art,
An earthly lover lurking at her heart.
Amazed, confused, he found his power expired, 145
Resigned to fate, and with a sigh retired.
    The Peer now spreads the glittering forfex wide,
To enclose the Lock; now joins it, to divide.
Even then, before the fatal engine closed,
A wretched Sylph too fondly interposed; 150
Fate urged the shears, and cut the Sylph in twain
(But airy substance soon unites again):
The meeting points the sacred hair dissever
From the fair head, forever, and forever!

8. Scylla was changed into a sea bird that is forever chased by an eagle because she betrayed her father, Nisus.

Then flashed the living lightning from her eyes,   155
And screams of horror rend the affrighted skies.
Not louder shrieks to pitying heaven are cast,
When husbands, or when lapdogs breathe their last;
Or when rich china vessels fallen from high,
In glittering dust and painted fragments lie!   160
"Let wreaths of triumph now my temples twine,"
The victor cried, "the glorious prize is mine!
While fish in streams, or birds delight in air,
Or in a coach and six the British Fair,
As long as *Atalantis*[9] shall be read,   165
Or the small pillow grace a lady's bed,
While visits shall be paid on solemn days,
When numerous wax-lights in bright order blaze,
While nymphs take treats, or assignations give,
So long my honor, name, and praise shall live!   170
What Time would spare, from Steel receives its date,
And monuments, like men, submit to fate!
Steel could the labor of the Gods destroy,
And strike to dust the imperial towers of Troy;
Steel could the works of mortal pride confound,   175
And hew triumphal arches to the ground.
What wonder then, fair nymph! thy hairs should feel,
The conquering force of unresisted Steel?"

CANTO IV

But anxious cares the pensive nymph oppressed,
And secret passions labored in her breast.
Not youthful kings in battle seized alive,
Not scornful virgins who their charms survive,
Not ardent lovers robbed of all their bliss,   5
Not ancient ladies when refused a kiss,
Not tyrants fierce that unrepenting die,
Not Cynthia when her manteau's pinned awry,
E'er felt such rage, resentment, and despair,
As thou, sad virgin! for thy ravished hair.   10
For, that sad moment, when the Sylphs withdrew
And Ariel weeping from Belinda flew,
Umbriel, a dusky, melancholy sprite
As ever sullied the fair face of light,
Down to the central earth, his proper scene,   15
Repaired to search the gloomy Cave of Spleen.
Swift on his sooty pinions flits the Gnome,
And in a vapor reached the dismal dome.
No cheerful breeze this sullen region knows,
The dreaded east is all the wind that blows.   20

9. A scandalous book of memoirs.

Here in a grotto, sheltered close from air,
And screened in shades from day's detested glare,
She sighs forever on her pensive bed,
Pain at her side, and Megrim at her head.
     Two handmaids wait the throne: alike in place   25
But differing far in figure and in face.
Here stood Ill-Nature like an ancient maid,
Her wrinkled form in black and white arrayed;
With store of prayers for mornings, nights, and noons,
Her hand is filled; her bosom with lampoons.   30
     There Affectation, with a sickly mien,
Shows in her cheek the roses of eighteen,
Practiced to lisp, and hang the head aside,
Faints into airs, and languishes with pride,
On the rich quilt sinks with becoming woe,   35
Wrapped in a gown, for sickness and for show.
The fair ones feel such maladies as these,
When each new nightdress gives a new disease.
     A constant vapor o'er the palace flies,
Strange phantoms rising as the mists arise;   40
Dreadful as hermit's dreams in haunted shades,
Or bright as visions of expiring maids.
Now glaring fiends, and snakes on rolling spires,
Pale specters, gaping tombs, and purple fires;
Now lakes of liquid gold, Elysian scenes,   45
And crystal domes, and angels in machines.
     Unnumbered throngs on every side are seen
Of bodies changed to various forms by Spleen.
Here living teapots stand, one arm held out,
One bent; the handle this, and that the spout: 50
A pipkin there, like Homer's tripod, walks;
Here sighs a jar, and there a goose pie talks;
Men prove with child, as powerful fancy works,
And maids, turned bottles, call aloud for corks.
     Safe passed the Gnome through this fantastic band,   55
A branch of healing spleenwort in his hand.
Then thus addressed the Power: "Hail, wayward Queen!
Who rule the sex to fifty from fifteen:
Parent of vapors and of female wit,
Who give the hysteric or poetic fit,   60
On various tempers act by various ways,
Make some take physic, others scribble plays;
Who cause the proud their visits to delay,
And send the godly in a pet to pray.
A nymph there is that all your power disdains,   65
And thousands more in equal mirth maintains.
But oh! if e'er thy Gnome could spoil a grace,
Or raise a pimple on a beauteous face,
Like citron-waters matrons' cheeks inflame,

Or change complexions at a losing game;   70
If e'er with airy horns I planted heads,
Or rumpled petticoats, or tumbled beds,
Or caused suspicion when no soul was rude,
Or discomposed the headdress of a prude,
Or e'er to costive lapdog gave disease,   75
Which not the tears of brightest eyes could ease,
Hear me, and touch Belinda with chagrin:
That single act gives half the world the spleen."
      The Goddess with a discontented air
Seems to reject him though she grants his prayer.   80
A wondrous bag with both her hands she binds,
Like that where once Ulysses held the winds;
There she collects the force of female lungs,
Sighs, sobs, and passions, and the war of tongues.
A vial next she fills with fainting fears,   85
Soft sorrows, melting griefs, and flowing tears.
The Gnome rejoicing bears her gifts away,
Spreads his black wings, and slowly mounts to day.
      Sunk in Thalestris[10] arms the nymph he found,
Her eyes dejected and her hair unbound.   90
Full o'er their heads the swelling bag he rent,
And all the Furies issued at the vent.
Belinda burns with more than mortal ire,
And fierce Thalestris fans the rising fire.
"O wretched maid!" she spreads her hands, and cried   95
(While Hampton's echoes, "Wretched maid!" replied),
"Was it for this you took such constant care
The bodkin, comb, and essence to prepare?
For this your locks in paper durance bound,
For this with torturing irons wreathed around?   100
For this with fillets strained your tender head,
And bravely bore the double loads of lead?
Gods! shall the ravisher display your hair,
While the fops envy, and the ladies stare!
Honor forbid! at whose unrivaled shrine   105
Ease, pleasure, virtue, all, our sex resign.
Methinks already I your tears survey,
Already hear the horrid things they say,
Already see you a degraded toast,
And all your honor in a whisper lost!   110
How shall I, then, your helpless fame defend?
'Twill then be infamy to seem your friend!
And shall this prize, the inestimable prize,
Exposed through crystal to the gazing eyes,
And heightened by the diamond's circling rays,   115
On that rapacious hand forever blaze?

---

10. Common name for an Amazon.

Sooner shall grass in Hyde Park Circus grow,
And wits take lodgings in the sound of Bow;[11]
Sooner let earth, air, sea, to chaos fall,
Men, monkeys, lapdogs, parrots, perish all!"   120
      She said; then raging to Sir Plume repairs,
And bids her beau demand the precious hairs
(Sir Plume of amber snuffbox justly vain,
And the nice conduct of a clouded cane).
With earnest eyes, and round unthinking face,   125
He first the snuffbox opened, then the case,
And thus broke out—"My Lord, why, what the devil!
Zounds! damn the lock! 'fore Gad, you must be civil!
Plague on't! 'tis past a jest—nay prithee, pox!
Give her the hair"—he spoke, and rapped his box.   130
      "It grieves me much," replied the Peer again,
"Who speaks so well should ever speak in vain.
But by this Lock, this sacred Lock I swear
(Which never more shall join its parted hair;
Which never more its honors shall renew,   135
Clipped from the lovely head where late it grew),
That while my nostrils draw the vital air,
This hand, which won it, shall forever wear."
He spoke, and speaking, in proud triumph spread
The long-contended honors of her head.   140
      But Umbriel, hateful Gnome, forbears not so;
He breaks the vial whence the sorrows flow.
Then see! the nymph in beauteous grief appears,
Her eyes half languishing, half drowned in tears;
On her heaved bosom hung her drooping head,   145
Which with a sigh she raised, and thus she said:
      "Forever cursed be this detested day,
Which snatched my best, my favorite curl away!
Happy! ah, ten times happy had I been,
If Hampton Court these eyes had never seen!   150
Yet am not I the first mistaken maid,
By love of courts to numerous ills betrayed.
Oh, had I rather unadmired remained
In some lone isle, or distant northern land;
Where the gilt chariot never marks the way,   155
Where none learn ombre, none e'er taste bohea!
There kept my charms concealed from mortal eye,
Like roses that in deserts blooms and die.
What moved my mind with youthful lords to roam?
Oh, had I stayed, and said my prayers at home!   160
'Twas this the morning omens seemed to tell,
Thrice from my trembling hand the patch box fell;
The tottering china shook without a wind,

11. Bowchurch bells.

Nay, Poll sat mute, and Shock was most unkind!
A Sylph too warned me of the threats of fate,   165
In mystic visions, now believed too late!
See the poor remnants of these slighted hairs!
My hands shall rend what e'en thy rapine spares.
These in two sable ringlets taught to break,
Once gave new beauties to the snowy neck;   170
The sister lock now sits uncouth, alone,
And in its fellow's fate foresees its own;
Uncurled it hangs, the fatal shears demands,
And tempts once more thy sacrilegious hands.
Oh, hadst thou, cruel! been content to seize   175
Hairs less in sight, or any hairs but these!"

CANTO V

She said: the pitying audience melt in tears.
But Fate and Jove had stopped the Baron's ears.
In vain Thalestris with reproach assails,
For who can move when fair Belinda fails?
Not half so fixed the Trojan could remain,   5
While Anna begged and Dido raged in vain.[12]
Then grave Clarissa graceful waved her fan;
Silence ensued, and thus the nymph began:
      "Say why are beauties praised and honored most,
The wise man's passion, and the vain man's toast?   10
Why decked with all that land and sea afford,
Why angels called, and angel-like adored?
Why round our coaches crowd the white-gloved beaux,
Why bows the side box from its inmost rows?
How vain are all these glories, all our pains,   15
Unless good sense preserve what beauty gains;
That men may say when we the front box grace,
'Behold the first in virtue as in face!'
Oh! if to dance all night, and dress all day,
Charmed the smallpox, or chased old age away,   20
Who would not scorn what housewife's cares produce,
Or who would learn one earthly thing of use?
To patch, nay ogle, might become a saint,
Nor could it sure be such a sin to paint.
But since, alas! frail beauty must decay,   25
Curled or uncurled, since locks will turn to gray;
Since painted, or not painted, all shall fade,
And she who scorns a man must die a maid;
What then remains but well our power to use,
And keep good humor still whate'er we lose?   30

12. Dido loved Aeneas, and complained when he wanted to leave Carthage; Anna was Dido's
sister.

And trust me, dear, good humor can prevail
When airs, and flights, and screams, and scolding fail.
Beauties in vain their pretty eyes may roll;
Charms strike the sight, but merit wins the soul."
  So spoke the dame, but no applause ensued;   35
Belinda frowned, Thalestris called her prude.
"To arms, to arms!" the fierce virago cries,
And swift as lightning to the combat flies.
All side in parties, and begin the attack;
Fans clap, silks rustle, and tough whalebones crack; 40
Heroes' and heroines' shouts confusedly rise,
And bass and treble voices strike the skies.
No common weapons in their hands are found,
Like Gods they fight, nor dread a mortal wound.
  So when bold Homer makes the Gods engage,   45
And heavenly breasts with human passions rage;
'Gainst Pallas, Mars; Latona, Hermes arms;
And all Olympus rings with loud alarms:
Jove's thunder roars, heaven trembles all around,
Blue Neptune storms, the bellowing deeps resound: 50
Earth shakes her nodding towers, the ground gives way,
And the pale ghosts start at the flash of day!
  Triumphant Umbriel on a sconce's height
Clapped his glad wings, and sat to view the fight:
Propped on the bodkin spears, the sprites survey 55
The growing combat, or assist the fray.
  While through the press enraged Thalestris flies,
And scatters death around from both her eyes,
A beau and witling perished in the throng,
One died in metaphor, and one in song. 60
"O cruel nymph! a living death I bear,"
Cried Dapperwit, and sunk beside his chair.
A mournful glance Sir Fopling upwards cast,
"Those eyes are made so killing"—was his last.
Thus on Maeander's flowery margin lies 65
The expiring swan, and as he sings he dies.
  When bold Sir Plume had drawn Clarissa down,
Chloe stepped in, and killed him with a frown;
She smiled to see the doughty hero slain,
But, at her smile, the beau revived again. 70
  Now Jove suspends his golden scales in air,
Weighs the men's wits against the lady's hair;
The doubtful beam long nods from side to side;
At length the wits mount up, the hairs subside.
  See, fierce Belinda on the Baron flies, 75
With more than usual lightning in her eyes;
Nor feared the chief the unequal fight to try,
Who sought no more than on his foe to die.
  But this bold lord with manly strength endued,

She with one finger and a thumb subdued: 80
Just where the breath of life his nostrils drew,
A charge of snuff the wily virgin threw;
The Gnomes direct, to every atom just,
The pungent grains of titillating dust.
Sudden, with starting tears each eye o'erflows,   85
And the high dome re-echoes to his nose.
    "Now meet thy fate," incensed Belinda cried,
And drew a deadly bodkin from her side.
(The same, his ancient personage to deck,
Her great-great-grandsire wore about his neck,   90
In three seal rings, which after, melted down,
Formed a vast buckle for his widow's gown:
Her infant grandame's whistle next it grew,
The bells she jingled, and the whistle blew;
Then in a bodkin graced her mother's hairs,   95
Which long she wore, and now Belinda wears.)
    "Boast not my fall," he cried, "insulting foe!
Thou by some other shalt be laid as low.
Nor think to die dejects my lofty mind:
All that I dread is leaving you behind!   100
Rather than so, ah, let me still survive,
And burn in Cupid's flames—but burn alive."
    "Restore the Lock!" she cries; and all around
"Restore the Lock!" the vaulted roofs rebound.
Not fierce Othello in so loud a strain   105
Roared for the handkerchief that caused his pain.
But see how oft ambitious aims are crossed,
And chiefs contend till all the prize is lost!
The lock, obtained with guilt, and kept with pain,
In every place is sought, but sought in vain: 110
With such a prize no mortal must be blessed,
So Heaven decrees! with Heaven who can contest?
    Some thought it mounted to the lunar sphere,
Since all things lost on earth are treasured there.
There heroes' wits are kept in ponderous vases,   115
And beaux' in snuffboxes and tweezer cases.
There broken vows and deathbed alms are found,
And lovers' hearts with ends of riband bound,
The courtier's promises, and sick man's prayers,
The smiles of harlots, and the tears of heirs,   120
Cages for gnats, and chains to yoke a flea,
Dried butterflies, and tomes of casuistry.
    But trust the Muse—she saw it upward rise,
Though marked by none but quick, poetic eyes
(So Rome's great founder to the heavens withdrew,   125
To Proculus alone confessed in view);
A sudden star, it shot through liquid air,
And drew behind a radiant trail of hair.

Not Berenice's locks first rose so bright,[13]
The heavens bespangling with disheveled light.   130
The Sylphs behold it kindling as it flies,
And pleased pursue its progress through the skies.
          This the beau monde shall from the Mall survey,
And hail with music its propitious ray.
This the blest lover shall for Venus take,   135
And send up vows from Rosamonda's Lake.
This Partridge soon shall view in cloudless skies,
When next he looks through Galileo's eyes;
And hence the egregious wizard shall foredoom
The fate of Louis, and the fall of Rome.   140
          Then cease, bright nymph! to mourn thy ravished hair,
Which adds new glory to the shining sphere!
Not all the tresses that fair head can boast,
Shall draw such envy as the Lock you lost.
For, after all the murders of your eye,   145
When, after millions slain, yourself shall die:
When those fair suns shall set, as set they must,
And all those tresses shall be laid in dust,
This Lock the Muse shall consecrate to fame,
And 'midst the stars inscribe Belinda's name.   150

13. Berenice was an Egyptian queen; her locks were made into a constellation.

Fact Questions and Exercises

1. What kind of lock is the poet speaking about?
2. Describe some of the powers the Sylphs possess.
3. According to Ariel, of whom or what should the "pious maid" be most aware?
4. Describe the "toilet" that "stands displayed" in Belinda's bedroom.
5. What does the "adventurous Baron" admire and wish to "ravish"?
6. In Canto III, what must happen so that "jurymen may dine"?
7. What is the name of the card game Belinda plays? How does Pope describe this game?
8. How does the Baron manage to steal the lock?
9. In Canto IV, what now "sits uncouth, alone"?
10. Ultimately, what happens to the stolen lock?

For Discussion and Writing

1. "The Rape of the Lock" is a satire; what values or standards is Pope criticizing by making fun of them? Is the "rape" really very significant? By implication or omission, what values and standards is Pope advocating?
2. What part do the supernatural creatures play in the poem? What are their duties? Do their powers prevent man from doing harm? What mood or tone does their inclusion give to the poem?

3. Characterize Belinda. What is her social status? What is her attitude toward men? How does her playing card games suggest a hidden part of her character? Is she coy? Sincere? What are her values? Is she a victim? Does she victimize others?

Thomas Gray [1716–1771]

Gray was born in England, and was educated at Eton College and Cambridge. He was devoted to scholarship, and spent most of his life as a professor at Cambridge. He wrote very little poetry, but was a prolific letter writer—his letters reveal wit and a wide range of interests. "Elegy Written in a Country Churchyard" (ca. 1742) is by far his most famous poem, perhaps one of the most widely read poems in the world. A deceptively simple poem, it is filled with imagery, subtle language, and echoes from other poems—all of which give the poem its universal appeal.

Elegy Written in a Country Churchyard

The curfew tolls the knell of parting day;
    The lowing herd wind slowly o'er the lea,
The plowman homeward plods his weary way,
    And leaves the world to darkness and to me.

Now fades the glimmering landscape on the sight,   5
    And all the air a solemn stillness holds,
Save where the beetle wheels his droning flight,
    And drowsy tinklings lull the distant folds;

Save that from yonder ivy-mantled tower
    The moping owl does to the moon complain   10
Of such, as wandering near her secret bower,
    Molest her ancient solitary reign.

Beneath those rugged elms, that yew tree's shade,
    Where heaves the turf in many a moldering heap,
Each in his narrow cell forever laid,   15
    The rude forefathers of the hamlet sleep.

The breezy call of incense-breathing morn,
    The swallow twittering from the straw-built shed,
The cock's shrill clarion, or the echoing horn,
    No more shall rouse them from their lowly bed.   20

For them no more the blazing hearth shall burn,
    Or busy housewife ply her evening care;

No children run to lisp their sire's return,
    Or climb his knees the envied kiss to share.

Oft did the harvest to their sickle yield,   25
    Their furrow oft the stubborn glebe[1] has broke;
How jocund did they drive their team afield!
    How bowed the woods beneath their sturdy stroke!

Let not Ambition mock their useful toil,
    Their homely joys, and destiny obscure;   30
Nor Grandeur hear with a disdainful smile
    The short and simple annals of the poor.

The boast of heraldry, the pomp of power,
    And all that beauty, all that wealth e'er gave,
Awaits alike the inevitable hour.   35
    The paths of glory lead but to the grave.

Nor you, ye proud, impute to these the fault,
    If Memory o'er their tomb no trophies raise,
Where through the long-drawn aisle and fretted[2] vault
    The pealing anthem swells the note of praise.   40

Can storied urn or animated bust
    Back to its mansion call the fleeting breath?
Can Honor's voice provoke the silent dust,
    Or Flattery soothe the dull cold ear of Death?

Perhaps in this neglected spot is laid   45
    Some heart once pregnant with celestial fire;
Hands that the rod of empire might have swayed,
    Or waked to ecstasy the living lyre.

But Knowledge to their eyes her ample page
    Rich with the spoils of time did ne'er unroll;   50
Chill Penury repressed their noble rage,
    And froze the genial current of the soul.

Full many a gem of purest ray serene,
    The dark unfathomed caves of ocean bear:
Full many a flower is born to blush unseen,   55
    And waste its sweetness on the desert air.

Some village Hampden,[3] that with dauntless breast
    The little tyrant of his fields withstood;
Some mute inglorious Milton here may rest,
    Some Cromwell guiltless of his country's blood.   60

1. Soil.   2. Decorated, ornamented.   3. A citizen soldier who fought against the tyranny of
Charles I.

The applause of listening senates to command,
　　The threats of pain and ruin to despise,
To scatter plenty o'er a smiling land,   *personification*
　　And read their history in a nation's eyes,

Their lot forbade: nor circumscribed alone   65
　　Their growing virtues, but their crimes confined;
Forbade to wade through slaughter to a throne,
　　And shut the gates of mercy on mankind,

The struggling pangs of conscious truth to hide,   *pains*
　　To quench the blushes of ingenuous shame,   70
Or heap the shrine of Luxury and Pride
　　With incense kindled at the Muse's flame.

Far from the madding[4] crowd's ignoble strife,
　　Their sober wishes never learned to stray;
Along the cool sequestered vale of life   *Separated farewell*   75
　　They kept the noiseless tenor of their way.

Yet even these bones from insult to protect
　　Some frail memorial still erected nigh,
With uncouth rhymes and shapeless sculpture decked,
　　Implores the passing tribute of a sigh.   80

Their names, their years, spelt by the unlettered Muse,
　　The place of fame and elegy supply:
And many a holy text around she strews,
　　That teach the rustic moralist to die.

For who to dumb Forgetfulness a prey,   85
　　This pleasing anxious being e'er resigned,
Left the warm precincts of the cheerful day,   *alliteration*
　　Nor cast one longing lingering look behind?

On some fond breast the parting soul relies,
　　Some pious drops the closing eye requires;   90
Even from the tomb the voice of Nature cries,
　　Even in our ashes live their wonted fires.

For thee, who mindful of the unhonored dead
　　Dost in these lines their artless tale relate;
If chance, by lonely contemplation led,   95
　　Some kindred spirit shall inquire thy fate,

Perhaps Haply some hoary-headed swain may say,   *death*
　　"Oft have we seen him at the peep of dawn

4. Milling.

Brushing with hasty steps the dews away
    To meet the sun upon the upland lawn.   100

"There at the foot of yonder nodding beech
    That wreathes its old fantastic roots so high,
His listless length at noontide would he stretch,
    And pore upon the brook that babbles by.

"Hard by yon wood, now smiling as in scorn,   105
    Muttering his wayward fancies he would rove,
Now drooping, woeful wan, like one forlorn,
    Or crazed with care, or crossed in hopeless love.

"One morn I missed him on the customed hill,
    Along the heath and near his favorite tree;   110
Another came; nor yet beside the rill,
    Nor up the lawn, nor at the wood was he;

"The next with dirges due in sad array
    Slow through the churchyard path we saw him borne.
Approach and read (for thou canst read) the lay,   115
    Graved on the stone beneath yon aged thorn."

THE EPITAPH

Here rests his head upon the lap of Earth
    A youth to Fortune and to Fame unknown.
Fair Science frowned not on his humble birth,
    And Melancholy marked him for her own.   120

Large was his bounty, and his soul sincere,
    Heaven did a recompense as largely send:
He gave to Misery all he had, a tear,
    He gained from Heaven ('twas all he wished) a friend.

No farther seek his merits to disclose,   125
    Or draw his frailties from their dread abode
(There they alike in trembling hope repose),
    The bosom of his Father and his God.

Fact Questions and Exercises

1. In line 1, what does "curfew" mean? In line 11, what does "bower" mean?
2. What phrase does Gray use to mean "grave," in line 15?
3. Gray alludes to a famous poet. Who is the poet?
4. Describe the kind of people that are praised in the poem.
5. Define "elegy."

For Discussion and Writing

1. Discuss the speaker's attitude toward the dead. Is it cynical? Sentimental? What? Does the speaker really know who the people are in the churchyard? What is the speaker's attitude toward famous people and city dwellers?

William Blake [1757–1827]

Blake was born in London, England. He studied at the Royal Academy of Arts, preparing himself for a career as an engraver and illustrator. He became interested in poetry early, and later he illustrated and printed many of his own poems. In general, his work shows Blake's dissatisfaction with the poetic tradition of his day, and a desire to discover new poetic technique and form of expression. Blake was considered radical; much of his poetry is obscured by his "visions" and the highly personal application of his symbols. In the shorter lyrics presented here, however, the visions are simpler, the symbols less personal. His poems of "innocence" present the vision of happy childhood; his poems of "experience" present the vision of that innocence corrupted by the ugliness and social ills of the world. *Songs of Innocence* was first published in 1789, *Songs of Experience* in 1794.

The Lamb

```
        Little Lamb, who made thee?
        Dost thou know who made thee?
Gave thee life & bid thee feed,
By the stream & o'er the mead;
Gave thee clothing of delight,                    5
Softest clothing wooly bright;
Gave thee such a tender voice,
Making all the vales rejoice!
        Little Lamb who made thee?
        Dost thou know who made thee?          10

        Little Lamb I'll tell thee,
        Little Lamb I'll tell thee!
He is callèd by thy name,
For he calls himself a Lamb:
He is meek & he is mild,                          15
He became a little child:
I a child & thou a lamb,
We are callèd by his name.
        Little Lamb God bless thee.
        Little Lamb God bless thee.              20
```

The Little Black Boy

My mother bore me in the southern wild,
And I am black, but O! my soul is white;
White as an angel is the English child:
But I am black as if bereav'd of light.

My mother taught me underneath a tree,   5
And sitting down before the heat of day,
She took me on her lap and kisséd me,
And pointing to the east, began to say:

"Look on the rising sun: there God does live,
And gives his light, and gives his heat away;   10
And flowers and trees and beasts and men receive
Comfort in morning, joy in the noon day.

"And we are put on earth a little space,
That we may learn to bear the beams of love,
And these black bodies and this sun-burnt face   15
Is but a cloud, and like a shady grove.

"For when our souls have learn'd the heat to bear,
The cloud will vanish; we shall hear his voice,
Saying: 'Come out from the grove, my love & care,
And round my golden tent like lambs rejoice.'"   20

Thus did my mother say, and kisséd me;
And thus I say to little English boy:
When I from black and he from white cloud free,
And round the tent of God like lambs we joy,

I'll shade him from the heat till he can bear   25
To lean in joy upon our father's knee;
And then I'll stand and stroke his silver hair,
And be like him, and he will then love me.

The Tyger

Tyger! Tyger! burning bright
In the forests of the night,
What immortal hand or eye
Could frame thy fearful symmetry?

In what distant deeps or skies
Burnt the fire of thine eyes?

On what wings dare he aspire?   *who created it*
What the hand, dare seize the fire?

And what shoulder, & what art,
Could twist the sinews of thy heart?   10
And when thy heart began to beat,
What dread hand? & what dread feet?   *Who gave thee life?*

What the hammer? what the chain?
In what furnace was thy brain?
What the anvil? what dread grasp   15
Dare its deadly terrors clasp?

When the stars threw down their spears,
And water'd heaven with their tears,
Did he smile his work to see?   *Did He who created*
Did he who made the Lamb make thee?   20   *the Lamb create the*
                                                                         Tyger

Tyger! Tyger! burning bright
In the forests of the night,
What immortal hand or eye   *trying to understand*
Dare frame thy fearful symmetry?   *why there is bad*

4 line stanza

The SICK ROSE

O Rose, thou art sick.
The invisible worm
That flies in the night
In the howling storm

Has found out thy bed   5
Of crimson joy,
And his dark secret love
Does thy life destroy.

Fact Questions and Exercises

1. What question does the speaker ask in "The Lamb"? Does he answer it?
2. What is it, according to the speaker in "Little Black Boy," that "we may learn
   to bear"? What does the speaker promise to give the "little English boy"?
3. In "The Tyger," what words or lines indicate that the tiger is "fearful" or
   dreadful?
4. In "The SICK ROSE," what has found out the rose's "bed / Of crimson joy"?

For Discussion and Writing

1. Compare "The Lamb" and "The Tyger." What traits does the lamb possess that the tiger does not? The tiger that the lamb does not? Do these two poems represent the good and bad forces of life? Does Blake imply that God made both the lamb and tiger? Do similar opposing forces appear in Blake's other poems?
2. Analyze "The SICK ROSE." What does the rose symbolize? What does the worm symbolize? Do you see this poem as a Freudian or sexual statement, or is Blake commenting again on the more general forces of good and evil?

Robert Burns [1759–1796]

Burns was born in Ayshire, Scotland, the son of a poor farmer. As a child, Burns was forced to work excessively hard to help his father; this contributed to Burns's early death. The poet once said that his abiding interests were "Love and Poesy," and he constantly pursued both. Before he had reached twenty-seven, he sired a number of illegitimate children, and wrote all of his best poems. His first collection of poems, *Poems, Chiefly in the Scottish Dialect* (1786), was very popular, and established him as a "natural" genius—a plowman poet. However, his scandalous sex life and radical politics (he supported the colonies during the American Revolution), lost Burns his popularity; his later collections were not successful. Many of his poems are written in the common tongue of the Scottish peasant, a northern English dialect called Scots.

To a Mouse

On Turning Her Up in Her Nest with the Plough, November, 1785

Wee, sleekit, cowrin, tim'rous beastie,
O, what a panic's in thy breastie!
Thou need na start awa sae hasty,
   Wi' bickering brattle!
I wad be laith to rin an' chase thee,   5
   Wi' murd'ring pattle![1]

I'm truly sorry Man's dominion
Has broken Nature's social union,
An' justifies that ill opinion

---

1. Plow.

Which makes thee startle,   10
At me, thy poor, earth-born companion,
An' fellow-mortal!

I doubt na, whyles, but thou may thieve.
What then? poor beastie, thou maun live!
A daimen icker in a thrave[2]   15
'S a sma' request.
I'll get a blessin wi' the lave,[3]
And never miss't!

Thy wee bit housie, too, in ruin!
Its silly wa's the win's are strewin!   20
An' naething, now, to big[4] a new ane,
O' foggage[5] green!
An' bleak December's winds ensuin,
Baith snell[6] and keen!

Thou saw the fields laid bare an' waste,   25
An' weary Winter comin fast,
An' cozie here, beneath the blast,
Thou thought to dwell,
Till crash! the cruel coulter past
Out thro' thy cell.   30

That wee bit heap o' leaves an' stibble,
Has cost thee mony a weary nibble!
Now thou's turned out, for a' thy trouble,
But house or hald,
To thole[7] the Winter's sleety dribble,   35
An' cranreuch[8] cauld!

But, Mousie, thou are no thy lane,[9]
In proving foresight may be vain:
The best-laid schemes o' Mice an' Men,
Gang aft a-gley,   40
An' lea'e us nought but grief and pain,
For promised joy.

Still thou art blest, compared wi' me!
The present only toucheth thee;
But, Och! I backward cast my e'e,   45
On prospects drear!
An' forward, tho' I canna see,
I guess an' fear!

2. An occasional ear, in twenty-four sheaves.   3. Leavings, remainder.
4. Build. 5. Moss. 6. Harsh. 7. Endure. 8. Frost. 9. Not alone.

To a Louse, *person regarded as ones*

On Seeing One on a Lady's Bonnet at Church

Ha! where ye gaun, ye crowlan ferlie![10]
Your impudence protects you sairly.
I canna say but ye strunt rarely,
      Owre gawze and lace;
Tho' faith, I fear ye dine but sparely,   5
      On sic a place.

Ye ugly, creepan, blastet wonner,
Detested, shunn'd, by saunt an' sinner,
How daur ye set your fit upon her,
      Sae fine a Lady!   10
Gae somewhere else and seek your dinner,
      On some poor body.

Swith,[11] in some beggar's haffet[12] squattle;
There ye may creep, and sprawl, and sprattle,[13]
Wi' ither kindred, jumping cattle,   15
      In shoals and nations;
Whare horn nor bane[14] ne'er daur unsettle,
      Your thick plantations.

Now haud you there, ye're out o' sight,
Below the fatt'rels,[15] snug and tight,   20
Na faith ye yet! ye'll no be right,
      Till ye've got on it,
The vera tapmost, towrin height
      O' Miss's bonnet.

My sooth! right bauld ye set your nose out,   25
As plump an' gray as onie grozet:[16]
O for some rank, mercurial rozet,[17]
      Or fell, red smeddum,[18]
I'd gie you sic a hearty dose o't,
      Wad dress your droddum![19]   30

I wad na been surpriz'd to spy
You on an auld wife's flainen toy;[20]
Or aiblins[21] some bit duddie[22] boy,
      On's wylecoat;[23]
But Miss's fine Lunardi,[24] fye!   35
      How daur ye do't?

10. Wonder. 11. Fast. 12. Temples. 13. Work, struggle. 14. Bone. 15. Ribbons.
16. Berry. 17. Rosin. 18. Powder. 19. Buttocks. 20. Cap. 21. Maybe. 22. Ragged.
23. Vest. 24. Large bonnet.

O Jenny dinna toss your head,
An' set your beauties a' abroad!²⁵
Ye little ken what cursed speed
   The blastie's makin!   40
Thae winks and finger-ends, I dread,
   Are notice takin!

   O wad some Pow'r the giftie gie us
To see oursels as others see us!
It wad frae monie a blunder free us   45
   An' foolish notion:
What airs in dress an' gait wad lea'e us,
   And ev'n Devotion!

Holy Willie's Prayer

O Thou, wha in the heavens dost dwell,
Wha, as it pleases best thysel',
Sends ane to heaven and ten to hell,
   A' for thy glory,
And no for ony guid or ill   5
   They've done afore thee!

I bless and praise thy matchless might,
Whan thousands thou hast left in night,
That I am here afore thy sight,
   For gifts an' grace   10
A burnin' an' a shinin' light,
   To a' this place.

What was I, or my generation,
That I should get sic exaltation?
I, wha deserve most just damnation,   15
   For broken laws,
Sax thousand years 'fore my creation,
   Thro' Adam's cause.

When frae my mither's womb I fell,
Thou might hae plungéd me in hell,   20
To gnash my gums, to weep and wail,
   In burnin lakes,
Where damnéd devils roar and yell,
   Chained to their stakes;

Yet I am here a chosen sample,   25
To show thy grace is great and ample;

25. Abroad.

I'm here a pillar in thy temple,
　　　　Strong as a rock,
A guide, a buckler, an example
　　　　To a' thy flock.　　　　　　30

O Lord, thou kens what zeal I bear,
When drinkers drink, and swearers swear.
And singin' there and dancin' here,
　　　　Wi' great an' sma':
For I am keepit by thy fear　　　　35
　　　　Free frae them a'.

But yet, O Lord! confess I must
At times I'm fashed[26] wi' fleshy lust;
An' sometimes too, wi' warldly trust,
　　　　Vile self gets in;　　　　40
But thou remembers we are dust,
　　　　Defiled in sin.

O Lord! yestreen, thou kens, wi' Meg—
Thy pardon I sincerely beg;
O! may't ne'er be a livin' plague　　　45
　　　　To my dishonour,
An' I'll ne'er lift a lawless leg
　　　　Again upon her.

Besides I farther maun allow,
Wi' Lizzie's lass, three times I trow—　　50
But, Lord, that Friday I was fou,[27]
　　　　When I cam near her,
Or else thou kens thy servant true
　　　　Wad never steer her.

May be thou lets this fleshly thorn　　55
Beset thy servant e'en and morn
Lest he owre high and proud should turn,
　　　　That he's sae gifted;
If sae, thy hand maun e'en be borne,
　　　　Until thou lift it.　　　　60

Lord, bless thy chosen in this place,
For here thou hast a chosen race;
But God confound their stubborn face,
　　　　And blast their name,
Wha bring thy elders to disgrace　　　65
　　　　An' public shame.

26. Bothered.　27. Drunk.

Lord, mind Gawn Hamilton's[28] deserts,
He drinks, an' swears, an' plays at cartes,
Yet has sae mony takin arts
   Wi' great an' sma',   70
Frae God's ain priest the people's hearts
   He steals awa'.

An' when we chastened him therefor,
Thou kens how he bred sic a splore [29]
As set the warld in a roar   75
   O' laughin' at us;
Curse thou his basket and his store,
   Kail and potatoes.

Lord, hear my earnest cry an' pray'r,
Against that presbytery o' Ayr;   80
Thy strong right hand, Lord, make it bare
   Upo' their heads;
Lord, weigh it down, and dinna spare,
   For their misdeeds.

O Lord my God, that glib-tongued Aiken,[30]   85
My very heart and soul are quakin',
To think how we stood sweatin, shakin,
   An' pissed wi' dread,
While he, wi' hingin[31] lips and snakin,[32]
   Held up his head.   90

Lord in the day of vengeance try him;
Lord, visit them wha did employ him,
And pass not in thy mercy by them,
   Nor hear their pray'r:
But, for thy people's sake, destroy them,   95
   And dinna spare.

But, Lord, remember me and mine
Wi' mercies temp'ral and divine,
That I for gear[33] and grace may shine
   Excelled by nane,   100
And a' the glory shall be thine,
   Amen, Amen!

---

28. Hamilton, a lawyer friend of Burns's, was accused of breaking the Sabbath; he was cleared by the Presbytery of Ayr. **29.** Uproar. **30.** Robert Aiken defended Hamilton (see Note 28, above). **31.** Hanging. **32.** Sneering. **33.** Material goods, wealth.

Fact Questions and Exercises

1. In "To a Mouse," why does the mouse have an "ill opinion" of humans? Why is the mouse "blest" when compared with the man who has disturbed the nest?

2. In "To a Louse," where should the louse be instead of on the lady, according to the speaker of the poem?
3. What are some of the sins that Holy Willie has committed?
4. What are some of the sins for which Willie asks God to condemn others?
5. What does Willie mean when he refers to "Adam's cause"?
6. Why does Willie condemn the presbytery of Ayr and Aiken?

For Discussion and Writing

1. In "To a Mouse," what is the speaker's attitude toward nature? What represents nature? Do human beings have dominance over nature? What facts indicate that they work under the same laws as does the mouse? Why is the mouse luckier than they are?
2. Discuss Burns's theme of hypocrisy as it appears in "Holy Willie's Prayer" and "To a Louse." Does Willie commit greater "sins" than do the other men he condemns? What is implied about Willie's character in the manner that he addresses God? Explain. Does the lady with the louse have other than Christian motives for being in church? If so, what are these motives? What facts in the poem support your answer?

William Wordsworth [1770–1850]

Wordsworth was born in the West Cumberland district of England, and was educated at Cambridge. He was in France during the early stages of the French Revolution; while there, he had an affair with Annette Vallon. He was never able to marry her or to acknowledge their illegitimate daughter—a fact that caused Wordsworth considerable guilt. By 1797 he was back in England and settled in Somersetshire with his sister Dorothy, who figures prominently in some of his poems. In 1798, with his close friend Samuel Taylor Coleridge, Wordsworth published *Lyrical Ballads*, one of the most influential books in English literature. It is the bible of the romantic movement—a book that, as Wordsworth said, was based on "incidents and situations from common life," and that demonstrated Wordsworth's idea of poetry as "the spontaneous overflow of powerful feelings."

Lines

Composed a Few Miles above Tintern Abbey, on Revisiting the Banks of the Wye During a Tour. July 13, 1798.

Five years have past; five summers, with the length
Of five long winters! and again I hear
These waters, rolling from their mountain-springs
With a soft inland murmur.—Once again

Do I behold these steep and lofty cliffs, 5
That on a wild secluded scene impress
Thoughts of more deep seclusion, and connect
The landscape with the quiet of the sky.
The day is come when I again repose
Here, under this dark sycamore, and view 10
These plots of cottage-ground, these orchard-tufts,
Which at this season, with their unripe fruits,
Are clad in one green hue, and lose themselves
'Mid groves and copses. Once again I see
These hedge-rows, hardly hedge-rows, little lines 15
Of sportive wood run wild: these pastoral farms,
Green to the very door; and wreaths of smoke
Sent up, in silence, from among the trees!
With some uncertain notice, as might seem
Of vagrant dwellers in the houseless woods, 20
Or of some hermit's cave, where by his fire
The hermit sits alone.
　　　　　　　　These beauteous forms,
Through a long absence, have not been to me
As is a landscape to a blind man's eye:
But oft, in lonely rooms, and 'mid the din 25
Of towns and cities, I have owed to them
In hours of weariness, sensations sweet,
Felt in the blood, and felt along the heart;
And passing even into my purer mind,
With tranquil restoration:—feelings too 30
Of unremembered pleasure: such, perhaps,
As have no slight or trivial influence
On that best portion of a good man's life,
His little, nameless, unremembered, acts
Of kindness and of love. Nor less, I trust, 35
To them I may have owed another gift,
Of aspect more sublime; that blessed mood,
In which the burthen of the mystery,
In which the heavy and the weary weight
Of all this unintelligible world, 40
Is lightened:—that serene and blessed mood,
In which the affections gently lead us on,—
Until, the breath of this corporeal frame
And even the motion of our human blood
Almost suspended, we are laid asleep 45
In body, and become a living soul:
While with an eye made quiet by the power
Of harmony, and the deep power of joy,
We see into the life of things.
　　　　　　　　　　If this
Be but a vain belief, yet, oh! how oft— 50
In darkness and amid the many shapes
Of joyless daylight; when the fretful stir

past - present - future

Unprofitable, and the fever of the world,
Have hung upon the beatings of my heart—
How oft, in spirit, have I turned to thee,
O sylvan Wye! thou wanderer thro' the woods,   55
How often has my spirit turned to thee!
          And now, with gleams of half-extinguished thought,
With many recognitions dim and faint,
And somewhat of a sad perplexity,   60
The picture of the mind revives again:
While here I stand, not only with the sense
Of present pleasure, but with pleasing thoughts
That in this moment there is life and food
For future years. And so I dare to hope,   65
Though changed, no doubt, from what I was when first
I came among these hills; when like a roe
I bounded o'er the mountains, by the sides
Of the deep rivers, and the lonely streams,
Wherever nature led: more like a man   70
Flying from something that he dreads, than one
Who sought the thing he loved. For nature then
(The coarser pleasures of my boyish days,
And their glad animal movements all gone by)
To me was all in all. I cannot paint   75
What then I was. The sounding cataract
Haunted me like a passion: the tall rock,
The mountain, and the deep and gloomy wood,
Their colors and their forms, were then to me
An appetite; a feeling and a love,   80
That had no need of a remoter charm,
By thought supplied, nor any interest
Unborrowed from the eye.—That time is past,
And all its aching joys are now no more,
And all its dizzy raptures. Not for this   85
Faint I, nor mourn nor murmur; other gifts
Have followed; for such loss, I would believe,
Abundant recompense. For I have learned
To look on nature, not as in the hour
Of thoughtless youth; but hearing oftentimes   90
The still, sad music of humanity,
Nor harsh nor grating, though of ample power
To chasten and subdue. And I have felt
A presence that disturbs me with the joy
Of elevated thoughts; a sense sublime   95
Of something far more deeply interfused,
Whose dwelling is the light of setting suns,
And the round ocean and the living air,
And the blue sky, and in the mind of man:
A motion and a spirit, that impels   100
All thinking things, all objects of all thought,
And rolls through all things. Therefore am I still

A lover of the meadows and the woods,
And mountains; and of all that we behold
From this green earth; of all the mighty world   105
Of eye, and ear—both what they half create,
And what perceive; well pleased to recognize
In nature and the language of the sense
The anchor of my purest thoughts, the nurse,
The guide, the guardian of my heart, and soul   110
Of all my moral being.

               Nor perchance,
If I were not thus taught, should I the more
Suffer my genial spirits to decay:
For thou art with me here upon the banks
Of this fair river; thou my dearest Friend,[1]   115
My dear, dear Friend; and in thy voice I catch
The language of my former heart, and read
My former pleasures in the shooting lights
Of thy wild eyes. Oh! yet a little while
May I behold in thee what I was once,   120
My dear, dear Sister! and this prayer I make,
Knowing that Nature never did betray
The heart that loved her; 'tis her privilege,
Through all the years of this our life, to lead
From joy to joy: for she can so inform   125
The mind that is within us, so impress
With quietness and beauty, and so feed
With lofty thoughts, that neither evil tongues,
Rash judgments, nor the sneers of selfish men,
Nor greetings where no kindness is, nor all   130
The dreary intercourse of daily life,
Shall e'er prevail against us, or disturb
Our cheerful faith, that all which we behold
Is full of blessings. Therefore let the moon
Shine on thee in thy solitary walk;   135
And let the misty mountain winds be free
To blow against thee: and, in after years,
When these wild ecstasies shall be matured
Into a sober pleasure; when thy mind
Shall be a mansion for all lovely forms,   140
Thy memory be as a dwelling place
For all sweet sounds and harmonies; oh! then,
If solitude, or fear, or pain, or grief
Should be thy portion, with what healing thoughts
Of tender joy wilt thou remember me,   145
And these my exhortations! Nor, perchance—
If I should be where I no more can hear
Thy voice, nor catch from thy wild eyes these gleams

1. Wordsworth's sister, Dorothy.

Of past existence—wilt thou then forget
That on the banks of this delightful stream   150
We stood together; and that I, so long
A worshiper of Nature, hither came
Unwearied in that service; rather say
With warmer love—oh! with far deeper zeal
Of holier love. Nor wilt thou then forget,   155
That after many wanderings, many years
Of absence, these steep woods and lofty cliffs,
And this green pastoral landscape, were to me
More dear, both for themselves and for thy sake!

I Wandered Lonely as a Cloud

I wandered lonely as a cloud
That floats on high o'er vales and hills,
When all at once I saw a crowd,
A host, of golden daffodils;
Beside the lake, beneath the trees,   5
Fluttering and dancing in the breeze.

Continuous as the stars that shine
And twinkle on the milky way,
They stretched in never-ending line
Along the margin of a bay: 10
Ten thousand saw I at a glance,
Tossing their heads in sprightly dance.

The waves beside them danced; but they
Outdid the sparkling waves in glee;
A poet could not but be gay,   15
In such a jocund company;
I gazed—and gazed—but little thought
What wealth the show to me had brought:

For oft, when on my couch I lie
In vacant or in pensive mood,   20
They flash upon that inward eye
Which is the bliss of solitude;
And then my heart with pleasure fills,
And dances with the daffodils.

She Dwelt among the Untrodden Ways

She dwelt among the untrodden ways
　　Beside the springs of Dove,

A maid whom there were none to praise,
    And very few to love.

A violet by a mossy stone   5
    Half-hidden from the eye!
—Fair as a star, when only one
    Is shining in the sky.

She lived unknown, and few could know
    When Lucy ceased to be;   10
But she is in her grave, and, oh,
    The difference to me!

My Heart Leaps Up When I Behold

My heart leaps up when I behold
    A rainbow in the sky:
So was it when my life began;
So is it now I am a man;
So be it when I shall grow old,   5
    Or let me die!
The Child is father of the Man;
And I could wish my days to be
Bound each to each by natural piety.

Surprised by Joy

Surprised by joy—impatient as the Wind
I turned to share the transport—Oh! with whom
But thee,[2] deep buried in the silent tomb,
That spot which no vicissitude can find?
Love, faithful love, recalled thee to my mind—   5
But how could I forget thee? Through what power,
Even for the least division of an hour,
Have I been so beguiled as to be blind
To my most grievous loss!—That thought's return
Was the worst pang that sorrow ever bore,   10
Save one, only one, when I stood forlorn,
Knowing my heart's best treasure was no more;
That neither present time, nor years unborn
Could to my sight that heavenly face restore.

2. Wordsworth's daughter, who died when she was four years old.

Mutability

From low to high doth dissolution climb,
And sink from high to low, along a scale
Of awful notes, whose concord shall not fail;
A musical but melancholy chime,
Which they can hear who meddle not with crime,   5
Nor avarice, nor over-anxious care.
Truth fails not; but her outward forms that bear
The longest date do melt like frosty rime,[3]
That in the morning whitened hill and plain
And is no more; drop like the tower sublime   10
Of yesterday, which royally did wear
His crown of weeds, but could not even sustain
Some casual shout that broke the silent air,
Or the unimaginable touch of Time.

Scorn Not the Sonnet

Scorn not the sonnet; critic, you have frowned,
Mindless of its just honors; with this key
Shakespeare unlocked his heart; the melody
Of this small lute gave ease to Petrarch's[4] wound;
A thousand times this pipe did Tasso[5] sound;   5
With it Camöens[6] soothed an exile's grief;
The sonnet glittered a gay myrtle leaf
Amid the cypress with which Dante crowned
His visionary brow; a glow-worm lamp,
It cheered mild Spenser, called from Faeryland   10
To struggle through dark ways; and, when a damp[7]
Fell round the path of Milton, in his hand
The thing became a trumpet; whence he blew
Soul-animating strains—alas, too few!

The World Is Too Much with Us

The world is too much with us; late and soon,
Getting and spending, we lay waste our powers;
Little we see in Nature that is ours;
We have given our hearts away, a sordid boon!
This Sea that bares her bosom to the moon,   5
The winds that will be howling at all hours,
And are up-gathered now like sleeping flowers,

---

3. A light covering of ice crystals.   4. Fourteenth-century Italian poet.   5. Sixteenth-century
Italian poet.   6. Sixteenth-century Portuguese poet.   7. Dark mist.

For this, for everything, we are out of tune;
It moves us not.—Great God! I'd rather be
A Pagan suckled in a creed outworn;   10
So might I, standing on this pleasant lea,
Have glimpses that would make me less forlorn;
Have sight of Proteus[8] rising from the sea;
Or hear old Triton[9] blow his wreathed horn.[10]

Ode to Duty

Jam non consilio bonus, sed more eo
perductus, ut non tantum recte facere
possim, sed nisi recte facere non possim.[11]
                                          SENECA

Stern Daughter of the Voice of God!
O Duty! if that name thou love
Who are a light to guide, a rod
To check the erring, and reprove;
Thou, who art victory and law   5
When empty terrors overawe;
From vain temptations dost set free;
And calm'st the weary strife of frail humanity!

There are who ask not if thine eye
Be on them; who, in love and truth,   10
Where no misgiving is, rely
Upon the genial sense of youth:
Glad Hearts! without reproach or blot;
Who do thy work, and know it not:
Oh! if through confidence misplaced   15
They fail, thy saving arms, dread Power! around them cast.

Serene will be our days and bright,
And happy will our nature be,
When love is an unerring light,
And joy its own security.   20
And they a blissful course may hold
Even now, who, not unwisely bold,
Live in the spirit of this creed;
Yet seek thy firm support, according to their need.

I, loving freedom, and untried,   25
No sport of every random gust,

8. A mythological sea god.   9. The son of Neptune, god of the sea.   10. Conch shell.
11. Freely translated, this epigraph from Seneca's *Moral Epistles* reads: "I am not good
because of thought, but by habit I have reached the point that it is not so much that I act
rightly, but that I am unable to act except rightly."

Yet being to myself a guide,
Too blindly have reposed my trust;
And oft, when in my heart was heard
Thy timely mandate, I deferred   30
The task, in smoother walks to stray;
But thee I now would serve more strictly, if I may.

Through no disturbance of my soul,
Or strong compunction in me wrought,
I supplicate for thy control;   35
But in the quietness of thought:
Me this unchartered freedom tires;
I feel the weight of chance desires:
My hopes no more must change their name,
I long for a repose that ever is the same.   40

Stern Lawgiver! yet thou dost wear
The Godhead's most benignant grace;
Now know we anything so fair
As is the smile upon thy face:
Flowers laugh before thee on their beds   45
And fragrance in thy footing treads;
Thou dost preserve the stars from wrong
And the most ancient heavens, through thee, are fresh and
        strong.

To humbler functions, awful Power!
I call thee: I myself commend   50
Unto thy guidance from this hour;
Oh, let my weakness have an end!
Give unto me, made lowly wise,
The spirit of self-sacrifice;
The confidence of reason give;   55
And in the light of truth thy Bondman let me live!

Fact Questions and Exercises

1. Where is the speaker of "Tintern Abbey" when he relates the poem? What is his description of himself on his first visit to the Wye? To whom is he speaking when he asks to "behold in thee what I was once"?
2. What is the name of the girl who "dwelt among the untrodden ways"?
3. In "Surprised by Joy," what is the speaker's "most grievous loss"?
4. What does "mutability" mean as it's used in the poem of that name? What is it that "do melt like frosty rime"?
5. In "Scorn Not the Sonnet," what is the "thing" in line 13?
6. In "Ode to Duty," what does the speaker ask that Duty "give unto me"?
7. Point out an example of allegory or personification in Wordsworth's poems.

For Discussion and Writing

ss the theme of change or mutability as it appears in the poems. How
this change relate to time? What changes within the individual? What
the person lose? Gain? Does Wordsworth accept this change with no
regrets, or is he disturbed by it?

2. How does Wordsworth use nature? How do nature and its forces affect the
personas of these poems? What happens when the individual loses contact
with nature? Does Wordsworth's view of nature change from the time he
wrote "Tintern Abbey" to the time he wrote "Ode to Duty"? How is this
change indicated in the poems?

Samuel Taylor Coleridge [1772–1834]

Coleridge was born in rural Devonshire, England. He attended
Cambridge, where he established a reputation for loneliness,
scholarship, and eloquence. Bored with college, he enlisted in the
cavalry, but was soon rescued by his brother. About 1796 he
moved to Somersetshire, where he worked closely with Wordsworth, and shared in the momentous publication of Lyrical Ballads
in 1798. By 1806, however, his life was shattered; he was a
confirmed drug addict, and suffered from nightmares, guilt, and
despair. Still, he somehow managed to write and to present public
lectures in London. Ultimately, with the help of friends, he
managed to order his life; he spent his last twenty years quietly,
with some degree of happiness.

The Rime of the Ancient Mariner

PART I

*An ancient Mariner
meeteth three Gallants
bidden to a wedding-
feast, and detaineth one.*

It is an ancient Mariner,
And he stoppeth one of three.
"By thy long gray beard and glittering eye,
Now wherefore stopp'st thou me?

The Bridegroom's doors are opened wide,   5
And I am next of kin;
The guests are met, the feast is set:
May'st hear the merry din."

He holds him with his skinny hand,
"There was a ship," quoth he.   10

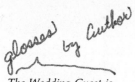

glosses by author

"Hold off! unhand me, gray-beard loon!"
Eftsoons his hand dropt he.

The Wedding-Guest is spellbound by the eye of the old seafaring man, and constrained to hear his tale.

He holds him with his glittering eye—
The Wedding-Guest stood still,
And listens like a three years' child: 15
The Mariner hath his will.

The Wedding-Guest sat on a stone:
He cannot choose but hear;
And thus spake on that ancient man,
The bright-eyed Mariner.   20

"The ship was cheered, the harbor cleared,
Merrily did we drop
Below the kirk, below the hill,
Below the lighthouse top.

church   *3 elements reversed @ end of poem*

The Mariner tells how the ship sailed southward with a good wind and fair weather, till it reached the Line.

The Sun came up upon the left,   25
Out of the sea came he!
And he shone bright, and on the right
Went down into the sea.

Higher and higher every day,
Till over the mast at noon—"
The Wedding-Guest here beat his breast,   30
For he heard the loud bassoon.

pulled back to present time

The Wedding-Guest heareth the bridal music; but the Mariner continueth his tale.

The bride hath paced into the hall,
Red as a rose is she;
Nodding their heads before her goes   35
The merry minstrelsy.

The Wedding-Guest he beat his breast,
Yet he cannot choose but hear;
And thus spake on that ancient man,
The bright-eyed Mariner.   40

The ship driven by a storm toward the south pole.

"And now the storm-blast came, and he
Was tyrannous and strong:
He struck with his o'ertaking wings,
And chased us south along.

With sloping masts and dipping prow,   45
As who pursued with yell and blow
Still treads the shadow of his foe,
And forward bends his head,
The ship drove fast, loud roared the blast,
And southward aye we fled.   50

And now there came both mist and snow,
And it grew wondrous cold:
And ice, mast high, came floating by,
As green as emerald.

The land of ice, and of
fearful sounds where no
living thing was to be
seen.

And through the drifts the snowy clifts   55
Did send a dismal sheen:
Nor shapes of men nor beasts we ken—
The ice was all between.

The ice was here, the ice was there,
The ice was all around: 60
It cracked and growled, and roared and howled,
Like noises in a swound!

Till a great sea-bird,
called the Albatross,
came through the snow-
fog, and was received
with great joy and hospi-
tality.

At length did cross an Albatross,   *Represents*
Thorough the fog it came;   *absolute honest.*
As if it had been a Christian soul,   65
We hailed it in God's name.

It ate the food it ne'er had eat,
And round and round it flew.
The ice did split with a thunder-fit;
The helmsman steered us through!   70

And lo! the Albatross
proveth a bird of good
omen, and followeth the
ship as it returned north-
ward through fog and
floating ice.

And a good south wind sprung up behind;
The Albatross did follow,
And every day, for food or play,
Came to the mariners' hollo!

In mist or cloud, on mast or shroud,   75
It perched for vespers nine;
Whiles all the night, through fog-smoke white,
Glimmered the white moon-shine."

The ancient Mariner in-
hospitably killeth the
pious bird of good omen.

violates
the trust between
the [ ] mariner
and the Albatross)

"God save thee, ancient Mariner!
From the fiends, that plague thee thus!—   80
Why look'st thou so?"—"With my crossbow
I shot the ALBATROSS."

PART II

"The Sun now rose upon the right:
Out of the sea came he,
Still hid in mist, and on the left   85
Went down into the sea.

And the good south wind still blew behind
But no sweet bird did follow,

(handwritten: worried about themselves)

*His shipmates cry out
against the ancient Mari-
ner, for killing the bird
of good luck.*

Nor any day for food or play
Came to the mariners' hollo!   90

And I had done a hellish thing,
And it would work 'em woe:
For all averred, I had killed the bird
That made the breeze to blow.
'Ah wretch!' said they, 'the bird to slay,   95
That made the breeze to blow!'

*But when the fog cleared
off, they justify the
same, and thus make
themselves accomplices
in the crime.*

Nor dim nor red, like God's own head,
The glorious Sun uprist:
Then all averred, I had killed the bird
That brought the fog and mist.   100
''Twas right,' said they, 'such birds to slay,
That bring the fog and mist.'

*The fair breeze contin-
ues; the ship enters the
Pacific Ocean, and sails
northward, even till it
reaches the Line. The
ship hath been suddenly
becalmed.*

The fair breeze blew, the white foam flew,
The furrow followed free;
We were the first that ever burst   105
Into that silent sea.

Down dropt the breeze, the sails dropt down,
'Twas sad as sad could be;
And we did speak only to break
The silence of the sea!   110

All in a hot and copper sky,
The bloody Sun, at noon,
Right up above the mast did stand,
No bigger than the Moon.

Day after day, day after day,   115
We stuck, nor breath nor motion;
As idle as a painted ship
Upon a painted ocean.

*And the Albatross begins
to be avenged.*

Water, water, everywhere,
And all the boards did shrink;   120
Water, water, everywhere *} ironic*
Nor any drop to drink.

The very deep did rot: O Christ!
That ever this should be!
Yea, slimy things did crawl with legs   125
Upon the slimy sea.

*A Spirit had followed
them; one of the invisible*

About, about, in reel and rout
The death-fires danced at night;

inhabitants of this planet, neither departed souls nor angels; concerning whom the learned Jew, Josephus, and the Platonic Constantinopolitan, Michael Psellus, may be consulted. They are very numerous, and there is no climate or element without one or more.

The water, like a witch's oils,
Burnt green, and blue, and white.   *not pleasant*   130

And some in dreams assuréd were
Of the Spirit that plagued us so:
Nine fathom deep he had followed us
From the land of mist and snow.

And every tongue, through utter drought,   135
Was withered at the root;
We could not speak, no more than if
We had been choked with soot.

The ship-mates, in their sore distress, would fain throw the whole guilt on the ancient Mariner: in sign whereof they hang the dead sea-bird round his neck.

Ah! well-a-day! what evil looks
Had I from old and young!   140
Instead of the cross, the Albatross
About my neck was hung.''

PART III

The ancient Mariner beholdeth a sign in the element afar off.

''There passed a weary time. Each throat
Was parched, and glazed each eye.
A weary time! a weary time!   145
How glazed each weary eye,
When looking westward, I beheld
A something in the sky.

At first it seemed a little speck,
And then it seemed a mist;   150
It moved and moved, and took at last
A certain shape, I wist.

A speck, a mist, a shape, I wist!
And still it neared and neared:
As if it dodged a water-sprite,   155
It plunged and tacked and veered.

At its nearer approach, it seemeth him to be a ship; and at a dear ransom he freeth his speech from the bonds of thirst.

With throats unslaked, with black lips baked,   *REPRESE[NT]*
We could nor laugh nor wail;   *HELL*
Through utter drought all dumb we stood!   *(symbol)*
I bit my arm, I sucked the blood,
And cried, 'A sail! a sail!'   160

With throats unslaked, with black lips baked,
Agape they heard me call;
A flash of joy;   Gramercy! they for joy did grin,
And all at once their breath drew in,   165
As they were drinking all.

And horror follows. For can it be a ship that comes onward without wind or tide?	'See! see! (I cried) she tacks no more! Hither to work us weal; Without a breeze, without a tide, She steadies with upright keel!'	170

The western wave was all a-flame;
The day was well nigh done!
Almost upon the western wave
Rested the broad bright Sun;
When that strange shape drove suddenly   175
Betwixt us and the Sun.

It seemeth him but the skeleton of a ship:

And straight the Sun was flecked with bars
(Heaven's Mother send us grace!)
As if through a dungeon-grate he peered
With broad and burning face.   180

Alas! (thought I, and my heart beat loud)
How fast she nears and nears!
Are those her sails that glance in the Sun,
Like restless gossameres?

And its ribs are seen as bars on the face of the setting Sun. The Spectre-Woman and her Death-mate, and no other on board the skeleton-ship. Like vessel, like crew!

Are those her ribs through which the Sun   185
Did peer, as through a grate?
And is that Woman all her crew?
Is that a Death? and are there two?
Is Death that woman's mate?

Her lips were red, her looks were free,   190
Her locks were yellow as gold:
Her skin was as white as leprosy,
The nightmare Life-in-Death was she,
Who thicks man's blood with cold.

Death and Life-in-Death have diced for the ship's crew, and she (the latter) winneth the ancient Mariner.

The naked hulk alongside came,   195
And the twain were casting dice;
'The game is done! I've won! I've won!'
Quoth she, and whistles thrice.

DEATH WINS
the CREW
LIFE-IN-
DEATH WINS
the MARINER

No twilight within the courts of the Sun.

The Sun's rim dips; the stars rush out:
At one stride comes the dark;   200
With far-heard whisper, o'er the sea,
Off shot the spectre-bark.

At the rising of the Moon,

We listened and looked sideways up!
Fear at my heart, as at a cup,
My lifeblood seemed to sip!   205
The stars were dim, and thick the night,
The steersman's face by his lamp gleamed white;

From the sails the dew did drip—
Till clomb above the eastern bar
The horned Moon, with one bright star   210
Within the nether tip.

One after another,

One after one, by the star-dogged Moon,
Too quick for groan or sigh,
Each turned his face with a ghastly pang,
And cursed me with his eye.   215

ship's crew of 200 men die, one-by-one

*His ship-mates drop
down dead.*

Four times fifty living men
(And I heard nor sigh nor groan)
With heavy thump, a lifeless lump,
They dropped down one by one.

*But Life-in-Death begins
her work on the ancient
Mariner.*

The souls did from their bodies fly—   220
They fled to bliss or woe!
And every soul, it passed me by,
Like the whizz of my cross-bow!"

PART IV

Back to PRESENT Time

*The Wedding-Guest
feareth that a Spirit is
talking to him;*

"I fear thee, ancient Mariner!
I fear thy skinny hand!
And thou art long, and lank, and brown,   225
As is the ribbed sea-sand.

*But the ancient Mariner
assureth him of his bodi-
ly life, and proceedeth to
relate his horrible pen-
ance.*

I fear thee and thy glittering eye,
And thy skinny hand, so brown."—
"Fear not, fear not, thou Wedding-Guest!   230
This body dropt not down.

Alone, alone, all, all alone,
Alone on a wide, wide sea!
And never a saint took pity on
My soul in agony.   235

*He despiseth the crea-
tures of the calm.*

The many men, so beautiful!
And they all dead did lie:
And a thousand thousand slimy things
Lived on; and so did I.

identify himself w/the slimy things

*And envieth that they
should live, and so many
lie dead.·*

I looked upon the rotting sea,   240
And drew my eyes away;
I looked upon the rotting deck,
And there the dead men lay.

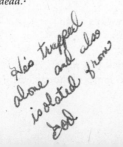
He's trapped alone and also isolated from God

I looked to heaven, and tried to pray;
But or ever a prayer had gusht,   245

A wicked whisper came, and made
My heart as dry as dust.

I closed my lids, and kept them close,
And the balls like pulses beat;
For the sky and the sea, and the sea and
    the sky   250
Lay like a load on my weary eye,
And the dead were at my feet.

But the curse liveth for
him in the eye of the
dead men.

The cold sweat melted from their limbs,
Nor rot nor reek did they:
The look with which they looked on me   255
Had never passed away.

An orphan's curse would drag to hell
A spirit from on high;
But oh! more horrible than that
Is the curse in a dead man's eye!   260
Seven days, seven nights, I saw that curse,
And yet I could not die.

In his loneliness and fix-
edness he yearneth to-
ward the journeying
Moon, and the stars that
still sojourn, yet still
move onward; and
everywhere the blue sky
belongs to them, and is
their appointed rest, and
their native country and
their own natural homes,
which they enter unan-
nounced, as lords that
are certainly expected
and yet there is a silent
joy at their arrival.

The moving Moon went up the sky,
And nowhere did abide:
Softly she was going up,   265
And a star or two beside—

Her beams bemocked the sultry main,
Like April hoar-frost spread;
But where the ship's huge shadow lay,
The charmèd water burnt alway   270
A still and awful red.

Beyond the shadow of the ship,
I watched the water-snakes:
They moved in tracks of shining white,
And when they reared, the elfish light   275
Fell off in hoary flakes.

By the light of the Moon
he beholdeth God's crea-
tures of the great calm.

Within the shadow of the ship
I watched their rich attire:
Blue, glossy green, and velvet black,
They coiled and swam; and every track   280
Was a flash of golden fire.

Their beauty and their
happiness.

O happy living things! no tongue
Their beauty might declare:
A spring of love gushed from my heart,

The turning point of story [handwritten]

He blesseth them in his heart.	And I blessed them unaware: Sure my kind saint took pity on me, And I blessed them unaware.

That frees him, barrier between him & God & he "can" pray [handwritten]

285

The spell begins to break.	The selfsame moment I could pray; And from my neck so free The Albatross fell off, and sank Like lead into the sea."

290

PART V

Oh sleep! it is a gentle thing,
Beloved from pole to pole!
To Mary Queen the praise be given!
She sent the gentle sleep from Heaven,
That slid into my soul.

He sleeps & dreams [handwritten]

By grace of the holy Mother, the ancient Mariner is refreshed with rain.

The silly buckets on the deck,
That had so long remained,
I dreamt that they were filled with dew;
And when I awoke, it rained.

It Rains, [handwritten]

300

My lips were wet, my throat was cold,
My garments all were dank;
Sure I had drunken in my dreams,
And still my body drank.

I moved, and could not feel my limbs; 305
I was so light—almost
I thought that I had died in sleep,
And was a blessèd ghost.

He heareth sounds and seeth strange sights and commotions in the sky and the element.

And soon I heard a roaring wind:
It did not come anear; 310
But with its sound it shook the sails,
That were so thin and sere.

The upper air burst into life!
And a hundred fire-flags sheen,
To and fro they were hurried about! 315
And to and fro, and in and out,
The wan stars danced between.

And the coming wind did roar more loud,
And the sails did sigh like sedge;
And the rain poured down from one black
cloud; 320
The moon was at its edge.

The thick black cloud was cleft, and still
The Moon was at its side:
Like waters shot from some high crag,
The lightning fell with never a jag,   325
A river steep and wide.

The loud wind never reached the ship,
Yet now the ship moved on!
Beneath the lightning and the Moon
The dead men gave a groan.   330

The bodies of the ship's
crew are inspired and the
ship moves on;

They groaned, they stirred, they all uprose,
Nor spake, nor moved their eyes;
It had been strange, even in a dream,
To have seen those dead men rise.

The helmsman steered, the ship moved on;   335
Yet never a breeze up blew;
The mariners all 'gan work the ropes,
Where they were wont to do;
They raised their limbs like lifeless tools—
We were a ghastly crew.   340

The body of my brother's son
Stood by me, knee to knee:
The body and I pulled at one rope
But he said nought to me."

But not by the souls of
the men, nor by daemons
of earth or middle air,
but by a blessed troop of
angelic spirits, sent down
by the invocation of the
guardian saint.

"I fear thee, ancient Mariner!"   345
"Be calm, thou Wedding-Guest!
'Twas not those souls that fled in pain,
Which to their corses came again,
But a troop of spirits blest:

For when it dawned—they dropped their arms,   350
And clustered round the mast;
Sweet sounds rose slowly through their mouths,
And from their bodies passed.

Around, around, flew each sweet sound,
Then darted to the Sun;   355
Slowly the sounds came back again,
Now mixed, now one by one.

Sometimes a-dropping from the sky
I heard the sky-lark sing;
Sometimes all little birds that are,   360
How they seemed to fill the sea and air
With their sweet jargoning!

And now 'twas like all instruments,
Now like a lonely flute;
And now it is an angel's song,   365
That makes the heavens be mute.

It ceased; yet still the sails made on
A pleasant noise till noon,
A noise like of a hidden brook
In the leafy month of June,   370
That to the sleeping woods all night
Singeth a quiet tune.

Till noon we quietly sailed on,
Yet never a breeze did breathe:
Slowly and smoothly went the ship,   375
Moved onward from beneath.

The lonesome Spirit from the South Pole carries on the ship as far as the Line, in obedience to the angelic troop, but still requireth vengeance.

Under the keel nine fathom deep,
From the land of mist and snow,
The spirit slid: and it was he
That made the ship to go.   380
The sails at noon left off their tune,
And the ship stood still also.

The Sun, right up above the mast,
Had fixed her to the ocean:
But in a minute she 'gan stir,   385
With a short uneasy motion—
Backwards and forwards half her length
With a short uneasy motion.

Then like a pawing horse let go,
She made a sudden bound: 390
It flung the blood into my head,
And I fell down in a swound.

The Polar Spirit's fellow-daemons, the invisible inhabitants of the element, take part in his wrong; and two of them relate one to the other, that penance long and heavy for the ancient Mariner hath been accorded to the Polar Spirit, who returneth southward.

How long in that same fit I lay,
I have not to declare;
But ere my living life returned,   395
I heard and in my soul discerned
Two voices in the air.

'Is it he?' quoth one, 'Is this the man? ✳
By Him who died on cross, ✳
With his cruel bow he laid full low ✳   400
The harmless Albatross. ✳

The Spirit who bideth by himself
In the land of mist and snow,

[handwritten marginalia:] ✳ Spirit world commentation on phy world

[handwritten marginalia:] ✳ Symbol Christ dying on cross

He loved the bird that loved the man *violation*
Who shot him with his bow.'   405

The other was a softer voice,
As soft as honey-dew:
Quoth he, 'The man hath penance done,
And penance more will do.'''   *(not punishment)*

PART VI

FIRST VOICE
"'But tell me, tell me! speak again,   410
Thy soft response renewing—
What makes that ship drive on so fast?
What is the ocean doing?'

SECOND VOICE
'Still as a slave before his lord,
The ocean hath no blast;   415
His great bright eye most silently
Up to the Moon is cast—

If he may know which way to go;
For she guides him smooth or grim.
See, brother, see! how graciously   420
She looketh down on him.'

FIRST VOICE
'But why drives on that ship so fast,
Without or wave or wind?'

SECOND VOICE
'The air is cut away before,
And closes from behind.   425

Fly, brother, fly, more high, more high!
Or we shall be belated:
For slow and slow that ship will go,
When the Mariner's trance is abated.'

I woke, and we were sailing on   430
As in a gentle weather:
'Twas night, calm night, the Moon was high,
The dead men stood together.

All stood together on the deck,
For a charnel-dungeon fitter: 435
All fixed on me their stony eyes,
That in the Moon did glitter.

The Mariner hath been cast into a trance; for the angelic power causeth the vessel to drive northward faster than human life could endure.

The supernatural motion is retarded; the Mariner awakes, and his penance begins anew.

The pang, the curse, with which they died,
Had never passed away:
I could not draw my eyes from theirs,   440
Nor turn them up to pray.

The curse is finally
expiated. ~~broken~~,

but penance goes

on

And now this spell was snapped: once more
I viewed the ocean green,
And looked far forth, yet little saw
Of what had else been seen—   445

Like one, that on a lonesome road
Doth walk in fear and dread,
And having once turned round walks on,
And turns no more his head;
Because he knows, a frightful fiend   450
Doth close behind him tread.

But soon there breathed a wind on me,
Nor sound nor motion made:
Its path was not upon the sea,
In ripple or in shade.   455

It raised my hair, it fanned my cheek
Like a meadow-gale of spring—
It mingled strangely with my fears,
Yet it felt like a welcoming.

Swiftly, swiftly flew the ship,   460
Yet she sailed softly too:
Sweetly, sweetly blew the breeze—
On me alone it blew.

And the ancient Mariner
beholdeth his native
country.

backward sequence
compare: @ beg.
of story

Oh! dream of joy! is this indeed
The lighthouse top I see?   465
Is this the hill? is this the kirk?—*church*
Is this mine own countree?

We drifted o'er the harbor-bar,
And I with sobs did pray—
O let me be awake, my God!   470
Or let me sleep alway.

The harbor-bay was clear as glass,
So smoothly it was strewn!
And on the bay the moonlight lay,
And the shadow of the Moon.   475

The rock shone bright, the kirk no less,
That stands above the rock:

The moonlight steeped in silentness
The steady weathercock.

And the bay was white with silent light   480
Til rising from the same,
Full many shapes, that shadows were,
In crimson colors came.

The angelic spirits leave
the dead bodies,

A little distance from the prow
Those crimson shadows were: 485
I turned my eyes upon the deck—
Oh, Christ, what saw I there!

And appear in their own
forms of light.

Each corse lay flat, lifeless and flat,
And, by the holy rood!
A man all light, a seraph-man,   490
On every corse there stood.

This seraph-band, each waved his hand;
It was a heavenly sight!
They stood as signals to the land
Each one a lovely light;   495

This seraph-band, each waved his hand,
No voice did they impart—
No voice; but oh! the silence sank
Like music on my heart.

But soon I heard the dash of oars,   500
I heard the Pilot's cheer;
My heard was turned perforce away,
And I saw a boat appear.

The Pilot and the Pilot's boy,
I heard them coming fast: 505
Dear Lord in Heaven! it was a joy
The dead men could not blast.

I saw a third—I heard his voice:
It is the Hermit good!
He singeth loudly his godly hymns   510
That he makes in the wood.
He'll shrieve my soul; he'll wash away
The Albatross's blood."

bring forgiveness
for Mariner's
sins.

PART VII

The Hermit of the Wood,

"This Hermit good lives in that wood
Which slopes down to the sea.   515

How loudly his sweet voice he rears!
He loves to talk with marineres
That come from a far countree.

He kneels at morn, and noon, and eve—
He hath a cushion plump: 520
It is the moss that wholly hides
The rotted old oak-stump.

The skiff-boat neared: I heard them talk,
'Why, this is strange, I trow!
Where are those lights so many and fair,   525
That signal made but now?'

Approacheth the ship   'Strange, by my faith!' the Hermit said—
with wonder.   'And they answered not our cheer!
The planks look warped! and see those sails,
How thin they are and sere!   530
I never saw aught like to them,
Unless perchance it were

Brown skeletons of leaves that lag
My forest-brook along;
When the ivy-tod is heavy with snow,   535
And the owlet whoops to the wolf below,
That eats the she-wolf's young.'

'Dear Lord! it hath a fiendish look—
(The Pilot made reply)
I am a-feared'—'Push on, push on!'   540
Said the Hermit cheerily.

The boat came closer to the ship,
But I nor spake nor stirred;
The boat came close beneath the ship,
And straight a sound was heard.   545

The ship suddenly sink-   Under the water it rumbled on,
eth.   Still louder and more dread:
It reached the ship, it split the bay;
The ship went down like lead.

The ancient Mariner is   Stunned by that loud and dreadful sound,   550
saved in the Pilot's boat. Which sky and ocean smote,
Like one that hath been seven days drowned
My body lay afloat;
But swift as dreams, myself I found
Within the Pilot's boat.   555

Upon the whirl, where sank the ship,
The boat spun round and round;
And all was still, save that the hill
Was telling of the sound.

I moved my lips—the Pilot shrieked   560
And fell down in a fit;
The holy Hermit raised his eyes,
And prayed where he did sit.

I took the oars: the Pilot's boy,
Who now doth crazy go,   565
Laughed loud and long, and all the while
His eyes went to and fro.
'Ha! ha!' quoth he, 'full plain I see,
The Devil knows how to row.'

And now, all in my own countree,   570
I stood on the firm land!
The Hermit stepped forth from the boat,
And scarcely he could stand.

The ancient Mariner ear-   'O shrieve me, shrieve me, holy man!'
nestly entreateth the   The Hermit crossed his brow.   575
Hermit to shrieve him;   'Say quick,' quoth he, 'I bid thee say—
and the penance of life   What manner of man art thou?'
falls on him.

Forthwith this frame of mine was wrenched
With a woeful agony,
Which forced me to begin my tale;   580
And then it left me free.

And ever and anon   Since then, at an uncertain hour,
throughout his future life That agony returns:
an agony constraineth   And till my ghastly tale is told,
him to travel from land   This heart within me burns.   585
to land,

I pass, like night, from land to land;
I have strange power of speech;
That moment that his face I see,
I know the man that must hear me:
To him my tale I teach.   590

What loud uproar bursts from that door!
The wedding-guests are there:
But in the garden-bower the bride
And bride-maids singing are:
And hark the little vesper bell   595
Which biddeth me to prayer!

[handwritten margin note:] Mariner must wander the land until he finds the one who is to listen to the mariners story (tale)

[handwritten: Mariners summerizes his experience]

O Wedding-Guest! this soul hath been
Alone on a wide, wide sea;
So lonely 'twas, that God himself
Scarce seeméd there to be.   600

O sweeter than the marriage-feast,
'Tis sweeter far to me,
To walk together to the kirk
With a goodly company!—

To walk together to the kirk,   605
And all together pray,
While each to his great Father bends,
Old men, and babes, and loving friends,
And youths and maidens gay!

And to teach, by his own example, love and reverence to all things that God made and loveth.

Farewell, farewell! but this I tell   610
To thee, thou Wedding-Guest!
He prayeth well, who loveth well
Both man and bird and beast.

[handwritten: moral of story]

He prayeth best, who loveth best
All things both great and small;   615
For the dear God who loveth us,
He made and loveth all."

The Mariner, whose eye is bright,
Whose beard with age is hoar,
Is gone: and now the Wedding-Guest   620
Turned from the Bridegroom's door.

He went like one that hath been stunned,
And is of sense forlorn:
A sadder and a wiser man,
He rose the morrow morn.   625

Fact Questions and Exercises
1. Describe the setting in which the ancient mariner tells his story. *[handwritten: On the road, to attend a wedding feast]*
2. How does the mariner kill the albatross? What do his shipmates do with the dead bird? *[handwritten: Bow & Arrow (CROSS BOW) Hang it around his head]*
3. Describe the conditions that follow the killing of the albatross. *[handwritten: Crew was fir... angry, then forgive]*
4. Of whom is this a description: "Her lips were red, her looks were free, / Her locks were yellow as gold"? *[handwritten: Spectre Woman / Life-In-Death]*
5. How does the mariner react when he first sees the water snakes? *[handwritten: Anger, envy]*
6. Identify the Hermit of the Wood. What does he do for the ancient mariner? *[handwritten left margin: HOLY MAN, HEARS the mariners confession]*
7. Define the word "shrieve." *[handwritten: CONFESSION OF ONE'S SINS]*
8. Why does the mariner have to travel "from land to land" and retell his story?

[handwritten: AGONY or burning in his heart, penance]

For Discussion and Writing

To LOVE ALL THINGS GOD HAS MADE BOTH GREAT AND SMALL, IMPLIED @ first

1. What is the moral of the poem? Is this moral clearly stated, or implied? What does this moral suggest about Coleridge's view of nature? Of the individual's place in nature? Does the moral say that people should have dominion over other forms of life or that they should strive to be an integral part of all life? In the poem, what happens when the moral is not upheld?

2. Discuss Coleridge's use of symbols. Which of his symbols are the most effective or clearest in meaning? Is each a distinct symbol?

3. Discuss the themes of melancholy and joy in the poem. For example, the mariner tells his story at a wedding; why? Which events in the poem seem to bring joy? Which seem to create melancholy or despair? Does joy or does despair dominate the poem?

George Gordon, Lord Byron [1788–1824]

Byron was born in England, but was reared in Scotland by his Scottish mother, an ignorant, unpredictable woman of strong Calvinist belief, with whom Byron fought violently, but affectionately. Although he was descended from aristocrats, Byron was brought up in near poverty. Not until the death of his uncle, in 1798, was Byron made the sixth Lord Byron; thereafter, he enjoyed the status that the title brought. Byron led a wild, turbulent, and often scandalous life that even today is the subject of much discussion and conjecture. *Don Juan* (1818), a great comic, satirical poem, is one of the longest poems in the English language; in its entirety, it expresses Byron's views on just about every aspect of society.

She Walks in Beauty

young lovely lady

1

She walks in beauty, like the night
   Of cloudless climes and starry skies;
And all that's best of dark and bright
   Meet in her aspect and her eyes:
Thus mellowed to that tender light   5
   Which heaven to gaudy day denies.

2

One shade the more, one ray the less,
   Had half impaired the nameless grace
Which waves in every raven tress,
   Or softly lightens o'er her face;   10
Where thoughts serenely sweet express
   How pure, how dear their dwelling place.

3

And on that cheek, and o'er that brow,
    So soft, so calm, yet eloquent,
The smiles that win, the tints that glow,   15
    But tell of days in goodness spent,
A mind at peace with all below,
    A heart whose love is innocent!

So We'll Go No More A-Roving

1

So we'll go no more a-roving
    So late into the night,
Though the heart be still as loving,
    And the moon be still as bright.

2

For the sword outwears its sheath,   5
    And the soul wears out the breast,
And the heart must pause to breathe,
    And Love itself have rest.

3

Though the night was made for loving,
    And the day returns too soon,   10
Yet we'll go no more a-roving
    By the light of the moon.

Don Juan

From *Canto the First*

1

I want a hero: an uncommon want,
    When every year and month sends forth a new one,
Till, after cloying the gazettes with cant,
    The age discovers he is not the true one;
Of such as these I should not care to vaunt,   5
    I'll therefore take our ancient friend Don Juan—
We all have seen him, in the pantomime,
Sent to the Devil somewhat ere his time.

    .   .   .   .

6

Most epic poets plunge *"in medias res"*[1]
    (Horace makes this the heroic turnpike road),

---

1. "Into the middle of things."

And then your hero tells, when'er you please,
　　What went before—by way of episode,
While seated after dinner at his ease,   45
　　Beside his mistress in some soft abode,
Palace, or garden, paradise, or cavern,
Which serves the happy couple for a tavern.

7

That is the usual method, but not mine—
　　My way is to begin with the beginning;   50
The regularity of my design
　　Forbids all wandering as the worst of sinning,
And therefore I shall open with a line
　　(Although it cost me half an hour in spinning),
Narrating somewhat of Don Juan's father,   55
And also of his mother, if you'd rather.

8

In Seville was he born, a pleasant city,
　　Famous for oranges and women—he
Who has not seen it will be much to pity,
　　So says the proverb—and I quite agree;   60
Of all the Spanish towns is none more pretty,
　　Cadiz perhaps—but that you soon may see;
Don Juan's parents lived beside the river,
A noble stream, and called the Guadalquivir.

9

His father's name was José—*Don,* of course,—   65
　　A true Hidalgo,[2] free from every stain
Of Moor or Hebrew blood, he traced his source
　　Through the most Gothic gentlemen of Spain;
A better cavalier ne'er mounted horse,
　　Or, being mounted, e'er got down again,   70
Than José, who begot our hero, who
Begot—but that's to come—Well, to renew:

10

His mother was a learned lady, famed
　　For every branch of every science known—
In every Christian language ever named,   75
　　With virtues equaled by her wit alone:
She made the cleverest people quite ashamed,
　　And even the good with inward envy groan,
Finding themselves so very much exceeded,
In their own way, by all the things that she did.   80

　　　　　　·　·　·　·　·

2. Minor Spanish nobleman.

18

Perfect she was, but as perfection is
    Insipid in this naughty world of ours,
Where our first parents never learned to kiss
    Till they were exiled from their earlier bowers,   140
Where all was peace, and innocence, and bliss,
    (I wonder how they got through the twelve hours),
Don José, like a lineal son of Eve,
Went plucking various fruit without her leave.

19

He was a mortal of the careless kind,   145
    With no great love for learning, or the learned,
Who chose to go where'er he had a mind,
    And never dreamed his lady was concerned;
The world, as usual, wickedly inclined
    To see a kingdom or a house o'erturned,   150
Whispered he had a mistress, some said *two.*
But for domestic quarrels *one* will do.

20

Now Donna Inez had, with all her merit,
    A great opinion of her own good qualities;
Neglect, indeed, requires a saint to bear it,   155
    And such, indeed, she was in her moralities;
But then she had a devil of a spirit,
    And sometimes mixed up fancies with realities,
And let few opportunities escape
Of getting her liege lord into a scrape.   160

21

This was an easy matter with a man
    Oft in the wrong, and never on his guard;
And even the wisest, do the best they can,
    Have moments, hours, and days, so unprepared,
That you might "brain them with their lady's fan";[3]   165
    And sometimes ladies hit exceeding hard,
And fans turn into falchions[4] in fair hands,
And why and wherefore no one understands.

22

'Tis pity learned virgins ever wed
    With persons of no sort of education,   170
Or gentlemen, who, though well born and bred,
    Grow tired of scientific conversation:
I don't choose to say much upon this head,
    I'm a plain man, and in a single station,

3. From *Henry IV,* Part I, Act 2, Sc. 3.   **4.** Swords.

But—Oh! ye lords of ladies intellectual,   175
Inform us truly, have they not hen-pecked you all?

. . . .

54

Young Juan now was sixteen years of age,   425
 Tall, handsome, slender, but well knit; he seemed
Active, though not so sprightly, as a page;
 And everybody but his mother deemed
Him almost man; but she flew in a rage
 And bit her lips (for else she might have screamed)   430
If any said so—for to be precocious
Was in her eyes a thing the most atrocious.

55

Amongst her numerous acquaintance, all
 Selected for discretion and devotion,
There was the Donna Julia, whom to call   435
 Pretty were but to give a feeble notion
Of many charms in her as natural
 As sweetness to the flower, or salt to Ocean,
Her zone[5] to Venus, or his bow to Cupid,
(But this last simile is trite and stupid.)   440

56

The darkness of her Oriental eye
 Accorded with her Moorish origin;
(Her blood was not all Spanish; by the by,
 In Spain, you know, this is a sort of sin;)
When proud Granada fell, and, forced to fly,   445
 Boabdil[6] wept: of Donna Julia's kin
Some went to Africa, some stayed in Spain—
Her great great grandmamma chose to remain.

57

She married (I forget the pedigree)
 With an Hidalgo, who transmitted down   450
His blood less noble than such blood should be;
 At such alliances his sires would frown,
In that point so precise in each degree
 That they bred *in and in*, as might be shown,
Marrying their cousins—nay, their aunts, and nieces,   455
Which always spoils the breed, if it increases.

58

This heathenish cross restored the breed again,
 Ruined its blood, but much improved its flesh;

5. Waist.   6. The last Mohammedan ruler of Granada.

For from a root the ugliest in Old Spain
    Sprung up a branch as beautiful as fresh;   460
The sons no more were short, the daughters plain:
    But there's a rumour which I fain would hush,
'Tis said that Donna Julia's grandmamma
Produced her Don more heirs at love than law.

59

However this might be, the race went on   465
    Improving still through every generation,
Until it centered in an only son,
    Who left an only daughter; my narration
May have suggested that this single one
    Could be but Julia (whom on this occasion   470
I shall have much to speak about), and she
Was married, charming, chaste, and twenty-three.

60

Her eye (I'm very fond of handsome eyes)
    Was large and dark, suppressing half its fire
Until she spoke, then through its soft disguise   475
    Flashed an expression more of pride than ire,
And love than either; and there would arise
    A something in them which was not desire,
But would have been, perhaps, but for the soul
Which struggled through and chastened down the whole.   480

61

Her glossy hair was clustered o'er a brow
    Bright with intelligence, and fair, and smooth:
Her eyebrow's shape was like the aerial bow,[7]
    Her cheek all purple with the beam of youth,
Mounting, at times, to a transparent glow,   485
    As if her veins ran lightning; she, in sooth,
Possessed an air and grace by no means common:
Her stature tall—I hate a dumpy woman.

62

Wedded she was some years, and to a man
    Of fifty, and such husbands are in plenty;   490
And yet, I think, instead of such a ONE
    'Twere better to have TWO of five-and-twenty,
Especially in countries near the sun:
    And now I think on't, *"mi vien in mente,"*[8]
Ladies even of the most uneasy virtue   495
Prefer a spouse whose age is short of thirty.

7. rainbow. 8. "It comes to my mind."

63

'Tis a sad thing, I cannot choose but say,
 And all the fault of that indecent sun,
Who cannot leave alone our helpless clay,
 But will keep baking, broiling, burning on,   500
That howsoever people fast and pray,
 The flesh is frail, and so the soul undone:
What men call gallantry, and gods adultery,
Is much more common where the climate's sultry.

. . . .

65

Alfonso was the name of Julia's lord,
 A man well looking for his years, and who
Was neither much beloved nor yet abhorred: 515
 They lived together as most people do,
Suffering each other's foibles by accord,
 And not exactly either *one* or *two;*
Yet he was jealous, though he did not show it,
For Jealousy dislikes the world to know it.   520

66

Julia was—yet I never could see why—
 With Donna Inez quite a favorite friend;
Between their tastes there was small sympathy,
 For not a line had Julia ever penned:
Some people whisper (but, no doubt, they lie,   525
 For Malice still imputes some private end)
That Inez had, ere Don Alfonso's marriage,
Forgot with him her very prudent carriage,[9]

67

And that still keeping up with the old connection,
 Which Time had lately rendered much more chaste,   530
She took his lady also in affection,
 And certainly this course was much the best:
She flattered Julia with her sage protection,
 And complimented Don Alfonso's taste;
And if she could not (who can?) silence scandal,   535
At least she left it a more slender handle.

68

I can't tell whether Julia saw the affair
 With other people's eyes, or if her own
Discoveries made, but none could be aware
 Of this, at least no symptom e'er was shown;   540

9. Behavior.

Perhaps she did not know, or did not care,
    Indifferent from the first, or callous grown:
I'm really puzzled what to think or say,
She kept her counsel in so close a way.

69

Juan she saw, and, as a pretty child,   545
    Caressed him often—such a thing might be
Quite innocently done, and harmless styled,
    When she had twenty years, and thirteen he;
But I am not so sure I should have smiled
    When he was sixteen, Julia twenty-three;   550
These few short years make wondrous alterations,
Particularly amongst sun-burnt nations.

70

Whate'er the cause might be, they had become
    Changed; for the dame grew distant, the youth shy,
Their looks cast down, their greetings almost dumb,   555
    And much embarrassment in either eye;
There surely will be little doubt with some
    That Donna Julia knew the reason why,
But as for Juan, he had no more notion
Than he who never saw the sea of Ocean.   560

71

Yet Julia's very coldness still was kind,
    And tremulously gentle her small hand
Withdrew itself from his, but left behind
    A little pressure, thrilling, and so bland
And slight, so very slight, that to the mind   565
    'Twas but a doubt; but ne'er magician's wand
Wrought change with all Armida's[10] fairy art
Like what this light touch left on Juan's heart.

72

And if she met him, though she smiled no more,
    She looked a sadness sweeter than her smile,   570
As if her heart had deeper thoughts in store
    She must not own, but cherished more the while
For that compression in its burning core;
    Even Innocence itself has many a wile,
And will not dare to trust itself with truth,   575
And Love is taught hypocrisy from youth.

---

10. A reference to *Jerusalem Delivered,* by the sixteenth-century Italian poet Tasso; Armida
seduced Christian knights.

73

But Passion most dissembles, yet betrays
　　　Even by its darkness; as the blackest sky
Foretells the heaviest tempest, it displays
　　　Its workings through the vainly guarded eye,　　　　580
And in whatever aspect it arrays
　　　Itself, 'tis still the same hypocrisy;
Coldness or Anger, even Disdain or Hate,
Are masks it often wears, and still too late.

74

Then there were sighs, the deeper for suppression,　　　585
　　　And stolen glances, sweeter for the theft,
And burning blushes, though for no transgression,
　　　Tremblings when met, and restlessness when left;
All these are little preludes to possession,
　　　Of which young Passion cannot be bereft,　　　　590
And merely tend to show how greatly Love is
Embarrassed at first starting with a novice.

75

Poor Julia's heart was in an awkward state;
　　　She felt it going, and resolved to make
The noblest efforts for herself and mate,　　　　595
　　　For Honor's, Pride's, Religion's, Virtue's sake:
Her resolutions were most truly great,
　　　And almost might have made a Tarquin[11] quake:
She prayed the Virgin Mary for her grace,
As being the best judge of a lady's case.　　　　600

76

She vowed she never would see Juan more,
　　　And next day paid a visit to his mother,
And looked extremely at the opening door,
　　　Which, by the Virgin's grace, let in another;
Grateful she was, and yet a little sore—　　　　605
　　　Again it opens, it can be no other,
'Tis surely Juan now—No! I'm afraid
That night the Virgin was no further prayed.

77

She now determined that a virtuous woman
　　　Should rather face and overcome temptation,　　　610
That flight was base and dastardly, and no man
　　　Should ever give her heart the least sensation,

---

11. In Shakespeare's *Rape of Lucrece*, Tarquin rapes a very chaste woman.

That is to say, a thought beyond the common
      Preference, that we must feel, upon occasion,
For people who are pleasanter than others,   615
But then they only seem so many brothers.

     78
And even if by chance—and who can tell?
      The Devil's so very sly—she should discover
That all within was not so very well,
      And, if still free, that such or such a lover   620
Might please perhaps, a virtuous wife can quell
      Such thoughts, and be the better when they're over;
And if the man should ask, 'tis but denial:
I recommend young ladies to make trial.

     79
And, then, there are such things as Love divine,   625
      Bright and immaculate, unmixed and pure,
Such as the angels think so very fine,
      And matrons, who would be no less secure,
Platonic, perfect, "just such love as mine;"
      Thus Julia said—and thought so, to be sure;   630
And so I'd have her think, were *I* the man
On whom her reveries celestial ran.

     80
Such love is innocent, and may exist
      Between young persons without any danger.
A hand may first, and then a lip be kissed;   635
      For my part, to such doings I'm a stranger,
But *hear* these freedoms form the utmost list
      Of all o'er which such love may be a ranger:
If people go beyond, 'tis quite a crime,
But not my fault—I tell them all in time.   640

     81
Love, then, but Love within its proper limits,
      Was Julia's innocent determination
In young Don Juan's favour, and to him its
      Exertion might be useful on occasion;
And, lighted at too pure a shrine to dim its   645
      Ethereal luster, with what sweet persuasion
He might be taught, by Love and her together—
I really don't know what, nor Julia either.

     82
Frought with this fine intention, and well fenced
      In mail of proof—her purity of soul—   650
She, for the future, of her strength convinced,

And that her honor was a rock, or mole,[12]
Exceeding sagely from that hour dispensed
    With any kind of troublesome control;
But whether Julia to the task was equal   655
Is that which must be mentioned in the sequel.

      83
Her plan she deemed both innocent and feasible,
    And, surely, with a stripling of sixteen
Not Scandal's fangs could fix on much that's seizable,
    Or if they did so, satisfied to mean   660
Nothing but what was good, her breast was peaceable—
    A quiet conscience makes one so serene!
Christians have burnt each other, quite persuaded
That all the Apostles would have done as they did.

    . . . .

      90
Young Juan wandered by the glassy brooks,
    Thinking unutterable things; he threw
Himself at length within the leafy nooks   715
    Where the wild branch of the cork forest grew;
There poets find materials for their books,
    And every now and then we read them through,
So that their plan and prosody are eligible,
Unless, like Wordsworth, they prove unintelligible.   720

      91
He, Juan (and not Wordsworth), so pursued
    His self-communion with his own high soul,
Until his mighty heart, in its great mood,
    Had mitigated part, though not the whole
Of its disease; he did the best he could   725
    With things not very subject to control,
And turned, without perceiving his condition,
Like Coleridge, into a metaphysician.

      92
He thought about himself, and the whole earth,
    Of man the wonderful, and of the stars,   730
And how the deuce they ever could have birth;
    And then he thought of earthquakes, and of wars,
How many miles the moon might have in girth,
    Of air-balloons, and of the many bars
To perfect knowledge of the boundless skies;—   735
And then he thought of Donna Julia's eyes.

---

12. Pier, breakwater.

93

In thoughts like these true Wisdom may discern
　　　Longings sublime, and aspirations high,
Which some are born with, but the most part learn
　　　To plague themselves withal, they know not why: 740
'Twas strange that one so young should thus concern
　　　His brain about the action of the sky;
If *you* think 'twas Philosophy that this did,
I can't help thinking puberty assisted.

94

He pored upon the leaves, and on the flowers,   745
　　　And heard a voice in all the winds; and then
He thought of wood-nymphs and immortal bowers,
　　　And how the goddesses came down to men:
He missed the pathway, he forgot the hours,
　　　And when he looked upon his watch again,   750
He found how much old Time had been a winner—
He also found that he had lost his dinner.

95

Sometimes he turned to gaze upon his book,
　　　Boscan, or Garcilasso;[13]—by the wind
Even as the page is rustled while we look,   755
　　　So by the poesy of his own mind
Over the mystic leaf his soul was shook,
　　　As if 'twere one whereon magicians bind
Their spells, and give them to the passing gale,
According to some good old woman's tale.   760

96

Thus would he while his lonely hours away
　　　Dissatisfied, not knowing what he wanted;
Nor glowing reverie, nor poet's lay,
　　　Could yield his spirit that for which it panted,
A bosom whereon he his head might lay,   765
　　　And hear the heart beat with the love it granted,
With——several other things, which I forget,
Or which, at least, I need not mention yet.

97

Those lonely walks, and lengthening reveries,
　　　Could not escape the gentle Julia's eyes;   770
She saw that Juan was not at his ease;
　　　But that which chiefly may, and must surprise,
Is, that the Donna Inez did not tease
　　　Her only son with question or surmise;

13. Sixteenth-century Spanish poets.

Whether it was she did not see, or would not,   775
Or, like all very clever people, could not.

98

This may seem strange, but yet 'tis very common;
    For instance—gentlemen, whose ladies take
Leave to o'erstep the written rights of Woman,
    And break the——Which commandment is't they break?   780
(I have forgot the number, and think no man
    Should rashly quote, for fear of a mistake;)
I say, when these same gentlemen are jealous,
They make some blunder, which their ladies tell us.

99

A real husband always is suspicious,   785
    But still no less suspects in the wrong place,
Jealous of some one who had no such wishes,
    Or pandering blindly to his own disgrace,
By harboring some dear friend extremely vicious;
    The last indeed's infallibly the case: 790
And when the spouse and friend are gone off wholly,
He wonders at their vice, and not his folly.

100

Thus parents also are at times short-sighted:
    Though watchful as the lynx, they ne'er discover,
The while the wicked world beholds delighted,   795
    Young Hopeful's mistress, or Miss Fanny's lover,
Till some confounded escapade has blighted
    The plan of twenty years, and all is over;
And then the mother cries, the father swears,
And wonders why the devil he got heirs.   800

101

But Inez was so anxious, and so clear
    Of sight, that I must think, on this occasion,
She had some other motive much more near
    For leaving Juan to this new temptation,
But what that motive was, I shan't say here;   805
    Perhaps to finish Juan's education,
Perhaps to open Don Alfonso's eyes,
In case he thought his wife too great a prize.

102

It was upon a day, a summer's day—
    Summer's indeed a very dangerous season,   810
And so is spring about the end of May;
    The sun, no doubt, is the prevailing reason;

But whatsoe'er the cause is, one may say,
    And stand convicted of more truth than treason,
That there are months which nature grows more merry in,—   815
March has its hares, and May must have its heroine.

      103
'Twas on a summer's day—the sixth of June:
    I like to be particular in dates,
Not only of the age, and year, but moon;
    They are a sort of post-house, where the Fates   820
Change horses, making History change its tune,
    Then spur away o'er empires and o'er states,
Leaving at last not much besides chronology,
Excepting the post-obits[14] of theology.

      104
'Twas on the sixth of June, about the hour   825
    Of half-past six—perhaps still nearer seven—
When Julia sate within as pretty a bower
    As e'er held houri[15] in that heathenish heaven
Described by Mahomet, and Anacreon Moore,[16]
    To whom the lyre and laurels have been given,   830
With all the trophies of triumphant song—
He won them well, and may he wear them long!

      105
She sate, but not alone; I know not well
    How this same interview had taken place,
And even if I knew, I should not tell—   835
    People should hold their tongues in any case;
No matter how or why the thing befell,
    But there were she and Juan, face to face—
When two such faces are so, 'twould be wise,
But very difficult, to shut their eyes.   840

      106
How beautiful she looked! her conscious heart
    Glowed in her cheek, and yet she felt no wrong:
Oh Love! how perfect is thy mystic art,
    Strengthening the weak, and trampling on the strong!
How self-deceitful is the sagest part   845
    Of mortals whom thy lure hath led along!
The precipice she stood on was immense,
So was her creed[17] in her own innocence.

---

14. Debts paid from the estate of a dead person. **15.** In the Muslim concept of paradise, houris are beautiful girls who entertain those who go to heaven. **16.** Thomas Moore, Byron's friend, translated the love poems of the ancient Greek poet Anacreon. **17.** Belief, trust.

107

She thought of her own strength, and Juan's youth,
    And of the folly of all prudish fears,   850
Victorious Virtue, and domestic Truth,
    And then of Don Alfonso's fifty years:
I wish these last had not occurred, in sooth,
    Because that number rarely much endears,
And through all climes, the snowy and the sunny,   855
Sounds ill in love, whate'er it may in money.

108

When people say, "I've told you *fifty* times,"
    They mean to scold, and very often do;
When poets say, "I've written *fifty* rhymes,"
    They make you dread that they'll recite them too;   860
In gangs of *fifty*, thieves commit their crimes;
    At *fifty* love for love is rare, 'tis true,
But then, no doubt, it equally as true is,
A good deal may be bought for *fifty* Louis.[18]

109

Julia had honor, virtue, truth, and love   865
    For Don Alfonso; and she inly swore,
By all the vows below to Powers above,
    She never would disgrace the ring she wore,
Nor leave a wish which wisdom might reprove;
    And while she pondered this, besides much more,   870
One hand on Juan's carelessly was thrown,
Quite by mistake—she thought it was her own;

110

Unconsciously she leaned upon the other,
    Which played within the tangles of her hair;
And to contend with thoughts she could not smother
    She seemed by the distraction of her air.   875
'Twas surely very wrong in Juan's mother
    To leave together this imprudent pair,
She who for many years had watched her son so—
I'm very certain *mine* would not have done so.   880

. . . .

115

And Julia sate with Juan, half embraced
    And half retiring from the glowing arm,
Which trembled like the bosom where 'twas placed;   915
    Yet still she must have thought there was no harm,
Or else 'twere easy to withdraw her waist;

18. French coins.

But then the situation had its charm,
And then——God knows what next—I can't go on;
I'm almost sorry that I e'er begun.   920

116

Oh Plato! Plato! you have paved the way,
    With your confounded fantasies, to more
Immoral conduct by the fancied sway
    Your system feigns o'er the controlless core
Of human hearts, than all the long array   925
    Of poets and romancers:—You're a bore,
A charlatan, a coxcomb—and have been,
At best, no better than a go-between.

117

And Julia's voice was lost, except in sighs,
    Until too late for useful conversation;   930
The tears were gushing from her gentle eyes,
    I wish, indeed, they had not had occasion;
But who, alas! can love, and then be wise?
    Not that Remorse did not oppose Temptation;
A little still she strove, and much repented,   935
And whispering "I will ne'er consent"—consented.

118

'Tis said that Xerxes[19] offered a reward
    To those who could invent him a new pleasure:
Methinks the requisition's rather hard,
    And must have cost his Majesty a treasure: 940
For my part, I'm a moderate-minded bard,
    Fond of a little love (which I call leisure);
I care not for new pleasures, as the old
Are quite enough for me, so they but hold.

119

Oh Pleasure! you're indeed a pleasant thing,   945
    Although one must be damned for you, no doubt:
I make a resolution every spring
    Of reformation, ere the year run out,
But somehow, this my vestal vow takes wing,
    Yet still, I trust, it may be kept throughout: 950
I'm very sorry, very much ashamed,
And mean, next winter, to be quite reclaimed.

19. Persian king, fifth century B.C.

Fact Questions and Exercises

1. According to the narrator of *Don Juan,* what is his "method" for telling the story?

2. What country serves as the setting for *Don Juan*?
3. Who is described as "Perfect she was"?
4. In line 144, what does the narrator mean when he says that Don José went "plucking various fruit"?
5. Identify Donna Julia.
6. What is "much more common where the climate's sultry"?
7. Describe Don Juan at age sixteen.

For Discussion and Writing

1. Characterize the narrator of *Don Juan*. What is his attitude toward women? Toward Juan? Toward his own verse? Is the narrator's "shocked" attitude toward immorality sincere? Ironic? How does the narrator reveal his own character?
2. What are some of the things that Byron is satirizing in *Don Juan*? Is Byron really upset by these things, or does he look on them with a mild, humorous attitude? Is Byron upholding conventional morality and society, or is he in favor of the unorthodox or free individual? Byron once wrote that if he laughed at any mortal thing, it was so that he would not weep: Could this statement apply to *Don Juan*? Explain your answer.

Percy Bysshe Shelley [1792–1822]

Shelley was born in Sussex, England. A member of an old, aristocratic family, Shelley rebelled against his heritage and devoted himself to poetry and radical politics. In 1811 he was expelled from Oxford because of his avowed atheism. In 1818 he left England for Italy; he never returned to his homeland. During the following year he wrote most of his best poems, including "Ode to the West Wind." In the past, many critics have viewed Shelley's poetry as the work of an immature and shoddy writer; more recently, however, Shelley's poems have received greater appreciation, especially for their adept handling of symbolism.

Ode to the West Wind

1

O wild West Wind, thou breath of Autumn's being,
Thou, from whose unseen presence the leaves dead
Are driven, like ghosts from an enchanter fleeing,

Yellow, and black, and pale, and hectic red,
Pestilence-stricken multitudes: O thou,   5
Who chariotest to their dark wintry bed

The wingèd seeds, where they lie cold and low,
Each like a corpse within its grave, until
Thine azure sister of the Spring shall blow

Her clarion o'er the dreaming earth, and fill   10
(Driving sweet buds like flocks to feed in air)
With living hues and odors plain and hill:

Wild Spirit, which art moving everywhere;
Destroyer and preserver; hear, oh, hear!

2

Thou on whose stream, mid the steep sky's commotion,   15
Loose clouds like earth's decaying leaves are shed,
Shook from the tangled boughs of Heaven and Ocean,

Angels of rain and lightning: there are spread
On the blue surface of thine aëry surge,
Like the bright hair uplifted from the head   20

Of some fierce Maenad,[1] even from the dim verge
Of the horizon to the zenith's height,
The locks of the approaching storm. Thou dirge

Of the dying year, to which this closing night
Will be the dome of a vast sepulcher,   25
Vaulted with all thy congregated might

Of vapors, from whose solid atmosphere
Black rain, and fire, and hail will burst: oh, hear!

3

Thou who didst waken from his summer dreams
The blue Mediterranean, where he lay,   30
Lulled by the coil of his crystálline streams,

Beside a pumice isle in Baiae's bay,[2]
And saw in sleep old palaces and towers
Quivering within the wave's intenser day,

All overgrown with azure moss and flowers   35
So sweet, the sense faints picturing them! Thou
For whose path the Atlantic's level powers

Cleave themselves into chasms, while far below
The sea-blooms and the oozy woods which wear
The sapless foliage of the ocean, know   40

Thy voice, and suddenly grow gray with fear,
And tremble and despoil themselves: oh, hear!

---

1. A woman who danced wildly at the worship of Dionysus. 2. Location of the villas of Roman emperors, near Naples.

4

If I were a dead leaf thou mightest bear;
If I were a swift cloud to fly with thee;
A wave to pant beneath thy power, and share   45

The impulse of thy strength, only less free
Than thou, O uncontrollable! If even
I were as in my boyhood, and could be

The comrade of thy wanderings over Heaven,
As then, when to outstrip thy skyey speed   50
Scarce seem a vision; I would ne'er have striven

As thus with thee in prayer in my sore need.
Oh, lift me as a wave, a leaf, a cloud!
I fall upon the thorns of life! I bleed!

A heavy weight of hours has chained and bowed   55
One too like thee: tameless, and swift, and proud.

5

Make me thy lyre, even as the forest is:
What if my leaves are falling like its own!
The tumult of thy mighty harmonies

Will take from both a deep, autumnal tone,   60
Sweet though in sadness. Be thou, Spirit fierce,
My spirit! Be thou me, impetuous one!

Drive my dead thoughts over the universe
Like withered leaves to quicken a new birth!
And, by the incantation of this verse,   65

Scatter, as from an unextinguished hearth
Ashes and sparks, my words among mankind!
Be through my lips to unawakened earth

The trumpet of a prophecy! O Wind,
If Winter comes, can Spring be far behind?   70

To a Skylark *

Hail to thee, blithe Spirit!   a
   Bird thou never wert,   b
 That from Heaven, or near it,   a
   Pourest thy full heart   b
In profuse strains of unpremeditated art.   b   5

* A common largely brown Old World lark, noted for its song esp. as uttered in vertical flight.

Higher still and higher
    From the earth thou springest
Like a cloud of fire;
    The blue deep thou wingest,
And singing still dost soar, and soaring ever singest.   10

In the golden lightning
    Of the sunken sun,
O'er which clouds are bright'ning,
    Thou dost float and run;
Like an unbodied joy whose race is just begun.   15

The pale purple even
    Melts around thy flight;
Like a star of Heaven,
    In the broad daylight
Thou art unseen, but yet I hear thy shrill delight,   20

Keen as are the arrows
    Of that silver sphere,[3]
Whose intense lamp narrows
    In the white dawn clear
Until we hardly see—we feel that it is there.   25

All the earth and air
    With thy voice is loud,
As, when night is bare,
    From one lonely cloud
The moon rains out her beams, and Heaven is overflowed.   30

What thou art we know not;
    What is most like thee?
From rainbow clouds there flow not
    Drops so bright to see
As from thy presence showers a rain of melody.   35

Like a Poet hidden
    In the light of thought,
Singing hymns unbidden,
    Till the world is wrought
To sympathy with hopes and fears it heeded not: 40

Like a high-born maiden
    In a palace tower,
Soothing her love-laden
    Soul in secret hour
With music sweet as love, which overflows her bower: 45

3. A star.

Simile ⟵ Like a glowworm golden
          In a <u>dell</u> of dew, *small valley*
       Scattering <u>unbeholden</u> *under no obligation*
          Its aërial hue *color emitted in the air*
Among the flowers and grass, which screen it from the view!   50

11   ⟵—Like a rose embowered *to shelter or enclose*
          In its own green leaves,
       By warm winds deflowered,
          Till the scent it gives
Makes faint with too much sweet those heavy-wingéd thieves: 55

12   Sound of <u>vernal</u> showers *fresh, new like spring*
          On the twinkling grass,
       Rain-awakened flowers,
          All that ever was
Joyous, and clear, and fresh, thy music doth <u>surpass</u>: *go beyond*   60

Apostrophe 13 Teach us, Sprite or Bird, *disembodied spirit, soul*
          What sweet thoughts are thine:
       I have never heard
          Praise of love or wine
That <u>panted</u> forth a flood of rapture so divine.   65
breathe quickly

14 Chorus Hymeneal,[4]
          Or triumphal chant,
       Matched with thine would be all
          But an empty <u>vaunt</u>, *Brag, Boast*
A thing wherein we feel there is some hidden want.   70

15 What objects are the fountains
          Of thy happy strain?
       What fields, or waves, or mountains?
          What shapes of sky or plain?
What love of thine own kind? what ignorance of pain?   75

16 With thy clear keen joyance
          <u>Languor</u> cannot be: *weakness or weariness of body or mind*
       Shadow of annoyance
          Never came near thee:
Thou lovest—but ne'er knew love's sad <u>satiety</u>. *overindulgence*   80

17 Waking or asleep,
          Thou of death must <u>deem</u> *to judge*
       Things more true and deep,
          Than we mortals dream,
Or how could thy notes flow in such a crystal stream?   85

4. A wedding chorus.
clear unbroken flow

We look before and after,
　　And pine for what is not: *yearn intensely*
Our sincerest laughter
　　With some pain is fraught; *full of-loaded*
Our sweetest songs are those that tell of saddest thought. 　90

Yet if we could scorn *a feeling of extreme contempt*
　　Hate, and pride, and fear;
If we were things born
　　Not to shed a tear,
I know not how thy joy we ever should come near. 　95

Better than all measures
　　Of delightful sound,
Better than all treasures
　　That in books are found,
Thy skill to poet were, thou scorner of the ground! 　100

Teach me half the gladness
　　That thy brain must know,
Such harmonious madness
　　From my lips would flow
The world should listen then—as I am listening now. 　105

Stanzas Written in Dejection, Near Naples

1
The sun is warm, the sky is clear,
　　The waves are dancing fast and bright,
Blue isles and snowy mountains wear
　　The purple noon's transparent might,
　　The breath of the moist earth is light, 　5
Around its unexpanded buds;
　　Like many a voice of one delight,
The winds, the birds, the ocean floods,
The City's voice itself is soft like Solitude's.

2
I see the Deep's untrampled floor 　10
　　With green and purple seaweeds strown:
I see the waves upon the shore,
　　Like light dissolved in star-showers, thrown:
　　I sit upon the sands alone—
The lightning of the noontide ocean 　15
　　Is flashing round me, and a tone
Arises from its measured motion;
How sweet! did any heart now share in my emotion.

3

Alas! I have nor hope nor health,   20
　　Nor peace within nor calm around,
Nor that content surpassing wealth
　　The sage in meditation found,
　　And walked with inward glory crowned—
Nor fame, nor power, nor love, nor leisure.
　　Others I see whom these surround—   25
Smiling they live, and call life pleasure;
To me that cup has been dealt in another measure.

4

Yet now despair itself is mild,
　　Even as the winds and waters are;
I could lie down like a tired child,   30
　　And weep away the life of care
　　Which I have borne and yet must bear,
Till death like sleep might steal on me,
　　And I might feel in the warm air
My cheek grow cold, and hear the sea   35
Breathe o'er my dying brain its last monotony.

5

Some might lament that I were cold,
　　As I, when this sweet day is gone,
Which my lost heart, too soon grown old,
　　Insults with this untimely moan;   40
　　They might lament—for I am one
Whom men love not—and yet regret,
　　Unlike this day, which, when the sun
　　Shall on its stainless glory set,
Will linger, though enjoyed, like joy in memory yet.   45

Hymn to Intellectual Beauty

1

The awful shadow of some unseen Power
　　Floats through unseen among us—visiting
　　This various world with as inconstant wing
As summer winds that creep from flower to flower.
Like moonbeams that behind some piny mountain shower,   5
　　It visits with inconstant glance
　　Each human heart and countenance;
Like hues and harmonies of evening—
　　Like clouds in starlight widely spread—
　　Like memory of music fled—   10
　　Like aught that for its grace may be
Dear, and yet dearer for its mystery.

2

Spirit of BEAUTY, that dost consecrate
    With thine own hues all thou dost shine upon
    Of human thought or form—where art thou gone?
Why dost thou pass away and leave our state,   15
This dim vast vale of tears, vacant and desolate?
        Ask why the sunlight not forever
        Weaves rainbows o'er yon mountain river,
Why aught should fail and fade that once is shown,   20
        Why fear and dream and death and birth
        Cast on the daylight of this earth
        Such gloom—why man has such a scope
For love and hate, despondency and hope?

3

No voice from some sublimer world hath ever   25
    To sage or poet these responses given—
    Therefore the names of Daemon, Ghost, and Heaven,
Remain the records of their vain endeavor,
Frail spells—whose uttered charm might not avail to sever,
        From all we hear and all we see,   30
        Doubt, chance, and mutability.
Thy light alone—like mist o'er mountains driven,
        Or music by the night wind sent
        Through strings of some still instrument,
        Or moonlight on a midnight stream,   35
Gives grace and truth to life's unquiet dream.

4

Love, Hope, and Self-esteem, like clouds depart
    And come, for some uncertain moments lent.
    Man were immortal, and omnipotent,
Didst thou, unknown and awful as thou art,   40
Keep with thy glorious train firm state within his heart.
        Thou messenger of sympathies,
        That wax and wane in lovers' eyes—
Thou—that to human thought art nourishment,
        Like darkness to a dying flame!   45
        Depart not as thy shadow came,
        Depart not—lest the grave should be,
Like life and fear, a dark reality.

5

While yet a boy I sought for ghosts, and sped
    Through many a listening chamber, cave and ruin,   50
    And starlight wood, with fearful steps pursuing
Hopes of high talk with the departed dead.
I called on poisonous names with which our youth is fed;
        I was not heard—I saw them not—
        When musing deeply on the lot   55

Of life, at that sweet time when winds are wooing
        All vital things that wake to bring
        News of birds and blossoming—
        Sudden, thy shadow fell on me;
I shrieked, and clasped my hands in ecstasy!   60

6

I vowed that I would dedicate my powers
        To thee and thine—have I not kept the vow?
        With beating heart and streaming eyes, even now
I call the phantoms of a thousand hours
Each from his voiceless grave: they have in visioned bowers   65
        Of studious zeal or love's delight
        Outwatched with me the envious night—
They know that never joy illumed my brow
        Unlinked with hope that thou wouldst free
        This world from its dark slavery,   70
        That thou—O awful LOVELINESS,
Wouldst give whate'er these words cannot express.

7

The day becomes more solemn and serene
        When noon is past—there is a harmony
        In autumn, and a luster in its sky,   75
Which through the summer is not heard or seen,
As if it could not be, as if it had not been!
        Thus let thy power, which like the truth
        Of nature on my passive youth
Descended, to my onward life supply   80
        Its calm—to one who worships thee,
        And every form containing thee,
        Whom, SPIRIT fair, thy spells did bind
To fear himself, and love all human kind.

Fact Questions and Exercises

1. What are the powers that Shelley attributes to the West Wind? What does the speaker ask the wind to do for him?
2. In "To a Skylark," what do our "sweetest songs" tell of? What does the speaker ask the skylark to teach him?
3. In "Stanzas Written in Dejection, Near Naples," why is the speaker in despair?
4. In "Hymn to Intellectual Beauty," what questions does the speaker ask of Beauty? What happened to the speaker when he was "yet a boy"?

For Discussion and Writing

1. Discuss the themes of despair and hope in Shelley's poems. Would you say that the personas of Shelley's poems are idealists or realists? Or, are they

somewhere between the two? What factors seem to cause despair? Hope? Joy?

2. How do you interpret the various symbols Shelley uses—the wind and the skylark, for example? What do these symbols represent? Is there any particular significance to the fact that most of Shelley's symbols are taken from nature? Does Shelley use these symbols effectively?

John Keats [1795–1821]

Keats was born in London, England, the son of a livery stable worker. Keats studied to be an apothecary, but in 1816 he abandoned medicine to devote himself to poetry. Keats's mother had died of tuberculosis, and Keats correctly suspected that he, too, would soon die of the same disease; consequently, he applied himself desperately to his writing—in one year, 1819, he wrote almost all of his greatest poems. His poems are characterized by concrete description, intense application of the human senses, and the exploration of the meaning of art and the artist in a temporal world.

When I Have Fears

When I have fears that I may cease to be   a
    Before my pen has gleaned my teeming brain,   b
Before high-piled books, in charact'ry,[1]   a
    Hold like rich garners the full-ripened grain;   b
When I behold, upon the night's starred face,   c   5
    Huge cloudy symbols of a high romance,   d
And think that I may never live to trace   c
    Their shadows, with the magic hand of chance;   d
And when I feel, fair creature of an hour,   e
    That I shall never look upon thee more,   f   10
Never have relish in the faery[2] power   e
    Of unreflecting love!—then on the shore   f
Of the wide world I stand alone, and think   g
Till Love and Fame to nothingness do sink.   g

The Eve of St. Agnes

1

St. Agnes' Eve—Ah, bitter chill it was!
The owl, for all his feathers, was a-cold;

1. Written symbols or letters. 2. Magic.

The hare limped trembling through the frozen grass,
And silent was the flock in woolly fold:
Numb were the Beadsman's[3] fingers, while he told   5
His rosary, and while his frosted breath,
Like pious incense from a censer old,
Seemed taking flight for heaven, without a death,
Past the sweet Virgin's picture, while his prayer he saith.

2

His prayer he saith, this patient, holy man;   10
Then takes his lamp, and riseth from his knees,
And back returneth, meager, barefoot, wan,
Along the chapel aisle by slow degrees:
The sculptured dead, on each side, seem to freeze,
Imprisoned in black, purgatorial rails: 15
Knights, ladies, praying in dumb orat'ries,
He passeth by; and his weak spirit fails
To think how they may ache in icy hoods and mails.

3

Northward he turneth through a little door,
And scarce three steps, ere Music's golden tongue   20
Flattered to tears this aged man and poor;
But no—already had his deathbell rung:
The joys of all his life were said and sung:
His was harsh penance on St. Agnes' Eve:
Another way he went, and soon among   25
Rough ashes sat he for his soul's reprieve,
And all night kept awake, for sinners' sake to grieve.

4

That ancient Beadsman heard the prelude soft;
And so it chanced, for many a door was wide,
From hurry to and fro. Soon, up aloft,   30
The silver, snarling trumpets 'gan to chide:
The level chambers, ready with their pride,
Where glowing to receive a thousand guests:
The carvéd angels, ever eager-eyed,
Stared, where upon their heads the cornice rests,   35
With hair blown back, and wings put crosswise on their breasts.

5

At length burst in the argent revelry,
With plume, tiara, and all rich array,
Numerous as shadows haunting faerily
The brain, new stuffed, in youth, with triumphs gay   40
Of old romance. These let us wish away,

3. A man paid to pray for someone else.

And turn, sole-thoughted, to one Lady there,
Whose heart had brooded, all that wintry day,
On love, and winged St. Agnes' saintly care,
As she had heard old dames full many times declare.   45

6

They told her how, upon St. Agnes' Eve,
Young virgins might have visions of delight,
And soft adorings from their loves receive
Upon the honeyed middle of the night,
If ceremonies due they did aright;   50
As, supperless to bed they must retire,
And couch supine their beauties, lily white;
Nor look behind, nor sideways, but require
Of Heaven with upward eyes for all that they desire.

7

Full of this whim was thoughtful Madeline: 55
The music, yearning like a God in pain,
She scarcely heard: her maiden eyes divine,
Fixed on the floor, saw many a sweeping train
Pass by—she heeded not at all: in vain
Came many a tiptoe, amorous cavalier,   60
And back retired; not cooled by high disdain;
But she saw not: her heart was otherwhere:
She sighed for Agnes' dreams, the sweetest of the year.

8

She danced along with vague, regardless eyes,
Anxious her lips, her breathing quick and short: 65
The hallowed hour was near at hand: she sighs
Amid the timbrels,⁴ and the thronged resort
Of whisperers in anger, or in sport;
'Mid looks of love, defiance, hate, and scorn,
Hoodwinked with faery fancy; all amort,⁵   70
Save to St. Agnes and her lambs unshorn,
And all the bliss to be before tomorrow morn.

9

So, purposing each moment to retire,
She lingered still. Meantime, across the moors,
Had come young Porphyro, with heart on fire   75
For Madeline. Beside the portal doors,
Buttressed from moonlight, stands he, and implores
All saints to give him sight of Madeline,
But for one moment in the tedious hours,
That he might gaze and worship all unseen;   80

4. Drums.   5. Dead.

Perchance speak, kneel, touch, kiss—in sooth such things have
      been.

10
    He ventures in: let no buzzed whisper tell:
    All eyes be muffled, or a hundred swords
    Will storm his heart, Love's fev'rous citadel:
    For him, those chambers held barbarian hordes,   85
    Hyena foemen, and hot-blooded lords,
    Whose very dogs would execrations howl
    Against his lineage: not one breast affords
    Him any mercy, in that mansion foul,
Save one old beldame,[6] weak in body and in soul.   90

11
    Ah, happy chance! the aged creature came,
    Shuffling along with ivory-headed wand,
    To where he stood, hid from the torch's flame,
    Behind a broad hall-pillar, far beyond
    The sound of merriment and chorus bland: 95
    He startled her; but soon she knew his face,
    And grasped his fingers in her palsied hand,
    Saying, "Mercy, Porphyro! hie thee from this place;
They are all here tonight, the whole bloodthirsty race!

12
    "Get hence! get hence! there's dwarfish Hildebrand;   100
    He had a fever late, and in the fit
    He curséd thee and thine, both house and land:
    Then there's that old Lord Maurice, not a whit
    More tame for his gray hairs—Alas me! flit!
    Flit like a ghost away."—"Ah, Gossip dear,   105
    We're safe enough; here in this armchair sit,
    And tell me how"—"Good Saints! not here, not here;
Follow me, child, or else these stones will be thy bier."

13
    He followed through a lowly archéd way,
    Brushing the cobwebs with his lofty plume,   110
    And as she muttered "Well-a—well-a-day!"
    He found him in a little moonlight room,
    Pale, latticed, chill, and silent as a tomb.
    "Now tell me where is Madeline," said he,
    "O tell me, Angela, by the holy loom   115
    Which none but secret sisterhood may see,
When they St. Agnes' wool are weaving piously."

6. Old woman.

14

"St. Agnes! Ah! it is St. Agnes' Eve—
Yet men will murder upon holy days:
Thou must hold water in a witch's sieve,   120
And be liege lord of all the Elves and Fays,[7]
To venture so: it fills me with amaze
To see thee, Porphyro!—St. Agnes' Eve!
God's help! my lady fair the conjuror plays
This very night: good angels her deceive!
But let me laugh awhile, I've mickle[8] time to grieve."   125

15

Feebly she laugheth in the languid moon,
While Porphyro upon her face doth look,
Like puzzled urchin on an aged crone
Who keepeth closed a wondrous riddle-book,   130
As spectacled she sits in chimney nook.
But soon his eyes grew brilliant, when she told
His lady's purpose: and he scarce could brook
Tears, as the thought of those enchantments cold,
And Madeline asleep in lap of legends old.   135

16

Sudden a thought came like a full-blown rose,
Flushing his brow, and in his painéd heart
Made purple riot: then doth he propose
A stratagem, that makes the beldame start:
"A cruel man and impious thou art: 140
Sweet lady, let her pray, and sleep, and dream
Alone with her good angels, far apart
From wicked men like thee. Go, go!—I deem
Thou canst not surely be the same that thou didst seem."

17

"I will not harm her, by all saints I swear,"   145
Quoth Porphyro: "O may I ne'er find grace
When my weak voice shall whisper its last prayer,
If one of her soft ringlets I displace,
Or look with ruffian passion in her face:
Good Angela, believe me by these tears;   150
Or I will, even in a moment's space,
Awake, with horrid shout, my foemen's ears,
And beard them, though they be more fanged than wolves and
      bears."

18

"Ah! why wilt thou affright a feeble soul?
A poor, weak, palsy-stricken, churchyard thing,   155

7. Fairies. 8. Much.

Whose passing bell may ere the midnight toll;
Whose prayers for thee, each morn and evening,
Were never missed."—Thus plaining,[9] doth she bring
A gentler speech from burning Porphyro;
So woeful and of such deep sorrowing,   160
That Angela gives promise she will do
Whatever he shall wish, betide her weal or woe.

19

Which was, to lead him, in close secrecy,
Even to Madeline's chamber, and there hide
Him in a closet, of such privacy   165
That he might see her beauty unespied,
And win perhaps that night a peerless bride,
While legioned faeries paced the coverlet,
And pale enchantment held her sleepy-eyed.
Never on such a night have lovers met,   170
Since Merlin paid his Demon all the monstrous debt.[10]

20

"It shall be as thou wishest," said the Dame:
"All cates and dainties shall be storéd there
Quickly on this feast night: by the tambour frame[11]
Her own lute thou wilt see: no time to spare,   175
For I am slow and feeble, and scarce dare
On such a catering trust my dizzy head.
Wait here, my child, with patience; kneel in prayer
The while: Ah! thou must needs the lady wed,
Or may I never leave my grave among the dead."   180

21

So saying, she hobbled off with busy fear.
The lover's endless minutes slowly passed:
The dame returned, and whispered in his ear
To follow her; with aged eyes aghast
From fright of dim espial. Safe at last,   185
Through many a dusky gallery, they gain
The maiden's chamber, silken, hushed, and chaste;
Where Porphyro took covert, pleased amain.
His poor guide hurried back with agues in her brain.

22

Her falt'ring hand upon the balustrade,   190
Old Angela was feeling for the stair,
When Madeline, St. Agnes' charméd maid,
Rose, like a missioned spirit, unaware:
With silver taper's light, and pious care,
She turned, and down the aged gossip led   195

---

9. Complaining.   **10.** Merlin, a wizard in the legends of King Arthur, lost his life when an evil woman turned one of his own spells against him.   **11.** An embroidery hoop.

To a safe level matting. Now prepare,
   Young Porphyro, for gazing on that bed;
She comes, she comes again, like ringdove frayed and fled.

23

   Out went the taper as she hurried in;
   Its little smoke, in pallid moonshine, died: 200
   She closed the door, she panted, all akin
   To spirits of the air, and visions wide:
   No uttered syllable, or, woe betide!
   But to her heart, her heart was voluble,
   Paining with eloquence her balmy side;   205
   As though a tongueless nightingale should swell
Her throat in vain, and die, heart-stifled, in her dell.

24

   A casement high and triple-arched there was,
   All garlanded with carven imag'ries
   Of fruits, and flowers, and bunches of knot-grass,   210
   And diamonded with panes of quaint device,
   Innumerable of stains and splendid dyes,
   As are the tiger-moth's deep-damasked wings;
   And in the midst, 'mong thousand heraldries,
   And twilight saints, and dim emblazonings,   215
A shielded scutcheon blushed with blood of queens and kings.

25

   Full on this casement shone the wintry moon,
   And threw warm gules[12] on Madeline's fair breast,
   As down she knelt for heaven's grace and boon;
   Rose-bloom fell on her hands, together pressed,
   And on her silver cross soft amethyst,
   And on her hair a glory, like a saint:
   She seemed a splendid angel, newly dressed,
   Save wings, for heaven—Porphyro grew faint:
She knelt, so pure a thing, so free from mortal taint.   225

26

   Anon his heart revives: her vespers done,
   Of all its wreathéd pearls her hair she frees;
   Unclasps her warméd jewels one by one;
   Loosens her fragrant bodice; by degrees
   Her rich attire creeps rustling to her knees;   230
   Half-hidden, like a mermaid in sea-weed,
   Pensive awhile she dreams awake, and sees,
   In fancy, fair St. Agnes in her bed,
But dares not look behind, or all the charm is fled.

12. The color red as it appears in a coat of arms. Here, the moon shines through a stained-glass window, projecting the red pattern onto Madeline.

27

Soon, trembling in her soft and chilly nest,   235
In sort of wakeful swoon, perplexed she lay,
Until the poppied warmth of sleep oppressed
Her soothéd limbs, and soul fatigued away;
Flown, like a thought, until the morrow-day;
Blissfully havened both from joy and pain;   240
Clasped like a missal where swart Paynims[13] pray;
Blinded alike from sunshine and from rain,
As though a rose should shut, and be a bud again.

28

Stol'n to this paradise, and so entranced,
Porphyro gazed upon her empty dress,   245
And listened to her breathing, if it chanced
To wake into a slumberous tenderness;
Which when he heard, that minute did he bless,
And breathed himself: then from the closet crept,
Noiseless as fear in a wide wilderness,   250
And over the hushed carpet, silent, stepped,
And 'tween the curtains peeped, where, lo!—how fast she slept.

29

Then by the bedside, where the faded moon
Made a dim, silver twilight, soft he set
A table, and, half anguished, threw thereon   255
A cloth of woven crimson, gold, and jet—
O for some drowsy Morphean amulet!
The boisterous, midnight, festive clarion,
The kettledrum, and far-heard clarinet,
Affray his ears, though but in dying tone—   260
The hall door shuts again, and all the noise is gone.

30

And still she slept an azure-lidded sleep,
In blanchéd linen, smooth, and lavendered,
While he from forth the closet brought a heap
Of candied apple, quince, and plum, and gourd;   265
With jellies soother than the creamy curd,
And lucent syrups, tinct with cinnamon:
Manna and dates, in argosy transferred
From Fez; and spicéd dainties, every one,
From silken Samarcand to cedared Lebanon.   270

31

These delicates he heaped with glowing hand
On golden dishes and in baskets bright

13. Pagans.

Of wreathéd silver: sumptuous they stand
In the retiréd quiet of the night,
Filling the chilly room with perfume light.—   275
"And now, my love, my seraph fair, awake!
Thou art my heaven, and I thine eremite:
Open thine eyes, for meek St. Agnes' sake,
Or I shall drowse beside thee, so my soul doth ache."

32
Thus whispering, his warm, unnervéd arm   280
Sank in her pillow. Shaded was her dream
By the dusk curtains: 'twas a midnight charm
Impossible to melt as icéd stream:
The lustrous salvers in the moonlight gleam;
Broad golden fringe upon the carpet lies: 285
It seemed he never, never could redeem
From such a steadfast spell his lady's eyes;
So mused awhile, entoiled in wooféd fantasies.

33
Awakening up, he took her hollow lute—
Tumultuous—and, in chords that tenderest be,   290
He played an ancient ditty, long since mute,
In Provence called "La belle dame sans merci"[14]
Close to her ear touching the melody;
Wherewith disturbed, she uttered a soft moan:
He ceased—she panted quick—and suddenly   295
Her blue affrayéd eyes wide open shone:
Upon his knees he sank, pale as smooth-sculptured stone.

34
Her eyes were open, but she still beheld,
Now wide awake, the vision of her sleep:
There was a painful change, that nigh expelled   300
The blisses of her dream so pure and deep,
At which fair Madeline began to weep,
And moan forth witless words with many a sigh;
While still her gaze on Porphyro would keep,
Who knelt, with joinéd hands and piteous eye,   305
Fearing to move or speak, she looked so dreamingly.

35
"Ah, Porphyro!" said she, "but even now
Thy voice was at sweet tremble in mine ear,
Made tunable with every sweetest vow;
And those sad eyes were spiritual and clear: 310
How changed thou art! how pallid, chill, and drear!
Give me that voice again, my Porphyro,

14. "The beautiful lady without mercy."

Those looks immortal, those complainings dear!
Oh leave me not in this eternal woe,
For if thou diest, my Love, I know not where to go."   315

36
Beyond a mortal man impassioned far
At these voluptuous accents, he arose,
Ethereal, flushed, and like a throbbing star
Seen mid the sapphire heaven's deep repose;
Into her dream he melted, as the rose   320
Blendeth its odor with the violet—
Solution sweet: meantime the frost-wind blows
Like Love's alarum pattering the sharp sleet
Against the windowpanes; St. Agnes' moon hath set.

37
'Tis dark: quick pattereth the flaw-blown sleet: 325
"This is no dream, my bride, my Madeline!"
'Tis dark: the icéd gusts still rave and beat:
"No dream, alas! alas! and woe is mine!
Porphyro will leave me hear to fade and pine.—
Cruel! what traitor could thee hither bring?   330
I curse not, for my heart is lost in thine,
Though thou forsakest a deceivéd thing—
A dove forlorn and lost with sick unprunéd wing."

38
"My Madeline! sweet dreamer! lovely bride!
Say, may I be for aye thy vassal blest?   335
Thy beauty's shield, heart-shaped and vermcil[15] dyed:
Ah, silver shrine, here will I take my rest
After so many hours of toil and quest,
A famished pilgrim—saved by miracle.
Though I have found, I will not rob thy nest   340
Saving of thy sweet self; if thou think'st well
To trust, fair Madeline, to no rude infidel.

39
"Hark! 'tis an elfin-storm from faery land,
Of haggard seeming, but a boon indeed:
Arise—arise! the morning is at hand—   345
The bloated wassaillers will never heed—
Let us away, my love, with happy speed;
There are no ears to hear, or eyes to see—
Drowned all in Rhenish and the sleepy mead:[16]
Awake! arise! my love, and fearless be,   350
For o'er the southern moors I have a home for thee."

15. Vermilion.   16. Wine from the Rhine, and a drink made of water and honey.

40

She hurried at his words, beset with fears,
For there were sleeping dragons all around,
At glaring watch, perhaps, with ready spears—
Down the wide stairs a darkling way they found.—   355
In all the house was heard no human sound.
A chain-drooped lamp was flickering by each door;
The arias, rich with horseman, hawk, and hound,
Fluttered in the besieging wind's uproar;
And the long carpets rose along the gusty floor.   360

41

They glide, like phantoms, into the wide hall;
Like phantoms, to the iron porch, they glide;
Where lay the Porter, in uneasy sprawl,
With a huge empty flagon by his side:
The wakeful bloodhound rose, and shook his hide,   365
But his sagacious eye an inmate owns.[17]
By one, and one, the bolts full easy slide:
The chains lie silent on the footworn stones;
The key turns, and the door upon its hinges groans.

42

And they are gone: aye, ages long ago   370
These lovers fled away into the storm.
That night the Baron dreamt of many a woe,
And all his warrior-guests, with shade and form
Of witch, and demon, and large coffin-worm,
Were long be-nightmared. Angela the old   375
Died palsy-twitched, with meager face deform;
The Beadsman, after thousand aves told,
For aye unsought for slept among his ashes cold.

Ode to a Nightingale

1

My heart aches, and a drowsy numbness pains
    My sense, as though of hemlock I had drunk,
Or emptied some dull opiate to the drains
    One minute past, and Lethe-wards[18] had sunk:
'Tis not through envy of thy happy lot,   5
    But being too happy in thine happiness—
        That thou, light-wingéd Dryad[19] of the trees,
            In some melodious plot
Of beechen green, and shadows numberless,
        Singest of summer in full-throated ease.   10

17. Sees, recognizes. 18. Lethe is the river of forgetfulness in Hades. 19. In Greek
mythology, a nymph or fairy presiding over trees.

What leaf-fringed legend haunts about thy shape
    Of deities or mortals, or of both, 5
        In Tempe or the dales of Arcady?[26]
    What men or gods are these? What maidens loath?
What mad pursuit? What struggle to escape?
        What pipes and timbrels? What wild ecstasy? 10

      2

Heard melodies are sweet, but those unheard
    Are sweeter; therefore, ye soft pipes, play on;
Not to the sensual ear, but, more endeared,
    Pipe to the spirit ditties of no tone:
Fair youth, beneath the trees, thou canst not leave 15
    Thy song, nor ever can those trees be bare;
        Bold Lover, never, never canst thou kiss,
Though winning near the goal—yet, do not grieve;
        She cannot fade, though thou hast not thy bliss,
    Forever wilt thou love, and she be fair! 20

      3

Ah, happy, happy boughs! that cannot shed
    Your leaves, nor ever bid the Spring adieu;
And, happy melodist, unweariéd,
    Forever piping songs forever new;
More happy love! more happy, happy love! 25
    Forever warm and still to be enjoyed,
        Forever panting, and forever young;
All breathing human passion far above,
    That leaves a heart high-sorrowful and cloyed,
        A burning forehead, and a parching tongue. 30

      4

Who are these coming to the sacrifice?
    To what green altar, O mysterious priest,
Lead'st thou that heifer lowing at the skies,
    And all her silken flanks with garlands dressed?
What little town by river or sea shore, 35
    Or mountain-built with peaceful citadel,
        Is emptied of this folk, this pious morn?
And, little town, thy streets forevermore
    Will silent be; and not a soul to tell
        Why thou art desolate, can e'er return. 40

     5

O Attic[27] shape! Fair attitude! with brede[28]
    Of marble men and maidens overwrought,

26. Arcadia in Greece; the "dales" represent rural beauty. 27. That is, Greek shape. 28. A woven pattern.

With forest branches and the trodden weed;
    Thou, silent form, dost tease us out of thought
As doth eternity: Cold Pastoral! *natural, simple*   45
    When old age shall this generation waste,
      Thou shalt remain, in midst of other woe
Than ours, a friend to man, to whom thou say'st: *to urn*
"Beauty is truth, truth beauty,"—that is all — *inscription*
    Ye know on earth, and all ye need to know. *urn*   50

He's growing old & he knows the urn won't grow old

La Belle Dame sans Merci

O what can ail thee, Knight at arms,
    Alone and palely loitering?
The sedge has withered from the Lake
    And no birds sing!

O what can ail thee, Knight at arms,   5
    So haggard, and so woebegone?
The squirrel's granary is full
    And the harvest's done.

I see a lily on thy brow
    With anguish moist and fever dew,   10
And on thy cheeks a fading rose
    Fast withereth too.

"I met a Lady in the Meads,[29]
    Full beautiful, a faery's child,
Her hair was long, her foot was light   15
    And her eyes were wild.

"I made a Garland for her head,
    And bracelets too, and fragrant Zone;[30]
She looked at me as she did love
    And made sweet moan.   20

"I set her on my pacing steed
    And nothing else saw all day long,
For sidelong would she bend and sing
    A faery's song.

"She found me roots of relish sweet,   25
    And honey wild, and manna dew,
And sure in language strange she said
    'I love thee true.'

29. Meadows. **30.** Girdle.

"She took me to her elfin grot
    And there she wept and sighed full sore,   30
And there I shut her wild wild eyes
    With kisses four.

"And there she lulléd me asleep,
    And there I dreamed, Ah Woe betide!
The latest dream I ever dreamt   35
    On the cold hill side.

"I saw pale Kings, and Princes too,
    Pale warriors, death-pale were they all;
They cried, 'La belle dame sans merci[31]
    Thee hath in thrall!'   40

"I saw their starved lips in the gloam
    With horrid warning gapéd wide,
And I awoke, and found me here
    On the cold hill's side.

"And this is why I sojourn here,   45
    Alone and palely loitering;
Though the sedge is withered from the Lake
    And no birds sing."

To Autumn

I

Season of mists and mellow fruitfulness,
    Close bosom-friend of the maturing sun;
Conspiring with him how to load and bless
    With fruit the vines that round the thatch-eves run;   5
To bend with apples the mossed cottage-trees,
    And fill all fruit with ripeness to the core;
        To swell the gourd, and plump the hazel shells
With a sweet kernel; to set budding more,
    And still more, later flowers for the bees,   10
    Until they think warm days will never cease,
        For Summer has o'er-brimmed their clammy cells.

II

Who hath not seen thee oft amid thy store?
    Sometimes whoever seeks abroad may find
Thee sitting careless on a granary floor,   15
    Thy hair soft-lifted by the winnowing wind;

---

31. See Note 14, above.

Or on a half-reaped furrow sound asleep,
    Drowsed with the fume of poppies, while thy hook[32]
        Spares the next swath and all its twinéd flowers:
And sometimes like a gleaner thou dost keep
    Steady thy laden head across a brook;   20
    Or by a cider-press, with patient look,
        Thou watchest the last oozings hours by hours.

                III
Where are the songs of Spring? Ay, where are they?
    Think not of them, thou hast thy music too—
While barréd clouds bloom the soft-dying day,   25
    And touch the stubble-plains with rosy hue;
Then in a wailful choir the small gnats mourn
    Among the river sallows,[33] borne aloft
        Or sinking as the light wind lives or dies;
And full-grown lambs loud bleat from hilly bourn;[34]   30
    Hedge-crickets sing; and now with treble soft
    The red-breast whistles from a garden-croft;[35]
        And gathering swallows twitter in the skies.

32. Sickle.   **33.** Small willows.   **34.** Field.   **35.** Garden plot, small field.

Fact Questions and Exercises

1. What does the speaker fear in "When I Have Fears"?
2. In "The Eve of St. Agnes," why does Porphyro have to sneak into the mansion to see Madeline? Who helps Porphyro in his efforts to see Madeline? Ultimately, what happens to Madeline and Porphyro?
3. Describe the mood of the speaker in "Ode to a Nightingale." The speaker says that he has been "half in love"—with what?
4. Describe the scenes that are on the Grecian urn.
5. What does the knight of "La Belle Dame sans Merci" make for the Lady in the Mead? Eventually, what happens to the knight?

For Discussion and Writing

1. What is the poet's attitude toward art? What does he want his own art to accomplish? According to Keats, can art make a person "eternal"? What are the various symbols of art or creativity that Keats uses in his poems?
2. Discuss the imagery in "The Eve of St. Agnes." Does Keats present contrasting images—for instance, images of sensuality/coldness? Of smoothness/roughness? If so, how do these contrasts strengthen the various images? (See An Introduction to Reading Literature, pages 15–16.)
3. Analyze the last five lines of "Ode on a Grecian Urn." What do you think the lines mean? From this poem and the others, can you define what Keats means by "truth" and "beauty"?

Ralph Waldo Emerson [1803–1882]

Emerson was born in Boston, Massachusetts, the son of a Unitarian minister. After his father's death in 1811, the Emersons were left in poverty; nevertheless, Emerson worked his way through Harvard and Harvard Divinity School. He served as a Unitarian minister for several years, but left the church because of philosophical disagreements. In 1836 he published *Nature*, an expression of his idealism. Philosophically, Emerson insisted upon individual freedom, promoted the belief in a universal divinity that he called the Over-Soul, and spoke for the virtues of energy and genius. Overall, however, his writings are vague and contradictory; his great influence on nineteenth-century American writing is as much the result of his pithy, aphoristic style as of his idealism. Though noted primarily as an essayist, Emerson has become more and more respected as a poet.

Concord Hymn

Sung at the Completion of the
Battle Monument, July 4, 1837

By the rude bridge that arched the flood,
　　Their flag to April's breeze unfurled,
Here once the embattled farmers stood
　　And fired the shot heard round the world.

The foe long since in silence slept;　　　　　　　　　5
　　Alike the conqueror silent sleeps;
And Time the ruined bridge has swept
　　Down the dark stream which seaward creeps.

On this green bank, by this soft stream,
　　We set to-day a votive stone;　　　　　　　　　　10
That memory may their deed redeem,
　　When, like our sires, our sons are gone.

Spirit, that made those heroes dare
　　To die, and leave their children free,
Bid Time and Nature gently spare　　　　　　　　　15
　　The shaft we raise to them and thee.

The Rhodora

On Being Asked, Whence is the Flower?

In May, when sea-winds pierced our solitudes,
I found the fresh Rhodora in the woods,

Spreading its leafless blooms in a damp nook,
To please the desert and the sluggish brook.
The purple petals, fallen in the pool,   5
Made the black water with their beauty gay;
Here might the red-bird come his plumes to cool,
And court the flower that cheapens his array.
Rhodora! if the sages ask thee why
This charm is wasted on the earth and sky,   10
Tell them, dear, that if eyes were made for seeing,
Then Beauty is its own excuse for being:
Why thou wert there, O rival of the rose!
I never thought to ask, I never knew;
But, in my simple ignorance, suppose   15
The self-same Power that brought me there brought you.

Brahma[1]

If the red slayer think he slays,
    Or if the slain think he is slain,
They know not well the subtle ways
    I keep, and pass, and turn again.

Far or forgot to me is near;   5
    Shadow and sunlight are the same;
The vanished gods to me appear;
    And one to me are shame and fame.

They reckon ill who leave me out;
    When me they fly, I am the wings;   10
I am the doubter and the doubt,
    And I the hymn the Brahmin sings.

The strong gods pine for my abode,
    And pine in vain the sacred Seven,[2]
But thou, meek lover of the good!   15
    Find me, and turn thy back on heaven.

1. The universal soul of the Hindu religion.   2. The Brahmin saints.

Fact Questions and Exercises

1. Where is Concord? How does this location relate to the "Concord Hymn"?
2. Who "fired the shot heard round the world"? How is Emerson using the word "heard"? What happens to the "rude bridge"?
3. What color is the rhodora?
4. Point out the contradictory elements that are enumerated in "Brahma."

For Discussion and Writing

1. Discuss Emerson's view of nature, particularly as it is presented in "Rhodora." How does the individual fit into nature? Dominate? Subserve? Become a part of it? What qualities does Emerson seem to admire most?

Edgar Allan Poe [1809–1849]

To Helen

Helen, thy beauty is to me
    Like those Nicean[1] barks of yore,
That gently, o'er a perfumed sea,
    The weary, way-worn wanderer bore
    To his own native shore.   5

On desperate seas long wont to roam,
    Thy hyacinth hair,[2] thy classic face,
Thy Naiad[3] airs have brought me home
    To the glory that was Greece
And the grandeur that was Rome.   10

Lo! in yon brilliant window-niche
    How statue-like I see thee stand!
    The agate lamp within thy hand,
Ah! Psyche,[4] from the regions which
    Are Holy Land!   15

Annabel Lee

It was many and many a year ago,
    In a kingdom by the sea,
That a maiden there lived whom you may know
    By the name of Annabel Lee;
And this maiden she lived with no other thought   5
    Than to love and be loved by me.

She was a child and I was a child,
    In this kingdom by the sea,

---

1. Poe's meaning here is uncertain; perhaps he is alluding to the sea travels of Ulysses and other ancient wanderers. 2. Again, Poe's meaning is uncertain; he may simply mean black hair. 3. In mythology, water sprites or nymphs. 4. In mythology, the maiden loved by Eros.

But we loved with a love that was more than love—
    I and my Annabel Lee—   10
With a love that the wingéd seraphs of Heaven
    Coveted her and me.

And this was the reason that, long ago,
    In this kingdom by the sea,
A wind blew out of a cloud by night   15
    Chilling my Annabel Lee;
So that her highborn kinsmen came
    And bore her away from me,
To shut her up in a sepulchre *grave, tomb*
    In this kingdom by the sea.   20

The angels, not half so happy in Heaven,
    Went envying her and me:
Yes! that was the reason (as all men know,
    In this kingdom by the sea)
That the wind came out of the cloud, chilling   25
    And killing my Annabel Lee.

But our love it was stronger by far than the love
    Of those who were older than we—
    Of many far wiser than we—
And neither the angels in Heaven above   30
    Nor the demons down under the sea,
Can ever dissever my soul from the soul
    Of the beautiful Annabel Lee:

For the moon never beams without bringing me dreams
    Of the beautiful Annabel Lee;   35
And the stars never rise but I see the bright eyes
    Of the beautiful Annabel Lee;
And so, all the night-tide, I lie down by the side
Of my darling, my darling, my life and my bride,
    In her sepulchre there by the sea—   40
    In her tomb by the side of the sea.

* Internal Rhyme

The Raven

Once upon a midnight dreary, while I pondered, weak and
    weary,   *a*
Over many a quaint and curious volume of forgotten lore—   *b*
While I nodded, nearly napping, suddenly there came a tapping,   *c*
As of some one gently rapping, rapping at my chamber door.   *b*
"'Tis some visitor," I muttered, "tapping at my chamber door—   *b* 5
    Only this and nothing more."   *b*

irregular meter
fits back into

Trochaic Octameter

Ah, distinctly I remember it was in the bleak December;
And each separate dying ember wrought its ghost upon the floor.
Eagerly I wished the morrow;—vainly I had sought to borrow
From my books surcease of sorrow—sorrow for the lost Lenore—
For the rare and radiant maiden whom the angels name Lenore—
  Nameless here for evermore.

Caesura

a enjambement
b end-stopped
c
b
b
b

And the silken, sad, uncertain rustling of each purple curtain
Thrilled me—filled me with fantastic terrors never felt before;
So that now, to still the beating of my heart, I stood repeating,
"'Tis some visitor entreating entrance at my chamber door—
Some late visitor entreating entrance at my chamber door;—
  This it is and nothing more."

15

a
b
c
b
b
b

Presently my soul grew stronger; hesitating then no longer,
"Sir," said I, "or Madam, truly your forgiveness I implore;
But the fact is I was napping, and so gently you came rapping,
And so faintly you came tapping, tapping at my chamber door,
That I scarce was sure I heard you"—here I opened wide the
      door;—
  Darkness there and nothing more.

20

not enjambement
enjambement

Deep into that darkness peering, long I stood there wondering,
      fearing,
Doubting, dreaming dreams no mortal ever dared to dream
      before;
But the silence was unbroken, and the stillness gave no token,
And the only word there spoken was the whispered word,
      "Lenore!"
This I whispered, and an echo murmured back the word,
      "Lenore!"
  Merely this and nothing more.

25

30

Back into the chamber turning, all my soul within me burning,
Soon again I heard a tapping somewhat louder than before.
"Surely," said I, "surely that is something at my window lattice;
Let me see, then, what thereat is, and this mystery explore—
Let my heart be still a moment and this mystery explore;—
  'Tis the wind and nothing more!"

35

Open here I flung the shutter, when, with many a flirt and
      flutter,
In there stepped a stately raven of the saintly days of yore.
Not the least obeisance made he; not a minute stopped or stayed
      he;
But, with mien of lord or lady, perched above my chamber
      door—

40

Perched upon a bust of Pallas[5] just above my chamber door—
      Perched, and sat, and nothing more.

Then this ebony bird beguiling my sad fancy into smiling,
By the grave and stern decorum of the countenance it wore,
"Though thy crest be shorn and shaven, thou," I said, "art sure
      no craven,   45
Ghastly grim and ancient raven wandering from the nightly
      shore—
Tell me what thy lordly name is on the night's Plutonian[6]
      shore!"
      Quoth the raven, "Nevermore."

Much I marvelled this ungainly fowl to hear discourse so plainly,
Though its answer little meaning—little relevancy bore;   50
For we cannot help agreeing that no living human being
Ever yet was blessed with seeing bird above his chamber door—
Bird or beast upon the sculptured bust above his chamber door,
      With such name as "Nevermore."

But the raven, sitting lonely on the placid bust, spoke only   55
That one word, as if his soul in that one word he did outpour.
Nothing farther then he uttered—not a feather then he
      fluttered—
Till I scarcely more than muttered, "Other friends have flown
      before—
On the morrow he will leave me, as my hopes have flown
      before."
      Then the bird said, "Nevermore."   60

Startled at the stillness broken by reply so aptly spoken,
"Doubtless," said I, "what it utters is its only stock and store
Caught from some unhappy master whom unmerciful disaster
Followed fast and followed faster till his songs one burden bore—
Till the dirges of his hope that melancholy burden bore   65
      Of 'Never—nevermore.'"

But the raven still beguiling my sad fancy into smiling,
Straight I wheeled a cushioned seat in front of bird and bust and
      door;
Then, upon the velvet sinking, I betook myself to linking
Fancy unto fancy, thinking what this ominous bird of yore—   70
What this grim, ungainly, ghastly, gaunt, and ominous bird of
      yore
      Meant in croaking "Nevermore."

5. Pallas Athena, the Greek goddess of wisdom.   6. Pluto, the Roman god of the dead and
ruler of the underworld.

This I sat engaged in guessing, but no syllable expressing
To the fowl whose fiery eyes now burned into my bosom's core;
This and more I sat divining, with my head at ease reclining   75
On the cushion's velvet lining that the lamplight gloated o'er,
But whose velvet-violet lining with the lamplight gloating o'er,
   She shall press, ah, nevermore!

Then, methought, the air grew denser, perfumed from an unseen
   censer
Swung by seraphim whose foot-falls tinkled on the tufted floor.   80
"Wretch," I cried, "thy God hath lent thee—by these angels he
   hath sent thee
Respite—respite and nepenthe[7] from thy memories of Lenore;
Quaff, oh, quaff this kind nephenthe and forget this lost
   Lenore!"
   Quoth the raven, "Nevermore."

"Prophet!" said I, "thing of evil!—prophet still, if bird or devil!—   85
Whether tempter sent, or whether tempest tossed thee here
   ashore,
Desolate yet all undaunted, on this desert land enchanted—
On this home by horror haunted—tell me truly, I implore—
Is there—is there balm in Gilead?[8]—tell me—tell me, I implore!"
   Quoth the raven, "Nevermore."   90

"Prophet!" said I, "thing of evil!—prophet still, if bird or devil!
By that Heaven that bends above us—by that God we both
   adore—
Tell this soul with sorrow laden if, within the distant Aidenn,[9]
It shall clasp a sainted maiden whom the angels name Lenore—
Clasp a rare and radiant maiden whom the angels name Lenore."   95
   Quoth the raven, "Nevermore."

"Be that word our sign of parting, bird or fiend!" I shrieked,
   upstarting—
"Get thee back into the tempest and the Night's Plutonian shore!
Leave no black plume as a token of that lie thy soul hath spoken!
Leave my loneliness unbroken!—quit the bust above my door!   100
Take thy beak from out my heart, and take thy form from off my
   door!"
   Quoth the Raven "Nevermore."

And the Raven, never flitting, still is sitting, still is sitting
On the pallid bust of Pallas just above my chamber door;
And his eyes have all the seeming of a demon's that is dreaming,   105
And the lamp-light o'er him streaming throws his shadow on the
   floor;

7. A drink that prevents sorrow.   8. See Jer. 8:22.   9. Eden.

And my soul from out that shadow that lies floating on the floor
    Shall be lifted—nevermore!

Fact Questions and Exercises

1. Who is being addressed in "To Helen"?
2. Why did the wind blow "out of a cloud" to kill Annabel Lee? How does the narrator react to her death?
3. What is the speaker doing when the raven first taps on the door?
4. Where does the raven perch? What word does the raven repeat, again and again?
5. Who is Lenore?

For Discussion and Writing

1. Discuss the raven as a symbol. Would another kind of bird have been as effective in the poem—a parrot, for instance? What do you think the raven symbolizes? What things do you think of when you think of a raven? Are these things present in Poe's poem? (You might want to look at "Brainstorm" by Nemerov, on page 1215. This is another poem concerning crows or ravens.)
2. Is there any one theme that appears in all these poems? What is the theme? How is it presented in each poem? Does the theme also appear in "The Cask of Amontillado," Poe's short story (page 19)?

Alfred, Lord Tennyson   [1809–1892]

Tennyson was born in Lincolnshire, England, the fourth of twelve children. Tennyson became interested in poetry, in part, to escape the unrest of a sometimes violent family. He left home to attend Cambridge, where he overcame many of his personal problems and developed his poetic skills. In 1850, with the publication of *In Memoriam*, an elegy in tribute to his close friend Arthur Henry Hallam, his fame was established and Tennyson was appointed poet laureate; thereafter, he lived a comfortable, busy life. In general, Tennyson's poetry reflects not only his interests in the problems of his time, but his attempts to find solutions for them.

The Lotos-Eaters

"Courage!" he[1] said, and pointed toward the land,
"This mounting wave will roll us shoreward soon."
In the afternoon they came unto a land

---

1. Ulysses; in the *Odyssey*, the Greek soldiers wanted to give up their attempt to return to Greece after the Trojan War.

In which it seeméd always afternoon.
All round the coast the languid air did swoon,   5
Breathing like one that hath a weary dream.
Full-faced above the valley stood the moon;
And, like a downward smoke, the slender stream
Along the cliff to fall and pause and fall did seem.

A land of streams! some, like a downward smoke,   10
Slow-dropping veils of thinnest lawn,[2] did go;
And some through wavering lights and shadows broke,
Rolling a slumbrous sheet of foam below.
They saw the gleaming river seaward flow
From the inner land; far off, three mountain-tops,   15
Three silent pinnacles of aged snow,
Stood sunset-flushed; and, dewed with showery drops,
Up-clomb the shadowy pine above the woven copse.

The charméd sunset lingered low adown
In the red West; through mountain clefts the dale   20
Was seen far inland, and the yellow down
Bordered with palm, and many a winding vale
And meadow, set with slender galingale;[3]
A land where all things always seemed the same!
And round about the keel with faces pale,   25
Dark faces pale against that rosy flame,
The mild-eyed melancholy Lotos-eaters[4] came.

Branches they bore of that enchanted stem,
Laden with flower and fruit, whereof they gave
To each, but whoso did receive of them   30
And taste, to him the gushing of the wave
Far away did seem to mourn and rave
On alien shores; and if his fellow spake,
His voice was thin, as voices from the grave;
And deep-asleep he seemed, yet all awake,   35
And music in his ears his beating heart did make.

They sat them down upon the yellow sand,
Between the sun and moon upon the shore;
And sweet it was to dream of fatherland,
Of child, and wife, and slave; but evermore   40
Most weary seemed the sea, weary the oar,
Weary the wandering fields of barren foam.
Then someone said, "We will return no more;"
And all at once they sang, "Our island home
Is far beyond the wave; we will no longer roam."   45

2. Linen cloth.   3. Tall, grasslike plant.   4. The land of the Lotos-eaters is a stop on the way
to Greece. Those who eat the Lotos are unwilling to leave the island.

CHORIC SONG

1

There is sweet music here that softer falls
Than petals from blown roses on the grass,
Or night-dews on still waters between walls
Of shadowy granite, in a gleaming pass;
Music that gentlier on the spirit lies,   50
Than tired eyelids upon tired eyes;
Music that brings sweet sleep down from the blissful skies.
Here are cool mosses deep,
And through the moss the ivies creep,
And in the stream the long-leaved flowers weep,   55
And from the craggy ledge the poppy hangs in sleep.

2

Why are we weighed upon with heaviness,
And utterly consumed with sharp distress,
While all things else have rest from weariness?
All things have rest: why should we toil alone,   60
We only toil, who are the first of things,
And make perpetual moan,
Still from one sorrow to another thrown;
Nor ever fold our wings,
And cease from wanderings,   65
Nor steep our brows in slumber's holy balm;
Nor harken what the inner spirit sings,
"There is no joy but calm!"—
Why should we only toil, the roof and crown of things?

3

Lo! in the middle of the wood,   70
The folded leaf is wooed from out the bud
With winds upon the branch, and there
Grows green and broad, and takes no care,
Sun-steeped at noon, and in the moon
Nightly dew-fed; and turning yellow   75
Falls, and floats adown the air.
Lo! sweetened with the summer light,
The full-juiced apple, waxing over-mellow,
Drops in a silent autumn night.   80
All its allotted length of days
The flower ripens in its place,
Ripens and fades, and falls, and hath no toil,
Fast-rooted in the fruitful soil.

4

Hateful is the dark-blue sky,
Vaulted o'er the dark-blue sea.   85

Death is the end of life; ah, why
Should life all labor be?
Let us alone. Time driveth onward fast
And in a little while our lips are dumb.
Let us alone. What is it that will last?   90
All things are taken from us, and become
Portions and parcels of the dreadful past.
Let us alone. What pleasure can we have
To war with evil? Is there any peace
In ever climbing up the climbing wave?   95
All things have rest, and ripen toward the grave
In silence—ripen, fall, and cease:
Give us long rest or death, dark death, or dreamful ease.

        5
How sweet it were, hearing the downward stream,
With half-shut eyes ever to seem   100
Falling asleep in a half-dream!
To dream and dream, like yonder amber light,
Which will not leave the myrrh-bush on the height;
To hear each other's whispered speech;
Eating the Lotos day by day,   105
To watch the crisping ripples on the beach,
And tender curving lines of creamy spray;
To lend our hearts and spirits wholly
To the influence of mild-minded melancholy;
To muse and brood and live again in memory,   110
With those old faces of our infancy
Heaped over with a mound of grass,
Two handfuls of white dust, shut in an urn of brass!

        6
Dear is the memory of our wedded lives,
And dear the last embraces of our wives   115
And their warm tears; but all hath suffered change;
For surely now our household hearths are cold,
Our sons inherit us, our looks are strange,
And we should come like ghosts to trouble joy.
Or else the island princes over-bold   120
Have eat our substance, and the minstrel sings
Before them of the ten years' war in Troy,
And our great deeds, as half-forgotten things.
Is there confusion in the little isle?
Let what is broken so remain.   125
The Gods are hard to reconcile;
'Tis hard to settle order once again.
There *is* confusion worse than death,
Trouble on trouble, pain on pain,
Long labor unto aged breath,   130

Sore tasks to hearts worn out by many wars
And eyes grown dim with gazing on the pilot-stars.

    7

But, propt on beds of amaranth[5] and moly,[6]
How sweet—while warm airs lull us, blowing lowly—
With half-dropt eyelid still,   135
Beneath a heaven dark and holy,
To watch the long bright river drawing slowly
His waters from the purple hill—
To hear the dewy echoes calling
From cave to cave through the thick-twined vine—   140
To watch the emerald-colored water falling
Through many a woven acanthus-wreath divine!
Only to hear and see the far-off sparkling brine,
Only to hear were sweet, stretched out beneath the pine.

    8

The Lotos blooms below the barren peak,   145
The Lotos blows by every winding creek;
All day the wind breathes low with mellower tone;
Through every hollow cave and alley lone
Round and round the spicy downs the yellow Lotos-dust is blown
We have had enough of action, and of motion we,   150
Rolled to starboard, rolled to larboard, when the surge was
            seething free,
Where the wallowing monster spouted his foam-fountains in the sea
Let us swear an oath, and keep it with an equal mind,
In the hollow Lotos-land to live and lie reclined
On the hills like Gods together, careless of mankind.   155
For they lie beside their nectar, and the bolts are hurled
Far below them in the valleys, and the clouds are lightly curled
Round their golden houses, girdled with the gleaming world;
Where they smile in secret, looking over wasted lands,
Blight and famine, plague and earthquake, roaring deeps and
            fiery sands,   160
Clanging fights, and flaming towns, and sinking ships, and
            praying hands.
But they smile, they find a music centered in a doleful song
Steaming up, a lamentation and an ancient tale of wrong,
Like a tale of little meaning though the words are strong;
Chanted from an ill-used race of men that cleave the soil,   165
Sow the seed, and reap the harvest with enduring toil,
Storing yearly little dues of wheat, and wine and oil;
Till they perish and they suffer—some, 'tis whispered—down in hell
Suffer endless anguish, others in Elysian valleys dwell,

5. A flower that, according to legend, never fades.   **6.** A magic herb.

Resting weary limbs at last on beds of asphodel.[7]   170
Surely, surely, slumber is more sweet than toil, the shore
Than labor in the deep mid-ocean, wind and wave and oar;
O, rest ye, brother mariners, we will not wander more.

Ulysses

It little profits that an idle king,
By this still hearth, among these barren crags,
Matched with an aged wife, I mete and dole
Unequal laws unto a savage race,
That hoard, and sleep, and feed, and know not me.   5
I cannot rest from travel; I will drink
Life to the lees. All times I have enjoyed
Greatly, have suffered greatly, both with those
That loved me, and alone; on shore, and when
Through scudding drifts the rainy Hyades[8]   10
Vext the dim sea. I am become a name;
For always roaming with a hungry heart
Much have I seen and known—cities of men
And manners, climates, councils, governments,
Myself not least, but honored of them all,—   15
And drunk delight of battle with my peers,
Far on the ringing plains of windy Troy.
I am a part of all that I have met;
Yet all experience is an arch wherethrough
Gleams that untraveled world whose margin fades   20
For ever and for ever when I move.
How dull it is to pause, to make an end,
To rust unburnished, not to shine in use!
As though to breathe were life! Life piled on life
Were all too little, and of one to me   25
Little remains; but every hour is saved
From that eternal silence, something more,
A bringer of new things; and vile it were
For some three suns to store and hoard myself,
And this gray spirit yearning in desire   30
To follow knowledge like a sinking star,
Beyond the utmost bound of human thought.
         This is my son, mine own Telemachus,
To whom I leave the scepter and the isle,
Well-loved of me, discerning to fulfill   35
This labor, by slow prudence to make mild
A rugged people, and through soft degrees

7. A yellow lily.   8. A group of stars used for forecasting rain.

Subdue them to the useful and the good.
Most blameless is he, centered in the sphere
Of common duties, decent not to fail   40
In offices of tenderness, and pay
Meet adoration to my household gods,
When I am gone. He works his work, I mine.
                    There lies the port; the vessel puffs her sail;
There gloom the dark, broad seas. My mariners,   45
Souls that have toiled, and wrought, and thought with me,
That ever with a frolic welcome took
The thunder and the sunshine, and opposed
Free hearts, free foreheads—you and I are old;
Old age hath yet his honor and his toil.   50
Death closes all; but something ere the end,
Some work of noble note, may yet be done,
Not unbecoming men that strove with gods.
The lights begin to twinkle from the rocks;
The long day wanes; the slow moon climbs; the deep   55
Moans round with many voices. Come, my friends,
'Tis not too late to seek a newer world.
Push off, and sitting well in order smite
The sounding furrows; for my purpose holds
To sail beyond the sunset, and the baths   60
Of all the western stars, until I die.
It may be that the gulfs will wash us down;
It may be we shall touch the Happy Isles,[9]
And see the great Achilles, whom we knew.
Though much is taken, much abides; and though   65
We are not now that strength which in old days
Moved earth and heaven, that which we are, we are,
One equal temper of heroic hearts,
Made weak by time and fate, but strong in will
To strive, to seek, to find, and not to yield.   70

Break, Break, Break

Break, break, break,
        On thy cold gray stones, O Sea!
And I would that my tongue could utter
        The thoughts that arise in me.

O well for the fisherman's boy,   5
        That he shouts with his sister at play!
O well for the sailor lad,
        That he sings in his boat on the bay!

9. Elysium, or heaven.

And the stately ships go on
    To their haven under the hill;   10
But O for the touch of a vanished hand,
    And the sound of a voice that is still!

Break, break, break,
    At the foot of thy crags, O Sea!
But the tender grace of a day that is dead   15
    Will never come back to me.

Morte d'Arthur

So all day long the noise of battle rolled
Among the mountains by the winter sea,
Until King Arthur's table, man by man,
Had fallen in Lyonnesse[10] about their lord,
King Arthur; then, because his wound was deep,   5
The bold Sir Bedivere uplifted him,
Sir Bedivere, the last of all his knights,
And bore him to a chapel nigh the field,
A broken chancel with a broken cross,
That stood on a dark strait of barren land.   10
On one side lay the ocean, and on one
Lay a great water, and the moon was full.
    Then spake King Arthur to Sir Bedivere:
"The sequel of to-day unsolders all
The goodliest fellowship of famous knights   15
Whereof this world holds record. Such a sleep
They sleep—the men I loved. I think that we
Shall never more, at any future time,
Delight out souls with talk of knightly deeds,
Walking about the gardens and the halls   20
Of Camelot, as in the days that were.
I perish by this people which I made—
Though Merlin sware that I should come again
To rule once more—but let what will be be,
I am so deeply smitten through the helm   25
That without help I cannot last till morn.
Thou therefore take my brand Excalibur,[11]
Which was my pride; for thou rememberest how
In those old days, one summer noon, an arm
Rose up from out the bosom of the lake,   30
Clothed in white samite,[12] mystic, wonderful,
Holding the sword—and how I rowed across

---

10. A land that, according to legend, sank into the ocean. **11.** Arthur's sword. **12.** Heavy silk.

And took it, and have worn it, like a king;
And, wheresoever I am sung or told
In aftertime, this also shall be known.   35
But now delay not; take Excalibur,
And fling him far into the middle mere;
Watch what thou seest, and lightly bring me word."
     To him replied the bold Sir Bedivere:
"It is not meet, Sir King, to leave thee thus,   40
Aidless, alone, and smitten through the helm.
A little thing may harm a wounded man.
Yet I thy hest will all perform at full,
Watch what I see, and lightly bring thee word."
     So saying, from the ruined shrine he stept   45
And in the moon athwart the place of tombs,
Where lay the mighty bones of ancient men,
Old knights, and over them the sea-wind sang
Shrill, chill, with flakes of foam. He, stepping down
By zigzag paths and juts of pointed rock,   50
Came on the shining levels of the lake.
     There drew he forth the brand Excalibur,
And o'er him, drawing it, the winter moon,
Brightening the skirts of a long cloud, ran forth
And sparkled keen with frost against the hilt;   55
For all the haft twinkled with diamond sparks,
Myriads of topaz-lights, and jacinth-work
Of subtlest jewelry. He gazed so long
That both his eyes were dazzled, as he stood,
This way and that dividing the swift mind,   60
In act to throw; but at the last it seemed
Better to leave Excalibur concealed
There in the many-knotted water-flags,
That whistled stiff and dry about the marge.
So strode he back slow to the wounded king.   65
     Then spake King Arthur to Sir Bedivere:
"Hast thou performed my mission which I gave?
What is it thou hast seen, or what hast heard?"
     And answer made the bold Sir Bedivere:
"I heard the ripple washing in the reeds,   70
And the wild water lapping on the crag."
     To whom replied King Arthur, faint and pale:
"Thou hast betrayed thy nature and thy name,
Not rendering true answer, as beseemed
Thy fealty, nor like a noble knight;   75
For surer sign had followed, either hand,
Or voice, or else a motion of the mere.
This is a shameful thing for men to lie.
Yet now, I charge thee, quickly go again
As thou art lief and dear, and do the thing   80
I bade thee, watch, and lightly bring me word."

Then went Sir Bedivere the second time
Across the ridge, and paced beside the mere,
Counting the dewy pebbles, fixed in thought;
But when he saw the wonder of the hilt,   85
How curiously and strangely chased, he smote
His palms together, and he cried aloud:
          "And if indeed I cast the brand away,
Surely a precious thing, one worthy note,
Should thus be lost forever from the earth,   90
Which might have pleased the eyes of many men.
What good should follow this, if this were done?
What harm, undone? deep harm to disobey,
Seeing obedience is the bond of rule.
Were it well to obey then, if a king demand   95
An act unprofitable, against himself?
The king is sick, and knows not what he does.
What record, or what relic of my lord
Should be to aftertime, but empty breath
And rumors of a doubt? but were this kept,   100
Stored in some treasure-house of mighty kings,
Someone might show it at a joust of arms,
Saying, 'King Arthur's sword, Excalibur,
Wrought by the lonely maiden of the lake.
Nine years she wrought it, sitting in the deeps   105
Upon the hidden bases of the hills.'
So might some old man speak in the aftertime
To all the people, winning reverence;
But now much honor and much fame were lost."
          So spake he, clouded with his own conceit,   110
And hid Excalibur the second time,
And so strode back slow to the wounded king.
          Then spoke King Arthur, breathing heavily:
"What is it thou hast seen, or what hast heard?"
          And answer made the bold Sir Bedivere: 115
"I heard the water lapping on the crag,
And the long ripple washing in the reeds."
          To whom replied King Arthur, much in wrath:
"Ah, miserable and unkind, untrue,
Unknightly, traitor-hearted! Woe is me!   120
Authority forgets a dying king,
Laid widowed of the power in his eye
That bowed the will. I see thee what thou art,
For thou, the latest-left of all my knights,
In whom should meet the offices of all,   125
Thou wouldst betray me for the precious hilt;
Either from lust of gold, or like a girl
Valuing the giddy pleasure of the eyes.
Yet, for a man may fail in duty twice,
And the third time may prosper, get thee hence;   130

But, if thou spare to fling Excalibur,
I will arise and slay thee with my hands."
    Then quickly rose Sir Bedivere, and ran,
And, leaping down the ridges lightly, plunged
Among the bulrush-beds, and clutched the sword,   135
And strongly wheeled and threw it. The great brand
Made lightnings in the splendor of the moon,
And flashing round and round, and whirled in an arch,
Shot like a streamer of the northern morn,
Seen where the moving isles of winter shock   140
By night, with noises of the northern sea.
So flashed and fell the brand Excalibur;
But ere he dipped the surface, rose an arm
Clothed in white samite, mystic, wonderful,
And caught him by the hilt, and brandished him   145
Three times, and drew him under in the mere.
And lightly went the other to the king.
    Then spoke King Arthur, drawing thicker breath:
"Now see I by thine eyes that this is done.
Speak out; what is it thou hast heard, or seen?"   150
    And answer made the bold Sir Bedivere:
"Sir King, I closed mine eyelids, lest the gems
Should blind my purpose, for I never saw,
Nor shall see, here or elsewhere, till I die,
Not though I live three lives of mortal men,   155
So great a miracle as yonder hilt.
Then with both hands I flung him, wheeling him;
But when I looked again, behold an arm,
Clothed in white samite, mystic, wonderful,
That caught him by the hilt, and brandished him   160
Three times, and drew him under in the mere."
    And answer made King Arthur, breathing hard:
"My end draws nigh; 'tis time that I were gone.
Make broad thy shoulders to receive my weight,
And bear me to the margin; yet I fear   165
My wound hath taken cold, and I shall die."
    So saying, from the pavement he half rose,
Slowly, with pain, reclining on his arm,
And looking wistfully with wide blue eyes
As in a picture. Him Sir Bedivere   170
Remorsefully regarded through his tears,
And would have spoken, but he found not words,
Then took with care, and kneeling on one knee,
O'er both his shoulders drew the languid hands,
And rising bore him through the place of tombs.   175
    But, as he walked, King Arthur panted hard,
Like one that feels a nightmare on his bed
When all the house is mute. So sighed the king,

Muttering and murmuring at his ear, "Quick, quick!
I fear it is too late, and I shall die." 180
But the other swiftly strode from ridge to ridge,
Clothed with his breath, and looking, as he walked,
Larger than human on the frozen hills.
He heard the deep behind him, and a cry
Before. His own thought drove him like a goad. 185
Dry clashed his harness in the icy caves
And barren chasms, and all to left and right
The bare black cliff clanged round him, as he based
His feet on juts of slippery crag that rang
Sharp-smitten with the dint of arméd heels— 190
And on a sudden, lo! the level lake,
And the long glories of the winter moon.
　　　　Then saw they how there hove a dusky barge,
Dark as a funeral scarf from stem to stern,
Beneath them; and descending they were ware 195
That all the decks were dense with stately forms
Black-stoled, black-hooded, like a dream—by these
Three queens with crowns of gold—and from them rose
A cry that shivered to the tingling stars,
And, as it were one voice, an agony 200
Of lamentation, like a wind that shrills
All night in a waste land, where no one comes,
Or hath come, since the making of the world.
　　　　Then murmured Arthur, "Place me in the barge,"
And to the barge they came. There those three queens 205
Put forth their hands, and took the king, and wept.
But she that rose the tallest of them all
And fairest laid his head upon her lap,
And loosed the shattered casque,[13] and chafed his hands,
And called him by his name, complaining loud, 210
And dropping bitter tears against his brow
Striped with dark blood; for all his face was white
And colorless, and like the withered moon
Smote by the fresh beam of the springing east;
And all his greaves and cuisses[14] dashed with drops 215
Of onset;[15] and the light and lustrous curls—
That made his forehead like a rising sun
High from the dais-throne—were parched with dust;
Or, clotted into points and hanging loose,
Mixed with the knightly growth that fringed his lips. 220
So like a shattered column lay the king;
Not like that Arthur who, with lance in rest,
From spur to plume a star of tournament,

---

13. Helmet.　14. Armor.　15. Blood.

Shot through the lists at Camelot, and charged
Before the eyes of ladies and of kings.   225
   Then loudly cried the bold Sir Bedivere:
"Ah! my Lord Arthur, whither shall I go?
Where shall I hide my forehead and my eyes?
For now I see the true old times are dead,
When every morning brought a noble chance,   230
And every chance brought out a noble knight.
Such times have been not since the light that led
The holy Elders with the gift of myrrh.
But now the whole Round Table is dissolved
Which was an image of the mighty world;   235
And I, the last, go forth companionless,
And the days darken round me, and the years,
Among new men, strange faces, other minds."
   And slowly answered Arthur from the barge:
"The old order changeth, yielding place to new,   240
And God fulfills himself in many ways,
Lest one good custom should corrupt the world.
Comfort thyself: what comfort is in me?
I have lived my life, and that which I have done
May He within Himself make pure! but thou,   245
If thou shouldst never see my face again,
Pray for my soul. More things are wrought by prayer
Than this world dreams of. Wherefore, let thy voice
Rise like a fountain for me night and day.
For what are men better than sheep or goats   250
That nourish a blind life within the brain,
If, knowing God, they lift not hands of prayer
Both for themselves and those who call them friend?
For so the whole round earth is every way
Bound by gold chains about the feet of God.   255
But now farewell. I am going a long way
With these thou seest—if indeed I go—
For all my mind is clouded with a doubt—
To the island-valley of Avilion;[16]
Where falls not hail, or rain, or any snow,   260
Nor ever wind blows loudly, but it lies
Deep-meadowed, happy, fair with orchard lawns
And bowery hollows crowned with summer sea,
Where I will heal me of my grievous wound."
   So said he, and the barge with oar and sail   265
Moved from the brink, like some full-breasted swan
That, fluting a wild carol ere her death,
Ruffles her pure cold plume, and takes the flood
With swarthy webs. Long stood Sir Bedivere

16. Avalon, an earthly paradise.

Revolving many memories, till the hull   270
Looked one black dot against the verge of dawn,
And on the mere the wailing died away.

Tithonus

The woods decay, the woods decay and fall,
The vapors weep their burthen to the ground,
Man comes and tills the field and lies beneath,
And after many a summer dies the swan.
Me only cruel immortality[17]   5
Consumes; I wither slowly in thine arms,
Here at the quiet limit of the world,
A white-haired shadow roaming like a dream
The ever-silent spaces of the East,
Far-folded mists, and gleaming halls of morn.   10
        Alas! for this gray shadow, once a man—
So glorious in his beauty and thy choice,
Who madest him thy chosen, that he seemed
To his great heart none other than a God!
I asked thee, "Give me immortality."   15
Then didst thou grant mine asking with a smile,
Like wealthy men who care not how they give.
But thy strong Hours indignant worked their wills,
And beat me down and marred and wasted me,
And though they could not end me, left me maimed   20
To dwell in presence of immortal youth,
Immortal age beside immortal youth,
And all I was in ashes. Can thy love,
Thy beauty, make amends, though even now,
Close over us, the silver star thy guide,   25
Shines in those tremulous eyes that fill with tears
To hear me? Let me go; take back thy gift.
Why should a man desire in any way
To vary from the kindly race of men,
Or pass beyond the goal of ordinance   30
Where all should pause, as is most meet for all?
        A soft air fans the cloud apart; there comes
A glimpse of that dark world where I was born.
Once more the old mysterious glimmer steals
From thy pure brows, and from thy shoulders pure,   35
And bosom beating with a heart renewed.
Thy cheek begins to redden through the gloom,

---

17. In Greek mythology, Tithonus was granted eternal life by Eos, goddess of the dawn. Tithonus, however, failed to ask for eternal youth; thus he becomes an eternally old man.

Thy sweet eyes brighten slowly close to mine,
Ere yet they blind the stars, and the wild team
Which love thee, yearning for thy yoke, arise,   40
And shake the darkness from their loosened manes,
And beat the twilight into flakes of fire.
      Lo! ever thus thou growest beautiful
In silence, then before thine answer given
Departest, and thy tears are on my cheek.   45
      Why wilt thou ever scare me with thy tears,
And make me tremble lest a saying learnt,
In days far-off, on that dark earth, be true?
"The Gods themselves cannot recall their gifts."
      Ay me! ay me! with what another heart   50
In days far-off, and with what other eyes
I used to watch—if I be he that watched—
The lucid outline forming round thee; saw
The dim curls kindle into sunny rings;
Changed with thy mystic change, and felt my blood   55
Glow with the glow that slowly crimsoned all
Thy presence and thy portals, while I lay,
Mouth, forehead, eyelids, growing dewy-warm
With kisses balmier than half-opening buds
Of April, and could hear the lips that kissed   60
Whispering I knew not what of wild and sweet,
Like that strange song I heard Apollo sing,
While Ilion like a mist rose into towers.
      Yet hold me not for ever in thine East;
How can my nature longer mix with thine?   65
Coldly thy rosy shadows bathe me, cold
Are all thy lights, and cold my wrinkled feet
Upon thy glimmering thresholds, when the steam
Floats up from those dim fields about the homes
Of happy men that have the power to die,   70
And grassy barrows of the happier dead.
Release me, and restore me to the ground.
Thou seest all things, thou wilt see my grave;
Thou wilt renew thy beauty morn by morn,
I earth in earth forget these empty courts,   75
And thee returning on thy silver wheels.

The Charge of the Light Brigade[18]

1

Half a league, half a league,
Half a league onward,

18. This poem was written about a battle that took place at Balaklava, during the Crimean War (1854). Russian artillery killed more than five hundred charging British soldiers.

All in the valley of Death
    Rode the six hundred.
"Forward the Light Brigade!   5
Charge for the guns!" he said.
Into the valley of Death
    Rode the six hundred.

      2
"Forward, the Light Brigade!"
Was there a man dismayed?   10
Not though the soldier knew
    Someone had blundered.
Theirs not to make reply,
Theirs not to reason why,
Theirs but to do and die.   15
Into the valley of Death
    Rode the six hundred.

      3
Cannon to right of them,
Cannon to left of them,
Cannon in front of them   20
    Volleyed and thundered;
Stormed at with shot and shell,
Boldly they rode and well,
Into the jaws of Death,
Into the mouth of hell   25
    Rode the six hundred.

      4
Flashed all their sabers bare,
Flashed as they turned in air
Sab'ring the gunners there,
Charging an army, while   30
    All the world wondered.
Plunged in the battery smoke
Right through the line they broke;
Cossack and Russian
Reeled from the saber stroke   35
    Shattered and sundered.
Then they rode back, but not,
    Not the six hundred.

      5
Cannon to right of them,
Cannon to left of them,   40
Cannon behind them
    Volleyed and thundered;
Stormed at with shot and shell,

While horse and hero fell,
They that had fought so well   45
Came through the jaws of Death,
Back from the mouth of hell,
All that was left of them,
    Left of six hundred.

6

When can their glory fade?   50
O the wild charge they made!
    All the world wondered.
Honor the charge they made!
Honor the Light Brigade,
    Noble six hundred!

Crossing the Bar[19]

Sunset and evening star,
    And one clear call for me!
And may there be no moaning of the bar,
    When I put out to sea,

But such a tide as moving seems asleep,   5
    Too full for sound and foam,
When that which drew from out the boundless deep
    Turns again home.

Twilight and evening bell,
    And after that the dark!   10
And may there be no sadness of farewell,
    When I embark;

For though from out our bourne of Time and Place
    The flood may bear me far,
I hope to see my Pilot face to face   15
    When I have crossed the bar.[20]

19. Tennyson requested that this poem be placed as the last poem in any collection of his
work. 20. The sand bar that stretches across the entrance to a harbor.

Fact Questions and Exercises

1. Describe the land of the Lotos-eaters.
2. What effect does the Lotos have on those who eat it? What argument do the
   Lotos-eaters present against work and striving?
3. In "Ulysses," what is the speaker's attitude toward idleness?
4. Check the definition of "dramatic monologue" in the Guide to Literary Terms.
   Is "Ulysses" a dramatic monologue? Explain.
5. In "Break, Break, Break," what will "never come back" to the speaker?

6. In "Morte D'Arthur," who is "the last of all" Arthur's knights? How does he betray Arthur?
7. Identify Excalibur. How did Arthur acquire Excalibur?
8. Why is Tithonus unhappy with immortality?
9. In "The Charge of the Light Brigade," what must the men do? How must they do it?

For Discussion and Writing

1. In the poems, point out the elements that relate to the theme of work and effort by the individual. According to the poems, why should a person work? Is there a sense of fatalism in the poems—"Morte d'Arthur," for instance? If so, how does this fatalism affect the question of work?
2. Tennyson uses a number of myths in the poems; how do these serve to comment on his contemporary society? For example, what values does Ulysses uphold? How are his values applicable to modern life? Do the poems imply that there are no modern heroes of the caliber of Ulysses and Arthur? How do the soldiers of "The Charge of the Light Brigade" compare with the mythical heroes?
3. Weariness or death is a theme common in these poems. What is Tennyson's attitude toward death? Does the death theme reflect any attitudes toward change, both for the individual and for society? Are there values left unchanged by death? Or is everything in a constant state of change? (Note, for instance, Tennyson's use of ships or sailing as symbols of movement or change.)

Robert Browning [1812–1889]

Browning was born in London, England, the son of a bank clerk and a loving mother, whom he would not leave until he was thirty-four. He attended the University of London for a short period, but most of his education was received from private tutors, at home. His early poems received little attention; Browning was past fifty before his stature as a poet was recognized. (He was married to the popular poet Elizabeth Barrett Browning, and was often referred to as "Mrs. Browning's husband.") Today, he is appreciated most for his work with the dramatic monologue—a form he employed to involve a triangle of participants (the reader, the poet, and the poem's speaker) in a subtle, psychological examination of human motivation.

Home-Thoughts, from Abroad

1

Oh, to be in England
Now that April's there,
And whoever wakes in England
Sees, some morning, unaware,

That the lowest boughs and the brushwood sheaf   5
Round the elm-tree bole are in tiny leaf,
While the chaffinch sings on the orchard bough
In England—now!

      2

And after April, when May follows,
And the whitethroat builds, and all the swallows!   10
Hark, where my blossomed peartree in the hedge
Leans to the field and scatters on the clover
Blossoms and dewdrops—at the bent spray's edge—
That's the wise thrush; he sings each song twice over,
Lest you should think he never could recapture   15
The first fine careless rapture!
And though the fields look rough with hoary dew,
All will be gay when noontide wakes anew
The buttercups, the little children's dower
—Far brighter than this gaudy melon-flower!   20

My Last Duchess

Dramatic Monologue

Ferrara

That's my last duchess painted on the wall, *a*
Looking as if she were alive. I call *a*
That piece a wonder, now: Frà Pandolf's hands *b*
Worked busily a day, and there she stands. *b*
Will't please you sit and look at her? I said *c*   5
"Frà Pandolf" by design, for never read *c*
Strangers like you that pictured countenance, *slant rhyme*
The depth and passion of its earnest glance,
But to myself they turned (since none puts by *e*
The curtain I have drawn for you, but I) *e*   10
And seemed as they would ask me, if they durst, *f*
How such a glance came there; so, not the first *f*
Are you to turn and ask thus. Sir, 'twas not *g*
Her husband's presence only, called that spot *g*
Of joy into the Duchess' cheek: perhaps   15
Frà Pandolf chanced to say "Her mantle laps
"Over my lady's wrist too much," or "Paint
"Must never hope to reproduce the faint
"Half-flush that dies along her throat": such stuff
Was courtesy, she thought, and cause enough   20
For calling up that spot of joy. She had
A heart—how shall I say?—too soon made glad,
Too easily impressed; she liked whate'er
She looked on, and her looks went everywhere.
Sir, 'twas all one! My favor at her breast!   25
Changed The dropping of the daylight in the West,

The bough of cherries some officious fool
Broke in the orchard for her, the white mule
She rode with round the terrace—all and each
Would draw from her alike the approving speech,   30
Or blush, at least. She thanked men—good! but thanked
Somehow—I know not how—as if she ranked
My gift of a nine-hundred-years-old name
With anybody's gift. Who'd stoop to blame
This sort of trifling? Even had you skill   35
In speech—which I have not—to make your will
Quite clear to such an one, and say, "Just this
Or that in you disgusts me; here you miss,
Or there exceed the mark"—and if she let
Herself be lessoned so, nor plainly set   40
Her wits to yours, forsooth, and made excuse,
—E'en then would be some stooping; and I choose
Never to stoop. Oh sir, she smiled, no doubt,
Whene'er I passed her; but who passed without
Much the same smile? This grew; I gave commands;   45
Then all smiles stopped together. There she stands
As if alive. Will't please you rise? We'll meet
The company below, then. I repeat,
The Count your master's known munificence
Is ample warrant that no just pretense   50
Of mine for dowry will be disallowed;
Though his fair daughter's self, as I avowed
At starting, is my object. Nay, we'll go
Together down, sir. Notice Neptune, though,
Taming a sea-horse, thought a rarity,   55
Which Claus of Innsbruck cast in bronze for me!

Soliloquy of the Spanish Cloister

1

Gr-r-r—there go, my heart's abhorrence!
    Water your damned flower-pots, do!
If hate killed men, Brother Lawrence,
    God's blood, would not mine kill you!
What? your myrtle-bush wants trimming?   5
    Oh, that rose has prior claims—
Needs its leaden vase filled brimming?
    Hell dry you up with its flames!

2

At the meal we sit together:
    Salve tibi![1] I must hear   10

1. Hail to thee!

Wise talk of the kind of weather,
    Sort of season, time of year:
Not a plenteous cork-crop: scarcely
    Dare we hope oak-galls,[2] *I doubt:*
What's the Latin name for "parsley"?   15
    What's the Greek name for Swine's Snout?

3

Whew! We'll have out platter burnished,
    Laid with care on our own shelf!
With a fire-new spoon we're furnished,
    And a goblet for ourself,   20
Rinsed like something sacrificial
    Ere 'tis fit to touch our chaps—
Marked with L for our initial!
    (He-he! There his lily snaps!)

4

Saint, forsooth! While brown Dolores
    Squats outside the Convent bank   25
With Sanchicha, telling stories,
    Steeping tresses in the tank,
Blue-black, lustrous, thick like horsehairs,
    —Can't I see his dead eye glow,   30
Bright as 'twere a Barbary corsair's?[3]
    (That is, if he'd let it show!)

5

When he finishes refection,[4]
    Knife and fork he never lays
Cross-wise, to my recollection,   35
    As do I, in Jesu's praise.
I the Trinity illustrate,
    Drinking watered orange pulp—
In three sips the Arian[5] frustrate;
    While he drains his at one gulp.   40

6

Oh, those melons? If he's able
    We're to have a feast! so nice!
One goes to the Abbot's table,
    All of us get each a slice.
How go on your flowers? None double?   45
    Not one fruit-sort can you spy?
Strange!—And I, too, at such trouble,
    Keep them close-nipped on the sly!

---

2. Diseased growths on oak trees. **3.** African pirates, noted for their viciousness. **4.** Dinner. **5.** The heretic Arius.

7

There's a great text in Galatians,[6]
    Once you trip on it, entails   50
Twenty-nine distinct damnations,
    One sure, if another fails:
If I trip him just a-dying,
    Sure of heaven as sure can be,
Spin him round and send him flying
    Off to hell, a Manichee?[7]   55

8

Or, my scrofulous French novel
    On gray paper with blunt type!
Simply glance at it, you grovel
    Hand and foot in Belial's gripe: 60
If I double down its pages
    At the woeful sixteenth print,
When he gathers his greengages,
    Ope a sieve and slip it in't?

9

Or, there's Satan!—one might venture   65
    Pledge one's soul to him, yet leave
Such a flaw in the indenture
    As he'd miss till, past retrieve,
Blasted lay that rose-acacia
    We're so proud of! *Hy, Zy, Hine* . . .[8]   70
'St, there's Vespers! *Plena gratá*
    Ave, Virgo![9] Gr-r-r—you swine!

The Bishop Orders His Tomb at Saint Praxed's Church

Rome, 15—

Vanity, saith the preacher, vanity!
Draw round my bed: is Anselm keeping back?
Nephews—sons mine . . . ah God, I know not! Well—
She, men would have to be your mother once,
Old Gandolf envied me, so fair she was!   5
What's done is done, and she is dead beside,
Dead long ago, and I am Bishop since,
And as she died so much we die ourselves,
And thence ye may perceive the world's a dream.

6. Probably Gal. 3:10. 7. The Manichees believed good and evil existed equally in the world. 8. Browning's meaning is unclear; perhaps, a Satanic curse. 9. Literally, "Full of grace, Hail Virgin [Mary]!"

Life, how and what is it? As here I lie   10
In this state-chamber, dying by degrees,
Hours and long hours in the dead night, I ask
"Do I live, am I dead?" Peace, peace seems all.
Saint Praxed's ever was the church for peace;
And so, about this tomb of mine. I fought   15
With tooth and nail to save my niche, ye know:
—Old Gandolf cozened[10] me, despite my care;
Shrewd was that snatch from out the corner south
He graced his carrion with, God curse the same!
Yet still my niche is not so cramped but thence   20
One sees the pulpit o' the epistle-side,[11]
And somewhat of the choir, those silent seats,
And up into the aery dome where live
The angels, and a sunbeam's sure to lurk:
And I shall find my slab of basalt there,   25
And 'neath my tabernacle take my rest,
With those nine columns round me, two and two,
The odd one at my feet where Anselm stands:
Peach-blossom marble all, the rare, the ripe
As fresh-poured red wine of a mighty pulse.   30
—Old Gandolf with his paltry onion-stone,
Put me where I may look at him! True peach,
Rosy and flawless: how I earned the prize!
Draw close: that conflagration of my church
—What then? So much was saved if aught were missed!   35
My sons, ye would not be my death? Go dig
The white-grape vineyard where the oil-press stood,
Drop water gently till the surface sink,
And if ye find . . . Ah God, I know not, I! . . .
Bedded in store of rotten fig-leaves soft,   40
And corded up in a tight olive-frail,
Some lump, ah God, of *lapis lazuli*,[12]
Big as a Jew's head cut off at the nape,
Blue as a vein o'er the Madonna's breast . . .
Sons, all have I bequeathed you, villas, all,   45
That brave Frascati[13] villa with its bath,
So, let the blue lump poise between my knees,
Like God the Father's globe on both his hands
Ye worship in the Jesu Church so gay,
For Gandolf shall not choose but see and burst!   50
Swift as a weaver's shuttle fleet our years:
Man goeth to the grave, and where is he?
Did I say basalt for my slab, sons? Black—
'Twas ever antique-black I meant! How else
Shall ye contrast my frieze to come beneath?   55

---

10. Cheated. 11. Right-hand side. 12. A deep blue, semiprecious stone. 13. Roman
town, famous as a resort.

The bas-relief in bronze ye promised me,
Those Pans and Nymphs ye wot of, and perchance
Some tripod, thyrsus,[14] with a vase or so,
The Saviour at his sermon on the mount,
Saint Praxed in a glory, and one Pan   60
Ready to twitch the Nymph's last garment off,
And Moses with the tables . . . but I know
Ye mark me not! What do they whisper thee,
Child of my bowels, Anselm? Ah, ye hope
To revel down my villas while I gasp   65
Bricked o'er with beggar's moldy travertine[15]
Which Gandolf from his tomb-top chuckles at!
Nay, boys, ye love me—all of jasper, then!
'T is jasper ye stand pledged to, lest I grieve
My bath must needs be left behind, alas!   70
One block, pure green as a pistachio-nut,
There's plenty jasper somewhere in the world—
And have I not Saint Praxed's ear to pray
Horses for ye, and brown Greek manuscripts,
And mistresses with great smooth marbly limbs?   75
—That's if ye carve my epitaph aright,
Choice Latin, picked phrase, Tully's[16] every word,
No gaudy ware like Gandolf's second line—
Tully, my masters? Ulpian[17] serves his need!
And then how I shall lie through centuries,   80
And hear the blessed mutter of the mass,
And see God made and eaten all day long,
And feel the steady candle-flame, and taste
Good strong thick stupefying incense-smoke!
For as I lie here, hours of the dead night,   85
Dying in state and by such slow degrees,
I fold my arms as if they clasped a crook,
And stretch my feet forth straight as stone can point,
And let the bedclothes, for a mortcloth, drop
Into great laps and folds of sculptor's-work: 90
And as yon tapers dwindle, and strange thoughts
Grow, with a certain humming in my ears,
About the life before I lived this life,
And this life too, popes, cardinals and priests,
Saint Praxed at his sermon on the mount,[18]   95
Your tall pale mother with her talking eyes,
And new-found agate urns as fresh as day,
And marble's language, Latin pure, discreet,
—Aha, ELUCESCEBAT[19] quoth our friend?
No Tully, said I, Ulpian at the best!   100

14. An ornamented staff. 15. Limestone. 16. Cicero, a classical Latin writer. 17.
Another Latin writer, who did not write as well as Cicero. 18. The Bishop is confusing St.
Praxed, a woman, with Christ. 19. A poor form of the Latin verb "elucebat," meaning "he
shone forth."

Evil and brief hath been my pilgrimage.
All *lapis*, all, sons! Else I give the Pope
My villas! Will ye ever eat my heart?
Ever your eyes were as a lizard's quick,
They glitter like your mother's for my soul,   105
Or ye would heighten my impoverished frieze,
Piece out its starved design, and fill my vase
With grapes, and add a vizor[20] and a Term,[21]
And to the tripod ye would tie a lynx
That in his struggle throws the thyrsus down,   110
To comfort me on my entablature
Whereon I am to lie till I must ask
"Do I live, am I dead?" There, leave me, there!
For ye have stabbed me with ingratitude
To death—ye wish it—God, ye wish it! Stone—   115
Gritstone, a-crumble! Clammy squares which sweat
As if the corpse they keep were oozing through—
And no more *lapis* to delight the world!
Well, go! I bless ye. Fewer tapers there,
But in a row: and, going, turn your backs   120
—Ay, like departing altar-ministrants,
And leave me in my church, the church for peace,
That I may watch at leisure if he leers—
Old Gandolf, at me, from his onion-stone,
As still he envied me, so fair she was!   125

"Childe Roland to the Dark Tower Came"[22]

1

My first thought was, he lied in every word,
        That hoary cripple, with malicious eye
        Askance to watch the working of his lie
On mine, and mouth scarce able to afford
Suppression of the glee, that pursed and scored   5
        Its edge, at one more victim gained thereby.

2

What else should he be set for, with his staff?
        What, save to waylay with his lies, ensnare
        All travelers who might find him posted there,
And ask the road? I guessed what skull-like laugh   10
Would break, what crutch 'gin write my epitaph
        For pastime in the dusty thoroughfare,

---

20. A helmet. **21.** Probably, a column with a statue or a bust at the top. **22.** *King Lear,* act
2, sc. 4. "Childe" means an apprentice knight.

3

If at his counsel I should turn aside
     Into that ominous tract which, all agree,
     Hides the Dark Tower. Yet acquiescingly   15
I did turn as he pointed: neither pride
Nor hope rekindling at the end described,
     So much as gladness that some end might be.

4

For, what with my whole world-wide wandering,
     What with my search drawn out through years, my hope   20
     Dwindled into a ghost not fit to cope
With that obstreperous joy success would bring,—
I hardly tried now to rebuke the spring
     My heart made, finding failure in its scope.

5

As when a sick man very near to death   25
     Seems dead indeed, and feels begin and end
     The tears, and takes the farewell of each friend,
And hears one bid the other go, draw breath
Freelier outside, ("since all is o'er," he saith,
     "And the blow fallen no grieving can amend;")   30

6

While some discuss if near the other graves
     Be room enough for this, and when a day
     Suits best for carrying the corpse away,
With care about the banners, scarves and staves:
And still the man hears all, and only craves   35
     He may not shame such tender love and stay.

7

Thus, I had so long suffered in this quest,
     Heard failure prophesied so oft, been writ
     So many times among "The Band"—to wit,
The knights who to the Dark Tower's search addressed   40
Their steps—that just to fail as they, seemed best,
     And all the doubt was now—should I be fit?

8

So, quiet as despair, I turned from him,
     That hateful cripple, out of his highway
     Into the path he pointed. All the day   45
Had been a dreary one at best, and dim
Was settling to its close, yet shot one grim
     Red leer to see the plain catch its estray.[23]

23. Stray animal.

9

For mark! no sooner was I fairly found
    Pledged to the plain, after a pace or two,   50
    Than, pausing to throw backward a last view
O'er the safe road, 'twas gone; gray plain all round:
Nothing but plain to the horizon's bound.
    I might go on; naught else remained to do.

10

So, on I went. I think I never saw   55
    Such starved ignoble nature; nothing throve:
    For flowers—as well expect a cedar grove!
But cockle, spurge, according to their law
Might propagate their kind, with none to awe,
    You'd think; a burr had been a treasure trove.   60

11

No! penury, inertness and grimace,
    In some strange sort, were the land's portion. "See
    Or shut your eyes," said Nature peevishly,
"It nothing skills: I cannot help my case;
'Tis the Last Judgment's fire must cure this place,   65
    Calcine its clods and set my prisoners free."

12

If there pushed any ragged thistle stalk
    Above its mates, the head was chopped; the bents[24]
    Were jealous else. What made those holes and rents
In the dock's[25] harsh swarth leaves, bruised as to balk   70
All hope of greenness? 'tis a brute must walk
    Pashing their life out, with a brute's intents.

13

As for the grass, it grew as scant as hair
    In leprosy; thin dry blades pricked the mud
    Which underneath looked kneaded up with blood.   75
One stiff blind horse, his every bone a-stare,
Stood stupefied, however he came there:
    Thrust out past service from the devil's stud!

14

Alive? he might be dead for aught I know,
    With that red gaunt and colloped neck a-strain,   80
    And shut eyes underneath the rusty mane;
Seldom went such grotesqueness with such woe;
I never saw a brute I hated so;
    He must be wicked to deserve such pain.

24. Reeds.   25. Weeds.

15

I shut my eyes and turned them on my heart.   85
    As a man calls for wine before he fights,
    I asked one draught of earlier, happier sights,
Ere fitly I could hope to play my part.
Think first, fight afterwards—the soldier's art:
    One taste of the old time sets all to rights.   90

16

Not it! I fancied Cuthbert's reddening face
    Beneath its garniture of curly gold,
    Dear fellow, till I almost felt him fold
An arm in mine to fix me to the place,
That way he used. Alas, one night's disgrace!   95
    Out went my heart's new fire and left it cold.

17

Giles then, the soul of honor—there he stands
    Frank as ten years ago when knighted first.
    What honest man should dare (he said) he durst.
Good—but the scene shifts—faugh! what hangman hands   100
Pin to his breast a parchment? His own bands
    Read it. Poor traitor, spit upon and curst!

18

Better this present than a past like that;
    Back therefore to my darkening path again!
    No sound, no sight as far as eye could strain.   105
Will the night send a howlet[26] or a bat?
I asked: when something on the dismal flat
    Came to arrest my thoughts and change their train.

19

A sudden little river crossed my path
    As unexpected as a serpent comes.   110
    No sluggish tide congenial to the glooms;
This, as it frothed by, might have been a bath
For the fiend's glowing hoof—to see the wrath
    Of its black eddy bespate with flakes and spumes.

20

So petty yet so spiteful! All along,   115
    Low scrubby alders kneeled down over it;
    Drenched willows flung them headlong in a fit
Of mute despair, a suicidal throng:
The river which had done them all the wrong,
    Whate'er that was, rolled by, deterred no whit.   120

26. Owl.

21

Which, while I forded,—good saints, how I feared
  To set my foot upon a dead man's cheek,
  Each step, or feel the spear I thrust to seek
For hollows, tangled in his hair or beard!
—It may have been a water-rat I speared,   125
  But, ugh! it sounded like a baby's shriek.

22

Glad was I when I reached the other bank.
  Now for a better country. Vain presage!
  Who were the strugglers, what war did they wage,
Whose savage trample thus could pad the dank   130
Soil to a plash? Toads in a poisoned tank,
  Or wild cats in a red-hot iron cage—

23

The fight must so have seemed in that fell cirque.[27]
  What penned them there, with all the plain to choose?
  No footprint leading to that horrid mews,[28]   135
None out of it. Mad brewage set to work
Their brains, no doubt, like galley slaves the Turk
  Pits for his pastime, Christians against Jews.

24

And more than that—a furlong on—why, there!
  What bad use was that engine for, that wheel,   140
  Or brake, not wheel—that harrow fit to reel
Men's bodies out like silk? with all the air
Of Tophet's tool, on earth left unaware,
  Or brought to sharpen its rusty teeth of steel.

25

Then came a bit of stubbed ground, once a wood,   145
  Next a marsh, it would seem, and now mere earth
  Desperate and done with; (so a fool finds mirth,
Makes a thing and then mars it, till his mood
Changes and off he goes!) within a rood[29]—
  Bog, clay and rubble, sand and stark black dearth. 150

26

Now blotches rankling, colored gay and grim,
  Now patches where some leanness of the soil's
  Broke into moss or substances like boils;
Then came some palsied oak, a cleft in him
Like a distorted mouth that splits its rim   155
  Gaping at death, and dies while it recoils.

27. A hollow place surrounded by hills. 28. Stables. 29. A measure of about seven yards.

27

And just as far as ever from the end!
     Naught in the distance but the evening, naught
     To point my footstep further! At the thought,
A great black bird, Apollyon's[30] bosom friend,   160
Sailed past, nor beat his wide wing dragon-penned
     That brushed my cap—perchance the guide I sought.

28

For, looking up, aware I somehow grew,
     'Spite of the dusk, the plain had given place
     All round to mountains—with such name to grace   165
Mere ugly heights and heaps now stolen in view.
How thus they had surprised me,—solve it, you!
     How to get from them was no clearer case.

29

Yet half I seemed to recognize some trick
     Of mischief happened to me, God knows when—   170
     In a bad dream perhaps. Here ended, then,
Progress this way. When, in the very nick
Of giving up, one time more, came a click
     As when a trap shuts—you're inside the den!

30

Burningly it came on me all at once,   175
     This was the place! those two hills on the right,
     Crouched like two bulls locked horn in horn in fight;
While to the left, a tall scalped mountain . . . Dunce,
Dotard, a-dozing at the very nonce,[31]
     After a life spent training for the sight!   180

31

What in the midst lay but the Tower itself?
     The round squat turret, blind as the fool's heart,
     Built of brown stone, without a counterpart
In the whole world. The tempest's mocking elf
Points to the shipman thus the unseen shelf   185
     He strikes on, only when the timbers start.

32

Not see? because of night perhaps?—why, day
     Came back again for that! before it left,
     The dying sunset kindled through a cleft:
The hills, like giants at a hunting, lay,   190
Chin upon hand, to see the game at bay,—
     "Now stab and end the creature—to the heft!"[32]

30. An angel of the bottomless pit, mentioned in Revelations. **31.** Moment. **32.** Sword's handle.

33

Not hear? when noise was everywhere! it tolled
    Increasing like a bell. Names in my ears
    Of all the lost adventurers my peers,—   195
How such a one was strong, and such was bold,
And such was fortunate, yet each of old
    Lost, lost! one moment knelled the woe of years.

34

There they stood, ranged along the hillsides, met
    To view the last of me, a living frame   200
    For one more picture! in a sheet of flame
I saw them and I knew them all. And yet
Dauntless the slug-horn to my lips I set,
    And blew. *"Childe Roland to the Dark Tower came."*

Fact Questions and Exercises

1. In "Home-Thoughts, from Abroad," why does the speaker long to be in England?
2. What do you think has happened to the "Last Duchess"? Which lines in the poem support your conclusion?
3. In "Soliloquy of the Spanish Cloister," who is Dolores? List some of the ways in which the speaker reveals his dislike of Brother Lawrence.
4. In what ways does the bishop in "The Bishop Orders His Tomb" show non-Christian attitudes?
5. Identify Gandolf and Anselm. Why, according to the bishop, does Gandolf envy him?
6. Describe the plain that Childe Roland crosses.

For Discussion and Writing

1. Discuss the characterizations of the speakers in Browning's dramatic monologues. In "My Last Duchess," for instance, what does the duke reveal about himself? Is he an egotist? Is he compassionate? Of what is he proudest? Similarly, what do the other speakers in the dramatic monologues reveal about themselves?
2. Discuss Browning's use of symbols in "Childe Roland to the Dark Tower Came." What are some of the prominent symbols? What do they symbolize? Are symbols as prevelent in any of the other poems?
3. Are any of Browning's poems satirical? If so, which ones? What do they satirize? In contrast, what values are upheld, either explicitly or implicitly?

Walt Whitman [1819–1892]

Whitman was born in West Hills, Long Island, New York; in 1823 Whitman's family moved to Brooklyn so that his father could pursue his trade as a carpenter. Although Whitman received little formal education, he taught school for a short while; he also worked as a printer, carpenter, and editor. In 1855 he published the first edition of *Leaves of Grass*, a collection of poems that he would expand and revise through nine editions. "Song of Myself," selections of which are presented here, is the best-known poem in the collection. Few people paid any attention to the book; only Emerson seems to have recognized the influence it would have on American poetry. Whitman was the first American poet to praise the idea of democracy and the democratic individual; he was the first American poet to talk openly about human sexuality and other formerly taboo subjects; and, he was the first American poet to break completely with past poetic traditions of rhyme, rhythm, stanzaic pattern, and language. Today, there are those who view Whitman as America's national poet; there are those who agree with Whitman's own estimation of his work as "barbaric yawp"; but there are few who would disagree with the significance of Whitman's poetic influence.

Song of Myself

1

I celebrate myself, and sing myself,
And what I assume you shall assume,
For every atom belonging to me as good belongs to you.

I loafe and invite my soul,
I lean and loafe at my ease observing a spear of summer grass.   5

My tongue, every atom of my blood, form'd from this soil, this air,
Born here of parents born here from parents the same, and their parents
              the same,
I, now thirty-seven years old in perfect health begin,
Hoping to cease not till death.

Creeds and schools in abeyance,   10
Retiring back a while sufficed at what they are, but never forgotten,
I harbor for good or bad, I permit to speak at every hazard,
Nature without check with original energy.

2

Houses and rooms are full of perfumes, the shelves are crowded with
              perfumes,
I breathe the fragrance myself and know it and like it,   15
The distillation would intoxicate me also, but I shall not let it.

The atmosphere is not a perfume, it has no taste of the distillation, it is
              odorless,

It is for my mouth forever, I am in love with it,
I will go to the bank by the wood and become undisguised and naked,
I am mad for it to be in contact with me.   20

The smoke of my own breath,
Echoes, ripples, buzz'd whispers, love-root, silk-thread, crotch and vine,
My respiration and inspiration, the beating of my heart, the passing of
        blood and air through my lungs,
The sniff of green leaves and dry leaves, and of the shore and
        dark-color'd sea-rocks, and of hay in the barn,
The sound of the belch'd words of my voice loos'd to the eddies of the
        wind,   25
A few light kisses, a few embraces, a reaching around of arms,
The play of shine and shade on the trees as the supple boughs wag,
The delight alone or in the rush of the streets, or along the fields and
        hill-sides,
The feeling of health, the full-noon trill, the song of me rising from bed
        and meeting the sun.

Have you reckon'd a thousand acres much? have you reckon'd the earth
        much?   30
Have you practis'd so long to learn to read?
Have you felt so proud to get at the meaning of poems?

Stop this day and night with me and you shall possess the origin of all
        poems,
You shall possess the good of the earth and sun, (there are millions of
        suns left,)
You shall no longer take things at second or third hand, nor look through
        the eyes of the dead, nor feed on the spectres in books,   35
You shall not look through my eyes either, nor take things from me,
You shall listen to all sides and filter them from your self.

                        . . . .

                6
A child said *What is the grass?* fetching it to me with full hands;
How could I answer the child? I do not know what it is any more than
        he.   100

I guess it must be the flag of my disposition, out of hopeful green stuff
        woven.

Or I guess it is the handkerchief of the Lord,
A scented gift and remembrancer designedly dropt,
Bearing the owner's name someway in the corners, that we may see and
        remark, and say *Whose?*

Or I guess the grass is itself a child, the produced babe of the
        vegetation.   105

Or I guess it is a uniform hieroglyphic,
And it means, Sprouting alike in broad zones and narrow zones,
Growing among black folks as among white,
Kanuck, Tuckahoe, Congressman, Cuff,[1] I give them the same, I receive
        them the same.

And now it seems to me the beautiful uncut hair of graves.   110

Tenderly will I use you curling grass,
It may be you transpire from the breasts of young men,
It may be if I had known them I would have loved them,
It may be you are from old people, or from offspring taken soon out of
        their mothers' laps,
And here you are the mothers' laps.   115

This grass is very dark to be from the white heads of old mothers,
Darker than the colorless beards of old men,
Dark to come from under the faint red roofs of mouths.

O I perceive after all so many uttering tongues,
And I perceive they do not come from the roofs of mouths for nothing.   120

I wish I could translate the hints about the dead young men and women.
And the hints about old men and mothers, and the offspring taken soon
        out of their laps.

What do you think has become of the young and old men?
And what do you think has become of the women and children?
They are alive and well somewhere,   125
The smallest sprout shows there is really no death,
And if ever there was it led forward life, and does not wait at the end to
        arrest it,
And ceas'd the moment life appear'd.
All goes onward and outward, nothing collapses,
And to die is different from what any one supposed, and luckier.

        . . . .

      11
Twenty-eight young men bathe by the shore,
Twenty-eight young men and all so friendly;   200
Twenty-eight years of womanly life and all so lonesome.

She owns the fine house by the rise of the bank,
She hides handsome and richly drest aft the blinds of the window.

Which of the young men does she like the best?
Ah the homeliest of them is beautiful to her.   205

    1. Kanuck, a French Canadian; Tuckahoe, a tidewater Virginian; Cuff, a Negro

Where are you off to, Lady? for I see you,
You splash in the water there, yet stay stock still in your room.

Dancing and laughing along the beach came the twenty-ninth bather,
The rest did not see her, but she saw them and loved them.

The beards of the young men glisten'd with wet, it ran from their long
          hair,   210
Little streams pass'd all over their bodies.

An unseen hand also pass'd over their bodies,
It descended tremblingly from their temples and ribs.

The young men float on their backs, their white bellies bulge to the sun,
          they do not ask who seizes fast to them,
They do not know who puffs and declines with pendant and bending
          arch,   215
They do not think whom they souse with spray.

. . . .

21
I am the poet of the Body and I am the poet of the Soul,
The pleasures of heaven are with me and the pains of hell are with me,
The first I graft and increase upon myself, the latter I translate into a
          new tongue.

I am the poet of the woman the same as the man,   425
And I say it is as great to be a woman as to be a man,
And I say there is nothing greater than the mother of men.

I chant the chant of dilation or pride,
We have had ducking and deprecating about enough,
I show that size is only development.   430

Have you outstript the rest? are you the President?
It is a trifle, they will more than arrive there every one, and still pass on.

I am he that walks with the tender and growing night,
I call to the earth and sea half-held by the night.

Press close bare-bosom'd night—press close magnetic nourishing
          night!   435
Night of south winds—night of the large few stars!
Still nodding night—mad naked summer night.

Smile O voluptuous cool-breath'd earth!
Earth of the slumbering and liquid trees!
Earth of departed sunset—earth of the mountains misty-topt!   440
Earth of the vitreous pour of the full moon just tinged with blue!

Earth of shine and dark mottling the tide of the river!
Earth of the limpid gray of clouds brighter and clearer for my sake!
Far-swooping elbow'd earth—rich apple-blossom'd earth!
Smile, for your lover comes.   445

Prodigal, you have given me love—therefore I to you give love!
O unspeakable passionate love.

                    .   .   .   .

          24
Walt Whitman, a kosmos, of Manhattan the son,
Turbulent, fleshly, sensual, eating, drinking and breeding,
No sentimentalist, no stander above men and women or apart from them,
No more modest than immodest.   500

Unscrew the locks from the doors!
Unscrew the doors themselves from their jambs!

Whoever degrades another degrades me,
And whatever is done or said returns at last to me.

Through me the afflatus surging and surging, through me the current
          and index.   505

I speak the pass-word primeval, I give the sign of democracy,
By God! I will accept nothing which all cannot have their counterpart of
          on the same terms.

Through me many long dumb voices,
Voices of the interminable generations of prisoners and slaves,
Voices of the diseas'd and despairing and of thieves and dwarfs,   510
Voices of cycles of preparation and accretion,
And of the threads that connect the stars, and of wombs and of the
          father-stuff,
And of the rights of them the others are down upon,
Of the deform'd, trivial, flat, foolish, despised,
Fog in the air, beetles rolling balls of dung.   515

Through me forbidden voices,
Voices of sexes and lusts, voices veil'd and I remove the veil,
Voices indecent by me clarified and transfigur'd.

I do not press my fingers across my mouth,
I keep as delicate around the bowels as around the head and heart,   520
Copulation is no more rank to me than death is.

I believe in the flesh and the appetites,
Seeing, hearing, feeling, are miracles, and each part and tag of me is a
          miracle.

Divine am I inside and out, and I make holy whatever I touch or am
       touch'd from,
The scent of these arm-pits aroma finer than prayer,   525
This head more than churches, bibles, and all the creeds.

If I worship one thing more than another it shall be the spread of my
       own body, or any part of it,
Translucent mould of me it shall be you!
Shaded ledges and rests it shall be you!
Firm masculine colter it shall be you!   530
Whatever goes to the tilth of me it shall be you!
You my rich blood! your milky stream pale strippings of my life!
Breast that presses against other breasts it shall be you!
My brain it shall be your occult convolutions!   534
Root of wash'd sweet-flag! timorous pond-snipe! nest of guarded
       duplicate eggs! it shall be you!
Mix'd tussled hay of head, beard, brawn, it shall be you!
Trickling sap of maple, fibre of manly wheat, it shall be you!
Sun so generous it shall be you!
Vapors lighting and shading my face it shall be you!
You sweaty brooks and dews it shall be you!   540
Winds whose soft-tickling genitals rub against me it shall be you!
Broad muscular fiends, branches of live oak, loving lounger in my
       winding paths, it shall be you!
Hands I have taken, face I have kiss'd, mortal I have ever touch'd, it
       shall be you.

I dote on myself, there is that lot of me and all so luscious,
Each moment and whatever happens thrills me with joy,   545
I cannot tell how my ankles bend, nor whence the cause of my faintest
       wish,
Nor the cause of the friendship I emit, nor the cause of the friendship I
       take again.

That I walk up my stoop, I pause to consider if it really be,
A morning-glory at my window satisfies me more than the metaphysics
       of books.

To behold the day-break!   550
The little light fades the immense and diaphanous shadows,
The air tastes good to my palate.

Hefts of the moving world at innocent gambols silently rising, freshly
       exuding,
Scooting obliquely high and low.

Something I cannot see puts upward libidinous prongs,   555
Seas of bright juice suffuse heaven.

The earth by the sky staid with, the daily close of their junction,
The heav'd challenge from the east that moment over my head,
The mocking taunt, See then whether you shall be master!

.   .   .   .

28
Is this then a touch? quivering me to a new identity,
Flames and ether making a rush for my veins,   620
Treacherous tip of me reaching and crowding to help them,
My flesh and blood playing out lightning to strike what is hardly
            different from myself,
On all sides prurient provokers stiffening my limbs,
Straining the udder of my heart for its withheld drip,
Behaving licentious toward me, taking no denial,   625
Depriving me of my best as for a purpose,
Unbuttoning my clothes, holding me by the bare waist,
Deluding my confusion with the calm of the sunlight and pasture-fields,
Immodestly sliding the fellow-senses away,
They bribed to swap off with touch and go and graze at the edges of
            me,   630
No consideration, no regard for my draining strength or my anger,
Fetching the rest of the herd around to enjoy them a while,
Then all uniting to stand on a headland and worry me.

The sentries desert every other part of me,
They have left me helpless to a red marauder,   635
They all come to the headland to witness and assist against me.

I am given up by traitors,
I talk wildly, I have lost my wits, I and nobody else am the greatest
            traitor,
I went myself first to the headland, my own hands carried me there.

You villain touch! what are you doing? my breath is tight in its throat,   640
Unclench your floodgates, you are too much for me.

.   .   .   .

32
I think I could turn and live with animals, they are so placid and
            self-contain'd,
I stand and look at them long and long.   685

They do not sweat and whine about their condition,
They do not lie awake in the dark and weep for their sins,
They do not make me sick discussing their duty to God,
Not one is dissatisfied, not one is demented with the mania of owning
            things,
Not one kneels to another, nor to his kind that lived thousands of years
            ago,   690
Not one is respectable or unhappy over the whole earth.

So they show their relations to me and I accept them,
They bring me tokens of myself, they evince them plainly in their
          possession.

I wonder where they get those tokens,
Did I pass that way huge times ago and negligently drop them?   695

Myself moving forward then and now and forever,
Gathering and showing more always and with velocity,
Infinite and omnigenous, and the like of these among them,
Not too exclusive toward the reachers of my remembrancers,
Picking out here one that I love, and now go with him on brotherly
          terms.   700

A gigantic beauty of a stallion, fresh and responsive to my caresses,
Head high in the forehead, wide between the ears,
Limbs glossy and supple, tail dusting the ground,
Eyes full of sparkling wickedness, ears finely cut, flexibly moving.

His nostrils dilate as my heels embrace him,   705
His well-built limbs tremble with pleasure as we race around and return.

I but use you a minute, then I resign you, stallion,
Why do I need your paces when I myself out-gallop them?
Even as I stand or sit passing faster than you.

.   .   .   .

48
I have said that the soul is not more than the body,
And I have said that the body is not more than the soul,   1270
And nothing, not God, is greater to one than one's self is,
And whoever walks a furlong without sympathy walks to his own
          funeral drest in his shroud,
And I or you pocketless of a dime may purchase the pick of the earth,
And to glance with an eye or show a bean in its pod confounds the
          learning of all times,
And there is no trade or employment but the young man following it
          may become a hero,   1275
And there is no object so soft but it makes a hub for the wheel'd universe,
And I say to any man or woman, Let your soul stand cool and
          composed before a million universes.

And I say to mankind, Be not curious about God,
For I who am curious about each am not curious about God,
(No array of terms can say how much I am at peace about God and
          about death.)   1280

I hear and behold God in every object, yet understand God not in the
          least,
Nor do I understand who there can be more wonderful than myself.

Why should I wish to see God better than this day?
I see something of God each hour of the twenty-four, and each moment
            then,
In the faces of men and women I see God, and in my own face in the
            glass,   1285
I find letters from God dropt in the street, and every one is sign'd by
            God's name,
And I leave them where they are, for I know that wheresoe'er I go,
Others will punctually come for ever and ever.

            51
The past and present wilt—I have fill'd them, emptied them,
And proceed to fill my next fold of the future.   1320

Listener up there! what have you to confide to me?
Look in my face while I snuff the sidle of evening,
(Talk honestly, no one else hears you, and I stay only a minute longer.)

Do I contradict myself?
Very well then I contradict myself,   1325
(I am large, I contain multitudes.)
I concentrate toward them that are nigh, I wait on the door-slab.

Who has done his day's work? who will soonest be through with his
            supper?
Who wishes to walk with me?

Will you speak before I am gone? will you prove already too late?

            52
The spotted hawk swoops by and accuses me, he complains of my gab
            and my loitering.   1331

I too am not a bit tamed, I too am untranslatable,
I sound my barbaric yawp over the roofs of the world.

The last scud of day holds back for me,
It flings my likeness after the rest and true as any on the shadow'd
            wilds,   1335
It coaxes me to the vapor and the dusk.

I depart as air, I shake my white locks at the runaway sun,
I effuse my flesh in eddies, and drift it in lacy jags.

I bequeath myself to the dirt to grow from the grass I love,
If you want me again look for me under your boot-soles.   1340

You will hardly know who I am or what I mean,
But I shall be good health to you nevertheless,
And filter and fibre your blood.

Failing to fetch me at first keep encouraged,
Missing me one place search another,   1345
I stop somewhere waiting for you.

When Lilacs Last in the Dooryard Bloom'd[2]

1

When lilacs last in the dooryard bloom'd
And the great star early droop'd in the western sky in the night,
I mourn'd, and yet shall mourn with ever-returning spring.

Ever-returning spring, trinity sure to me you bring,
Lilac blooming perennial and drooping star in the west,   5
And thought of him I love.

2

O powerful western fallen star!
O shades of night—O moody, tearful night!
O great star disappear'd—O the black murk that hides the star!
O cruel hands that hold me powerless—O helpless soul of me!   10
O harsh surrounding cloud that will not free my soul.

3

In the dooryard fronting an old farm-house near the white-wash'd palings,
Stands the lilac-bush tall-growing with heart-shaped leaves of rich green,
With many a pointed blossom rising delicate, with the perfume strong I
            love,
With every leaf a miracle—and from this bush in the dooryard,   15
With delicate-color'd blossoms and heart-shaped leaves of rich green,
A sprig with its flower I break.

4

In the swamp in secluded recesses,
A shy and hidden bird is warbling a song.

Solitary the thrush,   20
The hermit withdrawn to himself, avoiding the settlements,
Sings by himself a song.

Song of the bleeding throat,
Death's outlet song of life, (for well dear brother I know,
If thou wast not granted to sing thou would'st surely die.)   25

5

Over the breast of the spring, the land, amid cities,

---

2. This poem expresses Whitman's reactions to the death of Abraham Lincoln.

Amid lanes and through old woods, where lately the violets peep'd from
            the ground, spotting the gray debris,
Amid the grass in the fields each side of the lanes, passing the endless
            grass,
Passing the yellow-spear'd wheat, every grain from its shroud in the
            dark-brown fields uprisen,
Passing the apple-tree blows of white and pink in the orchards,   30
Carrying a corpse to where it shall rest in the grave,
Night and day journeys a coffin.

6

Coffin that passes through lanes and streets,[3]
Through day and night with the great cloud darkening the land,
With the pomp of the inloop'd flags with the cities draped in black,   35
With the show of the States themselves as of crape-veil'd women
            standing,
With processions long and winding and the flambeaus of the night,
With the countless torches lit, with the silent sea of faces and the
            unbared heads,
With the waiting depot, the arriving coffin, and the sombre faces,
With dirges through the night, with the thousand voices rising strong
            and solemn,   40
With all the mournful voices of the dirges pour'd around the coffin,
The dim-lit churches and the shuddering organs—where amid these you
            journey,
With the tolling tolling bells' perpetual clang,
Here, coffin that slowly passes,
I give you my sprig of lilac.   45

7

(Nor for you, for one alone,
Blossoms and branches green to coffins all I bring,
For fresh as the morning, thus would I chant a song for you O sane and
            sacred death.

All over bouquets of roses,
O death, I cover you over with roses and early lilies,   50
But mostly and now the lilac that blooms the first,
Copious I break, I break the sprigs from the bushes,
With loaded arms I come, pouring for you,
For you and the coffins all of you O death.)

8

O western orb sailing the heaven,   55
Now I know what you must have meant as a month since I walk'd,
As I walk'd in silence the transparent shadowy night,
As I saw you had something to tell as you bent to me night after night,

3. The funeral procession that took Lincoln's body to Illinois.

As you droop'd from the sky low down as if to my side, (while the other
      stars all look'd on,)
As we wander'd together the solemn night, (for something I know not
      what kept me from sleep,)   60
As the night advanced, and I saw on the rim of the west how full you
      were of woe,
As I stood on the rising ground in the breeze in the cool transparent
      night,
As I watch'd where you pass'd and was lost in the netherward black of
      the night,
As my soul in its trouble dissatisfied sank, as where you sad orb,
Concluded, dropt in the night, and was gone.   65

9
Sing on there in the swamp,
O singer bashful and tender, I hear your notes, I hear your call,
I hear, I come presently, I understand you,
But a moment I linger, for the lustrous star has detain'd me,
The star my departing comrade holds and detains me.   70

10
O how shall I warble myself for the dead one there I loved?
And how shall I deck my song for the large sweet soul that has gone?
And what shall my perfume be for the grave of him I love?
Sea-winds blown from east to west,
Blown from the Eastern sea and blown from the Western sea, till there
      on the prairies meeting,   75
These and with these and the breath of my chant,
I'll perfume the grave of him I love.

11
O what shall I hang on the chamber walls?
And what shall the pictures be that I hang on the walls,
To adorn the burial-house of him I love?   80

Pictures of growing spring and farms and homes,
With the Fourth-month eve at sundown, and the gray smoke lucid and
      bright,
With floods of the yellow gold of the gorgeous, indolent, sinking sun,
      burning, expanding the air,
With the fresh sweet herbage under foot, and the pale green leaves of
      the trees prolific,
In the distance the flowing glaze, the breast of the river, with a   85
      wind-dapple here and there,
With ranging hills on the banks, with many a line against the sky, and
      shadows,
And the city at hand with dwellings so dense, and stacks of chimneys,
And all the scenes of life and the workshops, and the workmen
      homeward returning.

12

Lo, body and soul—this land,
My own Manhattan with spires, and the sparkling and hurrying tides,   90
        and the ships,
The varied and ample land, the South and the North in the light, Ohio's
        shores and flashing Missouri,
And ever the far-spreading prairies cover'd with grass and corn.

Lo, the most excellent sun so calm and haughty,
The violet and purple morn with just-felt breezes,
The gentle soft-born measureless light,   95
The miracle spreading bathing all, the fulfill'd noon,
The coming eve delicious, the welcome night and the stars,
Over my cities shining all, enveloping man and land.

13

Sing on, sing on you gray-brown bird,
Sing from the swamps, the recesses, pour your chant from the   100
        bushes,
Limitless out of the dusk, out of the cedars and pines.

Sing on dearest brother, warble your reedy song,
Loud human song, with voice of uttermost woe.

O liquid and free and tender!
O wild and loose to my soul—O wondrous singer!   105
You only I hear—yet the star holds me, (but will soon depart,)
Yet the lilac with mastering odor holds me.

14

Now while I sat in the day and look'd forth,
In the close of the day with its light and the fields of spring, and the
        farmers preparing their crops,
In the large unconscious scenery of my land with its lakes and forests   110
In the heavenly aerial beauty, (after the perturb'd winds and the storms,)
Under the arching heavens of the afternoon swift passing, and the
        voices of children and women.
The many-moving sea-tides, and I saw the ships how they sail'd,
And the summer approaching with richness, and the fields all busy with
        labor,
And the infinite separate houses, how they all went on, each with its
        meals and minutia of daily usages,   115
And the streets how their throbbings throbb'd, and the cities pent—lo,
        then and there,
Falling upon them all and among them all, enveloping me with the rest,
Appear'd the cloud, appear'd the long black trail,
And I knew death, its thought, and the sacred knowledge of death.

Then with the knowledge of death as walking one side of me,   120
And the thought of death close-walking the other side of me,

And I in the middle as with companions, and as holding the hands of
        companions,
I fled forth to the hiding receiving night that talks not,
Down to the shores of the water, the path by the swamp in the dimness,
To the solemn shadowy cedars and ghostly pines so still.   125

And the singer so shy to the rest receiv'd me,
The gray-brown bird I know receiv'd us comrades three,
And he sang the carol of death, and a verse for him I love.

From deep secluded recesses,
From the fragrant cedars and the ghostly pines so still,   130
Came the carol of the bird.

And the charm of the carol rapt me,
As I held as if by their hands my comrades in the night,
And the voice of my spirit tallied the song of the bird.

Come lovely and soothing death,   135
Undulate round the world, serenely arriving, arriving,
In the day, in the night, to all, to each,
Sooner or later delicate death.

Prais'd be the fathomless universe,
For life and joy, and for objects and knowledge curious,   140
And for love, sweet love—but praise! praise! praise!
For the sure-enwinding arms of cool-enfolding death.

Dark mother always gliding near with soft feet,
Have none chanted for thee a chant of fullest welcome?
Then I chant it for thee, I glorify thee above all,   145
I bring thee a song that when thou must indeed come, come unfalteringly.

Approach strong deliveress,
When it is so, when thou hast taken them I joyously sing the dead,
Lost in the loving floating ocean of thee,
Laved in the flood of thy bliss O death.   150

From me to thee glad serenades,
Dances for thee I propose saluting thee, adornments and feastings for thee,
And the sights of the open landscape and the high-spread sky are fitting,
And life and the fields, and the huge and thoughtful night.

The night in silence under many a star,   155
The ocean shore and the husky whispering wave whose voice I know,
And the soul turning to thee O vast and well-veil'd death,
And the body gratefully nestling close to thee.

Over the tree-tops I float thee a song,
Over the rising and sinking waves, over the myriad fields and the prairies
        wide,   160
Over the dense-pack'd cities all and the teeming wharves and ways,
I float this carol with joy, with joy to thee O death.

15
To the tally of my soul,
Loud and strong kept up the gray-brown bird,
With pure deliberate notes spreading filling the night.   165

Loud in the pines and cedars dim,
Clear in the freshness moist and the swamp-perfume,
And I with my comrades there in the night.

While my sight that was bound in my eyes unclosed,
As to long panoramas of visions.   170

And I saw askant the armies,
I saw as in noiseless dreams hundreds of battle-flags,
Borne through the smoke of the battles and pierc'd with missiles I saw
        them,
And carried hither and yon through the smoke, and torn and bloody,
And at last but a few shreds left on the staffs, (and all in silence,)   175
And the staffs all splinter'd and broken.

I saw battle-corpses, myriads of them,
And the white skeletons of young men, I saw them,
I saw the debris and debris of all the slain soldiers of the war,
But I saw they were not as was thought,   180
They themselves were fully at rest, they suffer'd not,
The living remain'd and suffer'd, the mother suffer'd,
And the wife and the child and the musing comrade suffer'd,
And the armies that remain'd suffer'd.

16
Passing the visions, passing the night,   185
Passing, unloosing the hold of my comrades' hands,
Passing the song of the hermit bird and the tallying song of my soul,
Victorious song, death's outlet song, yet varying ever-altering song,
As low and wailing, yet clear the notes, rising and falling, flooding the
        night,
Sadly sinking and fainting, as warning and warning, and yet again
        bursting with joy,   190
Covering the earth and filling the spread of the heaven,
As that powerful psalm in the night I heard from recesses,
Passing, I leave thee lilac with heart-shaped leaves,
I leave thee there in the door-yard, blooming, returning with spring.

I cease from my song for thee,   195
From my gaze on thee in the west, fronting the west, communing with
      thee,
O comrade lustrous with silver face in the night.

Yet each to keep and all, retrievements out of the night,
The song, the wondrous chant of the gray-brown bird,
And the tallying chant, the echo arous'd in my soul,   200
With the lustrous and drooping star with the countenance full of woe,
With the holders holding my hand nearing the call of the bird,
Comrades mine and I in the midst, and their memory ever to keep, for
      the dead I loved so well,
For the sweetest, wisest soul of all my days and lands—and this for his
      dear sake,
Lilac and star and bird twined with the chant of my soul,   205
There in the fragrant pines and the cedars dusk and dim.

Fact Questions and Exercises

1. According to the speaker in "Song of Myself," how does a person learn to "possess the origin of all poems"?
2. In Section 6, what is "the handkerchief of the Lord"?
3. Point out specific lines that express the speaker's attitude toward dying.
4. In Section 11, who is watching the "twenty-eight young men"?
5. Point out specific lines that show Whitman's attitude toward books and schools.
6. What is the speaker's attitude toward contradicting himself in Section 51?
7. What kind of bird appears in "When Lilacs Last in the Dooryard Bloom'd"? What is the message in the bird's song?
8. What visions does the speaker have in Section 15?
9. What three things are "twined with the chant of my soul"?

For Discussion and Writing

1. Characterize the speaker of "Song of Myself." Is Whitman the "I"? Does Whitman speak for himself alone, or is he speaking for the universal person or poet? What does the speaker admire? Of what does he disapprove? What makes him a true "democrat"?
2. Discuss Whitman's use of symbols. What symbols appear prominently in each of the poems? What do these various symbols represent? Does Whitman use the symbols effectively? For the most part, are they private or universal symbols?
3. The speaker of "Song of Myself" says: "I am the poet of the Body and I am the poet of the Soul." Discuss the "body and soul" aspects of the poem. Which elements in the poem show each of these two sides of life? Are the elements equally balanced, or does one outweigh the other? Explain.

Matthew Arnold [1822–1888]

Arnold was born in Laleham, England, and attended Oxford, where he established a reputation as an elegant and dandified merrymaker. In 1851 he was appointed inspector of schools, a post he kept for most of his life; and, in 1857 he was elected Professor of Poetry at Oxford. Arnold's prose is as noteworthy as his poetry—in fact, after 1860 he wrote more essays than poems; *Culture and Anarchy* (1869), for instance, is a significant document of social criticism. In describing his own poetry, Arnold said that its primary aim was to "rejoice the reader."

Requiescat[1]

Strew on her roses, roses,
    And never a spray of yew!
In quiet she reposes;
    Ah, would that I did too!

Her mirth the world required;
    She bathed it in smiles of glee   5
But her heart was tired, tired,
    And now they let her be.

Her life was turning, turning,
    In mazes of heat and sound.   10
But for peace her soul was yearning,
    And now peace laps her round.

Her cabined, ample spirit,
    It fluttered and failed for breath.
Tonight it doth inherit   15
    The vasty hall of death.

Dover Beach

The sea is calm tonight.
The tide is full, the moon lies fair
Upon the straits; on the French coast the light
Gleams and is gone; the cliffs of England stand,
Glimmering and vast, out in the tranquil bay.   5
Come to the window, sweet is the night-air!

1. "May she rest."

Only, from the long line of spray
Where the sea meets the moon-blanched land,
Listen! you hear the grating roar
Of pebbles which the waves draw back, and fling,   10
At their return, up the high strand,
Begin, and cease, and then again begin,
With tremulous cadence slow, and bring
The eternal note of sadness in.

Sophocles long ago   15
Heard it on the Aegean, and it brought
Into his mind the turbid ebb and flow
Of human misery; we
Find also in the sound a thought,
Hearing it by this distant northern sea.   20

The Sea of Faith
Was once, too, at the full, and round earth's shore
Lay like the folds of a bright girdle furled.
But now I only hear
Its melancholy, long, withdrawing roar,   25
Retreating, to the breath
Of the night-wind, down the vast edges drear
And naked shingles² of the world.

Ah, love, let us be true
To one another! for the world, which seems   30
To lie before us like a land of dreams,
So various, so beautiful, so new,
Hath really neither joy, nor love, nor light,
Nor certitude, nor peace, nor help for pain;
And we are here as on a darkling plain   35
Swept with confused alarms of struggle and flight,
Where ignorant armies clash by night.

The Forsaken Merman

Come, dear children, let us away;
Down and away below!
Now my brothers call from the bay,
Now the great winds shoreward blow,
Now the salt tides seaward flow;   5
Now the wild white horses play,
Champ and chafe and toss in the spray.
Children dear, let us away!
This way, this way!

2. Small pebbles.

Call her once before you go—   10
Call once yet!
In a voice that she will know:
"Margaret! Margaret!"
Children's voices should be dear
(Call once more) to a mother's ear;   15
Children's voices, wild with pain—
Surely she will come again!
Call her once and come away;
This way, this way!
"Mother dear, we cannot stay!   20
The wild white horses foam and fret."
Margaret! Margaret!

Come, dear children, come away down;
Call no more!
One last look at the white-walled town,   25
And the little gray church on the windy shore;
Then come down!
She will not come though you call all day;
Come away, come away!

Children dear, was it yesterday   30
We heard the sweet bells over the bay?
In the caverns where we lay,
Through the surf and through the swell,
The far-off sound of a silver bell?
Sand-strewn caverns, cool and deep,   35
Where the winds are all asleep;
Where the spent lights quiver and gleam,
Where the salt weed sways in the stream,
Where the sea-beasts, ranged all round,
Feed in the ooze of their pasture-ground;   40
Where the sea-snakes coil and twine,
Dry their mail and bask in the brine;
Where great whales come sailing by,
Sail and sail, with unshut eye,
Round the world for ever and aye?   45
When did music come this way?
Children dear, was it yesterday?

Children dear, was it yesterday
(Call yet once) that she went away?
Once she sate with you and me,   50
On a red gold throne in the heart of the sea,
And the youngest sate on her knee.
She combed its bright hair, and she tended it well,
When down swung the sound of a far-off bell.
She sighed, she looked up through the clear green sea;   55

She said: "I must go, for my kinsfolk pray
In the little gray church on the shore today.
'Twill be Easter-time in the world—ah me!
And I lose my poor soul, Merman! here with thee."
I said: "Go up, dear heart, through the waves;   60
Say thy prayer, and come back to the kind sea-caves!"
She smiled, she went up through the surf in the bay.
Children dear, was it yesterday?

      Children dear, were we long alone?
"The sea grows stormy, the little ones moan;   65
Long prayers," I said, "in the world they say;
Come!" I said; and we rose through the surf in the bay.
We went up the beach, by the sandy down
Where the sea-stocks bloom, to the white-walled town;
Through the narrow paved'streets, where all was still,   70
To the little gray church on the windy hill.
From the church came a murmur of folk at their prayers,
But we stood without in the cold blowing airs.
We climbed on the graves, on the stones worn with rains,
And we gazed up the aisle through the small leaded panes.   75
She sate by the pillar; we saw her clear:
"Margaret, hist! come quick, we are here!
Dear heart," I said, "we are long alone;
The sea grows stormy, the little ones moan."
But, ah, she gave me never a look,   80
For her eyes were sealed to the holy book!
Loud prays the priest; shut stands the door.
Come away, children, call no more!
Come away, come down, call no more!

      Down, down, down!   85
Down to the depths of the sea!
She sits at her wheel in the humming town,
Singing most joyfully.
Hark what she sings: "O joy, O joy,
For the humming street, and the child with its toy!   90
For the priest, and the bell, and the holy well;
For the wheel where I spun,
And the blessed light of the sun!"
And so sings her fill.
Singing most joyfully,   95
Till the spindle drops from her hand,
And the whizzing wheel stands still.
She steals to the window, and looks at the sand,
And over the sand at the sea;
And her eyes are set in a stare;   100
And anon there breaks a sigh,
And anon there drops a tear,

From a sorrow-clouded eye,
And a heart sorrow-laden,
A long, long sigh;   105
For the cold strange eyes of a little mermaiden
And the gleam of her golden hair.

      Come away, away children;
Come children, come down!
The hoarse wind blows coldly;   110
Lights shine in the town.
She will start from her slumber
When gusts shake the door;
She will hear the winds howling,
Will hear the waves roar.   115
We shall see, while above us
The waves roar and whirl,
A ceiling of amber,
A pavement of pearl.
Singing: "Here came a mortal,   120
But faithless was she!
And alone dwell for ever
The kings of the sea."

But, children, at midnight,
When soft the winds blow,   125
When clear falls the moonlight,
When spring-tides are low;
When sweet airs come seaward
From heaths starred with broom,
And high rocks throw mildly   130
On the blanched sands a gloom;
Up the still, glistening beaches,
Up the creeks we will hie,
Over banks of bright seaweed
The ebb-tide leaves dry.   135
We will gaze, from the sand-hills,
At the white, sleeping town;
At the church on the hill-side—
And then come back down.
Singing: "There dwells a loved one,   140
But cruel is she!
She left lonely for ever
The kings of the sea."

Fact Questions and Exercises

1. In "Requiescat," in which line does the reader learn that the speaker wishes to join the woman in death?

2. What brings the "eternal note of sadness in" on Dover Beach? What two kinds of "sea" does Arnold mention in the poem?
3. To whom is the forsaken merman talking in the poem? What is a "merman"?
4. What is the name of the wife and mother who has had to return to the "white-walled town"? What is the mother doing when the merman and children see her through the windows of the church?
5. Point out the lines in the poem that let the reader know the woman is unhappy about leaving the merman and her children.

For Discussion and Writing

1. In "Dover Beach," what is the speaker's philosophy of life? That is, is the speaker optimistic or pessimistic? What has happened to his faith? Has anything replaced it? Is this same philosophy present in either of the other two poems?
2. Analyze the woman's conflict in "The Forsaken Merman." Why must she leave her husband and children and return to live in the town? What is she giving up by leaving them? What forces make her stay in the town, even though she would like to return to the sea? Is the merman justified in calling her cruel? If the poem has a theme, what do you think it is?

Emily Dickinson [1830–1866]

Dickinson was born in Amherst, Massachusetts, and with the exception of a few brief visits and a year at nearby Mount Holyoke College, she never left her house in Amherst. Her father was a congressman and a staunch churchman, a man whom Dickinson would later describe as "pure" and "terrible." Not much is known about Dickinson's personal life; she was a reclusive individual who used poetry as her "letter to the world/That never wrote to me." Few of her more than seventeen-hundred poems were published in her lifetime; today, however, her poetry is much admired for its concreteness, symbolism, and clever, often unorthodox, language and form. Although some of her lyrics are obscure and awkward, at their best, her poems are among the finest in the English language. The poems presented here are numbered as they appear in *The Complete Poems of Emily Dickinson*, edited by Thomas H. Johnson.

Poem 214

I taste a liquor never brewed—
From Tankards scooped in Pearl—
Not all the Vats upon the Rhine
Yield such an Alcohol!

Inebriate of Air—am I—   5
And Debauchee of Dew—
Reeling—thro endless summer days—
From inns of Molten Blue—

When "Landlords" turn the drunken Bee
Out of the Foxglove's door—   10
When Butterflies—renounce their "drams"—
I shall but drink the more!

Till Seraphs swing their snowy Hats—
And Saints—to windows run—
To see the little Tippler   15
Leaning against the—Sun—

Poem 258

There's a certain Slant of light,
Winter Afternoons—
That oppresses, like the Heft
Of Cathedral Tunes—

Heavenly Hurt, it gives us—   5
We can find no scar,
But internal difference,
Where the Meanings, are—

None may teach it—Any—
'Tis the Seal Despair—   10
An imperial affliction
Sent us of the Air—

When it comes, the Landscape listens—
Shadows—hold their breath—
When it goes, 'tis like the Distance   15
On the look of Death—

Poem 435

Much Madness is divinest Sense—
To a discerning Eye—
Much Sense—the starkest Madness—
'Tis the Majority
In this, as All, prevail—   5
Assent—and you are sane—

Demur—you're straightway dangerous—
And handled with a Chain—

Poem 465

I heard a Fly buzz—when I died—
The stillness in the Room
Was like the Stillness in the Air—
Between the Heaves of Storm—

The Eyes around—had wrung them dry—   5
And Breaths were gathering firm
For that last Onset—when the King
Be witnessed—in the Room—

I willed my Keepsakes—Signed away
What portion of me be   10
Assignable—and then it was
There interposed a Fly—

With Blue—uncertain stumbling Buzz—
Between the light—and me—
And then the Windows failed—and then   15
I could not see to see—

Poem 520

I started Early—Took my Dog—
And visited the Sea—
The Mermaids in the Basement
Came out to look at me—

And Frigates—in the Upper Floor   5
Extended Hempen Hands—
Presuming Me to be a Mouse—
Aground—upon the Sands—

But no Man moved Me—till the Tide
Went past my simple Shoe—   10
And past my Apron—and my Belt
And past my Bodice—too—

And made as He would eat me up—
As wholly as a Dew
Upon a Dandelion's Sleeve—   15
And then—I started—too—

And He—He followed—close behind—
I felt His Silver Heel
Upon my Ankle—Then my Shoes
Would overflow with Pearl—   20

Until We met the Solid Town—
No One He seemed to know—
And bowing—with a Mighty look—
At me—The Sea withdrew—

Poem 585

I like to see it lap the Miles—
And lick the Valleys up—
And stop to feed itself at Tanks—
And then—prodigious step

Around a Pile of Mountains—   5
And supercilious peer
In Shanties—by the sides of Roads—
And then a Quarry pare

To fit its ribs
And crawl between   10
Complaining all the while
In horrid—hooting stanza—
Then chase itself down Hill—

And neigh like Boanerges[1]
Then—prompter than a Star   15
Stop—docile and omnipotent
At its own stable door—

Poem 712

Because I could not stop for Death—   *iambic, tetrameter*
He kindly stopped for me—
The Carriage held but just Ourselves—
And Immortality.

We slowly drove—He knew no haste   5
And I had put away,
My labor and my leisure too,
For His Civility—   *Iambic,*

1. Usually, a very loud preacher.

[handwritten: ? Symbolic - compares to 3 mains in life childhood, maturity, death. Iambic, trimeter " Iambic, tetrameter " Iambic, Trimeter]

We passed the School, where Children strove   *[handwritten: struGGLiNG]*
At Recess—in the Ring—
We passed the Fields of Gazing Grain—   10
We passed the Setting Sun—   *[handwritten: her perspective changes]*

Or rather—He passed Us—   *[handwritten: symbolic for death]*
The Dews drew quivering and chill—
For only Gossamer, my Gown—   *[handwritten: not dressed for the weather, so she's chilly]*
My Tippet[2]—only Tulle—   15

We paused before a House that seemed   *[handwritten: cemetery]*
A Swelling of the Ground—
The Roof was scarcely visible—
The Cornice—in the Ground—   20

Since then—'tis Centuries—and yet   *[handwritten: Summary. Been centuries since she died, but seems much shorter]*
Feels shorter than the Day
I first surmised the Horses' Heads
Were toward Eternity—

Poem 986

[handwritten: euphemism]

A narrow Fellow in the Grass
Occasionally rides—
You may have met Him—did you not
His notice sudden is—

The Grass divides as with a Comb—   5
A spotted shaft is seen—
And then it closes at your feet
And opens further on—

He likes a Boggy Acre
A Floor too cool for Corn—   10
Yet when a Boy, and Barefoot—
I more than once at Noon

Have passed, I thought, a Whip lash
Unbraiding in the Sun
When stooping to secure it   15
It wrinkled, and was gone—

Several of Nature's People
I know, and they know me—
I feel for them a transport
Of cordiality—   20

2. A short cape.

But never met this Fellow
Attended, or alone
Without a tighter breathing
And Zero at the Bone—

Fact Questions and Exercises

1. In Poem 214, what do "inebriate" and "debauchee" mean?
2. In Poem 258, what "oppresses" and gives "Heavenly Hurt"?
3. In Poem 435, what must a person do to be considered "sane"?
4. What comes "Between the light—and me," in Poem 465? Point out all the examples of metaphor in the poem.
5. What does the poetess like to see "lap the Miles," in Poem 585?
6. In poem 986, what is the "narrow Fellow in the Grass"? How does the speaker react to it?

For Discussion and Writing

1. Select any one of these poems and write an interpretational analysis of it. Discuss the denotation and connotation of words, the use of figurative language, and any other aspect of the poem that you feel is noteworthy.
2. Is there a repeated theme in Dickinson's poems? Loneliness, isolation, or sexuality, for example? If so, discuss this common theme. In what ways is it expressed in the various poems?

Thomas Hardy [1840–1928]

Hardy was born in Dorchester, England. He quit school at fifteen and worked for six years as an architect's helper. In the early 1870s, Hardy gave up his architectural career to concentrate on writing; between 1872 and 1896 he wrote a series of novels that established him as one of England's leading novelists. However, when *Jude the Obscure* (1896), the story of a man destroyed by his sexuality, received scathing criticism, Hardy abandoned the novel form and devoted himself to poetry. In both his novels and poems, Hardy displays pessimism, a term that he did not accept; it is clear, however, that his work does reflect his awareness of the waste in human life, and an ironic concern for a world that has no benevolent god working for its betterment. *Tess of the D'Urbervilles* (1891) is another of his best-known novels.

The Ruined Maid

"O'Melia, my dear, this does everything crown!
Who could have supposed I should meet you in Town?
And whence such fair garments, such prosperi-ty?"
"O didn't you know I'd been ruined?" said she.

"You left us in tatters, without shoes or socks,   5
Tired of digging potatoes, and spudding up docks;[1]
And now you've gay bracelets and bright feathers three!"
"Yes: that's how we dress when we're ruined," said she.

"At home in the barton[2] you said 'thee' and 'thou,'
And 'thik oon,' and 'theäs oon' and 't'other'; but now   10
Your talking quite fits 'ee for high compa-ny!"
"Some polish is gained with one's ruin," said she.

"Your hands were like paws then, your face blue and bleak
But now I'm bewitched by your delicate cheek,
And your little gloves fit as on any la-dy!"   15
"We never do work when we're ruined," said she.

"You used to call home-life a hag-ridden dream,
And you'd sigh, and you'd sock; but at present you seem
To know not of megrims[3] or melancho-ly!"
"True. One's pretty lively when ruined," said she.   20

"I wish I had feathers, a fine sweeping gown,
And a delicate face, and could strut about Town!"
"My dear—a raw country girl, such as you be,
Cannot quite expect that. You ain't ruined," said she.

The Darkling Thrush

I leant upon a coppice[4] gate
    When Frost was specter-gray,
And Winter's dregs made desolate
    The weakening eye of day.
The tangled bine-stems[5] scored the sky   5
    Like strings of broken lyres,
And all mankind that haunted nigh
    Had sought their household fires.

The land's sharp features seemed to be
    The Century's corpse outleant,   10
His crypt the cloudy canopy,
    The wind his death-lament.
The ancient pulse of germ and birth
    Was shrunken hard and dry,
And every spirit upon earth   15
    Seemed fervorless as I.

1. Digging weeds.   2. Farm.   3. Depressions, "blue" feelings.   4. A small wood.
5. Twining plants, as ivy.

At once a voice arose among
    The bleak twigs overhead
In a full-hearted evensong
    Of joy illimited;   20
An aged thrush, frail, gaunt, and small,
    In blast-beruffled plume,
Had chosen thus to fling his soul
    Upon the growing gloom.

So little cause for carolings   25
    Of such ecstatic sound
Was written on terrestrial things
    Afar or nigh around,
That I could think there trembled through
    His happy good-night air   30
Some blessed Hope, whereof he knew
    And I was unaware.

Channel Firing

That night your great guns, unawares,
Shook all our coffins as we lay,
And broke the chancel window-squares,
We thought it was the Judgement-day

And sat upright. While drearisome   5
Arose the howl of wakened hounds:
The mouse let fall the altar-crumb,
The worms drew back into the mounds,

The glebe cow[6] drooled. Till God called, "No;
It's gunnery practice out at sea   10
Just as before you went below;
The world is as it used to be:

"All nations striving strong to make
Red war yet redder. Mad as hatters
They do no more for Christés sake   15
Than you who are helpless in such matters.

"That this is not the judgment-hour
For some of them's a blessed thing,
For if it were they'd have to scour
Hell's floor for so much threatening. . . .   20

6. A cow kept in a small plot of land or near a rectory.

"Ha, ha. It will be warmer when
I blow the trumpet (if indeed
I ever do; for you are men,
And rest eternal sorely need)."

So down we lay again. "I wonder,   25
Will the world ever saner be,"
Said one, "than when He sent us under
In our indifferent century!"

And many a skeleton shook his head.
"Instead of preaching forty year,"   30
My neighbor Parson Thirdly said,
"I wish I had stuck to pipes and beer."

Again the guns disturbed the hour,
Roaring their readiness to avenge,
As far inland as Stourton Tower,[7]   35
And Camelot, and starlit Stonehenge.

Afterwards

When the Present has latched its postern behind my tremulous
          stay,
     And the May month flaps its glad green leaves like wings,
Delicate-filmed as new-spun silk, will the neighbors say,
     "He was a man who used to notice such things"?

If it be in the dusk when, like an eyelid's soundless blink,   5
     The dewfall-hawk comes crossing the shades to alight
Upon the wind-warped upland thorn, a gazer may think,
     "To him this must have been a familiar sight."

If I pass during some nocturnal blackness, mothy and warm,
     When the hedgehog travels furtively over the lawn,   10
One may say, "He strove that such innocent creatures should
          come to no harm,
     But he could do little for them; and now he is gone."

If, when hearing that I have been stilled at last, they stand at the
          door,
     Watching the full-starred heavens that winter sees,

---

7. Located near the Somersetshire border.

Will this thought rise on those who will meet my face no more,   15
  "He was one who had an eye for such mysteries"?

And will any say when my bell of quittance is head in the gloom,
  And a crossing breeze cuts a pause in its outrollings,
Till they rise again, as they were a new bell's boom,
  "He hears it not now, but used to notice such things"?   20

The Man He Killed

  "Had he and I but met
  By some old ancient inn,
We should have sat us down to wet
  Right many a nipperkin!

  "But ranged as infantry,   5
  And staring face to face,
I shot at him as he at me,
  And killed him in his place.

  "I shot him dead because—
  Because he was my foe,   10
Just so: my foe of course he was;
  That's clear enough; although

  "He thought he'd 'list, perhaps,
  Off-hand-like—just as I—
Was out of work—had sold his traps—   15
  No other reason why.

  "Yes; quaint and curious war is!
  You shoot a fellow down
You'd treat, if met where any bar is,
  Or help to half-a-crown."   20

Fact Questions and Exercises

1. Which lines in "The Ruined Maid" let the reader know that both speakers are female?
2. In what ways has the maid been "improved" by being "ruined"? What does Hardy mean by "ruined"?
3. What does the darkling thrush know that the speaker does not?
4. Who is the speaker in "Channel Firing"? In the poem, who wishes he "had stuck to pipes and beer"?
5. In the context of "Afterwards," what does "stay" mean?

6. In "The Man He Killed," how do you know that the speaker is talking about war?

For Discussion and Writing

1. Discuss Hardy's use of irony or satire. In "The Man He Killed," for instance, what is ironic about the killing? What is ironic in "The Ruined Maid"? What is ironic in "Channel Firing"? What things or values is Hardy condemning in his poems? What values is he advocating, either overtly or by implication?

2. In these poems, does Hardy have an optimistic or pessimistic view of life? How do the various speakers of the poems reflect his view of life? That is, are the speakers flippant? Bitter? Resigned? Explain.

Gerard Manley Hopkins [1844–1889]

Hopkins was born in London, England. He studied at Oxford, where he was converted to Roman Catholicism; in 1877 he was ordained, serving thereafter as a devoted and faithful priest. Despite his religious devotion, he fluctuated between periods of great happiness and deep depression; these moods are reflected in his poetry. None of his poems was published during his life, primarily because Hopkins did not wish to offend his superiors. His poetry is noted for its innovation, particularly for its use of "sprung rhythm"—a method that breaks with the fixed stressed and unstressed syllables of conventional poetic meter, and applies the freer time and tempo controls of music.

God's Grandeur

The world is charged with the grandeur of God.   a
   It will flame out, like shining from shook foil;   b
   It gathers to a greatness, like the ooze of oil   b
Crushed.[1] Why do men then now not reck his rod?   a
Generations have trod, have trod, have trod;   a
   And all is seared with trade; bleared, smeared with toil;   b
   And wears man's smudge and shares man's smell: the soil   b
Is bare now, nor can foot feel, being shod.   a

And for all this, nature is never spent;   c
   There lives the dearest freshness deep down things;   c   10
And though the last lights off the black West went   c
   Oh, morning, at the brown brink eastward, springs—   d

1. Crushing oil from olives.

sestet

Because the Holy Ghost over the bent
  World broods with warm breast and with ah! bright wings.

Symbol (the dove)

The Windhover[2]

To Christ our Lord

I caught this morning morning's minion,[3] king-
    dom of daylight's dauphin,[4] dapple-dawn-drawn Falcon, in his riding
    Of the rolling level underneath him steady air, and striding
High there, how he rung upon the rein of a wimpling wing
In his ecstasy! then off, off forth on swing,   5
    As a skate's heel sweeps smooth on a bow-bend: the hurl and gliding
    Rebuffed the big wind. My heart in hiding
Stirred for a bird,—the achieve of, the mastery of the thing!

Brute beauty and valour and act, oh, air, pride, plume, here
    Buckle! AND the fire that breaks from thee then, a billion
Times told lovelier, more dangerous, O my chevalier!   10

    No wonder of it: shéer plód makes plough down sillion[5]
Shine, and blue-bleak embers, ah my dear,
    Fall, gall themselves, and gash gold-vermilion.

Sound device - alliteration

Carrion Comfort

Not, I'll not, carrion comfort, Despair, not feast on thee;
Not untwist—slack they may be—these last strands of man
In me ór, most weary, cry *I can no more.* I can;
Can something, hope, wish day come, not choose not to be.
But ah, but O thou terrible, why wouldst thou rude on me   5
Thy wring-world right foot rock? lay a lionlimb against me? scan
With darksome devouring eyes my bruised bones? and fan,
O in turns of tempest, me heaped there; me frantic to avoid thee
            and flee?

Why? That my chaff might fly; my grain lie, sheer and clear.
Nay in all that toil, that coil, since (seems) I kissed the rod,   10
Hand rather, my heart lo! lapped strength, stole joy, would
            laugh, chéer.
Cheer whom though? The hero whose heaven-handling flung
            me, fóot tród

---

2. A small falcon or hawk.   3. Darling.   4. Literally, heir.   5. Furrow.

Me? or me that fought him? O which one? is it each one? That
        night, that year
Of now done darkness I wretch lay wrestling with (my God!) my
        God.

Thou Art Indeed Just, Lord

*Justus quidem tu es, Domine, si disputem tecum: verumtamen justa loquar
ad te: Quare via impiorum prosperatur? &c.*[6]

Thou art indeed just, Lord, if I contend
With thee; but, sir, so what I plead is just.
Why do sinners' ways prosper? and why must
Disappointment all I endeavour end?
      Wert thou my enemy, O thou my friend,   5
How wouldst thou worse, I wonder, than thou dost
Defeat, thwart me? Oh, the sots and thralls of lust
Do in spare hours more thrive than I that spend,
Sir, life upon thy cause. See, banks and brakes[7]
Now, leavèd how thick! lacèd they are again   10
With fretty chervil,[8] look, and fresh wind shakes
Them; birds build—but not I build; no, but strain,
Time's eunuch, and not breed one work that wakes.
Mine, O thou lord of life, send my roots rain.

6. See Jeremiah 12:1   7. Ferns.   8. A parsleylike herb, with curled or "fretty" leaves.

Fact Questions and Exercises

1. According to the speaker of "God's Grandeur," why can't "foot feel"? What "broods with warm breast" over the world?
2. In "The Windhover," what stirs the speaker's heart? What does "gall" mean?
3. Define the word "carrion" as it is used in Hopkins's poem. Point out one or two allusions to the Bible in the poem. With whom is the speaker wrestling? What is his reaction?
4. In "Thou Art Indeed Just, Lord," whose ways prosper? To what has the speaker devoted his life?

For Discussion and Writing

1. Does any one theme run throughout these poems? If so, what is it? A theme of happiness? Doubt? Despair? Does the speaker have unwavering faith? What specific lines or phrases support your answer? Do the first two poems here differ from the second two, so far as this theme is concerned?
2. Discuss the poetic style. Does Hopkins use unusual similes or metaphors? Does he use certain words in new or unusual ways ("buckle," for instance)? Do you see any significant differences or similarities between Hopkins's sonnets and those of some of the earlier poets—Shakespeare, for instance?

A. E. Housman [1859–1936]

Alfred Edward Housman was born in Fockbury, England, and studied at Oxford. In 1892 he was given the Chair of Latin at University College; in 1911 he was made Professor of Latin at Cambridge. He devoted most of his time to his classical studies, and led a quiet, solitary life. He wrote very little poetry, but those lyrics that he did write are marked by wit and pathos. Typically, his poems deal with youth facing the tragedy of a brief life and the underlying idea that life must be led here and now, while there is time.

Loveliest of Trees, the Cherry Now

Loveliest of trees, the cherry now
Is hung with bloom along the bough,
And stands about the woodland ride
Wearing white for Eastertide.

Now, of my threescore years and ten,   5
Twenty will not come again,
And take from seventy springs a score,
It only leaves me fifty more.

And since to look at things in bloom
Fifty springs are little room,   10
About the woodlands I will go
To see the cherry hung with snow.

To an Athlete Dying Young

The time you won your town the race
We chaired you through the market-place;
Man and boy stood cheering by,
And home we brought you shoulder-high.

Today, the road all runners come,   5
Shoulder-high we bring you home,
And set you at your threshold down,
Townsman of a stiller town.

Smart lad, to slip betimes away
From fields where glory does not stay   10
And early though the laurel grows
It withers quicker than the rose.

[handwritten: popularity doesn't last that long]

Eyes the shady night has shut
Cannot see the record cut,
And silence sounds no worse than cheers   15
After earth has stopped the ears:

Now you will not swell the rout
Of lads that wore their honors out,
Runners whom renown outran
And the name died before the man.   20

So set, before it echoes fade,
The fleet foot on the sill of shade,
And hold to the low lintel up
The still-defended challenge-cup.

And round that early-laureled head   25
Will flock to gaze the strengthless dead,
And find unwithered on its curls
The garland briefer than a girl's.

[handwritten: CONTRADICTION of STYLE: light, humorous approach; CONTENT: life & death; serious]

Terence, This Is Stupid Stuff

"Terence, this is stupid stuff:
You eat your victuals fast enough;
There can't be much amiss, 'tis clear,
To see the rate you drink your beer.
But oh, good Lord, the verse you make,   5
It gives a chap the belly-ache.
The cow, the old cow, she is dead;   *[handwritten: mocking]*
It sleeps well, the hornéd head:
We poor lads, 'tis our turn now
To hear such tunes as killed the cow.   10
Pretty friendship 'tis to rhyme
Your friends to death before their time
Moping melancholy mad:
Come, pipe a tune to dance to, lad."

        Why, if 'tis dancing you would be,   15
There's brisker pipes than poetry.
Say, for what were hop-yards meant,
Or why was Burton built on Trent?[1]
Oh many a peer of England brews
Livelier liquor than the Muse,   *   20
And malt does more than Milton can
To justify God's ways to man.

[handwritten: answer to above criticism]

1. Burton-on-Trent, a town famous for its breweries.

*[handwritten: * Symbol — author of Paradise Lost]*

Ale, man, ale's the stuff to drink
For fellows whom it hurts to think:
Look into the pewter pot
To see the world as the world's not.
And faith, 'tis pleasant till 'tis past:
The mischief is that 'twill not last.
Oh I have been to Ludlow[2] fair
And left my necktie God knows where,
And carried halfway home, or near,
Pints and quarts of Ludlow beer:
Then the world seemed none so bad,
And I myself a sterling lad;
And down in lovely muck I've lain,
Happy till I woke again.
Then I saw the morning sky:
Heigho, the tale was all a lie;
The world, it was the old world yet,
I was I, my things were wet,
And nothing now remained to do
But begin the game anew.

    Therefore, since the world has still
Much good, but much less good than ill,
And while the sun and moon endure
Luck's a chance, but trouble's sure,
I'd face it as a wise man would,
And train for ill and not for good.
'Tis true, the stuff I bring for sale
Is not so brisk a brew as ale:
Out of a stem that scored the hand
I wrung it in a weary land.
But take it: if the smack is sour,
The better for the embittered hour;
It should do good to heart and head
When your soul is in my soul's stead;
And I will friend you, if I may,
In the dark and cloudy day.

    There was a king reigned in the East:
There, when kings will sit to feast,
They get their fill before they think
With poisoned meat and poisoned drink.
He gathered all that springs to birth
From the many-venomed earth;
First a little, thence to more,
He sampled all her killing store;

30

40

45

50

55

60

65

Handwritten annotations:

"Personal testimony" (left margin)

If your hurt, drink to forget

Drink to make the world seem brighter 25

Faith is not lasting

Being drunk numerous times; makes the world seem better until the morning, when you wake and find nothing's changed. Then, the process of starting over begins. 35

Much good in the world exists, but less than the bad.

The wise man learns how to deal with the bad; for sure he will need the knowledge.

Take the bitter (hard) and learn from it, pay off in the end.

Example of the lesson he's trying to tell.

hand in briar patch (left margin)

a friend in the cloudy days is a better friend than... (left margin)

---

2. A town in Shropshire, England.

And easy, smiling, seasoned sound,
Sate the king when healths went round.
They put arsenic in his meat
And stared aghast to watch him eat;   70
They poured strychnine in his cup
And shook to see him drink it up:
They shook, they stared as white's their shirt:
Them it was their poison hurt.
—I tell the tale that I heard told.   75
Mithridates,[3] he died old.

(margin note, left) Summation: The wise men protect themselves from bad with the knowledge & experience of bad!

(margin note, right) "They" were flabergasted & shocked that their plan to murder the king did not succeed

3. Mithridates was an Asian king (first century, B.C.) who drank small doses of poison so that he would become immune to them.

Fact Questions and Exercises

1. In "Loveliest of Trees," how old is the speaker? How many years does he calculate that he will live? What season of the year is the setting for the poem?
2. What are some of the reasons that the athlete was a "smart lad" for dying young? In stanza 1, the athlete is being carried in triumph through the town. Where is he being carried in stanza 2?
3. In "Terence, This Is Stupid Stuff" Housman makes an allusion to a famous English poet—who? Are there other allusions in the poem?
4. What has Terence "carried halfway home, or near"? What is the geographical setting of the poem? How do you know?
5. According to Terence, for what must a person train? How did Mithridates survive to old age?

For Discussion and Writing

1. One of the themes of these poems is an awareness of life's brevity. How is the theme presented? In "To an Athlete Dying Young," the poet points out some advantages to an early death—yet in "Terence, This Is Stupid Stuff," he shows how one can live to be very old. Are these two poems contradictory, or is Housman being ironic in the latter? Does he say, in fact, that there is no real purpose to living a long life? How does "Loveliest of Trees" fit into these themes, if at all?
2. Consider the style of Housman's poems. Particularly in "Terence, This Is Stupid Stuff," Housman uses a light, humorous approach, yet his subject matter is hardly "light." What qualities does Housman gain by this contradiction of style and content? Does the contrast present interesting tensions or conflicts? Or do you see the contrast as a weakness in the poems? Explain.

William Butler Yeats [1865–1939]

Yeats was born in Dublin, Ireland, where he attended art school. He intended to become an artist, but by 1885 he had given up painting for poetry. Yeats was also instrumental in founding the Irish National Theatre, and even served for six years as a senator.

Yeats, like his father, did not believe in orthodox Christianity; he tried to find a replacement for it in various kinds of mysticism, folklore, and spiritualism. Much of his poetic symbolism lies in these different systems. His verse is varied and powerful. He is generally considered to be one of the greatest of modern poets.

The Lake Isle of Innisfree

I will arise and go now, and go to Innisfree,
And a small cabin build there, of clay and wattles[1] made:
Nine bean-rows will I have there, a hive for the honey-bee,
And live alone in the bee-loud glade.

And I shall have some peace there, for peace comes dropping
        slow,   5
Dropping from the veils of the morning to where the cricket
        sings;
There midnight's all a glimmer, and noon a purple glow,
And evening full of the linnet's wings.

I will arise and go now, for always night and day
I hear lake water lapping with low sounds by the shore;   10
While I stand on the roadway, or on the pavements gray,
I hear it in the deep heart's core.

The Second Coming

Turning and turning in the widening gyre[2]
The falcon cannot hear the falconer;
Things fall apart; the center cannot hold;
Mere anarchy is loosed upon the world,
The blood-dimmed tide is loosed, and everywhere   5
The ceremony of innocence is drowned;
The best lack all conviction, while the worst
Are full of passionate intensity.

Surely some revelation is at hand;
Surely the Second Coming is at hand;   10
The Second Coming! Hardly are those words out
When a vast image out of *Spiritus Mundi*
Troubles my sight: somewhere in sands of the desert
A shape with lion body and the head of a man,
A gaze blank and pitiless as the sun,   15

1. Interwoven poles and branches. 2. See "An Introduction to Reading Literature," p. 14, for comments about "gyre" and other aspects of this poem.

Is moving its slow thighs, while all about it
Reel shadows of the indignant desert birds.
The darkness drops again; but now I know
That twenty centuries of stony sleep
Were vexed to nightmare by a rocking cradle,   20
And what rough beast, its hour come round at last,
Slouches towards Bethlehem to be born?

Sailing to Byzantium

1

That is no country for old men. The young
In one another's arms, birds in the trees
—Those dying generations—at their song,
The salmon-falls, the mackerel-crowded seas,
Fish, flesh, or fowl, commend all summer long   5
Whatever is begotten, born, and dies.
Caught in that sensual music all neglect
Monuments of unaging intellect.

2

An aged man is but a paltry thing,
A tattered coat upon a stick, unless   10
Soul clap its hands and sing, and louder sing
For every tatter in its mortal dress,
Nor is there singing school but studying
Monuments of its own magnificence;
And therefore I have sailed the seas and come   15
To the holy city of Byzantium.[3]

3

O sages standing in God's holy fire
As in the gold mosaic of a wall,
Come from the holy fire, perne in a gyre,
And be the singing-masters of my soul.   20
Consume my heart away; sick with desire
And fastened to a dying animal
It knows not what it is; and gather me
Into the artifice of eternity.

4

Once out of nature I shall never take   25
My bodily form from any natural thing,
But such a form as Grecian goldsmiths make
Of hammered gold and gold enameling

3. The eastern capital of the Roman Empire, Byzantium, now Istanbul, was famous as a center
of art and culture.

To keep a drowsy Emperor awake;
Or set upon a golden bough to sing   30
To lords and ladies of Byzantium
Of what is past, or passing, or to come.

Lapis Lazuli

(For Harry Clifton)

I have heard that hysterical women say
They are sick of the palette and fiddle-bow,
Of poets that are always gay,
For everybody knows or else should know
That if nothing drastic is done   5
Aeroplane and Zeppelin will come out,
Pitch like King Billy[4] bomb-balls in
Until the town lie beaten flat.

All perform their tragic play,
There struts Hamlet, there is Lear,   10
That's Ophelia, that Cordelia;
Yet they, should the last scene be there,
The great stage curtain about to drop,
If worthy their prominent part in the play,
Do not break up their lines to weep.   15
They know that Hamlet and Lear are gay;
Gaiety transfiguring all that dread.
All men have aimed at, found and lost;
Black out; Heaven blazing into the head:
Tragedy wrought to its uttermost.   20
Though Hamlet rambles and Lear rages,
And all the drop-scenes drop at once
Upon a hundred thousand stages,
It cannot grow by an inch or an ounce.

On their own feet they came, or on shipboard,   25
Camelback, horseback, ass-back, mule-back,
Old civilizations put to the sword.
Then they and their wisdom went to rack:
No handiwork of Callimachus,[5]
Who handled marble as if it were bronze,   30
Made draperies that seemed to rise
When sea-wind swept the corner, stands;
His long lamp-chimney shaped like the stem
Of a slender palm, stood but a day;

4. Probably King William III, who defeated James II at the Battle of the Boyne (1690).
5. Fifth-century B.C. Greek sculptor.

All things fall and are built again,   35
And those that build them again are gay.

Two Chinamen, behind them a third,
Are carved in lapis lazuli,[6]
Over them flies a long-legged bird,
A symbol of longevity;   40
The third, doubtless a serving-man,
Carries a musical instrument.

Every discoloration of the stone,
Every accidental crack or dent,
Seems a water-course or an avalanche,   45
Of lofty slope where it still snows
Though doubtless plum or cherry-branch
Sweetens the little half-way house
Those Chinamen climb towards, and I
Delight to imagine them seated there;   50
There, on the mountain and the sky,
On all the tragic scene they stare.
One asks for mournful melodies;
Accomplished fingers begin to play.
Their eyes mid many wrinkles, their eyes,   55
Their ancient, glittering eyes, are gay.

6. A semiprecious, dark blue stone.

Fact Questions and Exercises

1. "The Second Coming" was written near the time of World War I and the Irish rebellion. What are some of the lines that possibly refer to this general historical period? Point out some of the biblical allusions that appear in the poem.
2. Which line in "The Second Coming" refers to the Sphinx?
3. In "Sailing to Byzantium," what, according to the speaker, is neglected? Which line in the poem compares an old man to a scarecrow?
4. Point out the allusions to Shakespeare's works that appear in "Lapis Lazuli." Describe the scene that is "carved" in the stone. What is lapis lazuli?

For Discussion and Writing

1. "Lapis Lazuli" and "Sailing to Byzantium" are, in part, statements about the creative or artistic process. What is Yeats's attitude toward art as expressed in these poems? Can it make a person immortal? Which other poems have you read that make similar statements?
2. How would you characterize the speakers or personas of these poems? Does the romantic, escapist attitude expressed in "The Lake Isle of Innisfree" carry

through into the other poems? If not, how does the speaker change? What
forces cause the change?

3. Write an interpretation of one of Yeats's poems. Suggest meanings for his
symbols. Discuss those aspects of the poem that you like. Explain those
aspects you dislike. (See An Introduction to Reading Literature, page 14, for
comments about Yeats's poetry.)

Edwin Arlington Robinson [1869–1935]

Robinson was born in Head Tide, Maine, and was reared in
Gardiner. He attended Harvard for two years, but was forced to
leave when family fortunes disintegrated. Although he wrote
poems from age eleven, he received no public recognition until
1927, when he won the Pulitzer Prize. Theodore Roosevelt, one of
the first to appreciate Robinson, got him a job in the New York
Customs House so that he could support himself while writing his
poetry; still, for most of his life, Robinson was poverty stricken
and prone to alcoholism. Among his collections of poems are *The
Man Against the Sky* (1916), *Merlin* (1917), and *Tristam* (1927).

Cliff Klingenhagen

Cliff Klingenhagen had me in to dine
With him one day; and after soup and meat,
And all the other things there were to eat,
Cliff took two glasses and filled one with wine
And one with wormwood. Then, without a sign   5
For me to choose at all, he took the draught
Of bitterness himself, and lightly quaffed
It off, and said the other one was mine.

And when I asked him what the deuce he meant
By doing that, he only looked at me   10
And smiled, and said it was a way of his.
And though I know the fellow, I have spent
Long time a-wondering when I shall be
As happy as Cliff Klingenhagen is.

Richard Cory

Whenever Richard Cory went down town,
We people on the pavement looked at him:
He was a gentleman from sole to crown,
Clean favored, and imperially slim.

And he was always quietly arrayed,   5
And he was always human when he talked;
But still he fluttered pulses when he said,
'Good-morning,' and he glittered when he walked.

And he was rich—yes, richer than a king—
And admirably schooled in every grace: 10
In fine, we thought that he was everything
To make us wish that we were in his place.

So on we worked, and waited for the light,
And went without the meat, and cursed the bread;
And Richard Cory, one calm summer night,   15
Went home and put a bullet through his head.

Miniver Cheevy

Miniver Cheevy, child of scorn,
        Grew lean while he assailed the seasons;
He wept that he was ever born,
        And he had reasons.

Miniver loved the days of old   5
        When swords were bright and steeds were prancing;
The vision of a warrior bold
        Would set him dancing.

Miniver sighed for what was not,
        And dreamed, and rested from his labors;   10
He dreamed of Thebes[1] and Camelot,[2]
        And Priam's[3] neighbors.

Miniver mourned the ripe renown
        That made so many a name so fragrant;
He mourned Romance, now on the town,   15
        And Art, a vagrant.

Miniver loved the Medici,[4]
        Albeit he had never seen one;
He would have sinned incessantly
        Could he have been one.   20

Miniver cursed the commonplace
        And eyed a khaki suit with loathing;

1. Ancient Greek city (see *Oedipus Rex,* page 433).   2. Site of King Arthur's court.
3. Priam, king of ancient Troy.   4. A famous family of the Italian Renaissance, noted both
for their cruelty and their work in advancing the arts.

He missed the medieval grace
    Of iron clothing.

Miniver scorned the gold he sought,   25
    But sore annoyed was he without it;
Miniver thought, and thought, and thought,
    And thought about it.

Miniver Cheevy, born too late,
    Scratched his head and kept on thinking;   30
Miniver coughed, and called it fate,
    And kept on drinking.

Flammonde

The man Flammonde, from God knows where,
With firm address and foreign air,
With news of nations in his talk
And something royal in his walk,
With glint of iron in his eyes,
But never doubt, nor yet surprise,   5
Appeared, and stayed, and held his head
As one by kings accredited.

Erect, with his alert repose
About him, and about his clothes,
He pictured all tradition hears   10
Of what we owe to fifty years.
His cleansing heritage of taste
Paraded neither want nor waste;
And what he needed for his fee
To live, he borrowed graciously.   15

He never told us what he was,
Or what mischance, or other cause,
Had banished him from better days
To play the Prince of Castaways.
Meanwhile he played surpassing well   20
A part, for most, unplayable;
In fine, one pauses, half afraid
To say for certain that he played.

For that, one may as well forego
Conviction as to yes or no;   25
Nor can I say just how intense
Would then have been the difference
To several, who, having striven

In vain to get what he was given,   30
Would see the stranger taken on
By friends not easy to be won.

Moreover, many a malcontent
He soothed and found munificent;
His courtesy beguiled and foiled   35
Suspicion that his years were soiled;
His mien distinguished any crowd,
His credit strengthened when he bowed;
And women, young and old, were fond
Of looking at the man Flammonde.   40

There was a woman in our town
On whom the fashion was to frown;
But while our talk renewed the tinge
Of a long-faded scarlet fringe,
The man Flammonde saw none of that,   45
And what he saw we wondered at—
That none of us, in her distress,
Could hide or find our littleness.

There was a boy that all agreed
Had shut within him the rare seed   50
Of learning. We could understand,
But none of us could lift a hand.
The man Flammonde appraised the youth,
And told a few of us the truth;
And thereby, for a little gold,   55
A flowered future was unrolled.

There were two citizens who fought
For years and years, and over nought;
They made life awkward for their friends,
And shortened their own dividends.   60
The man Flammonde said what was wrong
Should be made right; nor was it long
Before they were again in line,
And had each other in to dine.

And these I mention are but four   65
Of many out of many more.
So much for them. But what of him—
So firm in every look and limb?
What small satanic sort of kink
Was in his brain? What broken link   70
Withheld him from the destinies
That came so near to being his?

What was he, when we came to sift
His meaning, and to note the drift
Of incommunicable ways   75
That make us ponder while we praise?

Why was it that his charm revealed
Somehow the surface of a shield?
What was it that we never caught?
What was he, and what was he not?   80

How much it was of him we met
We cannot ever know; nor yet
Shall all he gave us quite atone
For what was his, and his alone;
Nor need we now, since he knew best,   85
Nourish an ethical unrest:
Rarely at once will nature give
The power to be Flammonde and live.

We cannot know how much we learn
From those who never will return,   90
Until a flash of unforeseen
Remembrance falls on what has been.
We've each a darkening hill to climb;
And this is why, from time to time
In Tilbury Town, we look beyond   95
Horizons for the man Flammonde.

Mr. Flood's Party

Old Eben Flood, climbing alone one night
Over the hill between the town below
And the forsaken upland hermitage
That held as much as he should ever know
On earth again of home, paused warily.   5
The road was his with not a native near;
And Eben, having leisure, said aloud,
For no man else in Tilbury Town to hear:

"Well, Mr. Flood, we have the harvest moon
Again, and we may not have many more;   10
The bird is on the wing, the poet says,
And you and I have said it here before.
Drink to the bird." He raised up to the light
The jug that he had gone so far to fill,
And answered huskily: "Well, Mr. Flood,   15
Since you propose it, I believe I will."

Alone, as if enduring to the end
A valiant armor of scarred hopes outworn,
He stood there in the middle of the road
Like Roland's ghost winding a silent horn.   20
Below him, in the town among the trees,
Where friends of other days had honored him,
A phantom salutation of the dead
Rang thinly till old Eben's eyes were dim.

Then, as a mother lays her sleeping child   25
Down tenderly, fearing it may awake,
He set the jug down slowly at his feet
With trembling care, knowing that most things break;
And only when assured that on firm earth
It stood, as the uncertain lives of men   30
Assuredly did not, he paced away,
And with his hand extended paused again:

"Well, Mr. Flood, we have not met like this
In a long time; and many a change has come
To both of us, I fear, since last it was   35
We had a drop together. Welcome home!"
Convivially returning with himself,
Again he raised the jug up to the light;
And with an acquiescent quaver said:
"Well, Mr. Flood, if you insist, I might.   40

"Only a very little, Mr. Flood—
For auld lang syne. No more, sir; that will do."
So, for the time, apparently it did,
And Eben evidently thought so too;
For soon amid the silver loneliness   45
Of night he lifted up his voice and sang,
Secure, with only two moons listening,
Until the whole harmonious landscape rang—

"For auld lang syne." The weary throat gave out,
The last word wavered; and the song being done,   50
He raised again the jug regretfully
And shook his head, and was again alone.
There was not much that was ahead of him,
And there was nothing in the town below—
Where strangers would have shut the many doors   55
That many friends had opened long ago.

Fact Questions and Exercises

1. In "Cliff Klingenhagen," what does "wormwood" mean?
2. In line 24 of "Miniver Cheevy," what does "iron clothing" mean? What are

some of the things that Miniver Cheevy misses because he was "born too late"?

3. Point out the good deeds that Flammonde performs. In what town is the poem set? Does this same town appear in any of the other Robinson poems? If so, which poem?

4. To whom is Eben Flood speaking? Which lines in the poem support your answer? What song does Eben Flood sing at the end of the poem?

5. In which of these poems does a rich man go "home and put a bullet through his head"?

6. Which of Robinson's characters drinks a bitter drink, but remains "happy"?

7. Which of Robinson's characters has a "satanic sort of kink"?

For Discussion and Writing

1. In "Flammonde," Robinson says: "We've each a darkening hill to climb." Could this serve as a statement of the theme for all of Robinson's poems? Does each of Robinson's personas have a skeptical outlook on life? How does Robinson show this skepticism? Does any force or value counteract this skepticism?

2. Do Robinson's characters share any common traits? If so, what are they? How, for instance, do the various characters relate to their fellow beings? Do the characters prefer the past, the present, or the future? Could you compare Robinson's characters with the characters of other writers you have studied?

Robert Frost [1874–1963]

Frost was born in San Francisco, California; at the age of eleven, he returned to the New England of his ancestors. He briefly attended Dartmouth and Harvard, but soon gave up formal education to work at a variety of jobs—mill worker, shoemaker, teacher, and farmer. He published his first poems when he was twenty, but they attracted no attention. In 1912 he left America and settled in England, where his poetry was appreciated, and where, in 1913, he published his first collection, *A Boy's Will.* He returned to America in 1915, an established poet. Before his death, he had become one of the most famous American poets. His poetry is often conventional in form (the sonnet, the couplet, the ballad), and simple in subject and language; but it is very modern in content, displaying a philosophical complexity and a concern for the social problems of a fragmented urban society. Among his poetry collections are *North of Boston* (1914) and *New Hampshire* (1923), which won Frost his first of four Pulitzer Prizes.

Mending Wall

Something there is that doesn't love a wall,
That sends the frozen-ground-swell under it

And spills the upper boulders in the sun,
And makes gaps even two can pass abreast.
The work of hunters is another thing: 5
I have come after them and made repair
Where they have left not one stone on a stone,
But they would have the rabbit out of hiding,
To please the yelping dogs. The gaps I mean,
No one has seen them made or heard them made,   10
But at spring mending-time we find them there.
I let my neighbor know beyond the hill;
And on a day we meet to walk the line
And set the wall between us once again.
We keep the wall between us as we go.   15
To each the boulders that have fallen to each.
And some are loaves and some so nearly balls
We have to use a spell to make them balance:
"Stay where you are until our backs are turned!"
We wear our fingers rough with handling them.   20
Oh, just another kind of outdoor game,
One on a side. It comes to little more:
There where it is we do not need the wall:
He is all pine and I am apple orchard.
My apple trees will never get across   25
And eat the cones under his pines, I tell him.
He only says, "Good fences make good neighbors."
Spring is the mischief in me, and I wonder
If I could put a notion in his head:
"*Why* do they make good neighbors? Isn't it   30
Where there are cows? But here there are no cows.
Before I built a wall I'd ask to know
What I was walling in or walling out,
And to whom I was like to give offense.
Something there is that doesn't love a wall,   35
That wants it down." I could say "Elves" to him,
But it's not elves exactly, and I'd rather
He said it for himself. I see him there,
Bringing a stone grasped firmly by the top
In each hand, like an old-stone savage armed.   40
He moves in darkness as it seems to me,
Not of woods only and the shade of trees.
He will not go behind his father's saying,
And he likes having thought of it so well
He says again, "Good fences make good neighbors."   45

Stopping by Woods
on a Snowy Evening

Whose woods these are I think I know.   *a*
His house is in the village, though;   *a*

[handwritten: iambic tetrameter]

He will not see me stopping here   b
To watch his woods fill up with snow.   a

My little horse must think it queer   b   5
To stop without a farmhouse near   b
Between the woods and frozen lake   c
The darkest evening of the year.   b

He gives his harness bells a shake   c
To ask if there is some mistake.   c   10
The only other sound's the sweep   d
Of easy wind and downy flake.   d

The woods are lovely, dark, and deep,   d
But I have promises to keep,   d
And miles to go before I sleep,   d   15
And miles to go before I sleep.   d

Acquainted with the Night

I have been one acquainted with the night. a
I have walked out in rain—and back in rain. b
I have outwalked the furthest city light. a
good things, etc.

I have looked down the saddest city lane. b
I have passed by the watchman on his beat c   5
And dropped my eyes, unwilling to explain. b

I have stood still and stopped the sound of feet c
When far away an interrupted cry d
Came over houses from another street, c

But not to call me back or say good-by; d   10
And further still at an unearthly height a
One luminary clock against the sky d
moon

Proclaimed the time was neither wrong nor right. a
I have been one acquainted with the night. a

mysteries of life; loneliness, death, etc.

He's lived, seen all the sadness of life

Fact Questions and Exercises

1. Which facts in "Mending Wall" indicate that the poem is set in New England?
2. Describe the circumstances that bring the two neighbors together. What does the neighbor say when asked why the wall must be repaired?
3. Who or what "must think it queer" to stop by the woods? What must the speaker of "Stopping by Woods on a Snowy Evening" do before he can rest?
4. In line 12 of "Acquainted with the Night," what does "luminary" mean?
5. Which of Frost's poems is a sonnet?

For Discussion and Writing

1. In "Mending Wall," what does the wall symbolize? That is, does the poem merely tell the story of two neighbors fixing a stone fence, or does it say something more important than that? Note, for instance, lines 32 through 34 of the poem.

2. In Frost's poems, what values or forces seem to bring happiness or contentment to the speaker? What seems to cause unhappiness or despair? Is Frost either totally optimistic or totally pessimistic about life? Explain.

Wallace Stevens [1879–1955]

Stevens was born in Reading, Pennsylvania. He attended Harvard for three years. He then received a law degree from New York Law school and was admitted to the bar in 1904. For a decade he lived the dual life of daytime lawyer and nighttime poet-artist, before leaving New York and moving to Hartford, Connecticut, where he became the vice president of a large insurance company—a position he would hold until his death. One of the interesting anecdotes told about Stevens is that he composed poetry in the back seat of his limousine, while being driven to work! His poetry is characterized by its wit and its contrast of appearance to reality, of the mundane to the artistic. Among his collections are *Harmonium* (1923) and *The Man with the Blue Guitar* (1937).

The Idea of Order at Key West

She sang beyond the genius of the sea.
The water never formed to mind or voice,
Like a body wholly body, fluttering
Its empty sleeves; and yet its mimic motion
Made constant cry, caused constantly a cry,   5
That was not ours although we understood,
Inhuman, of the veritable ocean.

The sea was not a mask. No more was she.
The song and water were not medleyed sound
Even if what she sang was what she heard,   10
Since what she sang was uttered word by word.
It may be that in all her phrases stirred
The grinding water and the gasping wind;
But it was she and not the sea we heard.
For she was the maker of the song she sang.   15
The ever-hooded, tragic-gestured sea
Was merely a place by which she walked to sing.

Whose spirit is this? we said, because we knew
It was the spirit that we sought and knew
That we should ask this often as she sang.   20

If it was only the dark voice of the sea
That rose, or even colored by many waves;
If it was only the outer voice of sky
And cloud, of the sunken coral water-walled,
However clear, it would have been deep air,   25
The heaving speech of air, a summer sound
Repeated in a summer without end
And sound alone. But it was more than that,
More even than her voice, and ours, among
The meaningless plungings of water and the wind,   30
Theatrical distances, bronze shadows heaped
On high horizons, mountainous atmospheres
Of sky and sea.
             It was her voice that made
The sky acutest at its vanishing.   35
She measured to the hour its solitude.
She was the single artificer of the world
In which she sang. And when she sang, the sea,
Whatever self it had, became the self
That was her song, for she was the maker. Then we,   40
As we beheld her striding there alone,
Knew that there never was a world for her
Except the one she sang and, singing, made.

Ramon Fernandez, tell me, if you know,
Why, when the singing ended and we turned   45
Toward the town, tell why the glassy lights,
The lights in the fishing boats at anchor there,
As the night descended, tilting in the air,
Mastered the night and portioned out the sea,
Fixing emblazoned zones and fiery poles,   50
Arranging, deepening, enchanting night.

Oh! Blessed rage for order, pale Ramon,
The maker's rage to order words of the sea,
Words of the fragrant portals, dimly-starred,
And of ourselves and of our origins,   55
In ghostlier demarcations, keener sounds.

The Emperor of Ice-Cream

Call the roller of big cigars,
The muscular one, and bid him whip

In kitchen cups concupiscent curds.
Let the wenches dawdle in such dress
As they are used to wear, and let the boys   5
Bring flowers in last month's newspapers.
Let be be finale of seem.
The only emperor is the emperor of ice-cream.

Take from the dresser of deal.
Lacking the three glass knobs, that sheet   10
On which she embroidered fantails once
And spread it so as to cover her face.
If her horny feet protrude, they come
To show how cold she is, and dumb.
Let the lamp affix its beam.   15
The only emperor is the emperor of ice-cream.

Anecdote of the Jar

I placed a jar in Tennessee,
And round it was, upon a hill.
It made the slovenly wilderness
Surround that hill.

The wilderness rose up to it,   5
And sprawled around, no longer wild.
The jar was round upon the ground
And tall and of a port in air.

It took dominion everywhere.
The jar was gray and bare.   10
It did not give of bird or bush,
Like nothing else in Tennessee.

Fact Questions and Exercises

1. In "The Idea of Order at Key West," where is the woman walking as she
   sings? In line 37, what does "artificer" mean? What person other than the
   singer is mentioned in the poem?
2. In "The Emperor of Ice-Cream," which line indicates that the "boys" are
   poor? Which lines suggest that the dead woman was a prostitute?
3. In "Anecdote of the Jar," in what state does the speaker place the jar? Exactly
   where does he place it?

For Discussion and Writing

1. Look again at "The Idea of Order at Key West." What represents nature in the
   poem? How does the singer contrast to nature? How is the poem a statement
   about the importance of the creative process? Do any of the other poems by

Stevens make a similar statement about man's creativity? What force in the poem represents "order"?

2. Write an analysis of "The Emperor of Ice-Cream." Note, for instance, the vocabulary. What are the denotations and connotations of "concupiscent"? Of "curds"? In line 1, how is "roller" used? Is there a double-entendre in the word "horny"? Also, *who* is the emperor? And what is the implication of there being no other "emperor"? In short, by noting any and all relevant aspects of the poem, present a logical argument for what you think the poem means.

William Carlos Williams [1883–1963]

Williams was born in Rutherford, New Jersey, the town in which he would eventually make his home. He was educated in Europe, took his M.D. at the University of Pennsylvania, and later studied pediatrics at the University of Leipzig. His life was primarily devoted to medicine; he remained a practicing physician almost until his death. Still, he managed to write a prolific amount of prose and poetry, beginning with *Poems,* in 1909. Although Williams himself rejected the term "imagist," his work stands nonetheless at the forefront of imagist poetry. Among his many writings are *Sour Grapes* (1921) and *Paterson* (1946–1958).

The Red Wheelbarrow

so much depends
upon

a red wheel
barrow

glazed with rain   5
water

beside the white
chickens.

Portrait of a Lady

Your thighs are appletrees
whose blossoms touch the sky.
Which sky? The sky
where Watteau[1] hung a lady's

1. A French painter (1684–1721).

slipper. Your knees   5
are a southern breeze—or
a gust of snow. Agh! what
sort of man was Fragonard?[2]
—as if that answered
anything. Ah, yes—below   10
the knees, since the tune
drops that way, it is
one of those white summer days,
the tall grass of your ankles
flickers upon the shore—   15
Which shore?—
the sand clings to my lips—
Which shore?
Agh, petals maybe. How
should I know?   20
Which shore? Which shore?
I said petals from an appletree.

2. Another French painter (1732–1806). Actually, it was Fragonard, not Watteau, who painted "The Swing," which depicts a girl kicking her shoe into the air.

The Yachts

contend in a sea which the land partly encloses
shielding them from the too-heavy blows
of an ungoverned ocean which when it chooses

tortures the biggest hulls, the best man knows
to pit against its beatings, and sinks them pitilessly.   5
Mothlike in mists, scintillant in the minute

brilliance of cloudless days, with broad bellying sails
they glide to the wind tossing green water
from their sharp prows while over them the crew crawls

ant-like, solicitously grooming them, releasing,   10
making fast as they turn, lean far over and having
caught the wind again, side by side, head for the mark.

In a well guarded area of open water surrounded by
lesser and greater craft which, sycophant, lumbering
and flittering follow them, they appear youthful, rare   15

as the light of a happy eye, live with the grace
of all that in the mind is fleckless, free and
naturally to be desired. Now the sea which holds them

is moody, lapping their glossy sides, as if feeling
for some slightest flaw but fails completely.   20
Today no race. Then the wind comes again. The yachts

move, jockeying for a start, the signal is set and they
are off. Now the waves strike at them but they are too
well made, they slip through, though they take in canvas.

Arms with hands grasping seek to clutch at the prows.   25
Bodies thrown recklessly in the way are cut aside.
It is a sea of faces about them in agony, in despair

until the horror of the race dawns staggering the mind,
the whole sea become an entanglement of watery bodies
lost to the world bearing what they cannot hold. Broken,   30

beaten, desolate, reaching from the dead to be taken up
they cry out, failing, failing! their cries rising
in waves still as the skillful yachts pass over.

Fact Questions and Exercises

1. With what is the red wheelbarrow glazed? What does the wheelbarrow stand beside?
2. In "Portrait of a Lady," Williams says: "Your thighs are appletrees"; point out other elements of nature that he uses to describe the lady. In the poem, what "drops that way"?
3. In line 14 of "The Yachts," what does "sycophant" mean? What happens to the sea after the race begins?
4. Point out an example of personification in "The Yachts."

For Discussion and Writing

1. Review the discussion of imagery in An Introduction to Reading Literature, pages 15–16, and then discuss Williams's use of imagery. Is it limited to "The Red Wheelbarrow"? Or, is it used just as effectively in his other poems?
2. In "The Yachts," note the progression of the description of the sea. How is the sea described in the first part of the poem (to line 18)? How is the sea described in the last part of the poem? Do the yachts also change? Ultimately, which is dominant, the sea or the yachts? Is Williams using the sea and yachts symbolically? If so, what do they symbolize?

T. S. Eliot [1888–1965]

Thomas Stearns Eliot was born in St. Louis, Missouri, a member of one of the most distinguished families in America. He graduated from Harvard, where two of his ancestors—Charles Eliot Norton and Charles William Eliot—had been very influential. Eliot eventually completed the work for a Ph.D., but never returned to Harvard to take the degree; instead he moved to London, where he would spend most of his life, and eventually become a British citizen. Eliot devoted his entire adult life to writing; he is as highly respected for his plays and literary criticism as for his poetry. *The Waste Land* (1922) established Eliot as the most influential poet writing in English; few would dispute the fact that he remains one of the most powerful voices in world literature. His writing is complex, intellectual, and diverse; it forbids any simple characterization. He was awarded the Nobel Prize in 1948.

The Love Song of J. Alfred Prufrock

> S'io credesse che mia risposta fosse
> A persona che mai tornasse al mondo,
> Questa fiamma staria senza piu scosse.
> Ma perciocche giammai di questo fondo
> Non torno vivo alcun, s'i'odo il vero,
> Senza tema d'infamia ti rispondo.[1]

Let us go then, you and I,
When the evening is spread out against the sky
Like a patient etherized upon a table;
Let us go, through certain half-deserted streets,
The muttering retreats   5
Of restless nights in one-night cheap hotels
And sawdust restaurants with oyster-shells:
Streets that follow like a tedious argument
Of insidious intent
To lead you to an overwhelming question. . .   10
Oh, do not ask, "What is it?"
Let us go and make our visit.

In the room the women come and go
Talking of Michelangelo.

The yellow fog that rubs its back upon the window-panes   15
The yellow smoke that rubs its muzzle on the window-panes
Licked its tongue into the corners of the evening,

---

1. See Question 1, For Discussion and Writing, page 1193, for an explanation of this epigraph.

Lingered upon the pools that stand in drains,
Let fall upon its back the soot that falls from chimneys,
Slipped by the terrace, made a sudden leap,   20
And seeing that it was a soft October night,
Curled once about the house, and fell asleep.

And indeed there will be time
For the yellow smoke that slides along the street,
Rubbing its back upon the window-panes;   25
There will be time, there will be time
To prepare a face to meet the faces that you meet;
There will be time to murder and create,
And time for all the works and days of hands
That lift and drop a question on your plate;   30
Time for you and time for me,
And time yet for a hundred indecisions,
And for a hundred visions and revisions,
Before the taking of a toast and tea.

In the room the women come and go   35
Talking of Michelangelo.

And indeed there will be time
To wonder, "Do I dare?" and, "Do I dare?"
Time to turn back and descend the stair,
With a bald spot in the middle of my hair—   40
[They will say: "How his hair is growing thin!"]
My morning coat, my collar mounting firmly to the chin,
My necktie rich and modest, but asserted by a simple pin—
[They will say: "But how his arms and legs are thin!"]
Do I dare   45
Disturb the universe?
In a minute there is time
For decisions and revisions which a minute will reverse.

For I have known them all already, known them all:
Have known the evenings, mornings, afternoons,   50
I have measured out my life with coffee spoons;
I know the voices dying with a dying fall
Beneath the music from a farther room.
          So how should I presume?

And I have known the eyes already, known them all—   55
The eyes that fix you in a formulated phrase,
And when I am formulated, sprawling on a pin,
When I am pinned and wriggling on the wall,
Then how should I begin
To spit out all the butt-ends of my days and ways?   60
          And how should I presume?

And I have known the arms already, known them all—
Arms that are braceleted and white and bare
[But in the lamplight, downed with light brown hair!]
Is it perfume from a dress   65
That makes me so digress?
Arms that lie along a table, or wrap about a shawl.
          And should I then presume?
          And how should I begin?

                    . . . . .

Shall I say, I have gone at dusk through narrow streets   70
And watched the smoke that rises from the pipes
Of lonely men in shirt-sleeves, leaning out of windows? . . .

I should have been a pair of ragged claws
Scuttling across the floors of silent seas.

                    . . . . .

And the afternoon, the evening, sleeps so peacefully!   75
Smoothed by long fingers,
Asleep . . . tired . . . or it malingers,
Stretched on the floor, here beside you and me.
Should I, after tea and cakes and ices,
Have the strength to force the moment to its crisis?   80
But though I have wept and fasted, wept and prayed,
Though I have seen my head [grown slightly bald] brought in
              upon a platter,[2]
I am no prophet—and here's no great matter;
I have seen the moment of my greatness flicker,
And I have seen the eternal Footman hold my coat, and snicker,   85
And in short, I was afraid.

And would it have been worth it, after all,
After the cups, the marmalade, the tea,
Among the porcelain, among some talk of you and me,
Would it have been worth while,   90
To have bitten off the matter with a smile,
To have squeezed the universe into a ball
To roll it toward some overwhelming question,
To say: "I am Lazarus,[3] come from the dead,
Come back to tell you all, I shall tell you all"—   95
If one, settling a pillow by her head,
          Should say: "That is not what I meant at all.
          That is not it, at all."

And would it have been worth it, after all,
Would it have been worth while,   100
After the sunsets and the dooryards and the sprinkled streets,

2. See Matt. 14:1-12. Herod beheaded John the Baptist at the request of Salome.   3. See John
11:1-44.

After the novels, after the teacups, after the skirts that trail along
        the floor—
And this, and so much more?—
It is impossible to say just what I mean!
But as if a magic lantern threw the nerves in patterns on a screen: 105
Would it have been worth while
If one, settling a pillow or throwing off a shawl,
And turning toward the window, should say:
      "That is not it at all,
      That is not what I meant, at all."   110

      .   .   .   .   .

No! I am not Prince Hamlet, nor was meant to be;
Am an attendant lord, one that will do
To swell a progress, start a scene or two,
Advise the prince; no doubt, an easy tool,
Deferential, glad to be of use,   115
Politic, cautious, and meticulous;
Full of high sentence, but a bit obtuse;
At times, indeed, almost ridiculous—
Almost, at times, the Fool.

I grow old . . . I grow old . . .   120
I shall wear the bottoms of my trousers rolled.

Shall I part my hair behind? Do I dare to eat a peach?
I shall wear white flannel trousers, and walk upon the beach.
I have heard the mermaids singing, each to each.

I do not think that they will sing to me.   125

I have seen them riding seaward on the waves
Combing the white hair of the waves blown back
When the wind blows the water white and black.

We have lingered in the chambers of the sea
By sea-girls wreathed with seaweed red and brown   130
Till human voices wake us, and we drown.

The Hippopotamus

    And when this epistle is read among
    you, cause that it be read also in the
    church of the Laodiceans.

The broad-backed hippopotamus
Rests on his belly in the mud;
Although he seems so firm to us
He is merely flesh and blood.

Flesh and blood is weak and frail,   5
Susceptible to nervous shock;
While the True Church can never fail
For it is based upon a rock.

The hippo's feeble steps may err
In compassing material ends,   10
While the True Church need never stir
To gather in its dividends.

The 'potamus can never reach
The mango on the mango-tree;
But fruits of pomegranate and peach   15
Refresh the Church from over sea.

At mating time the hippo's voice
Betrays inflexions hoarse and odd,
But every week we hear rejoice
The Church, at being one with God.   20

The hippopotamus's day
Is passed in sleep; at night he hunts;
God works in a mysterious way—
The Church can sleep and feed at once.

I saw the 'potamus take wing   25
Ascending from the damp savannas,
And quiring angels round him sing
The praise of God, in loud hosannas.

Blood of the Lamb shall wash him clean
And him shall heavenly arms enfold,   30
Among the saints he shall be seen
Performing on a harp of gold.

He shall be washed as white as snow,
By all the martyr'd virgins kist,
While the True Church remains below   35
Wrapt in the old miasmal mist.

Fact Questions and Exercises

1. When the "women come and go" in "The Love Song of J. Alfred Prufrock," of whom do they talk?
2. When Prufrock turns back to "descend the stair," what does he fear "they" will say about him?
3. With what has Prufrock "measured out" his life?
4. Eliot alludes to Hamlet in the poem; point out the other allusions that appear.
5. Who or what has Prufrock heard "singing, each to each"?

6. In "The Hippopotamus," what is "based upon a rock"?
7. What two things are being compared in the poem?
8. What remains wrapped in "the old miasmal mist"?

For Discussion and Writing

1. The epigraph that introduces "Prufrock" is taken from Dante's *Divine Comedy,* a fourteenth-century allegory about the human being's descent into hell and ultimate discovery of paradise. In the quotation, the speaker is Guido da Montefeltro, a man damned in the Inferno, the first part of hell. Guido believes that Dante (to whom he is speaking) is also damned, and will never leave the underworld. Thus Guido tells Dante that since Dante will never return to the world above, then he (Guido) is not afraid to confess; if he knew that Dante would return to the world to repeat his story, then Guido would never reveal his shameful secrets to him. How does this epigraph relate to Eliot's poem?
2. Characterize Prufrock. What facts does the reader know about him? How does he dress? Approximately how old is he? What kind of life has he led? What is his attitude toward women? Does he ever ask the "question"?
3. Eliot develops an analogy in "The Hippopotamus." What is it? How do the hippopotamus and the Church differ? Are they similar in any ways? Look at lines 25 to 36; is Eliot being ironic here? What is Eliot implying here by the animal going to heaven and the True Church remaining below?

e. e. cummings [1894–1962]

Edward Estlin Cummings was born in Cambridge, Massachusetts. His father taught at Harvard, and cummings was later educated there. In 1916 he joined the ambulance corps and went to France; while there, cummings was arrested and served a brief prison term—an experience he uses in his novel *The Enormous Room* (1922). He originally wanted to be a painter, but soon abandoned that idea to devote his time to writing. His poems are famous for their unconventional form and appearance—the absence of punctuation and capitalization, for instance—and for their rebellious attitude toward a society that too often manipulates the individual. Among his many works are *Tulips and Chimneys* (1923), *him* (1927), and *XAIPE* (1950).

All in green went my love riding[1]

All in green went my love riding
on a great horse of gold
into the silver dawn.

four lean hounds crouched low and smiling
the merry deer ran before.   5

1. See "An Introduction to Reading Literature" (pages 6–7) for comments about this poem.

Fleeter be they than dappled dreams
the swift sweet deer
the red rare deer.

Four red roebuck at a white water
the cruel bugle sang before.   10

Horn at hip went my love riding
riding the echo down
into the silver dawn.

four lean hounds crouched low and smiling
the level meadows ran before.   15

Softer be they than slippered sleep
the lean lithe deer
the fleet flown deer.

Four fleet does at a gold valley
the famished arrow sang before.   20

Bow at belt went my love riding
riding the mountain down
into the silver dawn.

four lean hounds crouched low and smiling
the sheer peaks ran before.   25

Paler be they than daunting death
the sleek slim deer
the tall tense deer.

Four tall stags at a green mountain
the lucky hunter sang before.   30

All in green went my love riding
on a great horse of gold
into the silver dawn.

four lean hounds crouched low and smiling
my heart fell dead before.   35

How anyone lived in a pretty how town.
• — pretty I lived in a
" how pretty town.

anyone lived in a pretty how town

anyone lived in a pretty <u>how</u> town
(with up so floating many <u>bells</u> down)
spring summer autumn winter
he sang his didn't he danced his did.

Important events (weddings, death
all year, all season etc

without to many regrets things one doesn't get to do
Happy with & " one does "

[handwritten top left: Syntax up and down in lines]

[handwritten: (big) opposite? answer: not just little but small, small.]

Women and men(both little and small) 5
cared for anyone not at all
[handwritten: PERSON ≠ no one else]
they sowed their isn't they reaped their same,
[handwritten right: Reap their profits which are nothing (Negations)]
sun moon stars rain
[handwritten: day nite fair foul weather]

children guessed(but only a few
and down they forgot as up they grew 10
autumn winter spring summer) *[handwritten: cycle of seasons]*
that noone loved him more by more.
*[handwritten left: a character → noone *]*
*[handwritten: Rather than addition, multiplication * DOUBLE MEANING]*
when by now and tree by leaf
she laughed his joy she cried his grief
[handwritten: SPRING WINTER]
[handwritten: Thru a series of "nows" one 15 gets to "when"]
bird by snow and stir by still *[handwritten: opposites,]*
anyone's any was all to her. *[handwritten: again.]*
[handwritten: Thru a series of leaves you get to the tree (totality of their lives)]
[handwritten left: they shared everything]

someones married their everyones
[handwritten left: contrast]
laughed their cryings and did their dance.
[handwritten left: all the]
(sleep wake hope and then)they *[handwritten: (cycle)]*
said their nevers they slept their dream. 20

[handwritten left: how people — the town]
stars rain sun moon *[handwritten: (cycle) (smaller)]*
(and only the snow can begin to explain
how children are apt to forget to remember
with up so floating many bells down).

one day anyone died i guess 25
(and noone stooped to kiss his face). *[handwritten: * double meaning]*
busy folk buried them side by side
little by little and was by was,
[handwritten: contrast]
[handwritten: Townspeople perspective]
all by all and deep by deep
[handwritten: Anyone's and noone's perspective (also, outside)]
and more by more they dream their sleep. " " 30 " sleep
noone and anyone earth by april
[handwritten: SPRINGTIME, Newness of life]
wish by spirit and if by yes.

Women and men(both dong and ding)
summer autumn winter spring
reaped their sowing and went their came 35
sun moon stars rain

somewhere i have never travelled,gladly beyond

somewhere i have never travelled,gladly beyond
any experience,your eyes have their silence:
in your most frail gesture are things which enclose me,
or which i cannot touch because they are too near

your slightest look easily will unclose me 5
though i have closed myself as fingers,

you open always petal by petal myself as Spring opens
(touching skilfully,mysteriously)her first rose

or if your wish be to close me,i and
my life will shut very beautifully,suddenly,   10
as when the heart of this flower imagines
the snow carefully everywhere descending;

nothing which we are to perceive in this world equals
the power of your intense fragility:whose texture
compels me with the colour of its countries,   15
rendering death and forever with each breathing

(i do not know what it is about you that closes
and opens;only something in me understands
the voice of your eyes is deeper than all roses)
nobody,not even the rain,has such small hands   20

Buffalo Bill's *(uncomparable)*

Irony —
Buffalo Bill
is invincible,
(the blue-eyed
all American boy)
but he is dead.

Buffalo Bill's
defunct *dead, dead*
            who used to
            ride a watersmooth-silver
                                    stallion;   5
and break onetwothreefourfive pigeonsjustlikethat.
                                    Jesus!

He was a handsome man;
                    and what i want to know is,
how do you like your blueeyed boy   10
Mister Death?

Fact Questions and Exercises

1. Remembering that cummings does not usually follow conventional spelling
and spacing of words, what does "noone" in line 12 of "anyone lived in a
pretty how town" mean? That is, how would "noone" be written in
conventional English? In the poem, what eventually happens to "anyone"?

   none
   he dies

2. Point out an example of personification in "Buffalo Bill's."
3. In "somewhere i have never travelled,gladly beyond" what opened "petal by
petal"? What flower is used prominently in the poem?

For Discussion and Writing

1. Is cummings being satirical? Is he poking fun at something or someone? If
so, what is the object of his satire? Is he satirical in a constructive way?

2. Discuss the poet's style. Do you think his unconventional technique (the refusal to use capital letters and such) is effective? What do you think he is trying to convey? Would the meaning change significantly in any one of his poems if conventional punctuation, spelling, and capitalization were used?

W. H. Auden [1907–1973]

Wystan Hugh Auden was born in England, educated at Oxford, and taught school from 1930 to 1935. In 1939 he emigrated to the United States and became an American citizen, leaving in 1956 to return to England as the Professor of Poetry at Oxford. Auden was noted during the 1930s for his Marxist thoughts and activities, but his philosophy gradually changed—his later poetry reflects a distinctly Christian-centered ideology. The influence of Freudian thought is also perceptible in Auden's poetry, and Auden often combines the Christian and Freudian ideas to explore the confusion that results when people have no definite sense of identity.

Musée des Beaux Arts

About suffering they were never wrong,
The Old Masters: how well they understood
Its human position; how it takes place
While someone else is eating or opening a window or just
        walking dully along;
How, when the aged are reverently, passionately waiting   5
For the miraculous birth, there always must be
Children who did not specially want it to happen, skating
On a pond at the edge of the wood·
They never forgot
That even the dreadful martyrdom must run its course   10
Anyhow in a corner, some untidy spot
Where the dogs go on with their doggy life and the torturer's
        horse
Scratches its innocent behind on a tree.

In Brueghel's *Icarus,* for instance: how everything turns away
Quite leisurely from the disaster; the ploughman may   15
Have heard the splash, the forsaken cry,
But for him it was not an important failure; the sun shone
As it had to on the white legs disappearing into the green
Water; and the expensive delicate ship that must have seen
Something amazing, a boy falling out of the sky,   20
Had somewhere to get to and sailed calmly on.

The Unknown Citizen

(To JS/07/M/378 This Marble Monument Is Erected by the State)

He was found by the Bureau of Statistics to be
One against whom there was no official complaint,
And all the reports on his conduct agree
That, in the modern sense of an old-fashioned word, he was a
       saint,
For in everything he did he served the Greater Community.   5
Except for the War till the day he retired
He worked in a factory and never got fired,
But satisfied his employers, Fudge Motors Inc.
Yet he wasn't a scab or odd in his views,
For his Union reports that he paid his dues,   10
(Our report on his Union shows it was sound)
And our Social Psychology workers found
That he was popular with his mates and liked a drink.
The Press are convinced that he bought a paper every day
And that his reactions to advertisements were normal in every
       way.   15
Policies taken out in his name prove that he was fully insured,
And his Health-card shows he was once in hospital but left it
       cured.
Both Producers Research and High-Grade Living declare
He was fully sensible to the advantages of the Installment Plan
And had everything necessary to the Modern Man,   20
A phonograph, a radio, a car and a frigidaire.
Our researchers into Public Opinion are content
That he held the proper opinions for the time of year;
When there was peace, he was for peace; when there was war,
       he went.
He was married and added five children to the population,   25
Which our Eugenist says was the right number for a parent of his
       generation,
And our teachers report that he never interfered with their
       education.
Was he free? Was he happy? The question is absurd:
Had anything been wrong, we should certainly have heard.

As I Walked Out One Evening

As I walked out one evening,
    Walking down Bristol Street,
The crowds upon the pavement
    Were fields of harvest wheat.

And down by the brimming river   5
    I heard a lover sing
Under an arch of the railway:
    "Love has no ending.

"I'll love you, dear, I'll love you
    Till China and Africa meet,   10
And the river jumps over the mountain
    And the salmon sing in the street,

"I'll love you until the ocean
    Is folded and hung up to dry
And the seven stars go squawking   15
    Like geese about the sky.

"The years shall run like rabbits,
    For in my arms I hold
The Flower of the Ages,
    And the first love of the world."   20

But all the clocks in the city
    Began to whirr and chime:
"O let not Time deceive you,
    You cannot conquer Time.

"In the burrows of the Nightmare   25
    Where Justice naked is,
Time watches from the shadow
    And coughs when you would kiss.

"In headaches and in worry
    Vaguely life leaks away,   30
And Time will have his fancy
    Tomorrow or today.

"Into many a green valley
    Drifts the appalling snow;
Time breaks the threaded dances   35
    And the diver's brilliant bow.

"O plunge your hands in water,
    Plunge them in up to the wrist;
Stare, stare in the basin
    And wonder what you've missed.   40

"The glacier knocks in the cupboard,
    The desert sighs in the bed,
And the crack in the teacup opens
    A lane to the land of the dead.

"Where the beggars raffle the banknotes   45
        And the Giant is enchanting to Jack,
And the Lily-white Boy is a Roarer,
        And Jill goes down on her back.

"O look, look in the mirror,
        O look in your distress;   50
Life remains a blessing
        Although you cannot bless.

"O stand, stand at the window
        As the tears scald and start;
You shall love your crooked neighbor   55
        With your crooked heart."

It was late, late in the evening
        The lovers they were gone;
The clocks had ceased their chiming,
        And the deep river ran on.   60

Fact Questions and Exercises

1. In "Musée des Beaux Arts," point out a Biblical allusion. Point out an allusion to a famous painting.
2. For what company did the Unknown Citizen work? What else does the poem reveal about this man?
3. Point out the metaphor in the first stanza of "As I Walked Out One Evening." How do the "clocks in the city" reply to the lover's song? What does the river do after the lovers are gone and the clocks no longer chime?

Questions for Discussion and Writing

1. In general, what seems to be Auden's attitude toward humanity or society? Does he feel that human beings have compassion? Love of beauty? Freedom of choice? Other admirable qualities? Is human life brief and transitory, or does it have factors that give it permanence? Specifically, how does Auden reveal these attitudes in his poems?
2. Discuss Auden's use of irony or·satire. In "The Unknown Citizen," what is Auden saying? Is the·citizen admirable? Why, when many facts are known about him, is the citizen "unknown"? In "As I Walked Out One Evening," is the lover's song realistic? Do the clocks mock the song? Have you read any other poems in which a lover makes exaggerated promises?

Elizabeth Bishop [1911–   ]

Elizabeth Bishop was born in Worcester, Massachusetts, and was educated at Vassar. At various times, she has lived in Nova Scotia, Key West, and Brazil; travel has been a significant part of her life and is a theme often reflected in her poetry. In 1934 she met and

became friends with Marianne Moore, whose poetry has had a
noticeable influence on Bishop's work. Bishop published her first
volume of poems, *North and South*, in 1946; in 1955 she won the
Pulitzer Prize for *Poems*. In general, her poetry expresses a kind of
cool detachment; it avoids overt emotion but is rich in suggested
feelings and responses.

The Man-Moth[1]

     Here, above,
cracks in the buildings are filled with battered moonlight.
The whole shadow of Man is only as big as his hat.
It lies at his feet like a circle for a doll to stand on,
and he makes an inverted pin, the point magnetized to the moon.   5
He does not see the moon; he observes only her vast properties,
feeling the queer light on his hands, neither warm nor cold,
of a temperature impossible to record in thermometers.

     But when the Man-Moth
pays his rare, although occasional, visits to the surface,   10
the moon looks rather different to him. He emerges
from an opening under the edge of one of the sidewalks
and nervously begins to scale the faces of the buildings.
He thinks the moon is a small hole at the top of the sky,
proving the sky quite useless for protection.   15
He trembles, but must investigate as high as he can climb.

     Up the façades,
his shadow dragging like a photographer's cloth behind him,
he climbs fearfully, thinking that this time he will manage
to push his small head through that round clean opening   20
and be forced through, as from a tube, in black scrolls on the light.
(Man, standing below him, has no such illusions.)
But what the Man-Moth fears most he must do, although
he fails, of course, and falls back scared but quite unhurt.

     Then he returns   25
to the pale subways of cement he calls his home. He flits,
he flutters, and cannot get aboard the silent trains
fast enough to suit him. The doors close swiftly.
The Man-Moth always seats himself facing the wrong way
and the train starts at once at its full, terrible speed,   30
without a shift in gears or a gradation of any sort.
He cannot tell the rate at which he travels backwards.

1. Bishop's note: "Newspaper misprint for 'mammoth.'"

Each night he must
be carried through artificial tunnels and dream recurrent dreams.
Just as the ties recur beneath his train, these underlie   35
his rushing brain. He does not dare look out the window,
for the third rail, the unbroken draught of poison,
runs there beside him. He regards it as a disease
he has inherited the susceptibility to. He has to keep
his hands in his pockets, as others must wear mufflers.   40

If you catch him,
hold up a flashlight to his eye. It's all dark pupil,
an entire night itself, whose haired horizon tightens
as he stares back, and closes up the eye. Then from the lids
one tear, his only possession, like the bee's sting, slips.   45
Slyly he palms it, and if you're not paying attention
he'll swallow it. However, if you watch, he'll hand it over,
cool as from underground springs and pure enough to drink.

The Fish

I caught a tremendous fish
and held him beside the boat
half out of water, with my hook
fast in a corner of his mouth.
He didn't fight.   5
He hadn't fought at all.
He hung a grunting weight,
battered and venerable
and homely. Here and there
his brown skin hung in strips   10
like ancient wallpaper,
and its pattern of darker brown
was like wallpaper:
shapes like full-blown roses
stained and lost through age.   15
He was speckled with barnacles,
fine rosettes of lime,
and infested
with tiny white sea-lice,
and underneath two or three   20
rags of green weed hung down.
While his gills were breathing in
the terrible oxygen
—the frightening gills,
fresh and crisp with blood,   25
that can cut so badly—
I thought of the coarse white flesh

packed in like feathers,
the big bones and the little bones,
the dramatic reds and blacks   30
of his shiny entrails,
and the pink swim-bladder
like a big peony.
I looked into his eyes
which were far larger than mine   35
but shallower, and yellowed,
the irises backed and packed
with tarnished tinfoil
seen through the lenses
of old scratched isinglass.   40
They shifted a little, but not
to return my stare.
—It was more like the tipping
of an object toward the light.
I admired his sullen face,   45
the mechanism of his jaw,
and then I saw
that from his lower lip
—if you could call it a lip—
grim, wet, and weaponlike,   50
hung five old pieces of fish-line,
or four and a wire leader
with the swivel still attached,
with all their five big hooks
grown firmly in his mouth.   55
A green line, frayed at the end
where he broke it, two heavier lines,
and a fine black thread
still crimped from the strain and snap
when it broke and he got away.   60
Like medals with their ribbons
frayed and wavering,
a five-haired beard of wisdom
trailing from his aching jaw.
I stared and stared   65
and victory filled up
the little rented boat,
from the pool of bilge
where oil had spread a rainbow
around the rusted engine   70
to the bailer rusted orange,
the sun-cracked thwarts,
the oarlocks on their strings,
the gunnels—until everything
was rainbow, rainbow, rainbow!   75
And I let the fish go.

Some Dreams They Forgot

The dead birds fell, but no one had seen them fly,
or could guess from where. They were black, their eyes were shut,
and no one knew what kind of birds they were. But
all held them and looked up through the new far-funneled sky.
Also, dark drops fell. Night-collected on the eaves,   5
or congregated on the ceilings over their beds,
they hung, mysterious drop-shapes, all night over their heads,
now rolling off their careless fingers quick as dew off leaves.
Where had they seen wood-berries perfect black as these,
shining just so in early morning? Dark-hearted decoys on   10
upper-bough or below-leaf. Had they thought *poison*
and left? or—remember—eaten them from the loaded trees?
What flowers shrink to seeds like these, like columbine?
But their dreams are all inscrutable by eight or nine.

Fact Questions and Exercises

1. What does the Man-Moth think the moon is? What is the Man-Moth's "only possession"?
2. Point out several characteristics of the Man-Moth that parallel human characteristics.
3. In "The Fish," what does the speaker do with the fish at the end of the poem? What hangs from the fish's "lower lip"?
4. What form or type of poem is "Some Dreams They Forgot"? What has happened to the birds? Which lines or facts in the poem give you this information?

For Discussion and Writing

1. Each of these poems centers on a small animal. Is Bishop merely describing these creatures, or does she have a more significant purpose in mind? In "The Fish," for instance, what does the "rainbow" suggest? Why does it affect the poem's speaker as it does? What is suggested by the fact that the fish "hadn't fought at all"?
2. Compare the ways in which Bishop uses nature's creatures with the ways in which other poets use similar animals. Look, for instance, at Wilbur's "A Grasshopper" (p. 1219) or perhaps Hardy's "The Darkling Thrush" (p. 1158).

Randall Jarrell [1914–1965]

Jarrell was born in Tennessee, and was educated at Vanderbilt University. In 1942 he joined the air force and served throughout World War II, an experience that bears directly on his poetry. He later taught at several different universities, including the University of Texas and the University of North Carolina. In contrast to his poetry, Jarrell also wrote several books for children and a satirical novel, *Pictures from an Institution* (1954); he is best-known, however, for his war poems.

The Death of the Ball Turret Gunner

From my mother's sleep I fell into the State,
And I hunched in its belly till my wet fur froze.
Six miles from earth, loosed from its dream of life,
I woke to black flak and the nightmare fighters.
When I died they washed me out of the turret with a hose.   5

Losses

It was not dying: everybody died.
It was not dying: we had died before
In the routine crashes—and our fields
Called up the papers, wrote home to our folks,   5
And the rates rose, all because of us.
We died on the wrong page of the almanac,
Scattered on mountains fifty miles away;
Diving on haystacks, fighting with a friend,
We blazed up on the lines we never saw.
We died like aunts or pets or foreigners.   10
(When we left high school nothing else had died
For us to figure we had died like.)

In our new planes, with our new crews, we bombed
The ranges by the desert or the shore,
Fired at towed targets, waited for our scores—   15
And turned into replacements and woke up
One morning, over England, operational.
It wasn't different: but if we died
It was not an accident but a mistake
(But an easy one for anyone to make).   20
We read our mail and counted up our missions—
In bombers named for girls, we burned
The cities we had learned about in school—
Till our lives wore out; our bodies lay among
The people we had killed and never seen.   25
When we lasted long enough they gave us medals;
When we died they said, "Our casualties were low."
They said, "Here are the maps"; we burned the cities.

It was not dying—no, not ever dying;
But the night I died I dreamed that I was dead,   30
And the cities said to me: "Why are you dying?
We are satisfied, if you are; but why did I die?"

Fact Questions and Exercises

1. What is a "ball turret"?
2. To what does the speaker awake "six miles from earth"? How is the speaker removed from the turret?
3. In "Losses," what happens to the cities that "we had learned about in school"?
4. In both of these poems, what facts reveal that the speakers are referring to war?
5. What happens to the speakers of both poems?
6. The poems were published in 1944 and 1945; consequently, about which war is Jarrell writing?

For Discussion and Writing

1. Examine "The Death of the Ball Turret Gunner." How does its brevity relate to its content? That is, does the length of the poem say anything about the length or significance of human life? Does the length of the poem emphasize the "nightmare" in line 4? Note that within the space of five lines, the speaker progresses from birth to death.
2. What seem to be the speakers' attitudes toward war in the poems? Do the speakers approve of war? If not, why do they participate? Is there irony in the poems? What, for instance, is "lost" in "Losses"?

Dylan Thomas [1914–1953]

Thomas was born in Swansea, Wales, and attended public schools there. In 1934 he published *Eighteen Poems*, a collection of verse noted for its intriguing imagery; his later verse showed him to be a careful craftsman as well, able to create orderly poetic images and symbols. Thomas was an excellent speaker; his poetry readings were extremely popular, especially in America. In fact, Robert Zimmerman, an American singer, later used Thomas's name, and became known as Bob Dylan. Thomas led a bohemian life: he drank heavily, lived recklessly, and died young.

The Force That Through
the Green Fuse Drives the Flower

The force that through the green fuse drives the flower
Drives my green age; that blasts the roots of trees

Is my destroyer.
And I am dumb to tell the crooked rose
My youth is bent by the same wintry fever.   5

The force that drives the water through the rocks
Drives my red blood; that dries the mouthing streams
Turns mine to wax.
And I am dumb to mouth unto my veins
How at the mountain spring the same mouth sucks.   10

The hand that whirls the water in the pool
Stirs the quicksand; that ropes the blowing wind
Hauls my shroud sail.
And I am dumb to tell the hanging man
How of my clay is made the hangman's lime.   15

The lips of time leech to the fountain head;
Love drips and gathers, but the fallen blood
Shall calm her sores.
And I am dumb to tell a weather's wind
How time has ticked a heaven round the stars.   20

And I am dumb to tell the lover's tomb
How at my sheet goes the same crooked worm.

Fern Hill

Now as I was young and easy under the apple boughs
About the lilting house and happy as the grass was green,
    The night above the dingle starry,
        Time let me hail and climb
    Golden in the heydays of his eyes,   5
And honored among wagons I was a prince of the apple towns
And once below a time I lordly had the trees and leaves
        Trail with daisies and barley
    Down the rivers of the windfall light.

And as I was green and carefree, famous among the barns   10
About the happy yard and singing as the farm was home,
    In the sun that is young once only,
        Time let me play and be
    Golden in the mercy of his means,
And green and golden I was huntsman and herdsman, the calves   15
Sang to my horn, the foxes on the hills barked clear and cold,
        And the sabbath rang slowly
    In the pebbles of the holy streams.

All the sun long it was running, it was lovely, the hay
Fields high as the house, the tunes from the chimneys, it was air   20
  And playing, lovely and watery
    And fire green as grass.
  And nightly under the simple stars
As I rode to sleep the owls were bearing the farm away,
All the moon long I heard, blessed among stables, the night-jars   25
  Flying with the ricks, and the horses
    Flashing into the dark.

And then to awake, and the farm, like a wanderer white
With the dew, come back, the cock on his shoulder: it was all
  Shining, it was Adam and maiden,   30
    The sky gathered again
  And the sun grew round that very day.
So it must have been after the birth of the simple light
In the first, spinning place, the spellbound horses walking warm
  Out of the whinnying green stable   35
    On to the fields of praise.

And honored among foxes and pheasants by the gay house
Under the new made clouds and happy as the heart was long,
  In the sun born over and over,
    I ran my heedless ways,   40
  My wishes raced through the house high hay
And nothing I cared, at my sky blue trades, that time allows
In all his tuneful turning so few and such morning songs
  Before the children green and golden
    Follow him out of grace,   45

Nothing I cared, in the lamb white days, that time would take
    me
Up to the swallow thronged loft by the shadow of my hand,
  In the moon that is always rising,
    Nor that riding to sleep
  I should hear him fly with the high fields   50
And wake to the farm forever fled from the childless land.
Oh as I was young and easy in the mercy of his means,
    Time held me green and dying
  Though I sang in my chains like the sea.

In My Craft or Sullen Art

In my craft or sullen art
Exercised in the still night
When only the moon rages
And the lovers lie abed

With all their griefs in their arms,   5
I labor by singing light
Not for ambition or bread
Or the strut and trade of charms
On the ivory stages
But for the common wages   10
Of their most secret heart.

Not for the proud man apart
From the raging moon I write
On these spindrift pages
Nor for the towering dead   15
With their nightingales and psalms
But for the lovers, their arms
Round the griefs of the ages,
Who pay no praise or wages
Nor heed my craft or art.   20

Fact Questions and Exercises

1. Point out lines in "The Force That Through the Green Fuse Drives the Flower" that show the speaker's connection with nature or natural forces. What phrase is repeated in the poem?
2. In "Fern Hill," of what was the speaker once "prince"? In line 14, to what does "his" refer? What held the speaker in "chains"?
3. In "Fern Hill," which stanza or lines allude to the Bible?
4. In "My Craft or Sullen Art," for whom does the poet "write / On these spindrift pages"? What does "sullen" mean?

For Discussion and Writing

1. Thomas seems to see a certain "unity" that connects all life. How is this unity presented in "The Force That Through the Green Fuse Drives the Flower" and "Fern Hill"? What things do all people share—both good and bad? How does time affect people? Is there continuity to life, even though individuals die? If so, what form does this continuity take?
2. In relation to the previous question, does Thomas seem to be an optimist or a pessimist? Explain.

Robert Lowell [1917–   ]

Lowell was born in Boston, Massachusetts. After a brief and unhappy stay at Harvard, he transferred to Kenyon College. During World War II, he refused to serve in the army, and was imprisoned; after his release, he moved to Maine to devote his time to writing. His first collection of poems, *Land of Unlikeness*, was published in 1944; in 1946 *Lord Weary's Castle* won the Pulitzer Prize. Particularly during the period just after World War II, Lowell was troubled by personal and psychological problems—much of his poetry reflects his efforts to understand and overcome these traumas.

Skunk Hour

(For Elizabeth Bishop)

Nautilus Island's hermit
heiress still lives through winter in her Spartan cottage;
her sheep still graze above the sea.
Her son's a bishop. Her farmer
is first selectman in our village;   5
she's in her dotage.

Thirsting for
the hierarchic privacy
of Queen Victoria's century,
she buys up all   10
the eyesores facing her shore,
and lets them fall.

The season's ill—
we've lost our summer millionaire,
who seemed to leap from an L. L. Bean[1]   15
catalogue. His nine-knot yawl
was auctioned off to lobstermen.
A red fox stain covers Blue Hill.[2]

And now our fairy
decorator brightens his shop for fall;   20
his fishnet's filled with orange cork,
orange, his cobbler's bench and awl;
there is no money in his work,
he'd rather marry.

---

1. A well-known mail-order house in Maine, specializing in sportsman's gear.   2. A mountain in Maine.

One dark night,   25
my Tudor Ford climbed the hill's skull;
I watched for love-cars. Lights turned down,
they lay together, hull to hull,
where the graveyard shelves on the town. . . .
My mind's not right.   30

A car radio bleats,
"Love, O careless Love. . . ." I hear
my ill-spirit sob in each blood cell,
as if my hand were at its throat. . . .
I myself am hell;   35
nobody's here—

only skunks, that search
in the moonlight for a bite to eat.
They march on their soles up Main Street:
white stripes, moonstruck eyes' red fire   40
under the chalk-dry and spar spire
of the Trinitarian Church.

I stand on top
of our back steps and breathe the rich air—
a mother skunk with her column of kittens swills the garbage pail.   45
She jabs her wedge-head in a cup
of sour cream, drops her ostrich tail,
and will not scare.

Mr. Edwards and The Spider

I saw the spiders marching through the air,
Swimming from tree to tree that mildewed day
        In latter August when the hay
        Came creaking to the barn. But where
                The wind is westerly,   5
Where gnarled November makes the spiders fly
Into the apparitions of the sky,
        They purpose nothing but their ease and die
Urgently beating east to sunrise and the sea;

What are we in the hands of the great God?   10
It was in vain you set up thorn and briar
        In battle array against the fire
        And treason crackling in your blood;
                For the wild thorns grow tame
        And will do nothing to oppose the flame;   15
        Your lacerations tell the losing game

You play against a sickness past your cure.
How will the hands be strong? How will the heart endure?

A very little thing, a little worm,
Or hourglass-blazoned spider, it is said,   20
    Can kill a tiger. Will the dead
    Hold up his mirror and affirm
        To the four winds the smell
And flash of his authority? It's well
If God who holds you to the pit of hell,   25
Much as one holds a spider, will destroy,
Baffle and dissipate your soul. As a small boy

On Windsor Marsh, I saw the spider die
When thrown into the bowels of fierce fire:
    There's no long struggle, no desire   30
    To get up on its feet and fly—
        It stretches out its feet
And dies. This is the sinner's last retreat;
Yes, and no strength exerted on the heat
Then sinews the abolished will, when sick   35
And full of burning, it will whistle on a brick.

But who can plumb the sinking of that soul?
Josiah Hawley, picture yourself cast
    Into a brick-kiln where the blast
    Fans your quick vitals to a coal—   40
        If measured by a glass,
How long would it seem burning! Let there pass
A minute, ten, ten trillion; but the blaze
Is infinite, eternal: this is death,
To die and know it. This is the Black Widow, death.   45

Fact Questions and Exercises

1. In "Skunk Hour," for what is the hermit "thirsting"? Explain the phrase "fairy decorator" as it appears in lines 19 and 20 of the poem.
2. What is the speaker looking for as he goes up "the hill's skull"? What "swills the garbage pail"?
3. In "Mr. Edwards and the Spider," what can "kill a tiger"? "Black Widow" in line 45 refers to or echoes a previous line in the poem. What is the line?

For Discussion and Writing

1. Discuss the analogy that Lowell develops in "Mr. Edwards and the Spider." What two things are being compared? What seems to be Lowell's message? According to the poem, what type of deity controls human life?
2. Lowell begins both of these poems with a statement about a real thing; he then moves from reality to a symbolic, moral, or philosophical statement.

Discuss this technique. How, for instance, do Lowell's comments about the skunks relate to the hermit, the lovers, and the persona in "Skunk Hour"? Are the skunks used symbolically?

Gwendolyn Brooks [1917–   ]

Brooks was born in Topeka, Kansas, but grew up in Chicago, her present home. She graduated from Wilson Junior College, where she developed an interest in poetry. By the time she was seventeen, many of her poems had been published in the *Chicago Defender*, a well-known Negro newspaper. Her first collection of poems, *A Street in Bronzeville*, was published in 1945; her second collection, *Annie Allen*, won the 1950 Pulitzer Prize—she was the first black poet ever to win the award.

The Birth in a Narrow Room

Weeps out of western country something new.
Blurred and stupendous. Wanted and unplanned.
    Winks. Twines, and weakly winks
Upon the milk-glass fruit bowl, iron pot,
The bashful china child tipping forever   5
Yellow apron and spilling pretty cherries.

Now, weeks and years will go before she thinks
"How pinchy is my room! how can I breathe!
I am not anything and I have got
Not anything, or anything to do!"—   10

But prances nevertheless with gods and fairies
Blithely about the pump and then beneath
The elms and grapevines, then in darling endeavor
By privy foyer, where the screenings stand
And where the bugs buzz by in private cars   15
Across old peach cans and old jelly beans.

Pygmies Are Pygmies Still, Though Percht on Alps

—EDWARD YOUNG[1]

But can see better there, and laughing there
Pity the giants wallowing on the plain.
Giants who bleat and chafe in their small grass,
Seldom to spread the palm; to spit; come clean.

---

1. The title is from a poem by Edward Young (1683–1765), an English poet.

Pygmies expand in cold impossible air,   5
Cry fie on giantshine, poor glory which
Pounds breast-bone punily, screeches, and has
Reached no Alps: or, knows no Alps to reach.

We Real Cool

> The Pool Players.
> Seven at the Golden Shovel.

We real cool. We
Left school. We

Lurk late. We   5
Strike straight. We

Sing sin. We
Thin gin. We

Jazz June. We
Die soon.   10

Fact Questions and Exercises

1. What common household items are mentioned in "The Birth in a Narrow Room"? In the poem, what is both "wanted and unplanned"?
2. Point out an example of alliteration in "Pygmies Are Pygmies Still Though Percht on Alps." In the poem, who or what will "bleat and chafe in their small grass"?
3. In "We Real Cool," how many pool players are mentioned? What is the name of the pool room where they hang out? Ultimately, what is going to happen to the pool players?

For Discussion and Writing

1. Analyze "The Birth in a Narrow Room." Who is being born? How does the statuette of the "bashful china child" relate to the birth? What is suggested by the fact that the room is "narrow"? Are there symbols of aging or decay in the poem? If so, what are they? And, do they contrast with the other symbols in the poem? What do you think Brooks is saying in the poem?
2. Does Brooks develop any one theme that is common to all three poems? If so, discuss this theme (or themes) and explain how it is developed in each poem.

Howard Nemerov [1920–   ]

Nemerov was born in New York City, and was educated at Harvard. He has taught at the University of Minnesota and several other universities, and is presently a professor of English at Washington University in St. Louis. In addition to his poetry, Nemerov has published several novels and numerous critical essays. His first collection of poems, *The Image and the Law*, was published in 1947; since then, he has established himself as one of America's leading contemporary poets.

Brainstorm

The house was shaken by a rising wind
That rattled window and door. He sat alone
In an upstairs room and heard these things: a blind
Ran up with a bang, a door slammed, a groan
Came from some hidden joist, a leaky tap,   5
At any silence of the wind walked like
A blind man through the house. Timber and sap
Revolt, he thought, from washer, baulk and spike.
Bent to his book, continued unafraid
Until the crows came down from their loud flight   10
To walk along the rooftree overhead.
Their horny feet, so near but out of sight,
Scratched on the slate; when they were blown away
He heard their wings beat till they came again,
While the wind rose, and the house seemed to sway,   15
And window panes began to blind with rain.
The house was talking, not to him, he thought,
But to the crows; the crows were talking back
In their black voices. The secret might be out:
Houses are only trees stretched on the rack.   20
And once the crows knew, all nature would know.
Fur, leaf and feather would invade the form,
Nail rust with rain and shingle warp with snow,
Vine tear the wall, till any straw-borne storm
Could rip both roof and rooftree off and show   25
Naked to nature what they had kept warm.
He came to feel the crows walk on his head
As if he were the house, their crooked feet
Scratched, through the hair, his scalp. He might be dead,
It seemed, and all the noises underneath   30
Be but the cooling of the sinews, veins,
Juices, and sodden sacks suddenly let go;
While in his ruins of wiring, his burst mains,
The rainy wind had been set free to blow
Until the green uprising and mob rule   35
That ran the world had taken over him,
Split him like seed, and set him in the school
Where any crutch can learn to be a limb.

Inside his head he heard the stormy crows.

The Goose Fish

On the long shore, lit by the moon
To show them properly alone,
Two lovers suddenly embraced
So that their shadows were as one.
The ordinary night was graced   5
For them by the swift tide of blood
That silently they took at flood,
And for a little time they prized
        Themselves emparadised.

Then, as if shaken by stage-fright   10
Beneath the hard moon's bony light,
They stood together on the sand
Embarrassed in each other's sight
But still conspiring hand in hand,
Until they saw, there underfoot,   15
As though the world had found them out,
The goose fish turning up, though dead,
        His hugely grinning head.

There in the china light he lay,
Most ancient and corrupt and gray   20
They hesitated at his smile,
Wondering what it seemed to say
To lovers who a little while
Before had thought to understand,
By violence upon the sand,   25
The only way that could be known
        To make a world their own.

It was a wide and moony grin
Together peaceful and obscene;
They knew not what he would express,   30
So finished a comedian
He might mean failure or success,
But took it for an emblem of
Their sudden, new and guilty love
To be observed by, when they kissed,   35
        That rigid optimist.

So he became their patriarch,
Dreadfully mild in the half-dark.
His throat that the sand seemed to choke,
His picket teeth, these left their mark   40
But never did explain the joke
That so amused him, lying there
While the moon went down to disappear

Along the still and tilted track
    That bears the zodiac.   45

Fact Questions and Exercises

1. In "Brainstorm," what has "shaken" the house? What comes and walks "on the slate" of the house?
2. Describe the speaker's brainstorm.
3. In "The Goose Fish," who "stood together on the sand"?
4. Describe the goose fish. Where is he? What does his head look like? What does Nemerov mean when he refers to the goose fish as a "rigid optimist"?

For Discussion and Writing

1. Discuss Nemerov's use of symbols in the poems. What symbols are found in "Brainstorm"? What do they mean? Are they universal or private symbols? What does the goose fish symbolize? How does it contrast with the other elements of the poem—the lovers, for instance?

Richard Wilbur [1921–   ]

Wilbur, the son of an artist, was born in New York City, but grew up in New Jersey in pleasant, cultivated surroundings. He was educated at Amherst and Harvard, and served in the infantry during World War II. He has taught at several universities, and is presently a professor of English at Wesleyan University in Connecticut. In 1957 he won the Pulitzer Prize for his collection entitled *Poems*. In addition to his poetry, Wilbur has also written music and translated plays; it is his translation of *The Misanthrope* that appears in this text.

Potato

for André du Bouchet

An underground grower, blind and a common brown;
Got a misshapen look, it's nudged where it could;
Simple as soil yet crowded as earth with all.

Cut open raw, it looses a cool clean stench,
Mineral acid seeping from pores of prest meal;   5
It is like breaching a strangely refreshing tomb:

Therein the taste of first stones, the hands of dead slaves,
Waters men drank in the earliest frightful woods,
Flint chips, and peat, and the cinders of buried camps.

Scrubbed under faucet water the planet skin   10
Polishes yellow, but tears to the plain insides;
Parching, the white's blue-hearted like hungry hands.

All of the cold dark kitchens, and war-frozen gray
Evening at window; I remember so many
Peeling potatoes quietly into chipt pails.   15

"It was potatoes saved us, they kept us alive."
Then they had something to say akin to praise
For the mean earth-apples, too common to cherish or steal.

Times being hard, the Sikh and the Senegalese,
Hobo and Okie, the body of Jesus the Jew,   20
Vestigial virtues, are eaten; we shall survive.

What has not lost its savor shall hold us up,
And we are praising what saves us, what fills the need.
(Soon there'll be packets again, with Algerian fruits.)

Oh, it will not bear polish, the ancient potato,   25
Needn't be nourished by Caesars, will blow anywhere,
Hidden by nature, counted-on, stubborn and blind.

You may have noticed the bush that it pushes to air,
Comical-delicate, sometimes with second-rate flowers
Awkward and milky and beautiful only to hunger.   30

The Death of a Toad

A toad the power mower caught,
Chewed and clipped of a leg, with a hobbling hop has got
To the garden verge, and sanctuaried him
Under the cineraria leaves, in the shade
Of the ashen heartshaped leaves, in a dim,   5
Low, and a final glade.

The rare original heartsblood goes,
Spends on the earthen hide, in the folds and wizening, flows
In the gutters of the banked and staring eyes. He lies
As still as if he would return to stone,   10
And soundlessly attending, dies
Toward some deep monotone,

Toward misted and ebullient seas
And cooling shores, toward lost Amphibia's emperies.[1]

1. That is, the places where amphibians live.

Day dwindles, drowning, and at length is gone
In the wide and antique eyes, which still appear
  To watch, across the castrate lawn,
    The haggard daylight steer.

A Grasshopper

But for a brief
Moment, a poised minute,
He paused on the chicory-leaf;
Yet within it

The sprung perch   5
Had time to absorb the shock,
Narrow its pitch and lurch,
Cease to rock.

A quiet spread
Over the neighbor ground;   10
No flower swayed its head
For yards around;

The wind shrank
Away with a swallowed hiss;
Caught in a widening, blank   15
Parenthesis,

Cry upon cry
Faltered and faded out;
Everything seemed to die.
Oh, without doubt   20

Peace like a plague
Had gone to the world's verge,
But that an aimless, vague
Grasshopper-urge

Leapt him aloft,   25
Giving the leaf a kick,
Starting the grasses' soft
Chafe and tick,

So that the sleeping
Crickets resumed their chimes,   30
And all things wakened, keeping
Their several times.

In gay release
The whole field did what it did,
Peaceful now that its peace   35
Lay busily hid.

Fact Questions and Exercises

1. What does the potato "taste of"? What kind of flowers does the potato have?
2. What causes the death of the toad? What does "castrate" mean, in line 17 of
   the poem?
3. In "A Grasshopper," what "resumed their chimes"? What is caught in a
   "parenthesis"?

For Discussion and Writing

1. In each of these poems Wilbur talks about very common things. Is his purpose
   merely to describe a potato or a dead frog? If not, is he using these things
   symbolically? What do they represent?

W. D. Snodgrass [1926–   ]

Snodgrass, a native of Pennsylvania, served for two years in the
navy, during World War II; afterward, he took three degrees from
the University of Iowa, where he studied under Robert Lowell. It
is sometimes assumed that Snodgrass's poems are influenced by
the older poet. He taught sporadically at several universities
before receiving the Pulitzer Prize for *Heart's Needle*, in 1959. In
addition to the collections published under his own name, Snodgrass has published several poems under the name of S. S.
Gardons—an anagram of his own name.

The Campus on the Hill

Up the reputable walks of old established trees
They stalk, children of the *nouveaux riches*: chimes
Of the tall Clock Tower drench their heads in blessing:
"I don't wanna play at your house;
I don't like you any more."   5
My house stands opposite, on the other hill,
Among meadows, with the orchard fences down and falling;
Deer come almost to the door.
You cannot see it, even in this clearest morning.
White birds hang in the air between   10
Over the garbage landfill and those homes thereto adjacent,
Hovering slowly, turning, settling down

Like the flakes sifting imperceptibly onto the little town
In a waterball of glass.
And yet, this morning, beyond this quiet scene,   15
The floating birds, the backyards of the poor,
Beyond the shopping plaza, the dead canal, the hillside lying
                    tilted in the air,
Tomorrow has broken out today:
Riot in Algeria, in Cyprus, in Alabama;
Aged in wrong, the empires are declining,   20
And China gathers, soundlessly, like evidence.
What shall I say to the young on such a morning?—
Mind is the one salvation?—also grammar?—
No; my little ones lean not toward revolt. They
Are the Whites, the vaguely furiously driven, who resist   25
Their souls with such passivity
As would make Quakers swear. All day, dear Lord, all day
They wear their godhead lightly.
They look out from their hill and say,
To themselves, "We have nowhere to go but down: 30
The great destination is to stay."
Surely the nations will be reasonable;
They look at the world—don't they?—the world's way?
The clock just now has nothing more to say.

April Inventory

The green catalpa tree has turned
All White; the cherry blooms once more.
In one whole year I haven't learned
A blessed thing they pay you for.
The blossoms snow down in my hair;   5
The trees and I will soon be bare.

The trees have more than I to spare.
The sleek, expensive girls I teach,
Younger and pinker every year,
Bloom gradually out of reach.   10
The pear tree lets its petals drop
Like dandruff on a tabletop.

The girls have grown so young by now
I have to nudge myself to stare.
This year they smile and mind me how   15
My teeth are falling with my hair.
In thirty years I may not get
Younger, shrewder, or out of debt.

The tenth time, just a year ago,
I made myself a little list   20
Of all the things I'd ought to know,
Then told my parents, analyst,
And everyone who's trusted me
I'd be substantial, presently.

I haven't read one book about   25
A book or memorized one plot.
Or found a mind I did not doubt.
I learned one date. And then forgot.
And one by one the solid scholars
Get the degrees, the jobs, the dollars.   30

And smile above their starchy collars.
I taught my classes Whitehead's notions;
One lovely girl, a song of Mahler's.
Lacking a source-book or promotions,
I showed one child the colors of   35
A luna moth and how to love.

I taught myself to name my name,
To bark back, loosen love and crying;
To ease my woman so she came,
To ease an old man who was dying.   40
I have not learned how often I
Can win, can love, but choose to die.

I have not learned there is a lie
Love shall be blonder, slimmer, younger;
That my equivocating eye   45
Loves only by my body's hunger;
That I have forces, true to feel,
Or that the lovely world is real.

While scholars speak authority
And wear their ulcers on their sleeves,   50
My eyes in spectacles shall see
These trees procure and spend their leaves.
There is a value underneath
The gold and silver in my teeth.

Though trees turn bare and girls turn wives,   55
We shall afford our costly seasons;
There is a gentleness survives
That will outspeak and has its reasons.
There is a loveliness exists,
Preserves us, not for specialists.   60

Fact Questions and Exercises

1. In line 2 of "The Campus on the Hill," what does "nouveaux riches" mean? In the poem, who are the speaker's "little ones"?
2. Where is the speaker's house located in relation to the campus?
3. In "April Inventory," what is the profession of the speaker? Does the speaker of "The Campus on the Hill" have the same profession? Which lines support your answer?
4. Who or what reminds the speaker of "April Inventory" that his "teeth are falling with my hair"? In the poem, who gets "the jobs, the dollars"?

For Discussion and Writing

1. In these two poems, what is the speaker's attitude toward students and campus life? Does he have a sense of humor about himself and his profession? What qualities about the students does he seem to admire most? Least? Do you agree with his view of campus life?
2. How does Snodgrass use symbols in these poems? Are the trees in "April Inventory" used symbolically? If so, what do they symbolize? How are they like the speaker? How do they differ? What about the clock and the birds that hover over the garbage in "The Campus on the Hill"?

Anne Sexton [1928–1974]

Anne Sexton was born in Newton, Massachusetts, and attended Garland Junior College. She was married, had two daughters, and for a short while taught in a high school; most of her time, however, was devoted to her poetry and to coping with the personal traumas that are reflected in her poems and that led to her suicide. In general, she writes intimately—sometimes suggesting the confessional quality of Robert Lowell, with whom she studied. Her poetry collections include *To Bedlam and Part Way Back* (1960) and *All My Pretty Ones* (1962).

Lullaby

It is a summer evening.
The yellow moths sag
against the locked screens
and the faded curtains
suck over the window sills   5
and from another building
a goat calls in his dreams.
This is the TV parlour
in the best ward at Bedlam.

The night nurse is passing   10
out the evening pills.
She walks on two erasers,
padding by us one by one.

My sleeping pill is white.
It is a splendid pearl;   15
it floats me out of myself,
my stung skin as alien
as a loose bolt of cloth.
I will ignore the bed.
I am linen on a shelf.   20
Let the others moan in secret;
let each lost butterfly
go home. Old woollen head,
take me like a yellow moth
while the goat calls hush-   25
a-bye.

Woman with Girdle

Your Midriff sags toward your knees;
your breasts lie down in air,
their nipples as uninvolved
as warm starfish.
You stand in your elastic case,   5
still not giving up the new-born
and the old-born cycle.
Moving, you roll down the garment,
down that pink snapper and hoarder,
as your belly, soft as pudding,   10
slops into the empty space;
down, over the surgeon's careful mark,
down over hips, those head cushions
and mouth cushions,
slow motion like a rolling pin,   15
over crisp hairs, that amazing field
that hides your genius from your patron;
over thighs, thick as young pigs,
over knees like saucers,
over calves, polished as leather,   20
down toward the feet.
You pause for a moment,
tying your ankles into knots.
Now you rise,
a city from the sea,   25

born long before Alexandria was,
straightway from God you have come
into your redeeming skin.

The Addict

Sleepmonger,
deathmonger,
with capsules in my palms each night,
eight at a time from sweet
      pharmaceutical bottles
I make arrangements for a pint-sized
      journey.   5
I'm the queen of this condition.
I'm an expert on making the trip
and now they say I'm an addict.
Now they ask why.
Why!   10

Don't they know
that I promised to die!
I'm keeping in practice.
I'm merely staying in shape.
The pills are a mother, but better,   15
every color and as good as sour balls.
I'm on a diet from death.

Yes, I admit
it has gotten to be a bit of a habit—
blows eight at a time, socked in the
      eye,   20
hauled away by the pink, the orange,
the green and the white goodnights.
I'm becoming something of a chemical
mixture
That's it!   25

My supply
of tablets
has got to last for years and years.
I like them more than I like me.
Stubborn as hell, they won't let go.   30
It's a kind of marriage.
It's a kind of war
where I plant bombs inside
of myself.

Yes   35
I try
to kill myself in small amounts,
an innocuous occupation.
Actually I'm hung up on it.
But remember I don't make too much
            noise.   40
And frankly no one has to lug me out

and I don't stand there in my winding
            sheet.
I'm a little buttercup in my yellow
            nightie
eating my eight loaves in a row
and in a certain order as in   45
the laying on of hands
or the black sacrament.

It's a ceremony
but like any other sport
it's full of rules.   50
It's like a musical tennis match where
my mouth keeps catching the ball.
Then I lie on my altar
elevated by the eight chemical kisses.

What a lay me down this is   55
with two pink, two orange,
two green, two white goodnights.
Fee-fi-fo-fum—
Now I'm borrowed.
Now I'm numb.   60

Wanting to Die

Since you ask, most days I cannot remember.
I walk in my clothing, unmarked by that voyage.
Then the almost unnameable lust returns.

Even then I have nothing against life.
I know well the grass blades you mention,   5
the furniture you have placed under the sun.

But suicides have a special language.
Like carpenters they want to know *which tools*.
They never ask *why build*.

Twice I have so simply declared myself,   10
have possessed the enemy, eaten the enemy,
have taken on his craft, his magic.

In this way, heavy and thoughtful,
warmer than oil or water,
I have rested, drooling at the mouth-hole.   15

I did not think of my body at needle point.
Even the cornea and the leftover urine were gone.
Suicides have already betrayed the body.

Still-born, they don't always die,
but dazzled, they can't forget a drug so sweet   20
that even children would look on and smile.

To thrust all that life under your tongue!—
that, all by itself, becomes a passion.
Death's a sad bone; bruised, you'd say,

and yet she waits for me, year after year,   25
to so delicately undo an old wound,
to empty my breath from its bad prison.

Balanced there, suicides sometimes meet,
raging at the fruit, a pumped-up moon,
leaving the bread they mistook for a kiss,   30

leaving the page of the book carelessly open,
something unsaid, the phone off the hook
and the love, whatever it was, an infection.

Fact Questions and Exercises

1. In "Lullaby," where does the poem take place? What are the "two erasers" in
   line 12?
2. What is as "soft as pudding" in "Woman with Girdle"? What does the speaker
   mean when she says that the woman is tying her "ankles into knots"?
3. In "The Addict," why is the speaker "keeping in practice" and "staying in
   shape"? What is as "stubborn as hell" and "won't let go"?
4. In line 25 of "Wanting to Die," to what does "she" refer? In the poem, who or
   what "have a special language"?

For Discussion and Writing

1. Can you discern a central theme or motif that runs throughout these poems?
   If so, what is it? How is it displayed in each poem? Does "Woman with
   Girdle," for instance, express the same theme as "The Addict"?

2. Discuss Sexton's allusions to nursery rhymes and fairytales. For instance,
from what source does she take line 58 in "The Addict"? What other
references appear? (Note the poem titles.) Does her use of these references
bear on the meaning of the poems? That is, is she being ironic? If so, what
does the irony suggest?

Sylvia Plath [1932–1963]

Plath was born in Boston, Massachusetts, the daughter of an
Austrian mother, and a Prussian father who died when she was
ten. His death created a serious crisis for Plath; although she had
published her first poems before she was nine, after her father's
death, she began to write compulsively. She won a scholarship to
Smith College; during her stay there she tried to commit suicide
by swallowing sleeping pills. After graduating summa cum laude,
she traveled to England, where she met and married Ted Hughes,
the poet. In 1960 she published her first collection of poems, *The
Colossus*; her only novel, *The Bell Jar* (1968), is a fictional account
of her unhappy life. In 1963 she placed her head in the oven of her
kitchen stove, turned the jets on, and died.

Point Shirley

From Water-Tower Hill to the brick prison
The shingle booms, bickering under
The sea's collapse.
Snowcakes break and welter. This year
The gritted wave leaps   5
The seawall and drops onto a bier
Of quahog chips,
Leaving a salty mash of ice to whiten

In my grandmother's sand yard. She is dead,
Whose laundry snapped and froze here, who   10
Kept house against
What the sluttish, rutted sea could do.
Squall waves once danced
Ship timbers in through the cellar window;
A thresh-tailed, lanced   15
Shark littered in the geranium bed—

Such collusion of mulish elements
She wore her broom straws to the nub.
Twenty years out

Of her hand, the house still hugs in each drab   20
Stucco socket
The purple egg-stones: from Great Head's knob
To the filled-in Gut
The sea in its cold gizzard ground those rounds.

Nobody wintering now behind   25
The planked-up windows where she set
Her wheat loaves
And apple cakes to cool. What is it
Survives, grieves
So, over this battered, obstinate spit   30
Of gravel? The waves'
Spewed relics clicker masses in the wind,

Gray waves the stub-necked eiders ride.
A labor of love, and that labor lost.
Steadily the sea   35
East at Point Shirley. She died blessed,
And I come by
Bones, bones only, pawed and tossed,
A dog-faced sea.
The sun sinks under Boston, bloody red.   40

I would get from these dry-papped stones
The milk your love instilled in them.
The black ducks dive.
And though your graciousness might stream,
And I contrive,   45
Grandmother, stones are nothing of home
To that spumiest dove.
Against both bar and tower the black sea runs.

Medallion

By the gate with star and moon
Worked into the peeled orange wood
The bronze snake lay in the sun

Inert as a shoelace; dead
But pliable still, his jaw   5
Unhinged and his grin crooked,

Tongue a rose-colored arrow.
Over my hand I hung him.
His little vermilion eye

Ignited with a glassed flame   10
As I turned him in the light;
When I split a rock one time

The garnet bits burned like that.
Dust dulled his back to ochre
The way sun ruins a trout.   15

Yet his belly kept its fire
Going under the chainmail,
The old jewels smoldering there

In each opaque belly-scale:
Sunset looked at through milk glass.   20
And I saw white maggots coil

Thin as pins in the dark bruise
Where his innards bulged as if
He were digesting a mouse.

Knifelike, he was chaste enough,   25
Pure death's-metal. The yardman's
Flung brick perfected his laugh.

The Rival

If the moon smiled, she would resemble you.
You leave the same impression
Of something beautiful, but annihilating.
Both of you are great light borrowers.
Her O-mouth grieves at the world; yours is unaffected,   5

And your first gift is making stone out of everything.
I wake to a mausoleum; you are here,
Ticking your fingers on the marble table, looking for
          cigarettes,
Spiteful as a woman, but not so nervous,
And dying to say something unanswerable.   10

The moon, too, abases her subjects,
But in the daytime she is ridiculous.
Your dissatisfactions, on the other hand,
Arrive through the mailslot with loving regularity,
White and blank, expansive as carbon monoxide.   15

No day is safe from news of you,
Walking about in Africa maybe, but thinking of me.

Two Views of a Cadaver Room

1

The day she visited the dissecting room
They had four men laid out, black as burnt turkey,
Already half unstrung. A vinegary fume
Of the death vats clung to them;
The white-smocked boys started working.   5
The head of his cadaver had caved in,
And she could scarcely make out anything
In that rubble of skull plates and old leather.
A sallow piece of string held it together.

In their jars the snail-nosed babies moon and glow.   10
He hands her the cut-out heart like a cracked heirloom.

2

In Brueghel's panorama of smoke and slaughter
Two people only are blind to the carrion army:
He, afloat in the sea of her blue satin
Skirts, sings in the direction   15
Of her bare shoulder, while she bends,
Fingering a leaflet of music, over him,
Both of them deaf to the fiddle in the hands
Of the death's-head shadowing their song.
These Flemish lovers flourish; not for long.   20

Yet desolation, stalled in paint, spares the little country
Foolish, delicate, in the lower right-hand corner.

Fact Questions and Exercises

1. What is the setting described in "Point Shirley"? In line 9, to whom does "she" refer? What "sinks under Boston, bloody red"?
2. In "Medallion," what "lay in the sun"? What has the "yardman" done?
3. In "The Rival," whose "O-mouth grieves at the world"? What does "abases" mean, in line 11? Which line in the poem indicates that the speaker receives mail from the person being addressed?
4. Describe the two views of a cadaver room as presented in the poem.

For Discussion and Writing

1. The subject of death is in at least three of these poems. How does Plath present this theme? What symbols in the poems relate to death? What are the speakers' attitudes toward death?
2. Look at "The Goose Fish" (page 1216) and "The Death of a Toad" (page 1218).

Is "Medallion" similar to these poems? If so, what qualities do the poems share? Do they convey similar messages? How are they different?

Nikki Giovanni [1943–   ]

Giovanni was born in Knoxville, Tennessee, but grew up in Lincoln Heights, a black suburb of Cincinnati. When she was sixteen, Giovanni entered Fisk University, but was soon expelled; she was later readmitted and finished her degree in 1967. She also attended graduate school at the University of Pennsylvania, organized Cincinnati's first Black Arts Festival, and taught at Rutgers University. She is an outspoken, direct individualist whose poetry reflects her experiences as a black woman in America. Her poetry collections include *Black Feelings, Black Talk* (1968) and *Re: Creation* (1970).

Nikki-Rosa

childhood rememberances are always a drag
if you're Black
you always remember things like living in Woodlawn
with no inside toilet
and if you become famous or something   5
they never talk about how happy you were to have your mother
all to yourself and
how good the water felt when you got your bath from one of those
big tubs that folk in chicago barbecue in
and somehow when you talk about home   10
it never gets across how much you
understood their feelings
as the whole family attended meetings about Hollydale
and even though you remember
your biographers never understand   15
your father's pain as he sells his stock
and another dream goes
and though you're poor it isn't poverty that
concerns you
and though they fought a lot   20
it isn't your father's drinking that makes any difference
but only that everybody is together and you
and your sister have happy birthdays and very good christmasses
and I really hope no white person ever has cause to write about me
because they never understand Black love is Black wealth and   25
                    they'll
probably talk about my hard childhood and never understand that
all the while I was quite happy

Kidnap Poem

ever been kidnapped
by a poet
if i were a poet
i'd kidnap you
put you in my phrases and meter   5
you to jones beach
or maybe coney island
or maybe just to my house
lyric you in lilacs
dash you in the rain   10
blend into the beach
to complement my see
play the lyre for you
ode you with my love song
anything to win you   15
wrap you in the red Black green
show you off to mama
yeah if i were a poet i'd kid
nap you

Ego Tripping

(there may be a reason why)

I was born in the congo
I walked to the fertile crescent and built
        the sphinx
I designed a pyramid so tough that a star
        that only glows every one hundred years falls   5
        into the center giving divine perfect light
I am bad

I sat on the throne
        drinking nectar with allah
I got hot and sent an ice age to europe   10
        to cool my thirst
My oldest daughter is nefertiti
        the tears from my birth pains
        created the nile
I am a beautiful woman   15

I gazed on the forest and burned
        out the sahara desert
        with a packet of goat's meat
        and a change of clothes

I crossed it in two hours   20
I am a gazelle so swift
       so swift you can't catch me

       For a birthday present when he was three
I gave my son hannibal an elephant
       He gave me rome for mother's day   25
My strength flows ever on

My son noah built new/ark and
I stood proudly at the helm
       as we sailed on a soft summer day
I turned myself into myself and was   30
       jesus
         men intone my loving name
         All praises All praises
I am the one who would save

I sowed diamonds in my back yard   35
My bowels deliver uranium
       the filings from my fingernails are
       semi-precious jewels
        On a trip north
I caught a cold and blew   40
My nose giving oil to the arab world
I am so hip even my errors are correct
I sailed west to reach east and had to round off
       the earth as I went
        The hair from my head thinned and gold was laid   45
       across three continents

I am so perfect so divine so ethereal so surreal
I cannot be comprehended
       except by my permission

I mean . . . I . . . can fly   50
       like a bird in the sky . . .

Fact Questions and Exercises

1. In "Nikki-Rosa," what specific things make the speaker feel "good" or "happy"? What specific facts are revealed about her father? Why does the speaker hope that no "white person" will write about her?
2. In "Kidnap Poem," what poetic terms does Giovanni use? Which terms is she using as double-entendres?
3. In line 47 of "Ego Tripping," what do "ethereal" and "surreal" mean? Point out the several Biblical or historical allusions that are made in the poem.

For Discussion and Writing

1. Particularly in "Nikki-Rosa" and "Kidnap Poem," how does Giovanni's style help convey the meanings of the poems? What is the importance of her disregarding the usual conventions of capitalization and punctuation? What is the importance of the way she prints "kidnap" in the last two lines of the poem? Do these poetic devices remind you of any other poet that appears in this text? If so, what is the significance of these similarities of style?

2. Do you think Giovanni is serious when she says that she hopes "no white person ever has cause to write about me"? Or, is she being ironic? In the last line of "Nikki-Rosa," is she being factual? Or, again, is she being ironic? Is Giovanni ironic in any of the other poems?

Absurd: In its simplest form, the meaninglessness of human life; the term is most often associated with the philosophy developed by Albert Camus. It is closely related to **existentialism**. (See **existentialism**.)

Act: A division in the action of a play.

Allegory: A work of literature in which ideas, moral concepts, or other abstractions are presented in the form of living characters or, occasionally, in the form of places. The character (or place) is given the name of the concept. There are allegorical elements in Hawthorne's "Young Goodman Brown"—for example, Faith (the wife) represents faith (the moral concept).

Alliteration: In its simplest form, the repetition of consonants or consonant sounds at the beginning of words. These lines from Coleridge's *The Rime of the Ancient Mariner* are a good example: "The western wave was all aflame. / The day was well nigh done!" An even more obvious example is this line from Stevens's "The Emperor of Ice-Cream": "In kitchen cups concupiscent curds."

Allusion: In literature, a reference to a person, historical event, myth, or to another work of literature. In Eliot's poem, Prufrock says "No! I am not Prince Hamlet, nor was meant to be"—the allusion is to Shakespeare's *Hamlet*.

Analogy: The comparison of two things that share certain attributes but that are basically dissimilar. The comparison usually consists of a familiar object and a less familiar object—the purpose being to explain the unfamiliar object. John Donne begins Holy Sonnet 5 with an analogy: "I am a little world made cunningly." Two common analogies are the comparison of a country's government to a ship, and the vice president of the United States to the copilot of an airplane. An analogy is more extended than a **simile** or a **metaphor**.

Anapest: A common metrical **foot** in poetry, consisting of two unstressed syllables followed by one stressed syllable: intercept—iñ/tĕr/cépt.

Antagonist: In fiction, the character who opposes the hero or **protagonist**. Though not necessarily, the antagonist more often than not will be the villain of the story. In *Hamlet*, Claudius is the antagonist. (See **protagonist**.)

Anticlimax: The effect that results when an event of lesser importance immediately follows an event of greater importance; or, when a serious statement is immediately followed by an unimportant statement. It can be intentional or unintentional: Albee has an intentional anticlimatic line in *The American Dream* when Grandma announces that "old people have colitis and lavender perfume"; and Byron frequently uses anticlimax in *Don Juan*.

Antistrophe: In Greek drama, the **chorus** moved right, left, or stood still as it chanted its lines. The antistrophe is the part of the lines that was chanted as the chorus moved from left to right on stage. (See **epode** and **strophe**.)

Apostrophe: In literature, a figure of speech in which an abstraction or nonexistent person is addressed or spoken to as if present. Most often found in poetry, apostrophe is usually used to express serious emotions, although, it does lend itself easily to **satire**. Pope used it humorously in "The Rape of the Lock," lines 7 and following.

Archetype: In its simplest form, the religious beliefs, the myths, and the folklore of a nation or nations. Archetypal concepts are so commonly known that they form part of a people's heritage. The story of Adam and Eve is an archetype, as is the story of Christ and the legend of Santa Claus. C. G. Jung, the psychologist, used the term in connection with a people's inherited experiences: these ancestral experiences become part of the human race's collective unconscious, and are revealed in literature, dreams, religion, and other forms of human expression. *The Rime of the Ancient Mariner* contains archetypes in the form of the journey theme and Christian salvation, among others. (See **myth**.)

Ballad: A verse form that usually tells an exciting, uncomplicated story and that is written in a simple fashion. Ballads originated as songs. The common ballad **stanza** consists of four **iambic** lines, with the second and fourth lines rhyming, as in "Sir Patrick Spens." As a rule, the ballad does not concentrate on in-depth characterization and description; its impact comes from its overall simplicity. The ballad relies on stock phrases, the **refrain**, and incremental repetition (i.e., a line is repeated, but with a slight addition or change each time it appears). The ballad is a very old form of poetry, but it remains popular; it can be seen today in numerous folk songs—for instance, those sung by Joan Baez.

Blank Verse: Verse consisting of unrhymed **iambic** pentameter lines. Wordsworth's "Tintern Abbey" is written in blank verse.

Burlesque: In fiction, a comic device characterized by extreme exaggeration or imitation. All or part of a work may be burlesque; but it is used most often as a satirical device. (See **mock epic**.)

Canto: A subdivision of a long poem, comparable to a chapter in a book. A canto is not a **stanza**, and may, in fact, be made up of many stanzas, as in Byron's *Don Juan*.

Caricature: In literature, the exaggeration of certain character traits for the purpose of **satire** or **burlesque**.

Carpe Diem: Literally, "seize the day." The phrase is applied most often to short poems that express the "live for today, because tomorrow we may be dead" philosophy. Marvell's "To His Coy Mistress" is an excellent example of carpe diem poetry.

Catastrophe: A dramatic term used most often to designate the death or destruction of the hero of a tragedy. Technically, it refers to the last of the four divisions of a classic tragedy.

Catharsis: The emotional release or "cleansing" that the spectator is meant to experience while watching a tragedy; the term is often used synonymously with purgation. In watching *Oedipus Rex*, for example, the spectator is supposed to be purged of evil (momentarily or permanently) by seeing what happens to the unfortunate Oedipus.

Chorus: In Greek drama, a group of dancers that usually assumes the part of society by speaking for or representing the thinking of the people—most often, expressing traditional moral and social values. In later plays, the chorus changed by taking on various forms and functions, among them the role of narrator. For example, Tom in *The Glass Menagerie*, serves a function quite similar to that of the Greek chorus.

Climax: In fiction, usually the turning point in the action, or the point at which the reader or viewer experiences the highest degree of emotion. The climax in *Hamlet*, for instance, is often considered to be in Act 3, when Hamlet learns that Claudius has slain Hamlet's father; the climax of *The Metamorphosis*, according to many readers, comes in the very first line of the story.

Comedy: See the Introduction to Reading Literature, pages 9–10.

Comedy of Humors: A play based on the theory of four humors—an ancient theory that a person's character was determined by the four humors—blood, phlegm, yellow bile (choler), and black bile (melancholy). Depending on which of these humors dominated, a person would be passionate or cheerful (blood), unemotional (phlegm), bad tempered (yellow bile), or sad and gloomy (black bile). In this type of play, the central characters suffer from an imbalance of the humors, and are thus characterized by the specific attributes that result from the various humors. Ben Jonson's comedy *The Alchemist* (not included in this text) is a prime example of the comedy of humors.

Comedy of Manners: A play that satirizes the manners or actions of society, usually the upper classes of society. A later version of the type is *Major Barbara*. The term is sometimes applied in a broader sense to forms of fiction other than drama: parts of Roth's *Goodbye, Columbus* could be considered a comedy of manners.

Conceit: In poetry, a protracted **metaphor** that draws a comparison between two dissimilar things. Two types of conceit are usually distinguished: the Petrarchan and the metaphysical. The Petrarchan conceit, named for the Italian poet Petrarch, usually consists of strained comparisons in which, for instance, love is likened to a sinking ship; Shakespeare's Sonnet 130 (page 971) satirizes the Petrarchan conceit. The metaphysical conceit is usually very intellectual and presents witty, unexpected comparisons; John Donne is most commonly associated with the metaphysical conceit, and "The Flea" (page 976) and "A Valediction: Forbidding Mourning" (page 978) are excellent examples of its use.

Conflict: The tension or animosity that develops between the **protagonist** and the **antagonist**. Often, there is a conflict between the protagonist and an inanimate object or, occasionally, between forces within the protagonist. "Roman Fever" demonstrates a conflict between two characters, while "The Love Song of J. Alfred Prufrock" shows a conflict primarily between the forces within Prufrock. In "Barn Burning," Sarty also suffers inner conflict in determining right from wrong.

Couplet: Usually, two lines of poetry that contain a complete thought. Pope's "The Rape of the Lock" (page 994) has many couplets.

Crisis: In fiction, that moment when the forces of **conflict** join to decide which force will be dominant; it is commonly called the turning point.

Dénouement: In drama, the portion of the play that comes late in the action and clarifies the plot or resolves any unexplained situations—the term is sometimes applied to forms of fiction other than drama. Dénouement may be translated as "untying," and is pronounced dáy-new-mah or dáy-new-mahn.

Deus ex Machina: Generally, any suddenly introduced method an author uses to solve problems of plot, which does not grow logically out of what has already taken place; it is also used to solve problems that cannot logically be resolved on the human level. Literally, the term means "god from the machine," and refers to the use, in classic Greek drama, of an actual machine to lower the actor who was playing a god onto the stage. In old western movies, the cavalry usually shows up at the last second to save the hero from the Indians—this is deus ex machina. Today, the device is a sign of poor writing, unless it is used intentionally for comic effect.

Dialogue: The written version of speech between two or more characters.

Domestic Tragedy: A play that is based on the lives of common, everyday people, instead of on the lives of kings, princes, or other great persons. *Desire Under the Elms* is a domestic tragedy.

Double-entendre: A word or phrase that has two or more possible interpretations, one of which is often bawdy.

Dramatic Irony: Generally, the situation that results when a character in a work of fiction is unaware of facts known to the audience, and these facts are both about and important to the character. In *Oedipus Rex*, there is dramatic irony in Oedipus's pledging to revenge the killing of his father—the audience knows that Oedipus is the killer, but Oedipus is unaware of this fact and, consequently, is unaware that he is threatening himself.

Dramatic Monologue: In poetry, the use of a speaker who talks to an audience in the poem that does not answer—or at least the reader does not hear the audience answer. Usually, the intent of this device is to reveal the character of the speaker. Both Donne's "The Canonization" and Browning's "The Bishop Orders His Tomb at Saint Praxed's Church" are examples of the type; Eliot's "The Love Song of J. Alfred Prufrock" is a later example.

Elegy: A usually long, somewhat formal or somber poem that mourns the death of a particular individual or, occasionally, of humanity in general. Both Gray's "Elegy Written in a Country Churchyard" and Whitman's "When Lilacs Last in the Dooryard Bloom'd" are elegies.

Epic: A very long poem that tells a serious story. Its central character is a "superman," usually of divine or semidivine birth, whose fate determines the fate of a people or country. The hero takes part in great and important action, often covering a wide geographical area—facing and, usually, triumphing over many dangers and problems. The style of the epic is "elevated" or very serious. Perhaps the most famous epics are Homer's *Odyssey* and Vergil's *Aeneid*; English epics include *Beowulf* and Milton's *Paradise Lost*. (See **mock epic**.)

Epode: In Greek drama, the part of the **chorus's** song that was chanted while the chorus stood still. (See **antistrophe** and **strophe**.)

Euphemism: The substitution of an indirect or mild statement to avoid the use of a more direct or blunt statement. Today, euphemisms are, usually, considered inappropriate, since they are an attempt by the writer to be less than frank with the reader. Common euphemisms are "pass on" for "die," "got sick" for "vomited," and "with child" for "pregnant."

Existentialism: In its basic form, the philosophy that views each individual as isolated and alone, struggling for survival in a universe that has no god, truth, or value. In this universe, the individual comes from nothing and moves back toward nothing—and life is thus **absurd**. There are, however, some positive elements in the philosophy: personal freedom, the making or shaping of the self, and self-honesty. In literature, the philosophy has been stated most clearly by Jean-Paul Sartre and Albert Camus. (See **absurd**.)

Figurative Language: In literature, the use of language to achieve special effects. The most common forms of figurative language are **metaphor**, **simile**, and **personification**. (See the definitions for these specific terms.)

Flashback: In fiction, a device to let the reader or audience know about an event that has taken place before the action of the story. Hemingway uses the flashback in "The Snows of Kilimanjaro."

Foot: In poetry, the unit of rhythm; it is made up of stressed and unstressed syllables. (See **iamb**, for example.)

Foreshadowing: In fiction, the hints the author gives to build suspense and to indicate to the reader some of what is to come in the story. In "The Rocking-Horse Winner," for example, the emphasis on the family's lack of money foreshadows the story's development.

Free Verse: A verse form that does not adhere to regular rhythm, pattern, or rhyme. In contrast to conventional forms, free verse can attain a wide range of effects, avoiding the mechanical effects that can result from too close adherence to the traditional forms. It can, however, lead to self-indulgence and mere formlessness. The psalms of the Bible are written in free verse, as is Whitman's "Song of Myself" (page 1131); also many of cummings's poems are free-verse poems.

Genre: A designation of types of literature. The fiction in this book is divided into four genres—short story, novel, play, and poem.

Hamartia: See **tragic flaw**.

Hubris: (Sometimes spelled hybris.) Excessive pride. For example, this is Oedipus's fatal flaw and leads to his downfall. (See **tragic flaw**.)

Humor: See **Comedy of Humors**.

Hyperbole: Generally, overstatement. In literature, often it is the use of high-flown language to describe a situation that does not justify such speech. The speaker's promises to his lady in "To His Coy Mistress" may be thought of as hyperbole although, here, the use of hyperbole is more serious than in most verse.

Iamb: The most common **foot** in English poetry, consisting of an unstressed syllable followed by a stressed syllable. The first line of Keats's "When I Have Fears" is a good example of an iambic foot: "Whĕn Í/ hăve feárs/ thăt Í/ măy ceáse/ tŏ bé/ . . ."; the opening line of Gray's "Elegy Written in a Country Churchyard" is another example.

Imagery: See the Introduction to Reading Literature, pages 15–16.

Irony: Saying one thing while meaning the opposite—sarcasm is a low form of irony. The subtleties of irony are complex: it is often easier to detect irony when it is presented orally, for the inflection of the voice conveys meaning more readily than does the written word. For example, a person can say "That was really a beautiful thing you did for me," and the hearer knows immediately whether the speaker really means what is said. There are no sure-fire signs to mark irony in the written language, but there are certain hints that suggest the reader should suspect irony: when a speaker praises a person, thing, or event excessively; when a character says or does something that her or his previous actions and statements contradict; when an author presents an argument in favor of a course of action that is absurd or totally out of keeping with society's accepted behavior; or when a character greatly understates the importance of something. Pope's "The Rape of the Lock" and Byron's *Don Juan* are famous for their irony; Browning's "Soliloquy of the Spanish Cloister" and Roth's *Goodbye, Columbus* also contain considerable irony. Auden's "The Unknown Citizen" is a very ironic poem, particularly in the last two lines. (See **Dramatic Irony**.)

Litotes: Generally, understatement, although litotes technically means making a positive statement by stating the opposite or negative of that statement. "Alaska does not have the warmest climate in the world" and "He is not the world's handsomest man" are examples. (See **understatement**.)

Lyric: Originally, any song that was sung to the accompaniment of a lyre. Today, the term refers to any short poem that expresses the personal emotions of the poet or of the poet's **persona**. The lyric is a very old and diverse form of poetry. In this text, Thomas Wyatt's poems are lyrics, as are Shakespeare's **sonnets**, Donne's "The Canonization," and Yeats's "Sailing to Byzantium."

Melodrama: A type of drama, common in the nineteenth century, in which the characters are simple and stereotyped, and the plot is based on sensationalism—its primary aim, to play on the emotions of the audience. A typical melodrama has a hero and heroine, both unfailingly pure and virtuous; a villain, unfailingly mean and cruel, who in some way threatens the heroine (the picture of a black-dressed villain with a long mustache binding a heroine to railroad tracks comes from melodrama); and a plot that hinges on whether the hero will save the heroine and overcome the evil villain. Of course, the hero ultimately prevails. Many movies and television programs derive from melodrama, and animated cartoons, such as "Popeye," satirize it.

Metaphor: An implied comparison between two or more things, different from a **simile** in that it does not use the words "like" or "as." These lines from Keats's "La Belle Dame sans Merci" are a metaphor: "And on thy cheeks a fading rose / Fast withereth too"; the lines, by implication, compare cheeks to roses.

Meter: Generally, the stressed and unstressed syllables that form a more or less regular pattern in a line of poetry. Meter is measured by the **foot**, and may be thought of as the measurement of rhythm in poetry—just as notes measure the rhythm of music.

Mock Epic: A poem that imitates or makes fun of the **epic** by using nonheroic heroes and insignificant events. Its purpose is not to ridicule the epic form, but to ridicule the trivial and overemphasized actions of society. This is accomplished by greatly overplaying the importance of such actions within the epic pattern—a pattern that includes asking a deity for help, the presence of supernatural beings, the high-flown speech of the heroes, the description of great battles and warriors, and the division of the poem into cantos. (See **epic**.)

Monologue: In fiction, a speech given by one person, either to himself or to an audience. *Hamlet* contains numerous monologues, the most famous being Hamlet's "to be or not to be".

Myth: Stories, usually anonymous, that deal with supernatural figures and events, that form a common part of a people's history or background. More generally, myth may refer to a race's imaginative interpretation of its past. Stories about the Greek gods, Adam and Eve, Paul Revere's ride, and the romance of the pre-Civil War South are all forms of myth. Marvell alludes to the Adam and Eve myth in "The Garden"; Coleridge uses various myths in *The Rime of the Ancient Mariner*; and even the American Civil War is used in a mythical way by both Faulkner and Warren in their stories. (See **archetype.**)

Naturalism: In fiction, the scientific (rather than supernatural) interpretation of the universe in which the human being is viewed as an animal who is formed by heredity and environment, and is thus at the mercy of the forces of nature—neither controlling nor totally understanding these determining forces. The individual is merely another animal trying to survive. Crane's "The Open Boat" is an outstanding example of naturalism. His term for nature is "willy-nilly," implying that there is little or no purpose to life and no god that controls the forces of the universe. Hemingway's "The Snows of Kilimanjaro" is also naturalistic, in that the protagonist's death is caused by the insignificant but unavoidable fact that he is scratched by a thorn.

Novella: See the Introduction to Reading Literature, page 5.

Ode: A lyric poem, usually long, that is concerned with a serious subject—death or beauty, for instance. In its original form, the ode was an imitation of the songs the **chorus** sang in Greek drama: its stanzas, arranged so as to imitate the dance movements of the chorus, were very formal and complex. More recent odes, called "irregular odes," are looser in form and do not necessarily attempt to imitate the Greek chorus. Keats's "Ode to a Nightingale" is an irregular ode.

Pastoral Elegy: A variation of the **elegy**, using shepherds to represent the mourner and the one who is mourned. The pastoral elegy is a very old form of poetry, dating back to the early Greek poets. It usually contains these elements or conventions: an address to the muses, numerous references to classical mythology, blame for the shepherd's death placed on nymphs or other supernatural figures, mourning by all nature at the death, divine providence questioned, the presentation of numerous mourners, and the final resolution that the shepherd's death is part of a divine purpose and, thus, is not a dreadful thing. Milton's "Lycidas" (not included in this text) is a pastoral elegy, in which Milton mourns the death of a poet friend; Shelley's "Adonais" (also not included in this text) is another example of the pastoral elegy, in which Shelley mourns the death of John Keats. (See **elegy.**)

Persona: Generally, whoever is speaking, or the **voice,** in a work of fiction. The persona is not actually the author; instead, it is the author's creation, often in the form of a first-person narrator. The persona in Marvell's "To His Coy Mistress" is the man who argues with the lady that they do not have "world enough and time" to waste; the persona in *Don Juan* is the unidentified speaker, whom the reader assumes to be Byron; and the persona in Melville's "Bartleby the Scrivener" is the lawyer who cannot escape from Bartleby.

Personification: The giving of human characteristics to nonhuman things, such as animals, inanimate objects, or ideas. In her poem "Because I could not stop for Death," Dickinson personifies death; and, in "The Sun Rising," Donne personifies the sun by addressing it as a human being.

Point of View: See the Introduction to Reading Literature, pages 11–13.

Proscenium: In a theater, that part of the stage between the orchestra pit and the curtain. More generally, proscenium can mean the entire stage.

Protagonist: The main character in a work of fiction, usually, the hero—it is generally correct to use the terms "hero" and "protagonist" synonymously. In some fiction, however, a nonheroic figure can be the main character, and, in this case, the hero would be the **antagonist**. "Protagonist" usually implies goodness or champion qualities, whereas "antagonist" usually implies the opposite. Hamlet is a protagonist, as is Neil Klugman of *Goodbye, Columbus*; in O'Connor's "The Life You Save May Be Your Own," however, Shiftlet is neither heroic nor admirable, yet he is the protagonist of the story. In some modern works it is difficult to determine who is the protagonist and who is the antagonist, if indeed either is present: note, for example, *The American Dream* or *Desire Under the Elms*.

Realism: In literature, writing that attempts to present an objective picture of life—the mud, the warts, the sores, and the sorrows, as well as the less unpleasant aspects. Realism usually concentrates on the lower or middle classes, and it strives to present the everyday, commonplace happenings of daily living. Although realism has appeared in literature of all periods, it is most commonly associated with modern nineteenth- and twentieth-century writing: Anthony Trollope and Thomas Hardy are well-known English realist writers, while William Dean Howells and Mark Twain are famous American realists. In this text, *Goodbye, Columbus* is a realistic work, whereas "Young Goodman Brown" is not, because it attempts to present an allegorical or symbolic statement rather than an objective account of life.

Refrain: See **ballad**.

Rhyme Scheme: The pattern of rhymed words in a poem. Rhyme scheme is designated by letters of the alphabet, as shown in this example from Gray's "Elegy Written in a Country Churchyard":

> The curfew tolls the knell of parting day,   **(a)**
> The lowing herd wind slowly o'er the lea,   **(b)**
> The plowman homeward plods his weary way,   **(a)**
> And leaves the world to darkness and to me.   **(b)**

Satire: In its simplest form, a method of belittling a subject by making it appear ridiculous. Although satire may be humorous, the author's intent is usually serious—a hope that through laughter the audience will see an evil and rectify it. There are numerous methods and types of satire. The following works are all satires, either completely or in part: Molière's *The Misanthrope*, Twain's "The Man That Corrupted Hadleyburg," Burns's "Holy Willie's Prayer," and Albee's *The American Dream*. (See **irony**.)

Sentimentalism: In literature, an author's overuse of emotion to evoke an emotional response from the reader and an overly optimistic belief in the goodness of the human being. In modern writing, sentimentalism is considered a sign of the author's poor taste or lack of ability, unless, of course, it is being used intentionally. In eighteenth-century English writing, however, sentimentalism was a common and acceptable part of literature. Gray's "Elegy Written in a Country Churchyard" is sentimental; and, to a lesser degree, so is Blake's "Little Black Boy." More recent examples are Segal's novel *Love Story*, some of McKuen's poems, and some popular songs by singers such as John Denver.

Simile: A comparison between two things, distinguished by the words "like" or "as." Here is an example from Frost's "Birches": "It's when I'm weary of consideration, / And life is too much like a pathless wood . . ." (See **metaphor**.)

Sonnet: In modern poetry, a lyric poem consisting of fourteen lines. More traditionally, there are two types of sonnet: the Italian and the English (or Shakespearean). The Italian sonnet divides into two parts, one consisting of eight lines (octave) and the second of six lines (sestet); the octave usually raises a question that is answered or resolved in the sestet. The English sonnet also divides into parts—three four-line divisions and a **couplet**, which usually comments on or closes the rest of the poem. In addition to those of Shakespeare, Donne, and Milton, other sonnets that appear in this text are Robinson's "Cliff Klingenhagen," and all of Hopkins's poems.

Stanza: One of the units into which a poem is divided, usually consisting of at least two lines. Other than a single line, the stanza is the smallest complete unit into which a poem may be divided.

Stock Character: A type of character that appears so often in a particular **genre** that it is immediately recognizable and readily associated with the genre. **Melodrama**, for instance, depends heavily on stock characters. Even Hamlet is a stock character—he is the vengeful hero of a revenge tragedy. Often used stock characters include: the "gull," a person who is easily fooled or who is stupidly susceptible to other people; the "miles gloriosus," a braggard soldier, such as Shakespeare's Falstaff; and the "buffoon," a clown. The brave, moral private detective seen in many television shows is also a stock character.

Stream of Consciousness: A method of writing in which an author attempts to convey what goes on in the mind of a fictional character. The technique tries to duplicate the thought processes or mental associations of the character, and usually does not adhere to traditional punctuation or grammatical conventions. James Joyce's novel *Ulysses* uses this technique, as do many of William Faulkner's novels and short stories (see, for example, the italicized passages in "Barn Burning"); Hemingway also uses stream of consciousness passages in "The Snows of Kilimanjaro."

Strophe: In Greek drama, the part of the **chorus's** song that was chanted as the chorus moved from right to left on stage. (See **antistrophe** and **epode**.)

Style: The ways in which an author uses the language to say what he or she wants to say. Style includes any element that relates to the author's use of language: the choice of words, the kinds of sentences, the punctuation, for instance. Hemingway's style is characterized by short, uncomplicated sentences, and an adherence to the rules of conventional English. Faulkner's style, on the other hand, is noted for its long, complicated sentences, its difficult vocabulary, and an apparent disregard for conventional grammar.

Theme: A major idea that is developed in a work of literature. A work may contain more than one theme, and any two readers may not discover the same major themes in any one work. Currently, the word "motif" is often used for "theme."

Tone: Generally, the mood that a work of fiction conveys—somber, happy, serious, lighthearted, and so forth. Almost all aspects of a work go into creating its tone.

Tragedy: See the Introduction to Reading Literature, pages 9–10.

Tragic Flaw: In a tragedy, the insurmountable fault in the character of the hero. This tragic or fatal flaw may be pride or poor judgment or any number of character weaknesses, but it is not the result of intentional evil on the hero's part—it is a weakness over which the hero has little or no control, and of which he is perhaps unaware. The flaw leads to the hero's downfall by preventing him from doing what is right. Oedipus and Hamlet are examples of heroes with tragic flaws. Hamartia is often called the tragic flaw.

Understatement: Writing that underplays the importance of something. The device is often used to achieve ironic effect. The last line of Fitzgerald's "Babylon Revisited" is an understatement. (See **litotes**.)

Unity: In literature, generally any device or element that connects all the various parts of the work to each other. Unity may result from plot, character, theme, symbols, or any number of other elements. When applied specifically to drama, unity most often refers to the mechanical considerations of time, place, and action. *Oedipus Rex*, for example, is a play in which the action centers on one person (Oedipus), and in which the events happen during a brief period of time, in one location. More recent plays, however, seldom adhere strictly to such unity.

Voice: See **persona**.

INDEX